1998
Sports Collectors
ALMANAC

From the Editors of

Published by

700 E. State Street • Iola, WI 54990-0001
Telephone: 715/445-2214

Please call or write for our free catalog.
Our toll-free number to place an order or obtain a free catalog is 800-258-0929
or please use our regular business telephone 715-445-2214
for editorial comment and further information.

ISBN: 0-87341-548-5

Printed in the United States of America

TABLE OF CONTENTS

BASEBALL

FOOTBALL

AUTO RACING

MULTI-SPORTS

MVP CHECKLISTS

1998
Sports Collectors
ALMANAC

What were the hottest issues, inserts and innovations in trading cards in 1997?

The first annual *Sports Collectors Almanac* has the answers to all of your sports collecting questions.

This one-of-a-kind reference book, created by the Price Guide Editors of *Sports Collectors Digest*, contains timely information on every sports trading card produced in 1997.

Baseball? The *Almanac* dedicates 81 pages to pricing everything from Ken Griffey Refractors to Cal Ripken die-cuts. Manufacturers featured include Topps, Pinnacle, Donruss, Fleer, Upper Deck and Pacific.

Basketball? All of the hottest 1997 releases are included in the *Almanac*, with 43 pages of coverage on manufacturers such as SkyBox, Upper Deck, Topps and Fleer.

Football? The *Almanac* features a comprehensive look at the NFL card market, including more than 75 pages of information and pricing on sets produced by Upper Deck, Pinnacle, Donruss, Fleer, Topps, SkyBox, Collector's Edge, Press Pass, The Score Board, Pacific and Playoff.

Looking for more? *Sports Collectors Almanac* includes complete coverage of all hockey, racing and multi-sport card issues, as well as a summary of all sports figurines produced in 1997.

As a bonus, we've included a sport-by-sport summary of the trading card market and our popular "Top 10" lists, which detail the hottest cards, inserts and sets in the hobby today. We polish the book off with player checklists for the MVPs in each of the five sports.

In summary, *Sports Collectors Almanac* provides "one-stop shopping" for the collector seeking comprehensive checklists, photos, pricing and detailed information on all basketball, baseball, football, hockey, motorsports and multi-sport cards issued in 1997.

Enjoy the book – and keep enjoying your sports collecting hobby!

Steve Bloedow
New products coordinator,
Sports Collectors Digest
December 31, 1997

1997 The Year in Baseball Cards

Baseball cards were bigger than ever in 1997. The hobby itself may not have been bigger, but some cards certainly were — and some were smaller. Having just about reached the limits of technology for putting a baseball player's picture on a piece of cardboard, plastic, wood, metal or any combination thereof, most of the major manufacturers in 1997 tinkered with the physical dimensions to give the collector another reason to buy.

In recent years, most of the major card companies – Topps, Donruss, Fleer, Score and especially Upper Deck, have pro-duced various baseball cards in sizes larger than the 1957 present standard of $2\frac{1}{2}$ by $3\frac{1}{2}$ inches. Known to collectors as "jumbos" or "supers," these large format cards most frequently were reproductions of regular cards, sometimes with the addition of an individual serial number. Quite often the sizes chosen were exact multiples of the standard size.

The jumbos were issued via virtually every conceivable manner of distribution. A few were sold individually in wax or cello packs. In 1992, Topps became the first major company to produce a special oversized version of its cards exclusively for a large retail chain when it packed a 5 by 7 inch Stadium Club Master Photo in boxes sold at Wal-Mart. Within a short time, all of the major chain stores were pressuring the card companies for such exclusives and collectors soon learned to carefully study the packaging of cards in the big chain stores to find hidden treasures.

For instance, in Wal-Mart boxes of Bowman's Best in 1996, a jumbo refractor of one of 10 top stars was included. Bowman used a similar concept for 1997, producing an edition of just 900 sets of jumbo Bowman's Best stars. Each 16 card set included 13 regular finish cards, plus two randomly selected Refractor cards and one Atomic Refractor.

Anderson News Co., through its Treat Entertainment arm, teamed with Topps and Wal-Mart to create specially boxed packages containing from 6 to 15 foil packs and a large reproduction of a 1997 Topps card. Visible through a cello window in the display box, collectors could get a large 1952 Topps reprint card of Willie Mays with Series I packs, or one of a handful of top stars, also in large format reproductions in Series II. Oversize versions of Topps Chrome cards were featured in boxes containing a half-dozen Chrome packs.

Score was the second of the big card companies to issue a version of its cards in a size larger than 5 by 7. As an exclusive in a $30 collectors' kit sold at K-Mart stores, Score included a $7\frac{1}{2}$ by $10\frac{1}{2}$ version of its "Score Rules" insert in each kit.

Upper Deck has been the most active in the production of oversize cards. In 1997, special retail packaging of various Upper Deck products included $3\frac{1}{2}$ by 5 versions of the Griffey Hot Shots subset, a select group of Collector's Choice stars, Power Package inserts and the Griffey Clearly Dominant inserts.

It was also in 1997 that extremely large-format cards became a regular pack insert. When Studio introduced its 1997 issue, it was in packaging such as collectors had never previously seen. Instead of the traditional wax or foil pack, the '97 Studio was sold in an $8\frac{1}{2}$ by 12 cardboard envelope, complete with zip-strip opener, very much like an express mail envelope. Inside, each "pack" of Studio was a cello-wrapped group of five regular-size cards and one 8 by 10 Portrait or Master Strokes card.

The cards of 24 of the top players made up the super size Portraits parallels, while each of the 24 Master Strokes inserts could also be found in a serial numbered edition of 5,000. (This is one case where the large format card is more common than the regular, since only 2,000 numbered Master Strokes cards were issued in $2\frac{1}{2}$ by $3\frac{1}{2}$ size.)

As the baseball season drew to a close, Pinnacle's Zenith brand introduced its own 8x10 cards, and upped the ante on technology for supers. In packaging similar to Studio, two of the four types of 8x10 cards were found along with a pack of five standard size cards. There the similarities end, however, as suggested retail price on the Zenith packs was $9.99 – four times Studio's issue price.

For the extra money, collectors opening packs of Zenith could look for four different styles of 8x10s. The most common are regular oversize versions of the standard card in a 24 player parallel edition, and a version printed on metallic foil in Pinnacle's Dufex technology. Both the regular and Dufex 8x10s were seeded one per pack.

Lucky collectors, however, had a chance to find the hobby's first 8x10 motion card. Eight top stars were produced in the V2 chase set which combines foil technology, die-cutting and a motion-vision background. The V2 cards were reportedly inserted at an average rate of one per 47 packs – those odds mean a collector would have to buy nearly $470 worth of packs to find one of the V2 motion cards.

At the top of the line, bearing the prestigious Z-Team name, was a set of nine top players rendered in an 8x10 format and printed on "Mirror Gold Holographic Mylar Foil," in a numbered edition of just 1,000 each.

At the opposite end of the size scale, there have also been numerous attempts to downsize from the standard of 2½ by 3½ inches.

Long known as an innovative company in the use of metallic foils and die-cutting, Pacific revived the mini-card in 1997 with its Card-supial issue. As a one-per-box insert in Pacific Crown Collection baseball, the Card-supial chase cards feature 36 top stars and hot rookies. Each Card-supial consists of two cards: a standard size card which in a die-cut "pouch" on its back holds a 1¼ by 1¾ inch card.

Pacific's concept did eliminate one of the hobby's greatest objections to minis. Since the small card was carried on the back of the large card, the pair could be housed in the standard nine-pocket plastic sheet.

Much as the addition of a little gold foil to card fronts in 1992 spawned an eye-popping new generation of flashy cards, the size variations which have proliferated in 1997 may one day result in the contemporary 2½ by 3½ inch baseball card format no longer being the "standard."

> *Since many collectors find it difficult or impossible to "cash in" the chase cards they may be lucky enough to pull from packs, some companies in 1997 took the lottery to the next step, offering cash awards.*

Packaging became collectible in '97

As mentioned, the issue of 8x10 cards by Studio and Zenith required a new type of packaging, the zip-strip cardboard envelope. However, that was just one of the card manufacturers' packaging innovations of 1997. In an effort to get their product to stand out among the dozens of similar products on retail shelves, two of Pinnacle's baseball card brands were packaged in containers which were designed to be collectibles themselves. "Inside Pinnacle" debuted in early summer as the first "cards in a can."

About the size of a can of vegetables, the steel cans were lithographed with pictures of one of 24 major stars or hot rookies. Sealed inside — requiring a can opener to extract — was a cello pack containing an assortment of cards from the regular Inside Pinnacle set and inserts. Collectors were faced with the decision of ruining the can's "Mint" status as a collectible by opening it, or never seeing the cards inside. Suggested retail price was about $4 a can, and dealers quickly scooped up the top-shelf players at that price and marked them up on the collector market. Putting together a complete set of 24 cans could easily cost $200. Some collectors compromised by opening the cans from the

bottom to get at the cards while still allowing the cans to be displayed with their tops intact.

Later in the season, Donruss Preferred debuted in another type of steel container, a 3¼ by 4½ inch box. The box had a hinged top on which was lithographed the photograph of one of 25 stars or rookies. In addition to the individual tins, the "case" in which the tins were packaged was also a tin box featuring a player picture. Shrink wrapping of the tins preserved their mint status, but they could still be easily removed to retrieve the cello wrapped pack of cards inside without harming the display appeal of the player tins. There was even a set of "chase" tins produced. Each of the 25 player tins can also be found in a gold colored version serially numbered to 1,200 each.

When Topps' Screen Play issue made its long-delayed debut in late October, it too was packaged in a "tin." In the case of Screen Play, the cards were sold in one-card "packs" which were 5 inch diameter round lithographed steel, resembling a film canister.

The hobby jury is still out on whether these non-standard packagings will become real collectors items. By the end of 1997, prices for both the cans and the Preferred tins had dropped considerably from their peaks. It may be that the space required to store or display these bulky items is not easy to come by for most collectors. Expect to see the card companies continue to experiment with collectible packaging for 1998.

Built-in scarcity challenges collectors

Another trend which gathered momentum in 1997 was the issue of baseball card sets in a "fractured matrix." Few in the hobby can explain the phrase or even fully understand the concept, because each of the companies takes a slightly different approach to the concept of creating varying levels of scarcity within a particular card set.

Between 1974-90, most regular baseball card sets were issued in a single series. Theoretically, each card was issued in the same quantity, so the only variables in placing a value on a card became the player depicted and the card's condition.

All that changed in 1996 when Topps Finest was issued in three different tiers of scarcity for the cards in the basic 359 card set. Various cards were labeled as "Common" (bronze), Uncommon" (silver) or "Rare" (gold) in appropriate degrees of scarcity. Naturally the rarest, thus most expensive, cards were also those likely to be in highest demand, the top superstars and hottest rookies.

On top of this "fracture" of the base set, the same diversity was carried over to the parallel Refractor version, with selling prices in the hobby market up to 20 times that of the corresponding "regular" Finest card. Finest returned for '97 with the same three-tiered base set, but added differing levels of scarcity with embossed silver cards and die-cut/embossed gold cards.

The 1997 Leaf set carried the concept a step further by issuing cards in three metallic finishes – bronze, silver and gold – in non-die cut version and in one of three die-cut variations labeled X, Y, and Z. At the time of issue, the manufacturer did not reveal the relative levels of scarcity among the variations, requiring collectors and dealers to figure out for themselves which cards were the scarcest.

Donruss Preferred (in the "cough drop" tins) also was issued with varying levels of scarcity. The 200-card set was divided into 100 bronze cards, 60 silver, 30 gold and 10 platinum. Again the best/most popular players were in the higher levels of scarcity, but at least the concept was straightforward.

The closing months of 1997 also saw the first-ever product to be completely serially numbered. Pinnacle's Totally Certified Baseball offered three parallel issues of 150 cards each. The base cards, dubbed "Platinum Red," were numbered on back within an edition of 3,999 each; Platinum Blue cards were issued to a total of 1,999 each, and Platinum Gold cards were numbered only to 30 apiece. Cases were individually numbered to 999.

While the Totally Certified concept has not yet been totally embraced by the hobby, it has a lot going for it that collectors and dealers have been seeking from the card companies. First and foremost, everything is numbered, there is no question about production quantities and, thus, scarcity or rarity. Secondly, the set is very straightforward while still offering each collector a price-point option. Persons can collect a base set of red cards at minimal prices, step-up to the blues for a greater challenge, or go for the gold in what could become a years-long quest. The set size of 150 players means that every card is either an established star or a hot prospect.

It has taken only seven years since Donruss introduced the first serially numbered baseball cards (1991 Elite Series) until the first all-numbered set was created. It is a virtual certainty that numbering of individual cards will become more prevalent in the coming years as collectors seek to get the most perceived value for their card buying dollars.

Renaming its premium priced product Flair Showcase for 1997, Fleer took the concept of base set scarcity to a new — and much more complex — level. The base set(s) of Flair Showcase consisted of 160 cards in each of three different designs. Fronts are labeled either Style, Grace or Showcase. Backs are labeled Showtime, Show Stopper or Showpiece. This creates nine different front-back combinations in varying levels of scarcity which are also affected by the player's card number within the ranges of 1-60, 61-120 and 121-160. No wonder the Flair boxes carry a warning label indicating the issue is for the serious collector only.

Regardless of whether collectors understood the Flair Showcase set system, the product earned a place in hobby history by taking the chase card to its ultimate level — one, single, solitary card. Among the inserts in Flair Showcase was a 180 player Legacy Collection parallel set, with each player represented in Style, Grace and Showcase versions, enhanced with metallic blue foil.

For all practical purposes, the completion of a 540 card Legacy set would be an impossibility. Even if a collector had the inclination and the money, it would require a lifetime of searching. But even that quest pales in comparison to the hunt for the ultimate insert card, Legacy Masterpiece.

One-of-a-kind inserts issued

A parallel set of the Legacy parallel set, Masterpiece cards were produced in an edition of exactly one card each. Like the Legacy cards, the Masterpiece can be found in Style, Grace and Showcase versions. They differ from the "common" Legacy cards in that they are foil enhanced on front with metallic purple and have the notation printed on back, "The Only 1 of 1 Masterpiece". Found on average of about one per 3,000 packs, these cards set off a frenzy of flying foil as collectors tore through the five card, $4.99 suggested retail.

At the top end of the Legacy Masterpiece scale is Ken Griffey, Jr. All three of his Masterpiece versions have been found. One collector bought up two of them for a reported $12,000 apiece, and the third is held by a man who has turned down $10,000.

Since many collectors find it difficult or impossible to "cash in" the chase cards they may be lucky enough to pull from packs, some companies in 1997 took the lottery to the next step, offering cash awards. Fleer's "Million Dollar Moments" sweepstakes began in 1997 and will continue into 1998 across the company's brands in all sports. Any collector who assembles all 50 Moments cards of a particular sport will win a million dollars. Other cash awards are also available. The catch is, again, only one card of No. 50, Jeff Bagwell, was released, and severely limited numbers of the other cards Nos. 45-49 which could be redeemed for lesser cash prizes.

Another cash award angle was instituted by Pinnacle with the introduction of its New Pinnacle brand in mid-season. As random pack inserts, the actual color plates used to print the fronts and backs of the cards were cut up, autographed by company president Jerry Meyer and inserted. If any collector accumulated all four different color plates (red, blue, yellow, black) for either the front or back of any card, the set could be exchanged for a prize that began at $30,000 prior to Aug. 29, dropped to $25,000 before Sept. 5, then stood at $20,000 through the end of the year. As of press time, nobody had yet claimed the prize. Again, by spreading the press plate pieces all over the country, the chance of any one person being able to assemble a complete set was very remote. Pinnacle did offer a spot on its web site where collectors who found any of the press-plates could list them in hopes that those who had the others might contact them.

Motion, new materials lead technology

As has been the case once Topps tapped on a bit of gold foil for its 1991 Stadium Club premiere, the technology of card production made major advances in 1997.

The most impressive steps forward in card technology in 1997 were the various "motion" cards. Most of the major manufacturers issued products which offered several seconds of game action on a card as the viewer changed the angle of its perspective. Pitchers threw the ball, batters hit the ball and base-runners slid into second. Motion technology had been experimented with as far back as 1986 by Sportflics, which offered a two-frame action sequence when tilted. The current generation, represented by such issues as Topps Screen Plays, Premier Concepts Instant Replay, Upper Deck's Highlight Reel and Zenith V2 can have two dozen or more individual frames sandwiched together to create the action.

Besides creating a nearly seamless flow of action, the most recent generation of motion cards is brighter, requiring less light from behind to see and appreciate the movement on the card. Similar strides have been made in the clarity of holographic action cards, such as Stadium Club's Instavision.

The motion technology did not come cheaply, however. Top-of-the-line products such as Screen Plays have a suggested retail price of $10 per card, while the large format Instant Replay cards retail for nearly $30.

Collectors can rest assured that the limits of this technology have not yet been reached. The research and development arms of all card companies are hard at work to improve what exists and create even better forms of motion cards. The current generation of hobbyists will surely see the day when a card held in the hand will project a 3-D holographic image of a ballplayer in action, complete with sound.

While not a new process, the printing of cards on metal or embossed metallic foil was again very much in evidence in 1997's baseball card issues. Generally reserved for long-odds inserts, the latest generation of metal printed cards represents an incremental step forward in detailing.

Among the metallic cards in 1997 was Pinnacle X Press' Metal Works silver and gold inserts, with prices running as high as $100. Insert odds of one per 470 packs for a silver redemption card and one per 950 packs for a gold redemption card were advertised.

Pinnacle also introduced a "two-part" baseball card in 1997 with its Mint Collection. Each of the 30 players cards in the set were issued in four versions. Three of the parallels were cards highlighted by bronze, silver or gold foil team logos. The fourth was die-cut with a quarter-sized hole in which to theoretically fit a "coin" of the same player. The pure gold coins were minted in an edition of just one each, and the stated odds of finding a redemption card for a gold coin were one per 47,200 packs.

The Donruss division of Pinnacle also had redemption cards inserted into its Preferred "tin" packs which could be exchanged for a top-of-the-line partial parallel set of cards printed on silver, gold and platinum in an edition of no more than 100 each. Values there range from $50 for a "common" silver player to more than $750 for a gold superstar.

The use of non-cardboard stock for cards was not limited to metal in 1997. Donruss Limited produced a set of inserts with each player represented on wood, leather and canvas cards as varying levels of rarity. Over at Leaf, the Frank Thomas Collection was inserted with cards made from all manners of his game used equipment: hat, home and away jerseys, batting gloves, bats and sweat bands.

With such exotic production techniques proliferating in 1997, one of the most innovative technologies of the year was pretty much overlooked and under-appreciated by collectors because it was "only" a card printed on die-cut cardboard and plastic. SkyBox E-X2000's base set consisted of cards with a die-cut player photo centered on an acetate background of blue sky and clouds.

It may be an arguable point, but 1997 may one day be seen as the year in which despite greatly reduced numbers of both card collectors and baseball fans – the issue of baseball cards became a year-round effort, and a rather prodigious one at that. All told, the major companies produced more than 50 full-size sets in 1997, and literally hundreds of insert sets spawned from that number.

For the average collector, though, 1997 wasn't so bad. There were lots of choices of available product, generally at favorable prices (if the collector was patient enough to wait for the price softening which inevitably followed virtually every new issue), and in exciting new technologies.

In 1997 the baseball card hobby went as far as it could go with year-round issue of new cards, scarcity of inserts and serial numbering of cards within a set. Whether 1998 will bring similar superlatives remains to be seen.

INSERT SINGLES

THE FOLLOWING LIST OF CARDS HAVE GENERATED THE MOST DEMAND WITHIN THE HOBBY OVER THE LAST YEAR. THE RANKINGS ARE DETERMINED BY COLLECTORS AND DEALERS FROM THE HOBBY.

No. 1 — KEN GRIFFEY JR.

'96 Select Certified Mirror Gold #47
Junior's MVP award should be the first of many more to come. No other player in the baseball card hobby commands the nationwide demand from collectors as Junior does, which is why this one remains perched at the No.1 position this month. Expect to pay $3,200 for this hot single, which is limited to only 30.

No. 2 — KEN GRIFFEY JR.
'97 Upper Deck Game Jersey #GJ1
This game-used jersey insert would be a welcome addition to any Junior collection. The odds are long (1:2,500 packs) and the price tag is steep at $600.

No. 3 — KEN GRIFFEY JR.

'97 Flair Showcase Legacy #24
Only 100 serially numbered versions exist of this one, and die-hard Junior collectors are clamoring to get their hands on this $600 insert.

No. 4 — KEN GRIFFEY JR.

'97 Pinnacle Certified Mirror Gold #53
This Mirror Gold insert jumps one spot this month due to strong demand. Reports have this one retailing in the $2,500 range.

No. 5 — KEN GRIFFEY JR.

'97 SkyBox E-X2000 Essential Credentials #40
Junior's first MVP award, along with his drive to break Maris' home run mark, has fueled demand for his top inserts, including this one for $600.

No. 6 — NOMAR GARCIAPARRA

'97 Totally Certified Platinum Gold #114
Garciaparra proved that he is already one of the top players in all of baseball as he was the unanimous Rookie of the Year winner. This one goes for $600.

No. 7 — KEN GRIFFEY JR.

'97 Circa Rave #24
Only 150 serially numbered versions of this Junior insert exist, which helps explain the strong demand for it. Dealers report getting $300 to $350 for this one.

No. 8 — KEN GRIFFEY JR.

'97 Pinnacle Certified Mirror Blue #53
This is the seventh Junior insert in our Top 10s for the year, but not without good reason. Collectors are demanding this hot $1,000 insert.

No. 9 — SCOTT ROLEN

'95 Bowman's Best Refractor #87
His unanimous selection as NL Rookie of the Year has solidified his spot as one of the top young third basemen in baseball. This one currently books at $120.

No. 10 — FRANK THOMAS

'97 Flair Showcase Legacy #35
The Big Hurt's huge season was lost in Junior's and McGwire's shadow. He continues to punish opposing pitchers, as this one moves in the $500 range.

INSERT SETS

THE FOLLOWING LIST OF SETS HAVE GENERATED THE MOST DEMAND WITHIN THE HOBBY OVER THE LAST YEAR. THE RANKINGS ARE DETERMINED BY COLLECTORS AND DEALERS FROM THE HOBBY.

No. 1 — 1997 TOTALLY CERTIFIED PLATINUM GOLD

Platinum Golds catapult to the No. 1 spot for the year, as strong secondary activity and strong retail sales have fueled demand for the Platinum Golds. Collectors love to chase this set, which is serially numbered to 30 and seeded at 1:79 packs.

No. 2 — 1996 SELECT CERTIFIED MIRROR GOLD

You just don't find many of these singles sitting in dealers' showcases. The few star singles out there command strong prices.

No. 3 — 1997 FLAIR SHOWCASE LEGACY COLLECTION

Dealers report strong activity for any of the star singles, with the Clemens vaulting to $175 and the Garciaparra to $250.

No. 4 — 1997 PINNACLE CERTIFIED MIRROR GOLD

Collectors love the thrill of the chase of these 1:299-pack parallel inserts. The Griffey is the most sought after, at around $2,500.

No. 5 — 1997 SKYBOX E-X 2000 ESSENTIAL CREDENTIALS

Although this set has cooled off recently, Essential Credentials are experiencing continued strong demand.

No. 6 — 1997 DONRUSS LIMITED EXPOSURE

These Refractor-like inserts are stirring demand, as only 40 sets of the Star Factors are thought to exist. The Junior is priced at $800.

No. 7 — 1997 PINNACLE CERTIFIED MIRROR BLUE

These 1:199-pack Mirror Blues are almost as fun as getting the Mirror Golds, which is why it's No. 7 on our Top Ten lists.

No. 8 — 1997 CIRCA RAVES

As a number of new products have hit the market the past few months, these have been lost in the mix. But that doesn't dismiss the fact that Raves are serially numbered to 150 sets.

No. 9 — 1996 SELECT CERTIFIED MIRROR BLUE

Only 60 sets are thought to exist, which makes for a lot of pack-busting. The Clemens jumps to $350 this month.

No. 10 — 1996 LEAF SIGNATURE SERIES EXTENDED AUTOGRAPHS

The strong checklist, which includes Clemens, Gwynn, Maddux, Puckett and Thomas, helps fuel demand for this set.

REGULAR-ISSUE SINGLES

THE FOLLOWING LIST OF CARDS HAVE GENERATED THE MOST DEMAND WITHIN THE HOBBY OVER THE LAST YEAR. THE RANKINGS ARE DETERMINED BY COLLECTORS AND DEALERS FROM THE HOBBY.

No. 1
LAST MONTH No. 2

NOMAR GARCIAPARRA
'92 Topps Traded #39T
This card has climbed all the way to No. 1 as dealers report strong demand for this Topps Traded issue. Most of the year, collectors could have picked up this single for a mere $4, but his unanimous Rookie of the Year award and big year at the plate has propelled this one to a $25 price tag.

1996 BOWMAN LIVAN HERNANDEZ #286

A World Series MVP award has done wonders for this rookie card, as Hernandez helped to lead the Florida Marlins past the Cleveland Indians. This one was priced at 50 cents a year ago, but has since catapulted to its current price tag of $4.

No. 2
KEN GRIFFEY JR.
'89 Upper Deck #1
This rookie card should be the cornerstone of any serious Junior collection. Demand remains strong following another huge season, as this one is priced at $90.

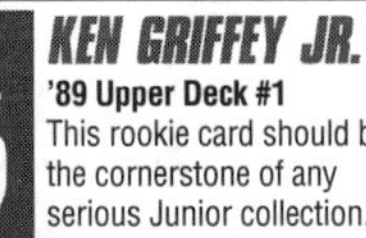

No. 3
JOSE CRUZ JR.
'97 Bowman #100
Although it's not ranked No. 1, that doesn't diminish the impact Cruz had on the Toronto Blue Jays. Cruz's most popular rookie card moves for $20.

No. 4
JOSE CRUZ JR.
'97 Bowman's Best #188
Cruz is already considered one of the top hitting outfielders in the A.L. This rookie card continues to be popular and remains a fast mover in the $25 range.

No. 5
SCOTT ROLEN
'95 Bowman's Best #87
You can't argue with a unanimous Rookie of the Year selection for Rolen, who should become the cornerstone of the Phillie infield. This one jumps up to $25.

No. 6
TRAVIS LEE
'97 Bowman #389
After dominating the minor leagues with 32 homers and 109 RBI, Lee is expected to start at first base for the expansion Arizona Diamondbacks. His rookie remains at

No. 7
TONY GWYNN
'83 Topps #482
Gwynn is finally getting well-deserved recognition after winning his eighth batting title. This rookie is one of the best bargains in the hobby right now, at $50.

No. 8
MARK MCGWIRE
'85 Topps #401
The best power-hitter in the game, McGwire will hit the long ball to parts unknown as long as he stays healthy. This slugger's rookie currently sells for $25.

No. 9
ROGER CLEMENS
'85 Donruss #273/ '85 Fleer #155
Behind his dominating Cy Young season, Clemens is solidifying his spot in the Hall of Fame. Dealers are getting a strong $25 each for both cards.

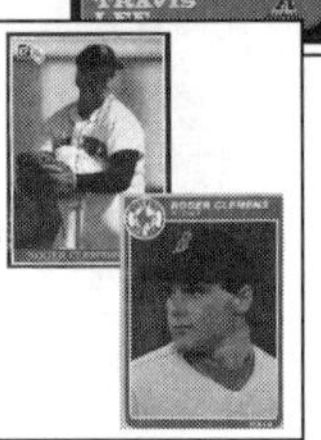

No. 10
TRAVIS LEE
'97 Bowman's Best #187
He's one of the hottest players in the hobby, and he hasn't played a major league game yet. That will change next year, though, as this one remains priced at $20.

REGULAR-ISSUE SETS

THE FOLLOWING LIST OF SETS HAVE GENERATED THE MOST DEMAND WITHIN THE HOBBY OVER THE LAST YEAR. THE RANKINGS ARE DETERMINED BY COLLECTORS AND DEALERS FROM THE HOBBY.

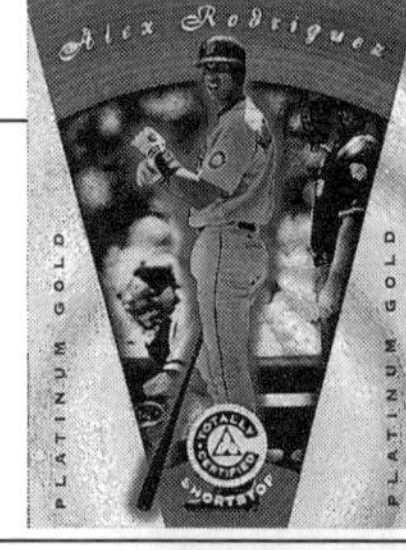

No. 1
1997 TOTALLY CERTIFIED
Collectors have the utmost confidence in this product, as every card is serially numbered. The Platinum Reds are numbered to 3,999, Platinum Blues to 1,999 and the Platinum Golds to 30. Dealers report strong demand for Totally Certified, with packs retailing for $10 to $12 and boxes in the $200 range. The Platinum Red set books for $500, and the Platinum Blue for $1,000.

1992 BOWMAN

This is one of those products that will always hold its value. The '92 Bowman has become the standard by which all ensuing Bowman issues have followed. The strong rookie selection, which includes Mike Piazza, Manny Ramirez and Chipper Jones, has led to a steady set price in the last year of $325.

No. 2
1997 BOWMAN
Rookie cards is the name of the game in Bowman. The Jose Cruz Jr. and Travis Lee singles are among the hottest singles in the market. The 441-card set carries a $150 price tag.

No. 3
1997 FLAIR SHOWCASE
The Legacy Collection inserts and the one-of-a-kind Legacy Masterpieces continue to be the driving force behind this Showcase. Packs sell for $7-$8.

No. 4
1997 PINNACLE CERTIFIED
Although it drops one spot this month, dealers report strong pack sales, as collectors love to gamble on getting a Mirror Gold.

No. 5
1997 DONRUSS LIMITED
The Limited Exposures are helping fuel demand, along with the Fabric of the Game inserts. Packs are retailing for $5 and boxes for around $100.

No. 6
1997 BOWMAN'S BEST
With a strong selection of rookies, and for the first time offering autographs, Bowman's Best continues to be a hot seller. The set is booking for $100.

No. 7
1997 SKYBOX E-X2000
With two serially numbered inserts (Credentials, Essential Credentials) it should be no surprise why E-X2000 is faring so well.

No. 8
1997 FLEER SPORTS ILLUSTRATED
The partnership of SI and Fleer is already paying big dividends, as collectors love this debut offering. Packs are at $2, with the set at $40.

No. 9
1997 PINNACLE ZENITH
Collectors like getting two 8x10 cards in every pack, which has five base cards. Packs are selling for around $10, with the 50-card set priced at $50.

No. 10
1995 BOWMAN
Scott Rolen's rookie card has climbed to $25, while Garciaparra's first Bowman card has risen to $25. Ben Grieve's card is also active, as the 439-card set currently carries a $175 price tag.

1996 Bowman's Best

Bowman's Best returns in its traditional format of 180 cards, including 90 established stars and 90 up-and-coming prospects and rookies. There are three types of insert sets found in Bowman's Best - Mirror Image, Bowman's Best Cuts and the 1952 Bowman Mickey Mantle reprint. Mirror Image features four top players and 10 different positions, pairing an American League veteran and a prospect on one side, and a National League veteran and a prospect on the other. These cards are seeded one per 48 packs. Bowman's Best Cuts are die-cut chromium cards of 15 top stars; they are seeded one per 24 packs. There is also a 1952 Bowman Mickey Mantle chromium reprint found in every 24th pack. This is No. 20 in the Mantle reprint series from 1996 Topps Baseball. There are also Refractors and Atomic Refractors randomly seeded in packs. They form parallel sets. Regular issue Refractors are seeded one per every 12 packs; Atomic Refractors are seeded one per every 48 packs. Mirror Image Refractors are found one per every 96 packs, while Mirror Image Atomic Refractors are seeded one per every 192 packs. Bowman's Best Cuts Refractors are seeded in every 48th pack, while Bowman's Best Cuts Atomic Refractors are in every 96th pack. Refractor versions of the Mantle reprint are seeded one per every 96 packs; Atomic Refractor Mantle reprints are seeded in every 192nd pack.

		MT
Complete Set (180):		100.00
Common Player:		.25
Complete Refractor Set (180):		2000.
Veteran Star Refractors:		5x to 10x
Young Stars and RCs:		4x to 8x
Veteran Star Atomics:		40x to 50x
Young Stars and RCs Atomics:		25x to 35x
1952 Mickey Mantle:		8.00
1952 Mantle Refractor:		20.00
1952 Mantle Atomic Refractor:		40.00
Wax Box:		160.00
1	Hideo Nomo	1.25
2	Edgar Martinez	.25
3	Cal Ripken Jr.	5.00
4	Wade Boggs	.50
5	Cecil Fielder	.50
6	Albert Belle	1.75
7	Chipper Jones	4.00
8	Ryne Sandberg	1.50
9	Tim Salmon	.75
10	Barry Bonds	1.50
11	Ken Caminiti	.75
12	Ron Gant	.25
13	Frank Thomas	6.00
14	Dante Bichette	.75
15	Jason Kendall	.25
16	Mo Vaughn	1.50
17	Rey Ordonez	.40
18	Henry Rodriguez	.25
19	Ryan Klesko	.75
20	Jeff Bagwell	2.00
21	Randy Johnson	1.00
22	Jim Edmonds	.50
23	Kenny Lofton	1.50
24	Andy Pettitte	1.50
25	Brady Anderson	.40
26	Mike Piazza	4.00
27	Greg Vaughn	.25
28	Joe Carter	.40
29	Jason Giambi	.25
30	Ivan Rodriguez	1.25
31	Jeff Conine	.25
32	Rafael Palmeiro	.40
33	Roger Clemens	2.00
34	Chuck Knoblauch	.50
35	Reggie Sanders	.25
36	Andres Galarraga	.50
37	Paul O'Neill	.50
38	Tony Gwynn	3.00
39	Paul Wilson	.25
40	Garret Anderson	.25
41	David Justice	.40
42	Eddie Murray	.75
43	*Mike Grace*	.50
44	Marty Cordova	.40
45	Kevin Appier	.25
46	Raul Mondesi	.50
47	Jim Thome	.75
48	Sammy Sosa	.75
49	Craig Biggio	.35
50	Marquis Grissom	.25
51	Alan Benes	.25
52	Manny Ramirez	1.50
53	Gary Sheffield	.75
54	Mike Mussina	1.00
55	Robin Ventura	.25
56	Johnny Damon	.25
57	Jose Canseco	.50
58	Juan Gonzalez	3.00
59	Tino Martinez	.65
60	Brian Hunter	.25
61	Fred McGriff	.60
62	Jay Buhner	.40
63	Carlos Delgado	.25
64	Moises Alou	.35
65	Roberto Alomar	1.00
66	Barry Larkin	.50
67	Vinny Castilla	.25
68	Ray Durham	.25
69	Travis Fryman	.25
70	Jason Isringhausen	.25
71	Ken Griffey Jr.	6.00
72	John Smoltz	.40
73	Matt Williams	.50
74	Chan Ho Park	.25
75	Mark McGwire	2.00
76	Jeffrey Hammonds	.25
77	Will Clark	.50
78	Kirby Puckett	2.00
79	Derek Jeter	4.00
80	Derek Bell	.25
81	Eric Karros	.25
82	Lenny Dykstra	.25
83	Larry Walker	.75
84	Mark Grudzielanek	.25
85	Greg Maddux	3.50
86	Carlos Baerga	.25
87	Paul Molitor	.50
88	John Valentin	.25
89	Mark Grace	.40
90	Ray Lankford	.25
91	Andruw Jones	8.00
92	Nomar Garciaparra	4.00
93	Alex Ochoa	.25
94	Derrick Gibson	.25
95	Jeff D'Amico	.25
96	Ruben Rivera	.50
97	Vladimir Guerrero	5.00
98	Calvin Reese	.25
99	Richard Hidalgo	.25
100	Bartolo Colon	1.00
101	Karim Garcia	1.25
102	Ben Davis	1.00
103	Jay Powell	.25
104	Chris Snopek	.25
105	*Glendon Rusch*	.40
106	Enrique Wilson	.25
107	*Antonio Alfonseca*	.25
108	Wilton Guerrero	2.00
109	*Jose Guillen*	10.00
110	*Miguel Mejia*	.25
111	Jay Payton	.75
112	Scott Elarton	.50
113	Brooks Kieschnick	.25
114	Dustin Hermanson	.25
115	Roger Cedeno	.25
116	Matt Wagner	.25
117	Lee Daniels	.25
118	Ben Grieve	4.00
119	Ugueth Urbina	.25
120	Danny Graves	.50
121	*Dan Donato*	.25
122	*Matt Ruebel*	.25
123	*Mark Sievert*	.25
124	Chris Stynes	.25
125	Jeff Abbott	.25
126	*Rocky Coppinger*	.75
127	Jermaine Dye	.50
128	Todd Greene	.25
129	Chris Carpenter	.25
130	Edgar Renteria	.75
131	Matt Drews	.25
132	*Edgard Velazquez*	3.00
133	Casey Whitten	.25
134	*Ryan Jones*	.75
135	Todd Walker	2.00
136	*Geoff Jenkins*	2.50
137	*Matt Morris*	2.50
138	Richie Sexson	.25
139	*Todd Dunwoody*	1.00
140	*Gabe Alvarez*	1.00
141	J.J. Johnson	.25
142	Shannon Stewart	.25
143	Brad Fullmer	.50
144	Julio Santana	.25
145	Scott Rolen	4.00
146	Amaury Telemaco	.25
147	Trey Beamon	.25
148	Billy Wagner	.25
149	Todd Hollandsworth	.25
150	Doug Million	.25
151	*Jose Valentin*	2.00
152	*Wes Helms*	6.00
153	Jeff Suppan	.25
154	*Luis Castillo*	2.00
155	Bob Abreu	.25
156	Paul Konerko	3.00
157	Jamey Wright	.25
158	Eddie Pearson	.25
159	Jimmy Haynes	.25
160	Derrek Lee	.75
161	Damian Moss	.75
162	*Carlos Guillen*	.25
163	*Chris Fussell*	1.00
164	*Mike Sweeney*	1.00
165	Donnie Sadler	.25
166	Desi Relaford	.25
167	Steve Gibralter	.25
168	Neifi Perez	.30
169	Antone Williamson	.25
170	*Marty Janzen*	.25
171	Todd Helton	8.00
172	*Raul Ibanez*	.25
173	Bill Selby	.25
174	*Shane Monahan*	1.50
175	*Robin Jennings*	.25
176	*Bobby Chouinard*	.25
177	Einar Diaz	.25
178	Jason Thompson	.25
179	*Rafael Medina*	1.00
180	Kevin Orie	1.00

1996 Bowman's Best Cuts

Bowman's Best Cuts give collectors the first die-cut chromium cards in a 15-card set of top stars. The cards were seeded one per every 24 packs. Refractor versions were also made; they are seeded one per every 48 packs. Atomic Refractor versions were seeded one per every 96 packs.

		MT
Complete Set (15):		200.00
Common Player:		4.00
1	Ken Griffey Jr.	30.00
2	Jason Isringhausen	4.00
3	Derek Jeter	20.00
4	Andruw Jones	25.00
5	Chipper Jones	20.00
6	Ryan Klesko	6.00
7	Raul Mondesi	4.00
8	Hideo Nomo	8.00
9	Mike Piazza	20.00
10	Manny Ramirez	8.00
11	Cal Ripken Jr.	25.00
12	Ruben Rivera	4.00
13	Tim Salmon	5.00
14	Frank Thomas	30.00
15	Jim Thome	6.00

1996 Bowman's Best Cuts Refractors

Two Refractor versions are made of these die-cut chromium cards - regular Refractors and Atomic Refractors. The regular versions are seeded one per every 48 packs; Atomic Refractors appear in every 96th pack.

		MT
Complete Set (15):		325.00
Common Player:		8.00
Atomics:		2x
1	Ken Griffey Jr.	60.00
2	Jason Isringhausen	8.00
3	Derek Jeter	40.00
4	Andruw Jones	40.00
5	Chipper Jones	40.00
6	Ryan Klesko	10.00
7	Raul Mondesi	10.00
8	Hideo Nomo	15.00
9	Mike Piazza	40.00
10	Manny Ramirez	15.00
11	Cal Ripken Jr.	50.00
12	Ruben Rivera	10.00
13	Tim Salmon	10.00
14	Frank Thomas	60.00
15	Jim Thome	12.00

1996 Bowman's Best Mirror Image

Mirror Image inserts feature four top players at 10 different positions, pairing an American League veteran and a prospect on one side and a National League veteran and prospect on the other. These cards are seeded one per every 48 packs. Mirror Image Refractors (one in every 96 packs) and Mirror Image Atomic Refractors (one in every 192 packs) were also produced.

		MT
Complete Set (10):		200.00
Common Player:		8.00
Refractors:		1.5x to 2x
Atomics:		2x to 4x
1	Jeff Bagwell, Todd Helton, Frank Thomas, Richie Sexson	30.00
2	Craig Biggio, Luis Castillo, Roberto Alomar, Desi Relaford	10.00
3	Chipper Jones, Scott Rolen, Wade Boggs, George Arias	25.00
4	Barry Larkin, Neifi Perez, Cal Ripken Jr., Mark Bellhorn	25.00
5	Larry Walker, Karim Garcia, Albert Belle, Ruben Rivera	10.00

6	Barry Bonds, Andruw Jones, Kenny Lofton, Donnie Sadler	20.00
7	Tony Gwynn, Vladimir Guerrero, Ken Griffey Jr., Ben Grieve	40.00
8	Mike Piazza, Ben Davis, Ivan Rodriguez, Jose Valentin	20.00
9	Greg Maddux, Jamey Wright, Mike Mussina, Bartolo Colon	20.00
10	Tom Glavine, Billy Wagner, Randy Johnson, Jarrod Washburn	10.00

1996 Circa

This hobby exclusive product is limited to 2,000 sequentially numbered cases. The regular issue set has 196 player cards, including 18 top prospects and four prospects. Circa also has a 200-card parallel set called Rave which is limited to 150 sets. Each Rave card is sequentially numbered from 1-150. Two other insert sets were also produced - Boss, and Access.

		MT
Complete Set (200):		25.00
Common Player:		.10
1	Roberto Alomar	.75
2	Brady Anderson	.20
3	*Rocky Coppinger*	.10
4	Eddie Murray	.40
5	Mike Mussina	.75
6	Randy Myers	.10
7	Rafael Palmeiro	.25
8	Cal Ripken Jr.	2.50
9	Jose Canseco	.30
10	Roger Clemens	1.00
11	Mike Greenwell	.10
12	Tim Naehring	.10
13	John Valentin	.15
14	Mo Vaughn	1.00
15	Tim Wakefield	.10
16	Jim Abbott	.10
17	Garret Anderson	.10
18	Jim Edmonds	.25
19	*Darin Erstad*	2.50
20	Chuck Finley	.10
21	Troy Percival	.10
22	Tim Salmon	.20
23	J.T. Snow	.15
24	Wilson Alvarez	.10
25	Harold Baines	.12
26	Ray Durham	.10
27	Alex Fernandez	.20
28	Tony Phillips	.15
29	Frank Thomas	3.00
30	Robin Ventura	.15
31	Sandy Alomar Jr.	.15
32	Albert Belle	1.00
33	Kenny Lofton	1.00
34	Dennis Martinez	.10
35	Jose Mesa	.10
36	Charles Nagy	.10
37	Manny Ramirez	.75
37p	Manny Ramirez (overprinted "PROMOTIONAL SAMPLE")	3.00
38	Jim Thome	.50
39	Travis Fryman	.10
40	Bob Higginson	.20
41	Melvin Nieves	.10

42	Alan Trammell	.10
43	Kevin Appier	.10
44	Johnny Damon	.10
45	Keith Lockhart	.10
46	Jeff Montgomery	.10
47	Joe Randa	.10
48	Bip Roberts	.10
49	Ricky Bones	.10
50	Jeff Cirillo	.10
51	Marc Newfield	.10
52	Dave Nilsson	.10
53	Kevin Seitzer	.10
54	Ron Coomer	.10
55	Marty Cordova	.20
56	Roberto Kelly	.10
57	Chuck Knoblauch	.30
58	Paul Molitor	.50
59	Kirby Puckett	1.00
60	Scott Stahoviak	.10
61	Wade Boggs	.25
62	David Cone	.20
63	Cecil Fielder	.20
64	Dwight Gooden	.15
65	Derek Jeter	1.50
66	Tino Martinez	.30
67	Paul O'Neill	.20
68	Andy Pettitte	1.00
69	Ruben Rivera	.30
70	Bernie Williams	.50
71	Geronimo Berroa	.10
72	Jason Giambi	.20
73	Mark McGwire	1.00
74	Terry Steinbach	.10
75	Todd Van Poppel	.10
76	Jay Buhner	.20
77	Norm Charlton	.10
78	Ken Griffey Jr.	3.00
79	Randy Johnson	.50
80	Edgar Martinez	.10
81	Alex Rodriguez	3.00
82	Paul Sorrento	.10
83	Dan Wilson	.10
84	Will Clark	.30
85	Kevin Elster	.10
86	Juan Gonzalez	1.50
87	Rusty Greer	.10
88	Ken Hill	.10
89	Mark McLemore	.10
90	Dean Palmer	.10
91	Roger Pavlik	.10
92	Ivan Rodriguez	.75
93	Joe Carter	.20
94	Carlos Delgado	.15
95	Juan Guzman	.10
96	John Olerud	.15
97	Ed Sprague	.10
98	Jermaine Dye	.20
99	Tom Glavine	.20
100	Marquis Grissom	.10
101	Andruw Jones	2.50
102	Chipper Jones	2.00
103	David Justice	.25
104	Ryan Klesko	.50
105	Greg Maddux	2.00
106	Fred McGriff	.40
107	John Smoltz	.25
108	Brant Brown	.10
109	Mark Grace	.25
110	Brian McRae	.10
111	Ryne Sandberg	.75
112	Sammy Sosa	.30
113	Steve Trachsel	.10
114	Bret Boone	.10
115	Eric Davis	.12
116	Steve Gibralter	.10
117	Barry Larkin	.25
118	Reggie Sanders	.15
119	John Smiley	.10
120	Dante Bichette	.25
121	Ellis Burks	.15
122	Vinny Castilla	.10
123	Andres Galarraga	.20
124	Larry Walker	.40
125	Eric Young	.10
126	Kevin Brown	.10
127	Greg Colbrunn	.10
128	Jeff Conine	.15
129	Charles Johnson	.15
130	Al Leiter	.10
131	Gary Sheffield	.40
132	Devon White	.10
133	Jeff Bagwell	1.25
134	Derek Bell	.15
135	Craig Biggio	.20
136	Doug Drabek	.10
137	Brian Hunter	.10
138	Darryl Kile	.10
139	Shane Reynolds	.10
140	Brett Butler	.10
141	Eric Karros	.15
142	Ramon Martinez	.10

143	Raul Mondesi	.25
144	Hideo Nomo	.75
145	Chan Ho Park	.12
146	Mike Piazza	2.00
147	Moises Alou	.20
148	Yamil Benitez	.10
149	Mark Grudzielanek	.10
150	Pedro Martinez	.20
151	Henry Rodriguez	.10
152	David Segui	.10
153	Rondell White	.20
154	Carlos Baerga	.10
155	John Franco	.10
156	Bernard Gilkey	.10
157	Todd Hundley	.20
158	Jason Isringhausen	.15
159	Lance Johnson	.10
160	Alex Ochoa	.10
161	Rey Ordonez	.25
162	Paul Wilson	.20
163	Ron Blazier	.10
164	Ricky Bottalico	.10
165	Jim Eisenreich	.10
166	Pete Incaviglia	.10
167	Mickey Morandini	.10
168	Ricky Otero	.10
169	Curt Schilling	.10
170	Jay Bell	.10
171	Charlie Hayes	.10
172	Jason Kendall	.15
173	Jeff King	.10
174	Al Martin	.10
175	Alan Benes	.20
176	Royce Clayton	.10
177	Brian Jordan	.10
178	Ray Lankford	.10
179	John Mabry	.10
180	Willie McGee	.10
181	Ozzie Smith	.50
182	Todd Stottlemyre	.10
183	Andy Ashby	.10
184	Ken Caminiti	.25
185	Steve Finley	.10
186	Tony Gwynn	1.50
187	Rickey Henderson	.10
188	Wally Joyner	.15
189	Fernando Valenzuela	.10
190	Greg Vaughn	.10
191	Rod Beck	.10
192	Barry Bonds	1.00
193	Shawon Dunston	.15
194	Chris Singleton	.10
195	Robby Thompson	.10
196	Matt Williams	.25
197	Checklist (Barry Bonds)	.30
198	Checklist (Ken Griffey Jr.)	1.00
199	Checklist (Cal Ripken Jr.)	.75
200	Checklist (Frank Thomas)	1.00

1996 Circa Rave

Circa also has a 200-card parallel set called Rave which is limited to 150 sets. Each Rave card is sequentially numbered from 1-150.

		MT
Common Player:		25.00
Raves:		75x to 120x
1	Roberto Alomar	90.00
2	Brady Anderson	30.00
3	*Rocky Coppinger*	25.00
4	Eddie Murray	75.00
5	Mike Mussina	75.00
6	Randy Myers	25.00
7	Rafael Palmeiro	40.00
8	Cal Ripken Jr.	350.00
9	Jose Canseco	40.00
10	Roger Clemens	120.00
11	Mike Greenwell	25.00
12	Tim Naehring	25.00
13	John Valentin	25.00
14	Mo Vaughn	100.00
15	Tim Wakefield	25.00
16	Jim Abbott	25.00
17	Garret Anderson	25.00
18	Jim Edmonds	35.00
19	Darin Erstad	150.00
20	Chuck Finley	25.00
21	Troy Percival	25.00
22	Tim Salmon	40.00
23	J.T. Snow	25.00
24	Wilson Alvarez	25.00
25	Harold Baines	25.00
26	Ray Durham	25.00
27	Alex Fernandez	25.00
28	Tony Phillips	25.00
29	Frank Thomas	400.00
30	Robin Ventura	25.00

31	Sandy Alomar Jr.	40.00
32	Albert Belle	125.00
33	Kenny Lofton	90.00
34	Dennis Martinez	25.00
35	Jose Mesa	25.00
36	Charles Nagy	25.00
37	Manny Ramirez	90.00
38	Jim Thome	50.00
39	Travis Fryman	25.00
40	Bob Higginson	25.00
41	Melvin Nieves	25.00
42	Alan Trammell	25.00
43	Kevin Appier	25.00
44	Johnny Damon	25.00
45	Keith Lockhart	25.00
46	Jeff Montgomery	25.00
47	Joe Randa	25.00
48	Bip Roberts	25.00
49	Ricky Bones	25.00
50	Jeff Cirillo	25.00
51	Marc Newfield	25.00
52	Dave Nilsson	25.00
53	Kevin Seitzer	25.00
54	Ron Coomer	25.00
55	Marty Cordova	25.00
56	Roberto Kelly	25.00
57	Chuck Knoblauch	50.00
58	Paul Molitor	80.00
59	Kirby Puckett	160.00
60	Scott Stahoviak	25.00
61	Wade Boggs	40.00
62	David Cone	30.00
63	Cecil Fielder	35.00
64	Dwight Gooden	25.00
65	Derek Jeter	225.00
66	Tino Martinez	50.00
67	Paul O'Neill	40.00
68	Andy Pettitte	100.00
69	Ruben Rivera	50.00
70	Bernie Williams	70.00
71	Geronimo Berroa	25.00
72	Jason Giambi	35.00
73	Mark McGwire	140.00
74	Terry Steinbach	25.00
75	Todd Van Poppel	25.00
76	Jay Buhner	40.00
77	Norm Charlton	25.00
78	Ken Griffey Jr.	500.00
79	Randy Johnson	50.00
80	Edgar Martinez	25.00
81	Alex Rodriguez	350.00
82	Paul Sorrento	25.00
83	Dan Wilson	25.00
84	Will Clark	40.00
85	Kevin Elster	25.00
86	Juan Gonzalez	175.00
87	Rusty Greer	25.00
88	Ken Hill	25.00
89	Mark McLemore	25.00
90	Dean Palmer	25.00
91	Roger Pavlik	25.00
92	Ivan Rodriguez	80.00
93	Joe Carter	35.00
94	Carlos Delgado	25.00
95	Juan Guzman	25.00
96	John Olerud	25.00
97	Ed Sprague	25.00
98	Jermaine Dye	30.00
99	Tom Glavine	40.00
100	Marquis Grissom	25.00
101	Andruw Jones	275.00
102	Chipper Jones	225.00
103	David Justice	40.00
104	Ryan Klesko	50.00
105	Greg Maddux	225.00
106	Fred McGriff	40.00
107	John Smoltz	50.00
108	Brant Brown	25.00
109	Mark Grace	40.00
110	Brian McRae	25.00
111	Ryne Sandberg	90.00
112	Sammy Sosa	50.00
113	Steve Trachsel	25.00
114	Bret Boone	25.00
115	Eric Davis	25.00
116	Steve Gibralter	25.00
117	Barry Larkin	40.00
118	Reggie Sanders	25.00
119	John Smiley	25.00
120	Dante Bichette	40.00
121	Ellis Burks	25.00
122	Vinny Castilla	25.00
123	Andres Galarraga	40.00
124	Larry Walker	80.00
125	Eric Young	25.00
126	Kevin Brown	25.00
127	Greg Colbrunn	25.00
128	Jeff Conine	25.00
129	Charles Johnson	25.00
130	Al Leiter	25.00
131	Gary Sheffield	50.00

#	Player	MT
132	Devon White	25.00
133	Jeff Bagwell	150.00
134	Derek Bell	25.00
135	Craig Biggio	35.00
136	Doug Drabek	25.00
137	Brian Hunter	25.00
138	Darryl Kile	25.00
139	Shane Reynolds	25.00
140	Brett Butler	25.00
141	Eric Karros	25.00
142	Ramon Martinez	25.00
143	Raul Mondesi	35.00
144	Hideo Nomo	80.00
145	Chan Ho Park	25.00
146	Mike Piazza	240.00
147	Moises Alou	35.00
148	Yamil Benitez	25.00
149	Mark Grudzielanek	25.00
150	Pedro Martinez	35.00
151	Henry Rodriguez	25.00
152	David Segui	25.00
153	Rondell White	35.00
154	Carlos Baerga	25.00
155	John Franco	25.00
156	Bernard Gilkey	25.00
157	Todd Hundley	35.00
158	Jason Isringhausen	25.00
159	Lance Johnson	25.00
160	Alex Ochoa	25.00
161	Rey Ordonez	35.00
162	Paul Wilson	25.00
163	Ron Blazier	25.00
164	Ricky Bottalico	25.00
165	Jim Eisenreich	25.00
166	Pete Incaviglia	25.00
167	Mickey Morandini	25.00
168	Ricky Otero	25.00
169	Curt Schilling	25.00
170	Jay Bell	25.00
171	Charlie Hayes	25.00
172	Jason Kendall	25.00
173	Jeff King	25.00
174	Al Martin	25.00
175	Alan Benes	35.00
176	Royce Clayton	25.00
177	Brian Jordan	25.00
178	Ray Lankford	25.00
179	John Mabry	25.00
180	Willie McGee	25.00
181	Ozzie Smith	100.00
182	Todd Stottlemyre	25.00
183	Andy Ashby	25.00
184	Ken Caminiti	50.00
185	Steve Finley	25.00
186	Tony Gwynn	150.00
187	Rickey Henderson	25.00
188	Wally Joyner	25.00
189	Fernando Valenzuela	25.00
190	Greg Vaughn	25.00
191	Rod Beck	25.00
192	Barry Bonds	90.00
193	Shawon Dunston	25.00
194	Chris Singleton	25.00
195	Robby Thompson	25.00
196	Matt Williams	40.00
197	Checklist (Barry Bonds)	45.00
198	Checklist (Ken Griffey Jr.)	175.00
199	Checklist (Cal Ripken Jr.)	125.00
200	Checklist (Frank Thomas)	150.00

1996 Circa Access

This 1996 Fleer Circa insert set highlights 30 players on a three-panel design that includes multiple photographs, personal information and statistics. The cards were seeded one per every 12 packs.

#	Player	MT
	Complete Set (30):	125.00
	Common Player:	2.00
1	Cal Ripken Jr.	15.00
2	Mo Vaughn	5.00
3	Tim Salmon	2.50
4	Frank Thomas	20.00
5	Albert Belle	6.00
6	Kenny Lofton	5.00
7	Manny Ramirez	5.00
8	Paul Molitor	3.00
9	Kirby Puckett	8.00
10	Paul O'Neill	2.00
11	Mark McGwire	6.00
12	Ken Griffey Jr.	20.00
13	Randy Johnson	4.00
14	Greg Maddux	12.00
15	John Smoltz	3.00
16	Sammy Sosa	3.00
17	Barry Larkin	3.00
18	Gary Sheffield	4.00
19	Jeff Bagwell	8.00
20	Hideo Nomo	4.00
21	Mike Piazza	12.00
22	Moises Alou	2.00
23	Henry Rodriguez	2.00
24	Rey Ordonez	2.00
25	Jay Bell	2.00
26	Ozzie Smith	4.00
27	Tony Gwynn	8.00
28	Rickey Henderson	2.00
29	Barry Bonds	5.00
30	Matt Williams	3.00
30p	Matt Williams (overprinted "PROMOTIONAL SAMPLE")	3.00

1996 Circa Boss

This 1996 Fleer Circa insert set showcases the game's top stars on an embossed design. Cards were seeded one per every six packs.

#	Player	MT
	Complete Set (50):	125.00
	Common Player:	1.00
1	Roberto Alomar	3.00
2	Cal Ripken Jr.	12.00
2p	Cal Ripken Jr. (overprinted "PROMOTIONAL SAMPLE")	8.00
3	Jose Canseco	1.50
4	Mo Vaughn	4.00
5	Tim Salmon	1.50
6	Frank Thomas	15.00
7	Robin Ventura	1.00
8	Albert Belle	5.00
9	Kenny Lofton	4.00
10	Manny Ramirez	4.00
11	Dave Nilsson	1.00
12	Chuck Knoblauch	1.50
13	Paul Molitor	2.50
14	Kirby Puckett	6.00
15	Wade Boggs	1.50
16	Dwight Gooden	1.00
17	Paul O'Neill	1.00
18	Mark McGwire	5.00
19	Jay Buhner	1.50
20	Ken Griffey Jr.	15.00
21	Randy Johnson	2.50
22	Will Clark	1.50
23	Juan Gonzalez	8.00
24	Joe Carter	1.00
25	Tom Glavine	1.00
26	Ryan Klesko	2.50
27	Greg Maddux	10.00
28	John Smoltz	1.50
29	Ryne Sandberg	5.00
30	Sammy Sosa	2.00
31	Barry Larkin	2.00
32	Reggie Sanders	1.00
33	Dante Bichette	1.50
34	Andres Galarraga	1.50
35	Charles Johnson	1.00
36	Gary Sheffield	2.50
37	Jeff Bagwell	8.00
38	Hideo Nomo	3.00
39	Mike Piazza	10.00
40	Moises Alou	1.00
41	Henry Rodriguez	1.00
42	Rey Ordonez	1.00
43	Ricky Otero	1.00
44	Jay Bell	1.00
45	Royce Clayton	1.00
46	Ozzie Smith	2.50
47	Tony Gwynn	6.00
48	Rickey Henderson	1.00
49	Barry Bonds	4.00
50	Matt Williams	2.00

1996 Leaf/Limited

Leaf's 1996 Limited set contains 90 of the top rookies and veterans in baseball. There is also a 100-card Limited Gold parallel set which includes the 90 main cards, plus 10 cards from a Limited Rookies insert set. The gold parallel cards are seeded one per every 11 packs. Regular Limited Rookies inserts were seeded one per every seven packs. Two other insert sets were also made - two versions of Lumberjacks and Pennant Craze.

#	Player	MT
	Complete Set (90):	50.00
	Common Player:	.25
	Limited Gold Comp. Set (90):	400.00
	Limited Golds:	4x to 10x
	Wax Box:	100.00
1	Ivan Rodriguez	1.50
2	Roger Clemens	2.50
3	Gary Sheffield	1.00
4	Tino Martinez	.25
5	Sammy Sosa	.75
6	Reggie Sanders	.25
7	Ray Lankford	.25
8	Manny Ramirez	2.00
9	Jeff Bagwell	3.00
10	Greg Maddux	5.00
11	Ken Griffey Jr.	8.00
12	Rondell White	.25
13	Mike Piazza	5.00
14	Marc Newfield	.25
15	Cal Ripken Jr.	6.00
16	Carlos Delgado	.25
17	Tim Salmon	.50
18	Andres Galarraga	.50
19	Chuck Knoblauch	.50
20	Matt Williams	.50
21	Mark McGwire	2.50
22	Ben McDonald	.25
23	Frank Thomas	8.00
24	Johnny Damon	.25
25	Gregg Jefferies	.25
26	Travis Fryman	.25
27	Chipper Jones	5.00
28	David Cone	.40
29	Kenny Lofton	2.00
30	Mike Mussina	1.00
31	Alex Rodriguez	8.00
32	Carlos Baerga	.25
33	Brian Hunter	.25
34	Juan Gonzalez	4.00
35	Bernie Williams	1.50
36	Wally Joyner	.25
37	Fred McGriff	.75
38	Randy Johnson	1.00
39	Marty Cordova	.25
40	Garret Anderson	.25
41	Albert Belle	2.50
42	Edgar Martinez	.25
43	Barry Larkin	.75
44	Paul O'Neill	.25
45	Cecil Fielder	.50
46	Rusty Greer	.25
47	Mo Vaughn	2.50
48	Dante Bichette	.75
49	Ryan Klesko	1.00
50	Roberto Alomar	2.00
51	Raul Mondesi	.75
52	Robin Ventura	.25
53	Tony Gwynn	3.00
54	Mark Grace	.50
55	Jim Thome	1.00
56	Jason Giambi	.25
57	Tom Glavine	.50
58	Jim Edmonds	.50
59	Pedro Martinez	.25
60	Charles Johnson	.25
61	Wade Boggs	.50
62	Orlando Merced	.25
63	Craig Biggio	.25
64	Brady Anderson	.50
65	Hideo Nomo	1.50
66	Ozzie Smith	1.00
67	Eddie Murray	.75
68	Will Clark	.75
69	Jay Buhner	.50
70	Kirby Puckett	3.00
71	Barry Bonds	2.00
72	Ray Durham	.25
73	Sterling Hitchcock	.25
74	John Smoltz	.75
75	Andre Dawson	.25
76	Joe Carter	.50
77	Ryne Sandberg	1.50
78	Rickey Henderson	.25
79	Brian Jordan	.40
80	Greg Vaughn	.25
81	Andy Pettitte	2.00
82	Dean Palmer	.25
83	Paul Molitor	1.00
84	Rafael Palmeiro	.50
85	Henry Rodriguez	.25
86	Larry Walker	.75
87	Ismael Valdes	.25
88	Derek Bell	.25
89	J.T. Snow	.25
90	Jack McDowell	.25

1996 Leaf/Limited Lumberjacks

Lumberjacks inserts return to Leaf Limited, but the 1996 versions feature an improved maple stock that puts wood grains on both sides of the card. Ten different Lumberjacks are available in two different versions. Regular versions are serial numbered to 5,000, while a special black-bordered Limited Edition version is numbered to 500.

#	Player	MT
	Complete Set (10):	250.00
	Common Player:	8.00
	Lumberjack Blacks (500):	3x to 5x
1	Ken Griffey Jr.	45.00
2	Sammy Sosa	12.00
3	Cal Ripken Jr.	40.00

4	Frank Thomas	45.00
5	Alex Rodriguez	45.00
6	Mo Vaughn	15.00
7	Chipper Jones	25.00
8	Mike Piazza	25.00
9	Jeff Bagwell	20.00
10	Mark McGwire	15.00

1996 Leaf/Limited Pennant Craze

Each card in this insert set is sequentially numbered to 2,500 in silver foil on the back. The top-front of the cards have a die-cut pennant shape and is felt-textured.

		MT
Complete Set (10):		500.00
Common Player:		15.00
1	Juan Gonzalez	50.00
2	Cal Ripken Jr.	80.00
3	Frank Thomas	100.00
4	Ken Griffey Jr.	100.00
5	Albert Belle	30.00
6	Greg Maddux	60.00
7	Paul Molitor	15.00
8	Alex Rodriguez	80.00
9	Barry Bonds	25.00
10	Chipper Jones	60.00

1996 Leaf/Limited Rookies

There are two versions of this 1996 Limited insert set. The cards are reprinted as part of a Limited Gold parallel set, which also includes the regular issue's 90 cards. The gold cards are seeded one per every 11 packs. The top young players are also featured on regular Limited Rookies inserts; these versions are seeded one per every seven packs.

		MT
Complete Set (10):		60.00
Common Player:		3.00
1	Alex Ochoa	3.00
2	Darin Erstad	15.00
3	Ruben Rivera	5.00
4	Derek Jeter	20.00

5	Jermaine Dye	3.00
6	Jason Kendall	3.00
7	Mike Grace	3.00
8	Andruw Jones	25.00
9	Rey Ordonez	4.00
10	George Arias	3.00

1996 Leaf/Signature Series

There were 245 Major League Baseball players who autographed cards for Leaf's 1996 Signature Series. At least one authentic signature is guaranteed in every pack. There were 235 players who signed cards in these quantities: Gold (500 autographs), Silver (1,000) and Bronze (3,500). The other 10 players signed fewer autographs - 100 Gold, 200 Silver and 700 Bronze. They are: Kenny Lofton, Mo Vaughn, Frank Thomas, Wade Boggs, Derek Jeter, Manny Ramirez, Paul Molitor, Alex Rodriguez, Raul Mondesi and Roberto Alomar. Each major leaguer signed his cards, including an affidavit that was notarized to guarantee each signature was authentic. In addition, Pinnacle used team clubhouse officials to witness autographs. One out of every 48 packs is a super pack containing nothing but autographed cards. In addition, the regular-issue set, which has 100 cards, is paralleled in a Press Proof insert set. These gold version cards are seeded one per every 12 packs.

		MT
Complete Set (150):		75.00
Complete 1st Series Set (100):		50.00
Complete Extended Series Set (50):		25.00
Common Player:		.20
Complete Gold PP Set (150):		1000.
Gold Press Proofs:		8x to 15x
Complete Platinum Set (150):		3000.
Platinum PP Ser.1 Stars:		30x to 40x
Platinum PP Ser.2 Stars:		12x to 25x
Platinum PP Ser. 1 Yng Stars:		20x to 30x
Platinum PP Ser. 2 Yng Stars:		8x to 20x
Wax Box:		100.00
1	Mike Piazza	3.00
2	Juan Gonzalez	2.50
3	Greg Maddux	3.00
4	Marc Newfield	.20
5	Wade Boggs	.40
6	Ray Lankford	.20
7	Frank Thomas	5.00
8	Rico Brogna	.20
9	Tim Salmon	.40
10	Ken Griffey Jr.	5.00
11	Manny Ramirez	1.25
12	Cecil Fielder	.40
13	Gregg Jefferies	.20
14	Rondell White	.40
15	Cal Ripken Jr.	4.00
16	Alex Rodriguez	4.00
17	Bernie Williams	1.00
18	Andres Galarraga	.40
19	Mike Mussina	1.00
20	Chuck Knoblauch	.20
21	Joe Carter	.40
22	Jeff Bagwell	2.50
23	Mark McGwire	1.75
24	Sammy Sosa	.50
25	Reggie Sanders	.20

26	Chipper Jones	3.00
27	Jeff Cirillo	.20
28	Roger Clemens	1.25
29	Craig Biggio	.20
30	Gary Sheffield	.50
31	Paul O'Neill	.20
32	Johnny Damon	.50
33	Jason Isringhausen	.20
34	Jay Bell	.20
35	Henry Rodriguez	.20
36	Matt Williams	.40
37	Randy Johnson	.75
38	Fred McGriff	.50
39	Jason Giambi	.20
40	Ivan Rodriguez	.75
41	Raul Mondesi	.50
42	Barry Larkin	.75
43	Ryan Klesko	1.25
44	Joey Hamilton	.20
45	Todd Hundley	.20
46	Jim Edmonds	.50
47	Dante Bichette	.50
48	Roberto Alomar	1.25
49	Mark Grace	.40
50	Brady Anderson	.40
51	Hideo Nomo	1.25
52	Ozzie Smith	1.00
53	Robin Ventura	.20
54	Andy Pettitte	1.50
55	Kenny Lofton	1.50
56	John Mabry	.20
57	Paul Molitor	.75
58	Rey Ordonez	.75
59	Albert Belle	2.00
60	Charles Johnson	.20
61	Edgar Martinez	.20
62	Derek Bell	.20
63	Carlos Delgado	.20
64	Raul Casanova	.20
65	Ismael Valdes	.20
66	J.T. Snow	.20
67	Derek Jeter	3.00
68	Jason Kendall	.20
69	John Smoltz	.50
70	Chad Mottola	.20
71	Jim Thome	.75
72	Will Clark	.50
73	Mo Vaughn	2.00
74	John Wasdin	.20
75	Rafael Palmeiro	.40
76	Mark Grudzielanek	.20
77	Larry Walker	.30
78	Alan Benes	.40
79	Michael Tucker	.20
80	Billy Wagner	.20
81	Paul Wilson	.50
82	Greg Vaughn	.20
83	Dean Palmer	.20
84	Ryne Sandberg	1.25
85	Eric Young	.20
86	Jay Buhner	.40
87	Tony Clark	.50
88	Jermaine Dye	.40
89	Barry Bonds	1.25
90	Ugueth Urbina	.20
91	Charles Nagy	.20
92	Ruben Rivera	.75
93	Todd Hollandsworth	.20
94	*Darin Erstad*	4.00
95	Brooks Kieschnick	.20
96	Edgar Renteria	.50
97	Lenny Dykstra	.20
98	Tony Gwynn	2.00
99	Kirby Puckett	1.50
100	Checklist	.20
101	Andruw Jones	4.00
102	Alex Ochoa	.20
103	David Cone	.20
104	Rusty Greer	.20
105	Jose Canseco	.40
106	Ken Caminiti	.40
107	Mariano Rivera	.50
108	Ron Gant	.20
109	Darryl Strawberry	.20
110	Vladimir Guerrero	3.00
111	George Arias	.20
112	Jeff Conine	.20
113	Bobby Higginson	.20
114	Eric Karros	.20
115	Brian Hunter	.20
116	Eddie Murray	.50
117	Todd Walker	.75
118	Chan Ho Park	.20
119	John Jaha	.20
120	David Justice	.30
121	Makoto Suzuki	.20
122	Scott Rolen	1.50
123	Tino Martinez	.20
124	Kimera Bartee	.20
125	Garret Anderson	.20
126	Brian Jordan	.20

127	Andre Dawson	.20
128	Javier Lopez	.30
129	Bill Pulsipher	.20
130	Dwight Gooden	.20
131	Al Martin	.20
132	Terrell Wade	.20
133	Steve Gibralter	.20
134	Tom Glavine	.30
135	Kevin Appier	.20
136	Tim Raines	.20
137	Curtis Pride	.20
138	Todd Greene	.20
139	Bobby Bonilla	.20
140	Trey Beamon	.20
141	Marty Cordova	.20
142	Rickey Henderson	.20
143	Ellis Burks	.20
144	Dennis Eckersley	.20
145	Kevin Brown	.20
146	Carlos Baerga	.20
147	Brett Butler	.20
148	Marquis Grissom	.20
149	Karim Garcia	.75
150	Checklist	.20

1996 Leaf/Signature Series Autographs

Every pack of 1996 Leaf Signature Series product includes at least one authentically signed card from one of 245 players. There were 235 players who signed three versions in these quantities - 500 Gold, 1,000 Silver and 3,500 Bronze. There are also short-printed autographs for 10 players in quantities of 100 Gold, 200 Silver and 700 Bronze. The short-printed players are designated with an "SP" in the checklist. Cards are numbered alphabetically in the checklist since the autographed cards are unnumbered. Each major leaguer signed a notarized affidavit to guarantee each signature was authentic. Series I style cards of Carlos Delgado, Brian Hunter, Phil Plantier, Jim Thome, Terrell Wade and Ernie Young were signed too late for inclusion in Series 1 packs, and were inserted with Extended. No Bronze cards of Thome were signed.

		MT
Complete Bronze Set (251):		2000.
Common Bronze Player:		4.00
Silver:		2x
Gold:		3x-4x
SP Signatures: 100 Gold, 200 Silver, 700 Bronze		
(1)	Kurt Abbott	4.00
(2)	Juan Acevedo	4.00
(3)	Terry Adams	4.00
(4)	Manny Alexander	4.00
(5)	Roberto Alomar (SP)	80.00
(6)	Moises Alou	12.00
(7)	Wilson Alvarez	4.00
(8)	Garret Anderson	6.00
(9)	Shane Andrews	4.00
(10)	Andy Ashby	4.00
(11)	Pedro Astacio	4.00
(12)	Brad Ausmus	4.00
(13)	Bobby Ayala	4.00
(14)	Carlos Baerga	6.00
(15)	Harold Baines	6.00
(16)	Jason Bates	4.00
(17)	Allen Battle	4.00

(18) Rich Becker	5.00
(19) David Bell	4.00
(20) Rafael Belliard	4.00
(21) Andy Benes	6.00
(22) Armando Benitez	4.00
(23) Jason Bere	4.00
(24) Geronimo Berroa	4.00
(25) Willie Blair	4.00
(26) Mike Blowers	4.00
(27) Wade Boggs (SP)	80.00
(28) Ricky Bones	4.00
(29) Mike Bordick	4.00
(30) Toby Borland	4.00
(31) Ricky Bottalico	4.00
(32) Darren Bragg	4.00
(33) Jeff Branson	4.00
(34) Tilson Brito	4.00
(35) Rico Brogna	4.00
(36) Scott Brosius	4.00
(37) Damon Buford	4.00
(38) Mike Busby	4.00
(39) Tom Candiotti	4.00
(40) Frank Castillo	4.00
(41) Andujar Cedeno	4.00
(42) Domingo Cedeno	4.00
(43) Roger Cedeno	4.00
(44) Norm Charlton	4.00
(45) Jeff Cirillo	4.00
(46) Will Clark	20.00
(47) Jeff Conine	6.00
(48) Steve Cooke	4.00
(49) Joey Cora	6.00
(50) Marty Cordova	4.00
(51) Rheal Cormier	4.00
(52) Felipe Crespo	4.00
(53) Chad Curtis	4.00
(54) Johnny Damon	12.00
(55) Russ Davis	4.00
(56) Andre Dawson	20.00
(57a) Carlos Delgado (black autograph)	8.00
(57b) Carlos Delgado (blue autograph)	8.00
(58) Doug Drabek	4.00
(59) Darren Dreifort	4.00
(60) Shawon Dunston	4.00
(61) Ray Durham	4.00
(62) Jim Edmonds	5.00
(63) Joey Eischen	4.00
(64) Jim Eisenreich	4.00
(65) Sal Fasano	4.00
(66) Jeff Fassero	4.00
(67) Alex Fernandez	7.50
(68) Darrin Fletcher	4.00
(69) Chad Fonville	4.00
(70) Kevin Foster	4.00
(71) John Franco	4.00
(72) Julio Franco	5.00
(73) Marvin Freeman	4.00
(74) Travis Fryman	6.00
(75) Gary Gaetti	5.00
(76) Carlos Garcia	4.00
(77) Jason Giambi	6.00
(78) Benji Gil	4.00
(79) Greg Gohr	4.00
(80) Chris Gomez	4.00
(81) Leo Gomez	4.00
(82) Tom Goodwin	4.00
(83) Mike Grace	1.00
(84) Mike Greenwell	4.00
(85) Rusty Greer	5.00
(86) Mark Grudzielanek	7.50
(87) Mark Gubicza	4.00
(88) Juan Guzman	4.00
(89) Darryl Hamilton	4.00
(90) Joey Hamilton	5.00
(91) Chris Hammond	4.00
(92) Mike Hampton	4.00
(93) Chris Haney	4.00
(94) Todd Haney	4.00
(95) Erik Hanson	4.00
(96) Pete Harnisch	4.00
(97) LaTroy Hawkins	4.00
(98) Charlie Hayes	4.00
(99) Jimmy Haynes	4.00
(100) Roberto Hernandez	4.00
(101) Bobby Higginson	9.00
(102) Glenallen Hill	4.00
(103) Ken Hill	4.00
(104) Sterling Hitchcock	4.00
(105) Trevor Hoffman	4.00
(106) Dave Hollins	4.00
(107) Dwayne Hosey	4.00
(108) Thomas Howard	4.00
(109) Steve Howe	4.00
(110) John Hudek	4.00
(111) Rex Hudler	4.00
(112) Brian Hunter	5.00
(113) Butch Huskey	5.00
(114) Mark Hutton	4.00
(115) Jason Jacome	4.00

(116) John Jaha	4.00
(117) Reggie Jefferson	4.00
(118) Derek Jeter (SP)	160.00
(119) Bobby Jones	4.00
(120) Todd Jones	4.00
(121) Brian Jordan	4.00
(122) Kevin Jordan	4.00
(123) Jeff Juden	4.00
(124) Ron Karkovice	4.00
(125) Roberto Kelly	4.00
(126) Mark Kiefer	4.00
(127) Brooks Kieschnick	5.00
(128) Jeff King	4.00
(129) Mike Lansing	4.00
(130) Matt Lawton	4.00
(131) Al Leiter	4.00
(132) Mark Leiter	4.00
(133) Curtis Leskanic	4.00
(134) Darren Lewis	4.00
(135) Mark Lewis	4.00
(136) Felipe Lira	4.00
(137) Pat Listach	4.00
(138) Keith Lockhart	4.00
(139) Kenny Lofton (SP)	100.00
(140) John Mabry	4.00
(141) Mike Macfarlane	4.00
(142) Kirt Manwaring	4.00
(143) Al Martin	4.00
(144) Norberto Martin	4.00
(145) Dennis Martinez	6.00
(146) Pedro Martinez	15.00
(147) Sandy Martinez	4.00
(148) Mike Matheny	4.00
(149) T.J. Mathews	4.00
(150) David McCarty	4.00
(151) Ben McDonald	4.00
(152) Pat Meares	4.00
(153) Orlando Merced	4.00
(154) Jose Mesa	4.00
(155) Matt Mieske	4.00
(156) Orlando Miller	4.00
(157) Mike Mimbs	4.00
(158) Paul Molitor (SP)	90.00
(159) Raul Mondesi (SP)	50.00
(160) Jeff Montgomery	4.00
(161) Mickey Morandini	4.00
(162) Lyle Mouton	4.00
(163) James Mouton	4.00
(164) Jamie Moyer	4.00
(165) Rodney Myers	4.00
(166) Denny Neagle	5.00
(167) Robb Nen	4.00
(168) Marc Newfield	4.00
(169) Dave Nilsson	4.00
(170) Jon Nunnally	4.00
(171) Chad Ogea	4.00
(172) Troy O'Leary	4.00
(173) Rey Ordonez	6.00
(174) Jayhawk Owens	4.00
(175) Tom Pagnozzi	4.00
(176) Dean Palmer	4.00
(177) Roger Pavlik	4.00
(178) Troy Percival	4.00
(179) Carlos Perez	4.00
(180) Robert Perez	4.00
(181) Andy Pettitte	30.00
(182) Phil Plantier	4.00
(183) Mike Potts	4.00
(184) Curtis Pride	4.00
(185) Ariel Prieto	6.00
(186) Bill Pulsipher	4.00
(187) Brad Radke	4.00
(188) Manny Ramirez (SP)	60.00
(189) Joe Randa	4.00
(190) Pat Rapp	4.00
(191) Bryan Rekar	4.00
(192) Shane Reynolds	4.00
(193) Arthur Rhodes	4.00
(194) Mariano Rivera	4.00
(195a) Alex Rodriguez (SP, black autograph)	275.00
(195b) Alex Rodriguez (SP, blue autograph)	275.00
(196) Frank Rodriguez	4.00
(197) Mel Rojas	4.00
(198) Ken Ryan	4.00
(199) Bret Saberhagen	6.00
(200) Tim Salmon	6.00
(201) Rey Sanchez	4.00
(202) Scott Sanders	4.00
(203) Steve Scarsone	4.00
(204) Curt Schilling	4.00
(205) Jason Schmidt	4.00
(206) David Segui	4.00
(207) Kevin Seitzer	4.00
(208) Scott Servais	4.00
(209) Don Slaught	4.00
(210) Zane Smith	4.00
(211) Paul Sorrento	4.00
(212) Scott Stahoviak	4.00
(213) Mike Stanley	4.00

(214) Terry Steinbach	4.00
(215) Kevin Stocker	4.00
(216) Jeff Suppan	4.00
(217) Bill Swift	4.00
(218) Greg Swindell	4.00
(219) Kevin Tapani	4.00
(220) Danny Tartabull	4.00
(221) Julian Tavarez	4.00
(222) Frank Thomas (SP)	275.00
(223) Ozzie Timmons	4.00
(224a) Michael Tucker (black autograph)	4.00
(224b) Michael Tucker (blue autograph)	4.00
(225) Ismael Valdez	4.00
(226) Jose Valentin	4.00
(227) Todd Van Poppel	4.00
(228) Mo Vaughn (SP)	80.00
(229) Quilvio Veras	4.00
(230) Fernando Vina	4.00
(231) Joe Vitiello	4.00
(232) Jose Vizcaino	4.00
(233) Omar Vizquel	5.00
(234) Terrell Wade	4.00
(235) Paul Wagner	4.00
(236) Matt Walbeck	4.00
(237) Jerome Walton	4.00
(238) Turner Ward	4.00
(239) Allen Watson	4.00
(240) David Weathers	4.00
(241) Walt Weiss	4.00
(242) Turk Wendell	4.00
(243) Rondell White	5.00
(244) Brian Williams	4.00
(245) George Williams	4.00
(246) Paul Wilson	4.00
(247) Bobby Witt	4.00
(248) Bob Wolcott	4.00
(249) Eric Young	4.00
(250) Ernie Young	4.00
(251) Greg Zaun	4.00
--- Frank Thomas (Autographed jumbo)	200.00

1996 Leaf/Signature Series Extended Autographs

Leaf Signature Series Extended Autograph cards consist of 31 stars and rising prospects, six autographs from Series I that were late inclusions and 186 other major leaguers. The 186 regular players signed 5,000 each, while other signees' totals are listed in parentheses. Signature cards for Alex Rodriguez, Juan Gonzalez and Andruw Jones were only available through redemption cards. Autographed versions are different designs from the regular-issue cards, with two available in each pack. The unnumbered cards are checklisted here in alphabetical order.

	MT
Complete Set (217):	2600.
Common Player:	4.00
(1) Scott Aldred	4.00
(2) Mike Aldrete	4.00
(3) Rich Amaral	4.00
(4) Alex Arias	4.00
(5) Paul Assenmacher	4.00
(6) Roger Bailey	4.00
(7) Erik Bennett	4.00
(8) Sean Bergman	4.00
(9) Doug Bochtler	4.00
(10) Tim Bogar	4.00
(11) Pat Borders	4.00
(12) Pedro Borbon	4.00

(13) Shawn Boskie	4.00
(14) Rafael Bournigal	4.00
(15) Mark Brandenburg	4.00
(16) John Briscoe	4.00
(17) Jorge Brito	4.00
(18) Doug Brocail	4.00
(19) Jay Buhner (SP, 1000)	50.00
(20) Scott Bullett	4.00
(21) Dave Burba	4.00
(22) Ken Caminiti (SP, 1000)	50.00
(23) John Cangelosi	4.00
(24) Cris Carpenter	4.00
(25) Chuck Carr	4.00
(26) Larry Casian	4.00
(27) Tony Castillo	4.00
(28) Jason Christiansen	4.00
(29) Archi Cianfrocco	4.00
(30) Mark Clark	4.00
(31) Terry Clark	4.00
(32) Roger Clemens (SP, 1000)	150.00
(33) Jim Converse	4.00
(34) Dennis Cook	4.00
(35) Francisco Cordova	5.00
(36) Jim Corsi	4.00
(37) Tim Crabtree	4.00
(38) Doug Creek (SP, 1950)	6.00
(39) John Cummings	4.00
(40) Omar Daal	4.00
(41) Rich DeLucia	4.00
(42) Mark Dewey	4.00
(43) Alex Diaz	4.00
(44) Jermaine Dye (SP, 2500)	16.00
(45) Ken Edenfield	4.00
(46) Mark Eichhorn	4.00
(47) John Ericks	4.00
(48) Darin Erstad	50.00
(49) Alvaro Espinoza	4.00
(50) Jorge Fabregas	4.00
(51) Mike Fetters	4.00
(52) John Flaherty	4.00
(53) Bryce Florie	4.00
(54) Tony Fossas	4.00
(55) Lou Frazier	4.00
(56) Mike Gallego	4.00
(57) Karim Garcia (SP, 2500)	40.00
(58) Jason Giambi	4.00
(59) Ed Giovanola	4.00
(60) Tom Glavine (SP, 1250)	40.00
(61) Juan Gonzalez (SP, 1000)	150.00
(62) Craig Grebeck	4.00
(63) Buddy Groom	4.00
(64) Kevin Gross	4.00
(65) Eddie Guardado	4.00
(66) Mark Guthrie	4.00
(67) Tony Gwynn (SP, 1000)	120.00
(68) Chip Hale	4.00
(69) Darren Hall	4.00
(70) Lee Hancock	4.00
(71) Dave Hansen	4.00
(72) Bryan Harvey	4.00
(73) Bill Haselman	4.00
(74) Mike Henneman	4.00
(75) Doug Henry	4.00
(76) Gil Heredia	4.00
(77) Carlos Hernandez	4.00
(78) Jose Hernandez	4.00
(79) Darren Holmes	4.00
(80) Mark Holzemer	4.00
(81) Rick Honeycutt	4.00
(82) Chris Hook	4.00
(83) Chris Howard	4.00
(84) Jack Howell	4.00
(85) David Hulse	4.00
(86) Edwin Hurtado	4.00
(87) Jeff Huson	4.00
(88) Mike James	4.00
(89) Derek Jeter (SP, 1000)	140.00
(90) Brian Johnson	4.00
(91) Randy Johnson (SP, 1000)	60.00
(92) Mark Johnson	4.00
(93) Andruw Jones (SP, 2000)	120.00
(94) Chris Jones	4.00
(95) Ricky Jordan	4.00
(96) Matt Karchner	4.00
(97) Scott Karl	4.00
(98) Jason Kendall (SP, 2500)	15.00
(99) Brian Keyser	4.00
(100) Mike Kingery	4.00
(101) Wayne Kirby	4.00
(102) Ryan Klesko (SP, 1000)	50.00
(103) Chuck Knoblauch (SP, 1000)	60.00
(104) Chad Kreuter	4.00
(105) Tom Lampkin	4.00
(106) Scott Leius	4.00
(107) Jon Lieber	4.00
(108) Nelson Liriano	4.00
(109) Scott Livingstone	4.00
(110) Graeme Lloyd	4.00
(111) Kenny Lofton (SP, 1000)	60.00
(112) Luis Lopez	4.00

(113)Torey Lovullo	4.00
(114)Greg Maddux (SP, 500)	250.00
(115)Mike Maddux	4.00
(116)Dave Magadan	4.00
(117)Mike Magnante	4.00
(118)Joe Magrane	4.00
(119)Pat Mahomes	4.00
(120)Matt Mantei	4.00
(121)John Marzano	4.00
(122)Terry Matthews	4.00
(123)Chuck McElroy	4.00
(124)Fred McGriff (SP, 1000)	30.00
(125)Mark McLemore	4.00
(126)Greg McMichael	4.00
(127)Blas Minor	4.00
(128)Dave Mlicki	4.00
(129)Mike Mohler	4.00
(130)Paul Molitor (SP, 1000)	80.00
(131)Steve Montgomery	4.00
(132)Mike Mordecai	4.00
(133)Mike Morgan	4.00
(134)Mike Munoz	4.00
(135)Greg Myers	4.00
(136)Jimmy Myers	4.00
(137)Mike Myers	4.00
(138)Bob Natal	4.00
(139)Dan Naulty	4.00
(140)Jeff Nelson	4.00
(141)Warren Newson	4.00
(142)Chris Nichting	4.00
(143)Melvin Nieves	4.00
(144)Charlie O'Brien	4.00
(145)Alex Ochoa	4.00
(146)Omar Olivares	4.00
(147)Joe Oliver	4.00
(148)Lance Painter	4.00
(149)Rafael Palmeiro (SP, 2000)	35.00
(150)Mark Parent	4.00
(151)Steve Parris (SP, 1800)	12.00
(152)Bob Patterson	4.00
(153)Tony Pena	4.00
(154)Eddie Perez	4.00
(155)Yorkis Perez	4.00
(156)Robert Person	4.00
(157)Mark Petkovsek	4.00
(158)Andy Pettitte (SP, 1000)	60.00
(159)J.R. Phillips	4.00
(160)Hipolito Pichardo	4.00
(161)Eric Plunk	4.00
(162)Jimmy Poole	4.00
(163)Kirby Puckett (SP, 1000)	150.00
(164)Paul Quantrill	4.00
(165)Tom Quinlan	4.00
(166)Jeff Reboulet	4.00
(167)Jeff Reed	4.00
(168)Steve Reed	4.00
(169)Carlos Reyes	4.00
(170)Bill Risley	4.00
(171)Kevin Ritz	4.00
(172)Kevin Roberson	4.00
(173)Rich Robertson	4.00
(174)Alex Rodriguez (SP, 500)	300.00
(175)Ivan Rodriguez (SP, 1250)	80.00
(176)Bruce Ruffin	4.00
(177)Juan Samuel	4.00
(178)Tim Scott	4.00
(179)Kevin Sefcik	4.00
(180)Jeff Shaw	4.00
(181)Danny Sheaffer	4.00
(182)Craig Shipley	4.00
(183)Dave Silvestri	4.00
(184)Aaron Small	4.00
(185)John Smoltz (SP, 1000)	50.00
(186)Luis Sojo	4.00
(187)Sammy Sosa (SP, 1000)	50.00
(188)Steve Sparks	4.00
(189)Tim Spehr	4.00
(190)Russ Springer	4.00
(191)Matt Stairs	4.00
(192)Andy Stankiewicz	4.00
(193)Mike Stanton	4.00
(194)Kelly Stinnett	4.00
(195)Doug Strange	4.00
(196)Mark Sweeney	4.00
(197)Jeff Tabaka	4.00
(198)Jesus Tavarez	4.00
(199)Frank Thomas (SP, 1000)	200.00
(200)Larry Thomas	4.00
(201)Mark Thompson	4.00
(202)Mike Timlin	4.00
(203)Steve Trachsel	4.00
(204)Tom Urbani	4.00
(205)Julio Valera	4.00
(206)Dave Valle	4.00
(207)William VanLandingham	4.00
(208)Mo Vaughn (SP, 1000)	60.00
(209)Dave Veres	4.00
(210)Ed Vosberg	4.00
(211)Don Wengert	4.00
(212)Matt Whiteside	4.00
(213)Bob Wickman	4.00
(214)Matt Williams (SP, 1250)	45.00
(215)Mike Williams	4.00
(216)Woody Williams	4.00

(217)Craig Worthington	4.00
--- Frank Thomas	200.00
(Autographed jumbo)	

1996 Leaf/Signature Extended Autographs - Century Marks

Century Marks consisted of the first 100 autographs by the 31 stars and top prospects, and are designated with a "Century Marks" blue holographic foil logo. Several players' autographed cards were available only by mail-in redemption cards.

		MT
Common Player:		80.00
(1)	Jay Buhner	125.00
(2)	Ken Caminiti	125.00
(3)	Roger Clemens	300.00
(4)	Jermaine Dye	80.00
(5)	Darin Erstad	175.00
(6)	Karim Garcia	100.00
(7)	Jason Giambi	80.00
(8)	Tom Glavine	100.00
(9)	Juan Gonzalez	300.00
(10)	Tony Gwynn	275.00
(11)	Derek Jeter	300.00
(12)	Randy Johnson	150.00
(13)	Andruw Jones	300.00
(14)	Jason Kendall	80.00
(15)	Ryan Klesko	125.00
(16)	Chuck Knoblauch	140.00
(17)	Kenny Lofton	175.00
(18)	Greg Maddux	600.00
(19)	Fred McGriff	125.00
(20)	Paul Molitor	175.00
(21)	Alex Ochoa	80.00
(22)	Rafael Palmeiro	80.00
(23)	Andy Pettitte	150.00
(24)	Kirby Puckett	400.00
(25)	Alex Rodriguez	600.00
(26)	Ivan Rodriguez	175.00
(27)	John Smoltz	125.00
(28)	Sammy Sosa	140.00
(29)	Frank Thomas	600.00
(30)	Mo Vaughn	175.00
(31)	Matt Williams	100.00

1996 Certified

This hobby-exclusive set has 144 cards in its regular issue, plus six parallel versions and two insert sets. The parallel sets are: Certified Red (one per five packs), Certified Blue (one per 50), Artist's Proofs (one per 12), Mirror Red (one per 100), Mirror Blue (one per 200), and Mirror Gold (one per 300). Breaking down the numbers, there are 1,800 Certified Red sets, 180 Certified Blue, 500 Artist's Proofs, 90 Mirror Red Mirror Blue and 30 Mirror Gold sets. The insert sets are Interleague Preview cards and Select Few. Cards #135-144 are a "Pastime Power" subset.

		MT
Complete Set (144):		40.00
Common Player:		.20
Wax Box:		200.00
1	Frank Thomas	5.00
2	Tino Martinez	.40

3	Gary Sheffield	.75
4	Kenny Lofton	1.50
5	Joe Carter	.40
6	Alex Rodriguez	4.00
7	Chipper Jones	3.00
8	Roger Clemens	1.50
9	Jay Bell	.20
10	Eddie Murray	.50
11	Will Clark	.50
12	Mike Mussina	1.25
13	Hideo Nomo	1.25
14	Andres Galarraga	.40
15	Marc Newfield	.20
16	Jason Isringhausen	.20
17	Randy Johnson	.75
18	Chuck Knoblauch	.40
19	J.T. Snow	.20
20	Mark McGwire	1.75
21	Tony Gwynn	2.00
22	Albert Belle	1.50
23	Gregg Jefferies	.20
24	Reggie Sanders	.20
25	Bernie Williams	1.00
26	Ray Lankford	.20
27	Johnny Damon	.20
28	Ryne Sandberg	1.25
29	Rondell White	.40
30	Mike Piazza	3.00
31	Barry Bonds	1.25
32	Greg Maddux	3.00
33	Craig Biggio	.20
34	John Valentin	.20
35	Ivan Rodriguez	1.25
36	Rico Brogna	.20
37	Tim Salmon	.40
38	Sterling Hitchcock	.20
39	Charles Johnson	.20
40	Travis Fryman	.20
41	Barry Larkin	.60
42	Tom Glavine	.40
43	Marty Cordova	.20
44	Shawn Green	.20
45	Ben McDonald	.20
46	Robin Ventura	.20
47	Ken Griffey Jr.	5.00
48	Orlando Merced	.20
49	Paul O'Neill	.40
50	Ozzie Smith	1.00
51	Manny Ramirez	1.25
52	Ismael Valdes	.20
53	Cal Ripken Jr.	4.00
54	Jeff Bagwell	2.00
55	Greg Vaughn	.20
56	Juan Gonzalez	2.00
57	Raul Mondesi	.50
58	Carlos Baerga	.20
59	Sammy Sosa	.60
60	Mike Kelly	.20
61	Edgar Martinez	.20
62	Kirby Puckett	1.50
63	Cecil Fielder	.35
64	David Cone	.30
65	Moises Alou	.40
66	Fred McGriff	.50
67	Mo Vaughn	1.25
68	Edgardo Alfonzo	.20
69	Jim Thome	.75
70	Rickey Henderson	.20
71	Dante Bichette	.40
72	Lenny Dykstra	.20
73	Benji Gil	.20
74	Wade Boggs	.40
75	Jim Edmonds	.20
76	Michael Tucker	.20
77	Carlos Delgado	.20
78	Butch Huskey	.20
79	Billy Ashley	.20
80	Dean Palmer	.20
81	Paul Molitor	.50
82	Ryan Klesko	1.00
83	Brian Hunter	.20
84	Jay Buhner	.40
85	Larry Walker	.60
86	Mike Bordick	.20
87	Matt Williams	.40
88	Jack McDowell	.30
89	Hal Morris	.20
90	Brian Jordan	.20
91	Andy Pettitte	1.50
92	Melvin Nieves	.20
93	Pedro Martinez	.40
94	Mark Grace	.40
95	Garret Anderson	.20
96	Andre Dawson	.30
97	Ray Durham	.20
98	Jose Canseco	.50
99	Roberto Alomar	1.25
100	Derek Jeter	2.50
101	Alan Benes	.40
102	Karim Garcia	.60
103	*Robin Jennings*	.20

104	Bob Abreu	.20
105	Sal Fasano (Card front has Livan Hernandez' name)	.20
106	Steve Gibralter	.20
107	Jermaine Dye	.30
108	Jason Kendall	.20
109	*Mike Grace*	.50
110	Jason Schmidt	.20
111	Paul Wilson	.30
112	Rey Ordonez	.75
113	*Wilton Guerrero*	1.00
114	Brooks Kieschnick	.20
115	George Arias	.20
116	*Osvaldo Fernandez*	.20
117	Todd Hollandsworth	.30
118	John Wasdin	.20
119	Eric Owens	.20
120	Chan Ho Park	.20
121	Mark Loretta	.20
122	Richard Hidalgo	.20
123	Jeff Suppan	.20
124	Jim Pittsley	.20
125	LaTroy Hawkins	.20
126	Chris Snopek	.20
127	Justin Thompson	.20
128	Jay Powell	.20
129	Alex Ochoa	.20
130	Felipe Crespo	.20
131	*Matt Lawton*	.20
132	Jimmy Haynes	.20
133	Terrell Wade	.20
134	Ruben Rivera	.60
135	Frank Thomas (Pastime Power)	3.00
136	Ken Griffey Jr. (Pastime Power)	3.00
137	Greg Maddux (Pastime Power)	2.00
138	Mike Piazza (Pastime Power)	2.00
139	Cal Ripken Jr. (Pastime Power)	2.50
140	Albert Belle (Pastime Power)	1.00
141	Mo Vaughn (Pastime Power)	.75
142	Chipper Jones (Pastime Power)	2.00
143	Hideo Nomo (Pastime Power)	.60
144	Ryan Klesko (Pastime Power)	.60

1996 Certified Artist's Proofs

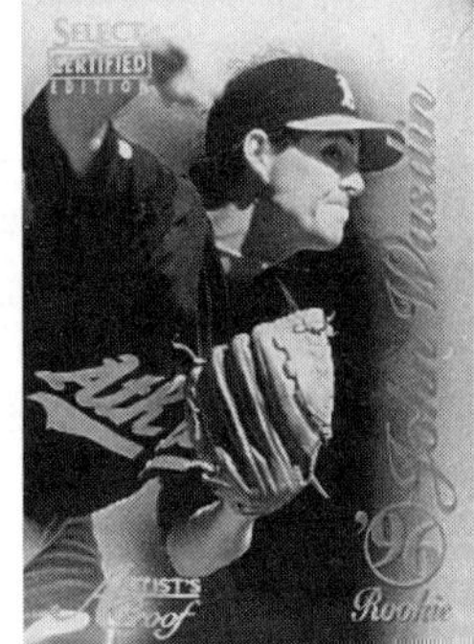

These 1996 Select Certified insert cards are among the most common of the parallel cards issued; there are 500 of each card produced, identified by a special logo on the card front.

		MT
Complete Set (144):		1800.
Common Player:		3.00
Artist's Proofs:		8x to 20x
1	Frank Thomas	100.00
2	Tino Martinez	8.00
3	Gary Sheffield	12.00
4	Kenny Lofton	25.00
5	Joe Carter	4.00
6	Alex Rodriguez	80.00
7	Chipper Jones	60.00
8	Roger Clemens	25.00
9	Jay Bell	3.00
10	Eddie Murray	15.00
11	Will Clark	8.00
12	Mike Mussina	20.00
13	Hideo Nomo	20.00

#	Player	MT
14	Andres Galarraga	8.00
15	Marc Newfield	3.00
16	Jason Isringhausen	4.00
17	Randy Johnson	20.00
18	Chuck Knoblauch	8.00
19	J.T. Snow	3.00
20	Mark McGwire	35.00
21	Tony Gwynn	45.00
22	Albert Belle	30.00
23	Gregg Jefferies	3.00
24	Reggie Sanders	3.00
25	Bernie Williams	20.00
26	Ray Lankford	3.00
27	Johnny Damon	5.00
28	Ryne Sandberg	25.00
29	Rondell White	5.00
30	Mike Piazza	60.00
31	Barry Bonds	25.00
32	Greg Maddux	60.00
33	Craig Biggio	5.00
34	John Valentin	3.00
35	Ivan Rodriguez	20.00
36	Rico Brogna	3.00
37	Tim Salmon	8.00
38	Sterling Hitchcock	3.00
39	Charles Johnson	3.00
40	Travis Fryman	3.00
41	Barry Larkin	8.00
42	Tom Glavine	5.00
43	Marty Cordova	3.00
44	Shawn Green	3.00
45	Ben McDonald	3.00
46	Robin Ventura	3.00
47	Ken Griffey Jr.	110.00
48	Orlando Merced	3.00
49	Paul O'Neill	6.00
50	Ozzie Smith	15.00
51	Manny Ramirez	25.00
52	Ismael Valdes	3.00
53	Cal Ripken Jr.	80.00
54	Jeff Bagwell	30.00
55	Greg Vaughn	3.00
56	Juan Gonzalez	50.00
57	Raul Mondesi	6.00
58	Carlos Baerga	3.00
59	Sammy Sosa	10.00
60	Mike Kelly	3.00
61	Edgar Martinez	3.00
62	Kirby Puckett	25.00
63	Cecil Fielder	5.00
64	David Cone	5.00
65	Moises Alou	6.00
66	Fred McGriff	8.00
67	Mo Vaughn	25.00
68	Edgardo Alfonzo	3.00
69	Jim Thome	15.00
70	Rickey Henderson	3.00
71	Dante Bichette	6.00
72	Lenny Dykstra	3.00
73	Benji Gil	3.00
74	Wade Boggs	6.00
75	Jim Edmonds	3.00
76	Michael Tucker	3.00
77	Carlos Delgado	5.00
78	Butch Huskey	3.00
79	Billy Ashley	3.00
80	Dean Palmer	3.00
81	Paul Molitor	10.00
82	Ryan Klesko	15.00
83	Brian Hunter	3.00
84	Jay Buhner	6.00
85	Larry Walker	8.00
86	Mike Bordick	3.00
87	Matt Williams	8.00
88	Jack McDowell	3.00
89	Hal Morris	3.00
90	Brian Jordan	3.00
91	Andy Pettitte	20.00
92	Melvin Nieves	3.00
93	Pedro Martinez	6.00
94	Mark Grace	8.00
95	Garret Anderson	8.00
96	Andre Dawson	5.00
97	Ray Durham	3.00
98	Jose Canseco	8.00
99	Roberto Alomar	20.00
100	Derek Jeter	60.00
101	Alan Benes	6.00
102	Karim Garcia	10.00
103	Robin Jennings	3.00
104	Bob Abreu	3.00
105	Sal Fasano (Card front has Livan Hernandez' name)	3.00
106	Steve Gibralter	3.00
107	Jermaine Dye	3.00
108	Jason Kendall	3.00
109	Mike Grace	5.00
110	Jason Schmidt	3.00
111	Paul Wilson	3.00
112	Rey Ordonez	5.00
113	Wilton Guerrero	3.00
114	Brooks Kieschnick	3.00
115	George Arias	3.00
116	Osvaldo Fernandez	3.00
117	Todd Hollandsworth	3.00
118	John Wasdin	3.00
119	Eric Owens	3.00
120	Chan Ho Park	3.00
121	Mark Loretta	3.00
122	Richard Hidalgo	3.00
123	Jeff Suppan	3.00
124	Jim Pittsley	3.00
125	LaTroy Hawkins	3.00
126	Chris Snopek	3.00
127	Justin Thompson	3.00
128	Jay Powell	3.00
129	Alex Ochoa	3.00
130	Felipe Crespo	3.00
131	Matt Lawton	3.00
132	Jimmy Haynes	3.00
133	Terrell Wade	3.00
134	Ruben Rivera	8.00
135	Frank Thomas (Pastime Power)	50.00
136	Ken Griffey Jr. (Pastime Power)	60.00
137	Greg Maddux (Pastime Power)	30.00
138	Mike Piazza (Pastime Power)	30.00
139	Cal Ripken Jr. (Pastime Power)	40.00
140	Albert Belle (Pastime Power)	15.00
141	Mo Vaughn (Pastime Power)	12.00
142	Chipper Jones (Pastime Power)	30.00
143	Hideo Nomo (Pastime Power)	10.00
144	Ryan Klesko (Pastime Power)	8.00

1996 Certified Interleague Preview

These 1996 Select Certified insert cards feature 21 prospective match-ups from when interleague play begins. The cards were seeded one per every 42 packs.

#	Players	MT
Complete Set (25):		475.00
Common Player:		8.00
1	Ken Griffey Jr., Hideo Nomo	60.00
2	Greg Maddux, Mo Vaughn	40.00
3	Frank Thomas, Sammy Sosa	60.00
4	Mike Piazza, Jim Edmonds	40.00
5	Ryan Klesko, Roger Clemens	15.00
6	Derek Jeter, Rey Ordonez	25.00
7	Johnny Damon, Ray Lankford	15.00
8	Manny Ramirez, Reggie Sanders	25.00
9	Barry Bonds, Jay Buhner	18.00
10	Jason Isringhausen, Wade Boggs	10.00
11	David Cone, Chipper Jones	40.00
12	Jeff Bagwell, Will Clark	30.00
13	Tony Gwynn, Randy Johnson	25.00
14	Cal Ripken Jr., Tom Glavine	50.00
15	Kirby Puckett, Alan Benes	20.00
16	Gary Sheffield, Mike Mussina	15.00
17	Raul Mondesi, Tim Salmon	12.00
18	Rondell White, Carlos Delgado	8.00
19	Cecil Fielder, Ryne Sandberg	20.00
20	Kenny Lofton, Brian Hunter	25.00
21	Paul Wilson, Paul O'Neill	8.00
22	Ismael Valdes, Edgar Martinez	8.00
23	Matt Williams, Mark McGwire	15.00
24	Albert Belle, Barry Larkin	20.00
25	Brady Anderson, Marquis Grissom	8.00

1996 Certified Mirror Gold

These 1996 Select Certified inserts are the scarcest of the set; cards were seeded one per every 300 packs. Only 30 Mirror Gold sets were made. Due to the improbability of completing the collection, no complete set price is given.

#	Player	MT
Common Player:		100.00
1	Frank Thomas	2400.
2	Tino Martinez	400.00
3	Gary Sheffield	175.00
4	Kenny Lofton	600.00
5	Joe Carter	125.00
6	Alex Rodriguez	2400.
7	Chipper Jones	1400.
8	Roger Clemens	800.00
9	Jay Bell	100.00
10	Eddie Murray	400.00
11	Will Clark	150.00
12	Mike Mussina	300.00
13	Hideo Nomo	400.00
14	Andres Galarraga	100.00
15	Marc Newfield	100.00
16	Jason Isringhausen	100.00
17	Randy Johnson	300.00
18	Chuck Knoblauch	100.00
19	J.T. Snow	100.00
20	Mark McGwire	900.00
21	Tony Gwynn	1100.
22	Albert Belle	1200.
23	Gregg Jefferies	100.00
24	Reggie Sanders	100.00
25	Bernie Williams	250.00
26	Ray Lankford	100.00
27	Johnny Damon	125.00
28	Ryne Sandberg	450.00
29	Rondell White	100.00
30	Mike Piazza	1500.
31	Barry Bonds	750.00
32	Greg Maddux	1400.
33	Craig Biggio	100.00
34	John Valentin	100.00
35	Ivan Rodriguez	600.00
36	Rico Brogna	100.00
37	Tim Salmon	125.00
38	Sterling Hitchcock	100.00
39	Charles Johnson	100.00
40	Travis Fryman	100.00
41	Barry Larkin	150.00
42	Tom Glavine	100.00
43	Marty Cordova	100.00
44	Shawn Green	100.00
45	Ben McDonald	100.00
46	Robin Ventura	100.00
47	Ken Griffey Jr.	3200.
48	Orlando Merced	100.00
49	Paul O'Neill	100.00
50	Ozzie Smith	200.00
51	Manny Ramirez	500.00
52	Ismael Valdes	100.00
53	Cal Ripken Jr.	2200.
54	Jeff Bagwell	1200.
55	Greg Vaughn	100.00
56	Juan Gonzalez	1200.
57	Raul Mondesi	150.00
58	Carlos Baerga	100.00
59	Sammy Sosa	200.00
60	Mike Kelly	100.00
61	Edgar Martinez	100.00
62	Kirby Puckett	1000.
63	Cecil Fielder	125.00
64	David Cone	100.00
65	Moises Alou	100.00
66	Fred McGriff	250.00
67	Mo Vaughn	600.00
68	Edgardo Alfonzo	100.00
69	Jim Thome	450.00
70	Rickey Henderson	100.00
71	Dante Bichette	150.00
72	Lenny Dykstra	100.00
73	Benji Gil	100.00
74	Wade Boggs	150.00
75	Jim Edmonds	100.00
76	Michael Tucker	100.00
77	Carlos Delgado	100.00
78	Butch Huskey	100.00
79	Billy Ashley	100.00
80	Dean Palmer	100.00
81	Paul Molitor	200.00
82	Ryan Klesko	350.00
83	Brian Hunter	100.00
84	Jay Buhner	150.00
85	Larry Walker	400.00
86	Mike Bordick	100.00
87	Matt Williams	125.00
88	Jack McDowell	100.00
89	Hal Morris	100.00
90	Brian Jordan	100.00
91	Andy Pettitte	250.00
92	Melvin Nieves	100.00
93	Pedro Martinez	125.00
94	Mark Grace	125.00
95	Garret Anderson	100.00
96	Andre Dawson	100.00
97	Ray Durham	100.00
98	Jose Canseco	150.00
99	Roberto Alomar	450.00
100	Derek Jeter	1200.
101	Alan Benes	100.00
102	Karim Garcia	200.00
103	Robin Jennings	100.00
104	Bob Abreu	100.00
105	Sal Fasano (Card front has Livan Hernandez' name)	100.00
106	Steve Gibralter	100.00
107	Jermaine Dye	125.00
108	Jason Kendall	100.00
109	Mike Grace	125.00
110	Jason Schmidt	100.00
111	Paul Wilson	150.00
112	Rey Ordonez	200.00
113	Wilton Guerrero	300.00
114	Brooks Kieschnick	100.00
115	George Arias	100.00
116	Osvaldo Fernandez	100.00
117	Todd Hollandsworth	100.00
118	John Wasdin	100.00
119	Eric Owens	100.00
120	Chan Ho Park	100.00
121	Mark Loretta	100.00
122	Richard Hidalgo	100.00
123	Jeff Suppan	100.00
124	Jim Pittsley	100.00
125	LaTroy Hawkins	100.00
126	Chris Snopek	100.00
127	Justin Thompson	100.00
128	Jay Powell	100.00
129	Alex Ochoa	100.00
130	Felipe Crespo	100.00
131	Matt Lawton	100.00
132	Jimmy Haynes	100.00
133	Terrell Wade	100.00
134	Ruben Rivera	200.00
135	Frank Thomas (Pastime Power)	1200.
136	Ken Griffey Jr. (Pastime Power)	1600.
137	Greg Maddux (Pastime Power)	700.00
138	Mike Piazza (Pastime Power)	700.00
139	Cal Ripken Jr. (Pastime Power)	900.00
140	Albert Belle (Pastime Power)	500.00
141	Mo Vaughn (Pastime Power)	300.00
142	Chipper Jones (Pastime Power)	700.00

143	Hideo Nomo (Pastime Power)	200.00
144	Ryan Klesko (Pastime Power)	175.00

1996 Certified Mirror Red, Blue

Cards in these 1996 Select Certified insert sets were seeded one every 100 packs. There were 90 sets made of the Mirror Red cards and just 60 sets made of the Mirror Blue inserts. Because of the improbability of completing the set, no complete set value is quoted.

		MT
Common Mirror Red:		20.00
Mirror Blue (144):		2x
Common Mirror Blues:		50.00
1	Frank Thomas	500.00
2	Tino Martinez	50.00
3	Gary Sheffield	60.00
4	Kenny Lofton	125.00
5	Joe Carter	30.00
6	Alex Rodriguez	450.00
7	Chipper Jones	300.00
8	Roger Clemens	175.00
9	Jay Bell	20.00
10	Eddie Murray	100.00
11	Will Clark	50.00
12	Mike Mussina	100.00
13	Hideo Nomo	100.00
14	Andres Galarraga	40.00
15	Marc Newfield	20.00
16	Jason Isringhausen	30.00
17	Randy Johnson	100.00
18	Chuck Knoblauch	60.00
19	J.T. Snow	20.00
20	Mark McGwire	200.00
21	Tony Gwynn	250.00
22	Albert Belle	150.00
23	Gregg Jefferies	20.00
24	Reggie Sanders	20.00
25	Bernie Williams	100.00
26	Ray Lankford	20.00
27	Johnny Damon	30.00
28	Ryne Sandberg	125.00
29	Rondell White	40.00
30	Mike Piazza	300.00
31	Barry Bonds	125.00
32	Greg Maddux	300.00
33	Craig Biggio	40.00
34	John Valentin	20.00
35	Ivan Rodriguez	100.00
36	Rico Brogna	20.00
37	Tim Salmon	40.00
38	Sterling Hitchcock	20.00
39	Charles Johnson	20.00
40	Travis Fryman	20.00
41	Barry Larkin	50.00
42	Tom Glavine	40.00
43	Marty Cordova	20.00
44	Shawn Green	20.00
45	Ben McDonald	20.00
46	Robin Ventura	20.00
47	Ken Griffey Jr.	600.00
48	Orlando Merced	20.00
49	Paul O'Neill	40.00
50	Ozzie Smith	75.00
51	Manny Ramirez	120.00
52	Ismael Valdes	20.00
53	Cal Ripken Jr.	400.00
54	Jeff Bagwell	200.00
55	Greg Vaughn	20.00
56	Juan Gonzalez	250.00
57	Raul Mondesi	40.00
58	Carlos Baerga	20.00
59	Sammy Sosa	60.00
60	Mike Kelly	20.00
61	Edgar Martinez	20.00
62	Kirby Puckett	175.00
63	Cecil Fielder	40.00
64	David Cone	30.00
65	Moises Alou	40.00
66	Fred McGriff	50.00
67	Mo Vaughn	125.00
68	Edgardo Alfonzo	20.00
69	Jim Thome	75.00
70	Rickey Henderson	20.00
71	Dante Bichette	50.00
72	Lenny Dykstra	20.00
73	Benji Gil	20.00
74	Wade Boggs	50.00
75	Jim Edmonds	30.00
76	Michael Tucker	20.00
77	Carlos Delgado	20.00

78	Butch Huskey	20.00
79	Billy Ashley	20.00
80	Dean Palmer	20.00
81	Paul Molitor	100.00
82	Ryan Klesko	75.00
83	Brian Hunter	20.00
84	Jay Buhner	50.00
85	Larry Walker	60.00
86	Mike Bordick	20.00
87	Matt Williams	50.00
88	Jack McDowell	20.00
89	Hal Morris	20.00
90	Brian Jordan	20.00
91	Andy Pettitte	125.00
92	Melvin Nieves	20.00
93	Pedro Martinez	40.00
94	Mark Grace	40.00
95	Garret Anderson	20.00
96	Andre Dawson	30.00
97	Ray Durham	20.00
98	Jose Canseco	40.00
99	Roberto Alomar	100.00
100	Derek Jeter	250.00
101	Alan Benes	20.00
102	Karim Garcia	50.00
103	Robin Jennings	20.00
104	Bob Abreu	20.00
105	Livan Hernandez	40.00
106	Steve Gibralter	20.00
107	Jermaine Dye	20.00
108	Jason Kendall	20.00
109	Mike Grace	30.00
110	Jason Schmidt	20.00
111	Paul Wilson	30.00
112	Rey Ordonez	40.00
113	Wilton Guerrero	50.00
114	Brooks Kieschnick	20.00
115	George Arias	20.00
116	Osvaldo Fernandez	20.00
117	Todd Hollandsworth	20.00
118	John Wasdin	20.00
119	Eric Owens	20.00
120	Chan Ho Park	20.00
121	Mark Loretta	20.00
122	Richard Hidalgo	20.00
123	Jeff Suppan	20.00
124	Jim Pittsley	20.00
125	LaTroy Hawkins	20.00
126	Chris Snopek	20.00
127	Justin Thompson	20.00
128	Jay Powell	20.00
129	Alex Ochoa	20.00
130	Felipe Crespo	20.00
131	Matt Lawton	20.00
132	Jimmy Haynes	20.00
133	Terrell Wade	20.00
134	Ruben Rivera	40.00
135	Frank Thomas (Pastime Power)	250.00
136	Ken Griffey Jr. (Pastime Power)	300.00
137	Greg Maddux (Pastime Power)	150.00
138	Mike Piazza (Pastime Power)	150.00
139	Cal Ripken Jr. (Pastime Power)	200.00
140	Albert Belle (Pastime Power)	75.00
141	Mo Vaughn (Pastime Power)	60.00
142	Chipper Jones (Pastime Power)	150.00
143	Hideo Nomo (Pastime Power)	50.00
144	Ryan Klesko (Pastime Power)	40.00

1996 Certified Red, Blue

These 1996 Select Certified insert cards were the most common of the parallel cards issued; they were seeded one per every five packs. There were 1,800 Certified Red sets produced, with the number of Certified Blue sets at 180. Cards are essentially the same as regular-issue Select Certified except for the color of the foil background on front.

		MT
Complete Set, Red (144):		800.00
Common Player, Red:		2.00
Certified Blues (144):		5x to 7x
1	Frank Thomas	40.00
2	Tino Martinez	4.00

3	Gary Sheffield	6.00
4	Kenny Lofton	10.00
5	Joe Carter	3.00
6	Alex Rodriguez	30.00
7	Chipper Jones	25.00
8	Roger Clemens	12.00
9	Jay Bell	2.00
10	Eddie Murray	8.00
11	Will Clark	4.00
12	Mike Mussina	8.00
13	Hideo Nomo	8.00
14	Andres Galarraga	5.00
15	Marc Newfield	2.00
16	Jason Isringhausen	2.00
17	Randy Johnson	8.00
18	Chuck Knoblauch	5.00
19	J.T. Snow	2.00
20	Mark McGwire	18.00
21	Tony Gwynn	25.00
22	Albert Belle	12.00
23	Gregg Jefferies	2.00
24	Reggie Sanders	2.00
25	Bernie Williams	8.00
26	Ray Lankford	2.00
27	Johnny Damon	3.00
28	Ryne Sandberg	10.00
29	Rondell White	4.00
30	Mike Piazza	25.00
31	Barry Bonds	10.00
32	Greg Maddux	25.00
33	Craig Biggio	4.00
34	John Valentin	2.00
35	Ivan Rodriguez	8.00
36	Rico Brogna	2.00
37	Tim Salmon	5.00
38	Sterling Hitchcock	2.00
39	Charles Johnson	2.00
40	Travis Fryman	2.00
41	Barry Larkin	5.00
42	Tom Glavine	4.00
43	Marty Cordova	3.00
44	Shawn Green	2.00
45	Ben McDonald	2.00
46	Robin Ventura	2.00
47	Ken Griffey Jr.	45.00
48	Orlando Merced	2.00
49	Paul O'Neill	4.00
50	Ozzie Smith	8.00
51	Manny Ramirez	10.00
52	Ismael Valdes	2.00
53	Cal Ripken Jr.	30.00
54	Jeff Bagwell	20.00
55	Greg Vaughn	2.00
56	Juan Gonzalez	20.00
57	Raul Mondesi	5.00
58	Carlos Baerga	2.00
59	Sammy Sosa	6.00
60	Mike Kelly	2.00
61	Edgar Martinez	2.00
62	Kirby Puckett	12.00
63	Cecil Fielder	4.00
64	David Cone	3.00
65	Moises Alou	3.00
66	Fred McGriff	4.00
67	Mo Vaughn	10.00
68	Edgardo Alfonzo	2.00
69	Jim Thome	8.00
70	Rickey Henderson	2.00
71	Dante Bichette	4.00
72	Lenny Dykstra	2.00
73	Benji Gil	2.00
74	Wade Boggs	5.00
75	Jim Edmonds	4.00
76	Michael Tucker	2.00
77	Carlos Delgado	2.00
78	Butch Huskey	2.00
79	Billy Ashley	2.00
80	Dean Palmer	2.00
81	Paul Molitor	8.00
82	Ryan Klesko	8.00
83	Brian Hunter	2.00

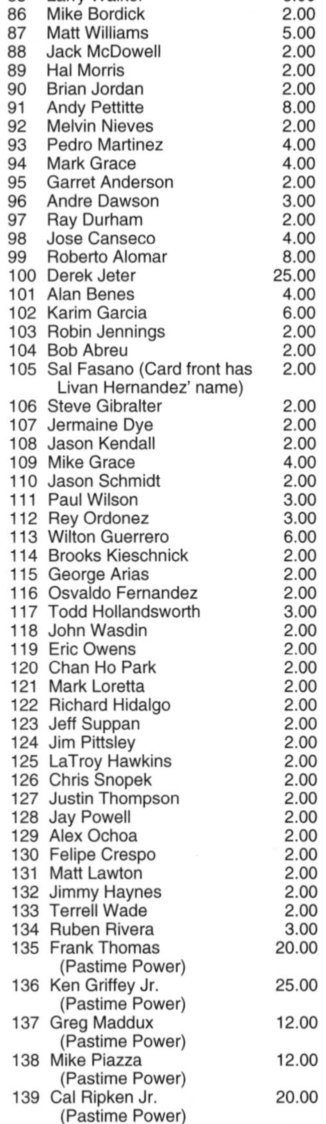

84	Jay Buhner	5.00
85	Larry Walker	6.00
86	Mike Bordick	2.00
87	Matt Williams	5.00
88	Jack McDowell	2.00
89	Hal Morris	2.00
90	Brian Jordan	2.00
91	Andy Pettitte	8.00
92	Melvin Nieves	2.00
93	Pedro Martinez	4.00
94	Mark Grace	4.00
95	Garret Anderson	2.00
96	Andre Dawson	3.00
97	Ray Durham	2.00
98	Jose Canseco	4.00
99	Roberto Alomar	8.00
100	Derek Jeter	25.00
101	Alan Benes	4.00
102	Karim Garcia	6.00
103	Robin Jennings	2.00
104	Bob Abreu	2.00
105	Sal Fasano (Card front has Livan Hernandez' name)	2.00
106	Steve Gibralter	2.00
107	Jermaine Dye	2.00
108	Jason Kendall	2.00
109	Mike Grace	4.00
110	Jason Schmidt	2.00
111	Paul Wilson	3.00
112	Rey Ordonez	3.00
113	Wilton Guerrero	6.00
114	Brooks Kieschnick	2.00
115	George Arias	2.00
116	Osvaldo Fernandez	2.00
117	Todd Hollandsworth	3.00
118	John Wasdin	2.00
119	Eric Owens	2.00
120	Chan Ho Park	2.00
121	Mark Loretta	2.00
122	Richard Hidalgo	2.00
123	Jeff Suppan	2.00
124	Jim Pittsley	2.00
125	LaTroy Hawkins	2.00
126	Chris Snopek	2.00
127	Justin Thompson	2.00
128	Jay Powell	2.00
129	Alex Ochoa	2.00
130	Felipe Crespo	2.00
131	Matt Lawton	2.00
132	Jimmy Haynes	2.00
133	Terrell Wade	2.00
134	Ruben Rivera	3.00
135	Frank Thomas (Pastime Power)	20.00
136	Ken Griffey Jr. (Pastime Power)	25.00
137	Greg Maddux (Pastime Power)	12.00
138	Mike Piazza (Pastime Power)	12.00
139	Cal Ripken Jr. (Pastime Power)	20.00
140	Albert Belle (Pastime Power)	6.00
141	Mo Vaughn (Pastime Power)	5.00
142	Chipper Jones (Pastime Power)	12.00
143	Hideo Nomo (Pastime Power)	4.00
144	Ryan Klesko (Pastime Power)	3.00

1996 Certified Select Few

Eighteen top players are featured on these 1996 Select Certified inserts, which utilize holographic technology with a dot matrix hologram. Cards were seeded one per every 60 packs.

		MT
Complete Set (18):		550.00
Common Player:		10.00
1	Sammy Sosa	15.00
2	Derek Jeter	30.00
3	Ken Griffey Jr.	75.00
4	Albert Belle	30.00
5	Cal Ripken Jr.	60.00
6	Greg Maddux	50.00
7	Frank Thomas	75.00
8	Mo Vaughn	25.00
9	Chipper Jones	50.00
10	Mike Piazza	50.00
11	Ryan Klesko	20.00
12	Hideo Nomo	25.00
13	Alan Benes	10.00
14	Manny Ramirez	30.00
15	Gary Sheffield	15.00
16	Barry Bonds	20.00
17	Matt Williams	15.00
18	Johnny Damon	15.00

1996 Zenith

Pinnacle's 1996 Zenith set has 150 cards in the regular set, including 30 Rookies, 20 Honor roll and two checklist cards. Each card in the set has a parallel Artist's Proof version (seeded one per every 35 packs). Insert sets include Z Team, Mozaics and two versions of Diamond Club. Normal Dufex versions of Diamond Club appear one per every 24 packs; parallel versions, which have an actual diamond chip incorporated into the card design, were seeded one per every 350 packs.

		MT
Complete Set (150):		40.00
Common Player:		.25
Wax Box:		100.00
1	Ken Griffey Jr.	4.00
2	Ozzie Smith	.75
3	Greg Maddux	2.50
4	Rondell White	.40
5	Mark McGwire	1.50
6	Jim Thome	.75
7	Ivan Rodriguez	.75
8	Marc Newfield	.25
9	Travis Fryman	.25
10	Fred McGriff	.50
11	Shawn Green	.25
12	Mike Piazza	2.50
13	Dante Bichette	.40
14	Tino Martinez	.50
15	Sterling Hitchcock	.25
16	Ryne Sandberg	1.00
17	Rico Brogna	.25
18	Roberto Alomar	.75
19	Barry Larkin	.40
20	Bernie Williams	.75
21	Gary Sheffield	.50
22	Frank Thomas	4.00
23	Gregg Jefferies	.25
24	Jeff Bagwell	1.75
25	Marty Cordova	.25
26	Jim Edmonds	.40
27	Jay Bell	.25
28	Ben McDonald	.25
29	Barry Bonds	1.00
30	Mo Vaughn	1.00
31	Johnny Damon	.25
32	Dean Palmer	.25
33	Ismael Valdes	.25
34	Manny Ramirez	1.00
35	Edgar Martinez	.25
36	Cecil Fielder	.40
37	Ryan Klesko	.75
38	Ray Lankford	.25
39	Tim Salmon	.40
40	Joe Carter	.30
41	Jason Isringhausen	.25
42	Rickey Henderson	.25
43	Lenny Dykstra	.25
44	Andre Dawson	.25
45	Paul O'Neill	.40
46	Ray Durham	.25
47	Raul Mondesi	.50
48	Jay Buhner	.40
49	Eddie Murray	.75
50	Henry Rodriguez	.25
51	Hal Morris	.25
52	Mike Mussina	.75
53	Wally Joyner	.25
54	Will Clark	.50
55	Chipper Jones	2.50
56	Brian Jordan	.25
57	Larry Walker	.50
58	Wade Boggs	.40
59	Melvin Nieves	.25
60	Charles Johnson	.25
61	Juan Gonzalez	2.00
62	Carlos Delgado	.25
63	Reggie Sanders	.25
64	Brian Hunter	.25
65	Edgardo Alfonzo	.25
66	Kenny Lofton	1.00
67	Paul Molitor	.75
68	Mike Bordick	.25
69	Garret Anderson	.25
70	Orlando Merced	.25
71	Craig Biggio	.40
72	Chuck Knoblauch	.50
73	Mark Grace	.40
74	Jack McDowell	.25
75	Randy Johnson	.75
76	Cal Ripken Jr.	3.00
77	Matt Williams	.50
78	Benji Gil	.25
79	Moises Alou	.40
80	Robin Ventura	.25
81	Greg Vaughn	.25
82	Carlos Baerga	.25
83	Roger Clemens	1.00
84	Hideo Nomo	.75
85	Pedro Martinez	.40
86	John Valentin	.25
87	Andres Galarraga	.40
88	Andy Pettitte	1.00
89	Derek Bell	.25
90	Kirby Puckett	1.25
91	Tony Gwynn	2.00
92	Brady Anderson	.30
93	Derek Jeter	2.50
94	Michael Tucker	.25
95	Albert Belle	1.25
96	David Cone	.35
97	J.T. Snow	.25
98	Tom Glavine	.40
99	Alex Rodriguez	3.50
100	Sammy Sosa	.50
101	Karim Garcia	.60
102	Alan Benes	.30
103	Chad Mottola	.25
104	*Robin Jennings*	.25
105	Bob Abreu	.25
106	Tony Clark	1.00
107	George Arias	.25
108	Jermaine Dye	.25
109	Jeff Suppan	.25
110	*Ralph Milliard*	.25
111	Ruben Rivera	.40
112	Billy Wagner	.25
113	Jason Kendall	.25
114	*Mike Grace*	.50
115	Edgar Renteria	.40
116	Jason Schmidt	.25
117	Paul Wilson	.40
118	Rey Ordonez	.40
119	*Rocky Coppinger*	.40
120	*Wilton Guerrero*	1.00
121	Brooks Kieschnick	.25
122	Raul Casanova	.25
123	Alex Ochoa	.25
124	Chan Ho Park	.25
125	John Wasdin	.25
126	Eric Owens	.25
127	Justin Thompson	.25
128	Chris Snopek	.25
129	Terrell Wade	.25
130	*Darin Erstad*	4.00
131	Albert Belle (Honor Roll)	.60
132	Cal Ripken Jr. (Honor Roll)	1.50
133	Frank Thomas (Honor Roll)	2.00
134	Greg Maddux (Honor Roll)	1.25
135	Ken Griffey Jr. (Honor Roll)	2.00
136	Mo Vaughn (Honor Roll)	.50
137	Chipper Jones (Honor Roll)	1.25
138	Mike Piazza (Honor Roll)	1.25
139	Ryan Klesko (Honor Roll)	.35
140	Hideo Nomo (Honor Roll)	.40
141	Roberto Alomar (Honor Roll)	.40
142	Manny Ramirez (Honor Roll)	.50
143	Gary Sheffield (Honor Roll)	.30
144	Barry Bonds (Honor Roll)	.50
145	Matt Williams (Honor Roll)	.25
146	Jim Edmonds (Honor Roll)	.25
147	Derek Jeter (Honor Roll)	1.25
148	Sammy Sosa (Honor Roll)	.35
149	Kirby Puckett (Honor Roll)	.75
150	Tony Gwynn (Honor Roll)	1.00

1996 Zenith Artist's Proofs

This 150-card parallel set featured each card from the regular-issue set with the additon of a gold Artist's Proof logo on the front of the card. These inserts were seeded one per 35 packs.

	MT
Complete Set (150):	2000.
Common Player:	4.00
Stars:	15x to 25x
Yng. Stars & RC's:	8x to 15x

1996 Zenith Diamond Club

Twenty different players are featured on these two 1996 Pinnacle Zenith insert cards. Normal Dufex versions are inserted one per every 24 packs. Parallel versions of these cards, containing an actual diamond chip incorporated into the design, were seeded one per every 350 packs.

		MT
Complete Set (20):		180.00
Common Player:		4.00
Diamond Versions:		3x to 5x
1	Albert Belle	10.00
2	Mo Vaughn	8.00
3	Ken Griffey Jr.	30.00
4	Mike Piazza	20.00
5	Cal Ripken Jr.	25.00
6	Jermaine Dye	4.00
7	Jeff Bagwell	12.00
8	Frank Thomas	30.00
9	Alex Rodriguez	25.00
10	Ryan Klesko	6.00
11	Roberto Alomar	6.00
12	Sammy Sosa	6.00
13	Matt Williams	4.00
14	Gary Sheffield	6.00
15	Ruben Rivera	4.00
16	Darin Erstad	20.00
17	Randy Johnson	6.00
18	Greg Maddux	20.00
19	Karim Garcia	8.00
20	Chipper Jones	20.00

1996 Zenith Mozaics

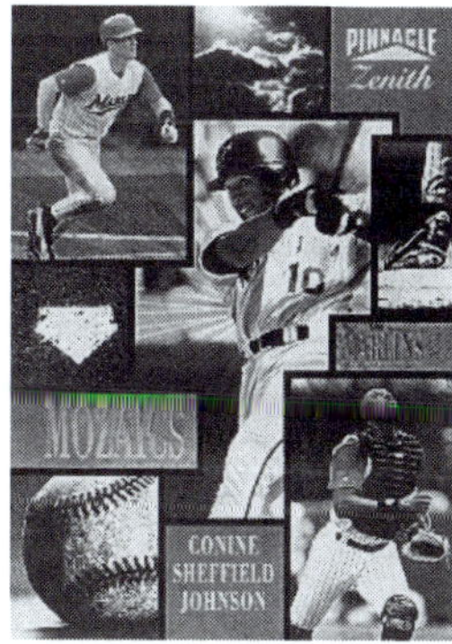

Each of these 1996 Pinnacle Zenith cards contains multiple player images for the team represented on the card. The cards were inserted one per every 10 packs.

		MT
Complete Set (25):		175.00
Common Player:		3.00
1	Greg Maddux, Chipper Jones, Ryan Klesko	20.00
2	Juan Gonzalez, Will Clark, Ivan Rodriguez	8.00
3	Frank Thomas, Robin Ventura, Ray Durham	20.00
4	Matt Williams, Barry Bonds, Osvaldo Fernandez	6.00
5	Ken Griffey Jr., Randy Johnson, Alex Rodriguez	25.00
6	Sammy Sosa, Ryne Sandberg, Mark Grace	8.00
7	Jim Edmonds, Tim Salmon, Garret Anderson	3.00
8	Cal Ripken Jr., Roberto Alomar, Mike Mussina	18.00
9	Mo Vaughn, Roger Clemens, John Valentin	8.00
10	Barry Larkin, Reggie Sanders, Hal Morris	3.00
11	Ray Lankford, Brian Jordan, Ozzie Smith	4.00
12	Dante Bichette, Larry Walker, Andres Galarraga	3.00
13	Mike Piazza, Hideo Nomo, Raul Mondesi	15.00
14	Ben McDonald, Greg Vaughn, Kevin Seitzer	3.00
15	Joe Carter, Carlos Delgado, Alex Gonzalez	3.00
16	Gary Sheffield, Charles Johnson, Jeff Conine	3.00
17	Rondell White, Moises Alou, Henry Rodriguez	3.00
18	Albert Belle, Manny Ramirez, Carlos Baerga	10.00
19	Kirby Puckett, Paul Molitor, Chuck Knoblauch	10.00
20	Tony Gwynn, Rickey Henderson, Wally Joyner	10.00
21	Mark McGwire, Mike Bordick, Scott Brosius	8.00
22	Paul O'Neill, Bernie Williams, Wade Boggs	4.00
23	Jay Bell, Orlando Merced, Jason Kendall	3.00
24	Rico Brogna, Paul Wilson, Jason Isringhausen	3.00
25	Jeff Bagwell, Craig Biggio, Derek Bell	12.00

1996 Zenith Z-Team

Pinnacle's 1996 Zenith baseball continues the Z Team insert concept with a new clear plastic treatment that is micro-etched for a see-through design that allows light to shine through etched highlights and a green baseball field background. The 18 cards were seeded one per every 72 packs.

	MT
Complete Set (18):	600.00
Common Player:	10.00
1 Ken Griffey Jr.	100.00
2 Albert Belle	40.00
3 Cal Ripken Jr.	80.00
4 Frank Thomas	100.00
5 Greg Maddux	60.00
6 Mo Vaughn	30.00
7 Chipper Jones	60.00
8 Mike Piazza	60.00
9 Ryan Klesko	20.00
10 Hideo Nomo	20.00
11 Roberto Alomar	20.00
12 Manny Ramirez	25.00
13 Gary Sheffield	15.00
14 Barry Bonds	25.00
15 Matt Williams	15.00
16 Jim Edmonds	10.00
17 Kirby Puckett	35.00
18 Sammy Sosa	15.00

1996 Topps/Chrome

In conjunction with baseball's postseason, Topps introduced the premier edition of Chrome Baseball. The set has 165 of the elite players from 1996 Topps Baseball Series I and II. Card #7 is a Mickey Mantle tribute card, similar to Topps' Series I card. There are four insert sets: Masters of the Game and Wrecking Crew, and scarcer Refractor versions for both types.

	MT
Complete Set (165):	75.00
Common Player:	.25
Complete Refractor Set (165):	2500.
Common Refractor:	5.00
Refractors:	10x to 20x
Wax Box:	60.00
1 Tony Gwynn (Star Power)	2.00
2 Mike Piazza (Star Power)	2.50
3 Greg Maddux (Star Power)	2.50
4 Jeff Bagwell (Star Power)	1.50
5 Larry Walker (Star Power)	.75
6 Barry Larkin (Star Power)	.50
7 Mickey Mantle (Commemorative)	10.00
8 Tom Glavine (Star Power)	.40
9 Craig Biggio (Star Power)	.25
10 Barry Bonds (Star Power)	1.00
11 Heathcliff Slocumb (Star Power)	.25
12 Matt Williams (Star Power)	.50
13 Todd Helton (Draft Pick)	3.00
14 Paul Molitor	1.50
15 Glenallen Hill	.25
16 Troy Percival	.25
17 Albert Belle	2.50
18 Mark Wohlers	.25
19 Kirby Puckett	3.00
20 Mark Grace	.50
21 J.T. Snow	.25
22 David Justice	.50
23 Mike Mussina	1.50
24 Bernie Williams	1.50
25 Ron Gant	.25
26 Carlos Baerga	.25
27 Gary Sheffield	1.00
28 Cal Ripken Jr. (Tribute Card)	8.00
29 Frank Thomas	8.00
30 Kevin Seitzer	.25
31 Joe Carter	.40
32 Jeff King	.25
33 David Cone	.40

	MT
34 Eddie Murray	.75
35 Brian Jordan	.25
36 Garret Anderson	.25
37 Hideo Nomo	1.50
38 Steve Finley	.25
39 Ivan Rodriguez	1.50
40 Quilvio Veras	.25
41 Mark McGwire	3.00
42 Greg Vaughn	.25
43 Randy Johnson	1.50
44 David Segui	.25
45 Derek Bell	.25
46 John Valentin	.25
47 Steve Avery	.25
48 Tino Martinez	.75
49 Shane Reynolds	.25
50 Jim Edmonds	.40
51 Raul Mondesi	.60
52 Chipper Jones	5.00
53 Gregg Jefferies	.25
54 Ken Caminiti	1.00
55 Brian McRae	.25
56 Don Mattingly	2.50
57 Marty Cordova	.25
58 Vinny Castilla	.25
59 John Smoltz	.60
60 Travis Fryman	.25
61 Ryan Klesko	1.00
62 Alex Fernandez	.25
63 Dante Bichette	.50
64 Eric Karros	.25
65 Roger Clemens	2.50
66 Randy Myers	.25
67 Cal Ripken Jr.	6.00
68 Rod Beck	.25
69 Jack McDowell	.25
70 Ken Griffey Jr.	8.00
71 Ramon Martinez	.25
72 Jason Giambi (Future Star)	.50
73 Nomar Garciaparra (Future Star)	5.00
74 Billy Wagner (Future Star)	.50
75 Todd Greene (Future Star)	.25
76 Paul Wilson (Future Star)	.40
77 Johnny Damon (Future Star)	.25
78 Alan Benes (Future Star)	.50
79 Karim Garcia (Future Star)	.75
80 Derek Jeter (Future Star)	2.50
81 Kirby Puckett (Star Power)	1.50
82 Cal Ripken Jr. (Star Power)	3.00
83 Albert Belle (Star Power)	1.25
84 Randy Johnson (Star Power)	.50
85 Wade Boggs (Star Power)	.40
86 Carlos Baerga (Star Power)	.25
87 Ivan Rodriguez (Star Power)	.60
88 Mike Mussina (Star Power)	.75
89 Frank Thomas (Star Power)	4.00
90 Ken Griffey Jr. (Star Power)	4.00
91 Jose Mesa (Star Power)	.25
92 *Matt Morris* (Draft Pick)	1.00
93 Mike Piazza	5.00
94 Edgar Martinez	.25
95 Chuck Knoblauch	.50
96 Andres Galarraga	.50
97 Tony Gwynn	4.00
98 Lee Smith	.25
99 Sammy Sosa	.75
100 Jim Thome	1.00
101 Bernard Gilkey	.25
102 Brady Anderson	.40
103 Rico Brogna	.25
104 Lenny Dykstra	.25
105 Tom Glavine	.40
106 John Olerud	.25
107 Terry Steinbach	.25
108 Brian Hunter	.25
109 Jay Buhner	.50
110 Mo Vaughn	2.00
111 Jose Mesa	.25
112 Brett Butler	.25
113 Chili Davis	.25
114 Paul O'Neill	.40
115 Roberto Alomar	1.50
116 Barry Larkin	.50
117 Marquis Grissom	.25
118 Will Clark	.50
119 Barry Bonds	2.00
120 Ozzie Smith	1.00
121 Pedro Martinez	.40
122 Craig Biggio	.40
123 Moises Alou	.40
124 Robin Ventura	.25
125 Greg Maddux	5.00
126 Tim Salmon	.50
127 Wade Boggs	.50
128 Ismael Valdes	.25
129 Juan Gonzalez	3.50
130 Ray Lankford	.25

	MT
131 Bobby Bonilla	.40
132 Reggie Sanders	.25
133 Alex Ochoa (Now Appearing)	.25
134 Mark Loretta (Now Appearing)	.25
135 Jason Kendall (Now Appearing)	.25
136 Brooks Kieschnick (Now Appearing)	.25
137 Chris Snopek (Now Appearing)	.25
138 Ruben Rivera (Now Appearing)	.50
139 Jeff Suppan (Now Appearing)	.25
140 John Wasdin (Now Appearing)	.25
141 Jay Payton (Now Appearing)	.40
142 Rick Krivda (Now Appearing)	.25
143 Jimmy Haynes (Now Appearing)	.25
144 Ryne Sandberg	1.50
145 Matt Williams	.50
146 Jose Canseco	.50
147 Larry Walker	.75
148 Kevin Appier	.25
149 Javy Lopez	.40
150 Dennis Eckersley	.25
151 Jason Isringhausen	.25
152 Dean Palmer	.25
153 Jeff Bagwell	3.00
154 Rondell White	.40
155 Wally Joyner	.25
156 Fred McGriff	.50
157 Cecil Fielder	.40
158 Rafael Palmeiro	.40
159 Rickey Henderson	.25
160 Shawon Dunston	.25
161 Manny Ramirez	2.00
162 Alex Gonzalez	.25
163 Shawn Green	.25
164 Kenny Lofton	2.00
165 Jeff Conine	.25

1996 Topps/Chrome Masters of the Game

These 1996 Topps Chrome inserts were seeded one per every 12 packs. Each of the cards is also reprinted in a Refractor version; these cards are seeded one per every 36 packs.

	MT
Complete Set (20):	75.00
Common Player:	2.00
Refractors:	1.5x to 3x
1 Dennis Eckersley	2.00
2 Denny Martinez	2.00
3 Eddie Murray	4.00
4 Paul Molitor	5.00
5 Ozzie Smith	5.00
6 Rickey Henderson	2.00
7 Tim Raines	2.00
8 Lee Smith	2.00
9 Cal Ripken Jr.	15.00
10 Chili Davis	2.00
11 Wade Boggs	3.00
12 Tony Gwynn	10.00
13 Don Mattingly	8.00
14 Bret Saberhagen	2.00

	MT
15 Kirby Puckett	8.00
16 Joe Carter	3.00
17 Roger Clemens	8.00
18 Barry Bonds	6.00
19 Greg Maddux	12.00
20 Frank Thomas	20.00

1996 Topps/Chrome Wrecking Crew

Wrecking Crew insert cards were inserted one per every 24 packs of 1996 Topps Chrome Baseball. Refractor versions were also made for these cards; they are seeded one per every 72 packs.

	MT
Complete Set (15):	90.00
Common Player:	3.00
Refractors:	1.5x to 3x
WC1 Jeff Bagwell	10.00
WC2 Albert Belle	8.00
WC3 Barry Bonds	6.00
WC4 Jose Canseco	4.00
WC5 Joe Carter	3.00
WC6 Cecil Fielder	3.00
WC7 Ron Gant	3.00
WC8 Juan Gonzalez	12.00
WC9 Ken Griffey Jr.	25.00
WC10 Fred McGriff	4.00
WC11 Mark McGwire	10.00
WC12 Mike Piazza	15.00
WC13 Frank Thomas	25.00
WC14 Mo Vaughn	6.00
WC15 Matt Williams	4.00

1996 SPX

Upper Deck's 1996 SPX set has 60 players in it, which are each paralleled as a Gold version (one per every seven packs). Base cards feature a new look with a different perimeter die-cut design from those used in the past for basketball and football sets. A 10-card insert set, Bound for Glory, was also produced. Tribute cards were also made for Ken Griffey Jr. and Mike Piazza, with scarcer autographed versions also produced for each player.

		MT
	Complete Set (60):	100.00
	Common Player:	1.00
	Complete Gold Set (60):	300.00
	Golds:	1.5x to 3x
	Wax Box:	80.00
1	Greg Maddux	6.00
2	Chipper Jones	6.00
3	Fred McGriff	1.50
4	Tom Glavine	1.00
5	Cal Ripken Jr.	8.00
6	Roberto Alomar	2.00
7	Rafael Palmeiro	1.00
8	Jose Canseco	1.50
9	Roger Clemens	3.00
10	Mo Vaughn	2.50
11	Jim Edmonds	1.00
12	Tim Salmon	1.50
13	Sammy Sosa	2.00
14	Ryne Sandberg	2.50
15	Mark Grace	1.00
16	Frank Thomas	10.00
17	Barry Larkin	1.50
18	Kenny Lofton	2.50
19	Albert Belle	3.00
20	Eddie Murray	1.50
21	Manny Ramirez	2.50
22	Dante Bichette	1.50
23	Larry Walker	1.50
24	Vinny Castilla	1.00
25	Andres Galarraga	1.50
26	Cecil Fielder	1.00
27	Gary Sheffield	1.50
28	Craig Biggio	1.00
29	Jeff Bagwell	3.00
30	Derek Bell	1.00
31	Johnny Damon	1.00
32	Eric Karros	1.00
33	Mike Piazza	6.00
34	Raul Mondesi	1.50
35	Hideo Nomo	2.00
36	Kirby Puckett	3.00
37	Paul Molitor	2.00
38	Marty Cordova	1.00
39	Rondell White	1.00
40	Jason Isringhausen	1.00
41	Paul Wilson	1.00
42	Rey Ordonez	1.00
43	Derek Jeter	6.00
44	Wade Boggs	1.50
45	Mark McGwire	3.00
46	Jason Kendall	1.00
47	Ron Gant	1.00
48	Ozzie Smith	2.00
49	Tony Gwynn	5.00
50	Ken Caminiti	1.50
51	Barry Bonds	2.50
52	Matt Williams	1.50
53	Osvaldo Fernandez	1.00
54	Jay Buhner	1.00
55	Ken Griffey Jr.	12.00
55p	Ken Griffey Jr. (overprinted "For Promotional Use Only")	15.00
56	Randy Johnson	2.00
57	Alex Rodriguez	10.00
58	Juan Gonzalez	5.00
59	Joe Carter	1.00
60	Carlos Delgado	1.00

1996 SPX Bound for Glory

Some of baseball's best players are highlighted on these 1996 Upper Deck SPX insert cards. The cards were seeded one per every 24 packs.

		MT
	Complete Set (10):	150.00
	Common Player:	8.00
1	Ken Griffey Jr.	30.00
2	Frank Thomas	30.00
3	Barry Bonds	8.00
4	Cal Ripken Jr.	25.00
5	Greg Maddux	20.00
6	Chipper Jones	20.00
7	Roberto Alomar	7.00
8	Manny Ramirez	8.00
9	Tony Gwynn	15.00
10	Mike Piazza	20.00

1996 SPX Ken Griffey Jr. Commemorative

Seattle Mariners' star Ken Griffey Jr. has this tribute card in Upper Deck's 1996 SPX set. The card was seeded one per every 75 packs. Autographed versions were also produced; these cards were seeded one per every 2,000 packs.

	MT
Ken Griffey Jr. (KG1)	20.00
Ken Griffey Jr. Autograph:	350.00

1996 SPX Mike Piazza Tribute

Los Angeles Dodgers' star catcher Mike Piazza is featured on this 1996 Upper Deck SPX insert card. Normal versions of the card are found one per every 95 packs, making it scarcer than the Ken Griffey Jr. inserts. Autographed Piazza cards are seeded one per every 2,000 packs.

	MT
Mike Piazza (MP1)	10.00
Mike Piazza Autograph:	250.00

1997 Bowman

The 1997 Bowman set consists of 440 base cards, an increase of 55 cards from the '96 set. Card fronts consist of a player photo within a red frame, with the players name and team logo at the bottom of the frame. A black border surrounds the outside of the card. Card backs feature another color photo, along with the player's 1996 statistics broken down by opponent. Players making their first appearance in a Bowman set have a "1st Bowman Card" designation on the card. Cards of prospects contain either silver or red foil on the fronts. Inserts within the set include Certified Autographs (found in gold, blue and black ink versions), Scouts Honor Roll, and Bowman's Best Previews. Cards were sold in 10-card packs for a suggested retail price of $2.50 each, and Topps offered collectors a $125 guarantee on the value of the set by the year 2000.

		MT
	Complete Set (440):	150.00
	Complete Series 1 Set (221):	80.00
	Complete Series 2 Set (219):	70.00
	Common Player:	.15
	Foil Stars:	2x to 4x
	Foil Yng. Stars:	1.5x to 3x
	Wax Box:	120.00
1	Derek Jeter	2.50
2	Edgar Renteria	.15
3	Chipper Jones	2.50
4	Hideo Nomo	.75
5	Tim Salmon	.25
6	Jason Giambi	.15
7	Robin Ventura	.15
8	Tony Clark	.75
9	Barry Larkin	.25
10	Paul Molitor	.50
11	Bernard Gilkey	.15
12	Jack McDowell	.15
13	Andy Benes	.15
14	Ryan Klesko	.75
15	Mark McGwire	1.50
16	Ken Griffey Jr.	4.00
17	Robb Nen	.15
18	Cal Ripken Jr.	3.00
19	John Valentin	.15
20	Ricky Bottalico	.15
21	Mike Lansing	.15
22	Ryne Sandberg	1.00
23	Carlos Delgado	.15
24	Craig Biggio	.20
25	Eric Karros	.15
26	Kevin Appier	.15
27	Mariano Rivera	.20
28	Vinny Castilla	.15
29	Juan Gonzalez	1.75
30	Al Martin	.15
31	Jeff Cirillo	.15
32	Eddie Murray	.50
33	Ray Lankford	.15
34	Manny Ramirez	1.00
35	Roberto Alomar	.75
36	Will Clark	.25
37	Chuck Knoblauch	.20
38	Harold Baines	.15
39	Trevor Hoffman	.15
40	Edgar Martinez	.15
41	Geronimo Berroa	.15
42	Rey Ordonez	.15
43	Mike Stanley	.15
44	Mike Mussina	.75
45	Kevin Brown	.15
46	Dennis Eckersley	.15
47	Henry Rodriguez	.15
48	Tino Martinez	.25
49	Eric Young	.15
50	Bret Boone	.15
51	Raul Mondesi	.25
52	Sammy Sosa	.40
53	John Smoltz	.25
54	Billy Wagner	.15
55	Jeff D'Amico	.15
56	Ken Caminiti	.25
57	Jason Kendall	.15
58	Wade Boggs	.25
59	Andres Galarraga	.25
60	Jeff Brantley	.15
61	Mel Rojas	.15
62	Brian Hunter	.15
63	Bobby Bonilla	.15
64	Roger Clemens	1.00
65	Jeff Kent	.15
66	Matt Williams	.40
67	Albert Belle	1.50
68	Jeff King	.15
69	John Wetteland	.15
70	Deion Sanders	.40
71	Bubba Trammell	3.00
72	Felix Heredia	.60
73	Billy Koch	.40
74	Sidney Ponson	.40
75	Ricky Ledee	5.00
76	Brett Tomko	.15
77	Braden Looper	.40
78	Damian Jackson	.15
79	Jason Dickson	.50
80	Chad Green	1.00
81	R.A. Dickey	.40
82	Jeff Liefer	.40
83	Matt Wagner	.15
84	Richard Hidalgo	.15
85	Adam Riggs	.15
86	Robert Smith	.15
87	Chad Hermansen	5.00
88	Felix Martinez	.15
89	J.J. Johnson	.15
90	Todd Dunwoody	.20
91	Katsuhiro Maeda	.15
92	Darin Erstad	3.00
93	Elieser Marrero	.15
94	Bartolo Colon	.15
95	Chris Fussell	.25
96	Ugueth Urbina	.15
97	Josh Paul	.50
98	Jaime Bluma	.15
99	Seth Greisinger	.50
100	Jose Cruz	20.00
101	Todd Dunn	.15
102	Joe Young	.40
103	Jonathan Johnson	.15
104	Justin Towle	.40
105	Brian Rose	.20
106	Jose Guillen	1.50
107	Andruw Jones	2.50
108	Mark Kotsay	4.00
109	Wilton Guerrero	.15
110	Jacob Cruz	.15
111	Mike Sweeney	.35
112	Julio Mosquera	.15
113	Matt Morris	.50
114	Wendell Magee	.15
115	John Thomson	.15
116	Javier Valentin	.40
117	Tom Fordham	.15
118	Ruben Rivera	.15
119	Mike Drumright	.50
120	Chris Holt	.15
121	Sean Maloney	.40
122	Michael Barrett	.15
123	Tony Saunders	.50
124	Kevin Brown	.15
125	Richard Almanzar	.15
126	Mark Redman	.15
127	Anthony Sanders	.40
128	Jeff Abbott	.15
129	Eugene Kingsale	.15
130	Paul Konerko	1.00
131	Randall Simon	.40
132	Andy Larkin	.15
133	Rafael Medina	.25
134	Mendy Lopez	.15
135	Freddy Garcia	.15
136	Karim Garcia	.40
137	Larry Rodriguez	.50
138	Carlos Guillen	.15
139	Aaron Boone	.15
140	Donnie Sadler	.15
141	Brooks Kieschnick	.15
142	Scott Spiezio	.15
143	Everett Stull	.15
144	Enrique Wilson	.15
145	Milton Bradley	.40

#	Player	Price
146	Kevin Orie	.20
147	Derek Wallace	.15
148	Russ Johnson	.15
149	*Joe Lagarde*	.40
150	Luis Castillo	.40
151	Jay Payton	.25
152	Joe Long	.15
153	Livan Hernandez	.25
154	*Vladimir Nunez*	1.50
155	Calvin Reese	.15
156	George Arias	.15
157	Homer Bush	.15
158	Chris Carpenter	.15
159	*Eric Milton*	1.00
160	Richie Sexson	.15
161	Carl Pavano	1.00
162	*Chris Gissell*	.40
163	Mac Suzuki	.15
164	Pat Cline	.15
165	Ron Wright	1.00
166	Dante Powell	.40
167	Mark Bellhorn	.25
168	George Lombard	.50
169	*Pee Wee Lopez*	.40
170	*Paul Wilder*	2.00
171	Brad Fullmer	.15
172	*Willie Martinez*	.75
173	*Dario Veras*	.40
174	Dave Coggin	.15
175	*Kris Benson*	3.00
176	Torii Hunter	.15
177	D.T. Cromer	.40
178	Nelson Figueroa	1.25
179	*Hiram Bocachica*	1.50
180	Shane Monahan	.25
181	*Jimmy Anderson*	.75
182	Juan Melo	.15
183	*Pablo Ortega*	1.00
184	Calvin Pickering	.40
185	Reggie Taylor	.15
186	*Jeff Farnsworth*	.40
187	Terrence Long	.15
188	Geoff Jenkins	.15
189	*Steve Rain*	.40
190	*Nerio Rodriguez*	1.00
191	Derrick Gibson	.40
192	Darin Blood	.40
193	Ben Davis	.15
194	*Adrian Beltre*	10.00
195	*Damian Sapp*	1.50
196	*Kerry Wood*	4.00
197	Nate Rolison	1.50
198	Fernando Tatis	4.00
199	*Brad Penny*	.40
200	*Jake Westbrook*	.75
201	Edwin Diaz	.15
202	*Joe Fontenot*	.60
203	*Matt Halloran*	.75
204	Blake Stein	.40
205	Onan Masaoka	.15
206	Ben Petrick	.15
207	Matt Clement	.75
208	Todd Greene	.15
209	Ray Ricken	.15
210	*Eric Chavez*	5.00
211	Edgard Velazquez	.40
212	*Bruce Chen*	1.50
213	*Danny Patterson*	.40
214	Jeff Yoder	.15
215	*Luis Ordaz*	.40
216	Chris Widger	.15
217	Jason Brester	.15
218	Carlton Loewer	.15
219	*Chris Reitsma*	1.50
220	Neifi Perez	.15
221	*Hideki Irabu*	5.00
222	Ellis Burks	.15
223	Pedro J. Martinez	.30
224	Kenny Lofton	1.00
225	Randy Johnson	.75
226	Terry Steinbach	.15
227	Bernie Williams	.75
228	Dean Palmer	.15
229	Alan Benes	.15
230	Marquis Grissom	.15
231	Gary Sheffield	.40
232	Curt Schilling	.15
233	Reggie Sanders	.15
234	Bobby Higginson	.15
235	Moises Alou	.25
236	Tom Glavine	.30
237	Mark Grace	.30
238	Ramon Martinez	.15
239	Rafael Palmeiro	.30
240	John Olerud	.15
241	Dante Bichette	.30
242	Greg Vaughn	.15
243	Jeff Bagwell	1.50
244	Barry Bonds	1.00
245	Pat Hentgen	.15
246	Jim Thome	.75

#	Player	Price
247	Jermaine Allensworth	.15
248	Andy Pettitte	1.00
249	Jay Bell	.15
250	John Jaha	.15
251	Jim Edmonds	.15
252	Ron Gant	.15
253	David Cone	.30
254	Jose Canseco	.40
255	Jay Buhner	.30
256	Greg Maddux	2.50
257	Brian McRae	.15
258	Lance Johnson	.15
259	Travis Fryman	.15
260	Paul O'Neill	.30
261	Ivan Rodriguez	.75
262	Gregg Jefferies	.15
263	Fred McGriff	.30
264	Derek Bell	.15
265	Jeff Conine	.15
266	Mike Piazza	2.50
267	Mark Grudzielanek	.15
268	Brady Anderson	.15
269	Marty Cordova	.15
270	Ray Durham	.15
271	Joe Carter	.15
272	Brian Jordan	.15
273	David Justice	.40
274	Tony Gwynn	2.00
275	Larry Walker	.40
276	Cecil Fielder	.30
277	Mo Vaughn	1.00
278	Alex Fernandez	.15
279	Michael Tucker	.15
280	Jose Valentin	.15
281	Sandy Alomar	.15
282	Todd Hollandsworth	.15
283	Rico Brogna	.15
284	Rusty Greer	.15
285	Roberto Hernandez	.15
286	Hal Morris	.15
287	Johnny Damon	.15
288	Todd Hundley	.30
289	Rondell White	.30
290	Frank Thomas	4.00
291	*Don Denbow*	.15
292	Derrek Lee	.15
293	Todd Walker	.50
294	Scott Rolen	1.50
295	Wes Helms	1.50
296	Bob Abreu	.15
297	John Patterson	.15
298	Alex Gonzalez	.15
299	*Grant Roberts*	3.00
300	Jeff Suppan	.15
301	Luke Wilcox	.15
302	Marlon Anderson	.15
303	Ray Brown	.15
304	*Mike Caruso*	1.50
305	Sam Marsonek	.40
306	*Brady Raggio*	.40
307	*Kevin McGlinchy*	.75
308	Roy Halladay	.50
309	*Jeremi Gonzalez*	1.00
310	Aramis Ramirez	1.25
311	Dermal Brown	.50
312	Justin Thompson	.15
313	Jay Tessmer	.15
314	Mike Johnson	.15
315	Danny Clyburn	.15
316	Bruce Aven	.15
317	*Keith Foulke*	.40
318	*Jimmy Osting*	.40
319	*Valerio DeLosSantos*	.40
320	Shannon Stewart	.15
321	Willie Adams	.15
322	Larry Barnes	.15
323	Mark Johnson	.15
324	*Chris Stowers*	.40
325	Brandon Reed	.15
326	Randy Winn	.15
327	Steven Chavez	.15
328	Nomar Garciaparra	1.50
329	*Jacque Jones*	2.00
330	Chris Clemons	.15
331	Todd Helton	1.50
332	Ryan Brannan	.40
333	Alex Sanchez	.15
334	Arnold Gooch	.15
335	Russell Branyan	1.00
336	Daryle Ward	.15
337	*John LeRoy*	.40
338	Steve Cox	.15
339	Kevin Witt	.15
340	Norm Hutchins	.15
341	Gabby Martinez	.15
342	Kris Detmers	.15
343	*Mike Villano*	.50
344	Preston Wilson	.15
345	*Jim Manias*	.40
346	*Deivi Cruz*	.25
347	*Donzell McDonald*	.40

#	Player	Price
348	*Rod Myers*	.40
349	*Shawn Chacon*	.40
350	*Elvin Hernandez*	.40
351	*Orlando Cabrera*	1.00
352	Brian Banks	.15
353	Robbie Bell	.15
354	Brad Rigby	.15
355	Scott Elarton	.15
356	*Kevin Sweeney*	.75
357	Steve Soderstrom	.15
358	Ryan Nye	.15
359	*Marlon Allen*	.40
360	*Donny Leon*	.40
361	*Garrett Neubart*	.40
362	*Abraham Nunez*	.75
363	*Adam Eaton*	.40
364	*Octavio Dotel*	.40
365	*Dean Crow*	.40
366	*Jason Baker*	.40
367	Sean Casey	.50
368	*Joe Lawrence*	.40
369	*Adam Johnson*	.40
370	*Scott Schoeneweis*	.40
371	Gerald Witasick, Jr.	.15
372	*Ronnie Belliard*	.40
373	Russ Ortiz	.15
374	*Robert Stratton*	.40
375	Bobby Estalella	.15
376	*Corey Lee*	.40
377	Carlos Beltran	.15
378	Mike Cameron	.50
379	*Scott Randall*	.40
380	*Corey Erickson*	1.50
381	Jay Canizaro	.15
382	*Kerry Robinson*	.40
383	*Todd Noel*	.40
384	*A.J. Zapp*	1.50
385	Jarrod Washburn	.15
386	Ben Grieve	1.50
387	*Javier Vazquez*	.40
388	Tony Graffanino	.15
389	*Travis Lee*	15.00
390	DaRond Stovall	.15
391	*Dennis Reyes*	.40
392	Danny Buxbaum	.15
393	Marc Lewis	1.50
394	Kelvim Escobar	1.00
395	Danny Klassen	.15
396	Ken Cloude	.50
397	Gabe Alvarez	.15
398	*Jaret Wright*	2.50
399	Raul Casanova	.15
400	*Clayton Brunner*	.40
401	*Jason Marquis*	.75
402	Marc Kroon	.15
403	Jamey Wright	.15
404	*Matt Snyder*	.40
405	*Josh Garrett*	1.00
406	Juan Encarnacion	.75
407	Heath Murray	.15
408	*Brett Herbison*	.50
409	*Brent Butler*	1.00
410	*Danny Peoples*	.50
411	*Miguel Tejada*	4.00
412	Damian Moss	.15
413	Jim Pittsley	.15
414	Dmitri Young	.15
415	Glendon Rusch	.15
416	Vladimir Guerrero	2.00
417	Cole Liniak	1.50
418	Ramon Hernandez	.75
419	*Cliff Politte*	.50
420	Mel Rosario	.50
421	*Jorge Carrion*	.50
422	*John Barnes*	.40
423	*Chris Stowe*	.40
424	*Vernon Wells*	.40
425	*Brett Caradonna*	.50
426	*Scott Hodges*	.50
427	*Jon Garland*	.40
428	*Nathan Haynes*	.50
429	*Geoff Goetz*	.50
430	*Adam Kennedy*	.50
431	*T.J. Tucker*	.50
432	*Aaron Akin*	.50
433	*Jayson Werth*	.50
434	Glenn Davis	.50
435	*Mark Mangum*	.50
436	*Troy Cameron*	.50
437	*J.J. Davis*	.50
438	*Lance Berkman*	.40
439	*Jason Standridge*	.75
440	*Jason Dellaero*	1.00

1997 Bowman Autographs

A total of 90 players signed autographs for inclusion in both Series I and II packs. Each autograph card is printed on 16-point stock and features a special Certified Autograph stamp. Every autograph card can be found in one of three versions. A blue ink version was inserted 1:96 packs; black ink 1:503 packs; gold ink 1:1,509 packs.

	MT
Complete Set (90):	2000.
Complete Series 1 Set (46):	900.00
Complete Series 2 Set (44):	1200.
Common Blue Ink:	
Black Ink Autos:	1.5x to 2.5x
Gold Ink Autos:	4x to 6x
Multipliers doesn't apply to Jeter	

#	Player	Price
1	Jeff Abbott	15.00
2	Bob Abreu	20.00
3	Willie Adams	15.00
4	Brian Banks	15.00
5	Kris Benson	50.00
6	Darin Blood	15.00
7	Jaime Bluma	15.00
8	Kevin Brown	20.00
9	Ray Brown	15.00
10	Homer Bush	15.00
11	Mike Cameron	25.00
12	Jay Canizaro	15.00
13	Luis Castillo	15.00
14	Dave Coggin	20.00
15	Bartolo Colon	20.00
16	Rocky Coppinger	15.00
17	Jacob Cruz	25.00
18	Jose Cruz	140.00
19	Jeff D'Amico	20.00
20	Ben Davis	25.00
21	Mike Drumbright	15.00
22	Scott Elarton	15.00
23	Darin Erstad	50.00
24	Bobby Estalella	20.00
25	Joe Fontenot	15.00
26	Tom Fordham	15.00
27	Brad Fullmer	20.00
28	Chris Fussell	15.00
29	Karim Garcia	25.00
30	Kris Detmers	15.00
31	Todd Greene	25.00
32	Ben Grieve	50.00
33	Vladimir Guerrero	75.00
34	Jose Guillen	60.00
35	Roy Halladay	15.00
36	Wes Helms	40.00
37	Chad Hermansen	40.00
38	Richard Hidalgo	20.00
39	Todd Hollandsworth	20.00
40	Damian Jackson	15.00
41	Derek Jeter	125.00
42	Andruw Jones	125.00
43	Brooks Kieschnick	20.00
44	Eugene Kingsale	15.00
45	Paul Konerko	50.00
46	Marc Kroon	15.00
47	Derrek Lee	40.00
48	Travis Lee	100.00
49	Terrence Long	15.00
50	Curt Lyons	15.00
51	Elieser Marrero	20.00
52	Rafael Medina	15.00
53	Juan Melo	20.00
54	Shane Monahan	20.00
55	Julio Mosquera	15.00
56	Heath Murray	15.00
57	Ryan Nye	15.00
58	Kevin Orie	25.00
59	Russ Ortiz	15.00
60	Carl Pavano	30.00
61	Jay Payton	25.00
62	Neifi Perez	25.00
63	Sidney Ponson	15.00
64	Calvin Reese	15.00
65	Ray Ricken	15.00
66	Brad Rigby	15.00
67	Adam Riggs	15.00
68	Ruben Rivera	25.00
69	J.J. Johnson	15.00
70	Scott Rolen	75.00
71	Tony Saunders	15.00
72	Donnie Sadler	15.00
73	Richie Sexson	25.00
74	Scott Spiezio	25.00
75	Everett Stull	15.00
76	Mike Sweeney	15.00
77	Fernando Tatis	40.00
78	Miguel Tejada	50.00
79	Justin Thompson	25.00
80	Justin Towle	25.00
81	Billy Wagner	25.00
82	Todd Walker	35.00
83	Luke Wilcox	15.00
84	Paul Wilder	25.00

85	Enrique Wilson	15.00
86	Kerry Wood	35.00
87	Jamey Wright	20.00
88	Ron Wright	25.00
89	Dmitri Young	20.00
90	Nelson Figueroa	15.00

1997 Bowman International Best

This 220-card parallel set features a flag design on the background of each card front depicting the player's country of origin. One International Best card was inserted in every pack.

		MT
Complete Set (20):		100.00
Common Player:		2.00
Refractors:		2x to 3x
Atomic Refractors:		3x to 5x
BBI1	Frank Thomas	20.00
BBI2	Ken Griffey Jr.	20.00
BBI3	Juan Gonzalez	10.00
BBI4	Bernie Williams	4.00
BBI5	Hideo Nomo	4.00
BBI6	Sammy Sosa	3.00
BBI7	Larry Walker	3.00
BBI8	Vinny Castilla	2.00
BBI9	Mariano Rivera	2.00
BBI10	Rafael Palmeiro	2.00
BBI11	Nomar Garciaparra	10.00
BBI12	Todd Walker	3.00
BBI13	Andruw Jones	12.00
BBI14	Vladimir Guerrero	10.00
BBI15	Ruben Rivera	2.00
BBI16	Bob Abreu	2.00
BBI17	Karim Garcia	2.00
BBI18	Katsuhiro Maeda	2.00
BBI19	Jose Cruz	20.00
BBI20	Damian Moss	3.00

1997 Bowman's Best Preview

This 20-card set, featuring 10 veterans and 10 prospects, features a preview of the design used on the Bowman's Best product. Three different versions of the Preview cards were available: Regular version (1:12 packs), Refractors (1:48) and Atomic Refractors (1:96).

		MT
Complete Set (20):		125.00
Common Player:		2.00
Refractors:		2x to 3x
Atomic Refractors:		3x to 5x
1	Frank Thomas	20.00
2	Ken Griffey Jr.	20.00
3	Barry Bonds	5.00
4	Derek Jeter	12.00
5	Chipper Jones	12.00
6	Mark McGwire	8.00
7	Cal Ripken Jr.	15.00
8	Kenny Lofton	5.00
9	Gary Sheffield	3.00
10	Jeff Bagwell	10.00
11	Wilton Guerrero	3.00
12	Scott Rolen	8.00
13	Todd Walker	5.00
14	Ruben Rivera	2.00
15	Andruw Jones	12.00
16	Nomar Garciaparra	8.00
17	Vladimir Guerrero	10.00
18	Miguel Tejada	5.00
19	Bartolo Colon	2.00
20	Katsuhiro Maeda	2.00

1997 Bowman Rookie of the Year Candidates

This 15-card insert was inserted in one per 12 packs of Bowman Series II. Fronts featured a color shot of the player over a textured foil background, with the player's name across the bottom and the words "Rookie of the Year Favorites" across the top with the word "Rookie" in large script letters. Card numbers carried a "ROY" prefix.

		MT
Complete Set (15):		30.00
Common Player:		1.50
ROY1	Jeff Abbott	1.50
ROY2	Karim Garcia	2.50
ROY3	Todd Helton	4.00
ROY4	Richard Hidalgo	1.50
ROY5	Geoff Jenkins	2.00
ROY6	Russ Johnson	1.50
ROY7	Paul Konerko	4.00
ROY8	Mark Kotsay	5.00
ROY9	Ricky Ledee	5.00
ROY10	Travis Lee	12.00
ROY11	Derrek Lee	2.00
ROY12	Elieser Marrero	1.50
ROY13	Juan Melo	1.50
ROY14	Brian Rose	1.50
ROY15	Fernando Tatis	3.00

1997 Bowman Scouts' Honor Roll

This insert features 15 prospects deemed to have the most potential by Topps' scouts. Each card features a double-etched foil design and is inserted 1:12 packs.

		MT
Complete Set (15):		75.00
Common Player:		1.50
1	Dmitri Young	1.50
2	Bob Abreu	1.50
3	Vladimir Guerrero	10.00
4	Paul Konerko	5.00

5	Kevin Orie	2.00
6	Todd Walker	0.00
7	Ben Grieve	3.00
8	Darin Erstad	8.00
9	Derrek Lee	2.00
10	Jose Cruz	20.00
11	Scott Rolen	8.00
12	Travis Lee	15.00
13	Andruw Jones	12.00
14	Wilton Guerrero	1.50
15	Nomar Garciaparra	8.00

1997 Bowman's Best

The 200-card base set is divided into a 100-card subset featuring current super-stars on a gold chromium stock, and 100 cards of top prospects on a silver chromium stock. Packs contained six cards each and carried a suggested retail price of $5 each. Autographed cards of 10 different players were randomly inserted into packs, with each player signing regular, Refractor and Atomic Refractor versions of their cards. Bowman's Best Laser Cuts and Mirror Image are the two other inserts, each with Refractor and Atomic Refractor editions.

		MT
Complete Set (200):		100.00
Common Player:		.25
Star Refractors:		6x to 10x
Young Star & RC Refractors:		4x to 8x
Star Atomics:		12x to 20x
Yng Star & RC Atomics:		8x to 15x
1	Ken Griffey Jr.	8.00
2	Cecil Fielder	.40
3	Albert Belle	2.50
4	Todd Hundley	.50
5	Mike Piazza	5.00
6	Matt Williams	.75
7	Mo Vaughn	2.00
8	Ryne Sandberg	2.00
9	Chipper Jones	5.00
10	Edgar Martinez	.25
11	Kenny Lofton	2.00
12	Ron Gant	.25
13	Moises Alou	.25
14	Pat Hentgen	.25
15	Steve Finley	.25
16	Mark Grace	.50
17	Jay Buhner	.50
18	Jeff Conine	.25
19	Jim Edmonds	.25
20	Todd Hollandsworth	.25
21	Andy Petitte	2.00
22	Jim Thome	1.50
23	Eric Young	.25
24	Ray Lankford	.25
25	Marquis Grissom	.25
26	Tony Clark	2.00
27	Jermaine Allensworth	.25
28	Ellis Burks	.25
29	Tony Gwynn	3.00
30	Barry Larkin	.50
31	John Olerud	.25
32	Mariano Rivera	.40
33	Paul Molitor	1.25
34	Ken Caminiti	.50
35	Gary Sheffield	.75
36	Al Martin	.25
37	John Valentin	.25
38	Frank Thomas	8.00
39	John Jaha	.25
40	Greg Maddux	5.00
41	Alex Fernandez	.25
42	Dean Palmer	.25
43	Bernie Williams	1.50
44	Deion Sanders	.75
45	Mark McGwire	2.50
46	Brian Jordan	.25
47	Bernard Gilkey	.25
48	Will Clark	.50
49	Kevin Appier	.25
50	Tom Glavine	.40
51	Chuck Knoblauch	.50
52	Rondell White	.25
53	Greg Vaughn	.25
54	Mike Mussina	1.50
55	Brian McRae	.25
56	Chili Davis	.25
57	Wade Boggs	.50
58	Jeff Bagwell	3.00
59	Roberto Alomar	1.50
60	Dennis Eckersley	.25
61	Ryan Klesko	1.00
62	Manny Ramirez	2.00
63	John Wetteland	.25
64	Cal Ripken Jr.	6.00
65	Edgar Renteria	.25
66	Tino Martinez	.75
67	Larry Walker	.75
68	Gregg Jefferies	.25
69	Lance Johnson	.25
70	Carlos Delgado	.25
71	Craig Biggio	.40
72	Jose Canseco	.60
73	Barry Bonds	2.00
74	Juan Gonzalez	3.00
75	Eric Karros	.25
76	Reggie Sanders	.25
77	Robin Ventura	.25
78	Hideo Nomo	1.50
79	David Justice	.50
80	Vinny Castilla	.25
81	Travis Fryman	.25
82	Derek Jeter	5.00
83	Sammy Sosa	1.00
84	Ivan Rodriguez	1.50
85	Rafael Palmeiro	.50
86	Roger Clemens	2.00
87	Jason Giambi	.25
88	Andres Galarraga	.50
89	Jermaine Dye	.25
90	Joe Carter	.25
91	Brady Anderson	.25
92	Derek Bell	.25
93	Randy Johnson	1.50
94	Fred McGriff	.50
95	John Smoltz	.40
96	Harold Baines	.25
97	Raul Mondesi	.50
98	Tim Salmon	.50
99	Carlos Baerga	.25
100	Dante Bichette	.50
101	Vladimir Guerrero	5.00
102	Richard Hidalgo	.25
103	Paul Konerko	1.00
104	Alex Gonzalez	.25
105	Jason Dickson	.50
106	Jose Rosado	.25
107	Todd Walker	2.00
108	*Seth Greisinger*	.50
109	Todd Helton	2.00
110	Ben Davis	.25
111	Bartolo Colon	.25
112	Elieser Marrero	.25
113	Jeff D'Amico	.25
114	*Miguel Tejada*	7.00
115	Darin Erstad	4.00
116	*Kris Benson*	4.00
117	*Adrian Beltre*	10.00
118	Neifi Perez	.25
119	Calvin Reese	.25
120	Carl Pavano	1.25
121	Juan Melo	.25
122	*Kevin McGlinchy*	.25
123	Pat Cline	.25

124	*Felix Heredia*	.60
125	Aaron Boone	.25
126	Glendon Rusch	.25
127	Mike Cameron	.75
128	Justin Thompson	.25
129	*Chad Hermansen*	5.00
130	*Sidney Ponson*	.50
131	*Willie Martinez*	1.00
132	*Paul Wilder*	2.00
133	Geoff Jenkins	.25
134	*Roy Halladay*	.50
135	Carlos Guillen	.25
136	Tony Batista	.25
137	Todd Greene	.25
138	Luis Castillo	.25
139	*Jimmy Anderson*	.75
140	Edgard Velazquez	.40
141	Chris Snopek	.25
142	Ruben Rivera	.25
143	*Javier Valentin*	.40
144	Brian Rose	.35
145	*Fernando Tatis*	4.00
146	*Dean Crow*	.25
147	Karim Garcia	.40
148	Dante Powell	.25
149	*Hideki Irabu*	5.00
150	Matt Morris	.50
151	Wes Helms	2.00
152	Russ Johnson	.25
153	Jarrod Washburn	.25
154	*Kerry Wood*	5.00
155	*Joe Fontenot*	.60
156	Eugene Kingsale	.25
157	Terrence Long	.25
158	Calvin Maduro	.25
159	Jeff Suppan	.25
160	DaRond Stovall	.25
161	Mark Redman	.25
162	*Ken Cloude*	.50
163	Bobby Estalella	.25
164	*Abraham Nunez*	.25
165	Derrick Gibson	.40
166	*Mike Drumright*	.75
167	Katsuhiro Maeda	.25
168	Jeff Liefer	.40
169	Ben Grieve	.75
170	Bob Abreu	.25
171	Shannon Stewart	.25
172	*Braden Looper*	.50
173	Brant Brown	.25
174	Marlon Anderson	.25
175	Brad Fullmer	.25
176	Carlos Beltran	.25
177	Nomar Garciaparra	4.00
178	Derrek Lee	.25
179	*Valerio DeLosSantos*	.25
180	Dmitri Young	.25
181	Jamey Wright	.25
182	*Hiram Bocachica*	1.50
183	Wilton Guerrero	.25
184	Chris Carpenter	.25
185	Scott Spiezio	.25
186	Andruw Jones	5.00
187	*Travis Lee*	20.00
188	*Jose Cruz Jr.*	25.00
189	Jose Guillen	1.50
190	Jeff Abbott	.25
191	*Ricky Ledee*	6.00
192	Mike Sweeney	.25
193	Donnie Sadler	.25
194	Scott Rolen	4.00
195	Kevin Orie	.25
196	*Jason Conti*	.75
197	*Mark Kotsay*	5.00
198	*Eric Milton*	1.50
199	Russell Branyan	1.50
200	Alex Sanchez	.25

1997 Bowman's Best Autographs

Ten different players each signed 10 regular versions of their respective Bowman's Best cards (1:170 packs), 10 of their Bowman's Best Refractors (1:2,036 packs) and 10 of their Bowman's Best Atomic Refractors (1:6,107 packs). Each autograph card features a special Certified Autograph stamp.

		MT
Complete Set (10):		600.00
Common Player:		25.00
Refractors		1.5x to 2x
Atomics		5x to 8x
29	Tony Gwynn	125.00
33	Paul Molitor	40.00
82	Derek Jeter	140.00

91	Brady Anderson	30.00
98	Tim Salmon	35.00
107	Todd Walker	30.00
183	Wilton Guerrero	25.00
185	Scott Spiezio	25.00
188	Jose Cruz Jr.	150.00
194	Scott Rolen	75.00

1997 Bowman's Best Cuts

Each card in this 20-card insert features a laser-cut design on Chromium stock. Again, three versions of each card are available: Regular (1:24 packs), Refractor (1:48 packs) and Atomic Refractors (1:96 packs).

		MT
Complete Set (20):		300.00
Common Player:		4.00
Refractors:		1.5x to 2x
Atomic Refractors:		2.5x to 4x
BC1	Derek Jeter	25.00
BC2	Chipper Jones	25.00
BC3	Frank Thomas	40.00
BC4	Cal Ripken Jr.	30.00
BC5	Mark McGwire	15.00
BC6	Ken Griffey Jr.	40.00
BC7	Jeff Bagwell	18.00
BC8	Mike Piazza	25.00
BC9	Ken Caminiti	4.00
BC10	Albert Belle	15.00
BC11	Jose Cruz Jr.	40.00
BC12	Wilton Guerrero	4.00
BC13	Darin Erstad	15.00
BC14	Andruw Jones	25.00
BC15	Scott Rolen	15.00
BC16	Jose Guillen	8.00
BC17	Bob Abreu	4.00
BC18	Vladimir Guerrero	20.00
BC19	Todd Walker	8.00
BC20	Nomar Garciaparra	15.00

1997 Bowman's Best Jumbos

This large-format (4" x 5-5/8") version of 1997 Bowman's Best features 16 of the season's top stars and hottest rookies. Utilizing Topps chromium, Refractor and Atomic Refractor technologies, the cards are identical in every way except size to the regular-issue Bowman's Best. The jumbos were sold only through Topps Stadium Club. Each of the sets consists of 12 chromium cards, plus three randomly packaged Refractors and one Atomic Refractor. Only 900 sets were produced according to Topps sales literature.

		MT
Complete Set (16):		125.00
Common Player:		3.00
Refractor:		5x-7Xx
Atomic Refractor:		8x-12x
1	Ken Griffey Jr.	17.50
5	Mike Piazza	12.50
9	Chipper Jones	12.50
11	Kenny Lofton	7.50
29	Tony Gwynn	12.50
33	Paul Molitor	12.50
38	Frank Thomas	18.00
45	Mark McGwire	12.50
64	Cal Ripken Jr.	16.00
73	Barry Bonds	7.50
74	Juan Gonzalez	10.00
82	Derek Jeter	10.00
101	Vladimir Guerrero	10.00
177	Nomar Garciaparra	10.00
186	Andruw Jones	12.50
188	Jose Cruz, Jr.	25.00

1997 Bowman's Best Mirror Image

This 10-card insert features four players on each double-sided card - two veterans and two rookies - utilizing Finest technology. Regular Mirror Image cards are found 1:48 packs, while Refractor versions are seeded 1:96 packs and Atomic Refractors are found 1:192 packs.

		MT
Complete Set (10):		160.00
Common Card:		12.00
Refractors:		1.5x
Atomic Refractors:		2x to 4x
MI1	Nomar Garciaparra, Derek Jeter, Hiram Bocachica, Barry Larkin	20.00
MI2	Travis Lee, Frank Thomas, Derrek Lee, Jeff Bagwell	25.00
MI3	Kerry Wood, Greg Maddux, Kris Benson, John Smoltz	20.00
MI4	Kevin Brown, Ivan Rodriguez, Elieser Marrero, Mike Piazza	20.00
MI5	Jose Cruz Jr., Ken Griffey Jr., Andruw Jones, Barry Bonds	30.00
MI6	Jose Guillen, Juan Gonzalez, Richard Hidalgo, Gary Sheffield	15.00
MI7	Paul Konerko, Mark McGwire, Todd Helton, Rafael Palmeiro	15.00
MI8	Wilton Guerrero, Craig Biggio, Donnie Sadler, Chuck Knoblauch	12.00
MI9	Russell Branyan, Matt Williams, Adrian Beltre, Chipper Jones	20.00
MI10	Bob Abreu, Kenny Lofton, Vladimir Guerrero, Albert Belle	20.00

1997 Donruss

Donruss' 1997 regular-issue Series I set has 300 cards, including 30 Rated Rookies (1 in 8). Each regular

card has a full-bleed color action photo on the front; the player's name, team logo and position are in the lower-left corner. The Donruss logo is in the upper-left corner. The horizontal back has a photo on one side, flanked on the opposite side by a chart of career statistics and a brief player profile. The two sides are separated by five tilted capsules, each containing a biographical tidbit. The player's name, team logo and card number are in the upper right-hand corner. A Press Proofs parallel set was also made of 270 cards, excluding the 30 Rated Rookies. There were 2,000 of these sets made. Other Series I inserts include the annual Diamond Kings, 12 Elite inserts, 15 Armed and Dangerous cards, 15 Longball Leaders and 15 Rocket Launchers. A 180-card Donruss Update set was released later, designed as a follow-up to the regular '97 Donruss series. Regular cards are numbered #271-450. Like the first series, Press Proofs and Gold Press Proof parallel inserts were available. Other update inserts include Dominators, Franchise Futures, Power Alley, Rookie Diamond Kings and a special Cal Ripken Jr. set.

		MT
Complete Set (450):		45.00
Complete Series 1 Set (270):		25.00
Complete Series 2 Set (180):		20.00
Common Player:		.10
Wax Box:		45.00
1	Juan Gonzalez	1.25
2	Jim Edmonds	.15
3	Tony Gwynn	1.00
4	Andres Galarraga	.20
5	Joe Carter	.20
6	Raul Mondesi	.20
7	Greg Maddux	1.50
8	Travis Fryman	.10
9	Brian Jordan	.10
10	Henry Rodriguez	.10
11	Manny Ramirez	.75
12	Mark McGwire	1.00
13	Marc Newfield	.10
14	Craig Biggio	.10
15	Sammy Sosa	.20
16	Brady Anderson	.10
17	Wade Boggs	.15
18	Charles Johnson	.10
19	Matt Williams	.20
20	Denny Neagle	.10
21	Ken Griffey Jr.	2.50
22	Robin Ventura	.10
23	Barry Larkin	.20
24	Todd Zeile	.10
25	Chuck Knoblauch	.10
26	Todd Hundley	.10
27	Roger Clemens	.75
28	Michael Tucker	.10
29	Rondell White	.10
30	Osvaldo Fernandez	.10
31	Ivan Rodriguez	.50
32	Alex Fernandez	.10
33	Jason Isringhausen	.10
34	Chipper Jones	1.50
35	Paul O'Neill	.10
36	Hideo Nomo	.60
37	Roberto Alomar	.75
38	Derek Bell	.10
39	Paul Molitor	.25
40	Andy Benes	.10

No.	Player	Value
41	Steve Trachsel	.10
42	J.T. Snow	.10
43	Jason Kendall	.10
44	Alex Rodriguez	2.50
45	Joey Hamilton	.10
46	Carlos Delgado	.10
47	Jason Giambi	.10
48	Larry Walker	.30
49	Derek Jeter	1.25
50	Kenny Lofton	.75
51	Devon White	.10
52	Matt Mieske	.10
53	Melvin Nieves	.10
54	Jose Canseco	.25
55	Tino Martinez	.30
56	Rafael Palmeiro	.15
57	Edgardo Alfonzo	.10
58	Jay Buhner	.15
59	Shane Reynolds	.10
60	Steve Finley	.10
61	Bobby Higginson	.10
62	Dean Palmer	.10
63	Terry Pendleton	.10
64	Marquis Grissom	.10
65	Mike Stanley	.10
66	Moises Alou	.10
67	Ray Lankford	.10
68	Marty Cordova	.15
69	John Olerud	.10
70	David Cone	.10
71	Benito Santiago	.10
72	Ryne Sandberg	.60
73	Rickey Henderson	.10
74	Roger Cedeno	.10
75	Wilson Alvarez	.10
76	Tim Salmon	.20
77	Orlando Merced	.10
78	Vinny Castilla	.10
79	Ismael Valdes	.10
80	Dante Bichette	.20
81	Kevin Brown	.10
82	Andy Pettitte	.60
83	Scott Stahoviak	.10
84	Mickey Tettleton	.10
85	Jack McDowell	.10
86	Tom Glavine	.10
87	Gregg Jefferies	.10
88	Chili Davis	.10
89	Randy Johnson	.35
90	John Mabry	.10
91	Billy Wagner	.10
92	Jeff Cirillo	.10
93	Trevor Hoffman	.10
94	Juan Guzman	.10
95	Geronimo Berroa	.10
96	Bernard Gilkey	.10
97	Danny Tartabull	.10
98	Johnny Damon	.20
99	Charlie Hayes	.10
100	Reggie Sanders	.10
101	Robby Thompson	.10
102	Bobby Bonilla	.10
103	Reggie Jefferson	.10
104	John Smoltz	.20
105	Jim Thome	.35
106	Ruben Rivera	.40
107	Darren Oliver	.10
108	Mo Vaughn	1.00
109	Roger Pavlik	.10
110	Terry Steinbach	.10
111	Jermaine Dye	.25
112	Mark Grudzielanek	.10
113	Rick Aguilera	.10
114	Jamey Wright	.10
115	Eddie Murray	.35
116	Brian Hunter	.10
117	Hal Morris	.10
118	Tom Pagnozzi	.10
119	Mike Mussina	.35
120	Mark Grace	.20
121	Cal Ripken Jr.	2.00
122	Tom Goodwin	.10
123	Paul Sorrento	.10
124	Jay Bell	.10
125	Todd Hollandsworth	.10
126	Edgar Martinez	.10
127	George Arias	.10
128	Greg Vaughn	.10
129	Roberto Hernandez	.10
130	Delino DeShields	.10
131	Bill Pulsipher	.10
132	Joey Cora	.10
133	Mariano Rivera	.25
134	Mike Piazza	1.50
135	Carlos Baerga	.15
136	Jose Mesa	.10
137	Will Clark	.25
138	Frank Thomas	2.50
139	John Wetteland	.10
140	Shawn Estes	.10
141	Garret Anderson	.10
142	Andre Dawson	.10
143	Eddie Taubensee	.10
144	Ryan Klesko	.50
145	Rocky Coppinger	.10
146	Jeff Bagwell	1.25
147	Donovan Osborne	.10
148	Greg Myers	.10
149	Brant Brown	.10
150	Kevin Elster	.10
151	Bob Wells	.10
152	Wally Joyner	.10
153	Rico Brogna	.10
154	Dwight Gooden	.10
155	Jermaine Allensworth	.10
156	Ray Durham	.10
157	Cecil Fielder	.20
158	Ryan Hancock	.10
159	Gary Sheffield	.20
160	Albert Belle	1.00
161	Tomas Perez	.10
162	David Doster	.10
163	John Valentin	.10
164	Danny Graves	.10
165	Jose Paniagua	.10
166	Brian Giles	.10
167	Barry Bonds	.75
168	Sterling Hitchcock	.10
169	Bernie Williams	.50
170	Fred McGriff	.25
171	George Williams	.10
172	Amaury Telemaco	.10
173	Ken Caminiti	.10
174	Ron Gant	.10
175	David Justice	.15
176	James Baldwin	.10
177	Pat Hentgen	.10
178	Ben McDonald	.10
179	Tim Naehring	.10
180	Jim Eisenreich	.10
181	Ken Hill	.10
182	Paul Wilson	.10
183	Marvin Benard	.10
184	Alan Benes	.10
185	Ellis Burks	.10
186	Scott Servais	.10
187	David Segui	.10
188	Scott Brosius	.10
189	Jose Offerman	.10
190	Eric Davis	.10
191	Brett Butler	.10
192	Curtis Pride	.10
193	Yamil Benitez	.10
194	Chan Ho Park	.10
195	Bret Boone	.10
196	Omar Vizquel	.10
197	Orlando Miller	.10
198	Ramon Martinez	.10
199	Harold Baines	.10
200	Eric Young	.10
201	Fernando Vina	.10
202	Alex Gonzalez	.10
203	Fernando Valenzuela	.10
204	Steve Avery	.10
205	Ernie Young	.10
206	Kevin Appier	.10
207	Randy Myers	.10
208	Jeff Suppan	.10
209	James Mouton	.10
210	Russ Davis	.10
211	Al Martin	.10
212	Troy Percival	.10
213	Al Leiter	.10
214	Dennis Eckersley	.10
215	Mark Johnson	.10
216	Eric Karros	.10
217	Royce Clayton	.10
218	Tony Phillips	.10
219	Tim Wakefield	.10
220	Alan Trammell	.10
221	Eduardo Perez	.10
222	Butch Huskey	.10
223	Tim Belcher	.10
224	Jamie Moyer	.10
225	F.P. Santangelo	.10
226	Rusty Greer	.10
227	Jeff Brantley	.10
228	Mark Langston	.10
229	Ray Montgomery	.10
230	Rich Becker	.10
231	Ozzie Smith	.50
232	Rey Ordonez	.30
233	Ricky Otero	.10
234	Mike Cameron	.10
235	Mike Sweeney	.10
236	Mark Lewis	.10
237	Luis Gonzalez	.10
238	Marcus Jensen	.10
239	Ed Sprague	.10
240	Jose Valentin	.10
241	Jeff Frye	.10
242	Charles Nagy	.10
243	Carlos Garcia	.10
244	Mike Hampton	.10
245	B.J. Surhoff	.10
246	Wilton Guerrero	.10
247	Frank Rodriguez	.10
248	Gary Gaetti	.10
249	Lance Johnson	.10
250	Darren Bragg	.10
251	Darryl Hamilton	.10
252	John Jaha	.10
253	Craig Paquette	.10
254	Jaime Navarro	.10
255	Shawon Dunston	.10
256	Ron Wright	.75
257	Tim Belk	.10
258	Jeff Darwin	.10
259	Ruben Sierra	.10
260	Chuck Finley	.10
261	Darryl Strawberry	.10
262	Shannon Stewart	.10
263	Pedro Martinez	.10
264	Neifi Perez	.10
265	Jeff Conine	.10
266	Orel Hershiser	.10
267	Checklist 1-90 (Eddie Murray) (500 Career HR)	
268	Checklist 91-180 (Paul Molitor) (3,000 Career Hits)	.10
269	Checklist 181-270 (Barry Bonds) (300 Career HR)	.30
270	Checklist - inserts (Mark McGwire) (300 Career HR)	.20
271	Matt Williams	.30
272	Todd Zeile	.10
273	Roger Clemens	.75
274	Michael Tucker	.10
275	J.T. Snow	.10
276	Kenny Lofton	.75
277	Jose Canseco	.25
278	Marquis Grissom	.10
279	Moises Alou	.10
280	Benito Santiago	.10
281	Willie McGee	.10
282	Chili Davis	.10
283	Ron Coomer	.10
284	Orlando Merced	.10
285	Delino DeShields	.10
286	John Wetteland	.10
287	Darren Daulton	.10
288	Lee Stevens	.10
289	Albert Belle	1.00
290	Sterling Hitchcock	.10
291	David Justice	.20
292	Eric Davis	.10
293	Brian Hunter	.10
294	Darryl Hamilton	.10
295	Steve Avery	.10
296	Joe Vitiello	.10
297	Jaime Navarro	.10
298	Eddie Murray	.30
299	Randy Myers	.10
300	Francisco Cordova	.10
301	Javier Lopez	.15
302	Geronimo Berroa	.10
303	Jeffrey Hammonds	.10
304	Deion Sanders	.25
305	Jeff Fassero	.10
306	Curt Schilling	.10
307	Robb Nen	.10
308	Mark McLemore	.10
309	Jimmy Key	.10
310	Quilvio Veras	.10
311	Bip Roberts	.10
312	Esteban Loaiza	.10
313	Andy Ashby	.10
314	Sandy Alomar Jr.	.10
315	Shawn Green	.10
316	Luis Castillo	.10
317	Benji Gil	.10
318	Otis Nixon	.10
319	Aaron Sele	.10
320	Brad Ausmus	.10
321	Troy O'Leary	.10
322	Terrell Wade	.10
323	Jeff King	.10
324	Kevin Seitzer	.10
325	Mark Wohlers	.10
326	Edgar Renteria	.10
327	Dan Wilson	.10
328	Brian McRae	.10
329	Rod Beck	.10
330	Julio Franco	.10
331	Dave Nilsson	.10
332	Glenallen Hill	.10
333	Kevin Elster	.10
334	Joe Girardi	.10
335	David Wells	.10
336	Jeff Blauser	.10
337	Darryl Kile	.10
338	Jeff Kent	.10
339	Jim Leyritz	.10
340	Todd Stottlemyre	.10
341	Tony Clark	.50
342	Chris Hoiles	.10
343	Mike Lieberthal	.10
344	Matt Lawton	.10
345	Alex Ochoa	.10
346	Chris Snopek	.10
347	Rudy Pemberton	.10
348	Eric Owens	.10
349	Joe Randa	.10
350	John Olerud	.10
351	Steve Karsay	.10
352	Mark Whiten	.10
353	Bob Abreu	.10
354	Bartolo Colon	.10
355	Vladimir Guerrero	1.50
356	Darin Erstad	1.25
357	Scott Rolen	1.25
358	Andruw Jones	2.00
359	Scott Spiezio	.10
360	Karim Garcia	.10
361	*Hideki Irabu*	2.00
362	Nomar Garciaparra	1.25
363	Dmitri Young	.10
364	*Bubba Trammell*	1.00
365	Kevin Orie	.10
366	Jose Rosado	.10
367	Jose Guillen	1.00
368	Brooks Kieschnick	.10
369	Pokey Reese	.10
370	Glendon Rusch	.10
371	Jason Dickson	.20
372	Todd Walker	.60
373	Justin Thompson	.10
374	Todd Greene	.10
375	Jeff Suppan	.10
376	Trey Beamon	.10
377	Damon Mashore	.10
378	Wendell Magee	.10
379	Shigetosi Hasegawa	.10
380	Bill Mueller	.10
381	Chris Widger	.10
382	Tony Grafannino	.10
383	Derrek Lee	.10
384	Brian Moehler	.10
385	Quinton McCracken	.10
386	Matt Morris	.20
387	Marvin Benard	.10
388	*Deivi Cruz*	.10
389	*Javier Valentin*	.20
390	Todd Dunwoody	.10
391	Derrick Gibson	.20
392	*Raul Casanova*	.10
393	George Arias	.10
394	*Tony Womack*	.25
395	Antone Williamson	.10
396	*Jose Cruz, Jr.*	7.00
397	Desi Relaford	.10
398	Frank Thomas (Hit List)	1.50
399	Ken Griffey Jr. (Hit List)	1.50
400	Cal Ripken Jr. (Hit List)	1.25
401	Chipper Jones (Hit List)	1.00
402	Mike Piazza (Hit List)	1.00
403	Gary Sheffield (Hit List)	.15
404	Alex Rodriguez (Hit List)	1.50
405	Wade Boggs (Hit List)	.15
406	Juan Gonzalez (Hit List)	.60
407	Tony Gwynn (Hit List)	.60
408	Edgar Martinez (Hit List)	.10
409	Jeff Bagwell (Hit List)	.60
410	Larry Walker (Hit List)	.15
411	Kenny Lofton (Hit List)	.35
412	Manny Ramirez (Hit List)	.35
413	Mark McGwire (Hit List)	.50
414	Roberto Alomar (Hit List)	.25
415	Derek Jeter (Hit List)	1.00
416	Brady Anderson (Hit List)	.10
417	Paul Molitor (Hit List)	.20
418	Dante Bichette (Hit List)	.15
419	Jim Edmonds (Hit List)	.10
420	Mo Vaughn (Hit List)	.35
421	Barry Bonds (Hit List)	.35
422	Rusty Greer (Hit List)	.10
423	Greg Maddux (King of the Hill)	1.00
424	Andy Pettitte (King of the Hill)	.35
425	John Smoltz (King of the Hill)	.10
426	Randy Johnson (King of the Hill)	.25
427	Hideo Nomo (King of the Hill)	.25
428	Roger Clemens (King of the Hill)	.35
429	Tom Glavine (King of the Hill)	.15
430	Pat Hentgen (King of the Hill)	.10

		MT
431	Kevin Brown	.10
	(King of the Hill)	
432	Mike Mussina	.25
	(King of the Hill)	
433	Alex Fernandez	.10
	(King of the Hill)	
434	Kevin Appier	.10
	(King of the Hill)	
435	David Cone	.15
	(King of the Hill)	
436	Jeff Fassero	.10
	(King of the Hill)	
437	John Wetteland	.10
	(King of the Hill)	
438	Barry Bonds, Ivan Rodriguez	.25
	(Interleague Showdown)	
439	Ken Griffey Jr., Andres Galarraga	1.00
	(Interleague Showdown)	
440	Fred McGriff, Rafael Palmeiro	.15
	(Interleague Showdown)	
441	Barry Larkin, Jim Thome	.20
	(Interleague Showdown)	
442	Sammy Sosa, Albert Belle	.30
	(Interleague Showdown)	
443	Bernie Williams, Todd Hundley	.20
	(Interleague Showdown)	
444	Chuck Knoblauch, Brian Jordan	.15
	(Interleague Showdown)	
445	Mo Vaughn, Jeff Conine	.25
	(Interleague Showdown)	
446	Ken Caminiti, Jason Giambi	.15
	(Interleague Showdown)	
447	Raul Mondesi, Tim Salmon	.15
	(Interleague Showdown)	
448	Checklist (Cal Ripken Jr.)	.75
449	Checklist (Greg Maddux)	.60
450	Checklist (Ken Griffey Jr.)	1.00

1997 Donruss Press Proofs

Each of the 270 cards in the Donruss Series I base set was also produced in a Press Proof parallel edition of 2,000 cards. Virtually identical in design to the regular cards, the Press Proofs are printed on a metallic background with silver-foil highlights. Each regular Press Proof back carries the notation "1 of 2000". Stated odds of finding a press proof are one per eight packs. A special "gold" press proof chase set features cards with gold-foil highlights, a notch die-cut at top and bottom, and numbered "1 of 500" on the back. Gold press proofs are found on average of once per 32 packs.

	MT
Press Proof Set (450):	1000.
Press Proof:	8x to 12x
Press Proof Yng Stars & RC's:	4x to 8x
Press Proof Gold Set (450):	2500.
Press Proof Gold Stars:	30x to 40x
PP Gold Yng Stars & RCs:	15x to 30x

1997 Donruss Armed and Dangerous

These 15 cards are numbered up to 5,000. They were inserted in 1997 Donruss Series I retail packs only.

		MT
Complete Set (15):		140.00
Common Player:		3.00
1	Ken Griffey Jr.	30.00
2	Raul Mondesi	5.00
3	Chipper Jones	20.00
4	Ivan Rodriguez	8.00
5	Randy Johnson	6.00
6	Alex Rodriguez	25.00
7	Larry Walker	5.00
8	Cal Ripken Jr.	25.00
9	Kenny Lofton	8.00
10	Barry Bonds	8.00
11	Derek Jeter	18.00
12	Charles Johnson	3.00
13	Greg Maddux	20.00
14	Roberto Alomar	6.00
15	Barry Larkin	3.00

1997 Donruss Diamond Kings

Diamond Kings this year are sequentially numbered from 1 to 10,000. To celebrate 15 years of this popular insert set, Donruss is offering collectors a one-of-a-kind piece of artwork if they find one of the 10 cards with the serial number 1,982 (1982 was the first year of the Diamond Kings). Those who find these cards can redeem them for an original artwork provided by artist Dan Gardiner. In addition, Donruss is printing the first 500 of each card on canvas stock.

		MT
Complete Set (10):		140.00
Common Player:		5.00
Canvas (1st 500):		5x to 10x
1	Ken Griffey Jr.	30.00
2	Cal Ripken Jr.	25.00
3	Mo Vaughn	10.00
4	Chuck Knoblauch	5.00
5	Jeff Bagwell	15.00
6	Henry Rodriguez	5.00
7	Mike Piazza	20.00
8	Ivan Rodriguez	10.00
9	Frank Thomas	30.00
10	Chipper Jones	20.00

1997 Donruss Elite Inserts

There were 2,500 sets of these insert cards made. The cards were randomly included in 1997 Donruss Series I packs.

		MT
Complete Set (12):		450.00
Common Player:		10.00
1	Frank Thomas	80.00
2	Paul Molitor	15.00
3	Sammy Sosa	10.00
4	Barry Bonds	20.00
5	Chipper Jones	50.00
6	Alex Rodriguez	65.00
7	Ken Griffey Jr.	80.00
8	Jeff Bagwell	30.00
9	Cal Ripken Jr.	65.00
10	Mo Vaughn	20.00
11	Mike Piazza	50.00
12	Juan Gonzalez	40.00

1997 Donruss Longball Leaders

These 1997 Donruss Series I inserts were limited to 5,000 each. They were seeded in retail packs only.

		MT
Complete Set (15):		90.00
Common Player:		2.00
1	Frank Thomas	25.00
2	Albert Belle	7.00
3	Mo Vaughn	6.00
4	Brady Anderson	2.00
5	Greg Vaughn	2.00
6	Ken Griffey Jr.	25.00
7	Jay Buhner	2.00
8	Juan Gonzalez	12.00
9	Mike Piazza	15.00
10	Jeff Bagwell	8.00
11	Sammy Sosa	4.00
12	Mark McGwire	8.00
13	Cecil Fielder	2.00
14	Ryan Klesko	4.00
15	Jose Canseco	4.00

1997 Donruss Rated Rookies

Although numbered more like an insert set, Rated Rookies were part of the regular-issue set. Cards are numbered 1-30, with no ratio given on packs. The cards are differentiated by a large silver-foil strip on the top right side with the words Rated Rookie.

		MT
Complete Set (30):		50.00
Common Player:		1.50
1	Jason Thompson	1.50
2	LaTroy Hawkins	1.50
3	Scott Rolen	10.00
4	Trey Beamon	1.50
5	Kimera Bartee	1.50
6	Nerio Rodriguez	1.50
7	Jeff D'Amico	1.50
8	Quinton McCracken	1.50
9	John Wasdin	1.50
10	Robin Jennings	1.50
11	Steve Gibralter	1.50
12	Tyler Houston	1.50
13	Tony Clark	4.00
14	Ugueth Urbina	1.50
15	Billy McMillon	1.50
16	Raul Casanova	1.50
17	Brooks Kieschnick	1.50
18	Luis Castillo	1.50
19	Edgar Renteria	2.50
20	Andruw Jones	15.00
21	Chad Mottola	1.50
22	Makoto Suzuki	1.50
23	Justin Thompson	1.50
24	Darin Erstad	8.00
25	Todd Walker	5.00
26	Todd Greene	1.50
27	Vladimir Guerrero	12.00
28	Darren Dreifort	1.50
29	John Burke	1.50
30	Damon Mashore	1.50

1997 Donruss Rocket Launchers

These 1997 Donruss Series I inserts are limited to 5,000 each. They were only included in magazine packs.

		MT
Complete Set (15):		100.00
Common Player:		3.00
1	Frank Thomas	25.00
2	Albert Belle	7.00
3	Chipper Jones	15.00
4	Mike Piazza	15.00
5	Mo Vaughn	6.00
6	Juan Gonzalez	12.00
7	Fred McGriff	4.00
8	Jeff Bagwell	8.00
9	Matt Williams	4.00
10	Gary Sheffield	3.00
11	Barry Bonds	6.00
12	Manny Ramirez	6.00
13	Henry Rodriguez	3.00
14	Jason Giambi	3.00
15	Cal Ripken Jr.	20.00

1997 Donruss Team Sets

A total of 165 cards were part of the Donruss Team Set issue. Packs consisted solely of players from one of 11 different teams. In addition, a full 150-card parallel set called Pennant Edition was available, featuring red and gold foil and a special "Pennant Edition" logo. Cards were sold in five-card packs for $1.99 each.

		MT
Comp. Angels Set (1-15):		2.50
Comp. Braves Set (16-30):		6.00
Comp. Orioles Set (31-45):		3.50
Comp. Red Sox Set (46-60):		3.00
Comp. White Sox Set (61-75):		4.00
Comp. Indians Set (76-90):		3.00
Comp. Rockies Set (91-105):		2.50
Comp. Dodgers Set (106-120):		0.50
Comp. Yankees Set (121-135):		5.00
Comp. Mariners Set (136-150):		10.00
Common Player:		.10
Pennant Edition Stars:		10x to 15x
Pennant Edit. Yng Stars & RC:		5x to 10x
1	Jim Edmonds	.15
2	Tim Salmon	.25
3	Tony Phillips	.10
4	Garret Anderson	.10
5	Troy Percival	.10
6	Mark Langston	.10
7	Chuck Finley	.10
8	Eddie Murray	.40
9	Jim Leyritz	.10
10	Darin Erstad	1.00
11	Jason Dickson	.10
12	Allen Watson	.10
13	Shigetosi Hasegawa	.10
14	Dave Hollins	.10
15	Gary DiSarcina	.10
16	Greg Maddux	2.00
17	Denny Neagle	.15
18	Chipper Jones	2.00
19	Tom Glavine	.20
20	John Smoltz	.20
21	Ryan Klesko	.40
22	Fred McGriff	.30
23	Michael Tucker	.10
24	Kenny Lofton	.75
25	Javier Lopez	.20
26	Mark Wohlers	.10
27	Jeff Blauser	.10
28	Andruw Jones	2.00
29	Tony Graffanino	.10
30	Terrell Wade	.10
31	Brady Anderson	.15
32	Roberto Alomar	.60
33	Rafael Palmeiro	.20
34	Mike Mussina	.60
35	Cal Ripken Jr.	2.50
36	Rocky Coppinger	.10
37	Randy Myers	.10
38	B.J. Surhoff	.10
39	Eric Davis	.10
40	Armando Benitez	.10
41	Jeffrey Hammonds	.10
42	Jimmy Key	.10
43	Chris Hoiles	.10
44	Mike Bordick	.10
45	Pete Incaviglia	.10
46	Mike Stanley	.10
47	Reggie Jefferson	.10
48	Mo Vaughn	.75
49	John Valentin	.10
50	Tim Naehring	.10
51	Jeff Suppan	.10
52	Tim Wakefield	.10
53	Jeff Frye	.10
54	Darren Bragg	.10
55	Steve Avery	.10
56	Shane Mack	.10
57	Aaron Sele	.10
58	Troy O'Leary	.10
59	Rudy Pemberton	.10
60	Nomar Garciaparra	2.00
61	Robin Ventura	.10
62	Wilson Alvarez	.10
63	Roberto Hernandez	.10
64	Frank Thomas	3.00
65	Ray Durham	.10
66	James Baldwin	.10
67	Harold Baines	.10
68	Doug Drabek	.10
69	Mike Cameron	.10
70	Albert Belle	1.00
71	Jaime Navarro	.10
72	Chris Snopek	.10
73	Lyle Mouton	.10
74	Dave Martinez	.10
75	Ozzie Guillen	.10
76	Manny Ramirez	.75
77	Jack McDowell	.10

78	Jim Thome	.50
79	Jose Mesa	.10
80	Brian Giles	.10
81	Omar Vizquel	.10
82	Charles Nagy	.10
83	Orel Hershiser	.10
84	Matt Williams	.25
85	Marquis Grissom	.15
86	David Justice	.20
87	Sandy Alomar	.10
88	Kevin Seitzer	.10
89	Julio Franco	.10
90	Bartolo Colon	.10
91	Andres Galarraga	.20
92	Larry Walker	.30
93	Vinny Castilla	.10
94	Dante Bichette	.20
95	Jamey Wright	.10
96	Ellis Burks	.10
97	Eric Young	.10
98	Neifi Perez	.10
99	Quinton McCracken	.10
100	Bruce Ruffin	.10
101	Walt Weiss	.10
102	Roger Bailey	.10
103	Jeff Reed	.10
104	Bill Swift	.10
105	Kirt Manwaring	.10
106	Raul Mondesi	.20
107	Hideo Nomo	.60
108	Roger Cedeno	.10
109	Ismael Valdes	.10
110	Todd Hollandsworth	.10
111	Mike Piazza	2.00
112	Brett Butler	.10
113	Chan Ho Park	.10
114	Ramon Martinez	.10
115	Eric Karros	.10
116	Wilton Guerrero	.10
117	Todd Zeile	.10
118	Karim Garcia	.20
119	Greg Gagne	.10
120	Darron Droifort	.10
121	Wade Boggs	.25
122	Paul O'Neill	.20
123	Derek Jeter	2.00
124	Tino Martinez	.25
125	David Cone	.20
126	Andy Pettitte	.75
127	Charlie Hayes	.10
128	Mariano Rivera	.20
129	Dwight Gooden	.20
130	Cecil Fielder	.20
131	Not Issued	.10
132	Darryl Strawberry	.15
133	Joe Girardi	.10
134	David Wells	.10
135	Hideki Irabu	1.50
136	Ken Griffey Jr.	3.00
137	Alex Rodriguez	2.50
138	Jay Buhner	.20
139	Randy Johnson	.50
140	Paul Sorrento	.10
141	Edgar Martinez	.10
142	Joey Cora	.10
143	Bob Wells	.10
144	Not Issued	.10
145	Jamie Moyer	.10
146	Jeff Fassero	.10
147	Dan Wilson	.10
148	Jose Cruz, Jr.	5.00
149	Scott Sanders	.10
150	Rich Amaral	.10
151	Brian Jordan	.10
152	Andy Benes	.10
153	Ray Lankford	.10
154	John Mabry	.10
155	Tom Pagnozzi	.10
156	Ron Gant	.10
157	Alan Benes	.10
158	Dennis Eckersley	.10
159	Royce Clayton	.10
160	Todd Stottlemyre	.10
161	Gary Gaetti	.10
162	Willie McGee	.10
163	Delino DeShields	.10
164	Dmitri Young	.10
165	Matt Morris	.10

1997 Donruss Team Sets MVP

The top players at each position were available in this 18-card insert set. Each card is sequentially numbered to 1,000.

		MT
Complete Set (18):		500.00
Common Player:		4.00
1	Ivan Rodriguez	15.00
2	Mike Piazza	45.00
3	Frank Thomas	75.00
4	Jeff Bagwell	35.00
5	Chuck Knoblauch	6.00
6	Eric Young	4.00
7	Alex Rodriguez	60.00
8	Barry Larkin	4.00
9	Cal Ripken Jr.	60.00
10	Chipper Jones	45.00
11	Albert Belle	20.00
12	Barry Bonds	15.00
13	Ken Griffey Jr.	75.00
14	Kenny Lofton	15.00
15	Juan Gonzalez	40.00
16	Larry Walker	4.00
17	Roger Clemens	25.00
18	Greg Maddux	45.00

1997 Donruss Update Cal Ripken

This 10-card set salutes Cal Ripken Jr. and is printed on an all-foil stock with foil stamping. Photos and text are taken from Ripken's autobiography, "The Only Way I Know." The first nine cards of the set were randomly inserted into packs. The 10th card was only available inside the book. Each card found within packs was numbered to 5,000.

	MT
Complete Set (10):	120.00
Common Ripken:	15.00

1997 Donruss Update Dominators

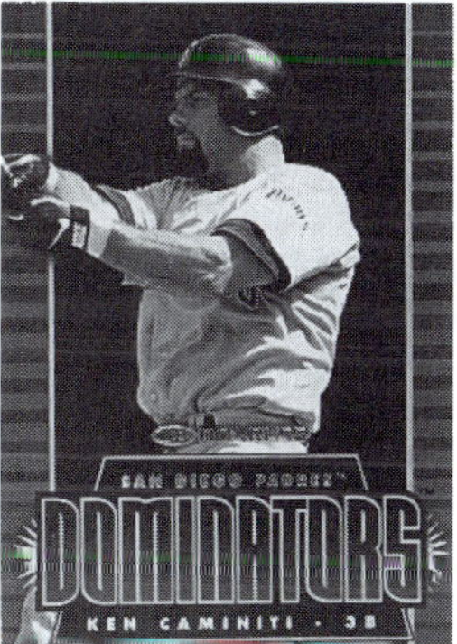

This 20-card insert highlights players known for being able to "take over a game." Each card features a special silver foil stamping.

		MT
Complete Set (20):		80.00
Common Player:		2.00
1	Frank Thomas	15.00
2	Ken Griffey Jr.	15.00
3	Greg Maddux	9.00
4	Cal Ripken Jr.	12.00
5	Alex Rodriguez	12.00
6	Albert Belle	5.00
7	Mark McGwire	6.00
8	Juan Gonzalez	7.00
9	Chipper Jones	9.00
10	Hideo Nomo	3.00
11	Roger Clemens	4.00
12	John Smoltz	2.00
13	Mike Piazza	9.00
14	Sammy Sosa	2.50
15	Matt Williams	2.50
16	Kenny Lofton	4.00
17	Barry Larkin	2.00
18	Rafael Palmeiro	2.00
19	Ken Caminiti	2.00
20	Gary Sheffield	2.00

1997 Donruss Update Franchise Features

This hobby-exclusive insert consists of 15 cards designed with a movie poster theme. The double-front design highlights a top veteran player on one side with an up-and-coming rookie on the other. The side featuring the veteran has the designation "Now Playing," while the rookie side carries the banner "Coming Attraction." Each card is printed on an all-foil stock and numbered to 3,000.

		MT
Complete Set (15):		500.00
Common Player:		10.00
1	Ken Griffey Jr., Andruw Jones	75.00
2	Frank Thomas, Darin Erstad	60.00
3	Alex Rodriguez, Nomar Garciaparra	60.00
4	Chuck Knoblauch, Wilton Guerrero	10.00
5	Juan Gonzalez, Jose Cruz, Jr.	60.00
6	Chipper Jones, Todd Walker	40.00
7	Barry Bonds, Vladimir Guerrero	25.00
8	Mark McGwire, Dmitri Young	25.00
9	Mike Piazza, Mike Sweeney	40.00
10	Mo Vaughn, Tony Clark	20.00
11	Gary Sheffield, Jose Guillen	15.00
12	Kenny Lofton, Shannon Stewart	20.00
13	Cal Ripken Jr., Scott Rolen	50.00
14	Derek Jeter, Pokey Reese	40.00
15	Tony Gwynn, Bob Abreu	30.00

1997 Donruss Update Power Alley

This 24-card insert is fractured into three different styles: Gold, Blue and Green. Each card is micro-etched and printed on holographic foil board. All cards are sequentially numbered, with the first 250 cards in each level being die-cut. The first 12 players feature a Green finish and are numbered to 4,000. The next eight players are printed on Blue cards that are numbered to 2,000. The final four players are found on Gold cards numbered to 1,000.

		MT
Complete Set (24):		600.00
Common Gold (1-4):		20.00
Common Blue (5-12):		10.00
Common Green (13-24):		5.00
1	Frank Thomas	100.00
2	Ken Griffey Jr.	120.00
3	Cal Ripken Jr.	80.00
4	Jeff Bagwell	50.00
5	Mike Piazza	40.00
6	Andruw Jones	40.00
7	Alex Rodriguez	60.00
8	Albert Belle	25.00
9	Mo Vaughn	20.00

10	Chipper Jones	40.00
11	Juan Gonzalez	30.00
12	Ken Caminiti	10.00
13	Manny Ramirez	10.00
14	Mark McGwire	18.00
15	Kenny Lofton	10.00
16	Barry Bonds	10.00
17	Gary Sheffield	7.50
18	Tony Gwynn	18.00
19	Vladimir Guerrero	20.00
20	Ivan Rodriguez	8.00
21	Paul Molitor	6.00
22	Sammy Sosa	6.00
23	Matt Williams	5.00
24	Derek Jeter	25.00

1997 Donruss Update Rookie Diamond Kings

This popular Donruss insert set features a new twist - all 10 cards feature promising rookies. Each card is sequentially numbered to 10,000, with the first 500 cards of each player printed on actual canvas.

		MT
Complete Set (10):		75.00
Common Player:		4.00
1	Andruw Jones	20.00
2	Vladimir Guerrero	15.00
3	Scott Rolen	15.00
4	Todd Walker	6.00
5	Bartolo Colon	4.00
6	Jose Guillen	7.00
7	Nomar Garciaparra	20.00
8	Darin Erstad	12.00
9	Dmitri Young	4.00
10	Wilton Guerrero	5.00

1997 Donruss Elite

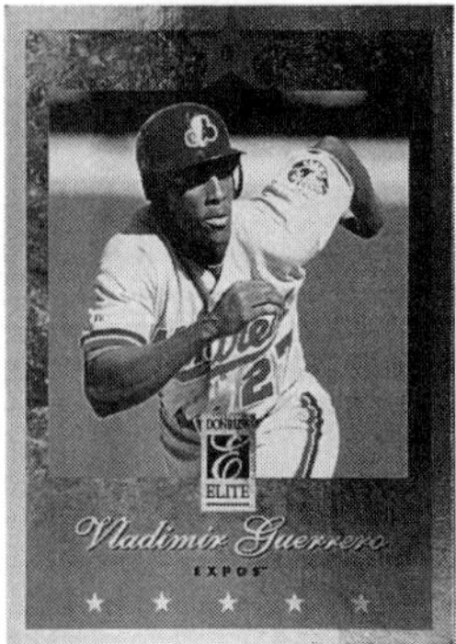

Donruss Elite Baseball is a 150-card, single-series set distributed as a hobby-only product. The regular-issue cards feature a silver border around the entire card, with a marbleized look around the inside and a player photo at center. Backs feature a color player photo and minimal statistics and personal data. Elite was accompanied by an Elite Stars parallel set and three inserts, called Leather and Lumber, Passing the Torch and Turn of the Century.

		MT
Complete Set (150):		40.00
Common Player:		.15
Complete Elite Star Set (150):		750.00
Common Elite Star:		2.00
Elite Veteran Stars:		15x to 25x
Young Stars & RC's:		5x to 10x
Wax Box:		75.00
1	Juan Gonzalez	1.75
2	Alex Rodriguez	4.00
3	Frank Thomas	4.00
4	Greg Maddux	2.50
5	Ken Griffey Jr.	4.00
6	Cal Ripken Jr.	3.00
7	Mike Piazza	2.50
8	Chipper Jones	2.50
9	Albert Belle	1.25
10	Andruw Jones	2.50
11	Vladimir Guerrero	2.00
12	Mo Vaughn	1.00
13	Ivan Rodriguez	.75
14	Andy Pettitte	1.00
15	Tony Gwynn	2.00
16	Barry Bonds	1.00
17	Jeff Bagwell	1.75
18	Manny Ramirez	1.00
19	Kenny Lofton	1.00
20	Roberto Alomar	.75
21	Mark McGwire	1.50
22	Ryan Klesko	.50
23	Tim Salmon	.30
24	Derek Jeter	2.00
25	Eddie Murray	.50
26	Jermaine Dye	.20
27	Ruben Rivera	.25
28	Jim Edmonds	.15
29	Mike Mussina	.75
30	Randy Johnson	.50
31	Sammy Sosa	.40
32	Hideo Nomo	.75
33	Chuck Knoblauch	.30
34	Paul Molitor	.50
35	Rafael Palmeiro	.25
36	Brady Anderson	.20
37	Will Clark	.30
38	Craig Biggio	.25
39	Jason Giambi	.15
40	Roger Clemens	1.50
41	Jay Buhner	.25
42	Edgar Martinez	.15
43	Gary Sheffield	.40
44	Fred McGriff	.40
45	Bobby Bonilla	.15
46	Tom Glavine	.25
47	Wade Boggs	.25
48	Jeff Conine	.15
49	John Smoltz	.25
50	Jim Thome	.60
51	Billy Wagner	.15
52	Jose Canseco	.30
53	Javy Lopez	.15
54	Cecil Fielder	.25
55	Garret Anderson	.15
56	Alex Ochoa	.15
57	Scott Rolen	1.50
58	Darin Erstad	1.25
59	Rey Ordonez	.30
60	Dante Bichette	.25
61	Joe Carter	.25
62	Moises Alou	.25
63	Jason Isringhausen	.15
64	Karim Garcia	.50
65	Brian Jordan	.15
66	Ruben Sierra	.15
67	Todd Hollandsworth	.25
68	Paul Wilson	.15
69	Ernie Young	.15
70	Ryne Sandberg	1.25
71	Raul Mondesi	.30
72	George Arias	.15
73	Ray Durham	.15
74	Dean Palmer	.15
75	Shawn Green	.15
76	Eric Young	.15
77	Jason Kendall	.15
78	Greg Vaughn	.15
79	Terrell Wade	.15
80	Bill Pulsipher	.15
81	Bobby Higginson	.15
82	Mark Grudzielanek	.15
83	Ken Caminiti	.40
84	Todd Greene	.15
85	Carlos Delgado	.15
86	Mark Grace	.25
87	Rondell White	.25
88	Barry Larkin	.35
89	J.T. Snow	.15
90	Alex Gonzalez	.15
91	Raul Casanova	.15
92	Marc Newfield	.15
93	Jermaine Allensworth	.15
94	John Mabry	.15
95	Kirby Puckett	1.50
96	Travis Fryman	.15
97	Kevin Brown	.15
98	Andres Galarraga	.25
99	Marty Cordova	.15
100	Henry Rodriguez	.15
101	Sterling Hitchcock	.15
102	Trey Beamon	.15
103	Brett Butler	.15
104	Rickey Henderson	.15
105	Tino Martinez	.40
106	Kevin Appier	.15
107	Brian Hunter	.15
108	Eric Karros	.15
109	Andre Dawson	.15
110	Darryl Strawberry	.15
111	James Baldwin	.15
112	Chad Mottola	.15
113	Dave Nilsson	.15
114	Carlos Baerga	.15
115	Chan Ho Park	.15
116	John Jaha	.15
117	Alan Benes	.25
118	Mariano Rivera	.25
119	Ellis Burks	.15
120	Tony Clark	.75
121	Todd Walker	.75
122	Dwight Gooden	.15
123	Ugueth Urbina	.15
124	David Cone	.25
125	Ozzie Smith	.60
126	Kimera Bartee	.15
127	Rusty Greer	.15
128	Pat Hentgen	.15
129	Charles Johnson	.15
130	Quinton McCracken	.15
131	Troy Percival	.15
132	Shane Reynolds	.15
133	Charles Nagy	.15
134	Tom Goodwin	.15
135	Ron Gant	.15
136	Dan Wilson	.15
137	Matt Williams	.35
138	LaTroy Hawkins	.15
139	Kevin Seitzer	.15
140	Michael Tucker	.15
141	Todd Hundley	.25
142	Alex Fernandez	.15
143	Marquis Grissom	.15
144	Steve Finley	.15
145	Curtis Pride	.15
146	Derek Bell	.15
147	Butch Huskey	.15
148	Dwight Gooden	.15
149	Al Leiter	.15
150	Hideo Nomo	.50

1997 Donruss Elite Leather & Lumber

Leather and Lumber is a 10-card insert set filled with veterans. Genuine leather is featured on one side of the card, while wood card stock is on the other. There are 500 sequentially numbered sets that were produced.

		MT
Complete Set (10):		900.00
Common Player:		20.00
1	Ken Griffey Jr.	200.00
2	Alex Rodriguez	150.00
3	Frank Thomas	175.00
4	Chipper Jones	120.00
5	Ivan Rodriguez	40.00
6	Cal Ripken Jr.	140.00
7	Barry Bonds	50.00
8	Chuck Knoblauch	25.00
9	Manny Ramirez	40.00
10	Mark McGwire	75.00

1997 Donruss Elite Passing the Torch

Passing the Torch was a 12-card insert that was limited to 1,500 individually numbered sets. It featured eight different stars, each with their own cards and then featured on a double-sided card with another player from the set.

		MT
Complete Set (12):		700.00
Common Player:		15.00
1	Cal Ripken Jr.	80.00
2	Alex Rodriguez	80.00
3	Cal Ripken Jr., Alex Rodriguez	125.00
4	Kirby Puckett	50.00
5	Andruw Jones	70.00
6	Kirby Puckett, Andruw Jones	80.00
7	Cecil Fielder	15.00
8	Frank Thomas	100.00
9	Cecil Fielder, Frank Thomas	80.00
10	Ozzie Smith	25.00
11	Derek Jeter	50.00
12	Ozzie Smith, Derek Jeter	50.00

1997 Donruss Elite Passing the Torch Autographs

The first 150 individually numbered sets of the Passing the Torch insert were autographed. This means that cards 3, 6, 9 and 12 are dual-autographed on their double-sided format.

		MT
Complete Set (12):		4500.
Common Autograph:		100.00
1	Cal Ripken Jr.	500.00
2	Alex Rodriguez	500.00
3	Cal Ripken Jr., Alex Rodriguez	1000.
4	Kirby Puckett	400.00
5	Andruw Jones	300.00
6	Kirby Puckett, Andruw Jones	600.00
7	Cecil Fielder	100.00
8	Frank Thomas	450.00
9	Cecil Fielder, Frank Thomas	550.00
10	Ozzie Smith	250.00
11	Derek Jeter	300.00
12	Ozzie Smith, Derek Jeter	500.00

1997 Donruss Elite Turn of the Century

Turn of the Century included 20 potential year 2000 superstars on an insert set numbered to 3,500. The first 500 of these sets feature an external die-cut design. Cards feature the player over a framed background image on silver foil board, with black strips down each side. Backs have a color photo, a few words about the player and the serial number.

	MT
Complete Set (20):	175.00
Common Player:	4.00
Complete Die-Cut Set (20):	500.00
Die-Cuts:	3x to 4x
1 Alex Rodriguez	30.00
2 Andruw Jones	25.00
3 Chipper Jones	25.00
4 Todd Walker	8.00
5 Scott Rolen	15.00
6 Trey Beamon	4.00
7 Derek Jeter	25.00
7S Derek Jeter ("SAMPLE" overprint)	15.00
8 Darin Erstad	20.00
9 Tony Clark	8.00
10 Todd Greene	6.00
11 Jason Giambi	4.00
12 Justin Thompson	6.00
13 Ernie Young	4.00
14 Jason Kendall	4.00
15 Alex Ochoa	4.00
16 Brooks Kieschnick	4.00
17 Bobby Higginson	4.00
18 Ruben Rivera	4.00
19 Chan Ho Park	4.00
20 Chad Mottola	4.00

1997 Donruss Limited

Each of the 200 base cards in this set features a double-front design showcasing an action photo on each side. The set is divided into four different subsets: Counterparts (100 cards) highlights two different players from the same position; Double Team (40 cards) features some of the majors' top teammate duos; Star Factor (40 cards) consists of two photos of some of the hobby's favorite players; and Unlimited Potential/Talent (20 cards) combines a top veteran with a top rookie prospect. The set also consisted of one Limited Exposure parallel set and one multi-tiered insert called Fabric of the Game. Odds of finding any insert card were 1:5 packs. Less than 1,100 base sets were available. Cards were sold in five-card packs for $4.99 each.

	MT
Complete Set (200):	1500.
Common Counterpart:	.50
Common Double Team:	5.00
Common Star Factor:	15.00
Common Unlimited Potential:	15.00
1 Ken Griffey Jr., Rondell White (Counterparts)	5.00
2 Greg Maddux, David Cone (Counterparts)	3.00
3 Gary Sheffield, Moises Alou (Double Team)	6.00
4 Frank Thomas (Star Factor)	90.00
5 Cal Ripken Jr., Kevin Orie (Counterparts)	4.00
6 Vladimir Guerrero, Barry Bonds (Unlimited Potential/Talent)	50.00
7 Eddie Murray, Reggie Jefferson (Counterparts)	.75
8 Manny Ramirez, Marquis Grissom (Double Team)	10.00
9 Mike Piazza (Star Factor)	60.00
10 Barry Larkin, Rey Ordonez (Counterparts)	.75
11 Jeff Bagwell, Eric Karros (Counterparts)	2.00
12 Chuck Knoblauch, Ray Durham (Counterparts)	.75
13 Alex Rodriguez, Edgar Renteria (Counterparts)	4.00
14 Matt Williams, Vinny Castilla (Counterparts)	.75
15 Todd Hollandsworth, Bob Abreu (Counterparts)	.50
16 John Smoltz, Pedro Martinez (Counterparts)	.75
17 Jose Canseco, Chili Davis (Counterparts)	.75
18 Jose Cruz, Jr., Ken Griffey Jr. (Unlimited Potential/Talent)	100.00
19 Ken Griffey Jr. (Star Factor)	100.00
20 Paul Molitor, John Olerud (Counterparts)	1.00
21 Roberto Alomar, Luis Castillo (Counterparts)	1.00
22 Derek Jeter, Lou Collier (Counterparts)	3.00
23 Chipper Jones, Robin Ventura (Counterparts)	3.00
24 Gary Sheffield, Ron Gant (Counterparts)	.75
25 Ramon Martinez, Bobby Jones (Counterparts)	.50
26 Mike Piazza, Raul Mondesi (Double Team)	20.00
27 Darin Erstad, Jeff Bagwell (Unlimited Potential/Talent)	40.00
28 Ivan Rodriguez (Star Factor)	25.00
29 J.T. Snow, Kevin Young (Counterparts)	.50
30 Ryne Sandberg, Julio Franco (Counterparts)	1.50
31 Travis Fryman, Chris Snopek (Counterparts)	.50
32 Wade Boggs, Russ Davis (Counterparts)	.75
33 Brooks Kieschnick, Marty Cordova (Counterparts)	.50
34 Andy Pettitte, Denny Neagle (Counterparts)	1.50
35 Paul Molitor, Matt Lawton (Double Team)	8.00
36 Scott Rolen, Cal Ripken Jr. (Unlimited Potential/Talent)	75.00
37 Cal Ripken Jr. (Star Factor)	75.00
38 Jim Thome, Dave Nilsson (Counterparts)	1.00
39 Tony Womack, Carlos Baerga (Counterparts)	.50
40 Nomar Garciaparra, Mark Grudzielanek (Counterparts)	2.50
41 Todd Greene, Chris Widger (Counterparts)	.50
42 Deion Sanders, Bernard Gilkey (Counterparts)	.75
43 Hideo Nomo, Charles Nagy (Counterparts)	1.25
44 Ivan Rodriguez, Rusty Greer (Double Team)	10.00
45 Todd Walker, Chipper Jones (Unlimited Potential/Talent)	50.00
46 Greg Maddux (Star Factor)	60.00
47 Mo Vaughn, Cecil Fielder (Counterparts)	1.50
48 Craig Biggio, Scott Spiezio (Counterparts)	.50
49 Pokey Reese, Jeff Blauser (Counterparts)	.50
50 Ken Caminiti, Joe Randa (Counterparts)	.75
51 Albert Belle, Shawn Green (Counterparts)	1.75
52 Randy Johnson, Jason Dickson (Counterparts)	1.25
53 Hideo Nomo, Chan Ho Park (Double Team)	10.00
54 Scott Spiezio, Chuck Knoblauch (Unlimited Potential/Talent)	20.00
55 Chipper Jones (Star Factor)	60.00
56 Tino Martinez, Ryan McGuire (Counterparts)	.75
57 Eric Young, Wilton Guerrero (Counterparts)	.50
58 Ron Coomer, Dave Hollins (Counterparts)	.50
59 Sammy Sosa, Angel Echevarria (Counterparts)	.75
60 *Dennis Reyes*, Jimmy Key (Counterparts)	.50
61 Barry Larkin, Deion Sanders (Double Team)	6.00
62 Wilton Guerrero, Roberto Alomar (Unlimited Potential/Talent)	20.00
63 Albert Belle (Star Factor)	35.00
64 Mark McGwire, Andres Galarraga (Counterparts)	2.00
65 Edgar Martinez, Todd Walker (Counterparts)	.75
66 Steve Finley, Rich Becker (Counterparts)	.50
67 Tom Glavine, Andy Ashby (Counterparts)	.75
68 Sammy Sosa, Ryne Sandberg (Double Team)	12.00
69 Nomar Garciaparra, Alex Rodriguez (Unlimited Potential/Talent)	75.00
70 Jeff Bagwell (Star Factor)	40.00
71 Darin Erstad, Mark Grace (Counterparts)	2.00
72 Scott Rolen, Edgardo Alfonzo (Counterparts)	2.00
73 Kenny Lofton, Lance Johnson (Counterparts)	1.50
74 Joey Hamilton, Brett Tomko (Counterparts)	.50
75 Eddie Murray, Tim Salmon (Double Team)	7.00
76 Dmitri Young, Mo Vaughn (Unlimited Potential/Talent)	25.00
77 Juan Gonzalez (Star Factor)	50.00
78 Frank Thomas, Tony Clark (Counterparts)	5.00
79 Shannon Stewart, Bip Roberts (Counterparts)	.50
80 Shawn Estes, Alex Fernandez (Counterparts)	.50
81 John Smoltz, Javier Lopez (Double Team)	.75
82 Todd Greene, Mike Piazza (Unlimited Potential/Talent)	60.00
83 Derek Jeter (Star Factor)	60.00
84 Dmitri Young, Antone Williamson (Counterparts)	.50
85 Rickey Henderson, Darryl Hamilton (Counterparts)	.50
86 Billy Wagner, Dennis Eckersley (Counterparts)	.50
87 Larry Walker, Eric Young (Double Team)	7.50
88 Mark Kotsay, Juan Gonzalez (Unlimited Potential/Talent)	50.00
89 Barry Bonds (Star Factor)	25.00
90 Will Clark, Jeff Conine (Counterparts)	.75
91 Tony Gwynn, Brett Butler (Counterparts)	2.50
92 John Wetteland, Rod Beck (Counterparts)	.50
93 Bernie Williams, Tino Martinez (Double Team)	8.00
94 Andruw Jones, Kenny Lofton (Unlimited Potential/Talent)	55.00
95 Mo Vaughn (Star Factor)	25.00
96 Joe Carter, Derek Lee (Counterparts)	.50
97 John Mabry, F.P. Santangelo (Counterparts)	.50
98 Esteban Loaiza, Wilson Alvarez (Counterparts)	.50
99 Matt Williams, David Justice (Double Team)	7.00
100 Derek Lee, Frank Thomas (Unlimited Potential/Talent)	90.00
101 Mark McGwire (Star Factor)	35.00
102 Fred McGriff, Paul Sorrento (Counterparts)	.75
103 Jermaine Allensworth, Bernie Williams (Counterparts)	1.25
104 Ismael Valdes, Chris Holt (Counterparts)	.50
105 Fred McGriff, Ryan Klesko (Double Team)	7.00
106 Tony Clark, Mark McGwire (Unlimited Potential/Talent)	40.00
107 Tony Gwynn (Star Factor)	50.00
108 Jeffrey Hammonds, Ellis Burks (Counterparts)	.50
109 Shane Reynolds, Andy Benes (Counterparts)	.50
110 Roger Clemens, Carlos Delgado (Double Team)	12.00
111 Karim Garcia, Albert Belle (Unlimited Potential/Talent)	25.00
112 Paul Molitor (Star Factor)	20.00
113 Trey Beamon, Eric Owens (Counterparts)	.50
114 Curt Schilling, Darryl Kile (Counterparts)	.50
115 Tom Glavine, Michael Tucker (Double Team)	6.00
116 Pokey Reese, Derek Jeter (Unlimited Potential/Talent)	60.00
117 Manny Ramirez (Star Factor)	25.00
118 Juan Gonzalez, Brant Brown (Counterparts)	2.50
119 Juan Guzman, Francisco Cordova (Counterparts)	.50
120 Randy Johnson, Edgar Martinez (Double Team)	8.00
121 Hideki Irabu, Greg Maddux (Unlimited Potential/Talent)	60.00
122 Alex Rodriguez (Star Factor)	75.00
123 Barry Bonds, Quinton McCracken (Counterparts)	1.50
124 Roger Clemens, Alan Benes (Counterparts)	1.50
125 Wade Boggs, Paul O'Neill (Double Team)	6.00
126 Mike Cameron, Larry Walker (Unlimited Potential/Talent)	20.00
127 Gary Sheffield (Star Factor)	20.00
128 Andruw Jones, Raul Mondesi (Counterparts)	3.00
129 Brian Anderson, Terrell Wade (Counterparts)	.50
130 Brady Anderson, Rafael Palmeiro (Double Team)	5.00
131 Neifi Perez, Barry Larkin (Unlimited Potential/Talent)	15.00
132 Ken Caminiti (Star Factor)	15.00
133 Larry Walker, Rusty Greer (Counterparts)	.75
134 Mariano Rivera, Mark Wohlers (Counterparts)	.50
135 Hideki Irabu, Andy Pettitte (Double Team)	12.00
136 Jose Guillen, Tony Gwynn (Unlimited Potential/Talent)	50.00
137 Hideo Nomo (Star Factor)	20.00
138 Vladimir Guerrero, Jim Edmonds (Counterparts)	2.00
139 Justin Thompson, Dwight Gooden (Counterparts)	.50
140 Andres Galarraga, Dante Bichette (Double Team)	6.00
141 Kenny Lofton (Star Factor)	25.00
142 Tim Salmon, Manny Ramirez (Counterparts)	1.50
143 Kevin Brown, Matt Morris (Counterparts)	.50
144 Craig Biggio, Bob Abreu (Double Team)	.50
145 Roberto Alomar (Star Factor)	20.00
146 Jose Guillen, Brian Jordan (Counterparts)	1.50
147 Bartolo Colon, Kevin Appier (Counterparts)	.50
148 Ray Lankford, Brian Jordan (Double Team)	.50
149 Chuck Knoblauch (Star Factor)	20.00

150	Henry Rodriguez, Ray Lankford (Counterparts)	.50
151	*Jaret Wright*, Ben McDonald (Counterparts)	2.00
152	Bobby Bonilla, Kevin Brown (Double Team)	5.00
153	Barry Larkin (Star Factor)	15.00
154	David Justice, Reggie Sanders (Counterparts)	.75
155	Mike Mussina, Ken Hill (Counterparts)	1.25
156	Mark Grace, Brooks Kieschnick (Double Team)	6.00
157	Jim Thome (Star Factor)	20.00
158	Michael Tucker, Curtis Goodwin (Counterparts)	.50
159	Jeff Suppan, Jeff Fassero (Counterparts)	.50
160	Mike Mussina, Jeffrey Hammonds (Double Team)	10.00
161	John Smoltz (Star Factor)	15.00
162	Moises Alou, Eric Davis (Counterparts)	.50
163	Sandy Alomar Jr., Dan Wilson (Counterparts)	.50
164	Rondell White, Henry Rodriguez (Double Team)	5.00
165	Roger Clemens (Star Factor)	30.00
166	Brady Anderson, Al Martin (Counterparts)	.50
167	Jason Kendall, Charles Johnson (Counterparts)	.50
168	Jason Giambi, Jose Canseco (Double Team)	6.00
169	Larry Walker (Star Factor)	20.00
170	Jay Buhner, Geronimo Berroa (Counterparts)	.75
171	Ivan Rodriguez, Mike Sweeney (Counterparts)	1.25
172	Kevin Appier, Jose Rosado (Double Team)	5.00
173	Bernie Williams (Star Factor)	20.00
174	Todd Dunwoody, Brian Giles (Counterparts)	.50
175	Javier Lopez, Scott Hatteberg (Counterparts)	.60
176	John Jaha, Jeff Cirillo (Double Team)	5.00
177	Andy Pettitte (Star Factor)	25.00
178	Dante Bichette, Butch Huskey (Counterparts)	.75
179	Raul Casanova, Todd Hundley (Counterparts)	.75
180	Jim Edmonds, Garret Anderson (Double Team)	5.00
181	Deion Sanders (Star Factor)	15.00
182	Ryan Klesko, Paul O'Neill (Counterparts)	.75
183	Joe Carter, Pat Hentgen (Double Team)	5.00
184	Brady Anderson (Star Factor)	15.00
185	Carlos Delgado, Wally Joyner (Counterparts)	.50
186	Jermaine Dye, Johnny Damon (Double Team)	5.00
187	Randy Johnson (Star Factor)	20.00
188	Todd Hundley, Carlos Baerga (Double Team)	5.00
189	Tom Glavine (Star Factor)	15.00
190	Damon Mashore, Jason McDonald (Double Team)	5.00
191	Wade Boggs (Star Factor)	15.00
192	Al Martin, Jason Kendall (Double Team)	5.00
193	Matt Williams (Star Factor)	15.00
194	Will Clark, Dean Palmer (Double Team)	6.00
195	Sammy Sosa (Star Factor)	20.00
196	Jose Cruz, Jr., Jay Buhner (Double Team)	35.00
197	Eddie Murray (Star Factor)	15.00
198	Darin Erstad, Jason Dickson (Double Team)	12.00
199	Fred McGriff (Star Factor)	15.00
200	Bubba Trammell, Bobby Higginson (Double Team)	10.00

1997 Donruss Limited Exposure

A complete 200-card parallel set printed on Holographic Poly-Chromium technology on both sides and featuring a special "Limited Exposure" stamp. Less than 40 sets of the Star Factor Limited Exposures are thought to exist.

		MT
	Complete Set (200):	12000.
	Common Counterpart:	4.00
	Common Double Team:	10.00
	Common Star Factor:	40.00
	Common Unlimited Potential:	25.00
1	Ken Griffey Jr., Rondell White (Counterparts)	75.00
2	Greg Maddux, David Cone (Counterparts)	40.00
3	Gary Sheffield, Moises Alou (Double Team)	12.00
4	Frank Thomas (Star Factor)	700.00
5	Cal Ripken Jr., Kevin Orie (Counterparts)	50.00
6	Vladimir Guerrero, Barry Bonds (Unlimited Potential/Talent)	160.00
7	Eddie Murray, Reggie Jefferson (Counterparts)	8.00
8	Manny Ramirez, Marquis Grissom (Double Team)	20.00
9	Mike Piazza (Star Factor)	400.00
10	Barry Larkin, Rey Ordonez (Counterparts)	6.00
11	Jeff Bagwell, Eric Karros (Counterparts)	25.00
12	Chuck Knoblauch, Ray Durham (Counterparts)	8.00
13	Alex Rodriguez, Edgar Renteria (Counterparts)	50.00
14	Matt Williams, Vinny Castilla (Counterparts)	8.00
15	Todd Hollandsworth, Bob Abreu (Counterparts)	4.00
16	John Smoltz, Pedro Martinez (Counterparts)	6.00
17	Jose Canseco, Chili Davis (Counterparts)	6.00
18	Jose Cruz, Jr., Ken Griffey Jr. (Unlimited Potential/Talent)	700.00
19	Ken Griffey Jr. (Star Factor)	800.00
20	Paul Molitor, John Olerud (Counterparts)	12.00
21	Roberto Alomar, Luis Castillo (Counterparts)	12.00
22	Derek Jeter, Lou Collier (Counterparts)	30.00
23	Chipper Jones, Robin Ventura (Counterparts)	40.00
24	Gary Sheffield, Ron Gant (Counterparts)	8.00
25	Ramon Martinez, Bobby Jones (Counterparts)	4.00
26	Mike Piazza, Raul Mondesi (Double Team)	120.00
27	Darin Erstad, Jeff Bagwell (Unlimited Potential/Talent)	200.00
28	Ivan Rodriguez (Star Factor)	175.00
29	J.T. Snow, Kevin Young (Counterparts)	4.00
30	Ryne Sandberg, Julio Franco (Counterparts)	15.00
31	Travis Fryman, Chris Snopek (Counterparts)	4.00
32	Wade Boggs, Russ Davis (Counterparts)	6.00
33	Brooks Kieschnick, Marty Cordova (Counterparts)	4.00
34	Andy Pettitte, Denny Neagle (Counterparts)	15.00
35	Paul Molitor, Matt Lawton (Double Team)	20.00
36	Scott Rolen, Cal Ripken Jr. (Unlimited Potential/Talent)	400.00
37	Cal Ripken Jr. (Star Factor)	500.00
38	Jim Thome, Dave Nilsson (Counterparts)	8.00
39	Tony Womack, Carlos Baerga (Counterparts)	4.00
40	Nomar Garciaparra, Mark Grudzielanek (Counterparts)	50.00
41	Todd Greene, Chris Widger (Counterparts)	4.00
42	Deion Sanders, Bernard Gilkey (Counterparts)	6.00
43	Hideo Nomo, Charles Nagy (Counterparts)	25.00
44	Ivan Rodriguez, Rusty Greer (Double Team)	50.00
45	Todd Walker, Chipper Jones (Unlimited Potential/Talent)	250.00
46	Greg Maddux (Star Factor)	400.00
47	Mo Vaughn, Cecil Fielder (Counterparts)	15.00
48	Craig Biggio, Scott Spiezio (Counterparts)	4.00
49	Pokey Reese, Jeff Blauser (Counterparts)	4.00
50	Ken Caminiti, Joe Randa (Counterparts)	6.00
51	Albert Belle, Shawn Green (Counterparts)	20.00
52	Randy Johnson, Jason Dickson (Counterparts)	12.00
53	Hideo Nomo, Chan Ho Park (Double Team)	75.00
54	Scott Spiezio, Chuck Knoblauch (Unlimited Potential/Talent)	35.00
55	Chipper Jones (Star Factor)	400.00
56	Tino Martinez, Ryan McGuire (Counterparts)	6.00
57	Eric Young, Wilton Guerrero (Counterparts)	4.00
58	Ron Coomer, Dave Hollins (Counterparts)	4.00
59	Sammy Sosa, Angel Echevarria (Counterparts)	8.00
60	*Dennis Reyes*, Jimmy Key (Counterparts)	4.00
61	Barry Larkin, Deion Sanders (Double Team)	15.00
62	Wilton Guerrero, Roberto Alomar (Unlimited Potential/Talent)	35.00
63	Albert Belle (Star Factor)	200.00
64	Mark McGwire, Andres Galarraga (Counterparts)	25.00
65	Edgar Martinez, Todd Walker (Counterparts)	8.00
66	Steve Finley, Rich Becker (Counterparts)	4.00
67	Tom Glavine, Andy Ashby (Counterparts)	6.00
68	Sammy Sosa, Ryne Sandberg (Double Team)	50.00
69	Nomar Garciaparra, Alex Rodriguez (Unlimited Potential/Talent)	400.00
70	Jeff Bagwell (Star Factor)	250.00
71	Darin Erstad, Mark Grace (Counterparts)	18.00
72	Scott Rolen, Edgardo Alfonzo (Counterparts)	25.00
73	Kenny Lofton, Lance Johnson (Counterparts)	15.00
74	Joey Hamilton, Brett Tomko (Counterparts)	4.00
75	Eddie Murray, Tim Salmon (Double Team)	12.00
76	Dmitri Young, Mo Vaughn (Unlimited Potential/Talent)	100.00
77	Juan Gonzalez (Star Factor)	350.00
78	Frank Thomas, Tony Clark (Counterparts)	50.00
79	Shannon Stewart, Bip Roberts (Counterparts)	4.00
80	Shawn Estes, Alex Fernandez (Counterparts)	4.00
81	John Smoltz, Javier Lopez (Double Team)	10.00
82	Todd Greene, Mike Piazza (Unlimited Potential/Talent)	250.00
83	Derek Jeter (Star Factor)	350.00
84	Dmitri Young, Antone Williamson (Counterparts)	4.00
85	Rickey Henderson, Darryl Hamilton (Counterparts)	4.00
86	Billy Wagner, Dennis Eckersley (Counterparts)	4.00
87	Larry Walker, Eric Young (Double Team)	12.00
88	Mark Kotsay, Juan Gonzalez (Unlimited Potential/Talent)	250.00
89	Barry Bonds (Star Factor)	175.00
90	Will Clark, Jeff Conine (Counterparts)	6.00
91	Tony Gwynn, Brett Butler (Counterparts)	10.00
92	John Wetteland, Rod Beck (Counterparts)	4.00
93	Bernie Williams, Tino Martinez (Double Team)	15.00
94	Andruw Jones, Kenny Lofton (Unlimited Potential/Talent)	200.00
95	Mo Vaughn (Star Factor)	175.00
96	Joe Carter, Derrek Lee (Counterparts)	4.00
97	John Mabry, F.P. Santangelo (Counterparts)	4.00
98	Esteban Loaiza, Wilson Alvarez (Counterparts)	4.00
99	Matt Williams, David Justice (Double Team)	10.00
100	Derrek Lee, Frank Thomas (Unlimited Potential/Talent)	400.00
101	Mark McGwire (Star Factor)	250.00
102	Fred McGriff, Paul Sorrento (Counterparts)	5.00
103	Jermaine Allensworth, Bernie Williams (Counterparts)	8.00
104	Ismael Valdes, Chris Holt (Counterparts)	4.00
105	Fred McGriff, Ryan Klesko (Double Team)	12.00
106	Tony Clark, Mark McGwire (Unlimited Potential/Talent)	175.00
107	Tony Gwynn (Star Factor)	350.00
108	Jeffrey Hammonds, Ellis Burks (Counterparts)	4.00
109	Shane Reynolds, Andy Benes (Counterparts)	4.00
110	Roger Clemens, Carlos Delgado (Double Team)	80.00
111	Karim Garcia, Albert Belle (Unlimited Potential/Talent)	100.00
112	Paul Molitor (Star Factor)	75.00
113	Trey Beamon, Eric Owens (Counterparts)	4.00
114	Curt Schilling, Darryl Kile (Counterparts)	4.00
115	Tom Glavine, Michael Tucker (Double Team)	10.00
116	Pokey Reese, Derek Jeter (Unlimited Potential/Talent)	200.00
117	Manny Ramirez (Star Factor)	100.00
118	Juan Gonzalez, Brant Brown (Counterparts)	35.00
119	Juan Guzman, Francisco Cordova (Counterparts)	4.00
120	Randy Johnson, Edgar Martinez (Double Team)	10.00
121	Hideki Irabu, Greg Maddux (Unlimited Potential/Talent)	250.00
122	Alex Rodriguez (Star Factor)	500.00
123	Barry Bonds, Quinton McCracken (Counterparts)	15.00
124	Roger Clemens, Alan Benes (Counterparts)	25.00
125	Wade Boggs, Paul O'Neill (Double Team)	10.00
126	Mike Cameron, Larry Walker (Unlimited Potential/Talent)	25.00
127	Gary Sheffield (Star Factor)	50.00
128	Andruw Jones, Raul Mondesi (Counterparts)	40.00
129	Brian Anderson, Terrell Wade (Counterparts)	4.00
130	Brady Anderson, Rafael Palmeiro (Double Team)	10.00
131	Neifi Perez, Barry Larkin (Unlimited Potential/Talent)	25.00
132	Ken Caminiti (Star Factor)	40.00

133	Larry Walker, Rusty Greer (Counterparts)	5.00
134	Mariano Rivera, Mark Wohlers (Counterparts)	4.00
135	Hideki Irabu, Andy Pettitte (Double Team)	30.00
136	Jose Guillen, Tony Gwynn (Unlimited Potential/Talent)	200.00
137	Hideo Nomo (Star Factor)	300.00
138	Vladimir Guerrero, Jim Edmonds (Counterparts)	30.00
139	Justin Thompson, Dwight Gooden (Counterparts)	4.00
140	Andres Galarraga, Dante Bichette (Double Team)	10.00
141	Kenny Lofton (Star Factor)	150.00
142	Tim Salmon, Manny Ramirez (Counterparts)	12.00
143	*Kevin Brown, Matt Morris* (Counterparts)	4.00
144	Craig Biggio, Bob Abreu (Double Team)	4.00
145	Roberto Alomar (Star Factor)	100.00
146	Jose Guillen, Brian Jordan (Counterparts)	10.00
147	Bartolo Colon, Kevin Appier (Counterparts)	4.00
148	Ray Lankford, Brian Jordan (Double Team)	10.00
149	Chuck Knoblauch (Star Factor)	60.00
150	Henry Rodriguez, Ray Lankford (Counterparts)	4.00
151	*Jaret Wright*, Ben McDonald (Counterparts)	8.00
152	Bobby Bonilla, Kevin Brown (Double Team)	10.00
153	Barry Larkin (Star Factor)	40.00
154	David Justice, Reggie Sanders (Counterparts)	5.00
155	Mike Mussina, Ken Hill (Counterparts)	8.00
156	Mark Grace, Brooks Kieschnick (Double Team)	10.00
157	Jim Thome (Star Factor)	75.00
158	Michael Tucker, Curtis Goodwin (Counterparts)	4.00
159	Jeff Suppan, Jeff Fassero (Counterparts)	4.00
160	Mike Mussina, Jeffrey Hammonds (Double Team)	15.00
161	John Smoltz (Star Factor)	40.00
162	Moises Alou, Eric Davis (Counterparts)	4.00
163	Sandy Alomar Jr., Dan Wilson (Counterparts)	4.00
164	Rondell White, Henry Rodriguez (Double Team)	10.00
165	Roger Clemens (Star Factor)	250.00
166	Brady Anderson, Al Martin (Counterparts)	4.00
167	Jason Kendall, Charles Johnson (Counterparts)	4.00
168	Jason Giambi, Jose Canseco (Double Team)	12.00
169	Larry Walker (Star Factor)	50.00
170	Jay Buhner, Geronimo Berroa (Counterparts)	4.00
171	Ivan Rodriguez, Mike Sweeney (Counterparts)	12.00
172	Kevin Appier, Jose Rosado (Double Team)	10.00
173	Bernie Williams (Star Factor)	75.00
174	Todd Dunwoody, Brian Giles (Counterparts)	4.00
175	Javier Lopez, Scott Hatteberg (Counterparts)	4.00
176	John Jaha, Jeff Cirillo (Double Team)	10.00
177	Andy Pettitte (Star Factor)	90.00
178	Dante Bichette, Butch Huskey (Counterparts)	6.00
179	Raul Casanova, Todd Hundley (Counterparts)	4.00
180	Jim Edmonds, Garret Anderson (Double Team)	10.00
181	Deion Sanders (Star Factor)	50.00
182	Ryan Klesko, Paul O'Neill (Counterparts)	6.00
183	Joe Carter, Pat Hentgen (Double Team)	10.00
184	Brady Anderson (Star Factor)	40.00
185	Carlos Delgado, Wally Joyner (Counterparts)	4.00
186	Jermaine Dye, Johnny Damon (Double Team)	10.00
187	Randy Johnson (Star Factor)	80.00
188	Todd Hundley, Carlos Baerga (Double Team)	10.00
189	Tom Glavine (Star Factor)	40.00
190	Damon Mashore, Jason McDonald (Double Team)	10.00
191	Wade Boggs (Star Factor)	50.00
192	Al Martin, Jason Kendall (Double Team)	10.00
193	Matt Williams (Star Factor)	50.00
194	Will Clark, Dean Palmer (Double Team)	15.00
195	Sammy Sosa (Star Factor)	60.00
196	Jose Cruz, Jr., Jay Buhner (Double Team)	125.00
197	Eddie Murray (Star Factor)	60.00
198	Darin Erstad, Jason Dickson (Double Team)	60.00
199	Fred McGriff (Star Factor)	50.00
200	Bubba Trammell, Bobby Higginson (Double Team)	15.00

1997 Donruss Limited Fabric of the Game

This fractured insert set consists of 69 different cards highlighting three different technologies representing three statistical categories: Canvas (stolen bases), Leather (doubles) and Wood (home runs). Each of the 23 cards in each category are found in varying levels of scarcity: Legendary Material (one card per theme; numbered to 100), Hall of Fame Material (four cards numbered to 250), Superstar Material (five cards numbered to 500), Star Material (six cards numbered to 750), and Major League Material (seven cards numbered to 1,000).

	MT
Complete Set (69):	
Complete Canvas Set (23):	1800.00
Rickey Henderson (100)	60.00
Barry Bonds (250)	60.00
Kenny Lofton (250)	60.00
Roberto Alomar (250)	50.00
Ryne Sandberg (250)	60.00
Tony Gwynn (500)	60.00
Barry Larkin (500)	25.00
Brady Anderson (500)	20.00
Chuck Knoblauch (500)	25.00
Craig Biggio (500)	20.00
Sammy Sosa (750)	25.00
Gary Sheffield (750)	25.00
Eric Young (750)	15.00
Larry Walker (750)	30.00
Ken Griffey Jr. (750)	125.00
Deion Sanders (750)	20.00
Raul Mondesi (1,000)	20.00
Rondell White (1,000)	15.00
Derek Jeter (1,000)	50.00
Nomar Garciaparra (1,000)	40.00
Wilton Guerrero (1,000)	10.00
Pokey Reese (1,000)	10.00
Darin Erstad (1,000)	35.00
Complete Leather Set (23):	
Paul Molitor (100)	125.00
Wade Boggs (250)	30.00
Cal Ripken Jr. (250)	160.00
Tony Gwynn (250)	100.00
Joe Carter (250)	25.00
Rafael Palmeiro (500)	25.00
Mark Grace (500)	25.00
Bobby Bonilla (500)	20.00
Andres Galarraga (500)	25.00
Edgar Martinez (500)	20.00
Ken Caminiti (750)	25.00
Ivan Rodriguez (750)	35.00
Frank Thomas (750)	100.00
Jeff Bagwell (750)	50.00
Albert Belle (750)	40.00
Bernie Williams (750)	35.00
Chipper Jones (1,000)	50.00
Rusty Greer (1,000)	10.00
Todd Walker (1,000)	20.00
Scott Rolen (1,000)	40.00
Bob Abreu (1,000)	10.00
Jose Guillen (1,000)	30.00
Jose Cruz, Jr. (1,000)	90.00

Complete Wood Set (23):	
Eddie Murray (100)	100.00
Cal Ripken Jr. (250)	160.00
Barry Bonds (250)	60.00
Mark McGwire (250)	75.00
Fred McGriff (250)	25.00
Ken Griffey Jr. (500)	140.00
Albert Belle (500)	40.00
Frank Thomas (500)	120.00
Juan Gonzalez (500)	60.00
Matt Williams (500)	25.00
Mike Piazza (750)	60.00
Jeff Bagwell (750)	45.00
Mo Vaughn (750)	35.00
Gary Sheffield (750)	25.00
Tim Salmon (750)	20.00
David Justice (750)	20.00
Manny Ramirez (1,000)	25.00
Jim Thome (1,000)	20.00
Tino Martinez (1,000)	20.00
Andruw Jones (1,000)	50.00
Vladimir Guerrero (1,000)	40.00
Tony Clark (1,000)	25.00
Dmitri Young (1,000)	10.00

1997 Donruss Preferred

Each of the 200 base cards is printed on an all-foil-micro-etched stock. The set is fractured into three different scarcities: 100 Bronze cards, 70 Silver cards, 20 Gold cards and 10 Platinum cards. Instead of traditional packs, cards were sold in five-card collectible tins. A total of 25 different tins were available, and each tin was numbered to 1,200. Four different inserts were included with the product: Staremaster, X-Ponential Power, Cut To The Chase, and Precious Metals. Odds of finding any insert were 1:4 packs.

		MT
Complete Set (200):		800.00
Common Bronze:		.10
Common Silver:		1.50
Common Gold:		8.00
Wax Box:		140.00
1	Frank Thomas P	80.00
2	Ken Griffey Jr. P	80.00
3	Cecil Fielder B	.20
4	Chuck Knoblauch G	8.00
5	Garret Anderson B	.10
6	Greg Maddux P	50.00
7	Matt Williams S	2.00
8	Marquis Grissom S	1.50
9	Jason Isringhausen B	.10
10	Larry Walker S	2.50
11	Charles Nagy B	.10
12	Dan Wilson B	.10
13	Albert Belle G	15.00
14	Javier Lopez B	.20
15	David Cone B	.20
16	Bernard Gilkey B	.10
17	Andres Galarraga S	2.00
18	Bill Pulsipher B	.10
19	Alex Fernandez B	.10
20	Andy Pettitte B	5.00
21	Mark Grudzielanek B	.10
22	Juan Gonzalez P	40.00
23	Reggie Sanders B	.10
24	Kenny Lofton G	10.00
25	Andy Ashby B	.10
26	John Wetteland B	.10
27	Bobby Bonilla B	.10
28	Hideo Nomo G	12.00
29	Joe Carter B	.20
30	Jose Canseco B	.25
31	Ellis Burks B	.10
32	Edgar Martinez S	1.50
33	Chan Ho Park B	.10
34	David Justice B	.40
35	Carlos Delgado B	.10
36	Jeff Cirillo S	1.50
37	Charles Johnson B	.10
38	Manny Ramirez G	10.00
39	Greg Vaughn B	.10
40	Henry Rodriguez B	.10
41	Darryl Strawberry B	.10
42	Jim Thome G	6.00
43	Ryan Klesko S	3.00
44	Jermaine Allensworth B	.10
45	Brian Jordan G	8.00
46	Tony Gwynn P	40.00
47	Rafael Palmeiro G	10.00
48	Dante Bichette S	2.00
49	Ivan Rodriguez G	15.00
50	Mark McGwire G	20.00
51	Tim Salmon S	2.00
52	Roger Clemens B	1.00
53	Matt Lawton B	.10
54	Wade Boggs S	2.00
55	Travis Fryman B	.10
56	Bobby Higginson S	1.50
57	John Jaha S	1.50
58	Rondell White S	1.50
59	Tom Glavine S	2.00
60	Eddie Murray S	4.00
61	Vinny Castilla B	.10
62	Todd Hundley B	.40
63	Jay Buhner S	2.00
64	Paul O'Neill B	.20
65	Steve Finley B	.10
66	Kevin Appier B	.10
67	Ray Durham B	.10
68	Dave Nilsson B	.10
69	Jeff Bagwell G	20.00
70	Al Martin S	1.50
71	Paul Molitor G	10.00
72	Kevin Brown S	1.50
73	Ron Gant B	.10
74	Dwight Gooden B	.10
75	Quinton McCracken B	.10
76	Rusty Greer S	1.50
77	Juan Guzman B	.10
78	Fred McGriff S	1.50
79	Tino Martinez B	.40
80	Ray Lankford B	.10
81	Ken Caminiti G	8.00
82	James Baldwin B	.10
83	Jermaine Dye G	8.00
84	Mark Grace S	2.00
85	Pat Hentgen S	1.50
86	Jason Giambi S	1.50
87	Brian Hunter B	.10
88	Andy Benes B	.10
89	Jose Rosado B	.10
90	Shawn Green B	.10
91	Jason Kendall B	.10
92	Alex Rodriguez P	70.00
93	Chipper Jones P	50.00
94	Barry Bonds G	10.00
95	Brady Anderson G	8.00
96	Ryne Sandberg S	5.00
97	Lance Johnson B	.10
98	Cal Ripken Jr. P	60.00
99	Craig Biggio S	1.50
100	Dean Palmer B	.10
101	Gary Sheffield G	8.00
102	Johnny Damon B	.10
103	Mo Vaughn G	10.00
104	Randy Johnson S	3.00
105	Raul Mondesi S	1.50
106	Roberto Alomar G	10.00
107	Mike Piazza P	50.00
108	Rey Ordonez B	.10
109	Barry Larkin G	8.00
110	Tony Clark S	5.00
111	Bernie Williams S	4.00
112	John Smoltz G	8.00
113	Moises Alou B	.10
114	Will Clark B	.25
115	Sammy Sosa G	8.00
116	Jim Edmonds S	1.50
117	Jeff Conine B	.10
118	Joey Hamilton B	.10
119	Todd Hollandsworth B	.10
120	Troy Percival B	.10
121	Paul Wilson B	.10
122	Ken Hill B	.10
123	Mariano Rivera S	1.50
124	Eric Karros B	.10
125	Derek Jeter G	30.00
126	Eric Young S	1.50
127	John Mabry B	.10
128	Gregg Jefferies B	.10
129	Ismael Valdes S	1.50

130	Marty Cordova B	.10
131	Omar Vizquel B	.10
132	Mike Mussina S	4.00
133	Darin Erstad B	2.00
134	Edgar Renteria S	1.50
135	Billy Wagner B	.10
136	Alex Ochoa B	.10
137	Luis Castillo B	.10
138	Rocky Coppinger B	.10
139	Mike Sweeney B	.10
140	Michael Tucker B	.10
141	Chris Snopek B	.10
142	Dmitri Young S	1.50
143	Andruw Jones P	40.00
144	Mike Cameron S	1.50
145	Brant Brown B	.10
146	Todd Walker G	8.00
147	Nomar Garciaparra G	30.00
148	Glendon Rusch B	.10
149	Karim Garcia S	1.50
150	*Bubba Trammell S*	5.00
151	Todd Greene B	.10
152	Wilton Guerrero G	8.00
153	Scott Spiezio B	.10
154	Brooks Kieschnick B	.10
155	Vladimir Guerrero G	25.00
156	Brian Giles S	1.50
157	Pokey Reese B	.10
158	Jason Dickson G	8.00
159	Kevin Orie S	1.50
160	Scott Rolen G	20.00
161	Bartolo Colon S	1.50
162	Shannon Stewart G	8.00
163	Wendell Magee B	.10
164	Jose Guillen S	4.00
165	Bob Abreu S	1.50
166	Deivi Cruz B	.10
167	Alex Rodriguez B	2.00
	(National Treasures)	
168	Frank Thomas B	2.00
	(National Treasures)	
169	Cal Ripken Jr. B	1.50
	(National Treasures)	
170	Chipper Jones B	1.00
	(National Treasures)	
171	Mike Piazza B	1.00
	(National Treasures)	
172	Tony Gwynn S	8.00
	(National Treasures)	
173	Juan Gonzalez B	.75
	(National Treasures)	
174	Kenny Lofton S	5.00
	(National Treasures)	
175	Ken Griffey Jr. B	2.00
	(National Treasures)	
176	Mark McGwire B	.75
	(National Treasures)	
177	Jeff Bagwell B	.75
	(National Treasures)	
178	Paul Molitor S	3.00
	(National Treasures)	
179	Andruw Jones B	1.00
	(National Treasures)	
180	Manny Ramirez S	4.00
	(National Treasures)	
181	Ken Caminiti S	2.00
	(National Treasures)	
182	Barry Bonds B	.50
	(National Treasures)	
183	Mo Vaughn B	.50
	(National Treasures)	
184	Derek Jeter B	1.00
	(National Treasures)	
185	Barry Larkin S	2.00
	(National Treasures)	
186	Ivan Rodriguez B	.30
	(National Treasures)	
187	Albert Belle S	5.00
	(National Treasures)	
188	John Smoltz S	1.50
	(National Treasures)	
189	Chuck Knoblauch S	2.00
	(National Treasures)	
190	Brian Jordan S	1.50
	(National Treasures)	
191	Gary Sheffield S	2.00
	(National Treasures)	
192	Jim Thome S	4.00
	(National Treasures)	
193	Brady Anderson S	1.50
	(National Treasures)	
194	Hideo Nomo S	6.00
	(National Treasures)	
195	Sammy Sosa S	2.50
	(National Treasures)	
196	Greg Maddux B	1.00
	(National Treasures)	
197	Checklist	1.50
	(Vladimir Guerrero B)	
198	Checklist (Scott Rolen B)	1.00
199	Checklist (Todd Walker B)	.25

200	Checklist	1.00
	(Nomar Garciaparra B)	

1997 Donruss Preferred Cut To The Chase

Each of the cards in the Donruss Preferred series can also be found in this parallel set with die-cut borders, in the same bronze, silver, gold and platinum finishes. Multiplier values of the die-cuts are inverse to that usually found, with platinum cards the lowest, followed by gold, silver and bronze. Besides die-cutting, the chase cards feature a "CUT TO THE CHASE" designation at bottom.

	MT
Complete Set (200):	4000.
Cut totheChaseGolds:	2.5x to 3x
Common Gold:	12.00
Cut to the Chase Silvers:	3x to 4x
Common Silver:	6.00
Cut to the Chase Bronze:	5x to 10x
Common Bronze:	1.50
Cut to the Chase Platinum:	2x to 3x
Common Platinum:	100.00

1997 Donruss Preferred Precious Metals

This 25-card partial parallel set features cards printed on actual silver, gold and platinum stock. Only 100 of each card were produced.

		MT
Complete Set (25):		6000.
Common Player:		80.00
1	Frank Thomas	700.00
2	Ken Griffey Jr.	700.00
3	Greg Maddux	400.00
4	Albert Belle	250.00
5	Juan Gonzalez	325.00
6	Kenny Lofton	175.00
7	Tony Gwynn	350.00
8	Ivan Rodriguez	150.00
9	Mark McGwire	250.00
10	Matt Williams	80.00
11	Wade Boggs	80.00
12	Eddie Murray	100.00
13	Jeff Bagwell	250.00
14	Ken Caminiti	100.00
15	Alex Rodriguez	500.00
16	Chipper Jones	400.00
17	Barry Bonds	175.00
18	Cal Ripken Jr.	500.00
19	Mo Vaughn	175.00
20	Mike Piazza	400.00
21	Derek Jeter	400.00
22	Bernie Williams	125.00
23	Andruw Jones	350.00
24	Vladimir Guerrero	250.00
25	Jose Guillen	100.00

1997 Donruss Preferred Staremasters

A 20-card insert printed on foil stock and accented with holographic foil stamping, Staremasters is de-signed to show up-close "game-face" photography. Each card is sequentially numbered to 1,500.

		MT
Complete Set (20):		900.00
Common Player:		20.00
1	Alex Rodriguez	80.00
2	Frank Thomas	100.00
3	Chipper Jones	65.00
4	Cal Ripken Jr.	80.00
5	Mike Piazza	65.00
6	Juan Gonzalez	40.00
7	Derek Jeter	65.00
8	Jeff Bagwell	40.00
9	Ken Griffey Jr.	125.00
10	Tony Gwynn	50.00
11	Barry Bonds	30.00
12	Albert Belle	35.00
13	Greg Maddux	65.00
14	Mark McGwire	40.00
15	Ken Caminiti	20.00
16	Hideo Nomo	25.00
17	Gary Sheffield	20.00
18	Andruw Jones	60.00
19	Mo Vaughn	30.00
20	Ivan Rodriguez	25.00

1997 Donruss Preferred Tins

A total of 25 different players are featured on the lithographed steel tins which were the "packs" of Donruss Preferred baseball. The tins measure 3" x 4-1/2" x 5/8" and are hinged along the left side. Tins were produced in two versions. Predominantly blue tins are the standard package. A premium parallel version is gold-colored and serially numbered within an edition of 1,200. Gold tins were packed one per 24-pack box of Preferred.

		MT
Complete Set, Blue (25):		20.00
Common Tin:		.50
Gold:		5x-10x
1	Frank Thomas	2.00
2	Ken Griffey Jr.	2.00
3	Andruw Jones	1.25
4	Cal Ripken Jr.	1.50
5	Mike Piazza	1.25
6	Chipper Jones	1.25
7	Alex Rodriguez	1.50
8	Derek Jeter	1.00
9	Juan Gonzalez	.75
10	Albert Belle	.50
11	Tony Gwynn	.75
12	Greg Maddux	.75
13	Jeff Bagwell	.50
14	Roger Clemens	.75
15	Mark McGwire	.75
16	Gary Sheffield	.50
17	Manny Ramirez	.50
18	Hideo Nomo	.60
19	Kenny Lofton	.50
20	Mo Vaughn	.50
21	Ryne Sandberg	.60
22	Barry Bonds	.75
23	Sammy Sosa	.50
24	John Smoltz	.50
25	Ivan Rodriguez	.60

1997 Donruss Preferred X-Ponential Power

This 20-card die-cut insert contains two top hitters from 10 different teams. Placing the cards of teammates together forms an "X" shape. Cards are printed on thick plastic stock and gold holographic foil stamping and are sequentially numbered to 3,000.

		MT
Complete Set (20):		300.00
Common Player:		5.00
1A	Manny Ramirez	12.00
1B	Jim Thome	10.00
2A	Paul Molitor	8.00
2B	Chuck Knoblauch	5.00
3A	Ivan Rodriguez	10.00
3B	Juan Gonzalez	20.00
4A	Albert Belle	18.00
4B	Frank Thomas	50.00
5A	Roberto Alomar	10.00
5B	Cal Ripken Jr.	40.00
6A	Tim Salmon	5.00
6B	Jim Edmonds	5.00
7A	Ken Griffey Jr.	50.00
7B	Alex Rodriguez	40.00
8A	Chipper Jones	30.00
8B	Andruw Jones	25.00
9A	Mike Piazza	30.00
9B	Raul Mondesi	5.00
10A	Tony Gwynn	20.00
10B	Ken Caminiti	5.00

1997 Studio

Innovations in both product and packaging marked the seventh annual issue of Donruss' Studio brand. As in the past, the 165 cards in the base set rely on high-quality front photos to bring out the players' personalities. For '97, the photos are set against a background of variously shaded gray horizontal stripes. Backs have a second player photo, often an action shot, along with a short career summary. The "pack" for '97 Studio is something totally new to the hobby. An 8-1/2" x 12" cardboard envelope, complete with a zip strip opener in the style of an express-mail envelope, contains a cello pack of five standard-size cards plus either an 8" x 10" Studio Portrait card or an 8" x 10" version of the Master Strokes insert. Suggested retail price at issue was $2.49 per pack. Regular-size Master Strokes cards are one of several insert series which includes silver and gold press proofs and die-cut plastic Hard Hats.

		MT
Complete Set (165):		30.00
Common Player:		.10
Wax Box:		45.00
1	Frank Thomas	3.00
2	Gary Sheffield	.30
3	Jason Isringhausen	.10
4	Ron Gant	.10
5	Andy Pettitte	.75
6	Todd Hollandsworth	.10
7	Troy Percival	.10
8	Mark McGwire	1.00
9	Barry Larkin	.20
10	Ken Caminiti	.20
11	Paul Molitor	.40
12	Travis Fryman	.10
13	Kevin Brown	.10
14	Robin Ventura	.10
15	Andres Galarraga	.20
16	Ken Griffey Jr.	3.00
17	Roger Clemens	1.00
18	Alan Benes	.20
19	David Justice	.25
20	Damon Buford	.10
21	Mike Piazza	2.00
22	Ray Durham	.10
23	Billy Wagner	.10
24	Dean Palmer	.10
25	David Cone	.20
26	Ruben Sierra	.10
27	Henry Rodriguez	.10
28	Ray Lankford	.10
29	Jamey Wright	.10
30	Brady Anderson	.15
31	Tino Martinez	.20
32	Manny Ramirez	.75
33	Jeff Conine	.10
34	Dante Bichette	.20
35	Jose Canseco	.25
36	Mo Vaughn	.75
37	Sammy Sosa	.30
38	Mark Grudzielanek	.10
39	Mike Mussina	.60
40	Bill Pulsipher	.10
41	Ryne Sandborg	.75
42	Rickey Henderson	.10
43	Alex Rodriguez	3.00
44	Eddie Murray	.40
45	Ernie Young	.10
46	Joey Hamilton	.10
47	Wade Boggs	.20
48	Rusty Greer	.10
49	Carlos Delgado	.10
50	Ellis Burks	.10
51	Cal Ripken Jr.	2.50
52	Alex Fernandez	.10
53	Wally Joyner	.10
54	James Baldwin	.10
55	Juan Gonzalez	1.25
56	John Smoltz	.20
57	Omar Vizquel	.10
58	Shane Reynolds	.10
59	Barry Bonds	.75
60	Jason Kendall	.10
61	Marty Cordova	.10
62	Charles Johnson	.10
63	John Jaha	.10
64	Chan Ho Park	.10
65	Jermaine Allensworth	.10
66	Mark Grace	.20
67	Tim Salmon	.20
68	Edgar Martinez	.10
69	Marquis Grissom	.10
70	Craig Biggio	.20
71	Bobby Higginson	.10
72	Kevin Seitzer	.10
73	Hideo Nomo	.60
74	Dennis Eckersley	.10
75	Bobby Bonilla	.10
76	Dwight Gooden	.10
77	Jeff Cirillo	.10
78	Brian McRae	.10
79	Chipper Jones	2.00
80	Jeff Fassero	.10
81	Fred McGriff	.25
82	Garret Anderson	.10
83	Eric Karros	.10
84	Derek Bell	.10
85	Kenny Lofton	.75
86	John Mabry	.10
87	Pat Hentgen	.10
88	Greg Maddux	2.00
89	Jason Giambi	.10
90	Al Martin	.10
91	Derek Jeter	2.00
92	Rey Ordonez	.10
93	Will Clark	.25
94	Kevin Appier	.10
95	Roberto Alomar	.50
96	Joe Carter	.15
97	Bernie Williams	.50
98	Albert Belle	1.00
99	Greg Vaughn	.10
100	Tony Clark	.50
101	Matt Williams	.30
102	Jeff Bagwell	1.25
103	Reggie Sanders	.10
104	Mariano Rivera	.20
105	Larry Walker	.35
106	Shawn Green	.10
107	Alex Ochoa	.10
108	Ivan Rodriguez	.60
109	Eric Young	.10
110	Javier Lopez	.20
111	Brian Hunter	.10
112	Raul Mondesi	.25
113	Randy Johnson	.60
114	Tony Phillips	.10
115	Carlos Garcia	.10
116	Moises Alou	.10
117	Paul O'Neill	.10
118	Jim Thome	.40
119	Jermaine Dye	.10
120	Wilson Alvarez	.10
121	Rondell White	.10
122	Michael Tucker	.10
123	Mike Lansing	.10
124	Tony Gwynn	1.25
125	Ryan Klesko	.50
126	Jim Edmonds	.10
127	Chuck Knoblauch	.20
128	Rafael Palmeiro	.20
129	Jay Buhner	.20
130	Tom Glavine	.20
131	Julio Franco	.10
132	Cecil Fielder	.20
133	Paul Wilson	.10
134	Deion Sanders	.25
135	Alex Gonzalez	.10
136	Charles Nagy	.10
137	Andy Ashby	.10
138	Edgar Renteria	.10
139	Pedro Martinez	.20
140	Brian Jordan	.10
141	Todd Hundley	.20
142	Marc Newfield	.10
143	Darryl Strawberry	.10
144	Dan Wilson	.10
145	Brian Giles	.10
146	Bartolo Colon	.10
147	Shannon Stewart	.10
148	Scott Spiezio	.10
149	Andruw Jones	2.00
150	Karim Garcia	.10
151	Vladimir Guerrero	1.50
152	George Arias	.10
153	Brooks Kieschnick	.10
154	Todd Walker	.50
155	Scott Rolen	1.50
156	Todd Greene	.10
157	Dmitri Young	.10
158	Ruben Rivera	.10
159	Trey Beamon	.10
160	Nomar Garciaparra	2.00
161	Bob Abreu	.15
162	Darin Erstad	1.25
163	Ken Griffey Jr. CL	1.00
164	Frank Thomas CL	1.00
165	Alex Rodriguez CL	1.00

1997 Studio Press Proofs

Each of the 165 cards in the base set of '97 Studio was also produced in a pair of Press Proof versions as random pack inserts. Fronts of the Press Proofs have either silver or gold holographic foil replacing the silver foil graphics found on regular cards, as well as foil strips down each side. Backs are identical to the regular issue. The silver Press Proofs were issued in an edition of 1,500 of each player; the golds are limited to 500 of each.

	MT
Complete Set, Silver (165):	650.00
Complete Set, Gold (165):	850.00
Common Player, Silver:	1.50
Common Player, Gold:	4.00
Silver Press Proof Stars:	10x to 15x
Silver Yng Stars & RCs:	5x to 10x
Gold Press Proof Stars:	25x to 40x
Gold Yng Stars & RCs:	15x to 30x

1997 Studio Hard Hats

Die-cut plastic is used to represent a player's batting helmet in this set of '97 Studio inserts. A player action photo appears in the foreground with his name and other graphic elements in silver foil. Backs feature a small portrait photo, short career summary and a serial number from within the edition of 5,000 of each card.

		MT
Complete Set (24):		275.00
Common Player:		4.00
1	Ivan Rodriguez	10.00
2	Albert Belle	12.00
3	Ken Griffey Jr.	35.00
4	Chuck Knoblauch	6.00
5	Frank Thomas	35.00
6	Cal Ripken Jr.	30.00
7	Todd Walker	8.00
8	Alex Rodriguez	35.00
9	Jim Thome	8.00
10	Mike Piazza	20.00
11	Barry Larkin	6.00
12	Chipper Jones	20.00
13	Derek Jeter	20.00
14	Jermaine Dye	4.00
15	Jason Giambi	4.00
16	Tim Salmon	6.00
17	Brady Anderson	4.00
18	Rondell White	4.00
19	Bernie Williams	8.00
20	Juan Gonzalez	18.00
21	Karim Garcia	4.00
22	Scott Rolen	15.00
23	Darin Erstad	12.00
24	Brian Jordan	4.00

1997 Studio Master Strokes

The look and feel of a painting on canvas is the effect presented by '97 Studio's Master Strokes inserts. Card fronts feature unique player action art and are highlighted by gold-foil graph-

ics. Each card has a facsimile autograph on front. UV-coated backs are team-color coordinated and have a few sentences about the player. Gold-foil serial numbering identifies the card from an edition of 2,000 of each player.

		MT
Complete Set (24):		600.00
Common Player:		10.00
1	Derek Jeter	40.00
2	Jeff Bagwell	30.00
3	Ken Griffey Jr.	70.00
4	Barry Bonds	18.00
5	Frank Thomas	60.00
6	Andy Pettitte	18.00
7	Mo Vaughn	15.00
8	Alex Rodriguez	50.00
9	Andruw Jones	40.00
10	Kenny Lofton	15.00
11	Cal Ripken Jr.	50.00
12	Greg Maddux	40.00
13	Manny Ramirez	15.00
14	Mike Piazza	40.00
15	Vladimir Guerrero	30.00
16	Albert Belle	20.00
17	Chipper Jones	40.00
18	Hideo Nomo	12.00
19	Sammy Sosa	10.00
20	Tony Gwynn	30.00
21	Gary Sheffield	10.00
22	Mark McGwire	25.00
23	Juan Gonzalez	30.00
24	Paul Molitor	12.00

1997 Studio Master Strokes 8x10

The look and feel of a painting on canvas is the effect presented by the 8" x 10" version of '97 Studio's Master Strokes inserts. Card fronts feature unique player action art and are highlighted by gold-foil graphics. Each card has a facsimile autograph on front. UV-coated backs are team-color coordinated and have a few sentences about the player. Gold-foil serial numbering identifies the card from an edition of 5,000 of each player - making the super-size version more than twice as common as the 2-1/2" x 3-1/2" version.

		MT
Complete Set (24):		220.00
Common Player:		4.00
1	Derek Jeter	15.00
2	Jeff Bagwell	10.00
3	Ken Griffey Jr.	25.00
4	Barry Bonds	6.00
5	Frank Thomas	25.00
6	Andy Pettitte	6.00
7	Mo Vaughn	6.00
8	Alex Rodriguez	25.00
9	Andruw Jones	15.00
10	Kenny Lofton	6.00
11	Cal Ripken Jr.	20.00
12	Greg Maddux	15.00
13	Manny Ramirez	6.00
14	Mike Piazza	15.00
15	Vladimir Guerrero	12.00
16	Albert Belle	8.00
17	Chipper Jones	15.00
18	Hideo Nomo	6.00

		MT
19	Sammy Sosa	4.00
20	Tony Gwynn	10.00
21	Gary Sheffield	4.00
22	Mark McGwire	8.00
23	Juan Gonzalez	10.00
24	Paul Molitor	6.00

1997 Studio Portrait Collection

In a departure from traditional sportscard marketing, the 1997 Studio program offered a pair of specially framed editions directly to consumers. The offer was made in a color brochure found in about half the packs advertising the "Portrait Collection." The offer includes one standard-size card and an 8" x 10" Portrait or Master card similar to those in the regular issue. These cards differ from the regular issue in that they are trimmed in platinum holographic foil, individually hand-numbered and signed by the photographer. The cards were sold framed with a metal plaque, also numbered, attesting to the limited-edition status. The framed Studio Portrait piece was produced in an edition of 500 of each player; the Master Strokes piece was limited to 100 for each player on the checklist. The former was issued at $159; the latter at $299.

		MT
Complete Set, Studio Portrait (24):		3800.
Complete Set, Master Strokes (24):		7000.
Common Plaque, Studio Portrait:		159.00
Common Plaque, Master Strokes:		299.00
P1	Ken Griffey Jr.	159.00
P2	Frank Thomas	159.00
P3	Alex Rodriquez	159.00
P4	Andruw Jones	159.00
P5	Cal Ripken Jr.	159.00
P6	Greg Maddux	159.00
P7	Mike Piazza	159.00
P8	Chipper Jones	159.00
P9	Albert Belle	159.00
P10	Derek Jeter	159.00
P11	Juan Gonzalez	159.00
P12	Todd Walker	159.00
P13	Mark McGwire	159.00
P14	Barry Bonds	159.00
P15	Jeff Bagwell	159.00
P16	Manny	159.00
P17	Kenny Lofton	159.00
P18	Mo Vaughn	159.00
P19	Hideo Nomo	159.00
P20	Tony Gwynn	159.00
P21	Vladimir Guerrero	159.00
P22	Gary Sheffield	159.00
P23	Ryne Sandberg	159.00
P24	Scott Rolen	159.00
M1	Derek Jeter	299.00
M2	Jeff Bagwell	299.00
M3	Ken Griffey Jr.	299.00
M4	Barry Bonds	299.00
M5	Frank Thomas	299.00
M6	Andy Pettitte	299.00
M7	Mo Vaughn	299.00
M8	Alex Rodriguez	299.00
M9	Andruw Jones	299.00
M10	Kenny Lofton	299.00
M11	Cal Ripken Jr.	299.00
M12	Greg Maddux	299.00
M13	Manny Ramirez	299.00
M14	Mike Piazza	299.00
M15	Vladimir Guerrero	299.00
M16	Albert Belle	299.00
M17	Chipper Jones	299.00
M18	Hideo Nomo	299.00
M19	Sammy Sosa	299.00
M20	Tony Gwynn	299.00
M21	Gary Sheffield	299.00
M22	Mark McGwire	299.00
M23	Juan Gonzalez	299.00
M24	Paul Molitor	299.00

1997 Studio Portraits

Perhaps the most innovative feature of '97 Studio is the 8" x 10" Portrait cards which come one per pack (except when a pack contains a Master Strokes 8x10). Virtually identical to the player's regular-size Studio card, the jumbo version has the word "PORTRAIT" in black beneath the team name on front. Backs have different card numbers than the same player's card in the regular set. The Portrait cards are produced with a special UV coating on front to facilitate autographing. Pre-autographed cards of three youngsters in the series were included as random pack inserts.

		MT
Complete Set (24):		40.00
Common Player:		.50
1	Ken Griffey Jr.	5.00
1s	Frank Thomas (overprinted "SAMPLE")	.50
2	Frank Thomas	5.00
3	Alex Rodriguez	5.00
4	Andruw Jones	3.00
5	Cal Ripken Jr.	4.00
6	Greg Maddux	3.00
7	Mike Piazza	3.00
8	Chipper Jones	3.00
9	Albert Belle	1.50
10	Derek Jeter	3.00
11	Juan Gonzalez	2.00
12	Todd Walker	1.00
12a	Todd Walker (autographed edition of 1,250)	40.00
13	Mark McGwire	1.50
14	Barry Bonds	1.00
15	Jeff Bagwell	2.00
16	Manny Ramirez	1.00
17	Kenny Lofton	1.00
18	Mo Vaughn	1.00
19	Hideo Nomo	.75
20	Tony Gwynn	2.00
21	Vladimir Guerrero	2.00
21a	Vladimir Guerrero (autographed edition of 500)	100.00
22	Gary Sheffield	.50
23	Ryne Sandberg	1.00
24	Scott Rolen	1.50
24a	Scott Rolen (autographed edition of 1,000)	75.00

1997 Fleer

Fleer maintained its matte-finish coating for 1997 after it debuted in the 1996 product. The regular-issue set had 500 cards equipped with icons designating All-Stars, League Leaders and World Series cards. There were also 10 checklist cards in the regular-issue set, featuring stars on the front. Fleer arrived in 10-card packs and had a Tiffany Collection parallel set and six different insert sets, including Rookie Sensations, Golden Memories, Team Leaders, Night and Day, Zone and Lumber Company.

		MT
Complete Set (761):		65.00
Complete Series 1 Set (500):		40.00
Complete Series 2 Set (261):		25.00
Common Player:		.05
Complete Tiffany Set (1-761):		3500.
Ser. 1 Tiffany Veteran Stars:		25x to 40x
Ser. 1 Young Stars & RC's:		15x to 25x
Ser. 2 Tiffany Veteran Stars:		20x to 30x
Ser. 2 Yng. Stars & RC's:		10x to 15x
Wax Box:		50.00
1	Roberto Alomar	.60
2	Brady Anderson	.10
3	Bobby Bonilla	.10
4	Rocky Coppinger	.05
5	Cesar Devarez	.05
6	Scott Erickson	.05
7	Jeffrey Hammonds	.05
8	Chris Hoiles	.05
9	Eddie Murray	.40
10	Mike Mussina	.60
11	Randy Myers	.05
12	Rafael Palmeiro	.15
13	Cal Ripken Jr.	2.50
14	B.J. Surhoff	.05
15	David Wells	.05
16	Todd Zeile	.05
17	Darren Bragg	.05
18	Jose Canseco	.25
19	Roger Clemens	.75
20	Wil Cordero	.05
21	Jeff Frye	.05
22	Nomar Garciaparra	2.00
23	Tom Gordon	.05
24	Mike Greenwell	.05
25	Reggie Jefferson	.05
26	Jose Malave	.05
27	Tim Naehring	.05
28	Troy O'Leary	.05
29	Heathcliff Slocumb	.05
30	Mike Stanley	.05
31	John Valentin	.05
32	Mo Vaughn	1.00
33	Tim Wakefield	.05
34	Garret Anderson	.05
35	George Arias	.05
36	Shawn Boskie	.05
37	Chili Davis	.05
38	Jason Dickson	.25
39	Gary DiSarcina	.05
40	Jim Edmonds	.05
41	Darin Erstad	1.25
42	Jorge Fabregas	.05
43	Chuck Finley	.05
44	Todd Greene	.05
45	*Mike Holtz*	.10
46	Rex Hudler	.05
47	Mike James	.05
48	Mark Langston	.05
49	Troy Percival	.05
50	Tim Salmon	.20
51	Jeff Schmidt	.05
52	J.T. Snow	.05
53	Randy Velarde	.05
54	Wilson Alvarez	.05
55	Harold Baines	.05
56	James Baldwin	.05
57	Jason Bere	.05
58	Mike Cameron	.05
59	Ray Durham	.05
60	Alex Fernandez	.05
61	Ozzie Guillen	.05
62	Roberto Hernandez	.05
63	Ron Karkovice	.05
64	Darren Lewis	.05
65	Dave Martinez	.05
66	Lyle Mouton	.05
67	Greg Norton	.05
68	Tony Phillips	.05
69	Chris Snopek	.05
70	Kevin Tapani	.05
71	Danny Tartabull	.05
72	Frank Thomas	3.00
73	Robin Ventura	.05
74	Sandy Alomar Jr.	.05
75	Albert Belle	1.00
76	Mark Carreon	.05
77	Julio Franco	.05
78	Brian Giles	.05
79	Orel Hershiser	.05
80	Kenny Lofton	.75
81	Dennis Martinez	.05
82	Jack McDowell	.05
83	Jose Mesa	.05
84	Charles Nagy	.05
85	Chad Ogea	.05
86	Eric Plunk	.05
87	Manny Ramirez	.75
88	Kevin Seitzer	.05
89	Julian Tavarez	.05
90	Jim Thome	.25
91	Jose Vizcaino	.05
92	Omar Vizquel	.05
93	Brad Ausmus	.05
94	Kimera Bartee	.05
95	Raul Casanova	.05
96	Tony Clark	.60
97	John Cummings	.05
98	Travis Fryman	.05
99	Bob Higginson	.05
100	Mark Lewis	.05
101	Felipe Lira	.05
102	Phil Nevin	.05
103	Melvin Nieves	.05
104	Curtis Pride	.05
105	A.J. Sager	.05
106	Ruben Sierra	.05
107	Justin Thompson	.05
108	Alan Trammell	.05
109	Kevin Appier	.05
110	Tim Belcher	.05
111	Jaime Bluma	.05
112	Johnny Damon	.15
113	Tom Goodwin	.05
114	Chris Haney	.05
115	Keith Lockhart	.05
116	Mike Macfarlane	.05
117	Jeff Montgomery	.05
118	Jose Offerman	.05
119	Craig Paquette	.05
120	Joe Randa	.05
121	Bip Roberts	.05
122	Jose Rosado	.05
123	Mike Sweeney	.05
124	Michael Tucker	.05
125	Jeromy Burnitz	.05
126	Jeff Cirillo	.05
127	Jeff D'Amico	.05
128	Mike Fetters	.05
129	John Jaha	.05
130	Scott Karl	.05
131	Jesse Levis	.05
132	Mark Loretta	.05
133	Mike Matheny	.05
134	Ben McDonald	.05
135	Matt Mieske	.05
136	Marc Newfield	.05
137	Dave Nilsson	.05
138	Jose Valentin	.05
139	Fernando Vina	.05
140	Bob Wickman	.05
141	Gerald Williams	.05
142	Rick Aguilera	.05
143	Rich Becker	.05
144	Ron Coomer	.05
145	Marty Cordova	.10
146	Roberto Kelly	.05
147	Chuck Knoblauch	.10
148	Matt Lawton	.05
149	Pat Meares	.05
150	Travis Miller	.05
151	Paul Molitor	.30
152	Greg Myers	.05
153	Dan Naulty	.05
154	Kirby Puckett	1.00
155	Brad Radke	.05
156	Frank Rodriguez	.05
157	Scott Stahoviak	.05
158	Dave Stevens	.05
159	Matt Walbeck	.05
160	Todd Walker	.50
161	Wade Boggs	.15
162	David Cone	.10
163	Mariano Duncan	.05
164	Cecil Fielder	.15
165	Joe Girardi	.05
166	Dwight Gooden	.05
167	Charlie Hayes	.05
168	Derek Jeter	1.50
169	Jimmy Key	.05
170	Jim Leyritz	.05
171	Tino Martinez	.30
172	*Ramiro Mendoza*	.05
173	Jeff Nelson	.05
174	Paul O'Neill	.05
175	Andy Pettitte	.75
176	Mariano Rivera	.15
177	Ruben Rivera	.35
178	Kenny Rogers	.05
179	Darryl Strawberry	.05
180	John Wetteland	.05

#	Player	Value
181	Bernie Williams	.40
182	Willie Adams	.05
183	Tony Batista	.05
184	Geronimo Berroa	.05
185	Mike Bordick	.05
186	Scott Brosius	.05
187	Bobby Chouinard	.05
188	Jim Corsi	.05
189	Brent Gates	.05
190	Jason Giambi	.05
191	Jose Herrera	.05
192	*Damon Mashore*	.05
193	Mark McGwire	1.00
194	Mike Mohler	.05
195	Scott Spiezio	.05
196	Terry Steinbach	.05
197	Bill Taylor	.05
198	John Wasdin	.05
199	Steve Wojciechowski	.05
200	Ernie Young	.05
201	Rich Amaral	.05
202	Jay Buhner	.15
203	Norm Charlton	.05
204	Joey Cora	.05
205	Russ Davis	.05
206	Ken Griffey Jr.	3.00
207	Sterling Hitchcock	.05
208	Brian Hunter	.05
209	Raul Ibanez	.05
210	Randy Johnson	.30
211	Edgar Martinez	.05
212	Jamie Moyer	.05
213	Alex Rodriguez	3.00
214	Paul Sorrento	.05
215	Matt Wagner	.05
216	Bob Wells	.05
217	Dan Wilson	.05
218	Damon Buford	.05
219	Will Clark	.25
220	Kevin Elster	.05
221	Juan Gonzalez	1.50
222	Rusty Greer	.05
223	Kevin Gross	.05
224	Darryl Hamilton	.05
225	Mike Henneman	.05
226	Ken Hill	.05
227	Mark McLemore	.05
228	Darren Oliver	.05
229	Dean Palmer	.05
230	Roger Pavlik	.05
231	Ivan Rodriguez	.50
232	Mickey Tettleton	.05
233	Bobby Witt	.05
234	Jacob Brumfield	.05
235	Joe Carter	.20
236	Tim Crabtree	.05
237	Carlos Delgado	.05
238	Huck Flener	.05
239	Alex Gonzalez	.05
240	Shawn Green	.05
241	Juan Guzman	.05
242	Pat Hentgen	.05
243	Marty Janzen	.05
244	Sandy Martinez	.05
245	Otis Nixon	.05
246	Charlie O'Brien	.05
247	John Olerud	.05
248	Robert Perez	.05
249	Ed Sprague	.05
250	Mike Timlin	.05
251	Steve Avery	.05
252	Jeff Blauser	.05
253	Brad Clontz	.05
254	Jermaine Dye	.20
255	Tom Glavine	.10
256	Marquis Grissom	.05
257	Andruw Jones	2.00
258	Chipper Jones	2.00
259	David Justice	.15
260	Ryan Klesko	.40
261	Mark Lemke	.05
262	Javier Lopez	.10
263	Greg Maddux	2.00
264	Fred McGriff	.35
265	Greg McMichael	.05
266	Denny Neagle	.05
267	Terry Pendleton	.05
268	Eddie Perez	.05
269	John Smoltz	.15
270	Terrell Wade	.05
271	Mark Wohlers	.05
272	Terry Adams	.05
273	Brant Brown	.05
274	Leo Gomez	.05
275	Luis Gonzalez	.05
276	Mark Grace	.15
277	Tyler Houston	.05
278	Robin Jennings	.05
279	Brooks Kieschnick	.05
280	Brian McRae	.05
281	Jaime Navarro	.05
282	Ryne Sandberg	.75
283	Scott Servais	.05
284	Sammy Sosa	.20
285	*Dave Swartzbaugh*	.05
286	Amaury Telemaco	.05
287	Steve Trachsel	.05
288	*Pedro Valdes*	.05
289	Turk Wendell	.05
290	Bret Boone	.05
291	Jeff Branson	.05
292	Jeff Brantley	.05
293	Eric Davis	.05
294	Willie Greene	.05
295	Thomas Howard	.05
296	Barry Larkin	.20
297	Kevin Mitchell	.05
298	Hal Morris	.05
299	Chad Mottola	.05
300	Joe Oliver	.05
301	Mark Portugal	.05
302	Roger Salkeld	.05
303	Reggie Sanders	.05
304	Pete Schourek	.05
305	John Smiley	.05
306	Eddie Taubensee	.05
307	Dante Bichette	.20
308	Ellis Burks	.05
309	Vinny Castilla	.05
310	Andres Galarraga	.15
311	Curt Leskanic	.05
312	Quinton McCracken	.05
313	Neifi Perez	.05
314	Jeff Reed	.05
315	Steve Reed	.05
316	Armando Reynoso	.05
317	Kevin Ritz	.05
318	Bruce Ruffin	.05
319	Larry Walker	.30
320	Walt Weiss	.05
321	Jamey Wright	.05
322	Eric Young	.05
323	Kurt Abbott	.05
324	Alex Arias	.05
325	Kevin Brown	.05
326	Luis Castillo	.15
327	Greg Colbrunn	.05
328	Jeff Conine	.05
329	Andre Dawson	.05
330	Charles Johnson	.05
331	Al Leiter	.05
332	Ralph Milliard	.05
333	Robb Nen	.05
334	Pat Rapp	.05
335	Edgar Renteria	.25
336	Gary Sheffield	.25
337	Devon White	.05
338	Bob Abreu	.05
339	Jeff Bagwell	1.25
340	Derek Bell	.05
341	Sean Berry	.05
342	Craig Biggio	.05
343	Doug Drabek	.05
344	Tony Eusebio	.05
345	Ricky Gutierrez	.05
346	Mike Hampton	.05
347	Brian Hunter	.05
348	Todd Jones	.05
349	Darryl Kile	.05
350	Derrick May	.05
351	Orlando Miller	.05
352	James Mouton	.05
353	Shane Reynolds	.05
354	Billy Wagner	.05
355	Donne Wall	.05
356	Mike Blowers	.05
357	Brett Butler	.05
358	Roger Cedeno	.05
359	Chad Curtis	.05
360	Delino DeShields	.05
361	Greg Gagne	.05
362	Karim Garcia	.50
363	Wilton Guerrero	.25
364	Todd Hollandsworth	.15
365	Eric Karros	.05
366	Ramon Martinez	.05
367	Raul Mondesi	.25
368	Hideo Nomo	.60
369	Antonio Osuna	.05
370	Chan Ho Park	.05
371	Mike Piazza	2.00
372	Ismael Valdes	.05
373	Todd Worrell	.05
374	Moises Alou	.05
375	Shane Andrews	.05
376	Yamil Benitez	.05
377	Jeff Fassero	.05
378	Darrin Fletcher	.05
379	Cliff Floyd	.05
380	Mark Grudzielanek	.05
381	Mike Lansing	.05
382	Barry Manuel	.05
383	Pedro J. Martinez	.05
384	Henry Rodriguez	.05
385	Mel Rojas	.05
386	F.P. Santangelo	.05
387	David Segui	.05
388	Ugueth Urbina	.05
389	Rondell White	.05
390	Edgardo Alfonzo	.05
391	Carlos Baerga	.10
392	Mark Clark	.05
393	Alvaro Espinoza	.05
394	John Franco	.05
395	Bernard Gilkey	.05
396	Pete Harnisch	.05
397	Todd Hundley	.05
398	Butch Huskey	.05
399	Jason Isringhausen	.10
400	Lance Johnson	.05
401	Bobby Jones	.05
402	Alex Ochoa	.05
403	Rey Ordonez	.10
404	Robert Person	.05
405	Paul Wilson	.15
406	Matt Beech	.05
407	Ron Blazier	.05
408	Ricky Bottalico	.05
409	Lenny Dykstra	.05
410	Jim Eisenreich	.05
411	Bobby Estalella	.05
412	Mike Grace	.15
413	Gregg Jefferies	.05
414	Mike Lieberthal	.05
415	Wendell Magee Jr.	.05
416	Mickey Morandini	.05
417	Ricky Otero	.05
418	Scott Rolen	1.50
419	Ken Ryan	.05
420	Benito Santiago	.05
421	Curt Schilling	.05
422	Kevin Sefcik	.05
423	Jermaine Allensworth	.05
424	Trey Beamon	.05
425	Jay Bell	.05
426	Francisco Cordova	.10
427	Carlos Garcia	.05
428	Mark Johnson	.05
429	Jason Kendall	.05
430	Jeff King	.05
431	Jon Lieber	.05
432	Al Martin	.05
433	Orlando Merced	.05
434	Ramon Morel	.05
435	Matt Ruebel	.05
436	Jason Schmidt	.05
437	*Marc Wilkins*	.05
438	Alan Benes	.15
439	Andy Benes	.05
440	Royce Clayton	.05
441	Dennis Eckersley	.05
442	Gary Gaetti	.05
443	Ron Gant	.10
444	Aaron Holbert	.05
445	Brian Jordan	.05
446	Ray Lankford	.05
447	John Mabry	.05
448	T.J. Mathews	.05
449	Willie McGee	.05
450	Donovan Osborne	.05
451	Tom Pagnozzi	.05
452	Ozzie Smith	.40
453	Todd Stottlemyre	.05
454	Mark Sweeney	.05
455	Dmitri Young	.05
456	Andy Ashby	.05
457	Ken Caminiti	.15
458	Archi Cianfrocco	.05
459	Steve Finley	.05
460	John Flaherty	.05
461	Chris Gomez	.05
462	Tony Gwynn	1.25
463	Joey Hamilton	.05
464	Rickey Henderson	.05
465	Trevor Hoffman	.05
466	Brian Johnson	.05
467	Wally Joyner	.05
468	Jody Reed	.05
469	Scott Sanders	.05
470	Bob Tewksbury	.05
471	Fernando Valenzuela	.05
472	Greg Vaughn	.05
473	Tim Worrell	.05
474	Rich Aurilia	.05
475	Rod Beck	.05
476	Marvin Benard	.05
477	Barry Bonds	.75
478	Jay Canizaro	.05
479	Shawon Dunston	.05
480	Shawn Estes	.05
481	Mark Gardner	.05
482	Glenallen Hill	.05
483	Stan Javier	.05
484	Marcus Jensen	.05
485	*Bill Mueller*	.05
486	William VanLandingham	.05
487	Allen Watson	.05
488	Rick Wilkins	.05
489	Matt Williams	.25
489p	Matt Williams ("PROMOTIONAL SAMPLE")	3.00
490	Desi Wilson	.05
491	Checklist (Albert Belle)	.40
492	Checklist (Ken Griffey Jr.)	1.00
493	Checklist (Andruw Jones)	.50
494	Checklist (Chipper Jones)	.60
495	Checklist (Mark McGwire)	.40
496	Checklist (Paul Molitor)	.15
497	Checklist (Mike Piazza)	.60
498	Checklist (Cal Ripken Jr.)	.75
499	Checklist (Alex Rodriguez)	1.00
500	Checklist (Frank Thomas)	1.00
501	Kenny Lofton	.75
502	Carlos Perez	.05
503	Tim Raines	.05
504	*Danny Patterson*	.20
505	Derrick May	.05
506	Dave Hollins	.05
507	Felipe Crespo	.05
508	Brian Banks	.05
509	Jeff Kent	.05
510	*Bubba Trammell*	.75
511	Robert Person	.05
512	David Arias	.05
513	Ryan Jones	.05
514	David Justice	.15
515	Will Cunnane	.05
516	Russ Johnson	.05
517	John Burkett	.05
518	*Robinson Checo*	.20
519	*Ricardo Rincon*	.15
520	Woody Williams	.05
521	Rick Helling	.05
522	Jorge Posada	.05
523	Kevin Orie	.05
524	*Fernando Tatis*	1.00
525	Jermaine Dye	.05
526	Brian Hunter	.05
527	Greg McMichael	.05
528	Matt Wagner	.05
529	Richie Sexson	.05
530	Scott Ruffcorn	.05
531	Luis Gonzalez	.05
532	Mike Johnson	.05
533	Mark Petkovsek	.05
534	Doug Drabek	.05
535	Jose Canseco	.25
536	Bobby Bonilla	.05
537	J.T. Snow	.05
538	Shawon Dunston	.05
539	John Ericks	.05
540	Terry Steinbach	.05
541	Jay Bell	.05
542	Joe Borowski	.05
543	David Wells	.05
544	*Justin Towle*	.05
545	Mike Blowers	.05
546	Shannon Stewart	.05
547	Rudy Pemberton	.05
548	Bill Swift	.05
549	Osvaldo Fernandez	.05
550	Eddie Murray	.35
551	Don Wengert	.05
552	Brad Ausmus	.05
553	Carlos Garcia	.05
554	Jose Guillen	1.00
555	Rheal Cormier	.05
556	Doug Brocail	.05
557	Rex Hudler	.05
558	Armando Benitez	.05
559	Elieser Marrero	.05
560	*Ricky Ledee*	1.50
561	Bartolo Colon	.05
562	Quilvio Veras	.05
563	Alex Fernandez	.05
564	Darren Dreifort	.05
565	Benji Gil	.05
566	Kent Mercker	.05
567	Glendon Rusch	.05
568	Ramon Tatis	.05
569	Roger Clemens	1.25
570	Mark Lewis	.05
571	*Emil Brown*	.15
572	Jaime Navarro	.05
573	Sherman Obando	.05
574	John Wasdin	.05
575	Calvin Maduro	.05
576	Todd Jones	.05
577	Orlando Merced	.05
578	Cal Eldred	.05
579	Mark Gubicza	.05
580	Michael Tucker	.05
581	*Tony Saunders*	.15

		MT
582	Garvin Alston	.05
583	Joe Roa	.05
584	*Brady Raggio*	.05
585	Jimmy Key	.05
586	*Marc Sagmoen*	.05
587	Jim Bullinger	.05
588	Yorkis Perez	.05
589	*Jose Cruz*	7.50
590	Mike Stanton	.05
591	*Deivi Cruz*	.05
592	Steve Karsay	.05
593	Mike Trombley	.05
594	Doug Glanville	.05
595	Scott Sanders	.05
596	Thomas Howard	.05
597	T.J. Staton	.05
598	Garrett Stephenson	.05
599	Rico Brogna	.05
600	Albert Belle	1.00
601	Jose Vizcaino	.05
602	Chili Davis	.05
603	Shane Mack	.05
604	Jim Eisenreich	.05
605	Todd Zeile	.05
606	Brian Boehringer	.05
607	Paul Shuey	.05
608	Kevin Tapani	.05
609	John Wetteland	.05
610	Jim Leyritz	.05
611	Ray Montgomery	.05
612	Doug Bochtler	.05
613	Wady Almonte	.05
614	Danny Tartabull	.05
615	Orlando Miller	.05
616	Bobby Ayala	.05
617	Tony Graffanino	.05
618	Marc Valdes	.05
619	Ron Villone	.05
620	Derrek Lee	.05
621	Greg Colbrunn	.05
622	*Felix Heredia*	.25
623	Carl Everett	.05
624	Mark Thompson	.05
625	Jeff Granger	.05
626	Damian Jackson	.05
627	Mark Leiter	.05
628	Chris Holt	.05
629	*Dario Veras*	.15
630	Dave Burba	.05
631	Darryl Hamilton	.05
632	Mark Acre	.05
633	Fernando Hernandez	.05
634	Terry Mulholland	.05
635	Dustin Hermanson	.05
636	Delino DeShields	.05
637	Steve Avery	.05
638	*Tony Womack*	.25
639	Mark Whiten	.05
640	Marquis Grissom	.05
641	Xavier Hernandez	.05
642	Eric Davis	.05
643	Bob Tewksbury	.05
644	Dante Powell	.05
645	Carlos Castillo	.05
646	Chris Widger	.05
647	Moises Alou	.05
648	Pat Listach	.05
649	Edgar Ramos	.05
650	Deion Sanders	.20
651	John Olerud	.05
652	Todd Dunwoody	.05
653	*Randall Simon*	.05
654	Dan Carlson	.05
655	Matt Williams	.25
656	Jeff King	.05
657	Luis Alicea	.05
658	Brian Moehler	.05
659	Ariel Prieto	.05
660	Kevin Elster	.05
661	Mark Hutton	.05
662	Aaron Sele	.05
663	Graeme Lloyd	.05
664	John Burke	.05
665	Mel Rojas	.05
666	Sid Fernandez	.05
667	Pedro Astacio	.05
668	Jeff Abbott	.05
669	Darren Daulton	.05
670	Mike Bordick	.05
671	Sterling Hitchcock	.05
672	Damion Easley	.05
673	Armando Reynoso	.05
674	Pat Cline	.05
675	*Orlando Cabrera*	.30
676	Alan Embree	.05
677	Brian Bevil	.05
678	David Weathers	.05
679	Cliff Floyd	.05
680	Joe Randa	.05
681	Bill Haselman	.05
682	Jeff Fassero	.05

		MT
683	Matt Morris	.05
684	Mark Portugal	.05
685	Lee Smith	.05
686	Pokey Reese	.05
687	Benito Santiago	.05
688	Brian Johnson	.05
689	*Brent Brede*	.05
690	Shigetosi Hasegawa	.05
691	Julio Santana	.05
692	Steve Kline	.05
693	Julian Tavarez	.05
694	John Hudek	.05
695	Manny Alexander	.05
696	Roberto Alomar (Encore)	.30
697	Jeff Bagwell (Encore)	.60
698	Barry Bonds (Encore)	.40
699	Ken Caminiti (Encore)	.10
700	Juan Gonzalez (Encore)	.60
701	Ken Griffey Jr. (Encore)	1.50
702	Tony Gwynn (Encore)	.60
703	Derek Jeter (Encore)	1.00
704	Andruw Jones (Encore)	1.00
705	Chipper Jones (Encore)	1.00
706	Barry Larkin (Encore)	.05
707	Greg Maddux (Encore)	1.00
708	Mark McGwire (Encore)	.50
709	Paul Molitor (Encore)	.15
710	Hideo Nomo (Encore)	.30
711	Andy Pettitte (Encore)	.40
712	Mike Piazza (Encore)	1.00
713	Manny Ramirez (Encore)	.40
714	Cal Ripken Jr. (Encore)	1.25
715	Alex Rodriguez (Encore)	1.50
716	Ryne Sandberg (Encore)	.40
717	John Smoltz (Encore)	.05
718	Frank Thomas (Encore)	1.50
719	Mo Vaughn (Encore)	.40
720	Bernie Williams (Encore)	.30
721	Checklist (Tim Salmon)	.05
722	Checklist (Greg Maddux)	.50
723	Checklist (Cal Ripken Jr.)	.75
724	Checklist (Mo Vaughn)	.25
725	Checklist (Ryne Sandberg)	.25
726	Checklist (Frank Thomas)	1.00
727	Checklist (Barry Larkin)	.05
728	Checklist (Manny Ramirez)	.25
729	Checklist (Andres Galarraga)	.05
730	Checklist (Tony Clark)	.25
731	Checklist (Gary Sheffield)	.15
732	Checklist (Jeff Bagwell)	.35
733	Checklist (Kevin Appier)	.05
734	Checklist (Mike Piazza)	.50
735	Checklist (Jeff Cirillo)	.05
736	Checklist (Paul Molitor)	.15
737	Checklist (Henry Rodriguez)	.05
738	Checklist (Todd Hundley)	.10
739	Checklist (Derek Jeter)	.50
740	Checklist (Mark McGwire)	.35
741	Checklist (Curt Schilling)	.05
742	Checklist (Jason Kendall)	.05
743	Checklist (Tony Gwynn)	.40
744	Checklist (Barry Bonds)	.25
745	Checklist (Ken Griffey Jr.)	1.00
746	Checklist (Brian Jordan)	.05
747	Checklist (Juan Gonzalez)	.40
748	Checklist (Joe Carter)	.05
749	Arizona Diamondbacks	.05
750	Tampa Bay Devil Rays	.05
751	*Hideki Irabu*	2.00
752	*Jeremi Gonzalez*	.60
753	*Mario Valdez*	.25
754	Aaron Boone	.05
755	Brett Tomko	.05
756	*Jaret Wright*	.75
757	Ryan McGuire	.05
758	Jason McDonald	.05
759	*Adrian Brown*	.20
760	*Keith Foulke*	.25
761	Checklist	.05

1997 Fleer Bleacher Blasters

This 10-card insert features some of the game's top power hitters and was found in retail packs only. Cards featured a die-cut "burst" pattern on an etched foil background. Cards were inserted 1:36 packs.

		MT
	Complete Set (10):	60.00
	Common Player:	2.00
1	Albert Belle	5.00
2	Barry Bonds	4.00

3	Juan Gonzalez	7.00
4	Ken Griffey Jr.	15.00
5	Mark McGwire	6.00
6	Mike Piazza	9.00
7	Alex Rodriguez	15.00
8	Frank Thomas	15.00
9	Mo Vaughn	4.00
10	Matt Williams	2.00

1997 Fleer Decade of Excellence

A 12-card insert found only 1:36 hobby shop packs. Cards feature a design similar to the 1987 Fleer set and feature players who started their careers no later than the '87 season. Ten percent of the press run received a special foil treatment and designated as "Rare Traditions."

		MT
	Complete Set (12):	70.00
	Common Player:	3.00
1	Wade Boggs	3.00
2	Barry Bonds	6.00
3	Roger Clemens	8.00
4	Tony Gwynn	10.00
5	Rickey Henderson	3.00
6	Greg Maddux	15.00
7	Mark McGwire	8.00
8	Paul Molitor	4.00
9	Eddie Murray	4.00
10	Cal Ripken Jr.	20.00
11	Ryne Sandberg	6.00
12	Matt Williams	4.00

1997 Fleer Diamond Tribute

Twelve of the game's top stars are highlighted in this set. Cards feature an embossed foil design and were inserted 1:288 packs.

		MT
	Complete Set (12):	650.00
	Common Player:	15.00
1	Albert Belle	30.00
2	Barry Bonds	25.00
3	Juan Gonzalez	50.00
4	Ken Griffey Jr.	120.00
5	Tony Gwynn	40.00
6	Greg Maddux	65.00
7	Mark McGwire	35.00
8	Eddie Murray	15.00
9	Mike Piazza	65.00
10	Cal Ripken Jr.	80.00
11	Alex Rodriguez	80.00
12	Frank Thomas	100.00

1997 Fleer Golden Memories

Golden Memories captures 10 different highlights from the 1996 season, and is inserted one per 16 packs. Moments like Dwight Gooden's no hitter, Paul Molitor's 3000th hit and Eddie Murray's 500th home run are highlighted on a horizontal format.

		MT
	Complete Set (10):	20.00
	Common Player:	.75
1	Barry Bonds	2.00
2	Dwight Gooden	.75
3	Todd Hundley	1.00
4	Mark McGwire	2.50
5	Paul Molitor	1.25
6	Eddie Murray	1.00
7	Hideo Nomo	2.00
8	Mike Piazza	5.00
9	Cal Ripken Jr.	6.00
10	Ozzie Smith	2.00

1997 Fleer Goudey Greats

Using the 1933 Goudey design, this 15-card insert offers today's top players in classic old-time design. Cards were inserted 1:8 packs. A limited number (1% of press run) of cards received a special foil treatment and were found only in hobby packs.

		MT
Complete Set (15):		30.00
Common Player:		.50
Foils:		20x to 40x
1	Barry Bonds	1.00
2	Ken Griffey Jr.	5.00
3	Tony Gwynn	2.00
4	Derek Jeter	3.00
5	Chipper Jones	3.00
6	Kenny Lofton	1.00
7	Greg Maddux	3.00
8	Mark McGwire	1.50
9	Eddie Murray	.50
10	Mike Piazza	3.00
11	Cal Ripken Jr.	4.00
12	Alex Rodriguez	5.00
13	Ryne Sandberg	1.00
14	Frank Thomas	5.00
15	Mo Vaughn	1.00

1997 Fleer Headliners

This 20-card insert highlights the personal achievements of each of the players depicted. Cards were inserted 1:2 packs and feature multi-color foil stamping on the fronts and a newspaper-style account of the player's achievement on the back.

		MT
Complete Set (20):		12.00
Common Player:		.20
1	Jeff Bagwell	.75
2	Albert Belle	.75
3	Barry Bonds	.50
4	Ken Caminiti	.20
5	Juan Gonzalez	.75
6	Ken Griffey Jr.	2.00
7	Tony Gwynn	.75
8	Derek Jeter	1.25
9	Andruw Jones	1.25
10	Chipper Jones	1.25
11	Greg Maddux	1.25
12	Mark McGwire	.60
13	Paul Molitor	.30
14	Eddie Murray	.30
15	Mike Piazza	1.25
16	Cal Ripken Jr.	1.50
17	Alex Rodriguez	2.00
18	Ryne Sandberg	.50
19	John Smoltz	.20
20	Frank Thomas	2.00

1997 Fleer Lumber Company

Lumber Company inserts were found every 48 retail packs. The cards were printed on a die-cut, spherical wood-like pattern, with the player imposed on the left side. Eighteen of the top power hitters in baseball are highlighted.

		MT
Complete Set (18):		175.00
Common Player:		4.00
1	Brady Anderson	4.00
2	Jeff Bagwell	15.00
3	Albert Belle	12.00
4	Barry Bonds	10.00
5	Jay Buhner	4.00
6	Ellis Burks	4.00
7	Andres Galarraga	4.00
8	Juan Gonzalez	18.00
9	Ken Griffey Jr.	60.00
10	Todd Hundley	5.00
11	Ryan Klesko	6.00
12	Mark McGwire	12.00
13	Mike Piazza	20.00
14	Alex Rodriguez	30.00
15	Gary Sheffield	6.00
16	Sammy Sosa	6.00
17	Frank Thomas	35.00
18	Mo Vaughn	10.00

1997 Fleer New Horizons

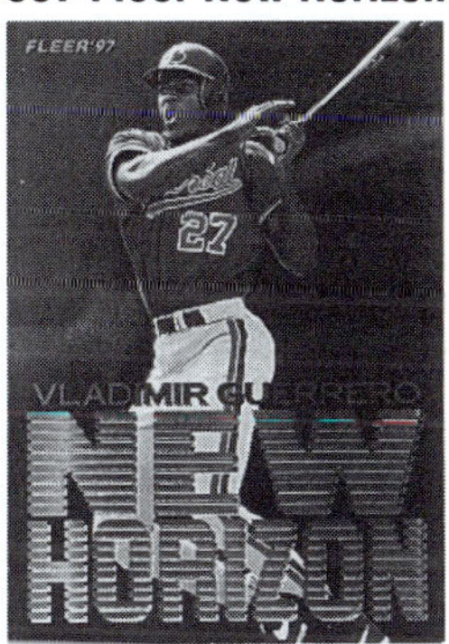

Rookies and prospects expected to make an impact during the 1996 season were featured in this 15-card insert set. Card fronts feature a rainbow foil background with the words "New Horizon" featured prominently on the bottom under the player's name. Cards were inserted 1:4 packs.

		MT
Complete Set (15):		15.00
Common Player:		.25
1	Bob Abreu	.25
2	Jose Cruz Jr.	4.00
3	Darin Erstad	2.00
4	Nomar Garciaparra	2.50
5	Vladimir Guerrero	2.50
6	Wilton Guerrero	.25
7	Jose Guillen	1.00
8	Hideki Irabu	2.00
9	Andruw Jones	2.50
10	Kevin Orie	.25
11	Scott Rolen	2.00
12	Scott Spiezio	.25
13	Bubba Trammell	.75
14	Todd Walker	.50
15	Dmitri Young	.25

1997 Fleer Night & Day

Night and Day spotlighted 10 stars with unusual prowess during night or day games. These lenticular cards carried the toughest insert ratios in Fleer Baseball at one per 288 packs.

		MT
Complete Set (10):		375.00
Common Player:		10.00
1	Barry Bonds	18.00
2	Ellis Burks	10.00
3	Juan Gonzalez	35.00

4	Ken Griffey Jr.	75.00
5	Mark McGwire	30.00
6	Mike Piazza	50.00
7	Manny Ramirez	15.00
8	Alex Rodriguez	60.00
9	John Smoltz	10.00
10	Frank Thomas	75.00

1997 Fleer Rookie Sensations

Rookies Sensations showcased 20 of the top up-and-coming stars in baseball. Appearing every six packs, these inserts have the feaured player in the foreground, with the background look of painted brush strokes.

		MT
Complete Set (20):		18.00
Common Player:		.40
1	Jermaine Allensworth	.40
2	James Baldwin	.40
3	Alan Benes	.60
4	Jermaine Dye	.50
5	Darin Erstad	2.50
6	Todd Hollandsworth	.75
7	Derek Jeter	4.00
8	Jason Kendall	.60
9	Alex Ochoa	.50
10	Rey Ordonez	.75
11	Edgar Renteria	.60
12	Bob Abreu	1.00
13	Nomar Garciaparra	3.00
14	Wilton Guerrero	1.00
15	Andruw Jones	4.00
16	Wendell Magee	1.00
17	Neifi Perez	.40
18	Scott Rolen	3.00
19	Scott Spiezio	.40
20	Todd Walker	1.00

1997 Fleer Soaring Stars

A 12-card insert found 1:12 packs designed to profile players with outstanding statistical performances during their careers.

		MT
Complete Set (12):		40.00
Common Player:		.75
1	Albert Belle	2.50
2	Barry Bonds	2.00
3	Juan Gonzalez	3.00
4	Ken Griffey Jr.	8.00
5	Derek Jeter	5.00

6	Andruw Jones	5.00
7	Chipper Jones	5.00
8	Greg Maddux	5.00
9	Mark McGwire	3.00
10	Mike Piazza	5.00
11	Alex Rodriguez	6.00
12	Frank Thomas	8.00

1997 Fleer Team Leaders

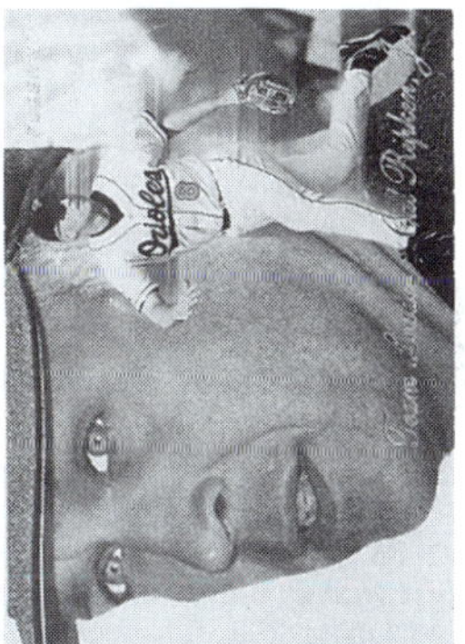

Team Leaders captured the statistical and/or inspirational leaders from all 28 teams. Inserted every 20 packs, these inserts were printed on a horizontal format, with the player's face die-cut in the perimeter of the card.

		MT
Complete Set (28):		120.00
Common Player:		2.00
1	Cal Ripken Jr.	15.00
2	Mo Vaughn	6.00
3	Jim Edmonds	2.00
4	Frank Thomas	20.00
5	Albert Belle	7.00
6	Bob Higginson	2.00
7	Kevin Appier	2.00
8	John Jaha	2.00
9	Paul Molitor	3.00
10	Andy Pettitte	5.00
11	Mark McGwire	8.00
12	Ken Griffey Jr.	20.00
13	Juan Gonzalez	10.00
14	Pat Hentgen	2.00
15	Chipper Jones	12.00
16	Mark Grace	2.50
17	Barry Larkin	2.50
18	Ellis Burks	2.00
19	Gary Sheffield	3.00
20	Jeff Bagwell	10.00
21	Mike Piazza	12.00
22	Henry Rodriguez	2.00
23	Todd Hundley	2.00
24	Curt Schilling	2.00
25	Jeff King	2.00
26	Brian Jordan	2.00
27	Tony Gwynn	12.00
28	Barry Bonds	5.00

1997 Fleer Zone

Twenty of the top hitters in baseball are featured on these holographic cards with the words Zone printed across the front. Zone inserts were found only in hobby packs at a rate of one per 80.

		MT
Complete Set (20):		275.00
Common Player:		5.00
1	Jeff Bagwell	15.00
2	Albert Belle	12.00
3	Barry Bonds	10.00
4	Ken Caminiti	5.00
5	Andres Galarraga	5.00
6	Juan Gonzalez	20.00
7	Ken Griffey Jr.	40.00
8	Tony Gwynn	20.00
9	Chipper Jones	25.00
10	Greg Maddux	25.00
11	Mark McGwire	15.00
12	Dean Palmer	5.00
13	Andy Pettitte	10.00
14	Mike Piazza	25.00
15	Alex Rodriguez	30.00
16	Gary Sheffield	8.00
17	John Smoltz	5.00
18	Frank Thomas	40.00
19	Jim Thome	8.00
20	Matt Williams	6.00

1997 Circa

Circa baseball returned for the second year in 1997, with a 400-card set, including 393 player cards and seven checklists. The cards feature an art-type look, similar to Z-Force in basketball, and arrived in eight-card packs. The set was paralleled in a Rave insert and was accompanied by five inserts: Boss, Fast Track, Icons, Limited Access and Rave Reviews.

		MT
Complete Set (400):		40.00
Common Player:		.10
Wax Box:		60.00
1	Kenny Lofton	.75
2	Ray Durham	.10
3	Mariano Rivera	.20
4	Jon Lieber	.10
5	Tim Salmon	.20
6	Mark Grudzielanek	.10
7	Neifi Perez	.10
8	Cal Ripken Jr.	2.50
9	John Olerud	.10
10	Edgar Renteria	.10
11	Jose Rosado	.10
12	Mickey Morandini	.10
13	Orlando Miller	.10
14	Ben McDonald	.10
15	Hideo Nomo	.75
16	Fred McGriff	.25
17	Sean Berry	.10
18	Roger Pavlik	.10
19	Aaron Sele	.10
20	Joey Hamilton	.10
21	Roger Clemens	1.00
22	Jose Herrera	.10
23	Ryne Sandberg	.75
24	Ken Griffey Jr.	3.00
25	Barry Bonds	.75
26	Dan Naulty	.10
27	Wade Boggs	.20
28	Ray Lankford	.10
29	Rico Brogna	.10
30	Wally Joyner	.10
31	F.P. Santangelo	.10
32	Vinny Castilla	.10
33	Eddie Murray	.40
34	Kevin Elster	.10
35	Mike Macfarlane	.10
36	Jeff Kent	.10
37	Orlando Merced	.10
38	Jason Isringhausen	.10
39	Chad Ogea	.10
40	Greg Gagne	.10
41	Curt Lyons	.25
42	Mo Vaughn	.75
43	Rusty Greer	.10
44	Shane Reynolds	.10
45	Frank Thomas	3.00
46	Chris Hoiles	.10
47	Scott Sanders	.10
48	Mark Lemke	.10
49	Fernando Vina	.10
50	Mark McGwire	1.00
51	Bernie Williams	.50
52	Bobby Higginson	.10
53	Kevin Tapani	.10
54	Rich Becker	.10
55	*Felix Heredia*	.40
56	Delino DeShields	.10
57	Rick Wilkins	.10
58	Edgardo Alfonzo	.10
59	Brett Butler	.10
60	Ed Sprague	.10
61	Joe Randa	.10
62	Ugueth Urbina	.10
63	Todd Greene	.10
64	Devon White	.10
65	Bruce Ruffin	.10
66	Mark Gardner	.10
67	Omar Vizquel	.10
68	Luis Gonzalez	.10
69	Tom Glavine	.20
70	Cal Eldred	.10
71	William VanLandingham	.10
72	Jay Buhner	.20
73	James Baldwin	.10
74	Robin Jennings	.10
75	Terry Steinbach	.10
76	Billy Taylor	.10
77	Armando Benitez	.10
78	Joe Girardi	.10
79	Jay Bell	.10
80	Damon Buford	.10
81	Deion Sanders	.40
82	Bill Haselman	.10
83	John Flaherty	.10
84	Todd Stottlemyre	.10
85	J.T. Snow	.10
86	Felipe Lira	.10
87	Steve Avery	.10
88	Trey Beamon	.10
89	Alex Gonzalez	.10
90	Mark Clark	.10
91	Shane Andrews	.10
92	Randy Myers	.10
93	Gary Gaetti	.10
94	Jeff Blauser	.10
95	Tony Batista	.10
96	Todd Worrell	.10
97	Jim Edmonds	.10
98	Eric Young	.10
99	Roberto Kelly	.10
100	Alex Rodriguez	3.00
100p	Alex Rodriguez (overprinted "PROMOTIONAL SAMPLE")	5.00
101	Julio Franco	.10
102	Jeff Bagwell	1.25
103	Bobby Witt	.10
104	Tino Martinez	.25
105	Shannon Stewart	.10
106	Brian Banks	.10
107	Eddie Taubensee	.10
108	Terry Mulholland	.10
109	Lyle Mouton	.10
110	Jeff Conine	.10
111	Johnny Damon	.10
112	Quilvio Veras	.10
113	Wilton Guerrero	.20
114	Dmitri Young	.10
115	Garret Anderson	.10
116	Bill Pulsipher	.10
117	Jacob Brumfield	.10
118	Mike Lansing	.10
119	Jose Canseco	.30
120	Mike Bordick	.10
121	Kevin Stocker	.10
122	Frank Rodriguez	.10
123	Mike Cameron	.10
124	*Tony Womack*	.25
125	Bret Boone	.10
126	Moises Alou	.10
127	Tim Naehring	.10
128	Brant Brown	.20
129	Todd Zeile	.10
130	Dave Nilsson	.10
131	Donne Wall	.10
132	Jose Mesa	.10
133	Mark McLemore	.10
134	Mike Stanton	.10
135	Dan Wilson	.10
136	Jose Offerman	.10
137	David Justice	.30
138	Kirt Manwaring	.10
139	Raul Casanova	.10
140	Ron Coomer	.10
141	Dave Hollins	.10
142	Shawn Estes	.10
143	Darren Daulton	.10
144	Turk Wendell	.10
145	Darrin Fletcher	.10
146	Marquis Grissom	.10
147	Andy Benes	.10
148	Nomar Garciaparra	2.00
149	Andy Pettitte	.75
150	Tony Gwynn	1.50
151	Robb Nen	.10
152	Kevin Seitzer	.10
153	Ariel Prieto	.10
154	Scott Karl	.10
155	Carlos Baerga	.10
156	Wilson Alvarez	.10
157	Thomas Howard	.10
158	Kevin Appier	.10
159	Russ Davis	.10
160	Justin Thompson	.10
161	Pete Schourek	.10
162	John Burkett	.10
163	Roberto Alomar	.75
164	Darren Holmes	.10
165	Travis Miller	.10
166	Mark Langston	.10
167	Juan Guzman	.10
168	Pedro Astacio	.10
169	Mark Johnson	.10
170	Mark Leiter	.10
171	Heathcliff Slocumb	.10
172	Dante Bichette	.20
173	Brian Giles	.10
174	Paul Wilson	.10
175	Eric Davis	.10
176	Charles Johnson	.10
177	Willie Greene	.10
178	Geronimo Berroa	.10
179	Mariano Duncan	.10
180	Robert Person	.10
181	David Segui	.10
182	Ozzie Guillen	.10
183	Osvaldo Fernandez	.10
184	Dean Palmer	.10
185	Bob Wickman	.10
186	Eric Karros	.10
187	Travis Fryman	.10
188	Andy Ashby	.10
189	Scott Stahoviak	.10
190	Norm Charlton	.10
191	Craig Paquette	.10
192	John Smoltz	.25
193	Orel Hershiser	.10
194	Glenallen Hill	.10
195	George Arias	.10
196	Brian Jordan	.10
197	Greg Vaughn	.10
198	Rafael Palmeiro	.20
199	Darryl Kile	.10
200	Derek Jeter	2.00
201	Jose Vizcaino	.10
202	Rick Aguilera	.10
203	Jason Schmidt	.10
204	Trot Nixon	.10
205	Tom Pagnozzi	.10
206	Mark Wohlers	.10
207	Lance Johnson	.10
208	Carlos Delgado	.10
209	Cliff Floyd	.10
210	Kent Mercker	.10
211	Matt Mieske	.10
212	Ismael Valdes	.10
213	Shawon Dunston	.10
214	Melvin Nieves	.10
215	Tony Phillips	.10
216	Scott Spiezio	.10
217	Michael Tucker	.10
218	Matt Williams	.25
219	Ricky Otero	.10
220	Kevin Ritz	.10
221	Darryl Strawberry	.10
222	Troy Percival	.10
223	Eugene Kingsale	.10
224	Julian Tavarez	.10
225	Jermaine Dye	.10
226	Jason Kendall	.10
227	Sterling Hitchcock	.10
228	Jeff Cirillo	.10
229	Roberto Hernandez	.10
230	Ricky Bottalico	.10
231	Bobby Bonilla	.10
232	Edgar Martinez	.10
233	John Valentin	.10
234	Ellis Burks	.10
235	Benito Santiago	.10
236	Terrell Wade	.10
237	Armando Reynoso	.10
238	Danny Graves	.10
239	Ken Hill	.10
240	Dennis Eckersley	.10
241	Darin Erstad	1.25
242	Lee Smith	.10
243	Cecil Fielder	.20
244	Tony Clark	.50
245	Scott Erickson	.10
246	Bob Abreu	.10
247	Ruben Sierra	.10
248	Chili Davis	.10
249	Darryl Hamilton	.10
250	Albert Belle	1.00
251	Todd Hollandsworth	.10
252	Terry Adams	.10
253	Rey Ordonez	.10
254	Steve Finley	.10
255	Jose Valentin	.10
256	Royce Clayton	.10
257	Sandy Alomar	.10
258	Mike Lieberthal	.10
259	Ivan Rodriguez	.50
260	Rod Beck	.10
261	Ron Karkovice	.10
262	Mark Gubicza	.10
263	Chris Holt	.10
264	Jaime Bluma	.10
265	Francisco Cordova	.15
266	Javy Lopez	.20
267	Reggie Jefferson	.10
268	Kevin Brown	.10
269	Scott Brosius	.10
270	Dwight Gooden	.10
271	Marty Cordova	.10
272	Jeff Brantley	.10
273	Joe Carter	.10
274	Todd Jones	.10
275	Sammy Sosa	.40
276	Randy Johnson	.50
277	B.J. Surhoff	.10
278	Chan Ho Park	.10
279	Jamey Wright	.10
280	Manny Ramirez	.75
281	John Franco	.10
282	Tim Worrell	.10
283	Scott Rolen	1.25
284	Reggie Sanders	.10
285	Mike Fetters	.10
286	Tim Wakefield	.10
287	Trevor Hoffman	.10
288	Donovan Osborne	.10
289	Phil Nevin	.10
290	Jermaine Allensworth	.10
291	Rocky Coppinger	.10
292	Tim Raines	.10
293	Henry Rodriguez	.10
294	Paul Sorrento	.10
295	Tom Goodwin	.10
296	Raul Mondesi	.25
297	Allen Watson	.10
298	Derek Bell	.10
299	Gary Sheffield	.40
300	Paul Molitor	.40
301	Shawn Green	.10
302	Darren Oliver	.10
303	Jack McDowell	.10
304	Denny Neagle	.10
305	Doug Drabek	.10
306	Mel Rojas	.10
307	Andres Galarraga	.20
308	Alex Ochoa	.10
309	Gary DiSarcina	.10
310	Ron Gant	.10
311	Gregg Jefferies	.10
312	Ruben Rivera	.10
313	Vladimir Guerrero	1.50
314	Willie Adams	.10
315	Bip Roberts	.10
316	Mark Grace	.20
317	Bernard Gilkey	.10
318	Marc Newfield	.10
319	Al Leiter	.10
320	Otis Nixon	.10
321	Tom Candiotti	.10
322	Mike Stanley	.10
323	Jeff Fassero	.10
324	Billy Wagner	.10
325	Todd Walker	.75
326	Chad Curtis	.10
327	Quinton McCracken	.10
328	Will Clark	.25
329	Andruw Jones	2.00
330	Robin Ventura	.10
331	Curtis Pride	.10
332	Barry Larkin	.30
333	Jimmy Key	.10
334	David Wells	.10
335	Mike Holtz	.10
336	Paul Wagner	.10
337	Greg Maddux	2.00

#	Player	Price
338	Curt Schilling	.10
339	Steve Trachsel	.10
340	John Wetteland	.10
341	Rickey Henderson	.10
342	Ernie Young	.10
343	Harold Baines	.10
344	Bobby Jones	.10
345	Jeff D'Amico	.10
346	John Mabry	.10
347	Pedro Martinez	.10
348	Mark Lewis	.10
349	Dan Miceli	.10
350	Chuck Knoblauch	.10
351	John Smiley	.10
352	Brady Anderson	.10
353	Jim Leyritz	.10
354	Al Martin	.10
355	Pat Hentgen	.10
356	Mike Piazza	2.00
357	Charles Nagy	.10
358	Luis Castillo	.15
359	Paul O'Neill	.10
360	Steve Reed	.10
361	Tom Gordon	.10
362	Craig Biggio	.10
363	Jeff Montgomery	.10
364	Jamie Moyer	.10
365	Ryan Klesko	.40
366	Todd Hundley	.20
367	Bobby Estalella	.10
368	Jason Giambi	.10
369	Brian Hunter	.10
370	Ramon Martinez	.10
371	Carlos Garcia	.10
372	Hal Morris	.10
373	Juan Gonzalez	1.25
374	Brian McRae	.10
375	Mike Mussina	.60
376	John Ericks	.10
377	Larry Walker	.35
378	Chris Gomez	.10
379	John Jaha	.10
380	Rondell White	.20
381	Chipper Jones	2.00
382	David Cone	.20
383	Alan Benes	.20
384	Troy O'Leary	.10
385	Ken Caminiti	.30
386	Jeff King	.10
387	Mike Hampton	.10
388	Jaime Navarro	.10
389	Brad Radke	.10
390	Joey Cora	.10
391	Jim Thome	.40
392	Alex Fernandez	.20
393	Chuck Finley	.10
394	Andruw Jones CL	1.00
395	Ken Griffey Jr. CL	1.50
396	Frank Thomas CL	1.50
397	Alex Rodriguez CL	1.50
398	Cal Ripken Jr. CL	1.25
399	Mike Piazza CL	1.00
400	Greg Maddux CL	1.00

1997 Circa Rave

In its second year, the Rave parallel inserts for Circa baseball were limited to inclusion only in hobby packs, with a stated insertion rate of one card per "30 to 40" packs. Rave cards are distinguished from regular-edition Circa cards by the use of purple metallic foil for the brand name and player identification on the front of the card. Rave backs also carry a silver-foil serial number detailing its position from within a production run of just 150 for each card.

#	Player	MT
	Complete Set (400):	NA
	Common Player:	15.00
1	Kenny Lofton	75.00
2	Ray Durham	15.00
3	Mariano Rivera	25.00
4	Jon Lieber	15.00
5	Tim Salmon	30.00
6	Mark Grudzielanek	15.00
7	Neifi Perez	15.00
8	Cal Ripken Jr.	200.00
9	John Olerud	15.00
10	Edgar Renteria	15.00
11	Jose Rosado	15.00
12	Mickey Morandini	15.00
13	Orlando Miller	15.00
14	Ben McDonald	15.00
15	Hideo Nomo	75.00
16	Fred McGriff	25.00
17	Sean Berry	15.00
18	Roger Pavlik	15.00
19	Aaron Sele	15.00
20	Joey Hamilton	15.00
21	Roger Clemens	90.00
22	Jose Herrera	15.00
23	Ryne Sandberg	75.00
24	Ken Griffey Jr.	350.00
25	Barry Bonds	75.00
26	Dan Naulty	15.00
27	Wade Boggs	30.00
28	Ray Lankford	15.00
29	Rico Brogna	15.00
30	Wally Joyner	15.00
31	F.P. Santangelo	15.00
32	Vinny Castilla	15.00
33	Eddie Murray	50.00
34	Kevin Elster	15.00
35	Mike Macfarlane	15.00
36	Jeff Kent	15.00
37	Orlando Merced	15.00
38	Jason Isringhausen	15.00
39	Chad Ogea	15.00
40	Greg Gagne	15.00
41	Curt Lyons	15.00
42	Mo Vaughn	75.00
43	Rusty Greer	15.00
44	Shane Reynolds	15.00
45	Frank Thomas	275.00
46	Chris Hoiles	15.00
47	Scott Sanders	15.00
48	Mark Lemke	15.00
49	Fernando Vina	15.00
50	Mark McGwire	120.00
51	Bernie Williams	60.00
52	Bobby Higginson	15.00
53	Kevin Tapani	15.00
54	Rich Becker	15.00
55	Felix Heredia	20.00
56	Delino DeShields	15.00
57	Rick Wilkins	15.00
58	Edgardo Alfonzo	15.00
59	Brett Butler	15.00
60	Ed Sprague	15.00
61	Joe Randa	15.00
62	Ugueth Urbina	15.00
63	Todd Greene	15.00
64	Devon White	15.00
65	Bruce Ruffin	15.00
66	Mark Gardner	15.00
67	Omar Vizquel	15.00
68	Luis Gonzalez	15.00
69	Tom Glavine	25.00
70	Cal Eldred	15.00
71	William VanLandingham	15.00
72	Jay Buhner	25.00
73	James Baldwin	15.00
74	Robin Jennings	15.00
75	Terry Steinbach	15.00
76	Billy Taylor	15.00
77	Armando Benitez	15.00
78	Joe Girardi	15.00
79	Jay Bell	15.00
80	Damon Buford	15.00
81	Deion Sanders	40.00
82	Bill Haselman	15.00
83	John Flaherty	15.00
84	Todd Stottlemyre	15.00
85	J.T. Snow	15.00
86	Felipe Lira	15.00
87	Steve Avery	15.00
88	Trey Beamon	15.00
89	Alex Gonzalez	15.00
90	Mark Clark	15.00
91	Shane Andrews	15.00
92	Randy Myers	15.00
93	Gary Gaetti	15.00
94	Jeff Blauser	15.00
95	Tony Batista	15.00
96	Todd Worrell	15.00
97	Jim Edmonds	15.00
98	Eric Young	15.00
99	Roberto Kelly	15.00
100	Alex Rodriguez	200.00
101	Julio Franco	15.00
102	Jeff Bagwell	125.00
103	Bobby Witt	15.00
104	Tino Martinez	30.00
105	Shannon Stewart	15.00
106	Brian Banks	15.00
107	Eddie Taubensee	15.00
108	Terry Mulholland	15.00
109	Lyle Mouton	15.00
110	Jeff Conine	15.00
111	Johnny Damon	15.00
112	Quilvio Veras	15.00
113	Wilton Guerrero	25.00
114	Dmitri Young	15.00
115	Garret Anderson	15.00
116	Bill Pulsipher	15.00
117	Jacob Brumfield	15.00
118	Mike Lansing	15.00
119	Jose Canseco	30.00
120	Mike Bordick	15.00
121	Kevin Stocker	15.00
122	Frank Rodriguez	15.00
123	Mike Cameron	15.00
124	Tony Womack	20.00
125	Bret Boone	15.00
126	Moises Alou	15.00
127	Tim Naehring	15.00
128	Brant Brown	20.00
129	Todd Zeile	15.00
130	Dave Nilsson	15.00
131	Donne Wall	15.00
132	Jose Mesa	15.00
133	Mark McLemore	15.00
134	Mike Stanton	15.00
135	Dan Wilson	15.00
136	Jose Offerman	15.00
137	David Justice	30.00
138	Kirt Manwaring	15.00
139	Raul Casanova	15.00
140	Ron Coomer	15.00
141	Dave Hollins	15.00
142	Shawn Estes	15.00
143	Darren Daulton	15.00
144	Turk Wendell	15.00
145	Darrin Fletcher	15.00
146	Marquis Grissom	25.00
147	Andy Benes	15.00
148	Nomar Garciaparra	125.00
149	Andy Pettitte	75.00
150	Tony Gwynn	125.00
151	Robb Nen	15.00
152	Kevin Seitzer	15.00
153	Ariel Prieto	15.00
154	Scott Karl	15.00
155	Carlos Baerga	15.00
156	Wilson Alvarez	15.00
157	Thomas Howard	15.00
158	Kevin Appier	15.00
159	Russ Davis	15.00
160	Justin Thompson	15.00
161	Pete Schourek	15.00
162	John Burkett	15.00
163	Roberto Alomar	60.00
164	Darren Holmes	15.00
165	Travis Miller	15.00
166	Mark Langston	15.00
167	Juan Guzman	15.00
168	Pedro Astacio	15.00
169	Mark Johnson	15.00
170	Mark Leiter	15.00
171	Heathcliff Slocumb	15.00
172	Dante Bichette	30.00
173	Brian Giles	15.00
174	Paul Wilson	15.00
175	Eric Davis	15.00
176	Charles Johnson	15.00
177	Willie Greene	15.00
178	Geronimo Berroa	15.00
179	Mariano Duncan	15.00
180	Robert Person	15.00
181	David Segui	15.00
182	Ozzie Guillen	15.00
183	Osvaldo Fernandez	15.00
184	Dean Palmer	20.00
185	Bob Wickman	15.00
186	Eric Karros	15.00
187	Travis Fryman	20.00
188	Andy Ashby	15.00
189	Scott Stahoviak	15.00
190	Norm Charlton	15.00
191	Craig Paquette	15.00
192	John Smoltz	30.00
193	Orel Hershiser	15.00
194	Glenallen Hill	15.00
195	George Arias	15.00
196	Brian Jordan	20.00
197	Greg Vaughn	15.00
198	Rafael Palmeiro	25.00
199	Darryl Kile	15.00
200	Derek Jeter	160.00
201	Jose Vizcaino	15.00
202	Rick Aguilera	15.00
203	Jason Schmidt	15.00
204	Trot Nixon	15.00
205	Tom Pagnozzi	15.00
206	Mark Wohlers	15.00
207	Lance Johnson	15.00
208	Carlos Delgado	15.00
209	Cliff Floyd	15.00
210	Kent Mercker	15.00
211	Matt Mieske	15.00
212	Ismael Valdes	15.00
213	Shawon Dunston	15.00
214	Melvin Nieves	15.00
215	Tony Phillips	15.00
216	Scott Spiezio	15.00
217	Michael Tucker	15.00
218	Matt Williams	40.00
219	Ricky Otero	15.00
220	Kevin Hill	15.00
221	Darryl Strawberry	15.00
222	Troy Percival	15.00
223	Eugene Kingsale	15.00
224	Julian Tavarez	15.00
225	Jermaine Dye	15.00
226	Jason Kendall	15.00
227	Sterling Hitchcock	15.00
228	Jeff Cirillo	15.00
229	Roberto Hernandez	15.00
230	Ricky Bottalico	15.00
231	Bobby Bonilla	20.00
232	Edgar Martinez	20.00
233	John Valentin	15.00
234	Ellis Burks	20.00
235	Benito Santiago	15.00
236	Terrell Wade	15.00
237	Armando Reynoso	15.00
238	Danny Graves	15.00
239	Ken Hill	15.00
240	Dennis Eckersley	20.00
241	Darin Erstad	100.00
242	Lee Smith	15.00
243	Cecil Fielder	25.00
244	Tony Clark	60.00
245	Scott Erickson	15.00
246	Bob Abreu	15.00
247	Ruben Sierra	15.00
248	Chili Davis	15.00
249	Darryl Hamilton	15.00
250	Albert Belle	80.00
251	Todd Hollandsworth	15.00
252	Terry Adams	15.00
253	Rey Ordonez	20.00
254	Steve Finley	15.00
255	Jose Valentin	15.00
256	Royce Clayton	15.00
257	Sandy Alomar	15.00
258	Mike Lieberthal	15.00
259	Ivan Rodriguez	60.00
260	Rod Beck	15.00
261	Ron Karkovice	15.00
262	Mark Gubicza	15.00
263	Chris Holt	15.00
264	Jaime Bluma	15.00
265	Francisco Cordova	20.00
266	Javy Lopez	25.00
267	Reggie Jefferson	15.00
268	Kevin Brown	15.00
269	Scott Brosius	15.00
270	Dwight Gooden	20.00
271	Marty Cordova	15.00
272	Jeff Brantley	15.00
273	Joe Carter	20.00
274	Todd Jones	15.00
275	Sammy Sosa	40.00
276	Randy Johnson	60.00
277	B.J. Surhoff	15.00
278	Chan Ho Park	15.00
279	Jamey Wright	15.00
280	Manny Ramirez	75.00
281	John Franco	15.00
282	Tim Worrell	15.00
283	Scott Rolen	100.00
284	Reggie Sanders	15.00
285	Mike Fetters	15.00
286	Tim Wakefield	15.00
287	Trevor Hoffman	15.00
288	Donovan Osborne	15.00
289	Phil Nevin	15.00
290	Jermaine Allensworth	15.00
291	Rocky Coppinger	15.00
292	Tim Raines	15.00
293	Henry Rodriguez	15.00
294	Paul Sorrento	15.00
295	Tom Goodwin	15.00
296	Raul Mondesi	30.00
297	Allen Watson	15.00
298	Derek Bell	15.00
299	Gary Sheffield	40.00
300	Paul Molitor	50.00

#	Player	MT
301	Shawn Green	15.00
302	Darren Oliver	15.00
303	Jack McDowell	20.00
304	Denny Neagle	15.00
305	Doug Drabek	15.00
306	Mel Rojas	15.00
307	Andres Galarraga	25.00
308	Alex Ochoa	15.00
309	Gary DiSarcina	15.00
310	Ron Gant	20.00
311	Gregg Jefferies	15.00
312	Ruben Rivera	20.00
313	Vladimir Guerrero	125.00
314	Willie Adams	15.00
315	Bip Roberts	15.00
316	Mark Grace	25.00
317	Bernard Gilkey	15.00
318	Marc Newfield	15.00
319	Al Leiter	15.00
320	Otis Nixon	15.00
321	Tom Candiotti	15.00
322	Mike Stanley	15.00
323	Jeff Fassero	15.00
324	Billy Wagner	15.00
325	Todd Walker	40.00
326	Chad Curtis	15.00
327	Quinton McCracken	15.00
328	Will Clark	30.00
329	Andruw Jones	150.00
330	Robin Ventura	15.00
331	Curtis Pride	15.00
332	Barry Larkin	30.00
333	Jimmy Key	15.00
334	David Wells	15.00
335	Mike Holtz	15.00
336	Paul Wagner	15.00
337	Greg Maddux	150.00
338	Curt Schilling	15.00
339	Steve Trachsel	15.00
340	John Wetteland	15.00
341	Rickey Henderson	20.00
342	Ernie Young	15.00
343	Harold Baines	15.00
344	Bobby Jones	15.00
345	Jeff D'Amico	15.00
346	John Mabry	15.00
347	Pedro Martinez	25.00
348	Mark Lewis	15.00
349	Dan Miceli	15.00
350	Chuck Knoblauch	30.00
351	John Smiley	15.00
352	Brady Anderson	25.00
353	Jim Leyritz	15.00
354	Al Martin	15.00
355	Pat Hentgen	15.00
356	Mike Piazza	150.00
357	Charles Nagy	15.00
358	Luis Castillo	15.00
359	Paul O'Neill	20.00
360	Steve Reed	15.00
361	Tom Gordon	15.00
362	Craig Biggio	25.00
363	Jeff Montgomery	15.00
364	Jamie Moyer	15.00
365	Ryan Klesko	40.00
366	Todd Hundley	30.00
367	Bobby Estalella	15.00
368	Jason Giambi	15.00
369	Brian Hunter	15.00
370	Ramon Martinez	20.00
371	Carlos Garcia	15.00
372	Hal Morris	15.00
373	Juan Gonzalez	125.00
374	Brian McRae	15.00
375	Mike Mussina	60.00
376	John Ericks	15.00
377	Larry Walker	60.00
378	Chris Gomez	15.00
379	John Jaha	15.00
380	Rondell White	25.00
381	Chipper Jones	150.00
382	David Cone	25.00
383	Alan Benes	20.00
384	Troy O'Leary	15.00
385	Ken Caminiti	30.00
386	Jeff King	15.00
387	Mike Hampton	15.00
388	Jaime Navarro	15.00
389	Brad Radke	15.00
390	Joey Cora	15.00
391	Jim Thome	50.00
392	Alex Fernandez	20.00
393	Chuck Finley	15.00
394	Andruw Jones CL	60.00
395	Ken Griffey Jr. CL	150.00
396	Frank Thomas CL	125.00
397	Alex Rodriguez CL	125.00
398	Cal Ripken Jr. CL	80.00
399	Mike Piazza CL	60.00
400	Greg Maddux CL	60.00

1997 Circa Autograph Redemptions

These box topper cards were found only in hobby boxes and offered the chance to acquire autographed bats, gloves and cards from one of six major leaguers: Alex Rodriguez, Scott Rolen, Darin Erstad, Todd Walker, Todd Hollandsworth and Alex Ochoa.

		MT
Complete Set (6):		400.00
Common Autograph:		30.00
AU1	Darin Erstad	75.00
AU2	Todd Hollandsworth	30.00
AU3	Alex Ochoa	30.00
AU4	Alex Rodriguez	250.00
AU5	Scott Rolen	90.00
AU6	Todd Walker	40.00

1997 Circa Boss

Boss was the easiest insert to get in Circa. These 20 embossed cards were seeded one per six packs. The insert displayed some of baseball's best players. A Super Boss parallel insert set features metallic-foil background and graphics on front, and is inserted at a rate of one per 36 packs.

		MT
Complete Set (20):		50.00
Common Player:		1.00
Super Boss:		2x-3x
1	Jeff Bagwell	3.00
2	Albert Belle	2.50
3	Barry Bonds	2.00
4	Ken Caminiti	1.00
5	Juan Gonzalez	3.00
6	Ken Griffey Jr.	8.00
7	Tony Gwynn	3.00
8	Derek Jeter	5.00
9	Andruw Jones	5.00
10	Chipper Jones	5.00
11	Greg Maddux	5.00
12	Mark McGwire	2.50
13	Mike Piazza	5.00
14	Manny Ramirez	2.00
15	Cal Ripken Jr.	6.00
16	Alex Rodriguez	8.00
17	John Smoltz	1.00
18	Frank Thomas	8.00
19	Mo Vaughn	2.00
20	Bernie Williams	1.50

1997 Circa Fast Track

Fast Track highlighted 10 top rookies and young stars on a flocked design that showed grass raised fabric. Cards featured the insert name in the top left corner and were inserted every 24 packs.

		MT
Complete Set (10):		60.00
Common Player:		2.50
1	Vladimir Guerrero	10.00
2	Todd Hollandsworth	2.50
3	Derek Jeter	12.00
4	Andruw Jones	12.00
5	Chipper Jones	12.00
6	Andy Pettitte	5.00
7	Mariano Rivera	3.00
8	Alex Rodriguez	20.00
9	Scott Rolen	10.00
10	Todd Walker	4.00

1997 Circa Icons

Twelve of baseball's top sluggers were displayed on 100-percent holofoil cards in Icons. Icons were found at a rate of one per 36 packs.

		MT
Complete Set (12):		125.00
Common Player:		3.00
1	Juan Gonzalez	12.00
2	Ken Griffey Jr.	25.00
3	Tony Gwynn	12.00
4	Derek Jeter	15.00
5	Chipper Jones	15.00
6	Greg Maddux	15.00
7	Mark McGwire	10.00
8	Mike Piazza	15.00
9	Cal Ripken Jr.	20.00
10	Alex Rodriguez	25.00
11	Frank Thomas	25.00
12	Matt Williams	4.00

1997 Circa Limited Access

Limited Access was a retail-only insert found every 18 packs. Cards featured an in-depth, statistical analysis including the player's favorite pitcher to hit and each pitcher's least favorite hitter to face. Limited Access contained a die-cut, bi-fold design resembling a book, and featured 15 different players.

		MT
Complete Set (15):		125.00
Common Player:		2.00
1	Jeff Bagwell	8.00
2	Albert Belle	6.00
3	Barry Bonds	5.00
4	Juan Gonzalez	8.00
5	Ken Griffey Jr.	20.00
6	Tony Gwynn	8.00
7	Derek Jeter	12.00
8	Chipper Jones	12.00
9	Greg Maddux	12.00
10	Mark McGwire	6.00
11	Mike Piazza	12.00
12	Cal Ripken Jr.	15.00
13	Alex Rodriguez	20.00
14	Frank Thomas	20.00
15	Mo Vaughn	5.00

1997 Circa Rave Reviews

Hitters that continually put up great numbers were selected in Rave Reviews. The insert was found every 288 packs, contained 12 stars and was printed on 100-percent holofoil.

		MT
Complete Set (12):		600.00
Common Player:		20.00
1	Albert Belle	35.00
2	Barry Bonds	25.00
3	Juan Gonzalez	50.00
4	Ken Griffey Jr.	100.00
5	Tony Gwynn	50.00
6	Greg Maddux	60.00
7	Mark McGwire	35.00
8	Eddie Murray	20.00
9	Mike Piazza	60.00
10	Cal Ripken Jr.	80.00
11	Alex Rodriguez	80.00
12	Frank Thomas	100.00

1997 Metal Universe

Metal Universe Baseball arrived in a 250-card set, including three checklists. Each card is printed on 100-percent etched foil with "comic book" art full-bleed backgrounds, with the player's name, team, position and the Metal Universe logo near the bottom of the card. Backs contain another player photo and key statistics. Metal Universe sold in eight-card packs and contained six different insert sets. They included: Blast Furnace, Magnetic Field, Mining for Gold, Mother Lode, Platinum Portraits and Titanium.

		MT
Complete Set (250):		35.00
Common Player:		.10
Wax Box:		50.00
1	Roberto Alomar	.60
2	Brady Anderson	.15
3	Rocky Coppinger	.10
4	Chris Hoiles	.10
5	Eddie Murray	.40
6	Mike Mussina	.50
7	Rafael Palmeiro	.20
8	Cal Ripken Jr.	2.50
9	B.J. Surhoff	.10
10	Brant Brown	.10
11	Mark Grace	.20
12	Brian McRae	.10
13	Jaime Navarro	.10
14	Ryne Sandberg	.75
15	Sammy Sosa	.40
16	Amaury Telemaco	.10
17	Steve Trachsel	.10
18	Darren Bragg	.10
19	Jose Canseco	.25
20	Roger Clemens	1.00
21	Nomar Garciaparra	2.00
22	Tom Gordon	.10
23	Tim Naehring	.10
24	Mike Stanley	.10
25	John Valentin	.10
26	Mo Vaughn	.75
27	Jermaine Dye	.20
28	Tom Glavine	.20
29	Marquis Grissom	.10
30	Andruw Jones	2.00
31	Chipper Jones	2.00
32	Ryan Klesko	.50
33	Greg Maddux	2.00
34	Fred McGriff	.30
35	John Smoltz	.25
36	Garret Anderson	.10
37	George Arias	.10
38	Gary DiSarcina	.10
39	Jim Edmonds	.10
40	Darin Erstad	1.50
41	Chuck Finley	.10
42	Troy Percival	.10
43	Tim Salmon	.25
44	Bret Boone	.10
45	Jeff Brantley	.10
46	Eric Davis	.10
47	Barry Larkin	.25
48	Hal Morris	.10
49	Mark Portugal	.10
50	Reggie Sanders	.10
51	John Smiley	.10
52	Wilson Alvarez	.10
53	Harold Baines	.10
54	James Baldwin	.10
55	Albert Belle	1.00
56	Mike Cameron	.10
57	Ray Durham	.10
58	Alex Fernandez	.10
59	Roberto Hernandez	.10
60	Tony Phillips	.10
61	Frank Thomas	3.00
62	Robin Ventura	.10
63	Jeff Cirillo	.10
64	Jeff D'Amico	.10
65	John Jaha	.10
66	Scott Karl	.10
67	Ben McDonald	.10
68	Marc Newfield	.10
69	Dave Nilsson	.10
70	Jose Valentin	.10
71	Dante Bichette	.25
72	Ellis Burks	.10
73	Vinny Castilla	.10
74	Andres Galarraga	.20
75	Kevin Ritz	.10
76	Larry Walker	.40
77	Walt Weiss	.10
78	Jamey Wright	.10
79	Eric Young	.10
80	Julio Franco	.10
81	Orel Hershiser	.10
82	Kenny Lofton	.75
83	Jack McDowell	.20
84	Jose Mesa	.10
85	Charles Nagy	.10
86	Manny Ramirez	.75
87	Jim Thome	.40
88	Omar Vizquel	.10
89	Matt Williams	.25
90	Kevin Appier	.10
91	Johnny Damon	.10
92	Chili Davis	.10

93	Tom Goodwin	.10
94	Keith Lockhart	.10
95	Jeff Montgomery	.10
96	Craig Paquette	.10
97	Jose Rosado	.10
98	Michael Tucker	.10
99	Wilton Guerrero	.20
100	Todd Hollandsworth	.10
101	Eric Karros	.10
102	Ramon Martinez	.10
103	Raul Mondesi	.25
104	Hideo Nomo	.75
105	Mike Piazza	2.00
106	Ismael Valdes	.10
107	Todd Worrell	.10
108	Tony Clark	.60
109	Travis Fryman	.10
110	Bob Higginson	.10
111	Mark Lewis	.10
112	Melvin Nieves	.10
113	Justin Thompson	.10
114	Wade Boggs	.20
115	David Cone	.15
116	Cecil Fielder	.20
117	Dwight Gooden	.10
118	Derek Jeter	1.75
119	Tino Martinez	.40
120	Paul O'Neill	.10
121	Andy Pettitte	.75
122	Mariano Rivera	.20
123	Darryl Strawberry	.10
124	John Wetteland	.10
125	Bernie Williams	.40
126	Tony Batista	.10
127	Geronimo Berroa	.10
128	Scott Brosius	.10
129	Jason Giambi	.10
130	Jose Herrera	.10
131	Mark McGwire	1.00
132	John Wasdin	.10
133	Bob Abreu	.10
134	Jeff Bagwell	1.25
135	Derek Bell	.10
136	Craig Biggio	.10
137	Brian Hunter	.10
138	Darryl Kile	.10
139	Orlando Miller	.10
140	Shane Reynolds	.10
141	Billy Wagner	.10
142	Donne Wall	.10
143	Jay Buhner	.20
144	Jeff Fassero	.10
145	Ken Griffey Jr.	3.00
146	Sterling Hitchcock	.10
147	Randy Johnson	.40
148	Edgar Martinez	.10
149	Alex Rodriguez	3.00
149p	Alex Rodriguez (overprinted "PROMOTIONAL SAMPLE")	5.00
150	Paul Sorrento	.10
151	Dan Wilson	.10
152	Moises Alou	.10
153	Darrin Fletcher	.10
154	Cliff Floyd	.10
155	Mark Grudzielanek	.10
156	Vladimir Guerrero	1.50
157	Mike Lansing	.10
158	Pedro Martinez	.10
159	Henry Rodriguez	.10
160	Rondell White	.10
161	Will Clark	.25
162	Juan Gonzalez	1.25
163	Rusty Greer	.10
164	Ken Hill	.10
165	Mark McLemore	.10
166	Dean Palmer	.10
167	Roger Pavlik	.10
168	Ivan Rodriguez	.50
169	Mickey Tettleton	.10
170	Bobby Bonilla	.10
171	Kevin Brown	.10
172	Greg Colbrunn	.10
173	Jeff Conine	.10
174	Jim Eisenreich	.10
175	Charles Johnson	.10
176	Al Leiter	.10
177	Robb Nen	.10
178	Edgar Renteria	.20
179	Gary Sheffield	.40
180	Devon White	.10
181	Joe Carter	.20
182	Carlos Delgado	.10
183	Alex Gonzalez	.10
184	Shawn Green	.10
185	Juan Guzman	.10
186	Pat Hentgen	.10
187	Orlando Merced	.10
188	John Olerud	.10
189	Robert Perez	.10

190	Ed Sprague	.10
191	Mark Clark	.10
192	John Franco	.10
193	Bernard Gilkey	.10
194	Todd Hundley	.10
195	Lance Johnson	.10
196	Bobby Jones	.10
197	Alex Ochoa	.10
198	Rey Ordonez	.20
199	Paul Wilson	.10
200	Ricky Bottalico	.10
201	Gregg Jefferies	.10
202	Wendell Magee Jr.	.10
203	Mickey Morandini	.10
204	Ricky Otero	.10
205	Scott Rolen	1.25
206	Benito Santiago	.10
207	Curt Schilling	.10
208	Rich Becker	.10
209	Marty Cordova	.10
210	Chuck Knoblauch	.10
211	Pat Meares	.10
212	Paul Molitor	.40
213	Frank Rodriguez	.10
214	Terry Steinbach	.10
215	Todd Walker	.60
216	Andy Ashby	.10
217	Ken Caminiti	.25
218	Steve Finley	.10
219	Tony Gwynn	1.00
220	Joey Hamilton	.10
221	Rickey Henderson	.10
222	Trevor Hoffman	.10
223	Wally Joyner	.10
224	Scott Sanders	.10
225	Fernando Valenzuela	.10
226	Greg Vaughn	.10
227	Alan Benes	.10
228	Andy Benes	.10
229	Dennis Eckersley	.10
230	Ron Gant	.10
231	Brian Jordan	.10
232	Ray Lankford	.10
233	John Mabry	.10
234	Tom Pagnozzi	.10
235	Todd Stottlemyre	.10
236	Jermaine Allensworth	.10
237	Francisco Cordova	.15
238	Jason Kendall	.10
239	Jeff King	.10
240	Al Martin	.10
241	Rod Beck	.10
242	Barry Bonds	.75
243	Shawn Estes	.10
244	Mark Gardner	.10
245	Glenallen Hill	.10
246	Bill Mueller	.10
247	J.T. Snow	.10
248	Checklist	.10
249	Checklist	.10
250	Checklist	.10

1997 Metal Universe Blast Furnace

Blast Furnace inserts were found only in hobby packs, at a rate of one per 48 packs. The 12-card set was printed on a red-tinted plastic, with the words "Blast Furnace" near the bottom in gold foil with a fire-like border.

		MT
Complete Set (12):		150.00
Common Player:		3.00
1	Jeff Bagwell	12.00
2	Albert Belle	10.00
3	Barry Bonds	7.00

4	Andres Galarraga	4.00
5	Juan Gonzalez	15.00
6	Ken Griffey Jr.	30.00
7	Todd Hundley	3.00
8	Mark McGwire	12.00
9	Mike Piazza	20.00
10	Alex Rodriguez	25.00
11	Frank Thomas	30.00
12	Mo Vaughn	8.00

1997 Metal Universe Emerald Autographs

Six different young stars were featured in this insert, which was found every 480 hobby packs of Metal Universe. The cards are similar to regular-issue cards, but have a green foil finish and autograph on the front. Cards are numbered AU1-AU6 and were available via redemption cards.

	MT
Complete Set (6):	400.00
Common Autograph:	25.00
AU1 Darin Erstad	75.00
AU2 Todd Hollandsworth	30.00
AU3 Alex Ochoa	25.00
AU4 Alex Rodriguez	200.00
AU5 Scott Rolen	70.00
AU6 Todd Walker	40.00

1997 Metal Universe Magnetic Field

Magnetic Field inserts are printed in a horizontal format with prismatic foil backgrounds. This 10-card insert was found every 12 packs of Metal Universe.

		MT
Complete Set (10)		10.00
Common Player:		1.00
1	Roberto Alomar	2.00
2	Jeff Bagwell	4.00
3	Barry Bonds	2.50
4	Ken Griffey Jr.	10.00
5	Derek Jeter	5.00
6	Kenny Lofton	2.50
7	Edgar Renteria	1.00
8	Cal Ripken Jr.	8.00
9	Alex Rodriguez	10.00
10	Matt Williams	1.50

1997 Metal Universe Mining for Gold

Mining for Gold was a 10-card insert that featured some of baseball's brightest stars on a die-cut "ingot" design with pearlized gold coating. This insert was found every nine packs.

		MT
Complete Set (10):		20.00
Common Player:		.75
1	Bob Abreu	1.00
2	Kevin Brown	.75
3	Nomar Garciaparra	5.00

		MT
4	Vladimir Guerrero	4.00
5	Wilton Guerrero	1.25
6	Andruw Jones	7.00
7	Curt Lyons	.75
8	Neifi Perez	.75
9	Scott Rolen	3.00
10	Todd Walker	2.00

1997 Metal Universe Mother Lode

Mother lode was the most difficult insert out of Metal Universe with a one per 288 pack insertion ratio. Each card in this 10-card inert was printed on etched foil with a plant-type monument in back of the player.

		MT
Complete Set (12):		750.00
Common Player:		20.00
1	Roberto Alomar	25.00
2	Jeff Bagwell	50.00
3	Barry Bonds	30.00
4	Ken Griffey Jr.	120.00
5	Andruw Jones	75.00
6	Chipper Jones	75.00
7	Kenny Lofton	35.00
8	Mike Piazza	75.00
9	Cal Ripken Jr.	90.00
10	Alex Rodriguez	90.00
11	Frank Thomas	120.00
12	Matt Williams	20.00

1997 Metal Universe Platinum Portraits

Each card in the Platinum Portraits insert is printed on a background of platinum-colored etched foil. The 10-card set includes some of the top prospects and rising stars in baseball, and is included every 36 packs.

		MT
Complete Set (10):		60.00
Common Player:		2.50
1	James Baldwin	2.50
2	Jermaine Dye	2.00
3	Todd Hollandsworth	2.50
4	Derek Jeter	15.00
5	Chipper Jones	15.00
6	Jason Kendall	2.50
7	Rey Ordonez	3.00
8	Andy Pettitte	6.00
9	Edgar Renteria	4.00
10	Alex Rodriguez	25.00

1997 Metal Universe Titanium

These retail exclusive inserts include 10 cards and were found every 24 packs. Each card is die-cut on the top-left and bottom-right corner with a silver foil background. Titanium includes some of the most popular players in baseball on cards that are also embossed.

		MT
Complete Set (10):		90.00
Common Player:		2.00
1	Jeff Bagwell	7.00
2	Albert Belle	5.00
3	Ken Griffey Jr.	18.00
4	Chipper Jones	10.00
5	Greg Maddux	10.00
6	Mark McGwire	6.00
7	Mike Piazza	10.00
8	Cal Ripken Jr.	14.00
9	Alex Rodriguez	15.00
10	Frank Thomas	18.00

1997 SkyBox E-X2000

The premier issue of E-X2000 consists of 100 base cards designed with "SkyView" technology, utilizing a die-cut holofoil border and the player silhouetted in front of a transparent "window" featuring a variety of sky patterns. Inserts include two sequentially-numbered parallel sets - Credentials (1:50 packs) and Essential Credentials (1:200 packs) - as well as Emerald Autograph Exchange Cards, A Cut Above, Hall of Nothing, and Star Date. Cards were sold in two-card packs for $3.99 each.

		MT
Complete Set (100):		100.00
Common Player:		1.00
Wax Box:		90.00
1	Jim Edmonds	1.00
2	Darin Erstad	4.00
3	Eddie Murray	2.00
4	Roberto Alomar	2.00
5	Brady Anderson	1.00
6	Mike Mussina	2.00
7	Rafael Palmeiro	1.50
8	Cal Ripken Jr.	8.00
9	Steve Avery	1.00
10	Nomar Garciaparra	6.00
11	Mo Vaughn	2.50
12	Albert Belle	3.00
13	Mike Cameron	1.00
14	Ray Durham	1.00
15	Frank Thomas	10.00
16	Robin Ventura	1.00
17	Manny Ramirez	2.50
18	Jim Thome	2.00
19	Matt Williams	1.50
20	Tony Clark	2.00
21	Travis Fryman	1.00
22	Bob Higginson	1.00
23	Kevin Appier	1.00
24	Johnny Damon	1.00
25	Jermaine Dye	1.00
26	Jeff Cirillo	1.00
27	Ben McDonald	1.00
28	Chuck Knoblauch	1.50
29	Paul Molitor	2.50
30	Todd Walker	2.00
31	Wade Boggs	1.50
32	Cecil Fielder	1.25
33	Derek Jeter	6.00
34	Andy Pettitte	2.50
35	Ruben Rivera	1.00
36	Bernie Williams	2.00
37	Jose Canseco	1.50
38	Mark McGwire	4.00
39	Jay Buhner	1.50
40	Ken Griffey Jr.	10.00
41	Randy Johnson	2.00
42	Edgar Martinez	1.00
43	Alex Rodriguez	8.00
44	Dan Wilson	1.00
45	Will Clark	1.50
46	Juan Gonzalez	5.00
47	Ivan Rodriguez	2.50
48	Joe Carter	1.00
49	Roger Clemens	3.00
50	Juan Guzman	1.00
51	Pat Hentgen	1.00
52	Tom Glavine	1.50
53	Andruw Jones	6.00
54	Chipper Jones	6.00
55	Ryan Klesko	1.50
56	Kenny Lofton	2.50
57	Greg Maddux	6.00
58	Fred McGriff	1.50
59	John Smoltz	1.25
60	Mark Wohlers	1.00
61	Mark Grace	1.50
62	Ryne Sandberg	2.50
63	Sammy Sosa	1.50
64	Barry Larkin	1.50
65	Deion Sanders	1.50
66	Reggie Sanders	1.00
67	Dante Bichette	1.50
68	Ellis Burks	1.00
69	Andres Galarraga	1.50
70	Moises Alou	1.00
71	Kevin Brown	1.00
72	Cliff Floyd	1.00
73	Edgar Renteria	1.00
74	Gary Sheffield	1.50
75	Bob Abreu	1.00
76	Jeff Bagwell	4.00
77	Craig Biggio	1.50
78	Todd Hollandsworth	1.00
79	Eric Karros	1.00
80	Raul Mondesi	1.50
81	Hideo Nomo	2.50
82	Mike Piazza	6.00
83	Vladimir Guerrero	5.00
84	Henry Rodriguez	1.00
85	Todd Hundley	1.50
86	Rey Ordonez	1.00
87	Alex Ochoa	1.00
88	Gregg Jefferies	1.00
89	Scott Rolen	5.00
90	Jermaine Allensworth	1.00
91	Jason Kendall	1.00
92	Ken Caminiti	1.50
93	Tony Gwynn	5.00
94	Rickey Henderson	1.00
95	Barry Bonds	2.50
96	J.T. Snow	1.00
97	Dennis Eckersley	1.00
98	Ron Gant	1.00
99	Brian Jordan	1.00
100	Ray Lankford	1.00

1997 SkyBox E-X2000 Credentials

This parallel set features different colored foils from the base cards, as well as different images on the "window." Cards were inserted 1:50 packs.

	MT
Common Player:	12.00
Credentials Stars:	12x to 20x
Yng Stars & RC's:	8x to 12x

1997 SkyBox E-X2000 Essential Credentials

A sequentially-numbered parallel set, found one per 200 packs, and limited to 99 total sets.

		MT
Common Player:		25.00
Essential Credentials:		25x to 50x
1	Jim Edmonds	25.00
2	Darin Erstad	175.00
3	Eddie Murray	100.00
4	Roberto Alomar	100.00
5	Brady Anderson	35.00
6	Mike Mussina	100.00
7	Rafael Palmeiro	50.00
8	Cal Ripken Jr.	350.00
9	Steve Avery	25.00
10	Nomar Garciaparra	250.00
11	Mo Vaughn	125.00
12	Albert Belle	150.00
13	Mike Cameron	25.00
14	Ray Durham	25.00
15	Frank Thomas	450.00
16	Robin Ventura	25.00
17	Manny Ramirez	100.00
18	Jim Thome	100.00
19	Matt Williams	75.00
20	Tony Clark	100.00
21	Travis Fryman	25.00
22	Bob Higginson	25.00
23	Kevin Appier	25.00
24	Johnny Damon	25.00
25	Jermaine Dye	25.00
26	Jeff Cirillo	25.00
27	Ben McDonald	25.00
28	Chuck Knoblauch	50.00
29	Paul Molitor	100.00
30	Todd Walker	75.00
31	Wade Boggs	50.00
32	Cecil Fielder	50.00
33	Derek Jeter	275.00
34	Andy Pettitte	125.00
35	Ruben Rivera	25.00
36	Bernie Williams	100.00
37	Jose Canseco	50.00

38	Mark McGwire	175.00
39	Jay Buhner	50.00
40	Ken Griffey Jr.	600.00
41	Randy Johnson	100.00
42	Edgar Martinez	25.00
43	Alex Rodriguez	450.00
44	Dan Wilson	25.00
45	Will Clark	50.00
46	Juan Gonzalez	220.00
47	Ivan Rodriguez	100.00
48	Joe Carter	40.00
49	Roger Clemens	175.00
50	Juan Guzman	25.00
51	Pat Hentgen	25.00
52	Tom Glavine	40.00
53	Andruw Jones	250.00
54	Chipper Jones	275.00
55	Ryan Klesko	60.00
56	Kenny Lofton	125.00
57	Greg Maddux	275.00
58	Fred McGriff	50.00
59	John Smoltz	50.00
60	Mark Wohlers	25.00
61	Mark Grace	50.00
62	Ryne Sandberg	125.00
63	Sammy Sosa	60.00
64	Barry Larkin	40.00
65	Deion Sanders	60.00
66	Reggie Sanders	25.00
67	Dante Bichette	40.00
68	Ellis Burks	25.00
69	Andres Galarraga	40.00
70	Moises Alou	50.00
71	Kevin Brown	25.00
72	Cliff Floyd	25.00
73	Edgar Renteria	25.00
74	Gary Sheffield	60.00
75	Bob Abreu	25.00
76	Jeff Bagwell	200.00
77	Craig Biggio	50.00
78	Todd Hollandsworth	25.00
79	Eric Karros	25.00
80	Raul Mondesi	50.00
81	Hideo Nomo	125.00
82	Mike Piazza	275.00
83	Vladimir Guerrero	200.00
84	Henry Rodriguez	25.00
85	Todd Hundley	50.00
86	Rey Ordonez	25.00
87	Alex Ochoa	25.00
88	Gregg Jefferies	25.00
89	Scott Rolen	200.00
90	Jermaine Allensworth	25.00
91	Jason Kendall	25.00
92	Ken Caminiti	50.00
93	Tony Gwynn	200.00
94	Rickey Henderson	25.00
95	Barry Bonds	125.00
96	J.T. Snow	25.00
97	Dennis Eckersley	25.00
98	Ron Gant	35.00
99	Brian Jordan	25.00
100	Ray Lankford	25.00

1997 SkyBox E-X2000 A Cut Above

Some of the game's elite players are featured in this 10-card insert (1:288) that features a die-cut design resembling a saw blade.

		MT
Complete Set (10):		500.00
Common Player:		20.00
1	Frank Thomas	120.00
2	Ken Griffey Jr.	120.00
3	Alex Rodriguez	100.00
4	Albert Belle	40.00

5	Juan Gonzalez	60.00
6	Mark McGwire	50.00
7	Mo Vaughn	30.00
8	Manny Ramirez	30.00
9	Barry Bonds	30.00
10	Fred McGriff	20.00

1997 SkyBox E-X2000 Emerald Autograph Redemptions

Inserted 1:480 packs, these cards can be exchanged for autographed cards or memorabilia from one to six different major leaguers.

		MT
Complete Set (6):		450.00
Common Player:		25.00
AU1	Darin Erstad	80.00
AU2	Todd Hollandsworth	25.00
AU3	Alex Ochoa	25.00
AU4	Alex Rodriguez	250.00
AU5	Scott Rolen	90.00
AU6	Todd Walker	40.00

1997 SkyBox E-X2000 Hall or Nothing

This 20-card insert, featuring players who are candidates for the Hall of Fame, utilizes a die-cut design on plastic stock. Cards were inserted 1:20 packs.

		MT
Complete Set (20):		300.00
Common Player:		3.00
1	Frank Thomas	40.00
2	Ken Griffey Jr.	40.00
3	Eddie Murray	6.00
4	Cal Ripken Jr.	30.00
5	Ryne Sandberg	10.00
6	Wade Boggs	3.00
7	Roger Clemens	10.00
8	Tony Gwynn	20.00
9	Alex Rodriguez	30.00
10	Mark McGwire	15.00
11	Barry Bonds	10.00
12	Greg Maddux	25.00
13	Juan Gonzalez	20.00
14	Albert Belle	15.00
15	Mike Piazza	25.00
16	Jeff Bagwell	20.00
17	Dennis Eckersley	3.00
18	Mo Vaughn	10.00
19	Roberto Alomar	8.00
20	Kenny Lofton	10.00

1997 SkyBox E-X2000 Star Date 2000

A 15-card set highlighting young stars that are likely to be the game's top players in the year 2000. Cards were inserted 1:9 packs.

		MT
Complete Set (15):		80.00
Common Player:		2.00
1	Alex Rodriguez	15.00
2	Andruw Jones	12.00
3	Andy Pettitte	5.00
4	Brooks Kieschnick	2.00
5	Chipper Jones	12.00
6	Darin Erstad	10.00
7	Derek Jeter	12.00
8	Jason Kendall	2.00
9	Jermaine Dye	2.00
10	Neifi Perez	2.00
11	Scott Rolen	10.00
12	Todd Hollandsworth	2.00
13	Todd Walker	5.00
14	Tony Clark	5.00
15	Vladimir Guerrero	10.00

1997 Fleer Sports Illustrated

Fleer teamed up with Sports Illustrated to produce a 180-card World Series Fever set. The regular set is divided into six different subsets: 96 Player Cards, 27 Fresh Faces, 18 Inside Baseball, 18 Slber Vision, 12 covers and 9 Newsmakers. Inserts included the Extra Edition parallel set, Great Shots, Cooperstown Collection and Autographed Mini-Cover Redemption Cards. Cards were sold in six-card packs for $1.99 each.

		MT
Complete Set (180):		40.00
Common Player:		.10
1	Bob Abreu (Fresh Faces)	.10
2	Jaime Bluma (Fresh Faces)	.10
3	Emil Brown (Fresh Faces)	.10
4	Jose Cruz, Jr. (Fresh Faces)	8.00
5	Jason Dickson (Fresh Faces)	.10
6	Nomar Garciaparra (Fresh Faces)	2.50
7	Todd Greene (Fresh Faces)	.20
8	Vladimir Guerrero (Fresh Faces)	2.00
9	Wilton Guerrero (Fresh Faces)	.10
10	Jose Guillen (Fresh Faces)	1.00
11	Hideki Irabu (Fresh Faces)	3.00
12	Russ Johnson (Fresh Faces)	.10
13	Andruw Jones (Fresh Faces)	2.50
14	Damon Mashore (Fresh Faces)	.10
15	Jason McDonald (Fresh Faces)	.10
16	Ryan McGuire (Fresh Faces)	.10
17	Matt Morris (Fresh Faces)	.10
18	Kevin Orie (Fresh Faces)	.10
19	Dante Powell (Fresh Faces)	.10
20	Pokey Reese (Fresh Faces)	.10
21	Joe Roa (Fresh Faces)	.10
22	Scott Rolen (Fresh Faces)	2.00
23	Glendon Rusch (Fresh Faces)	.10
24	Scott Spiezio (Fresh Faces)	.10
25	Bubba Trammell (Fresh Faces)	1.00
26	Todd Walker (Fresh Faces)	.75
27	Jamey Wright (Fresh Faces)	.10
28	Ken Griffey Jr. (Season Highlights)	2.00
29	Tino Martinez (Season Highlights)	.20
30	Roger Clemens (Season Highlights)	.50
31	Hideki Irabu (Season Highlights)	1.50
32	Kevin Brown (Season Highlights)	.10
33	Chipper Jones, Cal Ripken Jr. (Season Highlights)	1.25
34	Sandy Alomar (Season Highlights)	.10
35	Ken Caminiti (Season Highlights)	.20
36	Randy Johnson (Season Highlights)	.40
37	Andy Ashby (Inside Baseball)	.10
38	Jay Buhner (Inside Baseball)	.20
39	Joe Carter (Inside Baseball)	.10
40	Darren Daulton (Inside Baseball)	.10
41	Jeff Fassero (Inside Baseball)	.10
42	Andres Galarraga (Inside Baseball)	.20
43	Rusty Greer (Inside Baseball)	.10
44	Marquis Grissom (Inside Baseball)	.10
45	Joey Hamilton (Inside Baseball)	.10
46	Jimmy Key (Inside Baseball)	.10
47	Ryan Klesko (Inside Baseball)	.50
48	Eddie Murray (Inside Baseball)	.40
49	Charles Nagy (Inside Baseball)	.10
50	Dave Nilsson (Inside Baseball)	.10
51	Ricardo Rincon (Inside Baseball)	.10
52	Billy Wagner (Inside Baseball)	.10
53	Dan Wilson (Inside Baseball)	.10
54	Dmitri Young (Inside Baseball)	.10
55	Roberto Alomar (S.I.BER Vision)	.60
56	Sandy Alomar Jr. (S.I.BER Vision)	.10
57	Scott Brosius (S.I.BER Vision)	.10
58	Tony Clark (S.I.BER Vision)	.60
59	Carlos Delgado (S.I.BER Vision)	.10
60	Jermaine Dye (S.I.BER Vision)	.10
61	Darin Erstad (S.I.BER Vision)	2.00
62	Derek Jeter (S.I.BER Vision)	1.25
63	Jason Kendall (S.I.BER Vision)	.10
64	Hideo Nomo (S.I.BER Vision)	.40
65	Rey Ordonez (S.I.BER Vision)	.10
66	Andy Pettitte (S.I.BER Vision)	.50

67	Manny Ramirez (S.I.BER Vision)	.40
68	Edgar Renteria (S.I.BER Vision)	.10
69	Shane Reynolds (S.I.BER Vision)	.10
70	Alex Rodriguez (S.I.BER Vision)	1.50
71	Ivan Rodriguez (S.I.BER Vision)	.40
72	Jose Rosado (S.I.BER Vision)	.10
73	John Smoltz	.20
74	Tom Glavine	.20
75	Greg Maddux	2.50
76	Chipper Jones	2.50
77	Kenny Lofton	1.00
78	Fred McGriff	.30
79	Kevin Brown	.10
80	Alex Fernandez	.10
81	Al Leiter	.10
82	Bobby Bonilla	.10
83	Gary Sheffield	.30
84	Moises Alou	.20
85	Henry Rodriguez	.10
86	Mark Grudzielanek	.10
87	Pedro Martinez	.20
88	Todd Hundley	.20
89	Bernard Gilkey	.10
90	Bobby Jones	.10
91	Curt Schilling	.10
92	Ricky Bottalico	.10
93	Mike Lieberthal	.10
94	Sammy Sosa	.40
95	Ryne Sandberg	1.00
96	Mark Grace	.30
97	Deion Sanders	.30
98	Reggie Sanders	.10
99	Barry Larkin	.20
100	Craig Biggio	.20
101	Jeff Bagwell	1.50
102	Derek Bell	.10
103	Brian Jordan	.10
104	Ray Lankford	.10
105	Ron Gant	.10
106	Al Martin	.10
107	Kevin Elster	.10
108	Jermaine Allensworth	.10
109	Vinny Castilla	.10
110	Dante Bichette	.20
111	Larry Walker	.30
112	Mike Piazza	2.50
113	Eric Karros	.10
114	Todd Hollandsworth	.10
115	Raul Mondesi	.25
116	Hideo Nomo	.75
117	Ramon Martinez	.10
118	Ken Caminiti	.25
119	Tony Gwynn	2.00
120	Steve Finley	.10
121	Barry Bonds	1.00
122	J.T. Snow	.10
123	Rod Beck	.10
124	Cal Ripken Jr.	3.00
125	Mike Mussina	.75
126	Brady Anderson	.10
127	Bernie Williams	.75
128	Derek Jeter	2.50
129	Tino Martinez	.30
130	Andy Pettitte	1.00
131	David Cone	.20
132	Mariano Rivera	.20
133	Roger Clemens	1.50
134	Pat Hentgen	.10
135	Juan Guzman	.10
136	Bob Higginson	.10
137	Tony Clark	1.00
138	Travis Fryman	.10
139	Mo Vaughn	1.00
140	Tim Naehring	.10
141	John Valentin	.10
142	Matt Williams	.30
143	David Justice	.30
144	Jim Thome	.60
145	Chuck Knoblauch	.25
146	Paul Molitor	.30
147	Marty Cordova	.10
148	Frank Thomas	4.00
149	Albert Belle	1.25
150	Robin Ventura	.10
151	John Jaha	.10
152	Jeff Cirillo	.10
153	Jose Valentin	.10
154	Jay Bell	.10
155	Jeff King	.10
156	Kevin Appier	.10
157	Ken Griffey Jr.	4.00

158	Alex Rodriguez	3.00
158p	Alex Rodriguez (overprinted "PROMOTIONAL SAMPLE")	3.00
159	Randy Johnson	.60
160	Juan Gonzalez	2.00
161	Will Clark	.25
162	Dean Palmer	.10
163	Tim Salmon	.25
164	Jim Edmonds	.10
165	Jim Leyritz	.10
166	Jose Canseco	.30
167	Jason Giambi	.10
168	Mark McGwire	1.50
169	Barry Bonds	1.00
170	Alex Rodriguez	1.50
171	Roger Clemens	.60
172	Ken Griffey Jr.	2.00
173	Greg Maddux	1.25
174	Mike Piazza	1.25
175	Will Clark, Mark McGwire	.75
176	Hideo Nomo	.40
177	Cal Ripken Jr.	1.50
178	Ken Griffey Jr., Frank Thomas	2.00
179	Alex Rodriguez, Derek Jeter	1.50
180	John Wetteland	.10

1997 Fleer Sports Illustrated Extra Edition

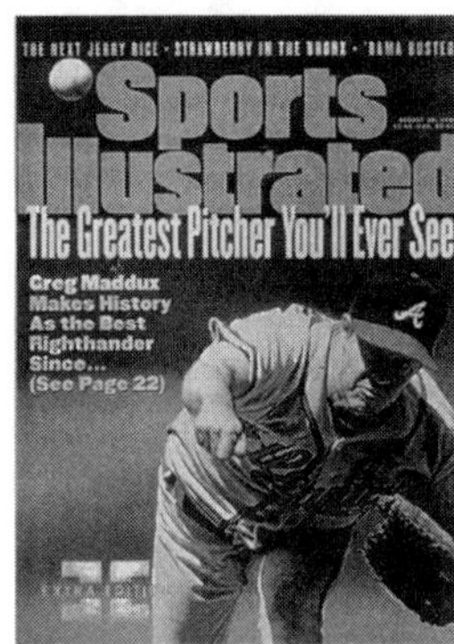

Each of the regular cards in the premiere Fleer SI issue is also found in a parallel set designated on front in gold holographic foil as "Extra Edition". Backs of the cards carry a serial number from within a production of 500 of each card.

	MT
Complete Set (180):	850.00
Common Player:	2.50
Extra Edition Stars:	35x-50x
Extra Edition Yng Stars & RC's:	25x-35x

1997 Fleer Sports Illustrated Auto Mini-Covers

Six different players autographed 250 magazine mini-covers that were available through randomly seeded redemption cards. The players who autographed cards were Hank Aaron, Willie Mays, Frank Robinson, Kirby Puckett, Cal Ripken Jr., and Alex Rodriguez.

	MT
Complete Set (6):	500.00
Common Player:	50.00
Alex Rodriguez	150.00
Cal Ripken Jr.	150.00
Kirby Puckett	80.00
Willie Mays	75.00
Frank Robinson	50.00
Hank Aaron	75.00

1997 Fleer Sports Illustrated Box Topper

This special version of A-Rod's card was packaged one per box of foil packs. It was intended to be inserted into die-cuts on the box to create a sample display for the new issue. The card measures 2-1/2" x 4-1/16". The back is in black-and-white with instructions on how to insert the card into the box.

	MT
Alex Rodriguez	6.00

1997 Fleer Sports Illustrated Cooperstown Collection

This 12-card insert (found 1:12 packs) lets collectors relive classic SI baseball covers with a description of each issue on the back.

		MT
Complete Set (12):		75.00
Common Player:		5.00
1	Hank Aaron	15.00
2	Yogi Berra	8.00
3	Lou Brock	5.00
4	Rod Carew	5.00
5	Juan Marichal	5.00
6	Al Kaline	5.00
7	Joe Morgan	5.00
8	Brooks Robinson	10.00
9	Willie Stargell	5.00
10	Kirby Puckett	15.00
11	Willie Mays	15.00
12	Frank Robinson	8.00

1997 Fleer Sports Illustrated Great Shots

A 25-card insert, found one per pack, designed to highlight Sports Illustrated's classic photography. Each card in the set folds out to a 5" x 7" format to showcase a larger photo.

		MT
Complete Set (25):		5.00
Common Player:		.10
	Chipper Jones	.60
	Ryan Klesko	.15
	Kenny Lofton	.25

	Greg Maddux	.60
	John Smoltz	.10
	Roberto Alomar	.20
	Cal Ripken Jr.	.75
	Mo Vaughn	.25
	Albert Belle	.30
	Frank Thomas	1.00
	Ryne Sandberg	.25
	Deion Sanders	.15
	Vinny Castilla, Andres Galarraga	.10
	Eric Karros	.10
	Mike Piazza	.60
	Derek Jeter	.60
	Mark McGwire	.35
	Darren Daulton	.10
	Andy Ashby	.10
	Barry Bonds	.25
	Jay Buhner	.10
	Randy Johnson	.15
	Alex Rodriguez	.75
	Juan Gonzalez	.40
	Ken Griffey Jr.	1.00

1997 Flair Showcase

This 540-card set is actually a 180-card set printed in three different versions, all on a super-glossy thick stock. Card fronts feature holographic foil with an action photo of the player silhouetted over a larger head-shot image in the background. Each of the 180 base cards has three versions - Style, Grace and Showcase. There are two different parallel sets (Legacy Collection and Legacy Collection Masterpiece) as well as five other inserts: Wave of the Future, Diamond Cuts, Hot Gloves, Emerald, and Million Dollar Moments. Cards were sold exclusively at hobby shops in five-card packs for $4.99.

		MT
Complete Set (180):		2000.
Common Style/Showtime (1-60):		.25
Grace/Showtime (1-60):		1.5x to 2x
Showcase/Showpiece (1-60):		10x to 15x
Common Style/Showpiece (61-120):		.35
Grace/Showtime (61-120):		1x to 2x
Showcase/Showstopper (61-120):		4x
Common Style/Showstopper (121-180):		.25
Grace/Showpiece (121-180):		2x
Showcase/Showtime (121-180):		3x
Wax Box:		140.00
1	Andruw Jones	5.00
2	Derek Jeter	5.00
3	Alex Rodriguez	8.00
4	Paul Molitor	1.50
5	Jeff Bagwell	3.00
6	Scott Rolen	4.00
7	Kenny Lofton	2.00
8	Cal Ripken Jr.	6.00
9	Brady Anderson	.25
10	Chipper Jones	5.00
11	Todd Greene	.25
12	Todd Walker	1.50
13	Billy Wagner	.25
14	Craig Biggio	.25
15	Kevin Orie	.25
16	Hideo Nomo	1.50
17	Kevin Appier	.25
18	*Bubba Trammell*	2.00
19	Juan Gonzalez	4.00
20	Randy Johnson	1.50
21	Roger Clemens	3.00

#	Player	MT
22	Johnny Damon	.25
23	Ryne Sandberg	2.00
24	Ken Griffey Jr.	10.00
25	Barry Bonds	2.00
26	Nomar Garciaparra	5.00
27	Vladimir Guerrero	5.00
28	Ron Gant	.25
29	Joe Carter	.25
30	Tim Salmon	.75
31	Mike Piazza	5.00
32	Barry Larkin	.50
33	Manny Ramirez	2.00
34	Sammy Sosa	.75
35	Frank Thomas	8.00
36	Melvin Nieves	.25
37	Tony Gwynn	4.00
38	Gary Sheffield	.75
39	Darin Erstad	3.50
40	Ken Caminiti	.50
41	Jermaine Dye	.25
42	Mo Vaughn	2.00
43	Raul Mondesi	.75
44	Greg Maddux	5.00
45	Chuck Knoblauch	.75
46	Andy Pettitte	2.00
47	Deion Sanders	.75
48	Albert Belle	2.50
49	Jamey Wright	.25
50	Rey Ordonez	.25
51	Bernie Williams	1.50
52	Mark McGwire	2.50
53	Mike Mussina	1.50
54	Bob Abreu	.25
55	Reggie Sanders	.25
56	Brian Jordan	.25
57	Ivan Rodriguez	1.50
58	Roberto Alomar	1.50
59	Tim Naehring	.25
60	Edgar Renteria	.25
61	Dean Palmer	.35
62	Benito Santiago	.25
63	David Cone	.50
64	Carlos Delgado	.50
65	Brian Giles	.35
66	Alex Ochoa	.35
67	Rondell White	.35
68	Robin Ventura	.35
69	Eric Karros	.35
70	Jose Valentin	.35
71	Rafael Palmeiro	.50
72	Chris Snopek	.35
73	David Justice	.75
74	Tom Glavine	.50
75	Rudy Pemberton	.35
76	Larry Walker	1.00
77	Jim Thome	1.50
78	Charles Johnson	.35
79	Dante Powell	.35
80	Derek Lee	.35
81	Jason Kendall	.35
82	Todd Hollandsworth	.35
83	Bernard Gilkey	.35
84	Mel Rojas	.35
85	Dmitri Young	.35
86	Bret Boone	.35
87	Pat Hentgen	.35
88	Bobby Bonilla	.35
89	John Wetteland	.35
90	Todd Hundley	.50
91	Wilton Guerrero	.50
92	Geronimo Berroa	.05
93	Al Martin	.35
94	Danny Tartabull	.35
95	Brian McRae	.35
96	Steve Finley	.35
97	Todd Stottlemyre	.35
98	John Smoltz	.50
99	Matt Williams	1.00
100	Eddie Murray	1.00
101	Henry Rodriguez	.35
102	Marty Cordova	.35
103	Juan Guzman	.05
104	Chili Davis	.35
105	Eric Young	.35
106	Jeff Abbott	.35
107	Shannon Stewart	.35
108	Rocky Coppinger	.35
109	Jose Canseco	.75
110	Dante Bichette	.60
111	Dwight Gooden	.35
112	Scott Brosius	.35
113	Steve Avery	.35
114	Andres Galarraga	.60
115	Sandy Alomar Jr.	.35
116	Ray Lankford	.35
117	Jorge Posada	.35
118	Ryan Klesko	1.00
119	Jay Buhner	.60
120	Jose Guillen	1.50
121	Paul O'Neill	.25
122	Jimmy Key	.25
123	Hal Morris	.25
124	Travis Fryman	.25
125	Jim Edmonds	.25
126	Jeff Cirillo	.25
127	Fred McGriff	.60
128	Alan Benes	.50
129	Derek Bell	.25
130	Tony Graffanino	.25
131	Shawn Green	.25
132	Denny Neagle	.25
133	Alex Fernandez	.25
134	Mickey Morandini	.25
135	Royce Clayton	.25
136	Jose Mesa	.25
137	Edgar Martinez	.25
138	Curt Schilling	.25
139	Lance Johnson	.25
140	Andy Benes	.25
141	Charles Nagy	.25
142	Mariano Rivera	.50
143	Mark Wohlers	.25
144	Ken Hill	.25
145	Jay Bell	.25
146	Bob Higginson	.40
147	Mark Grudzielanek	.25
148	Ray Durham	.25
149	John Olerud	.25
150	Joey Hamilton	.25
151	Trevor Hoffman	.25
152	Dan Wilson	.25
153	J.T. Snow	.25
154	Marquis Grissom	.40
155	Yamil Benitez	.25
156	Rusty Greer	.25
157	Darryl Kile	.25
158	Ismael Valdes	.25
159	Jeff Conine	.25
160	Darren Daulton	.25
161	Chan Ho Park	.25
162	Troy Percival	.25
163	Wade Boggs	.50
164	Dave Nilsson	.25
165	Vinny Castilla	.25
166	Kevin Brown	.25
167	Dennis Eckersley	.25
168	Wendell Magee Jr.	.25
169	John Jaha	.25
170	Garret Anderson	.25
171	Jason Giambi	.25
172	Mark Grace	.50
173	Tony Clark	1.50
174	Moises Alou	.40
175	Brett Butler	.25
176	Cecil Fielder	.50
177	Chris Widger	.25
178	Doug Drabek	.25
179	Ellis Burks	.25
180	Shigetosi Hasegawa	.25

1997 Flair Showcase Legacy Collection

This 540-card parallel set is printed on different stock than the regular cards and is sequentially numbered in gold foil. Odds of finding a card is 1:30 packs. Less than 100 complete Legacy Collection sets are available.

#	Player	MT
	Common Player:	25.00
1	Andruw Jones	300.00
2	Derek Jeter	300.00
3	Alex Rodriguez	450.00
4	Paul Molitor	100.00
5	Jeff Bagwell	200.00
6	Scott Rolen	200.00
7	Kenny Lofton	140.00
8	Cal Ripken Jr.	400.00
9	Brady Anderson	40.00
10	Chipper Jones	300.00
11	Todd Greene	25.00
12	Todd Walker	90.00
13	Billy Wagner	25.00
14	Craig Biggio	40.00
15	Kevin Orie	35.00
16	Hideo Nomo	100.00
17	Kevin Appier	25.00
18	Bubba Trammell	75.00
19	Juan Gonzalez	250.00
20	Randy Johnson	100.00
21	Roger Clemens	175.00
22	Johnny Damon	25.00
23	Ryne Sandberg	140.00
24	Ken Griffey Jr.	600.00
25	Barry Bonds	140.00
26	Nomar Garciaparra	250.00
27	Vladimir Guerrero	200.00
28	Ron Gant	25.00
29	Joe Carter	25.00
30	Tim Salmon	50.00
31	Mike Piazza	300.00
32	Barry Larkin	50.00
33	Manny Ramirez	100.00
34	Sammy Sosa	75.00
35	Frank Thomas	500.00
36	Melvin Nieves	25.00
37	Tony Gwynn	250.00
38	Gary Sheffield	75.00
39	Darin Erstad	175.00
40	Ken Caminiti	50.00
41	Jermaine Dye	25.00
42	Mo Vaughn	140.00
43	Raul Mondesi	60.00
44	Greg Maddux	300.00
45	Chuck Knoblauch	60.00
46	Andy Pettitte	140.00
47	Deion Sanders	90.00
48	Albert Belle	150.00
49	Jamey Wright	25.00
50	Rey Ordonez	25.00
51	Bernie Williams	100.00
52	Mark McGwire	200.00
53	Mike Mussina	100.00
54	Bob Abreu	25.00
55	Reggie Sanders	25.00
56	Brian Jordan	25.00
57	Ivan Rodriguez	100.00
58	Roberto Alomar	100.00
59	Tim Naehring	25.00
60	Edgar Renteria	25.00
61	Dean Palmer	25.00
63	David Cone	40.00
64	Carlos Delgado	40.00
65	Brian Giles	25.00
66	Alex Ochoa	25.00
67	Rondell White	25.00
68	Robin Ventura	25.00
69	Eric Karros	25.00
70	Jose Valentin	25.00
71	Rafael Palmeiro	40.00
72	Chris Snopek	25.00
73	David Justice	50.00
74	Tom Glavine	50.00
75	Rudy Pemberton	25.00
76	Larry Walker	100.00
77	Jim Thome	100.00
78	Charles Johnson	25.00
79	Dante Powell	25.00
80	Derek Lee	25.00
81	Jason Kendall	25.00
82	Todd Hollandsworth	26.00
83	Bernard Gilkey	25.00
84	Mel Rojas	25.00
85	Dmitri Young	25.00
86	Bret Boone	25.00
87	Pat Hentgen	25.00
88	Bobby Bonilla	40.00
89	John Wetteland	25.00
90	Todd Hundley	50.00
91	Wilton Guerrero	40.00
92	Geronimo Berroa	25.00
93	Al Martin	25.00
94	Danny Tartabull	25.00
95	Brian McRae	25.00
96	Steve Finley	25.00
97	Todd Stottlemyro	25.00
98	John Smoltz	50.00
99	Matt Williams	75.00
100	Eddie Murray	75.00
101	Henry Rodriguez	25.00
102	Marty Cordova	25.00
103	Juan Guzman	25.00
104	Chili Davis	25.00
105	Eric Young	25.00
106	Jeff Abbott	25.00
107	Shannon Stewart	25.00
108	Rocky Coppinger	25.00
109	Jose Canseco	50.00
110	Dante Bichette	50.00
111	Dwight Gooden	25.00
112	Scott Brosius	25.00
113	Steve Avery	25.00
114	Andres Galarraga	50.00
115	Sandy Alomar Jr.	25.00
116	Ray Lankford	25.00
117	Jorge Posada	25.00
118	Ryan Klesko	80.00
119	Jay Buhner	50.00
120	Jose Guillen	75.00
121	Paul O'Neill	40.00
122	Jimmy Key	25.00
123	Hal Morris	25.00
124	Travis Fryman	25.00
125	Jim Edmonds	25.00
126	Jeff Cirillo	25.00
127	Fred McGriff	40.00
128	Alan Benes	50.00
129	Derek Bell	25.00
130	Tony Graffanino	25.00
131	Shawn Green	25.00
132	Denny Neagle	25.00
133	Alex Fernandez	40.00
134	Mickey Morandini	25.00
135	Royce Clayton	25.00
136	Jose Mesa	25.00
137	Edgar Martinez	40.00
138	Curt Schilling	25.00
139	Lance Johnson	25.00
140	Andy Benes	25.00
141	Charles Nagy	25.00
142	Mariano Rivera	50.00
143	Mark Wohlers	25.00
144	Ken Hill	25.00
145	Jay Bell	25.00
146	Bob Higginson	25.00
147	Mark Grudzielanek	25.00
148	Ray Durham	25.00
149	John Olerud	25.00
150	Joey Hamilton	25.00
151	Trevor Hoffman	25.00
152	Dan Wilson	25.00
153	J.T. Snow	25.00
154	Marquis Grissom	40.00
155	Yamil Benitez	25.00
156	Rusty Greer	25.00
157	Darryl Kile	25.00
158	Ismael Valdes	25.00
159	Jeff Conine	25.00
160	Darren Daulton	25.00
161	Chan Ho Park	25.00
162	Troy Percival	25.00
163	Wade Boggs	60.00
164	Dave Nilsson	25.00
165	Vinny Castilla	25.00
166	Kevin Brown	25.00
167	Dennis Eckersley	25.00
168	Wendell Magee Jr.	25.00
169	John Jaha	25.00
170	Garret Anderson	25.00
171	Jason Giambi	25.00
172	Mark Grace	50.00
173	Tony Clark	100.00
174	Moises Alou	40.00
175	Brett Butler	25.00
176	Cecil Fielder	40.00
177	Chris Widger	25.00
178	Doug Drabek	25.00
179	Ellis Burks	25.00
180	Shigetosi Hasegawa	25.00

1997 Flair Showcase Legacy Masterpieces

The insert card chase reached its inevitable zenith with the creation of this series of one-of-a-kind inserts. Each of the 180 players' three cards (Style, Grace, Showpiece) in the '97 Flair Legacy Collection (100 of each) was also produced in an edition of one card and inserted at a rate of about one per 3,000 packs. Instead of the blue metallic foil on front and highlights on back of the regular Legacy cards, the one-of-a-kind cards are highlighted in purple and carry a notation on back that they are "The Only 1 of 1 Masterpiece". Because of the unique nature of each card, current market values cannot be quoted.

MT

(Recently observed buy/sell asking prices range from $250 for a common player to $10,000 for Ken Griffey, Jr.)

1997 Flair Showcase Diamond Cuts

This 20-card insert, found 1:20 packs, features a die-cut design with an action photo of the player appearing above a baseball diamond in the lower background of the cards.

		MT
Complete Set (20):		300.00
Common Player:		5.00
1	Jeff Bagwell	18.00
2	Albert Belle	12.00
3	Ken Caminiti	5.00
4	Juan Gonzalez	20.00
5	Ken Griffey Jr.	45.00
6	Tony Gwynn	18.00
7	Todd Hundley	5.00
8	Andruw Jones	25.00
9	Chipper Jones	30.00
10	Greg Maddux	30.00
11	Mark McGwire	15.00
12	Mike Piazza	30.00
13	Derek Jeter	30.00
14	Manny Ramirez	10.00
15	Cal Ripken Jr.	35.00
16	Alex Rodriguez	35.00
17	Frank Thomas	40.00
18	Mo Vaughn	10.00
19	Bernie Williams	8.00
20	Matt Williams	6.00

1997 Flair Showcase Hot Gloves

Inserted 1:90 packs, Hot Gloves features 15 cards with a die-cut "flame" design saluting some of baseball's best defensive players.

		MT
Complete Set (15):		700.00
Common Player:		10.00
1	Roberto Alomar	20.00
2	Barry Bonds	25.00
3	Juan Gonzalez	50.00
4	Ken Griffey Jr.	125.00
5	Marquis Grissom	10.00
6	Derek Jeter	65.00
7	Chipper Jones	60.00
8	Barry Larkin	10.00
9	Kenny Lofton	25.00
10	Greg Maddux	65.00
11	Mike Piazza	65.00
12	Cal Ripken Jr.	80.00
13	Alex Rodriguez	80.00
14	Ivan Rodriguez	20.00
15	Frank Thomas	100.00

1997 Flair Showcase Wave of the Future

This 27-card insert focuses on some of the up-and-coming young stars in the game. Cards were seeded 1:4 packs. A large ocean wave makes up the background of each card front.

		MT
Complete Set (27):		100.00
Common Player:		1.50
1	Todd Greene	1.50
2	Andruw Jones	12.00
3	Randall Simon	1.50
4	Wady Almonte	1.50
5	Pat Cline	1.50
6	Jeff Abbott	1.50
7	Justin Towle	1.50
8	Richie Sexson	1.50
9	Bubba Trammell	5.00
10	Bob Abreu	1.50
11	David Arias	1.50
12	Todd Walker	4.00
13	Orlando Cabrera	1.50

		MT
14	Vladimir Guerrero	10.00
15	Ricky Ledee	10.00
16	Jorge Posada	1.50
17	Ruben Rivera	1.50
18	Scott Spiezio	1.50
19	Scott Rolen	10.00
20	Emil Brown	1.50
21	Jose Guillen	5.00
22	T.J. Staton	1.50
23	Elieser Marrero	1.50
24	Fernando Tatis	4.00
25	Ryan Jones	1.50
WF1	Hideki Irabu	12.00
WF2	Jose Cruz Jr.	45.00

1997 Ultra

Ultra arrived in a 300-card Series I issue with two parallel sets, Gold and Platinum, which featured "G" and "P" prefixes on the card number, respectively. The cards arrived in 10-card packs and featured the player's name in holographic foil in simulated logo script. Backs contained complete year-by-year statistics, plus two photos of the player. This also marked the first time that the Gold and Platinum parallel sets displayed a different photo than the base cards. Inserts in Ultra included: Rookie Reflections, Double Trouble, Checklists, Season Crowns, RBI Kings, Power Plus, Fielder's Choice, Diamond Producers, HR Kings and Baseball Rules.

		MT
Complete Set (553):		55.00
Complete Series 1 Set (300):		30.00
Complete Series 2 Set (253):		25.00
Common Player:		.10
Unlisted Stars:		.20 to .35
Series I & II Wax Box:		60.00
1	Roberto Alomar	.75
2	Brady Anderson	.10
3	Rocky Coppinger	.10
4	Jeffrey Hammonds	.10
5	Chris Hoiles	.10
6	Eddie Murray	.40
7	Mike Mussina	.60
8	Jimmy Myers	.10
9	Randy Myers	.10
10	Arthur Rhodes	.10
11	Cal Ripken Jr.	2.50
12	Jose Canseco	.25
13	Roger Clemens	1.00
14	Tom Gordon	.10
15	Jose Malave	.10
16	Tim Naehring	.10
17	Troy O'Leary	.10
18	Bill Selby	.10
19	Heathcliff Slocumb	.10
20	Mike Stanley	.10
21	Mo Vaughn	.75
22	Garret Anderson	.10
23	George Arias	.10
24	Chili Davis	.10
25	Jim Edmonds	.20
26	Darin Erstad	1.25
27	Chuck Finley	.10
28	Todd Greene	.10
29	Troy Percival	.10
30	Tim Salmon	.20
31	Jeff Schmidt	.10
32	Randy Velarde	.10
33	Shad Williams	.10
34	Wilson Alvarez	.10

		MT
35	Harold Baines	.10
36	James Baldwin	.10
37	Mike Cameron	.10
38	Ray Durham	.10
39	Ozzie Guillen	.10
40	Roberto Hernandez	.10
41	Darren Lewis	.10
42	Jose Munoz	.10
43	Tony Phillips	.10
44	Frank Thomas	3.00
45	Sandy Alomar Jr.	.10
46	Albert Belle	1.00
47	Mark Carreon	.10
48	Julio Franco	.10
49	Orel Hershiser	.10
50	Kenny Lofton	.75
51	Jack McDowell	.15
52	Jose Mesa	.10
53	Charles Nagy	.10
54	Manny Ramirez	.75
55	Julian Tavarez	.10
56	Omar Vizquel	.10
57	Raul Casanova	.10
58	Tony Clark	.60
59	Travis Fryman	.10
60	Bob Higginson	.10
61	Melvin Nieves	.10
62	Curtis Pride	.10
63	Justin Thompson	.10
64	Alan Trammell	.10
65	Kevin Appier	.10
66	Johnny Damon	.30
67	Keith Lockhart	.10
68	Jeff Montgomery	.10
69	Jose Offerman	.10
70	Bip Roberts	.10
71	Jose Rosado	.10
72	Chris Stynes	.10
73	Mike Sweeney	.10
74	Jeff Cirillo	.10
75	Jeff D'Amico	.10
76	John Jaha	.10
77	Scott Karl	.10
78	Mike Matheny	.10
79	Ben McDonald	.10
80	Matt Mieske	.10
81	Marc Newfield	.10
82	Dave Nilsson	.10
83	Jose Valentin	.10
84	Fernando Vina	.10
85	Rick Aguilera	.10
86	Marty Cordova	.10
87	Chuck Knoblauch	.10
88	Matt Lawton	.10
89	Pat Meares	.10
90	Paul Molitor	.25
91	Greg Myers	.10
92	Dan Naulty	.10
93	Kirby Puckett	1.00
94	Frank Rodriguez	.10
95	Wade Boggs	.20
96	Cecil Fielder	.15
97	Joe Girardi	.10
98	Dwight Gooden	.15
99	Derek Jeter	1.50
100	Tino Martinez	.30
101	*Ramiro Mendoza*	.10
102	Andy Pettitte	.75
103	Mariano Rivera	.20
104	Ruben Rivera	.20
105	Kenny Rogers	.10
106	Darryl Strawberry	.10
107	Bernie Williams	.50
108	Tony Batista	.10
109	Geronimo Berroa	.10
110	Bobby Chouinard	.10
111	Brent Gates	.10
112	Jason Giambi	.10
113	*Damon Mashore*	.10
114	Mark McGwire	1.25
115	Scott Spiezio	.10
116	John Wasdin	.10
117	Steve Wojciechowski	.10
118	Ernie Young	.10
119	Norm Charlton	.10
120	Joey Cora	.10
121	Ken Griffey Jr.	3.00
122	Sterling Hitchcock	.10
123	Raul Ibanez	.10
124	Randy Johnson	.50
125	Edgar Martinez	.10
126	Alex Rodriguez	3.00
127	Matt Wagner	.10
128	Bob Wells	.10
129	Dan Wilson	.10
130	Will Clark	.25
131	Kevin Elster	.10
132	Juan Gonzalez	1.25
133	Rusty Greer	.10
134	Darryl Hamilton	.10
135	Mike Henneman	.10

		MT
136	Ken Hill	.10
137	Mark McLemore	.10
138	Dean Palmer	.10
139	Roger Pavlik	.10
140	Ivan Rodriguez	.60
141	Joe Carter	.20
142	Carlos Delgado	.10
143	Alex Gonzalez	.10
144	Juan Guzman	.10
145	Pat Hentgen	.10
146	Marty Janzen	.10
147	Otis Nixon	.10
148	Charlie O'Brien	.10
149	John Olerud	.10
150	Robert Perez	.10
151	Jermaine Dye	.15
152	Tom Glavine	.15
153	Andruw Jones	2.00
154	Chipper Jones	2.00
155	Ryan Klesko	.50
156	Javier Lopez	.20
157	Greg Maddux	2.00
158	Fred McGriff	.35
159	Wonderful Monds	.10
160	John Smoltz	.20
161	Terrell Wade	.10
162	Mark Wohlers	.10
163	Brant Brown	.10
164	Mark Grace	.20
165	Tyler Houston	.10
166	Robin Jennings	.10
167	Jason Maxwell	.10
168	Ryne Sandberg	.75
169	Sammy Sosa	.20
170	Amaury Telemaco	.10
171	Steve Trachsel	.10
172	*Pedro Valdes*	.10
173	Tim Belk	.10
174	Bret Boone	.10
175	Jeff Brantley	.10
176	Eric Davis	.10
177	Barry Larkin	.25
178	Chad Mottola	.10
179	Mark Portugal	.10
180	Reggie Sanders	.10
181	John Smiley	.10
182	Eddie Taubensee	.10
183	Dante Bichette	.20
184	Ellis Burks	.10
185	Andres Galarraga	.20
186	Curt Leskanic	.10
187	Quinton McCracken	.10
188	Jeff Reed	.10
189	Kevin Ritz	.10
190	Walt Weiss	.10
191	Jamey Wright	.10
192	Eric Young	.10
193	Kevin Brown	.10
194	Luis Castillo	.25
195	Jeff Conine	.10
196	Andre Dawson	.10
197	Charles Johnson	.10
198	Al Leiter	.10
199	Ralph Milliard	.10
200	Robb Nen	.10
201	Edgar Renteria	.15
202	Gary Sheffield	.35
203	Bob Abreu	.10
204	Jeff Bagwell	1.25
205	Derek Bell	.10
206	Sean Berry	.10
207	Richard Hidalgo	.10
208	Todd Jones	.10
209	Darryl Kile	.10
210	Orlando Miller	.10
211	Shane Reynolds	.10
212	Billy Wagner	.10
213	Donne Wall	.10
214	Roger Cedeno	.10
215	Greg Gagne	.10
216	Karim Garcia	.35
217	Wilton Guerrero	.15
218	Todd Hollandsworth	.10
219	Ramon Martinez	.10
220	Raul Mondesi	.20
221	Hideo Nomo	.60
222	Chan Ho Park	.10
223	Mike Piazza	2.00
224	Ismael Valdes	.10
225	Moises Alou	.15
226	Derek Aucoin	.10
227	Yamil Benitez	.10
228	Jeff Fassero	.10
229	Darrin Fletcher	.10
230	Mark Grudzielanek	.10
231	Barry Manuel	.10
232	Pedro Martinez	.10
233	Henry Rodriguez	.10
234	Ugueth Urbina	.10
235	Rondell White	.10
236	Carlos Baerga	.15

#	Player	Price
237	John Franco	.10
238	Bernard Gilkey	.10
239	Todd Hundley	.10
240	Butch Huskey	.10
241	Jason Isringhausen	.15
242	Lance Johnson	.10
243	Bobby Jones	.10
244	Alex Ochoa	.10
245	Rey Ordonez	.20
246	Paul Wilson	.20
247	Ron Blazier	.10
248	David Doster	.10
249	Jim Eisenreich	.10
250	Mike Grace	.30
251	Mike Lieberthal	.10
252	Wendell Magee	.10
253	Mickey Morandini	.10
254	Ricky Otero	.10
255	Scott Rolen	1.50
256	Curt Schilling	.10
257	Todd Zeile	.10
258	Jermaine Allensworth	.10
259	Trey Beamon	.10
260	Carlos Garcia	.10
261	Mark Johnson	.10
262	Jason Kendall	.10
263	Jeff King	.10
264	Al Martin	.10
265	Denny Neagle	.10
266	Matt Ruebel	.10
267	*Marc Wilkins*	.10
268	Alan Benes	.10
269	Dennis Eckersley	.10
270	Ron Gant	.10
271	Aaron Holbert	.10
272	Brian Jordan	.10
273	Ray Lankford	.10
274	John Mabry	.10
275	T.J. Mathews	.10
276	Ozzie Smith	.40
277	Todd Stottlemyre	.10
278	Mark Sweeney	.10
279	Andy Ashby	.10
280	Steve Finley	.10
281	John Flaherty	.10
282	Chris Gomez	.10
283	Tony Gwynn	1.25
284	Joey Hamilton	.10
285	Rickey Henderson	.10
286	Trevor Hoffman	.10
287	Jason Thompson	.10
288	Fernando Valenzuela	.10
289	Greg Vaughn	.10
290	Barry Bonds	.75
291	Jay Canizaro	.10
292	Jacob Cruz	.10
293	Shawon Dunston	.10
294	Shawn Estes	.10
295	Mark Gardner	.10
296	Marcus Jensen	.10
297	*Bill Mueller*	.10
298	Chris Singleton	.10
299	Allen Watson	.10
300	Matt Williams	.25
301	Rod Beck	.10
302	Jay Bell	.10
303	Shawon Dunston	.10
304	Reggie Jefferson	.10
305	Darren Oliver	.10
306	Benito Santiago	.10
307	Gerald Williams	.10
308	Damon Buford	.10
309	Jeromy Burnitz	.10
310	Sterling Hitchcock	.10
311	Dave Hollins	.10
312	Mel Rojas	.10
313	Robin Ventura	.10
314	David Wells	.10
315	Cal Eldred	.10
316	Gary Gaetti	.10
317	John Hudek	.10
318	Brian Johnson	.10
319	Denny Neagle	.10
320	Larry Walker	.35
321	Russ Davis	.10
322	Delino DeShields	.10
323	Charlie Hayes	.10
324	Jermaine Dye	.10
325	John Ericks	.10
326	Jeff Fassero	.10
327	Nomar Garciaparra	2.00
328	Willie Greene	.10
329	Greg McMichael	.10
330	Damion Easley	.10
331	Ricky Bones	.10
332	John Burkett	.10
333	Royce Clayton	.10
334	Greg Colbrunn	.10
335	Tony Eusebio	.10
336	Gregg Jefferies	.10
337	Wally Joyner	.10

#	Player	Price
338	Jim Leyritz	.10
339	Paul O'Neill	.10
340	Bruce Ruffin	.10
341	Michael Tucker	.10
342	Andy Benes	.10
343	Craig Biggio	.20
344	Rex Hudler	.10
345	Brad Radke	.10
346	Deion Sanders	.25
347	Moises Alou	.10
348	Brad Ausmus	.10
349	Armando Benitez	.10
350	Mark Gubicza	.10
351	Terry Steinbach	.10
352	Mark Whiten	.10
353	Ricky Bottalico	.10
354	Brian Giles	.10
355	Eric Karros	.10
356	Jimmy Key	.10
357	Carlos Perez	.10
358	Alex Fernandez	.10
359	J.T. Snow	.10
360	Bobby Bonilla	.15
361	Scott Brosius	.10
362	Greg Swindell	.10
363	Jose Vizcaino	.10
364	Matt Williams	.30
365	Darren Daulton	.10
366	Shane Andrews	.10
367	Jim Eisenreich	.10
368	Ariel Prieto	.10
369	Bob Tewksbury	.10
370	Mike Bordick	.10
371	Rheal Cormier	.10
372	Cliff Floyd	.10
373	David Justice	.20
374	John Wetteland	.10
375	Mike Blowers	.10
376	Jose Canseco	.30
377	Roger Clemens	1.00
378	Kevin Mitchell	.10
379	Todd Zeile	.10
380	Jim Thome	.50
381	Turk Wendell	.10
382	Rico Brogna	.10
383	Eric Davis	.10
384	Mike Lansing	.10
385	Devon White	.10
386	Marquis Grissom	.10
387	Todd Worrell	.10
388	Jeff Kent	.10
389	Mickey Tettleton	.10
390	Steve Avery	.10
391	David Cone	.20
392	Scott Cooper	.10
393	Lee Stevens	.10
394	Kevin Elster	.10
395	Tom Goodwin	.10
396	Shawn Green	.10
397	Pete Harnisch	.10
398	Eddie Murray	.40
399	Joe Randa	.10
400	Scott Sanders	.10
401	John Valentin	.10
402	Todd Jones	.10
403	Terry Adams	.10
404	Brian Hunter	.10
405	Pat Listach	.10
406	Kenny Lofton	.75
407	Hal Morris	.10
408	Ed Sprague	.10
409	Rich Becker	.10
410	Edgardo Alfonzo	.10
411	Albert Belle	1.00
412	Jeff King	.10
413	Kirt Manwaring	.10
414	Jason Schmidt	.10
415	Allen Watson	.10
416	Lee Tinsley	.10
417	Brett Butler	.10
418	Carlos Garcia	.10
419	Mark Lemke	.10
420	Jaime Navarro	.10
421	David Segui	.10
422	Ruben Sierra	.10
423	B.J. Surhoff	.10
424	Julian Tavarez	.10
425	Billy Taylor	.10
426	Ken Caminiti	.25
427	Chuck Carr	.10
428	Benji Gil	.10
429	Terry Mulholland	.10
430	Mike Stanton	.10
431	Wil Cordero	.10
432	Chili Davis	.10
433	Mariano Duncan	.10
434	Orlando Merced	.10
435	Kent Mercker	.10
436	John Olerud	.10
437	Quilvio Veras	.10
438	Mike Fetters	.10

#	Player	Price
439	Glenallen Hill	.10
440	Bill Swift	.10
441	Tim Wakefield	.10
442	Pedro Astacio	.10
443	Vinny Castilla	.10
444	Doug Drabek	.10
445	Alan Embree	.10
446	Lee Smith	.10
447	Darryl Hamilton	.10
448	Brian McRae	.10
449	Mike Timlin	.10
450	Bob Wickman	.10
451	Jason Dickson	.20
452	Chad Curtis	.10
453	Mark Leiter	.10
454	Damon Berryhill	.10
455	Kevin Orie	.10
456	Dave Burba	.10
457	Chris Holt	.10
458	*Ricky Ledee*	1.50
459	Mike Devereaux	.10
460	Pokey Reese	.10
461	Tim Raines	.10
462	Ryan Jones	.10
463	Shane Mack	.10
464	Darren Dreifort	.10
465	Mark Parent	.10
466	Mark Portugal	.10
467	Dante Powell	.20
468	Craig Grebeck	.10
469	Ron Villone	.10
470	Dmitri Young	.10
471	Shannon Stewart	.10
472	Rick Helling	.10
473	Bill Haselman	.10
474	Albie Lopez	.10
475	Glendon Rusch	.10
476	Derrick May	.10
477	Chad Ogea	.10
478	Kirk Reuter	.10
479	Chris Hammond	.10
480	Russ Johnson	.10
481	James Mouton	.10
482	Mike Macfarlane	.10
483	Scott Ruffcorn	.10
484	Jeff Frye	.10
485	Richie Sexson	.10
486	*Emil Brown*	.20
487	Desi Wilson	.10
488	Brent Gates	.10
489	Tony Graffanino	.10
490	Dan Miceli	.10
491	*Orlando Cabrera*	.50
492	*Tony Womack*	.25
493	Jerome Walton	.10
494	Mark Thompson	.10
495	Jose Guillen	1.00
496	Willie Blair	.10
497	T.J. Staton	.10
498	Scott Kamieniecki	.10
499	Vince Coleman	.10
500	Jeff Abbott	.10
501	Chris Widger	.10
502	Kevin Tapani	.10
503	Carlos Castillo	.10
504	Luis Gonzalez	.10
505	Tim Belcher	.10
506	Armando Reynoso	.10
507	Jamie Moyer	.10
508	*Randall Simon*	.10
509	Vladimir Guerrero	1.50
510	Wady Almonte	.10
511	Dustin Hermanson	.10
512	*Deivi Cruz*	.10
513	Luis Alicea	.10
514	*Felix Heredia*	.25
515	Don Slaught	.10
516	Shigetosi Hasegawa	.10
517	Matt Walbeck	.10
518	David Arias	.10
519	*Brady Raggio*	.10
520	Rudy Pemberton	.10
521	Wayne Kirby	.10
522	Calvin Maduro	.10
523	Mark Lewis	.10
524	Mike Jackson	.10
525	Sid Fernandez	.10
526	Mike Bielecki	.10
527	*Bubba Trammell*	1.00
528	*Brent Brede*	.10
529	Matt Morris	.15
530	Joe Borowski	.10
531	Orlando Miller	.10
532	Jim Bullinger	.10
533	Robert Person	.10
534	Doug Glanville	.10
535	Terry Pendleton	.10
536	Jorge Posada	.10
537	*Marc Sagmoen*	.10
538	*Fernando Tatis*	1.50
539	Aaron Sele	.10

#	Player	Price
540	Brian Banks	.10
541	Derrek Lee	.10
542	John Wasdin	.10
543	*Justin Towle*	.10
544	Pat Cline	.10
545	Dave Magadan	.10
546	Jeff Blauser	.10
547	Phil Nevin	.10
548	Todd Walker	.75
549	Elieser Marrero	.10
550	Bartolo Colon	.10
551	*Jose Cruz, Jr.*	8.00
552	Todd Dunwoody	.10
553	*Hideki Irabu*	2.00

1997 Ultra Gold Medallion Edition

A new concept in parallel editions was debuted by Ultra in Series I. While sharing the card numbers with regular-issue Ultra cards, the Gold Medallion Edition features a "G" prefix to the card number and gold-foil highlights on front. Unlike past parallels, however, the '97 Ultra Gold Medallion and Platinum Medallion inserts share a photograph which is entirely different from the regular Ultra base cards. Gold Medallion Edition cards are identified as such in the lower-right corner and were inserted at a rate of one per pack.

	MT
Complete Set (553):	175.00
Common Player:	.25
Complete Gold Medallion Set (553):	220.00
Gold Stars:	3x to 6x
Gold Rks & Young Stars:	2x to 4x

1997 Ultra Platinum Medallion Edition

A new concept in parallel editions was debuted by Ultra in Series I. While sharing the card numbers with regular-issue Ultra cards, the Platinum Medallion Edition features a "P" prefix to the card number and holographic-foil highlights on front. Unlike past parallels, however, the '97 Ultra Gold Medallion and Platinum Medallion inserts share a photograph which is entirely different from the regular Ultra base cards are identified as such in the lower-right corner and were inserted at a rate of one per 100 packs.

	MT
Complete Set (553):	3,000.00
Common Player:	3.00
Platinum Stars:	35x to 60x
Platinum Rks & Young Stars:	20x to 35x

1997 Ultra Baseball "Rules"!

Baseball Rules was a 10-card insert that was found only in retail packs at a rate of one per 36 packs. The cards are die-cut with a player in front of a mound of baseballs with embossed seams on the front, while each card back explains a baseball term or rule.

		MT
Complete Set (10):		100.00
Common Player:		3.00
1	Barry Bonds	6.00
2	Ken Griffey Jr.	25.00
3	Derek Jeter	10.00
4	Chipper Jones	15.00
5	Greg Maddux	15.00
6	Mark McGwire	9.00
7	Troy Percival	3.00
8	Mike Piazza	15.00
9	Cal Ripken Jr.	20.00
10	Frank Thomas	25.00

1997 Ultra Checklists

There were 10 Checklist cards in Ultra Baseball covering all regular-issue cards and inserts. The front of the card features a superstar, while the back contains a portion of the set checklist. The cards contain the word CHECKLIST in bold, all caps across the bottom in silver foil.

		MT
Complete Set (10):		8.00
Common Player:		.25
1	Dante Bichette	.25
2	Barry Bonds	.50
3	Ken Griffey Jr.	2.00
4	Greg Maddux	1.25
5	Mark McGwire	.75
6	Mike Piazza	1.25
7	Cal Ripken Jr.	1.50
8	John Smoltz	.25
9	Sammy Sosa	.40
10	Frank Thomas	2.00

1997 Ultra II Checklists

This 10-card insert features photos of some of the game's top stars on the fronts, with checklist information on the back. Fronts feature the word "Checklist" in large foil-stamped letters. Odds of finding a card were 1:4 packs.

		MT
Complete Set (10):		10.00
Common Player:		.25
1	Andruw Jones	1.25
2	Ken Griffey Jr.	2.00
3	Frank Thomas	2.00
4	Alex Rodriguez	2.00
5	Cal Ripken Jr.	1.50
6	Mike Piazza	1.25
7	Greg Maddux	1.25
8	Chipper Jones	1.25
9	Derek Jeter	1.25
10	Juan Gonzalez	1.00

1997 Ultra Diamond Producers

Printed on a flannel-like material, this 12-card insert contains some of the most consistent producers in baseball. This insert was the most difficult insert in Ultra to pull from packs, with a ratio of one per 288.

		MT
Complete Set (12):		700.00
Common Player:		15.00
1	Jeff Bagwell	50.00
2	Barry Bonds	30.00
3	Ken Griffey Jr.	140.00
4	Chipper Jones	80.00
5	Kenny Lofton	30.00
6	Greg Maddux	80.00
7	Mark McGwire	50.00
8	Mike Piazza	80.00
9	Cal Ripken Jr.	100.00
10	Alex Rodriguez	120.00
11	Frank Thomas	120.00
12	Matt Williams	15.00

1997 Ultra Double Trouble

Double Trouble is a 20-card, team color coded set pairing two stars from the same team on a horizontal front. These inserts were found every four packs.

		MT
Complete Set (20):		20.00
Common Player:		.50
1	Roberto Alomar, Cal Ripken Jr.	2.50
2	Mo Vaughn, Jose Canseco	1.00
3	Jim Edmonds, Tim Salmon	.50
4	Harold Baines, Frank Thomas	3.00
5	Albert Belle, Kenny Lofton	1.25
6	Chuck Knoblauch, Marty Cordova	.50
7	Andy Pettitte, Derek Jeter	2.00
8	Jason Giambi, Mark McGwire	1.50
9	Ken Griffey Jr., Alex Rodriguez	4.00
10	Juan Gonzalez, Will Clark	2.00
11	Greg Maddux, Chipper Jones	2.50
12	Mark Grace, Sammy Sosa	.50
13	Dante Bichette, Andres Galarraga	.50
14	Jeff Bagwell, Derek Bell	1.50
15	Hideo Nomo, Mike Piazza	2.00
16	Henry Rodriguez, Moises Alou	.50
17	Rey Ordonez, Alex Ochoa	.75
18	Ray Lankford, Ron Gant	.50
19	Tony Gwynn, Rickey Henderson	1.50
20	Barry Bonds, Matt Williams	1.00

1997 Ultra Fielder's Choice

Fielder's Choice highlights 18 of the top defensive players in baseball on leather, horizontal cards. Fielder's Choice inserts were found every 144 packs.

		MT
Complete Set (18):		300.00
Common Player:		10.00
1	Roberto Alomar	15.00
2	Jeff Bagwell	35.00
3	Wade Boggs	10.00
4	Barry Bonds	20.00
5	Mark Grace	10.00
6	Ken Griffey Jr.	80.00
7	Marquis Grissom	10.00
8	Charles Johnson	10.00
9	Chuck Knoblauch	10.00
10	Barry Larkin	15.00
11	Kenny Lofton	20.00
12	Greg Maddux	50.00
13	Raul Mondesi	15.00
14	Rey Ordonez	15.00
15	Cal Ripken Jr.	60.00
16	Alex Rodriguez	80.00
17	Ivan Rodriguez	12.00
18	Matt Williams	10.00

1997 Ultra Golden Prospects

This 10-card set was exclusive to hobby shop packs and highlighted the top young players in baseball. Cards were inserted 1:4 packs.

		MT
Complete Set (10):		8.00
Common Player:		.25
1	Andruw Jones	3.00
2	Vladimir Guerrero	2.00
3	Todd Walker	.75
4	Karim Garcia	.25
5	Kevin Orie	.25
6	Brian Giles	.25
7	Jason Dickson	.50
8	Jose Guillen	1.00
9	Ruben Rivera	.50
10	Derek Lee	.50

1997 Ultra Hitting Machines

This 36-card insert was only found in hobby packs and showcases the game's top hitters. Cards were inserted at a ratio of 1:36 packs.

		MT
Complete Set (18):		220.00
Common Player:		3.00
1	Andruw Jones	18.00
2	Ken Griffey Jr.	30.00
3	Frank Thomas	30.00
4	Alex Rodriguez	30.00
5	Cal Ripken Jr.	25.00
6	Mike Piazza	18.00
7	Derek Jeter	18.00
8	Albert Belle	10.00
9	Tony Gwynn	12.00
10	Jeff Bagwell	12.00
11	Mark McGwire	10.00
12	Kenny Lofton	8.00
13	Manny Ramirez	8.00
14	Roberto Alomar	6.00
15	Ryne Sandberg	8.00
16	Eddie Murray	4.00
17	Sammy Sosa	3.00
18	Ken Caminiti	3.00

1997 Ultra Homerun Kings

HR Kings are printed on clear plastic with transparent refractive holofoil crowns and other objects in the plastic. The backs of the cards contain a white cutout of the player, with words contained in the white. HR Kings were exclusive to hobby packs, appearing one per 36.

		MT
Complete Set (12):		100.00
Common Player:		3.00
1	Albert Belle	8.00
2	Barry Bonds	6.00
3	Juan Gonzalez	10.00
4	Ken Griffey Jr.	25.00
5	Todd Hundley	3.00
6	Ryan Klesko	5.00
7	Mark McGwire	9.00
8	Mike Piazza	15.00
9	Sammy Sosa	3.00
10	Frank Thomas	25.00
11	Mo Vaughn	8.00
12	Matt Williams	3.00

1997 Ultra Leather Shop

Baseball's best fielders are honored in this 12-card hobby-exclusive insert. Cards were inserted at a ratio of 1:6 packs and feature an embossed grain-like finish on the fronts.

		MT
Complete Set (12):		20.00
Common Player:		.50
1	Ken Griffey Jr.	5.00
2	Alex Rodriguez	5.00
3	Cal Ripken Jr.	4.00
4	Derek Jeter	3.00
5	Juan Gonzalez	2.00
6	Tony Gwynn	2.00
7	Jeff Bagwell	2.00
8	Roberto Alomar	1.00
9	Ryne Sandberg	1.25
10	Ken Caminiti	.75
11	Kenny Lofton	1.25
12	John Smoltz	.50

1997 Ultra Power Plus

Power Plus was a 12-card insert utilizing silver rainbow holofoil in the background, with the featured player in the foreground. The insert captures power hitters that also excel in other areas of the game. Power Plus inserts can be found every 24 packs of Ultra I.

		MT
Complete Set (12):		100.00
Common Player:		2.50
1	Jeff Bagwell	8.00
2	Barry Bonds	5.00
3	Juan Gonzalez	8.00
4	Ken Griffey Jr.	18.00
5	Chipper Jones	12.00
6	Mark McGwire	7.00
7	Mike Piazza	12.00
8	Cal Ripken Jr.	15.00
9	Alex Rodriguez	18.00
10	Sammy Sosa	2.50
11	Frank Thomas	18.00
12	Matt Williams	3.00

1997 Ultra II Power Plus

Similar in design to the Power Plus insert in Series I, this 12-card insert salutes the game's top sluggers

and was found only in hobby packs. Cards were inserted at a ratio of 1:8 packs.

		MT
Complete Set (12):		40.00
Common Player:		.75
1	Ken Griffey Jr.	7.00
2	Frank Thomas	7.00
3	Alex Rodriguez	7.00
4	Cal Ripken Jr.	5.00
5	Mike Piazza	4.00
6	Chipper Jones	4.00
7	Albert Belle	2.50
8	Juan Gonzalez	3.00
9	Jeff Bagwell	3.00
10	Mark McGwire	2.50
11	Mo Vaughn	1.75
12	Barry Bonds	1.75

1997 Ultra RBI Kings

Ten different players are featured in RBI Kings, which contain a metallic paisley background, with an English shield of armor and latin words in the background. RBI Kings were inserted every 18 packs of Series I.

		MT
Complete Set (10):		50.00
Common Player:		2.00
1	Jeff Bagwell	6.00
2	Albert Belle	5.00
3	Dante Bichette	2.00
4	Barry Bonds	4.00
5	Jay Buhner	2.00
6	Juan Gonzalez	6.00
7	Ken Griffey Jr.	15.00
8	Sammy Sosa	2.00
9	Frank Thomas	15.00
10	Mo Vaughn	5.00

1997 Ultra Rookie Reflections

Rookie Reflections features 10 of the 1996 season's top first-year stars. Cards are inserted every four packs and feature a unique black and silver foil design.

		MT
Complete Set (10):		10.00
Common Player:		.25
1	James Baldwin	.25
2	Jermaine Dye	.75

3	Darin Erstad	3.00
4	Todd Hollandsworth	.25
5	Derek Jeter	4.00
6	Jason Kendall	.50
7	Alex Ochoa	.25
8	Rey Ordonez	.50
9	Edgar Renteria	.75
10	Scott Rolen	2.00

1997 Ultra Season Crowns

Season Crowns were found at a rate of one per eight packs of Ultra I Baseball. This etched, silver-foil insert contained 12 statistical leaders and award winners from the 1996 season.

		MT
Complete Set (12):		25.00
Common Player:		.75
1	Albert Belle	2.50
2	Dante Bichette	.50
3	Barry Bonds	2.00
4	Kenny Lofton	2.00
5	Edgar Martinez	.50
6	Mark McGwire	2.50
7	Andy Pettitte	2.00
8	Mike Piazza	5.00
9	Alex Rodriguez	8.00
10	John Smoltz	.50
11	Sammy Sosa	.75
12	Frank Thomas	8.00

1997 Ultra Starring Role

Another hobby-exclusive insert, these 12 cards salute baseball's clutch performers and were found 1:288 packs.

		MT
Complete Set (12):		850.00
Common Player:		15.00
1	Andruw Jones	75.00
2	Ken Griffey Jr.	140.00
3	Frank Thomas	120.00
4	Alex Rodriguez	120.00
5	Cal Ripken Jr.	100.00
6	Mike Piazza	75.00
7	Greg Maddux	75.00
8	Chipper Jones	75.00
9	Derek Jeter	75.00
10	Juan Gonzalez	60.00
11	Albert Belle	40.00
12	Tony Gwynn	50.00

1997 Ultra The Fame Game

This eight-card hobby-exclusive insert showcases players who have displayed Hall of Fame potential. Cards were inserted 1:8 packs.

		MT
Complete Set (18):		65.00
Common Player:		.75
1	Ken Griffey Jr.	10.00
2	Frank Thomas	10.00
3	Alex Rodriguez	10.00
4	Cal Ripken Jr.	8.00
5	Mike Piazza	6.00
6	Greg Maddux	6.00
7	Derek Jeter	6.00

8	Jeff Bagwell	4.00
9	Juan Gonzalez	4.00
10	Albert Belle	0.00
11	Tony Gwynn	4.00
12	Mark McGwire	3.00
13	Andy Pettitte	2.50
14	Kenny Lofton	2.50
15	Roberto Alomar	2.00
16	Ryne Sandberg	2.50
17	Barry Bonds	2.50
18	Eddie Murray	1.00

1997 Ultra Thunderclap

This 10-card hobby-exclusive insert showcases hitters who strike fear in opposing pitchers. Cards were inserted 1:18 packs.

		MT
Complete Set (10):		70.00
Common Player:		2.00
1	Barry Bonds	4.00
2	Mo Vaughn	4.00
3	Mark McGwire	5.00
4	Jeff Bagwell	6.00
5	Juan Gonzalez	6.00
6	Alex Rodriguez	15.00
7	Chipper Jones	9.00
8	Ken Griffey Jr.	15.00
9	Mike Piazza	9.00
10	Frank Thomas	15.00

1997 Ultra Top 30

This 30-card insert was found only in retail store packs and salutes the 30 most collectible players in the game.

Cards were inserted one per pack. A Top 30 Gold Medallion parallel set was also produced and inserted 1:18 packs.

		MT
Complete Set (30):		18.00
Common Player:		.25
Gold Medallions:		10x
1	Andruw Jones	1.50
2	Ken Griffey Jr.	2.50
3	Frank Thomas	2.50
4	Alex Rodriguez	2.50
5	Cal Ripken Jr.	2.00
6	Mike Piazza	1.50
7	Greg Maddux	1.50
8	Chipper Jones	1.50
9	Derek Jeter	1.50
10	Juan Gonzalez	1.00
11	Albert Belle	1.00
12	Tony Gwynn	1.00
13	Jeff Bagwell	1.00
14	Mark McGwire	.75
15	Andy Pettitte	.50
16	Mo Vaughn	.50
17	Kenny Lofton	.50
18	Manny Ramirez	.50
19	Roberto Alomar	.40
20	Ryne Sandberg	.50
21	Hideo Nomo	.40
22	Barry Bonds	.50
23	Eddie Murray	.30
24	Ken Caminiti	.25
25	John Smoltz	.25
26	Pat Hentgen	.25
27	Todd Hollandsworth	.25
28	Matt Williams	.30
29	Bernie Williams	.40
30	Brady Anderson	.25

1997 Leaf

Leaf produced a 200-card set for the first series in 1997. The cards featured a grey border, with the featured player in the center. The player's name, team and a Leaf logo were displayed at the bottom center with silver foil, with the team logo in the upper-right hand corner. Cards numbered 188-200 were part of a subset called Legacy Collection. Leaf was the first installment of the Fractal Matrix system, and also included the following inserts: Banner Season, Dress for Success, Get-A-Grip, Knot-hole Gang and Statistical Standouts.

		MT
Complete Set (400):		50.00
Complete Series I Set (200):		25.00
Complete Series II Set (200):		25.00
Common Player:		.10
Jackie Robinson 1948 Leaf Reprint:		60.00
Wax Box:		45.00
1	Wade Boggs	.20
2	Brian McRae	.10
3	Jeff D'Amico	.10
4	George Arias	.10
5	Billy Wagner	.10
6	Ray Lankford	.10
7	Will Clark	.25
8	Edgar Renteria	.10
9	Alex Ochoa	.10
10	Roberto Hernandez	.10
11	Joe Carter	.20
12	Gregg Jefferies	.10

13	Mark Grace	.20
14	Roberto Alomar	.75
15	Joe Randa	.10
16	Alex Rodriguez	3.00
17	Tony Gwynn	1.25
18	Steve Gibralter	.10
19	Scott Stahoviak	.10
20	Matt Williams	.25
21	Quinton McCracken	.10
22	Ugueth Urbina	.10
23	Jermaine Allensworth	.10
24	Paul Molitor	.40
25	Carlos Delgado	.15
26	Bob Abreu	.10
27	John Jaha	.10
28	Rusty Greer	.10
29	Kimera Bartee	.10
30	Ruben Rivera	.20
31	Jason Kendall	.10
32	Lance Johnson	.10
33	Robin Ventura	.10
34	Kevin Appier	.10
35	John Mabry	.10
36	Ricky Otero	.10
37	Mike Lansing	.10
38	Mark McGwire	1.00
39	Tim Naehring	.10
40	Tom Glavine	.20
41	Rey Ordonez	.15
42	Tony Clark	.50
43	Rafael Palmeiro	.20
44	Pedro Martinez	.20
45	Keith Lockhart	.10
46	Dan Wilson	.10
47	John Wetteland	.10
48	Chan Ho Park	.10
49	Gary Sheffield	.40
50	Shawn Estes	.10
51	Royce Clayton	.10
52	Jaime Navarro	.10
53	Raul Casanova	.10
54	Jeff Bagwell	1.25
55	Barry Larkin	.30
56	Charles Nagy	.10
57	Ken Caminiti	.30
58	Todd Hollandsworth	.10
59	Pat Hentgen	.10
60	Jose Valentin	.10
61	Frank Rodriguez	.10
62	Mickey Tettleton	.10
63	Marty Cordova	.10
64	Cecil Fielder	.20
65	Barry Bonds	.75
66	Scott Servais	.10
67	Ernie Young	.10
68	Wilson Alvarez	.10
69	Mike Grace	.10
70	Shane Reynolds	.10
71	Henry Rodriguez	.10
72	Eric Karros	.10
73	Mark Langston	.10
74	Scott Karl	.10
75	Trevor Hoffman	.10
76	Orel Hershiser	.10
77	John Smoltz	.20
78	Raul Mondesi	.25
79	Jeff Brantley	.10
80	Donne Wall	.10
81	Joey Cora	.10
82	Mel Rojas	.10
83	Chad Mottola	.10
84	Omar Vizquel	.10
85	Greg Maddux	2.00
86	Jamey Wright	.10
87	Chuck Finley	.10
88	Brady Anderson	.10
89	Alex Gonzalez	.10
90	Andy Benes	.10
91	Reggie Jefferson	.10
92	Paul O'Neill	.10
93	Javier Lopez	.20
94	Mark Grudzielanek	.10
95	Marc Newfield	.10
96	Kevin Ritz	.10
97	Fred McGriff	.25
98	Dwight Gooden	.10
99	Hideo Nomo	.75
100	Steve Finley	.10
101	Juan Gonzalez	1.25
102	Jay Buhner	.20
103	Paul Wilson	.10
104	Alan Benes	.10
105	Manny Ramirez	.75
106	Kevin Elster	.10
107	Frank Thomas	3.00
108	Orlando Miller	.10
109	Ramon Martinez	.10
110	Kenny Lofton	.75
111	Bernie Williams	.50
112	Robby Thompson	.10
113	Bernard Gilkey	.10

114	Ray Durham	.10
115	Jeff Cirillo	.10
116	Brian Jordan	.10
117	Rich Becker	.10
118	Al Leiter	.10
119	Mark Johnson	.10
120	Ellis Burks	.10
121	Sammy Sosa	.40
122	Willie Greene	.10
123	Michael Tucker	.10
124	Eddie Murray	.40
125	Joey Hamilton	.10
126	Antonio Osuna	.10
127	Bobby Higginson	.10
128	Tomas Perez	.10
129	Tim Salmon	.25
130	Mark Wohlers	.10
131	Charles Johnson	.10
132	Randy Johnson	.50
133	Brooks Kieschnick	.10
134	Al Martin	.10
135	Dante Bichette	.20
136	Andy Pettitte	.75
137	Jason Giambi	.10
138	James Baldwin	.10
139	Ben McDonald	.10
140	Shawn Green	.10
141	Geronimo Berroa	.10
142	Jose Offerman	.10
143	Curtis Pride	.10
144	Terrell Wade	.10
145	Ismael Valdes	.10
146	Mike Mussina	.60
147	Mariano Rivera	.20
148	Ken Hill	.10
149	Darin Erstad	1.25
150	Jay Bell	.10
151	Mo Vaughn	.75
152	Ozzie Smith	.50
153	Jose Mesa	.10
154	Osvaldo Fernandez	.10
155	Vinny Castilla	.10
156	Jason Isringhausen	.10
157	B.J. Surhoff	.10
158	Robert Perez	.10
159	Ron Coomer	.10
160	Darren Oliver	.10
161	Mike Mohler	.10
162	Russ Davis	.10
163	Bret Boone	.10
164	Ricky Bottalico	.10
165	Derek Jeter	2.00
166	Orlando Merced	.10
167	John Valentin	.10
168	Andruw Jones	2.00
169	Angel Echevarria	.10
170	Todd Walker	.75
171	Desi Relaford	.10
172	Trey Beamon	.10
173	Brian Giles	.10
174	Scott Rolen	1.25
175	Shannon Stewart	.10
176	Dmitri Young	.10
177	Justin Thompson	.10
178	Trot Nixon	.10
179	Josh Booty	.10
180	Robin Jennings	.10
181	Marvin Benard	.10
182	Luis Castillo	.25
183	Wendell Magee	.10
184	Vladimir Guerrero	1.50
185	Nomar Garciaparra	2.00
186	Ryan Hancock	.10
187	Mike Cameron	.10
188	Cal Ripken Jr. (Legacy)	1.25
189	Chipper Jones (Legacy)	1.00
190	Albert Belle (Legacy)	.60
191	Mike Piazza (Legacy)	1.00
192	Chuck Knoblauch (Legacy)	.10
193	Ken Griffey Jr. (Legacy)	1.50
194	Ivan Rodriguez (Legacy)	.25
195	Jose Canseco (Legacy)	.20
196	Ryne Sandberg (Legacy)	.35
197	Jim Thome (Legacy)	.20
198	Andy Pettitte (Checklist)	.35
199	Andruw Jones (Checklist)	.75
200	Derek Jeter (Checklist)	.60
201	Chipper Jones	2.00
202	Albert Belle	1.00
203	Mike Piazza	2.00
204	Ken Griffey Jr.	3.00
205	Ryne Sandberg	.75
206	Jose Canseco	.25
207	Chili Davis	.10
208	Roger Clemens	1.00
209	Deion Sanders	.25
210	Darryl Hamilton	.10
211	Jermaine Dye	.10
212	Matt Williams	.25
213	Kevin Elster	.10
214	John Wetteland	.10

215	Garret Anderson	.10
216	Kevin Brown	.10
217	Matt Lawton	.10
218	Cal Ripken Jr.	2.50
219	Moises Alou	.10
220	Chuck Knoblauch	.20
221	Ivan Rodriguez	.60
222	Travis Fryman	.10
223	Jim Thome	.40
224	Eddie Murray	.35
225	Eric Young	.10
226	Ron Gant	.10
227	Tony Phillips	.10
228	Reggie Sanders	.10
229	Johnny Damon	.10
230	Bill Pulsipher	.10
231	Jim Edmonds	.10
232	Melvin Nieves	.10
233	Ryan Klesko	.40
234	David Cone	.20
235	Derek Bell	.10
236	Julio Franco	.10
237	Juan Guzman	.10
238	Larry Walker	.25
239	Delino DeShields	.10
240	Troy Percival	.10
241	Andres Galarraga	.20
242	Rondell White	.15
243	John Burkett	.10
244	J.T. Snow	.10
245	Alex Fernandez	.10
246	Edgar Martinez	.10
247	Craig Biggio	.10
248	Todd Hundley	.15
249	Jimmy Key	.10
250	Cliff Floyd	.10
251	Jeff Conine	.10
252	Curt Schilling	.10
253	Jeff King	.10
254	Tino Martinez	.20
255	Carlos Baerga	.10
256	Jeff Fassero	.10
257	Dean Palmer	.10
258	Robb Nen	.10
259	Sandy Alomar Jr.	.10
260	Carlos Perez	.10
261	Rickey Henderson	.10
262	Bobby Bonilla	.10
263	Darren Daulton	.10
264	Jim Leyritz	.10
265	Dennis Martinez	.10
266	Butch Huskey	.10
267	Joe Vitiello	.10
268	Steve Trachsel	.10
269	Glenallen Hill	.10
270	Terry Steinbach	.10
271	Mark McLemore	.10
272	Devon White	.10
273	Jeff Kent	.10
274	Tim Raines	.10
275	Carlos Garcia	.10
276	Hal Morris	.10
277	Gary Gaetti	.10
278	John Olerud	.10
279	Wally Joyner	.10
280	Brian Hunter	.10
281	Steve Karsay	.10
282	Denny Neagle	.10
283	Jose Herrera	.10
284	Todd Stottlemyre	.10
285	Bip Roberts	.10
286	Kevin Seitzer	.10
287	Benji Gil	.10
288	Dennis Eckersley	.10
289	Brad Ausmus	.10
290	Otis Nixon	.10
291	Darryl Strawberry	.10
292	Marquis Grissom	.10
293	Darryl Kile	.10
294	Quilvio Veras	.10
295	Tom Goodwin	.10
296	Benito Santiago	.10
297	Mike Bordick	.10
298	Roberto Kelly	.10
299	David Justice	.20
300	Carl Everett	.10
301	Mark Whiten	.10
302	Aaron Sele	.10
303	Darren Dreifort	.10
304	Bobby Jones	.10
305	Fernando Vina	.10
306	Ed Sprague	.10
307	Andy Ashby	.10
308	Tony Fernandez	.10
309	Roger Pavlik	.10
310	Mark Clark	.10
311	Mariano Duncan	.10
312	Tyler Houston	.10
313	Eric Davis	.10
314	Greg Vaughn	.10
315	David Segui	.10

#	Player	MT
316	Dave Nilsson	.10
317	F.P. Santangelo	.10
318	Wilton Guerrero	.10
319	Jose Guillen	1.00
320	Kevin Orie	.10
321	Derrek Lee	.10
322	Bubba Trammell	.75
323	Pokey Reese	.10
324	Hideki Irabu	2.00
325	Scott Spiezio	.10
326	Bartolo Colon	.10
327	Damon Mashore	.10
328	Ryan McGuire	.10
329	Chris Carpenter	.10
330	Jose Cruz, Jr.	6.00
331	Todd Greene	.10
332	Brian Moehler	.10
333	Mike Sweeney	.10
334	Neifi Perez	.10
335	Matt Morris	.10
336	Marvin Benard	.10
337	Karim Garcia	.10
338	Jason Dickson	.10
339	Brant Brown	.10
340	Jeff Suppan	.10
341	Deivi Cruz	.10
342	Antone Williamson	.10
343	Curtis Goodwin	.10
344	Brooks Kieschnick	.10
345	Tony Womack	.10
346	Rudy Pemberton	.10
347	Todd Dunwoody	.10
348	Frank Thomas (Legacy)	1.50
349	Andruw Jones (Legacy)	1.00
350	Alex Rodriguez (Legacy)	1.25
351	Greg Maddux (Legacy)	1.00
352	Jeff Bagwell (Legacy)	.75
353	Juan Gonzalez (Legacy)	.75
354	Barry Bonds (Legacy)	.40
355	Mark McGwire (Legacy)	.50
356	Tony Gwynn (Legacy)	.75
357	Gary Sheffield (Legacy)	.20
358	Derek Jeter (Legacy)	1.00
359	Manny Ramirez (Legacy)	.40
360	Hideo Nomo (Legacy)	.30
361	Sammy Sosa (Legacy)	.20
362	Paul Molitor (Legacy)	.20
363	Kenny Lofton (Legacy)	.40
364	Eddie Murray (Legacy)	.20
365	Barry Larkin (Legacy)	.10
366	Roger Clemens (Legacy)	.50
367	John Smoltz (Legacy)	.10
368	Alex Rodriguez (Gamers)	1.25
369	Frank Thomas (Gamers)	1.50
370	Cal Ripken Jr. (Gamers)	1.25
371	Ken Griffey Jr. (Gamers)	1.50
372	Greg Maddux (Gamers)	1.00
373	Mike Piazza (Gamers)	1.00
374	Chipper Jones (Gamers)	1.00
375	Albert Belle (Gamers)	.50
376	Chuck Knoblauch (Gamers)	.15
377	Brady Anderson (Gamers)	.10
378	David Justice (Gamers)	.10
379	Randy Johnson (Gamers)	.20
380	Wade Boggs (Gamers)	.15
381	Kevin Brown (Gamers)	.10
382	Tom Glavine (Gamers)	.10
383	Raul Mondesi (Gamers)	.10
384	Ivan Rodriguez (Gamers)	.30
385	Larry Walker (Gamers)	.10
386	Bernie Williams (Gamers)	.00
387	Rusty Greer (Gamers)	.10
388	Rafael Palmeiro (Gamers)	.10
389	Matt Williams (Gamers)	.15
390	Eric Young (Gamers)	.10
391	Fred McGriff (Gamers)	.10
392	Ken Caminiti (Gamers)	.10
393	Roberto Alomar (Gamers)	.30
394	Brian Jordan (Gamers)	.10
395	Mark Grace (Gamers)	.10
396	Jim Edmonds (Gamers)	.10
397	Deion Sanders (Gamers)	.10
398	Checklist (Vladimir Guerrero)	.75
399	Checklist (Darin Erstad)	.60
400	Checklist (Nomar Garciaparra)	.75

1997 Leaf Fractal Matrix

Leaf introduced the Fractal Matrix system, a 200-card set broken down into three colors and three unique die-cuts for a parallel set. There were two Fractures, with the first breaking the cards down into colors only (40 Golds, 60 Silvers and 100 Bronze), and the second Fracture breaking the cards down into color and die-cuts. The Axis-X included five Golds, 20 Silver and 75 Bronze. Axis-Y had 10 Gold, 30 Silver and 20 Bronze, while Axis-Z included 25 Gold, 10 Silver and five Bronze. No actual production numbers or insert ratios were given for either Fracture.

#	Card	MT
	Common Bronze:	2.00
	Common Silver:	4.00
	Common Gold Z-Axis:	10.00
	Common Gold Y-Axis:	20.00
	Common Gold X-Axis:	40.00
1	Wade Boggs G/Y	35.00
2	Brian McRae B/Y	2.00
3	Jeff D'Amico B/Y	2.00
4	George Arias S/Y	4.00
5	Billy Wagner S/Y	4.00
6	Ray Lankford B/Z	2.00
7	Will Clark S/Y	10.00
8	Edgar Renteria S/Y	4.00
9	Alex Ochoa S/Y	4.00
11	Joe Carter S/Y	6.00
12	Gregg Jefferies B/Y	2.00
13	Mark Grace S/Y	8.00
14	Roberto Alomar G/Y	50.00
15	Joe Randa B/X	2.00
16	Alex Rodriguez G/Z	125.00
17	Tony Gwynn G/Z	75.00
18	Steve Gibralter B/Y	2.00
19	Scott Stahoviak B/X	2.00
20	Matt Williams S/Z	15.00
21	Quinton McCracken B/Y	2.00
22	Ugueth Urbina B/X	2.00
23	Jermaine Allensworth S/X	6.00
24	Paul Molitor G/Y	75.00
25	Carlos Delgado S/Y	8.00
26	Bob Abreu S/Y	6.00
27	John Jaha S/Y	6.00
28	Rusty Greer S/Z	4.00
29	Kimera Bartee B/X	2.00
30	Ruben Rivera S/Y	6.00
31	Jason Kendall S/Y	6.00
32	Lance Johnson B/X	2.00
33	Robin Ventura B/Y	2.00
34	Kevin Appier S/X	4.00
35	John Mabry S/Y	4.00
36	Ricky Otero B/X	2.00
37	Mike Lansing B/X	2.00
38	Mark McGwire G/Z	60.00
39	Tim Naehring B/X	2.00
40	Tom Glavine S/Z	6.00
41	Rey Ordonez S/Y	6.00
42	Tony Clark S/Y	20.00
43	Rafael Palmeiro S/Z	10.00
44	Pedro Martinez B/X	4.00
45	Keith Lockhart B/X	2.00
46	Dan Wilson B/Y	2.00
47	John Wetteland B/Y	2.00
48	Chan Ho Park B/X	2.00
49	Gary Sheffield G/Z	25.00
50	Shawn Estes B/X	2.00
51	Royce Clayton B/X	2.00
52	Jaime Navarro B/X	2.00
53	Raul Casanova B/X	2.00
54	Jeff Bagwell G/Z	60.00
55	Barry Larkin G/X	40.00
56	Charles Nagy B/Y	2.00
57	Ken Caminiti G/Y	40.00
58	Todd Hollandsworth S/Z	4.00
59	Pat Hentgen S/X	4.00
60	Jose Valentin B/X	2.00
61	Frank Rodriguez B/X	2.00
62	Mickey Tettleton B/X	2.00
63	Marty Cordova G/X	30.00
64	Cecil Fielder S/X	8.00
65	Barry Bonds G/Z	40.00
66	Scott Servais B/X	2.00
67	Ernie Young B/X	2.00
68	Wilson Alvarez B/X	2.00
69	Mike Grace B/X	2.00
70	Shane Reynolds S/Y	6.00
71	Henry Rodriguez S/Y	4.00
72	Eric Karros B/X	2.00
73	Mark Langston B/X	2.00
74	Scott Karl B/X	2.00
75	Trevor Hoffman B/X	2.00
76	Orel Hershiser S/X	4.00
77	John Smoltz G/Y	30.00
78	Raul Mondesi G/Z	25.00
79	Jeff Brantley B/X	2.00
80	Donne Wall B/X	2.00
81	Joey Cora B/X	2.00
82	Mel Rojas B/X	2.00
83	Chad Mottola B/X	2.00
84	Omar Vizquel B/X	2.00
85	Greg Maddux G/Z	120.00
86	Jamey Wright S/Y	6.00
87	Chuck Finley B/X	2.00
88	Brady Anderson G/Y	20.00
89	Alex Gonzalez S/X	6.00
90	Andy Benes B/X	2.00
91	Reggie Jefferson B/X	2.00
92	Paul O'Neill B/Y	4.00
93	Javier Lopez S/X	8.00
94	Mark Grudzielanek S/X	6.00
95	Marc Newfield B/X	2.00
96	Kevin Ritz B/X	2.00
97	Fred McGriff G/Y	25.00
98	Dwight Gooden S/X	6.00
99	Hideo Nomo S/Y	30.00
100	Steve Finley B/X	2.00
101	Juan Gonzalez G/Z	75.00
102	Jay Buhner S/Z	8.00
103	Paul Wilson S/Y	4.00
104	Alan Benes B/Y	4.00
105	Manny Ramirez G/Z	30.00
106	Kevin Elster B/X	2.00
107	Frank Thomas G/Z	160.00
108	Orlando Miller B/X	2.00
109	Ramon Martinez B/X	4.00
110	Kenny Lofton G/Z	45.00
111	Bernie Williams G/Z	50.00
112	Robby Thompson B/X	2.00
113	Bernard Gilkey B/Z	2.00
114	Ray Durham B/X	2.00
115	Jeff Cirillo S/Z	4.00
116	Brian Jordan G/Z	10.00
117	Rich Becker S/Y	4.00
118	Al Leiter B/X	2.00
119	Mark Johnson B/X	2.00
120	Ellis Burks B/Y	4.00
121	Sammy Sosa G/Z	30.00
122	Willie Greene B/X	2.00
123	Michael Tucker B/X	2.00
124	Eddie Murray G/Y	40.00
125	Joey Hamilton S/Y	4.00
126	Antonio Osuna B/X	2.00
127	Bobby Higginson S/Y	6.00
128	Tomas Perez B/X	2.00
129	Tim Salmon G/Z	20.00
130	Mark Wohlers B/X	2.00
131	Charles Johnson S/X	4.00
132	Randy Johnson S/Y	20.00
133	Brooks Kieschnick S/X	6.00
134	Al Martin S/Y	4.00
135	Dante Bichette B/X	4.00
136	Andy Pettitte G/Z	45.00
137	Jason Giambi G/Y	20.00
138	James Baldwin S/X	4.00
139	Ben McDonald B/X	2.00
140	Shawn Green S/X	4.00
141	Geronimo Berroa B/Y	2.00
142	Jose Offerman B/X	2.00
143	Curtis Pride B/X	2.00
144	Terrell Wade B/X	2.00
145	Ismael Valdes S/X	4.00
146	Mike Mussina S/Y	25.00
147	Mariano Rivera S/X	10.00
148	Ken Hill B/Y	2.00
149	Darin Erstad G/Z	75.00
150	Jay Bell B/X	2.00
151	Mo Vaughn G/Z	40.00
152	Ozzie Smith G/Y	60.00
153	Jose Mesa B/X	2.00
154	Osvaldo Fernandez B/X	2.00
155	Vinny Castilla B/Y	2.00
156	Jason Isringhausen S/Y	4.00
157	B.J. Surhoff B/X	2.00
158	Robert Perez B/X	2.00
159	Ron Coomer B/X	2.00
160	Darren Oliver B/X	2.00
161	Mike Mohler B/X	2.00
162	Russ Davis B/X	2.00
163	Bret Boone B/X	2.00
164	Ricky Bottalico D/X	2.00
165	Derek Jeter G/Z	100.00
166	Orlando Merced B/X	2.00
167	John Valentin D/X	2.00
168	Andruw Jones G/Z	100.00
169	Angel Echevarria B/X	2.00
170	Todd Walker G/Z	30.00
171	Desi Relaford B/Y	2.00
172	Trey Beamon S/X	4.00
173	Brian Giles S/Y	4.00
174	Scott Rolen G/Z	75.00
175	Shannon Stewart S/Z	4.00
176	Dmitri Young G/Z	10.00
177	Justin Thompson B/Y	2.00
178	Trot Nixon S/Y	4.00
179	Josh Booty S/Y	4.00
180	Robin Jennings B/X	2.00
181	Marvin Benard B/X	2.00
182	Luis Castillo B/Y	2.00
183	Wendell Magee B/X	2.00
184	Vladimir Guerrero G/X	150.00
185	Nomar Garciaparra G/X	120.00
186	Ryan Hancock B/X	2.00
187	Mike Cameron S/X	12.00
188	Cal Ripken Jr. B/Z (Legacy)	30.00
189	Chipper Jones S/Z (Legacy)	50.00
190	Albert Belle S/Z (Legacy)	25.00
191	Mike Piazza B/Z (Legacy)	25.00
192	Chuck Knoblauch S/Y (Legacy)	12.00
193	Ken Griffey Jr. B/Z (Legacy)	40.00
194	Ivan Rodriguez G/Z (Legacy)	30.00
195	Jose Canseco S/X (Legacy)	20.00
196	Ryne Sandberg S/X (Legacy)	40.00
197	Jim Thome G/Y (Legacy)	40.00
198	Checklist (Andy Pettitte B/Y)	12.00
199	Checklist (Andruw Jones B/Y)	25.00
200	Checklist (Derek Jeter S/Y)	60.00
201	Chipper Jones B/X	120.00
202	Albert Belle G/Y	60.00
203	Mike Piazza G/Y	100.00
204	Ken Griffey Jr. G/X	350.00
205	Ryne Sandberg G/Z	25.00
206	Jose Canseco S/Y	8.00
207	Chili Davis B/X	2.00
208	Roger Clemens G/Z	30.00
209	Deion Sanders G/Z	15.00
210	Darryl Hamilton B/X	2.00
211	Jermaine Dye S/X	4.00
212	Matt Williams G/Y	25.00
213	Kevin Elster B/X	2.00
214	John Wetteland S/X	4.00
215	Garret Anderson G/Z	10.00
216	Kevin Brown G/Y	20.00
217	Matt Lawton S/Y	4.00
218	Cal Ripken Jr. G/X	250.00
219	Moises Alou G/Y	20.00
220	Chuck Knoblauch G/Z	15.00
221	Ivan Rodriguez G/Y	40.00
222	Travis Fryman B/Y	2.00
223	Jim Thome G/Z	20.00
224	Eddie Murray S/Z	15.00
225	Eric Young G/Z	10.00
226	Ron Gant S/X	4.00
227	Tony Phillips B/X	2.00
228	Reggie Sanders B/Y	2.00
229	Johnny Damon S/Z	4.00
230	Bill Pulsipher B/X	2.00
231	Jim Edmonds G/Z	10.00
232	Melvin Nieves B/X	2.00
233	Ryan Klesko G/X	15.00
234	David Cone S/X	4.00
235	Derek Bell B/Y	2.00
236	Julio Franco S/X	4.00
237	Juan Guzman B/X	2.00
238	Larry Walker G/Z	15.00
239	Delino DeShields B/X	2.00
240	Troy Percival B/Y	2.00
241	Andres Galarraga G/Z	12.00
242	Rondell White G/Z	10.00
243	John Burkett B/X	2.00
244	J.T. Snow B/Y	2.00
245	Alex Fernandez S/Y	4.00
246	Edgar Martinez G/Z	10.00
247	Craig Biggio G/Z	10.00
248	Todd Hundley G/Y	20.00
249	Jimmy Key S/X	4.00
250	Cliff Floyd B/Y	2.00
251	Jeff Conine B/Y	2.00
252	Curt Schilling B/X	2.00
253	Jeff King B/X	2.00
254	Tino Martinez G/Z	15.00
255	Carlos Baerga S/Y	4.00
256	Jeff Fassero B/Y	2.00
257	Dean Palmer S/Y	4.00
258	Robb Nen B/X	2.00
259	Sandy Alomar Jr. S/Y	4.00
260	Carlos Perez B/X	2.00
261	Rickey Henderson S/Y	4.00
262	Bobby Bonilla S/Y	4.00
263	Darren Daulton B/X	2.00
264	Jim Leyritz B/X	2.00
265	Dennis Martinez B/X	2.00
266	Butch Huskey B/X	2.00
267	Joe Vitiello S/X	4.00
268	Steve Trachsel B/X	2.00
269	Glenallen Hill B/X	2.00
270	Terry Steinbach B/X	2.00
271	Mark McLemore B/X	2.00
272	Devon White B/X	2.00
273	Jeff Kent B/X	2.00
274	Tim Raines B/X	2.00
275	Carlos Garcia B/X	2.00
276	Hal Morris B/X	2.00
277	Gary Gaetti B/X	2.00

		MT
278	John Olerud S/Y	4.00
279	Wally Joyner B/X	2.00
280	Brian Hunter S/X	4.00
281	Steve Karsay B/X	2.00
282	Denny Neagle S/X	4.00
283	Jose Herrera B/X	2.00
284	Todd Stottlemyre B/X	2.00
285	Bip Roberts S/X	4.00
286	Kevin Seitzer B/X	2.00
287	Benji Gil B/X	2.00
288	Dennis Eckersley S/X	4.00
289	Brad Ausmus B/X	2.00
290	Otis Nixon B/X	2.00
291	Darryl Strawberry B/X	2.00
292	Marquis Grissom S/Y	4.00
293	Darryl Kile B/X	2.00
294	Quilvio Veras B/X	2.00
295	Tom Goodwin B/X	2.00
296	Benito Santiago B/X	2.00
297	Mike Bordick B/X	2.00
298	Roberto Kelly B/X	2.00
299	David Justice G/Z	15.00
300	Carl Everett B/X	2.00
301	Mark Whiten B/X	2.00
302	Aaron Sele B/X	2.00
303	Darren Dreifort B/X	2.00
304	Bobby Jones B/X	2.00
305	Fernando Vina B/X	2.00
306	Ed Sprague B/X	2.00
307	Andy Ashby S/X	4.00
308	Tony Fernandez B/X	2.00
309	Roger Pavlik B/X	2.00
310	Mark Clark B/X	2.00
311	Mariano Duncan B/X	2.00
312	Tyler Houston B/X	2.00
313	Eric Davis S/Y	4.00
314	Greg Vaughn B/Y	2.00
315	David Segui S/Y	4.00
316	Dave Nilsson S/X	4.00
317	F.P. Santangelo S/X	4.00
318	Wilton Guerrero G/Z	10.00
319	Jose Guillen G/Z	25.00
320	Kevin Orie S/Y	4.00
321	Derrek Lee G/Z	10.00
322	Bubba Trammell S/Y	15.00
323	Pokey Reese G/Z	10.00
324	Hideki Irabu G/X	100.00
325	Scott Spiezio S/Z	4.00
326	Bartolo Colon G/Z	10.00
327	Damon Mashore S/Y	4.00
328	Ryan McGuire S/Y	4.00
329	Chris Carpenter B/X	2.00
330	Jose Cruz, Jr. G/X	275.00
331	Todd Greene S/Z	6.00
332	Brian Moehler B/X	2.00
333	Mike Sweeney B/Y	2.00
334	Neifi Perez G/Z	10.00
335	Matt Morris S/Y	4.00
336	Marvin Benard B/Y	2.00
337	Karim Garcia S/Z	4.00
338	Jason Dickson S/Y	4.00
339	Brant Brown S/Y	4.00
340	Jeff Suppan S/Z	4.00
341	Deivi Cruz B/X	2.00
342	Antone Williamson G/Z	10.00
343	Curtis Goodwin B/X	2.00
344	Brooks Kieschnick S/Y	4.00
345	Tony Womack B/X	2.00
346	Rudy Pemberton B/X	2.00
347	Todd Dunwoody B/X	2.00
348	Frank Thomas S/Y (Legacy)	60.00
349	Andruw Jones S/X (Legacy)	30.00
350	Alex Rodriguez B/Y (Legacy)	30.00
351	Greg Maddux S/Y (Legacy)	40.00
352	Jeff Bagwell B/Y (Legacy)	20.00
353	Juan Gonzalez S/Y (Legacy)	30.00
354	Barry Bonds B/Y (Legacy)	10.00
355	Mark McGwire B/Y (Legacy)	15.00
356	Tony Gwynn B/Y (Legacy)	20.00
357	Gary Sheffield B/X (Legacy)	4.00
358	Derek Jeter S/X (Legacy)	30.00
359	Manny Ramirez S/Y (Legacy)	15.00
360	Hideo Nomo G/Z (Legacy)	20.00
361	Sammy Sosa B/X (Legacy)	5.00
362	Paul Molitor S/Z (Legacy)	8.00
363	Kenny Lofton B/Y (Legacy)	10.00
364	Eddie Murray B/Y (Legacy)	6.00
365	Barry Larkin S/Z (Legacy)	6.00
366	Roger Clemens S/Y (Legacy)	20.00
367	John Smoltz B/Z (Legacy)	2.00
368	Alex Rodriguez S/X (Gamers)	40.00
369	Frank Thomas B/X (Gamers)	35.00
370	Cal Ripken Jr. S/Y (Gamers)	50.00
371	Ken Griffey Jr. S/Y (Gamers)	70.00
372	Greg Maddux B/X (Gamers)	20.00
373	Mike Piazza S/X (Gamers)	30.00
374	Chipper Jones B/Y (Gamers)	20.00
375	Albert Belle B/X (Gamers)	12.00
376	Chuck Knoblauch B/X (Gamers)	4.00
377	Brady Anderson B/Z (Gamers)	2.00
378	David Justice S/X (Gamers)	8.00
379	Randy Johnson B/Z (Gamers)	8.00
380	Wade Boggs B/X (Gamers)	4.00
381	Kevin Brown B/X (Gamers)	2.00
382	Tom Glavine G/Y (Gamers)	20.00
383	Raul Mondesi S/X	6.00
384	Ivan Rodriguez S/X (Gamers)	10.00
385	Larry Walker B/Y (Gamers)	4.00
386	Bernie Williams B/Z (Gamers)	6.00
387	Rusty Greer G/Y (Gamers)	20.00
388	Rafael Palmeiro G/Y (Gamers)	20.00
389	Matt Williams B/X (Gamers)	4.00
390	Eric Young B/X (Gamers)	2.00
391	Fred McGriff B/X (Gamers)	4.00
392	Ken Caminiti B/X (Gamers)	3.00
393	Roberto Alomar B/Z (Gamers)	8.00
394	Brian Jordan B/X (Gamers)	2.00
395	Mark Grace G/Z (Gamers)	15.00
396	Jim Edmonds B/Y (Gamers)	2.00
397	Deion Sanders S/Y	6.00
398	Checklist (Vladimir Guerrero S/Z)	20.00
399	Checklist (Darin Erstad S/Y)	20.00
400	Checklist (Nomar Garciaparra S/Z)	25.00

1997 Leaf Fractal Matrix Die-Cut

A second parallel set to the Leaf product, the Fractal Matrix Die-Cuts offer three different die-cut designs with three different styles for each. The Axis-X die-cuts consist of 100 cards (75 bronze, 20 silver and 5 gold), the Axis-Y die-cuts consist of 60 cards (30 silver, 20 bronze, 10 gold), and the Axis-Z die-cuts consist of 40 cards (25 gold, 10 silver, 5 bronze). Odds of finding any of these inserts are 1:6 packs.

		MT
	Common X-Axis:	8.00
	Common Y-Axis:	12.00
	Common Z-Axis:	20.00
1	Wade Boggs G/Y	35.00
2	Brian McRae B/Y	12.00
3	Jeff D'Amico B/Y	12.00
4	George Arias S/Y	12.00
5	Billy Wagner S/Y	12.00
6	Ray Lankford B/Z	20.00
7	Will Clark S/Y	20.00
8	Edgar Renteria S/Y	12.00
9	Alex Ochoa S/Y	12.00
10	Joe Carter S/Y	12.00
11	Gregg Jefferies B/Y	12.00
12	Mark Grace S/Y	18.00
13	Roberto Alomar G/Y	50.00
14	Joe Randa B/X	8.00
15	Alex Rodriguez G/Z	250.00
16	Tony Gwynn G/Z	150.00
17	Steve Gibralter B/Y	12.00
18	Scott Stahoviak B/X	8.00
19	Matt Williams S/Z	50.00
20	Quinton McCracken B/Y	12.00
21	Ugueth Urbina B/Y	8.00
22	Jermaine Allensworth S/X	8.00
23	Paul Molitor G/X	25.00
24	Carlos Delgado S/Y	12.00
25	Bob Abreu S/Y	12.00
26	John Jaha S/Y	12.00
27	Rusty Greer S/Z	20.00
28	Kimera Bartee B/X	8.00
29	Ruben Rivera S/Y	12.00
30	Jason Kendall S/Y	12.00
31	Lance Johnson B/X	8.00
32	Robin Ventura B/Y	12.00
33	Kevin Appier S/X	8.00
34	John Mabry S/Y	12.00
35	Ricky Otero B/X	8.00
36	Mike Lansing B/X	8.00
37	Mark McGwire G/Z	125.00
38	Tim Naehring B/X	8.00
39	Tom Glavine S/Z	25.00
40	Rey Ordonez S/Y	12.00
41	Tony Clark S/Y	40.00
42	Rafael Palmeiro S/Z	25.00
43	Pedro Martinez B/X	10.00
44	Keith Lockhart B/X	8.00
45	Dan Wilson B/Y	12.00
46	John Wetteland B/Y	12.00
47	Chan Ho Park B/X	8.00
48	Gary Sheffield G/Z	60.00
49	Shawn Estes B/X	8.00
50	Royce Clayton B/X	8.00
51	Jaime Navarro B/X	8.00
52	Raul Casanova B/X	8.00
53	Jeff Bagwell G/Z	150.00
54	Barry Larkin G/X	12.00
55	Charles Nagy B/Y	12.00
56	Ken Caminiti G/Y	40.00
57	Todd Hollandsworth S/Z	20.00
58	Pat Hentgen S/X	8.00
59	Jose Valentin B/X	8.00
60	Frank Rodriguez B/X	8.00
61	Mickey Tettleton B/X	8.00
62	Marty Cordova G/X	10.00
63	Cecil Fielder S/X	12.00
64	Barry Bonds G/Z	80.00
65	Scott Servais B/X	8.00
66	Ernie Young B/X	8.00
67	Wilson Alvarez B/X	8.00
68	Mike Grace B/X	12.00
69	Shane Reynolds S/X	8.00
70	Henry Rodriguez S/Y	12.00
71	Eric Karros B/X	8.00
72	Mark Langston B/X	8.00
73	Scott Karl B/X	8.00
74	Trevor Hoffman B/X	8.00
75	Orel Hershiser S/X	8.00
76	John Smoltz G/Y	40.00
77	Raul Mondesi G/Z	30.00
78	Jeff Brantley B/X	8.00
79	Donne Wall B/X	8.00
80	Joey Cora B/X	8.00
81	Mel Rojas B/X	8.00
82	Chad Mottola B/X	8.00
83	Omar Vizquel B/X	8.00
84	Greg Maddux G/Z	200.00
85	Jamey Wright S/Y	12.00
86	Chuck Finley B/X	8.00
87	Brady Anderson G/Y	15.00
88	Alex Gonzalez S/X	8.00
89	Andy Benes B/X	8.00
90	Reggie Jefferson B/X	8.00
91	Paul O'Neill B/Y	15.00
92	Javier Lopez S/X	12.00
93	Mark Grudzielanek S/X	8.00
94	Marc Newfield B/X	8.00
95	Kevin Ritz B/X	8.00
96	Fred McGriff G/Y	20.00
97	Dwight Gooden S/X	10.00
98	Hideo Nomo S/Y	60.00
99	Steve Finley B/X	8.00
100	Juan Gonzalez G/Z	150.00
101	Jay Buhner S/Z	25.00
102	Paul Wilson S/Y	12.00
103	Alan Benes B/Y	12.00
104	Manny Ramirez G/Z	60.00
105	Kevin Elster B/X	8.00
106	Frank Thomas G/Z	300.00
107	Orlando Miller B/X	8.00
108	Ramon Martinez B/X	8.00
109	Kenny Lofton G/Z	80.00
110	Bernie Williams G/Y	50.00
111	Robby Thompson B/X	8.00
112	Bernard Gilkey B/Z	20.00
113	Ray Durham B/X	8.00
114	Jeff Cirillo S/Z	20.00
115	Brian Jordan B/X	20.00
116	Rich Becker S/Y	12.00
117	Al Leiter B/X	8.00
118	Mark Johnson B/X	8.00
119	Ellis Burks B/Y	12.00
120	Sammy Sosa G/Z	60.00
121	Willie Greene B/X	8.00
122	Michael Tucker B/X	8.00
123	Eddie Murray G/Y	40.00
124	Joey Hamilton S/Y	12.00
125	Antonio Osuna B/X	8.00
126	Bobby Higginson S/Y	15.00
127	Tomas Perez B/X	8.00
128	Tim Salmon G/Z	30.00
129	Mark Wohlers B/X	8.00
130	Charles Johnson S/X	8.00
131	Randy Johnson S/Y	40.00
132	Brooks Kieschnick S/X	8.00
133	Al Martin S/Y	8.00
134	Dante Bichette B/X	12.00
135	Andy Pettitte G/Y	60.00
136	Jason Giambi G/Y	20.00
137	James Baldwin S/X	8.00
138	Ben McDonald B/X	8.00
139	Shawn Green S/X	8.00
140	Geronimo Berroa B/Y	12.00
141	Jose Offerman B/X	8.00
142	Curtis Pride B/X	8.00
143	Terrell Wade B/X	8.00
144	Ismael Valdes S/X	8.00
145	Mike Mussina S/Y	40.00
146	Mariano Rivera S/X	15.00
147	Ken Hill B/Y	12.00
148	Darin Erstad G/Z	100.00
149	Jay Bell B/X	8.00
150	Mo Vaughn G/Z	80.00
151	Ozzie Smith G/Y	60.00
152	Jose Mesa B/X	8.00
153	Osvaldo Fernandez B/X	8.00
154	Vinny Castilla B/Y	12.00
155	Jason Isringhausen S/Y	12.00
156	B.J. Surhoff B/X	8.00
157	Robert Perez B/X	8.00
158	Ron Coomer B/X	8.00
159	Darren Oliver B/X	8.00
160	Mike Mohler B/X	8.00
161	Russ Davis B/X	8.00
162	Bret Boone B/X	8.00
163	Ricky Bottalico B/X	8.00
164	Derek Jeter G/Z	200.00
165	Orlando Merced B/X	8.00
166	John Valentin B/X	8.00
167	Andruw Jones G/Z	200.00
168	Angel Echevarria B/X	8.00
169	Todd Walker G/Z	50.00
170	Desi Relaford B/Y	12.00
171	Trey Beamon S/X	8.00
172	Brian Giles S/Y	12.00
173	Scott Rolen G/Z	100.00
174	Shannon Stewart S/Z	20.00
175	Dmitri Young S/Z	20.00
176	Justin Thompson B/X	8.00
177	Trot Nixon S/Y	12.00
178	Josh Booty S/Y	12.00
179	Robin Jennings B/X	8.00
180	Marvin Benard B/X	8.00
181	Luis Castillo B/Y	12.00
182	Wendell Magee B/X	8.00
183	Vladimir Guerrero G/X	60.00
184	Nomar Garciaparra G/X	60.00
185	Ryan Hancock B/X	8.00
186	Mike Cameron S/X	15.00
187	Cal Ripken Jr. B/Z (Legacy)	250.00
188	Chipper Jones S/Z (Legacy)	200.00
189	Albert Belle S/Z (Legacy)	100.00
190	Mike Piazza B/Z (Legacy)	200.00
191	Chuck Knoblauch S/Y (Legacy)	20.00
192	Ken Griffey Jr. B/Z (Legacy)	300.00
193	Ivan Rodriguez G/Z (Legacy)	60.00
194	Jose Canseco S/X (Legacy)	20.00
195	Ryne Sandberg S/X (Legacy)	40.00
196	Jim Thome G/Y (Legacy)	50.00
197	Checklist (Andy Pettitte B/Y)	40.00
198	Checklist (Andruw Jones B/Y)	120.00
199	Checklist (Derek Jeter S/Y)	120.00
200	Chipper Jones G/X	60.00
201	Albert Belle G/Y	75.00

203	Mike Piazza G/Y	120.00
204	Ken Griffey Jr. G/X	100.00
205	Ryne Sandberg G/Z	75.00
206	Jose Canseco S/Y	20.00
207	Chili Davis B/X	8.00
208	Roger Clemens G/Z	100.00
209	Deion Sanders G/Z	30.00
210	Darryl Hamilton B/X	8.00
211	Jermaine Dye S/X	8.00
212	Matt Williams G/Y	35.00
213	Kevin Elster B/X	8.00
214	John Wetteland S/X	8.00
215	Garret Anderson G/Z	20.00
216	Kevin Brown G/Y	12.00
217	Matt Lawton S/Y	12.00
218	Cal Ripken Jr. G/X	75.00
219	Moises Alou G/Y	15.00
220	Chuck Knoblauch G/Z	40.00
221	Ivan Rodriguez G/Y	50.00
222	Travis Fryman B/Y	12.00
223	Jim Thome G/Z	50.00
224	Eddie Murray S/Z	50.00
225	Eric Young G/Z	20.00
226	Ron Gant S/X	8.00
227	Tony Phillips B/X	8.00
228	Reggie Sanders B/Y	12.00
229	Johnny Damon S/Z	20.00
230	Bill Pulsipher B/X	8.00
231	Jim Edmonds G/Z	25.00
232	Melvin Nieves B/X	8.00
233	Ryan Klesko G/Z	50.00
234	David Cone S/X	8.00
235	Derek Bell B/Y	12.00
236	Julio Franco S/X	8.00
237	Juan Guzman B/X	8.00
238	Larry Walker G/Z	40.00
239	Delino DeShields B/X	8.00
240	Troy Percival B/Y	12.00
241	Andres Galarraga G/Z	30.00
242	Rondell White G/Z	20.00
243	John Burkett B/X	8.00
244	J.T. Snow B/Y	12.00
245	Alex Fernandez S/Y	12.00
246	Edgar Martinez G/Z	20.00
247	Craig Biggio G/Z	20.00
248	Todd Hundley G/Y	15.00
249	Jimmy Key S/X	8.00
250	Cliff Floyd B/Y	12.00
251	Jeff Conine B/Y	12.00
252	Curt Schilling B/X	8.00
253	Jeff King B/X	8.00
254	Tino Martinez G/Z	35.00
255	Carlos Baerga S/Y	12.00
256	Jeff Fassero B/X	12.00
257	Dean Palmer S/Y	12.00
258	Robb Nen B/X	8.00
259	Sandy Alomar Jr. S/Y	12.00
260	Carlos Perez B/X	8.00
261	Rickey Henderson S/Y	12.00
262	Bobby Bonilla S/Y	12.00
263	Darren Daulton B/X	8.00
264	Jim Leyritz B/X	8.00
265	Dennis Martinez B/X	8.00
266	Butch Huskey B/X	8.00
267	Joe Vitiello S/Y	12.00
268	Steve Trachsel B/X	8.00
269	Glenallen Hill B/X	8.00
270	Terry Steinbach B/X	8.00
271	Mark McLemore B/X	8.00
272	Devon White B/X	8.00
273	Jeff Kent B/X	8.00
274	Tim Raines B/X	8.00
275	Carlos Garcia B/X	8.00
276	Hal Morris B/X	8.00
277	Gary Gaetti B/X	8.00
278	John Olerud S/Y	12.00
279	Wally Joyner B/X	8.00
280	Brian Hunter S/X	8.00
281	Steve Karsay B/X	8.00
282	Denny Neagle S/X	8.00
283	Jose Herrera B/X	8.00
284	Todd Stottlemyre B/X	8.00
285	Bip Roberts S/X	8.00
286	Kevin Seitzer B/X	8.00
287	Benji Gil B/X	8.00
288	Dennis Eckersley S/X	8.00
289	Brad Ausmus B/X	8.00
290	Otis Nixon B/X	8.00
291	Darryl Strawberry B/X	8.00
292	Marquis Grissom S/Y	12.00
293	Darryl Kile B/X	8.00
294	Quilvio Veras B/X	8.00
295	Tom Goodwin B/X	8.00
296	Benito Santiago B/X	8.00
297	Mike Bordick B/X	8.00
298	Roberto Kelly B/X	8.00
299	David Justice G/Z	30.00
300	Carl Everett B/X	8.00
301	Mark Whiten B/X	8.00
302	Aaron Sele B/X	8.00
303	Darren Dreifort B/X	8.00

304	Bobby Jones B/X	8.00
305	Fernando Vina B/X	8.00
306	Ed Sprague B/X	8.00
307	Andy Ashby S/X	8.00
308	Tony Fernandez B/X	8.00
309	Roger Pavlik B/X	8.00
310	Mark Clark B/X	8.00
311	Mariano Duncan B/X	8.00
312	Tyler Houston B/X	8.00
313	Eric Davis S/Y	12.00
314	Greg Vaughn B/Y	12.00
315	David Segui S/Y	12.00
316	Dave Nilsson S/X	8.00
317	F.P. Santangelo S/X	8.00
318	Wilton Guerrero G/Z	20.00
319	Jose Guillen G/Z	70.00
320	Kevin Orie S/Y	12.00
321	Derrek Lee G/Z	20.00
322	Bubba Trammell S/Y	50.00
323	Pokey Reese G/Z	20.00
324	Hideki Irabu G/X	50.00
325	Scott Spiezio S/Z	20.00
326	Bartolo Colon G/Z	20.00
327	Damon Mashore S/Y	12.00
328	Ryan McGuire S/Y	12.00
329	Chris Carpenter B/X	8.00
330	Jose Cruz, Jr. G/X	80.00
331	Todd Greene S/Z	30.00
332	Brian Moehler B/X	8.00
333	Mike Sweeney B/Y	12.00
334	Neifi Perez G/Z	20.00
335	Matt Morris S/Y	12.00
336	Marvin Benard B/Y	12.00
337	Karim Garcia S/Z	25.00
338	Jason Dickson S/Y	12.00
339	Brant Brown S/Y	12.00
340	Jeff Suppan S/Z	20.00
341	Deivi Cruz B/X	8.00
342	Antone Williamson G/Z	20.00
343	Curtis Goodwin B/X	8.00
344	Brooks Kieschnick S/Y	12.00
345	Tony Womack B/X	8.00
346	Rudy Pemberton B/X	8.00
347	Todd Dunwoody D/X	8.00
348	Frank Thomas S/Y (Legacy)	150.00
349	Andruw Jones S/X (Legacy)	40.00
350	Alex Rodriguez B/Y (Legacy)	125.00
351	Greg Maddux S/Y (Legacy)	100.00
352	Jeff Bagwell B/Y (Legacy)	75.00
353	Juan Gonzalez S/Y (Legacy)	75.00
354	Barry Bonds B/Y (Legacy)	50.00
355	Mark McGwire B/Y (Legacy)	60.00
356	Tony Gwynn B/Y (Legacy)	75.00
357	Gary Sheffield B/X (Legacy)	12.00
358	Derek Jeter S/X (Legacy)	40.00
359	Manny Ramirez S/Y (Legacy)	35.00
360	Hideo Nomo G/Z (Legacy)	40.00
361	Sammy Sosa B/X (Legacy)	15.00
362	Paul Molitor S/Z (Legacy)	30.00
363	Kenny Lofton B/Y (Legacy)	50.00
364	Eddie Murray B/X (Legacy)	15.00
365	Barry Larkin S/Z (Legacy)	25.00
366	Roger Clemens S/Y (Legacy)	50.00
367	John Smoltz B/Z (Legacy)	20.00
368	Alex Rodriguez S/X (Gamers)	65.00
369	Frank Thomas B/X (Gamers)	75.00
370	Cal Ripken Jr. S/Y (Gamers)	125.00
371	Ken Griffey Jr. S/Y (Gamers)	175.00
372	Greg Maddux B/X (Gamers)	40.00
373	Mike Piazza C/X (Gamers)	40.00
374	Chipper Jones B/Y (Gamers)	90.00
375	Albert Belle B/X (Gamers)	20.00
376	Chuck Knoblauch B/X (Gamers)	15.00
377	Brady Anderson B/Z (Gamers)	20.00
378	David Justice S/X (Gamers)	12.00
379	Randy Johnson B/Z (Gamers)	40.00
380	Wade Boggs B/X (Gamers)	12.00
381	Kevin Brown B/X (Gamers)	8.00
382	Tom Glavine G/Y (Gamers)	12.00
383	Raul Mondesi S/X (Gamers)	12.00
384	Ivan Rodriguez S/X (Gamers)	15.00
385	Larry Walker B/Y (Gamers)	20.00

386	Bernie Williams B/Z (Gamers)	40.00
387	Rusty Greer G/Y (Gamers)	12.00
388	Rafael Palmeiro G/Y (Gamers)	15.00
389	Matt Williams B/X (Gamers)	12.00
390	Eric Young B/X (Gamers)	8.00
391	Fred McGriff B/X (Gamers)	12.00
392	Ken Caminiti B/X (Gamers)	10.00
393	Roberto Alomar B/Z (Gamers)	40.00
394	Brian Jordan B/X (Gamers)	8.00
395	Mark Grace G/Z (Gamers)	30.00
396	Jim Edmonds B/Y (Gamers)	12.00
397	Deion Sanders S/Y (Gamers)	18.00
398	Checklist (Vladimir Guerrero S/Z)	60.00
399	Checklist (Darin Erstad B/Y)	50.00
400	Checklist (Nomar Garciaparra S/Z)	75.00

1997 Leaf Banner Season

Banner Season was a 15-card insert set that was die-cut and printed on a canvas card stock. Only 2,500 individually numbered sets were produced, with cards only found in pre-priced packs.

		MT
Complete Set (15):		250.00
Common Player:		5.00
1	Jeff Bagwell	20.00
2	Ken Griffey Jr.	60.00
3	Juan Gonzalez	25.00
4	Frank Thomas	50.00
5	Alex Rodriguez	40.00
6	Kenny Lofton	12.00
7	Chuck Knoblauch	6.00
8	Mo Vaughn	12.00
9	Chipper Jones	30.00
10	Ken Caminiti	5.00
11	Craig Biggio	5.00
12	John Smoltz	5.00
13	Pat Hentgen	5.00
14	Derek Jeter	30.00
15	Todd Hollandsworth	5.00

1997 Leaf Dress for Success

Exclusive to retail packs was an insert called Dress for Success. It included 18 players printed on nylon and flocking card stock. Dress for Success was limited to 3,500 individually numbered sets.

		MT
Complete Set (18):		300.00
Common Player:		5.00
1	Greg Maddux	25.00
2	Cal Ripken Jr.	30.00
3	Albert Belle	12.00
4	Frank Thomas	40.00
5	Dante Bichette	5.00
6	Gary Sheffield	8.00
7	Jeff Bagwell	18.00
8	Mike Piazza	25.00
9	Mark McGwire	15.00
10	Ken Caminiti	8.00
11	Alex Rodriguez	30.00
12	Ken Griffey Jr.	40.00
13	Juan Gonzalez	18.00
14	Brian Jordan	5.00
15	Mo Vaughn	10.00
16	Ivan Rodriguez	8.00
17	Andruw Jones	25.00
18	Chipper Jones	25.00

1997 Leaf Get-A-Grip

Get a Grip included 16 double-sided cards, with a star hitter on one side and a star pitcher on the other. The card slated the two stars against each other and explained how the hitter would hit against the pitcher, while featuring the pitcher's top pitch. This insert was printed on silver foilboard with the right side die-cut, and limited to 3,500 numbered sets found only in hobby packs.

		MT
Complete Set (16):		300.00
Common Player:		8.00
1	Ken Griffey Jr., Greg Maddux	40.00
2	John Smoltz, Frank Thomas	35.00
3	Mike Piazza, Andy Pettitte	25.00
4	Randy Johnson, Chipper Jones	25.00
5	Tom Glavine, Alex Rodriguez	35.00
6	Pat Hentgen, Jeff Bagwell	15.00
7	Kevin Brown, Juan Gonzalez	15.00
8	Barry Bonds, Mike Mussina	12.00
9	Hideo Nomo, Albert Belle	15.00
10	Troy Percival, Andruw Jones	20.00
11	Roger Clemens, Brian Jordan	15.00
12	Paul Wilson, Ivan Rodriguez	10.00
13	Andy Benes, Mo Vaughn	12.00
14	Al Leiter, Derek Jeter	25.00
15	Bill Pulsipher, Cal Ripken Jr.	30.00
16	Mariano Rivera, Ken Caminiti	8.00

1997 Leaf Knot-Hole Gang

Knot-Hole Gang pictured 12 hitters against a wood picket fence in the background. Cards were die-cut along the top of the fence and printed on a wood card stock. Set production was limited to 5,000 and these inserts were found in all types of packs.

		MT
Complete Set (12):		140.00
Common Player:		4.00
1	Chuck Knoblauch	5.00
2	Ken Griffey Jr.	30.00
3	Frank Thomas	30.00
4	Tony Gwynn	15.00
5	Mike Piazza	20.00
6	Jeff Bagwell	15.00
7	Rusty Greer	4.00
8	Cal Ripken Jr.	25.00
9	Chipper Jones	20.00
10	Ryan Klesko	6.00
11	Barry Larkin	5.00
12	Paul Molitor	6.00

1997 Leaf Leagues of the Nation

A 15-card insert set featuring a double-sided die-cut design. The players on each card represent matchups from the initial rounds of interleague play. Cards were numbered to 2,500 and feature a flocked texture.

		MT
Complete Set (15):		400.00
Common Player:		10.00
1	Juan Gonzalez, Barry Bonds	25.00
2	Cal Ripken Jr., Chipper Jones	40.00
3	Mark McGwire, Ken Caminiti	20.00
4	Derek Jeter, Kenny Lofton	30.00
5	Ivan Rodriguez, Mike Piazza	30.00
6	Ken Griffey Jr., Larry Walker	60.00
7	Frank Thomas, Sammy Sosa	50.00
8	Paul Molitor, Barry Larkin	10.00
9	Albert Belle, Deion Sanders	18.00
10	Matt Williams, Jeff Bagwell	20.00
11	Mo Vaughn, Gary Sheffield	15.00
12	Alex Rodriguez, Tony Gwynn	50.00
13	Tino Martinez, Scott Rolen	30.00
14	Darin Erstad, Wilton Guerrero	25.00
15	Tony Clark, Vladimir Guerrero	30.00

1997 Leaf Statistical Standouts

Statistical Standouts were limited to only 1,000 individually numbered sets. Inserts were printed on leather and die-cut. The set included 15 top stars who excelled beyond their competition in many statistical categories.

		MT
Complete Set (15):		900.00
Common Player:		20.00
1	Albert Belle	40.00
2	Juan Gonzalez	60.00
3	Ken Griffey Jr.	125.00
4	Alex Rodriguez	100.00
5	Frank Thomas	125.00
6	Chipper Jones	75.00
7	Greg Maddux	75.00
8	Mike Piazza	75.00
9	Cal Ripken Jr.	100.00
10	Mark McGwire	50.00
11	Barry Bonds	30.00
12	Derek Jeter	75.00
13	Ken Caminiti	20.00
14	John Smoltz	20.00
15	Paul Molitor	25.00

1997 Leaf Thomas Collection

This six-card insert from Series II features pieces of various game-used Frank Thomas items built into the texture of each card. Jerseys, bats, hats, batting gloves and sweatbands are all featured on the various cards, which are numbered to 100 each.

		MT
Complete Set (6):		2000.
Common Thomas:		350.00
1	Frank Thomas Hat	350.00
2	Frank Thomas Home Jersey	500.00
3	Frank Thomas Batting Glove	350.00
4	Frank Thomas Bat	350.00
5	Frank Thomas Sweatband	350.00
6	Frank Thomas Away Jersey	500.00

1997 Leaf 22kt Gold Stars

A 36-card insert from Series II Leaf, each card features a special 22kt. gold foil stamping and is numbered to 2,500.

		MT
Complete Set (36):		750.00
Common Player:		10.00
1	Frank Thomas	60.00
2	Alex Rodriguez	50.00
3	Ken Griffey Jr.	70.00
4	Andruw Jones	35.00
5	Chipper Jones	35.00
6	Jeff Bagwell	25.00
7	Derek Jeter	35.00
8	Deion Sanders	10.00
9	Ivan Rodriguez	18.00
10	Juan Gonzalez	30.00

		MT
11	Greg Maddux	35.00
12	Andy Pettitte	18.00
13	Roger Clemens	25.00
14	Hideo Nomo	18.00
15	Tony Gwynn	30.00
16	Barry Bonds	18.00
17	Kenny Lofton	18.00
18	Paul Molitor	12.00
19	Jim Thome	10.00
20	Albert Belle	20.00
21	Cal Ripken Jr.	50.00
22	Mark McGwire	25.00
23	Barry Larkin	10.00
24	Mike Piazza	35.00
25	Darin Erstad	20.00
26	Chuck Knoblauch	10.00
27	Vladimir Guerrero	25.00
28	Tony Clark	18.00
29	Scott Rolen	30.00
30	Nomar Garciaparra	30.00
31	Eric Young	10.00
32	Ryne Sandberg	18.00
33	Roberto Alomar	15.00
34	Eddie Murray	12.00
35	Rafael Palmeiro	10.00
36	Jose Guillen	15.00

1997 Leaf Warning Track

A 12-card insert printed on embossed canvas depicting players who are known for making tough catches. Cards were numbered to 3,500.

		MT
Complete Set (18):		200.00
Common Player:		6.00
1	Ken Griffey Jr.	50.00
2	Albert Belle	18.00
3	Barry Bonds	15.00
4	Andruw Jones	30.00
5	Kenny Lofton	15.00
6	Tony Gwynn	20.00
7	Manny Ramirez	10.00
8	Rusty Greer	6.00
9	Bernie Williams	10.00
10	Gary Sheffield	8.00
11	Juan Gonzalez	20.00
12	Raul Mondesi	8.00
13	Brady Anderson	6.00
14	Rondell White	6.00
15	Sammy Sosa	8.00
16	Deion Sanders	6.00
17	David Justice	8.00
18	Jim Edmonds	6.00

1997 Pacific Crown

The 450-card, regular-sized set was available in 12-card packs. The card fronts feature the player's name in gold foil along the left border with the team logo in the bottom right corner. The card backs feature a head shot of the player in the lower left quadrant with a short highlight in both Spanish and English. Inserted in packs were: Card-Supials, Cramer's Choice, Latinos Of The Major Leagues, Fireworks Die-Cuts, Gold Crown Die-Cuts and Triple Crown Die-Cuts. A parallel silver version (67 sets) was available.

		MT
Complete Set (450):		35.00
Common Player:		.05
Silver Stars:		75x to 120x
Silver Yng Stars & RCs:		50x to 90x
Wax Box:		60.00
1	Garret Anderson	.05
2	George Arias	.05
3	Chili Davis	.05
4	Gary DiSarcina	.05
5	Jim Edmonds	.05
6	Darin Erstad	1.25
7	Jorge Fabregas	.05
8	Chuck Finley	.05
9	Rex Hudler	.05
10	Mark Langston	.05
11	Orlando Palmeiro	.05
12	Troy Percival	.05
13	Tim Salmon	.25
14	J.T. Snow	.05
15	Randy Velarde	.05
16	Manny Alexander	.05
17	Roberto Alomar	.60
18	Brady Anderson	.10
19	Armando Benitez	.05
20	Bobby Bonilla	.10
21	Rocky Coppinger	.15
22	Scott Erickson	.05
23	Jeffrey Hammonds	.05
24	Chris Hoiles	.05
25	Eddie Murray	.35
26	Mike Mussina	.60
27	Randy Myers	.05
28	Rafael Palmeiro	.10
29	Cal Ripken Jr.	2.50
30	B.J. Surhoff	.05
31	Tony Tarasco	.05
32	Esteban Beltre	.05
33	Darren Bragg	.05
34	Jose Canseco	.25
35	Roger Clemens	1.00
36	Wil Cordero	.05
37	Alex Delgado	.05
38	Jeff Frye	.05
39	Nomar Garciaparra	1.50
40	Tom Gordon	.05
41	Mike Greenwell	.05
42	Reggie Jefferson	.05
43	Tim Naehring	.05
44	Troy O'Leary	.05
45	Heathcliff Slocumb	.05
46	Lee Tinsley	.05
47	John Valentin	.05
48	Mo Vaughn	1.00
49	Wilson Alvarez	.05
50	Harold Baines	.05
51	Ray Durham	.05
52	Alex Fernandez	.05
53	Ozzie Guillen	.05
54	Roberto Hernandez	.05
55	Ron Karkovice	.05
56	Darren Lewis	.05
57	Norberto Martin	.05
58	Dave Martinez	.05
59	Lyle Mouton	.05
60	Jose Munoz	.05
61	Tony Phillips	.05
62	Rich Sauveur	.05
63	Danny Tartabull	.05
64	Frank Thomas	3.00
65	Robin Ventura	.05
66	Sandy Alomar Jr.	.05
67	Albert Belle	1.00
68	Julio Franco	.05
69	Brian Giles	.05
70	Danny Graves	.05
71	Orel Hershiser	.05
72	Jeff Kent	.05
73	Kenny Lofton	.75
74	Dennis Martinez	.05
75	Jack McDowell	.10
76	Jose Mesa	.05
77	Charles Nagy	.05

No.	Player	MT
78	Manny Ramirez	.75
79	Julian Tavarez	.05
80	Jim Thome	.30
81	Jose Vizcaino	.05
82	Omar Vizquel	.05
83	Brad Ausmus	.05
84	Kimera Bartee	.05
85	Raul Casanova	.05
86	Tony Clark	.40
87	Travis Fryman	.05
88	Bobby Higginson	.05
89	Mark Lewis	.05
90	Jose Lima	.05
91	Felipe Lira	.05
92	Phil Nevin	.05
93	Melvin Nieves	.05
94	Curtis Pride	.05
95	Ruben Sierra	.05
96	Alan Trammell	.05
97	Kevin Appier	.05
98	Tim Belcher	.05
99	Johnny Damon	.20
100	Tom Goodwin	.05
101	Bob Hamelin	.05
102	David Howard	.05
103	Jason Jacome	.05
104	Keith Lockhart	.05
105	Mike Macfarlane	.05
106	Jeff Montgomery	.05
107	Jose Offerman	.05
108	Hipolito Pichardo	.05
109	Joe Randa	.05
110	Bip Roberts	.05
111	Chris Stynes	.05
112	Mike Sweeney	.05
113	Joe Vitiello	.05
114	Jeromy Burnitz	.05
115	Chuck Carr	.05
116	Jeff Cirillo	.05
117	Mike Fetters	.05
118	David Hulse	.05
119	John Jaha	.05
120	Scott Karl	.05
121	Jesse Levis	.05
122	Mark Loretta	.05
123	Mike Matheny	.05
124	Ben McDonald	.05
125	Matt Mieske	.05
126	Angel Miranda	.05
127	Dave Nilsson	.05
128	Jose Valentin	.05
129	Fernando Vina	.05
130	Ron Villone	.05
131	Gerald Williams	.05
132	Rick Aguilera	.05
133	Rich Becker	.05
134	Ron Coomer	.05
135	Marty Cordova	.10
136	Eddie Guardado	.05
137	Denny Hocking	.05
138	Roberto Kelly	.05
139	Chuck Knoblauch	.05
140	Matt Lawton	.05
141	Pat Meares	.05
142	Paul Molitor	.25
143	Greg Myers	.05
144	Jeff Reboulet	.05
145	Scott Stahoviak	.05
146	Todd Walker	.50
147	Wade Boggs	.15
148	David Cone	.10
149	Mariano Duncan	.05
150	Cecil Fielder	.15
151	Dwight Gooden	.05
152	Derek Jeter	1.50
153	Jim Leyritz	.05
154	Tino Martinez	.20
155	Paul O'Neill	.05
156	Andy Pettitte	.75
157	Tim Raines	.05
158	Mariano Rivera	.15
159	Ruben Rivera	.35
160	Kenny Rogers	.05
161	Darryl Strawberry	.05
162	John Wetteland	.05
163	Bernie Williams	.50
164	Tony Batista	.05
165	Geronimo Berroa	.05
166	Mike Bordick	.05
167	Scott Brosius	.05
168	Brent Gates	.05
169	Jason Giambi	.05
170	Jose Herrera	.05
171	Brian Lesher	.05
172	*Damon Mashore*	.05
173	Mark McGwire	1.00
174	Ariel Prieto	.05
175	Carlos Reyes	.05
176	Matt Stairs	.05
177	Terry Steinbach	.05
178	John Wasdin	.05
179	Ernie Young	.05
180	Rich Amaral	.05
181	Bobby Ayala	.05
182	Jay Buhner	.15
183	Rafael Carmona	.05
184	Norm Charlton	.05
185	Joey Cora	.05
186	Ken Griffey Jr.	3.00
187	Sterling Hitchcock	.05
188	Dave Hollins	.05
189	Randy Johnson	.35
190	Edgar Martinez	.05
191	Jamie Moyer	.05
192	Alex Rodriguez	3.00
193	Paul Sorrento	.05
194	Salomon Torres	.05
195	Bob Wells	.05
196	Dan Wilson	.05
197	Will Clark	.25
198	Kevin Elster	.05
199	Rene Gonzales	.05
200	Juan Gonzalez	1.50
201	Rusty Greer	.05
202	Darryl Hamilton	.05
203	Mike Henneman	.05
204	Ken Hill	.05
205	Mark McLemore	.05
206	Darren Oliver	.05
207	Dean Palmer	.05
208	Roger Pavlik	.05
209	Ivan Rodriguez	.60
210	Kurt Stillwell	.05
211	Mickey Tettleton	.05
212	Bobby Witt	.05
213	Tilson Brito	.05
214	Jacob Brumfield	.05
215	Miguel Cairo	.05
216	Joe Carter	.20
217	Felipe Crespo	.05
218	Carlos Delgado	.05
219	Alex Gonzalez	.05
220	Shawn Green	.05
221	Juan Guzman	.05
222	Pat Hentgen	.05
223	Charlie O'Brien	.05
224	John Olerud	.05
225	Robert Perez	.05
226	Tomas Perez	.05
227	Juan Samuel	.05
228	Ed Sprague	.05
229	Mike Timlin	.05
230	Rafael Belliard	.05
231	Jermaine Dye	.30
232	Tom Glavine	.10
233	Marquis Grissom	.05
234	Andruw Jones	2.00
235	Chipper Jones	2.00
236	David Justice	.20
237	Ryan Klesko	.50
238	Mark Lemke	.05
239	Javier Lopez	.15
240	Greg Maddux	2.00
241	Fred McGriff	.35
242	Denny Neagle	.05
243	Eddie Perez	.05
244	John Smoltz	.15
245	Mark Wohlers	.05
246	Brant Brown	.05
247	Scott Bullett	.05
248	Leo Gomez	.05
249	Luis Gonzalez	.05
250	Mark Grace	.10
251	Jose Hernandez	.05
252	Brooks Kieschnick	.05
253	Brian McRae	.05
254	Jaime Navarro	.05
255	Mike Perez	.05
256	Rey Sanchez	.05
257	Ryne Sandberg	.75
258	Scott Servais	.05
259	Sammy Sosa	.20
260	*Pedro Valdes*	.05
261	Turk Wendell	.05
262	Bret Boone	.05
263	Jeff Branson	.05
264	Jeff Brantley	.05
265	Dave Burba	.05
266	Hector Carrasco	.05
267	Eric Davis	.05
268	Willie Greene	.05
269	Lenny Harris	.05
270	Thomas Howard	.05
271	Barry Larkin	.20
272	Hal Morris	.05
273	Joe Oliver	.05
274	Eric Owens	.05
275	Jose Rijo	.05
276	Reggie Sanders	.05
277	Eddie Taubensee	.05
278	Jason Bates	.05
279	Dante Bichette	.20
280	Ellis Burks	.05
281	Vinny Castilla	.05
282	Andres Galarraga	.15
283	Quinton McCracken	.05
284	Jayhawk Owens	.05
285	Jeff Reed	.05
286	Bryan Rekar	.05
287	Armando Reynoso	.05
288	Kevin Ritz	.05
289	Bruce Ruffin	.05
290	John Vander Wal	.05
291	Larry Walker	.25
292	Walt Weiss	.05
293	Eric Young	.05
294	Kurt Abbott	.05
295	Alex Arias	.05
296	Miguel Batista	.05
297	Kevin Brown	.05
298	Luis Castillo	.15
299	Greg Colbrunn	.05
300	Jeff Conine	.05
301	Charles Johnson	.05
302	Al Leiter	.05
303	Robb Nen	.05
304	Joe Orsulak	.05
305	Yorkis Perez	.05
306	Edgar Renteria	.25
307	Gary Sheffield	.25
308	Jesus Tavarez	.05
309	Quilvio Veras	.05
310	Devon White	.05
311	Jeff Bagwell	1.25
312	Derek Bell	.05
313	Sean Berry	.05
314	Craig Biggio	.05
315	Doug Drabek	.05
316	Tony Eusebio	.05
317	Ricky Gutierrez	.05
318	Xavier Hernandez	.05
319	Brian L. Hunter	.05
320	Darryl Kile	.05
321	Derrick May	.05
322	Orlando Miller	.05
323	James Mouton	.05
324	Bill Spiers	.05
325	Pedro Astacio	.05
326	Brett Butler	.05
327	Juan Castro	.05
328	Roger Cedeno	.05
329	Delino DeShields	.05
330	Karim Garcia	.50
331	Todd Hollandsworth	.10
332	Eric Karros	.05
333	Oreste Marrero	.05
334	Ramon Martinez	.05
335	Raul Mondesi	.25
336	Hideo Nomo	.60
337	Antonio Osuna	.05
338	Chan Ho Park	.05
339	Mike Piazza	2.00
340	Ismael Valdes	.05
341	Moises Alou	.05
342	Omar Daal	.05
343	Jeff Fassero	.05
344	Cliff Floyd	.05
345	Mark Grudzielanek	.05
346	Mike Lansing	.05
347	Pedro Martinez	.05
348	Sherman Obando	.05
349	Jose Paniagua	.05
350	Henry Rodriguez	.05
351	Mel Rojas	.05
352	F.P. Santangelo	.05
353	Dave Segui	.05
354	Dave Silvestri	.05
355	Ugueth Urbina	.05
356	Rondell White	.05
357	Edgardo Alfonzo	.05
358	Carlos Baerga	.10
359	Tim Bogar	.05
360	Rico Brogna	.05
361	Alvaro Espinoza	.05
362	Carl Everett	.05
363	John Franco	.05
364	Bernard Gilkey	.05
365	Todd Hundley	.05
366	Butch Huskey	.05
367	Jason Isringhausen	.10
368	Bobby Jones	.05
369	Lance Johnson	.05
370	Brent Mayne	.05
371	Alex Ochoa	.05
372	Rey Ordonez	.20
373	Ron Blazier	.05
374	Ricky Bottalico	.05
375	David Doster	.05
376	Lenny Dykstra	.05
377	Jim Eisenreich	.05
378	Bobby Estalella	.05
379	Gregg Jefferies	.05
380	Kevin Jordan	.05
381	Ricardo Jordan	.05
382	Mickey Morandini	.05
383	Ricky Otero	.05
384	Benito Santiago	.05
385	Gene Schall	.05
386	Curt Schilling	.05
387	Kevin Sefcik	.05
388	Kevin Stocker	.05
389	Jermaine Allensworth	.05
390	Jay Bell	.05
391	Jason Christiansen	.05
392	Francisco Cordova	.10
393	Mark Johnson	.05
394	Jason Kendall	.05
395	Jeff King	.05
396	Jon Lieber	.05
397	Nelson Liriano	.05
398	Esteban Loaiza	.10
399	Al Martin	.05
400	Orlando Merced	.05
401	Ramon Morel	.05
402	Luis Alicea	.05
403	Alan Benes	.15
404	Andy Benes	.05
405	Terry Bradshaw	.05
406	Royce Clayton	.05
407	Dennis Eckersley	.05
408	Gary Gaetti	.05
409	Mike Gallego	.05
410	Ron Gant	.10
411	Brian Jordan	.05
412	Ray Lankford	.05
413	John Mabry	.05
414	Willie McGee	.05
415	Tom Pagnozzi	.05
416	Ozzie Smith	.40
417	Todd Stottlemyre	.05
418	Mark Sweeney	.05
419	Andy Ashby	.05
420	Ken Caminiti	.10
421	Archi Cianfrocco	.05
422	Steve Finley	.05
423	Chris Gomez	.05
424	Tony Gwynn	1.25
425	Joey Hamilton	.05
426	Rickey Henderson	.05
427	Trevor Hoffman	.05
428	Brian Johnson	.05
429	Wally Joyner	.05
430	Scott Livingstone	.05
431	Jody Reed	.05
432	Craig Shipley	.05
433	Fernando Valenzuela	.05
434	Greg Vaughn	.05
435	Rich Aurilia	.05
436	Kim Batiste	.05
437	Jose Bautista	.05
438	Rod Beck	.05
439	Marvin Benard	.05
440	Barry Bonds	.75
441	Shawon Dunston	.05
442	Shawn Estes	.05
443	Osvaldo Fernandez	.05
444	Stan Javier	.05
445	David McCarty	.05
446	*Bill Mueller*	.05
447	Steve Scarsone	.05
448	Robby Thompson	.05
449	Rick Wilkins	.05
450	Matt Williams	.25

1997 Pacific Crown Card-Supials

The 36-card, regular-sized set was inserted every 37 packs of 1997 Pacific Crown baseball. The card fronts feature a gold-foil spiral with the player's name printed along a curve on the bottom edge. The team logo appears in the lower right corner. The card backs feature an action shot and are numbered "x of 36." The cards come with a mini (1-1/4" x 1-3/4") card that slides into a pocket on the back. The mini cards are of a different player, but depict the same action shot as the larger card backs.

	MT
Complete Set (72):	550.00
Complete Large Set (36):	350.00
Complete Small Set (36):	200.00
Common Large:	4.00
Small Cards:	Half Price

#	Player	Value
1	Roberto Alomar	6.00
2	Brady Anderson	4.00
3	Eddie Murray	6.00
4	Cal Ripken Jr.	25.00
5	Jose Canseco	5.00
6	Mo Vaughn	8.00
7	Frank Thomas	30.00
8	Albert Belle	10.00
9	Omar Vizquel	4.00
10	Chuck Knoblauch	4.00
11	Paul Molitor	6.00
12	Wade Boggs	4.00
13	Derek Jeter	20.00
14	Andy Pettitte	8.00
15	Mark McGwire	12.00
16	Jay Buhner	4.00
17	Ken Griffey Jr.	30.00
18	Alex Rodriguez	25.00
19	Juan Gonzalez	15.00
20	Ivan Rodriguez	6.00
21	Andruw Jones	20.00
22	Chipper Jones	20.00
23	Ryan Klesko	5.00
24	Greg Maddux	20.00
25	Ryne Sandberg	8.00
26	Andres Galarraga	4.00
27	Gary Sheffield	5.00
28	Jeff Bagwell	15.00
29	Todd Hollandsworth	4.00
30	Hideo Nomo	6.00
31	Mike Piazza	20.00
32	Todd Hundley	4.00
33	Dennis Eckersley	4.00
34	Ken Caminiti	4.00
35	Tony Gwynn	15.00
36	Barry Bonds	8.00

1997 Pacific Crown Cramer's Choice Awards

The 10-card, regular-sized set was inserted every 721 packs and features a die-cut pyramid design. A color player photo is imaged over silver foil with the player's name and position in gold foil over a green marble background along the bottom. The card backs feature a headshot with a brief career highlight in both Spanish and English. The cards are numbered with a "CC" prefix.

		MT
Complete Set (10):		1200.
Common Player:		50.00
1	Roberto Alomar	60.00
2	Frank Thomas	250.00
3	Albert Belle	80.00
4	Andy Pettitte	70.00
5	Ken Griffey Jr.	250.00
6	Alex Rodriguez	200.00
7	Chipper Jones	150.00
8	John Smoltz	50.00
9	Mike Piazza	150.00
10	Tony Gwynn	125.00

Values quoted in this guide reflect the retail price of a card — the price a collector can expect to pay when buying a card from a dealer. The wholesale price — that which a collector can expect to receive from a dealer when selling cards — will be significantly lower, depending on desirability and condition.

1997 Pacific Crown Fireworks Die-Cuts

The 20-card, regular-sized, die-cut set was inserted every 73 packs of 1997 Crown. The card fronts feature a color action shot with generic fireworks over a stadium on the upper half. The horizontal card backs contain close-up shots with highlights in Spanish and English. The cards are numbered with the "FW" prefix.

		MT
Complete Set (20):		400.00
Common Player:		6.00
1	Roberto Alomar	12.00
2	Brady Anderson	6.00
3	Eddie Murray	8.00
4	Cal Ripken Jr.	40.00
5	Frank Thomas	50.00
6	Albert Belle	15.00
7	Derek Jeter	30.00
8	Andy Pettitte	12.00
9	Bernie Williams	10.00
10	Mark McGwire	18.00
11	Ken Griffey Jr.	50.00
12	Alex Rodriguez	40.00
13	Juan Gonzalez	20.00
14	Andruw Jones	30.00
15	Chipper Jones	30.00
16	Hideo Nomo	10.00
17	Mike Piazza	30.00
18	Henry Rodriguez	6.00
19	Tony Gwynn	25.00
20	Barry Bonds	12.00

1997 Pacific Crown Gold Crown Die-Cuts

The 36-card, regular-sized, die-cut set was inserted every 37 packs. The card fronts feature a die-cut, gold-foil crown on the top border and the player's name appears in gold along the bottom edge. The card backs contain a headshot and a Spanish/English highlight and are numbered with the "GC" prefix.

		MT
Complete Set (36):		400.00
Common Player:		4.00

#	Player	Value
1	Roberto Alomar	10.00
2	Brady Anderson	4.00
3	Mike Mussina	8.00
4	Eddie Murray	8.00
5	Cal Ripken Jr.	35.00
6	Jose Canseco	5.00
7	Frank Thomas	40.00
8	Albert Belle	15.00
9	Omar Vizquel	4.00
10	Wade Boggs	4.00
11	Derek Jeter	20.00
12	Andy Pettitte	10.00
13	Mariano Rivera	4.00
14	Bernie Williams	8.00
15	Mark McGwire	12.00
16	Ken Griffey Jr.	40.00
17	Edgar Martinez	4.00
18	Alex Rodriquez	35.00
19	Juan Gonzalez	20.00
20	Ivan Rodriguez	12.00
21	Andruw Jones	25.00
22	Chipper Jones	25.00
23	Ryan Klesko	6.00
24	John Smoltz	5.00
25	Ryne Sandberg	10.00
26	Andres Galarraga	4.00
27	Edgar Renteria	6.00
28	Jeff Bagwell	18.00
29	Todd Hollandsworth	4.00
30	Hideo Nomo	8.00
31	Mike Piazza	25.00
32	Todd Hundley	4.00
33	Brian Jordan	4.00
34	Ken Caminiti	5.00
35	Tony Gwynn	15.00
36	Barry Bonds	10.00

1997 Pacific Crown Latinos of the Major Leagues

The 36-card, regular-sized set was inserted twice every 37 packs. The card fronts feature a color action shot over the player's name in gold foil. The card backs have another action shot and a Spanish/English highlight.

		MT
Complete Set (36):		80.00
Common Player:		1.50
1	George Arias	1.50
2	Roberto Alomar	4.00
3	Rafael Palmeiro	2.00
4	Bobby Bonilla	2.00
5	Jose Canseco	2.50
6	Wilson Alvarez	1.50
7	Dave Martinez	1.50
8	Julio Franco	1.50
9	Manny Ramirez	6.00
10	Omar Vizquel	1.50
11	Marty Cordova	1.50
12	Roberto Kelly	1.50
13	Tino Martinez	2.00
14	Mariano Rivera	2.00
15	Ruben Rivera	2.00
16	Bernie Williams	4.00
17	Geronimo Berroa	1.50
18	Joey Cora	1.50
19	Edgar Martinez	1.50
20	Alex Rodriguez	20.00
21	Juan Gonzalez	10.00
22	Ivan Rodriguez	5.00
23	Andruw Jones	12.00
24	Javier Lopez	2.00
25	Sammy Sosa	3.00
26	Vinny Castilla	1.50
27	Andres Galarraga	2.00
28	Ramon Martinez	1.50
29	Raul Mondesi	2.50
30	Ismael Valdes	1.50
31	Pedro Martinez	1.50
32	Henry Rodriguez	1.50
33	Carlos Baerga	2.00
34	Rey Ordonez	2.50
35	Fernando Valenzuela	1.50
36	Osvaldo Fernandez	1.50

1997 Pacific Crown Triple Crown Die-Cuts

The 20-card, regular-sized, die-cut set was inserted every 145 packs of Crown baseball. The horizontal card fronts feature the same gold-foil, die-cut crown as on the Gold Crown Die-Cut inserts. The card backs feature a headshot, Spanish/English text and are numbered with the "TC" prefix.

		MT
Complete Set (20):		750.00
Common Player:		10.00
1	Brady Anderson	10.00
2	Rafael Palmeiro	12.00
3	Mo Vaughn	25.00
4	Frank Thomas	100.00
5	Albert Belle	35.00
6	Jim Thome	20.00
7	Cecil Fielder	12.00
8	Mark McGwire	30.00
9	Ken Griffey Jr.	100.00
10	Alex Rodriguez	100.00
11	Juan Gonzalez	50.00
12	Andruw Jones	60.00
13	Chipper Jones	60.00
14	Dante Bichette	10.00
15	Ellis Burks	10.00
16	Andres Galarraga	10.00
17	Jeff Bagwell	40.00
18	Mike Piazza	60.00
19	Ken Caminiti	10.00
20	Barry Bonds	25.00

1997 Pacific Invincible

The 1997 Pacific Invincible 150-card set was sold in three-card packs. The card fronts feature gold foil parallel lines with a color action shot. The bottom right quadrant contains a transparent cel headshot. The card backs have Spanish/English text and another color action shot. The reverse cel has the player's hat team logo airbrushed off to prevent reverse print. Insert sets are: Sluggers & Hurlers, Sizzling Lumber, Gate Attractions, and a Platinum parallel set (2:37) and a bonus set, Gems Of The Diamond (2:1).

		MT
Complete Set (150):		150.00
Common Player:		1.00
Platinums:		3x to 5x
Wax Box:		75.00
1	Chili Davis	1.00
2	Jim Edmonds	1.50
3	Darin Erstad	6.00
4	Orlando Palmeiro	1.00
5	Tim Salmon	2.00
6	J.T. Snow	1.00
7	Roberto Alomar	2.50
8	Brady Anderson	1.50
9	Eddie Murray	2.00
10	Mike Mussina	2.50
11	Rafael Palmeiro	1.50
12	Cal Ripken Jr.	12.00
13	Jose Canseco	1.50
14	Roger Clemens	4.00
15	Nomar Garciaparra	7.00
16	Reggie Jefferson	1.00
17	Mo Vaughn	4.00
18	Wilson Alvarez	1.00
19	Harold Baines	1.00
20	Alex Fernandez	1.00
21	Danny Tartabull	1.00
22	Frank Thomas	15.00
23	Robin Ventura	1.00
24	Sandy Alomar Jr.	1.00
25	Albert Belle	6.00
26	Kenny Lofton	4.00
27	Jim Thome	2.50
28	Omar Vizquel	1.00
29	Raul Casanova	1.00
30	Tony Clark	3.00
31	Travis Fryman	1.00
32	Bobby Higginson	1.00
33	Melvin Nieves	1.00
34	Justin Thompson	1.00
35	Johnny Damon	1.00
36	Tom Goodwin	1.00
37	Jeff Montgomery	1.00
38	Jose Offerman	1.00
39	John Jaha	1.00
40	Jeff Cirillo	1.00
41	Dave Nilsson	1.00
42	Jose Valentin	1.00
43	Fernando Vina	1.00
44	Marty Cordova	1.00
45	Roberto Kelly	1.00
46	Chuck Knoblauch	1.50
47	Paul Molitor	2.50
48	Todd Walker	4.00
49	Wade Boggs	1.50
50	Cecil Fielder	2.00
51	Derek Jeter	8.00
52	Tino Martinez	1.50
53	Andy Pettitte	3.00
54	Mariano Rivera	1.50
55	Bernie Williams	2.50
56	Tony Batista	1.00
57	Geronimo Berroa	1.00
58	Jason Giambi	1.00
59	Mark McGwire	5.00
60	Terry Steinbach	1.00
61	Jay Buhner	1.50
62	Joey Cora	1.00
63	Ken Griffey Jr.	15.00
64	Edgar Martinez	1.00
65	Alex Rodriguez	12.00
66	Paul Sorrento	1.00
67	Will Clark	1.50
68	Juan Gonzalez	7.00
69	Rusty Greer	1.00
70	Dean Palmer	1.00
71	Ivan Rodriguez	3.00
72	Joe Carter	1.50
73	Carlos Delgado	1.50
74	Juan Guzman	1.00
75	Pat Hentgen	1.00
76	Ed Sprague	1.00
77	Jermaine Dye	1.50
78	Andruw Jones	10.00
79	Chipper Jones	10.00
80	Ryan Klesko	2.50
81	Javier Lopez	1.50
82	Greg Maddux	10.00
83	John Smoltz	2.00
84	Mark Grace	1.50
85	Luis Gonzalez	1.00
86	Brooks Kieschnick	1.00
87	Jaime Navarro	1.00
88	Ryne Sandberg	4.00
89	Sammy Sosa	2.00
90	Bret Boone	1.00
91	Jeff Brantley	1.00
92	Eric Davis	1.00
93	Barry Larkin	2.00
94	Reggie Sanders	1.00
95	Ellis Burks	1.00
96	Dante Bichette	2.00
97	Vinny Castilla	1.00
98	Andres Galarraga	1.50
99	Eric Young	1.00
100	Kevin Brown	1.00
101	Jeff Conine	1.00
102	Charles Johnson	1.00
103	Edgar Renteria	1.50
104	Gary Sheffield	2.00
105	Jeff Bagwell	7.00
106	Derek Bell	1.00
107	Sean Berry	1.00
108	Craig Biggio	1.00
109	Shane Reynolds	1.00
110	Karim Garcia	2.00
111	Todd Hollandsworth	1.50
112	Ramon Martinez	1.00
113	Raul Mondesi	2.00
114	Hideo Nomo	3.00
115	Mike Piazza	10.00
116	Ismael Valdes	1.00
117	Moises Alou	1.00
118	Mark Grudzielanek	1.00
119	Pedro Martinez	1.00
120	Henry Rodriguez	1.00
121	F.P. Santangelo	1.00
122	Carlos Baerga	1.00
123	Bernard Gilkey	1.00
124	Todd Hundley	1.50
125	Lance Johnson	1.00
126	Alex Ochoa	1.00
127	Rey Ordonez	1.50
128	Lenny Dykstra	1.00
129	Gregg Jefferies	1.00
130	Ricky Otero	1.00
131	Benito Santiago	1.00
132	Jermaine Allensworth	1.00
133	Francisco Cordova	1.25
134	Carlos Garcia	1.00
135	Jason Kendall	1.00
136	Al Martin	1.00
137	Dennis Eckersley	1.00
138	Ron Gant	1.50
139	Brian Jordan	2.00
140	John Mabry	1.00
141	Ozzie Smith	3.00
142	Ken Caminiti	2.00
143	Steve Finley	1.00
144	Tony Gwynn	6.00
145	Wally Joyner	1.00
146	Fernando Valenzuela	1.00
147	Barry Bonds	4.00
148	Jacob Cruz	2.00
149	Osvaldo Fernandez	1.00
150	Matt Williams	2.00

1997 Pacific Invincible Gate Attractions

The 32-card, regular-sized set was inserted every 73 packs of Pacific Invincible baseball. The card fronts feature a generic baseball glove background with the player's name and position in a gold-foil circle. The center of the card is a cel action shot within a common baseball image. The player's team logo appears in the upper right corner. The card backs contain a headshot in the upper left corner with highlights in Spanish and English. The player's image in the cel is etched in gray in reverse. The cards are numbered with the "GA" prefix.

		MT
Complete Set (32):		600.00
Common Player:		8.00
1	Roberto Alomar	12.00
2	Brady Anderson	8.00
3	Cal Ripken Jr.	50.00
4	Frank Thomas	60.00
5	Kenny Lofton	15.00
6	Omar Vizquel	8.00
7	Paul Molitor	12.00
8	Wade Boggs	10.00
9	Derek Jeter	40.00
10	Andy Pettitte	15.00
11	Bernie Williams	12.00
12	Geronimo Berroa	8.00
13	Mark McGwire	25.00
14	Ken Griffey Jr.	60.00
15	Alex Rodriguez	50.00
16	Juan Gonzalez	30.00
17	Andruw Jones	40.00
18	Chipper Jones	10.00
19	Greg Maddux	40.00
20	Ryne Sandberg	15.00
21	Sammy Sosa	10.00
22	Andres Galarraga	8.00
23	Jeff Bagwell	25.00
24	Todd Hollandsworth	8.00
25	Hideo Nomo	10.00
26	Mike Piazza	40.00
27	Todd Hundley	8.00
28	Lance Johnson	8.00
29	Ozzie Smith	15.00
30	Ken Caminiti	10.00
31	Tony Gwynn	30.00
32	Barry Bonds	15.00

1997 Pacific Invincible Sizzling Lumber

The 36-card, regular-sized, die-cut set was inserted every 37 packs of Ivincible. The cards have die-cut flames along the right border with a bat running parallel. The player's name appears in gold foil along the top border with his position in English and Spanish in gold foil along the bottom. The card backs feature a headshot in the upper half and contain Spanish and English text. The cards are numbered with the "SL" prefix.

		MT
Complete Set (36):		400.00
Common Player:		4.00
1A	Cal Ripken Jr.	40.00
1B	Rafael Palmeiro	5.00
1C	Roberto Alomar	10.00
2A	Frank Thomas	50.00
2B	Robin Ventura	4.00
2C	Harold Baines	4.00
3A	Albert Belle	15.00
3B	Manny Ramirez	10.00
3C	Kenny Lofton	10.00
4A	Derek Jeter	25.00
4B	Bernie Williams	10.00
4C	Wade Boggs	5.00
5A	Mark McGwire	15.00
5B	Jason Giambi	4.00
5C	Geronimo Berroa	4.00
6A	Ken Griffey Jr.	50.00
6B	Alex Rodriguez	50.00
6C	Jay Buhner	5.00
7A	Juan Gonzalez	20.00
7B	Dean Palmer	4.00
7C	Ivan Rodriguez	12.00
8A	Ryan Klesko	6.00
8B	Chipper Jones	30.00
8C	Andruw Jones	30.00
9A	Dante Bichette	6.00
9B	Andres Galarraga	5.00
9C	Vinny Castilla	4.00
10A	Jeff Bagwell	20.00
10B	Craig Biggio	4.00
10C	Derek Bell	4.00
11A	Mike Piazza	30.00
11B	Raul Mondesi	6.00
11C	Karim Garcia	6.00
12A	Tony Gwynn	20.00
12B	Ken Caminiti	6.00
12C	Greg Vaughn	4.00

1997 Pacific Invincible Sluggers & Hurlers

The 24-card, regular-sized set was inserted every 145 packs of Pacific Invincible baseball. The cards are numbered with an "SH-xA" or "SH-xaB." Each "A" card is the left half of a two-card set with the two players from the same team having their logo in the fit-together center. Each card has the player's name printed in gold foil along the bottom border with gold-foil swirls around the team logo. The card backs have a circular headshot with text in English and Spanish.

	MT
Complete Set (24):	1000.
Common Player:	15.00
SH-1a Cal Ripken Jr.	80.00
SH-1b Mike Mussina	20.00
SH-2a Jose Canseco	20.00
SH-2b Roger Clemens	25.00
SH-3a Frank Thomas	100.00
SH-3b Wilson Alvarez	15.00
SH-4a Kenny Lofton	25.00
SH-4b Orel Hershiser	15.00
SH-5a Derek Jeter	60.00
SH-5b Andy Pettitte	25.00
SH-6a Ken Griffey Jr.	100.00
SH-6b Randy Johnson	20.00
SH-7a Alex Rodriguez	80.00
SH-7b Jamie Moyer	15.00
SH-8a Andruw Jones	60.00
SH-8b Greg Maddux	60.00
SH-9a Chipper Jones	60.00
SH-9b John Smoltz	18.00
SH-10a Jeff Bagwell	40.00
SH-10b Shane Reynolds	15.00
SH-11a Mike Piazza	60.00
SH-11b Hideo Nomo	20.00
SH-12a Tony Gwynn	40.00
SH-12b Fernando Valenzuela	15.00

1997 Pinnacle

The '97 Pinnacle baseball set consists of 200 base cards. The card fronts consist of the player's name stamped within a foil baseball diamond-shape at the bottom of each card. Card backs contain summaries of the players' 1996 and lifetime statistics. Included within the base set is a

30-card Rookies subset, a 12-card Clout subset and three checklists. Inserts include two parallel sets (Artist's Proof and Museum Collection), Passport to the Majors, Shades, Team Pinnacle, Cardfrontations, and Home/Away. Cards were sold in 10-card packs for $2.49 each.

		MT
Complete Set (200):		20.00
Common Player:		.10
Wax Box:		45.00
1	Cecil Fielder	.15
2	Garret Anderson	.10
3	Charles Nagy	.10
4	Darryl Hamilton	.10
5	Greg Myers	.10
6	Eric Davis	.10
7	Jeff Frye	.10
8	Marquis Grissom	.10
9	Curt Schilling	.10
10	Jeff Fassero	.10
11	Alan Benes	.20
12	Orlando Miller	.10
13	Alex Fernandez	.10
14	Andy Pettitte	.75
15	Andre Dawson	.10
16	Mark Grudzielanek	.10
17	Joe Vitiello	.10
18	Juan Gonzalez	1.25
19	Mark Whiten	.10
20	Lance Johnson	.10
21	Trevor Hoffman	.10
22	Marc Newfield	.10
23	Jim Eisenreich	.10
24	Joe Carter	.20
25	Jose Canseco	.25
26	Bill Swift	.10
27	Ellis Burks	.10
28	Ben McDonald	.10
29	Edgar Martinez	.10
30	Jamie Moyer	.10
31	Chan Ho Park	.10
32	Carlos Delgado	.10
33	Kevin Mitchell	.10
34	Carlos Garcia	.10
35	Darryl Strawberry	.10
36	Jim Thome	.30
37	Jose Offerman	.10
38	Ryan Klesko	.40
39	Ruben Sierra	.10
40	Devon White	.10
41	Brian Jordan	.10
42	Tony Gwynn	1.25
43	Rafael Palmeiro	.15
44	Dante Bichette	.20
45	Scott Stahoviak	.10
46	Roger Cedeno	.10
47	Ivan Rodriguez	.50
48	Bob Abreu	.10
49	Darryl Kile	.10
50	Darren Dreifort	.10
51	Shawon Dunston	.10
52	Mark McGwire	1.00
53	Tim Salmon	.25
54	Gene Schall	.10
55	Roger Clemens	1.00
56	Rondell White	.20
57	Ed Sprague	.10
58	Craig Paquette	.10
59	David Segui	.10
60	Jaime Navarro	.10
61	Tom Glavine	.15
62	Jeff Brantley	.10
63	Kimera Bartee	.10
64	Fernando Vina	.10
65	Eddie Murray	.40
66	Lenny Dykstra	.10

67	Kevin Elster	.10
68	Vinny Castilla	.10
69	Todd Greene	.10
70	Brett Butler	.10
71	Robby Thompson	.10
72	Reggie Jefferson	.10
73	Todd Hundley	.10
74	Jeff King	.10
75	Ernie Young	.10
76	Jeff Bagwell	1.25
77	Dan Wilson	.10
78	Paul Molitor	.25
79	Kevin Seitzer	.10
80	Kevin Brown	.10
81	Ron Gant	.15
82	Dwight Gooden	.10
83	Todd Stottlemyre	.10
84	Ken Caminiti	.15
85	James Baldwin	.10
86	Jermaine Dye	.15
87	Harold Baines	.10
88	Pat Hentgen	.10
89	Frank Rodriguez	.10
90	Mark Johnson	.10
91	Jason Kendall	.10
92	Alex Rodriguez	3.00
93	Alan Trammell	.10
94	Scott Brosius	.10
95	Delino DeShields	.10
96	Chipper Jones	2.00
97	Barry Bonds	.75
98	Brady Anderson	.15
99	Ryne Sandberg	.75
100	Albert Belle	1.00
101	Jeff Cirillo	.10
102	Frank Thomas	3.00
103	Mike Piazza	2.00
104	Rickey Henderson	.10
105	Rey Ordonez	.20
106	Mark Grace	.15
107	Terry Steinbach	.10
108	Ray Durham	.10
109	Barry Larkin	.25
110	Tony Clark	.50
111	Bernie Williams	.50
112	John Smoltz	.15
113	Moises Alou	.10
114	Alex Gonzalez	.10
115	Rico Brogna	.10
116	Eric Karros	.10
117	Jeff Conine	.10
118	Todd Hollandsworth	.15
119	Troy Percival	.10
120	Paul Wilson	.15
121	Orel Hershiser	.10
122	Ozzie Smith	.40
123	Dave Hollins	.10
124	Ken Hill	.10
125	Rick Wilkins	.10
126	Scott Servais	.10
127	Fernando Valenzuela	.10
128	Mariano Rivera	.15
129	Mark Loretta	.10
130	Shane Reynolds	.10
131	Darren Oliver	.10
132	Steve Trachsel	.10
133	Darren Bragg	.10
134	Jason Dickson	.35
135	Darren Fletcher	.10
136	Gary Gaetti	.10
137	Joey Cora	.10
138	Terry Pendleton	.10
139	Derek Jeter	1.50
140	Danny Tartabull	.10
141	John Flaherty	.10
142	B.J. Surhoff	.10
143	Mark Sweeney	.10
144	Chad Mottola	.10
145	Andujar Cedeno	.10
146	Tim Belcher	.10
147	Mark Thompson	.10
148	Rafael Bournigal	.10
149	Marty Cordova	.10
150	Osvaldo Fernandez	.10
151	Mike Stanley	.10
152	Ricky Bottalico	.10
153	Donnie Wall	.10
154	Omar Vizquel	.10
155	Mike Mussina	.60
156	Brant Brown	.10
157	F.P. Santangelo	.10
158	Ryan Hancock	.10
159	Jeff D'Amico	.10
160	Luis Castillo	.20
161	Darin Erstad	1.25
162	Ugueth Urbina	.10
163	Andruw Jones	2.00
164	Steve Gibralter	.10
165	Robin Jennings	.10
166	Mike Cameron	.10
167	George Arias	.10

168	Chris Stynes	.10
169	Justin Thompson	.10
170	Jamey Wright	.10
171	Todd Walker	.50
172	Nomar Garciaparra	2.00
173	Jose Paniagua	.10
174	Marvin Benard	.10
175	Rocky Coppinger	.10
176	Quinton McCracken	.10
177	Amaury Telemaco	.10
178	Neifi Perez	.10
179	Todd Greene	.10
180	Jason Thompson	.10
181	Wilton Guerrero	.20
182	Edgar Renteria	.20
183	Billy Wagner	.10
184	Alex Ochoa	.10
185	Billy McMillon	.10
186	Kenny Lofton	.75
187	Andres Galarraga (Clout)	.15
188	Chuck Knoblauch (Clout)	.10
189	Greg Maddux (Clout)	2.00
190	Mo Vaughn (Clout)	1.00
191	Cal Ripken Jr. (Clout)	2.50
192	Hideo Nomo (Clout)	.60
193	Ken Griffey Jr. (Clout)	3.00
194	Sammy Sosa (Clout)	.20
195	Jay Buhner (Clout)	.15
196	Manny Ramirez (Clout)	.75
197	Matt Williams (Clout)	.25
198	Andruw Jones CL	.75
199	Darin Erstad CL	.50
200	Trey Beamon CL	.10

1997 Pinnacle Museum Collection

Each of the 200 cards in 1997 Pinnacle Series I was also issued in a graphically enhanced Museum Collection parallel set. The Museum cards utilize basically the same design as the regular-issue Pinnacle cards, but the front is printed in the company's Dufex foil technology. On back, a small rectangular seal beneath the team logo verifies the card's special status.

	MT
Museum Collection Complete Set (200):	600.00
Common Museum:	1.00
Museum Veteran Stars:	10x to 15x
Museum Young Stars & RCs:	4x to 8x

1997 Pinnacle Artist's Proofs

The 200-card, regular-sized parallel set was randomly inserted in packs of 1997 Pinnacle baseball. Of the 200 cards, 125 were done in bronze foil (common), 50 in silver (uncommon) and 25 gold (rare). The card fronts feature a color action shot over a foil background. "Artist's Proof" is stamped along the lower edge. The card backs contain a large headshot with stats and a brief highlight text.

		MT
Complete Set (200):		3000.
Common Bronze:		6.00
Common Silver:		10.00
Common Gold:		15.00
1	Cecil Fielder B	8.00
2	Garret Anderson B	5.00
3	Charles Nagy B	5.00
4	Darryl Hamilton B	5.00
5	Greg Myers B	5.00
6	Eric Davis B	5.00
7	Jeff Frye B	5.00
8	Marquis Grissom S	10.00
9	Curt Schilling B	5.00
10	Jeff Fassero B	5.00
11	Alan Benes S	15.00
12	Orlando Miller B	5.00
13	Alex Fernandez B	8.00
14	Andy Pettitte G	50.00
15	Andre Dawson B	5.00
16	Mark Grudzielanek B	5.00
17	Joe Vitiello B	5.00
18	Juan Gonzalez G	125.00
19	Mark Whiten B	5.00
20	Lance Johnson B	5.00
21	Trevor Hoffman B	5.00
22	Marc Newfield B	5.00
23	Jim Eisenreich B	5.00
24	Joe Carter S	12.00
25	Jose Canseco S	15.00
26	Bill Swift B	5.00
27	Ellis Burks B	5.00
28	Ben McDonald B	5.00
29	Edgar Martinez S	10.00
30	Jamie Moyer B	5.00
31	Chan Ho Park S	10.00
32	Carlos Delgado S	10.00
33	Kevin Mitchell B	5.00
34	Carlos Garcia B	5.00
35	Darryl Strawberry G	15.00
36	Jim Thome G	40.00
37	Jose Offerman B	5.00
38	Ryan Klesko S	30.00
39	Ruben Sierra B	5.00
40	Devon White B	5.00
41	Brian Jordan G	15.00
42	Tony Gwynn S	100.00
43	Rafael Palmeiro S	12.00
44	Dante Bichette B	8.00
45	Scott Stahoviak B	5.00
46	Roger Cedeno B	5.00
47	Ivan Rodriguez G	40.00
48	Bob Abreu S	10.00
49	Darryl Kile B	5.00
50	Darren Dreifort B	5.00
51	Shawon Dunston B	5.00
52	Mark McGwire S	80.00
53	Tim Salmon S	15.00
54	Gene Schall B	5.00
55	Roger Clemens B	50.00
56	Rondell White S	10.00
57	Ed Sprague B	5.00
58	Craig Paquette B	5.00
59	David Segui B	5.00
60	Jaime Navarro B	5.00
61	Tom Glavine S	12.00
62	Jeff Brantley B	5.00
63	Kimera Bartee B	5.00
64	Fernando Vina B	5.00
65	Eddie Murray S	20.00
66	Lenny Dykstra B	5.00
67	Kevin Elster B	5.00
68	Vinny Castilla B	5.00
69	Todd Greene S	10.00
70	Brett Butler B	5.00
71	Robby Thompson B	5.00
72	Reggie Jefferson B	5.00
73	Todd Hundley S	10.00
74	Jeff King B	5.00
75	Ernie Young S	5.00
76	Jeff Bagwell G	125.00
77	Dan Wilson B	5.00
78	Paul Molitor G	50.00
79	Kevin Seitzer B	5.00
80	Kevin Brown S	10.00
81	Ron Gant S	10.00
82	Dwight Gooden S	10.00

#	Player	Price
83	Todd Stottlemyre B	5.00
84	Ken Caminiti G	30.00
85	James Baldwin B	5.00
86	Jermaine Dye S	15.00
87	Harold Baines B	5.00
88	Pat Hentgen B	5.00
89	Frank Rodriguez B	5.00
90	Mark Johnson B	5.00
91	Jason Kendall S	10.00
92	Alex Rodriguez G	200.00
93	Alan Trammell B	5.00
94	Scott Brosius B	5.00
95	Delino DeShields B	5.00
96	Chipper Jones S	120.00
97	Barry Bonds S	50.00
98	Brady Anderson S	12.00
99	Ryne Sandberg S	50.00
100	Albert Belle G	80.00
101	Jeff Cirillo B	5.00
102	Frank Thomas G	200.00
103	Mike Piazza S	120.00
104	Rickey Henderson B	6.00
105	Rey Ordonez S	15.00
106	Mark Grace S	12.00
107	Terry Steinbach B	5.00
108	Ray Durham B	5.00
109	Barry Larkin S	15.00
110	Tony Clark S	40.00
111	Bernie Williams G	35.00
112	John Smoltz G	30.00
113	Moises Alou B	5.00
114	Alex Gonzalez B	5.00
115	Rico Brogna B	5.00
116	Eric Karros B	5.00
117	Jeff Conine S	10.00
118	Todd Hollandsworth G	20.00
119	Troy Percival S	10.00
120	Paul Wilson S	15.00
121	Orel Hershiser B	5.00
122	Ozzie Smith S	25.00
123	Dave Hollins B	5.00
124	Ken Hill B	5.00
125	Rick Wilkins B	5.00
126	Scott Servais B	5.00
127	Fernando Valenzuela B	5.00
128	Mariano Rivera G	25.00
129	Mark Loretta B	5.00
130	Shane Reynolds S	10.00
131	Darren Oliver B	5.00
132	Steve Trachsel B	5.00
133	Darren Bragg B	5.00
134	Jason Dickson B	10.00
135	Darren Fletcher B	5.00
136	Gary Gaetti B	5.00
137	Joey Cora B	5.00
138	Terry Pendleton B	5.00
139	Derek Jeter G	150.00
140	Danny Tartabull B	5.00
141	John Flaherty B	5.00
142	B.J. Surhoff B	5.00
143	Mark Sweeney B	5.00
144	Chad Mottola B	5.00
145	Andujar Cedeno B	5.00
146	Tim Belcher B	5.00
147	Mark Thompson B	5.00
148	Rafael Bournigal B	5.00
149	Marty Cordova S	10.00
150	Osvaldo Fernandez B	5.00
151	Mike Stanley B	5.00
152	Ricky Bottalico B	5.00
153	Donnie Wall B	5.00
154	Omar Vizquel B	5.00
155	Mike Mussina S	30.00
156	Brant Brown B	5.00
157	F.P. Santangelo S	10.00
158	Ryan Hancock B	5.00
159	Jeff D'Amico B	5.00
160	Luis Castillo B	10.00
161	Darin Erstad G	80.00
162	Uguoth Urbina B	5.00
163	Andruw Jones G	120.00
164	Steve Gibralter B	5.00
165	Robin Jennings S	10.00
166	Mike Cameron B	5.00
167	George Arias S	10.00
168	Chris Stynes B	5.00
169	Justin Thompson B	5.00
170	Jamey Wright B	5.00
171	Todd Walker G	30.00
172	Nomar Garciaparra B	75.00
173	Jose Paniagua B	5.00
174	Marvin Benard B	5.00
175	Rocky Coppinger B	5.00
176	Quinton McCracken B	5.00
177	Amaury Telemaco B	5.00
178	Neifi Perez B	5.00
179	Todd Greene B	5.00
180	Jason Thompson B	5.00
181	Wilton Guerrero B	10.00
182	Edgar Renteria S	15.00
183	Billy Wagner S	10.00
184	Alex Ochoa G	15.00
185	Billy McMillon B	5.00
186	Kenny Lofton B (Clout)	15.00
187	Andres Galarraga B (Clout)	8.00
188	Chuck Knoblauch G (Clout)	15.00
189	Greg Maddux S (Clout)	80.00
190	Mo Vaughn S (Clout)	40.00
191	Cal Ripken Jr. G (Clout)	125.00
192	Hideo Nomo S (Clout)	30.00
193	Ken Griffey Jr. G (Clout)	250.00
194	Sammy Sosa S (Clout)	15.00
195	Jay Buhner S (Clout)	10.00
196	Manny Ramirez G (Clout)	40.00
197	Matt Williams B (Clout)	8.00
198	Andruw Jones CL B	40.00
199	Darin Erstad CL B	25.00
200	Trey Beamon CL B	5.00

1997 Pinnacle Cardfrontations

The 20-card, regular-sized, hobby-only set was inserted every 23 packs of 1997 Pinnacle baseball. The card fronts depict a player headshot imaged over a foil rainbow background. The same player is then pictured in action shots with the "Cardfrontation" logo in gold foil in the lower right half. The player's name appears in gold foil below the gold-foil team logo. The card backs depict another player's headshot with a short text describing interaction between the two players. The cards are numbered as "x of 20."

		MT
Complete Set (20):		225.00
Common Player:		4.00
1	Greg Maddux, Mike Piazza	20.00
2	Tom Glavine, Ken Caminiti	4.00
3	Randy Johnson, Cal Ripken Jr.	25.00
4	Kevin Appier, Mark McGwire	12.00
5	Andy Pettitte, Juan Gonzalez	15.00
6	Pat Hentgen, Albert Belle	15.00
7	Hideo Nomo, Chipper Jones	20.00
8	Ismael Valdes, Sammy Sosa	4.00
9	Mike Mussina, Manny Ramirez	8.00
10	David Cone, Jay Buhner	4.00
11	Mark Wohlers, Gary Sheffield	5.00
12	Alan Benes, Barry Bonds	10.00
13	Roger Clemens, Ivan Rodriguez	8.00
14	Mariano Rivera, Ken Griffey Jr.	35.00
15	Dwight Gooden, Frank Thomas	35.00
16	John Wetteland, Darin Erstad	15.00
17	John Smoltz, Brian Jordan	4.00
18	Kevin Brown, Jeff Bagwell	15.00
19	Jack McDowell, Alex Rodriguez	35.00
20	Charles Nagy, Bernie Williams	4.00

1997 Pinnacle Home/Away

The 24-card, regular-sized, die-cut set was inserted every 33 retail packs. Included in the set are Alex Rodriguez, Derek Jeter, Ken Griffey Jr. and Chipper Jones.

		MT
Complete Set (12):		175.00
Common Player:		5.00
1	Chipper Jones	20.00
2	Ken Griffey Jr.	30.00
3	Mike Piazza	20.00
4	Frank Thomas	30.00
5	Jeff Bagwell	12.00
6	Alex Rodriguez	25.00
7	Barry Bonds	8.00
8	Mo Vaughn	8.00
9	Derek Jeter	20.00
10	Mark McGwire	12.00
11	Cal Ripken Jr.	25.00
12	Albert Belle	10.00

1997 Pinnacle Passport to the Majors

The 25-card, regular-sized set was inserted every 36 packs of 1997 Pinnacle baseball. The cards fold out and resemble a mini passport.

		MT
Complete Set (25):		160.00
Common Player:		3.00
1	Greg Maddux	15.00
1s	Greg Maddux ("SAMPLE" overprint)	15.00
2	Ken Griffey Jr.	25.00
3	Frank Thomas	25.00
4	Cal Ripken Jr.	20.00
5	Mike Piazza	15.00
6	Alex Rodriguez	25.00
7	Mo Vaughn	8.00
8	Chipper Jones	15.00
9	Roberto Alomar	6.00
10	Edgar Martinez	3.00
11	Javier Lopez	3.00
12	Ivan Rodriguez	5.00
13	Juan Gonzalez	12.00
14	Carlos Baerga	3.00
15	Sammy Sosa	4.00
16	Manny Ramirez	7.00
17	Raul Mondesi	4.00
18	Henry Rodriguez	3.00
19	Rafael Palmeiro	3.00
20	Rey Ordonez	4.00
21	Hideo Nomo	6.00
22	Makoto Suzuki	3.00
23	Chan Ho Park	3.00
24	Larry Walker	3.00
25	Ruben Rivera	5.00

1997 Pinnacle Shades

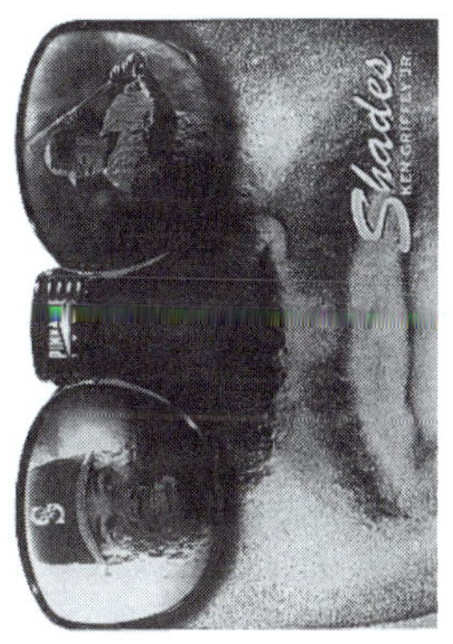

The 10-card, regular-sized set was inserted every 23 retail packs of Pinnacle baseball. The cards featured 10 headshots on horizontal cards wearing game sunglasses.

		MT
Complete Set (10):		110.00
Common Player:		3.00
1	Ken Griffey Jr.	25.00
2	Juan Gonzalez	10.00
3	John Smoltz	4.00
4	Gary Sheffield	5.00
5	Cal Ripken Jr.	20.00
6	Mo Vaughn	8.00
7	Brian Jordan	3.00
8	Mike Piazza	15.00
9	Frank Thomas	25.00
10	Alex Rodriguez	25.00

1997 Pinnacle Team Pinnacle

The 10-card, regular-sized set features top National League players from a position on one side with the best American League players on the other. One side of the card is in Dufex printing and there is actually two versions of each card, as either side will feature the Dufex foil. Team Pinnacle is inserted every 90 packs.

		MT
Complete Set (10):		250.00
Common Player:		10.00
1	Frank Thomas, Jeff Bagwell	50.00
2	Chuck Knoblauch, Eric Young	10.00
3	Ken Caminiti, Jim Thome	12.00
4	Alex Rodriguez, Chipper Jones	50.00

5	Mike Piazza, Ivan Rodriguez	30.00
6	Albert Belle, Barry Bonds	15.00
7	Ken Griffey Jr., Ellis Burks	50.00
8	Juan Gonzalez, Gary Sheffield	25.00
9	John Smoltz, Andy Pettitte	15.00
10	All Players	40.00

1997 New Pinnacle

In lieu of a second series of Pinnacle Baseball, the company offered collectors New Pinnacle, a 200-card set sold in 10-card packs for $2.99 each. Two parallel versions of the 200-card set exist in Museum Collection and Artist's Proof. Other inserts include Press Plates, Spellbound, Keeping the Pace and Interleague Encounter. Collectors who obtain four Press Plates of the same player's card back or front were eligible to win cash prizes.

		MT
Complete Set (200):		25.00
Common Player:		.10
Museum Collection Complete Set (200):		500.00
Common Museum:		1.50
Museum Veteran Stars:		10x to 15x
Museum Yng Stars & RCs:		5x to 10x
Wax Box:		50.00
1	Ken Griffey Jr.	3.00
2	Sammy Sosa	.35
3	Greg Maddux	2.00
4	Matt Williams	.35
5	Jason Isringhausen	.10
6	Gregg Jefferies	.10
7	Chili Davis	.10
8	Paul O'Neill	.10
9	Larry Walker	.35
10	Ellis Burks	.10
11	Cliff Floyd	.10
12	Albert Belle	1.00
13	Javier Lopez	.20
14	David Cone	.20
15	Jose Canseco	.30
16	Todd Zeile	.10
17	Bernard Gilkey	.10
18	Andres Galarraga	.20
19	Chris Snopek	.10
20	Tim Salmon	.25
21	Roger Clemens	1.00
22	Reggie Sanders	.10
23	John Jaha	.10
24	Andy Pettitte	.75
25	Kenny Lofton	.75
26	Robb Nen	.10
27	John Wetteland	.10
28	Bobby Bonilla	.10
29	Hideo Nomo	.60
30	Cecil Fielder	.20
31	Garret Anderson	.10
32	Pat Hentgen	.10
33	David Justice	.20
34	Billy Wagner	.10
35	Al Leiter	.10
36	Mark Wohlers	.10
37	Rondell White	.10
38	Charles Johnson	.10
39	Mark Grace	.20
40	Pedro Martinez	.20
41	Tom Goodwin	.10
42	Manny Ramirez	.75
43	Greg Vaughn	.10
44	Brian Jordan	.10
45	Mike Piazza	2.00
46	Roberto Hernandez	.10
47	Wade Boggs	.20
48	Scott Sanders	.10
49	Alex Gonzalez	.10
50	Kevin Brown	.10
51	Bob Higginson	.10
52	Ken Caminiti	.25
53	Derek Jeter	2.00
54	Carlos Baerga	.10
55	Jay Buhner	.20
56	Tim Naehring	.10
57	Jeff Bagwell	1.25
58	Steve Finley	.10
59	Kevin Appier	.10
60	Jay Bell	.10
61	Ivan Rodriguez	.60
62	Terrell Wade	.10
63	Rusty Greer	.10
64	Juan Guzman	.10
65	Fred McGriff	.30
66	Tino Martinez	.25
67	Ray Lankford	.10
68	Juan Gonzalez	1.25
69	Ron Gant	.10
70	Jack McDowell	.10
71	Tony Gwynn	1.25
72	Joe Carter	.10
73	Wilson Alvarez	.10
74	Jason Giambi	.10
75	Brian Hunter	.10
76	Michael Tucker	.10
77	Andy Benes	.10
78	Brady Anderson	.20
79	Ramon Martinez	.10
80	Troy Percival	.10
81	Alex Rodriguez	3.00
82	Jim Thome	.50
83	Denny Neagle	.10
84	Rafael Palmeiro	.20
85	Jose Valentin	.10
86	Marc Newfield	.10
87	Mariano Rivera	.20
88	Alan Benes	.20
89	Jimmy Key	.10
90	Joe Randa	.10
91	Cal Ripken Jr.	2.50
92	Craig Biggio	.20
93	Dean Palmer	.10
94	Gary Sheffield	.35
95	Ismael Valdez	.10
96	John Valentin	.10
97	Johnny Damon	.10
98	Mo Vaughn	.75
99	Paul Sorrento	.10
100	Randy Johnson	.60
101	Raul Mondesi	.20
102	Roberto Alomar	.60
103	Royce Clayton	.10
104	Mark Grudzielanek	.10
105	Wally Joyner	.10
106	Wil Cordero	.10
107	Will Clark	.25
108	Chuck Knoblauch	.25
109	Derek Bell	.10
110	Henry Rodriguez	.10
111	Edgar Renteria	.10
112	Travis Fryman	.10
113	Eric Young	.10
114	Sandy Alomar Jr.	.10
115	Darin Erstad	1.25
116	Barry Larkin	.10
117	Barry Bonds	.75
118	Frank Thomas	3.00
119	Carlos Delgado	.10
120	Jason Kendall	.10
121	Todd Hollandsworth	.10
122	Jim Edmonds	.10
123	Chipper Jones	2.00
124	Jeff Fassero	.10
125	Deion Sanders	.30
126	Matt Lawton	.10
127	Ryan Klesko	.50
128	Mike Mussina	.75
129	Paul Molitor	.50
130	Dante Bichette	.20
131	Bill Pulsipher	.10
132	Todd Hundley	.20
133	J.T. Snow	.10
134	Chuck Finley	.10
135	Shawn Green	.10
136	Charles Nagy	.10
137	Willie Greene	.10
138	Marty Cordova	.10
139	Eddie Murray	.40
140	Ryne Sandberg	.75
141	Alex Fernandez	.10
142	Mark McGwire	1.00
143	Eric Davis	.10
144	Jermaine Dye	.10
145	Ruben Sierra	.10
146	Damon Buford	.10
147	John Smoltz	.20
148	Alex Ochoa	.10
149	Moises Alou	.10
150	Rico Brogna	.10
151	Terry Steinbach	.10
152	Jeff King	.10
153	Carlos Garcia	.10
154	Tom Glavine	.20
155	Edgar Martinez	.10
156	Kevin Elster	.10
157	Darryl Hamilton	.10
158	Jason Dickson	.20
159	Kevin Orie	.10
160	*Bubba Trammell*	1.00
161	Jose Guillen	1.00
162	Brant Brown	.10
163	Wendell Magee	.10
164	Scott Spiezio	.10
165	Todd Walker	.50
166	*Rod Myers*	.10
167	Damon Mashore	.10
168	Wilton Guerrero	.20
169	Vladimir Guerrero	1.50
170	Nomar Garciaparra	2.00
171	Shannon Stewart	.10
172	Scott Rolen	1.50
173	Bob Abreu	.10
174	*Danny Patterson*	.20
175	Andruw Jones	2.00
176	Brian Giles	.10
177	Dmitri Young	.10
178	Cal Ripken Jr. (East Meets West)	1.25
179	Chuck Knoblauch (East Meets West)	.20
180	Alex Rodriguez (East Meets West)	1.50
181	Andres Galarraga (East Meets West)	.15
182	Pedro Martinez (East Meets West)	.15
183	Brady Anderson (East Meets West)	.10
184	Barry Bonds (East Meets West)	.40
185	Ivan Rodriguez (East Meets West)	.30
186	Gary Sheffield (East Meets West)	.20
187	Denny Neagle (East Meets West)	.10
188	Mark McGwire (Aura)	.50
189	Ellis Burks (Aura)	.10
190	Alex Rodriguez (Aura)	1.50
191	Mike Piazza (Aura)	1.00
192	Barry Bonds (Aura)	.40
193	Albert Belle (Aura)	.50
194	Chipper Jones (Aura)	1.00
195	Juan Gonzalez (Aura)	.60
196	Brady Anderson (Aura)	.10
197	Frank Thomas (Aura)	1.50
198	Checklist (Vladimir Guerrero)	.75
199	Checklist (Todd Walker)	.25
200	Checklist (Scott Rolen)	.60

1997 New Pinnacle Artist's Proof

This 200-card parallel set features a special foil treatment and is fractured into three levels of scarcity - Red (125 cards), Blue (50 cards) and Green (25 cards). Cards were inserted at a rate of 1:39 packs.

	MT
Common Red Artist's Proof:	5.00
Red Artist's Proofs:	15x to 20x
Common Blue Artist's Proof:	15.00
Blue Artist's Proofs:	35x to 50x
Common Green Artist's Proof:	30.00
Green Artist's Proofs:	50x to 75x

1997 New Pinnacle Interleague Encounter

Inserted 1:240 packs, this 10-card set showcases 20 American League and National League rivals with the date of their first interleague match-up on double-sided mirror mylar cards.

		MT
Complete Set (10):		700.00
Common Player:		20.00
1	Albert Belle, Brian Jordan	35.00
2	Andruw Jones, Brady Anderson	60.00
3	Ken Griffey Jr., Tony Gwynn	125.00
4	Cal Ripken Jr., Chipper Jones	80.00
5	Mike Piazza, Ivan Rodriguez	60.00
6	Derek Jeter, Vladimir Guerrero	75.00
7	Greg Maddux, Mo Vaughn	60.00
8	Alex Rodriguez, Hideo Nomo	100.00
9	Juan Gonzalez, Barry Bonds	50.00
10	Frank Thomas, Jeff Bagwell	100.00

1997 New Pinnacle Keeping the Pace

The top sluggers who are considered candidates to break Roger Maris' single-season record of 61 home runs are featured in this 18-card insert set. Cards feature Dot Matrix Holograms and were inserted 1:89 packs.

		MT
Complete Set (18):		750.00
Common Player:		15.00
1	Juan Gonzalez	50.00
2	Greg Maddux	60.00
3	Ivan Rodriguez	25.00
4	Ken Griffey Jr.	125.00
5	Alex Rodriguez	80.00
6	Barry Bonds	30.00
7	Frank Thomas	100.00
8	Chuck Knoblauch	20.00
9	Derek Jeter	60.00
10	Roger Clemens	35.00
11	Kenny Lofton	30.00

12	Tony Gwynn	50.00
13	Troy Percival	15.00
14	Cal Ripken Jr.	80.00
15	Andy Pettitte	30.00
16	Hideo Nomo	25.00
17	Randy Johnson	25.00
18	Mike Piazza	60.00

1997 New Pinnacle Press Plates

Just when collectors thought they had seen every type of pack insert chase card imaginable, New Pinnacle proved them wrong by cutting up and inserting into packs (about one per 1,250) the metal plates used to print the regular cards in the set. There are black, blue, red and yellow plates for the front and back of each card. Rather than touting the collector value of the plates, Pinnacle created a treasure hunt by offering $20,000-35,000 to anybody assembling a complete set of four plates for either the front or back of any card. The $35,000, which would have been awarded for completion prior to Aug. 22, was unclaimed. The amount decreased to $20,000 for any set redeemed by the end of 1997.

MT

(Because of the unique nature of each press plate, no current market value can be quoted.)

1997 New Pinnacle Spellbound

Each of the 50 cards in this insert features a letter of the alphabet as the basic card design. The letters can be used to spell out the names of nine players featured in the set. Cards featured micro-etched foil and are inserted 1:19 packs.

	MT
Common Griffey Jr. (1KG-6KG):	25.00
Common Andruw Jones (1AJ-6AJ):	15.00
Common Ripken Jr. (1CR-6CR):	20.00
Common Chipper Jones (1CJ-7CJ):	15.00
Common Frank Thomas (1FT-5FT):	25.00
Common Mike Piazza (1MP-6MP):	15.00
Common Ivan Rodriguez (1IR-5IR):	6.00
Common Alex Rodriguez (1AR-4AR):	25.00
Common Albert Belle (1AB-5AB):	8.00

1997 Pinnacle Certified

This 150-card base features a mirror-like mylar finish and a peel-off protector on each card front. Backs feature the player's 1996 statistics against each opponent. There are four different parallel sets, each with varying degrees of scarcity - Certified Red (1:5), Mirror Red (1:99), Mirror Blue (1:199) and Mirror Gold (1:299). Other inserts include Lasting Impressions, Certified Team, and Certified Gold Team. Cards were sold in six-card packs for a suggested price of $4.99.

		MT
Complete Set (150):		40.00
Common Player:		.15
Jose Cruz Jr. Redemption:		25.00
Wax Box:		100.00
1	Barry Bonds	1.25
2	Mo Vaughn	1.25
3	Matt Williams	.50
4	Ryne Sandberg	1.25
5	Jeff Bagwell	2.00
6	Alan Benes	.15
7	John Wetteland	.15
8	Fred McGriff	.40
9	Craig Biggio	.25
10	Bernie Williams	1.00
11	Brian L. Hunter	.15
12	Sandy Alomar Jr.	.15
13	Ray Lankford	.15
14	Ryan Klesko	.50
15	Jermaine Dye	.15
16	Andy Benes	.15
17	Albert Belle	.15
18	Tony Clark	1.00
19	Dean Palmer	.15
20	Bernard Gilkey	.15
21	Ken Caminiti	.30
22	Alex Rodriguez	4.00
23	Tim Salmon	.40
24	Larry Walker	.50
25	Barry Larkin	.30
26	Mike Piazza	3.00
27	Brady Anderson	.15
28	Cal Ripken Jr.	4.00
29	Charles Nagy	.15
30	Paul Molitor	.75
31	Darin Erstad	1.50
32	Rey Ordonez	.15
33	Wally Joyner	.15
34	David Cone	.25
35	Sammy Sosa	.50
36	Dante Bichette	.30
37	Eric Karros	.15
38	Omar Vizquel	.15
39	Roger Clemens	1.50
40	Joe Carter	.15
41	Frank Thomas	5.00
42	Javier Lopez	.15
43	Mike Mussina	1.00
44	Gary Sheffield	.50
45	Tony Gwynn	2.00
46	Jason Kendall	.15
47	Jim Thome	.75
48	Andres Galarraga	.30
49	Mark McGwire	1.75
50	Troy Percival	.15
51	Derek Jeter	3.00
52	Todd Hollandsworth	.15
53	Ken Griffey Jr.	5.00
54	Randy Johnson	.75
55	Pat Hentgen	.15
56	Rusty Greer	.15
57	John Jaha	.15
58	Kenny Lofton	1.25
59	Chipper Jones	3.00
60	Robb Nen	.15
61	Rafael Palmeiro	.30
62	Mariano Rivera	.25
63	Hideo Nomo	1.00
64	Greg Vaughn	.15
65	Ron Gant	.15
66	Eddie Murray	.40
67	John Smoltz	.30
68	Manny Ramirez	1.25
69	Juan Gonzalez	2.00
70	F.P. Santangelo	.15
71	Moises Alou	.15
72	Alex Ochoa	.15
73	Chuck Knoblauch	.30
74	Raul Mondesi	.30
75	J.T. Snow	.15
76	Rickey Henderson	.15
77	Bobby Bonilla	.15
78	Wade Boggs	.00
79	Ivan Rodriguez	1.00
80	Brian Jordan	.15
81	Al Leiter	.15
82	Jay Buhner	.30
83	Greg Maddux	3.00
84	Edgar Martinez	.15
85	Kevin Brown	.15
86	Eric Young	.15
87	Todd Hundley	.30
88	Ellis Burks	.15
89	Marquis Grissom	.15
90	Jose Canseco	.40
91	Henry Rodriguez	.15
92	Andy Pettitte	1.25
93	Mark Grudzielanek	.15
94	Dwight Gooden	.15
95	Roberto Alomar	1.00
96	Paul Wilson	.15
97	Will Clark	.30
98	Rondell White	.15
99	Charles Johnson	.15
100	Jim Edmonds	.15
101	Jason Giambi	.15
102	Billy Wagner	.15
103	Edgar Renteria	.15
104	Johnny Damon	.15
105	Jason Isringhausen	.15
106	Andruw Jones	3.00
107	Jose Guillen	.15
108	Kevin Orie	.15
109	Brian Giles	.15
110	Danny Patterson	.15
111	Vladimir Guerrero	2.00
112	Scott Rolen	2.00
113	Damon Mashore	.15
114	Nomar Garciaparra	2.50
115	Todd Walker	.75
116	Wilton Guerrero	.15
117	Bob Abreu	.15
118	Brooks Kieschnick	.15
119	Pokey Reese	.15
120	Todd Greene	.15
121	Dmitri Young	.15
122	Raul Casanova	.15
123	Glendon Rusch	.15
124	Jason Dickson	.15
125	Jorge Posada	.15
126	*Rod Myers*	.15
127	*Bubba Trammell*	1.50
128	Scott Spiezio	.15
129	*Hideki Irabu*	4.00
130	Wendell Magee	.15
131	Bartolo Colon	.15
132	Chris Holt	.15
133	Calvin Maduro	.15
134	Ray Montgomery	.15
135	Shannon Stewart	.15
136	Ken Griffey Jr. (Certified Stars)	2.50
137	Vladimir Guerrero (Certified Stars)	1.00
138	Roger Clemens (Certified Stars)	.75
139	Mark McGwire (Certified Stars)	.75
140	Albert Belle (Certified Stars)	.60
141	Derek Jeter (Certified Stars)	1.50
142	Juan Gonzalez (Certified Stars)	1.00
143	Greg Maddux (Certified Stars)	1.50
144	Alex Rodriguez (Certified Stars)	2.00
145	Jeff Bagwell (Certified Stars)	1.00
146	Cal Ripken Jr. (Certified Stars)	2.00
147	Tony Gwynn (Certified Stars)	1.00
148	Frank Thomas (Certified Stars)	2.50
149	Hideo Nomo (Certified Stars)	.50
150	Andruw Jones (Certified Stars)	1.50

1997 Pinnacle Certified Red

This parallel set features a red tint to the mylar background. Cards were inserted 1:5 packs.

	MT
Common Certified Red:	2.00
Certified Red Semistars:	4.00
Stars:	4x to 8x
Yng Stars & RC's:	3x to 6x

1997 Pinnacle Certified Mirror Red

This parallel set features a red design element on the front of each card. Cards were inserted 1:99 packs.

	MT
Common Mirror Red:	15.00
Mirror Red Semistars:	25.00
Stars:	40x to 75x
Young Stars & RCs:	30x to 50x

1997 Pinnacle Certified Mirror Blue

This parallel set features a blue design element on the front of each card. Cards were inserted 1:199 packs.

	MT
Common Mirror Blue:	30.00
Mirror Blue Semistars:	50.00
Mirror Blue Stars:	100x to 150x
Mirror Blue Yng Stars & RCs:	75x to 125x

1997 Pinnacle Certified Mirror Gold

This parallel set features a holographic gold design on the front of each card. Cards were inserted 1:299 packs.

	MT
Common Mirror Gold:	75.00
Mirror Gold Semistars:	150.00
Mirror Gold Stars:	300x to 450x
Yng Stars & RCs:	200x to 350x

1997 Pinnacle Certified Lasting Impression

This 20-card insert features a die-cut design and a mirror mylar finish and pictures some of baseball's top veteran stars. Cards were inserted 1:19 packs.

		MT
Complete Set (20):		220.00
Common Player:		4.00
1	Cal Ripken Jr.	30.00
2	Ken Griffey Jr.	40.00
3	Mo Vaughn	10.00
4	Brian Jordan	4.00
5	Mark McGwire	15.00
6	Chuck Knoblauch	6.00
7	Sammy Sosa	6.00
8	Brady Anderson	4.00
9	Frank Thomas	40.00
10	Tony Gwynn	18.00
11	Roger Clemens	10.00
12	Alex Rodriguez	30.00
13	Paul Molitor	8.00
14	Kenny Lofton	10.00
15	John Smoltz	4.00
16	Roberto Alomar	8.00
17	Randy Johnson	8.00
18	Ryne Sandberg	10.00
19	Manny Ramirez	10.00
20	Mike Mussina	8.00

1997 Pinnacle Certified Team

The top 20 players in the game are honored on cards with frosted silver mylar printing. Cards were inserted 1:19 packs. A parallel version of this set, Certified Gold Team, has a gold mylar design with each card numbered to 500.

		MT
Complete Set (20):		300.00
Common Player:		4.00
Gold Teams:		4x
1	Frank Thomas	40.00
2	Jeff Bagwell	18.00
3	Derek Jeter	25.00
4	Chipper Jones	25.00
5	Alex Rodriguez	30.00
6	Ken Caminiti	4.00
7	Cal Ripken Jr.	30.00
8	Mo Vaughn	10.00
9	Ivan Rodriguez	8.00
10	Mike Piazza	25.00
11	Juan Gonzalez	20.00
12	Barry Bonds	10.00
13	Ken Griffey Jr.	40.00
14	Andruw Jones	25.00
15	Albert Belle	12.00
16	Gary Sheffield	6.00
17	Andy Pettitte	10.00
18	Hideo Nomo	8.00
19	Greg Maddux	25.00
20	John Smoltz	4.00

A player's name in *italic type* indicates a rookie card.

1997 Pinnacle Inside

The first baseball card set to be sold within a sealed tin can, Inside Baseball consisted of a 150-card base set featuring both a color and black-and-white photo of the player on the front of the card. Included in the base set were 20 Rookies cards and three checklists. Inserts include the Club Edition and Diamond Edition parallel sets, Dueling Dugouts and Forty-something. In addition, 24 different cans, each featuring a different player, were available. Cans containing one pack of 10 cards were sold for $2.99 each.

		MT
Complete Set (150):		35.00
Common Player:		.10
Club Edition Complete Set (150):		500.00
Common Club Edition:		.75
Club Edition Stars:		5x to 10x
Club Edition Yng Stars & RC's:		3x to 6x
1	David Cone	.10
2	Sammy Sosa	.25
3	Joe Carter	.10
4	Juan Gonzalez	2.00
5	Hideo Nomo	.75
6	Moises Alou	.10
7	Marc Newfield	.10
8	Alex Rodriguez	4.00
9	Kimera Bartee	.10
10	Chuck Knoblauch	.25
11	Jason Isringhausen	.10
12	Jermaine Allensworth	.10
13	Frank Thomas	4.00
14	Paul Molitor	.75
15	John Mabry	.10
16	Greg Maddux	2.50
17	Rafael Palmeiro	.20
18	Brian Jordan	.10
19	Ken Griffey Jr.	4.00
20	Brady Anderson	.10
21	Ruben Sierra	.10
22	Travis Fryman	.10
23	Cal Ripken Jr.	3.00
24	Will Clark	.25
25	Todd Hollandsworth	.10
26	Kevin Brown	.10
27	Mike Piazza	2.50
28	Craig Biggio	.20
29	Paul Wilson	.10
30	Andres Galarraga	.20
31	Chipper Jones	2.50
32	Jason Giambi	.10
33	Ernie Young	.10
34	Marty Cordova	.10
35	Albert Belle	1.25
36	Roger Clemens	1.50
37	Ryne Sandberg	1.00
38	Henry Rodriguez	.10
39	Jay Buhner	.20
40	Raul Mondesi	.20
41	Jeff Fassero	.10
42	Edgar Martinez	.10
43	Trey Beamon	.10
44	Mo Vaughn	1.00
45	Gary Sheffield	.35
46	Ray Durham	.10
47	Brett Butler	.10
48	Ivan Rodriguez	.75
49	Fred McGriff	.25
50	Dean Palmer	.10
51	Rickey Henderson	.10
52	Andy Pettitte	1.00
53	Bobby Bonilla	.10
54	Shawn Green	.10
55	Tino Martinez	.40
56	Tony Gwynn	2.00
57	Tom Glavine	.20
58	Eric Young	.10
59	Kevin Appier	.10
60	Barry Bonds	1.00
61	Wade Boggs	.20
62	Jason Kendall	.10
63	Jeff Bagwell	2.00
64	Jeff Conine	.10
65	Greg Vaughn	.10
66	Eric Karros	.10
67	Manny Ramirez	1.00
68	John Smoltz	.20
69	Terrell Wade	.10
70	John Wetteland	.10
71	Kenny Lofton	1.00
72	Jim Thome	.75
73	Bill Pulsipher	.10
74	Darryl Strawberry	.10
75	Roberto Alomar	.75
76	Bobby Higginson	.10
77	James Baldwin	.10
78	Mark McGwire	1.50
79	Jose Canseco	.25
80	Mark Grudzielanek	.10
81	Ryan Klesko	.50
82	Javier Lopez	.10
83	Ken Caminiti	.20
84	Dave Nilsson	.10
85	Tim Salmon	.20
86	Cecil Fielder	.20
87	Derek Jeter	2.50
88	Garret Anderson	.10
89	Dwight Gooden	.10
90	Carlos Delgado	.10
91	Ugueth Urbina	.10
92	Chan Ho Park	.10
93	Eddie Murray	.40
94	Alex Ochoa	.10
95	Rusty Greer	.10
96	Mark Grace	.20
97	Pat Hentgen	.10
98	John Jaha	.10
99	Charles Johnson	.10
100	Jermaine Dye	.10
101	Quinton McCracken	.10
102	Troy Percival	.10
103	Shane Reynolds	.10
104	Rondell White	.10
105	Charles Nagy	.10
106	Alan Benes	.10
107	Tom Goodwin	.10
108	Ron Gant	.10
109	Dan Wilson	.10
110	Darin Erstad	1.50
111	Matt Williams	.25
112	Barry Larkin	.20
113	Mariano Rivera	.15
114	Larry Walker	.40
115	Jim Edmonds	.10
116	Michael Tucker	.10
117	Todd Hundley	.20
118	Alex Fernandez	.10
119	J.T. Snow	.10
120	Ellis Burks	.10
121	Steve Finley	.10
122	Mike Mussina	.75
123	Curtis Pride	.10
124	Derek Bell	.10
125	Dante Bichette	.20
126	Terry Steinbach	.10
127	Randy Johnson	.75
128	Andruw Jones	2.50
129	Vladimir Guerrero	2.00
130	Ruben Rivera	.10
131	Billy Wagner	.10
132	Scott Rolen	2.00
133	Rey Ordonez	.10
134	Karim Garcia	.10
135	George Arias	.10
136	Todd Greene	.10
137	Robin Jennings	.10
138	Raul Casanova	.10
139	Josh Booty	.10
140	Edgar Renteria	.10
141	Chad Mottola	.10
142	Dmitri Young	.10
143	Tony Clark	.75
144	Todd Walker	.75
145	Kevin Brown	.10
146	Nomar Garciaparra	2.50
147	Neifi Perez	.10
148	Derek Jeter, Todd Hollandsworth	.40
149	Pat Hentgen, John Smoltz	.10
150	Juan Gonzalez, Ken Caminiti	.30

1997 Pinnacle Inside Diamond Edition

A second parallel set, this time featuring a special die-cut design and gold holographic stamping. Cards were inserted 1:63 packs.

	MT
Common Diamond Edition:	15.00
Stars:	40x to 70x
Yng Stars & RCs:	30x to 50x

1997 Pinnacle Inside Cans

In addition to the cards, collectors had the option of collecting the 24 different player cans the cards were sold in.

		MT
Complete Opened Set (24):		20.00
Common Opened Can:		.40
Sealed Cans:		2x to 3x
1	Ken Griffey Jr.	2.50
2	Juan Gonzalez	1.25
3	Frank Thomas	2.50
4	Cal Ripken Jr.	2.00
5	Derek Jeter	1.50
6	Andruw Jones	1.50
7	Alex Rodriguez	2.50
8	Mike Piazza	1.50
9	Mo Vaughn	.75
10	Jeff Bagwell	1.00
11	Ken Caminiti	.40
12	Andy Pettitte	.75
13	Barry Bonds	.75
14	Mark McGwire	1.00
15	Ryan Klesko	.40
16	Manny Ramirez	.75
17	Ivan Rodriguez	.40
18	Chipper Jones	1.50
19	Albert Belle	1.00
20	Tony Gwynn	1.25
21	Kenny Lofton	.75
22	Greg Maddux	1.50
23	Hideo Nomo	.50
24	John Smoltz	.40

1997 Pinnacle Inside Dueling Dugouts

A 20-card insert that features a veteran player on one side, a rising star on the other, and a spinning wheel that reveals their respective achievements in various statistical categories. Cards were inserted 1:23 packs.

		MT
Complete Set (20):		325.00
Common Player:		8.00
1	Alex Rodriguez, Cal Ripken Jr.	50.00
2	Jeff Bagwell, Ken Caminiti	20.00
3	Barry Bonds, Albert Belle	20.00
4	Mike Piazza, Ivan Rodriguez	25.00
5	Chuck Knoblauch, Roberto Alomar	15.00
6	Ken Griffey Jr., Andruw Jones	50.00
7	Chipper Jones, Jim Thome	25.00
8	Frank Thomas, Mo Vaughn	40.00
9	Fred McGriff, Mark McGwire	15.00
10	Brian Jordan, Tony Gwynn	20.00
11	Barry Larkin, Derek Jeter	20.00
12	Kenny Lofton, Bernie Williams	15.00
13	Juan Gonzalez, Manny Ramirez	20.00
14	Will Clark, Rafael Palmeiro	10.00
15	Greg Maddux, Roger Clemens	20.00
16	John Smoltz, Andy Pettitte	15.00
17	Mariano Rivera, John Wetteland	8.00
18	Hideo Nomo, Mike Mussina	15.00
19	Todd Hollandsworth, Darin Erstad	15.00
20	Vladimir Guerrero, Karim Garcia	20.00

1997 Pinnacle
Inside Fortysomething

The top home run hitters in the game are pictured in this 16-card set. Cards were inserted 1:47 packs.

		MT
Complete Set (16):		300.00
Common Player:		8.00
1	Juan Gonzalez	40.00
2	Barry Bonds	20.00
3	Ken Caminiti	10.00
4	Mark McGwire	30.00
5	Todd Hundley	8.00
6	Albert Belle	25.00
7	Ellis Burks	8.00
8	Jay Buhner	8.00
9	Brady Anderson	8.00
10	Vinny Castilla	8.00
11	Mo Vaughn	20.00
12	Ken Griffey Jr.	80.00
13	Sammy Sosa	15.00
14	Andres Galarraga	10.00
15	Gary Sheffield	15.00
16	Frank Thomas	80.00

1997 Pinnacle
Mint Collection

The 30-card Mint Collection set came in three-card packs that also contained two coins. The cards came in two versions: die-cut and foil. Three foil versions appear with Bronze Act as the common with Silver (1:15) and Gold (1:48) also appearing. The coins that come with each pack arrive in brass, silver and gold and can be matched up with the corresponding player die-cut card. The card fronts feature a player action shot on the left side with a shadowed headshot on the right. On the die-cut versions, the coin-size hole is in the lower right quadrant while the foil team stamp for the common cards is in the same location. The card backs are numbered as "x of 30" and deliver a short text.

		MT
Complete Set (30):		20.00
Common Player:		.25
Bronze Cards: 2x		40.00
Silver Cards:		4x to 8x
Gold Cards:		10x to 20x
Wax Box:		50.00
1	Ken Griffey Jr.	2.50
2	Frank Thomas	2.50
3	Alex Rodriguez	2.50
4	Cal Ripken Jr.	2.00
5	Mo Vaughn	.75
6	Juan Gonzalez	1.25
7	Mike Piazza	1.75
8	Albert Belle	1.00
9	Chipper Jones	1.75
10	Andruw Jones	2.50
11	Greg Maddux	1.75
12	Hideo Nomo	.40
13	Jeff Bagwell	1.25
14	Manny Ramirez	.75
15	Mark McGwire	.75
16	Derek Jeter	1.75
17	Sammy Sosa	.40
18	Barry Bonds	.75
19	Chuck Knoblauch	.25
20	Dante Bichette	.25
21	Tony Gwynn	1.25
22	Ken Caminiti	.40
23	Gary Sheffield	.40
24	Tim Salmon	.25
25	Ivan Rodriguez	.50
26	Henry Rodriguez	.25
27	Barry Larkin	.25
28	Ryan Klesko	.50
29	Brian Jordan	.25
30	Jay Buhner	.25

1997 Pinnacle
Mint Collection Coins

Two coins from the 30-coin set were included in each three-card pack of 1997 Pinnacle Mint Collection. Brass coins are common while nickel-silver coins were inserted every 20 packs and gold-plated coins were inserted every 48 packs. Redemption cards for solid silver coins were found every 2,300 packs and a redemption card for a solid gold coin was inserted in 47,200 packs. The front of the coins feature the player's headshot while the backs have a baseball diamond with "Limited Edition, Pinnacle Mint Collection 1997" printed.

		MT
Complete Set (30):		65.00
Common Brass Coin:		1.00
Nickel Coins:		2x to 4x
Gold Plated Coins:		6x to 10x
1	Ken Griffey Jr.	10.00
2	Frank Thomas	10.00
3	Alex Rodriguez	10.00
4	Cal Ripken Jr.	8.00
5	Mo Vaughn	2.50
6	Juan Gonzalez	4.00
7	Mike Piazza	6.00
8	Albert Belle	3.00
9	Chipper Jones	6.00
10	Andruw Jones	10.00
11	Greg Maddux	6.00
12	Hideo Nomo	2.00
13	Jeff Bagwell	4.00
14	Manny Ramirez	2.50
15	Mark McGwire	2.50
16	Derek Jeter	4.00
17	Sammy Sosa	1.50
18	Barry Bonds	2.50
19	Chuck Knoblauch	1.00
20	Dante Bichette	1.50
21	Tony Gwynn	4.00
22	Ken Caminiti	1.50
23	Gary Sheffield	1.50
24	Tim Salmon	1.00
25	Ivan Rodriguez	2.00
26	Henry Rodriguez	1.00
27	Barry Larkin	1.00
28	Ryan Klesko	1.50
29	Brian Jordan	1.00
30	Jay Buhner	1.00

1997 Totally Certified
Platinum Red

Totally Certified doesn't have a true base set. Instead, the product consists of three different 150-card parallel sets. Packs consisted of three cards for $6.99 each. The first of three parallels is the Platinum Red set, inserted two per pack, and featuring micro-etched holographic mylar stock with red accents and foil stamping. Each card in the Red set is sequentially-numbered to 3,999.

		MT
Complete Set (150):		500.00
Common Player:		1.50
1	Barry Bonds	8.00
2	Mo Vaughn	8.00
3	Matt Williams	3.00
4	Ryne Sandberg	8.00
5	Jeff Bagwell	12.00
6	Alan Benes	1.50
7	John Wetteland	1.50
8	Fred McGriff	2.50
9	Craig Biggio	2.50
10	Bernie Williams	6.00
11	Brian Hunter	1.50
12	Sandy Alomar Jr.	1.50
13	Ray Lankford	1.50
14	Ryan Klesko	4.00
15	Jermaine Dye	1.50
16	Andy Benes	1.50
17	Albert Belle	10.00
18	Tony Clark	8.00
19	Dean Palmer	1.50
20	Bernard Gilkey	1.50
21	Ken Caminiti	4.00
22	Alex Rodriguez	25.00
23	Tim Salmon	4.00
24	Larry Walker	5.00
25	Barry Larkin	4.00
26	Mike Piazza	18.00
27	Brady Anderson	1.50
28	Cal Ripken Jr.	25.00
29	Charles Nagy	1.50
30	Paul Molitor	6.00
31	Darin Erstad	10.00
32	Rey Ordonez	1.50
33	Wally Joyner	1.50
34	David Cone	1.50
35	Sammy Sosa	4.00
36	Dante Bichette	3.00
37	Eric Karros	1.50
38	Omar Vizquel	1.50
39	Roger Clemens	12.00
40	Joe Carter	1.50
41	Frank Thomas	30.00
42	Javier Lopez	1.50
43	Mike Mussina	6.00
44	Gary Sheffield	4.00
45	Tony Gwynn	15.00
46	Jason Kendall	1.50
47	Jim Thome	8.00
48	Andres Galarraga	4.00
49	Mark McGwire	12.00
50	Troy Percival	1.50
51	Derek Jeter	18.00
52	Todd Hollandsworth	1.50
53	Ken Griffey Jr.	30.00
54	Randy Johnson	6.00
55	Pat Hentgen	1.50
56	Rusty Greer	1.50
57	John Jaha	1.50
58	Kenny Lofton	8.00
59	Chipper Jones	18.00
60	Robb Nen	1.50
61	Rafael Palmeiro	3.00
62	Mariano Rivera	2.50
63	Hideo Nomo	6.00
64	Greg Vaughn	1.50
65	Ron Gant	1.50
66	Eddie Murray	4.00
67	John Smoltz	3.00
68	Manny Ramirez	8.00
69	Juan Gonzalez	15.00
70	F.P. Santangelo	1.50
71	Moises Alou	2.50
72	Alex Ochoa	1.50
73	Chuck Knoblauch	3.00
74	Raul Mondesi	3.00
75	J.T. Snow	1.50
76	Rickey Henderson	1.50
77	Bobby Bonilla	2.50
78	Wade Boggs	3.00
79	Ivan Rodriguez	6.00
80	Brian Jordan	1.50
81	Al Leiter	1.50
82	Jay Buhner	3.00
83	Greg Maddux	18.00
84	Edgar Martinez	1.50
85	Kevin Brown	1.50
86	Eric Young	1.50
87	Todd Hundley	2.50
88	Ellis Burks	1.50
89	Marquis Grissom	1.50
90	Jose Canseco	3.00
91	Henry Rodriguez	1.50
92	Andy Pettitte	8.00
93	Mark Grudzielanek	1.50
94	Dwight Gooden	1.50
95	Roberto Alomar	6.00
96	Paul Wilson	1.50
97	Will Clark	3.00
98	Rondell White	2.50
99	Charles Johnson	1.50
100	Jim Edmonds	2.50
101	Jason Giambi	1.50
102	Billy Wagner	1.50
103	Edgar Renteria	1.50
104	Johnny Damon	1.50
105	Jason Isringhausen	1.50
106	Andruw Jones	15.00
107	Jose Guillen	8.00
108	Kevin Orie	1.50
109	Brian Giles	1.50
110	Danny Patterson	1.50
111	Vladimir Guerrero	15.00
112	Scott Rolen	15.00
113	Damon Mashore	1.50
114	Nomar Garciaparra	18.00
115	Todd Walker	5.00
116	Wilton Guerrero	1.50
117	Bob Abreu	1.50
118	Brooks Kieschnick	1.50
119	Pokey Reese	1.50
120	Todd Greene	1.50
121	Dmitri Young	1.50
122	Raul Casanova	1.50
123	Glendon Rusch	1.50
124	Jason Dickson	1.50
125	Jorge Posada	1.50
126	Rod Myers	1.50
127	Bubba Trammell	6.00
128	Scott Spiezio	1.50
129	Hideki Irabu	10.00
130	Wendell Magee	1.50
131	Bartolo Colon	1.50
132	Chris Holt	1.50
133	Calvin Maduro	1.50
134	Ray Montgomery	1.50
135	Shannon Stewart	1.50
136	Ken Griffey Jr. (Certified Stars)	15.00
137	Vladimir Guerrero (Certified Stars)	8.00
138	Roger Clemens (Certified Stars)	6.00
139	Mark McGwire (Certified Stars)	6.00
140	Albert Belle (Certified Stars)	5.00
141	Derek Jeter (Certified Stars)	9.00
142	Juan Gonzalez (Certified Stars)	8.00
143	Greg Maddux (Certified Stars)	9.00
144	Alex Rodriguez (Certified Stars)	12.00
145	Jeff Bagwell (Certified Stars)	6.00
146	Cal Ripken Jr. (Certified Stars)	12.00
147	Tony Gwynn (Certified Stars)	8.00
148	Frank Thomas (Certified Stars)	15.00
149	Hideo Nomo (Certified Stars)	3.00
150	Andruw Jones (Certified Stars)	8.00

1997 Totally Certified Platinum Blue

Featuring blue accents and foil stamping, the Platinum Blue cards are sequentially numbered to 1,999 and inserted one per pack.

		MT
Complete Set (150):		1000.
Common Player:		3.00
Minor Stars:		6.00
1	Barry Bonds	15.00
2	Mo Vaughn	15.00
3	Matt Williams	6.00
4	Ryne Sandberg	15.00
5	Jeff Bagwell	25.00
6	Alan Benes	3.00
7	John Wetteland	3.00
8	Fred McGriff	5.00
9	Craig Biggio	5.00
10	Bernie Williams	12.00
11	Brian Hunter	3.00
12	Sandy Alomar Jr.	3.00
13	Ray Lankford	3.00
14	Ryan Klesko	8.00
15	Jermaine Dye	3.00
16	Andy Benes	3.00
17	Albert Belle	20.00
18	Tony Clark	15.00
19	Dean Palmer	3.00
20	Bernard Gilkey	3.00
21	Ken Caminiti	8.00
22	Alex Rodriguez	50.00
23	Tim Salmon	8.00
24	Larry Walker	10.00
25	Barry Larkin	8.00
26	Mike Piazza	35.00
27	Brady Anderson	3.00
28	Cal Ripken Jr.	50.00
29	Charles Nagy	3.00
30	Paul Molitor	12.00
31	Darin Erstad	20.00
32	Rey Ordonez	3.00
33	Wally Joyner	3.00
34	David Cone	3.00
35	Sammy Sosa	8.00
36	Dante Bichette	6.00
37	Eric Karros	3.00
38	Omar Vizquel	3.00
39	Roger Clemens	25.00
40	Joe Carter	3.00
41	Frank Thomas	60.00
42	Javier Lopez	3.00
43	Mike Mussina	12.00
44	Gary Sheffield	8.00
45	Tony Gwynn	30.00
46	Jason Kendall	3.00
47	Jim Thome	12.00
48	Andres Galarraga	8.00
49	Mark McGwire	25.00
50	Troy Percival	3.00
51	Derek Jeter	35.00
52	Todd Hollandsworth	3.00
53	Ken Griffey Jr.	60.00
54	Randy Johnson	12.00
55	Pat Hentgen	3.00
56	Rusty Greer	3.00
57	John Jaha	3.00
58	Kenny Lofton	15.00
59	Chipper Jones	35.00
60	Robb Nen	3.00
61	Rafael Palmeiro	6.00
62	Mariano Rivera	5.00
63	Hideo Nomo	12.00
64	Greg Vaughn	3.00
65	Ron Gant	3.00
66	Eddie Murray	8.00
67	John Smoltz	6.00
68	Manny Ramirez	15.00
69	Juan Gonzalez	30.00
70	F.P. Santangelo	3.00
71	Moises Alou	5.00
72	Alex Ochoa	3.00
73	Chuck Knoblauch	6.00
74	Raul Mondesi	6.00
75	J.T. Snow	3.00
76	Rickey Henderson	3.00
77	Bobby Bonilla	5.00
78	Wade Boggs	6.00
79	Ivan Rodriguez	12.00
80	Brian Jordan	3.00
81	Al Leiter	3.00
82	Jay Buhner	6.00
83	Greg Maddux	35.00
84	Edgar Martinez	3.00
85	Kevin Brown	3.00
86	Eric Young	3.00
87	Todd Hundley	5.00
88	Ellis Burks	3.00
89	Marquis Grissom	3.00
90	Jose Canseco	6.00
91	Henry Rodriguez	3.00
92	Andy Pettitte	15.00
93	Mark Grudzielanek	3.00
94	Dwight Gooden	3.00
95	Roberto Alomar	12.00
96	Paul Wilson	3.00
97	Will Clark	6.00
98	Rondell White	5.00
99	Charles Johnson	3.00
100	Jim Edmonds	5.00
101	Jason Giambi	3.00
102	Billy Wagner	3.00
103	Edgar Renteria	3.00
104	Johnny Damon	3.00
105	Jason Isringhausen	3.00
106	Andruw Jones	30.00
107	Jose Guillen	15.00
108	Kevin Orie	3.00
109	Brian Giles	3.00
110	Danny Patterson	3.00
111	Vladimir Guerrero	30.00
112	Scott Rolen	30.00
113	Damon Mashore	3.00
114	Nomar Garciaparra	35.00
115	Todd Walker	10.00
116	Wilton Guerrero	3.00
117	Bob Abreu	3.00
118	Brooks Kieschnick	3.00
119	Pokey Reese	3.00
120	Todd Greene	3.00
121	Dmitri Young	3.00
122	Raul Casanova	3.00
123	Glendon Rusch	3.00
124	Jason Dickson	3.00
125	Jorge Posada	3.00
126	Rod Myers	3.00
127	Bubba Trammell	12.00
128	Scott Spiezio	3.00
129	Hideki Irabu	20.00
130	Wendell Magee	3.00
131	Bartolo Colon	3.00
132	Chris Holt	3.00
133	Calvin Maduro	3.00
134	Ray Montgomery	3.00
135	Shannon Stewart	3.00
136	Ken Griffey Jr. (Certified Stars)	30.00
137	Vladimir Guerrero (Certified Stars)	15.00
138	Roger Clemens (Certified Stars)	12.00
139	Mark McGwire (Certified Stars)	12.00
140	Albert Belle (Certified Stars)	10.00
141	Derek Jeter (Certified Stars)	18.00
142	Juan Gonzalez (Certified Stars)	15.00
143	Greg Maddux (Certified Stars)	18.00
144	Alex Rodriguez (Certified Stars)	25.00
145	Jeff Bagwell (Certified Stars)	12.00
146	Cal Ripken Jr. (Certified Stars)	25.00
147	Tony Gwynn (Certified Stars)	15.00
148	Frank Thomas (Certified Stars)	30.00
149	Hideo Nomo (Certified Stars)	6.00
150	Andruw Jones (Certified Stars)	15.00

1997 Totally Certified Platinum Gold

The most difficult to find of the Totally Certified cards, the Platinum Gold versions are sequentially-numbered to 30 per card and inserted 1:79 packs.

		MT
Complete Set (150):		NA
Common Player:		60.00
Minor Stars:		6.00
1	Barry Bonds	400.00
2	Mo Vaughn	400.00
3	Matt Williams	150.00
4	Ryne Sandberg	400.00
5	Jeff Bagwell	600.00
6	Alan Benes	60.00
7	John Wetteland	60.00
8	Fred McGriff	125.00
9	Craig Biggio	100.00
10	Bernie Williams	300.00
11	Brian Hunter	60.00
12	Sandy Alomar Jr.	60.00
13	Ray Lankford	60.00
14	Ryan Klesko	150.00
15	Jermaine Dye	60.00
16	Andy Benes	60.00
17	Albert Belle	500.00
18	Tony Clark	300.00
19	Dean Palmer	60.00
20	Bernard Gilkey	60.00
21	Ken Caminiti	150.00
22	Alex Rodriguez	900.00
23	Tim Salmon	150.00
24	Larry Walker	200.00
25	Barry Larkin	150.00
26	Mike Piazza	700.00
27	Brady Anderson	75.00
28	Cal Ripken Jr.	900.00
29	Charles Nagy	60.00
30	Paul Molitor	300.00
31	Darin Erstad	450.00
32	Rey Ordonez	60.00
33	Wally Joyner	60.00
34	David Cone	75.00
35	Sammy Sosa	250.00
36	Dante Bichette	125.00
37	Eric Karros	60.00
38	Omar Vizquel	60.00
39	Roger Clemens	600.00
40	Joe Carter	60.00
41	Frank Thomas	1200.
42	Javier Lopez	75.00
43	Mike Mussina	300.00
44	Gary Sheffield	200.00
45	Tony Gwynn	700.00
46	Jason Kendall	60.00
47	Jim Thome	300.00
48	Andres Galarraga	150.00
49	Mark McGwire	600.00
50	Troy Percival	60.00
51	Derek Jeter	750.00
52	Todd Hollandsworth	60.00
53	Ken Griffey Jr.	1400.
54	Randy Johnson	300.00
55	Pat Hentgen	60.00
56	Rusty Greer	60.00
57	John Jaha	60.00
58	Kenny Lofton	400.00
59	Chipper Jones	750.00
60	Robb Nen	60.00
61	Rafael Palmeiro	125.00
62	Mariano Rivera	75.00
63	Hideo Nomo	300.00
64	Greg Vaughn	60.00
65	Ron Gant	60.00
66	Eddie Murray	300.00
67	John Smoltz	100.00
68	Manny Ramirez	350.00
69	Juan Gonzalez	700.00
70	F.P. Santangelo	60.00
71	Moises Alou	75.00
72	Alex Ochoa	60.00
73	Chuck Knoblauch	150.00
74	Raul Mondesi	125.00
75	J.T. Snow	60.00
76	Rickey Henderson	60.00
77	Bobby Bonilla	75.00
78	Wade Boggs	150.00
79	Ivan Rodriguez	350.00
80	Brian Jordan	60.00
81	Al Leiter	60.00
82	Jay Buhner	125.00
83	Greg Maddux	750.00
84	Edgar Martinez	75.00
85	Kevin Brown	60.00
86	Eric Young	60.00
87	Todd Hundley	100.00
88	Ellis Burks	60.00
89	Marquis Grissom	75.00
90	Jose Canseco	125.00
91	Henry Rodriguez	60.00
92	Andy Pettitte	300.00
93	Mark Grudzielanek	60.00
94	Dwight Gooden	75.00
95	Roberto Alomar	300.00
96	Paul Wilson	60.00
97	Will Clark	150.00
98	Rondell White	100.00
99	Charles Johnson	60.00
100	Jim Edmonds	75.00
101	Jason Giambi	60.00
102	Billy Wagner	60.00
103	Edgar Renteria	60.00
104	Johnny Damon	60.00
105	Jason Isringhausen	60.00
106	Andruw Jones	600.00
107	Jose Guillen	250.00
108	Kevin Orie	60.00
109	Brian Giles	60.00
110	Danny Patterson	60.00
111	Vladimir Guerrero	500.00
112	Scott Rolen	500.00
113	Damon Mashore	60.00
114	Nomar Garciaparra	600.00
115	Todd Walker	150.00
116	Wilton Guerrero	60.00
117	Bob Abreu	60.00
118	Brooks Kieschnick	60.00
119	Pokey Reese	60.00
120	Todd Greene	60.00
121	Dmitri Young	60.00
122	Raul Casanova	60.00
123	Glendon Rusch	60.00
124	Jason Dickson	60.00
125	Jorge Posada	60.00
126	Rod Myers	60.00
127	Bubba Trammell	250.00
128	Scott Spiezio	60.00
129	Hideki Irabu	350.00
130	Wendell Magee	60.00
131	Bartolo Colon	60.00
132	Chris Holt	60.00
133	Calvin Maduro	60.00
134	Ray Montgomery	60.00
135	Shannon Stewart	60.00
136	Ken Griffey Jr. (Certified Stars)	700.00
137	Vladimir Guerrero (Certified Stars)	250.00
138	Roger Clemens (Certified Stars)	300.00
139	Mark McGwire (Certified Stars)	300.00
140	Albert Belle (Certified Stars)	250.00
141	Derek Jeter (Certified Stars)	400.00
142	Juan Gonzalez (Certified Stars)	350.00
143	Greg Maddux (Certified Stars)	400.00
144	Alex Rodriguez (Certified Stars)	450.00
145	Jeff Bagwell (Certified Stars)	300.00
146	Cal Ripken Jr. (Certified Stars)	450.00
147	Tony Gwynn (Certified Stars)	350.00
148	Frank Thomas (Certified Stars)	600.00
149	Hideo Nomo (Certified Stars)	150.00
150	Andruw Jones (Certified Stars)	300.00

1997 Pinnacle X-Press

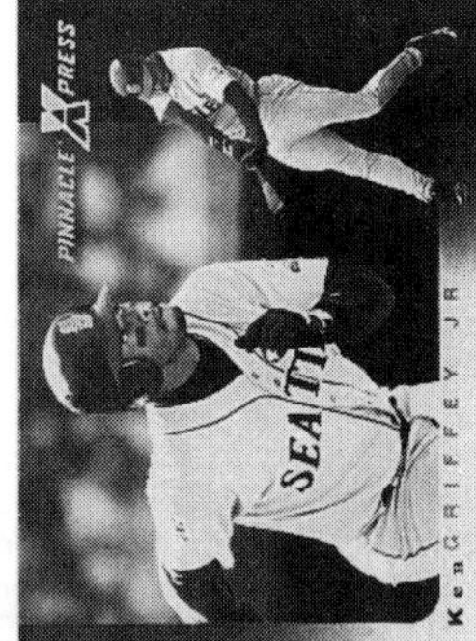

The 150-card set features 115 base cards, a 22-card Rookies subset, 10 Peak Performers and three checklist cards. Each of the regular cards features a horizontal design with two photos of each player on the front of the card and his name across the bottom. There are a number of inserts within this product, including Swing for the Fences (regular player cards as well as base and booster cards that can be used to accumulate points for a sweepstakes), Men of Summer, Far & Away, Melting Pot, Metal Works silver and Metal Works Gold. Cards were sold in eight-card packs for $1.00 each. X-Press Metal Works boxes were also available for $14.99 and contained a regular pack, one metal card and a master deck used to play the Swing for the Fences game.

		MT
Complete Set (150):		20.00
Common Player:		.05
Men of Summer:		3x to 5x
1	Larry Walker	.20
2	Andy Pettitte	.60
3	Matt Williams	.20
4	Juan Gonzalez	1.25
5	Frank Thomas	2.50
6	Kenny Lofton	.60
7	Ken Griffey Jr.	2.50
8	Andres Galarraga	.15
9	Greg Maddux	1.50
10	Hideo Nomo	.40
11	Cecil Fielder	.15
12	Jose Canseco	.15
13	Tony Gwynn	1.25
14	Eddie Murray	.20
15	Alex Rodriguez	2.00
16	Mike Piazza	1.50
17	Ken Hill	.05
18	Chuck Knoblauch	.15
19	Ellis Burks	.05
20	Rafael Palmeiro	.15
21	Vinny Castilla	.05
22	Rusty Greer	.05
23	Chipper Jones	1.50
24	Rey Ordonez	.05
25	Mariano Rivera	.15
26	Garret Anderson	.05
27	Edgar Martinez	.10
28	Dante Bichette	.15
29	Todd Hundley	.15
30	Barry Bonds	.60
31	Barry Larkin	.15
32	Derek Jeter	1.50
33	Marquis Grissom	.10
34	David Justice	.20
35	Ivan Rodriguez	.50
36	Jay Buhner	.15
37	Fred McGriff	.20
38	Brady Anderson	.15
39	Tony Clark	.60
40	Eric Young	.05
41	Charles Nagy	.05
42	Mark McGwire	1.00
43	Paul O'Neill	.15
44	Tino Martinez	.15
45	Ryne Sandberg	.60
46	Bernie Williams	.40
47	Albert Belle	.75
48	Jeff Cirillo	.05
49	Tim Salmon	.15
50	Steve Finley	.05
51	Lance Johnson	.05
52	John Smoltz	.15
53	Javier Lopez	.10
54	Roger Clemens	.60
55	Kevin Appier	.05
56	Ken Caminiti	.20
57	Cal Ripken Jr.	2.00
58	Moises Alou	.15
59	Marty Cordova	.05
60	David Cone	.15
61	Manny Ramirez	.50
62	Ray Durham	.05
63	Jermaine Dye	.05
64	Craig Biggio	.15
65	Will Clark	.20
66	Omar Vizquel	.05
67	Bernard Gilkey	.05
68	Greg Vaughn	.05
69	Wade Boggs	.15
70	Dave Nilsson	.05
71	Mark Grace	.15
72	Dean Palmer	.05
73	Sammy Sosa	.20
74	Mike Mussina	.50
75	Alex Fernandez	.05
76	Henry Rodriguez	.05
77	Travis Fryman	.05
78	Jeff Bagwell	1.00
79	Pat Hentgen	.05
80	Gary Sheffield	.20
81	Jim Edmonds	.15
82	Darin Erstad	1.25
83	Mark Grudzielanek	.05
84	Jim Thome	.40
85	Bobby Higginson	.15
86	Al Martin	.05
87	Jason Giambi	.05
88	Mo Vaughn	.60
89	Jeff Conine	.05
90	Edgar Renteria	.05
91	Andy Ashby	.05
92	Ryan Klesko	.30
93	John Jaha	.05
94	Paul Molitor	.40
95	Brian Hunter	.05
96	Randy Johnson	.40
97	Joey Hamilton	.05
98	Billy Wagner	.05
99	John Wetteland	.05
100	Jeff Fassero	.05
101	Rondell White	.15
102	Kevin Brown	.15
103	Andy Benes	.15
104	Raul Mondesi	.15
105	Todd Hollandsworth	.05
106	Alex Ochoa	.05
107	Bobby Bonilla	.15
108	Brian Jordan	.05
109	Tom Glavine	.15
110	Ron Gant	.15
111	Jason Kendall	.05
112	Roberto Alomar	.40
113	Troy Percival	.05
114	Michael Tucker	.05
115	Joe Carter	.15
116	Andruw Jones	1.50
117	Nomar Garciaparra	1.25
118	Todd Walker	.20
119	Jose Guillen	.75
120	Bubba Trammell	.75
121	Wilton Guerrero	.10
122	Bob Abreu	.05
123	Vladimir Guerrero	1.25
124	Dmitri Young	.05
125	Kevin Orie	.05
126	Glendon Rusch	.05
127	Brooks Kieschnick	.05
128	Scott Spiezio	.05
129	Brian Giles	.05
130	Jason Dickson	.15
131	Damon Mashore	.05
132	Wendell Magee	.05
133	Matt Morris	.05
134	Scott Rolen	1.25
135	Shannon Stewart	.05
136	Deivi Cruz	.05
137	Hideki Irabu	2.00
138	Larry Walker (Peak Performers)	.15
139	Ken Griffey Jr. (Peak Performers)	1.00
140	Frank Thomas (Peak Performers)	1.00
141	Ivan Rodriguez (Peak Performers)	.20
142	Randy Johnson (Peak Performers)	.20
143	Mark McGwire (Peak Performers)	.35
144	Tino Martinez (Peak Performers)	.10
145	Tony Clark (Peak Performers)	.25
146	Mike Piazza (Peak Performers)	.60
147	Alex Rodriguez (Peak Performers)	.75
148	Checklist (Roger Clemens)	.25
149	Checklist (Greg Maddux)	.50
150	Checklist (Hideo Nomo)	.20

> Post-1980 cards in Near Mint condition will generally sell for about 75% of the quoted Mint value. Excellent-condition cards bring no more than 40%.

1997 Pinnacle X-Press Far & Away

This 18-card insert highlights the top home run hitters in baseball and is printed with Dufex technology. Cards were inserted 1:19 packs.

		MT
Complete Set (18):		100.00
Common Player:		1.50
Men of Summer:		2x to 4x
1	Albert Belle	6.00
2	Mark McGwire	8.00
3	Frank Thomas	20.00
4	Mo Vaughn	5.00
5	Jeff Bagwell	8.00
6	Juan Gonzalez	10.00
7	Mike Piazza	12.00
8	Andruw Jones	12.00
9	Chipper Jones	12.00
10	Gary Sheffield	2.50
11	Sammy Sosa	2.50
12	Darin Erstad	8.00
13	Jay Buhner	1.50
14	Ken Griffey Jr.	20.00
15	Ken Caminiti	1.50
16	Brady Anderson	1.50
17	Manny Ramirez	4.00
18	Alex Rodriguez	15.00

1997 Pinnacle X-Press Melting Pot

This 20-card insert showcases the talents of major leaguers from various countries. Each card in the set is numbered to 500 and utilizes heliogram print technology.

		MT
Complete Set (20):		650.00
Common Player:		10.00
1	Jose Guillen	20.00
2	Vladimir Guerrero	40.00
3	Andruw Jones	60.00
4	Larry Walker	15.00
5	Manny Ramirez	20.00
6	Ken Griffey Jr.	100.00
7	Alex Rodriguez	75.00
7p	Alex Rodriguez (overprinted "SAMPLE")	6.00
8	Frank Thomas	100.00
9	Juan Gonzalez	50.00
10	Ivan Rodriguez	20.00
11	Hideo Nomo	20.00
12	Rafael Palmeiro	10.00
13	Dave Nilsson	10.00
14	Nomar Garciaparra	50.00
15	Wilton Guerrero	10.00
16	Sammy Sosa	15.00
17	Edgar Renteria	10.00
18	Cal Ripken Jr.	75.00
19	Derek Jeter	60.00
20	Rey Ordonez	10.00

1997 Pinnacle X-Press Metal Works

These randomly inserted redemption cards provide collectors with the opportunity to receive a metal card of one of 20 different players. Redemption cards for Silver Metal Works cards were inserted 1:470 packs, while redemptions cards for Gold Metal Works cards were inserted 1:950 packs.

		MT
Complete Set (20):		200.00
Common Player:		5.00
1	Ken Griffey Jr.	25.00
2	Frank Thomas	25.00
3	Andruw Jones	15.00
4	Alex Rodriguez	20.00
5	Derek Jeter	15.00
6	Cal Ripken Jr.	20.00
7	Mike Piazza	15.00
8	Chipper Jones	15.00
9	Juan Gonzalez	12.00
10	Greg Maddux	15.00
11	Tony Gwynn	12.00
12	Jeff Bagwell	10.00
13	Albert Belle	7.00
14	Mark McGwire	9.00
15	Nomar Garciaparra	12.00
16	Mo Vaughn	6.00
17	Andy Pettitte	6.00
18	Manny Ramirez	6.00
19	Kenny Lofton	6.00
20	Roger Clemens	8.00

1997 Pinnacle X-Press Swing for the Fences

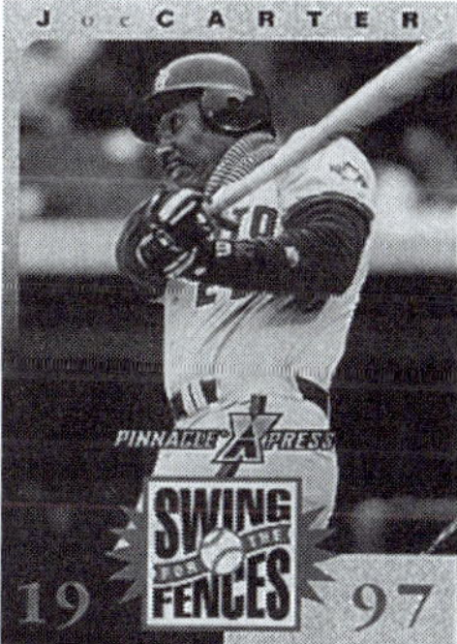

These inserts allow collectors to play an interactive game based on the number of home runs hit by the home run champions of each league. Player Cards feature 60 different players and were inserted 1:2 packs. Base Cards feature a number between 20-42 printed on them and are found one in every master deck. Booster Cards feature a plus-or-minus point total (i.e. +7, -2) that can be used to add or subtract points to get to the winning home run total. Booster Cards are found 1:2 packs, while Base Cards are found one per master deck. Collectors who accumulated the winning home run totals were eligible to win prizes ranging from autographs to a trip to the 1998 All-Star Game.

		MT
Complete Set (60):		5.00
Common Player:		.05
1	Ken Griffey Jr.	1.00
2	Tony Clark	.25
3	Tino Martinez	.10
4	Sandy Alomar Jr.	.05
5	Mark McGwire	.35
6	Jay Buhner	.05
7	Geronimo Berroa	.05
8	Tim Naehring	.05
9	Juan Gonzalez	.50
10	Frank Thomas	1.00
11	Jose Canseco	.15
12	Jim Thome	.15
13	Dean Palmer	.05
14	Albert Belle	.30
15	Matt Williams	.10
16	Brady Anderson	.05
17	Mo Vaughn	.25
18	Cal Ripken Jr.	.75
19	Cecil Fielder	.10
20	Jay Buhner	.10
21	Rafael Palmeiro	.05
22	Tim Salmon	.10
23	Edgar Martinez	.05

24	John Jaha	.05
25	Carlos Delgado	.05
26	Terry Steinbach	.05
27	David Justice	.10
28	Dave Nilsson	.05
29	Joe Carter	.05
30	Jim Edmonds	.05
31	Larry Walker	.10
32	Mike Lieberthal	.05
33	Raul Mondesi	.10
34	Vinny Castilla	.05
35	Moises Alou	.05
36	Ellis Burks	.05
37	Jeff Kent	.05
38	Henry Rodriguez	.05
39	Mike Piazza	.60
40	Barry Bonds	.25
41	Dante Bichette	.10
42	Jeff Bagwell	.40
43	Ken Caminiti	.05
44	Chipper Jones	.60
45	Ron Gant	.05
46	Barry Larkin	.05
47	Fred McGriff	.10
48	Andres Galarraga	.10
49	Gary Sheffield	.10
50	Todd Hundley	.10
51	Sammy Sosa	.10
52	Bernard Gilkey	.05
53	Vladimir Guerrero	.40
54	Bobby Bonilla	.05
55	Derek Bell	.05
56	Javier Lopez	.05
57	Rondell White	.10
58	Ryan Klesko	.15
59	Todd Zeile	.05
60	Brian Jordan	.05

1997 Zenith

This set combines standard size trading cards with cards in an 8" x 10" format. The standard size set consists of 60 cards. Card fronts feature full-bleed photos and the word "Zenith", but no reference to the player's name or team is found on the fronts. There are four inserts in the set, all of which are printed on the larger size format - 8" x 10", 8" x 10" Dufex, 8" x 10" V-2, and Z-Team. Each sale unit contained one pack of five standard-size cards and two larger size cards for a suggested retail price of $9.99.

		MT
Complete Set (50):		50.00
Common Player:		.50
1	Frank Thomas	6.00
2	Tony Gwynn	3.00
3	Jeff Bagwell	2.50
4	Paul Molitor	1.00
5	Roberto Alomar	1.00
6	Mike Piazza	4.00
7	Albert Belle	2.00
8	Greg Maddux	4.00
9	Barry Larkin	.50
10	Tony Clark	1.50
11	Larry Walker	1.00
12	Chipper Jones	4.00
13	Juan Gonzalez	3.00
14	Barry Bonds	1.50
15	Ivan Rodriguez	1.25
16	Sammy Sosa	1.00
17	Derek Jeter	4.00
18	Hideo Nomo	1.25
19	Roger Clemens	1.50

20	Ken Griffey Jr.	6.00
21	Andy Pettitte	1.50
22	Alex Rodriguez	5.00
23	Tino Martinez	.75
24	Bernie Williams	1.00
25	Ken Caminiti	.75
26	John Smoltz	.50
27	Javier Lopez	.50
28	Mark McGwire	2.00
29	Gary Sheffield	1.00
30	David Justice	.75
31	Randy Johnson	1.00
32	Chuck Knoblauch	.60
33	Mike Mussina	1.25
34	Deion Sanders	.75
35	Cal Ripken Jr.	5.00
36	Darin Erstad	2.50
37	Kenny Lofton	1.50
38	Jay Buhner	.50
39	Brady Anderson	.50
40	Edgar Martinez	.50
41	Mo Vaughn	1.50
42	Ryne Sandberg	1.50
43	Andruw Jones	4.00
44	Nomar Garciaparra	3.00
45	*Hideki Irabu*	5.00
46	Wilton Guerrero	.50
47	*Jose Cruz Jr.*	20.00
48	Vladimir Guerrero	2.50
49	Scott Rolen	2.50
50	Jose Guillen	1.50

1997 Zenith V-2

This eight-card die-cut insert utilizes motion technology as well as foil printing to create a very high-tech 8" x 10" card. Cards were inserted 1:47 packs.

		MT
Complete Set (8):		475.00
Common Player:		20.00
1	Ken Griffey Jr.	100.00
2	Andruw Jones	55.00
3	Frank Thomas	90.00
4	Mike Piazza	55.00
5	Alex Rodriguez	75.00
6	Cal Ripken Jr.	75.00
7	Derek Jeter	55.00
8	Vladimir Guerrero	40.00

1997 Zenith Z-Team

This nine-card 8" x 10" insert is printed on a mirror gold mylar foil stock with each card sequentially numbered to 1,000.

		MT
Complete Set (9):		675.00
Common Player:		25.00
1	Ken Griffey Jr.	150.00
2	Larry Walker	25.00
3	Frank Thomas	125.00
4	Alex Rodriguez	100.00
5	Mike Piazza	75.00
6	Cal Ripken Jr.	100.00
7	Derek Jeter	75.00
8	Andruw Jones	75.00
9	Roger Clemens	40.00

1997 Zenith 8x10

This 24-card insert takes select cards from the standard set and blows them up to an 8" x 10" format. Cards were inserted one per pack. A Dufex version of each 8" x 10" insert card was also available at a rate of one per pack (except in packs which contained either a Z-Team or V-2 card).

		MT
Complete Set (24):		80.00
Common Player:		1.00
Dufex versions:		1x to 1.5x
1	Frank Thomas	10.00
2	Tony Gwynn	5.00
3	Jeff Bagwell	4.00
4	Ken Griffey Jr.	10.00
5	Mike Piazza	6.00
6	Greg Maddux	6.00
7	Ken Caminiti	1.50
8	Albert Belle	3.00
9	Ivan Rodriguez	2.00
10	Sammy Sosa	2.00
11	Mark McGwire	3.50
12	Roger Clemens	3.00
13	Alex Rodriguez	8.00
14	Chipper Jones	6.00
15	Juan Gonzalez	5.00
16	Barry Bonds	2.50
17	Derek Jeter	6.00
18	Hideo Nomo	2.00
19	Cal Ripken Jr.	8.00
20	Hideki Irabu	5.00
21	Andruw Jones	6.00
22	Nomar Garciaparra	5.00
23	Vladimir Guerrero	5.00
24	Scott Rolen	5.00

1997 Score

A total of 551 cards make up the base set, with 330 cards sold in Series I and 221 making up Series II. The basic card design features a color action photo surrounded by a white border. The players name is above the photo, with the team name underneath. Backs feature text and statistics against a white background with the image of the team logo ghosted into the background. Two parallel insert sets - Artist's Proof and Showcase Series - were part of both series. Other inserts in Series I were Pitcher Perfect, The Franchise, The Glowing Franchise, Titanic Taters (retail exclusive), Stellar Season (magazine packs only), and The Highlight Zone (hobby exclusive). Series II inserts were Blastmasters, Heart of the Order and Stand and Deliver. Cards were sold in 10-card packs for 99 cents each.

A player's name in *italic type* indicates a rookie card.

		MT
Complete Set (551):		35.00
Complete Series 1 Set (330):		20.00
Complete Series 2 Set (221):		15.00
Common Player:		.05
Wax Box:		30.00
1	Jeff Bagwell	.75
2	Mickey Tettleton	.05
3	Johnny Damon	.15
4	Jeff Conine	.05
5	Bernie Williams	.40
6	Will Clark	.20
7	Ryan Klesko	.30
8	Cecil Fielder	.10
9	Paul Wilson	.05
10	Gregg Jefferies	.05
11	Chili Davis	.05
12	Albert Belle	.60
13	Ken Hill	.05
14	Cliff Floyd	.05
15	Jaime Navarro	.05
16	Ismael Valdes	.05
17	Jeff King	.05
18	Chris Bosio	.05
19	Reggie Sanders	.05
20	Darren Daulton	.05
21	Ken Caminiti	.05
22	Mike Piazza	1.25
23	Chad Mottola	.05
24	Darin Erstad	.75
25	Dante Bichette	.15
26	Frank Thomas	2.00
27	Ben McDonald	.05
28	Raul Casanova	.05
29	Kevin Ritz	.05
30	Garret Anderson	.05
31	Jason Kendall	.05
32	Billy Wagner	.05
33	David Justice	.05
34	Marty Cordova	.05
35	Derek Jeter	.75
36	Trevor Hoffman	.05
37	Geronimo Berroa	.05
38	Walt Weiss	.05
39	Kirt Manwaring	.05
40	Alex Gonzalez	.05
41	Sean Berry	.05
42	Kevin Appier	.05
43	Rusty Greer	.05
44	Pete Incaviglia	.05
45	Rafael Palmeiro	.10
46	Eddie Murray	.25
47	Moises Alou	.05
48	Mark Lewis	.05
49	Hal Morris	.05
50	Edgar Renteria	.25
51	Rickey Henderson	.05
52	Pat Listach	.05
53	John Wasdin	.05
54	James Baldwin	.05
55	Brian Jordan	.05
56	Edgar Martinez	.05
57	Wil Cordero	.05
58	Danny Tartabull	.05
59	Keith Lockhart	.05
60	Rico Brogna	.05
61	Ricky Bottalico	.05
62	Terry Pendleton	.05
63	Bret Boone	.05
64	Charlie Hayes	.05
65	Marc Newfield	.05
66	Sterling Hitchcock	.05
67	Roberto Alomar	.50
68	John Jaha	.05
69	Greg Colbrunn	.05
70	Sal Fasano	.05
71	Brooks Kieschnick	.05
72	Pedro Martinez	.05
73	Kevin Elster	.05
74	Ellis Burks	.05
75	Chuck Finley	.05
76	John Olerud	.05
77	Jay Bell	.05
78	Allen Watson	.05
79	Darryl Strawberry	.05
80	Orlando Miller	.05
81	Jose Herrera	.05
82	Andy Pettitte	.40
83	Juan Guzman	.05
84	Alan Benes	.05
85	Jack McDowell	.10
86	Ugueth Urbina	.05
87	Rocky Coppinger	.05
88	Jeff Cirillo	.05
89	Tom Glavine	.15
90	Robby Thompson	.05
91	Barry Bonds	.50
92	Carlos Delgado	.05
93	Mo Vaughn	.50
94	Ryne Sandberg	.40
95	Alex Rodriguez	2.00

#	Player	$	#	Player	$	#	Player	$	#	Player	$
96	Brady Anderson	.10	197	B.J. Surhoff	.05	298	Desi Relaford	.05	399	Hipolito Pichardo	.05
97	Scott Brosius	.05	198	Juan Gonzalez	.75	299	Jason Thompson	.05	400	Scott Erickson	.05
98	Dennis Eckersley	.05	199	Terrell Wade	.05	300	Osvaldo Fernandez	.05	401	Bobby Jones	.05
99	Brian McRae	.05	200	Jeff Frye	.05	301	Fernando Vina	.05	402	Jim Edmonds	.05
100	Rey Ordonez	.25	201	Joey Cora	.05	302	Jose Offerman	.05	403	Chad Ogea	.05
101	John Valentin	.05	202	Raul Mondesi	.15	303	Yamil Benitez	.05	404	Cal Eldred	.05
102	Brett Butler	.05	203	Ivan Rodriguez	.50	304	J.T. Snow	.05	405	Pat Listach	.05
103	Eric Karros	.05	204	Armando Reynoso	.05	305	Rafael Bournigal	.05	406	Todd Stottlemyre	.05
104	Harold Baines	.05	205	Jeffrey Hammonds	.05	306	Jason Isringhausen	.05	407	Phil Nevin	.05
105	Javier Lopez	.15	206	Darren Dreifort	.05	307	Bob Higginson	.05	408	Otis Nixon	.05
106	Alan Trammell	.05	207	Kevin Seitzer	.05	308	*Nerio Rodriguez*	.25	409	Billy Ashley	.05
107	Jim Thome	.25	208	Tino Martinez	.25	309	Brian Giles	.05	410	Jimmy Key	.05
108	Frank Rodriguez	.05	209	Jim Bruske	.05	310	Andruw Jones	1.25	411	Mike Timlin	.05
109	Bernard Gilkey	.05	210	Jeff Suppan	.05	311	Billy McMillon	.05	412	Joe Vitiello	.05
110	Reggie Jefferson	.05	211	Mark Carreon	.05	312	Arquimedez Pozo	.05	413	Rondell White	.05
111	Scott Stahoviak	.05	212	Wilson Alvarez	.05	313	Jermaine Allensworth	.05	414	Jeff Fassero	.05
112	Steve Gibralter	.05	213	John Burkett	.05	314	Luis Andujar	.05	415	Rex Hudler	.05
113	Todd Hollandsworth	.05	214	Tony Phillips	.05	315	Angel Echevarria	.05	416	Curt Schilling	.05
114	Ruben Rivera	.30	215	Greg Maddux	1.25	316	Karim Garcia	.30	417	Rich Becker	.05
115	Dennis Martinez	.05	216	Mark Whiten	.05	317	Trey Beamon	.05	418	William VanLandingham	.05
116	Mariano Rivera	.25	217	Curtis Pride	.05	318	Makoto Suzuki	.05	419	*Chris Snopek*	.05
117	John Smoltz	.20	218	Lyle Mouton	.05	319	Robin Jennings	.05	420	David Segui	.25
118	John Mabry	.05	219	Todd Hundley	.05	320	Dmitri Young	.05	421	Eddie Murray	.25
119	Tom Gordon	.05	220	Greg Gagne	.05	321	*Damon Mashore*	.05	422	Shane Andrews	.05
120	Alex Ochoa	.05	221	Rich Amaral	.05	322	Wendell Magee	.05	423	Gary DiSarcina	.05
121	Jamey Wright	.05	222	Tom Goodwin	.05	323	*Dax Jones*	.05	424	Brian Hunter	.05
122	Dave Nilsson	.05	223	Chris Hoiles	.05	324	Todd Walker	.40	425	Willie Greene	.05
123	Bobby Bonilla	.05	224	Jayhawk Owens	.05	325	Marvin Benard	.05	426	Felipe Crespo	.05
124	Al Leiter	.05	225	Kenny Rogers	.05	326	*Brian Raabe*	.05	427	Jason Bates	.05
125	Rick Aguilera	.05	226	Mike Greenwell	.05	327	Marcus Jensen	.05	428	Albert Belle	.60
126	Jeff Brantley	.05	227	Mark Wohlers	.05	328	Checklist	.05	429	Rey Sanchez	.05
127	Kevin Brown	.05	228	Henry Rodriguez	.05	329	Checklist	.05	430	Roger Clemens	.75
128	George Arias	.05	229	Robert Perez	.05	330	Checklist	.05	431	Deion Sanders	.20
129	Darren Oliver	.05	230	Jeff Kent	.05	331	Norm Charlton	.05	432	Ernie Young	.05
130	Bill Pulsipher	.05	231	Darryl Hamilton	.05	332	Bruce Ruffin	.05	433	Jay Bell	.05
131	Roberto Hernandez	.05	232	Alex Fernandez	.05	333	John Wetteland	.05	434	Jeff Blauser	.05
132	Delino DeShields	.05	233	Ron Karkovice	.05	334	Marquis Grissom	.05	435	Lenny Dykstra	.05
133	Mark Grudzielanek	.05	234	Jimmy Haynes	.05	335	Sterling Hitchcock	.05	436	Chuck Carr	.05
134	John Wetteland	.05	235	Craig Biggio	.05	336	John Olerud	.05	437	Russ Davis	.05
135	Carlos Baerga	.10	236	Ray Lankford	.05	337	David Wells	.05	438	Carl Everett	.05
136	Paul Sorrento	.05	237	Lance Johnson	.05	338	Chili Davis	.05	439	Damion Easley	.05
137	Leo Gomez	.05	238	Matt Williams	.20	339	Mark Lewis	.05	440	Pat Kelly	.05
138	Andy Ashby	.05	239	Chad Curtis	.05	340	Kenny Lofton	.50	441	Pat Rapp	.05
139	Julio Franco	.05	240	Mark Thompson	.05	341	Alex Fernandez	.05	442	David Justice	.15
140	Brian Hunter	.05	241	Jason Giambi	.05	342	Ruben Sierra	.05	443	Graeme Lloyd	.05
141	Jermaine Dye	.20	242	Barry Larkin	.20	343	Delino DeShields	.05	444	Damon Buford	.05
142	Tony Clark	.40	243	Paul Molitor	.20	344	John Wasdin	.05	445	Jose Valentin	.05
143	Ruben Sierra	.05	244	Sammy Sosa	.15	345	Dennis Martinez	.05	446	Jason Schmidt	.05
144	Donovan Osborne	.05	245	Kevin Tapani	.05	346	Kevin Elster	.05	447	Dave Martinez	.05
145	Mark McLemore	.05	246	Marquis Grissom	.05	347	Bobby Bonilla	.10	448	Danny Tartabull	.05
146	Terry Steinbach	.05	247	Joe Carter	.15	348	Jaime Navarro	.05	449	Jose Vizcaino	.05
147	Bob Wells	.05	248	Ramon Martinez	.05	349	Chad Curtis	.05	450	Steve Avery	.05
148	Chan Ho Park	.05	249	Tony Gwynn	.75	350	Terry Steinbach	.05	451	Mike Devereaux	.05
149	Tim Salmon	.20	250	Andy Fox	.05	351	Ariel Prieto	.05	452	Jim Eisenreich	.05
150	Paul O'Neill	.05	251	Troy O'Leary	.05	352	Jeff Kent	.05	453	Mark Leiter	.05
151	Cal Ripken Jr.	1.50	252	Warren Newson	.05	353	Carlos Garcia	.05	454	Roberto Kelly	.05
152	Wally Joyner	.05	253	Troy Percival	.05	354	Mark Whiten	.05	455	Benito Santiago	.05
153	Omar Vizquel	.05	254	Jamie Moyer	.05	355	Todd Zeile	.05	456	Steve Trachsel	.05
154	Mike Mussina	.40	255	Danny Graves	.05	356	Eric Davis	.05	457	Gerald Williams	.05
155	Andres Galarraga	.15	256	David Wells	.05	357	Greg Colbrunn	.05	458	Pete Schourek	.05
156	Ken Griffey Jr.	2.00	257	Todd Zeile	.05	358	Moises Alou	.05	459	Esteban Loaiza	.05
157	Kenny Lofton	.50	258	Raul Ibanez	.05	359	Allen Watson	.05	460	Mel Rojas	.05
158	Ray Durham	.05	259	Tyler Houston	.05	360	Jose Canseco	.20	461	Tim Wakefield	.05
159	Hideo Nomo	.40	260	LaTroy Hawkins	.05	361	Matt Williams	.25	462	Tony Fernandez	.05
160	Ozzie Guillen	.05	261	Joey Hamilton	.05	362	Jeff King	.05	463	Doug Drabek	.05
161	Roger Pavlik	.05	262	Mike Sweeney	.05	363	Darryl Hamilton	.05	464	Joe Girardi	.05
162	Manny Ramirez	.50	263	Brant Brown	.05	364	Mark Clark	.05	465	Mike Bordick	.05
163	Mark Lemke	.05	264	Pat Hentgen	.05	365	J.T. Snow	.05	466	Jim Leyritz	.05
164	Mike Stanley	.05	265	Mark Johnson	.05	366	Kevin Mitchell	.05	467	Erik Hanson	.05
165	Chuck Knoblauch	.05	266	Robb Nen	.05	367	Orlando Miller	.05	468	Michael Tucker	.05
166	Kimera Bartee	.05	267	Justin Thompson	.05	368	Rico Brogna	.05	469	*Tony Womack*	.15
167	Wade Boggs	.15	268	Ron Gant	.05	369	Mike James	.05	470	Doug Glanville	.05
168	Jay Buhner	.15	269	Jeff D'Amico	.05	370	Brad Ausmus	.05	471	Rudy Pemberton	.05
169	Eric Young	.05	270	Shawn Estes	.05	371	Darryl Kile	.05	472	Keith Lockhart	.05
170	Jose Canseco	.20	271	Derek Bell	.05	372	Edgardo Alfonzo	.05	473	Nomar Garciaparra	1.25
171	Dwight Gooden	.05	272	Fernando Valenzuela	.05	373	Julian Tavarez	.05	474	Scott Rolen	.75
172	Fred McGriff	.20	273	Luis Castillo	.10	374	Darren Lewis	.05	475	Jason Dickson	.15
173	Sandy Alomar Jr.	.05	274	Ray Montgomery	.05	375	Steve Karsay	.05	476	Glendon Rusch	.05
174	Andy Benes	.05	275	Ed Sprague	.05	376	Lee Stevens	.05	477	Todd Walker	.40
175	Dean Palmer	.05	276	F.P. Santangelo	.05	377	Albie Lopez	.05	478	Dmitri Young	.05
176	Larry Walker	.25	277	Todd Greene	.05	378	Orel Hershiser	.05	479	*Rod Myers*	.05
177	Charles Nagy	.05	278	Butch Huskey	.05	379	Lee Smith	.05	480	Wilton Guerrero	.15
178	David Cone	.05	279	Steve Finley	.05	380	Rick Helling	.05	481	Jorge Posada	.05
179	Mark Grace	.10	280	Eric Davis	.05	381	Carlos Perez	.05	482	Brant Brown	.05
180	Robin Ventura	.05	281	Shawn Green	.05	382	Tony Tarasco	.05	483	*Bubba Trammell*	.60
181	Roger Clemens	.60	282	Al Martin	.05	383	Melvin Nieves	.05	484	Jose Guillen	.60
182	Bobby Witt	.05	283	Michael Tucker	.05	384	Benji Gil	.05	485	Scott Spiezio	.05
183	Vinny Castilla	.05	284	Shane Reynolds	.05	385	Devon White	.05	486	Bob Abreu	.05
184	Gary Sheffield	.15	285	Matt Mieske	.05	386	Armando Benitez	.05	487	Chris Holt	.05
185	Dan Wilson	.05	286	Jose Rosado	.05	387	Bill Swift	.05	488	*Deivi Cruz*	.05
186	Roger Cedeno	.05	287	Mark Langston	.05	388	John Smiley	.05	489	Vladimir Guerrero	1.00
187	Mark McGwire	.60	288	Ralph Milliard	.05	389	Midre Cummings	.05	490	Julio Santana	.05
188	Darren Bragg	.05	289	Mike Lansing	.05	390	Tim Belcher	.05	491	Ray Montgomery	.05
189	Quinton McCracken	.05	290	Scott Servais	.05	391	Tim Raines	.05	492	Kevin Orie	.05
190	Randy Myers	.05	291	Royce Clayton	.05	392	Todd Worrell	.05	493	Todd Hundley (Goin' Yard)	.10
191	Jeromy Burnitz	.05	292	Mike Grace	.15	393	Quilvio Veras	.05	494	Tim Salmon (Goin' Yard)	.15
192	Randy Johnson	.25	293	James Mouton	.05	394	Matt Lawton	.05	495	Albert Belle (Goin' Yard)	.30
193	Chipper Jones	1.25	294	Charles Johnson	.05	395	Aaron Sele	.05	496	Manny Ramirez (Goin' Yard)	.25
194	Greg Vaughn	.05	295	Gary Gaetti	.05	396	Bip Roberts	.05	497	Rafael Palmeiro (Goin' Yard)	.10
195	Travis Fryman	.05	296	Kevin Mitchell	.05	397	Denny Neagle	.05			
196	Tim Naehring	.05	297	Carlos Garcia	.05	398	Tyler Green	.05			

		MT
498	Juan Gonzalez (Goin' Yard)	.40
499	Ken Griffey Jr. (Goin' Yard)	1.00
500	Andruw Jones (Goin' Yard)	.60
501	Mike Piazza (Goin' Yard)	.60
502	Jeff Bagwell (Goin' Yard)	.40
503	Bernie Williams (Goin' Yard)	.20
504	Barry Bonds (Goin' Yard)	.25
505	Ken Caminiti (Goin' Yard)	.10
506	Darin Erstad (Goin' Yard)	.50
507	Alex Rodriguez (Goin' Yard)	1.00
508	Frank Thomas (Goin' Yard)	1.00
509	Chipper Jones (Goin' Yard)	.60
510	Mo Vaughn (Goin' Yard)	.25
511	Mark McGwire (Goin' Yard)	.30
512	Fred McGriff (Goin' Yard)	.15
513	Jay Buhner (Goin' Yard)	.10
514	Jim Thome (Goin' Yard)	.15
515	Gary Sheffield (Goin' Yard)	.15
516	Dean Palmer (Goin' Yard)	.05
517	Henry Rodriguez (Goin' Yard)	.05
518	Andy Pettitte (Rock & Fire)	.25
519	Mike Mussina (Rock & Fire)	.20
520	Greg Maddux (Rock & Fire)	.60
521	John Smoltz (Rock & Fire)	.10
522	Hideo Nomo (Rock & Fire)	.20
523	Troy Percival (Rock & Fire)	.05
524	John Wetteland (Rock & Fire)	.05
525	Roger Clemens (Rock & Fire)	.25
526	Charles Nagy (Rock & Fire)	.05
527	Mariano Rivera (Rock & Fire)	.10
528	Tom Glavine (Rock & Fire)	.10
529	Randy Johnson (Rock & Fire)	.20
530	Jason Isringhausen (Rock & Fire)	.05
531	Alex Fernandez (Rock & Fire)	.05
532	Kevin Brown (Rock & Fire)	.05
533	Chuck Knoblauch (True Grit)	.10
534	Rusty Greer (True Grit)	.05
535	Tony Gwynn (True Grit)	.40
536	Ryan Klesko (True Grit)	.20
537	Ryne Sandberg (True Grit)	.25
538	Barry Larkin (True Grit)	.10
539	Will Clark (True Grit)	.10
540	Kenny Lofton (True Grit)	.25
541	Paul Molitor (True Grit)	.15
542	Roberto Alomar (True Grit)	.20
543	Rey Ordonez (True Grit)	.05
544	Jason Giambi (True Grit)	.05
545	Derek Jeter (True Grit)	.60
546	Cal Ripken Jr. (True Grit)	.75
547	Ivan Rodriguez (True Grit)	.20
548	Checklist (Ken Griffey Jr.)	.75
549	Checklist (Frank Thomas)	.75
550	Checklist (Mike Piazza)	.50
551	*Hideki Irabu*	1.50

1997 Score Showcase

A silver metallic-foil background distinguishes the cards in this parallel set, inserted at a rate of about one per seven packs of both hobby and retail.

	MT
Complete Set (551):	450.00
Common Player:	.50
Showcase Series:	4x to 8x
Common Showcase:	.50
Artist's Proofs:	20x to 40x
Common Artist's Proof:	1.50

1997 Score Premium Stock

This is an upscale version of Score's regular 1997 issue, designated for hobby sales only. The cards are basically the same as the regular issue, except for the use of gray borders on front and an embossed gold-foil "Premium Stock" logo.

	MT
Complete Set (551):	70.00
Common Player:	.10
Complete Premium Stock Set (330):	35.00
Premium Stocks:	1.5x to 2x

1997 Score Blastmasters

This 18-card set was inserted into every 35 Series II retail packs and every 23 hobby packs. The set displayed the top power hitters in the game over a gold prism background. The word "Blast" was printed across the top, while "Master" was printed across the bottom, both in red.

		MT
Complete Set (18):		125.00
Common Player:		2.00
1	Mo Vaughn	6.00
2	Mark McGwire	8.00
3	Juan Gonzalez	10.00
4	Albert Belle	8.00
5	Barry Bonds	6.00
6	Ken Griffey Jr.	25.00
7	Andruw Jones	15.00
8	Chipper Jones	15.00
9	Mike Piazza	15.00
10	Jeff Bagwell	10.00
11	Dante Bichette	2.00
12	Alex Rodriguez	25.00
13	Gary Sheffield	3.00
14	Ken Caminiti	2.00
15	Sammy Sosa	3.00
16	Vladimir Guerrero	12.00
17	Brian Jordan	2.00
18	Tim Salmon	3.00

1997 Score Heart of the Order

This 36-card set was distributed in both Series II retail and hobby packs, with cards 1-18 in retail (one per 23 packs) and cards 19-36 in hobby (one per 15). The cards are printed in a horizontal format, with some of the top hitters in the game included in the insert.

		MT
Complete Set (36):		170.00
Complete Retail Set (1-18):		100.00
Complete Hobby Set (19-36):		70.00
Common Player:		1.50
1	Ivan Rodriguez	4.00
2	Will Clark	2.00
3	Juan Gonzalez	10.00
4	Frank Thomas	20.00
5	Albert Belle	7.00
6	Robin Ventura	1.50
7	Alex Rodriguez	20.00
8	Ken Griffey Jr.	20.00
9	Jay Buhner	1.50
10	Roberto Alomar	4.00
11	Rafael Palmeiro	2.00
12	Cal Ripken Jr.	15.00
13	Manny Ramirez	5.00
14	Matt Williams	2.50
15	Jim Thome	3.00
16	Wade Boggs	2.00
17	Derek Jeter	12.00
18	Bernie Williams	4.00
19	Chipper Jones	12.00
20	Andruw Jones	12.00
21	Ryan Klesko	4.00
22	Wilton Guerrero	1.50
23	Mike Piazza	12.00
24	Raul Mondesi	2.50
25	Tony Gwynn	10.00
26	Ken Caminiti	2.00
27	Greg Vaughn	1.50
28	Brian Jordan	1.50
29	Ron Gant	1.50
30	Dmitri Young	1.50
31	Darin Erstad	8.00
32	Jim Edmonds	1.50
33	Tim Salmon	2.00
34	Chuck Knoblauch	2.00
35	Paul Molitor	3.00
36	Todd Walker	5.00

1997 Score Pitcher Perfect

Seattle Mariners' star pitcher Randy Johnson makes his picks for the top pitching talent in this 1997 Score Series I insert set. The cards were seeded one per 23 packs.

		MT
Complete Set (15):		70.00
Common Player:		1.50
1	Cal Ripken Jr.	12.00
2	Alex Rodriguez	15.00
3	Ken Griffey Jr.	15.00
4	Edgar Martinez	1.50
5	Ivan Rodriguez	2.00
6	Mark McGwire	6.00
7	Tim Salmon	2.50
8	Chili Davis	1.50
9	Joe Carter	2.00
10	Frank Thomas	15.00
11	Will Clark	2.50
12	Mo Vaughn	6.00
13	Wade Boggs	2.00
14	Randy Johnson	3.00
15	Alex Rodriguez, Cal Ripken Jr.	15.00

1997 Score Stand & Deliver

This 24-card insert was printed on a silver foil background, with the insert name in gold foil across the bottom. Cards were found in Series II packs one per 71 retail, one per 41 hobby. Card numbers 21-24 (Florida Marlins) were designated as the winning group, meaning the first 225 collectors

that mailed in the complete four card set received a gold upgrade version of the set framed in glass.

		MT
Complete Set (24):		375.00
Common Player:		4.00
1	Andruw Jones	30.00
2	Greg Maddux	30.00
3	Chipper Jones	30.00
4	John Smoltz	4.00
5	Ken Griffey Jr.	50.00
6	Alex Rodriguez	40.00
7	Jay Buhner	4.00
8	Randy Johnson	10.00
9	Derek Jeter	30.00
10	Andy Pettitte	15.00
11	Bernie Williams	12.00
12	Mariano Rivera	4.00
13	Mike Piazza	30.00
14	Hideo Nomo	12.00
15	Raul Mondesi	4.00
16	Todd Hollandsworth	4.00
17	Manny Ramirez	15.00
18	Jim Thome	12.00
19	David Justice	6.00
20	Matt Williams	8.00
21	Juan Gonzalez	25.00
22	Jeff Bagwell	20.00
23	Cal Ripken Jr.	40.00
24	Frank Thomas	50.00

1997 Score Stellar Season

These 1997 Score Series I inserts were seeded one per every 17 magazine packs.

		MT
Complete Set (18):		90.00
Common Player:		2.00
1	Juan Gonzalez	9.00
2	Chuck Knoblauch	4.00
3	Jeff Bagwell	7.50
4	John Smoltz	3.00
5	Mark McGwire	7.00
6	Ken Griffey Jr.	20.00
7	Frank Thomas	20.00
8	Alex Rodriguez	15.00
9	Mike Piazza	12.00
10	Albert Belle	6.00
11	Roberto Alomar	4.00
12	Sammy Sosa	3.00
13	Mo Vaughn	5.00
14	Brady Anderson	2.00
15	Henry Rodriguez	2.00
16	Eric Young	2.00
17	Gary Sheffield	2.00
18	Ryan Klesko	3.00

1997 Score Team Sets

Team sets consisting of 15 players from different teams were produced by Score. Only 10 different team sets were produced. Each card is similar in design to the regular 1997 Score set except for a special foil stamping at the bottom of the card that corresponds with the team colors for the specific player.

		MT
Common Player:		.25
Platinums:		5x to 8x
Braves Wax Box:		80.00
Orioles Wax Box:		70.00
Red Sox Wax Box:		60.00
White Sox Wax Box:		70.00
Indians Wax Box:		70.00
Rockies Wax Box:		55.00
Dodgers Wax Box:		70.00
Yankees Wax Box:		75.00
Mariners Wax Box:		120.00
Rangers Wax Box:		60.00
	Atlanta Braves	8.00
1	Ryan Klesko	.60
2	David Justice	.35
3	Terry Pendleton	.25
4	Tom Glavine	.35
5	Javier Lopez	.35
6	John Smoltz	.35
7	Jermaine Dye	.40
8	Mark Lemke	.25
9	Fred McGriff	.40
10	Chipper Jones	2.50
11	Terrell Wade	.25
12	Greg Maddux	2.50
13	Mark Wohlers	.25
14	Marquis Grissom	.25
15	Andruw Jones	4.00
	Baltimore Orioles	5.00
1	Rafael Palmeiro	.35
2	Eddie Murray	.50
3	Roberto Alomar	1.00
4	Rocky Coppinger	.25
5	Brady Anderson	.35
6	Bobby Bonilla	.35
7	Cal Ripken Jr.	3.00
8	Mike Mussina	.50
9	Nerio Rodriguez	.25
10	Randy Myers	.25
11	B.J. Surhoff	.25
12	Jeffrey Hammonds	.25
13	Chris Hoiles	.25
14	Jimmy Haynes	.25
15	David Wells	.25
	Boston Red Sox	4.00
1	Wil Cordero	.25
2	Mo Vaughn	1.50
3	John Valentin	.25
4	Reggie Jefferson	.25
5	Tom Gordon	.25
6	Mike Stanley	.25
7	Jose Canseco	.40
8	Roger Clemens	.75
9	Darren Bragg	.25
10	Jeff Frye	.25
11	Jeff Suppan	.25
12	Mike Greenwell	.25
13	Arquimedez Pozo	.25
14	Tim Naehring	.25
15	Troy O'Leary	.25
	Chicago White Sox	6.00
1	Frank Thomas	4.00
2	James Baldwin	.25
3	Danny Tartabull	.25
4	Jeff Darwin	.25
5	Harold Baines	.25
6	Roberto Hernandez	.25
7	Ray Durham	.25
8	Robin Ventura	.25
9	Wilson Alvarez	.25
10	Lyle Mouton	.25
11	Alex Fernandez	.30
12	Ron Karkovice	.25
13	Kevin Tapani	.25
14	Tony Phillips	.25
15	Mike Cameron	.25
	Cleveland Indians	6.00
1	Albert Belle	2.00
2	Jack McDowell	.30
3	Jim Thome	.60
4	Dennis Martinez	.25
5	Julio Franco	.25
6	Omar Vizquel	.25
7	Kenny Lofton	1.25
8	Manny Ramirez	1.25
9	Sandy Alomar Jr.	.25
10	Charles Nagy	.25
11	Kevin Seitzer	.25
12	Mark Carreon	.25
13	Jeff Kent	.25
14	Danny Graves	.25
15	Brian Giles	.25
	Colorado Rockies	4.00
1	Dante Bichette	.40
2	Kevin Ritz	.25
3	Walt Weiss	.25
4	Ellis Burks	.25
5	Jamey Wright	.25
6	Andres Galarraga	.35
7	Eric Young	.25
8	Larry Walker	.50
9	Vinny Castilla	.25
10	Quinton McCracken	.25
11	Armando Reynoso	.25
12	Jayhawk Owens	.25
13	Mark Thompson	.25
14	John Burke	.25
15	Bruce Ruffin	.25
	Los Angeles Dodgers	6.00
1	Ismael Valdez	.25
2	Mike Piazza	2.50
3	Todd Hollandsworth	.40
4	Delino DeShields	.25
5	Chan Ho Park	.25
6	Roger Cedeno	.25
7	Raul Mondesi	.40
8	Darren Dreifort	.25
9	Jim Bruske	.25
10	Greg Gagne	.25
11	Chad Curtis	.25
12	Ramon Martinez	.25
13	Brett Butler	.25
14	Eric Karros	.25
15	Hideo Nomo	.75
	New York Yankees	6.00
1	Bernie Williams	.75
2	Cecil Fielder	.40
3	Derek Jeter	2.50
4	Darryl Strawberry	.25
5	Andy Pettitte	1.00
6	Ruben Rivera	.50
7	Mariano Rivera	.40
8	John Wetteland	.25
9	Paul O'Neill	.25
10	Wade Boggs	.40
11	Dwight Gooden	.25
12	David Cone	.35
13	Tino Martinez	.25
14	Kenny Rogers	.25
15	Andy Fox	.25
	Seattle Mariners	12.00
1	Chris Bosio	.25
2	Edgar Martinez	.25
3	Alex Rodriguez	4.00
4	Paul Sorrento	.25
5	Bob Wells	.25
6	Ken Griffey Jr.	4.00
7	Jay Buhner	.10
8	Dan Wilson	.25
9	Randy Johnson	.40
10	Joey Cora	.25
11	Mark Whiten	.25
12	Rich Amaral	.25
13	Raul Ibanez	.25
14	Jamie Moyer	.25
15	Makoto Suzuki	.25
	Texas Rangers	5.00
1	Mickey Tettleton	.25
2	Will Clark	.40
3	Ken Hill	.25
4	Rusty Greer	.25
5	Kevin Elster	.25
6	Darren Oliver	.25
7	Mark McLemore	.25
8	Roger Pavlik	.25
9	Dean Palmer	.25
10	Bobby Witt	.25
11	Juan Gonzalez	2.00
12	Ivan Rodriguez	.50
13	Darryl Hamilton	.25
14	John Burkett	.25
15	Warren Newson	.25

1997 Score Team Sets Gold

A parallel gold version was also issued for each Score Team Sets card. The gold set also featured 15 players from each of 10 different teams.

		MT
Common Player:		10.00
Semistars:		25.00
	Atlanta Braves	600.00
1	Ryan Klesko	40.00
2	David Justice	15.00
3	Terry Pendleton	10.00
4	Tom Glavine	15.00
5	Javier Lopez	15.00
6	John Smoltz	15.00
7	Jermaine Dye	30.00
8	Mark Lemke	10.00
9	Fred McGriff	25.00
10	Chipper Jones	150.00
11	Terrell Wade	10.00
12	Greg Maddux	150.00
13	Mark Wohlers	10.00
14	Marquis Grissom	10.00
15	Andruw Jones	250.00
	Baltimore Orioles	350.00
1	Rafael Palmeiro	15.00
2	Eddie Murray	35.00
3	Roberto Alomar	75.00
4	Rocky Coppinger	10.00
5	Brady Anderson	15.00
6	Bobby Bonilla	15.00
7	Cal Ripken Jr.	175.00
8	Mike Mussina	30.00
9	Nerio Rodriguez	10.00
10	Randy Myers	10.00
11	B.J. Surhoff	10.00
12	Jeffrey Hammonds	10.00
13	Chris Hoiles	10.00
14	Jimmy Haynes	10.00
15	David Wells	10.00
	Boston Red Sox	250.00
1	Wil Cordero	10.00
2	Mo Vaughn	100.00
3	John Valentin	10.00
4	Reggie Jefferson	10.00
5	Tom Gordon	10.00
6	Mike Stanley	10.00
7	Jose Canseco	25.00
8	Roger Clemens	30.00
9	Darren Bragg	10.00
10	Jeff Frye	10.00
11	Jeff Suppan	10.00
12	Mike Greenwell	10.00
13	Arquimedez Pozo	10.00
14	Tim Naehring	10.00
15	Troy O'Leary	10.00
	Chicago White Sox	300.00
1	Frank Thomas	225.00
2	James Baldwin	10.00
3	Danny Tartabull	10.00
4	Jeff Darwin	10.00
5	Harold Baines	10.00
6	Roberto Hernandez	10.00
7	Ray Durham	10.00
8	Robin Ventura	10.00
9	Wilson Alvarez	10.00
10	Lyle Mouton	10.00
11	Alex Fernandez	15.00
12	Ron Karkovice	10.00
13	Kevin Tapani	10.00
14	Tony Phillips	10.00
15	Mike Cameron	10.00
	Cleveland Indians	400.00
1	Albert Belle	90.00
2	Jack McDowell	15.00
3	Jim Thome	25.00
4	Dennis Martinez	10.00
5	Julio Franco	10.00
6	Omar Vizquel	10.00
7	Kenny Lofton	75.00
8	Manny Ramirez	75.00
9	Sandy Alomar Jr.	10.00
10	Charles Nagy	10.00
11	Kevin Seitzer	10.00
12	Mark Carreon	10.00
13	Jeff Kent	10.00
14	Danny Graves	10.00
15	Brian Giles	10.00
	Colorado Rockies	200.00
1	Dante Bichette	25.00
2	Kevin Ritz	10.00
3	Walt Weiss	10.00
4	Ellis Burks	15.00
5	Jamey Wright	10.00
6	Andres Galarraga	25.00
7	Eric Young	10.00
8	Larry Walker	20.00
9	Vinny Castilla	10.00
10	Quinton McCracken	10.00
11	Armando Reynoso	10.00
12	Jayhawk Owens	10.00
13	Mark Thompson	10.00
14	John Burke	10.00
15	Bruce Ruffin	10.00
	Los Angeles Dodgers	300.00
1	Ismael Valdez	10.00
2	Mike Piazza	175.00
3	Todd Hollandsworth	20.00
4	Delino DeShields	10.00
5	Chan Ho Park	10.00
6	Roger Cedeno	10.00
7	Raul Mondesi	25.00
8	Darren Dreifort	10.00
9	Jim Bruske	10.00
10	Greg Gagne	10.00
11	Chad Curtis	10.00
12	Ramon Martinez	10.00
13	Brett Butler	10.00
14	Eric Karros	10.00
15	Hideo Nomo	50.00
	New York Yankees	350.00
1	Bernie Williams	40.00
2	Cecil Fielder	20.00
3	Derek Jeter	150.00
4	Darryl Strawberry	10.00
5	Andy Pettitte	75.00
6	Ruben Rivera	25.00
7	Mariano Rivera	20.00
8	John Wetteland	10.00
9	Paul O'Neill	10.00
10	Wade Boggs	20.00
11	Dwight Gooden	10.00
12	David Cone	15.00
13	Tino Martinez	10.00
14	Kenny Rogers	10.00
15	Andy Fox	10.00
	Seattle Mariners	500.00
1	Chris Bosio	10.00
2	Edgar Martinez	10.00
3	Alex Rodriguez	250.00
4	Paul Sorrento	10.00
5	Bob Wells	10.00
6	Ken Griffey Jr.	250.00
7	Jay Buhner	20.00
8	Dan Wilson	10.00
9	Randy Johnson	25.00
10	Joey Cora	10.00
11	Mark Whiten	10.00
12	Rich Amaral	10.00
13	Raul Ibanez	10.00
14	Jamie Moyer	10.00
15	Makoto Suzuki	10.00
	Texas Rangers	250.00
1	Mickey Tettleton	10.00
2	Will Clark	25.00
3	Ken Hill	10.00
4	Rusty Greer	10.00
5	Kevin Elster	10.00
6	Darren Oliver	10.00
7	Mark McLemore	10.00
8	Roger Pavlik	10.00
9	Dean Palmer	10.00
10	Bobby Witt	10.00
11	Juan Gonzalez	125.00
12	Ivan Rodriguez	40.00
13	Darryl Hamilton	10.00
14	John Burkett	10.00
15	Warren Newson	10.00

1997 Score The Franchise

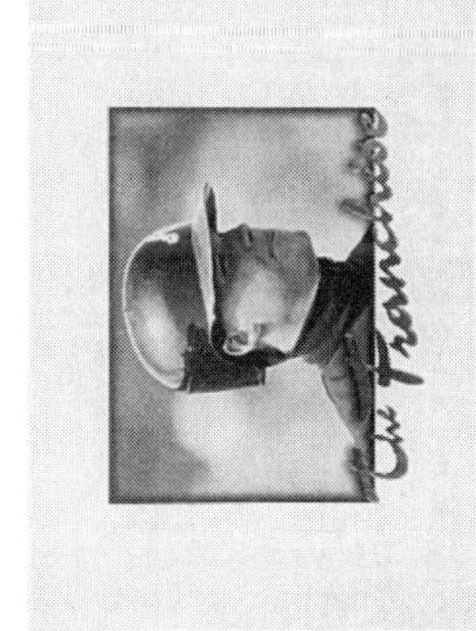

There were two versions made for these 1997 Score Series I inserts - regular and The Glowing Franchise, which has glow-in-the-dark highlights. The regular version is seeded one per 72 packs; glow-in-the-dark cards are seeded one per 240 packs, and generally valued about 2-3x regular.

		MT
Complete Set (9):		120.00
Common Player:		4.00
1	Ken Griffey Jr.	30.00
2	John Smoltz	4.00
3	Cal Ripken Jr.	25.00
4	Chipper Jones	20.00
5	Mike Piazza	20.00
6	Albert Belle	12.00
7	Frank Thomas	30.00
8	Sammy Sosa	6.00
9	Roberto Alomar	10.00

1997 Score The Highlight Zone

Exclusive to 1997 Score Series I hobby packs are these Highlight Zone inserts, seeded one per every 35 packs. Within the 18-card set, card numbers 1-9 are in regular hobby packs, while numbers 10-18 are found only in premium stock packs.

		MT
Complete Set (18):		120.00
Common Player:		2.00
1	Frank Thomas	20.00
2	Ken Griffey Jr.	20.00
3	Mo Vaughn	7.00
4	Albert Belle	8.00
5	Mike Piazza	12.00
6	Barry Bonds	5.00
7	Greg Maddux	12.00
8	Sammy Sosa	3.00
9	Jeff Bagwell	8.00
10	Alex Rodriguez	20.00
11	Chipper Jones	12.00
12	Brady Anderson	2.00
13	Ozzie Smith	4.00
14	Edgar Martinez	2.00
15	Cal Ripken Jr.	15.00
16	Ryan Klesko	5.00
17	Randy Johnson	4.00
18	Eddie Murray	3.50

1997 Score Titanic Taters

Some of the game's most powerful hitters are featured on these 1997 Score Series I inserts. The cards were seeded one per every 35 retail packs.

		MT
Complete Set (18):		120.00
Common Player:		3.00
1	Mark McGwire	8.00
2	Mike Piazza	15.00
3	Ken Griffey Jr.	25.00
4	Juan Gonzalez	12.00
5	Frank Thomas	25.00
6	Albert Belle	8.00
7	Sammy Sosa	4.00
8	Jeff Bagwell	10.00
9	Todd Hundley	3.00
10	Ryan Klesko	5.00
11	Brady Anderson	3.00
12	Mo Vaughn	8.00
13	Jay Buhner	3.00
14	Greg Vaughn	3.00
15	Barry Bonds	6.00
16	Gary Sheffield	4.00
17	Alex Rodriguez	25.00
18	Cecil Fielder	3.00

1997 Select

The base set is made up of 150 cards printed on a thick, 16-point stock. Each card in the regular set fea-tures a distinctive silver-foil treatment and either a red (100 cards) or blue (50 cards) foil accent. Subsets include 40 Rookies, 8 Super Stars and two checklists. Inserts include two parallel sets, (Artist's Proof and Registered Gold), Tools of the Trade, Mirror Blue Tools of the Trade, and Rookie Revolution. The cards were sold only at hobby shops in six-card packs for $2.99 each.

		MT
Complete Set (150):		45.00
Common Player:		.10
Prices listed for Red Cards:		
Blues 2x listed prices		
Wax Box:		60.00
1	Juan Gonzalez	1.25
2	Mo Vaughn	.75
3	Tony Gwynn	1.25
4	Manny Ramirez	.75
5	Jose Canseco	.25
6	David Cone	.15
7	Chan Ho Park	.10
8	Frank Thomas	3.00
9	Todd Hollandsworth	.10
10	Marty Cordova	.10
11	Gary Sheffield	.30
12	John Smoltz	.20
13	Mark Grudzielanek	.10
14	Sammy Sosa	.30
15	Paul Molitor	.40
16	Kevin Brown	.10
17	Albert Belle	1.00
18	Eric Young	.10
19	John Wetteland	.10
20	Ryan Klesko	.40
21	Joe Carter	.15
22	Alex Ochoa	.10
23	Greg Maddux	2.00
24	Roger Clemens	1.00
25	Ivan Rodriguez	.50
26	Barry Bonds	.75
27	Kenny Lofton	.75
28	Javy Lopez	.15
29	Hideo Nomo	.60
30	Rusty Greer	.10
31	Rafael Palmeiro	.15
32	Mike Piazza	2.00
33	Ryne Sandberg	.75
34	Wade Boggs	.20
35	Jim Thome	.40
36	Ken Caminiti	.20
37	Mark Grace	.15
38	Brian Jordan	.10
39	Craig Biggio	.15
40	Henry Rodriguez	.10
41	Dean Palmer	.10
42	Jason Kendall	.10
43	Bill Pulsipher	.10
44	Tim Salmon	.20
45	Marc Newfield	.10
46	Pat Hentgen	.10
47	Ken Griffey Jr.	3.00
48	Paul Wilson	.10
49	Jay Buhner	.20
50	Rickey Henderson	.10
51	Jeff Bagwell	1.25
52	Cecil Fielder	.15
53	Alex Rodriguez	3.00
54	John Jaha	.10
55	Brady Anderson	.10
56	Andres Galarraga	.20
57	Raul Mondesi	.25
58	Andy Pettitte	.75
59	Roberto Alomar	.50
60	Derek Jeter	2.00
61	Charles Johnson	.10
62	Travis Fryman	.10
63	Chipper Jones	2.00
64	Edgar Martinez	.10
65	Bobby Bonilla	.10
66	Greg Vaughn	.10
67	Bobby Higginson	.10
68	Garret Anderson	.10
69	Chuck Knoblauch	.15
70	Jermaine Dye	.10
71	Cal Ripken Jr.	2.50
72	Jason Giambi	.10
73	Trey Beamon	.10
74	Shawn Green	.10
75	Mark McGwire	1.00
76	Carlos Delgado	.10
77	Jason Isringhausen	.10
78	Randy Johnson	.60
79	Troy Percival	.10
80	Ron Gant	.15
81	Ellis Burks	.10
82	Mike Mussina	.50
83	Todd Hundley	.20
84	Jim Edmonds	.10
85	Charles Nagy	.10
86	Dante Bichette	.20
87	Mariano Rivera	.15
88	Matt Williams	.30
89	Rondell White	.10
90	Steve Finley	.10
91	Alex Fernandez	.15
92	Barry Larkin	.20
93	Tom Goodwin	.10
94	Will Clark	.30
95	Michael Tucker	.10
96	Derek Bell	.10
97	Larry Walker	.40
98	Alan Benes	.20
99	Tom Glavine	.20
100	Darin Erstad	1.25
101	Andruw Jones	2.00
102	Scott Rolen	1.50
103	Todd Walker	.50
104	Dmitri Young	.10
105	Vladimir Guerrero	1.75
106	Nomar Garciaparra	2.00
107	*Danny Patterson*	.20
108	Karim Garcia	.15
109	Todd Greene	.10
110	Ruben Rivera	.15
111	Raul Casanova	.10
112	Mike Cameron	.10
113	Bartolo Colon	.10
114	*Rod Myers*	.10
115	Todd Dunn	.10
116	Torii Hunter	.10
117	Jason Dickson	.20
118	*Gene Kingsale*	.20
119	Rafael Medina	.10
120	Raul Ibanez	.10
121	*Bobby Henley*	.20
122	Scott Spiezio	.10
123	*Bobby Smith*	.20
124	J.J. Johnson	.10
125	*Bubba Trammell*	1.00
126	Jeff Abbott	.10
127	Neifi Perez	.10
128	Derrek Lee	.10
129	*Kevin Brown*	.10
130	Mendy Lopez	.10
131	Kevin Orie	.10
132	Ryan Jones	.10
133	Juan Encarnacion	.50
134	Jose Guillen	1.00
135	Greg Norton	.10
136	Richie Sexson	.10
137	Jay Payton	.10
138	Bob Abreu	.10
139	*Ronnie Belliard*	.20
140	Wilton Guerrero	.10
141	Alex Rodriguez (Select Stars)	1.50
142	Juan Gonzalez (Select Stars)	.60
143	Ken Caminiti (Select Stars)	.15
144	Frank Thomas (Select Stars)	1.50
145	Ken Griffey Jr. (Select Stars)	1.50
146	John Smoltz (Select Stars)	.15
147	Mike Piazza (Select Stars)	1.00
148	Derek Jeter (Select Stars)	1.00
149	Frank Thomas CL	.75
150	Ken Griffey Jr. CL	.75

1997 Select Autographs

Four top candidates for the 1997 Rookie of the Year Award - Wilton Guerrero, Jose Guillen, Andruw Jones and Todd Walker - each signed a limited number of their Select Rookie cards. Jones signed 2,500 cards while each of the other players signed 3,000 each.

		MT
Complete Set (4):		180.00
Common Autograph:		35.00
AU1	Wilton Guerrero	35.00
AU2	Jose Guillen	60.00
AU3	Andruw Jones	75.00
AU4	Todd Walker	40.00

1997 Select Registered Gold

This parallel insert set, like the regular issue, can be found with 100 red-foil and 50 blue-foil enhanced cards. They differ from the regular issue in the use of gold foil instead of silver on the right side of the front. Also, the inserts have "Registered Gold" printed vertically on the right side of the photo. Backs are identical to the regular issue. Red-foil Registered Gold cards are found on average of once every 11 packs; blue-foiled cards are a 1 in 47 pick.

	MT
Complete Set (15):	1200.
Common Red Gold:	2.00
Common Blue Gold:	4.00
Registered Gold Reds:	5x to 10x
Registered Gold Blues:	20x to 35x
Artist's Proofs Reds:	25x to 50x
Artist's Proofs Blues:	80x to 100x

1997 Select Rookie Revolution

This 20-card insert highlights some of the top young stars in the game. Cards feature a micro-etched mylar design and are sequentially numbered. Odds of finding a card are 1:56 packs.

		MT
Complete Set (20):		200.00
Common Player:		6.00
1	Andruw Jones	45.00
2	Derek Jeter	45.00
3	Todd Hollandsworth	6.00
4	Edgar Renteria	6.00
5	Jason Kendall	6.00
6	Rey Ordonez	6.00
7	F.P. Santangelo	6.00
8	Jermaine Dye	6.00
9	Alex Ochoa	6.00
10	Vladimir Guerrero	25.00
11	Dmitri Young	6.00
12	Todd Walker	12.00
13	Scott Rolen	30.00
14	Nomar Garciaparra	30.00
15	Ruben Rivera	8.00
16	Darin Erstad	25.00
17	Todd Greene	6.00
18	Mariano Rivera	6.00
19	Trey Beamon	6.00
20	Karim Garcia	8.00

1997 Select Tools of the Trade

A 25-card insert featuring a double-front design saluting a top veteran player on one side and a promising youngster on the other. Cards feature a silver-foil card stock with gold-foil stamping. Cards were inserted 1:9 packs. A parallel to this set - Blue Mirror Tools of the Trade - features blue-foil stock with an insert ratio of 1:240 packs.

		MT
Complete Set (25):		200.00
Common Player:		3.00
Mirror Blues:		8x to 12x
1	Ken Griffey Jr., Andruw Jones	25.00
2	Greg Maddux, Andy Pettitte	15.00
3	Cal Ripken Jr., Chipper Jones	20.00
4	Mike Piazza, Jason Kendall	12.00
5	Albert Belle, Karim Garcia	10.00
6	Mo Vaughn, Dmitri Young	8.00
7	Juan Gonzalez, Vladimir Guerrero	15.00
8	Tony Gwynn, Jermaine Dye	12.00
9	Barry Bonds, Alex Ochoa	8.00
10	Jeff Bagwell, Jason Giambi	12.00
11	Kenny Lofton, Darin Erstad	15.00
12	Gary Sheffield, Manny Ramirez	8.00
13	Tim Salmon, Todd Hollandsworth	3.00
14	Sammy Sosa, Ruben Rivera	5.00
15	Paul Molitor, George Arias	6.00
16	Jim Thome, Todd Walker	6.00
17	Wade Boggs, Scott Rolen	8.00
18	Ryne Sandberg, Chuck Knoblauch	8.00

19	Mark McGwire, Frank Thomas	20.00
20	Ivan Rodriguez, Charles Johnson	7.00
21	Brian Jordan, Trey Beamon	3.00
22	Roger Clemens, Troy Percival	10.00
23	John Smoltz, Mike Mussina	6.00
24	Alex Rodriguez, Rey Ordonez	20.00
25	Derek Jeter, Nomar Garciaparra	15.00

1997 Score Board Mickey Mantle Shoe Box Collection

Yet another collectors' issue of Mickey Mantle cards, the Score Board "Shoe Box Collection" offered packs containing two of the 75 Mantle cards or seven-card insert set, along with a genuine - usually a low-grade common - Topps card from 1951-69. Several designs of Mantle cards are featured in the set, including color photos as well as blue-and-white duotones. Five of the cards are printed with gold-foil backgrounds and die-cut. Cards #51-69 are short-printed at a ratio of about 1-to-3 with cards #1-50. Suggested retail price was $6.50 per pack.

		MT
Complete Set (75):		125.00
Common Card:		1.00
1	Summary Of The Legend (foil die-cut)	10.00
1p	Summary of the Legend (promo card)	15.00
2	Triple Crown 1956	1.00
3	MVP 1956	1.00
4	MVP 1957	1.00
5	MVP 1962	1.00
6	Uniform #6 (foil die-cut)	10.00
6p	Uniform #6 (promo card)	20.00
7	Uniform #7 (foil die-cut)	10.00
7p	Uniform #7 (promo card)	20.00
7p	Uniform #7 (Marked as promo card on back)	4.00
8	Gold Glove Winner	1.00
9	17-time All-Star	1.00
10	4-time HR Champion	1.00
11	World Series Records	1.00
12	The Dirty Dozen (post seasons)	1.00
13	World Champion-1951	1.00
14	World Champion-1952	1.00
15	World Champion-1953	1.00
16	World Champion-1956	1.00
17	World Champion-1958	1.00
18	World Champion-1961	1.00
19	World Champion-1962	1.00
20	Replacing A Legend	1.00
21	Casey On Mantle	1.00
22	Mickey & The Media	1.00
23	Family Man	1.00
24	Fan Favorite	1.00
25	Playing Injured	1.00
26	Clubhouse Leader	1.00
27	Team Leader	1.00
28	M & M Boys	1.00
29	Legendary Friendships	1.00
30	Time Out	1.00
31	Mantle Is Born	1.00
32	Mutt Mantle	1.00

33	Growing Up	1.00
34	5-tool player-Arm	1.00
35	5-tool player-Defense	1.00
36	5-tool player-Average	1.00
37	5-tool player-Speed	1.00
38	5-tool player-Power	1.00
39	First Homer	1.00
40	100th Homer	1.00
41	200th Homer	1.00
42	300th Homer	1.00
43	400th Homer	1.00
44	500th Homer	1.00
45	536 Career Homers	1.00
46	Yankee Stadium Blasts	1.00
47	Switch-hit Home Runs	1.00
48	565-ft. Home Run	1.00
49	Signs 1st Pro Contract	1.00
50	Mickey In The Minors	1.00
51	1951 Trading Card	2.00
52	1952 Trading Card	2.00
53	1953 Trading Card	2.00
54	1954 Trading Card	2.00
55	1955 Trading Card	2.00
56A	1956 Trading Card	2.00
56B	1956 Trading Card	2.00
57	1957 Trading Card	2.00
58	1958 Trading Card	2.00
59	1959 Trading Card	2.00
60	1960 Trading Card	2.00
61	1961 Trading Card	2.00
62	1962 Trading Card	2.00
63	1963 Trading Card	2.00
64	1964 Trading Card	2.00
65	1965 Trading Card	2.00
66	1966 Trading Card	2.00
67	1967 Trading Card	2.00
68	1968 Trading Card	2.00
69	1969 Trading Card	2.00
70	Number Retired By Yankees (foil die-cut)	10.00
70p	Number Retired By Yankees (promo card)	15.00
71	Mickey Mantle Day (1965)	1.00
72	Mickey Mantle Day (1969)	1.00
73	Life After Baseball	1.00
74	Hall Of Fame Induction (foil die-cut)	10.00
74p	Hall of Fame Induction (promo card)	15.00

1997 Score Board Mickey Mantle Shoe Box Inserts

A set of seven insert cards, found on average of one per 16 packs, was part of the Mickey Mantle Shoe Box Collection. The inserts have a photo of Mantle on front, with blue metallic foil highlights. Contest rules on the back specify that the first seven persons to redeem a complete set of the seven insert cards will win a $7,000 Mantle phone card. All others redeeming the set of seven prior to July 7, 1998, received a $700 Mantle phone card. The #7 insert card was short-printed to limit the number of phone card winners.

		MT
Complete Set (7):		300.00
Common Card:		25.00
$700 Phone Card:		475.00
$7,000 Phone Card:		3500.
1	Mickey Mantle Insert #1	25.00
2	Mickey Mantle Insert #2	25.00
3	Mickey Mantle Insert #3	25.00
4	Mickey Mantle Insert #4	25.00
5	Mickey Mantle Insert #5	25.00
6	Mickey Mantle Insert #6	25.00
7	Mickey Mantle Insert #7 (short-print)	250.00

1997 Topps

Topps' 1997 set includes the first-ever player cards of the expansion Diamondbacks and Devil Rays; 16 Mickey Mantle reprints; a special Jackie Robinson tribute card; 27 Willie Mays Topps and Bowman reprints; randomly-inserted Willie Mays autographed reprint cards; and Inter-League Finest and Finest Refractors cards. The base set has 275 cards in each series. Each card front has a gloss coating on the photo and a spot matte finish on the outside border. Gold foil stamping is also used. Card backs have informative text, complete player stats and biographies, and a second photo. The Jackie Robinson card pays tribute to the 50th anniversary of his breaking the color line. This card is #42 in the regular issue. Mantle reprints, seeded one per every 12 packs, feature the 16 remaining Mantle cards which were not reprinted in 1996 Topps baseball. The cards, each stamped with a gold foil logo, are numbered from #21 to #36. Willie Mays has 27 of his cards reprinted and seeded one per every eight packs. Each card also has a gold foil stamp. As a special hobby-exclusive bonus, 1,000 randomly-selected Mays reprints will be autographed and randomly inserted in packs. Five other insert sets were made: All-Stars, Inter-League Finest and Inter-League Finest Refractors, Sweet Strokes and Hobby Masters.

		MT
Complete Set (496):		30.00
Complete Series 1 Set (276):		15.00
Complete Series 2 Set (220):		15.00
Common Player:		.05
Series I & II All-Star Box:		40.00
1	Barry Bonds	.50
2	Tom Pagnozzi	.05
3	Terrell Wade	.05
4	Jose Valentin	.05
5	Mark Clark	.05
6	Brady Anderson	.15
7	Not issued	
8	Wade Boggs	.20
9	Scott Stahoviak	.05
10	Andres Galarraga	.15
11	Steve Avery	.05
12	Rusty Greer	.05
13	Derek Jeter	1.25
14	Ricky Bottalico	.05
15	Andy Ashby	.05
16	Paul Shuey	.05
17	F.P. Santangelo	.05
18	Royce Clayton	.05
19	Mike Mohler	.05
20	Mike Piazza	1.50
21	Jaime Navarro	.05
22	Billy Wagner	.05
23	Mike Timlin	.05
24	Garret Anderson	.05

#	Player	Price
25	Ben McDonald	.05
26	Mel Rojas	.05
27	John Burkett	.05
28	Jeff King	.05
29	Reggie Jefferson	.05
30	Kevin Appier	.05
31	Felipe Lira	.05
32	Kevin Tapani	.05
33	Mark Portugal	.05
34	Carlos Garcia	.05
35	Joey Cora	.05
36	David Segui	.05
37	Mark Grace	.20
38	Erik Hanson	.05
39	Jeff D'Amico	.05
40	Jay Buhner	.15
41	B.J. Surhoff	.05
42	Jackie Robinson	3.00
43	Roger Pavlik	.05
44	Hal Morris	.05
45	Mariano Duncan	.05
46	Harold Baines	.08
47	Jorge Fabregas	.05
48	Jose Herrera	.05
49	Jeff Cirillo	.05
50	Tom Glavine	.10
51	Pedro Astacio	.05
52	Mark Gardner	.05
53	Arthur Rhodes	.05
54	Troy O'Leary	.05
55	Bip Roberts	.05
56	Mike Lieberthal	.05
57	Shane Andrews	.05
58	Scott Karl	.05
59	Gary DiSarcina	.05
60	Andy Pettitte	.60
61a	Kevin Elster	.05
61b	Mike Fetters (should be #84)	.05
62	Mark McGwire	.75
63	Dan Wilson	.05
64	Mickey Morandini	.05
65	Chuck Knoblauch	.12
66	Tim Wakefield	.05
67	Raul Mondesi	.25
68	Todd Jones	.05
69	Albert Belle	.75
70	Trevor Hoffman	.05
71	Eric Young	.05
72	Robert Perez	.05
73	Butch Huskey	.05
74	Brian McRae	.05
75	Jim Edmonds	.10
76	Mike Henneman	.05
77	Frank Rodriguez	.05
78	Danny Tartabull	.05
79	Robby Nen	.05
80	Reggie Sanders	.10
81	Ron Karkovice	.05
82	Benny Santiago	.08
83	Mike Lansing	.05
84	Not issued - see #61b	
85	Craig Biggio	.10
86	Mike Bordick	.05
87	Ray Lankford	.10
88	Charles Nagy	.05
89	Paul Wilson	.05
90	John Wetteland	.05
91	Tom Candiotti	.05
92	Carlos Delgado	.05
93	Derek Bell	.10
94	Mark Lemke	.05
95	Edgar Martinez	.08
96	Rickey Henderson	.20
97	Greg Myers	.05
98	Jim Leyritz	.05
99	Mark Johnson	.05
100	Dwight Gooden (Season Highlights)	.05
101	Al Leiter (Season Highlights)	.05
102	John Mabry (Season Highlights)	.05
103	Alex Ochoa (Season Highlights)	.05
104	Mike Piazza (Season Highlights)	.60
105	Jim Thome	.30
106	Ricky Otero	.05
107	Jamey Wright	.05
108	Frank Thomas	2.50
109	Jody Reed	.05
110	Orel Hershiser	.08
111	Terry Steinbach	.05
112	Mark Loretta	.05
113	Turk Wendell	.05
114	Marvin Benard	.05
115	Kevin Brown	.05
116	Robert Person	.05
117	Joey Hamilton	.05
118	Francisco Cordova	.10
119	John Smiley	.05
120	Travis Fryman	.05
121	Jimmy Key	.05
122	Tom Goodwin	.05
123	Mike Greenwell	.05
124	Juan Gonzalez	1.00
125	Pete Harnisch	.05
126	Roger Cedeno	.05
127	Ron Gant	.10
128	Mark Langston	.05
129	Tim Crabtree	.05
130	Greg Maddux	1.50
131	William VanLandingham	.05
132	Wally Joyner	.10
133	Randy Myers	.05
134	John Valentin	.10
135	Bret Boone	.05
136	Bruce Ruffin	.05
137	Chris Snopek	.05
138	Paul Molitor	.40
139	Mark McLemore	.05
140	Rafael Palmeiro	.10
141	Herb Perry	.05
142	Luis Gonzalez	.05
143	Doug Drabek	.05
144	Ken Ryan	.05
145	Todd Hundley	.10
146	Ellis Burks	.10
147	Ozzie Guillen	.05
148	Rich Becker	.05
149	Sterling Hitchcock	.05
150	Bernie Williams	.40
151	Mike Stanley	.05
152	Roberto Alomar	.50
153	Jose Mesa	.08
154	Steve Trachsel	.05
155	Alex Gonzalez	.05
156	Troy Percival	.05
157	John Smoltz	.20
158	Pedro Martinez	.05
159	Jeff Conine	.10
160	Bernard Gilkey	.08
161	Jim Eisenreich	.05
162	Mickey Tettleton	.05
163	Justin Thompson	.05
164	Jose Offerman	.05
165	Tony Phillips	.08
166	Ismael Valdes	.05
167	Ryne Sandberg	.50
168	Matt Mieske	.05
169	Geronimo Berroa	.05
170	Otis Nixon	.05
171	John Mabry	.05
172	Shawon Dunston	.10
173	Omar Vizquel	.05
174	Chris Holles	.05
175	Doc Gooden	.10
176	Wilson Alvarez	.05
177	Todd Hollandsworth	.10
178	Roger Salkeld	.05
179	Rey Sanchez	.05
180	Rey Ordonez	.30
181	Denny Martinez	.08
182	Ramon Martinez	.08
183	Dave Nilsson	.05
184	Marquis Grissom	.10
185	Randy Velarde	.05
186	Ron Coomer	.05
187	Tino Martinez	.25
188	Jeff Brantley	.05
189	Steve Finley	.05
190	Andy Benes	.08
191	Terry Adams	.05
192	Mike Blowers	.05
193	Russ Davis	.05
194	Darryl Hamilton	.05
195	Jason Kendall	.08
196	Johnny Damon	.15
197	Dave Martinez	.05
198	Mike Macfarlane	.05
199	Norm Charlton	.05
200	Doug Million, Damian Moss, Bobby Rodgers (Prospect)	.20
201	Geoff Jenkins, Raul Ibanez, Mike Cameron (Prospect)	.25
202	Sean Casey, Jim Bonnici, Dmitri Young (Prospect)	.10
203	Jed Hansen, Homer Bush, Felipe Crespo (Prospect)	.05
204	Kevin Orie, Gabe Alvarez, Aaron Boone (Prospect)	.25
205	Ben Davis, Kevin Brown, Bobby Estalella (Prospect)	.05
206	Billy McMillon, *Bubba Trammell*, Dante Powell (Prospect)	.75
207	Jarrod Washburn, *Marc Wilkins*, Glendon Rusch (Prospect)	.15
208	Brian Hunter	.05
209	Jason Giambi	.08
210	Henry Rodriguez	.05
211	Edgar Renteria	.20
212	Edgardo Alfonzo	.05
213	Fernando Vina	.05
214	Shawn Green	.05
215	Ray Durham	.05
216	Joe Randa	.05
217	Armando Reynoso	.05
218	Eric Davis	.08
219	Bob Tewksbury	.05
220	Jacob Cruz	.05
221	Glenallen Hill	.05
222	Gary Gaetti	.08
223	Donne Wall	.05
224	Brad Clontz	.05
225	Marty Janzen	.05
226	Todd Worrell	.05
227	John Franco	.05
228	David Wells	.05
229	Gregg Jefferies	.10
230	Tim Naehring	.05
231	Thomas Howard	.05
232	Roberto Hernandez	.05
233	Kevin Ritz	.05
234	Julian Tavarez	.05
235	Ken Hill	.05
236	Greg Gagne	.05
237	Bobby Chouinard	.05
238	Joe Carter	.10
239	Jermaine Dye	.15
240	Antonio Osuna	.05
241	Julio Franco	.05
242	Mike Grace	.05
243	Aaron Sele	.05
244	David Justice	.15
245	Sandy Alomar	.10
246	Jose Canseco	.25
247	Paul O'Neill	.05
248	Sean Berry	.05
249	Nick Bierbrodt, *Kevin Sweeney* (Diamond Backs)	.50
250	*Larry Rodriguez, Vladimir Nunez* (Diamond Backs)	.50
251	Ron Hartman, David Hayman (Diamond Backs)	.10
252	Alex Sanchez, Matt Quatraro (Devil Rays)	.10
253	Ronni Seberino, *Pablo Ortega* (Devil Rays)	.40
254	Rex Hudler	.05
255	Orlando Miller	.05
256	Mariano Rivera	.25
257	Brad Radke	.05
258	Bobby Higginson	.05
259	Jay Bell	.05
260	Mark Grudzielanek	.05
261	Lance Johnson	.05
262	Ken Caminiti	.10
263	J.T. Snow	.05
264	Gary Sheffield	.20
265	Darrin Fletcher	.05
266	Eric Owens	.05
267	Luis Castillo	.15
268	Scott Rolen	.75
269	Todd Noel, John Oliver (Draft Pick)	.05
270	*Robert Stratton*, Corey Lee (Draft Pick)	.20
271	Gil Meche, *Matt Halloran* (Draft Pick)	.30
272	*Eric Milton*, Dermal Brown (Draft Pick)	.40
273	*Josh Garrett, Chris Reitsma* (Draft Pick)	.50
274	A.J. Zapp, *Jason Marquis* (Draft Pick)	.25
275	Checklist	.05
276	Checklist	.05
277	Chipper Jones	1.50
278	Orlando Merced	.05
279	Ariel Prieto	.05
280	Al Leiter	.05
281	Pat Meares	.05
282	Darryl Strawberry	.08
283	Jamie Moyer	.05
284	Scott Servais	.05
285	Delino DeShields	.05
286	Danny Graves	.05
287	Gerald Williams	.05
288	Todd Greene	.05
289	Rico Brogna	.05
290	Derrick Gibson	.05
291	Joe Girardi	.05
292	Darren Lewis	.05
293	Nomar Garciaparra	1.00
294	Greg Colbrunn	.05
295	Jeff Bagwell	1.00
296	Brent Gates	.05
297	Jose Vizcaino	.05
298	Alex Ochoa	.05
299	Sid Fernandez	.05
300	Ken Griffey Jr.	2.50
301	Chris Gomez	.05
302	Wendell Magee	.10
303	Darren Oliver	.05
304	Mel Nieves	.05
305	Sammy Sosa	.25
306	George Arias	.05
307	Jack McDowell	.05
308	Stan Javier	.05
309	Kimera Bartee	.05
310	James Baldwin	.05
311	Rocky Coppinger	.05
312	Keith Lockhart	.05
313	C.J. Nitkowski	.05
314	Allen Watson	.05
315	Darryl Kile	.05
316	Amaury Telemaco	.05
317	Jason Isringhausen	.05
318	Manny Ramirez	.75
319	Terry Pendleton	.05
320	Tim Salmon	.15
321	Eric Karros	.10
322	Mark Whiten	.05
323	Rick Krivda	.05
324	Brett Butler	.10
325	Randy Johnson	.30
326	Eddie Taubensee	.05
327	Mark Leiter	.05
328	Kevin Gross	.05
329	Ernie Young	.05
330	Pat Hentgen	.05
331	Rondell White	.10
332	Bobby Witt	.05
333	Eddie Murray	.30
334	Tim Raines	.08
335	Jeff Fassero	.05
336	Chuck Finley	.05
337	Willie Adams	.05
338	Chan Ho Park	.05
339	Jay Powell	.05
340	Ivan Rodriguez	.30
341	Jermaine Allensworth	.05
342	Jay Payton	.15
343	T.J. Mathews	.05
344	Tony Batista	.05
345	Ed Sprague	.05
346	Jeff Kent	.05
347	Scott Erickson	.05
348	Jeff Suppan	.05
349	Pete Schourek	.05
350	Kenny Lofton	.75
351	Alan Benes	.10
352	Fred McGriff	.30
353	Charlie O'Brien	.05
354	Darren Bragg	.05
355	Alex Fernandez	.05
356	Al Martin	.05
357	Bob Wells	.05
358	Chad Mottola	.05
359	Devon White	.05
360	David Cone	.08
361	Bobby Jones	.05
362	Scott Sanders	.05
363	Karim Garcia	.40
364	Kirt Manwaring	.05
365	Chili Davis	.08
366	Mike Hampton	.05
367	Chad Ogea	.05
368	Curt Schilling	.05
369	Phil Nevin	.05
370	Roger Clemens	.50
371	Willie Greene	.05
372	Kenny Rogers	.05
373	Jose Rijo	.05
374	Bobby Bonilla	.08
375	Mike Mussina	.30
376	Curtis Pride	.05
377	Todd Walker	.40
378	Jason Bere	.05
379	Heathcliff Slocumb	.05
380	Dante Bichette	.20
381	Carlos Baerga	.10
382	Livan Hernandez	.10
383	Jason Schmidt	.05
384	Kevin Stocker	.05
385	Matt Williams	.25
386	Bartolo Colon	.15
387	Will Clark	.25
388	Dennis Eckersley	.08
389	Brooks Kieschnick	.12
390	Ryan Klesko	.40
391	Mark Carreon	.05
392	Tim Worrell	.05
393	Dean Palmer	.05

394	Wil Cordero	.05
395	Javy Lopez	.15
396	Rich Aurilla	.05
397	Greg Vaughn	.05
398	Vinny Castilla	.10
399	Jeff Montgomery	.05
400	Cal Ripken Jr.	2.00
401	Walt Weiss	.05
402	Brad Ausmus	.05
403	Ruben Rivera	.25
404	Mark Wohlers	.05
405	Rick Aguilera	.05
406	Tony Clark	.50
407	Lyle Mouton	.05
408	Bill Pulsipher	.05
409	Jose Rosado	.05
410	Tony Gwynn	1.00
411	Cecil Fielder	.15
412	John Flaherty	.05
413	Lenny Dykstra	.05
414	Ugueth Urbina	.05
415	Brian Jordan	.15
416	Bob Abreu	.05
417	Craig Paquette	.05
418	Sandy Martinez	.05
419	Jeff Blauser	.05
420	Barry Larkin	.25
421	Kevin Seitzer	.05
422	Tim Belcher	.05
423	Paul Sorrento	.05
424	Cal Eldred	.05
425	Robin Ventura	.10
426	John Olerud	.10
427	Bob Wolcott	.05
428	Matt Lawton	.05
429	Rod Beck	.05
430	Shane Reynolds	.05
431	Mike James	.05
432	Steve Wojciechowski	.05
433	Vladimir Guerrero	1.00
434	Dustin Hermanson	.10
435	Marty Cordova	.05
436	Marc Newfield	.05
437	Todd Stottlemyre	.05
438	Jeffrey Hammonds	.05
439	Dave Stevens	.05
440	Hideo Nomo	.50
441	Mark Thompson	.05
442	Mark Lewis	.05
443	Quinton McCracken	.05
444	Cliff Floyd	.05
445	Denny Neagle	.05
446	John Jaha	.05
447	Mike Sweeney	.05
448	John Wasdin	.05
449	Chad Curtis	.05
450	Mo Vaughn	.75
451	Donovan Osborne	.05
452	Ruben Sierra	.08
453	Michael Tucker	.05
454	Kurt Abbott	.05
455	Andruw Jones	2.00
456	Shannon Stewart	.05
457	Scott Brosius	.05
458	Juan Guzman	.05
459	Ron Villone	.05
460	Moises Alou	.10
461	Larry Walker	.30
462	Eddie Murray (Season Highlights)	.20
463	Paul Molitor (Season Highlights)	.20
464	Hideo Nomo (Season Highlights)	.25
465	Barry Bonds (Season Highlights)	.40
466	Todd Hundley (Season Highlights)	.05
467	Rheal Cormier	.05
468	*Jason Conti*	.40
469	Rod Barajas	.05
470	Jared Sandberg, Cedric Bowers	.05
471	Paul Wilders, Chie Gunner	.05
472	Mike Decelle, Marcus McCain	.05
473	Todd Zeile	.08
474	Neifi Perez	.05
475	Jeromy Burnitz	.05
476	Trey Beamon	.05
477	John Patterson, Braden Looper (Draft Picks)	.05
478	*Danny Peoples, Jake Westbrook* (Draft Picks)	.25
479	*Eric Chavez*, Adam Eaton (Draft Picks)	1.00
480	*Joe Lawrence*, Pete Tucci (Draft Picks)	.05
481	Kris Benson, Billy Koch (Draft Picks)	.05

482	John Nicholson, Andy Prater (Draft Picks)	.05
483	*Mark Kotsay*, Mark Johnson (Draft Picks)	1.50
484	Armando Benitez	.05
485	Mike Matheny	.05
486	Jeff Reed	.05
487	Mark Bellhorn, Russ Johnson, Enrique Wilson (Prospects)	.05
488	Ben Grieve, Richard Hidalgo, Scott Morgan (Prospects)	.30
489	Paul Konerko, Derrek Lee, Ron Wright (Prospects)	1.00
490	Wes Helms, *Bill Mueller*, Brad Seitzer (Prospects)	.75
491	Jeff Abbott, Shane Monahan, Edgard Velazquez (Prospects)	.20
492	*Jimmy Anderson*, Ron Blazier, Gerald Witasick, Jr. (Prospects)	.25
493	Darin Blood, Heath Murray, Carl Pavano (Prospects)	.05
494	Mark Redman, *Mike Villano*, Nelson Figueroa (Prospects)	.20
495	Checklist	.05
496	Checklist	.05

1997 Topps All-Stars

Topps' 1997 All-Stars insert cards, printed on a dazzling rainbow foilboard, feature the top players from each position. There are 22 cards, 11 from each league, which showcase the top three players from each position as voted by Topps' sports department. On the front of each card is a photo of a "first team" all-star player; the back has a different photo of that player, who appears alongside the "second team" and "third team" selections. These cards are seeded one per every 18 1997 Topps Series I packs.

		MT
	Complete Set (22):	75.00
	Common Player:	1.50
AS1	Ivan Rodriguez	2.00
AS2	Todd Hundley	1.50
AS3	Frank Thomas	15.00
AS4	Andres Galarraga	2.00
AS5	Chuck Knoblauch	1.50
AS6	Eric Young	1.50
AS7	Jim Thome	3.00
AS8	Chipper Jones	10.00
AS9	Cal Ripken Jr.	12.00
AS10	Barry Larkin	2.00
AS11	Albert Belle	5.00
AS12	Barry Bonds	4.00
AS13	Ken Griffey Jr.	15.00
AS14	Ellis Burks	1.50
AS15	Juan Gonzalez	7.00
AS16	Gary Sheffield	2.50
AS17	Andy Pettitte	4.00
AS18	Tom Glavine	1.50
AS19	Pat Hentgen	1.50
AS20	John Smoltz	2.00
AS21	Roberto Hernandez	1.50
AS22	Mark Wohlers	1.50

1997 Topps Hobby Masters

These 10 cards lead the way as dealers' top selections. The cards, printed on 28-point diffraction foilboard, replace two regular cards in every 36th pack of 1997 Topps Series I product.

		MT
	Complete Set (20):	100.00
	Complete Series 1 (10):	55.00
	Complete Series 2 (10):	45.00
	Common Player:	1.50
HM1	Ken Griffey Jr.	15.00
HM2	Cal Ripken Jr.	12.00
HM3	Greg Maddux	10.00
HM4	Albert Belle	4.00
HM5	Tony Gwynn	8.00
HM6	Jeff Bagwell	6.00
HM7	Randy Johnson	3.00
HM8	Raul Mondesi	1.50
HM9	Juan Gonzalez	8.00
HM10	Kenny Lofton	4.00
HM11	Frank Thomas	15.00
HM12	Mike Piazza	10.00
HM13	Chipper Jones	10.00
HM14	Brady Anderson	1.50
HM15	Ken Caminiti	2.00
HM16	Barry Bonds	4.00
HM17	Mo Vaughn	4.00
HM18	Derek Jeter	10.00
HM19	Sammy Sosa	2.50
HM20	Andres Galarraga	1.50

1997 Topps Inter-League Match Ups

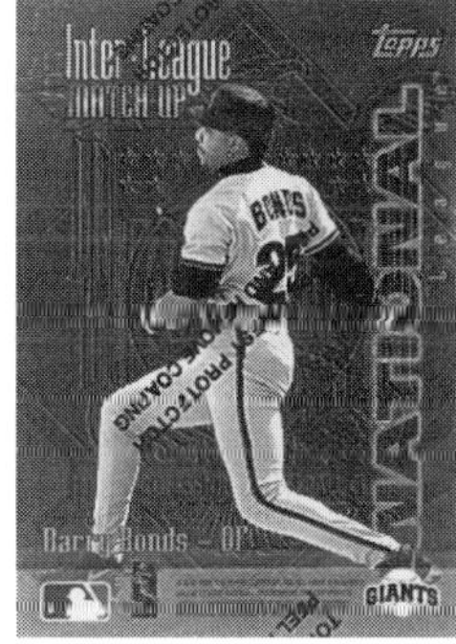

The double-sided Inter-League Finest and Inter-League Finest Refractors (seeded one in 36 and one in 210 Topps Series I packs respectively) feature top individual matchups from inter-league rivalries. One player from each major league team is represented, for a total of 28 players on 14 different cards. Each card is covered with a Finest clear protector.

		MT
	Complete Set (14):	70.00
	Common Player:	3.00
	Refractors:	3x to 4x
ILM1	Mark McGwire, Barry Bonds	5.00
ILM2	Tim Salmon, Mike Piazza	10.00
ILM3	Ken Griffey Jr., Dante Bichette	15.00
ILM4	Juan Gonzalez, Tony Gwynn	8.00
ILM5	Frank Thomas, Sammy Sosa	15.00
ILM6	Albert Belle, Barry Larkin	5.00
ILM7	Johnny Damon, Brian Jordan	3.00
ILM8	Paul Molitor, Jeff King	3.00
ILM9	John Jaha, Jeff Bagwell	6.00
ILM10	Bernie Williams, Todd Hundley	4.00
ILM11	Joe Carter, Henry Rodriguez	3.00
ILM12	Cal Ripken Jr., Gregg Jefferies	12.00
ILM13	Mo Vaughn, Chipper Jones	10.00
ILM14	Travis Fryman, Gary Sheffield	3.00

1997 Topps Mickey Mantle Finest

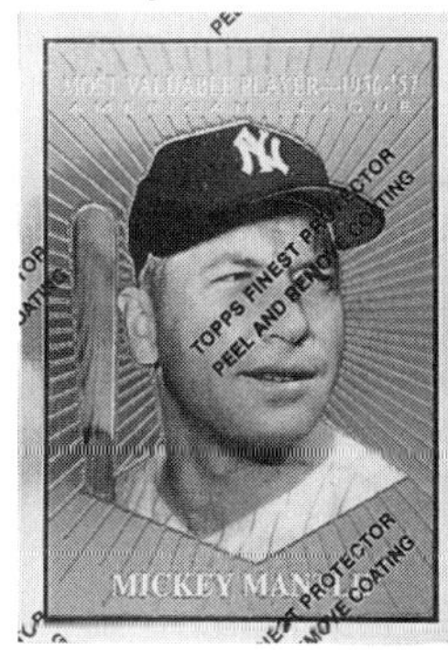

The 16-card Mickey Mantle reprints insert that was found in Series I was re-issued in Series II in the Topps Finest technology. The Finest versions are found on average of every 24 packs.

		MT
	Complete Set (16):	90.00
	Common Mantle:	6.00
21	1953 Bowman #44	6.00
22	1953 Bowman #59	9.00
23	1957 Topps #407	6.00
24	1958 Topps #418	6.00
25	1958 Topps #487	6.00
26	1959 Topps #461	6.00
27	1959 Topps #564	6.00
28	1960 Topps #160	6.00
29	1960 Topps #563	6.00
30	1961 Topps #406	6.00
31	1961 Topps #475	6.00
32	1961 Topps #578	6.00
33	1962 Topps #18	6.00
34	1962 Topps #318	6.00
35	1962 Topps #471	6.00
36	1964 Topps #331	6.00

1997 Topps Mickey Mantle Finest Refractors

Each of the 16 Mantle Finest reprints from Series II can also be found in a Refractor version. Refractors are found every 216 packs, on average.

		MT
	Complete Set (16):	450.00
	Common Mantle:	30.00
21	1953 Bowman #44	30.00
22	1953 Bowman #59	50.00
23	1957 Topps #407	30.00
24	1958 Topps #418	30.00
25	1958 Topps #487	30.00
26	1959 Topps #461	30.00
27	1959 Topps #564	30.00
28	1960 Topps #160	30.00
29	1960 Topps #563	30.00
30	1961 Topps #406	30.00
31	1961 Topps #475	30.00
32	1961 Topps #578	30.00
33	1962 Topps #18	30.00

34	1962 Topps #318	30.00
35	1962 Topps #471	30.00
36	1964 Topps #331	30.00

1997 Topps Mickey Mantle Reprints

All 16 remaining Mickey Mantle cards that were not reprinted in 1996 Topps Baseball are found in this insert, seeded every 12 packs of Series I Topps. The set starts off with No. 21 and runs through No. 36 since the '96 reprints were numbered 1-20.

		MT
Complete Set (16):		70.00
Common Card:		6.00
21	1953 Bowman #44	6.00
22	1953 Bowman #59	8.00
23	1957 Topps #407	6.00
24	1958 Topps #418	6.00
25	1958 Topps #487	6.00
26	1959 Topps #461	6.00
27	1959 Topps #564	6.00
28	1960 Topps #160	6.00
29	1960 Topps #563	6.00
30	1961 Topps #406	6.00
31	1961 Topps #475	6.00
32	1961 Topps #578	6.00
33	1962 Topps #18	6.00
34	1962 Topps #318	6.00
35	1962 Topps #471	6.00
36	1964 Topps #331	6.00

1997 Topps Porcelain

Six of 1997's most popular players are featured in this set of porcelain reproductions of their regular '97 Topps cards. Topps contracted with R&M China Co. to manufacture the ultra-thin ceramic "cards." Each porcelain card is trimmed in 22k gold and is limited to an edition of 500; a serial number appears on the back of each piece. Original issue price was $25 and the cards were available exclusively through Topps Stadium Club program.

		MT
Complete Set (6):		150.00
Common Player:		25.00
13	Derek Jeter	25.00
108	Frank Thomas	25.00
130	Greg Maddux	25.00
277	Chipper Jones	25.00
300	Ken Griffey Jr.	25.00
400	Cal Ripken	25.00

1997 Topps Season's Best

Season's Best features 25 players on prismatic illusion foilboard, and can be found every six packs. The set has the top five players from five statistical categories: home runs, RBIs, batting average, steals, and wins. Season's Best were found in packs of Topps Series II, and later reprinted on chromium stock as part of Topps Chrome.

		MT
Complete Set (25):		30.00
Common Player:		.50
1	Tony Gwynn	3.00
2	Frank Thomas	8.00
3	Ellis Burks	.50
4	Paul Molitor	1.50
5	Chuck Knoblauch	.75
6	Mark McGwire	3.00
7	Brady Anderson	.50
8	Ken Griffey Jr.	8.00
9	Albert Belle	3.00
10	Andres Galarraga	.50
11	Andres Galarraga	.50
12	Albert Belle	2.50
13	Juan Gonzalez	4.00
14	Mo Vaughn	2.00
15	Rafael Palmeiro	.50
16	John Smoltz	.50
17	Andy Pettitte	2.00
18	Pat Hentgen	.50
19	Mike Mussina	1.50
20	Andy Benes	.50
21	Kenny Lofton	2.00
22	Tom Goodwin	.50
23	Otis Nixon	.50
24	Eric Young	.50
25	Lance Johnson	.50

1997 Topps Series 2 Supers

At 3-3/4" x 5-1/4", these premium cards are nearly identical to the regular-issue versions except for size. Also, whereas the regular cards have a front format which combines a high-gloss central area with a matte finish near the borders, the supers have just one finish on the front which is a semi-gloss. The supers also have different card numbers on back. One of the supers was included in each boxed lot of 15 Series II foil packs sold at large retail outlets with a price tag of about $15.

		MT
Complete Set (3):		30.00
1	Chipper Jones	12.00
2	Ken Griffey Jr.	15.00
3	Cal Ripken Jr.	12.00

1997 Topps Sweet Strokes

These retail-exclusive Sweet Strokes insert cards consist of 15 Power Matrix foil cards of the top hitters in the game. These players have the swings to produce game winning-hits. The cards were seeded one per every 12 1997 Topps Series I retail packs.

		MT
Complete Set (15):		40.00
Common Player:		1.00
SS1	Roberto Alomar	2.00
SS2	Jeff Bagwell	4.00
SS3	Albert Belle	3.00
SS4	Barry Bonds	2.50
SS5	Mark Grace	1.00
SS6	Ken Griffey Jr.	10.00
SS7	Tony Gwynn	4.00
SS8	Chipper Jones	6.00
SS9	Edgar Martinez	1.00
SS10	Mark McGwire	3.50
SS11	Rafael Palmeiro	1.00
SS12	Mike Piazza	6.00
SS13	Gary Sheffield	1.50
SS14	Frank Thomas	10.00
SS15	Mo Vaughn	2.50

1997 Topps Team Timber

Team Timber was a 16-card insert that was exclusive to retail packs and inserted one per 36. The set displays the game's top sluggers on laminated litho wood cards.

		MT
Complete Set (16):		75.00
Common Player:		1.50
TT1	Ken Griffey Jr.	15.00
TT2	Ken Caminiti	2.00
TT3	Bernie Williams	3.00
TT4	Jeff Bagwell	6.00
TT5	Frank Thomas	15.00
TT6	Andres Galarraga	1.50
TT7	Barry Bonds	4.00
TT8	Rafael Palmeiro	1.50
TT9	Brady Anderson	1.50
TT10	Juan Gonzalez	8.00
TT11	Mo Vaughn	4.00
TT12	Mark McGwire	6.00
TT13	Gary Sheffield	2.50
TT14	Albert Belle	5.00
TT15	Chipper Jones	10.00
TT16	Mike Piazza	10.00

1997 Topps Willie Mays Commemorative Super

This oversize (4-1/4" x 5-3/4") version of card #2 (1952 Topps) in the Willie Mays Commemorative Reprint series was available exclusively in a special retail packaging of 10 1997 Topps Series I foil packs. Like the regular-size reprints, it has a gold-foil commemorative stamp on front.

		MT
2	Willie Mays (1952 Topps)	5.00

1997 Topps Willie Mays Finest

The introduction of Series II Topps offered collectors a chance to find Finest technology versions of each of the 27 commemorative reprint Topps and Bowman cards from throughout Mays' career. The Finest Mays reprints are found one in every 30 packs, on average.

		MT
Complete Set (27):		90.00
Common Card:		4.00
1	1951 Bowman #305	8.00
2	1952 Topps #261	6.00
3	1953 Topps #244	6.00
4	1954 Bowman #89	4.00
5	1954 Topps #90	4.00
6	1955 Bowman #184	4.00
7	1955 Topps #194	4.00
8	1956 Topps #130	4.00
9	1957 Topps #10	4.00
10	1958 Topps #5	4.00
11	1959 Topps #50	4.00
12	1960 Topps #200	4.00
13	1961 Topps #150	4.00
14	1961 Topps #579	4.00
15	1962 Topps #300	4.00
16	1963 Topps #300	4.00
17	1964 Topps #150	4.00
18	1965 Topps #250	4.00
19	1966 Topps #1	4.00
20	1967 Topps #200	4.00
21	1968 Topps #50	4.00
22	1969 Topps #190	4.00
23	1970 Topps #600	4.00
24	1971 Topps #600	4.00
25	1971 Topps #600	4.00
26	1972 Topps #49	4.00
27	1973 Topps #305	4.00

1997 Topps Willie Mays Finest Refractors

A high-end parallel set to the Willie Mays 27-card commemorative reprint issue is the Finest Refractor version issued in Series II. Refractors are found on average of once per 180 packs.

		MT
Complete Set (27):		500.00
Common Card:		20.00
1	1951 Bowman #305	50.00
2	1952 Topps #261	40.00
3	1953 Topps #244	40.00
4	1954 Bowman #89	30.00
5	1954 Topps #90	30.00
6	1955 Bowman #184	30.00
7	1955 Topps #194	30.00
8	1956 Topps #130	30.00
9	1957 Topps #10	30.00
10	1958 Topps #5	30.00
11	1959 Topps #50	30.00
12	1960 Topps #200	30.00
13	1961 Topps #150	30.00
14	1961 Topps #579	30.00
15	1962 Topps #300	30.00
16	1963 Topps #300	30.00
17	1964 Topps #150	30.00
18	1965 Topps #250	30.00
19	1966 Topps #1	30.00
20	1967 Topps #200	30.00
21	1968 Topps #50	30.00

		MT
22	1969 Topps #190	30.00
23	1970 Topps #600	30.00
24	1971 Topps #600	30.00
25	1971 Topps #600	30.00
26	1972 Topps #49	30.00
27	1973 Topps #305	30.00

1997 Topps Willie Mays Reprints

There are 27 different Willie Mays cards reprinted in Topps Series I and seeded every eight packs. The inserts form a collection of Topps and Bowman cards from throughout Mays' career and each is highlighted by a special commemorative gold foil stamp. Each of the Mays reprints can also be found in an autographed edition, bearing a special "Certified Autograph Issue" gold-foil logo.

		MT
Complete Set (27):		80.00
Common Card:		3.00
Autographed Card:		100.00
1	1951 Bowman #305	6.00
2	1952 Topps #261	4.00
3	1953 Topps #244	4.00
4	1954 Bowman #89	3.00
5	1954 Topps #90	3.00
6	1955 Bowman #184	3.00
7	1955 Topps #194	3.00
8	1956 Topps #130	3.00
9	1957 Topps #10	3.00
10	1958 Topps #5	3.00
11	1959 Topps #50	3.00
12	1960 Topps #200	3.00
13	1961 Topps #150	3.00
14	1961 Topps #579	3.00
15	1962 Topps #300	3.00
16	1963 Topps #300	3.00
17	1964 Topps #150	3.00
18	1965 Topps #250	3.00
19	1966 Topps #1	3.00
20	1967 Topps #200	3.00
21	1968 Topps #50	3.00
22	1969 Topps #190	3.00
23	1970 Topps #600	3.00
24	1971 Topps #600	3.00
25	1971 Topps #600	3.00
26	1972 Topps #49	3.00
27	1973 Topps #305	3.00

1997 Topps/Chrome

Chrome Baseball reprinted the top 165 cards from Topps Series I and II Baseball on a chromium, metallized stock. Chrome sold in four-card packs and included three insert sets - Diamond Duos, which was created exclusively for this product, Season's Best and Topps All-Stars, which were both reprinted from Topps products. Refractor versions of each card were found every 12 packs.

		MT
Complete Set (165):		70.00
Common Player:		.20
Common Refractors:		5.00
Star Refractors:		12x to 18x
Young Stars and RC's:		8x to 12x
Wax Box:		90.00
1	Barry Bonds	2.00
2	Jose Valentin	.20
3	Brady Anderson	.20
4	Wade Boggs	.40
5	Andres Galarraga	.50
6	Rusty Greer	.20
7	Derek Jeter	5.00
8	Ricky Bottalico	.20
9	Mike Piazza	5.00
10	Garret Anderson	.20
11	Jeff King	.20
12	Kevin Appier	.20
13	Mark Grace	.40
14	Jeff D'Amico	.20
15	Jay Buhner	.40
16	Hal Morris	.20
17	Harold Baines	.20
18	Jeff Cirillo	.20
19	Tom Glavine	.40
20	Andy Pettitte	2.00
21	Mark McGwire	2.50
22	Chuck Knoblauch	.40
23	Raul Mondesi	.50
24	Albert Belle	2.50
25	Trevor Hoffman	.20
26	Eric Young	.20
27	Brian McRae	.20
28	Jim Edmonds	.20
29	Robb Nen	.20
30	Reggie Sanders	.20
31	Mike Lansing	.20
32	Craig Biggio	.40
33	Ray Lankford	.20
34	Charles Nagy	.20
35	Paul Wilson	.20
36	John Wetteland	.20
37	Derek Bell	.20
38	Edgar Martinez	.20
39	Rickey Henderson	.20
40	Jim Thome	.75
41	Frank Thomas	8.00
42	Jackie Robinson (Tribute)	6.00
43	Terry Steinbach	.20
44	Kevin Brown	.20
45	Joey Hamilton	.20
46	Travis Fryman	.20
47	Juan Gonzalez	3.50
48	Ron Gant	.40
49	Greg Maddux	5.00
50	Wally Joyner	.20
51	John Valentin	.20
52	Bret Boone	.20
53	Paul Molitor	1.00
54	Rafael Palmeiro	.40
55	Todd Hundley	.50
56	Ellis Burks	.20
57	Bernie Williams	1.50
58	Roberto Alomar	1.50
59	Jose Mesa	.20
60	Troy Percival	.20
61	John Smoltz	.50
62	Jeff Conine	.20
63	Bernard Gilkey	.20
64	Mickey Tettleton	.20
65	Justin Thompson	.20
66	Tony Phillips	.20
67	Ryne Sandberg	1.50
68	Geronimo Berroa	.20
69	Todd Hollandsworth	.20
70	Rey Ordonez	.20
71	Marquis Grissom	.20
72	Tino Martinez	.50
73	Steve Finley	.20
74	Andy Benes	.20
75	Jason Kendall	.20
76	Johnny Damon	.20
77	Jason Giambi	.20
78	Henry Rodriguez	.20
79	Edgar Renteria	.20
80	Ray Durham	.20
81	Gregg Jefferies	.20
82	Roberto Hernandez	.20
83	Joe Carter	.40
84	Jermaine Dye	.20
85	Julio Franco	.20
86	David Justice	.50
87	Jose Canseco	.50
88	Paul O'Neill	.20
89	Mariano Rivera	.40
90	Bobby Higginson	.20
91	Mark Grudzielanek	.20
92	Lance Johnson	.20
93	Ken Caminiti	.60
94	Gary Sheffield	.60
95	Luis Castillo	.25
96	Scott Rolen	3.00
97	Chipper Jones	5.00
98	Darryl Strawberry	.20
99	Nomar Garciaparra	3.00
100	Jeff Bagwell	3.50
101	Ken Griffey Jr.	8.00
102	Sammy Sosa	.75
103	Jack McDowell	.20
104	James Baldwin	.20
105	Rocky Coppinger	.20
106	Manny Ramirez	1.75
107	Tim Salmon	.40
108	Eric Karros	.20
109	Brett Butler	.20
110	Randy Johnson	1.25
111	Pat Hentgen	.20
112	Rondell White	.20
113	Eddie Murray	.75
114	Ivan Rodriguez	1.50
115	Jermaine Allensworth	.20
116	Ed Sprague	.20
117	Kenny Lofton	2.00
118	Alan Benes	.40
119	Fred McGriff	.50
120	Alex Fernandez	.20
121	Al Martin	.20
122	Devon White	.20
123	David Cone	.40
124	Karim Garcia	.20
125	Chili Davis	.20
126	Roger Clemens	2.00
127	Bobby Bonilla	.20
128	Mike Mussina	1.50
129	Todd Walker	1.25
130	Dante Bichette	.40
131	Carlos Baerga	.20
132	Matt Williams	.60
133	Will Clark	.50
134	Dennis Eckersley	.20
135	Ryan Klesko	1.00
136	Dean Palmer	.20
137	Javy Lopez	.40
138	Greg Vaughn	.20
139	Vinny Castilla	.20
140	Cal Ripken Jr.	6.00
141	Ruben Rivera	.20
142	Mark Wohlers	.20
143	Tony Clark	1.25
144	Jose Rosado	.20
145	Tony Gwynn	3.50
146	Cecil Fielder	.40
147	Brian Jordan	.20
148	Bob Abreu	.20
149	Barry Larkin	.50
150	Robin Ventura	.20
151	John Olerud	.20
152	Rod Beck	.20
153	Vladimir Guerrero	4.00
154	Marty Cordova	.20
155	Todd Stottlemyre	.20
156	Hideo Nomo	1.50
157	Denny Neagle	.20
158	John Jaha	.20
159	Mo Vaughn	2.00
160	Andruw Jones	6.00
161	Moises Alou	.20
162	Larry Walker	.50
163	Eddie Murray (Season Highlights)	.50
164	Paul Molitor (Season Highlights)	.75
165	Checklist	.20

1997 Topps/Chrome All-Stars

Topps Chrome All-Stars display the same 22 cards found in Topps Series I, however these are reprinted on a Chrome stock. Regular versions are seeded every 24 packs, while Refractor versions arrive every 72 packs.

		MT
Complete Set (22):		150.00
Common Player:		2.00
Refractors:		2.5x to 3x
AS1	Ivan Rodriguez	8.00
AS2	Todd Hundley	5.00
AS3	Frank Thomas	30.00
AS4	Andres Galarraga	4.00
AS5	Chuck Knoblauch	2.00
AS6	Eric Young	2.00
AS7	Jim Thome	6.00
AS8	Chipper Jones	20.00
AS9	Cal Ripken Jr.	30.00
AS10	Barry Larkin	5.00
AS11	Albert Belle	12.00
AS12	Barry Bonds	10.00
AS13	Ken Griffey Jr.	35.00
AS14	Ellis Burks	2.00
AS15	Juan Gonzalez	15.00
AS16	Gary Sheffield	6.00
AS17	Andy Pettitte	10.00
AS18	Tom Glavine	4.00
AS19	Pat Hentgen	2.00
AS20	John Smoltz	4.00
AS21	Roberto Hernandez	2.00
AS22	Mark Wohlers	2.00

1997 Topps/Chrome Diamond Duos

Diamond Duos is the only one of the three insert sets in Chrome Baseball that was developed exclusively for this product. The set has 10 cards featuring two superstar teammates on double-sided chromium cards. Diamond Duos are found every 36 packs, while Refractor versions are found every 108 packs.

		MT
Complete Set (10):		120.00
Common Player:		3.00
Refractors:		2x to 3x
DD1	Chipper Jones, Andruw Jones	20.00
DD2	Derek Jeter, Bernie Williams	15.00
DD3	Ken Griffey Jr., Jay Buhner	25.00
DD4	Kenny Lofton, Manny Ramirez	10.00
DD5	Jeff Bagwell, Craig Biggio	10.00
DD6	Juan Gonzalez, Ivan Rodriguez	12.00
DD7	Cal Ripken Jr., Brady Anderson	20.00
DD8	Mike Piazza, Hideo Nomo	15.00
DD9	Andres Galarraga, Dante Bichette	5.00
DD10	Frank Thomas, Albert Belle	20.00

1997 Topps/Chrome Season's Best

Season's Best includes the 25 players found in Topps Series II, but in a chromium version. The top five players from five statistical categories, including Leading Looters, Bleacher Reachers and Kings of Swing. Regular versions are seeded every 18 packs, with Refractors every 54 packs.

		MT
Complete Set (25):		120.00
Common Player:		2.50
Refractors:		2.5x to 3x

#	Player	Price
1	Tony Gwynn	12.00
2	Frank Thomas	25.00
3	Ellis Burks	2.50
4	Paul Molitor	7.00
5	Chuck Knoblauch	2.50
6	Mark McGwire	10.00
7	Brady Anderson	2.50
8	Ken Griffey Jr.	30.00
9	Albert Belle	10.00
10	Andres Galarraga	4.00
11	Andres Galarraga	4.00
12	Albert Belle	10.00
13	Juan Gonzalez	12.00
14	Mo Vaughn	6.00
15	Rafael Palmeiro	4.00
16	John Smoltz	3.00
17	Andy Pettitte	6.00
18	Pat Hentgen	2.50
19	Mike Mussina	5.00
20	Andy Benes	2.50
21	Kenny Lofton	6.00
22	Tom Goodwin	2.50
23	Otis Nixon	2.50
24	Eric Young	2.50
25	Lance Johnson	2.50

1997 Finest

Finest returned for 1997 in its three-tiered format from 1996, but added several new twists. Cards numbered 1-100 were bronze, 101-150 were silver and 151-175 were gold. All cards fit into one of five different subsets, called Warriors, Blue Chips, Power, Hurlers and Masters. The bronze cards were the "common" card, while silvers were found every four packs and golds every 24 packs. Each card had a parallel Refractor version: bronze (1:12), silver (1:48) and gold (1:288). In addition, silver and gold cards had an additional parallel set. Silvers were found in an embossed version (1:16) and embossed Refractor version (1:192), while golds were found in a die-cut/embossed version (1:96) and a die-cut embossed Refractor (1:1152).

	MT
Complete Set (350):	1350.
Complete Series 1 Set (175):	700.00
Complete Series 2 Set (175):	650.00
Complete Bronze Set (200):	35.00
Common Bronze:	.25
Complete Silver Set (100):	350.00
Common Silver:	2.00
Embossed Silvers:	3x
Complete Gold Set (50):	900.00
Common Gold:	8.00
Embossed Die-Cut Golds:	2x to 3x
Wax Box:	125.00

#	Player	Price
1	Barry Bonds B	1.50
2	Ryne Sandberg B	1.50
3	Brian Jordan B	.25
4	Rocky Coppinger B	.25
5	Dante Bichette B	.50
6	Al Martin B	.25
7	Charles Nagy B	.25
8	Otis Nixon B	.25
9	Mark Johnson B	.25
10	Jeff Bagwell B	2.50
11	Ken Hill B	.25
12	Willie Adams B	.25
13	Raul Mondesi B	.50
14	Reggie Sanders B	.25
15	Derek Jeter B	3.00
16	Jermaine Dye B	.50
17	Edgar Renteria B	.50
18	Travis Fryman B	.25
19	Roberto Hernandez B	.25
20	Sammy Sosa B	.75
21	Garret Anderson B	.25
22	Rey Ordonez B	.50
23	Glenallen Hill B	.25
24	Dave Nilsson B	.25
25	Kevin Brown B	.25
26	Brian McRae B	.25
27	Joey Hamilton B	.25
28	Jamey Wright B	.25
29	Frank Thomas B	5.00
30	Mark McGwire B	2.00
31	Ramon Martinez B	.25
32	Jaime Bluma B	.25
33	Frank Rodriguez B	.25
34	Andy Benes B	.25
35	Jay Buhner B	.50
36	Justin Thompson B	.25
37	Darin Erstad B	2.50
38	Gregg Jefferies B	.25
39	Jeff D'Amico B	.40
40	Pedro Martinez B	.25
41	Nomar Garciaparra B	2.50
42	Jose Valentin B	.25
43	Pat Hentgen B	.25
44	Will Clark B	.50
45	Bernie Williams B	1.00
46	Luis Castillo B	.25
47	B.J. Surhoff B	.25
48	Greg Gagne B	.25
49	Pete Schourek B	.25
50	Mike Piazza B	3.00
51	Dwight Gooden B	.25
52	Javy Lopez B	.40
53	Chuck Finley B	.25
54	James Baldwin B	.25
55	Jack McDowell B	.25
56	Royce Clayton B	.25
57	Carlos Delgado B	.40
58	Neifi Perez B	.25
59	Eddie Taubensee B	.25
60	Rafael Palmeiro B	.50
61	Marty Cordova B	.25
62	Wade Boggs B	.50
63	Rickey Henderson B	.25
64	Mike Hampton B	.25
65	Troy Percival B	.25
66	Barry Larkin B	.75
67	Jermaine Allensworth B	.25
68	Mark Clark B	.25
69	Mike Lansing B	.25
70	Mark Grudzielanek B	.25
71	Todd Stottlemyre B	.25
72	Juan Guzman B	.25
73	John Burkett B	.25
74	Wilson Alvarez B	.25
75	Ellis Burks B	.40
76	Bobby Higginson B	.50
77	Ricky Bottalico B	.25
78	Omar Vizquel B	.25
79	Paul Sorrento B	.25
80	Denny Neagle B	.25
81	Roger Pavlik B	.25
82	Mike Lieberthal B	.25
83	Devon White B	.25
84	John Olerud B	.25
85	Kevin Appier B	.25
86	Joe Girardi B	.25
87	Paul O'Neill B	.40
88	Mike Sweeney B	.25
89	John Smiley B	.25
90	Ivan Rodriguez B	1.00
91	Randy Myers B	.25
92	Bip Roberts B	.25
93	Jose Mesa B	.25
94	Paul Wilson B	.40
95	Mike Mussina B	1.00
96	Ben McDonald B	.25
97	John Mabry B	.25
98	Tom Goodwin B	.25
99	Edgar Martinez B	.40
100	Andruw Jones B	3.00
101	Jose Canseco S	3.00
102	Billy Wagner S	3.00
103	Dante Bichette S	3.00
104	Curt Schilling S	2.00
105	Dean Palmer S	2.00
106	Larry Walker S	5.00
107	Bernie Williams S	6.00
108	Chipper Jones S	20.00
109	Gary Sheffield S	4.00
110	Randy Johnson S	5.00
111	Roberto Alomar S	6.00
112	Todd Walker S	5.00
113	Sandy Alomar S	2.00
114	John Jaha S	2.00
115	Ken Caminiti S	4.00
116	Ryan Klesko S	5.00
117	Mariano Rivera S	3.00
118	Jason Giambi S	2.00
119	Lance Johnson S	2.00
120	Robin Ventura S	2.00
121	Todd Hollandsworth S	2.50
122	Johnny Damon S	2.00
123	William VanLandingham S	2.00
124	Jason Kendall S	2.50
125	Vinny Castilla S	2.50
126	Harold Baines S	2.00
127	Joe Carter S	2.50
128	Craig Biggio S	2.50
129	Tony Clark S	6.00
130	Ron Gant S	2.50
131	David Segui S	2.00
132	Steve Trachsel S	2.00
133	Scott Rolen S	15.00
134	Mike Stanley S	2.00
135	Cal Ripken Jr. S	20.00
136	John Smoltz S	4.00
137	Bobby Jones S	2.00
138	Manny Ramirez S	6.00
139	Ken Griffey Jr. S	25.00
140	Chuck Knoblauch S	3.00
141	Mark Grace S	3.00
142	Chris Snopek S	2.00
143	Hideo Nomo S	6.00
144	Tim Salmon S	4.00
145	David Cone S	3.00
146	Eric Young S	2.50
147	Jeff Brantley S	2.00
148	Jim Thome S	5.00
149	Trevor Hoffman S	2.00
150	Juan Gonzalez S	12.00
151	Mike Piazza G	50.00
152	Ivan Rodriguez G	20.00
153	Mo Vaughn G	20.00
154	Brady Anderson G	12.00
155	Mark McGwire G	30.00
156	Rafael Palmeiro G	12.00
157	Barry Larkin G	12.00
158	Greg Maddux G	50.00
159	Jeff Bagwell G	35.00
160	Frank Thomas G	80.00
161	Ken Caminiti G	15.00
162	Andruw Jones G	50.00
163	Dennis Eckersley G	10.00
164	Jeff Conine G	10.00
165	Jim Edmonds G	10.00
166	Derek Jeter G	50.00
167	Vladimir Guerrero G	40.00
168	Sammy Sosa G	15.00
169	Tony Gwynn G	40.00
170	Andres Galarraga G	12.00
171	Todd Hundley G	12.00
172	Jay Buhner G	12.00
173	Paul Molitor G	15.00
174	Kenny Lofton G	20.00
175	Barry Bonds G	20.00
176	Gary Sheffield B	.50
177	Dmitri Young B	.25
178	Jay Bell B	.25
179	David Wells B	.25
180	Walt Weiss B	.25
181	Paul Molitor B	.75
182	Jose Guillen B	1.50
183	Al Leiter B	.25
184	Mike Fetters B	.25
185	Mark Langston B	.25
186	Fred McGriff B	.40
187	Darrin Fletcher B	.25
188	Brant Brown B	.25
189	Geronimo Berroa B	.25
190	Jim Thome B	1.00
191	Jose Vizcaino B	.25
192	Andy Ashby B	.25
193	Rusty Greer B	.25
194	Brian Hunter B	.25
195	Chris Hoiles B	.25
196	Orlando Merced B	.25
197	Brett Butler B	.25
198	Derek Bell B	.25
199	Bobby Bonilla B	.25
200	Alex Ochoa B	.25
201	Wally Joyner B	.25
202	Mo Vaughn B	1.25
203	Doug Drabek B	.25
204	Tino Martinez B	.50
205	Roberto Alomar B	1.00
206	Brian Giles B	.25
207	Todd Worrell B	.25
208	Alan Benes B	.25
209	Jim Leyritz B	.25
210	Darryl Hamilton B	.25
211	Jimmy Key B	.25
212	Juan Gonzalez B	2.50
213	Vinny Castilla B	.25
214	Chuck Knoblauch B	.40
215	Tony Phillips B	.25
216	Jeff Cirillo B	.25
217	Carlos Garcia B	.25
218	Brooks Kieschnick B	.25
219	Marquis Grissom B	.25
220	Dan Wilson B	.25
221	Greg Vaughn B	.25
222	John Wetteland B	.25
223	Andres Galarraga B	.40
224	Ozzie Guillen B	.25
225	Kevin Elster B	.25
226	Bernard Gilkey B	.25
227	Mike MacFarlane B	.25
228	Heathcliff Slocumb B	.25
229	Wendell Magee Jr. B	.25
230	Carlos Baerga B	.25
231	Kevin Seitzer B	.25
232	Henry Rodriguez B	.25
233	Roger Clemens B	1.50
234	Mark Wohlers B	.25
235	Eddie Murray B	.50
236	Todd Zeile B	.25
237	J.T. Snow B	.25
238	Ken Griffey Jr. B	5.00
239	Sterling Hitchcock B	.25
240	Albert Belle B	1.50
241	Terry Steinbach B	.25
242	Robb Nen B	.25
243	Mark McLemore B	.25
244	Jeff King B	.25
245	Tony Clark B	1.25
246	Tim Salmon B	.40
247	Benito Santiago B	.25
248	Robin Ventura B	.25
249	*Bubba Trammell B*	1.50
250	Chili Davis B	.25
251	John Valentin B	.25
252	Cal Ripken Jr. B	4.00
253	Matt Williams B	.50
254	Jeff Kent B	.25
255	Eric Karros B	.25
256	Ray Lankford B	.25
257	Ed Sprague B	.25
258	Shane Reynolds B	.25
259	Jaime Navarro B	.25
260	Eric Davis B	.25
261	Orel Hershiser B	.25
262	Mark Grace B	.40
263	Rod Beck B	.25
264	Ismael Valdes B	.25
265	Manny Ramirez B	1.25
266	Ken Caminiti B	.40
267	Tim Naehring B	.25
268	Jose Rosado B	.25
269	Greg Colbrunn B	.25
270	Dean Palmer B	.25
271	David Justice B	.50
272	Scott Spiezio B	.25
273	Chipper Jones B	3.00
274	Mel Rojas B	.25
275	Bartolo Colon B	.25
276	Darin Erstad S	12.00
277	Sammy Sosa S	4.00
278	Rafael Palmeiro S	3.00
279	Frank Thomas S	25.00
280	Ruben Rivera S	2.00
281	Hal Morris S	2.00
282	Jay Buhner S	3.00
283	Kenny Lofton S	8.00
284	Jose Canseco S	3.00
285	Alex Fernandez S	2.00
286	Todd Helton S	6.00
287	Andy Pettitte S	6.00
288	John Franco S	2.00
289	Ivan Rodriguez S	6.00
290	Ellis Burks S	2.00
291	Julio Franco S	2.00
292	Mike Piazza S	15.00
293	Brian Jordan S	2.00
294	Greg Maddux S	15.00
295	Bob Abreu S	2.00
296	Rondell White S	2.00
297	Moises Alou S	2.00
298	Tony Gwynn S	12.00
299	Deion Sanders S	3.00
300	Jeff Montgomery S	2.00
301	Ray Durham S	2.00
302	John Wasdin S	2.00
303	Ryne Sandberg S	6.00
304	Delino DeShields S	2.00
305	Mark McGwire S	10.00
306	Andruw Jones S	15.00
307	Kevin Orie S	2.00
308	Matt Williams S	3.00
309	Karim Garcia S	2.00
310	Derek Jeter S	15.00
311	Mo Vaughn S	8.00
312	Brady Anderson S	2.50
313	Barry Bonds S	8.00
314	Steve Finley S	2.00
315	Vladimir Guerrero S	12.00
316	Matt Morris S	2.00
317	Tom Glavine S	3.00

No.	Player		Price
318	Jeff Bagwell	S	12.00
319	Albert Belle	S	10.00
320	*Hideki Irabu*	S	15.00
321	Andres Galarraga	S	3.00
322	Cecil Fielder	S	3.00
323	Barry Larkin	S	3.00
324	Todd Hundley	S	3.00
325	Fred McGriff	S	3.00
326	Gary Sheffield	G	12.00
327	Craig Biggio	G	10.00
328	Raul Mondesi	G	12.00
329	Edgar Martinez	G	8.00
330	Chipper Jones	G	50.00
331	Bernie Williams	G	18.00
332	Juan Gonzalez	G	40.00
333	Ron Gant	G	8.00
334	Cal Ripken Jr.	G	60.00
335	Larry Walker	G	15.00
336	Matt Williams	G	12.00
337	Jose Cruz, Jr.	G	80.00
338	Joe Carter	G	8.00
339	Wilton Guerrero	G	8.00
340	Cecil Fielder	G	10.00
341	Todd Walker	G	15.00
342	Ken Griffey Jr.	G	80.00
343	Ryan Klesko	G	15.00
344	Roger Clemens	G	20.00
345	Hideo Nomo	G	18.00
346	Dante Bichette	G	8.00
347	Albert Belle	G	25.00
348	Randy Johnson	G	15.00
349	Manny Ramirez	G	20.00
350	John Smoltz	G	8.00

1997 Finest Refractors

Every card in the '97 Finest set - both regular and parallel - has a Refractor version. The Uncommon parallel set of Refractors feature a mosaic pattern in the background while the Rare embossed die-cut parallel set of Refractors are produced with a hyperplaid foil design. The number of cards and the insertion ratios for each level of Refractors is as follows: Common (100 cards, 1:12 packs), Uncommon (50, 1:48), Rare (25, 1:288), Embossed Uncommon (50, 1:192), Embossed Die-cut Rare (25, 1:1,152).

	MT
Complete Set (350):	7800.
Complete Series 1 Set (175):	4600.
Complete Series 2 Set (175):	3200.
Complete Bronze Set (200)	1100.
Common Bronze:	4.00
Complete Silver Set (100):	2000.
Common Silver:	10.00
Embossed Silver Refractors:	3x
Complete Gold Set (50):	4800.
Common Gold:	40.00
Embossed Die-Cut Gold Refractors:	3x
Wax Box:	95.00

No.	Player		Price
1	Barry Bonds	B	20.00
2	Ryne Sandberg	B	20.00
3	Brian Jordan	B	4.00
4	Rocky Coppinger	B	4.00
5	Dante Bichette	B	10.00
6	Al Martin	B	4.00
7	Charles Nagy	B	4.00
8	Otis Nixon	B	4.00
9	Mark Johnson	B	4.00
10	Jeff Bagwell	B	35.00
11	Ken Hill	B	4.00
12	Willie Adams	B	4.00
13	Raul Mondesi	B	10.00
14	Reggie Sanders	B	4.00
15	Derek Jeter	B	45.00
16	Jermaine Dye	B	4.00
17	Edgar Renteria	B	4.00
18	Travis Fryman	B	4.00
19	Roberto Hernandez	B	4.00
20	Sammy Sosa	B	10.00
21	Garret Anderson	B	4.00
22	Rey Ordonez	B	4.00
23	Glenallen Hill	B	4.00
24	Dave Nilsson	B	4.00
25	Kevin Brown	B	4.00
26	Brian McRae	B	4.00
27	Joey Hamilton	B	4.00
28	Jamey Wright	B	4.00
29	Frank Thomas	B	80.00
30	Mark McGwire	B	30.00
31	Ramon Martinez	B	4.00
32	Jaime Bluma	B	4.00
33	Frank Rodriguez	B	4.00
34	Andy Benes	B	4.00
35	Jay Buhner	B	8.00
36	Justin Thompson	B	4.00
37	Darin Erstad	B	30.00
38	Gregg Jefferies	B	4.00
39	Jeff D'Amico	B	6.00
40	Pedro Martinez	B	4.00
41	Nomar Garciaparra	B	30.00
42	Jose Valentin	B	4.00
43	Pat Hentgen	B	4.00
44	Will Clark	B	8.00
45	Bernie Williams	B	18.00
46	Luis Castillo	B	4.00
47	B.J. Surhoff	B	4.00
48	Greg Gagne	B	4.00
49	Pete Schourek	B	4.00
50	Mike Piazza	B	40.00
51	Dwight Gooden	B	4.00
52	Javy Lopez	B	6.00
53	Chuck Finley	B	4.00
54	James Baldwin	B	4.00
55	Jack McDowell	B	4.00
56	Royce Clayton	B	4.00
57	Carlos Delgado	B	4.00
58	Neifi Perez	B	4.00
59	Eddie Taubensee	B	4.00
60	Rafael Palmeiro	B	8.00
61	Marty Cordova	B	4.00
62	Wade Boggs	B	10.00
63	Rickey Henderson	B	4.00
64	Mike Hampton	B	4.00
65	Troy Percival	B	4.00
66	Barry Larkin	B	8.00
67	Jermaine Allensworth	B	4.00
68	Mark Clark	B	4.00
69	Mike Lansing	B	4.00
70	Mark Grudzielanek	B	4.00
71	Todd Stottlemyre	B	4.00
72	Juan Guzman	B	4.00
73	John Burkett	B	4.00
74	Wilson Alvarez	B	4.00
75	Ellis Burks	B	6.00
76	Bobby Higginson	B	6.00
77	Ricky Bottalico	B	4.00
78	Omar Vizquel	B	4.00
79	Paul Sorrento	B	4.00
80	Denny Neagle	B	4.00
81	Roger Pavlik	B	4.00
82	Mike Lieberthal	B	4.00
83	Devon White	B	4.00
84	John Olerud	B	4.00
85	Kevin Appier	B	4.00
86	Joe Girardi	B	4.00
87	Paul O'Neill	B	6.00
88	Mike Sweeney	B	4.00
89	John Smiley	B	4.00
90	Ivan Rodriguez	B	20.00
91	Randy Myers	B	4.00
92	Bip Roberts	B	4.00
93	Jose Mesa	B	4.00
94	Paul Wilson	B	4.00
95	Mike Mussina	B	15.00
96	Ben McDonald	B	4.00
97	John Mabry	B	4.00
98	Tom Goodwin	B	4.00
99	Edgar Martinez	B	6.00
100	Andruw Jones	B	60.00
101	Jose Canseco	S	20.00
102	Billy Wagner	S	15.00
103	Dante Bichette	S	20.00
104	Curt Schilling	S	12.00
105	Dean Palmer	S	12.00
106	Larry Walker	S	30.00
107	Bernie Williams	S	40.00
108	Chipper Jones	S	100.00
109	Gary Sheffield	S	25.00
110	Randy Johnson	S	30.00
111	Roberto Alomar	S	30.00
112	Todd Walker	S	25.00
113	Sandy Alomar	S	12.00
114	John Jaha	S	12.00
115	Ken Caminiti	S	20.00
116	Ryan Klesko	S	20.00
117	Mariano Rivera	S	12.00
118	Jason Giambi	S	10.00
119	Lance Johnson	S	10.00
120	Robin Ventura	S	10.00
121	Todd Hollandsworth	S	10.00
122	Johnny Damon	S	10.00
123	William VanLandingham	S	10.00
124	Jason Kendall	S	10.00
125	Vinny Castilla	S	12.00
126	Harold Baines	S	10.00
127	Joe Carter	S	12.00
128	Craig Biggio	S	12.00
129	Tony Clark	S	30.00
130	Ron Gant	S	10.00
131	David Segui	S	10.00
132	Steve Trachsel	S	10.00
133	Scott Rolen	S	70.00
134	Mike Stanley	S	10.00
135	Cal Ripken Jr.	S	125.00
136	John Smoltz	S	12.00
137	Bobby Jones	S	10.00
138	Manny Ramirez	S	30.00
139	Ken Griffey Jr.	S	160.00
140	Chuck Knoblauch	S	20.00
141	Mark Grace	S	20.00
142	Chris Snopek	S	12.00
143	Hideo Nomo	S	40.00
144	Tim Salmon	S	20.00
145	David Cone	S	15.00
146	Eric Young	S	12.00
147	Jeff Brantley	S	12.00
148	Jim Thome	S	35.00
149	Trevor Hoffman	S	12.00
150	Juan Gonzalez	S	90.00
151	Mike Piazza	G	250.00
152	Ivan Rodriguez	G	100.00
153	Mo Vaughn	G	125.00
154	Brady Anderson	G	50.00
155	Mark McGwire	G	175.00
156	Rafael Palmeiro	G	50.00
157	Barry Larkin	G	50.00
158	Greg Maddux	G	250.00
159	Jeff Bagwell	G	175.00
160	Frank Thomas	G	400.00
161	Ken Caminiti	G	60.00
162	Andruw Jones	G	250.00
163	Dennis Eckersley	G	40.00
164	Jeff Conine	G	40.00
165	Jim Edmonds	G	40.00
166	Derek Jeter	G	250.00
167	Vladimir Guerrero	G	200.00
168	Sammy Sosa	G	75.00
169	Tony Gwynn	G	200.00
170	Andres Galarraga	G	60.00
171	Todd Hundley	G	50.00
172	Jay Buhner	G	50.00
173	Paul Molitor	G	80.00
174	Kenny Lofton	G	125.00
175	Barry Bonds	G	125.00
176	Gary Sheffield	G	8.00
177	Dmitri Young	B	4.00
178	Jay Bell	B	4.00
179	David Wells	B	4.00
180	Walt Weiss	B	4.00
181	Paul Molitor	B	12.00
182	Jose Guillen	B	18.00
183	Al Leiter	B	4.00
184	Mike Fetters	B	4.00
185	Mark Langston	B	4.00
186	Fred McGriff	B	6.00
187	Darrin Fletcher	B	4.00
188	Brant Brown	B	4.00
189	Geronimo Berroa	B	4.00
190	Jim Thome	B	15.00
191	Jose Vizcaino	B	4.00
192	Andy Ashby	B	4.00
193	Rusty Greer	B	4.00
194	Brian L. Hunter	B	4.00
195	Chris Hoiles	B	4.00
196	Orlando Merced	B	4.00
197	Brett Butler	B	4.00
198	Derek Bell	B	4.00
199	Bobby Bonilla	B	4.00
200	Alex Ochoa	B	4.00
201	Wally Joyner	B	4.00
202	Mo Vaughn	B	20.00
203	Doug Drabek	B	4.00
204	Tino Martinez	B	8.00
205	Roberto Alomar	B	15.00
206	Brian Giles	B	4.00
207	Todd Worrell	B	4.00
208	Alan Benes	B	4.00
209	Jim Leyritz	B	4.00
210	Darryl Hamilton	B	4.00
211	Jimmy Key	B	4.00
212	Juan Gonzalez	B	40.00
213	Vinny Castilla	B	4.00
214	Chuck Knoblauch	B	6.00
215	Tony Phillips	B	4.00
216	Jeff Cirillo	B	4.00
217	Carlos Garcia	B	4.00
218	Brooks Kieschnick	B	4.00
219	Marquis Grissom	B	4.00
220	Dan Wilson	B	4.00
221	Greg Vaughn	B	4.00
222	John Wetteland	B	4.00
223	Andres Galarraga	B	6.00
224	Ozzie Guillen	B	4.00
225	Kevin Elster	B	4.00
226	Bernard Gilkey	B	4.00
227	Mike Macfarlane	B	4.00
228	Heathcliff Slocumb	B	4.00
229	Wendell Magee Jr.	B	4.00
230	Carlos Baerga	B	4.00
231	Kevin Seitzer	B	4.00
232	Henry Rodriguez	B	4.00
233	Roger Clemens	B	25.00
234	Mark Wohlers	B	4.00
235	Eddie Murray	B	8.00
236	Todd Zeile	B	4.00
237	J.T. Snow	B	4.00
238	Ken Griffey Jr.	B	80.00
239	Sterling Hitchcock	B	4.00
240	Albert Belle	B	25.00
241	Terry Steinbach	B	4.00
242	Robb Nen	B	4.00
243	Mark McLemore	B	4.00
244	Jeff King	B	4.00
245	Tony Clark	B	20.00
246	Tim Salmon	B	8.00
247	Benito Santiago	B	4.00
248	Robin Ventura	B	4.00
249	Bubba Trammell	B	15.00
250	Chili Davis	B	4.00
251	John Valentin	B	4.00
252	Cal Ripken Jr.	B	60.00
253	Matt Williams	B	8.00
254	Jeff Kent	B	4.00
255	Eric Karros	B	4.00
256	Ray Lankford	B	4.00
257	Ed Sprague	B	4.00
258	Shane Reynolds	B	4.00
259	Jaime Navarro	B	4.00
260	Eric Davis	B	4.00
261	Orel Hershiser	B	4.00
262	Mark Grace	B	8.00
263	Rod Beck	B	4.00
264	Ismael Valdes	B	4.00
265	Manny Ramirez	B	20.00
266	Ken Caminiti	B	6.00
267	Tim Naehring	B	4.00
268	Jose Rosado	B	4.00
269	Greg Colbrunn	B	4.00
270	Dean Palmer	B	4.00
271	David Justice	B	8.00
272	Scott Spiezio	B	4.00
273	Chipper Jones	B	50.00
274	Mel Rojas	B	4.00
275	Bartolo Colon	B	4.00
276	Darin Erstad	S	60.00
277	Sammy Sosa	S	20.00
278	Rafael Palmeiro	S	12.00
279	Frank Thomas	S	140.00
280	Ruben Rivera	S	10.00
281	Hal Morris	S	10.00
282	Jay Buhner	S	12.00
283	Kenny Lofton	S	35.00
284	Jose Canseco	S	12.00
285	Alex Fernandez	S	10.00
286	Todd Helton	S	20.00
287	Andy Pettitte	S	35.00
288	John Franco	S	10.00
289	Ivan Rodriguez	S	30.00
290	Ellis Burks	S	10.00
291	Julio Franco	S	10.00
292	Mike Piazza	S	90.00
293	Brian Jordan	S	10.00
294	Greg Maddux	S	90.00
295	Bob Abreu	S	10.00
296	Rondell White	S	10.00
297	Moises Alou	S	10.00
298	Tony Gwynn	S	60.00
299	Deion Sanders	S	15.00
300	Jeff Montgomery	S	10.00
301	Ray Durham	S	10.00
302	John Wasdin	S	10.00
303	Ryne Sandberg	S	35.00
304	Delino DeShields	S	10.00
305	Mark McGwire	S	60.00
306	Andruw Jones	S	90.00
307	Kevin Orie	S	10.00
308	Matt Williams	S	12.00
309	Karim Garcia	S	10.00
310	Derek Jeter	S	90.00
311	Mo Vaughn	S	35.00
312	Brady Anderson	S	10.00
313	Barry Bonds	S	35.00
314	Steve Finley	S	10.00
315	Vladimir Guerrero	S	70.00
316	Matt Morris	S	10.00
317	Tom Glavine	S	10.00
318	Jeff Bagwell	S	60.00
319	Albert Belle	S	50.00
320	Hideki Irabu	S	50.00
321	Andres Galarraga	S	12.00
322	Cecil Fielder	S	12.00
323	Barry Larkin	S	12.00
324	Todd Hundley	S	10.00
325	Fred McGriff	S	12.00
326	Gary Sheffield	G	60.00
327	Craig Biggio	G	40.00
328	Raul Mondesi	G	50.00
329	Edgar Martinez	G	40.00
330	Chipper Jones	G	250.00
331	Bernie Williams	G	75.00
332	Juan Gonzalez	G	200.00
333	Ron Gant	G	40.00
334	Cal Ripken Jr.	G	300.00
335	Larry Walker	G	60.00
336	Matt Williams	G	50.00

#	Player	MT
337	Jose Cruz G	300.00
338	Joe Carter G	40.00
339	Wilton Guerrero G	40.00
340	Cecil Fielder G	40.00
341	Todd Walker G	60.00
342	Ken Griffey Jr. G	450.00
343	Ryan Klesko G	60.00
344	Roger Clemens G	125.00
345	Hideo Nomo G	75.00
346	Dante Bichette G	50.00
347	Albert Belle G	140.00
348	Randy Johnson G	75.00
349	Manny Ramirez G	100.00
350	John Smoltz G	40.00

1997 Topps/Gallery

The second year of Gallery features 180 cards printed on extra-thick 24-point stock. Card fronts feature a player photo surrounded by an embossed foil "frame" to give each card the look of a piece of artwork. Backs contain career stats and biographical information on each player. Inserts include Peter Max Serigraphs, Signature Series Serigraphs, Player's Private Issue (parallel set), Photo Gallery and Gallery of Heroes. Cards were sold exclusively in hobby shops in eight-card packs for $4 each.

#	Player	MT
	Complete Set (180):	40.00
	Common Player:	.15
	Wax Box:	75.00
1	Paul Molitor	1.00
2	Devon White	.15
3	Andres Galarraga	.30
4	Cal Ripken Jr.	4.00
5	Tony Gwynn	2.00
6	Mike Stanley	.15
7	Orel Hershiser	.15
8	Jose Canseco	.40
9	Chili Davis	.15
10	Harold Baines	.15
11	Rickey Henderson	.15
12	Darryl Strawberry	.15
13	Todd Worrell	.15
14	Cecil Fielder	.30
15	Gary Gaetti	.15
16	Bobby Bonilla	.15
17	Will Clark	.40
18	Kevin Brown	.15
19	Tom Glavine	.30
20	Wade Boggs	.30
21	Edgar Martinez	.15
22	Lance Johnson	.15
23	Gregg Jefferies	.15
24	Bip Roberts	.15
25	Tony Phillips	.15
26	Greg Maddux	3.00
27	Mickey Tettleton	.15
28	Terry Steinbach	.15
29	Ryne Sandberg	1.50
30	Wally Joyner	.15
31	Joe Carter	.25
32	Ellis Burks	.15
33	Fred McGriff	.40
34	Barry Larkin	.40
35	John Franco	.15
36	Rafael Palmeiro	.30
37	Mark McGwire	1.75
38	Ken Caminiti	.40
39	David Cone	.25
40	Julio Franco	.15
41	Roger Clemens	1.50
42	Barry Bonds	1.50
43	Dennis Eckersley	.15
44	Eddie Murray	.50
45	Paul O'Neill	.15
46	Craig Biggio	.15
47	Roberto Alomar	1.00
48	Mark Grace	.30
49	Matt Williams	.50
50	Jay Buhner	.25
51	John Smoltz	.40
52	Randy Johnson	.75
53	Ramon Martinez	.15
54	Curt Schilling	.15
55	Gary Sheffield	.50
56	Jack McDowell	.15
57	Brady Anderson	.15
58	Dante Bichette	.30
59	Ron Gant	.30
60	Alex Fernandez	.30
61	Moises Alou	.15
62	Travis Fryman	.15
63	Dean Palmer	.15
64	Todd Hundley	.30
65	Jeff Brantley	.15
66	Bernard Gilkey	.15
67	Geronimo Berroa	.15
68	John Wetteland	.15
69	Robin Ventura	.15
70	Ray Lankford	.15
71	Kevin Appier	.15
72	Larry Walker	.40
73	Juan Gonzalez	2.50
74	Jeff King	.15
75	Greg Vaughn	.15
76	Steve Finley	.15
77	Brian McRae	.15
78	Paul Sorrento	.15
79	Ken Griffey Jr.	5.00
80	Omar Vizquel	.15
81	Jose Mesa	.15
82	Albert Belle	1.75
83	Glenallen Hill	.15
84	Sammy Sosa	.50
85	Andy Benes	.15
86	David Justice	.40
87	Marquis Grissom	.15
88	John Olerud	.15
89	Tino Martinez	.30
90	Frank Thomas	5.00
91	Raul Mondesi	.40
92	Steve Trachsel	.15
93	Jim Edmonds	.15
94	Rusty Greer	.15
95	Joey Hamilton	.15
96	Ismael Valdes	.15
97	Dave Nilsson	.15
98	John Jaha	.15
99	Alex Gonzalez	.15
100	Javy Lopez	.30
101	Ryan Klesko	.75
102	Tim Salmon	.30
103	Bernie Williams	1.00
104	Roberto Hernandez	.15
105	Chuck Knoblauch	.30
106	Mike Lansing	.15
107	Vinny Castilla	.15
108	Reggie Sanders	.15
109	Mo Vaughn	1.50
110	Rondell White	.15
111	Ivan Rodriguez	1.00
112	Mike Mussina	1.00
113	Carlos Baerga	.15
114	Jeff Conine	.15
115	Jim Thome	.50
116	Manny Ramirez	1.50
117	Kenny Lofton	1.50
118	Wilson Alvarez	.15
119	Eric Karros	.15
120	Robb Nen	.15
121	Mark Wohlers	.15
122	Ed Sprague	.15
123	Pat Hentgen	.15
124	Juan Guzman	.15
125	Derek Bell	.15
126	Jeff Bagwell	2.00
127	Eric Young	.15
128	John Valentin	.15
129	Al Martin (photo actually Javy Lopez)	.45
130	Trevor Hoffman	.15
131	Henry Rodriguez	.15
132	Pedro Martinez	.40
133	Mike Piazza	3.00
134	Brian Jordan	.15
135	Jose Valentin	.15
136	Jeff Cirillo	.15
137	Chipper Jones	3.00
138	Ricky Bottalico	.15
139	Hideo Nomo	1.00
140	Troy Percival	.15
141	Rey Ordonez	.15
142	Edgar Renteria	.15
143	Luis Castillo	.25
144	Vladimir Guerrero	3.00
145	Jeff D'Amico	.15
146	Andruw Jones	3.00
147	Darin Erstad	2.50
148	Bob Abreu	.15
149	Carlos Delgado	.15
150	Jamey Wright	.15
151	Nomar Garciaparra	2.50
152	Jason Kendall	.15
153	Jermaine Allensworth	.15
154	Scott Rolen	2.50
155	Rocky Coppinger	.15
156	Paul Wilson	.15
157	Garret Anderson	.15
158	Mariano Rivera	.30
159	Ruben Rivera	.40
160	Andy Pettitte	1.50
161	Derek Jeter	2.50
162	Neifi Perez	.15
163	Ray Durham	.15
164	James Baldwin	.15
165	Marty Cordova	.15
166	Tony Clark	.60
167	Michael Tucker	.15
168	Mike Sweeney	.15
169	Johnny Damon	.15
170	Jermaine Dye	.15
171	Alex Ochoa	.15
172	Jason Isringhausen	.15
173	Mark Grudzielanek	.15
174	Jose Rosado	.15
175	Todd Hollandsworth	.15
176	Alan Benes	.30
177	Jason Giambi	.15
178	Billy Wagner	.15
179	Justin Thompson	.15
180	Todd Walker	.75

1997 Topps/Gallery Private Issue

A foil-stamped parallel version to the regular set, the backs are sequentially numbered to 250, with some cards having been sent to players and the balance inserted in packs. The cards are spot UV coated on the photo only to allow for autographing. Cards were inserted 1:12 packs.

#	Player	MT
	Complete Set (180):	1700.
	Common Player:	5.00
	Stars:	25x to 35x
1	Paul Molitor	35.00
2	Devon White	5.00
3	Andres Galarraga	10.00
4	Cal Ripken Jr.	125.00
5	Tony Gwynn	80.00
6	Mike Stanley	5.00
7	Orel Hershiser	5.00
8	Jose Canseco	10.00
9	Chili Davis	5.00
10	Harold Baines	5.00
11	Rickey Henderson	5.00
12	Darryl Strawberry	5.00
13	Todd Worrell	5.00
14	Cecil Fielder	10.00
15	Gary Gaetti	5.00
16	Bobby Bonilla	5.00
17	Will Clark	10.00
18	Kevin Brown	5.00
19	Tom Glavine	10.00
20	Wade Boggs	10.00
21	Edgar Martinez	5.00
22	Lance Johnson	5.00
23	Gregg Jefferies	5.00
24	Bip Roberts	5.00
25	Tony Phillips	5.00
26	Greg Maddux	90.00
27	Mickey Tettleton	5.00
28	Terry Steinbach	5.00
29	Ryne Sandberg	40.00
30	Wally Joyner	5.00
31	Joe Carter	10.00
32	Ellis Burks	5.00
33	Fred McGriff	12.00
34	Barry Larkin	12.00
35	John Franco	5.00
36	Rafael Palmeiro	10.00
37	Mark McGwire	70.00
38	Ken Caminiti	15.00
39	David Cone	10.00
40	Julio Franco	5.00
41	Roger Clemens	50.00
42	Barry Bonds	50.00
43	Dennis Eckersley	5.00
44	Eddie Murray	30.00
45	Paul O'Neill	5.00
46	Craig Biggio	10.00
47	Roberto Alomar	35.00
48	Mark Grace	10.00
49	Matt Williams	15.00
50	Jay Buhner	10.00
51	John Smoltz	10.00
52	Randy Johnson	35.00
53	Ramon Martinez	5.00
54	Curt Schilling	5.00
55	Gary Sheffield	15.00
56	Jack McDowell	5.00
57	Brady Anderson	5.00
58	Dante Bichette	10.00
59	Ron Gant	10.00
60	Alex Fernandez	8.00
61	Moises Alou	5.00
62	Travis Fryman	5.00
63	Dean Palmer	5.00
64	Todd Hundley	10.00
65	Jeff Brantley	5.00
66	Bernard Gilkey	5.00
67	Geronimo Berroa	5.00
68	John Wetteland	5.00
69	Robin Ventura	5.00
70	Ray Lankford	5.00
71	Kevin Appier	5.00
72	Larry Walker	20.00
73	Juan Gonzalez	80.00
74	Jeff King	5.00
75	Greg Vaughn	5.00
76	Steve Finley	5.00
77	Brian McRae	5.00
78	Paul Sorrento	5.00
79	Ken Griffey Jr.	200.00
80	Omar Vizquel	5.00
81	Jose Mesa	5.00
82	Albert Belle	70.00
83	Glenallen Hill	5.00
84	Sammy Sosa	15.00
85	Andy Benes	5.00
86	David Justice	10.00
87	Marquis Grissom	5.00
88	John Olerud	5.00
89	Tino Martinez	10.00
90	Frank Thomas	150.00
91	Raul Mondesi	10.00
92	Steve Trachsel	5.00
93	Jim Edmonds	5.00
94	Rusty Greer	5.00
95	Joey Hamilton	5.00
96	Ismael Valdes	5.00
97	Dave Nilsson	5.00
98	John Jaha	5.00
99	Alex Gonzalez	5.00
100	Javy Lopez	10.00
101	Ryan Klesko	30.00
102	Tim Salmon	10.00
103	Bernie Williams	35.00
104	Roberto Hernandez	5.00
105	Chuck Knoblauch	10.00
106	Mike Lansing	5.00
107	Vinny Castilla	5.00
108	Reggie Sanders	5.00
109	Mo Vaughn	50.00
110	Rondell White	5.00
111	Ivan Rodriguez	35.00
112	Mike Mussina	35.00
113	Carlos Baerga	5.00
114	Jeff Conine	5.00
115	Jim Thome	20.00
116	Manny Ramirez	40.00
117	Kenny Lofton	50.00
118	Wilson Alvarez	5.00
119	Eric Karros	5.00
120	Robb Nen	5.00
121	Mark Wohlers	5.00
122	Ed Sprague	5.00
123	Pat Hentgen	5.00
124	Juan Guzman	5.00
125	Derek Bell	5.00
126	Jeff Bagwell	80.00
127	Eric Young	5.00
128	John Valentin	5.00
129	Al Martin	5.00
130	Trevor Hoffman	5.00
131	Henry Rodriguez	5.00
132	Pedro Martinez	10.00
133	Mike Piazza	100.00
134	Brian Jordan	5.00
135	Jose Valentin	5.00
136	Jeff Cirillo	5.00
137	Chipper Jones	100.00
138	Ricky Bottalico	5.00
139	Hideo Nomo	35.00
140	Troy Percival	5.00
141	Rey Ordonez	5.00
142	Edgar Renteria	5.00
143	Luis Castillo	8.00

Column 1

#	Player	MT
144	Vladimir Guerrero	75.00
145	Jeff D'Amico	5.00
146	Andruw Jones	110.00
147	Darin Erstad	60.00
148	Bob Abreu	5.00
149	Carlos Delgado	5.00
150	Jamey Wright	5.00
151	Nomar Garciaparra	50.00
152	Jason Kendall	5.00
153	Jermaine Allensworth	5.00
154	Scott Rolen	50.00
155	Rocky Coppinger	5.00
156	Paul Wilson	5.00
157	Garret Anderson	5.00
158	Mariano Rivera	10.00
159	Ruben Rivera	10.00
160	Andy Pettitte	50.00
161	Derek Jeter	100.00
162	Neifi Perez	5.00
163	Ray Durham	5.00
164	James Baldwin	5.00
165	Marty Cordova	5.00
166	Tony Clark	40.00
167	Michael Tucker	5.00
168	Mike Sweeney	5.00
169	Johnny Damon	5.00
170	Jermaine Dye	5.00
171	Alex Ochoa	5.00
172	Jason Isringhausen	5.00
173	Mark Grudzielanek	5.00
174	Jose Rosado	5.00
175	Todd Hollandsworth	5.00
176	Alan Benes	10.00
177	Jason Giambi	5.00
178	Billy Wagner	5.00
179	Justin Thompson	5.00
180	Todd Walker	20.00

1997 Topps/Gallery of Heroes

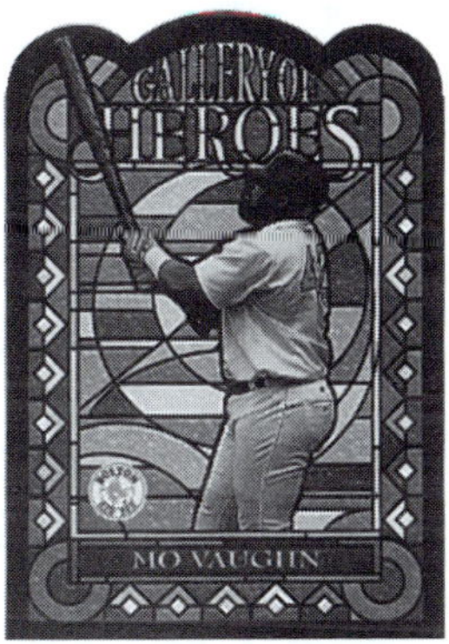

This 10-card die cut insert features a design resembling stained glass. Cards were inserted 1:36 packs.

	MT
Complete Set (10):	180.00
Common Player:	8.00
GH1 Derek Jeter	25.00
GH2 Chipper Jones	25.00
GH3 Frank Thomas	35.00
GH4 Ken Griffey Jr.	40.00
GH5 Cal Ripken Jr.	30.00
GH6 Mark McGwire	15.00
GH7 Mike Piazza	25.00
GH8 Jeff Bagwell	18.00
GH9 Tony Gwynn	18.00
GH10 Mo Vaughn	10.00

1997 Topps/Gallery Peter Max

Noted artist Peter Max has painted renditions of 10 superstar players and offered his commentary about those players on the backs. Cards were inserted 1:24 packs. In addition, Max autographed cards are inserted 1:1,200 packs.

Column 2

	MT
Complete Set (10):	90.00
Common Player:	4.00
Autographs	10x to 20x
1 Ken Griffey Jr.	20.00
2 Frank Thomas	20.00
3 Albert Belle	8.00
4 Barry Bonds	6.00
5 Derek Jeter	12.00
6 Ken Caminiti	4.00
7 Mike Piazza	12.00
8 Cal Ripken Jr.	15.00
9 Mark McGwire	8.00
10 Chipper Jones	12.00

1997 Topps/Gallery Photo Gallery

This 21-card set features full-bleed, high-gloss action photos of some of the game's top stars. Cards were inserted 1:24 packs.

	MT
Complete Set (16):	150.00
Common Player:	4.00
PG1 World Series	10.00
PG2 Paul Molitor	8.00
PG3 Eddie Murray	7.00
PG4 Ken Griffey Jr.	35.00
PG5 Chipper Jones	20.00
PG6 Derek Jeter	20.00
PG7 Frank Thomas	35.00
PG8 Mark McGwire	10.00
PG9 Kenny Lofton	8.00
PG10 Gary Sheffield	6.00
PG11 Mike Piazza	20.00
PG12 Vinny Castilla	4.00
PG13 Andres Galarraga	4.00
PG14 Andy Pettitte	8.00
PG15 Robin Ventura	4.00
PG16 Barry Larkin	4.00

1997 Stadium Club

Stadium Club totaled 390 cards in 1997, and was issued in two Series of 195 cards each. In Series I, card numbers 182-195 are a rookie subset called TSC 2000. In Series II, card numbers 376-390 form a subset called Stadium Slugger. Stadium Club, which arrived in nine-card hobby packs and six-card retail packs, is printed on an improved 20-point stock with Topps' Super Color process. Se-

Column 3

ries I included five Co-Signers, 11 Instavision, 20 Millennium, 10 Pure Gold, 60 TSC Matrix and 12 Firebrand inserts. Series II continued these inserts, except instead of Firebrand, Series II had Patent Leather.

#	Player	MT
	Complete Set (390):	80.00
	Complete Series I Set (195):	40.00
	Complete Series II Set (195):	40.00
	Common Player:	.10
	Wax Box:	65.00
1	Chipper Jones	2.00
2	Gary Sheffield	.40
3	Kenny Lofton	.60
4	Brian Jordan	.10
5	Mark McGwire	1.00
6	Charles Nagy	.10
7	Tim Salmon	.25
8	Cal Ripken Jr.	2.50
9	Jeff Conine	.10
10	Paul Molitor	.30
11	Mariano Rivera	.20
12	Pedro Martinez	.10
13	Jeff Bagwell	1.25
14	Bobby Bonilla	.10
15	Barry Bonds	.75
16	Ryan Klesko	.50
17	Barry Larkin	.20
18	Jim Thome	.30
19	Jay Buhner	.15
20	Juan Gonzalez	1.50
21	Mike Mussina	.30
22	Kevin Appier	.10
23	Eric Karros	.10
24	Steve Finley	.10
25	Ed Sprague	.10
26	Bernard Gilkey	.10
27	Tony Phillips	.10
28	Henry Rodriguez	.10
29	John Smoltz	.20
30	Dante Bichette	.20
31	Mike Piazza	2.00
32	Paul O'Neill	.10
33	Billy Wagner	.10
34	Reggie Sanders	.10
35	John Jaha	.10
36	Eddie Murray	.40
37	Eric Young	.10
38	Roberto Hernandez	.10
39	Pat Hentgen	.10
40	Sammy Sosa	.25
41	Todd Hundley	.10
42	Mo Vaughn	1.00
43	Robin Ventura	.10
44	Mark Grudzielanek	.10
45	Shane Reynolds	.10
46	Andy Pettitte	.75
47	Fred McGriff	.25
48	Rey Ordonez	.20
49	Will Clark	.25
50	Ken Griffey Jr.	3.00
51	Todd Worrell	.10
52	Rusty Greer	.10
53	Mark Grace	.20
54	Tom Glavine	.20
55	Derek Jeter	1.50
56	Rafael Palmeiro	.15
57	Bernie Williams	.60
58	Marty Cordova	.10
59	Andres Galarraga	.15
60	Ken Caminiti	.35
61	Garret Anderson	.10
62	Denny Martinez	.10
63	Mike Greenwell	.10
64	David Segui	.10
65	Julio Franco	.10
66	Rickey Henderson	.10
67	Ozzie Guillen	.10
68	Pete Harnisch	.10

Column 4

#	Player	MT
69	Chan Ho Park	.10
70	Harold Baines	.10
71	Mark Clark	.10
72	Steve Avery	.10
73	Brian Hunter	.10
74	Pedro Astacio	.10
75	Jack McDowell	.10
76	Gregg Jefferies	.10
77	Jason Kendall	.10
78	Todd Walker	.75
79	B.J. Surhoff	.10
80	Moises Alou	.20
81	Fernando Vina	.10
82	Darryl Strawberry	.10
83	Jose Rosado	.10
84	Chris Gomez	.10
85	Chili Davis	.10
86	Alan Benes	.10
87	Todd Hollandsworth	.10
88	Jose Vizcaino	.10
89	Edgardo Alfonzo	.10
90	Ruben Rivera	.30
91	Donovan Osborne	.10
92	Doug Glanville	.10
93	Gary DiSarcina	.10
94	Brooks Kieschnick	.10
95	Bobby Jones	.10
96	Raul Casanova	.10
97	Jermaine Allensworth	.10
98	Kenny Rogers	.10
99	Mark McLemore	.10
100	Jeff Fassero	.10
101	Sandy Alomar	.10
102	Chuck Finley	.10
103	Eric Owens	.10
104	Billy McMillon	.10
105	Dwight Gooden	.10
106	Sterling Hitchcock	.10
107	Doug Drabek	.10
108	Paul Wilson	.15
109	Chris Snopek	.10
110	Al Leiter	.10
111	Bob Tewksbury	.10
112	Todd Greene	.10
113	Jose Valentin	.10
114	Delino DeShields	.10
115	Mike Bordick	.10
116	Pat Meares	.10
117	Mariano Duncan	.10
118	Steve Trachsel	.10
119	Luis Castillo	.25
120	Andy Benes	.10
121	Donne Wall	.10
122	Alex Gonzalez	.10
123	Dan Wilson	.10
124	Omar Vizquel	.10
125	Devon White	.10
126	Darryl Hamilton	.10
127	Orlando Merced	.10
128	Royce Clayton	.10
129	William VanLandingham	.10
130	Terry Steinbach	.10
131	Jeff Blauser	.10
132	Jeff Cirillo	.10
133	Roger Pavlik	.10
134	Danny Tartabull	.10
135	Jeff Montgomery	.10
136	Bobby Higginson	.10
137	Mike Grace	.10
138	Kevin Elster	.10
139	Brian Giles	.10
140	Rod Beck	.10
141	Ismael Valdes	.10
142	Scott Brosius	.10
143	Mike Fetters	.10
144	Gary Gaetti	.10
145	Mike Lansing	.10
146	Glenallen Hill	.10
147	Shawn Green	.10
148	Mel Rojas	.10
149	Joey Cora	.10
150	John Smiley	.10
151	Marvin Benard	.10
152	Curt Schilling	.10
153	Dave Nilsson	.10
154	Edgar Renteria	.20
155	Joey Hamilton	.10
156	Carlos Garcia	.10
157	Nomar Garciaparra	2.00
158	Kevin Ritz	.10
159	Keith Lockhart	.10
160	Justin Thompson	.10
161	Terry Adams	.10
162	Jamey Wright	.10
163	Otis Nixon	.10
164	Michael Tucker	.10
165	Mike Stanley	.10
166	Ben McDonald	.10
167	John Mabry	.10
168	Troy O'Leary	.10
169	Mel Nieves	.10

170	Bret Boone	.10
171	Mike Timlin	.10
172	Scott Rolen	1.50
173	Reggie Jefferson	.10
174	Neifi Perez	.10
175	Brian McRae	.10
176	Tom Goodwin	.10
177	Aaron Sele	.10
178	Benny Santiago	.10
179	Frank Rodriguez	.10
180	Eric Davis	.10
181	Andruw Jones (TSC 2000)	4.00
182	Todd Walker (TSC 2000)	1.50
183	Wes Helms (TSC 2000)	1.00
184	*Nelson Figueroa* (TSC 2000)	.75
185	Vladimir Guerrero (TSC 2000)	4.00
186	Billy McMillon (TSC 2000)	.40
187	Todd Helton (TSC 2000)	2.00
188	Nomar Garciaparra (TSC 2000)	4.00
189	Katsuhiro Maeda (TSC 2000)	1.00
190	Russell Branyan (TSC 2000)	1.00
191	Glendon Rusch (TSC 2000)	.25
192	Bartolo Colon (TSC 2000)	.25
193	Scott Rolen (TSC 2000)	3.00
194	Angel Echevarria (TSC 2000)	.10
195	Bob Abreu (TSC 2000)	.25
196	Greg Maddux	2.00
197	Joe Carter	.20
198	Alex Ochoa	.20
199	Ellis Burks	.20
200	Ivan Rodriguez	.60
201	Marquis Grissom	.10
202	Trevor Hoffman	.10
203	Matt Williams	.30
204	Carlos Delgado	.15
205	Ramon Martinez	.10
206	Chuck Knoblauch	.20
207	Juan Guzman	.10
208	Derek Bell	.10
209	Roger Clemens	1.00
210	Vladimir Guerrero	1.50
211	Cecil Fielder	.20
212	Hideo Nomo	.60
213	Frank Thomas	3.00
214	Greg Vaughn	.10
215	Javy Lopez	.20
216	Raul Mondesi	.25
217	Wade Boggs	.20
218	Carlos Baerga	.10
219	Tony Gwynn	1.25
220	Tino Martinez	.25
221	Vinny Castilla	.20
222	Lance Johnson	.10
223	David Justice	.25
224	Rondell White	.20
225	Dean Palmer	.10
226	Jim Edmonds	.10
227	Albert Belle	1.00
228	Alex Fernandez	.20
229	Ryne Sandberg	.75
230	Jose Mesa	.10
231	David Cone	.20
232	Troy Percival	.10
233	Edgar Martinez	.10
234	Jose Canseco	.25
235	Kevin Brown	.10
236	Ray Lankford	.10
237	Karim Garcia	.20
238	J.T. Snow	.10
239	Dennis Eckersley	.10
240	Roberto Alomar	.60
241	John Valentin	.10
242	Ron Gant	.20
243	Geronimo Berroa	.10
244	Manny Ramirez	.75
245	Travis Fryman	.10
246	Denny Neagle	.10
247	Randy Johnson	.60
248	Darin Erstad	1.25
249	Mark Wohlers	.10
250	Ken Hill	.10
251	Larry Walker	.35
252	Craig Biggio	.10
253	Brady Anderson	.10
254	John Wetteland	.10
255	Andruw Jones	2.50
256	Turk Wendell	.10
257	Jason Isringhausen	.10
258	Jaime Navarro	.10
259	Sean Berry	.10
260	Albie Lopez	.10
261	Jay Bell	.10
262	Bobby Witt	.10
263	Tony Clark	.50
264	Tim Wakefield	.10
265	Brad Radke	.10

266	Tim Belcher	.10
267	Mark Lewis	.10
268	Roger Cedeno	.10
269	Tim Naehring	.10
270	Kevin Tapani	.10
271	Joe Randa	.10
272	Randy Myers	.10
273	Dave Burba	.10
274	Mike Sweeney	.10
275	Danny Graves	.10
276	Chad Mottola	.10
277	Ruben Sierra	.10
278	Norm Charlton	.10
279	Scott Servais	.10
280	Jacob Cruz	.10
281	Mike Macfarlane	.10
282	Rich Becker	.10
283	Shannon Stewart	.10
284	Gerald Williams	.10
285	Jody Reed	.10
286	Jeff D'Amico	.10
287	Walt Weiss	.10
288	Jim Leyritz	.10
289	Francisco Cordova	.15
290	F.P. Santangelo	.10
291	Scott Erickson	.10
292	Hal Morris	.10
293	Ray Durham	.10
294	Andy Ashby	.10
295	Darryl Kile	.10
296	Jose Paniagua	.10
297	Mickey Tettleton	.10
298	Joe Girardi	.10
299	Rocky Coppinger	.10
300	Bob Abreu	.20
301	John Olerud	.10
302	Paul Shuey	.10
303	Jeff Brantley	.10
304	Bob Wells	.10
305	Kevin Seitzer	.10
306	Shawon Dunston	.10
307	Jose Herrera	.10
308	Butch Huskey	.10
309	Jose Offerman	.10
310	Rick Aguilera	.10
311	Greg Gagne	.10
312	John Burkett	.10
313	Mark Thompson	.10
314	Alvaro Espinoza	.10
315	Todd Stottlemyre	.10
316	Al Martin	.10
317	James Baldwin	.10
318	Cal Eldred	.10
319	Sid Fernandez	.10
320	Mickey Morandini	.10
321	Robb Nen	.10
322	Mark Lemke	.10
323	Pete Schourek	.10
324	Marcus Jensen	.10
325	Rich Aurilia	.10
326	Jeff King	.10
327	Scott Stahoviak	.10
328	Ricky Otero	.10
329	Antonio Osuna	.10
330	Chris Hoiles	.10
331	Luis Gonzalez	.10
332	Wil Cordero	.10
333	Johnny Damon	.10
334	Mark Langston	.10
335	Orlando Miller	.10
336	Jason Giambi	.10
337	Damian Jackson	.10
338	David Wells	.10
339	Bip Roberts	.10
340	Matt Ruebel	.10
341	Tom Candiotti	.10
342	Wally Joyner	.10
343	Jimmy Key	.10
344	Tony Batista	.10
345	Paul Sorrento	.10
346	Ron Karkovice	.10
347	Wilson Alvarez	.10
348	John Flaherty	.10
349	Rey Sanchez	.10
350	John Vander Wal	.10
351	Jermaine Dye	.15
352	Mike Hampton	.10
353	Greg Colbrunn	.10
354	Heathcliff Slocumb	.10
355	Ricky Bottalico	.10
356	Marty Janzen	.10
357	Orel Hershiser	.10
358	Rex Hudler	.10
359	Amaury Telemaco	.10
360	Darrin Fletcher	.10
361	Robert Person	.10
362	Russ Davis	.10
363	Allen Watson	.10
364	Mike Lieberthal	.10
365	Dave Stevens	.10
366	Jay Powell	.10

367	Tony Fossas	.10
368	Bob Wolcott	.10
369	Mark Loretta	.10
370	Shawn Estes	.10
371	Sandy Martinez	.10
372	Wendell Magee Jr.	.10
373	John Franco	.10
374	Tom Pagnozzi	.10
375	Willie Adams	.10
376	Chipper Jones (Stadium Sluggers)	4.00
377	Mo Vaughn (Stadium Sluggers)	2.00
378	Frank Thomas (Stadium Sluggers)	6.00
379	Albert Belle (Stadium Sluggers)	2.00
380	Andres Galarraga (Stadium Sluggers)	.25
381	Gary Sheffield (Stadium Sluggers)	.25
382	Jeff Bagwell (Stadium Sluggers)	2.50
383	Mike Piazza (Stadium Sluggers)	4.00
384	Mark McGwire (Stadium Sluggers)	2.50
385	Ken Griffey Jr. (Stadium Sluggers)	6.00
386	Barry Bonds (Stadium Sluggers)	1.50
387	Juan Gonzalez (Stadium Sluggers)	3.00
388	Brady Anderson (Stadium Sluggers)	.10
389	Ken Caminiti (Stadium Sluggers)	.25
390	Jay Buhner (Stadium Sluggers)	.15

1997 Stadium Club Co-Signers

Each Series of Stadium Club included five different Co-Signers, with an insertion ratio of one per 168 hobby packs. These double-sided cards featured authentic autographs from each star, one per side.

		MT
	Complete Set (10):	650.00
	Complete Series 1 Set (5):	325.00
	Complete Series 2 Set (5):	350.00
	Common Autograph:	50.00
CO1	Andy Pettitte, Derek Jeter	125.00
CO2	Paul Wilson, Todd Hundley	50.00
CO3	Jermaine Dye, Mark Wohlers	50.00
CO4	Scott Rolen, Gregg Jefferies	100.00
CO5	Todd Hollandsworth, Jason Kendall	50.00
CO6	Alan Benes, Robin Ventura	50.00
CO7	Eric Karros, Raul Mondesi	50.00
CO8	Rey Ordonez, Nomar Garciaparra	125.00
CO9	Rondell White, Marty Cordova	50.00
CO10	Tony Gwynn, Karim Garcia	150.00

1997 Stadium Club Firebrand

This 12-card insert was found only in packs sold at retail chains. Cards were inserted 1:36 packs.

		MT
	Complete Set (12):	125.00
	Common Player:	4.00
F1	Jeff Bagwell	12.00
F2	Albert Belle	10.00
F3	Barry Bonds	8.00
F4	Andres Galarraga	4.00
F5	Ken Griffey Jr.	30.00
F6	Brady Anderson	4.00
F7	Mark McGwire	12.00
F8	Chipper Jones	20.00
F9	Frank Thomas	30.00
F10	Mike Piazza	20.00
F11	Mo Vaughn	8.00
F12	Juan Gonzalez	15.00

1997 Stadium Club Instavision

Instavision features holographic cards with exciting moments from the 1996 playoffs and World Series. Inserted one per 24 hobby packs and one per 36 retail packs, these cards are printed on a horizontal, plastic card. Cards carry an "I" prefix, with the first 10 found in Series I and the final 12 in Series II.

		MT
	Complete Set (22):	100.00
	Complete Series I Set (10):	40.00
	Complete Series II Set (12):	60.00
	Common Player:	3.00
11	Eddie Murray	4.00
12	Paul Molitor	6.00
13	Todd Hundley	4.00
14	Roger Clemens	8.00
15	Barry Bonds	6.00
16	Mark McGwire	10.00
17	Brady Anderson	3.00
18	Barry Larkin	5.00
19	Ken Caminiti	5.00
110	Hideo Nomo	8.00
111	Bernie Williams	6.00
112	Juan Gonzalez	12.00
113	Andy Pettitte	8.00
114	Albert Belle	10.00
115	John Smoltz	4.00
116	Brian Jordan	3.00
117	Derek Jeter	15.00
118	Ken Caminiti	5.00
119	John Wetteland	3.00
120	Brady Anderson	3.00
121	Andruw Jones	12.00
122	Jim Leyritz	3.00

1997 Stadium Club Members Only Basball

This boxed set was available only to members of Topps" Stadium Club for a price of $15, which included a year's membership in the club. Fronts feature action photos with a 2-1/2" circle behind the player, a gold-foil Members Only seal and the player's name, also in gold-foil. Backs feature another photo and a career summary on a red background which has the Members Only seal in a repeating pattern. Cards #51-55 are rookie stars and are printed in Topps Finest technologies.

		MT
Complete Set (55):		15.00
Common Player:		.25
1	Brady Anderson	.25
2	Carlos Baerga	.25
3	Jeff Bagwell	.40
4	Albert Belle	.40
5	Dante Bichette	.25
6	Craig Biggio	.25
7	Wade Boggs	.35
8	Barry Bonds	.75
9	Jay Buhner	.25
10	Ellis Burks	.25
11	Ken Caminiti	.25
12	Jose Canseco	.35
13	Joe Carter	.25
14	Roger Clemens	.40
15	Jeff Conine	.25
16	Andres Galarraga	.25
17	Ron Gant	.25
18	Juan Gonzalez	.60
19	Mark Grace	.25
20	Ken Griffey Jr.	3.00
21	Tony Gwynn	.75
22	Pat Hentgen	.25
23	Todd Hollandsworth	.25
24	Todd Hundley	.25
25	Derek Jeter	.60
26	Randy Johnson	.35
27	Chipper Jones	.75
28	Ryan Klesko	.25
29	Chuck Knoblauch	.25
30	Barry Larkin	.25
31	Kenny Lofton	.25
32	Greg Maddux	.50
33	Mark McGwire	.75
34	Paul Molitor	.25
35	Raul Mondesi	.25
36	Hideo Nomo	.25
37	Rafael Palmeiro	.25
38	Mike Piazza	.75
39	Manny Ramirez	.25
40	Cal Ripken Jr.	2.00
41	Ivan Rodriguez	.25
42	Tim Salmon	.25
43	Gary Sheffield	.25
44	John Smoltz	.25
45	Sammy Sosa	.25
46	Frank Thomas	3.00
47	Jim Thome	.25
48	Mo Vaughn	.25
49	Bernie Williams	.25
50	Matt Williams	.25
51	Darin Erstad (Finest)	2.00
52	Vladimir Guerrero (Finest)	3.00
53	Andruw Jones (Finest)	3.00
54	Scott Rolen (Finest)	2.00
55	Todd Walker (Finest)	2.00

1997 Stadium Club Millenium

Millennium was a 40-card insert that was released with 20 cards in Series I and Series II. The set featured 40 top prospects and rookies on a silver foil, holographic front, with a Future Forecast section on the back. Cards carried an "M" prefix and were numbered consecutively M1-M40. Millennium inserts were found every 24 hobby packs and every 36 retail packs.

		MT
Complete Set (40):		190.00
Complete Series I Set (20):		90.00
Complete Series II Set (20):		100.00
Common Player:		3.00
M1	Derek Jeter	25.00
M2	Mark Grudzielanek	3.00
M3	Jacob Cruz	3.00
M4	Ray Durham	3.00
M5	Tony Clark	8.00
M6	Chipper Jones	25.00
M7	Luis Castillo	3.00
M8	Carlos Delgado	4.00
M9	Brant Brown	3.00
M10	Jason Kendall	3.00
M11	Alan Benes	4.00
M12	Rey Ordonez	4.00
M13	Justin Thompson	4.00
M14	Jermaine Allensworth	3.00
M15	Brian Hunter	3.00
M16	Marty Cordova	3.00
M17	Edgar Renteria	4.00
M18	Karim Garcia	5.00
M19	Todd Greene	3.00
M20	Paul Wilson	4.00
M21	Andruw Jones	25.00
M22	Todd Walker	8.00
M23	Alex Ochoa	4.00
M24	Bartolo Colon	4.00
M25	Wendell Magee Jr.	4.00
M26	Jose Rosado	4.00
M27	Katsuhiro Maeda	3.00
M28	Bob Abreu	5.00
M29	Brooks Kieschnick	3.00
M30	Derrick Gibson	3.00
M31	Mike Sweeney	3.00
M32	Jeff D'Amico	4.00
M33	Chad Mottola	3.00
M34	Chris Snopek	3.00
M35	Jaime Bluma	3.00
M36	Vladimir Guerrero	15.00
M37	Nomar Garciaparra	20.00
M38	Scott Rolen	15.00
M39	Dmitri Young	3.00
M40	Neifi Perez	3.00

1997 Stadium Club Patent Leather

Patent Leather featured 13 of the top gloves in baseball on a leather, die-cut card. The cards carry a "PL" prefix and are inerted one per 36 retail packs.

		MT
Complete Set (13):		100.00
Common Player:		5.00
PL1	Ivan Rodriguez	8.00
PL2	Ken Caminiti	6.00
PL3	Barry Bonds	10.00
PL4	Ken Griffey Jr.	35.00
PL5	Greg Maddux	20.00
PL6	Craig Biggio	5.00
PL7	Andres Galarraga	5.00
PL8	Kenny Lofton	10.00
PL9	Barry Larkin	5.00
PL10	Mark Grace	5.00
PL11	Rey Ordonez	5.00
PL12	Roberto Alomar	8.00
PL13	Derek Jeter	20.00

1997 Stadium Club Pure Gold

Pure Gold featured 20 of the top players in baseball on gold, embossed foil cards. Cards carry a "PG" prefix and were inserted every 72 hobby packs and every 108 retail packs. The first 10 cards were in Series I packs, while the final 10 cards are exclusive to Series II.

		MT
Complete Set (20):		450.00
Complete Series I Set (10):		200.00
Complete Series II Set (10):		250.00
Common Player:		8.00
PG1	Brady Anderson	8.00
PG2	Albert Belle	20.00
PG3	Dante Bichette	8.00
PG4	Barry Bonds	15.00
PG5	Jay Buhner	8.00
PG6	Tony Gwynn	30.00
PG7	Chipper Jones	40.00
PG8	Mark McGwire	25.00
PG9	Gary Sheffield	12.00
PG10	Frank Thomas	60.00
PG11	Juan Gonzalez	30.00
PG12	Ken Caminiti	10.00
PG13	Kenny Lofton	15.00
PG14	Jeff Bagwell	30.00
PG15	Ken Griffey Jr.	60.00
PG16	Cal Ripken Jr.	50.00
PG17	Mo Vaughn	15.00
PG18	Mike Piazza	40.00
PG19	Derek Jeter	40.00
PG20	Andres Galarraga	8.00

1997 Stadium Club TSC Matrix

TSC Matrix consists of 120 cards from Series I and II reprinted with Power Matrix technology. In each Series, 60 of the 190 cards were selected for inclusion in TSC Matrix and inserted every 12 hobby packs and every 18 retail packs. Each insert carries the TSC Matrix logo in a top corner of the card.

		MT
Complete Set (120):		400.00
Complete Series I Set (60):		200.00
Complete Series II Set (60):		200.00
Common Player:		1.00
1	Chipper Jones	25.00
2	Gary Sheffield	5.00
3	Kenny Lofton	10.00
4	Brian Jordan	1.00
5	Mark McGwire	12.00
6	Charles Nagy	1.00
7	Tim Salmon	2.00
8	Cal Ripken Jr.	30.00
9	Jeff Conine	1.00
10	Paul Molitor	4.00
11	Mariano Rivera	2.00
12	Pedro Martinez	1.00
13	Jeff Bagwell	15.00
14	Bobby Bonilla	1.00
15	Barry Bonds	8.00
16	Ryan Klesko	5.00
17	Barry Larkin	2.00
18	Jim Thome	4.00
19	Jay Buhner	2.00
20	Juan Gonzalez	15.00
21	Mike Mussina	4.00
22	Kevin Appier	1.00
23	Eric Karros	1.00
24	Steve Finley	1.00
25	Ed Sprague	1.00
26	Bernard Gilkey	1.00
27	Tony Phillips	1.00
28	Henry Rodriguez	1.00
29	John Smoltz	2.00
30	Dante Bichette	2.00
31	Mike Piazza	25.00
32	Paul O'Neill	1.50
33	Billy Wagner	1.50
34	Reggie Sanders	1.00
35	John Jaha	1.00
36	Eddie Murray	4.00
37	Eric Young	1.00
38	Roberto Hernandez	1.00
39	Pat Hentgen	1.00
40	Sammy Sosa	4.00
41	Todd Hundley	1.00
42	Mo Vaughn	10.00
43	Robin Ventura	1.00
44	Mark Grudzielanek	1.00
45	Shane Reynolds	1.00
46	Andy Pettitte	10.00
47	Fred McGriff	2.50
48	Rey Ordonez	2.00
49	Will Clark	2.50
50	Ken Griffey Jr.	40.00
51	Todd Worrell	1.00
52	Rusty Greer	1.00
53	Mark Grace	2.00
54	Tom Glavine	1.50
55	Derek Jeter	20.00
56	Rafael Palmeiro	1.50
57	Bernie Williams	8.00
58	Marty Cordova	1.00
59	Andres Galarraga	2.00
60	Ken Caminiti	3.00
196	Greg Maddux	25.00
197	Joe Carter	2.00
198	Alex Ochoa	1.00
199	Ellis Burks	1.00
200	Ivan Rodriguez	8.00
201	Marquis Grissom	1.00
202	Trevor Hoffman	1.00
203	Matt Williams	4.00
204	Carlos Delgado	1.00
205	Ramon Martinez	1.00
206	Chuck Knoblauch	2.00
207	Juan Guzman	1.00
208	Derek Bell	1.00
209	Roger Clemens	8.00
210	Vladimir Guerrero	18.00
211	Cecil Fielder	2.00
212	Hideo Nomo	8.00
213	Frank Thomas	40.00
214	Greg Vaughn	1.00
215	Javy Lopez	2.00
216	Raul Mondesi	2.00
217	Wade Boggs	2.00
218	Carlos Baerga	1.00
219	Tony Gwynn	20.00
220	Tino Martinez	2.00
221	Vinny Castilla	1.00
222	Lance Johnson	1.00
223	David Justice	2.00

224	Rondell White	1.00
225	Dean Palmer	1.00
226	Jim Edmonds	1.00
227	Albert Belle	12.00
228	Alex Fernandez	2.00
229	Ryne Sandberg	12.00
230	Jose Mesa	1.00
231	David Cone	2.00
232	Troy Percival	1.00
233	Edgar Martinez	1.00
234	Jose Canseco	3.00
235	Kevin Brown	1.00
236	Ray Lankford	1.00
237	Karim Garcia	4.00
238	J.T. Snow	1.00
239	Dennis Eckersley	1.00
240	Roberto Alomar	8.00
241	John Valentin	1.00
242	Ron Gant	2.00
243	Geronimo Berroa	1.00
244	Manny Ramirez	10.00
245	Travis Fryman	1.00
246	Denny Neagle	1.00
247	Randy Johnson	6.00
248	Darin Erstad	18.00
249	Mark Wohlers	1.00
250	Ken Hill	1.00
251	Larry Walker	2.00
252	Craig Biggio	1.00
253	Brady Anderson	1.50
254	John Wetteland	1.00
255	Andruw Jones	25.00

1997 Upper Deck

The 520-card, regular-sized set was available in 12-card packs. The base card fronts feature a full action shot with the player's name near the bottom edge above a bronze-foil, wood-grain stripe. The player's team logo is in the lower left corner in silver foil. Each card front has the date of the game pictured with a brief description. The card backs contain more detailed game highlight descriptions and statistics, along with a small action shot in the upper left quadrant. Subsets are: Jackie Robinson Tribute (1-9), Strike Force (65-72), Defensive Gems (136-153), Global Impact (181-207), Season Highlights Checklist (214-222) and Star Rookies (223-240). Inserts are: Game Jerseys, Ticket To Stardom, Power Package, Amazing Greats and Rock Solid Foundation. A 30-card update to Series I was released early in the season featuring 1996 post-season highlights and star rookies. The card faces had red or purple borders and were numbered 241 to 270. A second update set of 30 was released near the end of the 1997 season, numbered 521-550 and featuring traded players and rookies in a format identical to Series I and II UD. Both of the update sets were available only via a mail-in redemption offer.

		MT
Complete Set (550):		110.00
Complete Series I Set (240):		30.00
Complete Update Set (241-270):		10.00
Complete Series II Set (250):		60.00
Complete Update Set (521-550):		12.00
Common Player:		.10
Hobby Box:		60.00
1	Jackie Robinson	1.00
2	Jackie Robinson	1.00
3	Jackie Robinson	1.00
4	Jackie Robinson	1.00
5	Jackie Robinson	1.00
6	Jackie Robinson	1.00
7	Jackie Robinson	1.00
8	Jackie Robinson	1.00
9	Jackie Robinson	1.00
10	Chipper Jones	2.00
11	Marquis Grissom	.10
12	Jermaine Dye	.20
13	Mark Lemke	.10
14	Terrell Wade	.10
15	Fred McGriff	.30
16	Tom Glavine	.15
17	Mark Wohlers	.10
18	Randy Myers	.10
19	Roberto Alomar	.75
20	Cal Ripken Jr.	2.50
21	Rafael Palmeiro	.15
22	Mike Mussina	.40
23	Brady Anderson	.10
24	Jose Canseco	.25
25	Mo Vaughn	1.00
26	Roger Clemens	1.00
27	Tim Naehring	.10
28	Jeff Suppan	.10
29	Troy Percival	.10
30	Sammy Sosa	.20
31	Amaury Telemaco	.10
32	Rey Sanchez	.10
33	Scott Servais	.10
34	Steve Trachsel	.10
35	Mark Grace	.20
36	Wilson Alvarez	.10
37	Harold Baines	.10
38	Tony Phillips	.10
39	James Baldwin	.10
40	Frank Thomas (wrong (Ken Griffey Jr.'s) vital data)	3.00
41	Lyle Mouton	.10
42	Chris Snopek	.10
43	Hal Morris	.10
44	Eric Davis	.10
45	Barry Larkin	.25
46	Reggie Sanders	.10
47	Pete Schourek	.10
48	Lee Smith	.10
49	Charles Nagy	.10
50	Albert Belle	1.00
51	Julio Franco	.10
52	Kenny Lofton	.75
53	Orel Hershiser	.10
54	Omar Vizquel	.10
55	Eric Young	.10
56	Curtis Leskanic	.10
57	Quinton McCracken	.10
58	Kevin Ritz	.10
59	Walt Weiss	.10
60	Dante Bichette	.25
61	Marc Lewis	.10
62	Tony Clark	.50
63	Travis Fryman	.10
64	John Smoltz (Strike Force)	.15
65	Greg Maddux (Strike Force)	1.00
66	Tom Glavine (Strike Force)	.15
67	Mike Mussina (Strike Force)	.20
68	Andy Pettitte (Strike Force)	.40
69	Mariano Rivera (Strike Force)	.15
70	Hideo Nomo (Strike Force)	.30
71	Kevin Brown (Strike Force)	.10
72	Randy Johnson (Strike Force)	.20
73	Felipe Lira	.10
74	Kimera Bartee	.10
75	Alan Trammell	.10
76	Kevin Brown	.10
77	Edgar Renteria	.25
78	Al Leiter	.10
79	Charles Johnson	.10
80	Andre Dawson	.10
81	Billy Wagner	.10
82	Donne Wall	.10
83	Jeff Bagwell	1.25
84	Keith Lockhart	.10
85	Jeff Montgomery	.10
86	Tom Goodwin	.10
87	Tim Belcher	.10

88	Mike Macfarlane	.10
89	Joe Randa	.10
90	Brett Butler	.10
91	Todd Worrell	.10
92	Todd Hollandsworth	.10
93	Ismael Valdes	.10
94	Hideo Nomo	.60
95	Mike Piazza	2.00
96	Jeff Cirillo	.10
97	Ricky Bones	.10
98	Fernando Vina	.10
99	Ben McDonald	.10
100	John Jaha	.10
101	Mark Loretta	.10
102	Paul Molitor	.50
103	Rick Aguilera	.10
104	Marty Cordova	.10
105	Kirby Puckett	.60
106	Dan Naulty	.10
107	Frank Rodriguez	.10
108	Shane Andrews	.10
109	Henry Rodriguez	.10
110	Mark Grudzielanek	.10
111	Pedro J. Martinez	.10
112	Ugueth Urbina	.10
113	David Segui	.10
114	Rey Ordonez	.25
115	Bernard Gilkey	.10
116	Butch Huskey	.10
117	Paul Wilson	.10
118	Alex Ochoa	.10
119	John Franco	.10
120	Dwight Gooden	.10
121	Ruben Rivera	.25
122	Andy Pettitte	.75
123	Tino Martinez	.30
124	Bernie Williams	.50
125	Wade Boggs	.15
126	Paul O'Neill	.10
127	Scott Brosius	.10
128	Ernie Young	.10
129	Doug Johns	.10
130	Geronimo Berroa	.10
131	Jason Giambi	.10
132	John Wasdin	.10
133	Jim Eisenreich	.10
134	Ricky Otero	.10
135	Ricky Bottalico	.10
136	Mark Langston (Defensive Gems)	.10
137	Greg Maddux (Defensive Gems)	1.00
138	Ivan Rodriguez (Defensive Gems)	.20
139	Charles Johnson (Defensive Gems)	.10
140	J.T. Snow (Defensive Gems)	.10
141	Mark Grace (Defensive Gems)	.15
142	Roberto Alomar (Defensive Gems)	.40
143	Craig Biggio (Defensive Gems)	.10
144	Ken Caminiti (Defensive Gems)	.10
145	Matt Williams (Defensive Gems)	.15
146	Omar Vizquel (Defensive Gems)	.10
147	Cal Ripken Jr. (Defensive Gems)	1.25
148	Ozzie Smith (Defensive Gems)	.25
149	Rey Ordonez (Defensive Gems)	.15
150	Ken Griffey Jr. (Defensive Gems)	1.50
151	Devon White (Defensive Gems)	.10
152	Barry Bonds (Defensive Gems)	.50
153	Kenny Lofton (Defensive Gems)	.40
154	Mickey Morandini	.10
155	Gregg Jefferies	.10
156	Curt Schilling	.10
157	Jason Kendall	.10
158	Francisco Cordova	.15
159	Dennis Eckersley	.12
160	Ron Gant	.12
161	Ozzie Smith	.20
162	Brian Jordan	.10
163	John Mabry	.10
164	Andy Ashby	.10
165	Steve Finley	.10
166	Fernando Valenzuela	.10
167	Archi Cianfrocco	.10
168	Wally Joyner	.10
169	Greg Vaughn	.10
170	Barry Bonds	.15

171	William VanLandingham	.10
172	Marvin Benard	.10
173	Rich Aurilia	.10
174	Jay Canizaro	.10
175	Ken Griffey Jr.	3.00
176	Bob Wells	.10
177	Jay Buhner	.20
178	Sterling Hitchcock	.10
179	Edgar Martinez	.10
180	Rusty Greer	.10
181	Dave Nilsson (Global Impact)	.10
182	Larry Walker (Global Impact)	.35
183	Edgar Renteria (Global Impact)	.15
184	Rey Ordonez (Global Impact)	.20
185	Rafael Palmeiro (Global Impact)	.10
186	Osvaldo Fernandez (Global Impact)	.10
187	Raul Mondesi (Global Impact)	.15
188	Manny Ramirez (Global Impact)	.50
189	Sammy Sosa (Global Impact)	.15
190	Robert Eenhoorn (Global Impact)	.10
191	Devon White (Global Impact)	.10
192	Hideo Nomo (Global Impact)	.30
193	Mac Suzuki (Global Impact)	.10
194	Chan Ho Park (Global Impact)	.10
195	Fernando Valenzuela (Global Impact)	.10
196	Andruw Jones (Global Impact)	1.00
197	Vinny Castilla (Global Impact)	.10
198	Dennis Martinez (Global Impact)	.10
199	Ruben Rivera (Global Impact)	.20
200	Juan Gonzalez (Global Impact)	.60
201	Roberto Alomar (Global Impact)	.40
202	Edgar Martinez (Global Impact)	.10
203	Ivan Rodriguez (Global Impact)	.20
204	Carlos Delgado (Global Impact)	.10
205	Andres Galarraga (Global Impact)	.15
206	Ozzie Guillen (Global Impact)	.10
207	Midre Cummings (Global Impact)	.10
208	Roger Pavlik	.10
209	Darren Oliver	.10
210	Dean Palmer	.10
211	Ivan Rodriguez	.60
212	Otis Nixon	.10
213	Pat Hentgen	.10
214	Ozzie Smith, Andre Dawson, Kirby Puckett CL (Season Highlights)	.25
215	Barry Bonds, Gary Sheffield, Brady Anderson CL (Season Highlights)	.25
216	Ken Caminiti CL (Season Highlights)	.10
217	John Smoltz CL (Season Highlights)	.10
218	Eric Young CL (Season Highlights)	.10
219	Juan Gonzalez CL (Season Highlights)	.60
220	Eddie Murray CL (Season Highlights)	.20
221	Tommy Lasorda CL (Season Highlights)	.25
222	Paul Molitor CL (Season Highlights)	.15
223	Luis Castillo	.25
224	Justin Thompson	.10
225	Rocky Coppinger	.10
226	Jermaine Allensworth	.10
227	Jeff D'Amico	.10
228	Jamey Wright	.10
229	Scott Rolen	1.25
230	Darin Erstad	1.25
231	Marty Janzen	.10
232	Jacob Cruz	.10
233	Raul Ibanez	.10

#	Player	Price
234	Nomar Garciaparra	2.00
235	Todd Walker	.60
236	Brian Giles	.10
237	Matt Beech	.10
238	Mike Cameron	.10
239	Jose Paniagua	.10
240	Andruw Jones	2.00
241	Brant Brown (Star Rookies)	.10
242	Robin Jennings (Star Rookies)	.10
243	Willie Adams (Star Rookies)	.10
244	Ken Caminiti (Division Series)	.20
245	Brian Jordan (Division Series)	.10
246	Chipper Jones (Division Series)	2.00
247	Juan Gonzalez (Division Series)	1.50
248	Bernie Williams (Division Series)	.50
249	Roberto Alomar (Division Series)	.50
250	Bernie Williams (Post-Season)	.50
251	David Wells (Post-Season)	.10
252	Cecil Fielder (Post-Season)	.15
253	Darryl Strawberry (Post-Season)	.10
254	Andy Pettitte (Post-Season)	.75
255	Javier Lopez (Post-Season)	.15
256	Gary Gaetti (Post-Season)	.10
257	Ron Gant (Post-Season)	.10
258	Brian Jordan (Post-Season)	.10
259	John Smoltz (Post-Season)	.20
260	Greg Maddux (Post-Season)	2.00
261	Tom Glavine (Post-Season)	.20
262	Chipper Jones (World Series)	2.00
263	Greg Maddux (World Series)	2.00
264	David Cone (World Series)	.15
265	Jim Leyritz (World Series)	.10
266	Andy Pettitte (World Series)	.75
267	John Wetteland (World Series)	.10
268	*Dario Veras* (Star Rookie)	.15
269	Neifi Perez (Star Rookie)	.10
270	Bill Mueller (Star Rookie)	.10
271	Vladimir Guerrero (Star Rookie)	1.50
272	Dmitri Young (Star Rookie)	.10
273	*Nerio Rodriguez* (Star Rookie)	.40
274	Kevin Orie (Star Rookie)	.25
275	Felipe Crespo (Star Rookie)	.10
276	Danny Graves (Star Rookie)	.10
277	Roderick Myers (Star Rookie)	.10
278	*Felix Heredia* (Star Rookie)	.40
279	Ralph Milliard (Star Rookie)	.10
280	Greg Norton (Star Rookie)	.10
281	Derek Wallace (Star Rookie)	.10
282	Trot Nixon (Star Rookie)	.10
283	Bobby Chouinard (Star Rookie)	.10
284	Jay Witasick (Star Rookie)	.10
285	Travis Miller (Star Rookie)	.10
286	Brian Bevil (Star Rookie)	.10
287	Bobby Estalella (Star Rookie)	.10
288	Steve Soderstrom (Star Rookie)	.10
289	Mark Langston	.10
290	Tim Salmon	.25
291	Jim Edmonds	.10
292	Garret Anderson	.10
293	George Arias	.10
294	Gary DiSarcina	.10
295	Chuck Finley	.10
296	Todd Greene	.10
297	Randy Velarde	.10
298	David Justice	.25
299	Ryan Klesko	.50
300	John Smoltz	.20
301	Javier Lopez	.15
302	Greg Maddux	2.00
303	Denny Neagle	.10
304	B.J. Surhoff	.10
305	Chris Hoiles	.10
306	Eric Davis	.10
307	Scott Erickson	.10
308	Mike Bordick	.10
309	John Valentin	.10
310	Heathcliff Slocumb	.10
311	Tom Gordon	.10
312	Mike Stanley	.10
313	Reggie Jefferson	.10
314	Darren Bragg	.10
315	Troy O'Leary	.10
316	John Mabry (Season Highlight)	.10
317	Mark Whiten (Season Highlight)	.10
318	Edgar Martinez (Season Highlight)	.10
319	Alex Rodriguez (Season Highlight)	1.50
320	Mark McGwire (Season Highlight)	.50
321	Hideo Nomo (Season Highlight)	.25
322	Todd Hundley (Season Highlight)	.15
323	Barry Bonds (Season Highlight)	.40
324	Andruw Jones (Season Highlight)	1.50
325	Ryne Sandberg	.75
326	Brian McRae	.10
327	Frank Castillo	.10
328	Shawon Dunston	.10
329	Ray Durham	.10
330	Robin Ventura	.10
331	Ozzie Guillen	.10
332	Roberto Hernandez	.10
333	Albert Belle	1.00
334	Dave Martinez	.10
335	Willie Greene	.10
336	Jeff Brantley	.10
337	Kevin Jarvis	.10
338	John Smiley	.10
339	Eddie Taubensee	.10
340	Bret Boone	.10
341	Kevin Seitzer	.10
342	Jack McDowell	.10
343	Sandy Alomar Jr.	.10
344	Chad Curtis	.10
345	Manny Ramirez	.75
346	Chad Ogea	.10
347	Jim Thome	.40
348	Mark Thompson	.10
349	Ellis Burks	.10
350	Andres Galarraga	.20
351	Vinny Castilla	.10
352	Kirt Manwaring	.10
353	Larry Walker	.25
354	Omar Olivares	.10
355	Bobby Higginson	.10
356	Melvin Nieves	.10
357	Brian Johnson	.10
358	Devon White	.10
359	Jeff Conine	.10
360	Gary Sheffield	.35
361	Robb Nen	.10
362	Mike Hampton	.10
363	Bob Abreu	.10
364	Luis Gonzalez	.10
365	Derek Bell	.10
366	Sean Berry	.10
367	Craig Biggio	.10
368	Darryl Kile	.10
369	Shane Reynolds	.10
370	Jeff Bagwell (Capture the Flag)	.60
371	Ron Gant (Capture the Flag)	.15
372	Andy Benes (Capture the Flag)	.10
373	Gary Gaetti (Capture the Flag)	.10
374	Ramon Martinez (Capture the Flag)	.10
375	Raul Mondesi (Capture the Flag)	.15
376	Steve Finley (Capture the Flag)	.10
377	Ken Caminiti (Capture the Flag)	.20
378	Tony Gwynn (Capture the Flag)	.75
379	Dario Veras (Capture the Flag)	.10
380	Andy Pettitte (Capture the Flag)	.40
381	Ruben Rivera (Capture the Flag)	.20
382	David Cone (Capture the Flag)	.10
383	Roberto Alomar (Capture the Flag)	.30
384	Edgar Martinez (Capture the Flag)	.10
385	Ken Griffey Jr. (Capture the Flag)	1.50
386	Mark McGwire (Capture the Flag)	.50
387	Rusty Greer (Capture the Flag)	.10
388	Jose Rosado	.10
389	Kevin Appier	.10
390	Johnny Damon	.10
391	Jose Offerman	.10
392	Michael Tucker	.10
393	Craig Paquette	.10
394	Bip Roberts	.10
395	Ramon Martinez	.10
396	Greg Gagne	.10
397	Chan Ho Park	.10
398	Karim Garcia	.20
399	Wilton Guerrero	.20
400	Eric Karros	.10
401	Raul Mondesi	.20
402	Matt Mieske	.10
403	Mike Fetters	.10
404	Dave Nilsson	.10
405	Jose Valentin	.10
406	Scott Karl	.10
407	Marc Newfield	.10
408	Cal Eldred	.10
409	Rich Becker	.10
410	Terry Steinbach	.10
411	Chuck Knoblauch	.20
412	Pat Meares	.10
413	Brad Radke	.10
414	not issued	.10
415a	Kirby Puckett (should be #414)	1.25
415b	Andruw Jones (Griffey Hot List)	6.00
416	Chipper Jones (Griffey Hot List)	6.00
417	Mo Vaughn (Griffey Hot List)	2.50
418	Frank Thomas (Griffey Hot List)	10.00
419	Albert Belle (Griffey Hot List)	3.00
420	Mark McGwire (Griffey Hot List)	4.00
421	Derek Jeter (Griffey Hot List)	6.00
422	Alex Rodriguez (Griffey Hot List)	10.00
423	Juan Gonzalez (Griffey Hot List)	5.00
424	Ken Griffey Jr. (Griffey Hot List)	12.00
425	Rondell White	.10
426	Darrin Fletcher	.10
427	Cliff Floyd	.10
428	Mike Lansing	.10
429	F.P. Santangelo	.10
430	Todd Hundley	.20
431	Mark Clark	.10
432	Pete Harnisch	.10
433	Jason Isringhausen	.10
434	Bobby Jones	.10
435	Lance Johnson	.10
436	Carlos Baerga	.10
437	Mariano Duncan	.10
438	David Cone	.20
439	Mariano Rivera	.20
440	Derek Jeter	2.00
441	Joe Girardi	.10
442	Charlie Hayes	.10
443	Tim Raines	.10
444	Darryl Strawberry	.10
445	Cecil Fielder	.20
446	Ariel Prieto	.10
447	Tony Batista	.10
448	Brent Gates	.10
449	Scott Spiezio	.10
450	Mark McGwire	1.00
451	Don Wengert	.10
452	Mike Lieberthal	.10
453	Lenny Dykstra	.10
454	Rex Hudler	.10
455	Darren Daulton	.10
456	Kevin Stocker	.10
457	Trey Beamon	.10
458	Midre Cummings	.10
459	Mark Johnson	.10
460	Al Martin	.10
461	Kevin Elster	.10
462	Jon Lieber	.10
463	Jason Schmidt	.10
464	Paul Wagner	.10
465	Andy Benes	.10
466	Alan Benes	.20
467	Royce Clayton	.10
468	Gary Gaetti	.10
469	Curt Lyons (Diamond Debuts)	.10
470	Eugene Kingsale (Diamond Debuts)	.10
471	Damian Jackson (Diamond Debuts)	.10
472	Wendell Magee (Diamond Debuts)	.10
473	Kevin L. Brown (Diamond Debuts)	.10
474	Raul Casanova (Diamond Debuts)	.10
475	Ramiro Mendoza (Diamond Debuts)	.10
476	Todd Dunn (Diamond Debuts)	.10
477	Chad Mottola (Diamond Debuts)	.10
478	Andy Larkin (Diamond Debuts)	.10
479	Jaime Bluma (Diamond Debuts)	.10
480	Mac Suzuki (Diamond Debuts)	.10
481	Brian Banks (Diamond Debuts)	.10
482	Desi Wilson (Diamond Debuts)	.10
483	Einar Diaz (Diamond Debuts)	.10
484	Tom Pagnozzi	.10
485	Ray Lankford	.10
486	Todd Stottlemyre	.10
487	Donovan Osborne	.10
488	Trevor Hoffman	.10
489	Chris Gomez	.10
490	Ken Caminiti	.30
491	John Flaherty	.10
492	Tony Gwynn	1.25
493	Joey Hamilton	.10
494	Rickey Henderson	.10
495	Glenallen Hill	.10
496	Rod Beck	.10
497	Osvaldo Fernandez	.10
498	Rick Wilkins	.10
499	Joey Cora	.10
500	Alex Rodriguez	3.00
501	Randy Johnson	.60
502	Paul Sorrento	.10
503	Dan Wilson	.10
504	Jamie Moyer	.10
505	Will Clark	.25
506	Mickey Tettleton	.10
507	John Burkett	.10
508	Ken Hill	.10
509	Mark McLemore	.10
510	Juan Gonzalez	1.25
511	Bobby Witt	.10
512	Carlos Delgado	.10
513	Alex Gonzalez	.10
514	Shawn Green	.10
515	Joe Carter	.20
516	Juan Guzman	.10
517	Charlie O'Brien	.10
518	Ed Sprague	.10
519	Mike Timlin	.10
520	Roger Clemens	1.00
521	Eddie Murray	.35
522	Jason Dickson	.20
523	Jim Leyritz	.10
524	Michael Tucker	.10
525	Kenny Lofton	1.00
526	Jimmy Key	.10
527	Mel Rojas	.10
528	Deion Sanders	.25
529	Bartolo Colon	.10
530	Matt Williams	.40
531	Marquis Grissom	.10
532	David Justice	.25
533	Bubba Trammell	1.00
534	Moises Alou	.10
535	Bobby Bonilla	.10
536	Alex Fernandez	.10
537	Jay Bell	.10
538	Chili Davis	.10
539	Jeff King	.10
540	Todd Zeile	.10
541	John Olerud	.10
542	Jose Guillen	1.50
543	Derrek Lee	.10
544	Dante Powell	.10
545	J.T. Snow	.10
546	Jeff Kent	.10
547	Jose Cruz	8.00
548	John Wetteland	.10
549	Orlando Merced	.10
550	Hideki Irabu	2.00

1997 Upper Deck Amazing Greats

The 20-card, regular-sized insert set was included every 138 packs of 1997 Upper Deck baseball. The cards include real wood with two player shots imaged on the card front. The team logo appears in the upper right corner of the horizontal card. The cards are numbered with the "AG" prefix.

	MT
Complete Set (20):	600.00
Common Player:	10.00
AG1 Ken Griffey Jr.	80.00
AG2 Roberto Alomar	15.00
AG3 Alex Rodriguez	70.00
AG4 Paul Molitor	15.00
AG5 Chipper Jones	50.00
AG6 Tony Gwynn	40.00
AG7 Kenny Lofton	20.00
AG8 Albert Belle	30.00
AG9 Matt Williams	10.00
AG10 Frank Thomas	80.00
AG11 Greg Maddux	50.00
AG12 Sammy Sosa	12.00
AG13 Kirby Puckett	30.00
AG14 Jeff Bagwell	30.00
AG15 Cal Ripken Jr.	60.00
AG16 Manny Ramirez	20.00
AG17 Barry Bonds	20.00
AG18 Mo Vaughn	20.00
AG19 Eddie Murray	15.00
AG20 Mike Piazza	50.00

1997 Upper Deck Blue Chip Prospects

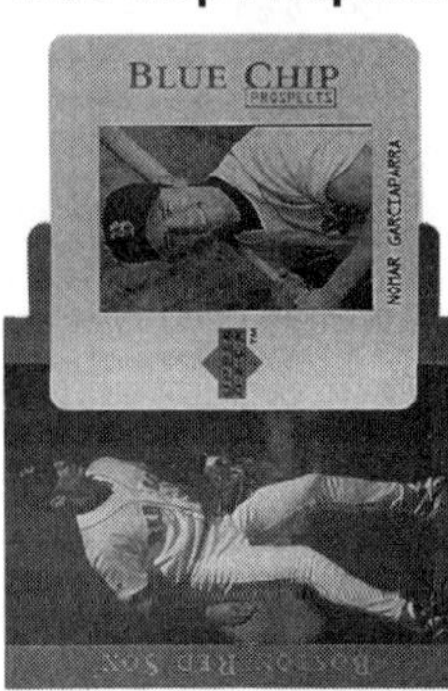

This 20-card insert was found in packs of Series II and features a die-cut design. Cards appear to have a photo slide attached to them featuring a portrait shot of the promising youngster depicted on the card. A total of 500 of each card were produced.

	MT
Complete Set (20):	800.00
Common Player:	10.00
BC1 Andruw Jones	100.00
BC2 Derek Jeter	100.00
BC3 Scott Rolen	90.00
BC4 Manny Ramirez	30.00
BC5 Todd Walker	25.00
BC6 Rocky Coppinger	10.00
BC7 Nomar Garciaparra	100.00
BC8 Darin Erstad	70.00
BC9 Jermaine Dye	10.00
BC10 Vladimir Guerrero	80.00
BC11 Edgar Renteria	10.00
BC12 Bob Abreu	10.00
BC13 Karim Garcia	20.00
BC14 Jeff D'Amico	10.00
BC15 Chipper Jones	100.00
BC16 Todd Hollandsworth	10.00
BC17 Andy Pettitte	30.00
BC18 Ruben Rivera	15.00
BC19 Jason Kendall	10.00
BC20 Alex Rodriguez	120.00

1997 Upper Deck Game Jersey

The three-card, regular-sized set was inserted every 800 packs of Upper Deck Series I. The cards contained a square of the player's game-used jersey, and carried a "GJ" card number prefix.

	MT
Complete Set (3):	800.00
Common Player:	100.00
GJ1 Ken Griffey Jr.	600.00
GJ2 Tony Gwynn	300.00
GJ3 Rey Ordonez	100.00

1997 Upper Deck Home Team Heroes

These large-format cards were issued both as a 12-card boxed set (original price about $20) and as a blister-pack insert to enhance the sales of special Collector's Choice team sets at Wal-Mart. Each $4.99 pack contains a 14-card team set and a Home Team Heroes card of one of 12 teams, plus a random assortment of Collector's Choice cards. The Heroes cards are 5" x 3-1/2" with a die-cut pattern at top. Fronts are rendered in team colors with two player action photos superimposed on a background of the players' home ballpark. The ballpark scene is executed in etched silver foil and there are silver-foil graphics around the card front. Backs are conventionally printed with small photos and a few sentences about each player.

		MT
Complete Set (12):		20.00
Common Player:		2.00
1	Alex Rodriguez, Ken Griffey Jr.	5.00
2	Bernie Williams, Derek Jeter	2.50
3	Bernard Gilkey, Randy Hundley	2.00
4	Hideo Nomo, Mike Piazza	3.50
5	Andruw Jones, Chipper Jones	3.50
6	John Smoltz, Greg Maddux	2.50
7	Mike Mussina, Cal Ripken Jr.	3.50
8	Andres Galarraga, Dante Bichette	2.00
9	Juan Gonzalez, Ivan Rodriguez	2.50
10	Albert Belle, Frank Thomas	5.00
11	Jim Thome, Manny Ramirez	2.00
12	Ken Caminiti, Tony Gwynn	2.50

1997 Upper Deck Hot Commodities

This 20-card insert from Series II features a flame pattern behind the image of the player depicted on the front of the card. Odds of finding a card were 1:13 packs.

	MT
Complete Set (20):	130.00
Common Player:	2.50
HC1 Alex Rodriguez	12.00
HC2 Andruw Jones	10.00
HC3 Derek Jeter	10.00
HC4 Frank Thomas	15.00
HC5 Ken Griffey Jr.	15.00
HC6 Chipper Jones	10.00
HC7 Juan Gonzalez	8.00
HC8 Cal Ripken Jr.	12.00
HC9 John Smoltz	2.50
HC10 Mark McGwire	6.00
HC11 Barry Bonds	4.00
HC12 Albert Belle	5.00
HC13 Mike Piazza	10.00
HC14 Manny Ramirez	4.00
HC15 Mo Vaughn	4.00
HC16 Tony Gwynn	8.00
HC17 Vladimir Guerrero	8.00
HC18 Hideo Nomo	3.50
HC19 Greg Maddux	10.00
HC20 Kirby Puckett	8.00

1997 Upper Deck Jackie Robinson Jumbos

The nine Jackie Robinson commemorative cards which lead off the '97 Upper Deck set were also issued in a large-format (3-1/2" x 5") version as a complete boxed set. The jumbos are printed in sepia tones on gold-foil backgrounds and, like the standard-size cards, are highlighted with silver-foil graphics on front. Backs are also identical to the regular cards. Complete sets only were sold in a gold-foil stamped box with the 50th anniversary logo.

		MT
Complete Set (10):		20.00
Common Player:		3.00
1	The Beginnings (Jackie Robinson)	3.00
2	Breaking the Barrier (Jackie Robinson)	3.00
3	The MVP Season (Jackie Robinson)	3.00
4	The '51 Season (Jackie Robinson)	3.00
5	The '52 and '53 Seasons (Jackie Robinson)	3.00
6	The '54 Season (Jackie Robinson)	3.00
7	The '55 Season (Jackie Robinson)	3.00
8	The '56 Season (Jackie Robinson)	3.00
9	The Hall of Fame (Jackie Robinson)	3.00
--	Checklist	.10

1997 Upper Deck Long Distance Connection

This 20-card insert from Series II features the top home run hitters in the game. Odds of finding a card were 1:35 packs.

	MT
Complete Set (20):	200.00
Common Player:	4.00
LD1 Mark McGwire	12.00
LD2 Brady Anderson	4.00
LD3 Ken Griffey Jr.	35.00
LD4 Albert Belle	10.00
LD5 Juan Gonzalez	18.00
LD6 Andres Galarraga	4.00
LD7 Jay Buhner	4.00
LD8 Mo Vaughn	8.00
LD9 Barry Bonds	8.00
LD10 Gary Sheffield	6.00
LD11 Todd Hundley	4.00
LD12 Frank Thomas	35.00
LD13 Sammy Sosa	6.00
LD14 Rafael Palmeiro	4.00
LD15 Alex Rodriguez	30.00
LD16 Mike Piazza	20.00
LD17 Ken Caminiti	6.00
LD18 Chipper Jones	20.00
LD19 Manny Ramirez	8.00
LD20 Andruw Jones	20.00

1997 Upper Deck Power Package

The 20-card, regular-sized, die-cut set was inserted every 23 packs of 1997 Upper Deck baseball. The player's name is printed in gold foil along the top border of the card face, which also features Light F/X. The die-cut cards have a silver-foil border and team-color frame with a "Power Package" logo in gold foil centered on the bottom border. The card backs have a short highlight in a brown box bordered by team colors and are numbered with the "PP" prefix.

	MT
Complete Set (20):	140.00
Common Player:	3.00
PP1 Ken Griffey Jr.	30.00
PP2 Joe Carter	3.00
PP3 Rafael Palmeiro	3.00
PP4 Jay Buhner	3.00
PP5 Sammy Sosa	4.00
PP6 Fred McGriff	3.00
PP7 Jeff Bagwell	12.00
PP8 Albert Belle	10.00
PP9 Matt Williams	3.00
PP10Mark McGwire	12.00
PP11Gary Sheffield	5.00
PP12Tim Salmon	3.00
PP13Ryan Klesko	4.00
PP14Manny Ramirez	8.00
PP15Mike Piazza	20.00
PP16Barry Bonds	8.00
PP17Mo Vaughn	8.00
PP18Jose Canseco	3.00
PP19Juan Gonzalez	15.00
PP20Frank Thomas	30.00

1997 Upper Deck Power Package Jumbos

Unlike the regular Power Package inserts found in Series I packs, these jumbo versions are not die-cut. The 5" x 7" jumbos are found one per retail foil box of Series I.

	MT
Complete Set (20):	130.00
Common Player:	3.00
PP1 Ken Griffey Jr.	15.00
PP2 Joe Carter	3.00
PP3 Rafael Palmeiro	3.00
PP4 Jay Buhner	3.00
PP5 Sammy Sosa	3.00
PP6 Fred McGriff	5.00
PP7 Jeff Bagwell	7.50
PP8 Albert Belle	8.00
PP9 Matt Williams	3.00
PP10Mark McGwire	6.00
PP11Gary Sheffield	3.00
PP12Tim Salmon	3.00
PP13Ryan Klesko	6.00
PP14Manny Ramirez	6.00
PP15Mike Piazza	12.00
PP16Barry Bonds	10.00
PP17Mo Vaughn	7.50
PP18Jose Canseco	5.00
PP19Juan Gonzalez	10.00
PP20Frank Thomas	15.00

1997 Upper Deck Predictor

A new concept in interactive cards was UD's Series II Predictor inserts. Each player's card has four scratch-off baseball bats at the top-right. Under each bat is printed a specific accomplishment - hit for cycle, CG shutout, etc. - If the player attained that goal during the '97 season, and if the collector had scratched off the correct bat among the four, the Predictor card could be redeemed (with $2) for a premium TV cel card of the player. Thus if the player made one of his goals, the collector had a 25% chance of choosing the right bat. Two goals

gave a 50% chance, etc. The Predictor cards have color action photos of the players at the left end of the horizontal format. The background at left and bottom is a red scorecard motif. Behind the bats is a black-and-white stadium scene. Backs repeat the red scorecard design with contest rules printed in white. A (W) in the checklist here indicates the player won one or more of his goals making his cards eligible for redemption. The redemption period ended Nov. 22, 1997. Values shown are for unscratched cards.

		MT
Complete Set (30):		40.00
Common Player:		.50
Prices for Unscratched Cards		
1	Andruw Jones	3.00
2	Chipper Jones	3.00
3	Greg Maddux (W)	3.00
4	Fred McGriff (W)	.75
5	John Smoltz (W)	.75
6	Brady Anderson (W)	.50
7	Cal Ripken Jr. (W)	4.00
8	Mo Vaughn (W)	1.25
9	Sammy Sosa	1.00
10	Albert Belle (W)	1.50
11	Frank Thomas	5.00
12	Kenny Lofton (W)	1.25
13	Jim Thome	.75
14	Dante Bichette (W)	.60
15	Andres Galarraga	.75
16	Gary Sheffield	1.00
17	Hideo Nomo (W)	1.00
18	Mike Piazza (W)	3.00
19	Derek Jeter (W)	3.00
20	Bernie Williams	1.00
21	Mark McGwire (W)	1.50
22	Ken Caminiti (W)	.75
23	Tony Gwynn (W)	2.50
24	Barry Bonds (W)	1.25
25	Jay Buhner (W)	.50
26	Ken Griffey Jr. (W)	5.00
27	Alex Rodriguez (W)	4.00
28	Juan Gonzalez (W)	2.50
29	Dean Palmer (W)	.50
30	Roger Clemens (W)	1.50

1997 Upper Deck Rock Solid Foundation

The 20-card, regular-sized set was inserted every seven packs of 1997 Upper Deck baseball. The card fronts feature rainbow foil with the player's name in silver foil along the top border. The team logo appears in gold foil in the lower right corner with "Rock Solid Foundation" also printed in gold foil over a marbled background. The card backs have the same marbled background with a close-up shot on the upper half. A short text is also included and the cards are numbered with the "RS" prefix.

	MT
Complete Set (20):	50.00
Common Player:	2.00
RS1 Alex Rodriguez	15.00
RS2 Rey Ordonez	3.00
RS3 Derek Jeter	10.00
RS4 Darin Erstad	10.00
RS5 Chipper Jones	10.00
RS6 Johnny Damon	3.00
RS7 Ryan Klesko	3.00
RS8 Charles Johnson	2.00
RS9 Andy Pettitte	6.00
RS10Manny Ramirez	5.00
RS11Ivan Rodriguez	3.00
RS12Jason Kendall	2.00
RS13Rondell White	2.00
RS14Alex Ochoa	2.00
RS15Javy Lopez	2.00
RS16Pedro J. Martinez	2.00
RS17Carlos Delgado	2.00
RS18Paul Wilson	3.00
RS19Alan Benes	2.00
RS20Raul Mondesi	3.00

1997 Upper Deck Run Producers

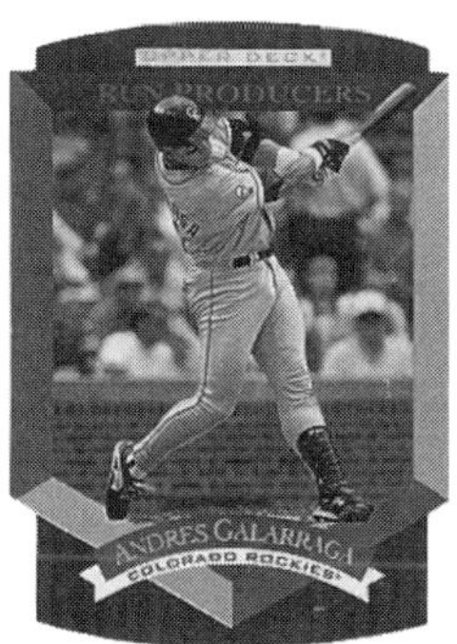

A 24-card insert found in Series II, Run Producers salutes the top offensive players in the game. Cards were inserted 1:69 packs.

	MT
Complete Set (24):	350.00
Common Player:	8.00
RP1 Ken Griffey Jr.	60.00
RP2 Barry Bonds	15.00
RP3 Albert Belle	20.00
RP4 Mark McGwire	25.00
RP5 Frank Thomas	60.00
RP6 Juan Gonzalez	30.00
RP7 Brady Anderson	8.00
RP8 Andres Galarraga	8.00
RP9 Rafael Palmeiro	8.00
RP10Alex Rodriguez	50.00
RP11Jay Buhner	8.00
RP12Gary Sheffield	10.00
RP13Sammy Sosa	10.00
RP14Dante Bichette	8.00
RP15Mike Piazza	40.00
RP16Manny Ramirez	15.00
RP17Kenny Lofton	15.00
RP18Mo Vaughn	15.00
RP19Tim Salmon	8.00
RP20Chipper Jones	40.00
RP21Jim Thome	12.00
RP22Ken Caminiti	10.00
RP23Jeff Bagwell	25.00
RP24Paul Molitor	12.00

1997 Upper Deck Ticket to Stardom

The 20-card, regular-sized, die-cut set was inserted every 34 packs of 1997 Upper Deck baseball. Card fronts have a gold-foil border on three sides with a portrait and action photo. Half of the player's league emblem appears on either the left or right border of the horizontal cards, as two cards can be placed together to form a "ticket." The card backs feature an in-depth text with the same headshot as the card front and are numbered with the "TS" prefix.

	MT
Complete Set (20):	150.00
Common Player:	4.00
TS1 Chipper Jones	25.00
TS2 Jermaine Dye	3.00
TS3 Rey Ordonez	4.00
TS4 Alex Ochoa	4.00
TS5 Derek Jeter	25.00
TS6 Ruben Rivera	5.00
TS7 Billy Wagner	4.00
TS8 Jason Kendall	4.00
TS9 Darin Erstad	20.00
TS10Alex Rodriguez	30.00
TS11Bob Abreu	4.00
TS12Richard Hidalgo	4.00
TS13Karim Garcia	5.00
TS14Andruw Jones	25.00
TS15Carlos Delgado	4.00
TS16Rocky Coppinger	4.00
TS17Jeff D'Amico	4.00
TS18Johnny Damon	4.00
TS19John Wasdin	4.00
TS20Manny Ramirez	8.00

1997 Collector's Choice

The 246-card, regular-sized set contained four subsets: Rookie Class (1-27), Leaders (56-63), Postseason (218-224) and Ken Griffey Jr. Checklists (244-246). Insert sets are: Stick'Ums, Premier Power, Clearly Dominant and The Big Show. The base card fronts feature a color action shot with the player's name appearing on the bottom edge. The team logo is located in the lower left corner and each card features a white border. The card backs contain another action shot on the upper half portion with bio, stat and career/season information included. The cards came in 12-card packs and retailed for 99 cents.

		MT
Complete Set (506):		30.00
Complete Series 1 Set (246):		15.00
Complete Series 2 Set (260):		18.00
Common Player:		.05
Series 1 Wax Box:		28.00
Series 2 Wax Box:		35.00
1	Andruw Jones (Rookie Class)	1.25
2	Rocky Coppinger (Rookie Class)	.05
3	Jeff D'Amico (Rookie Class)	.05
4	Dmitri Young (Rookie Class)	.05
5	Darin Erstad (Rookie Class)	.75
6	Jermaine Allensworth (Rookie Class)	.05
7	Damian Jackson (Rookie Class)	.05
8	Bill Mueller (Rookie Class)	.05
9	Jacob Cruz (Rookie Class)	.40
10	Vladimir Guerrero (Rookie Class)	.75
11	Marty Janzen (Rookie Class)	.05
12	Kevin L. Brown (Rookie Class)	.05
13	Willie Adams (Rookie Class)	.05
14	Wendell Magee (Rookie Class)	.05
15	Scott Rolen (Rookie Class)	1.00
16	Matt Beech (Rookie Class)	.05
17	Neifi Perez (Rookie Class)	.05

No.	Player	Value
18	Jamey Wright (Rookie Class)	.05
19	Jose Paniagua (Rookie Class)	.05
20	Todd Walker (Rookie Class)	.40
21	Justin Thompson (Rookie Class)	.05
22	Robin Jennings (Rookie Class)	.05
23	*Dario Veras* (Rookie Class)	.05
24	Brian Lesher (Rookie Class)	.05
25	Nomar Garciaparra (Rookie Class)	1.25
26	Luis Castillo (Rookie Class)	.10
27	Brian Giles (Rookie Class)	.05
28	Jermaine Dye	.15
29	Terrell Wade	.05
30	Fred McGriff	.25
31	Marquis Grissom	.05
32	Ryan Klesko	.30
33	Javier Lopez	.10
34	Mark Wohlers	.05
35	Tom Glavine	.15
36	Denny Neagle	.05
37	Scott Erickson	.05
38	Chris Hoiles	.05
39	Roberto Alomar	.50
40	Eddie Murray	.30
41	Cal Ripken Jr.	1.50
42	Randy Myers	.05
43	B.J. Surhoff	.05
44	Rick Krivda	.05
45	Jose Canseco	.20
46	Heathcliff Slocumb	.05
47	Jeff Suppan	.05
48	Tom Gordon	.05
49	Aaron Sele	.05
50	Mo Vaughn	.75
51	Darren Bragg	.05
52	Wil Cordero	.05
53	Scott Bullett	.05
54	Terry Adams	.05
55	Jackie Robinson	.05
56	Tony Gwynn, Alex Rodriguez (Batting Leaders)	.50
57	Andres Galarraga, Mark McGwire (Homer Leaders)	.20
58	Andres Galarraga, Albert Belle (RBI Leaders)	.30
59	Eric Young, Kenny Lofton (SB Leaders)	.15
60	John Smoltz, Andy Pettitte (Victory Leaders)	.25
61	John Smoltz, Roger Clemens (Strikout Leaders)	.30
62	Kevin Brown, Juan Guzman (ERA Leaders)	.05
63	John Wetteland, Todd Worrell, Jeff Brantley (Save Leaders)	.05
64	Scott Servais	.05
65	Sammy Sosa	.25
66	Ryne Sandberg	.60
67	Frank Castillo	.05
68	Rey Sanchez	.05
69	Steve Trachsel	.05
70	Robin Ventura	.05
71	Wilson Alvarez	.05
72	Tony Phillips	.05
73	Lyle Mouton	.05
74	Mike Cameron	.05
75	Harold Baines	.05
76	Albert Belle	.75
77	Chris Snopek	.05
78	Reggie Sanders	.05
79	Jeff Brantley	.05
80	Barry Larkin	.20
81	Kevin Jarvis	.05
82	John Smiley	.05
83	Pete Schourek	.05
84	Thomas Howard	.05
85	Lee Smith	.05
86	Omar Vizquel	.05
87	Julio Franco	.05
88	Orel Hershiser	.05
89	Charles Nagy	.05
90	Matt Williams	.20
91	Dennis Martinez	.05
92	Jose Mesa	.05
93	Sandy Alomar Jr.	.05
94	Jim Thome	.25
95	Vinny Castilla	.05
96	Armando Reynoso	.05
97	Kevin Ritz	.05
98	Larry Walker	.20
99	Eric Young	.05
100	Dante Bichette	.15
101	Quinton McCracken	.05
102	John Vander Wal	.05
103	Phil Nevin	.05
104	Tony Clark	.40
105	Alan Trammell	.05
106	Felipe Lira	.05
107	Curtis Pride	.05
108	Bobby Higginson	.05
109	Mark Lewis	.05
110	Travis Fryman	.05
111	Al Leiter	.05
112	Devon White	.05
113	Jeff Conine	.05
114	Charles Johnson	.05
115	Andre Dawson	.05
116	Edgar Renteria	.20
117	Robb Nen	.05
118	Kevin Brown	.05
119	Derek Bell	.05
120	Bob Abreu	.05
121	Mike Hampton	.05
122	Todd Jones	.05
123	Billy Wagner	.10
124	Shane Reynolds	.05
125	Jeff Bagwell	1.00
126	Brian L. Hunter	.05
127	Jeff Montgomery	.05
128	*Rod Myers*	.05
129	Tim Belcher	.05
130	Kevin Appier	.05
131	Mike Sweeney	.05
132	Craig Paquette	.05
133	Joe Randa	.05
134	Michael Tucker	.05
135	Raul Mondesi	.20
136	Tim Wallach	.05
137	Brett Butler	.05
138	Karim Garcia	.35
139	Todd Hollandsworth	.15
140	Eric Karros	.05
141	Hideo Nomo	.35
142	Ismael Valdes	.05
143	Cal Eldred	.05
144	Scott Karl	.05
145	Matt Mieske	.05
146	Mike Fetters	.05
147	Mark Loretta	.05
148	Fernando Vina	.05
149	Jeff Cirillo	.05
150	Dave Nilsson	.05
151	Kirby Puckett	1.00
152	Rich Becker	.05
153	Chuck Knoblauch	.15
154	Marty Cordova	.05
155	Paul Molitor	.25
156	Rick Aguilera	.05
157	Pat Meares	.05
158	Frank Rodriguez	.05
159	David Segui	.05
160	Henry Rodriguez	.05
161	Shane Andrews	.05
162	Pedro J. Martinez	.05
163	Mark Grudzielanek	.05
164	Mike Lansing	.05
165	Rondell White	.05
166	Ugueth Urbina	.05
167	Rey Ordonez	.20
168	Robert Person	.05
169	Carlos Baerga	.15
170	Bernard Gilkey	.05
171	John Franco	.05
172	Pete Harnisch	.05
173	Butch Huskey	.05
174	Paul Wilson	.15
175	Bernie Williams	.25
176	Dwight Gooden	.05
177	Wade Boggs	.15
178	Ruben Rivera	.20
179	Jim Leyritz	.05
180	Derek Jeter	1.00
181	Tino Martinez	.15
182	Tim Raines	.05
183	Scott Brosius	.05
184	Jason Giambi	.15
185	Geronimo Berroa	.05
186	Ariel Prieto	.05
187	Scott Spiezio	.05
188	John Wasdin	.05
189	Ernie Young	.05
190	Mark McGwire	.75
191	Jim Eisenreich	.05
192	Ricky Bottalico	.05
193	Darren Daulton	.05
194	David Doster	.05
195	Gregg Jefferies	.05
196	Lenny Dykstra	.05
197	Curt Schilling	.05
198	Todd Stottlemyre	.05
199	Willie McGee	.05
200	Ozzie Smith	.35
201	Dennis Eckersley	.05
202	Ray Lankford	.05
203	John Mabry	.05
204	Alan Benes	.05
205	Ron Gant	.10
206	Archi Cianfrocco	.05
207	Fernando Valenzuela	.05
208	Greg Vaughn	.05
209	Steve Finley	.05
210	Tony Gwynn	.75
211	Rickey Henderson	.05
212	Trevor Hoffman	.05
213	Jason Thompson	.05
214	Osvaldo Fernandez	.05
215	Glenallen Hill	.05
216	William VanLandingham	.05
217	Marvin Benard	.05
218	Juan Gonzalez (Postseason)	.40
219	Roberto Alomar (Postseason)	.25
220	Brian Jordan (Postseason)	.05
221	John Smoltz (Postseason)	.15
222	Javy Lopez (Postseason)	.05
223	Bernie Williams (Postseason)	.20
224	Jim Leyritz, John Wetteland (Postseason)	.05
225	Barry Bonds	.60
226	Rich Aurilia	.05
227	Jay Canizaro	.05
228	Dan Wilson	.05
229	Bob Wolcott	.05
230	Ken Griffey Jr.	2.00
231	Sterling Hitchcock	.05
232	Edgar Martinez	.05
233	Joey Cora	.05
234	Norm Charlton	.05
235	Alex Rodriguez	2.00
236	Bobby Witt	.05
237	Darren Oliver	.05
238	Kevin Elster	.05
239	Rusty Greer	.05
240	Juan Gonzalez	1.00
241	Will Clark	.20
242	Dean Palmer	.05
243	Ivan Rodriguez	.30
244	Checklist (Ken Griffey Jr.)	.50
245	Checklist (Ken Griffey Jr.)	.50
246	Checklist (Ken Griffey Jr.)	.50
247	Ken Griffey Jr. CL	.50
248	Ken Griffey Jr. CL	.50
249	Ken Griffey Jr. CL	.50
250	Eddie Murray	.25
251	Troy Percival	.05
252	Garret Anderson	.05
253	Allen Watson	.05
254	Jason Dickson	.15
255	Jim Edmonds	.10
256	Chuck Finley	.05
257	Randy Velarde	.05
258	Shigetosi Hasegawa	.05
259	Todd Greene	.05
260	Tim Salmon	.20
261	Mark Langston	.05
262	Dave Hollins	.05
263	Gary DiSarcina	.05
264	Kenny Lofton	.50
265	John Smoltz	.15
266	Greg Maddux	1.25
267	Jeff Blauser	.05
268	Alan Embree	.05
269	Mark Lemke	.05
270	Chipper Jones	1.25
271	Mike Mussina	.35
272	Rafael Palmeiro	.15
273	Jimmy Key	.05
274	Mike Bordick	.05
275	Brady Anderson	.10
276	Eric Davis	.05
277	Jeffrey Hammonds	.05
278	Reggie Jefferson	.05
279	Tim Naehring	.05
280	John Valentin	.05
281	Troy O'Leary	.05
282	Shane Mack	.05
283	Mike Stanley	.05
284	Tim Wakefield	.05
285	Brian McRae	.05
286	Brooks Kieschnick	.05
287	Shawon Dunston	.05
288	Kevin Foster	.05
289	Mel Rojas	.05
290	Mark Grace	.15
291	Brant Brown	.05
292	Amaury Telemaco	.05
293	Dave Martinez	.05
294	Jaime Navarro	.05
295	Ray Durham	.05
296	Ozzie Guillen	.05
297	Roberto Hernandez	.05
298	Ron Karkovice	.05
299	James Baldwin	.05
300	Frank Thomas	2.00
301	Eddie Taubensee	.05
302	Bret Boone	.05
303	Willie Greene	.05
304	Dave Burba	.05
305	Deion Sanders	.20
306	Reggie Sanders	.05
307	Hal Morris	.05
308	Pokey Reese	.05
309	Tony Fernandez	.05
310	Manny Ramirez	.50
311	Chad Ogea	.05
312	Jack McDowell	.05
313	Kevin Mitchell	.05
314	Chad Curtis	.05
315	Steve Kline	.05
316	Kevin Seitzer	.05
317	Kirt Manwaring	.05
318	Bill Swift	.05
319	Ellis Burks	.05
320	Andres Galarraga	.15
321	Bruce Ruffin	.05
322	Mark Thompson	.05
323	Walt Weiss	.05
324	Todd Jones	.05
325	Andruw Jones (Griffey Hot List)	.60
326	Chipper Jones (Griffey Hot List)	.60
327	Mo Vaughn (Griffey Hot List)	.25
328	Frank Thomas (Griffey Hot List)	1.00
329	Albert Belle (Griffey Hot List)	.35
330	Mark McGwire (Griffey Hot List)	.40
331	Derek Jeter (Griffey Hot List)	.60
332	Alex Rodriguez (Griffey Hot List)	1.00
333	Juan Gonzalez (Griffey Hot List)	.50
334	Ken Griffey Jr. (Griffey Hot List)	1.00
335	Brian L. Hunter	.05
336	Brian Johnson	.05
337	Omar Olivares	.05
338	*Deivi Cruz*	.05
339	Damion Easley	.05
340	Melvin Nieves	.05
341	Moises Alou	.05
342	Jim Eisenreich	.05
343	Mark Hutton	.05
344	Alex Fernandez	.05
345	Gary Sheffield	.15
346	Pat Rapp	.05
347	Brad Ausmus	.05
348	Sean Berry	.05
349	Darryl Kile	.05
350	Craig Biggio	.10
351	Chris Holt	.05
352	Luis Gonzalez	.05
353	Pat Listach	.05
354	Jose Rosado	.05
355	Mike Macfarlane	.05
356	Tom Goodwin	.05
357	Chris Haney	.05
358	Chili Davis	.05
359	Jose Offerman	.05
360	Johnny Damon	.05
361	Bip Roberts	.05
362	Ramon Martinez	.05
363	Pedro Astacio	.05
364	Todd Zeile	.05
365	Mike Piazza	1.25
366	Greg Gagne	.05
367	Chan Ho Park	.05
368	Wilton Guerrero	.15
369	Todd Worrell	.05
370	John Jaha	.05
371	Steve Sparks	.05
372	Mike Matheny	.05
373	Marc Newfield	.05
374	Jeromy Burnitz	.05
375	Jose Valentin	.05
376	Ben McDonald	.05
377	Roberto Kelly	.05
378	Bob Tewksbury	.05
379	Ron Coomer	.05
380	Brad Radke	.05
381	Matt Lawton	.05
382	Dan Naulty	.05
383	Scott Stahoviak	.05
384	Matt Wagner	.05
385	Jim Bullinger	.05

386	Carlos Perez	.05
387	Darrin Fletcher	.05
388	Chris Widger	.05
389	F.P. Santangelo	.05
390	Lee Smith	.05
391	Bobby Jones	.05
392	John Olerud	.05
393	Mark Clark	.05
394	Jason Isringhausen	.05
395	Todd Hundley	.15
396	Lance Johnson	.05
397	Edgardo Alfonzo	.05
398	Alex Ochoa	.05
399	Darryl Strawberry	.05
400	David Cone	.15
401	Paul O'Neill	.05
402	Joe Girardi	.05
403	Charlie Hayes	.05
404	Andy Pettitte	.50
405	Mariano Rivera	.10
406	Mariano Duncan	.05
407	Kenny Rogers	.05
408	Cecil Fielder	.10
409	George Williams	.05
410	Jose Canseco	.20
411	Tony Batista	.05
412	Steve Karsay	.05
413	Dave Telgheder	.05
414	Billy Taylor	.05
415	Mickey Morandini	.05
416	Calvin Maduro	.05
417	Mark Leiter	.05
418	Kevin Stocker	.05
419	Mike Lieberthal	.05
420	Rico Brogna	.05
421	Mark Portugal	.05
422	Rex Hudler	.05
423	Mark Johnson	.05
424	Esteban Loiaza	.05
425	Lou Collier	.05
426	Kevin Elster	.05
427	Francisco Cordova	.05
428	Marc Wilkins	.05
429	Joe Randa	.05
430	Jason Kendall	.05
431	Jon Lieber	.05
432	Steve Cooke	.05
433	*Emil Brown*	.10
434	*Tony Womack*	.15
435	Al Martin	.05
436	Jason Schmidt	.05
437	Andy Benes	.05
438	Delino DeShields	.05
439	Royce Clayton	.05
440	Brian Jordan	.05
441	Donovan Osborne	.05
442	Gary Gaetti	.05
443	Tom Pagnozzi	.05
444	Joey Hamilton	.05
445	Wally Joyner	.05
446	John Flaherty	.05
447	Chris Gomez	.05
448	Sterling Hitchcock	.05
449	Andy Ashby	.05
450	Ken Caminiti	.15
451	Tim Worrell	.05
452	Jose Vizcaino	.05
453	Rod Beck	.05
454	Wilson Delgado	.05
455	Darryl Hamilton	.05
456	Mark Lewis	.05
457	Mark Gardner	.05
458	Rick Wilkins	.05
459	Scott Sanders	.05
460	Kevin Orie	.05
461	Glendon Rusch	.05
462	Juan Melo	.05
463	Richie Sexson	.10
464	Bartolo Colon	.05
465	Jose Guillen	.50
466	Heath Murray	.05
467	Aaron Boone	.05
468	*Bubba Trammell*	.50
469	Jeff Abbott	.05
470	Derrick Gibson	.15
471	Matt Morris	.15
472	Ryan Jones	.05
473	Pat Cline	.05
474	Adam Riggs	.05
475	Jay Payton	.05
476	Derrek Lee	.15
477	Elieser Marrero	.05
478	Lee Tinsley	.05
479	Jamie Moyer	.05
480	Jay Buhner	.15
481	Bob Wells	.05
482	Jeff Fassero	.05
483	Paul Sorrento	.05
484	Russ Davis	.05
485	Randy Johnson	.40
486	Roger Pavlik	.05

487	Damon Buford	.05
488	Julio Santana	.05
489	Mark McLemore	.05
490	Mickey Tettleton	.05
491	Ken Hill	.05
492	Benji Gil	.05
493	Ed Sprague	.05
494	Mike Timlin	.05
495	Pat Hentgen	.05
496	Orlando Merced	.05
497	Carlos Garcia	.05
498	Carlos Delgado	.15
499	Juan Guzman	.05
500	Roger Clemens	.75
501	Erik Hanson	.05
502	Otis Nixon	.05
503	Shawn Green	.05
504	Charlie O'Brien	.05
505	Joe Carter	.15
506	Alex Gonzalez	.05

1997 Collector's Choice All-Star Connection

This 45-card insert from Series II highlights All-Star caliber players. Cards feature a large starburst pattern behind the player's photo and were inserted one per pack.

		MT
Complete Set (45):		18.00
Common Player:		.15
1	Mark McGwire	.75
2	Chuck Knoblauch	.20
3	Jim Thome	.35
4	Alex Rodriguez	2.50
5	Ken Griffey Jr.	2.50
6	Brady Anderson	.15
7	Albert Belle	1.00
8	Ivan Rodriguez	.40
9	Pat Hentgen (new)	.15
10	Frank Thomas	2.50
11	Roberto Alomar	.40
12	Robin Ventura	.15
13	Cal Ripken Jr.	2.00
14	Juan Gonzalez	1.00
15	Manny Ramirez	.50
16	Bernie Williams	.40
17	Terry Steinbach	.15
18	Andy Pettitte (new)	.50
19	Jeff Bagwell	1.00
20	Craig Biggio	.15
21	Ken Caminiti	.15
22	Barry Larkin	.15
23	Tony Gwynn	.75
24	Barry Bonds	.50
25	Kenny Lofton	.50
26	Mike Piazza	1.50
27	John Smoltz	.25
28	Andres Galarraga	.15
29	Ryne Sandberg	.50
30	Chipper Jones	1.50
31	Mark Grudzielanek	.15
32	Sammy Sosa	.25
33	Steve Finley	.15
34	Gary Sheffield	.25
35	Todd Hundley	.25
36	Greg Maddux	1.50
37	Mo Vaughn	.50
38	Eric Young	.15
39	Vinny Castilla	.15
40	Derek Jeter	1.50
41	Lance Johnson (new)	.15
42	Ellis Burks	.15
43	Bernard Gilkey	.15
44	Javy Lopez	.15
45	Hideo Nomo	.40

1997 Collector's Choice Big Shots

This 20-card insert depicts the game's top stars in unique photos. Cards were inserted 1:12 packs. Gold Signature Editions, featuring a gold foil-stamped facsimile autograph, were inserted 1:144 packs.

		MT
Complete Set (20):		60.00
Common Player:		.75
1	Ken Griffey Jr.	10.00
2	Nomar Garciaparra	5.00
3	Brian Jordan	.75
4	Scott Rolen	4.00
5	Alex Rodriguez	8.00
6	Larry Walker	1.00
7	Mariano Rivera	.75
8	Cal Ripken Jr.	8.00
9	Deion Sanders	1.00
10	Frank Thomas	10.00
11	Dean Palmer	.75
12	Ken Caminiti	1.00
13	Derek Jeter	6.00
14	Roger Clemens	3.00
15	Chipper Jones	6.00
16	Jay Buhner	.75
17	Jay Buhner	.75
18	Mike Piazza	6.00
19	Tony Gwynn	4.00
20	Barry Bonds	2.50

1997 Collector's Choice Big Show

The 45-card, regular-sized set was inserted in each pack of Series I 1997 Collector's Choice baseball. Backs feature player comments written by ESPN SportsCenter hosts Keith Olbermann and Dan Patrick, whose portraits appear both front and back. On front, printed on metallic foil, is an action shot of the player, with his name printed along the left border of the horizontal cards. The cards are numbered "x/45." A parallel set to this chase-card series carries a gold-foil "World Headquarters Edition" seal at lower-right.

		MT
Complete Set (45):		30.00
Common Player:		.25
1	Greg Maddux	2.50
2	Chipper Jones	2.50
3	Andruw Jones	2.50
4	John Smoltz	.40
5	Cal Ripken Jr.	3.00
6	Roberto Alomar	.75
7	Rafael Palmeiro	.25
8	Eddie Murray	.50
9	Jose Canseco	.25
10	Roger Clemens	.60
11	Mo Vaughn	1.00
12	Jim Edmonds	.25
13	Tim Salmon	.25
14	Sammy Sosa	.40
15	Albert Belle	1.50
16	Frank Thomas	4.00
17	Barry Larkin	.40
18	Kenny Lofton	.75
19	Manny Ramirez	.75
20	Matt Williams	.40

21	Dante Bichette	.25
22	Gary Sheffield	.40
23	Craig Biggio	.25
24	Jeff Bagwell	1.50
25	Todd Hollandsworth	.25
26	Raul Mondesi	.25
27	Hideo Nomo	.60
28	Mike Piazza	2.50
29	Paul Molitor	.75
30	Kirby Puckett	1.50
31	Rondell White	.25
32	Rey Ordonez	.25
33	Paul Wilson	.25
34	Derek Jeter	2.00
35	Andy Pettitte	.75
36	Mark McGwire	1.00
37	Jason Kendall	.25
38	Ozzie Smith	.75
39	Tony Gwynn	1.50
40	Barry Bonds	.75
41	Alex Rodriguez	4.00
42	Jay Buhner	.25
43	Ken Griffey Jr.	4.00
44	Randy Johnson	.40
45	Juan Gonzalez	1.50

1997 Collector's Choice Big Show/World HQ

The 45-card chase set inserted in each pack of Series I 1997 Collector's Choice is also found in a special parallel version which carries a "World Headquarters Edition" gold-foil seal on front at the lower-right.

	MT
Complete Set (45):	150.00
Common Player:	1.00
Stars:	4x to 8x

1997 Collector's Choice Clearly Dominant

The five-card, regular-sized set features Seattle outfielder Ken Griffey Jr. on each card and was inserted every 144 packs of 1997 Collector's Choice baseball.

	MT
Complete Set (5):	50.00
Common Griffey Jr.:	12.00
CD1 Ken Griffey Jr.	12.00
CD2 Ken Griffey Jr.	12.00
CD3 Ken Griffey Jr.	12.00

		MT
CD4	Ken Griffey Jr.	12.00
CD5	Ken Griffey Jr.	12.00

1997 Collector's Choice Hot List Jumbos

These 5" x 7" versions of the "Ken Griffey Jr.'s Hot List" subset from Series I are an exclusive box-topper in certain retail packaging of Series II Collector's Choice. Other than size, the jumbos are identical to the regular Hot List cards, including foil background printing on front.

		MT
Complete Set (10):		50.00
Common Player:		3.00
325	Andruw Jones	6.00
326	Chipper Jones	6.00
327	Mo Vaughn	3.00
328	Frank Thomas	8.00
329	Albert Belle	5.00
330	Mark McGwire	5.00
331	Derek Jeter	5.00
332	Alex Rodriguez	8.00
333	Juan Gonzalez	5.00
334	Ken Griffey Jr.	9.00

1997 Collector's Choice New Frontier

A 20-card insert in Series II highlighting anticipated interleague match-ups. Cards were inserted 1:69 packs.

		MT
Complete Set (20):		250.00
Common Player:		3.00
NF1	Alex Rodriguez, Tony Gwynn	35.00
NF3	Jose Canseco, Hideo Nomo	7.00
NF5	Mark McGwire, Barry Bonds	10.00
NF7	Juan Gonzalez, Ken Caminiti	15.00
NF9	Tim Salmon, Mike Piazza	25.00
NF11	Ken Griffey Jr., Andres Galarraga	35.00
NF13	Jay Buhner, Dante Bichette	3.00
NF15	Frank Thomas, Ryne Sandberg	35.00
NF17	Roger Clemens, Andruw Jones	25.00
NF19	Jim Thome, Sammy Sosa	6.00
NF21	David Justice, Deion Sanders	3.00
NF23	Todd Walker, Kevin Orie	8.00
NF25	Albert Belle, Jeff Bagwell	15.00
NF27	Manny Ramirez, Brian Jordan	8.00
NF29	Derek Jeter, Chipper Jones	25.00
NF31	Mo Vaughn, Gary Sheffield	8.00
NF33	Carlos Delgado, Vladimir Guerrero	15.00
NF35	Cal Ripken Jr., Greg Maddux	30.00
NF37	Cecil Fielder, Todd Hundley	3.00
NF39	Mike Mussina, Scott Rolen	12.00

1997 Collector's Choice Premier Power

The 20-card, regular-sized set was included every 15 packs of 1997 Upper Deck Collector's Choice baseball. The card fronts feature an action shot with the player's name, team and position on the lower card edge. The "Premier Power" logo appears in silver foil in the lower half with spotlights aiming out toward the card sides, also in silver foil. The bottom portion of the card, below the spotlights, is transparent red. The card backs are bordered in red with the same card front shot appearing in black and white above a

brief description and "Power Facts." The cards are numbered with a "PP" prefix. A parallel gold-foil version was available every 69 packs.

		MT
Complete Set (20):		75.00
Common Player:		1.00
Golds:		2x to 3x
PP1	Mark McGwire	6.00
PP2	Brady Anderson	1.50
PP3	Ken Griffey Jr.	15.00
PP4	Albert Belle	5.00
PP5	Juan Gonzalez	7.00
PP6	Andres Galarraga	1.50
PP7	Jay Buhner	1.00
PP8	Mo Vaughn	4.00
PP9	Barry Bonds	4.00
PP10	Gary Sheffield	2.50
PP11	Todd Hundley	1.50
PP12	Frank Thomas	15.00
PP13	Sammy Sosa	3.00
PP14	Ken Caminiti	2.00
PP15	Vinny Castilla	1.00
PP16	Ellis Burks	1.00
PP17	Rafael Palmeiro	1.00
PP18	Alex Rodriguez	12.00
PP19	Mike Piazza	10.00
PP20	Eddie Murray	2.50

1997 Collector's Choice Stick'Ums

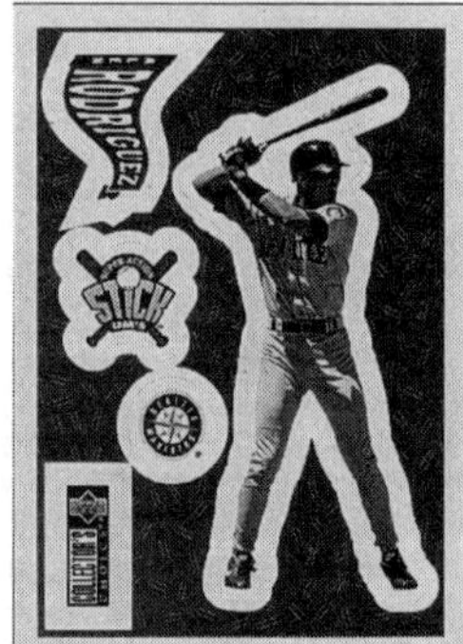

The 30-piece 2-1/2" x 3-1/2" sticker set was inserted every three packs of 1997 Collector's Choice. Fronts feature various bright background single colors and include five different peel-off stickers: An action shot of the player, a pennant in team colors featuring the player's name, a team logo, an Upper Deck Collector's Choice logo and a "Super Action Stick'Ums" decal. Backs feature the 20-player checklist in black ink over a gray background. An unnumbered version of the stickers (without Smith and Puckett) was sold in a special retail-only package.

		MT
Complete Set (30):		25.00
Common Player:		.25
1	Ozzie Smith	.50
2	Andruw Jones	2.00
3	Alex Rodriguez	3.00
4	Paul Molitor	.50
5	Jeff Bagwell	1.00

6	Manny Ramirez	.75
7	Kenny Lofton	.75
8	Albert Belle	1.00
9	Jay Buhner	.25
10	Chipper Jones	2.00
11	Barry Larkin	.40
12	Dante Bichette	.25
13	Mike Piazza	2.00
14	Andres Galarraga	.25
15	Barry Bonds	.75
16	Brady Anderson	.25
17	Gary Sheffield	.50
18	Jim Thome	.50
19	Tony Gwynn	1.25
20	Cal Ripken Jr.	2.50
21	Sammy Sosa	.50
22	Juan Gonzalez	1.00
23	Greg Maddux	2.00
24	Ken Griffey Jr.	3.00
25	Mark McGwire	.75
26	Kirby Puckett	1.00
27	Mo Vaughn	.75
28	Vladimir Guerrero	.75
29	Ken Caminiti	.40
30	Frank Thomas	3.00

1997 Collector's Choice Toast of the Town

This 30-card Series II insert features top stars on foil-enhanced cards. Odds of finding one of these inserts was 1:35 packs.

		MT
Complete Set (30):		240.00
Common Player:		2.50
T1	Andruw Jones	15.00
T2	Chipper Jones	15.00
T3	Greg Maddux	15.00
T4	John Smoltz	2.50
T5	Kenny Lofton	6.00
T6	Brady Anderson	2.50
T7	Cal Ripken Jr.	20.00
T8	Mo Vaughn	6.00
T9	Sammy Sosa	4.00
T10	Albert Belle	8.00
T11	Frank Thomas	25.00
T12	Barry Larkin	2.50
T13	Manny Ramirez	6.00
T14	Jeff Bagwell	10.00
T15	Mike Piazza	15.00
T16	Paul Molitor	4.00
T17	Vladimir Guerrero	12.00
T18	Todd Hundley	2.50
T19	Derek Jeter	15.00
T20	Andy Pettitte	6.00
T21	Bernie Williams	4.00
T22	Mark McGwire	8.00
T23	Scott Rolen	10.00
T24	Ken Caminiti	2.50
T25	Tony Gwynn	10.00
T26	Barry Bonds	6.00
T27	Ken Griffey Jr.	25.00
T28	Alex Rodriguez	25.00
T29	Juan Gonzalez	10.00
T30	Roger Clemens	6.00

1997 Collector's Choice Update

This update set was offered via a mail-in redemption offer. Traded players in their new uniforms and 1997 rookies are the focus of the set. Fronts

are color photos which are borderless at top and sides. Beneath each photo the player's name and team logo appear in a red (A.L.) or blue (N.L.) baseball design. Backs have another photo, major and minor league career stats and a trvia question.

		MT
Complete Set (30):		8.00
Common Player:		.25
U1	Jim Leyritz	.25
U2	Matt Perisho	.25
U3	Michael Tucker	.25
U4	Mike Johnson	.25
U5	Jaime Navarro	.25
U6	Doug Drabek	.25
U7	Terry Mulholland	.35
U8	Brett Tomko	.25
U9	Marquis Grissom	.40
U10	David Justice	.40
U11	Brian Moehler	.25
U12	Bobby Bonilla	.40
U13	Todd Dunwoody	.25
U14	Tony Saunders	.25
U15	Jay Bell	.25
U16	Jeff King	.25
U17	Terry Steinbach	.25
U18	Steve Bieser	.25
U19	Takashi Kashiwada	.40
U20	Hideki Irabu	1.50
U21	Damon Mashore	.25
U22	Quilvio Veras	.25
U23	Will Cunnane	.25
U24	Jeff Kent	.35
U25	J.T. Snow	.40
U26	Dante Powell	.25
U27	Jose Cruz, Jr.	4.00
U28	John Burkett	.25
U29	John Wetteland	.25
U30	Benito Santiago	.25

1997 Collector's Choice You Crash the Game

A 30-card interactive set found in Series II packs, featuring the game's top home run hitters. Cards were inserted 1:5 packs. Winning cards could be redeemed for prizes.

		MT
Complete Set (30):		35.00
Common Player:		.50
CG1	Ryan Klesko	.75
CG2	Chipper Jones	3.00
CG3	Andruw Jones	3.00
CG4	Brady Anderson	.50
CG5	Rafael Palmeiro	.50
CG6	Cal Ripken Jr.	4.00
CG7	Mo Vaughn	1.25
CG8	Sammy Sosa	.75
CG9	Albert Belle	2.00
CG10	Frank Thomas	5.00
CG11	Manny Ramirez	1.25
CG12	Jim Thome	.75
CG13	Matt Williams	.75
CG14	Dante Bichette	.50
CG15	Vinny Castilla	.50
CG16	Andres Galarraga	.50
CG17	Gary Sheffield	.75
CG18	Jeff Bagwell	2.00
CG19	Eric Karros	.50
CG20	Mike Piazza	3.00
CG21	Vladimir Guerrero	2.00
CG22	Cecil Fielder	.50
CG23	Jose Canseco	.75
CG24	Mark McGwire	1.50

CG25	Ken Caminiti	.50
CG26	Barry Bonds	1.25
CG27	Jay Buhner	.50
CG28	Ken Griffey Jr.	5.00
CG29	Alex Rodriguez	5.00
CG30	Juan Gonzalez	2.50

1997 Upper Deck UD3

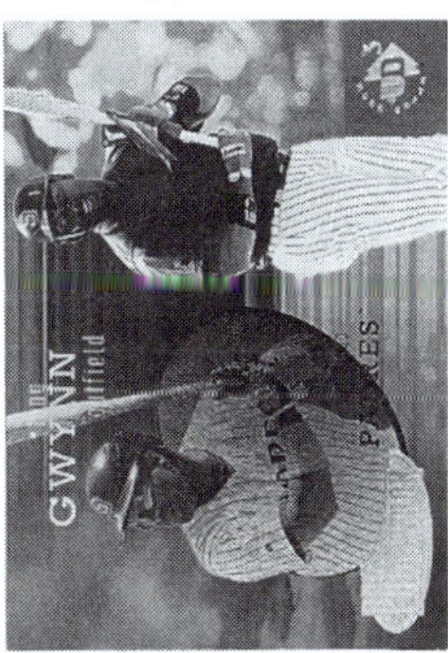

Released in April, this 60-card set is broken down into three different 20-card subsets, each utilizing a different print technology. There are 20 PROmotion cards (Light F/X cards featuring a special foil stock), 20 Future Impact cards (Cel-Chrome cards that feature a 3-D image on transparent chromium), and 20 Homerun Heroes (Electric Wood cards printed on an embossed wood/paper stock). Cards were sold in three-card packs (with one subset card per pack) for $3.99 each. Inserts include Superb Signatures, Generation Next and Marquee Attraction.

		MT
Complete Set (60):		50.00
Common Player:		.40
Wax Box:		80.00
1	Mark McGwire	1.75
2	Brady Anderson	.50
3	Ken Griffey Jr.	5.00
4	Albert Belle	1.50
5	Andres Galarraga	.60
6	Juan Gonzalez	2.50
7	Jay Buhner	.50
8	Mo Vaughn	1.25
9	Barry Bonds	1.25
10	Gary Sheffield	.75
11	Todd Hundley	.40
12	Ellis Burks	.40
13	Ken Caminiti	.75
14	Vinny Castilla	.40
15	Sammy Sosa	.60
16	Frank Thomas	5.00
17	Rafael Palmeiro	.60
18	Mike Piazza	3.00
19	Matt Williams	.75
20	Eddie Murray	1.00
21	Roger Clemens	1.50
22	Tim Salmon	.50
23	Robin Ventura	.40
24	Ron Gant	.40
25	Cal Ripken Jr.	4.00
26	Bernie Williams	1.00
27	Hideo Nomo	1.00
28	Ivan Rodriguez	1.00
29	John Smoltz	.50
30	Paul Molitor	1.00
31	Greg Maddux	3.00
32	Raul Mondesi	.60
33	Roberto Alomar	1.00
34	Barry Larkin	.60
35	Tony Gwynn	2.50
36	Jim Thome	.75
37	Kenny Lofton	1.25
38	Jeff Bagwell	2.00
39	Ozzie Smith	.75
40	Kirby Puckett	2.00
41	Andruw Jones	3.00
42	Vladimir Guerrero	2.50
43	Edgar Renteria	.40
44	Luis Castillo	.75
45	Darin Erstad	2.00
46	Nomar Garciaparra	3.50
47	Todd Greene	.40

48	Jason Kendall	.40
49	Rey Ordonez	.50
50	Alex Rodriguez	5.00
51	Manny Ramirez	1.25
52	Todd Walker	1.25
53	Ruben Rivera	.60
54	Andy Pettitte	1.25
55	Derek Jeter	3.00
56	Todd Hollandsworth	.40
57	Rocky Coppinger	.40
58	Scott Rolen	2.50
59	Jermaine Dye	.50
60	Chipper Jones	3.00

1997 Upper Deck UD3 Generation Next

A 20-card insert saluting the game's up-and-coming stars with two different photos of the player on each card front. Odds of finding these cards were 1:11 packs.

		MT
Complete Set (20):		150.00
Common Player:		4.00
GN1	Alex Rodriguez	25.00
GN2	Vladimir Guerrero	15.00
GN3	Luis Castillo	5.00
GN4	Rey Ordonez	6.00
GN5	Andruw Jones	20.00
GN6	Darin Erstad	15.00
GN7	Edgar Renteria	6.00
GN8	Jason Kendall	4.00
GN9	Jermaine Dye	4.00
GN10	Chipper Jones	18.00
GN11	Rocky Coppinger	4.00
GN12	Andy Pettitte	10.00
GN13	Todd Greene	4.00
GN14	Todd Hollandsworth	4.00
GN15	Derek Jeter	15.00
GN16	Ruben Rivera	6.00
GN17	Todd Walker	15.00
GN18	Nomar Garciaparra	15.00
GN19	Scott Rolen	12.00
GN20	Manny Ramirez	10.00

1997 Upper Deck UD3 Marquee Attraction

The game's top names are featured in this insert set, inserted 1:144 packs. Cards featured a peel-off protector that would expose a holographic image on the card fronts.

		MT
Complete Set (10):		500.00
Common Player:		15.00
MA1	Ken Griffey Jr.	100.00
MA2	Mark McGwire	30.00
MA3	Juan Gonzalez	40.00
MA4	Barry Bonds	20.00
MA5	Frank Thomas	90.00
MA6	Albert Belle	30.00
MA7	Mike Piazza	60.00
MA8	Cal Ripken Jr.	80.00
MA9	Mo Vaughn	20.00
MA10	Alex Rodriguez	100.00

1997 Upper Deck UD3 Superb Signatures

Autographed cards of Ken Griffey Jr., Ken Caminiti, Vladimir Guerrero and Derek Jeter were inserted 1:1,500 packs.

		MT
Complete Set (4):		1000.
Common Autograph:		100.00
1	Ken Caminiti	100.00
2	Ken Griffey Jr.	500.00
3	Vladimir Guerrero	200.00
4	Derek Jeter	250.00

1997 SP

The fifth anniversary edition of SP Baseball features 184 regular cards sold in eight-card packs for $4.39 each. Card fronts feature the player's name in gold foil-stamping at the bottom of the card, the team name and position running down one side of the card next to the player's photo. Inserts include Marquee Matchups, Special FX, Inside Info, Baseball Heroes, Game Film, SPx Force, and Autographed Vintage SP Cards.

		MT
Complete Set (184):		40.00
Common Player:		.15
Wax Box:		110.00
1	Andruw Jones (Great Futures)	2.50
2	Kevin Orie (Great Futures)	.15
3	Nomar Garciaparra (Great Futures)	1.50
4	Jose Guillen (Great Futures)	1.50
5	Todd Walker (Great Futures)	1.00
6	Derrick Gibson (Great Futures)	.25
7	Aaron Boone (Great Futures)	.25
8	Bartolo Colon (Great Futures)	.15
9	Derek Lee (Great Futures)	.25
10	Vladimir Guerrero (Great Futures)	2.00
11	Wilton Guerrero (Great Futures)	.15
12	Luis Castillo (Great Futures)	.15
13	Jason Dickson (Great Futures)	.15
14	*Bubba Trammell* (Great Futures)	1.50

15	*Jose Cruz Jr.* (Great Futures)	15.00
16	Eddie Murray	.50
17	Darin Erstad	1.50
18	Garret Anderson	.15
19	Jim Edmonds	.15
20	Tim Salmon	.40
21	Chuck Finley	.15
22	John Smoltz	.30
23	Greg Maddux	2.50
24	Kenny Lofton	1.00
25	Chipper Jones	2.50
26	Ryan Klesko	.60
27	Javier Lopez	.15
28	Fred McGriff	.40
29	Roberto Alomar	.75
30	Rafael Palmeiro	.30
31	Mike Mussina	.75
32	Brady Anderson	.15
33	Rocky Coppinger	.15
34	Cal Ripken Jr.	3.00
35	Mo Vaughn	1.00
36	Steve Avery	.15
37	Tom Gordon	.15
38	Tim Naehring	.15
39	Troy O'Leary	.15
40	Sammy Sosa	.60
41	Brian McRae	.15
42	Mel Rojas	.15
43	Ryne Sandberg	1.00
44	Mark Grace	.30
45	Albert Belle	1.50
46	Robin Ventura	.15
47	Roberto Hernandez	.15
48	Ray Durham	.15
49	Harold Baines	.15
50	Frank Thomas	4.00
51	Bret Boone	.15
52	Reggie Sanders	.15
53	Deion Sanders	.40
54	Hal Morris	.15
55	Barry Larkin	.30
56	Jim Thome	.75
57	Marquis Grissom	.15
58	David Justice	.50
59	Charles Nagy	.15
60	Manny Ramirez	1.00
61	Matt Williams	.40
62	Jack McDowell	.15
63	Vinny Castilla	.15
64	Dante Bichette	.25
65	Andres Galarraga	.25
66	Ellis Burks	.15
67	Larry Walker	.50
68	Eric Young	.15
69	Brian L. Hunter	.15
70	Travis Fryman	.15
71	Tony Clark	1.00
72	Bobby Higginson	.15
73	Melvin Nieves	.15
74	Jeff Conine	.15
75	Gary Sheffield	.50
76	Moises Alou	.15
77	Edgar Renteria	.15
78	Alex Fernandez	.15
79	Charles Johnson	.15
80	Bobby Bonilla	.15
81	Darryl Kile	.15
82	Derek Bell	.15
83	Shane Reynolds	.15
84	Craig Biggio	.25
85	Jeff Bagwell	2.00
86	Billy Wagner	.15
87	Chili Davis	.15
88	Kevin Appier	.15
89	Jay Bell	.15
90	Johnny Damon	.15
91	Jeff King	.15
92	Hideo Nomo	.75
93	Todd Hollandsworth	.15
94	Eric Karros	.15
95	Mike Piazza	2.50
96	Ramon Martinez	.15
97	Todd Worrell	.15
98	Raul Mondesi	.40
99	Dave Nilsson	.15
100	John Jaha	.15
101	Jose Valentin	.15
102	Jeff Cirillo	.15
103	Jeff D'Amico	.15
104	Ben McDonald	.15
105	Paul Molitor	.50
106	Rich Becker	.15
107	Frank Rodriguez	.15
108	Marty Cordova	.15
109	Terry Steinbach	.15
110	Chuck Knoblauch	.30
111	Mark Grudzielanek	.15
112	Mike Lansing	.15
113	Pedro J. Martinez	.30
114	Henry Rodriguez	.15
115	Rondell White	.15

116	Rey Ordonez	.15
117	Carlos Baerga	.15
118	Lance Johnson	.15
119	Bernard Gilkey	.15
120	Todd Hundley	.30
121	John Franco	.15
122	Bernie Williams	.75
123	David Cone	.30
124	Cecil Fielder	.25
125	Derek Jeter	2.50
126	Tino Martinez	.40
127	Mariano Rivera	.25
128	Andy Pettitte	1.00
129	Wade Boggs	.40
130	Mark McGwire	1.50
131	Jose Canseco	.40
132	Geronimo Berroa	.15
133	Jason Giambi	.15
134	Ernie Young	.15
135	Scott Rolen	1.50
136	Ricky Bottalico	.15
137	Curt Schilling	.15
138	Gregg Jefferies	.15
139	Mickey Morandini	.15
140	Jason Kendall	.15
141	Kevin Elster	.15
142	Al Martin	.15
143	Joe Randa	.15
144	Jason Schmidt	.15
145	Ray Lankford	.15
146	Brian Jordan	.15
147	Andy Benes	.15
148	Alan Benes	.25
149	Gary Gaetti	.15
150	Ron Gant	.15
151	Dennis Eckersley	.15
152	Rickey Henderson	.15
153	Joey Hamilton	.15
154	Ken Caminiti	.40
155	Tony Gwynn	2.00
156	Steve Finley	.15
157	Trevor Hoffman	.15
158	Greg Vaughn	.15
159	J.T. Snow	.15
160	Barry Bonds	1.00
161	Glenallen Hill	.15
162	William VanLandingham	.15
163	Jeff Kent	.15
164	Jay Buhner	.30
165	Ken Griffey Jr.	4.00
166	Alex Rodriguez	4.00
167	Randy Johnson	.75
168	Edgar Martinez	.15
169	Dan Wilson	.15
170	Ivan Rodriguez	.75
171	Roger Pavlik	.15
172	Will Clark	.30
173	Dean Palmer	.15
174	Rusty Greer	.15
175	Juan Gonzalez	2.00
176	John Wetteland	.15
177	Joe Carter	.15
178	Ed Sprague	.15
179	Carlos Delgado	.15
180	Roger Clemens	1.00
181	Juan Guzman	.15
182	Pat Hentgen	.15
183	Ken Griffey Jr.	4.00
184	*Hideki Irabu*	4.00

1997 SP Autographed Inserts

To celebrate the fifth anniversary of its premium SP brand, Upper Deck went into the hobby market to buy nearly 3,000 previous years' cards for a special insert program in 1997 SP packs. Various SP cards from 1993-96 issues and inserts were autographed by star players and a numbered holographic seal added on back. The number of each particular card signed ranged widely from fewer than 10 to more than 100. Numbers in parentheses in the checklist are the quantity reported signed for that card. All cards were inserted into foil packs except those of Mo Vaughn, which were a mail-in redemption.

		MT
Common Autograph (1-31):		25.00
1993 SP		
4	Ken Griffey Jr. (16)	2000.
28	Jeff Bagwell (7)	NA
167	Tony Gwynn (17)	700.00
280	Chipper Jones (34)	400.00
1993 SP Platinum Power		
PP9	Ken Griffey Jr. (5)	NA
1994 SP		
6	Todd Hollandsworth (167)	25.00
15	Alex Rodriguez (94)	350.00
105	Ken Griffey Jr. (103)	800.00
114	Gary Sheffield (130)	75.00
130	Tony Gwynn (367)	175.00
1994 SP Holoview Blue		
13	Tony Gwynn (31)	400.00
1994 SP Holoview Red		
35	Gary Sheffield (4)	NA
1995 SP		
34	Chipper Jones (60)	350.00
60	Jeff Bagwell (173)	160.00
105	Tony Gwynn (64)	300.00
188	Alex Rodriguez (63)	400.00
190	Ken Griffey Jr. (38)	1100.
195	Jay Buhner (57)	75.00
1996 SP		
1	Rey Ordonez (111)	25.00
18	Gary Sheffield (58)	80.00
26	Chipper Jones (102)	250.00
40	Mo Vaughn (250)	80.00
95	Jeff Bagwell (292)	120.00
160	Tony Gwynn (20)	500.00
170	Ken Griffey Jr. (312)	400.00
171	Alex Rodriguez (73)	400.00
173	Jay Buhner (79)	75.00
1996 SP Marquee Matchups		
MM13	Jeff Bagwell (23)	400.00
MM4	Rey Ordonez (40)	40.00
1996 SP Special F/X		
8	Jay Buhner (27)	100.00

1997 SP Baseball Heroes

First started in 1990, this single-player insert continues with a salute to Ken Griffey Jr. Each card in the set is numbered to 2,000.

		MT
Complete Set (10):		300.00
Common Griffey Jr.:		40.00
91	Ken Griffey Jr.	40.00
92	Ken Griffey Jr.	40.00
93	Ken Griffey Jr.	40.00
94	Ken Griffey Jr.	40.00
95	Ken Griffey Jr.	40.00
96	Ken Griffey Jr.	40.00
97	Ken Griffey Jr.	40.00
98	Ken Griffey Jr.	40.00
99	Ken Griffey Jr.	40.00
100	Ken Griffey Jr.	40.00

1997 SP Game Film

A 10-card insert utilizing pieces of actual game footage to highlight the top stars in the game. Only 500 of each card were available.

		MT
Complete Set (10):		1100.
Common Player:		25.00
GF1	Alex Rodriguez	150.00
GF2	Frank Thomas	200.00
GF3	Andruw Jones	125.00
GF4	Cal Ripken Jr.	150.00
GF5	Mike Piazza	125.00
GF6	Derek Jeter	125.00
GF7	Mark McGwire	75.00
GF8	Chipper Jones	125.00
GF9	Barry Bonds	50.00
GF10	Ken Griffey Jr.	200.00

1997 SP Inside Info

Each of the 25 cards in this insert feature a pull-out panel describing the player's major accomplishments. Cards were inserted one per box.

		MT
Complete Set (25):		250.00
Common Player:		4.00
1	Ken Griffey Jr.	30.00
2	Mark McGwire	12.00
3	Kenny Lofton	7.00
4	Paul Molitor	8.00
5	Frank Thomas	30.00
6	Greg Maddux	20.00
7	Mo Vaughn	7.00
8	Cal Ripken Jr.	25.00
9	Jeff Bagwell	12.00
10	Alex Rodriguez	25.00
11	John Smoltz	4.00
12	Manny Ramirez	7.00
13	Sammy Sosa	5.00
14	Vladimir Guerrero	15.00
15	Albert Belle	10.00
16	Mike Piazza	20.00
17	Derek Jeter	20.00
18	Scott Rolen	12.00
19	Tony Gwynn	12.00
20	Barry Bonds	7.00
21	Ken Caminiti	4.00
22	Chipper Jones	20.00
23	Juan Gonzalez	15.00
24	Roger Clemens	8.00
25	Andruw Jones	20.00

1997 SP Marquee Matchups

A 20-card die-cut set designed to highlight top interleague matchups. When the matching cards are put together, a third player is highlighted in the background. Cards were inserted 1:5 packs.

		MT
Complete Set (30):		80.00
Common Player:		1.50
MM1	Ken Griffey Jr.	10.00
MM2	Andres Galarraga	1.50
MM2	Juan Gonzalez	5.00
MM3	Barry Bonds	2.50
MM4	Mark McGwire	4.00
MM4	Jose Canseco	1.50
MM5	Mike Piazza	6.00
MM6	Tim Salmon	1.50
MM6	Hideo Nomo	2.50
MM7	Tony Gwynn	4.00
MM8	Alex Rodriguez	10.00
MM8	Ken Caminiti	1.50
MM9	Chipper Jones	6.00
MM10	Derek Jeter	6.00
MM10	Andruw Jones	6.00
MM11	Manny Ramirez	2.50
MM12	Jeff Bagwell	4.00
MM12	Matt Williams	1.50
MM13	Greg Maddux	6.00
MM14	Cal Ripken Jr.	8.00
MM14	Brady Anderson	1.50
MM15	Mo Vaughn	2.50
MM16	Gary Sheffield	2.00
MM16	Vladimir Guerrero	5.00
MM17	Jim Thome	2.50
MM18	Barry Larkin	1.50
MM18	Deion Sanders	1.50
MM19	Frank Thomas	10.00
MM20	Sammy Sosa	2.00
MM20	Albert Belle	3.00

1997 SP Special FX

Full-color, 3-D live motion images can be seen on these cards that also feature a die-cut design. The Alex Rodriguez card features the 1996 die-cut design since it was not available in the '96 set and is numbered 49 of 49. Cards were inserted 1:9 packs.

		MT
Complete Set (48):		300.00
Common Player:		3.00
1	Ken Griffey Jr.	25.00
2	Frank Thomas	25.00
3	Barry Bonds	6.00
4	Albert Belle	8.00
5	Mike Piazza	15.00
6	Greg Maddux	15.00
7	Chipper Jones	15.00
8	Cal Ripken Jr.	20.00
9	Jeff Bagwell	10.00
10	Alex Rodriguez	20.00
11	Mark McGwire	10.00
12	Kenny Lofton	6.00
13	Juan Gonzalez	12.00
14	Mo Vaughn	6.00
15	John Smoltz	3.00
16	Derek Jeter	15.00
17	Tony Gwynn	12.00
18	Ivan Rodriguez	6.00
19	Barry Larkin	3.00
20	Sammy Sosa	4.00
21	Mike Mussina	5.00
22	Gary Sheffield	4.00
23	Brady Anderson	3.00
24	Roger Clemens	8.00
25	Ken Caminiti	3.00
26	Roberto Alomar	5.00
27	Hideo Nomo	5.00
28	Bernie Williams	5.00
29	Todd Hundley	3.00
30	Manny Ramirez	6.00
31	Eric Karros	3.00
32	Tim Salmon	4.00
33	Jay Buhner	4.00
34	Andy Pettitte	6.00
35	Jim Thome	5.00
36	Ryne Sandberg	6.00
37	Matt Williams	4.00
38	Ryan Klesko	4.00
39	Jose Canseco	4.00
40	Paul Molitor	4.00

41	Eddie Murray	4.00
42	Darin Erstad	8.00
43	Todd Walker	5.00
44	Wade Boggs	3.00
45	Andruw Jones	15.00
46	Scott Rolen	12.00
47	Vladimir Guerrero	12.00
48	not issued	
49	Alex Rodriguez	20.00

1997 SP SPx Force

Each of the 10 cards in this set feature four different players. Cards are individually numbered to 500. In addition, a number of players signed 100 versions of their SPx Force cards that are also randomly inserted into packs.

		MT
Complete Set (10):		1000.
Common Player:		50.00
1	Ken Griffey Jr., Jay Buhner, Andres Galarraga, Dante Bichette	200.00
2	Albert Belle, Brady Anderson, Mark McGwire, Cecil Fielder	75.00
3	Mo Vaughn, Ken Caminiti, Frank Thomas, Jeff Bagwell	175.00
4	Gary Sheffield, Sammy Sosa, Barry Bonds, Jose Canseco	50.00
5	Greg Maddux, Roger Clemens, John Smoltz, Randy Johnson	125.00
6	Alex Rodriguez, Derek Jeter, Chipper Jones, Rey Ordonez	200.00
7	Todd Hollandsworth, Mike Piazza, Raul Mondesi, Hideo Nomo	100.00
8	Juan Gonzalez, Manny Ramirez, Roberto Alomar, Ivan Rodriguez	100.00
9	Tony Gwynn, Wade Boggs, Eddie Murray, Paul Molitor	90.00
10	Andruw Jones, Vladimir Guerrero, Todd Walker, Scott Rolen	125.00

1997 SP SPx Force Autographs

		MT
Complete Set (10):		3000.
Common Player:		125.00
1	Ken Griffey Jr.	1000.
2	Mark McGwire	250.00

3	Mo Vaughn	200.00
4	Gary Sheffield	150.00
5	Greg Maddux	500.00
6	Alex Rodriguez	500.00
7	Todd Hollandsworth	125.00
8	Roberto Alomar	200.00
9	Tony Gwynn	400.00
10	Andruw Jones	350.00

1997 SPx

Fifty cards, each featuring a perimeter die-cut design and a 3-D holoview photo, make up the SPx base set. Five different parallel sets - Steel (1:1 pack), Bronze (1:1), Silver (1:1), Gold (1:17) and Grand Finale (50 per card) - are also available, as are the Cornerstones of the Game, Bound for Glory and Bound for Glory Signature cards. Packs contained three cards and carried a suggested retail price of $5.99.

		MT
Complete Set (50):		60.00
Common Player:		.75
Silvers:		1.5x
Bronzes:		2x
Steels:		2x to 3x
Golds:		8x to 12x
1	Eddie Murray	1.00
2	Darin Erstad	5.00
3	Tim Salmon	1.00
4	Andruw Jones	4.00
5	Chipper Jones	4.00
6	John Smoltz	.75
7	Greg Maddux	4.00
8	Kenny Lofton	1.50
9	Roberto Alomar	1.25
10	Rafael Palmeiro	.75
11	Brady Anderson	.75
12	Cal Ripken Jr.	5.00
13	Nomar Garciaparra	2.50
14	Mo Vaughn	1.50

15	Ryne Sandberg	1.50
16	Sammy Sosa	1.00
17	Frank Thomas	6.00
18	Albert Belle	2.00
19	Barry Larkin	.75
20	Deion Sanders	.75
21	Manny Ramirez	1.50
22	Jim Thome	1.25
23	Dante Bichette	.75
24	Andres Galarraga	.75
25	Larry Walker	1.00
26	Gary Sheffield	1.00
27	Jeff Bagwell	2.50
28	Raul Mondesi	.75
29	Hideo Nomo	1.50
30	Mike Piazza	4.00
31	Paul Molitor	1.00
32	Todd Walker	1.00
33	Vladimir Guerrero	2.50
34	Todd Hundley	.75
35	Andy Pettitte	1.50
36	Derek Jeter	4.00
37	Jose Canseco	.75
38	Mark McGwire	2.50
39	Scott Rolen	2.50
40	Ron Gant	.75
41	Ken Caminiti	.75
42	Tony Gwynn	3.00
43	Barry Bonds	1.50
44	Jay Buhner	.75
45	Ken Griffey Jr.	6.00
46	Alex Rodriguez	6.00
47	Jose Cruz, Jr.	10.00
48	Juan Gonzalez	3.00
49	Ivan Rodriguez	1.25
50	Roger Clemens	1.50

1997 SPx Bound For Glory

A 20-card insert utilizing Holoview technology and sequentially numbered to 1,500 per card. Five players (Andruw Jones, Gary Sheffield, Alex Rodriguez, Ken Griffey Jr. and Jeff Bagwell) signed versions of their cards as part of the Bound For Glory Supreme Signatures set.

		MT
Complete Set (20):		550.00
Common Player:		15.00
1	Andruw Jones	40.00
2	Chipper Jones	40.00
3	Greg Maddux	40.00
4	Kenny Lofton	20.00
5	Cal Ripken Jr.	50.00
6	Mo Vaughn	20.00
7	Frank Thomas	60.00
8	Albert Belle	25.00
9	Manny Ramirez	15.00
10	Gary Sheffield	10.00
11	Jeff Bagwell	25.00
12	Mike Piazza	40.00
13	Derek Jeter	10.00
14	Mark McGwire	25.00
15	Tony Gwynn	30.00
16	Ken Caminiti	10.00
17	Barry Bonds	20.00
18	Alex Rodriguez	50.00
19	Ken Griffey Jr.	70.00
20	Juan Gonzalez	30.00

1997 SPx Cornerstones/Game

A 20-card insert utilizing a double-front design highlighting 40 of the top players in the game. Each card is sequentially numbered to 500.

		MT
Complete Set (10):		750.00
Common Player:		25.00
1	Ken Griffey Jr., Barry Bonds	150.00
2	Frank Thomas, Albert Belle	125.00
3	Chipper Jones, Greg Maddux	75.00
4	Tony Gwynn, Paul Molitor	60.00
5	Andruw Jones, Vladimir Guerrero	75.00
6	Jeff Bagwell, Ryne Sandberg	50.00
7	Mike Piazza, Ivan Rodriguez	75.00
8	Cal Ripken Jr., Eddie Murray	100.00
9	Mo Vaughn, Mark McGwire	50.00
10	Alex Rodriguez, Derek Jeter	100.00

1997 The Year in Basketball Cards

Basketball card collectors were hoping to score a slam dunk in 1997 as Michael Jordan led the Chicago Bulls to their fifth NBA title of the decade, but instead they had to settle for a simple tip-in.

While the NBA's popularity reached new heights in 1997, the basketball card market remained stagnant, unable to capitalize on the Bulls' popularity and the strong rookie class. On a per sport basis, basketball cards did see the biggest increase in sales from the previous year, but it was less than five percent. Still, according to a recent *Card Trade* survey, basketball card sales now account for 23.5 percent of the average dealer's gross sales, an increase of 2.4 percent from a year ago. Basketball card sales trail only baseball, which accounts for 29.7 percent of the average dealer's gross sales.

NEW RELEASES

The past year saw 29 new basketball card releases and a total of 202 new insert sets. Debut products in 1997 included SkyBox Z-Force, Topps Chrome, UD3, Flair Showcase, Bowman's Best and SkyBox E-X2000. Products that had been produced in the past which weren't produced in 1997 included Flair, SkyBox E-XL, Upper Deck SP Championship and Topps Gallery.

CARDS ON THE MOVE

The past year will be remembered for many things, but two trends really stand out for basketball card collectors. First of all, the introduction of SkyBox Autographics, an insert set that included autographed cards from over 95 NBA players, created a new interest in cards that has been duplicated by other manufacturers since its release. And secondly, the strong play of young stars like Grant Hill, Kevin Garnett and Kobe Bryant has reinvigorated the hobby's interest in rookie cards.

Last year's increased sales in the basketball card market can be directly attributed to the popular Autographics insert set. The innovative idea from Fleer/SkyBox wasn't just inserted into one set, which would have been an easy way to distribute these cards. Instead, they were inserted throughout all of the SkyBox products at a rate of one in every 72 packs. The star cards, which included future Hall of

Famers such as Clyde Drexler, Hakeem Olajuwon and Scottie Pippen, were scattered throughout the brands. SkyBox officials personally witnessed each of the signings and even videotaped every signing session.

However, there were a few glitches in the program which created even more interest in the Autographics cards. Players were asked to sign some of their cards in blue ink and the majority of their cards in black ink, creating a pair of parallel sets. The blue ink versions are worth 2-3x the black ink versions because of their scarcity. But two players – Olajuwon and Pippen – mistakenly signed all of their cards in blue ink, while Garnett signed two-thirds of his cards in blue ink. Pippen's cards lead the way at $400, while Garnett's black ink cards follow at $300 and his blue ink cards are at $275.

The second trend involved the renewed interest in rookie cards. Here's how it first began. While collectors were busy driving up the values of Hill's scarce insert cards two years ago, astute collectors began buying up his cheaper rookie cards. Leading the charge was his 1994-95 Topps Finest (#240), which in the last two years has gone from $20 to $80. Then last year when Garnett emerged as a budding superstar, collectors quickly found his 1995-96 Topps Finest (#115) was a bargain at only $10. Within 15 months, that rookie card had jumped to $70.

So naturally collectors noticed the trend and began investing in rookie cards of last year's talented class. They include stars such as Philadelphia's Allen Iverson – the 1996-97 Rookie of the Year – Boston's Antoine Walker, Minnesota's Stephon Marbury, Vancouver's Shareef Abdur-Rahim, Los Angeles' Kobe Bryant and Milwaukee's Ray Allen.

In the last year, collectors have been buying up the 1996-97 releases and speculating on the rookie cards of these prospects. Because of what happened to Hill and Garnett during the last two years, the big push is for cards from 1996-97 Topps Finest. Cards on the rise include those of

Abdur-Rahim (#54, $14), Iverson (#69, $20), Bryant (#74, $40) and Walker (#84, $15).

Other rookie cards which jumped in price last year included those of Los Angeles' Eddie Jones, Phoenix's Jason Kidd and Phoenix's Antonio McDyess. Jones emerged as a star for the Lakers last year and his 1994-95 Finest rookie card (#323) jumped from $4 to $25. Bryant's rookie card went on the same ride, increasing from $12 to $40. Kidd was traded from Dallas to Phoenix and the move to the Valley of the Sun helped all of his card values, especially his 1994-95 Finest (#286), which doubled from $12 to $25. McDyess also was traded from Denver to Phoenix and his 1995-96 Finest (#112) almost tripled in value from $5 to $14.

HOT PRODUCTS

Five regular issue sets stand out from the 29 that were released in 1997. Bowman's Best gets top honor as it was loaded with rookie cards and inserts and really grabbed the collector's attention. Topps wisely made Refractors and Atomic Refractors for every base and insert card, with the Refractors valued at 10-20x the base card and the Atomic Refractors going for 20-40x the base card. Boxes started selling for around $125, but were selling for $200 by the end of the calendar year.

Finest I was another hot product, although unlike Bowman's Best, it was red-hot from the very beginning. The rookie card craze fueled interest in this set, and boxes that began selling for $165 were going for $225 by season's end. As mentioned earlier, the biggest price jumps were in the rookie cards, led by Bryant. Abdur-Rahim's rookie card doubled from $7 to $14, while Walker's jumped from $2 to $14. The Refractors were also red-hot for many of the players. Collectors should also realize that many of the cards in both the base and the Refractor sets were tough to find centered, and many dealers are charging a premium for centered cards.

Flair Showcase was very similar to Finest. The debut product, which actually replaced Flair on Fleer's lineup, was an instant hit with collectors. Most collectors couldn't understand the concept of the product at first, but they didn't care. The base cards were beautiful and the Legacy insert, that had three versions of each player numbered to 150, were the hottest new inserts since the debut of Refractors. Packs were being sold at $6 because the Legacy cards were relatively easy to get at 1:30 packs. Only 90 players were in the set, so commons are few. Jordan's Showcase Legacy (#23) was one of the hottest insert cards in the hobby for most of the year, priced at $550.

> **Bowman's Best was one of the hot products of the year — loaded with rookie cards and inserts, it really grabbed the collector's attention.**

Other top sets of note were SkyBox E-X2000 and Topps Chrome. E-X2000 replaced E-XL in SkyBox's starting lineup and it was a popular brand. The base cards looked like inserts, which helped the two-card packs sell for $5. But it was the insert sets which drove this product, especially the parallel Credentials. The insert ratio wasn't given, but each card was numbered to 499, which again helped to create interest in another Fleer/SkyBox product.

Topps Chrome was a retail only product which didn't start out with a bang but finished that way. Packs and boxes debuted at $5 and $80, respectively, but by the end of the year they had increased to $10 and $200. Why the big increase in price? Rookie cards, once again. They have become the top rookie cards to get for Bryant (#138, $60), Abdur-Rahim (#128, $25), Iverson (#171, $40), Marbury (#177, $30) and Walker (#146, $25). Many of the cards in this set can be found off-center or with lines through them, so look at them closely.

But even though the rookies dominated the card market, Jordan is still the engine that drives this train. By leading the Bulls to their fifth title of the decade, Jordan wrote another chapter to his incredible NBA career. All of his cards remain popular and, of course, highly priced. His 1986-87 Fleer (#57) rookie card continues to be the best regular issue card in the basketball card market, priced at $1,000. That card rose $100 in the last year as Jordan led the Bulls past the Utah Jazz in the NBA Finals. Pippen's 1988-89 Fleer rookie card (#20) also rose $10 to $60, while Dennis Rodman's 1988-89 Fleer rookie card (#43) remained at $45.

Reaching the NBA Finals for the first time didn't hurt the Hall of Fame careers of John Stockton and Karl Malone, but it didn't help their rookie card values, however. Malone's 1986-87 Fleer (#68) and Stockton's 1988-89 Fleer (#115) remain priced at $60 and $25, respectively.

Also, Shaquille O'Neal's signing with Los Angeles created early interest in his rookie cards, but a late-season knee injury and an early exit from the playoffs kept Shaq's cards off the hot lists. Still, his move to the West Coast should be noted because having a superstar of Shaq's caliber in Los Angeles can be a boon to future basketball card sales.

This year should be an interesting one to watch for collectors involved in the basketball card market because it could be Jordan's last season. If Jordan decides to retire for good at the end of this year, can basketball cards maintain their share of the market? Only time will tell.

TOP TEN

INSERT SINGLES

THE FOLLOWING LIST OF CARDS HAVE GENERATED THE MOST DEMAND WITHIN THE HOBBY OVER THE LAST YEAR. THE RANKINGS ARE DETERMINED BY COLLECTORS AND DEALERS FROM THE HOBBY.

No. 1 — MICHAEL JORDAN
'96-97 Flair Showcase Legacy Collection #23
Serious collectors are going back and picking up Jordan's scarce inserts. Many of the numbered and low print run inserts, including this Legacy, are becoming harder to find. Jordan has three different Legacy cards with each numbered to 150 and each carrying a price tag of $550.

No. 2 — GRANT HILL
'94-95 Finest II Refractor #240
Some consider this card as Hill's top insert. It's hard to disagree, because this card has been on our list for the past two years. It now lists for $500.

No. 3 — MICHAEL JORDAN
'96-97 Finest II Refractor Gold #291
Out of all the Jordan Refractors, this is the one you see the least. It's every collector's dream to buy a pack for $5 and pull this $1,200 card.

No. 4 — GRANT HILL
'97-98 SkyBox Autographics
This is the second year Hill has been in the set and his card is once again the top card to get. This card is at $250, and its parallel Century Marks is worth almost $500.

No. 5 — KOBE BRYANT
'96-97 Finest Bronze Refractor #74
Kobe Bryant's top card is this Bronze Refractor from 1996-97 Finest, and it's a challenge to find centered. Mint ones will cost you $225.

No. 6 — TIM DUNCAN
'97 Press Pass Autograph
Duncan has made collectors very happy with his performance on the court. This $100 Autograph card is one of his top cards released this early in his career.

No. 7 — KOBE BRYANT
'96-97 Bowman's Best Refractor #R23
This Bryant Refractor isn't as hard to find as his Finest, but that's part of the reason this $120 card is so popular. All of Bryant's cards are on fire.

No. 8 — MICHAEL JORDAN
'96-97 Flair Showcase Hot Shots #1
If so many people broke down this product for all the inserts, then where is this card? Today you're lucky to find it for sale at $175.

No. 9 — KEVIN GARNETT
'96-97 SkyBox Autographics
This is a player that the NBA and the hobby needed at this time. The blue-ink version of this Autographics card is a great one to add to your collection for $275.

No. 10 — GRANT HILL
'96-97 SkyBox Autographics
This was Hill's first autographed card and continues to be one of the hottest collectibles out. He has both a black-ink version at $350 and a blue-ink version at $700.

TOP TEN

INSERT SETS

THE FOLLOWING LIST OF SETS HAVE GENERATED THE MOST DEMAND WITHIN THE HOBBY OVER THE LAST YEAR. THE RANKINGS ARE DETERMINED BY COLLECTORS AND DEALERS FROM THE HOBBY.

No. 1 — 1996-97 FLAIR SHOWCASE LEGACY COLLECTION
Many of the top singles in this set are on the rise, including Garnett, Hill and Jordan. Don't forget that top rookies Bryant, Marbury, Abdur-Rahim and Walker were also included. These cards can be found 1:30 packs, so building a set isn't impossible.

No. 2 — 1996-97 TOPPS CHROME REFRACTORS
This set is on fire! Six months ago, you could have found this 220-card set for $2,000, and today it's at $4,000. It looks as if it will continue to go up.

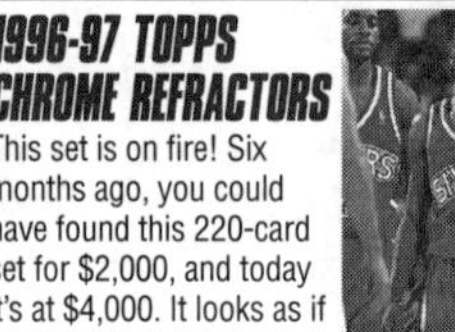

No. 3 — 1996-97 FINEST I BRONZE REFRACTORS
Abdur-Rahim, Bryant and Walker are all on the rise. Many cards are hard to find centered, so mint ones are drawing a premium in this $2,200 set.

No. 4 — 1997-98 SKYBOX Z-FORCE RAVES
Many collectors are trying to build this set, with these cards being pulled on an average of one-per-box. They are valued at 50x-100x the base card.

No. 5 — 1997-98 SKYBOX AUTOGRAPHICS
These cards are found throughout various SkyBox products. Top players include Hill and Drexler and each has a parallel Century Mark.

No. 6 — 1997-98 UPPER DECK GAME JERSEYS
These cards can be found in regular Upper Deck packs at a rate of 1:2,500. The 12-card set includes Garnett, Hill and Iverson and is selling for $2,500.

No. 7 — 1996-97 SKYBOX AUTOGRAPHICS
This set was one of the big reasons for the autograph boom. Now just about every product has some sort of autograph insert.

No. 8 — 1996-97 FLAIR SHOWCASE HOT SHOTS
This set may be losing ground on our list because of some of the newer inserts, but it's still popular with collectors. The 20-card set is priced at $700.

No. 9 — 1997-98 SKYBOX Z-FORCE RAVE REVIEWS
Rave Reviews are some of the hardest inserts to find at 1:288 packs. The set is loaded with Jordan, Garnett and Hardaway and is valued at $625.

No. 10 — 1997-98 METAL PLATINUM PORTRAITS
Each player is featured in a Hall of Fame plaque treatment on the front of the card. The 15-card set lists for $700 and includes both Jordan and Bryant.

REGULAR-ISSUE SINGLES

THE FOLLOWING LIST OF CARDS HAVE GENERATED THE MOST DEMAND WITHIN THE HOBBY OVER THE LAST YEAR. THE RANKINGS ARE DETERMINED BY COLLECTORS AND DEALERS FROM THE HOBBY.

No. 1 — MICHAEL JORDAN
'86-87 Fleer #57
This season could be Jordan's biggest challenge, with Pippen gone for half of the year and Rodman not knowing if he's coming or going. Look for Jordan to once again dominate like he did before he had a strong team around him. If he has that final big year, this rookie card could finally move from its $1,000 tag.

1994-95 EMBOSSED JASON KIDD #102
Kidd looks as if he has finally found a home in Phoenix. Most of his rookie cards have been a tough sell in the past, but that should all change soon as Kidd is off to a great start. All of his rookie cards should be on the rise, including this $3 item.

No. 2 — GRANT HILL
'94-95 Finest #240
Hill has picked up where he left off last year and there aren't any signs of this Finest rookie slowing down in the hobby as it holds at $80, up $60 in last two years.

No. 3 — KEVIN GARNETT
'95-96 Finest #115
This single has made the biggest move in the basketball card hobby in the last year. It has risen from $10 a little more than a year ago to $75 currently.

No. 4 — KOBE BRYANT
'96-97 Finest I #74
This card is jumping in price as collectors speculate on this rookie. Kobe isn't even starting yet, and collectors can't get enough of these cards. It's risen all the way to $40.

No. 5 — JASON KIDD
'94-95 Finest #286
This card has recently doubled in price, and is now up to $20 due to many collectors speculating that Kidd will have a big season with the Phoenix Suns.

No. 6 — ANFERNEE HARDAWAY
'93-94 Finest #189
There's been little movement in price over the last year, but this card is still a solid seller at its $40 tag. But a big season could turn this card around in the next few months.

No. 7 — STEPHON MARBURY
'96-97 Finest #62
Marbury has proven that with the help of Garnett and Gugliotta, they are a playoff team. Collectors love the maturity he has shown, and as a result, this card lists for $15.

No. 8 — EDDIE JONES
'94-95 Finest #323
It doesn't matter what team Jones plays for – he will produce. Many are jumping on this $25 card, as Jones began the year as one of the NBA's leading scorers.

No. 9 — SCOTTIE PIPPEN
'88-89 Fleer #20
It's a shame that Pippen started the year on the inactive list. But his rookie card is so under-valued that it's selling just as well now at $60 as it was when he was playing.

No. 10 — SHAREEF ABDUR-RAHIM
'96-97 Finest #54
One of the least known picks from last year's draft, but he may be the most talented player. This card is priced at $12 and will definitely go up by next month.

REGULAR-ISSUE SETS

THE FOLLOWING LIST OF SETS HAVE GENERATED THE MOST DEMAND WITHIN THE HOBBY OVER THE LAST YEAR. THE RANKINGS ARE DETERMINED BY COLLECTORS AND DEALERS FROM THE HOBBY.

No. 1 — 1996-97 FINEST I
The rookies in this set are making an impact in the NBA right now, which has made collectors pick up their top rookie cards. Abdur-Rahim, Bryant, Iverson, Marbury and Walker are as hot as anyone in the hobby. The 100-card set is a bargain to pick up for $100. Packs are selling for $10, with boxes selling for $225. Many of the Refractors are as hot as the base singles.

1995-96 TOPPS GALLERY
This was the first year Topps produced Gallery and the 144-card set ($40) was a mild success. The set was broken into four groups: The Classics, New Editions, The Modernists and The Masters. Each card was reported to have a parallel called the Player's Private Issue, but it was discovered that cards #1-18 did not exist. They were later added to '96/97 Stadium Club II.

No. 2 — 1996-97 FLAIR SHOWCASE
The same rookies who are in Finest are also driving this product. The 270-card set has climbed to $1,000, and boxes are tough to find for $160.

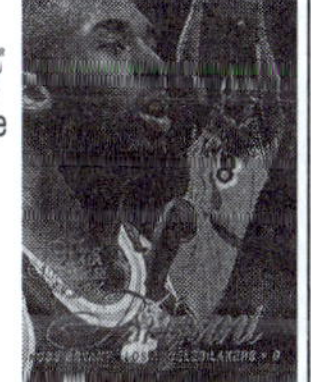

No. 3 — 1996-97 TOPPS CHROME
This product inches closer to the top spot as the rookie singles are hotter than the Finest singles. The 220-card set is at $160, and boxes at $90.

No. 4 — 1996-97 BOWMAN'S BEST
Many like this set, because it's a little more affordable than the previous three. All of the rookie cards are on the rise, and boxes are a hot mover at $200.

No. 5 — 1995-96 FINEST I
Rookie cards of Smith, Stackhouse, McDyess and Garnett have packs selling for $16 and boxes for $350. The 140-card set is a bargain at $140 as the Garnett single seems to rise every month.

No. 6 — 1994-95 FINEST II
The Jones and Kidd rookie cards have just added to the popularity of packs, which are selling for $18 and boxes for $380. The 166-card set is at $150.

No. 7 — 1996-97 E-X2000
This product may not be as strong as the first four, but it has all the top rookies and some beautiful insert sets. The 80-card set is priced at $100, while packs sell for $5, and boxes for $110.

No. 8 — 1986-87 FLEER
Collectors are always searching for any card from this set that is centered and mint, but it's very difficult to complete a near-mint set. This lists for $1,300, including the Jordan rookie.

No. 9 — 1993-94 TOPPS FINEST
Rookie cards of Baker and Webber have sparked this set. Packs are now selling for $12, with boxes at $240. The 220-card set is a bargain at $120.

No. 10 — 1997-98 METAL
Metal has done well, because it has some of the early rookies in the base set. Duncan, Mercer and Van Horn are three of the best in this $25 set. Packs are at $2.50, and boxes are at $55.

1996-97 Bowman's Best

The debut set for Bowman's Best Basketball arrived with 125 cards in the base set. Regular-issue cards are numbered 1-80, with a 25-card Rookies subset and 20 Throwbacks that are considered part of the regular-issue set, but numbered as inserts. We have listed them separately. The cards are printed with chromium technology and include a thick border on the left side along with a double border across the bottom that includes the player's and Throwbacks subsets, inserts include: Cuts, Shots, Picks and Honor Roll, along with Refractor and Atomic Refractor versions of the entire set and all the inserts.

		MT
Complete Set (80):		40.00
Common Player:		.25
Wax Box:		200.00
1	Scottie Pippen	2.00
2	Glen Rice	.50
3	Bryant Stith	.25
4	Dino Radja	.25
5	Horace Grant	.25
6	Mahmoud Abdul-Rauf	.25
7	Mookie Blaylock	.25
8	Clifford Robinson	.25
9	Vin Baker	.50
10	Grant Hill	4.00
11	Terrell Brandon	.25
12	P.J. Brown	.25
13	Kendall Gill	.25
14	Brent Barry	.25
15	Hakeem Olajuwon	1.50
16	Allan Houston	.25
17	Elden Campbell	.25
18	Latrell Sprewell	.75
19	Jerry Stackhouse	1.00
20	Robert Horry	.25
21	Mitch Richmond	.50
22	Gary Payton	.75
23	Rik Smits	.25
24	Jim Jackson	.25
25	Damon Stoudamire	1.50
26	Bobby Phills	.25
27	Chris Webber	1.00
28	Shawn Bradley	.25
29	Arvydas Sabonis	.25
30	John Stockton	.75
31	Anfernee Hardaway	4.00
32	Christian Laettner	.25
33	Juwan Howard	1.00
34	Anthony Mason	.25
35	Tom Gugliotta	.25
36	Avery Johnson	.25
37	Cedric Ceballos	.25
38	Patrick Ewing	.50
39	Joe Smith	1.00
40	Dennis Rodman	3.00
41	Alonzo Mourning	.50
42	Kevin Garnett	4.00
43	Antonio McDyess	.25
44	Detlef Schrempf	.25
45	Reggie Miller	.50
46	Charles Barkley	1.00
47	Derrick Coleman	.25
48	Brian Grant	.25
49	Kenny Anderson	.25
50	Otis Thorpe	.25
51	Rod Strickland	.25
52	Eric Williams	.25
53	Rony Seikaly	.25
54	Danny Manning	.25
55	Karl Malone	.75
56	B.J. Armstrong	.25
57	Greg Anthony	.25
58	Larry Johnson	.25
59	Loy Vaught	.25
60	Sean Elliott	.25
61	Dikembe Mutombo	.25
62	Clarence Weatherspoon	.25
63	Jamal Mashburn	.25
64	Bryant Reeves	.25
65	Vlade Divac	.25
66	Shawn Kemp	2.00
67	LaPhonso Ellis	.25
68	Tyrone Hill	.25
69	David Robinson	1.00
70	Shaquille O'Neal	4.00
71	Doug Christie	.25
72	Jayson Williams	.25
73	Michael Finley	.25
74	Tim Hardaway	.25
75	Clyde Drexler	.75
76	Joe Dumars	.25
77	Glenn Robinson	.50
78	Dana Barros	.25
79	Jason Kidd	.75
80	Michael Jordan	8.00

1996-97 Bowman's Best Refractors

All 125 cards in Bowman's Best Basketball had parallel Refractor versions. They were inserted every 12 packs of Hobby and every 20 packs of Retail. The fronts feature a refractive foil, while the backs contain the word "Refractor" within the white card number box.

	MT
Refractors:	10x-20x

1996-97 Bowman's Best Atomic Refractors

All 125 cards in Bowman's Best Basketball also had Atomic Refractor parallel versions. They were inserted every 24 packs of Hobby and every 40 packs of Retail. Atomic Refractors featured a prismatic refractive foil on the card fronts and the words "Atomic Refractor" on the back within the white card number box.

	MT
Atomic Refractors:	20x-40x

1996-97 Bowman's Best Cuts

Bowman's Best Cuts is a 20-card insert that is numbered BC1-BC20. The cards are die-cut on the right side and featured a gold strip down that side with the player's name in it. The insert name is in the upper left corner, with the player's facsimile signature along the left side. Regular versions are seeded every 24 hobby and 40 retail packs; Refractors are seeded every 96 hobby and 160 retail packs; and Atomic Refractors are seeded every 192 hobby and 320 retail packs.

	MT
Complete Set (20):	200.00
Common Player:	4.00
Refractors:	2x-3x
Atomic Refractors:	3x-6x
BC1 Karl Malone	4.00
BC2 Michael Jordan	60.00
BC3 Juwan Howard	6.00
BC4 Charles Barkley	6.00
BC5 Jerry Stackhouse	6.00
BC6 Anfernee Hardaway	30.00
BC7 Shaquille O'Neal	30.00
BC8 Alonzo Mourning	4.00
BC9 Shawn Kemp	15.00
BC10 Scottie Pippen	15.00
BC11 David Robinson	6.00
BC12 Kevin Garnett	30.00
BC13 Patrick Ewing	4.00
BC14 Hakeem Olajuwon	10.00
BC15 Damon Stoudamire	10.00
BC16 Grant Hill	30.00
BC17 Dennis Rodman	25.00
BC18 Chris Webber	6.00
BC19 Gary Payton	6.00
BC20 John Stockton	4.00

1996-97 Bowman's Best Honor Roll

Honor Roll is a 10-card, double-sided insert that highlights 20 top NBA draft picks dating back to 1984. The cards feature a mostly silver border, with the top corners in black. The cards are numbered HR1-HR10. Regular versions are seeded one per 48 hobby and one per 80 retail; Refractors are seeded one per 192 hobby and one per 320 retail; and Atomic Refractors are seeded one per 384 hobby and one per 640 retail.

	MT
Complete Set (10):	175.00
Common Player:	10.00
Refractors:	2x-3x
Atomic Refractors:	3x-6x
HR1 Charles Barkley, John Stockton	10.00
HR2 Michael Jordan, Hakeem Olajuwon	60.00
HR3 Patrick Ewing, Karl Malone	10.00
HR4 Dennis Rodman, Arvydas Sabonis	25.00
HR5 Scottie Pippen, David Robinson	15.00
HR6 Glen Rice, Shawn Kemp	15.00
HR7 Shaquille O'Neal, Alonzo Mourning	25.00
HR8 Anfernee Hardaway, Chris Webber	30.00
HR9 Grant Hill, Juwan Howard	30.00
HR10 Kevin Garnett, Jerry Stackhouse	25.00

1996-97 Bowman's Best Picks

This 10-card set is die-cut to resemble the Best Cuts insert; it has a die-cut on the right side at the bottom. The player's name appears in the silver strip on the right side, with the insert name in the upper left and a facsimile signature below it. Best Picks are numbered BP1-BP10, with regular versions seeded one per 24 hobby and one per 40 retail, Refractor versions every 96 hobby and 160 retail and Atomic Refractor versions seeded every 192 hobby and one per 320 retail.

	MT
Complete Set (10):	75.00
Common Player:	2.00
Refractors:	2x-3x
Atomic Refractors:	3x-6x
BP1 Stephon Marbury	18.00
BP2 Marcus Camby	14.00
BP3 Lorenzen Wright	2.00
BP4 John Wallace	4.00
BP5 Ray Allen	10.00
BP6 Kerry Kittles	7.00
BP7 Shareef Abdur-Rahim	14.00
BP8 Todd Fuller	2.00
BP9 Allen Iverson	25.00
BP10 Kobe Bryant	25.00

1996-97 Bowman's Best Rookies

Although considered a subset, Rookies were numbered as an insert set (R1-R25) and are listed separately. Rookies are identified by a silver strip down the left side of the card instead of the gold strip on regular-issue cards. Refractor versions are seeded one per 12 hobby and one per 20 retail, while Atomic Refractor versions are seeded one per 24 hobby and one per 40 retail packs.

	MT
Complete Set (25):	45.00
Common Player:	.25
Refractors:	5x-10x
Atomic Refractors:	10x-20x
R1	Allen Iverson	12.00
R2	Stephon Marbury	10.00
R3	Shareef Abdur-Rahim	8.00
R4	Marcus Camby	6.00
R5	Ray Allen	4.00
R6	Antoine Walker	8.00
R7	Lorenzen Wright	.50
R8	Kerry Kittles	3.00
R9	Samaki Walker	.50

R10	Tony Delk	.75
R11	Vitaly Potapenko	.50
R12	Jerome Williams	.25
R13	Todd Fuller	.25
R14	Erick Dampier	.75
R15	Derek Fisher	.50
R16	Donald Whiteside	.25
R17	John Wallace	3.00
R18	Steve Nash	.50
R19	Brian Evans	.25
R20	Jermaine O'Neal	3.00
R21	Roy Rogers	.50
R22	Priest Lauderdale	.25
R23	Kobe Bryant	14.00
R24	Martin Muursepp	.25
R25	Zydrunas Ilgauskas	2.50

1996-97 Bowman's Best Shots

Bowman's Best Shots are printed on clear plastic with a green tint, with the insert name in the upper left corner and the player's name in the lower left. The insert consists of 10 cards and is numbered with a "BS" prefix. Regular versions are seeded every 12 hobby and 20 retail packs, while Refractor versions are seeded every 48 hobby and 80 retail packs and Atomic Refractors are found every 96 hobby and 160 retail packs.

		MT
Complete Set (10):		65.00
Common Player:		2.00
Refractors:		2x-3x
Atomic Refractors:		3x-6x
BS1	Scottie Pippen	6.00
BS2	Gary Payton	2.00
BS3	Shaquille O'Neal	10.00
BS4	Hakeem Olajuwon	4.00
BS5	Kevin Garnett	10.00
BS6	Michael Jordan	25.00
BS7	Anfernee Hardaway	12.00
BS8	Grant Hill	12.00
BS9	Shawn Kemp	6.00
BS10	Dennis Rodman	8.00

1996-97 Bowman's Best Throwbacks

Retros was a 20-card subset that is actually considered part of the regular-issue set, but is numbered as an insert and listed as such. The cards featured a black border with green pinstripes and a black-and-white card. Numbered TB1-TB20, Refractor versions are seeded one per 12 hobby and one per 20 retail, while Atomic Refractor versions are seeded one per 24 hobby and one per 40 retail packs.

		MT
Complete Set (20):		10.00
Common Player:		.25
Refractors:		10x-20x
Atomic Refractors:		20x-40x
TB1	Avery Johnson	.25
TB2	Chris Webber	.50
TB3	Sean Elliott	.25
TB4	Joe Dumars	.25
TB5	Grant Hill	2.00
TB6	Gary Payton	.50
TB7	Shawn Kemp	1.00
TB8	Shaquille O'Neal	2.00
TB9	Eddie Jones	1.00
TB10	John Wallace	.50
TB11	Patrick Ewing	.50
TB12	Jerry Stackhouse	.50
TB13	Allen Iverson	4.00
TB14	Latrell Sprewell	.50
TB15	Dino Radja	.25
TB16	David Wesley	.25
TB17	Joe Smith	.50
TB18	Damon Stoudamire	.75
TB19	Marcus Camby	2.00
TB20	Juwan Howard	.50

1996 Collector's Edge Rookie Rage

Collector's Edge Rookie Rage Basketball Draft Picks has 48 different cards in the base set, plus two checklists. Each card front has a color action photo of the player in his collegiate uniform, against a metallic background with an orange basketball in the lower left corner. "Rookie Rage" and the player's name is stamped in silver foil along the sides of the card, which has a Collector's Edge logo in the lower right corner. The card back has a close-up shot of the player at the top, with his name above in an arch and his NBA team's city below. Biographical information and 1995-96 and career stats follow underneath. A basketball icon is in the lower right corner, with a Collector's Edge logo inside. A card number is in the lower left corner. Two parallel versions were also made, in silver and gold. Three insert sets, each with parallel versions, were also made - Key Kraze (normal and holofoil); Time Warp (normal, holofoil and gold); and Radical Recruits (normal and mosaic prism). A Scratch n' Win redemption card is also found in each pack. Prizes include an Ice Sculpture card (1:18), an uncut Rookie Rage sheet (1:36), an uncut Key Kraze sheet (1:72) and an uncut Time Warp sheet (1:108). Collectors can also send in for an 8" x 10" version of a Time Warp card by sending in 24 Rookie Rage wrappers and $3.95 for shipping and handling. An autographed version signed by an NBA legend may be found by including an upgrade card found in packs.

		MT
Complete Set (50):		10.00
Common Player:		.05
1	Shareef Abdur-Rahim	1.00
2	Ray Allen	1.00
3	Drew Barry	.05
4	Terrell Bell	.05
5	Joseph Blair	.05
6	Kobe Bryant	2.00
7	Marcus Camby	1.75
8	Erick Dampier	.30
9	Ben Davis	.05
10	Tony Delk	.50
11	Brian Evans	.10
12	Jamie Feick	.05
13	Dereck Fisher	.05
14	Todd Fuller	.10
15	Steve Hamer	.05
16	Othella Harrington	.10
17	Mark Hendrickson	.05
18	Reggie Geary	.05
19	Allen Iverson	2.50
20	Dontae Jones	.25
21	Kerry Kittles	.75
22	Travis Knight	.10
23	Priest Lauderdale	.05
24	Randy Livingston	.10
25	Marcus Mann	.05
26	Stephon Marbury	1.25
27	Walter McCarty	.50
28	Amal McCaskill	.05
29	Jeff McInnis	.05
30	Ryan Minor	.10
31	Darnell Robinson	.05
32	Steve Nash	.40
33	Moochie Norris	.05
34	Jormaino O'Neal	.50
35	Mark Pope	.05
36	Vitaly Potapenko	.15
37	Shandon Anderson	.05
38	Ron Riley	.05
39	Roy Rogers	.10
40	Malik Rose	.05
41	Jason Sasser	.05
42	Doron Sheffer	.05
43	Ronnie Henderson	.05
44	Antoine Walker	.50
45	Samaki Walker	.75
46	John Wallace	.40
47	Jerome Williams	.10
48	Lorenzen Wright	.40
49	Checklist	.05
50	Checklist	.05

1996 Collector's Edge Rookie Rage Key Kraze

Two versions of this 1996 Collector's Edge Rookie Rage were made - normal versions (seeded one every 56 packs) and holofoil versions (seeded one every 90 packs). The regular versions were limited to 3,200 sets; holofoils were limited to 2,000 sets. The basic card design has a color photo of the player in his college uniform, against a silver foiled, swirled pattern which has a ghosted image of the player in the background. "Key Kraze" is written along the left side of the card in silver foil, with the player's name at the top. An Edge logo is in the lower left corner. The card back has an artist's version of the photo from the front, with a square next to it containing a head shot. Biographical information and a recap of the player's collegiate accomplishments are written over the card. A card number is in the upper right corner; the serial number, out of 3,200, is along the lower right side.

		MT
Complete Set (25):		200.00
Common Player:		3.00
Holofoil Cards:		1.5x-3x
1	Shareef Abdur-Rahim	20.00
2	Ray Allen	12.00
3	Kobe Bryant	20.00
4	Marcus Camby	15.00
5	Erick Dampier	7.00
6	Tony Delk	6.00
7	Todd Fuller	3.00
8	Reggie Geary	3.00
9	Allen Iverson	30.00
10	Dontae Jones	3.00
11	Kerry Kittles	10.00
12	Stephon Marbury	25.00
13	Walter McCarty	10.00
14	Darnell Robinson	3.00
15	Steve Nash	8.00
16	Ben Davis	3.00
17	Mark Pope	3.00
18	Roy Rogers	3.00
19	Ronnie Henderson	3.00
20	Antoine Walker	20.00
21	Samaki Walker	10.00
22	John Wallace	12.00
23	Jerome Williams	3.00
24	Lorenzen Wright	3.00
25	Checklist	3.00

1996 Collector's Edge Rookie Rage Key Kraze Holofoil

This 25-card insert reprinted the Key Kraze insert with a holofoil finish and individually numbered up to 2,000. Holofoil Key Kraze versions were inserted every 90 packs of Rookie Rage.

	MT
Complete Set (25):	600.00
Holofoil Cards:	1.5x-3x

1996 Collector's Edge Rookie Rage Radical Recruits

Twenty-four top draft picks are showcased in this 1996 insert set. Normal versions are seeded one every 14 packs and are limited to 6,750, while mosaic prism versions are limited to 2,500 and are seeded one every 72 packs. The basic card front has a color photo against a basketball going through a net. The player's name is along the left side; Radical Recruits and Edge logos are in the bottom corners. The card back has a ghosted image of the player as a background, with a recap of the player's collegiate achievements and biographical information on it. A color photo is in the lower left corner. The player's name is at the top, with a card number in the upper right corner. A serial number (out of 6,750) is along the right side.

		MT
Complete Set (25):		100.00
Common Player:		2.00
1	Shareef Abdur-Rahim	10.00
2	Ray Allen	6.00
3	Kobe Bryant	15.00
4	Marcus Camby	8.00
5	Erick Dampier	4.00
6	Tony Delk	5.00
7	Todd Fuller	2.00
8	Allen Iverson	15.00
9	Dontae Jones	2.00
10	Kerry Kittles	5.00
11	Darnell Robinson	2.00
12	Stephon Marbury	12.00
13	Walter McCarty	4.00
14	Steve Nash	4.00
15	Ben Davis	2.00
16	Reggie Geary	2.00
17	Mark Pope	2.00
18	Roy Rogers	2.00
19	Ronnie Henderson	2.00
20	Antoine Walker	5.00
21	Samaki Walker	10.00
22	John Wallace	3.00
23	Jerome Williams	2.00
24	Lorenzen Wright	2.00
25	Checklist	2.00

1996 Collector's Edge Rookie Rage Radical Recruits Holofoil

This 25-card insert paralleled the Radical Recruits insert, but featured prismatic foil on the front, as well as individual hand-numbering. The back was also individually numbered to 2,500. Holofoil versions were inserted every 72 packs.

	MT
Complete Set (25):	300.00
Holofoil Cards:	1.5x-3x

1996 Collector's Edge Rookie Rage TimeWarp

These 1996 Collector's Edge Rookie Rage inserts pair an NBA legend with a 1996 draft pick. The background of the front is a blurred image of the same photo used for the draft pick. The players' two last names are in the bottom corners. The horizontal back has a hardwood court pattern, with photos of each player, plus biographical information and a comparison of the players' talents. A card number, using a "TW" prefix, is in the upper right corner. A serial number, out of 12,000, is also given along the

bottom. One of these inserts was seeded in every eighth pack, but two parallel versions also exist. Holofoil TimeWarps are found every 72 packs and are limited to 2,500 each; gold foil-stamped cards are limited to 1,000 and are seeded one per every 180 packs.

	MT
Complete Set (12):	40.00
Common Player:	1.50
TW1 Shareef Abdur-Rahim, David Robinson	4.00
TW2 Ray Allen, Alex English	4.00
TW3 Kobe Bryant, Alex English	6.00
TW4 Marcus Camby, Moses Malone	6.00
TW5 Erick Dampier, George Gervin	1.50
TW6 Allen Iverson, Isiah Thomas	8.00
TW7 Kerry Kittles, Isiah Thomas	4.00
TW8 Stephon Marbury, David Thompson	5.00
TW9 Antoine Walker, Moses Malone	3.00
TW10 Samaki Walker, Walter Frazier	3.00
TW11 John Wallace, George Gervin	3.00
TW12 Lorenzen Wright, Walter Frazier	1.50

1996 Collector's Edge Rookie Rage TimeWarp Holofoil

This 12-card insert reprinted each card in the TimeWarp insert, but was printed with a holofoil finish on the front and individually numbered to 2,500. This parallel version was seeded one per 72 packs.

	MT
Complete Set (12):	160.00
Holofoil Cards:	2x-4x

1996 Collector's Edge Rookie Rage TimeWarp Gold

This 12-card insert paralleled the TimeWarp insert, but was gold foil stamped on the front and individually numbered to 1,000. Gold foil stamped versions were inserted every 180 packs of Rookie Rage.

	MT
Complete Set (12):	160.00
Gold Cards:	2x-4x

1996-97 Fleer II

Fleer's 1996-97 basketball set was issued in two 150-card series. Card fronts featured full-bleed photos with the player's name in the lower left corner and the Fleer 1996-97 logo in the top right. Backs were horizontal and included another shot of the player and statistics over a basketball-like

background that includes the player's team logo. Series I had 119 regular-issue cards, 29 Hardwood Leaders and two checklists, while Series II had 118 regular cards, 20 All-Star Retro, 10 Crystal Ball and two checklists. Inserts in Series I include: Stackhouse's All-Fleer, Rookie Rewind, Lucky 13, Stackhouse's Scrapbook, Decade of Excellence, Franchise Futures and GameBreakers. Inserts in Series II include: Swing Shift, Towers of Power, Rookie Sensations, Decade of Excellence, Thrill Seekers and Total O.

		MT
Complete Series 2 (150):		15.00
Common Player:		.05
Series 2 Wax Box:		40.00
151	Alan Henderson	.05
152	*Priest Lauderdale*	.05
153	Dikembe Mutombo	.10
154	Dana Barros	.05
155	Todd Day	.05
156	*Brett Szabo*	.05
157	*Antoine Walker*	1.50
158	Scott Burrell	.05
159	*Tony Delk*	.25
160	Vlade Divac	.05
161	Matt Geiger	.05
162	Anthony Mason	.05
163	*Malik Rose*	.05
164	Ron Harper	.05
165	Steve Kerr	.05
166	Luc Longley	.05
167	Danny Ferry	.05
168	Tyrone Hill	.05
169	*Vitaly Potapenko*	.20
170	Tony Dumas	.05
171	Chris Gatling	.05
172	Oliver Miller	.05
173	Eric Montross	.05
174	*Samaki Walker*	.25
175	*Darvin Ham*	.05
176	Mark Jackson	.05
177	Ervin Johnson	.05
178	Stacey Augmon	.05
179	Joe Dumars	.05
180	Grant Hill	1.00
181	Grant Long	.05
182	Terry Mills	.05
183	Otis Thorpe	.05
184	*Jerome Williams*	.05
185	B.J. Armstrong	.05
186	*Todd Fuller*	.20
187	*Ray Owes*	.05
188	Mark Price	.05
189	Felton Spencer	.05
190	Charles Barkley	.40
191	Mario Elie	.05
192	*Othella Harrington*	.05
193	*Matt Maloney*	.50
194	Brent Price	.05
195	Kevin Willis	.05
196	Travis Best	.05
197	*Erick Dampier*	.25
198	Antonio Davis	.05
199	Jalen Rose	.05
200	Pooh Richardson	.05
201	Rodney Rogers	.05
202	*Lorenzen Wright*	.25
203	*Kobe Bryant*	3.00
204	*Derek Fisher*	.30
205	*Travis Knight*	.25
206	Shaquille O'Neal	1.25
207	Byron Scott	.05
208	P.J. Brown	.05
209	Sasha Danilovic	.05
210	Dan Majerle	.05
211	*Martin Muursepp*	.05
212	*Ray Allen*	1.25
213	Armon Gilliam	.05
214	Andrew Lang	.05
215	*Moochie Norris*	.05
216	Kevin Garnett	1.25
217	Tom Gugliotta	.05
218	*Shane Heal*	.05
219	Stephon Marbury	2.00
220	Stojko Vrankovic	.05
221	*Kerry Kittles*	1.25
222	Robert Pack	.05
223	Jayson Williams	.05
224	Allan Houston	.05
225	Larry Johnson	.10
226	*Dantae Jones*	.20
227	*Walter McCarty*	.05
228	*John Wallace*	.40
229	Charlie Ward	.05
230	*Brian Evans*	.05

231	*Amal McCaskill*	.05
232	Brian Shaw	.05
233	Mark Davis	.05
234	Lucious Harris	.05
235	Allen Iverson	3.00
236	Sam Cassell	.05
237	Robert Horry	.05
238	Danny Manning	.05
239	*Steve Nash*	.40
240	Kenny Anderson	.05
241	*Aleksandar Djordjevic*	.05
242	*Jermaine O'Neal*	.50
243	Isaiah Rider	.05
244	Rasheed Wallace	.05
245	Mahmoud Abdul-Rauf	.05
246	Michael Smith	.05
247	Corliss Williamson	.05
248	Vernon Maxwell	.05
249	Charles Smith	.05
250	Dominique Wilkins	.05
251	Craig Ehlo	.05
252	Jim McIlvaine	.05
253	Sam Perkins	.05
254	*Marcus Camby*	2.00
255	Popeye Jones	.05
256	*Donald Whiteside*	.05
257	Walt Williams	.05
258	Jeff Hornacek	.05
259	Karl Malone	.25
260	Bryon Russell	.05
261	John Stockton	.25
262	*Shareef Abdur-Rahim*	2.00
263	Anthony Peeler	.05
264	*Roy Rogers*	.20
265	Tim Legler	.05
266	Tracy Murray	.05
267	Rod Strickland	.05
268	*Ben Wallace*	.05
269	Kevin Garnett (Crystal Ball)	.60
270	Allan Houston (Crystal Ball)	.05
271	Eddie Jones (Crystal Ball)	.05
272	Jamal Mashburn (Crystal Ball)	.05
273	Antonio McDyess (Crystal Ball)	.05
274	Glenn Robinson (Crystal Ball)	.05
275	Joe Smith (Crystal Ball)	.20
276	Steve Smith (Crystal Ball)	.05
277	Jerry Stackhouse (Crystal Ball)	.30
278	Damon Stoudamire (Crystal Ball)	.40
279	Hakeem Olajuwon (All-Star Retro)	.30
280	Charles Barkley (All-Star Retro)	.20
281	Patrick Ewing (All-Star Retro)	.10
282	Michael Jordan (All-Star Retro)	1.50
283	Clyde Drexler (All-Star Retro)	.15
284	Karl Malone (All-Star Retro)	.10
285	John Stockton (All-Star Retro)	.10
286	David Robinson (All-Star Retro)	.20
287	Scottie Pippen (All-Star Retro)	.35
288	Shawn Kemp (All-Star Retro)	.35
289	Shaquille O'Neal (All-Star Retro)	.60
290	Mitch Richmond (All-Star Retro)	.05
291	Reggie Miller (All-Star Retro)	.05
292	Alonzo Mourning (All-Star Retro)	.05
293	Gary Payton (All-Star Retro)	.05
294	Anfernee Hardaway (All-Star Retro)	.75
295	Grant Hill (All-Star Retro)	.50
296	Dennis Rodman (All-Star Retro)	.60
297	Juwan Howard (All-Star Retro)	.05
298	Jason Kidd (All-Star Retro)	.15
299	Checklist	.05
300	Checklist	.05

1996-97 Fleer Decade of Excellence

These 20 cards feature reprints of active players' cards from Fleer's popular 1986-87 inaugural basketball set.

The set was issued with 10 cards in Series I and 10 in Series II, with both carrying a one in 72 hobby pack insertion ratio. The cards are identified by a gold foil stamp in the lower left corner that reads "Fleer Decade of Excellence 1986-96."

		MT
Complete Series 2 (10):		80.00
Common Player:		6.00
11	Charles Barkley	20.00
12	Patrick Ewing	16.00
13	Eddie Johnson	6.00
14	Hakeem Olajuwon	30.00
15	Robert Parish	6.00
16	Byron Scott	6.00
17	Wayman Tisdale	6.00
18	Gerald Wilkins	6.00
19	Herb Williams	6.00
20	Kevin Willis	6.00

1996-97 Fleer Rookie Sensations

This 15-card set highlighted the top rookies from the 1996-97 season, and were inserted one per 90 packs. The player's embossed image was cast over a copper foil background with silver foil around the border. In addition, the cards feature a Rookie Sensations logo in the lower right corner.

		MT
Complete Set (15):		200.00
Common Player:		3.00
1	Shareef Abdur-Rahim	30.00
2	Ray Allen	20.00
3	Kobe Bryant	45.00
4	Marcus Camby	30.00
5	Erick Dampier	3.00
6	Tony Delk	3.00
7	Allen Iverson	45.00
8	Kerry Kittles	18.00
9	Stephon Marbury	35.00
10	Steve Nash	6.00
11	Roy Rogers	3.00
12	Antoine Walker	20.00
13	Samaki Walker	3.00
14	John Wallace	8.00
15	Lorenzen Wright	3.00

1996-97 Fleer Swing Shift

This 15-card set was inserted into Series II packs at a rate of one per six packs. The cards feature a color shot of the player over the words "Swing Shift" that appear all over the background. The backs are white and include another color shot of the player.

		MT
Complete Set (15):		18.00
Common Player:		.50
1	Ray Allen	1.75
2	Charles Barkley	1.00
3	Michael Finley	.50
4	Anfernee Hardaway	5.00
5	Grant Hill	5.00
6	Jim Jackson	.50
7	Eddie Jones	.50
8	Kerry Kittles	1.75
9	Reggie Miller	.75
10	Gary Payton	.75
11	Scottie Pippen	2.50
12	Mitch Richmond	.50
13	Steve Smith	.50
14	Latrell Sprewell	.75
15	Jerry Stackhouse	1.25

1996-97 Fleer Thrill Seekers

Thrill Seekers included 15 cards on lenticular technology. This insert was found in every 240 hobby packs of Series II, and attempts to provide a three-dimensional look around the featured player.

		MT
Complete Set (15):		600.00
Common Player:		10.00
1	Shareef Abdur-Rahim	50.00
2	Charles Barkley	20.00
3	Anfernee Hardaway	90.00
4	Grant Hill	90.00
5	Allen Iverson	80.00
6	Michael Jordan	175.00
7	Shawn Kemp	40.00
8	Jason Kidd	15.00
9	Stephon Marbury	70.00
10	Antonio McDyess	10.00
11	Reggie Miller	10.00
12	Alonzo Mourning	10.00
13	Shaquille O'Neal	90.00
14	David Robinson	20.00
15	Damon Stoudamire	40.00

1996-97 Fleer Total "O"

This 10-card insert was found only in Series II retail packs, at a rate of one per 44 packs. The cards are printed on plastic with a large basketball in the background and the "Total O" logo in the upper left corner.

		MT
Complete Set (10):		125.00
Common Player:		3.00
1	Anfernee Hardaway	25.00
2	Grant Hill	25.00
3	Juwan Howard	5.00
4	Michael Jordan	50.00
5	Shawn Kemp	12.00
6	Karl Malone	3.00
7	Alonzo Mourning	3.00
8	Hakeem Olajuwon	8.00
9	Shaquille O'Neal	20.00
10	Jerry Stackhouse	6.00

1996-97 Fleer Towers of Power

Towers of Power displays 10 of the NBA top big men on a foil etched background. Inserted in one per 30 packs of Series II, these cards have a rough painting of a city skyline in the background with the insert name running up the left side. The backs are horizontal and include another shot of the player along with text in white print.

		MT
Complete Set (10):		70.00
Common Player:		3.00
1	Shareef Abdur-Rahim	12.00
2	Marcus Camby	12.00
3	Patrick Ewing	4.00
4	Kevin Garnett	18.00
5	Shawn Kemp	12.00
6	Hakeem Olajuwon	10.00
7	Shaquille O'Neal	20.00
8	David Robinson	5.00
9	Dennis Rodman	15.00
10	Joe Smith	3.00

1996-97 Flair Showcase

Flair Showcase features 90 different players, each with three different style card fronts - Grace, Style and Showcase. The set also has three different card backs - Showtime, Showstopper and Showpiece, with the entire set divided into 30-card segments of similar front and back designs. Each 30-card segment carried a different insert rate: Style Showtime 1:1; Style Showstopper 1:1.5; Style Showpiece 1:2; Grace Showtime 1:2; Grace Showstopper 1:2.5; Grace Showpiece 1:3.5; Showcase Showtime 1:5; Showcase Showstopper 1:10; and Showcase Showpiece 1:24. The cards are identified by a code in all four corners on the back: Row indicates the card front; Seat indicates the card number of 90, Section indicates if the card is regular-issue (1) or a parallel set (0) and the lower right corner indicates what type of card back the card is.

		MT
Complete Set (270):		1000.00
Comp. Style Set (90):		50.00
Common Style (A1-A90):		.25
Comp. Grace Set (90):		125.00
Common Grace (B1-B90):		.50
Comp. Showcase Set (90):		900.00
Common Showcase (C1-C90):		2.00
Wax Box:		160.00
A1	Anfernee Hardaway STY	4.00
A2	Mitch Richmond STY	.50
A3	*Allen Iverson STY*	8.00
A4	Charles Barkley STY	.75
A5	Juwan Howard STY	.75
A6	David Robinson STY	.75
A7	Gary Payton STY	.75
A8	*Kerry Kittles STY*	2.00
A9	Dennis Rodman STY	2.00
A10	Shaquille O'Neal STY	2.50
A11	*Stephon Marbury STY*	6.00
A12	John Stockton STY	.50
A13	Glenn Robinson STY	.50
A14	Hakeem Olajuwon STY	1.25
A15	Jason Kidd STY	.75
A16	Jerry Stackhouse STY	.75
A17	Joe Smith STY	.75
A18	Reggie Miller STY	.50
A19	Grant Hill STY	4.00
A20	Damon Stoudamire STY	1.25
A21	Kevin Garnett STY	4.00
A22	Clyde Drexler STY	.75
A23	Michael Jordan STY	8.00
A24	Antonio McDyess STY	.75
A25	Chris Webber STY	1.25
A26	*Antoine Walker STY*	4.00
A27	Scottie Pippen STY	2.00
A28	Karl Malone STY	.75
A29	*Shareef Abdur-Rahim STY*	5.00
A30	Shawn Kemp STY	2.00
A31	*Kobe Bryant STY*	10.00
A32	Derrick Coleman STY	.50
A33	Alonzo Mourning STY	.50
A34	Anthony Mason STY	.25
A35	*Ray Allen STY*	2.50
A36	Arvydas Sabonis STY	.25
A37	Brian Grant STY	.25
A38	Bryant Reeves STY	.25
A39	Christian Laettner STY	.25
A40	Tom Gugliotta STY	.25
A41	Latrell Sprewell STY	.75
A42	*Erick Dampier STY*	.75
A43	Gheorghe Muresan STY	.25
A44	Glen Rice STY	.50
A45	Patrick Ewing STY	.50
A46	Jim Jackson STY	.25
A47	Michael Finley STY	.50
A48	Toni Kukoc STY	.50
A49	*Marcus Camby STY*	4.00
A50	Kenny Anderson STY	.25
A51	Mark Price STY	.25
A52	Tim Hardaway STY	.50
A53	Mookie Blaylock STY	.25
A54	Steve Smith STY	.25
A55	Terrell Brandon STY	.50
A56	*Lorenzen Wright STY*	.75
A57	Sasha Danilovic STY	.25
A58	Jeff Hornacek STY	.25
A59	Eddie Jones STY	1.00
A60	Vin Baker STY	.50
A61	Chris Childs STY	.25
A62	Clifford Robinson STY	.25
A63	Anthony Peeler STY	.25
A64	Dino Radja STY	.25
A65	Joe Dumars STY	.25
A66	Loy Vaught STY	.25
A67	Rony Seikaly STY	.25
A68	*Vitaly Potapenko STY*	.50
A69	Chris Gatling STY	.25
A70	Dale Ellis STY	.25
A71	Allan Houston STY	.50
A72	Doug Christie STY	.25
A73	LaPhonso Ellis STY	.25
A74	Kendall Gill STY	.25
A75	Rik Smits STY	.25
A76	Bobby Phills STY	.25
A77	Malik Sealy STY	.25
A78	Sean Elliott STY	.25
A79	Vlade Divac STY	.25
A80	David Wesley STY	.25
A81	Dominique Wilkins STY	.25
A82	Danny Manning STY	.25
A83	Detlef Schrempf STY	.25
A84	Hersey Hawkins STY	.25
A85	Lindsey Hunter STY	.25
A86	Mahmoud Abdul-Rauf STY	.25
A87	Shawn Bradley STY	.25
A88	Horace Grant STY	.25
A89	Cedric Ceballos STY	.25
A90	Jamal Mashburn STY	.25
B1	Anfernee Hardaway GRA	5.00
B2	Mitch Richmond GRA	1.00

B3	Allen Iverson GRA	12.00
B4	Charles Barkley GRA	2.00
B5	Juwan Howard GRA	2.00
B6	David Robinson GRA	2.00
B7	Gary Payton GRA	2.00
B8	Kerry Kittles GRA	4.00
B9	Dennis Rodman GRA	4.00
B10	Shaquille O'Neal GRA	4.00
B11	Stephon Marbury GRA	10.00
B12	John Stockton GRA	1.00
B13	Glenn Robinson GRA	1.00
B14	Hakeem Olajuwon GRA	2.50
B15	Jason Kidd GRA	2.00
B16	Jerry Stackhouse GRA	2.00
B17	Joe Smith GRA	2.00
B18	Reggie Miller GRA	1.00
B19	Grant Hill GRA	6.00
B20	Damon Stoudamire GRA	2.50
B21	Kevin Garnett GRA	6.00
B22	Clyde Drexler GRA	1.25
B23	Michael Jordan GRA	16.00
B24	Antonio McDyess GRA	1.50
B25	Chris Webber GRA	2.50
B26	Antoine Walker GRA	8.00
B27	Scottie Pippen GRA	3.00
B28	Karl Malone GRA	1.00
B29	Shareef Abdur-Rahim GRA	8.00
B30	Shawn Kemp GRA	3.00
B31	Kobe Bryant GRA	15.00
B32	Derrick Coleman GRA	.50
B33	Alonzo Mourning GRA	1.00
B34	Anthony Mason GRA	.50
B35	Ray Allen GRA	3.00
B36	Arvydas Sabonis GRA	.50
B37	Brian Grant GRA	.50
B38	Bryant Reeves GRA	.50
B39	Christian Laettner GRA	.50
B40	Tom Gugliotta GRA	.50
B41	Latrell Sprewell GRA	1.50
B42	Erick Dampier GRA	1.50
B43	Gheorghe Muresan GRA	.50
B44	Glen Rice GRA	1.00
B45	Patrick Ewing GRA	1.00
B46	Jim Jackson GRA	.50
B47	Michael Finley GRA	1.00
B48	Toni Kukoc GRA	1.00
B49	Marcus Camby GRA	6.00
B50	Kenny Anderson GRA	.50
B51	Mark Price GRA	.50
B52	Tim Hardaway GRA	1.00
B53	Mookie Blaylock GRA	.50
B54	Steve Smith GRA	.50
B55	Terrell Brandon GRA	1.00
B56	Lorenzen Wright GRA	1.50
B57	Sasha Danilovic GRA	.50
B58	Jeff Hornacek GRA	.50
B59	Eddie Jones GRA	2.50
B60	Vin Baker GRA	1.00
B61	Chris Childs GRA	.50
B62	Clifford Robinson GRA	.50
B63	Anthony Peeler GRA	.50
B64	Dino Radja GRA	.50
B65	Joe Dumars GRA	.50
B66	Loy Vaught GRA	.50
B67	Rony Seikaly GRA	.50
B68	Vitaly Potapenko GRA	1.00
B69	Chris Gatling GRA	.50
B70	Dale Ellis GRA	.50
B71	Allan Houston GRA	1.00
B72	Doug Christie GRA	.50
B73	LaPhonso Ellis GRA	.50
B74	Kendall Gill GRA	.50
B75	Rik Smits GRA	.50
B76	Bobby Phills GRA	.50
B77	Malik Sealy GRA	.50
B78	Sean Elliott GRA	.50
B79	Vlade Divac GRA	.50
B80	David Wesley GRA	.50
B81	Dominique Wilkins GRA	.50
B82	Danny Manning GRA	.50
B83	Detlef Schrempf GRA	.50
B84	Hersey Hawkins GRA	.50
B85	Lindsey Hunter GRA	.50
B86	Mahmoud Abdul-Rauf GRA	.50
B87	Shawn Bradley GRA	.50
B88	Horace Grant GRA	.50
B89	Cedric Ceballos GRA	.50
B90	Jamal Mashburn GRA	1.00
C1	Anfernee Hardaway SHOW	40.00
C2	Mitch Richmond SHOW	10.00
C3	Allen Iverson SHOW	60.00
C4	Charles Barkley SHOW	20.00
C5	Juwan Howard SHOW	20.00
C6	David Robinson SHOW	20.00
C7	Gary Payton SHOW	20.00
C8	Kerry Kittles SHOW	20.00
C9	Dennis Rodman SHOW	30.00
C10	Shaquille O'Neal SHOW	40.00
C11	Stephon Marbury SHOW	50.00
C12	John Stockton SHOW	12.00
C13	Glenn Robinson SHOW	12.00

C14	Hakeem Olajuwon SHOW	30.00
C15	Jason Kidd SHOW	20.00
C16	Jerry Stackhouse SHOW	20.00
C17	Joe Smith SHOW	20.00
C18	Reggie Miller SHOW	15.00
C19	Grant Hill SHOW	60.00
C20	Damon Stoudamire SHOW	25.00
C21	Kevin Garnett SHOW	60.00
C22	Clyde Drexler SHOW	20.00
C23	Michael Jordan SHOW	125.00
C24	Antonio McDyess SHOW	15.00
C25	Chris Webber SHOW	25.00
C26	Antoine Walker SHOW	40.00
C27	Scottie Pippen SHOW	30.00
C28	Karl Malone SHOW	20.00
C29	Shareef Abdur-Rahim SHOW	40.00
C30	Shawn Kemp SHOW	30.00
C31	Kobe Bryant SHOW	50.00
C32	Derrick Coleman SHOW	4.00
C33	Alonzo Mourning SHOW	8.00
C34	Anthony Mason SHOW	2.00
C35	Ray Allen SHOW	10.00
C36	Arvydas Sabonis SHOW	2.00
C37	Brian Grant SHOW	2.00
C38	Bryant Reeves SHOW	2.00
C39	Christian Laettner SHOW	4.00
C40	Tom Gugliotta SHOW	4.00
C41	Latrell Sprewell SHOW	10.00
C42	Erick Dampier SHOW	6.00
C43	Gheorghe Muresan SHOW	2.00
C44	Glen Rice SHOW	8.00
C45	Patrick Ewing SHOW	8.00
C46	Jim Jackson SHOW	4.00
C47	Michael Finley SHOW	6.00
C48	Toni Kukoc SHOW	4.00
C49	Marcus Camby SHOW	20.00
C50	Kenny Anderson SHOW	4.00
C51	Mark Price SHOW	2.00
C52	Tim Hardaway SHOW	8.00
C53	Mookie Blaylock SHOW	2.00
C54	Steve Smith SHOW	2.00
C55	Terrell Brandon SHOW	6.00
C56	Lorenzen Wright SHOW	6.00
C57	Sasha Danilovic SHOW	2.00
C58	Jeff Hornacek SHOW	2.00
C59	Eddie Jones SHOW	15.00
C60	Vin Baker SHOW	8.00
C61	Chris Childs SHOW	2.00
C62	Clifford Robinson SHOW	2.00
C63	Anthony Peeler SHOW	2.00
C64	Dino Radja SHOW	2.00
C65	Joe Dumars SHOW	4.00
C66	Loy Vaught SHOW	2.00
C67	Rony Seikaly SHOW	2.00
C68	Vitaly Potapenko SHOW	6.00
C69	Chris Gatling SHOW	2.00
C70	Dale Ellis SHOW	2.00
C71	Allan Houston SHOW	4.00
C72	Doug Christie SHOW	2.00
C73	LaPhonso Ellis SHOW	2.00
C74	Kendall Gill SHOW	2.00
C75	Rik Smits SHOW	2.00
C76	Bobby Phills SHOW	2.00
C77	Malik Sealy SHOW	2.00
C78	Sean Elliott SHOW	2.00
C79	Vlade Divac SHOW	2.00
C80	David Wesley SHOW	2.00
C81	Dominique Wilkins SHOW	2.00
C82	Danny Manning SHOW	2.00
C83	Detlef Schrempf SHOW	2.00
C84	Hersey Hawkins SHOW	2.00
C85	Lindsey Hunter SHOW	4.00
C86	Mahmoud Abdul-Rauf SHOW	2.00
C87	Shawn Bradley SHOW	4.00
C88	Horace Grant SHOW	2.00
C89	Cedric Ceballos SHOW	2.00
C90	Jamal Mashburn SHOW	4.00

1996-97 Flair Showcase Legacy

Legacy Collection was a 270-card parallel set that featured purple foil on the front instead of gold foil, and a matte finish back with silver foil stamping, including individual numbering up to 150. The section number on the back is also 0 instead of 1, which appears on regular-issue cards.

		MT
Common Player:		10.00
Each Player Has Three Different Cards.		
1	Anfernee Hardaway	250.00

2	Mitch Richmond	40.00
3	Allen Iverson	275.00
4	Charles Barkley	60.00
5	Juwan Howard	60.00
6	David Robinson	60.00
7	Gary Payton	60.00
8	Kerry Kittles	80.00
9	Dennis Rodman	200.00
10	Shaquille O'Neal	225.00
11	Stephon Marbury	225.00
12	John Stockton	40.00
13	Glenn Robinson	40.00
14	Hakeem Olajuwon	100.00
15	Jason Kidd	50.00
16	Jerry Stackhouse	60.00
17	Joe Smith	60.00
18	Reggie Miller	40.00
19	Grant Hill	275.00
20	Damon Stoudamire	90.00
21	Kevin Garnett	275.00
22	Clyde Drexler	50.00
23	Michael Jordan	550.00
24	Antonio McDyess	50.00
25	Chris Webber	100.00
26	Antoine Walker	150.00
27	Scottie Pippen	125.00
28	Karl Malone	50.00
29	Shareef Abdur-Rahim	160.00
30	Shawn Kemp	125.00
31	Kobe Bryant	300.00
32	Derrick Coleman	20.00
33	Alonzo Mourning	40.00
34	Anthony Mason	10.00
35	Ray Allen	75.00
36	Arvydas Sabonis	10.00
37	Brian Grant	10.00
38	Bryant Reeves	10.00
39	Christian Laettner	20.00
40	Tom Gugliotta	20.00
41	Latrell Sprewell	50.00
42	Erick Dampier	20.00
43	Gheorghe Muresan	10.00
44	Glen Rice	40.00
45	Patrick Ewing	40.00
46	Jim Jackson	20.00
47	Michael Finley	30.00
48	Toni Kukoc	30.00
49	Marcus Camby	150.00
50	Kenny Anderson	20.00
51	Mark Price	10.00
52	Tim Hardaway	30.00
53	Mookie Blaylock	10.00
54	Steve Smith	10.00
55	Terrell Brandon	30.00
56	Lorenzen Wright	20.00
57	Sasha Danilovic	10.00
58	Jeff Hornacek	10.00
59	Eddie Jones	100.00
60	Vin Baker	40.00
61	Chris Childs	10.00
62	Clifford Robinson	10.00
63	Anthony Peeler	10.00
64	Dino Radja	10.00
65	Joe Dumars	20.00
66	Loy Vaught	10.00
67	Rony Seikaly	10.00
68	Vitaly Potapenko	20.00
69	Chris Gatling	10.00
70	Dale Ellis	10.00
71	Allan Houston	20.00
72	Doug Christie	10.00
73	LaPhonso Ellis	10.00
74	Kendall Gill	10.00
75	Rik Smits	10.00
76	Bobby Phills	10.00
77	Malik Sealy	10.00
78	Sean Elliott	10.00
79	Vlade Divac	10.00
80	David Wesley	10.00
81	Dominique Wilkins	10.00
82	Danny Manning	10.00
83	Detlef Schrempf	10.00

84	Hersey Hawkins	10.00
85	Lindsey Hunter	10.00
86	Mahmoud Abdul-Rauf	10.00
87	Shawn Bradley	10.00
88	Horace Grant	10.00
89	Cedric Ceballos	10.00
90	Jamal Mashburn	20.00

1996-97 Flair Showcase Class of '96

This 20-card insert features top rookies from the 1996 NBA Draft. The cards are extra thick and have a white background with an embossed foil player image to the right of the insert's name running up the left side in gold foil. Backs are black with another shot of the player in the upper right and the insert name along the left side. Class of 1996 inserts were seeded one per five packs.

		MT
Complete Set (20):		100.00
Common Player:		1.50
1	Shareef Abdur-Rahim	12.00
2	Ray Allen	5.00
3	Shandon Anderson	1.50
4	Kobe Bryant	20.00
5	Marcus Camby	10.00
6	Erick Dampier	2.00
7	Derek Fisher	2.00
8	Todd Fuller	1.50
9	Othella Harrington	1.50
10	Allen Iverson	20.00
11	Kerry Kittles	6.00
12	Travis Knight	2.00
13	Matt Maloney	3.00
14	Stephon Marbury	16.00
15	Steve Nash	2.00
16	Jermaine O'Neal	5.00
17	Vitaly Potapenko	1.50
18	Roy Rogers	1.50
19	Antoine Walker	10.00
20	Lorenzen Wright	1.50

1996-97 Flair Showcase Hot Shots

This 20-card insert features embossed cards die-cut around the shape of flames through the top and sides of the card. The player's image is cast over a Spalding basketball, which is all cast over orange/red flames, with the insert name in the upper right in gold foil. Inserted in one per 90 packs, each card appears to have a variation where the foil stamping doesn't match the player's picture on the front, however these variations carry no premium in price.

		MT
Complete Set (20):		700.00
Common Player:		12.00
1	Michael Jordan	175.00
2	Kevin Garnett	80.00
3	Damon Stoudamire	30.00
4	Anfernee Hardaway	75.00
5	Shaquille O'Neal	60.00
6	Grant Hill	75.00
7	Dennis Rodman	50.00
8	Shawn Kemp	40.00
9	Scottie Pippen	40.00
10	Juwan Howard	20.00
11	Jason Kidd	20.00
12	Hakeem Olajuwon	30.00
13	Karl Malone	12.00
14	Joe Smith	20.00
15	David Robinson	20.00
16	Jerry Stackhouse	20.00
17	Antonio McDyess	20.00
18	Clyde Drexler	12.00
19	Gary Payton	20.00
20	Eddie Jones	25.00

1996-97 Metal

Metal included 150 cards in Series I and 100 in Series II for 1996-97. Card fronts featured a color shot of the player cut out on a "metal" background that is made of silver foil. The player's name is embossed and runs up the right side with the Metal logo in the lower right corner. Backs are printed vertically with another shot of the player, and statistics printed horizontally on the right side. Series I includes 100 cards, 15 On the Move, 10 Metallized, five Fresh Foundations, 10 Metal Shredders and two checklists, while Series II included 73 regular cards, 10 Metal Shredders, 10 Metalized, five Fresh Foudations and two checklists. Insert sets in Series I include: Molten Metal, Power Tools, Steel Slammin', Metal Edge, Decade of Excellence, Maximum Metal and NBA Pick-Up Game. Inserts in Series II include: Cyber-Metal, Freshly Forged, Platinum Portraits, Maximum Metal, Molten Metal, Net Rageous and a 98-card parallel set (minus the two checklists) called Precious Metal.

		MT
Complete Set (250):		55.00
Complete Series 1 (150):		30.00
Complete Series 2 (100):		25.00
Common Player:		.10
Series 1 Wax Box:		50.00
Series 2 Wax Box:		55.00
1	Mookie Blaylock	.10
2	Christian Laettner	.10
3	Steve Smith	.10
4	Dana Barros	.10
5	Rick Fox	.10
6	Dino Radja	.10
7	Eric Williams	.10
8	Dell Curry	.10
9	Matt Geiger	.10
10	Glen Rice	.10
11	Michael Jordan	5.00
12	Toni Kukoc	.10
13	Luc Longley	.10
14	Scottie Pippen	1.25
15	Dennis Rodman	1.75
16	Terrell Brandon	.10
17	Danny Ferry	.10
18	Chris Mills	.10
19	Bobby Phills	.10
20	Bob Sura	.10
21	Jim Jackson	.30
22	Jason Kidd	1.00
23	Jamal Mashburn	.30
24	George McCloud	.10
25	LaPhonso Ellis	.10
26	Antonio McDyess	.50
27	Bryant Stith	.10
28	Joe Dumars	.10
29	Grant Hill	2.00
30	Theo Ratliff	.10
31	Otis Thorpe	.10
32	Chris Mullin	.10
33	Joe Smith	.50
34	Latrell Sprewell	.20
35	Sam Cassell	.10
36	Clyde Drexler	.40
37	Robert Horry	.10
38	Hakeem Olajuwon	1.00
39	Antonio Davis	.10
40	Dale Davis	.10
41	Derrick McKey	.10
42	Reggie Miller	.40
43	Rik Smits	.10
44	Brent Barry	.20
45	Malik Sealy	.10
46	Loy Vaught	.10
47	Elden Campbell	.10
48	Cedric Ceballos	.20
49	Eddie Jones	.30
50	Nick Van Exel	.20
51	Sasha Danilovic	.10
52	Tim Hardaway	.10
53	Alonzo Mourning	.30
54	Kurt Thomas	.10
55	Vin Baker	.30
56	Sherman Douglas	.10
57	Glenn Robinson	.30
58	Kevin Garnett	2.00
59	Tom Gugliotta	.10
60	Doug West	.10
61	Shawn Bradley	.10
62	Ed O'Bannon	.20
63	Jayson Williams	.10
64	Patrick Ewing	.40
65	Charles Oakley	.10
66	John Starks	.10
67	Nick Anderson	.10
68	Horace Grant	.10
69	Anfernee Hardaway	2.50
70	Dennis Scott	.10
71	Brian Shaw	.10
72	Derrick Coleman	.10
73	Jerry Stackhouse	1.00
74	Clarence Weatherspoon	.10
75	Charles Barkley	.50
76	Michael Finley	.75
77	Kevin Johnson	.10
78	Wesley Person	.10
79	Aaron McKie	.10
80	Clifford Robinson	.10
81	Arvydas Sabonis	.40
82	Gary Trent	.10
83	Tyus Edney	.20
84	Brian Grant	.10
85	Billy Owens	.10
86	Olden Polynice	.10
87	Mitch Richmond	.20
88	Vinny Del Negro	.10
89	Sean Elliott	.10
90	Avery Johnson	.10
91	David Robinson	.75
92	Hersey Hawkins	.10
93	Shawn Kemp	1.25
94	Gary Payton	.30
95	Sam Perkins	.10
96	Detlef Schrempf	.10
97	Doug Christie	.10
98	Damon Stoudamire	1.25
99	Sharone Wright	.10
100	Jeff Hornacek	.10
101	Karl Malone	.30
102	John Stockton	.30
103	Greg Anthony	.10
104	Blue Edwards	.10
105	Bryant Reeves	.30
106	Juwan Howard	.50
107	Gheorghe Muresan	.10
108	Chris Webber	.30
109	Kenny Anderson (On the Move)	.10
110	Stacey Augmon (On the Move)	.10
111	Chris Childs (On the Move)	.10
112	Vlade Divac (On the Move)	.10
113	Allan Houston (On the Move)	.10
114	Mark Jackson (On the Move)	.10
115	Larry Johnson (On the Move)	.10
116	Grant Long (On the Move)	.10
117	Anthony Mason (On the Move)	.10
118	Dikembe Mutombo (On the Move)	.10
119	Shaquille O'Neal (On the Move)	2.50
120	Isaiah Rider (On the Move)	.10
121	Rod Strickland (On the Move)	.10
122	Rasheed Wallace (On the Move)	.25
123	Jalen Rose (On the Move)	.10
124	Anfernee Hardaway (Metallized)	1.25
125	Tim Hardaway (Metallized)	.10
126	Allan Houston (Metallized)	.10
127	Eddie Jones (Metallized)	.10
128	Michael Jordan (Metallized)	2.50
129	Reggie Miller (Metallized)	.20
130	Glen Rice (Metallized)	.10
131	Mitch Richmond (Metallized)	.10
132	Steve Smith (Metallized)	.10
133	John Stockton (Metallized)	.10
134	*Stephon Marbury (Fresh Foundations)*	4.00
135	*Shareef Abdur-Rahim (Fresh Foundations)*	3.00
136	*Ray Allen (Fresh Foundations)*	2.00
137	*Kobe Bryant (Fresh Foundations)*	5.00
138	*Steve Nash (Fresh Foundations)*	.75
139	Grant Hill (Metal Shredders)	.75
140	Jason Kidd (Metal Shredders)	.50
141	Karl Malone (Metal Shredders)	.10
142	Hakeem Olajuwon (Metal Shredders)	.50
143	Shaquille O'Neal (Metal Shredders)	1.00
144	Gary Payton (Metal Shredders)	.10
145	Scottie Pippen (Metal Shredders)	.60
146	Jerry Stackhouse (Metal Shredders)	.50
147	Damon Stoudamire (Metal Shredders)	.60
148	Rod Strickland (Metal Shredders)	.10
149	Checklist	.10
150	Checklist	.10
151	Tyrone Corbin	.10
152	Dikembe Mutombo	.10
153	Antoine Walker	2.50
154	David Wesley	.10
155	Vlade Divac	.10
156	Anthony Mason	.10
157	Ron Harper	.10
158	Steve Kerr	.10
159	Robert Parish	.10
160	Tyrone Hill	.10
161	Vitaly Potapenko	.40
162	Sam Cassell	.10
163	Chris Gatling	.10
164	Samaki Walker	.40
165	Dale Ellis	.10
166	Mark Jackson	.10
167	Ervin Johnson	.10
168	Grant Hill	2.00
169	Lindsey Hunter	.10
170	Todd Fuller	.10
171	Mark Price	.10
172	Charles Barkley	.50
173	Othella Harrington	.10
174	Matt Maloney	.75
175	Kevin Willis	.10
176	Travis Best	.10
177	Erick Dampier	.50
178	Jalen Rose	.10
179	Rodney Rogers	.10
180	Lorenzen Wright	.50
181	Kobe Bryant	3.00
182	Robert Horry	.10
183	Shaquille O'Neal	2.00
184	P.J. Brown	.10
185	Dan Majerle	.10
186	Ray Allen	2.00
187	Armon Gilliam	.10
188	Andrew Lang	.10
189	Stephon Marbury	4.00
190	Stojko Vrankovic	.10
191	Kendall Gill	.10
192	Kerry Kittles	1.75
193	Robert Pack	.10
194	Chris Childs	.10
195	Allan Houston	.10
196	Larry Johnson	.10
197	John Wallace	.75
198	Rony Seikaly	.10
199	Gerald Wilkins	.10
200	Lucious Harris	.10
201	Allen Iverson	5.00
202	Cedric Ceballos	.10
203	Jason Kidd	.10
204	Danny Manning	.10
205	Steve Nash	.50
206	Kenny Anderson	.10
207	Isaiah Rider	.10
208	Rasheed Wallace	.10
209	Mahmoud Abdul-Rauf	.10
210	Corliss Williamson	.10
211	Vernon Maxwell	.10
212	Dominique Wilkins	.10
213	Craig Ehlo	.10
214	Jim McIlvaine	.10
215	Marcus Camby	3.00
216	Hubert Davis	.10
217	Walt Williams	.10
218	Shandon Anderson	.50
219	Bryon Russell	.10
220	Shareef Abdur-Rahim	2.50
221	Roy Rogers	.40
222	Tracy Murray	.10
223	Rod Strickland	.10
224	Kevin Garnett	1.00
225	Karl Malone	.10
226	Alonzo Mourning	.10
227	Hakeem Olajuwon	.50
228	Gary Payton	.10
229	Scottie Pippen	.75
230	David Robinson	.10
231	Dennis Rodman	1.00
232	Latrell Sprewell	.10
233	Jerry Stackhouse	.30
234	Marcus Camby	1.50
235	Todd Fuller	.10
236	Allen Iverson	2.50
237	Kerry Kittles	.75
238	Roy Rogers	.10
239	Anfernee Hardaway	1.00
240	Juwan Howard	.30
241	Michael Jordan	2.50
242	Shawn Kemp	.50
243	Gary Payton	.10
244	Mitch Richmond	.10
245	Glenn Robinson	.10
246	John Stockton	.10
247	Damon Stoudamire	.50
248	Chris Webber	.30
249	Checklist	.10
250	Checklist	.10

1996-97 Metal Precious Metal

This 98-card parallel set reprinted each card in Metal Series II, excluding the two checklists. Inserted at a rate of one per 36 hobby packs, Precious Metal cards were done with a fade in the etched foil and carried a "PM" prefix.

	MT
Complete Set (98):	1000.00
Precious Stars:	15x-30x
Precious Rookies:	6x-12x

1996-97 Metal Cyber-Metal

Cyber-Metal featured 20 cards and captured a color image of a player over a fantasy-like metallized background. This insert was exclusive to Series II Metal and was seeded one per six packs.

		MT
Complete Set (20):		45.00
Common Player:		1.00
CM1	Shareef Abdur-Rahim	6.00
CM2	Ray Allen	4.00
CM3	Vin Baker	2.00
CM4	Charles Barkley	3.00
CM5	Kobe Bryant	10.00
CM6	Patrick Ewing	2.00
CM7	Jason Kidd	2.00
CM8	Karl Malone	2.00
CM9	Stephon Marbury	7.50
CM10	Reggie Miller	2.00
CM11	Alonzo Mourning	1.00
CM12	Hakeem Olajuwon	4.00
CM13	Gary Payton	3.00
CM14	Scottie Pippen	5.00
CM15	Mitch Richmond	2.00
CM16	David Robinson	3.00
CM17	Joe Smith	3.00
CM18	Latrell Sprewell	2.00
CM19	John Stockton	2.00
CM20	Chris Webber	3.00

1996-97 Metal Decade of Excellence

These 1996-97 Fleer Metal inserts take the Decade of Excellence inserts from 1996-97 Fleer Basketball and add a metal touch to them. Cards were seeded one per every 100 packs, with 10 in Series I and 10 in Series II.

		MT
Complete Set (10):		100.00
Common Player:		6.00
1	Clyde Drexler	12.00
2	Joe Dumars	8.00
3	Derek Harper	6.00
4	Michael Jordan	80.00
5	Karl Malone	12.00
6	Chris Mullin	8.00
7	Charles Oakley	6.00
8	Sam Perkins	6.00
9	Ricky Pierce	6.00
10	Buck Williams	6.00

1996-97 Metal Freshly Forged

Freshly Forged gives attention to 15 young players on a sheet metal background, with the insert name printed across the bottom. This was inserted into every 24 packs of Series II Metal.

		MT
Complete Set (15):		120.00
Common Player:		3.00
FF1	Shareef Abdur-Rahim	15.00
FF2	Ray Allen	10.00
FF3	Kobe Bryant	20.00
FF4	Marcus Camby	15.00
FF5	Kevin Garnett	20.00
FF6	Anfernee Hardaway	20.00
FF7	Grant Hill	20.00
FF8	Allen Iverson	20.00
FF9	Jason Kidd	3.00
FF10	Stephon Marbury	17.00
FF11	Glenn Robinson	3.00
FF12	Joe Smith	6.00
FF13	Jerry Stackhouse	6.00
FF14	Damon Stoudamire	10.00
FF15	Antoine Walker	14.00

1996-97 Metal Maximum Metal

Maximum Metal was a 20-card insert set that included 10 cards in one per 180 hobby packs, the second 10 inserted in one per 120 retail packs. Although numbered consecutively, Series I cards are two layered with the foil basketball on the second layer, while Series II inserts are printed on a single layer.

		MT
Complete Set (20):		450.00
Complete Series 1 (10):		325.00
Complete Series 2 (10):		125.00
Common Player:		7.00
1	Charles Barkley	20.00
2	Anfernee Hardaway	70.00
3	Grant Hill	80.00
4	Michael Jordan	150.00
5	Jason Kidd	15.00
6	Karl Malone	15.00
7	Hakeem Olajuwon	25.00
8	Gary Payton	15.00
9	David Robinson	20.00
10	Damon Stoudamire	25.00
11	Juwan Howard	10.00
12	Shawn Kemp	20.00
13	Kerry Kittles	7.00
14	Stephon Marbury	30.00
15	Dennis Rodman	25.00
16	Joe Smith	10.00
17	Jerry Stackhouse	10.00
18	John Stockton	7.00
19	Antoine Walker	20.00
20	Chris Webber	12.00

1996-97 Metal Edge

These cards highlight players who have an edge over their opponents by using their distinct aggressiveness. The 15-card set includes five rookies who signed with their NBA teams before Aug. 15, 1996. Those players are Stephon Marbury, Shareef Abdur-Rahim, Ray Allen, Antoine Walker and Kobe Bryant. Cards were seeded one per every 36 packs of 1996-97 Fleer Metal.

		MT
Complete Set (15):		80.00
Common Player:		2.00
1	Charles Barkley	6.00
2	Jamal Mashburn	2.00
3	Alonzo Mourning	4.00
4	Gary Payton	4.00
5	Scottie Pippen	10.00
6	Steve Smith	2.00
7	Latrell Sprewell	2.00
8	John Stockton	4.00
9	Nick Van Exel	2.00
10	Chris Webber	7.00
11	Stephon Marbury	20.00
12	Shareef Abdur-Rahim	15.00
13	Ray Allen	10.00
14	Antoine Walker	10.00
15	Kobe Bryant	20.00

1996-97 Metal Minted Metal Redemption

This two-card insert was available in one per 720 Series II hobby packs. The redemption cards were available in both several different versions and could be sent in for Minted Metal cards from The Highland Mint. Each player was reproduced in an all-metal 14kt. gold, gold-plated, silver and bronze cards.

		MT
Complete Set (2):		100.00
Common Player:		40.00
1	Grant Hill Bronze	75.00
2	Jerry Stackhouse Bronze	40.00

1996-97 Metal Molten Metal

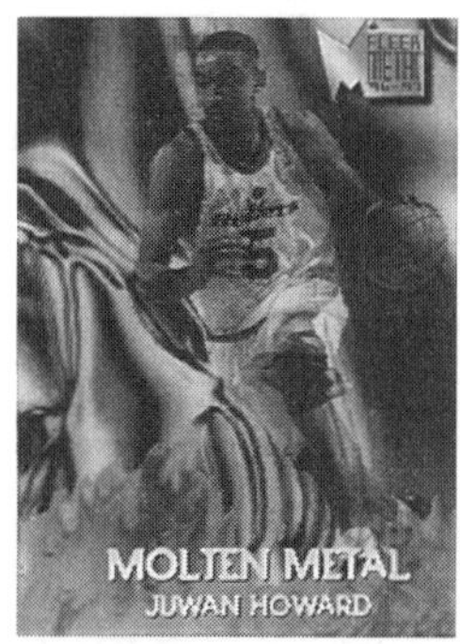

Molten Metal was a 30-card insert set that had cards numbered 1-10 inserted into packs of Series I at a rate

of one per 180 retail and 11-30 inserted into packs of Series II at a rate of one per 72 hobby packs. Series I inserts were printed on a lenticular design, while Series II cards were printed on a foil background.

		MT
Complete Set (30):		650.00
Complete Series 1 (10):		250.00
Complete Series 2 (20):		400.00
Common Player:		5.00
1	Michael Finley	10.00
2	Kevin Garnett	60.00
3	Anfernee Hardaway	60.00
4	Grant Hill	60.00
5	Juwan Howard	15.00
6	Jason Kidd	10.00
7	Antonio McDyess	10.00
8	Joe Smith	15.00
9	Jerry Stackhouse	15.00
10	Damon Stoudamire	25.00
11	Shareef Abdur-Rahim	35.00
12	Ray Allen	20.00
13	Charles Barkley	15.00
14	Terrell Brandon	5.00
15	Marcus Camby	35.00
16	Tom Gugliotta	5.00
17	Allen Iverson	60.00
18	Michael Jordan	120.00
19	Kerry Kittles	20.00
20	Karl Malone	8.00
21	Hakeem Olajuwon	20.00
22	Shaquille O'Neal	50.00
23	Gary Payton	12.00
24	Scottie Pippen	30.00
25	David Robinson	12.00
26	Glenn Robinson	8.00
27	Joe Smith	12.00
28	Latrell Spewell	12.00
29	Antoine Walker	25.00
30	Chris Webber	15.00

1996-97 Metal Net-Rageous

This 10-card die-cut insert features 10 top stars on a gold foil background. The word "Net" is printed in large letters down the left side, with the word "Rageous" printed horizontally on the right side. Net-Rageous inserts were found every 288 packs of Metal Series II.

		MT
Complete Set (10):		600.00
Common Player:		15.00
NR1	Kevin Garnett	90.00
NR2	Anfernee Hardaway	90.00
NR3	Grant Hill	90.00
NR4	Juwan Howard	15.00
NR5	Michael Jordan	200.00
NR6	Shawn Kemp	45.00
NR7	Shaquille O'Neal	75.00
NR8	Dennis Rodman	75.00
NR9	Jerry Stackhouse	20.00
NR10	Damon Stoudamire	30.00

1996-97 Metal Platinum Portraits

This 10-card set showcased some of the NBA's elite on a horizontal design, etched in silver foil. A close-up of the player's face was on the left side, with a large team logo. The player's name and insert name were printed across the bottom in gold foil. Platinum Portraits were available in one per 96 packs of Series II.

	MT
Complete Set (10):	225.00
Common Player:	4.00
PP1 Charles Barkley	8.00
PP2 Kevin Garnett	40.00
PP3 Anfernee Hardaway	40.00
PP4 Grant Hill	40.00
PP5 Michael Jordan	80.00
PP6 Shawn Kemp	20.00
PP7 Karl Malone	4.00
PP8 Shaquille O'Neal	30.00
PP9 Hakeem Olajuwon	15.00
PP10 Damon Stoudamire	15.00

1996-97 Metal Power Tools

These 1996-97 Fleer Metal cards spotlight some of the NBA's top forwards on 100 percent etched foil cards. The cards were seeded one per every 18 packs in Series I.

	MT
Complete Set (10):	40.00
Common Player:	1.00
1 Vin Baker	1.00
2 Charles Barkley	4.00
3 Horace Grant	1.00
4 Juwan Howard	4.00
5 Larry Johnson	1.00
6 Shawn Kemp	8.00
7 Karl Malone	2.00
8 Antonio McDyess	5.00
9 Dennis Rodman	14.00
10 Joe Smith	6.00

1996-97 Metal Steel Slammin

Several of the NBA's finest slam dunk artists are featured on these 1996-97 Fleer Metal embossed inserts. The cards were seeded one per every 72 packs in Series I.

	MT
Complete Set (10):	175.00
Common Player:	3.00
1 Brent Barry	3.00
2 Clyde Drexler	10.00
3 Michael Finley	8.00
4 Kevin Garnett	40.00
5 Eddie Jones	10.00
6 Michael Jordan	90.00
7 Shawn Kemp	25.00
8 Shaquille O'Neal	35.00
9 Joe Smith	12.00
10 Jerry Stackhouse	12.00

1996-97 Ultra

Ultra produced a 300-card set for 1996-97 that was released in two 150-card series. Card fronts feature an action shot of the player, with the player's name and team written in foil across the bottom, and the Fleer Ultra logo in either top corner (Rookie cards are noted under the Ultra logo). Series I included On the Block (124-138), Ultra Effort (139-147), Maxium Effort (148) and Checklists (149-150) subsets, while Series II included Rookie Encore (264-278), Step it Up (279-288), Play of the Game (289-298) and Checklists (299-300). Inserts in Series I include: Ultra Decade, Full Court Trap, Rookie Flashback, Fresh Faces, Rising Stars and Court Masters. Inserts in Series II include: All Rookie, Board Game, Ultra Decade, Starring Role, Scoring Kings and Give and Take. Both Series also included Gold Medallion and Platinum Medallion parallel sets.

	MT
Complete Set (300):	50.00
Complete Series 1 (150):	25.00
Complete Series 2 (150):	25.00
Common Player:	.10
Series 1 Wax Box:	50.00
Series 2 Wax Box:	50.00
1 Mookie Blaylock	.10
2 Alan Henderson	.10
3 Christian Laettner	.10
4 Dikembe Mutombo	.10
5 Steve Smith	.10
6 Dana Barros	.10
7 Rick Fox	.10
8 Dino Radja	.10
9 Antoine Walker	2.50
10 Eric Williams	.10
11 Dell Curry	.10
12 Tony Delk	.50
13 Matt Geiger	.10
14 Glen Rice	.10
15 Ron Harper	.10
16 Michael Jordan	4.00
17 Toni Kukoc	.20
18 Scottie Pippen	1.00
19 Dennis Rodman	1.50
20 Terrell Brandon	.10
21 Chris Mills	.10
22 Bobby Phills	.10
23 Bob Sura	.10
24 Jim Jackson	.20
25 Jason Kidd	.50
26 Jamal Mashburn	.20
27 George McCloud	.10
28 Samaki Walker	.50
29 LaPhonso Ellis	.10
30 Antonio McDyess	.50
31 Bryant Stith	.10
32 Joe Dumars	.10
33 Grant Hill	2.00
34 Theo Ratliff	.10
35 Otis Thorpe	.10
36 Chris Mullin	.10
37 Joe Smith	.75
38 Latrell Sprewell	.25
39 Charles Barkley	.50
40 Clyde Drexler	.50
41 Mario Elie	.10
42 Hakeem Olajuwon	.75
43 Erick Dampier	.40
44 Dale Davis	.10
45 Derrick McKey	.10
46 Reggie Miller	.30
47 Rik Smits	.10
48 Brent Barry	.20
49 Malik Sealy	.10
50 Loy Vaught	.10
51 Lorenzen Wright	.30
52 Kobe Bryant	5.00
53 Cedric Ceballos	.10
54 Eddie Jones	.50
55 Shaquille O'Neal	2.50
56 Nick Van Exel	.25
57 Tim Hardaway	.10
58 Alonzo Mourning	.30
59 Kurt Thomas	.10
60 Ray Allen	2.00
61 Vin Baker	.30
62 Sherman Douglas	.10
63 Glenn Robinson	.30
64 Kevin Garnett	2.00
65 Tom Gugliotta	.10
66 Stephon Marbury	4.00
67 Doug West	.10
68 Shawn Bradley	.10
69 Kendall Gill	.10
70 Kerry Kittles	1.25
71 Ed O'Bannon	.10
72 Patrick Ewing	.30
73 Larry Johnson	.20
74 Charles Oakley	.10
75 John Starks	.10
76 John Wallace	.50
77 Nick Anderson	.10
78 Horace Grant	.10
79 Anfernee Hardaway	2.50
80 Dennis Scott	.10
81 Derrick Coleman	.10
82 Allen Iverson	4.00
83 Jerry Stackhouse	.75
84 Clarence Weatherspoon	.10
85 Michael Finley	.50
86 Kevin Johnson	.10
87 Steve Nash	.50
88 Wesley Person	.10
89 Jermaine O'Neal	1.00
90 Clifford Robinson	.10
91 Arvydas Sabonis	.30
92 Gary Trent	.10
93 Tyus Edney	.10
94 Brian Grant	.10
95 Olden Polynice	.10
96 Mitch Richmond	.25
97 Corliss Williamson	.10
98 Vinny Del Negro	.10
99 Sean Elliott	.10
100 Avery Johnson	.10
101 David Robinson	.75
102 Hersey Hawkins	.10
103 Shawn Kemp	1.00
104 Gary Payton	.40
105 Sam Perkins	.10
106 Detlef Schrempf	.10
107 Marcus Camby	3.00
108 Doug Christie	.10
109 Damon Stoudamire	1.25
110 Sharone Wright	.10
111 Jeff Hornacek	.10
112 Karl Malone	.30
113 Chris Morris	.10
114 Bryon Russell	.10
115 John Stockton	.30
116 Shareef Abdur-Rahim	3.00
117 Greg Anthony	.10
118 Blue Edwards	.10
119 Bryant Reeves	.30
120 Calbert Cheaney	.10
121 Juwan Howard	.75
122 Gheorghe Muresan	.10
123 Chris Webber	.30
124 Vin Baker (On the Block)	.10
125 Charles Barkley (On the Block)	.25
126 Kevin Garnett (On the Block)	1.00
127 Juwan Howard (On the Block)	.40
128 Larry Johnson (On the Block)	.10
129 Shawn Kemp (On the Block)	.50
130 Karl Malone (On the Block)	.10
131 Anthony Mason (On the Block)	.10
132 Antonio McDyess (On the Block)	.25
133 Alonzo Mourning (On the Block)	.10
134 Hakeem Olajuwon (On the Block)	.40
135 Shaquille O'Neal (On the Block)	1.00
136 David Robinson (On the Block)	.40
137 Dennis Rodman (On the Block)	.75
138 Joe Smith (On the Block)	.30
139 Mookie Blaylock (Ultra Effort)	.10
140 Terrell Brandon (Ultra Effort)	.10
141 Anfernee Hardaway (Ultra Effort)	1.00
142 Grant Hill (Ultra Effort)	.75
143 Michael Jordan (Ultra Effort)	2.00
144 Jason Kidd (Ultra Effort)	.25
145 Gary Payton (Ultra Effort)	.10
146 Jerry Stackhouse (Ultra Effort)	.50
147 Damon Stoudamire (Ultra Effort)	.50
148 Robert Horry, Oliver Miller, Hakeem Olajuwon, David Robinson, Clarence Weatherspoon (Maximum Effort)	.30
149 Checklist	.10
150 Checklist	.10
151 Tyrone Corbin	.10
152 Priest Lauderdale	.10
153 Dikembe Mutombo	.10
154 Eldridge Recasner	.10
155 Todd Day	.10
156 Greg Minor	.10
157 David Wesley	.10
158 Vlade Divac	.10
159 Anthony Mason	.10
160 Malik Rose	.10
161 Jason Caffey	.10
162 Steve Kerr	.10
163 Luc Longley	.10
164 Danny Ferry	.10
165 Tyrone Hill	.10
166 Vitaly Potapenko	.25
167 Sam Cassell	.10
168 Michael Finley	.10
169 Chris Gatling	.10
170 A.C. Green	.10
171 Oliver Miller	.10
172 Eric Montross	.10
173 Dale Ellis	.10
174 Mark Jackson	.10
175 Ervin Johnson	.10
176 Sarunas Marciulionis	.10
177 Stacey Augmon	.10
178 Joe Dumars	.10
179 Grant Hill	2.00
180 Lindsey Hunter	.10
181 Grant Long	.10
182 Terry Mills	.10
183 Otis Thorpe	.10
184 Jerome Williams	.10
185 Todd Fuller	.20
186 Ray Owes	.10
187 Mark Price	.10
188 Felton Spencer	.10
189 Charles Barkley	.40

190	*Emanuel Davis*	.10
191	*Othella Harrington*	.25
192	*Matt Maloney*	.40
193	Brent Price	.10
194	Kevin Willis	.10
195	Travis Best	.10
196	Antonio Davis	.10
197	Jalen Rose	.10
198	Pooh Richardson	.10
199	Stanley Roberts	.10
200	Rodney Rogers	.10
201	Elden Campbell	.10
202	*Derek Fisher*	.25
203	*Travis Knight*	.20
204	Shaquille O'Neal	2.00
205	Byron Scott	.10
206	Sasha Danilovic	.10
207	Dan Majerle	.10
208	*Martin Muursepp*	.10
209	Armon Gilliam	.10
210	Andrew Lang	.10
211	Johnny Newman	.10
212	Kevin Garnett	2.00
213	Tom Gugliotta	.10
214	*Shane Heal*	.20
215	Stojko Vrankovic	.10
216	Robert Pack	.10
217	Khalid Reeves	.10
218	Jayson Williams	.10
219	Chris Childs	.10
220	Allan Houston	.10
221	Larry Johnson	.20
222	*Walter McCarty*	.25
223	Charlie Ward	.10
224	*Brian Evans*	.10
225	*Amal McCaskill*	.10
226	Rony Seikaly	.10
227	Gerald Wilkins	.10
228	Mark Davis	.10
229	Lucious Harris	.10
230	Don MacLean	.10
231	Cedric Ceballos	.10
232	Rex Chapman	.10
233	Jason Kidd	.30
234	Danny Manning	.10
235	Kenny Anderson	.10
236	Aaron McKie	.10
237	Isaiah Rider	.10
238	Rasheed Wallace	.10
239	Mahmoud Abdul-Rauf	.10
240	Billy Owens	.10
241	Michael Smith	.10
242	Vernon Maxwell	.10
243	Charles Smith	.10
244	Dominique Wilkins	.10
245	Craig Ehlo	.10
246	Jim McIlvaine	.10
247	Nate McMillan	.10
248	Hubert Davis	.10
249	Carlos Rogers	.10
250	Zan Tabak	.10
251	Walt Williams	.10
252	Jeff Hornacek	.10
253	Karl Malone	.25
254	Greg Ostertag	.10
255	Bryon Russell	.10
256	John Stockton	.25
257	George Lynch	.10
258	Lawrence Moten	.10
259	Anthony Peeler	.10
260	*Roy Rogers*	.25
261	Tracy Murray	.10
262	Rod Strickland	.10
263	*Ben Wallace*	.10
264	Shareef Abdur-Rahim (Rookie Encore)	2.50
265	Ray Allen (Rookie Encore)	1.50
266	Kobe Bryant (Rookie Encore)	3.00
267	Marcus Camby (Rookie Encore)	2.50
268	Erick Dampier (Rookie Encore)	.40
269	Tony Delk (Rookie Encore)	.40
270	Allen Iverson (Rookie Encore)	4.00
271	Kerry Kittles (Rookie Encore)	1.50
272	Stephon Marbury (Rookie Encore)	3.00
273	Steve Nash (Rookie Encore)	.30
274	Jermaine O'Neal (Rookie Encore)	1.00
275	Antoine Walker (Rookie Encore)	1.75
276	Samaki Walker (Rookie Encore)	.30
277	John Wallace (Rookie Encore)	.75

278	Lorenzen Wright (Rookie Encore)	.40
279	Anfernee Hardaway (Step It Up)	1.00
280	Michael Jordan (Step It Up)	2.00
281	Jason Kidd (Step It Up)	.10
282	Hakeem Olajuwon (Step It Up)	.40
283	Gary Payton (Step It Up)	.25
284	Mitch Richmond (Step It Up)	.10
285	David Robinson (Step It Up)	.25
286	John Stockton (Step It Up)	.10
287	Damon Stoudamire (Step It Up)	.40
288	Chris Webber (Step It Up)	.30
289	Clyde Drexler (Play of the Game)	.10
290	Kevin Garnett (Play of the Game)	1.00
291	Grant Hill (Play of the Game)	1.00
292	Shawn Kemp (Play of the Game)	.50
293	Karl Malone (Play of the Game)	.10
294	Antonio McDyess (Play of the Game)	.10
295	Alonzo Mourning (Play of the Game)	.10
296	Shaquille O'Neal (Play of the Game)	1.00
297	Scottie Pippen (Play of the Game)	.50
298	Jerry Stackhouse (Play of the Game)	.20
299	Checklist	.10
300	Checklist	.10

1996-97 Ultra Gold

Gold Medallion was a 296-card parallel set of the entire Series I and II Ultra set, except for the four checklists. Gold Medallions featured gold foil on the front instead of the silver used in regular-issue cards and carries a "G" prefix on the back (except for the subset cards in Series I, numbers 124-148). Series I Gold Medallion inserts were seeded one per 12 packs, while Series II inserts were found one per pack. Only the Series II cards contained the words "Gold Medallion Edition" on the front.

	MT
Complete Set (296):	600.00
Complete Series 1 (148):	500.00
Complete Series 2 (148):	100.00
Gold Cards (1-148):	7x-15x
Gold Cards (151-298):	2x-3x

1996-97 Ultra Platinum

This 296-card set paralleled each card in the 1996-97 Ultra set, except for the four checklist cards. Series I Platinums were inserted every 180 packs, while Series II cards were inserted every 100 packs. Series I inserts do not include the words "Platinum Medallion Edition" on the front, while Series II Platinum inserts do feature those words. In addition, cards 124-148 (subset cards from Series I) don't have a "P" prefix on the card number; all other Platinum contain this prefix.

	MT
Complete Set (296):	8000.00
Complete Ser.1 (148):	5500.00
Complete Ser.2 (148):	2500.00
Common Player (1-148):	10.00
Common Player (151-298):	7.00
Minor Stars (1-148):	20.00
Minor Stars (151-298):	14.00
1	Mookie Blaylock	10.00
2	Alan Henderson	20.00
3	Christian Laettner	20.00
4	Dikembe Mutombo	20.00
5	Steve Smith	10.00
6	Dana Barros	10.00
7	Rick Fox	10.00
8	Dino Radja	10.00
9	Antoine Walker	125.00
10	Eric Williams	10.00
11	Dell Curry	10.00
12	Tony Delk	20.00
13	Matt Geiger	10.00
14	Glen Rice	30.00
15	Ron Harper	10.00
16	Michael Jordan	500.00
17	Toni Kukoc	20.00
18	Scottie Pippen	125.00
19	Dennis Rodman	125.00
20	Terrell Brandon	20.00
21	Chris Mills	10.00
22	Bobby Phills	10.00
23	Bob Sura	20.00
24	Jim Jackson	20.00
25	Jason Kidd	30.00
26	Jamal Mashburn	20.00
27	George McCloud	10.00
28	Samaki Walker	20.00
29	LaPhonso Ellis	10.00
30	Antonio McDyess	30.00
31	Bryant Stith	10.00
32	Joe Dumars	20.00
33	Grant Hill	250.00
34	Theo Ratliff	10.00
35	Otis Thorpe	10.00
36	Chris Mullin	20.00
37	Joe Smith	50.00
38	Latrell Sprewell	40.00
39	Charles Barkley	50.00
40	Clyde Drexler	40.00
41	Mario Elie	10.00
42	Hakeem Olajuwon	75.00
43	Erick Dampier	20.00
44	Dale Davis	10.00
45	Derrick McKey	10.00
46	Reggie Miller	30.00
47	Rik Smits	10.00
48	Brent Barry	20.00
49	Malik Sealy	10.00
50	Loy Vaught	10.00
51	Lorenzen Wright	20.00
52	Kobe Bryant	225.00
53	Cedric Ceballos	10.00
54	Eddie Jones	75.00
55	Shaquille O'Neal	175.00
56	Nick Van Exel	25.00
57	Tim Hardaway	30.00
58	Alonzo Mourning	30.00
59	Kurt Thomas	10.00
60	Ray Allen	50.00
61	Vin Baker	40.00
62	Sherman Douglas	10.00
63	Glenn Robinson	30.00
64	Kevin Garnett	200.00
65	Tom Gugliotta	25.00
66	Stephon Marbury	175.00

67	Doug West	10.00
68	Shawn Bradley	20.00
69	Kendall Gill	10.00
70	Kerry Kittles	50.00
71	Ed O'Bannon	10.00
72	Patrick Ewing	30.00
73	Larry Johnson	20.00
74	Charles Oakley	10.00
75	John Starks	10.00
76	John Wallace	40.00
77	Nick Anderson	10.00
78	Horace Grant	10.00
79	Anfernee Hardaway	200.00
80	Dennis Scott	10.00
81	Derrick Coleman	10.00
82	Allen Iverson	200.00
83	Jerry Stackhouse	50.00
84	Clarence Weatherspoon	10.00
85	Michael Finley	30.00
86	Kevin Johnson	20.00
87	Steve Nash	25.00
88	Wesley Person	10.00
89	Jermaine O'Neal	50.00
90	Clifford Robinson	10.00
91	Arvydas Sabonis	10.00
92	Gary Trent	10.00
93	Tyus Edney	10.00
94	Brian Grant	10.00
95	Olden Polynice	10.00
96	Mitch Richmond	30.00
97	Corliss Williamson	10.00
98	Vinny Del Negro	10.00
99	Sean Elliott	10.00
100	Avery Johnson	10.00
101	David Robinson	50.00
102	Hersey Hawkins	10.00
103	Shawn Kemp	100.00
104	Gary Payton	50.00
105	Sam Perkins	10.00
106	Detlef Schrempf	10.00
107	Marcus Camby	100.00
108	Doug Christie	10.00
109	Damon Stoudamire	75.00
110	Sharone Wright	10.00
111	Jeff Hornacek	10.00
112	Karl Malone	30.00
113	Chris Morris	10.00
114	Bryon Russell	10.00
115	John Stockton	30.00
116	Shareef Abdur-Rahim	120.00
117	Greg Anthony	10.00
118	Blue Edwards	10.00
119	Bryant Reeves	20.00
120	Calbert Cheaney	10.00
121	Juwan Howard	50.00
122	Gheorghe Muresan	10.00
123	Chris Webber	70.00
124	Vin Baker (On the Block)	10.00
125	Charles Barkley (On the Block)	20.00
126	Kevin Garnett (On the Block)	100.00
127	Juwan Howard (On the Block)	20.00
128	Larry Johnson (On the Block)	10.00
129	Shawn Kemp (On the Block)	40.00
130	Karl Malone (On the Block)	20.00
131	Anthony Mason (On the Block)	10.00
132	Antonio McDyess (On the Block)	10.00
133	Alonzo Mourning (On the Block)	10.00
134	Hakeem Olajuwon (On the Block)	30.00
135	Shaquille O'Neal (On the Block)	80.00
136	David Robinson (On the Block)	20.00
137	Dennis Rodman (On the Block)	75.00
138	Joe Smith (On the Block)	20.00
139	Mookie Blaylock (Ultra Effort)	10.00
140	Terrell Brandon (Ultra Effort)	10.00
141	Anfernee Hardaway (Ultra Effort)	80.00
142	Grant Hill (Ultra Effort)	120.00
143	Michael Jordan (Ultra Effort)	250.00
144	Jason Kidd (Ultra Effort)	20.00
145	Gary Payton (Ultra Effort)	20.00
146	Jerry Stackhouse (Ultra Effort)	20.00
147	Damon Stoudamire (Ultra Effort)	20.00

148	Robert Horry, Oliver Miller, Hakeem Olajuwon, David Robinson, Clarence Weatherspoon (Maximum Effort)	20.00
151	Tyrone Corbin	7.00
152	Priest Lauderdale	14.00
153	Dikembe Mutombo	14.00
154	Eldridge Recasner	7.00
155	Todd Day	7.00
156	Greg Minor	7.00
157	David Wesley	7.00
158	Vlade Divac	7.00
159	Anthony Mason	14.00
160	Malik Rose	14.00
161	Jason Caffey	14.00
162	Steve Kerr	7.00
163	Luc Longley	7.00
164	Danny Ferry	7.00
165	Tyrone Hill	7.00
166	Vitaly Potapenko	14.00
167	Sam Cassell	7.00
168	Michael Finley	20.00
169	Chris Gatling	7.00
170	A.C. Green	7.00
171	Oliver Miller	7.00
172	Eric Montross	7.00
173	Dale Ellis	7.00
174	Mark Jackson	7.00
175	Ervin Johnson	7.00
176	Sarunas Marciulionis	7.00
177	Stacey Augmon	7.00
178	Joe Dumars	14.00
179	Grant Hill	175.00
180	Lindsey Hunter	14.00
181	Grant Long	7.00
182	Terry Mills	7.00
183	Otis Thorpe	7.00
184	Jerome Williams	7.00
185	Todd Fuller	14.00
186	Ray Owes	7.00
187	Mark Price	7.00
188	Felton Spencer	7.00
189	Charles Barkley	30.00
190	Emanuel Davis	7.00
191	Othella Harrington	14.00
192	Matt Maloney	20.00
193	Brent Price	7.00
194	Kevin Willis	7.00
195	Travis Best	7.00
196	Antonio Davis	7.00
197	Jalen Rose	7.00
198	Pooh Richardson	7.00
199	Stanley Roberts	7.00
200	Rodney Rogers	7.00
201	Elden Campbell	7.00
202	Derek Fisher	20.00
203	Travis Knight	20.00
204	Shaquille O'Neal	150.00
205	Byron Scott	7.00
206	Sasha Danilovic	7.00
207	Dan Majerle	7.00
208	Martin Muursepp	14.00
209	Armon Gilliam	7.00
210	Andrew Lang	7.00
211	Johnny Newman	7.00
212	Kevin Garnett	150.00
213	Tom Gugliotta	20.00
214	Shane Heal	14.00
215	Stojko Vrankovic	7.00
216	Robert Pack	7.00
217	Khalid Reeves	7.00
218	Jayson Williams	7.00
219	Chris Childs	7.00
220	Allan Houston	14.00
221	Larry Johnson	14.00
222	Walter McCarty	25.00
223	Charlie Ward	14.00
224	Brian Evans	7.00
225	Amal McCaskill	7.00
226	Rony Seikaly	7.00
227	Gerald Wilkins	7.00
228	Mark Davis	7.00
229	Lucious Harris	7.00
230	Don MacLean	7.00
231	Cedric Ceballos	7.00
232	Rex Chapman	7.00
233	Jason Kidd	30.00
234	Danny Manning	7.00
235	Kenny Anderson	14.00
236	Aaron McKie	7.00
237	Isaiah Rider	7.00
238	Rasheed Wallace	14.00
239	Mahmoud Abdul-Rauf	7.00
240	Billy Owens	7.00
241	Michael Smith	7.00
242	Vernon Maxwell	7.00
243	Charles Smith	7.00
244	Dominique Wilkins	14.00
245	Craig Ehlo	7.00
246	Jim McIlvaine	7.00

247	Nate McMillan	7.00
248	Hubert Davis	7.00
249	Carlos Rogers	7.00
250	Zan Tabak	7.00
251	Walt Williams	7.00
252	Jeff Hornacek	7.00
253	Karl Malone	30.00
254	Greg Ostertag	7.00
255	Bryon Russell	7.00
256	John Stockton	30.00
257	George Lynch	7.00
258	Lawrence Moten	7.00
259	Anthony Peeler	7.00
260	Roy Rogers	14.00
261	Tracy Murray	7.00
262	Rod Strickland	14.00
263	Ben Wallace	7.00
264	Shareef Abdur-Rahim (Rookie Encore)	40.00
265	Ray Allen (Rookie Encore)	20.00
266	Kobe Bryant (Rookie Encore)	100.00
267	Marcus Camby (Rookie Encore)	30.00
268	Erick Dampier (Rookie Encore)	14.00
269	Tony Delk (Rookie Encore)	14.00
270	Allen Iverson (Rookie Encore)	85.00
271	Kerry Kittles (Rookie Encore)	20.00
272	Stephon Marbury (Rookie Encore)	70.00
273	Steve Nash (Rookie Encore)	14.00
274	Jermaine O'Neal (Rookie Encore)	20.00
275	Antoine Walker (Rookie Encore)	50.00
276	Samaki Walker (Rookie Encore)	14.00
277	John Wallace (Rookie Encore)	20.00
278	Lorenzen Wright (Rookie Encore)	14.00
279	Anfernee Hardaway (Step It Up)	70.00
280	Michael Jordan (Step It Up)	200.00
281	Jason Kidd (Step It Up)	14.00
282	Hakeem Olajuwon (Step It Up)	25.00
283	Gary Payton (Step It Up)	14.00
284	Mitch Richmond (Step It Up)	7.00
285	David Robinson (Step It Up)	14.00
286	John Stockton (Step It Up)	14.00
287	Damon Stoudamire (Step It Up)	25.00
288	Chris Webber (Step It Up)	20.00
289	Clyde Drexler (Play of the Game)	14.00
290	Kevin Garnett (Play of the Game)	70.00
291	Grant Hill (Play of the Game)	80.00
292	Shawn Kemp (Play of the Game)	35.00
293	Karl Malone (Play of the Game)	14.00
294	Antonio McDyess (Play of the Game)	7.00
295	Alonzo Mourning (Play of the Game)	7.00
296	Shaquille O'Neal (Play of the Game)	70.00
297	Scottie Pippen (Play of the Game)	35.00
298	Jerry Stackhouse (Play of the Game)	14.00

1996-97 Ultra All-Rookie

All-Rookie highlights 15 of the top rookies in the NBA during the 1996-97 season and an embossed card. The player's color photo is shown over a crystal ball, with a black background. All-Rookie inserts were inserted in every four packs of Series II.

		MT
	Complete Set (15):	60.00
	Common Player:	1.00
1	Shareef Abdur-Rahim	8.00
2	Ray Allen	5.00
3	Kobe Bryant	12.00
4	Marcus Camby	8.00

5	Tony Delk	1.50
6	Derek Fisher	1.50
7	Allen Iverson	12.00
8	Kerry Kittles	4.00
9	Matt Maloney	1.50
10	Stephon Marbury	10.00
11	Vitaly Potapenko	1.00
12	Roy Rogers	1.00
13	Antoine Walker	8.00
14	Samaki Walker	1.00
15	John Wallace	4.00

1996-97 Ultra Board Game

This 20-card insert was found in packs of Series II Ultra at a rate of one per nine. Board Game highlights the top rebounders in the NBA on a checkerboard pattern, with cards numbered on the back "x of 20."

		MT
	Complete Set (20):	80.00
	Common Player:	1.00
1	Vin Baker	1.00
2	Charles Barkley	4.00
3	Dale Davis	1.00
4	Clyde Drexler	3.00
5	Patrick Ewing	2.00
6	Grant Hill	15.00
7	Michael Jordan	30.00
8	Shawn Kemp	8.00
9	Jason Kidd	2.00
10	Karl Malone	1.00
11	Alonzo Mourning	1.00
12	Dikembe Mutombo	1.00
13	Hakeem Olajuwon	6.00
14	Shaquille O'Neal	15.00
15	Scottie Pippen	8.00
16	David Robinson	4.00
17	Dennis Rodman	12.00
18	Loy Vaught	1.00
19	Chris Webber	3.00
20	Jayson Williams	1.00

1996-97 Ultra Court Masters

Court Masters was a 15-card insert found exclusively in retail packs at a rate of one per 180. This set was printed on plastic and contains the members of the 1st, 2nd and 3rd All-NBA teams.

		MT
	Complete Set (15):	475.00
	Common Player:	10.00
1	Anfernee Hardaway	70.00
2	Michael Jordan	140.00

3	Karl Malone	10.00
4	Scottie Pippen	35.00
5	David Robinson	18.00
6	Grant Hill	75.00
7	Shawn Kemp	35.00
8	Hakeem Olajuwon	25.00
9	Gary Payton	16.00
10	John Stockton	10.00
11	Charles Barkley	16.00
12	Juwan Howard	16.00
13	Reggie Miller	10.00
14	Shaquille O'Neal	60.00
15	Mitch Richmond	10.00

1996-97 Ultra Decade of Excellence

Ultra Decade was a 20-card insert that had 10 cards inserted into both Series I and II. The set salutes 20 players that were in the 1986-87 Fleer set and were still active in 1996-97. Inserted at one per 100 packs, Ultra Decade inserts are identified by a gold foil stamp in the lower left corner that reads "Ultra Decade 1986-1996." The same 20 Decade inserts were also inserted into packs of Fleer and Metal, and are marked Ultra Decade to distinguish them from others.

		MT
	Complete Set (20):	175.00
	Complete Series 1 (10):	100.00
	Complete Series 2 (10):	75.00
	Common Player:	6.00
U1	Clyde Drexler	10.00
U2	Joe Dumars	8.00
U3	Derek Harper	6.00
U4	Michael Jordan	75.00
U5	Karl Malone	10.00
U6	Chris Mullin	8.00
U7	Charles Oakley	6.00
U8	Sam Perkins	6.00
U9	Ricky Pierce	6.00
U10	Buck Williams	6.00
U11	Charles Barkley	16.00
U12	Patrick Ewing	12.00
U13	Eddie Johnson	6.00
U14	Hakeem Olajuwon	30.00
U15	Robert Parish	6.00
U16	Byron Scott	6.00
U17	Wayman Tisdale	6.00
U18	Gerald Wilkins	6.00
U19	Herb Williams	6.00
U20	Kevin Willis	6.00

1996-97 Ultra Fresh Faces

Fresh Faces showcased nine top rookies from the 1996 NBA Draft, and were inserted into packs of Series I at a rate of one per 72 packs. This insert featured an action shot of the player over the top of his die-cut jersey, with the position he was drafted in, in silver foil, in the lower right corner.

		MT
Complete Set (9):		150.00
Common Player:		4.00
1	Shareef Abdur-Rahim	20.00
2	Ray Allen	14.00
3	Kobe Bryant	35.00
4	Marcus Camby	20.00
5	Allen Iverson	35.00
6	Kerry Kittles	12.00
7	Stephon Marbury	30.00
8	Steve Nash	4.00
9	Antoine Walker	20.00

1996-97 Ultra Full Court Trap

Full Court Trap included the 10 players who were selected on the first and second All-Defensive Team. These inserts were found in every 15 packs of Series I, and contain a color shot of the player over a foil, spiral background with the player's name running up the left side and the insert name across the bottom. Parallel Gold versions of these inserts also exist with a more colorful foil background and an insertion rate of one per 180 packs.

		MT
Complete Set (10):		35.00
Common Player:		.75
1	Michael Jordan	20.00
2	Gary Payton	2.00
3	Scottie Pippen	6.00
4	David Robinson	3.00
5	Dennis Rodman	8.00
6	Mookie Blaylock	.75
7	Horace Grant	.75
8	Derrick McKey	.75
9	Hakeem Olajuwon	5.00
10	Bobby Phills	.75

1996-97 Ultra Full Court Trap Gold

Full Court Trap Gold inserts reprinted the 10-card Full Court Trap set in a thicker stock, gold foil card. This set was inserted into packs of Series I at a rate of one per 180 packs.

	MT
Complete Set (10):	210.00
Gold Cards:	3x-6x

1996-97 Ultra Give and Take

This 10-card insert was printed on a foil background divided into a gold and silver tone split equally from top to bottom. Give and Take inserts were found in every 18 retail packs of Ultra II, and includes players who produced assists and steals.

		MT
Complete Set (10):		60.00
Common Player:		2.00
1	Mookie Blaylock	2.00
2	Anfernee Hardaway	15.00
3	Tim Hardaway	2.00
4	Allen Iverson	15.00
5	Michael Jordan	30.00
6	Jason Kidd	4.00
7	Gary Payton	4.00
8	Scottie Pippen	8.00
9	John Stockton	3.00
10	Damon Stoudamire	6.00

1996-97 Ultra Rising Stars

This 10-card insert was found in hobby-only packs at a rate of one per 180. The cards feature top young stars on a canvas-like card with a rough white border surrounding it. Rising Stars inserts were exclusive to Series I.

		MT
Complete Set (10):		175.00
Common Player:		8.00
1	Shareef Abdur-Rahim	25.00
2	Kobe Bryant	30.00
3	Anfernee Hardaway	30.00
4	Grant Hill	35.00
5	Juwan Howard	10.00
6	Allen Iverson	35.00
7	Jason Kidd	8.00
8	Stephon Marbury	30.00
9	Joe Smith	10.00
10	Damon Stoudamire	15.00

1996-97 Ultra Rookie Flashback

This 11-card set captures the members of the 1995-96 NBA All-Rookie Team, and was inserted every 45 packs of Series I. These inserts show a color shot of the player over a foil-etched, basketball-like background.

		MT
Complete Set (11):		40.00
Common Player:		2.00
1	Michael Finley (First Team)	3.00
2	Antonio McDyess (First Team)	4.00
3	Arvydas Sabonis (First Team)	2.00
4	Joe Smith (First Team)	5.00
5	Jerry Stackhouse (First Team)	5.00
6	Damon Stoudamire (First Team)	10.00
7	Brent Barry (Second Team)	2.00
8	Tyus Edney (Second Team)	2.00
9	Kevin Garnett (Second Team)	20.00
10	Bryant Reeves (Second Team)	2.00
11	Rasheed Wallace (Second Team)	2.00

1996-97 Ultra Scoring Kings

This 29-card set was found every 24 hobby packs of Series II Ultra. Fronts captured a color action shot of the player over an ornamental background and a large foil stamped "K" in the lower left corner. There was also a Scoring Kings Plus version of this insert, found every 96 hobby packs, that was printed on 100-percent foil.

		MT
Complete Set (29):		300.00
Common Player:		3.00
1	Steve Smith	3.00
2	Dino Radja	3.00
3	Glen Rice	5.00
4	Michael Jordan	50.00
5	Terrell Brandon	3.00
6	Jim Jackson	3.00
7	Antonio McDyess	3.00
8	Grant Hill	25.00
9	Latrell Sprewell	6.00
10	Hakeem Olajuwon	10.00
11	Reggie Miller	6.00
12	Loy Vaught	3.00
13	Shaquille O'Neal	25.00
14	Alonzo Mourning	5.00
15	Vin Baker	5.00
16	Tom Gugliotta	3.00
17	Kendall Gill	3.00
18	Patrick Ewing	5.00
19	Anfernee Hardaway	25.00
20	Allen Iverson	25.00
21	Danny Manning	3.00
22	Kenny Anderson	3.00
23	Mitch Richmond	5.00
24	David Robinson	6.00
25	Shawn Kemp	12.00
26	Damon Stoudamire	10.00
27	Karl Malone	5.00
28	Shareef Abdur-Rahim	18.00
29	Chris Webber	8.00

1996-97 Ultra Scoring Kings Plus

Scoring Kings Plus reprints the 29 Scoring Kings inserts on 100-percent etched foil. This insert is seeded one per 96 hobby packs in Series II.

	MT
Complete Set (29):	900.00
Plus Cards:	1.5x-3x

1996-97 Ultra Starring Role

Starring Role inserts were found every 288 packs of Series II Ultra. The 10-card insert was printed on plastic with a color shot of the player over a darkened background with a large star and insert name running up the left side. The back contained the cutout of the player's image with text inserted.

		MT
Complete Set (10):		550.00
Common Player:		10.00
1	Kevin Garnett	80.00
2	Anfernee Hardaway	80.00
3	Grant Hill	80.00
4	Michael Jordan	160.00
5	Shawn Kemp	40.00
6	Karl Malone	10.00
7	Hakeem Olajuwon	30.00
8	Shaquille O'Neal	80.00
9	David Robinson	20.00
10	Damon Stoudamire	30.00

1996-97 Hoops II

NBA Hoops' 1996-97 was released in two series, with Series I containing 200 cards and Series II having 150 cards. Card fronts featured a full-bleed action shot of the player, with the bottom right corner colored in team colors with the team logo inside it. The player's name was stamped above it in gold foil, with a Hoops logo in the top left. Series I had 174 regular cards, 15 The Big Finish, nine Grant's Playback and two checklists, while Series II had 48 player updates, 40 rookies, 29 coaches, 10 Slam Talk, 20 Career Best Games, one Stackhouse Boys & Girls Clubs and two checklists. Inserts in Series I include: Hipnotized, Head to Head, Autographics, 10 Rookie Headliners and Superfeats. Inserts in Series II include: Autograph- ics, 1996-97 Rookies, Starting Five, Hot List, Fly With and Grant's All- Rookie Team.

		MT
Complete Series 2 (150):		15.00
Common Player:		.05
Series 2 Wax Box:		40.00
201	Dikembe Mutombo	.10
202	Dee Brown	.05
203	David Wesley	.05
204	Vlade Divac	.05
205	Anthony Mason	.05
206	Chris Gatling	.05
207	Eric Montross	.05
208	Ervin Johnson	.05
209	Stacey Augmon	.05
210	Joe Dumars	.05
211	Grant Hill	1.00
212	Charles Barkley	.30
213	Jalen Rose	.05
214	Lamond Murray	.05
215	Shaquille O'Neal	1.25
216	P.J. Brown	.05
217	Dan Majerle	.05
218	Armon Gilliam	.05
219	Andrew Lang	.05
220	Kevin Garnett	1.00
221	Tom Gugliotta	.05
222	Cherokee Parks	.05
223	Doug West	.05
224	Kendall Gill	.05
225	Robert Pack	.05
226	Allan Houston	.05
227	Larry Johnson	.05
228	Rony Seikaly	.05
229	Gerald Wilkins	.05
230	Michael Cage	.05
231	Lucious Harris	.05
232	Sam Cassell	.05
233	Robert Horry	.05
234	Kenny Anderson	.05
235	Isaiah Rider	.05
236	Rasheed Wallace	.05
237	Mahmoud Abdul-Rauf	.05
238	Vernon Maxwell	.05
239	Dominique Wilkins	.05
240	Jim McIlvaine	.05
241	Hubert Davis	.05
242	Popeye Jones	.05
243	Walt Williams	.05
244	Karl Malone	.20
245	John Stockton	.20
246	Anthony Peeler	.05
247	Tracy Murray	.05
248	Rod Strickland	.05
249	Len Wilkens	.05
250	M.L. Carr	.05
251	Dave Cowens	.05
252	Phil Jackson	.05
253	Mike Fratello	.05
254	Jim Cleamons	.05
255	Dick Motta	.05
256	Doug Collins	.05
257	Rick Adelman	.05
258	Rudy Tomjanovich	.05
259	Larry Brown	.05
260	Bill Fitch	.05
261	Del Harris	.05
262	Pat Riley	.05
263	Chris Ford	.05
264	Flip Saunders	.05
265	John Calipari	.05
266	Jeff Van Gundy	.05
267	Brian Hill	.05
268	Johnny Davis	.05
269	Danny Ainge	.05
270	P.J. Carlesimo	.05
271	Garry St. Jean	.05
272	Bob Hill	.05
273	George Karl	.05
274	Darrell Walker	.05
275	Jerry Sloan	.05
276	Brian Winters	.05
277	Jim Lynam	.05
278	Shareef Abdur-Rahim	2.00
279	Ray Allen	1.00
280	Shandon Anderson	.10
281	Kobe Bryant	3.00
282	Marcus Camby	2.00
283	Erick Dampier	.25
284	Emanuel Davis	.05
285	Tony Delk	.25
286	Brian Evans	.05
287	Derek Fisher	.30
288	Todd Fuller	.20
289	Dean Garrett	.20
290	Reggie Geary	.05
291	Darvin Ham	.25
292	Othella Harrington	.20
293	Shane Heal	.05
294	Mark Hendrickson	.05
295	Allen Iverson	3.00
296	Dontae Jones	.20
297	Kerry Kittles	1.25
298	Priest Lauderdale	.05
299	Matt Maloney	.50
300	Stephon Marbury	2.00
301	Walter McCarty	.05
302	Jeff McInnis	.05
303	Martin Muursepp	.05
304	Steve Nash	.40
305	Moochie Norris	.05
306	Jermaine O'Neal	.30
307	Vitaly Potapenko	.20
308	Virginius Praskevicius	.05
309	Roy Rogers	.20
310	Malik Rose	.05
311	James Scott	.05
312	Antoine Walker	1.50
313	Samaki Walker	.25
314	Ben Wallace	.05
315	John Wallace	.40
316	Jerome Williams	.05
317	Lorenzen Wright	.25
318	Charles Barkley	.15
319	Derrick Coleman	.05
320	Michael Finley	.05
321	Stephon Marbury	.75
322	Reggie Miller	.10
323	Alonzo Mourning	.05
324	Shaquille O'Neal	.50
325	Gary Payton	.10
326	Dennis Rodman	.50
327	Damon Stoudamire	.25
328	Vin Baker	.10
329	Clyde Drexler	.15
330	Patrick Ewing	.10
331	Anfernee Hardaway	.75
332	Grant Hill	.50
333	Juwan Howard	.20
334	Larry Johnson	.05
335	Michael Jordan	1.25
336	Shawn Kemp	.30
337	Jason Kidd	.05
338	Karl Malone	.10
339	Reggie Miller	.10
340	Hakeem Olajuwon	.30
341	Scottie Pippen	.30
342	Mitch Richmond	.05
343	David Robinson	.20
344	Dennis Rodman	.50
345	Joe Smith	.20
346	Jerry Stackhouse	.20
347	John Stockton	.10
348	Jerry Stackhouse	.10
349	Checklist	.05
350	Checklist	.05

3	Jason Kidd	4.00
4	Alonzo Mourning	3.00
5	Gary Payton	4.00
6	David Robinson	5.00
7	Dennis Rodman	12.00
8	Joe Smith	5.00
9	Jerry Stackhouse	5.00
10	Damon Stoudamire	7.00

1996-97 Hoops Grant's All-Rookie Team

Grant's All-Rookie Team features SkyView technology on 11 cards with individual numbering up to 1,996. Inserted only in packs of Series II, these two-layered cards feature a cut-out image of the selected rookie, with a plastic background that includes a head shot of Grant Hill. The mostly black border lists other members of the All-Rookie Team. The final card in the insert is of SkyBox spokesman Grant Hill, who the set is named for.

		MT
Complete Set (11):		500.00
Common Player:		10.00
1	Shareef Abdur-Rahim	60.00
2	Ray Allen	30.00
3	Kobe Bryant	100.00
4	Marcus Camby	60.00
5	Grant Hill	70.00
6	Allen Iverson	100.00
7	Kerry Kittles	30.00
8	Stephon Marbury	80.00
9	Antoine Walker	50.00
10	Samaki Walker	10.00
11	Lorenzen Wright	10.00

1996-97 Hoops Fly With

This 10-card insert was found ex- clusively in Series II retail packs at a rate of one per 24. The cards are print- ed on plastic with the words "Fly With" appearing in large letters across the top half, with the entire background providing a sky-like appearance with clouds. The player's image is cast over the top of the background, with his name and team, along with the in- sert name, printed in gold foil in the lower left corner.

		MT
Complete Set (10):		45.00
Common Player:		3.00
1	Charles Barkley	5.00
2	Juwan Howard	5.00

1996-97 Hoops Hot List

This 20-card insert is printed on clear plastic with rolling flames cover- ing the left side, while the right side is clear and the player's image lies on top. The words "Hot List" run down the left side in the flames. Hot List inserts were seeded one per 48 Series II hob- by packs.

		MT
Complete Set (20):		225.00
Common Player:		3.00
1	Vin Baker	6.00

2	Patrick Ewing	6.00
3	Michael Finley	0.00
4	Kevin Garnett	30.00
5	Anfernee Hardaway	30.00
6	Grant Hill	30.00
7	Allan Houston	3.00
8	Michael Jordan	60.00
9	Shawn Kemp	15.00
10	Christian Laettner	3.00
11	Karl Malone	6.00
12	Antonio McDyess	3.00
13	Reggie Miller	6.00
14	Hakeem Olajuwon	15.00
15	Shaquille O'Neal	25.00
16	Scottie Pippen	15.00
17	Mitch Richmond	6.00
18	Isaiah Rider	3.00
19	Rod Strickland	3.00
20	Chris Webber	8.00

1996-97 Hoops Rookies

This 30-card set captured the top rookies during the 1996-97 season on a gold foil background. The word "rookie" runs down the left side, with a silver stamped logo in the bottom right corner. 1996-97 Rookies were found every six packs of Hoops Series II.

		MT
Complete Set (30):		45.00
Common Player:		.50
1	Shareef Abdur-Rahim	6.00
2	Ray Allen	4.00
3	Kobe Bryant	10.00
4	Marcus Camby	6.00
5	Erick Dampier	.50
6	Emanuel Davis	.50
7	Tony Delk	1.00
8	Brian Evans	.50
9	Derek Fisher	1.00
10	Todd Fuller	.50
11	Othella Harrington	.50
12	Allen Iverson	10.00
13	Dontae Jones	.50
14	Kerry Kittles	3.00
15	Priest Lauderdale	.50
16	Matt Maloney	2.00
17	Stephon Marbury	8.00
18	Walter McCarty	.50
19	Jeff McInnis	.50
20	Martin Muursepp	.50
21	Steve Nash	1.00
22	Moochie Norris	.50
23	Jermaine O'Neal	2.00
24	Vitaly Potapenko	.50
25	Roy Rogers	1.00
26	Antoine Walker	5.00

27	Samaki Walker	1.00
28	John Wallace	2.00
29	Jerome Williams	.50
30	Lorenzen Wright	.50

1996-97 Hoops Starting Five

Starting Five was a 29-card insert that captured each NBA team's starting lineup. The star player was cast over the team's logo for the majority of the card, with the other four players appearing in boxes across the bottom. This insert was seeded every 12 packs of Hoops II.

		MT
Complete Set (29):		80.00
Common Player:		1.00
1	Atlanta Hawks Mookie Blaylock	1.00
2	Boston Celtics Dino Radja	1.00
3	Charlotte Hornets Glen Rice	1.00
4	Chicago Bulls Michael Jordan	15.00
5	Cleveland Cavaliers Tyrone Hill	1.00
6	Dallas Mavericks Jason Kidd	1.00
7	Denver Nuggets Antonio McDyess	1.00
8	Detroit Pistons Grant Hill	10.00
9	Golden State Warriors Joe Smith	1.00
10	Houston Rockets Hakeem Olajuwon	4.00
11	Indiana Pacers Reggie Miller	1.00
12	Los Angeles Clippers Rodney Rogers	1.00
13	Los Angeles Lakers Shaquille O'Neal	10.00
14	Miami Heat Alonzo Mourning	1.00
15	Milwaukee Bucks Ray Allen	1.00
16	Minnesota Timberwolves Kevin Garnett	8.00
17	New Jersey Nets Jayson Williams	1.00
18	New York Knicks Patrick Ewing	1.00
19	Orlando Magic Anfernee Hardaway	10.00
20	Philadelphia 76ers Jerry Stackhouse	5.00
21	Phoenix Suns Danny Manning	1.00
22	Portland Trail Blazers Isaiah Rider	1.00
23	Sacramento Kings Mitch Richmond	1.00
24	San Antonio Spurs David Robinson	1.00
25	Seattle Supersonics Shawn Kemp	4.00
26	Toronto Raptors Damon Stoudamire	6.00
27	Utah Jazz Karl Malone	1.00
28	Vancouver Grizzlies Bryant Reeves	5.00
29	Washington Bullets Juwan Howard	1.00

1996 Pacific Power Prism

This 54-card set included 42 top draft picks from 1996 and 12 pro players. The cards maintained Pacific's prism look, with solid gold foil backgrounds. Fronts included the player's name in large letters up the left side, with a Pacific Crown logo in the lower right corner. Each card in the regular-issue set carried a "PP" prefix. Metallic Silver and Presidential Gold parallel sets were also produced along with four insert sets, including Gold Crown Die-cut, Jump Ball Hoop-Cel, In the Paint and Regents of Roundball.

		MT
Complete Set (54):		20.00
Common Player:		.20
Metalic Silver:		8x-16x
Presidential Platinum:		75x-150x
1	Shareef Abdur-Rahim	2.00
2	Ray Allen	2.00
3	Terrell Bell	.20
4	Joseph Blair	.20
5	Marcus Brown	.20
6	Kobe Bryant	4.00
7	Marcus Camby	3.00
8	Erick Dampier	.50
9	Ben Davis	.20
10	Tony Delk	.75
11	Tyus Edney	.40
12	Brian Evans	.20
13	Michael Finley	1.00
14	Derek Fisher	.50
15	Todd Fuller	.20
16	Reggie Geary	.20
17	Steve Hamer	.20
18	Othella Harrington	.20
19	Mark Hendrickson	.20
20	Allen Iverson	4.00
21	Dontae Jones	.20
22	Jason Kidd	1.00
23	Kerry Kittles	1.50
24	Randy Livingston	.75
25	Stephon Marbury	3.00
26	Jamal Mashburn	.50
27	Walter McCarty	.20
28	Amal McCaskill	.20
29	Antonio McDyess	1.00
30	Jeff McInnis	.20
31	Russ Millard	.20
32	Ryan Minor	.20
33	Alonzo Mourning	.75
34	Dikembe Mutombo	.20
35	Steve Nash	.75
36	Moochie Norris	.20
37	Ed O'Bannon	.40
38	Jermaine O'Neal	.75
39	Mark Pope	.20
40	Vitaly Potapenko	.75
41	Ron Riley	.20
42	Darnell Robinson	.20
43	Glenn Robinson	.40
44	Roy Rogers	.20
45	Jason Sasser	.20
46	Doron Sheffer	.20
47	Joe Smith	1.00
48	Damon Stoudamire	2.00
49	Antoine Walker	1.00
50	Samaki Walker	.50
51	John Wallace	1.00
52	Rasheed Wallace	.20
53	Jerome Williams	.20
54	Lorenzen Wright	.20

1996 Pacific Power Prism Gold Crown Die-Cut

This 15-card insert continued Pacific's Gold Crown Die-cuts that were used previously in baseball and football. Cards were inserted three per 37 packs, with card numbers carrying a "GC" prefix.

		MT
Complete Set (15):		150.00
Common Player:		3.00
GC1	Shareef Abdur-Rahim	15.00
GC2	Ray Allen	15.00
GC3	Kobe Bryant	20.00
GC4	Marcus Camby	17.00
GC5	Erick Dampier	3.00
GC6	Tony Delk	8.00
GC7	Allen Iverson	25.00
GC8	Jason Kidd	10.00
GC9	Stephon Marbury	17.00
GC10	Steve Nash	8.00
GC11	Jermaine O'Neal	8.00
GC12	Joe Smith	10.00
GC13	Damon Stoudamire	12.00
GC14	Antoine Walker	8.00
GC15	John Wallace	8.00

1996 Pacific Power Prism In the Paint

In the Paint highlighted 20 future stars and was seeded three per 37 packs. The cards featured an action shot of the player over a gold foil background that includes the player's name in large letters. In the Paint cards carried an "IP" prefix.

		MT
Complete Set (20):		175.00
Common Player:		3.00
IP1	Shareef Abdur-Rahim	17.00
IP2	Ray Allen	17.00
IP3	Kobe Bryant	25.00
IP4	Marcus Camby	20.00
IP5	Erick Dampier	3.00
IP6	Tyus Edney	3.00
IP7	Michael Finley	7.00
IP8	Allen Iverson	30.00
IP9	Dontae Jones	3.00
IP10	Jason Kidd	12.00
IP11	Stephon Marbury	20.00
IP12	Antonio McDyess	7.00
IP13	Dikembe Mutombo	3.00
IP14	Steve Nash	10.00
IP15	Ed O'Bannon	3.00
IP16	Jermaine O'Neal	10.00
IP17	Joe Smith	12.00
IP18	Damon Stoudamire	15.00
IP19	Antoine Walker	10.00
IP20	John Wallace	10.00

1996 Pacific Power Prism Jump Ball Hoop-Cel

This 10-card set was printed on gold foil and contained a cel in the middle resembling a basketball net. The cel featured a shot of the player, while the background included basketballs. Inserted at one per 37 packs, this insert was numbered with a "JB" prefix.

		MT
Complete Set (10):		175.00
Common Player:		4.00
JB1	Shareef Abdur-Rahim	20.00
JB2	Ray Allen	20.00
JB3	Kobe Bryant	35.00
JB4	Marcus Camby	25.00
JB5	Erick Dampier	4.00
JB6	Allen Iverson	40.00
JB7	Dontae Jones	4.00
JB8	Stephon Marbury	25.00
JB9	Antoine Walker	10.00
JB10	Lorenzen Wright	4.00

1996 Pacific Power Prism Regents of Roundball

This 55-card set pictures all the top picks and was included at a rate of two per pack. The cards contain no foil and have a brushed border with an "RR" prefix on the card number.

		MT
Complete Set (55):		5.00
Regents of Roundball:		25%

1996 Press Pass

Press Pass' 1996 set contains 45 cards, plus seven different insert sets. Each regular card front has a full-bleed color action photo on it, with a gold-foiled banner at the bottom which includes the player's name, Press Pass logo, position and when the player was selected in the draft. The card back has a color photo, with the player's name, biographical information and a card number running down the left side. A box at the bottom of the card includes 1995-96 and career collegiate stats, plus a brief player profile. The insert sets include Net Burners, autographed cards, Jersey, Lotto, Pandemonium, Swisssh and Focused (acetate) cards. Swisssh and Net Burners cards are parallel to the main set and are each seeded one per pack. The Net Burners cards are die-cut, incorporating the net, backboard and rim of a basketball goal into the design. Swisssh cards feature a silver metallic foil in the design.

		MT
Complete Gold Set (45):		15.00
Common Gold Player:		.05
1	Allen Iverson	2.00
2	Marcus Camby	1.50
3	Shareef Abdur-Rahim	1.00
4	Stephon Marbury	1.25
5	Ray Allen	1.00
6	Antoine Walker	.75
7	Lorenzen Wright	.40
8	Kerry Kittles	.75
9	Samaki Walker	.75
10	Erick Dampier	.30
11	Todd Fuller	.25
12	Vitaly Potapenko	.25
13	Kobe Bryant	3.00
14	Steve Nash	.40
15	Tony Delk	.50
16	Jermaine O'Neal	.50
17	John Wallace	.40
18	Walter McCarty	.50
19	Dontae Jones	.25
20	Roy Rogers	.25
21	Jerome Williams	.25
22	Brian Evans	.25
23	Travis Knight	.25
24	Othella Harrington	.25
25	Ryan Minor	.25
26	Doron Sheffer	.05
27	Jeff McInnis	.10
28	Jason Sasser	.05
29	Randy Livingston	.10
30	Malik Rose	.05
31	Jamie Feick	.05
32	Mark Pope	.05
33	Damon Stoudamire (Rookie Team)	.30
34	Jerry Stackhouse (Rookie Team)	.20
35	Joe Smith (Rookie Team)	.15
36	Michael Finley (Rookie Team)	.10
37	Rasheed Wallace (Rookie Team)	.05
38	Antonio McDyess (Rookie Team)	.10
39	Ray Allen, Travis Knight, Chad Sheffer (UConn)	.50
40	Walter McCarty, Tony Delk, Antoine Walker, Mark Pope (Kentucky)	.50
41	Jerome Williams, Allen Iverson, Othella Harrington (Georgetown)	.50
42	Erick Dampier, Dontae Jones (Miss. State)	.25
43	Stephon Marbury, Drew Barry (Georgia Tech)	.50
44	Kobe Bryant, Jermaine O'Neal (High School Sensations)	.50
45	Checklist	.05

1996 Press Pass Autographs

More than 18,000 autographed cards, covering the top players drafted, are included as inserts in 1996 Press Pass packs. Cards were seeded one per every 72 packs and include a certificate of authenticity.

		MT
Complete Set (20):		400.00
Common Player:		10.00
(1)	Ray Allen	35.00
(2)	Kobe Bryant	80.00
(3)	Marcus Camby	60.00
(4)	Tony Delk	20.00
(5)	Brian Evans	10.00
(6)	Othella Harrington	10.00
(7)	Allen Iverson	70.00
(8)	Dantae Jones	20.00
(9)	Travis Knight	10.00
(10)	Randy Livingston	20.00
(11)	Stephon Marbury	45.00
(12)	Walter McCarty	20.00
(13)	Steve Nash	20.00
(14)	Vitaly Potapenko	10.00
(15)	Roy Rogers	10.00
(16)	Jason Sasser	10.00
(17)	Antoine Walker	25.00
(18)	Samaki Walker	25.00
(19)	Jerome Williams	10.00
(20)	Lorenzen Wright	20.00

1996 Press Pass Silver

Also referred to as Silver, Swissssh contained all 45 cards from the base set printed with a silver foil strip instead of gold foil from the regular-issue cards. These inserts were seeded one per pack.

	MT
Complete Set (45):	30.00
Silver Cards:	3x

1996 Press Pass Net Burners

Net Burners was a 45-card parallel set that included a die-cut basketball net and backboard with the player coming out of the rim. The insert and player's name is stamped across the bottom in gold foil. Net Burners parallel cards carry an "NB" prefix on the card number and were seeded one per pack.

	MT
Complete Set (45):	30.00
Net Burner Cards:	2x

1996 Press Pass Focused

Available only in 1996 Press Pass hobby packs, these acetate cards feature nine players in action, highlighted with gold foil stamping for their names. The player's name is also repeated in the background, using different colors for the letters. A Press Pass logo also appears on the front, as does a card number F1/9 (Focused) etc. The card back shows a white reversed image of the photo from the front.

		MT
Complete Set (9):		70.00
Common Player:		3.50
F1	Allen Iverson	20.00
F2	Marcus Camby	16.00
F3	Shareef Abdur-Rahim	12.00
F4	Stephon Marbury	12.00
F5	Ray Allen	10.00
F6	Antoine Walker	14.00
F7	Lorenzen Wright	3.50
F8	Kerry Kittles	7.00
F9	Samaki Walker	7.00

1996 Press Pass Jersey Cards

Jerseys of some of the NBA's top draft selections in 1996 are featured on these 1996 Press Pass inserts. Each individually-numbered jersey card includes a certificate of authenticity, an embedded piece of game-used jersey, and the likeness of the player who wore the jersey. The cards, numbered using a "J" prefix, were seeded one per every 640 hobby packs and one per every 720 retail packs.

		MT
Complete Set (4):		225.00
Common Player:		30.00
J1	Allen Iverson	125.00
J2	Marcus Camby	100.00
J3	Ray Allen	65.00
J4	Mystery Player	30.00

1996 Press Pass Lotto

This six-card holofoil progressive insert set highlights the top lottery picks. The card front uses silver foil for the border, the player's name (along the right side), Lottery Pick (in the upper left corner) and the year when the player was drafted (in a basketball in the upper right corner). The Press Pass logo is also on the front. The background is the surface of a basketball, with the numbers 1-6 running throughout it. The card back, numbered L1 of 6, etc., is divided into six parts; each part shows a mug shot of one of the top six picks. A basketball is in the middle; the Press Pass logo is at the bottom. The cards were seeded as such: #1 1:720; #2 1:360; #3 1:180; #4 1:90, #5 1:45 and #6 1:36.

		MT
Complete Set (6):		190.00
Common Player:		5.00
1	Allen Iverson	100.00
2	Marcus Camby	60.00
3	Shareef Abdur-Rahim	30.00
4	Stephon Marbury	25.00
5	Ray Allen	15.00
6	Antoine Walker	5.00

1996 Press Pass Pandemonium

Twelve of the draft's strongest players are featured on these techno-advanced NitroKrome all-foil cards. The cards were seeded one per every 12 packs. The card front has a color action photo against the NitroKrome foil background. "Pandemonium" can be spelled out from the jumbled letters in the background. The player's name is in silver foil along the bottom; the Press Pass logo is in the upper right corner. The card back has a full-bleed color action photo, except for the right border. The player's name and a card number (PM 1 of 12, etc.) are at the top. The Press Pass logo is in the lower right corner. A brief player profile is also given.

	MT
Complete Set (12):	65.00
Common Player:	2.00
PM1 Shareef Abdur-Rahim	10.00
PM2 Ray Allen	8.00
PM3 Kobe Bryant	20.00
PM4 Marcus Camby	12.00
PM5 Erick Dampier	3.00
PM6 Othella Harrington	2.00
PM7 Allen Iverson	18.00
PM8 Kerry Kittles	5.00
PM9 Stephon Marbury	10.00
PM10 Walter McCarty	2.00
PM11 Antoine Walker	10.00
PM12 John Wallace	4.00

1996 Score Board Basketball Rookies

Score Board's 1996 100-card basketball set includes the top picks from the 1996 NBA draft. Each card front features a full-bleed color action photo, with the player's name in block letters at the top. His name, college and position are along the bottom, next to a Basketball Rookies logo in the lower left-hand corner. The card back has a ghosted image of the player, with a frame around a full-color shot of his face. Draft data runs along each side of the frame. The left side of the card has a player profile; the right side has biographicial information and stats. The brand logo is in the upper right corner, opposite the card number. Subsets, each with 10 cards, include All American and Basketball Greats. Three insert sets were also created - College Jerseys, #1 Draft Picks and Vintage Rookie Cards. In all, there are 39 different, original, vintage rookie cards of top players seeded two per box of 1996 Basketball Rookies by Score Board. Among those vintage rookies found in packs are Michael Jordan and Magic Johnson (redemption cards are used for these two players), Patrick Ewing, Charles Barkley and Scottie Pippen.

		MT
Complete Set (100):		12.00
Common Player:		.05
1	Allen Iverson	2.00
2	Marcus Camby	1.50
3	Stephon Marbury	1.50
4	Shareef Abdur-Rahim	1.00
5	Ray Allen	1.00
6	Erick Dampier	.25
7	Antoine Walker	.75
8	John Wallace	.30
9	Kerry Kittles	.50
10	Lorenzen Wright	.30
11	Samaki Walker	.50
12	Todd Fuller	.25
13	Jaron Boone	.05
14	Roy Rogers	.20
15	Kobe Bryant	2.00
16	Walter McCarty	.40
17	Ryan Minor	.10
18	Steve Nash	.30
19	Jermaine O'Neal	.30
20	Vitaly Potapenko	.15
21	Kwame Evans	.05
22	Tony Delk	.40
23	Brian Evans	.05
24	Dion Cross	.05
25	Dontae Jones	.10
26	Travis Knight	.10
27	Priest Lauderdale	.10
28	Moochie Norris	.05
29	Efthimis Retzias	.05
30	Jerome Williams	.05
31	Jamie Feick	.05
32	Othella Harrington	.05
33	Mark Hendrickson	.05
34	Chris Robinson	.05
35	Randy Livingston	.05
36	Marcus Mann	.05
37	Darnell Robinson	.05
38	Jason Sasser	.05
39	Doron Sheffer	.05
40	Kevin Simpson	.05
41	Joseph Blair	.05
42	Eric Gingold	.05
43	Steve Hamer	.05
44	Ronnie Henderson	.05
45	Jeff McInnis	.05
46	Dante Calabria	.05
47	Martin Muursepp	.05
48	Mark Pope	.05
49	Ron Riley	.05
50	Shandon Anderson	.05
51	Derrick Battie	.05
52	Derek Fisher	.05
53	Kevin Granger	.05
54	Shawn Harvey	.05
55	Bernard Hopkins	.05
56	Raimonds Miglinieks	.05
57	Tim Moore	.05
58	Carlos Strong	.05
59	Chucky Atkins	.05
60	Drew Barry	.05
61	Terrell Bell	.05
62	Donta Bright	.05
63	Marcus Brown	.05
64	William Cunningham	.05
65	Katu Davis	.05
66	Ben Davis	.05
67	Adrian Griffin	.05
68	Darvin Ham	.05
69	Art Long	.05
70	Jerome Lambert	.05
71	Amal McCaskill	.05
72	Mingo Johnson	.05
73	Dametri Hill	.05
74	Michael Lloyd	.05
75	Malik Rose	.05
76	Jeff Nordgaard	.05
77	Duane Simpkins	.05
78	Russ Millard	.05
79	Allen Iverson	1.00
80	Marcus Camby	.75
81	Allen Iverson	1.00
82	Marcus Camby	.75
83	Stephon Marbury	.75
84	Ray Allen	.50
85	Kerry Kittles	.25
86	Erick Dampier	.05
87	Shareef Abdur-Rahim	.50
88	John Wallace	.05
89	Lorenzen Wright	.05
90	Tony Delk	.20
91	Shaquille O'Neal	.50
92	Hakeem Olajuwon	.05
93	Joe Smith	.05
94	Brent Barry	.05
95	Jason Kidd	.05
96	Scottie Pippen	.20
97	Damon Stoudamire	.30
98	Alonzo Mourning	.05
99	Rasheed Wallace	.05
100	Glenn Robinson	.05

1996 Score Board Basketball Rookies College Jerseys

This 30-card insert set showcases top 1995-96 college stars on special embossed cards that give the look and feel of an actual uniform. The horizontal front shows a picture of the player, and his college jersey. The cards are seeded one per every 10 packs.

		MT
Complete Set (30):		75.00
Common Player:		1.00
1	Allen Iverson	15.00
2	Stephon Marbury	12.00
3	Marcus Camby	12.00
4	Ray Allen	9.00
5	Erick Dampier	3.00
6	John Wallace	3.00
7	Antoine Walker	7.00
8	Lorenzen Wright	3.00
9	Kerry Kittles	5.00
10	Todd Fuller	3.00
11	Samaki Walker	5.00
12	Roy Rogers	1.00
13	Walter McCarty	4.00
14	Dontae Jones	1.00
15	Steve Nash	3.00
16	Jerome Williams	1.00
17	Ryan Minor	1.00
18	Shareef Abdur-Rahim	9.00
19	Brian Evans	1.00
20	Travis Knight	1.00
21	Mark Hendrickson	1.00
22	Tony Delk	4.00
23	Ronnie Henderson	1.00
24	Drew Barry	1.00
25	Damon Stoudamire	1.00
26	Shaquille O'Neal	1.00
27	Joe Smith	1.00
28	Jason Kidd	1.00
29	Alonzo Mourning	1.00
30	Rasheed Wallace	1.00

1996 Score Board Basketball Rookies #1 Die-Cuts

These 1996 Score Board Basketball Rookies inserts feature the first-round picks from the 1996 draft on cards printed on duplexed metallic stock. Each card is also die-cut around a #1 on the front. The cards are seeded one per every 50 packs.

		MT
Complete Set (30):		275.00
Common Player:		2.00
1	Allen Iverson	40.00
2	Marcus Camby	30.00
3	Shareef Abdur-Rahim	20.00
4	Stephon Marbury	30.00
5	Ray Allen	20.00
6	Antoine Walker	15.00
7	Lorenzen Wright	8.00
8	Kerry Kittles	10.00
9	Samaki Walker	10.00
10	Erick Dampier	5.00
11	Todd Fuller	5.00
12	Vitaly Potapenko	2.00
13	Kobe Bryant	45.00
14	Shaquille O'Neal	25.00
15	Steve Nash	8.00
16	Tony Delk	8.00
17	Jermaine O'Neal	8.00
18	John Wallace	8.00
19	Walter McCarty	8.00
20	Jason Kidd	12.00
21	Dontae Jones	2.00
22	Roy Rogers	2.00
23	Efthimis Retzias	2.00
24	Derek Fisher	2.00
25	Martin Muursepp	2.00
26	Jerome Williams	2.00
27	Brian Evans	2.00
28	Priest Lauderdale	2.00
29	Travis Knight	2.00
30	Damon Stoudamire	20.00

1996-97 SkyBox

SkyBox Premium in 1996-97 consisted of 290 cards, with 140 in Series I and 150 in Series II. Card fronts featured a mix of posed and action shots with a full bleed design. The SkyBox Premium logo was stamped in gold foil in the top right corner with the player's name in gold foil centered on the bottom. Backs displayed another shot of the player, with biographical information to the right and statistics across the bottom. Series I had 129 regular cards, two checklists and nine Triple Threats (three more Triple Threats Bulls cards exist, but are considered inserts), while Series II had 68 player updates, 40 Rookies, 20 Point Men, 20 Double Trouble and two checklists. Inserts in Series I include: Close-Ups, Rookie Prevue, Autographics, Standouts, Larger than Life, Bonus Triple Threats and Rubies parallel cards of the first 131 cards. Series II inserts include: Intimidators, Net Set, New Edition, Autographics, Thunder & Lightning, Golden Touch, 148 Rubies and five Emeralds autograph redemption.

		MT
Complete Set (290):		40.00
Complete Series 1 (140):		20.00
Complete Series 2 (150):		20.00
Common Player:		.05
Series 1 Wax Box:		60.00
Series 2 Wax Box:		60.00
1	Mookie Blaylock	.05
2	Alan Henderson	.05
3	Christian Laettner	.05
4	Dikembe Mutombo	.05
5	Steve Smith	.05
6	Dana Barros	.05
7	Rick Fox	.05
8	Dino Radja	.05
9	*Antoine Walker*	2.00
10	Eric Williams	.05
11	Dell Curry	.05
12	*Tony Delk*	.50
13	Matt Geiger	.05
14	Glen Rice	.05
15	Ron Harper	.05
16	Michael Jordan	4.00
17	Toni Kukoc	.05
18	Scottie Pippen	1.00
19	Dennis Rodman	1.50
20	Terrell Brandon	.05
21	Danny Ferry	.05
22	Chris Mills	.05
23	Bobby Phills	.05
24	*Vitaly Potapenko*	.25
25	Jim Jackson	.10
26	Jason Kidd	.40
27	Jamal Mashburn	.10
28	George McCloud	.05
29	*Samaki Walker*	.60
30	LaPhonso Ellis	.05
31	Antonio McDyess	.40
32	Bryant Stith	.05
33	Joe Dumars	.10
34	Grant Hill	2.00
35	Lindsey Hunter	.05
36	Theo Ratliff	.05
37	Otis Thorpe	.05
38	*Todd Fuller*	.25
39	Chris Mullin	.10
40	Joe Smith	.40
41	Latrell Sprewell	.20
42	Charles Barkley	.50

No.	Player	MT
43	Clyde Drexler	.40
44	Mario Elie	.05
45	Hakeem Olajuwon	.75
46	*Erick Dampier*	.30
47	Dale Davis	.05
48	Derrick McKey	.05
49	Reggie Miller	.30
50	Rik Smits	.05
51	Brent Barry	.10
52	Rodney Rogers	.05
53	Loy Vaught	.05
54	*Lorenzen White*	.40
55	*Kobe Bryant*	4.00
56	Cedric Ceballos	.05
57	Eddie Jones	.20
58	Shaquille O'Neal	2.00
59	Nick Van Exel	.20
60	Tim Hardaway	.05
61	Alonzo Mourning	.30
62	Kurt Thomas	.05
63	*Ray Allen*	1.50
64	Vin Baker	.25
65	Shawn Respert	.05
66	Glenn Robinson	.30
67	Kevin Garnett	2.00
68	Tom Gugliotta	.05
69	*Stephon Marbury*	3.00
70	Sam Mitchell	.05
71	Shawn Bradley	.05
72	Kendall Gill	.05
73	*Kerry Kittles*	1.00
74	Ed O'Bannon	.05
75	Patrick Ewing	.30
76	Larry Johnson	.10
77	Charles Oakley	.05
78	John Starks	.05
79	*John Wallace*	.75
80	Nick Anderson	.05
81	Horace Grant	.05
82	Anfernee Hardaway	2.00
83	Dennis Scott	.05
84	Derrick Coleman	.05
85	*Allen Iverson*	4.00
86	Jerry Stackhouse	.75
87	Clarence Weatherspoon	.05
88	Michael Finley	.40
89	Robert Horry	.05
90	Kevin Johnson	.05
91	*Steve Nash*	.40
92	Wesley Person	.05
93	Aaron McKie	.05
94	*Jermaine O'Neal*	1.00
95	Clifford Robinson	.05
96	Arvydas Sabonis	.25
97	Gary Trent	.05
98	Tyus Edney	.10
99	Brian Grant	.05
100	Mitch Richmond	.20
101	Billy Owens	.05
102	Corliss Williamson	.05
103	Vinny Del Negro	.05
104	Sean Elliot	.05
105	Avery Johnson	.05
106	Chuck Person	.05
107	David Robinson	.50
108	Hersey Hawkins	.05
109	Shawn Kemp	1.00
110	Gary Payton	.05
111	Sam Perkins	.05
112	Detlef Schrempf	.05
113	*Marcus Camby*	2.50
114	Carlos Rogers	.05
115	Damon Stoudamire	1.00
116	Zan Tabak	.05
117	Antoine Carr	.05
118	Jeff Hornacek	.05
119	Karl Malone	.30
120	Chris Morris	.05
121	John Stockton	.30
122	*Shareef Abdur-Rahim*	2.50
123	Greg Anthony	.05
124	Bryant Reeves	.25
125	*Roy Rogers*	.30
126	Calbert Cheaney	.05
127	Juwan Howard	.50
128	Gheorghe Muresan	.05
129	Chris Webber	.25
130	Checklist A	.05
131	Checklist B	.05
TT1	Chris Mullin (Triple Threats)	.05
TT2	Joe Smith (Triple Threats)	.10
TT3	Latrell Sprewell (Triple Threats)	.10
TT4	Avery Johnson (Triple Threats)	.05
TT5	Sean Elliot (Triple Threats)	.05
TT6	David Robinson (Triple Threats)	.10
TT7	John Stockton (Triple Threats)	.10
TT8	Karl Malone (Triple Threats)	.10
TT9	Jeff Hornacek (Triple Threats)	.05
132	Jon Barry	.05
133	Christian Laettner	.05
134	Dikembe Mutombo	.05
135	Dee Brown	.05
136	Todd Day	.05
137	David Wesley	.05
138	Vlade Divac	.05
139	Anthony Goldwire	.05
140	Anthony Mason	.05
141	Jason Caffey	.05
142	Luc Longley	.05
143	Tyrone Hill	.05
144	Antonio Lang	.05
145	Sam Cassell	.05
146	Chris Gatling	.05
147	Eric Montross	.05
148	Ervin Johnson	.05
149	Sarunas Marciulionis	.05
150	Stacey Augmon	.05
151	Grant Long	.05
152	Terry Mills	.05
153	Kenny Smith	.05
154	B.J. Armstrong	.05
155	Bimbo Coles	.05
156	Charles Barkley	.50
157	Brent Price	.05
158	Duane Ferrell	.05
159	Jalen Rose	.05
160	Terry Dehere	.05
161	Charles Outlaw	.05
162	Corie Blount	.05
163	Shaquille O'Neal	2.00
164	Rumeal Robinson	.05
165	P.J. Brown	.05
166	Ronnie Grandison	.05
167	Sherman Douglas	.05
168	Johnny Newman	.05
169	James Robinson	.05
170	Doug West	.05
171	Robert Pack	.05
172	Khalid Reeves	.05
173	Chris Childs	.05
174	Allan Houston	.05
175	Charlie Ward	.05
176	Darrell Armstrong	.05
177	Gerald Wilkins	.05
178	Lucious Harris	.05
179	Robert Horry	.05
180	Danny Manning	.05
181	Kenny Anderson	.05
182	Isaiah Rider	.05
183	Rasheed Wallace	.05
184	Mahmoud Abdul-Rauf	.05
185	Cory Alexander	.05
186	Vernon Maxwell	.05
187	Dominique Wilkins	.05
188	Nate McMillan	.05
189	Larry Stewart	.05
190	Doug Christie	.05
191	Hubert Davis	.05
192	Walt Williams	.05
193	Adam Keefe	.05
194	Greg Ostertag	.05
195	John Stockton	.30
196	George Lynch	.05
197	Lee Mayberry	.05
198	Tracy Murray	.05
199	Rod Strickland	.05
200	Shareef Abdur-Rahim	2.00
201	Ray Allen	1.25
202	Shandon Anderson	.05
203	Kobe Bryant	2.00
204	Marcus Camby	2.00
205	Erick Dampier	.25
206	Emanuel Davis	.05
207	Tony Delk	.25
208	Brian Evans	.05
209	Derek Fisher	.25
210	Todd Fuller	.05
211	Dean Garrett	.40
212	Reggie Geary	.05
213	Darvin Ham	.05
214	Othella Harrington	.30
215	Shane Heal	.05
216	Allen Iverson	3.00
217	Dontae Jones	.05
218	Kerry Kittles	1.00
219	Priest Lauderdale	.05
220	Randy Livingston	.25
221	Matt Maloney	.50
222	Stephon Marbury	2.50
223	Walter McCarty	.05
224	Amal McCaskill	.05
225	Jeff McInnis	.05
226	Martin Muursepp	.05
227	Steve Nash	.25
228	Ruben Nembhard	.05
229	Jermaine O'Neal	.75
230	Vitaly Potapenko	.25
231	Virginius Praskevicius	.05
232	Roy Rogers	.25
233	Malik Rose	.05
234	Antoine Walker	1.25
235	Samaki Walker	.05
236	Ben Wallace	.05
237	John Wallace	.40
238	Jerome Williams	.05
239	Lorenzen Wright	.25
240	Sam Cassell	.05
241	Anfernee Hardaway	1.00
242	Tim Hardaway	.05
243	Grant Hill	1.00
244	Allan Houston	.05
245	Juwan Howard	.05
246	Kevin Johnson	.05
247	Michael Jordan	2.00
248	Jason Kidd	.05
249	Karl Malone	.05
250	Reggie Miller	.05
251	Gary Payton	.05
252	Wesley Person	.05
253	Glen Rice	.05
254	David Robinson	.05
255	Steve Smith	.05
256	Latrell Sprewell	.05
257	Jerry Stackhouse	.05
258	Rod Strickland	.05
259	Nick Van Exel	.05
260	Charles Barkley	.25
261	Dale Davis	.05
262	Patrick Ewing	.05
263	Michael Finley	.05
264	Chris Gatling	.05
265	Armon Gilliam	.05
266	Tyrone Hill	.05
267	Robert Horry	.05
268	Mark Jackson	.05
269	Shawn Kemp	.50
270	Jamal Mashburn	.05
271	Anthony Mason	.05
272	Alonzo Mourning	.05
273	Dikembe Mutombo	.05
274	Shaquille O'Neal	1.00
275	Isaiah Rider	.05
276	Dennis Rodman	.50
277	Damon Stoudamire	.05
278	Chris Webber	.05
279	Jayson Williams	.05
280	Checklist	.05
281	Checklist	.05

1996-97 SkyBox Rubies

Rubies paralleled 279 cards from the SkyBox Series I and II set, and was inserted one per Series I and II hobby boxes. Rubies are identified by Ruby foil stamping in place of gold foil on regular-issue cards. The Ruby parallels are also twice as thick as regular-issue cards.

No.	Player	MT
Complete Set (279):		2400.00
Complete Series 1 (131):		1600.00
Complete Series 2 (148):		800.00
Common Player:		5.00
1	Mookie Blaylock	5.00
2	Alan Henderson	5.00
3	Christian Laettner	5.00
4	Dikembe Mutombo	5.00
5	Steve Smith	5.00
6	Dana Barros	5.00
7	Rick Fox	5.00
8	Dino Radja	5.00
9	Antoine Walker	40.00
10	Eric Williams	5.00
11	Dell Curry	5.00
12	Tony Delk	10.00
13	Matt Geiger	5.00
14	Glen Rice	15.00
15	Ron Harper	5.00
16	Michael Jordan	250.00
17	Toni Kukoc	10.00
18	Scottie Pippen	50.00
19	Dennis Rodman	70.00
20	Terrell Brandon	10.00
21	Danny Ferry	5.00
22	Chris Mills	5.00
23	Bobby Phills	5.00
24	Vitaly Potapenko	10.00
25	Jim Jackson	10.00
26	Jason Kidd	15.00
27	Jamal Mashburn	10.00
28	George McCloud	5.00
29	Samaki Walker	10.00
30	LaPhonso Ellis	5.00
31	Antonio McDyess	15.00
32	Bryant Stith	5.00
33	Joe Dumars	10.00
34	Grant Hill	100.00
35	Lindsey Hunter	5.00
36	Theo Ratliff	5.00
37	Otis Thorpe	5.00
38	Todd Fuller	10.00
39	Chris Mullin	10.00
40	Joe Smith	25.00
41	Latrell Sprewell	15.00
42	Charles Barkley	25.00
43	Clyde Drexler	20.00
44	Mario Elie	5.00
45	Hakeem Olajuwon	30.00
46	Erick Dampier	10.00
47	Dale Davis	5.00
48	Derrick McKey	5.00
49	Reggie Miller	15.00
50	Rik Smits	5.00
51	Brent Barry	5.00
52	Rodney Rogers	5.00
53	Loy Vaught	5.00
54	Lorenzen White	10.00
55	Kobe Bryant	100.00
56	Cedric Ceballos	5.00
57	Eddie Jones	30.00
58	Shaquille O'Neal	100.00
59	Nick Van Exel	15.00
60	Tim Hardaway	10.00
61	Alonzo Mourning	10.00
62	Kurt Thomas	5.00
63	Ray Allen	25.00
64	Vin Baker	15.00
65	Shawn Respert	5.00
66	Glenn Robinson	15.00
67	Kevin Garnett	90.00
68	Tom Gugliotta	10.00
69	Stephon Marbury	70.00
70	Sam Mitchell	5.00
71	Shawn Bradley	5.00
72	Kendall Gill	5.00
73	Kerry Kittles	25.00
74	Ed O'Bannon	5.00
75	Patrick Ewing	15.00
76	Larry Johnson	10.00
77	Charles Oakley	5.00
78	John Starks	5.00
79	John Wallace	15.00
80	Nick Anderson	5.00
81	Horace Grant	5.00
82	Anfernee Hardaway	100.00
83	Dennis Scott	5.00
84	Derrick Coleman	5.00
85	Allen Iverson	100.00
86	Jerry Stackhouse	20.00
87	Clarence Weatherspoon	5.00
88	Michael Finley	15.00
89	Robert Horry	5.00
90	Kevin Johnson	5.00
91	Steve Nash	10.00
92	Wesley Person	5.00
93	Aaron McKie	5.00
94	Jermaine O'Neal	25.00
95	Clifford Robinson	5.00
96	Arvydas Sabonis	5.00
97	Gary Trent	5.00
98	Tyus Edney	5.00
99	Brian Grant	5.00
100	Mitch Richmond	15.00
101	Billy Owens	5.00
102	Corliss Williamson	5.00
103	Vinny Del Negro	5.00
104	Sean Elliot	5.00
105	Avery Johnson	5.00
106	Chuck Person	5.00
107	David Robinson	25.00
108	Hersey Hawkins	5.00
109	Shawn Kemp	50.00
110	Gary Payton	20.00
111	Sam Perkins	5.00
112	Detlef Schrempf	5.00
113	Marcus Camby	60.00
114	Carlos Rogers	5.00
115	Damon Stoudamire	30.00
116	Zan Tabak	5.00
117	Antoine Carr	5.00
118	Jeff Hornacek	5.00
119	Karl Malone	15.00
120	Chris Morris	5.00
121	John Stockton	15.00
122	Shareef Abdur-Rahim	70.00
123	Greg Anthony	5.00
124	Bryant Reeves	10.00
125	Roy Rogers	10.00
126	Calbert Cheaney	5.00
127	Juwan Howard	25.00
128	Gheorghe Muresan	5.00
129	Chris Webber	25.00

130	Checklist A	5.00
131	Checklist B	5.00
132	Jon Barry	5.00
133	Christian Laettner	5.00
134	Dikembe Mutombo	5.00
135	Dee Brown	5.00
136	Todd Day	5.00
137	David Wesley	5.00
138	Vlade Divac	5.00
139	Anthony Goldwire	5.00
140	Anthony Mason	5.00
141	Jason Caffey	5.00
142	Luc Longley	5.00
143	Tyrone Hill	5.00
144	Antonio Lang	5.00
145	Sam Cassell	5.00
146	Chris Gatling	5.00
147	Eric Montross	5.00
148	Sarunas Marciulionis	5.00
149	Stacey Augmon	5.00
150	Grant Long	5.00
151	Terry Mills	5.00
152	Kenny Smith	5.00
153	B.J. Armstrong	5.00
154	Bimbo Coles	5.00
155	Charles Barkley	25.00
156	Brent Price	5.00
157	Duane Ferrell	5.00
158	Jalen Rose	5.00
159	Terry Dehere	5.00
160	Charles Outlaw	5.00
161	Corie Blount	5.00
162	Shaquille O'Neal	90.00
163	Rumeal Robinson	5.00
164	P.J. Brown	5.00
165	Ronnie Grandison	5.00
166	Sherman Douglas	5.00
167	Johnny Newman	5.00
168	James Robinson	5.00
169	Doug West	5.00
170	Robert Pack	5.00
171	Khalid Reeves	5.00
172	Chris Childs	5.00
173	Allan Houston	5.00
174	Charlie Ward	5.00
175	Darrell Armstrong	5.00
176	Gerald Wilkins	5.00
177	Lucious Harris	5.00
178	Sam Cassell	5.00
179	Robert Horry	5.00
180	Danny Manning	5.00
181	Kenny Anderson	5.00
182	Isaiah Rider	5.00
183	Rasheed Wallace	5.00
184	Mahmoud Abdul-Rauf	5.00
185	Cory Alexander	5.00
186	Vernon Maxwell	5.00
187	Dominique Wilkins	5.00
188	Nate McMillan	5.00
189	Larry Stewart	5.00
190	Doug Christie	5.00
191	Hubert Davis	5.00
192	Walt Williams	5.00
193	Adam Keefe	5.00
194	Greg Ostertag	5.00
195	John Stockton	15.00
196	George Lynch	5.00
197	Lee Mayberry	5.00
198	Tracy Murray	5.00
199	Rod Strickland	5.00
200	Shareef Abdur-Rahim	30.00
201	Ray Allen	15.00
202	Shandon Anderson	10.00
203	Kobe Bryant	50.00
204	Marcus Camby	30.00
205	Erick Dampier	10.00
206	Emanuel Davis	5.00
207	Tony Delk	5.00
208	Brian Evans	5.00
209	Derek Fisher	10.00
210	Todd Fuller	5.00
211	Dean Garrett	10.00
212	Reggie Geary	5.00
213	Darvin Ham	5.00
214	Othella Harrington	10.00
215	Shane Heal	5.00
216	Allen Iverson	50.00
217	Dontae Jones	5.00
218	Kerry Kittles	15.00
219	Priest Lauderdale	5.00
220	Randy Livingston	5.00
221	Matt Maloney	10.00
222	Stephon Marbury	30.00
223	Walter McCarty	5.00
224	Jeff McInnis	5.00
225	Martin Muursepp	5.00
226	Steve Nash	5.00
227	Moochie Norris	5.00
228	Jermaine O'Neal	12.00
229	Vitaly Potapenko	5.00
230	Virginius Praskevicius	5.00

231	Roy Rogers	5.00
232	Malik Rose	5.00
233	James Scott	5.00
234	Antoine Walker	20.00
235	Samaki Walker	5.00
236	Ben Wallace	5.00
237	John Wallace	10.00
238	Jerome Williams	5.00
239	Lorenzen Wright	5.00
240	Sam Cassell	5.00
241	Anfernee Hardaway	45.00
242	Tim Hardaway	5.00
243	Grant Hill	45.00
244	Allan Houston	5.00
245	Juwan Howard	5.00
246	Kevin Johnson	5.00
247	Michael Jordan	100.00
248	Jason Kidd	5.00
249	Karl Malone	5.00
250	Reggie Miller	5.00
251	Gary Payton	5.00
252	Wesley Person	5.00
253	Glen Rice	5.00
254	David Robinson	5.00
255	Steve Smith	5.00
256	Latrell Sprewell	5.00
257	Jerry Stackhouse	5.00
258	Rod Strickland	5.00
259	Nick Van Exel	5.00
260	Charles Barkley	5.00
261	Dale Davis	5.00
262	Patrick Ewing	5.00
263	Michael Finley	5.00
264	Chris Gatling	5.00
265	Armon Gilliam	5.00
266	Tyrone Hill	5.00
267	Robert Horry	5.00
268	Mark Jackson	5.00
269	Shawn Kemp	20.00
270	Jamal Mashburn	5.00
271	Anthony Mason	5.00
272	Alonzo Mourning	5.00
273	Dikembe Mutombo	5.00
274	Shaquille O'Neal	45.00
275	Isaiah Rider	5.00
276	Dennis Rodman	45.00
277	Damon Stoudamire	15.00
278	Chris Webber	5.00
279	Jayson Williams	5.00
280	Checklist	5.00
281	Checklist	5.00

1996-97 SkyBox Autographics

Autographics were inserted into each 1996-97 SkyBox basketball product at a rate of one per 72 packs. The cards were autographed in the more common black ink and a more limited blue ink, except for Scottie Pippen and Hakeem Olajuwon, who signed all of their cards in blue ink, and Kevin Garnett who signed two-thirds of his cards in blue ink. They were inserted into Hoops I and II, SkyBox I and II, Z-Force I and II and E-X2000. The set covered 95 players with certain players being exclusive to certain products, for example Antoine Walker, Damon Stoudamire and Kerry Kittles were only in E-X2000.

		MT
Blue Ink:		2x-3x
	Ray Allen	80.00
	Kenny Anderson	30.00

Nick Anderson	20.00
B.J. Armstrong	15.00
Vincent Askew	15.00
Dana Barros	15.00
Brent Barry	25.00
Travis Best	20.00
Muggsy Bogues	20.00
P.J. Brown	20.00
Randy Brown	20.00
Marcus Camby	100.00
Chris Childs	20.00
Dell Curry	15.00
Andrew DeClerq	15.00
Tony Delk	35.00
Sherman Douglas	15.00
Clyde Drexler	130.00
Tyus Edney	20.00
Michael Finley	45.00
Rick Fox	20.00
Kevin Garnett Black	300.00
Kevin Garnett Blue	275.00
Matt Geiger	15.00
Kendall Gill	30.00
Brian Grant	20.00
Tim Hardaway	60.00
Grant Hill	325.00
Tyrone Hill	20.00
Allan Houston	40.00
Juwan Howard	200.00
Jim Jackson	25.00
Mark Jackson	25.00
Eddie Jones	150.00
Adam Keefe	15.00
Steve Kerr	30.00
Toni Kukoc	50.00
Andrew Lang	15.00
Voshon Lenard	25.00
Grant Long	15.00
Luc Longley	30.00
George Lynch	20.00
Don MacLean	15.00
Stephon Marbury	175.00
Lee Mayberry	15.00
Walter McCarty	30.00
George McCloud	30.00
Antonio McDyess	80.00
Nate McMillan	15.00
Chris Mills	15.00
Sam Mitchell	15.00
Eric Montross	15.00
Chris Morris	15.00
Lawrence Moten	15.00
Alonzo Mourning	160.00
Gheorghe Muresan	25.00
Steve Nash	60.00
Ed O'Bannon	25.00
Charles Oakley	20.00
Hakeem Olajuwon Blue	175.00
Greg Ostertag	15.00
Billy Owens	15.00
Sam Perkins	15.00
Chuck Person	15.00
Wesley Person	20.00
Bobby Phills	15.00
Scottie Pippen Blue	325.00
Theo Ratliff	15.00
Glen Rice	75.00
Rodney Rogers	15.00
Byron Scott	15.00
Dennis Scott	20.00
Joe Smith	90.00
Kenny Smith	15.00
Rik Smits	25.00
Eric Snow	15.00
Latrell Sprewell	80.00
Jerry Stackhouse	80.00
John Starks	30.00
Bryant Stith	15.00
Damon Stoudamire	150.00
Rod Strickland	80.00
Bob Sura	25.00
Zan Tabak	15.00
Loy Vaught	15.00
Antoine Walker	150.00
Samaki Walker	30.00
John Wallace	60.00
Bill Wennington	20.00
David Wesley	20.00
Doug West	15.00
Monty Williams	15.00
Joe Wolf	15.00
Sharone Wright	15.00

1996-97 SkyBox Close-Ups

Close-Ups included nine die-cut cards with the featured player cast over a large globe with the insert

name on it. The team's logo is embossed in the lower right corner on the front. Inserted every 24 packs, this set is numbered CU1-CU9.

		MT
Complete Set (9):		60.00
Common Player:		3.00
CU1	Anfernee Hardaway	20.00
CU2	Grant Hill	20.00
CU3	Juwan Howard	7.00
CU4	Shawn Kemp	10.00
CU5	Jason Kidd	7.00
CU6	Alonzo Mourning	3.00
CU7	Hakeem Olajuwon	8.00
CU8	Jerry Stackhouse	6.00
CU9	Damon Stoudamire	8.00

1996-97 SkyBox Emerald Autographs

Emeralds were inserted every 20 hobby boxes as box toppers and were numbered E1-E5. The cards were available through redemption cards and captured the base cards for five players with Emerald foil treatment.

		MT
Complete Set (5):		600.00
Common Player:		75.00
E1	Ray Allen	90.00
E2	Marcus Camby	130.00
E3	Grant Hill	325.00
E4	Kerry Kittles	90.00
E5	Jerry Stackhouse	75.00

1996-97 SkyBox Golden Touch

This 10-card set highlighted some of the shooters in the NBA on gold and silver foil. The words "Golden Touch" are printed in fancy letters in the background and all cards are die-cut around three sides, with the bottom side the exclusion. Golden Touch inserts were seeded one per 240 packs of Series II.

		MT
Complete Set (10):		400.00
Common Player:		10.00
1	Vin Baker	15.00
2	Terrell Brandon	10.00

3	Allan Houston	10.00
4	Allen Iverson	80.00
5	Michael Jordan	160.00
6	Shawn Kemp	40.00
7	Karl Malone	20.00
8	Stephon Marbury	70.00
9	Latrell Sprewell	25.00
10	Damon Stoudamire	35.00

1996-97 SkyBox Intimidators

This 20-card insert was seeded one per eight Series II packs and captures some of the top big men in basketball. The cards are identified by featuring the players first and last name (first name runs up, last name runs down) printed in silver foil in the background.

		MT
Complete Set (20):		60.00
Common Player:		1.50
1	Shareef Abdur-Rahim	10.00
2	Charles Barkley	5.00
3	Marcus Camby	10.00
4	Elden Campbell	1.50
5	Derrick Coleman	1.50
6	Patrick Ewing	3.00
7	Michael Finley	1.50
8	Kevin Garnett	12.00
9	Jim Jackson	1.50
10	Anthony Mason	1.50
11	Antonio McDyess	1.50
12	Alonzo Mourning	3.00
13	Gheorghe Muresan	1.50
14	Dikembe Mutombo	1.50
15	Shaquille O'Neal	12.00
16	Isaiah Rider	1.50
17	Clifford Robinson	1.50
18	David Robinson	4.00
19	Dennis Rodman	12.00
20	Clarence Weatherspoon	1.50

1996-97 SkyBox Larger Than Life

Larger Than Life features 18 players on a horizontal foil design. Fronts contain an action shot of the player on the left side, with a foil close-up shot on the right side and the name of the insert printed across the bottom. This insert was seeded one per 180 Series I hobby packs, and was numbered L1-L18.

		MT
Complete Set (18):		650.00
Common Player:		6.00
L1	Shareef Abdur-Rahim	50.00
L2	Marcus Camby	50.00
L3	Kevin Garnett	60.00
L4	Anfernee Hardaway	60.00
L5	Grant Hill	60.00
L6	Allen Iverson	80.00
L7	Michael Jordan	175.00
L8	Shawn Kemp	35.00
L9	Stephon Marbury	60.00
L10	Jamal Mashburn	6.00
L11	Antonio McDyess	10.00
L12	Alonzo Mourning	6.00
L13	Dikembe Mutombo	6.00
L14	Hakeem Olajuwon	25.00
L15	Shaquille O'Neal	50.00
L16	Dennis Rodman	50.00
L17	Jerry Stackhouse	15.00
L18	Damon Stoudamire	25.00

1996-97 SkyBox Net Set

This 20-card insert was issued only in Series II hobby packs at a rate of one per 48. The fronts featured a color image of the player over the top of a gold and silver background that resembles the sun with rays reflecting down.

		MT
Complete Set (20):		300.00
Common Player:		4.00
1	Vin Baker	4.00
2	Clyde Drexler	10.00
3	Patrick Ewing	6.00
4	Anfernee Hardaway	40.00
5	Grant Hill	40.00
6	Juwan Howard	10.00
7	Allen Iverson	50.00
8	Michael Jordan	80.00
9	Shawn Kemp	25.00
10	Jason Kidd	8.00
11	Karl Malone	6.00
12	Stephon Marbury	50.00
13	Alonzo Mourning	4.00
14	Hakeem Olajuwon	20.00
15	Shaquille O'Neal	40.00
16	Scottie Pippen	30.00
17	David Robinson	12.00
18	Joe Smith	10.00
19	Damon Stoudamire	15.00
20	Chris Webber	12.00

1996-97 SkyBox New Editions

This 10-card, retail only insert has a green border with the player inset on a purple etched foil area inside. New Edition inserts were seeded one per 36 packs, and contained the words "New Editions" in yellow letters across the bottom.

		MT
Complete Set (10):		75.00
Common Player:		2.00
1	Shareef Abdur-Rahim	12.00
2	Ray Allen	8.00
3	Kobe Bryant	20.00
4	Marcus Camby	12.00
5	Allen Iverson	20.00
6	Kerry Kittles	6.00
7	Matt Maloney	4.00
8	Stephon Marbury	18.00
9	Steve Nash	8.00
10	Samaki Walker	2.00

1996-97 SkyBox Rookie Prevue

Rookie Prevue features the top 18 picks in the 1996 NBA Draft on a foil etched basketball background. Inserted at one per 54 packs, the insert name is stamped in gold foil across the bottom, with the player's name in the top right corner. Rookie Prevue inserts are numbered with an "R" prefix.

		MT
Complete Set (18):		250.00
Common Player:		3.00
R1	Shareef Abdur-Rahim	35.00
R2	Ray Allen	25.00
R3	Kobe Bryant	50.00
R4	Marcus Camby	35.00
R5	Erick Dampier	3.00
R6	Tony Delk	3.00
R7	Brian Evans	3.00
R8	Todd Fuller	3.00
R9	Allen Iverson	55.00
R10	Kerry Kittles	15.00
R11	Stephon Marbury	40.00
R12	Steve Nash	10.00
R13	Vitaly Potapenko	3.00
R14	Roy Rogers	3.00
R15	Antoine Walker	25.00
R16	Samaki Walker	6.00
R17	John Wallace	10.00
R18	Lorenzen Wright	3.00

1996-97 SkyBox Standouts

Standouts was a nine-card insert that was exclusive to Series I retail packs. Inserted one per 180 packs, the insert featured a multi-colored border with a basketball net in the background. The insert name is hard to find on the front, but does appear in the lower right corner along with the player's number.

		MT
Complete Set (9):		250.00
Common Player:		12.00
SO1	Grant Hill	70.00
SO2	Juwan Howard	25.00
SO3	Jason Kidd	20.00
SO4	Reggie Miller	20.00
SO5	Shaquille O'Neal	75.00
SO6	Gary Payton	20.00
SO7	Scottie Pippen	15.00
SO8	Mitch Richmond	12.00
SO9	Joe Smith	20.00

1996-97 SkyBox Thunder and Lightning

Thunder and Lightning was a 10-card, two-piece insert found in one per 144 Series II packs. The card included a Thunder part that contained a glossy front and back shell. Inside it, was the Lightning part, which could be pulled out to view. The set matched a star big man and guard from the same team and was numbered "x of 10".

		MT
Complete Set (10):		250.00
Common Player:		6.00
1	Michael Jordan, Scottie Pippen	100.00
2	Kevin Johnson, Danny Manning	6.00
3	Grant Hill, Joe Dumars	50.00
4	Latrell Sprewell, Joe Smith	20.00
5	Charles Barkley, Hakeem Olajuwon	25.00
6	Vin Baker, Glenn Robinson	15.00
7	Patrick Ewing, Larry Johnson	15.00
8	Shawn Kemp, Gary Payton	30.00
9	Karl Malone, John Stockton	15.00
10	Juwan Howard, Chris Webber	20.00

1996-97 SkyBox Bulls Triple Threat

This three-card set was inserted into packs of Series I at a rate of one per 240. Although these cards were inserts and called Bonus Triple Threats, they were numbered consecutively with the regular-issue subset. The regular-issue Triple Threats were numbered TT1-TT9, while the Bonus Triple Threats, which featured the Bulls, were numbered TT10-TT12.

	MT
Complete Set (3):	100.00
TT10 Dennis Rodman	25.00
TT11 Michael Jordan	75.00
TT12 Scottie Pippen	20.00

1996-97 SkyBox E-X2000

E-X2000 Basketball was an 80-card set featuring SkyView technology that had previously been used in 1995-96 NBA Hoops Series II Sky-View inserts. The technology utilized a die-cut holofoil border and the player silhouetted in front of a transparent window featuring a variety of sky patterns. Inserts include: Star Date 2000, Net Assets, Autographics, A Cut Above and the parallel Credentials insert. E-X2000 arrived in two-card packs and carried exclusive Autographics inserts of Damon Stoudamire, Antoine Walker and Kerry Kittles.

	MT
Complete Set (80):	100.00
Common Player:	.75
Wax Box:	110.00
1 Christian Laettner	.75
2 Dikembe Mutombo	.75
3 Steve Smith	.75
4 *Antoine Walker*	8.00
5 David Wesley	.75
6 *Tony Delk*	1.50
7 Anthony Mason	.75
8 Glen Rice	1.50
9 Michael Jordan	20.00
10 Scottie Pippen	4.00
11 Dennis Rodman	5.00
12 Terrell Brandon	.75
13 Chris Mills	.75
14 Shawn Bradley	.75
15 Michael Finley	.75
16 Dale Ellis	.75
17 Antonio McDyess	1.50
18 Joe Dumars	.75
19 Grant Hill	10.00
20 Chris Mullin	.75
21 Joe Smith	2.00
22 Latrell Sprewell	1.50
23 Charles Barkley	2.00
24 Clyde Drexler	1.50
25 Hakeem Olajuwon	4.00
26 *Erick Dampier*	.75
27 Reggie Miller	1.50
28 Loy Vaught	.75
29 *Lorenzen Wright*	.75
30 *Kobe Bryant*	12.00
31 Eddie Jones	3.00
32 Shaquille O'Neal	6.00
33 Nick Van Exel	.75
34 Tim Hardaway	.75
35 Jamal Mashburn	.75
36 Alonzo Mourning	1.50

37 *Ray Allen*	4.00
38 Vin Baker	1.50
39 Glenn Robinson	1.50
40 Kevin Garnett	10.00
41 Tom Gugliotta	.75
42 *Stephon Marbury*	10.00
43 Kendall Gill	.75
44 *Kerry Kittles*	3.00
45 Jim Jackson	.75
46 Patrick Ewing	1.50
47 Larry Johnson	.75
48 *John Wallace*	3.00
49 Nick Anderson	.75
50 Horace Grant	.75
51 Anfernee Hardaway	8.00
52 Derrick Coleman	.75
53 *Allen Iverson*	12.00
54 Jerry Stackhouse	2.00
55 Cedric Ceballos	.75
56 Kevin Johnson	.75
57 Jason Kidd	1.50
58 Clifford Robinson	.75
59 Arvydas Sabonis	.75
60 Rasheed Wallace	.75
61 Mahmoud Abdul-Rauf	.75
62 Brian Grant	.75
63 Mitch Richmond	1.50
64 Sean Elliott	.75
65 David Robinson	2.00
66 Dominique Wilkins	.75
67 Shawn Kemp	4.00
68 Gary Payton	2.00
69 Detlef Schrempf	.75
70 *Marcus Camby*	6.00
71 Damon Stoudamire	3.00
72 Walt Williams	.75
73 Shandon Anderson	.75
74 Karl Malone	2.00
75 John Stockton	2.00
76 *Shareef Abdul-Rahim*	8.00
77 Bryant Reeves	.75
78 Roy Rogers	.75
79 Juwan Howard	2.00
80 Chris Webber	2.00

1996-97 SkyBox E-X2000 Credentials

Credentials paralleled all 80 cards in the 1996-97 E-X2000 basketball set. These inserts are printed on holographic silver foil and sequentially numbered up to 499. The word "Credentials" is printed across the top of the card on these one-per-50-pack inserts.

	MT
Credential Rookies:	6x-12x
Credential Stars:	12x-24x

1996-97 SkyBox E-X2000 A Cut Above

This 10-card insert featured color shots of the player over a holographic foil saw blade, which was die-cut on the top in the saw blade shape. The words "Cut Above" and the player's name appears in the lower left corner and is slightly embossed. A Cut Above inserts were seeded every 288 packs of E-X2000.

	MT
Complete Set (10):	700.00
Common Player:	20.00
1 Allen Iverson	90.00
2 Anfernee Hardaway	90.00
3 Dennis Rodman	60.00
4 Glenn Robinson	20.00
5 Grant Hill	100.00
6 Hakeem Olajuwon	30.00
7 Kevin Garnett	90.00
8 Michael Jordan	225.00
9 Shaquille O'Neal	75.00
10 Shawn Kemp	40.00

1996-97 SkyBox E-X2000 Net Assets

Net Assets featured 20 cards die-cut in the shape of a basketball net, with the ball going through it. Sections of the net and the insert name, which runs across the top in yellow letters, are all die-cut. One per 20 packs included this insert, which was numbered "of 20".

	MT
Complete Set (20):	220.00
Common Player:	2.00
1 Ray Allen	10.00
2 Charles Barkley	6.00
3 Patrick Ewing	2.00
4 Kevin Garnett	25.00
5 Anfernee Hardaway	25.00
6 Grant Hill	30.00
7 Allen Iverson	25.00
8 Michael Jordan	50.00
9 Jason Kidd	2.00
10 Kerry Kittles	8.00
11 Karl Malone	4.00
12 Alonzo Mourning	4.00
13 Shaquille O'Neal	20.00
14 Gary Payton	4.00
15 Bryant Reeves	2.00
16 David Robinson	6.00
17 Dennis Rodman	20.00
18 Joe Smith	6.00
19 Damon Stoudamire	8.00
20 Chris Webber	6.00

1996-97 SkyBox E-X2000 Star Date 2000

Star Date 2000 showcased 15 top rookies from the 1996-97 season on an outer space background. The in-

sert name, player's name and team appeared in the lower left corner. Star Date 2000 inserts were found in every nine packs of E-X2000.

	MT
Complete Set (15):	100.00
Common Player:	1.50
1 Shareef Abdul-Rahim	12.00
2 Ray Allen	8.00
3 Kobe Bryant	18.00
4 Marcus Camby	12.00
5 Erick Dampier	1.50
6 Juwan Howard	5.00
7 Allen Iverson	20.00
8 Jason Kidd	3.00
9 Kerry Kittles	6.00
10 Stephon Marbury	16.00
11 Jamal Mashburn	1.50
12 Antonio McDyess	3.00
13 Joe Smith	5.00
14 Damon Stoudamire	7.00
15 Antoine Walker	10.00

1996-97 SkyBox Z-Force

SkyBox's 1996-97 Z-Force cards combine computer graphics and NBA action on each card; each card has a silhouetted action photo of the player against a surreal background featuring colorful graphics and the player's last name in bold type. Both Series I and II consisted of 100 cards. Series I inserts included Z-Cling, Vortex, Swat Team, Autographics and Slam Cam. Series II featured Zensations, Zebut, Little Big Men, BMOC, Autographics and a Grant Hill Total Z card. Series I marked the first installment of Autographics, which would run through all 1996-97 SkyBox releases, including Z-Force Series II.

	MT
Complete Set (200):	45.00
Complete Series 1 (100):	20.00
Complete Series 2 (100):	25.00
Common Player:	.10
Series 1 Wax Box:	50.00
Series 2 Wax Box:	55.00
1 Mookie Blaylock	.10
2 Alan Henderson	.10
3 Christian Laettner	.10
4 Steve Smith	.10
5 Rick Fox	.10
6 Dino Radja	.10
7 Eric Williams	.10
8 Tyrone Bogues	.10
9 Larry Johnson	.30
10 Glen Rice	.10
11 Michael Jordan	5.00
12 Toni Kukoc	.10
13 Scottie Pippen	1.25
14 Dennis Rodman	2.00
15 Terrell Brandon	.10
16 Bobby Phills	.10
17 Bob Sura	.10
18 Jim Jackson	.20
19 Jason Kidd	.75
20 Jamal Mashburn	.20
21 George McCloud	.10
22 Mahmoud Abdul-Rauf	.10
23 Antonio McDyess	.40
24 Dikembe Mutombo	.20
25 Joe Dumars	.10

26	Grant Hill	2.00
27	Allan Houston	.10
28	Otis Thorpe	.10
29	Chris Mullin	.10
30	Joe Smith	.50
31	Latrell Sprewell	.10
32	Sam Cassell	.10
33	Clyde Drexler	.40
34	Robert Horry	.10
35	Hakeem Olajuwon	.75
36	Travis Best	.10
37	Dale Davis	.10
38	Reggie Miller	.40
39	Rik Smits	.10
40	Brent Barry	.20
41	Loy Vaught	.10
42	Brian Williams	.10
43	Cedric Ceballos	.10
44	Eddie Jones	.20
45	Nick Van Exel	.25
46	Tim Hardaway	.10
47	Alonzo Mourning	.30
48	Kurt Thomas	.10
49	Walt Williams	.10
50	Vin Baker	.30
51	Glenn Robinson	.40
52	Kevin Garnett	2.00
53	Tom Gugliotta	.10
54	Isaiah Rider	.10
55	Shawn Bradley	.10
56	Chris Childs	.10
57	Jayson Williams	.10
58	Patrick Ewing	.30
59	Anthony Mason	.10
60	Charles Oakley	.10
61	Nick Anderson	.10
62	Horace Grant	.10
63	Anfernee Hardaway	2.50
64	Shaquille O'Neal	2.25
65	Dennis Scott	.10
66	Jerry Stackhouse	.75
67	Clarence Weatherspoon	.10
68	Charles Barkley	.50
69	Michael Finley	.50
70	Kevin Johnson	.20
71	Clifford Robinson	.10
72	Arvydas Sabonis	.30
73	Rod Strickland	.10
74	Tyus Edney	.20
75	Brian Grant	.10
76	Billy Owens	.10
77	Mitch Richmond	.20
78	Vinny Del Negro	.10
79	Sean Elliot	.10
80	Avery Johnson	.10
81	David Robinson	.75
82	Hersey Hawkins	.10
83	Shawn Kemp	1.25
84	Gary Payton	.40
85	Detlef Schrempf	.10
86	Doug Christie	.10
87	Damon Stoudamire	1.00
88	Sharone Wright	.10
89	Jeff Hornacek	.10
90	Karl Malone	.30
91	John Stockton	.30
92	Greg Anthony	.10
93	Bryant Reeves	.50
94	Byron Scott	.10
95	Juwan Howard	.50
96	Gheorghe Muresan	.10
97	Rasheed Wallace	.30
98	Chris Webber	.20
99	Checklist A	.10
100	Checklist B	.10
101	Dikembe Mutombo	.10
102	Dee Brown	.10
103	Dell Curry	.10
104	Vlade Divac	.10
105	Anthony Mason	.10
106	Robert Parish	.10
107	Oliver Miller	.10
108	Eric Montross	.10
109	Ervin Johnson	.10
110	Stacey Augmon	.10
111	Charles Barkley	.50
112	Jalen Rose	.10
113	Rodney Rogers	.10
114	Shaquille O'Neal	2.50
115	Dan Majerle	.10
116	Kendall Gill	.10
117	Khalid Reeves	.10
118	Allan Houston	.10
119	Larry Johnson	.20
120	John Starks	.10
121	Rony Seikaly	.10
122	Gerald Wilkins	.10
123	Michael Cage	.10
124	Derrick Coleman	.10
125	Sam Cassell	.10
126	Danny Manning	.10

127	Robert Horry	.10
128	Kenny Anderson	.10
129	Isaiah Rider	.10
130	Rasheed Wallace	.10
131	Mahmoud Abdul-Rauf	.10
132	Vernon Maxwell	.10
133	Dominique Wilkins	.10
134	Hubert Davis	.10
135	Popeye Jones	.10
136	Anthony Peeler	.10
137	Tracy Murray	.10
138	Rod Strickland	.10
139	*Shareef Abdur-Rahim*	2.50
140	*Ray Allen*	2.00
141	*Shandon Anderson*	.10
142	*Kobe Bryant*	4.00
143	*Marcus Camby*	3.00
144	*Erick Dampier*	.40
145	*Emanuel Davis*	.10
146	*Tony Delk*	.50
147	*Todd Fuller*	.10
148	*Darvin Ham*	.20
149	*Othella Harrington*	.20
150	*Shane Heal*	.10
151	*Allen Iverson*	4.00
152	*Dontae Jones*	.10
153	*Kerry Kittles*	1.50
154	*Priest Lauderdale*	.10
155	*Matt Maloney*	.40
156	*Stephon Marbury*	4.00
157	*Walter McCarty*	.10
158	*Steve Nash*	.30
159	*Jermaine O'Neal*	1.00
160	*Ray Owes*	.10
161	*Vitaly Potapenko*	.10
162	*Roy Rogers*	.10
163	*Antoine Walker*	1.50
164	*Samaki Walker*	.30
165	*Ben Wallace*	.10
166	*John Wallace*	.50
167	*Jerome Williams*	.10
168	*Lorenzen Wright*	.40
169	Vin Baker	.20
170	Charles Barkley	.25
171	Patrick Ewing	.20
172	Michael Finley	.10
173	Kevin Garnett	1.00
174	Anfernee Hardaway	1.00
175	Grant Hill	1.00
176	Juwan Howard	.25
177	Jim Jackson	.10
178	Eddie Jones	.25
179	Michael Jordan	2.00
180	Shawn Kemp	.50
181	Jason Kidd	.25
182	Karl Malone	.20
183	Antonio McDyess	.10
184	Reggie Miller	.20
185	Alonzo Mourning	.20
186	Hakeem Olajuwon	.50
187	Shaquille O'Neal	1.00
188	Gary Payton	.20
189	Mitch Richmond	.10
190	Clifford Robinson	.10
191	David Robinson	.25
192	Glenn Robinson	.20
193	Dennis Rodman	1.00
194	Joe Smith	.25
195	Jerry Stackhouse	.30
196	John Stockton	.20
197	Damon Stoudamire	.40
198	Chris Webber	.10
199	Checklist	.10
200	Checklist	.10

These 100 cards form a parallel set to SkyBox's 1996-97 Z-Force Series I set. Each card front uses a design similar to that which was used for the main issue, except the Z-Cling cards have a team logo on the front. The back has the player's name and team name at the bottom, along with a card number and the NBA and Sky-Box logos. If the back is peeled off, the card can cling to a wall, window or school locker. Three bonus cards were inserted into the Z-Cling insert that had no corresponding regular-issue card, and were numbered R1-R3.

		MT
	Complete Set (100):	60.00
	Common Player:	.20
	Z-Cling Cards:	2x
	#94 Never Printed	
64	Shaquille O'Neal LAK	10.00
R1	Ray Allen	7.00
R2	Stephon Marbury	12.00
R3	Shareef Abdur-Rahim	8.00

1996-97 SkyBox Z-Force Big Men On The Court

Known as its acronym, BMOC highlighted 10 top players on a die-cut format. The front included an action shot of the player over the words "big men on the court" in bold letters with "big" printed in red and the rest in blue. These cards were found every 240 packs, with parallel foil versions seeded every 1,120.

		MT
	Complete Set (10):	500.00
	Common Player:	15.00
1	Charles Barkley	25.00
2	Anfernee Hardaway	90.00
3	Grant Hill	90.00
4	Michael Jordan	200.00
5	Shawn Kemp	50.00
6	Alonzo Mourning	15.00
7	Hakeem Olajuwon	35.00
8	Shaquille O'Neal	75.00
9	Scottie Pippen	50.00
10	David Robinson	25.00

1996-97 SkyBox Z-Force BMOC Z-Peat

BMOC Z-Peats paralleled the BMOC insert, but added a foil finish to the entire card front, and the word "Z-Peat" in gold foil on the bottom right side. This parallel version was inserted one per 1,120 packs.

		MT
	Complete Set (10):	1800.00
	Common Player:	70.00
1	Charles Barkley	90.00
2	Anfernee Hardaway	300.00
3	Grant Hill	300.00
4	Michael Jordan	600.00
5	Shawn Kemp	150.00
6	Alonzo Mourning	70.00
7	Hakeem Olajuwon	125.00
8	Shaquille O'Neal	250.00
9	Scottie Pippen	175.00
10	David Robinson	90.00

1996-97 SkyBox Z-Force Little Big Men

Little Big Men was a 10-card retail-only insert that was seeded one per 36 packs. The fronts featured a foil-etched city skyline of large buildings, with a color shot of the player in front.

		MT
	Complete Set (10):	60.00
	Common Player:	2.00
1	Kenny Anderson	2.00
2	Mookie Blaylock	2.00
3	Tyrone Bogues	2.00
4	Terrell Brandon	2.00
5	Allen Iverson	25.00
6	Avery Johnson	2.00
7	Kevin Johnson	2.00
8	Stephon Marbury	20.00
9	Gary Payton	6.00
10	Nick Van Exel	2.00

1996-97 SkyBox Z-Force Slam Cam

These 1996-97 SkyBox inserts are some of the most limited ever; they are seeded one per every 240 Series I packs. Nine of the NBA's top slam dunkers are featured on the cards, which are printed in pastel tones and holographic foil, with the "Z-text" changes, resulting in the word rotating. Cards are numbered using an "SC" prefix.

1996-97 SkyBox Z-Force Z-Cling

	MT
Complete Set (9):	475.00
Common Player:	20.00
SC1 Clyde Drexler	30.00
SC2 Michael Finley	20.00
SC3 Anfernee Hardaway	125.00
SC4 Grant Hill	75.00
SC5 Michael Jordan	200.00
SC6 Shawn Kemp	60.00
SC7 Karl Malone	20.00
SC8 Antonio McDyess	20.00
SC9 Shaquille O'Neal	85.00

1996-97 SkyBox Z-Force Swat Team

These 1996-97 SkyBox Series I inserts showcase nine players who specialize in the art of rejecting shots. Each card features holographic foil, which makes the player look like he's popping off the card. Cards are numbered using an "ST" prefix and are seeded one per every 72 hobby packs only.

	MT
Complete Set (9):	100.00
Common Player:	3.00
ST1 Patrick Ewing	3.00
ST2 Kevin Garnett	35.00
ST3 Alonzo Mourning	3.00
ST4 Dikembe Mutombo	3.00
ST5 Hakeem Olajuwon	15.00
ST6 Shaquille O'Neal	30.00
ST7 David Robinson	10.00
ST8 Dennis Rodman	30.00
ST9 Joe Smith	10.00

1996-97 SkyBox Z-Force Vortex

These 1996-97 SkyBox Series I inserts showcase high-flying action from the likes of Anfernee Hardaway and Damon Stoudamire. They were seeded one per every 36 Series I retail packs only and are numbered using a "V" prefix.

	MT
Complete Set (15):	150.00
Common Player:	5.00
V1 Charles Barkley	10.00
V2 Anfernee Hardaway	30.00
V3 Grant Hill	25.00
V4 Juwan Howard	10.00
V5 Michael Jordan	60.00
V6 Jason Kidd	10.00

V7 Reggie Miller	7.00
V8 Gary Payton	7.00
V9 Scottie Pippen	15.00
V10 Mitch Richmond	5.00
V11 Glenn Robinson	5.00
V12 Arvydas Sabonis	5.00
V13 Jerry Stackhouse	10.00
V14 John Stockton	7.00
V15 Damon Stoudamire	15.00

1996-97 SkyBox Z-Force Zebut

Twenty rookies were included in this insert, which was seeded one per 24 hobby packs. The fronts featured the player over a gold, silver and copper foil background, with a large "Z" emblem in back of the player. The insert name, player and team name were stamped in gold foil across the bottom. Parallel versions were also printed and featured holographic foil. These were inserted one per 240 hobby packs.

	MT
Complete Set (20):	150.00
Common Player:	2.00
1 Shareef Abdur-Rahim	18.00
2 Ray Allen	12.00
3 Kobe Bryant	30.00
4 Marcus Camby	20.00
5 Erick Dampier	4.00
6 Todd Fuller	2.00
7 Othella Harrington	2.00
8 Allen Iverson	25.00
9 Kerry Kittles	8.00
10 Priest Lauderdale	2.00
11 Stephon Marbury	25.00
12 Steve Nash	4.00
13 Jermaine O'Neal	6.00
14 Ray Owes	2.00
15 Vitaly Potapenko	2.00
16 Roy Rogers	2.00
17 Antoine Walker	12.00
18 Samaki Walker	2.00
19 John Wallace	5.00
20 Lorenzen Wright	4.00

1996-97 SkyBox Z-Force Z-Peat Zebut

This insert paralleled the Zebut insert, but was printed in holographic foil and inserted one per 240 hobby packs.

	MT
Complete Set (20):	800.00
Z-Peat Cards:	3x-6x

1996-97 SkyBox Z-Force Zensations

Zenzations included 20 players featured in a spotlight-like design, with the team logo included across the bottom of the card. These inserts were seeded every six packs.

	MT
Complete Set (20):	40.00
Common Player:	.75
1 Shareef Abdur-Rahim	7.00
2 Ray Allen	5.00
3 Nick Anderson	.75
4 Vin Baker	2.00
5 Mookie Blaylock	.75
6 Calbert Cheaney	.75
7 Kevin Garnett	10.00
8 Horace Grant	.75
9 Tim Hardaway	.75
10 Allen Iverson	12.00
11 Avery Johnson	.75
12 Kevin Johnson	.75
13 Danny Manning	.75
14 Stephon Marbury	10.00
15 Jamal Mashburn	.75
16 Glen Rice	.75
17 Isaiah Rider	.75
18 Latrell Sprewell	2.00
19 Rod Strickland	.75
20 Nick Van Exel	1.50

1996-97 Topps II

Topps celebrates its 50th anniversary of basketball with its 1996-97 basketball set. Both Series I and Series II contain 110 cards each. Each regular card front has a color action photo with a white border. The Topps logo is stamped in gold in the upper right corner; the player's name is in gold along the bottom. The horizontal back also has a white border, with a card number in the upper right corner. In addition to a color mug shot, the back contains biographical information, statistics and a brief player profile. Series I inserts are Holding Court, Holding Court Refractors, Pro Files,

Season's Best, Hobby Masters, Super Team cards and NBA Draft Redemption (29 cards with a number corresponding to each draft position of the first round; seeded one per 18 packs). The regular set also has a parallel set which uses gold foil stamping to commemorate the NBA's 50th anniversary. These cards were seeded one per every three packs. Series II inserts include: Mystery Finest, Profiles, Youthquake, NBA Topps Stars Finest Reprints, 50th Anniversary parallels and Hobby Masters.

	MT
Complete Series 2 (110):	15.00
Common Player:	.05
Series 2 Wax Box:	55.00
112 Dikembe Mutombo	.10
113 Alonzo Mourning	.20
114 Hubert Davis	.05
115 Rony Seikaly	.05
116 Danny Manning	.05
117 Donyell Marshall	.05
118 Felton Spencer	.05
119 Efthimis Retzias	.05
120 Jalen Rose	.05
121 Dino Radja	.05
122 Glenn Robinson	.20
123 John Stockton	.25
124 Brent Price	.05
125 Clifford Robinson	.05
126 Steve Kerr	.05
127 Nate McMillan	.05
128 Shareef Abdur-Rahim	2.00
129 Loy Vaught	.05
130 Anthony Mason	.05
131 Kevin Garnett	1.25
132 Roy Rogers	.20
133 Erick Dampier	.25
134 Tyus Edney	.05
135 Chris Mills	.05
136 Cory Alexander	.05
137 Juwan Howard	.30
138 Kobe Bryant	3.00
139 Michael Jordan	2.50
140 Jayson Williams	.05
141 Rod Strickland	.05
142 Lorenzen Wright	.25
143 Will Perdue	.05
144 Derek Harper	.05
145 Predrag Stojakovic	.05
146 Antoine Walker	2.00
147 P.J. Brown	.05
148 Terrell Brandon	.05
149 Larry Johnson	.10
150 Steve Smith	.05
151 Eddie Jones	.20
152 Detlef Schrempf	.05
153 Dale Ellis	.05
154 Isaiah Rider	.05
155 Tony Delk	.25
156 Vincent Askew	.05
157 Jamal Mashburn	.10
158 Dennis Scott	.05
159 Dana Barros	.05
160 Martin Muursepp	.05
161 Marcus Camby	2.00
162 Jerome Williams	.05
163 Wesley Person	.05
164 Luc Longley	.05
165 Chris Childs	.05
166 Mark Jackson	.05
167 Derrick Coleman	.05
168 Dell Curry	.05
169 Armon Gilliam	.05
170 Vlade Divac	.05
171 Allen Iverson	3.00
172 Vitaly Potapenko	.20
173 Jon Koncak	.05
174 Lindsey Hunter	.05
175 Kevin Johnson	.05
176 Dennis Rodman	.75
177 Stephon Marbury	2.00
178 Karl Malone	.25
179 Charles Barkley	.40
180 Popeye Jones	.05
181 Samaki Walker	.25
182 Steve Nash	.40
183 Latrell Sprewell	.10
184 Kenny Anderson	.05
185 Tyrone Hill	.05
186 Robert Pack	.05
187 Greg Anthony	.05
188 Derrick McKey	.05
189 John Wallace	.40
190 Bryon Russell	.05
191 Jermaine O'Neal	.30

192	Clyde Drexler	.20
193	Mahmoud Abdul-Rauf	.05
194	Eric Montross	.05
195	Allan Houston	.05
196	Harvey Grant	.05
197	Rodney Rogers	.05
198	Kerry Kittles	1.25
199	Grant Hill	1.00
200	Lionel Simmons	.05
201	Reggie Miller	.20
202	Avery Johnson	.05
203	LaPhonso Ellis	.05
204	Brian Shaw	.05
205	Priest Lauderdale	.05
206	Jerome Kersey	.05
207	James Robinson	.05
208	Todd Fuller	.20
209	Hersey Hawkins	.05
210	Tim Legler	.05
211	Terry Dehere	.05
212	Gary Payton	.20
213	Stacey Augmon	.05
214	Don MacLean	.05
215	Greg Minor	.05
216	Tim Hardaway	.05
217	Ray Allen	1.25
218	Mario Elie	.05
219	Brooks Thompson	.05
220	Shaquille O'Neal	1.25
221	Checklist	.05

1996-97 Topps NBA 50th

This 220-card set paralleled the 1996-97 Topps Basketball Series I and II set and was inserted into Series I and II hobby and retail packs at a rate of one per three packs. The cards were identified by silver foil being added to the fronts, which gave the card a silver border, as well as an NBA 50th logo in the lower left corner.

	MT
NBA 50th Cards:	4x-8x

1996-97 Topps Finest Reprints

This 25-card set was included in one per 36 Series II Topps packs. It included 25 of the 50 Rookie Reprints from NBA Topps Stars printed in Finest technology, with the remainder of the set found in Stadium Club I. Refractor versions were also available.

	MT
Complete Set (25):	170.00
Common Player:	5.00
1	Kareem Abdul-Jabbar	15.00
3	Paul Arizin	5.00
9	Wilt Chamberlain	15.00
11	Dave Cowens	5.00
14	Clyde Drexler	10.00
16	Patrick Ewing	10.00
20	John Havlicek	10.00
21	Elvin Hayes	5.00
22	Magic Johnson	35.00
23	Sam Jones	5.00
25	Jerry Lucas	5.00
27	Moses Malone	5.00
30	George Mikan	12.00
31	Earl Monroe	5.00
32	Shaquille O'Neal	12.00
33	Hakeem Olajuwon	15.00
37	Willis Reed	5.00
38	Oscar Robertson	10.00
39	David Robinson	10.00
40	Bill Russell	15.00
42	Bill Sharman	5.00
43	John Stockton	8.00
45	Nate Thurmond	5.00
46	Wes Unseld	5.00
47	Bill Walton	5.00

1996-97 Topps Finest Reprints Refractors

Every card in the Series II Topps Finest Rookie Reprints insert was also available in a Refractor version. This 25- card set was seeded one per 144 packs. Refractor versions were easily identifiable by the fronts, and also included the word "Refractor" just below the bottom left side of the red box on the back.

	MT
Refractors:	2x-4x

1996-97 Topps Hobby Masters

These cards, printed on 28-point full-diffraction stock, were random inserts in 1996-97 Topps Series I hobby packs only, one every 36 packs. The card front has a color action photo on it, with a close-up shot of the player dominating the background. The Topps logo is in the upper left corner; "Hobby Masters," the player's name, position and team logo are along the bottom of the card. The horizontal card back, numbered in the upper right corner using an "HM" prefix, has a small rectangle under the card number which contains a color action photo. The left side has a photo as the background, with biographical and statistical information and a recap of why collectors pursue the player's cards.

	MT
Complete Set (20):	220.00
Complete Series 1 (10):	120.00
Complete Series 2 (10):	100.00
Common Player:	5.00
HM11 Shaquille O'Neal	25.00
HM12 Jerry Stackhouse	10.00
HM13 Dennis Rodman	20.00
HM14 Joe Smith	10.00
HM15 Damon Stoudamire	15.00
HM16 Gary Payton	8.00
HM17 Mitch Richmond	5.00
HM18 Reggie Miller	8.00
HM19 Chris Webber	8.00
HM20 Vin Baker	5.00
HM21 Grant Hill	30.00
HM22 Scottie Pippen	15.00
HM23 Karl Malone	5.00
HM24 Patrick Ewing	5.00
HM25 Shawn Kemp	15.00
HM26 Anfernee Hardaway	30.00
HM27 Charles Barkley	7.00
HM28 Jason Kidd	7.00
HM29 Hakeem Olajuwon	10.00
HM30 Larry Johnson	5.00

1996-97 Topps Mystery Finest Bordered

This 22-card insert arrived in packs hidden behind a black opaque seal that could be removed to reveal the player. Bordered versions were the most common type, arriving one per 36 packs, while Mystery Finest inserts also came in bordered Refractor, borderless and borderless Refractor versions.

	MT
Complete Set (22):	150.00
Common Player:	2.00
M1	Scottie Pippen	15.00
M2	Jason Kidd	6.00
M3	Anfernee Hardaway	30.00
M4	Gary Payton	6.00
M5	Juwan Howard	6.00
M6	Sean Elliott	2.00
M7	Dennis Rodman	20.00
M8	Shawn Kemp	15.00
M9	David Robinson	8.00
M10	Alonzo Mourning	2.00
M11	Dikembe Mutombo	2.00
M12	Shaquille O'Neal	25.00
M13	Clyde Drexler	6.00
M14	Michael Jordan	50.00
M15	Damon Stoudamire	10.00
M16	Mitch Richmond	2.00
M17	Patrick Ewing	5.00
M18	Vin Baker	5.00
M19	Hakeem Olajuwon	10.00
M20	Joe Smith	8.00
M21	Charles Barkley	6.00
M22	Reggie Miller	5.00

1996-97 Topps Mystery Finest Bordered Refractors

This insert captured all 22 Mystery Finest inserts in a bordered version with a Refractor finish. These cards were inserted exclusively in jumbo retail packs, and played off the production mistake of 1995-96 when bordered Refractors were not supposed to exist, but did surface in small quantities.

	MT
Refractors:	3x-6x

1996-97 Topps Mystery Finest Borderless

Borderless Mystery Finest inserts - as the name indicates - are identified by their borderless design in contrast to the more common bordered cards. Borderless versions of the 22-card set are seeded one per 72 packs.

	MT
Borderless Cards:	2x

1996-97 Topps Mystery Finest Borderless Refractors

All 22-cards in the Mystery Finest insert found in Topps Series II also arrived in Borderless Refractor versions. The cards featured Topps' familiar Refractor finish and were seeded one per 216 packs.

	MT
Refractors:	3x-6x

1996-97 Topps Pro Files

These foil board cards were seeded one per every 12 packs of 1996-97 Topps basketball. David Robinson, serving as Topps' spokesman, analyzes some of today's top stars; he wrote the backs for each card. The card front has a color action photo on it, with a ghosted image of the crowd in the background. "Pro Files" is written along the left side of the card, above a small mug shot of Robinson in the lower left corner. "By David Robinson" is written in an oval at the bottom of the card, below the action photo. The pictured player's name runs vertically in the upper right corner. The card back (numbered PF-1, etc.) has a color mug shot on the left, with a profile which recaps some of his achievements underneath. The right side provides Robinson's analysis of the player.

	MT
Complete Series 2 (10):	25.00
Common Player:	1.00
PF11 Anfernee Hardaway	6.00
PF12 Juwan Howard	2.00
PF13 Dikembe Mutombo	1.00
PF14 Dennis Rodman	5.00
PF15 Kevin Garnett	6.00
PF16 Jerry Stackhouse	3.00

PF17	Alonzo Mourning	1.00
PF18	Karl Malone	2.00
PF19	Hakeem Olajuwon	3.00
PF20	Gary Payton	2.00

1996-97 Topps Youthquake

Youthquake captured 15 top young players on a wood card stock with a glossy finish on the front. Inserted into Series II retail packs at a rate of one per 36 packs, the background contains a checkered look with a wood border and the insert name printed up the left side.

		MT
Complete Set (15):		100.00
Common Player:		1.50
U1	Allen Iverson	20.00
U2	Samaki Walker	1.50
U3	Stephon Marbury	16.00
U4	Damon Stoudamire	7.00
U5	John Wallace	4.00
U6	Michael Finley	3.00
U7	Marcus Camby	12.00
U8	Kerry Kittles	6.00
U9	Ray Allen	6.00
U10	Jerry Stackhouse	5.00
U11	Shareef Abdur-Rahim	12.00
U12	Antonio McDyess	3.00
U13	Joe Smith	5.00
U14	Brent Barry	1.50
U15	Kobe Bryant	25.00

1996-97 Topps Chrome

Topps Chrome reprinted the 220 cards from Series I and II of Topps Basketball with chromium technology. The base cards carried the identical design of Topps cards, except for this chromium upgrade. Three inserts - Profiles, Youth Quake and Season's Best - were also reprinted, along with each base card also available in a Refractor version.

		MT
Complete Set (220):		200.00
Common Player:		.25
Wax Box:		180.00
1	Patrick Ewing	1.00
2	Christian Laettner	.25
3	Mahmoud Abdul-Rauf	.25
4	Chris Webber	1.50
5	Jason Kidd	.75
6	Clifford Rozier	.25
7	Elden Campbell	.25
8	Chuck Person	.25
9	Jeff Hornacek	.25
10	Rik Smits	.25
11	Kurt Thomas	.25
12	Rod Strickland	.25
13	Kendall Gill	.25
14	Brian Williams	.25
15	Tom Gugliotta	.25
16	Ron Harper	.25
17	Eric Williams	.25
18	A.C. Green	.25
19	Scott Williams	.25
20	Damon Stoudamire	2.00
21	Bryant Reeves	.50
22	Bob Sura	.25
23	Mitch Richmond	.50
24	Larry Johnson	.50
25	Vin Baker	.75
26	Mark Bryant	.25
27	Horace Grant	.25
28	Allan Houston	.25
29	Sam Perkins	.25
30	Antonio McDyess	.75
31	Rasheed Wallace	.25
32	Malik Sealy	.25
33	Scottie Pippen	2.50
34	Charles Barkley	1.50
35	Hakeem Olajuwon	2.00
36	John Starks	.25
37	Byron Scott	.25
38	Arvydas Sabonis	.25
39	Vlade Divac	.25
40	Joe Dumars	.25
41	Danny Ferry	.25
42	Jerry Stackhouse	1.00
43	B.J. Armstrong	.25
44	Shawn Bradley	.25
45	Kevin Garnett	6.00
46	Dee Brown	.25
47	Michael Smith	.25
48	Doug Christie	.25
49	Mark Jackson	.25
50	Shawn Kemp	2.50
51	Predrag Danilovic	.25
52	Nick Anderson	.25
53	Matt Geiger	.25
54	Charles Smith	.25
55	Mookie Blaylock	.25
56	Johnny Newman	.25
57	George McCloud	.25
58	Greg Ostertag	.25
59	Reggie Williams	.25
60	Brent Barry	.25
61	Doug West	.25
62	Donald Royal	.25
63	Randy Brown	.25
64	Vincent Askew	.25
65	John Stockton	1.00
66	Joe Kleine	.25
67	Keith Askins	.25
68	Bobby Phills	.25
69	Chris Mullin	.50
70	Nick Van Exel	.75
71	Rick Fox	.25
72	Chicago Bulls Commemorative	4.00
73	Shawn Respert	.25
74	Hubert Davis	.25
75	Jim Jackson	.50
76	Olden Polynice	.25
77	Gheorghe Muresan	.25
78	Theo Ratliff	.25
79	Khalid Reeves	.25
80	David Robinson	1.50
81	Lawrence Moten	.25
82	Sam Cassell	.25
83	George Zidek	.25
84	Sharone Wright	.25
85	Clarence Weatherspoon	.25
86	Alan Henderson	.25
87	Chris Dudley	.25
88	Ed O'Bannon	.25
89	Calbert Cheaney	.25
90	Cedric Ceballos	.25
91	Michael Cage	.25
92	Ervin Johnson	.25
93	Gary Trent	.25
94	Sherman Douglas	.25
95	Joe Smith	1.25
96	Dale Davis	.25
97	Tony Dumas	.25
98	Muggsy Bogues	.25
99	Toni Kukoc	.50
100	Grant Hill	6.00
101	Michael Finley	.50
102	Isaiah Rider	.25
103	Bryant Stith	.25
104	Pooh Richardson	.25
105	Karl Malone	1.00
106	Brian Grant	.25
107	Sean Elliott	.25
108	Charles Oakley	.25
109	Pervis Ellison	.25
110	Anfernee Hardaway	5.00
111	Checklist	.25
112	Dikembe Mutombo	.25
113	Alonzo Mourning	.75
114	Hubert Davis	.25
115	Rony Seikaly	.25
116	Danny Manning	.25
117	Donyell Marshall	.25
118	Gerald Wilkins	.25
119	Ervin Johnson	.25
120	Jalen Rose	.25
121	Dino Radja	.25
122	Glenn Robinson	.75
123	John Stockton	1.00
124	*Matt Maloney*	2.00
125	Clifford Robinson	.25
126	Steve Kerr	.25
127	Nate McMillan	.25
128	*Shareef Abdur-Rahim*	25.00
129	Loy Vaught	.25
130	Anthony Mason	.25
131	Kevin Garnett	6.00
132	*Roy Rogers Jr.*	1.00
133	*Erick Dampier*	2.00
134	Tyus Edney	.25
135	Chris Mills	.25
136	Cory Alexander	.25
137	Juwan Howard	1.50
138	*Kobe Bryant*	90.00
139	Michael Jordan	18.00
140	Jayson Williams	.25
141	Rod Strickland	.25
142	*Lorenzen Wright*	2.00
143	Will Perdue	.25
144	Derek Harper	.25
145	Billy Owens	.25
146	*Antoine Walker*	30.00
147	P.J. Brown	.25
148	Terrell Brandon	.50
149	Larry Johnson	.50
150	Steve Smith	.25
151	Eddie Jones	1.75
152	Detlef Schrempf	.25
153	Dale Ellis	.25
154	Isaiah Rider	.25
155	*Tony Delk*	3.00
156	Adrian Caldwell	.25
157	Jamal Mashburn	.50
158	Dennis Scott	.25
159	Dana Barros	.25
160	Martin Muursepp	.25
161	*Marcus Camby*	15.00
162	Jerome Williams	.25
163	Wesley Person	.25
164	Luc Longley	.25
165	Charlie Ward	.25
166	Mark Jackson	.25
167	Derrick Coleman	.25
168	Dell Curry	.25
169	Armon Gilliam	.25
170	Vlade Divac	.25
171	*Allen Iverson*	30.00
172	*Vitaly Potapenko*	2.00
173	Jon Koncak	.25
174	Lindsey Hunter	.25
175	Kevin Johnson	.25
176	Dennis Rodman	3.00
177	*Stephon Marbury*	25.00
178	Karl Malone	1.00
179	Charles Barkley	1.50
180	Popeye Jones	.25
181	*Samaki Walker*	1.00
182	*Steve Nash*	3.00
183	Latrell Sprewell	1.00
184	Kenny Anderson	.25
185	Tyrone Hill	.25
186	Robert Pack	.25
187	Greg Anthony	.25
188	Derrick McKey	.25
189	*John Wallace*	5.00
190	Bryon Russell	.25
191	*Jermaine O'Neal*	5.00
192	Clyde Drexler	1.00
193	Mahmoud Abdul-Rauf	.25
194	Eric Montross	.25
195	Allan Houston	.25
196	Harvey Grant	.25
197	Rodney Rogers	.25
198	*Kerry Kittles*	6.00
199	Grant Hill	6.00
200	Lionel Simmons	.25
201	Reggie Miller	1.00
202	Avery Johnson	.25
203	LaPhonso Ellis	.25
204	Brian Shaw	.25
205	*Priest Lauderdale*	.25
206	*Derek Fisher*	3.00
207	Terry Porter	.25
208	*Todd Fuller*	.50
209	Hersey Hawkins	.25
210	Tim Legler	.25
211	Terry Dehere	.25
212	Gary Payton	1.25
213	Joe Dumars	.25
214	Don MacLean	.25
215	Greg Minor	.25
216	Tim Hardaway	.50
217	*Ray Allen*	10.00
218	Mario Elie	.25
219	Brooks Thompson	.25
220	Shaquille O'Neal	4.00

1996-97 Topps Chrome Refractors

All 220 cards in the Chrome Basketball set also arrived in a parallel Refractor set. Refractors were seeded every 12 packs.

		MT
Complete Set (220):		4250.00
Common Player:		10.00
1	Patrick Ewing	30.00
2	Christian Laettner	20.00
3	Mahmoud Abdul-Rauf	10.00
4	Chris Webber	50.00
5	Jason Kidd	40.00
6	Clifford Rozier	10.00
7	Elden Campbell	10.00
8	Chuck Person	10.00
9	Jeff Hornacek	10.00
10	Rik Smits	10.00
11	Kurt Thomas	10.00
12	Rod Strickland	10.00
13	Kendall Gill	10.00
14	Brian Williams	10.00
15	Tom Gugliotta	25.00
16	Ron Harper	10.00
17	Eric Williams	10.00
18	A.C. Green	10.00
19	Scott Williams	10.00
20	Damon Stoudamire	50.00
21	Bryant Reeves	10.00
22	Bob Sura	10.00
23	Mitch Richmond	30.00
24	Larry Johnson	20.00
25	Vin Baker	30.00
26	Mark Bryant	10.00
27	Horace Grant	10.00
28	Allan Houston	20.00
29	Sam Perkins	10.00
30	Antonio McDyess	30.00
31	Rasheed Wallace	10.00
32	Malik Sealy	10.00
33	Scottie Pippen	80.00
34	Charles Barkley	40.00
35	Hakeem Olajuwon	50.00
36	John Starks	10.00
37	Byron Scott	10.00
38	Arvydas Sabonis	10.00
39	Vlade Divac	10.00
40	Joe Dumars	10.00
41	Danny Ferry	10.00
42	Jerry Stackhouse	30.00
43	B.J. Armstrong	10.00
44	Shawn Bradley	20.00
45	Kevin Garnett	140.00
46	Dee Brown	10.00
47	Michael Smith	10.00
48	Doug Christie	10.00
49	Mark Jackson	10.00
50	Shawn Kemp	70.00
51	Predrag Danilovic	10.00
52	Nick Anderson	10.00
53	Matt Geiger	10.00
54	Charles Smith	10.00
55	Mookie Blaylock	10.00
56	Johnny Newman	10.00
57	George McCloud	10.00
58	Greg Ostertag	10.00
59	Reggie Williams	10.00
60	Brent Barry	20.00
61	Doug West	10.00
62	Donald Royal	10.00
63	Randy Brown	10.00

64	Vincent Askew	10.00
65	John Stockton	30.00
66	Joe Kleine	10.00
67	Keith Askins	10.00
68	Bobby Phills	10.00
69	Chris Mullin	20.00
70	Nick Van Exel	25.00
71	Rick Fox	10.00
72	Chicago Bulls Commemorative	150.00
73	Shawn Respert	10.00
74	Hubert Davis	10.00
75	Jim Jackson	20.00
76	Olden Polynice	10.00
77	Gheorghe Muresan	10.00
78	Theo Ratliff	10.00
79	Khalid Reeves	10.00
80	David Robinson	40.00
81	Lawrence Moten	10.00
82	Sam Cassell	10.00
83	George Zidek	10.00
84	Sharone Wright	10.00
85	Clarence Weatherspoon	10.00
86	Alan Henderson	10.00
87	Chris Dudley	10.00
88	Ed O'Bannon	10.00
89	Calbert Cheaney	10.00
90	Cedric Ceballos	10.00
91	Michael Cage	10.00
92	Ervin Johnson	10.00
93	Gary Trent	10.00
94	Sherman Douglas	10.00
95	Joe Smith	30.00
96	Dale Davis	10.00
97	Tony Dumas	10.00
98	Muggsy Bogues	10.00
99	Toni Kukoc	25.00
100	Grant Hill	140.00
101	Michael Finley	25.00
102	Isaiah Rider	10.00
103	Bryant Stith	10.00
104	Pooh Richardson	10.00
105	Karl Malone	30.00
106	Brian Grant	10.00
107	Sean Elliott	10.00
108	Charles Oakley	10.00
109	Pervis Ellison	10.00
110	Anfernee Hardaway	125.00
111	Checklist	10.00
112	Dikembe Mutombo	20.00
113	Alonzo Mourning	25.00
114	Hubert Davis	10.00
115	Rony Seikaly	10.00
116	Danny Manning	10.00
117	Donyell Marshall	10.00
118	Gerald Wilkins	10.00
119	Ervin Johnson	10.00
120	Jalen Rose	10.00
121	Dino Radja	10.00
122	Glenn Robinson	25.00
123	John Stockton	30.00
124	Matt Maloney	30.00
125	Clifford Robinson	10.00
126	Steve Kerr	10.00
127	Nate McMillan	10.00
128	Shareef Abdur-Rahim	130.00
129	Loy Vaught	10.00
130	Anthony Mason	10.00
131	Kevin Garnett	140.00
132	Roy Rogers Jr.	20.00
133	Erick Dampier	20.00
134	Tyus Edney	10.00
135	Chris Mills	10.00
136	Cory Alexander	10.00
137	Juwan Howard	40.00
138	Kobe Bryant	250.00
139	Michael Jordan	400.00
140	Jayson Williams	10.00
141	Rod Strickland	10.00
142	Lorenzen Wright	20.00
143	Will Perdue	10.00
144	Derek Harper	10.00
145	Billy Owens	10.00
146	Antoine Walker	150.00
147	P.J. Brown	10.00
148	Terrell Brandon	25.00
149	Larry Johnson	20.00
150	Steve Smith	10.00
151	Eddie Jones	60.00
152	Detlef Schrempf	10.00
153	Dale Ellis	10.00
154	Isaiah Rider	10.00
155	Tony Delk	20.00
156	Adrian Caldwell	10.00
157	Jamal Mashburn	20.00
158	Dennis Scott	10.00
159	Dana Barros	10.00
160	Martin Muursepp	10.00
161	Marcus Camby	100.00
162	Jerome Williams	10.00
163	Wesley Person	10.00

164	Luc Longley	10.00
165	Charlie Ward	10.00
166	Mark Jackson	10.00
167	Derrick Coleman	10.00
168	Dell Curry	10.00
169	Armon Gilliam	10.00
170	Vlade Divac	10.00
171	Allen Iverson	200.00
172	Vitaly Potapenko	20.00
173	Jon Koncak	10.00
174	Lindsey Hunter	10.00
175	Kevin Johnson	20.00
176	Dennis Rodman	80.00
177	Stephon Marbury	150.00
178	Karl Malone	30.00
179	Charles Barkley	30.00
180	Popeye Jones	10.00
181	Samaki Walker	20.00
182	Steve Nash	30.00
183	Latrell Sprewell	30.00
184	Kenny Anderson	20.00
185	Tyrone Hill	10.00
186	Robert Pack	10.00
187	Greg Anthony	10.00
188	Derrick McKey	10.00
189	John Wallace	40.00
190	Bryon Russell	10.00
191	Jermaine O'Neal	50.00
192	Clyde Drexler	30.00
193	Mahmoud Abdul-Rauf	10.00
194	Eric Montross	10.00
195	Allan Houston	20.00
196	Harvey Grant	10.00
197	Rodney Rogers	20.00
198	Kerry Kittles	50.00
199	Grant Hill	140.00
200	Lionel Simmons	10.00
201	Reggie Miller	25.00
202	Avery Johnson	10.00
203	LaPhonso Ellis	10.00
204	Brian Shaw	10.00
205	Priest Lauderdale	10.00
206	Derek Fisher	25.00
207	Terry Porter	10.00
208	Todd Fuller	10.00
209	Hersey Hawkins	10.00
210	Tim Legler	10.00
211	Terry Dehere	10.00
212	Gary Payton	35.00
213	Joe Dumars	20.00
214	Don MacLean	10.00
215	Greg Minor	10.00
216	Tim Hardaway	25.00
217	Ray Allen	60.00
218	Mario Elie	10.00
219	Brooks Thompson	10.00
220	Shaquille O'Neal	100.00

1996-97 Topps Chrome Pro Files

Pro Files reprinted the 20-card insert from Topps Basketball using chromium technology. These inserts were found every eight packs of Chrome.

		MT
Complete Set (20):		70.00
Common Player:		1.00
PF1	Grant Hill	10.00
PF2	Shawn Kemp	5.00
PF3	Michael Jordan	20.00
PF4	Vin Baker	2.00
PF5	Chris Webber	3.00
PF6	Joe Smith	3.00
PF7	Shaquille O'Neal	8.00
PF8	Patrick Ewing	1.50
PF9	Scottie Pippen	5.00
PF10	Damon Stoudamire	4.00
PF11	Anfernee Hardaway	10.00
PF12	Juwan Howard	3.00
PF13	Dikembe Mutombo	1.00
PF14	Dennis Rodman	8.00
PF15	Kevin Garnett	8.00
PF16	Jerry Stackhouse	3.00
PF17	Alonzo Mourning	1.50
PF18	Karl Malone	1.50
PF19	Hakeem Olajuwon	4.00
PF20	Gary Payton	2.00

1996-97 Topps Chrome Season's Best

This 25-card insert set reprinted the Season's Best insert from Topps

Basketball with chromium technology. The cards carried an "SB" prefix and were inserted every six packs.

		MT
Complete Set (25):		70.00
Common Player:		1.00
SB1	Michael Jordan	20.00
SB2	Hakeem Olajuwon	4.00
SB3	Shaquille O'Neal	8.00
SB4	Karl Malone	1.50
SB5	David Robinson	2.00
SB6	Dennis Rodman	8.00
SB7	David Robinson	2.00
SB8	Dikembe Mutombo	1.00
SB9	Charles Barkley	2.00
SB10	Shawn Kemp	5.00
SB11	John Stockton	1.50
SB12	Jason Kidd	2.00
SB13	Avery Johnson	1.00
SB14	Rod Strickland	1.00
SB15	Damon Stoudamire	4.00
SB16	Gary Payton	2.00
SB17	Mookie Blaylock	1.00
SB18	Michael Jordan	20.00
SB19	Jason Kidd	2.00
SB20	Alvin Robertson	1.00
SB21	Dikembe Mutombo	1.00
SB22	Shawn Bradley	1.00
SB23	David Robinson	2.00
SB24	Hakeem Olajuwon	4.00
SB25	Alonzo Mourning	1.50

1996-97 Topps Chrome Youthquake

This 15-card insert reprinted the Youthquake insert from Topps Basketball. The cards carried a "YQ" prefix and were inserted every 15 packs.

		MT
Complete Set (15):		80.00
Common Player:		1.50
YQ1	Allen Iverson	20.00
YQ2	Samaki Walker	1.50
YQ3	Stephon Marbury	16.00
YQ4	Damon Stoudamire	8.00
YQ5	John Wallace	3.00
YQ6	Michael Finley	1.50
YQ7	Marcus Camby	12.00
YQ8	Kerry Kittles	6.00
YQ9	Ray Allen	8.00
YQ10	Jerry Stackhouse	6.00
YQ11	Shareef Abdur-Rahim	12.00
YQ12	Antonio McDyess	3.00
YQ13	Joe Smith	5.00
YQ14	Brent Barry	1.50
YQ15	Kobe Bryant	20.00

1996-97 Finest

Finest Basketball consisted of 291 cards and was issued in two series, with Series I containing 146 cards and Series II containing 145 cards. Series I was broken into four subsets - Gladiators, Maestros, Apprentices and Sterling, while Series II was broken down into Heirs, Foundations, Mainstays and Sterling.

Both series were also broken down into Bronze (common), Silver (uncommon) and Gold (rare). Both included 100 Bronze and 27 Silver while Series I had 19 Golds and Series II had 18. The cards are easily identified by the bronze, silver or gold border surrounding the card, as well as the large subset heading in the top center. The backs include a small box in the lower right corner with the overall card number, subset number and common, uncommon or rare distinction. Bronze are considered the base cards, while Silvers are seeded one per four packs and Golds are seeded one per 24 packs. The only insert in either series is a parallel Refractor version of each card, which is also identified in the number box on the back.

		MT
Complete Set (291):		1400.
Complete Bronze 1 (100):		100.00
Complete Bronze 2 (100):		30.00
Common Bronze Player:		.50
Complete Silver 1 (27):		75.00
Complete Silver 2 (27):		150.00
Common Silver Player:		2.00
Complete Gold 1 (19):		500.00
Complete Gold 2 (18):		600.00
Common Gold Player:		15.00
Series 1 Wax Box:		225.00
Series 2 Wax Box:		150.00
1	Scottie Pippen	3.00
2	Tim Legler	.50
3	Rex Walters	.50
4	Calbert Cheaney	.50
5	Dennis Rodman	3.00
6	Tyrone Hill	.50
7	Christian Laettner #136	.50
8	Dell Curry	.50
9	Olden Polynice	.50
10	*John Wallace*	5.00
11	*Martin Muursepp*	.50
12	Chuck Person	.50
13	Grant Hill	4.00
14	Shawn Kemp	3.00
15	B.J. Armstrong	.50
16	Gary Trent	.50
17	Scott Williams	.50
18	Dino Radja	.50
19	*Roy Rogers*	1.00
20	*Tony Delk*	2.00
21	Clifford Robinson	.50
22	*Ray Allen*	6.00
23	Clyde Drexler	1.00
24	Elliott Perry	.50
25	Gary Payton	1.00
26	Dale Davis	.50
27	Horace Grant	.50
28	*Brian Evans*	.50
29	Joe Smith	1.00
30	Reggie Miller	1.00
31	*Jermaine O'Neal*	6.00
32	*Avery Johnson*	.50
33	Ed O'Bannon	.50
34	Cedric Ceballos	.50
35	Jamal Mashburn	.50
36	Michael Williams	.50
37	Detlef Schrempf	.50
38	Damon Stoudamire	2.00
39	Jason Kidd	1.00
40	Tom Gugliotta	.50
41	Arvydas Sabonis	.50
42	*Samaki Walker*	1.50
43	*Derek Fisher*	2.00
44	Patrick Ewing	1.00
45	Bryant Reeves	.50
46	Mookie Blaylock	.50
47	George Zidek	.50
48	Jerry Stackhouse	2.00
49	Vin Baker	1.00
50	Michael Jordan	12.00
51	Terrell Brandon	1.00
52	Karl Malone	1.00
53	*Lorenzen Wright*	1.50
54	*Shareef Abdur-Rahim*	16.00
55	Kurt Thomas	.50
56	Glen Rice	.50
57	Shawn Bradley	.50
58	*Todd Fuller*	.50
59	Dale Ellis	.50
60	David Robinson	1.00
61	Doug Christie	.50
62	*Stephon Marbury*	25.00
63	Hakeem Olajuwon	2.00

No.	Player	Price
64	Lindsey Hunter	.50
65	Anfernee Hardaway	5.00
66	Kevin Garnett	5.00
67	Kendall Gill	.50
68	Sean Elliott	.50
69	*Allen Iverson*	25.00
70	*Erick Dampier*	1.00
71	*Jerome Williams*	.50
72	Charles Jones	.50
73	Danny Manning	.50
74	*Kobe Bryant*	50.00
75	*Steve Nash*	3.00
76	Sam Perkins	.50
77	Horace Grant	.50
78	Alonzo Mourning	1.00
79	*Kerry Kittles*	6.00
80	LaPhonso Ellis	.50
81	Michael Finley	1.00
82	*Marcus Camby*	10.00
83	Antonio McDyess	1.00
84	*Antoine Walker*	20.00
85	Juwan Howard	1.00
86	Bryon Russell	.50
87	*Walter McCarty*	3.00
88	*Priest Lauderdale*	.50
89	Clarence Weatherspoon	.50
90	John Stockton	1.00
91	Mitch Richmond	1.00
92	*Dontae Jones*	.75
93	Michael Smith	.50
94	Brent Barry	.50
95	Chris Mills	.50
96	Dee Brown	.50
97	Terry Dehere	.50
98	Danny Ferry	.50
99	Gheorghe Muresan	.50
100	Checklist	.50
101	Jim Jackson (S)	3.00
102	Cedric Ceballos (S)	2.00
103	Glen Rice (S)	2.00
104	Tom Gugliotta (S)	2.00
105	Mario Elie (S)	2.00
106	Nick Anderson (S)	2.00
107	Glenn Robinson (S)	5.00
108	Terrell Brandon (S)	2.00
109	Tim Hardaway (S)	2.00
110	John Stockton (S)	5.00
111	Brent Barry (S)	2.00
112	Mookie Blaylock (S)	2.00
113	Tyus Edney (S)	2.00
114	Gary Payton (S)	6.00
115	Joe Smith (S)	6.00
116	Karl Malone (S)	5.00
117	Dino Radja (S)	2.00
118	Alonzo Mourning (S)	4.00
119	Bryant Stith (S)	2.00
120	Derrick McKey (S)	2.00
121	Clyde Drexler (S)	5.00
122	Michael Finley (S)	5.00
123	Sean Elliott (S)	2.00
124	Hakeem Olajuwon (S)	8.00
125	Joe Dumars (S)	2.00
126	Shawn Bradley (S)	2.00
127	Michael Jordan (S)	40.00
128	Latrell Sprewell (G)	25.00
129	Anfernee Hardaway (G)	60.00
130	Grant Hill (G)	75.00
131	Damon Stoudamire (G)	30.00
132	David Robinson (G)	25.00
133	Scottie Pippen (G)	40.00
134	Patrick Ewing (#136) (G)	20.00
135	Jason Kidd (G)	20.00
136	Jeff Hornacek (G)	15.00
137	Jerry Stackhouse (G)	20.00
138	Kevin Garnett (G)	60.00
139	Mitch Richmond (G)	15.00
140	Juwan Howard (G)	25.00
141	Reggie Miller (G)	20.00
142	Christian Laettner (G)	15.00
143	Vin Baker (G)	15.00
144	Shawn Kemp (G)	40.00
145	Dennis Rodman (G)	60.00
146	Shaquille O'Neal (G)	60.00
147	Mookie Blaylock	.50
148	Derek Harper	.50
149	Gerald Wilkins	.50
150	Adam Keefe	.50
151	Billy Owens	.50
152	Terrell Brandon	.50
153	Antonio Davis	.50
154	Muggsy Bogues	.50
155	Cherokee Parks	.50
156	Rasheed Wallace	.50
157	Lee Mayberry	.50
158	Craig Ehlo	.50
159	Todd Fuller	.50
160	Charles Barkley	1.00
161	Glenn Robinson	.75
162	Charles Oakley	.50
163	Chris Webber	1.25
164	Frank Brickowski	.50
165	Mark Jackson	.50
166	Jayson Williams	.50
167	Clarence Weatherspoon	.50
168	Toni Kukoc	.50
169	Alan Henderson	.50
170	Tony Delk	.75
171	Jamal Mashburn	.50
172	Vinny Del Negro	.50
173	Greg Ostertag	.50
174	Shawn Bradley	.50
175	Gheorghe Muresan	.50
176	Brent Price	.50
177	Rick Fox	.50
178	Stacey Augmon	.50
179	P.J. Brown	.50
180	Jim Jackson	.50
181	Hersey Hawkins	.50
182	Danny Manning	.50
183	Dennis Scott	.50
184	Tom Gugliotta	.50
185	Tyrone Hill	.50
186	Malik Sealy	.50
187	John Starks	.50
188	Mark Price	.50
189	Elden Campbell	.50
190	Mahmoud Abdul-Rauf	.50
191	Will Perdue	.50
192	Nate McMillan	.50
193	Robert Horry	.50
194	Dino Radja	.50
195	Loy Vaught	.50
196	Dikembe Mutombo	.50
197	Eric Montross	.50
198	Sasha Danilovic	.50
199	Kenny Anderson	.50
200	Sean Elliott	.50
201	Mark West	.50
202	Vlade Divac	.50
203	Joe Dumars	.50
204	Allan Houston	.50
205	Kevin Garnett	5.00
206	Rod Strickland	.50
207	Robert Parish	.50
208	Jalen Rose	.50
209	Armon Gilliam	.50
210	Kerry Kittles	3.00
211	Derrick Coleman	.50
212	Greg Anthony	.50
213	Joe Smith	1.00
214	Steve Smith	.50
215	Tim Hardaway	.50
216	Tyus Edney	.50
217	Steve Nash	.50
218	Anthony Mason	.50
219	Otis Thorpe	.50
220	Eddie Jones	1.00
221	Rik Smits	.50
222	Isaiah Rider	.50
223	Bobby Phills	.50
224	Antoine Walker	5.00
225	Rod Strickland	.50
226	Hubert Davis	.50
227	Eric Williams	.50
228	Danny Manning	.50
229	Dominique Wilkins	.50
230	Brian Shaw	.50
231	Larry Johnson	.50
232	Kevin Willis	.50
233	Bryant Stith	.50
234	Blue Edwards	.50
235	Robert Pack	.50
236	Brian Grant	.50
237	Latrell Sprewell	.75
238	Glen Rice	.75
239	Jerome Williams	.50
240	Allen Iverson	10.00
241	Popeye Jones	.50
242	Clifford Robinson	.50
243	Shaquille O'Neal	4.00
244	Vitaly Potapenko	.50
245	Ervin Johnson	.50
246	Checklist	.50
247	Scottie Pippen (S)	8.00
248	Jason Kidd (S)	4.00
249	Antonio McDyess (S)	3.00
250	Latrell Sprewell (S)	4.00
251	Lorenzen Wright (S)	2.00
252	Ray Allen (S)	5.00
253	Stephon Marbury (S)	16.00
254	Patrick Ewing (S)	3.00
255	Anfernee Hardaway (S)	14.00
256	Kenny Anderson (S)	2.00
257	David Robinson (S)	5.00
258	Marcus Camby (S)	10.00
259	Shareef Abdur-Rahim (S)	12.00
260	Dennis Rodman (S)	10.00
261	Juwan Howard (S)	5.00
262	Damon Stoudamire (S)	6.00
263	Shawn Kemp (S)	10.00
264	Mitch Richmond (S)	3.00
265	Jerry Stackhouse (S)	5.00
266	Horace Grant (S)	2.00
267	Kerry Kittles (S)	6.00
268	Vin Baker (S)	3.00
269	Kobe Bryant (G)	70.00
270	Reggie Miller (S)	3.00
271	Grant Hill (S)	16.00
272	Oliver Miller (S)	2.00
273	Chris Webber (S)	6.00
274	Dikembe Mutombo (G)	15.00
275	Antonio McDyess (G)	15.00
276	Clyde Drexler (G)	20.00
277	Brent Barry (G)	15.00
278	Tim Hardaway (G)	15.00
279	Glenn Robinson (G)	20.00
280	Allen Iverson (G)	70.00
281	Hakeem Olajuwon (G)	30.00
282	Marcus Camby (G)	35.00
283	John Stockton (G)	20.00
284	Shareef Abdur-Rahim (G)	35.00
285	Karl Malone (G)	20.00
286	Gary Payton (G)	20.00
287	Stephon Marbury (G)	55.00
288	Alonzo Mourning (G)	15.00
289	Shaquille O'Neal (S)	15.00
290	Charles Barkley (G)	25.00
291	Michael Jordan (G)	125.00

1996-97 Finest Refractors

Each card in the 291-card Finest Basketball set has a parallel Refractor version. Common Refractors were seeded every 12 packs, with Silvers every 48 packs and Gold Refractors every 288 packs. The fronts contain the familiar Refractor finish, while the backs have the word Refractor written in the number box in the lower right corner.

	MT
Complete Bronze 1 (100):	2200.00
Complete Bronze 2 (100):	700.00
Common Bronze Player:	5.00
Complete Silver 1 (27):	800.00
Complete Silver 2 (27):	1300.00
Common Silver Player:	15.00
Complete Gold 1 (19):	4500.00
Complete Gold 2 (18):	4500.00
Common Gold Player:	50.00

No.	Player	Price
1	Scottie Pippen	50.00
2	Tim Legler	5.00
3	Rex Walters	5.00
4	Calbert Cheaney	5.00
5	Dennis Rodman	80.00
6	Tyrone Hill	5.00
7	Christian Laettner #136	10.00
8	Dell Curry	5.00
9	Olden Polynice	5.00
10	John Wallace	30.00
11	Martin Muursepp	5.00
12	Chuck Person	5.00
13	Grant Hill	80.00
14	Shawn Kemp	60.00
15	B.J. Armstrong	5.00
16	Gary Trent	5.00
17	Scott Williams	5.00
18	Dino Radja	5.00
19	Roy Rogers	5.00
20	Tony Delk	15.00
21	Clifford Robinson	5.00
22	Ray Allen	60.00
23	Clyde Drexler	30.00
24	Elliott Perry	5.00
25	Gary Payton	25.00
26	Dale Davis	5.00
27	Horace Grant	5.00
28	Brian Evans	5.00
29	Joe Smith	35.00
30	Reggie Miller	20.00
31	Jermaine O'Neal	50.00
32	Avery Johnson	5.00
33	Ed O'Bannon	5.00
34	Cedric Ceballos	5.00
35	Jamal Mashburn	10.00
36	Michael Williams	5.00
37	Detlef Schrempf	5.00
38	Damon Stoudamire	50.00
39	Jason Kidd	20.00
40	Tom Gugliotta	5.00
41	Arvydas Sabonis	10.00
42	Samaki Walker	12.00
43	Derek Fisher	20.00
44	Patrick Ewing	20.00
45	Bryant Reeves	10.00
46	Mookie Blaylock	5.00
47	George Zidek	5.00
48	Jerry Stackhouse	30.00
49	Vin Baker	10.00
50	Michael Jordan	200.00
51	Terrell Brandon	5.00
52	Karl Malone	20.00
53	Lorenzen Wright	12.00
54	Shareef Abdur-Rahim	120.00
55	Kurt Thomas	5.00
56	Glen Rice	10.00
57	Shawn Bradley	5.00
58	Todd Fuller	5.00
59	Dale Ellis	5.00
60	David Robinson	25.00
61	Doug Christie	5.00
62	Stephon Marbury	150.00
63	Hakeem Olajuwon	40.00
64	Lindsey Hunter	5.00
65	Anfernee Hardaway	90.00
66	Kevin Garnett	100.00
67	Kendall Gill	5.00
68	Sean Elliott	5.00
69	Allen Iverson	175.00
70	Erick Dampier	5.00
71	Jerome Williams	5.00
72	Charles Jones	5.00
73	Danny Manning	5.00
74	Kobe Bryant	225.00
75	Steve Nash	20.00
76	Sam Perkins	5.00
77	Horace Grant	5.00
78	Alonzo Mourning	20.00
79	Kerry Kittles	60.00
80	LaPhonso Ellis	5.00
81	Michael Finley	20.00
82	Marcus Camby	75.00
83	Antonio McDyess	25.00
84	Antoine Walker	100.00
85	Juwan Howard	30.00
86	Bryon Russell	5.00
87	Walter McCarty	20.00
88	Priest Lauderdale	5.00
89	Clarence Weatherspoon	5.00
90	John Stockton	20.00
91	Mitch Richmond	5.00
92	Dontae Jones	10.00
93	Michael Smith	5.00
94	Brent Barry	5.00
95	Chris Mills	5.00
96	Dee Brown	5.00
97	Terry Dehere	5.00
98	Danny Ferry	5.00
99	Gheorghe Muresan	5.00
100	Checklist	5.00
101	Jim Jackson (S)	25.00
102	Cedric Ceballos (S)	15.00
103	Glen Rice (S)	15.00
104	Tom Gugliotta (S)	15.00
105	Mario Elie (S)	15.00
106	Nick Anderson (S)	15.00
107	Glenn Robinson (S)	30.00
108	Terrell Brandon (S)	15.00
109	Tim Hardaway (S)	15.00
110	John Stockton (S)	30.00
111	Brent Barry (S)	15.00
112	Mookie Blaylock (S)	15.00
113	Tyus Edney (S)	15.00
114	Gary Payton (S)	45.00
115	Joe Smith (S)	50.00
116	Karl Malone (S)	30.00
117	Dino Radja (S)	15.00
118	Alonzo Mourning (S)	30.00
119	Bryant Stith (S)	15.00
120	Derrick McKey (S)	15.00
121	Clyde Drexler (S)	40.00
122	Michael Finley (S)	30.00
123	Sean Elliott (S)	15.00
124	Hakeem Olajuwon (S)	60.00
125	Joe Dumars (S)	15.00
126	Shawn Bradley (S)	15.00
127	Michael Jordan (S)	275.00
128	Latrell Sprewell (G)	125.00
129	Anfernee Hardaway (G)	400.00
130	Grant Hill (G)	450.00
131	Damon Stoudamire (G)	175.00
132	David Robinson (G)	125.00
133	Scottie Pippen (G)	250.00
134	Patrick Ewing (#136) (G)	100.00
135	Jason Kidd (G)	100.00
136	Jeff Hornacek (G)	50.00
137	Jerry Stackhouse (G)	100.00
138	Kevin Garnett (G)	450.00
139	Mitch Richmond (G)	50.00
140	Juwan Howard (G)	125.00
141	Reggie Miller (G)	75.00
142	Christian Laettner (G)	50.00
143	Vin Baker (G)	50.00
144	Shawn Kemp (G)	225.00
145	Dennis Rodman (G)	325.00
146	Shaquille O'Neal (G)	350.00
147	Mookie Blaylock	5.00
148	Derek Harper	5.00
149	Gerald Wilkins	5.00

150	Adam Keefe	5.00
151	Billy Owens	5.00
152	Terrell Brandon	5.00
153	Antonio Davis	5.00
154	Muggsy Bogues	5.00
155	Cherokee Parks	5.00
156	Rasheed Wallace	5.00
157	Lee Mayberry	5.00
158	Craig Ehlo	5.00
159	Todd Fuller	5.00
160	Charles Barkley	25.00
161	Glenn Robinson	20.00
162	Charles Oakley	5.00
163	Chris Webber	30.00
164	Frank Brickowski	5.00
165	Mark Jackson	5.00
166	Jayson Williams	5.00
167	Clarence Weatherspoon	5.00
168	Toni Kukoc	5.00
169	Alan Henderson	5.00
170	Tony Delk	10.00
171	Jamal Mashburn	5.00
172	Vinny Del Negro	5.00
173	Greg Ostertag	5.00
174	Shawn Bradley	5.00
175	Gheorghe Muresan	5.00
176	Brent Price	5.00
177	Rick Fox	5.00
178	Stacey Augmon	5.00
179	P.J. Brown	5.00
180	Jim Jackson	5.00
181	Hersey Hawkins	5.00
182	Danny Manning	5.00
183	Dennis Scott	5.00
184	Tom Gugliotta	5.00
185	Tyrone Hill	5.00
186	Malik Sealy	5.00
187	John Starks	5.00
188	Mark Price	5.00
189	Elden Campbell	5.00
190	Mahmoud Abdul-Rauf	5.00
191	Will Perdue	5.00
192	Nate McMillan	5.00
193	Robert Horry	5.00
194	Dino Radja	5.00
195	Loy Vaught	5.00
196	Dikembe Mutombo	5.00
197	Eric Montross	5.00
198	Sasha Danilovic	5.00
199	Kenny Anderson	5.00
200	Sean Elliott	5.00
201	Mark West	5.00
202	Vlade Divac	5.00
203	Joe Dumars	5.00
204	Allan Houston	5.00
205	Kevin Garnett	100.00
206	Rod Strickland	5.00
207	Robert Parish	5.00
208	Jalen Rose	5.00
209	Armon Gilliam	5.00
210	Kerry Kittles	30.00
211	Derrick Coleman	5.00
212	Greg Anthony	5.00
213	Joe Smith	25.00
214	Steve Smith	5.00
215	Tim Hardaway	5.00
216	Tyus Edney	5.00
217	Steve Nash	5.00
218	Anthony Mason	5.00
219	Otis Thorpe	5.00
220	Eddie Jones	30.00
221	Rik Smits	5.00
222	Isaiah Rider	5.00
223	Bobby Phills	5.00
224	Antoine Walker	50.00
225	Rod Strickland	5.00
226	Hubert Davis	5.00
227	Eric Williams	5.00
228	Danny Manning	5.00
229	Dominique Wilkins	5.00
230	Brian Shaw	5.00
231	Larry Johnson	5.00
232	Kevin Willis	5.00
233	Bryant Stith	5.00
234	Blue Edwards	5.00
235	Robert Pack	5.00
236	Brian Grant	5.00
237	Latrell Sprewell	20.00
238	Glen Rice	20.00
239	Jerome Williams	5.00
240	Allen Iverson	100.00
241	Popeye Jones	5.00
242	Clifford Robinson	5.00
243	Shaquille O'Neal	75.00
244	Vitaly Potapenko	5.00
245	Ervin Johnson	5.00
246	Checklist	5.00
247	Scottie Pippen (S)	70.00
248	Jason Kidd (S)	25.00
249	Antonio McDyess (S)	15.00
250	Latrell Sprewell (S)	30.00
251	Lorenzen Wright (S)	15.00
252	Ray Allen (S)	35.00
253	Stephon Marbury (S)	100.00
254	Patrick Ewing (S)	25.00
255	Anfernee Hardaway (S)	120.00
256	Kenny Anderson (S)	15.00
257	David Robinson (S)	30.00
258	Marcus Camby (S)	60.00
259	Shareef Abdur-Rahim (S)	70.00
260	Dennis Rodman (S)	80.00
261	Juwan Howard (S)	30.00
262	Damon Stoudamire (S)	50.00
263	Shawn Kemp (S)	60.00
264	Mitch Richmond (S)	25.00
265	Jerry Stackhouse (S)	40.00
266	Horace Grant (S)	15.00
267	Kerry Kittles (S)	35.00
268	Vin Baker (S)	25.00
269	Kobe Bryant (S)	550.00
270	Reggie Miller (S)	25.00
271	Grant Hill (S)	130.00
272	Oliver Miller (S)	15.00
273	Chris Webber (S)	45.00
274	Dikembe Mutombo (G)	50.00
275	Antonio McDyess (G)	75.00
276	Clyde Drexler (G)	100.00
277	Brent Barry (G)	50.00
278	Tim Hardaway (G)	60.00
279	Glenn Robinson (G)	80.00
280	Allen Iverson (G)	550.00
281	Hakeem Olajuwon (G)	200.00
282	Marcus Camby (G)	200.00
283	John Stockton (G)	80.00
284	Shareef Abdur-Rahim (G)	275.00
285	Karl Malone (G)	100.00
286	Gary Payton (G)	120.00
287	Stephon Marbury (G)	400.00
288	Alonzo Mourning (G)	60.00
289	Shaquille O'Neal (S)	100.00
290	Charles Barkley (G)	150.00
291	Michael Jordan (G)	1200.

1996 Topps NBA Stars

In conjunction with the NBA's 50th anniversary, Topps secured the rights to produce this NBA Topps Stars set, a 150-card set featuring the NBA's 50 greatest players of all time. Each player is featured on three different cards - a Golden Season card, which highlights his best year, and two versions of a commemorative card. One version has an all text back; the other features complete career statistics which show why the player was selected to the team. The cards each feature a different photo on the front. Each of the 150 regular cards also has three parallel versions - Finest (one per six), Finest Refractor (one per 24 retail, one per 20 hobby) and Finest Atomic Refractor (one per 96). In addition, reprints of all 50 players' original Topps, Bowman or Star Co. basketball cards are included in every six hobby packs and every nine retail packs. The final insert set is called Imagine, which pits two players from a different era against each other. Also found in packs are High Five Favorites game cards, which allow collectors to use the ballot to vote on their all-time top five players. Those players receiving the most votes will be crowned Topps' High Five Favorites. Collectors who voted for all of those players will win special prizes.

		MT
Complete Set (150):		25.00
Common Player:		.10
Wax Box:		60.00
1	Kareem Abdul-Jabbar	.75
2	Nate Archibald	.10
3	Paul Arizin	.10
4	Charles Barkley	.60
5	Rick Barry	.30
6	Elgin Baylor	.30
7	Dave Bing	.10
8	Larry Bird	1.25
9	Wilt Chamberlain	1.00
10	Bob Cousy	.30
11	Dave Cowens	.10
12	Billy Cunningham	.10
13	Dave DeBusschere	.10
14	Clyde Drexler	.40
15	Julius Erving	.75
16	Patrick Ewing	.30
17	Walt Frazier	.20
18	George Gervin	.10
19	Hal Greer	.10
20	John Havlicek	.20
21	Elvin Hayes	.20
22	Magic Johnson	1.25
23	Sam Jones	.10
24	Michael Jordan	4.00
25	Jerry Lucas	.10
26	Karl Malone	.40
27	Moses Malone	.10
28	Pete Maravich	.50
29	Kevin McHale	.20
30	George Mikan	.50
31	Earl Monroe	.20
32	Shaquille O'Neal	1.50
33	Hakeem Olajuwon	.75
34	Robert Parish	.10
35	Bob Pettit	.20
36	Scottie Pippen	.75
37	Willis Reed	.10
38	Oscar Robertson	.50
39	David Robinson	.50
40	Bill Russell	.75
41	Dolph Schayes	.10
42	Bill Sharman	.10
43	John Stockton	.40
44	Isiah Thomas	.50
45	Nate Thurmond	.10
46	Wes Unseld	.10
47	Bill Walton	.10
48	Jerry West	.50
49	Len Wilkens	.10
50	James Worthy	.10
51	Kareem Abdul-Jabbar	.75
52	Nate Archibald	.10
53	Paul Arizin	.10
54	Charles Barkley	.60
55	Rick Barry	.30
56	Elgin Baylor	.30
57	Dave Bing	.10
58	Larry Bird	1.25
59	Wilt Chamberlain	1.00
60	Bob Cousy	.30
61	Dave Cowens	.10
62	Billy Cunningham	.10
63	Dave DeBusschere	.10
64	Clyde Drexler	.40
65	Julius Erving	.75
66	Patrick Ewing	.30
67	Walt Frazier	.20
68	George Gervin	.10
69	Hal Greer	.10
70	John Havlicek	.20
71	Elvin Hayes	.20
72	Magic Johnson	1.25
73	Sam Jones	.10
74	Michael Jordan	4.00
75	Jerry Lucas	.10
76	Karl Malone	.40
77	Moses Malone	.10
78	Pete Maravich	.50
79	Kevin McHale	.20
80	George Mikan	.50
81	Earl Monroe	.20
82	Shaquille O'Neal	1.50
83	Hakeem Olajuwon	.75
84	Robert Parish	.10
85	Bob Pettit	.20
86	Scottie Pippen	.75
87	Willis Reed	.10
88	Oscar Robertson	.50
89	David Robinson	.50
90	Bill Russell	.75
91	Dolph Schayes	.10
92	Bill Sharman	.10
93	John Stockton	.40
94	Isiah Thomas	.50
95	Nate Thurmond	.10
96	Wes Unseld	.10
97	Bill Walton	.10
98	Jerry West	.50
99	Len Wilkens	.10
100	James Worthy	.10
101	Kareem Abdul-Jabbar	.75
102	Nate Archibald	.10
103	Paul Arizin	.10
104	Charles Barkley	.60
105	Rick Barry	.30
106	Elgin Baylor	.30
107	Dave Bing	.10
108	Larry Bird	1.25
109	Wilt Chamberlain	1.00
110	Bob Cousy	.30
111	Dave Cowens	.10
112	Billy Cunningham	.10
113	Dave DeBusschere	.10
114	Clyde Drexler	.40
115	Julius Erving	.75
116	Patrick Ewing	.30
117	Walt Frazier	.20
118	George Gervin	.10
119	Hal Greer	.10
120	John Havlicek	.20
121	Elvin Hayes	.20
122	Magic Johnson	1.25
123	Sam Jones	.10
124	Michael Jordan	4.00
125	Jerry Lucas	.10
126	Karl Malone	.40
127	Moses Malone	.10
128	Pete Maravich	.50
129	Kevin McHale	.20
130	George Mikan	.50
131	Earl Monroe	.20
132	Shaquille O'Neal	1.50
133	Hakeem Olajuwon	.75
134	Robert Parish	.10
135	Bob Pettit	.20
136	Scottie Pippen	.75
137	Willis Reed	.10
138	Oscar Robertson	.50
139	David Robinson	.50
140	Bill Russell	.75
141	Dolph Schayes	.10
142	Bill Sharman	.10
143	John Stockton	.40
144	Isiah Thomas	.50
145	Nate Thurmond	.10
146	Wes Unseld	.10
147	Bill Walton	.10
148	Jerry West	.50
149	Len Wilkens	.10
150	James Worthy	.10

1996 Topps NBA Stars Finest

Each card in the 1996 NBA Topps Stars set also arrived in a Finest version. Inserted every six packs, this set utilized Finest technology for the 150-card set.

	MT
Finest Cards:	6x-12x

1996 Topps NBA Stars Refractors

Each card in the 150-card 1996 NBA Topps Stars set was also available in a Refractor version. The word

Refractor appeared on the back to identify it, and they were inserted every 20 hobby packs and 24 retail packs.

	MT
Refractors:	25x-50x

1996 Topps NBA Stars Atomic Refractors

Each card in the 1996 NBA Topps Stars set also arrived in a parallel Atomic Refractor version. This 150-card set was identified by a streaked, prismatic foil on the front.

	MT
Atomic Refractors:	50x-100x

1996 Topps NBA Stars Imagine

This 25-card insert set uses computer imagery to pit two players from different eras against each other. The glossy card front has "Imagine" written across the top inside some clouds. The players' last names are stamped in gold foil at the top. The NBA/Topps Stars logo is in the lower right corner. The card back is split into two halves, each with a brief player profile alongside a photo. "Battle of Wits" is written across the middle of the card. The card number, using an "I" prefix, is in the upper right corner. Cards were seeded one per every 18 packs.

		MT
Complete Set (25):		150.00
Common Player:		3.00
I1	Shaquille O'Neal, Wilt Chamberlain	20.00
I2	David Robinson, Dave Cowens	7.00
I3	Bill Russell, Kareem Abdul-Jabbar	10.00
I4	Scottie Pippen, Patrick Ewing	15.00
I5	Hakeem Olajuwon, Elvin Hayes	7.00
I6	Michael Jordan, Oscar Robertson	40.00
I7	Clyde Drexler, Earl Monroe	6.00
I8	Magic Johnson, Jerry West	12.00
I9	Larry Bird, Rick Barry	12.00
I10	Kevin McHale, Dave DeBusschere	3.00
I11	Moses Malone, Jerry Lucas	3.00
I12	Robert Parish, Nate Thurmond	3.00
I13	Pete Maravich, Sam Jones	6.00
I14	John Stockton, Bob Cousy	6.00
I15	Isiah Thomas, Bill Sharman	6.00
I16	Karl Malone, Bob Pettit	6.00
I17	Bill Walton, George Mikan	6.00
I18	Patrick Ewing, Willis Reed	6.00
I19	Billy Cunningham, James Worthy	3.00
I20	George Gervin, Hal Greer	3.00
I21	Wes Unseld, Dolph Schayes	3.00
I22	Nate Archibald, Len Wilkens	3.00
I23	Walt Frazier, Paul Arizin	3.00
I24	Charles Barkley, Elgin Baylor	7.00
I25	Dave Bing, John Havlicek	6.00

1996 Topps NBA Stars Reprints

The 50 players who were selected for Topps' set honoring the NBA's greatest players of all time are featured on this reprint set. Each of the players has his original Topps, Bowman or Star Co. card reprinted for the glossy set. Each card is identical in format to the original, except it is labeled on the back as being a reprint (1 of 50, etc.). Cards were seeded one per every six hobby packs and one per every nine retail packs.

		MT
Complete Set (50):		300.00
Common Player:		2.00
1	Kareem Abdul-Jabbar	12.00
2	Nate Archibald	2.00
3	Paul Arizin	2.00
4	Charles Barkley	10.00
5	Rick Barry	5.00
6	Elgin Baylor	5.00
7	Dave Bing	2.00
8	Larry Bird	25.00
9	Wilt Chamberlain	12.00
10	Bob Cousy	8.00
11	Dave Cowens	2.00
12	Billy Cunningham	2.00
13	Dave DeBusschere	2.00
14	Clyde Drexler	7.00
15	Julius Erving	12.00
16	Patrick Ewing	8.00
17	Walt Frazier	2.00
18	George Gervin	2.00
19	Hal Greer	2.00
20	John Havlicek	8.00
21	Elvin Hayes	2.00
22	Magic Johnson	25.00
23	Sam Jones	2.00
24	Michael Jordan	60.00
25	Jerry Lucas	2.00
26	Karl Malone	5.00
27	Moses Malone	4.00
28	Pete Maravich	8.00
29	Kevin McHale	2.00
30	George Mikan	8.00
31	Earl Monroe	4.00
32	Shaquille O'Neal	12.00
33	Hakeem Olajuwon	12.00
34	Robert Parish	2.00
35	Bob Pettit	4.00
36	Scottie Pippen	12.00
37	Willis Reed	2.00
38	Oscar Robertson	8.00
39	David Robinson	8.00
40	Bill Russell	12.00
41	Dolph Schayes	2.00
42	Bill Sharman	2.00
43	John Stockton	5.00
44	Isiah Thomas	5.00
45	Nate Thurmond	2.00
46	Wes Unseld	2.00
47	Bill Walton	2.00
48	Jerry West	10.00
49	Len Wilkens	2.00
50	James Worthy	4.00

1996 Topps NBA Stars Reprint Autographs

This 10-card set was available at a rate of one per retail box in NBA Topps Stars and one per 1996-97 Topps factory hobby set. The set consists of 10 player's rookie reprint cards from NBA Topps Stars in autographed versions with a Topps certified stamp.

		MT
Complete Set (10):		200.00
Common Player:		10.00
2	Nate Archibald	20.00
5	Rick Barry	25.00
17	Walt Frazier	20.00
18	George Gervin	25.00
21	Elvin Hayes	20.00
23	Sam Jones	10.00
30	George Mikan	80.00
31	Earl Monroe	20.00
37	Willis Reed	20.00
47	Bill Walton	25.00

1996-97 Stadium Club

Stadium Club's 1996-97 product consisted of 180 cards, which were issued in two 90-card series. The cards featured a full bleed color shot, with a silver holographic embossed strip down the right side that had the player's name. Backs included another shot of the player, stats and the card number in the bottom left corner in a red box. Inserts in Series I included: Fusion, Special Forces, Top Crop, NBA Topps Stars Finest Rookie Reprints, Player's Private Issue, Rookies, Shining Moments, Golden Moments and the parallel TSC Matrix. Inserts in Series II included: Mega Heroes, Fusion, Class Acts, High Risers, Rookie Showcase, Rookies, Welcome Additions and parallel TSC Matrix cards.

		MT
Complete Set (180):		26.00
Complete Series 1 (90):		14.00
Complete Series 2 (90):		12.00
Common Player:		.10
Series 1 Wax Box:		65.00
Series 2 Wax Box:		60.00
1	Scottie Pippen	1.00
2	Dale Davis	.10
3	Horace Grant	.10
4	Gheorghe Muresan	.10
5	Elliot Perry	.10
6	Carlos Rogers	.10
7	Glenn Robinson	.40
8	Avery Johnson	.10
9	Dee Brown	.10
10	Grant Hill	2.50
11	Tyus Edney	.20
12	Patrick Ewing	.40
13	Jason Kidd	1.00
14	Clifford Robinson	.10
15	Robert Horry	.10
16	Dell Curry	.10
17	Terry Porter	.10
18	Shaquille O'Neal	2.00
19	Bryant Stith	.10
20	Shawn Kemp	1.00
21	Kurt Thomas	.10
22	Pooh Richardson	.10

23	Bob Sura	.10
24	Olden Polynice	.10
25	Lawrence Moten	.10
26	Kendall Gill	.10
27	Cedric Ceballos	.20
28	Latrell Sprewell	.20
29	Christian Laettner	.10
30	Jamal Mashburn	.20
31	Jerry Stackhouse	.75
32	John Stockton	.40
33	Arvydas Sabonis	.30
34	Detlef Schrempf	.10
35	Toni Kukoc	.20
36	Sasha Danilovic	.10
37	Dana Barros	.10
38	Loy Vaught	.10
39	John Starks	.10
40	Marty Conlon	.10
41	Antonio McDyess	.50
42	Michael Finley	.60
43	Tom Gugliotta	.10
44	Terrell Brandon	.10
45	Derrick McKey	.10
46	Damon Stoudamire	1.25
47	Elden Campbell	.10
48	Luc Longley	.10
49	B.J. Armstrong	.10
50	Lindsey Hunter	.10
51	Glen Rice	.10
52	Shawn Respert	.10
53	Cory Alexander	.10
54	Tim Legler	.10
55	Bryant Reeves	.30
56	Anfernee Hardaway	2.50
57	Charles Barkley	.50
58	Mookie Blaylock	.10
59	Kevin Garnett	2.50
60	Hersey Hawkins	.10
61	Ed O'Bannon	.10
62	George Zidek	.10
63	Mitch Richmond	.20
64	Derrick Coleman	.10
65	Chris Webber	.75
66	Bobby Phills	.10
67	Rik Smits	.10
68	Jeff Hornacek	.10
69	Sam Cassell	.10
70	Gary Trent	.10
71	LaPhonso Ellis	.10
72	Oliver Miller	.10
73	Rex Chapman	.10
74	Jim Jackson	.20
75	Eric Williams	.10
76	Brent Barry	.20
77	Nick Anderson	.10
78	David Robinson	.75
79	Calbert Cheaney	.10
80	Joe Smith	.60
81	Steve Kerr	.10
82	Wayman Tisdale	.10
83	Steve Smith	.10
84	Clyde Drexler	.50
85	Theo Ratliff	.10
86	Charlie Ward	.10
87	Karl Malone	.40
88	Clarence Weatherspoon	.10
89	Greg Anthony	.10
90	Shawn Bradley	.10
91	Otis Thorpe	.10
92	Larry Johnson	.20
93	Sharone Wright	.10
94	Charles Barkley	.50
95	Wesley Person	.10
96	Dikembe Mutombo	.10
97	Eddie Jones	.20
98	Juwan Howard	.30
99	Grant Hill	2.50
100	Chris Carr	.10
101	Michael Jordan	4.00
102	Vincent Askew	.10
103	Gary Payton	.30
104	Chris Mills	.10
105	Reggie Miller	.30
106	Don MacLean	.10
107	John Stockton	.30
108	Mahmoud Abdul-Rauf	.10
109	P.J. Brown	.10
110	Kenny Anderson	.10
111	Mark Price	.10
112	Derek Harper	.10
113	Dino Radja	.10
114	Terry Dehere	.10
115	Mark Jackson	.10
116	Vin Baker	.25
117	Dennis Scott	.10
118	Sean Elliott	.10
119	Lee Mayberry	.10
120	Vlade Divac	.10
121	Joe Dumars	.10
122	Isaiah Rider	.10
123	Hakeem Olajuwon	.75

124	Robert Pack	.10
125	Jalen Rose	.10
126	Allan Houston	.10
127	Nate McMillan	.10
128	Rod Strickland	.10
129	Sean Rooks	.10
130	Dennis Rodman	2.00
131	Alonzo Mourning	.25
132	Danny Ferry	.10
133	Sam Cassell	.10
134	Brian Grant	.10
135	Karl Malone	.30
136	Chris Gatling	.10
137	Tom Gugliotta	.10
138	Hubert Davis	.10
139	Lucious Harris	.10
140	Rony Seikaly	.10
141	Alan Henderson	.10
142	Mario Elie	.10
143	Vinny Del Negro	.10
144	Harvey Grant	.10
145	Muggsy Bogues	.10
146	Rodney Rogers	.10
147	Kevin Johnson	.10
148	Anthony Peeler	.10
149	Jon Koncak	.10
150	Ricky Pierce	.10
151	Todd Day	.10
152	Tyrone Hill	.10
153	Nick Van Exel	.20
154	Rasheed Wallace	.10
155	Jayson Williams	.10
156	Sherman Douglas	.10
157	Bryon Russell	.10
158	Ron Harper	.10
159	Stacey Augmon	.10
160	Antonio Davis	.10
161	Tim Hardaway	.10
162	Charles Oakley	.10
163	Billy Owens	.10
164	Sam Perkins	.10
165	Chris Whitney	.10
166	Matt Geiger	.10
167	Andrew Lang	.10
168	Danny Manning	.10
169	Doug Christie	.10
170	George Lynch	.10
171	Malik Sealy	.10
172	Eric Montross	.10
173	Rick Fox	.10
174	Chris Mullin	.10
175	Ken Norman	.10
176	Sarunas Marciulionis	.10
177	Kevin Garnett	2.50
178	Brian Shaw	.10
179	Will Perdue	.10
180	Scott Williams	.10

1996-97 Stadium Club Matrix

Matrix parallel cards were produced for each card in Stadium Club Series I and inserted one per 12 hobby and one per 10 retail packs. The cards featured Topps' Matrix technology which consisted of a flashy, foil-etched background with highlights.

	MT
Complete Set (90):	140.00
Matrix Cards:	10x

1996-97 Stadium Club Class Acts

Class Acts was a 10-card insert that featured two stars from the same college on a double-sided Finest card. These cards were inserted every 24 packs of Series II. Refractor and Atomic Refractor versions are also available, with all three versions difficult to find on a perfectly centered card. Class Acts inserts carry a "CA" prefix.

		MT
Complete Set (10):		100.00
Common Player:		5.00
CA1	Michael Jordan, Jerry Stackhouse	30.00
CA2	Alonzo Mourning, Patrick Ewing	5.00
CA3	Brent Barry, Gary Payton	5.00
CA4	Juwan Howard, Chris Webber	10.00
CA5	Grant Hill, Christian Laettner	18.00
CA6	Jason Kidd, Shareef Abdur-Rahim	12.00
CA7	Clyde Drexler, Hakeem Olajuwon	10.00
CA8	Stephon Marbury, Kenny Anderson	16.00
CA9	Lorenzen Wright, Anfernee Hardaway	20.00
CA10	Dikembe Mutombo, Allen Iverson	18.00

1996-97 Stadium Club Class Acts Refractors

Class Acts Refractors parallel the regular Class Acts insert, but featured Topps' familiar Refractor finish. These cards were found in Series II packs at a rate of one per 96 packs.

	MT
Refractors:	2x-3x

1996-97 Stadium Club Class Acts Atomic Refractors

This 10-card set was inserted every 192 Series II hobby and retail packs. It paralleled the regular Class Acts insert, but featured a prismatic, streaked Refractor finish.

	MT
Atomic Refractors:	3x-6x

1996-97 Stadium Club Finest Reprints

This 25-card set included Finest Rookie Reprints from the NBA Topps Stars product. The set has a total of 50 cards, with 25 found in Stadium Club Series I (one per 24 hobby; one per 20 retail) and the other 25 in Topps Series II.

	MT
Complete Set (25):	125.00
Common Player:	3.00
2 Nate Archibald	3.00
4 Charles Barkley	10.00
5 Rick Barry	5.00
6 Elgin Baylor	5.00
7 Dave Bing	3.00
8 Larry Bird	20.00
10 Bob Cousy	8.00
12 Billy Cunningham	3.00
13 Dave DeBusschere	3.00
15 Julius Erving	8.00
17 Walt Frazier	5.00
18 George Gervin	3.00
19 Hal Greer	3.00
24 Michael Jordan	45.00
26 Karl Malone	5.00
28 Pete Maravich	5.00
29 Kevin McHale	5.00
34 Robert Parish	5.00
35 Bob Pettit	5.00
36 Scottie Pippen	10.00
41 Dolph Schayes	3.00
44 Isiah Thomas	5.00
48 Jerry West	8.00
49 Len Wilkens	5.00
50 James Worthy	3.00

1996-97 Stadium Club Finest Reprints Refractors

This insert paralleled the Finest Rookie Reprints from Stadium Club Series I, but featured Refractor technololgy. There were 25 cards in the set, and they were seeded every 96 hobby packs and 80 retail packs. The other 25 cards are found in Topps Series II.

	MT
Complete Set (25):	500.00
Refractors:	2x-4x

1996-97 Stadium Club Fusion

This 32-card set consisted of 16 cards from Series I and 16 cards from Series II, with both inserted one per 24 hobby packs. The card numbers carry an "F" prefix and feature two players from the same team on die-cut cards that fit together. Sixteen total match-ups are captured between the two series, with eight in each. The first eight cards in each are the right side of the die-cut, while the next eight are the left side; for example, F1 and F9 match-up to form one card.

		MT
Complete Set (32):		200.00
Complete Series 1 (16):		120.00
Complete Series 2 (16):		80.00
Common Player:		1.50
F1	Michael Jordan	60.00
F2	Chris Webber	7.00
F3	Glenn Robinson	5.00
F4	Glen Rice	1.50
F5	Gary Payton	5.00
F6	Rik Smits	1.50
F7	Grant Hill	20.00
F8	Horace Grant	1.50
F9	Scottie Pippen	10.00
F10	Gheorghe Muresan	1.50
F11	Vin Baker	1.50
F12	Dell Curry	1.50
F13	Shawn Kemp	15.00
F14	Reggie Miller	5.00
F15	Joe Dumars	1.50
F16	Anfernee Hardaway	30.00
F17	Charles Barkley	8.00
F18	Juwan Howard	8.00
F19	Patrick Ewing	6.00
F20	John Stockton	6.00
F21	David Robinson	8.00
F22	Cedric Ceballos	1.50
F23	Alonzo Mourning	6.00
F24	Mookie Blaylock	1.50
F25	Clyde Drexler	6.00
F26	Rod Strickland	1.50
F27	Larry Johnson	1.50
F28	Karl Malone	6.00
F29	Sean Elliott	1.50
F30	Shaquille O'Neal	20.00
F31	Tim Hardaway	1.50
F32	Dikembe Mutombo	1.50

1996-97 Stadium Club Player's Private Issue

This 18-card insert included the first 18 Player's Private Issue cards that were accidentally never printed in 1995-96 Topps Gallery. They were found in one per 96 hobby packs of Series II Stadium Club.

		MT
Complete Set (18):		700.00
Common Player:		10.00
1	Shaquille O'Neal	120.00
2	Shawn Kemp	70.00
3	Reggie Miller	25.00
4	Mitch Richmond	20.00
5	Grant Hill	120.00
6	Magic Johnson	50.00
7	Vin Baker	20.00
8	Charles Barkley	30.00
9	Hakeem Olajuwon	50.00
10	Michael Jordan	300.00
11	Patrick Ewing	20.00
12	David Robinson	30.00
13	Alonzo Mourning	20.00
14	Karl Malone	20.00
15	Chris Webber	40.00
16	Dikembe Mutombo	10.00
17	Larry Johnson	10.00
18	Jamal Mashburn	10.00

1996-97 Stadium Club High Risers

High Risers captured 15 players on a bright silver background that pictures skyscrapers and the insert name in the background. Inserted one per 36 Series II retail and hobby packs, this insert is numbered with an "HR" prefix.

	MT
Complete Set (15):	175.00
Common Player:	3.00
HR1 Scottie Pippen	15.00
HR2 Anfernee Hardaway	30.00
HR3 Vin Baker	3.00
HR4 Brent Barry	3.00
HR5 Clyde Drexler	8.00
HR6 Kevin Garnett	30.00
HR7 Grant Hill	30.00
HR8 Michael Finley	3.00
HR9 Jerry Stackhouse	10.00
HR10 Isaiah Rider	3.00
HR11 Shaquille O'Neal	25.00
HR12 Antonio McDyess	3.00
HR13 Shawn Kemp	15.00
HR14 Michael Jordan	60.00
HR15 Juwan Howard	7.00

1996-97 Stadium Club Moments

This five-card set carried a "GM" prefix in the card number and was inserted into packs of Series I. The cards were considered part of the regular-issue set but were numbered as an insert. They are known in the hobby as an insert set. Fronts carry a black border on the right side with gold lettering and the date of the "golden moment" in the lower right corner.

	MT
Complete Set (20):	14.00
Common Player:	.20
Minor Stars:	.40
GM1 Robert Parish	.20
GM2 John Stockton	.40
GM3 Michael Jordan, Dennis Rodman	3.50
GM4 Dennis Scott	.20
GM5 Hakeem Olajuwon	.75
SM1 Charles Barkley	.50
SM2 Michael Jordan	4.00
SM3 Karl Malone	.40
SM4 Hakeem Olajuwon	.75
SM5 John Stockton	.40
SM6 Patrick Ewing	.40
SM7 Reggie Miller	.40
SM8 David Robinson	.75
SM9 Dennis Rodman	2.00
SM10 Damon Stoudamire	1.00
SM11 Brent Barry	.20
SM12 Tim Legler	.20
SM13 Jason Kidd	.75
SM14 Terrell Brandon	.20
SM15 Allen Iverson	4.00

1996-97 Stadium Club Mega Heroes

This nine-card insert set was found in one per 20 retail packs of Series II Stadium Club. The cards featured an NBA star on a colorful, foil-etched background with the player's nickname printed across the bottom. The cards were numbered with an "MH" prefix.

	MT
Complete Set (9):	30.00
Common Player:	1.00
MH1 Dennis Rodman	10.00
MH2 David Robinson	4.00
MH3 Karl Malone	2.00
MH4 Clyde Drexler	2.50
MH5 Anfernee Hardaway	15.00
MH6 Hakeem Olajuwon	6.00
MH7 Charles Oakley	1.00
MH8 Joe Smith	4.00
MH9 Glenn Robinson	2.00

1996-97 Stadium Club Members Only

The 45 Stadium Club cards reflect the NBA's elite veteran players, showcasing at least one player from each team. The five Finest Cards represent Topps' selection of the top rookies from the 1995 NBA Draft.

		MT
Complete Set (50):		15.00
Common Player:		.10
1	Magic Johnson	1.50
2	Steve Smith	.10
3	Scottie Pippen	1.00
4	David Robinson	.75
5	Jason Kidd	.50
6	Dikembe Mutombo	.10
7	Sean Elliott	.10
8	Rik Smits	.10
9	Brian Grant	.10
10	Hakeem Olajuwon	1.00
11	Greg Anthony	.10
12	Mitch Richmond	.20
13	Clyde Drexler	.40
14	Mahmoud Abdul-Rauf	.10
15	Larry Johnson	.20
16	Mookie Blaylock	.10
17	Clarence Weatherspoon	.10
18	Grant Hill	2.00
19	Vin Baker	.30
20	Patrick Ewing	.30
21	Charles Barkley	.50
22	Glenn Robinson	.30
23	Dino Radja	.10
24	Charles Oakley	.10
25	Anfernee Hardaway	1.75
26	Jamal Mashburn	.10
27	John Stockton	.30
28	Isaiah Rider	.10
29	Cedric Ceballos	.10
30	Shaquille O'Neal	1.75
31	Shawn Kemp	1.00
32	Juwan Howard	.75
33	Alonzo Mourning	.20
34	Tom Gugliotta	.10
35	Karl Malone	.30
36	Cliff Robinson	.10
37	Chris Webber	.75
38	Latrell Sprewell	.40
39	Loy Vaught	.10
40	Michael Jordan	4.00
41	Reggie Miller	.30
42	Terrell Brandon	.20
43	Armon Gilliam	.10
44	Gary Payton	.30
45	Glen Rice	.20
46	Jerry Stackhouse	.40
47	Michael Finley	.20
48	Joe Smith	.40
49	Damon Stoudamire	.75
50	Brent Barry	.20

1996-97 Stadium Club Rookie Showcase

This 25-card insert set was found in Series II hobby and retail packs at a rate of one per 12 packs. The cards are printed on plastic with horizontal fronts and vertical backs. Fronts have a color picture of the player on the left third, with a holographic image taking up most of the remaining room, except for a strip on the right with basketballs containing the insert name. Backs carry an "RS" prefix on the card number.

	MT
Complete Set (25):	100.00
Common Player:	1.50
RS1 Marcus Camby	12.00
RS2 Shareef Abdur-Rahim	15.00
RS3 Stephon Marbury	20.00
RS4 Ray Allen	10.00
RS5 Antoine Walker	15.00
RS6 Lorenzen Wright	1.50
RS7 Kerry Kittles	8.00
RS8 Samaki Walker	1.50
RS9 Erick Dampier	1.50
RS10 Todd Fuller	1.50
RS11 Kobe Bryant	25.00
RS12 Steve Nash	1.50
RS13 Tony Delk	1.50
RS14 Jermaine O'Neal	5.00
RS15 John Wallace	4.00
RS16 Walter McCarty	1.50
RS17 Dontae Jones	1.50
RS18 Roy Rogers	1.50
RS19 Derek Fisher	1.50
RS20 Martin Muursepp	1.50
RS21 Jerome Williams	1.50
RS22 Brian Evans	1.50
RS23 Priest Lauderdale	1.50
RS24 Travis Knight	1.50
RS25 Allen Iverson	25.00

1996-97 Stadium Club Rookies I

Rookies I cards were inserted into packs of Series I Stadium Club and numbered R1-R25. Although they were an insert, Rookies were actually considered part of the regular-issue set, which is why no odds are listed. There is also a Rookies set in Series II, however Rookies I cards are identified by the word Rookie running up the right side of the card without a border and the Stadium Club logo is in the upper right corner.

	MT
Complete Set (25):	20.00
Common Player:	.20
R1 Allen Iverson	4.00
R2 Marcus Camby	3.00
R3 Shareef Abdur-Rahim	3.00
R4 Stephon Marbury	4.00
R5 Ray Allen	2.50
R6 Antoine Walker	3.00
R7 Lorenzen Wright	.50
R8 Kerry Kittles	1.50
R9 Samaki Walker	.75
R10 Erick Dampier	.75
R11 Todd Fuller	.40
R12 Kobe Bryant	6.00
R13 Steve Nash	.75
R14 Tony Delk	.50
R15 Jermaine O'Neal	1.00
R16 John Wallace	1.00
R17 Walter McCarty	.20
R18 Dontae Jones	.20
R19 Roy Rogers	.20
R20 Derek Fisher	.50
R21 Martin Muursepp	.20
R22 Jerome Williams	.20
R23 Brian Evans	.20
R24 Priest Lauderdale	.20
R25 Travis Knight	.50

1996-97 Stadium Club Rookies II

Rookies II, like Rookies I, was considered part of the regular-issue set but is numbered as an insert, which is why no insertion ratio is given. Rookies II cards were found in Series II Stadium Club packs, numbered R1-R20 and featured a thick strip running down the left side of the card with the word "Rookie" inside it and the Stadium Club logo in the lower left corner.

	MT
Complete Set (20):	20.00
Common Player:	.20
R1 Shareef Abdur-Rahim	3.00
R2 Tony Delk	.20
R3 Priest Lauderdale	.20
R4 Roy Rogers	.20
R5 Lorenzen Wright	.20
R6 Stephon Marbury	4.00
R7 Derek Fisher	.20
R8 John Wallace	.20
R9 Kobe Bryant	5.00
R10 Kerry Kittles	2.00
R11 Antoine Walker	3.00
R12 Steve Nash	.20
R13 Erick Dampier	.20
R14 Walter McCarty	.20
R15 Vitaly Potapenko	.20
R16 Allen Iverson	4.00
R17 Marcus Camby	3.00
R18 Todd Fuller	.20
R19 Ray Allen	2.00
R20 Jermaine O'Neal	1.00

1996-97 Stadium Club Special Forces

This 10-card insert set is numbered SF1-SF10 and was inserted one per 20 Series I retail packs. Fronts feature a foil-etched action shot with multi-colored stars in the background.

	MT
Complete Set (10):	130.00
Common Player:	5.00
SF1 Anfernee Hardaway	20.00
SF2 Grant Hill	20.00
SF3 Shawn Kemp	10.00
SF4 Michael Jordan	40.00
SF5 Shaquille O'Neal	20.00
SF6 Scottie Pippen	10.00
SF7 Damon Stoudamire	10.00
SF8 Jerry Stackhouse	8.00
SF9 Gary Payton	5.00
SF10 Dennis Rodman	18.00

1996-97 Stadium Club Top Crop

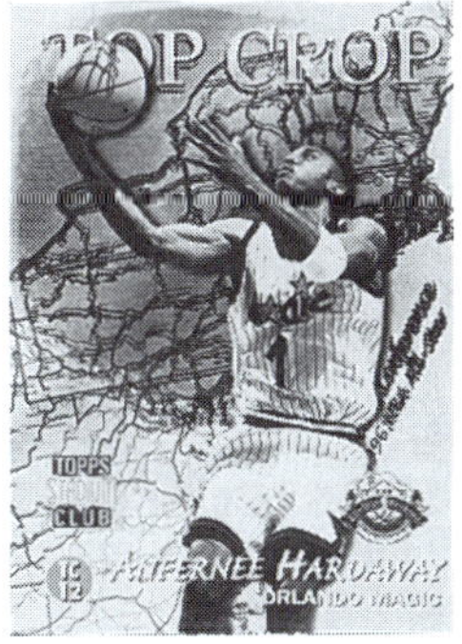

Top Crop matches two star players that play the same position on a holographic foil, double-sided card. Top Crop inserts are numbered TC1-TC10, and were inserted into Series I packs at a rate of one per 24 hobby packs and one per 20 retail packs.

	MT
Complete Set (12):	120.00
Common Player:	3.00
TC1 Shaquille O'Neal, Hakeem Olajuwon	20.00
TC2 Alonzo Mourning, Dikembe Mutombo	5.00
TC3 Patrick Ewing, David Robinson	7.00
TC4 Grant Hill, Sean Elliott	15.00
TC5 Scottie Pippen, Shawn Kemp	18.00
TC6 Vin Baker, Karl Malone	3.00
TC7 Juwan Howard, Charles Barkley	8.00
TC8 Glen Rice, Clyde Drexler	3.00
TC9 Michael Jordan, Gary Payton	40.00
TC10 Terrell Brandon, John Stockton	6.00
TC11 Reggie Miller, Mitch Richmond	6.00
TC12 Anfernee Hardaway, Jason Kidd	20.00

1996-97 Stadium Club Welcome Additions

Welcome Additions was a 25-card set that was considered part of the regular-issue set, but numbered as an insert set, which is why no insertion rate is given. Welcome Additions have a holographic purple strip down the left side with the insert name. Card numbers contain a "WA" prefix.

	MT
Complete Set (25):	5.00
Common Player:	.15
WA1 Charles Barkley	.75
WA2 Armon Gilliam	.15
WA3 Larry Johnson	.15
WA4 Felton Spencer	.15
WA5 Isaiah Rider	.15
WA6 Kevin Willis	.15
WA7 Mahmoud Abdul-Rauf	.15
WA8 Chris Childs	.15
WA9 Robert Horry	.15
WA10 Dan Majerle	.15
WA11 Robert Pack	.15
WA12 Rod Strickland	.15
WA13 Tyrone Corbin	.15
WA14 Anthony Mason	.15
WA15 Derek Harper	.15
WA16 Kenny Anderson	.15
WA17 Hubert Davis	.15
WA18 Allan Houston	.15
WA19 Shaquille O'Neal	2.50
WA20 Brent Price	.15
WA21 Ervin Johnson	.15
WA22 Craig Ehlo	.15
WA23 Jalen Rose	.15
WA24 Oliver Miller	.15
WA25 Mark West	.15

1996-97 Upper Deck

There were two 180-card series in Upper Deck's 1996-97 release. Each regular card front has a full-bleed color action photo, with a bronze and silver foil trimmed border on the left. The player's team logo is in silver in a bronze box in the lower left corner; the Upper Deck logo, also in silver, is in the upper right corner. The player's name and position are in white letters along the left side. White letters are used on the front to give a description of the game from which the photo was taken. Subsets in Series I include 29 Building a Winner and 15 The Game in Picture, while Series II had 15 Dateline: NBA and 29 Dan Patrick's From Way Downtown. There were six inserts sets in Series I - Generation Excitement, Fast Break Connections, Michael Jordan Greater Heights, Predictors, Meet the Stars (one per three packs) and NBA Pickup Game (one per seven packs). There were also six inserts in Series II - four Autographs, Rookie Exclusives, Smooth Grooves, Rookie of the Year Commemortive Collection, Michael's Viewpoints and Predictors.

	MT
Complete Set (360):	50.00
Complete Series 1 (180):	30.00
Complete Series 2 (180):	20.00
Common Player:	.10
Series 1 Wax Box:	50.00
Series 2 Wax Box:	55.00
1 Mookie Blaylock	.10
2 Alan Henderson	.10
3 Christian Laettner	.10
4 Ken Norman	.10
5 Dee Brown	.10
6 Todd Day	.10
7 Rick Fox	.10
8 Dino Radja	.10
9 Dana Barros	.10
10 Eric Williams	.10
11 Scott Burrell	.10
12 Dell Curry	.10
13 Matt Geiger	.10
14 Glen Rice	.10
15 Ron Harper	.10
16 Michael Jordan	4.00
17 Luc Longley	.10
18 Toni Kukoc	.10
19 Dennis Rodman	2.00
20 Danny Ferry	.10
21 Tyrone Hill	.10
22 Bobby Phills	.10
23 Bob Sura	.10
24 Tony Dumas	.10
25 George McCloud	.10
26 Jim Jackson	.20
27 Jamal Mashburn	.20
28 Loren Meyer	.10
29 Dale Ellis	.10
30 LaPhonso Ellis	.10
31 Tom Hammonds	.10
32 Antonio McDyess	.50
33 Joe Dumars	.10
34 Grant Hill	2.00
35 Lindsey Hunter	.10
36 Terry Mills	.10
37 Theo Ratliff	.10
38 B.J. Armstrong	.10
39 Donyell Marshall	.10
40 Chris Mullin	.10
41 Rony Seikaly	.10
42 Joe Smith	.50
43 Sam Cassell	.10
44 Clyde Drexler	.50
45 Mario Elie	.10
46 Robert Horry	.10
47 Travis Best	.10
48 Antonio Davis	.10
49 Dale Davis	.10
50 Eddie Johnson	.10
51 Derrick McKey	.10
52 Reggie Miller	.40
53 Brent Barry	.10
54 Lamond Murray	.10
55 Eric Piatkowski	.10
56 Rodney Rogers	.10
57 Loy Vaught	.10
58 Kobe Bryant	5.00
59 Eddie Jones	.20
60 Elden Campbell	.10
61 Shaquille O'Neal	2.00
62 Nick Van Exel	.20
63 Keith Askins	.10
64 Rex Chapman	.10
65 Sasha Danilovic	.10
66 Alonzo Mourning	.30
67 Kurt Thomas	.10
68 Tim Hardaway	.10
69 Ray Allen	2.00
70 Johnny Newman	.10
71 Shawn Respert	.10
72 Glenn Robinson	.40
73 Tom Gugliotta	.10
74 Stephon Marbury	4.00
75 Terry Porter	.10
76 Doug West	.10
77 Shawn Bradley	.10
78 Kevin Edwards	.10
79 Vern Fleming	.10
80 Ed O'Bannon	.10
83 Patrick Ewing	.40
84 Charlie Ward	.10
85 Nick Anderson	.10
86 Anfernee Hardaway	2.50
87 Jon Koncak	.10
88 Donald Royal	.10
89 Brian Shaw	.10
90 Derrick Coleman	.10
91 Allen Iverson	4.00
92 Jerry Stackhouse	.75
93 Clarence Weatherspoon	.20
94 Charles Barkley	.50
95 Kevin Johnson	.10
96 Danny Manning	.10
97 Elliot Perry	.10
98 Wayman Tisdale	.10
99 Randolph Childress	.10
100 Aaron McKie	.10
101 Arvydas Sabonis	.25
102 Gary Trent	.10
103 Chris Dudley	.10
104 Tyus Edney	.10
105 Brian Grant	.10
106 Bobby Hurley	.10
107 Olden Polynice	.10
108 Corliss Williamson	.10
109 Vinny Del Negro	.10
110 Avery Johnson	.10
111 Will Perdue	.10
112 David Robinson	.75
113 Hersey Hawkins	.10
114 Shawn Kemp	1.00
115 Nate McMillan	.10
116 Detlef Schrempf	.10
117 Gary Payton	.20
118 Marcus Camby	2.50
119 Zan Tabak	.10
120 Damon Stoudamire	1.25
121 Carlos Rogers	.10
122 Sharone Wright	.10
123 Antoine Carr	.10
124 Jeff Hornacek	.10
125 Adam Keefe	.10
126 Chris Morris	.10
127 John Stockton	.40
128 Blue Edwards	.10
129 Shareef Abdur-Rahim	2.50
130 Bryant Reeves	.30
131 Roy Rogers	.20
132 Calbert Cheaney	.10
133 Tim Legler	.10
134 Gheorghe Muresan	.10
135 Chris Webber	.30
136 Atlanta	.10
137 Boston	.10
138 Charlotte	.10
139 Chicago	1.00
140 Cleveland	.10
141 Dallas	.25
142 Denver	.25
143 Detroit	.50
144 Golden State	.20
145 Houston	.50
146 Indiana	.20
147 Los Angeles Clippers	.10
148 Los Angeles Lakers	.75
149 Miami	.10
150 Milwaukee	.10
151 Minnesota	.40
152 New Jersey	.10
153 New York	.10
154 Orlando	.50
155 Philadelphia	.25
156 Phoenix	.10
157 Portland	.10
158 Sacramento	.10
159 San Antonio	.30
160 Seattle	.40
161 Toronto	.30
162 Utah	.30
163 Vancouver	.40
164 Washington	.25
165 Michael Jordan	2.00
166 Corliss Williamson	.10
167 Dell Curry	.10
168 John Starks	.10
169 Clyde Drexler	.25
170 Chris Webber, Latrell Sprewell	.10
171 Cedric Ceballos	.10
172 Theo Ratliff	.10
173 Anfernee Hardaway	1.00
174 Grant Hill	.75
175 Alonzo Mourning	.10
176 Shawn Kemp	.50
177 Jason Kidd	.20
178 Avery Johnson	.10

179	Gary Payton	.10
180	Checklist	.10
181	*Priest Lauderdale*	.10
182	Dikembe Mutombo	.10
183	Eldridge Recasner	.10
184	Steve Smith	.10
185	Pervis Ellison	.10
186	Greg Minor	.10
187	*Antoine Walker*	2.00
188	David Wesley	.10
189	Muggsy Bogues	.10
190	*Tony Delk*	.50
191	Vlade Divac	.10
192	Anthony Mason	.10
193	George Zidek	.10
194	Jason Caffey	.10
195	Steve Kerr	.10
196	Robert Parish	.10
197	Scottie Pippen	1.00
198	Terrell Brandon	.10
199	Antonio Lang	.10
200	Chris Mills	.10
201	*Vitaly Potapenko*	.10
202	Mark West	.10
203	Chris Gatling	.10
204	Derek Harper	.10
205	Jason Kidd	.40
206	Eric Montross	.10
207	*Samaki Walker*	.40
208	Mark Jackson	.10
209	Ervin Johnson	.10
210	Sarunas Marciulionis	.10
211	Ricky Pierce	.10
212	Bryant Stith	.10
213	Stacey Augmon	.10
214	Grant Long	.10
215	Rick Mahorn	.10
216	Otis Thorpe	.10
217	*Jerome Williams*	.10
218	Bimbo Coles	.10
219	*Todd Fuller*	.20
220	Mark Price	.10
221	Felton Spencer	.10
222	Latrell Sprewell	.25
223	Charles Barkley	.50
224	*Othella Harrington*	.10
225	Hakeem Olajuwon	.75
226	*Matt Maloney*	.30
227	Kevin Willis	.10
228	*Erick Dampier*	.40
229	Duane Ferrell	.10
230	Jalen Rose	.10
231	Rik Smits	.10
232	Terry Dehere	.10
233	Charles Outlaw	.10
234	Pooh Richardson	.10
235	Malik Sealy	.10
236	*Lorenzen Wright*	.10
237	Cedric Ceballos	.10
238	*Derek Fisher*	.30
239	*Travis Knight*	.30
240	Sean Rooks	.10
241	Byron Scott	.10
242	P.J. Brown	.10
243	*Voshon Lenard*	.25
244	Dan Majerle	.10
245	*Martin Muursepp*	.10
246	Gary Grant	.10
247	Vin Baker	.30
248	Armon Gilliam	.10
249	Andrew Lang	.10
250	Elliot Perry	.10
251	Kevin Garnett	2.00
252	*Shane Heal*	.10
253	Cherokee Parks	.10
254	*Stojko Vrankovic*	.10
255	Kendall Gill	.10
256	*Kerry Kittles*	1.50
257	Xavier McDaniel	.10
258	Robert Pack	.10
259	Chris Childs	.10
260	Allan Houston	.10
261	Larry Johnson	.20
262	*Dontae Jones*	.25
263	*Walter McCarty*	.10
264	Charles Oakley	.10
265	*John Wallace*	.75
266	Buck Williams	.10
267	Brian Evans	.10
268	Horace Grant	.10
269	Dennis Scott	.10
270	Rony Seikaly	.10
271	David Vaughn	.10
272	Michael Cage	.10
273	Lucious Harris	.10
274	Don MacLean	.10
275	Mark Davis	.10
276	Sam Cassell	.10
277	Michael Finley	.25

278	A.C. Green	.10
279	Robert Horry	.10
280	*Steve Nash*	.40
281	Wesley Person	.10
282	Kenny Anderson	.10
283	*Aleksandar Djordjevic*	.10
284	*Jermaine O'Neal*	.75
285	Isaiah Rider	.10
296	Clifford Robinson	.10
287	Rasheed Wallace	.10
288	Mahmoud Abdul-Rauf	.10
289	Billy Owens	.10
290	Mitch Richmond	.25
291	Michael Smith	.10
292	Cory Alexander	.10
293	Sean Elliott	.10
294	Vernon Maxwell	.10
295	Dominique Wilkins	.10
296	Craig Ehlo	.10
297	Jim McIlvaine	.10
298	Sam Perkins	.10
299	Steve Scheffler	.10
300	Hubert Davis	.10
301	Popeye Jones	.10
302	Donald Whiteside	.10
303	Walt Williams	.10
304	Karl Malone	.30
305	Greg Ostertag	.10
306	Bryon Russell	.10
307	Jamie Watson	.10
308	Greg Anthony	.10
309	George Lynch	.10
310	Lawrence Moten	.10
311	Anthony Peeler	.10
312	Juwan Howard	.50
313	Tracy Murray	.10
314	Rod Strickland	.10
315	Harvey Grant	.10
316	Charles Barkley	.25
317	Clyde Drexler	.20
318	Dikembe Mutombo	.10
319	Larry Johnson	.10
320	Shaquille O'Neal	1.25
321	Mookie Blaylock	.10
322	Tim Hardaway	.10
323	Dennis Rodman	.75
324	Dan Majerle	.10
325	Stacey Augmon	.10
326	Anthony Mason	.10
327	Kenny Anderson	.10
328	Mahmoud Abdul-Rauf	.10
329	Chris Webber	.25
330	Dominique Wilkins	.10
331	Dikembe Mutombo	.10
332	Dana Barros	.10
333	Glen Rice	.10
334	Dennis Rodman	.75
335	Terrell Brandon	.10
336	Jason Kidd	.20
337	Antonio McDyess	.10
338	Grant Hill	1.00
339	Joe Smith	.25
340	Charles Barkley	.25
341	Reggie Miller	.20
342	Brent Barry	.10
343	Shaquille O'Neal	1.25
344	Alonzo Mourning	.20
345	Glenn Robinson	.10
346	Stephon Marbury	1.50
347	Kerry Kittles	.75
348	Patrick Ewing	.10
349	Anfernee Hardaway	1.00
350	Allen Iverson	2.00
351	Danny Manning	.10
352	Arvydas Sabonis	.10
353	Mitch Richmond	.10
354	David Robinson	.25
355	Shawn Kemp	.40
356	Marcus Camby	1.25
357	Karl Malone	.10
358	Shareef Abdur-Rahim	1.00
359	Gheorghe Muresan	.10
360	Checklist	.10

1996-97 Upper Deck Michael Jordan- Greater Heights

These 1996-97 Upper Deck Series I inserts focus on one of the greatest NBA players ever - Michael Jordan. Many of his spectacular drives to the hoop are featured on these cards, seeded one per every 71 packs. The card number uses a "GH" prefix.

	MT
Complete Set (10):	200.00
Common Player:	20.00
GH1 Michael Jordan	20.00
GH2 Michael Jordan	20.00
GH3 Michael Jordan	20.00
GH4 Michael Jordan	20.00
GH5 Michael Jordan	20.00
GH6 Michael Jordan	20.00
GH7 Michael Jordan	20.00
GH8 Michael Jordan	20.00
GH9 Michael Jordan	20.00
GH10 Michael Jordan	20.00

1996-97 Upper Deck Michael's Viewpoints

The 10-card, laser-engraved set is inserted every 34 packs and features Michael Jordan's views on different game subjects such as halftime, talking with the media, shooting free throws and handling pressure. The horizontal design has two color photos on the front with a Jordan quote and a die-cut image of Jordan flying toward the hoop in the upper left corner. The backs have another Jordan quote with an action shot. A silver-foil "MVP 23" logo is on the front with the same logo in gray print also found on the back.

	MT
Complete Set (10):	160.00
Common Player:	16.00
VP1 Michael Jordan	16.00
VP2 Michael Jordan	16.00
VP3 Michael Jordan	16.00
VP4 Michael Jordan	16.00
VP5 Michael Jordan	16.00
VP6 Michael Jordan	16.00
VP7 Michael Jordan	16.00
VP8 Michael Jordan	16.00
VP9 Michael Jordan	16.00
VP10 Michael Jordan	16.00

1996-97 Upper Deck Fast Break

Ten of the NBA's most exciting fast break triple threats are featured on these 1996-97 Upper Deck inserts. Each set of three die-cut cards, each numbered using an FB preifx, combines into one oversized card. This

30-card insert set is seeded one card per every four retail packs, and one per every two magazine packs. Cards are numbered with an "FB" prefix.

	MT
Complete Set (30):	70.00
Common Player:	.75
FB1 Jim Jackson	3.00
FB2 Jason Kidd	4.00
FB3 Jamal Mashburn	3.00
FB4 Mario Elie	.75
FB5 Hakeem Olajuwon	6.00
FB6 Clyde Drexler	4.00
FB7 Cedric Ceballos	.75
FB8 Nick Van Exel	3.00
FB9 Eddie Jones	3.00
FB10 Danny Manning	.75
FB11 Michael Finley	2.00
FB12 Kevin Johnson	.75
FB13 Tyus Edney	.75
FB14 Brian Grant	.75
FB15 Mitch Richmond	.75
FB16 Sean Elliott	.75
FB17 David Robinson	5.00
FB18 Avery Johnson	.75
FB19 Shawn Kemp	8.00
FB20 Gary Payton	4.00
FB21 Detlef Schrempf	.75
FB22 Scottie Pippen	8.00
FB23 Michael Jordan	30.00
FB24 Toni Kukoc	.75
FB25 Sherman Douglas	.75
FB26 Glenn Robinson	3.00
FB27 Vin Baker	3.00
FB28 Jeff Hornacek	.75
FB29 John Stockton	3.00
FB30 Karl Malone	3.00

1996-97 Upper Deck Generation Excitement

Some of the game's top young stars are featured on these 1996-97 Upper Deck Series I die-cut inserts. Each card front has a color action photo of the player, with a closeup shot of him as the background. "Generation" is in the upper left corner; "Excitement" is in the lower left corner. The player's name is along the bottom. "Generation Excitement" and the Upper Deck logo are at the top. Cards, numbered using a "GE" prefix, were seeded one per every 36 packs.

	MT
Complete Set (20):	200.00
Common Player:	2.00
GE1 Steve Smith	2.00
GE2 Eric Williams	2.00
GE3 Jason Kidd	10.00
GE4 Antonio McDyess	10.00
GE5 Grant Hill	45.00
GE6 Joe Smith	14.00
GE7 Brent Barry	2.00
GE8 Eddie Jones	12.00
GE9 Vin Baker	6.00
GE10 Kevin Garnett	45.00
GE11 Ed O'Bannon	2.00
GE12 Anfernee Hardaway	45.00
GE13 Jerry Stackhouse	14.00
GE14 Michael Finley	10.00
GE15 Gary Trent	2.00
GE16 Tyus Edney	2.00
GE17 Sean Elliott	2.00
GE18 Shawn Kemp	20.00
GE19 Damon Stoudamire	20.00
GE20 Gheorghe Muresan	2.00

1996-97 Upper Deck Predictor

This interactive insert is based on the above-average game output of 30 NBA players. If the player reaches the performance goal printed on the front of the card, the card is a winner and can be redeemed for an SP-quality replacement. Cards were seeded one per every 23 Series I packs.

	MT
Complete Set (20):	100.00
Common Player:	3.00
P1 Mookie Blaylock	3.00
P2 Dino Radja	3.00
P3 Michael Jordan	30.00
P4 Terrell Brandon	3.00
P5 Jason Kidd	6.00
P6 Joe Dumars	3.00
P7 Joe Smith	6.00
P8 Hakeem Olajuwon	10.00
P9 Rik Smits	3.00
P10 Brent Barry	3.00
P11 Kurt Thomas	3.00
P12 Anfernee Hardaway	20.00
P13 Clarence Weatherspoon	3.00
P14 Clifford Robinson	3.00
P15 Mitch Richmond	6.00
P16 David Robinson	10.00
P17 Shawn Kemp	10.00
P18 Damon Stoudamire	8.00
P19 Karl Malone	6.00
P20 Bryant Reeves	3.00

1996-97 Upper Deck Predictor II

The 20-card insert set parallels in design the first series Predictor cards. Inserted every 25 packs, the player cards feature a statistic (such as 35 points) that the player had to reach during the 1996-97 season. The winning cards could then be traded in for an SP-quality card of the same player.

	MT
Complete Set (20):	80.00
Common Player:	1.50
P1 Glen Rice	2.00
P2 Michael Jordan	30.00
P3 Jamal Mashburn	1.50
P4 Antonio McDyess	1.50
P5 Charles Barkley	5.00
P6 Reggie Miller	2.00
P7 Shaquille O'Neal	15.00
P8 Alonzo Mourning	2.00
P9 Vin Baker	2.00
P10 Kevin Garnett	15.00
P11 Kerry Kittles	3.00
P12 Patrick Ewing	2.00
P13 Anfernee Hardaway	15.00
P14 Allen Iverson	8.00
P15 Robert Horry	1.50
P16 Shawn Kemp	6.00
P17 Marcus Camby	3.00
P18 John Stockton	3.00
P19 Shareef Abdur-Rahim	5.00
P20 Juwan Howard	3.00

1996-97 Upper Deck Predictor TV Cels

TV Cels were available to collectors who redeemed their winning Predictor cards from Series I and II Upper Deck Basketball. The game ended 5/1/97, with cards redeemable if the player on the front equalled or exceeded the goal listed on the front of the card during the 1996-97 season.

	MT
TV Cels:	2x

1996-97 Upper Deck Rookie Exclusives

Inserted every four packs, the 20-card insert set features a basketball, leather-grain face with the player's last name featured in black in the upper right corner (the first name is in silver foil). "Exclusives 97" is printed in silver foil up the right edge. The backs feature Q & A and a player close-up and are numbered with an "R" prefix.

1996-97 Upper Deck Rookie of the Year

The die-cut Commemorative Collection cards feature silver-foil printing with "Rookie Of The Year" printed along the left border and "Commemorative Collection" printed down the right border. The card front features a player cut-out design with the backs having rookie season highlights the player's rookie campaign. The cards are numbered with an "RC" prefix.

	MT
Complete Set (14):	300.00
Common Player:	5.00
RC1 Damon Stoudamire	25.00
RC2 Grant Hill	60.00
RC3 Jason Kidd	10.00
RC4 Chris Webber	15.00
RC5 Shaquille O'Neal	50.00
RC6 Larry Johnson	5.00
RC7 Derrick Coleman	5.00
RC8 David Robinson	15.00
RC9 Mitch Richmond	5.00
RC10 Mark Jackson	5.00
RC11 Chuck Person	5.00
RC12 Patrick Ewing	10.00
RC13 Michael Jordan	120.00
RC14 Buck Williams	5.00

1996-97 Upper Deck Smooth Grooves

The 15-card insert set, inserted every 72 packs, honors the "slick" players of the league such as Jason Kidd, Damon Stoudamire, Allen Iverson, Vin Baker, Anfernee Hardaway and Kevin Garnett.

	MT
Complete Set (15):	350.00
Common Player:	5.00
SG1 Dennis Rodman	35.00
SG2 Jason Kidd	5.00
SG3 Grant Hill	40.00
SG4 Damon Stoudamire	10.00
SG5 Shaquille O'Neal	40.00
SG6 Clyde Drexler	10.00

	MT
Complete Set (20):	60.00
Common Player:	.75
R1 Allen Iverson	12.00
R2 John Wallace	2.00
R3 Kerry Kittles	4.00
R4 Roy Rogers	1.50
R5 Marcus Camby	8.00
R6 Antoine Walker	6.00
R7 Ray Allen	4.00
R8 Samaki Walker	1.50
R9 Walter McCarty	.75
R10 Kobe Bryant	15.00
R11 Shareef Abdur-Rahim	8.00
R12 Dontae Jones	.75
R13 Todd Fuller	.75
R14 Lorenzen Wright	.75
R15 Stephon Marbury	10.00
R16 Vitaly Potapenko	.75
R17 Tony Delk	1.50
R18 Steve Nash	1.50
R19 Jermaine O'Neal	2.50
R20 Erick Dampier	1.50

	MT
SG7 Shareef Abdur-Rahim	25.00
SG8 Michael Jordan	90.00
SG9 Alonzo Mourning	5.00
SG10 Allen Iverson	40.00
SG11 Vin Baker	5.00
SG12 Kevin Garnett	40.00
SG13 Anfernee Hardaway	40.00
SG14 Jerry Stackhouse	10.00
SG15 Shawn Kemp	25.00

1996-97 Collector's Choice II

Collector's Choice was issued in two, 200-card series in 1996-97. The cards feature an action shot of the player surrounded by a white border. The left side of the card has the player's name, position and team logo in a panel featuring black and the player's team's primary color. There is also a Collector's Choice logo in the upper right corner. Subsets in Series I include Anfernee Hardaway, Chicago Bulls' victory tour, 30 NBA Fundamentals and five checklists, while Series II included One on One, Assignment: Jordan, 30 NBA Playbook and five checklists. Inserts in Series I include: Mini Cards (reminiscent of the 1980-81 Topps set), Super Action Stick-Ums, You Crash the Game and an NBA Draft Trade Card. Inserts in Series II include: Super Action Stick-Ums, Mini Cards, You Crash the Game and an Update Trade Card.

	MT
Comp. Series 2 (200):	15.00
Common Player:	.05
Series 2 Wax Box:	30.00
201 Alan Henderson	.05
202 Steve Smith	.05
203 Donnie Boyce	.05
204 *Priest Lauderdale*	.10
205 Dikembe Mutombo	.05
206 Dee Brown	.05
207 Junior Burrough	.05
208 Todd Day	.05
209 Pervis Ellison	.05
210 Greg Minor	.05
211 *Antoine Walker*	1.00
212 Rafael Addison	.05
213 *Tony Delk*	.25
214 Vlade Divac	.05
215 Anthony Goldwire	.05
216 Anthony Mason	.05
217 Dickey Simpkins	.05
218 Randy Brown	.05
219 Jud Buechler	.05
220 Jason Caffey	.05
221 Scottie Pippen	.50
222 Bill Wennington	.05
223 Danny Ferry	.05
224 Antonio Lang	.05
225 Chris Mills	.05
226 *Vitaly Potapenko*	.15
227 Terry Davis	.05
228 Chris Gatling	.05
229 Jason Kidd	.30
230 George McCloud	.05
231 Eric Montross	.05
232 *Samaki Walker*	.20
233 Mark Jackson	.05
234 Ervin Johnson	.05
235 Sarunas Marciulionis	.05
236 Eric Murdock	.05

237	Ricky Pierce	.05
238	Bryant Stith	.05
239	Stacey Augmon	.05
240	Grant Hill	.75
241	Otis Thorpe	.05
242	*Jerome Williams*	.10
243	Andrew DeClerq	.05
244	*Todd Fuller*	.15
245	Mark Price	.05
246	Clifford Rozier	.05
247	Latrell Sprewell	.10
248	Charles Barkley	.25
249	Clyde Drexler	.20
250	*Othella Harrington*	.15
251	Sam Mack	.05
252	Kevin Willis	.05
253	*Erick Dampier*	.15
254	Antonio Davis	.05
255	Dale Davis	.05
256	Duane Ferrell	.05
257	Reggie Miller	.20
258	Jalen Rose	.05
259	Reggie Williams	.05
260	Terry Dehere	.05
261	Charles Outlaw	.05
262	Stanley Roberts	.05
263	Malik Sealy	.05
264	Loy Vaught	.05
265	*Lorenzen Wright*	.20
266	Corie Blount	.05
267	*Kobe Bryant*	2.00
268	Elden Campbell	.05
269	*Derek Fisher*	.25
270	Shaquille O'Neal	1.00
271	Nick Van Exel	.10
272	P.J. Brown	.05
273	Tim Hardaway	.05
274	*Voshon Lenard*	.15
275	Dan Majerle	.05
276	Alonzo Mourning	.10
277	*Martin Muursepp*	.10
278	*Ray Allen*	.75
279	Elliot Perry	.05
280	Glenn Robinson	.20
281	*Stephon Marbury*	1.25
282	Cherokee Parks	.05
283	Doug West	.05
284	Michael Williams	.05
285	*Kerry Kittles*	.50
286	Ed O'Bannon	.05
287	Robert Pack	.05
288	Khalid Reeves	.05
289	David Benoit	.05
290	Patrick Ewing	.20
291	Allan Houston	.05
292	Larry Johnson	.10
293	*Dontae Jones*	.10
294	*Walter McCarty*	.15
295	*John Wallace*	.30
296	Charlie Ward	.05
297	*Brian Evans*	.10
298	Horace Grant	.05
299	Jon Koncak	.05
300	Felton Spencer	.05
301	*Allen Iverson*	2.00
302	Don MacLean	.05
303	Scott Williams	.05
304	Sam Cassell	.05
305	Michael Finley	.20
306	Robert Horry	.05
307	Kevin Johnson	.05
308	Joe Kleine	.05
309	Danny Manning	.05
310	*Steve Nash*	.25
311	John Williams	.05
312	Kenny Anderson	.05
313	Randolph Childress	.05
314	Chris Dudley	.05
315	*Jermaine O'Neal*	.30
316	Isaiah Rider	.05
317	Clifford Robinson	.05
318	Rasheed Wallace	.10
319	Mahmoud Abdul-Rauf	.05
320	Duane Causwell	.05
321	Bobby Hurley	.05
322	Mitch Richmond	.10
323	Lionel Simmons	.05
324	Michael Smith	.05
325	Dominique Wilkins	.05
326	Cory Alexander	.05
327	Greg Anderson	.05
328	Carl Herrera	.05
329	David Robinson	.30
330	Charles Smith	.05
331	Craig Ehlo	.05
332	Sherell Ford	.05
333	Shawn Kemp	.50
334	Jim McIlvaine	.05
335	Gary Payton	.15
336	Sam Perkins	.05
337	Eric Snow	.05

338	David Wingate	.05
339	*Marcus Camby*	1.25
340	Acie Earl	.05
341	Carlos Rogers	.05
342	Greg Ostertag	.05
343	Bryon Russell	.05
344	John Stockton	.20
345	Jamie Watson	.05
346	*Shareef Abdur-Rahim*	1.25
347	Doug Edwards	.05
348	George Lynch	.05
349	Eric Mobley	.05
350	Anthony Peeler	.05
351	*Roy Rogers*	.25
352	Juwan Howard	.40
353	Harvey Grant	.05
354	Tracy Murray	.05
355	Rod Strickland	.05
356	One on One	1.00
357	One on One	.50
358	One on One	.40
359	One on One	.05
360	One on One	.25
361	NBA One on One	1.00
362	Nick Anderson, Michael Jordan	.50
363	Joe Dumars, Michael Jordan	.50
364	John Starks, Michael Jordan	.50
365	Reggie Miller, Michael Jordan	.50
366	Gary Payton, Michael Jordan	.50
367	Atlanta Hawks	.05
368	Boston Celtics	.05
369	Charlotte Hornets	.05
370	Chicago Bulls	.75
371	Cleveland Cavaliers	.05
372	Dallas Mavericks	.10
373	Denver Nuggets	.10
374	Detroit Pistons	.40
375	Golden State Warriors	.10
376	Houston Rockets	.75
377	Indiana Pacers	.10
378	Los Angeles Clippers	.05
379	Los Angeles Lakers	.05
380	Miami Heat	.05
381	Milwaukee Bucks	.30
382	Minnesota Timberwolves	.50
383	New Jersey Nets	.05
384	New York Knicks	.05
385	Orlando Magic	.75
386	Philadelphia 76ers	.20
387	Phoenix Suns	.05
388	Portland Trail Blazers	.05
389	Sacramento Kings	.05
390	San Antonio Spurs	.05
391	Seattle SuperSonics	.30
392	Toronto Raptors	.05
393	Utah Jazz	.05
394	Vancouver Grizzlies	.05
395	Washington Bullets	.05
396	Checklist #1	.05
397	Checklist #2	.05
398	Checklist #3	.05
399	Checklist #4	.05
400	Checklist #5	.05
NNO	NBA Update Trade Card	15.00
NNO	NBA Draft Trade Card	15.00

1996-97 Collector's Choice Mini-Cards II

Inserted in each pack of the second series, the 30-card insert set highlights three players on each horizontal card - identical to the first series mini cards. A gold -foil version was inserted very 35 packs.

		MT
	Complete Set (30):	10.00
	Common Player:	.10
1	Kevin Edwards, Doug West, Ken Norman	.10
2	B.J. Armstrong, Tim Hardaway, Steve Smith	.10
3	Sam Perkins, Danny Manning, Glen Rice	.10
4	Dana Barros, Reggie Miller, Steve Kerr	.10
5	Greg Minor, Lorenzen Wright, Samaki Walker	.40
6	Clarence Weatherspoon, Kevin Willis, LaPhonso Ellis	.10
7	Jason Caffey, Latrell Sprewell, Antonio McDyess	.10
8	Olden Polynice, Rodney Rogers, Bob Sura	.10
9	Kenny Anderson, Vinny Del Negro, Bryant Stith	.10
10	Ron Harper, Eddie Jones, Lindsey Hunter	.10
11	Antoine Carr, John Stockton, Otis Thorpe	.20
12	Gheorghe Muresan, Hakeem Olajuwon, Rik Smits	.50
13	Kevin Garnett, Jermaine O'Neal, Kobe Bryant	5.00
14	Patrick Ewing, Dikembe Mutombo, Alonzo Mourning	.30
15	Scottie Pippen, Jamal Mashburn, Vin Baker	.75
16	Wesley Person, Darrin Hancock, Stephon Marbury	.75
17	Kerry Kittles, Marcus Camby, Allan Houston	1.50
18	Antoine Walker, Walter McCarty, John Wallace	.75
19	Dale Davis, Elden Campbell, Horace Grant	.10
20	Mario Elie, Tim Legler, Donald Royal	.10
21	P.J. Brown, Antonio Davis, Brian Shaw	.10
22	Shaquille O'Neal, Joe Smith, Allen Iverson	3.00
23	Ray Allen, Scott Burrell, Clifford Robinson	.50
24	Hersey Hawkins, Will Perdue, Mitch Richmond	.10
25	Sean Elliott, Terrell Brandon, Gary Payton	.25
26	Tony Dumas, Johnny Newman, Doug Christie	.10
27	Khalid Reeves, Chris Mills, Shareef Abdur-Rahim	.50
28	Bryon Russell, Michael Smith, Lawrence Moten	.10
29	Damon Stoudamire, Michael Finley, Bryant Reeves	.50
30	Terry Mills, Loy Vaught, Juwan Howard	.10

1996-97 Collector's Choice Mini-Cards Gold

Gold versions of all 30 Series I Mini-cards were available at a rate of one per 35 packs. The gold versions featured gold foil stamping on the front.

	MT
Gold Cards:	4x-8x

1996-97 Collector's Choice Stick-Ums II

The 30-card insert set, found every three packs, featured decals of top players in a similar design with the first series Stick-Ums.

		MT
	Complete Set (30):	10.00
	Common Player:	.20
	Base Cards:	Half Price
S1	Steve Smith	.20
S2	Dino Radja	.20
S3	Glen Rice	.20
S4	Toni Kukoc	.20
S5	Bobby Phills	.20
S6	Jason Kidd	.50
S7	Antonio McDyess	.40
S8	Joe Dumars	.20
S9	Latrell Sprewell	.40
S10	Clyde Drexler	.75
S11	Reggie Miller	.50
S12	Loy Vaught	.20
S13	Eddie Jones	.40
S14	Alonzo Mourning	.40
S15	Glenn Robinson	.40
S16	Tom Gugliotta	.20
S17	Ed O'Bannon	.20
S18	John Starks	.20
S19	Anfernee Hardaway	2.00
S20	Jerry Stackhouse	1.00
S21	Kevin Johnson	.20
S22	Arvydas Sabonis	.20
S23	Brian Grant	.20
S24	Sean Elliott	.20
S25	Gary Payton	.40
S26	Zan Tabak	.20
S27	John Stockton	.40
S28	Greg Anthony	.20
S29	Juwan Howard	.40
S30	Michael Jordan	6.00

1996-97 Collector's Choice Crash the Game II

Inserted every five packs of second series Collector's Choice, the interactive cards rewarded collectors with prizes if the designated player scored over 30 points in the specified week. Gold versions were inserted every 49 packs.

		MT
	Complete Set (60):	60.00
	Common Player:	1.00
	Gold Cards:	2x-4x
C1	Steve Smith	1.00
C2	Dana Barros	1.00
C3	Tony Delk	1.00
C4	Toni Kukoc	1.00
C5	Bobby Phills	1.00
C6	Jamal Mashburn	1.00
C7	LaPhonso Ellis	1.00
C8	Jerome Williams	1.00
C9	Latrell Sprewell	2.00
C10	Clyde Drexler	2.00
C11	Dale Davis	1.00
C12	Brent Barry	1.00
C13	Nick Van Exel	1.00
C14	Sasha Danilovic	1.00
C15	Glenn Robinson	2.00
C16	Stephon Marbury	4.00
C17	Shawn Bradley	1.00
C18	John Wallace	1.00
C19	Anfernee Hardaway	5.00
C20	Jerry Stackhouse	2.00
C21	Danny Manning	1.00
C22	Arvydas Sabonis	1.00
C23	Brian Grant	1.00
C24	David Robinson	2.00
C25	Gary Payton	2.00
C26	Marcus Camby	3.00
C27	Karl Malone	2.00
C28	Shareef Abdur-Rahim	3.00
C29	Juwan Howard	1.00
C30	Michael Jordan	10.00

1996-97 SP

The 146-card, standard-size set was released in May of 1997 in eight-card packs retailing for $3.99 each. The base set includes the 20-card Premier Prospects subset with the remaining cards consisting of an average of five players from each team. Inserts in the set are Premium Collection Holoview, Inside-Info., NBA Game Film and SPx Force (with parallel autographed versions). The basic SP card has the set logo in the upper left corner and rainbow foil in a lower quadrant. The backs feature an action shot with a headshot inset, as well as bio and stat information.

		MT
Complete Set (146):		30.00
Common Player:		.10
Wax Box:		100.00
1	Mookie Blaylock	.10
2	Christian Laettner	.10
3	Dikembe Mutombo	.10
4	Steve Smith	.10
5	Dana Barros	.10
6	Rick Fox	.10
7	Dino Radja	.10
8	Eric Williams	.10
9	Dell Curry	.10
10	Vlade Divac	.10
11	Anthony Mason	.10
12	Glen Rice	.30
13	Scottie Pippen	1.25
14	Toni Kukoc	.20
15	Luc Longley	.10
16	Michael Jordan	5.00
17	Dennis Rodman	2.00
18	Terrell Brandon	.10
19	Tyrone Hill	.10
20	Bobby Phills	.10
21	Bob Sura	.10
22	Michael Finley	.30
23	A.C. Green	.10
24	Sam Cassell	.10
25	Derek Harper	.10
26	Dale Ellis	.10
27	LaPhonso Ellis	.10
28	Ervin Johnson	.10
29	Antonio McDyess	.30
30	Bryant Stith	.10
31	Joe Dumars	.20
32	Grant Hill	2.50
33	Lindsey Hunter	.10
34	Otis Thorpe	.10
35	Chris Mullin	.20
36	Mark Price	.10
37	Joe Smith	.60
38	Latrell Sprewell	.40
39	Charles Barkley	.50
40	Clyde Drexler	.40
41	Mario Elie	.10
42	Hakeem Olajuwon	1.00
43	Travis Best	.10
44	Dale Davis	.10
45	Reggie Miller	.30
46	Rik Smits	.10
47	Pooh Richardson	.10
48	Rodney Rogers	.10
49	Malik Sealy	.10
50	Loy Vaught	.10
51	Elden Campbell	.10
52	Robert Horry	.10
53	Eddie Jones	.75
54	Shaquille O'Neal	2.00
55	Nick Van Exel	.20
56	Sasha Danilovic	.10
57	Tim Hardaway	.20
58	Dan Majerle	.10
59	Alonzo Mourning	.30
60	Vin Baker	.30
61	Sherman Douglas	.10
62	Armon Gilliam	.10
63	Glenn Robinson	.30
64	Kevin Garnett	2.00
65	Tom Gugliotta	.10
66	Terry Porter	.10
67	Doug West	.10
68	Shawn Bradley	.10
69	Kendall Gill	.10
70	Robert Pack	.10
71	Jayson Williams	.10
72	Chris Childs	.10
73	Patrick Ewing	.30
74	Allan Houston	.10
75	Larry Johnson	.20
76	John Starks	.10
77	Nick Anderson	.10
78	Horace Grant	.10
79	Anfernee Hardaway	2.50
80	Dennis Scott	.10
81	Derrick Coleman	.10
82	Mark Davis	.10
83	Jerry Stackhouse	.40
84	Clarence Weatherspoon	.10
85	Cedric Ceballos	.10
86	Kevin Johnson	.10
87	Jason Kidd	.30
88	Danny Manning	.10
89	Wesley Person	.10
90	Kenny Anderson	.10
91	Isaiah Rider	.10
92	Clifford Robinson	.10
93	Arvydas Sabonis	.10
94	Rasheed Wallace	.10
95	Mahmoud Abdul-Rauf	.10
96	Brian Grant	.10
97	Olden Polynice	.10
98	Mitch Richmond	.30
99	Corliss Williamson	.10
100	Sean Elliott	.10
101	Avery Johnson	.10
102	David Robinson	.50
103	Dominique Wilkins	.10
104	Hersey Hawkins	.10
105	Jim McIlvaine	.10
106	Shawn Kemp	1.25
107	Gary Payton	.40
108	Detlef Schrempf	.10
109	Doug Christie	.10
110	Popeye Jones	.10
111	Damon Stoudamire	.75
112	Walt Williams	.10
113	Jeff Hornacek	.10
114	Karl Malone	.30
115	Greg Ostertag	.10
116	Bryon Russell	.10
117	John Stockton	.30
118	Greg Anthony	.10
119	Blue Edwards	.10
120	Anthony Peeler	.10
121	Bryant Reeves	.20
122	Calbert Cheaney	.10
123	Juwan Howard	.50
124	Gheorghe Muresan	.10
125	Rod Strickland	.10
126	Chris Webber	.60
127	Antoine Walker	2.00
	(Premier Prospects)	
128	Tony Delk	.40
	(Premier Prospects)	
129	Vitaly Potapenko	.20
	(Premier Prospects)	
130	Samaki Walker	.20
	(Premier Prospects)	
131	Todd Fuller	.20
	(Premier Prospects)	
132	Erick Dampier	.40
	(Premier Prospects)	
133	Lorenzen Wright	.20
	(Premier Prospects)	
134	Kobe Bryant	5.00
	(Premier Prospects)	
135	Derek Fisher	.60
	(Premier Prospects)	
136	Ray Allen	1.50
	(Premier Prospects)	
137	Stephon Marbury	3.00
	(Premier Prospects)	
138	Kerry Kittles	1.50
	(Premier Prospects)	
139	Walter McCarty	.20
	(Premier Prospects)	
140	John Wallace	.75
	(Premier Prospects)	
141	Allen Iverson	4.00
	(Premier Prospects)	
142	Steve Nash	.40
	(Premier Prospects)	
143	Jermaine O'Neal	1.00
	(Premier Prospects)	
144	Marcus Camby	2.50
	(Premier Prospects)	
145	Shareef Abdur-Rahim	2.50
	(Premier Prospects)	
146	Roy Rogers	.20
	(Premier Prospects)	

1996-97 SP Game Film

The 10-card insert set features actual slide photography and video film on the die-cut cards. Inserted every 120 packs, the cards feature two slides each with "NBA Game Film" printed in a lime green along the left border.

		MT
Complete Set (10):		350.00
Common Player:		8.00
GF1	Michael Jordan	120.00
GF2	Kevin Garnett	60.00
GF3	Charles Barkley	15.00
GF4	Anfernee Hardaway	60.00
GF5	Shaquille O'Neal	50.00
GF6	Jim Jackson	8.00
GF7	Dennis Rodman	50.00
GF8	Alonzo Mourning	8.00
GF9	Grant Hill	60.00
GF10	Shawn Kemp	30.00

1996-97 SP Holoviews

Inserted every 10 packs, the 40-card Holoview set features Upper Deck's Holoview technology. The cards are numbered with the "PC" prefix with a Light F/X action shot featured on the front.

		MT
Complete Set (40):		250.00
Common Player:		1.00
PC1	Mookie Blaylock	1.00
PC2	Antoine Walker	10.00
PC3	Eric Williams	1.00
PC4	Tony Delk	2.00
PC5	Michael Jordan	35.00
PC6	Dennis Rodman	15.00
PC7	Vitaly Potapenko	2.00
PC8	Bob Sura	1.00
PC9	Jamal Mashburn	2.00
PC10	Antonio McDyess	1.00
PC11	Grant Hill	15.00
PC12	Joe Smith	5.00
PC13	Latrell Sprewell	3.00
PC14	Charles Barkley	4.00
PC15	Hakeem Olajuwon	6.00
PC16	Erick Dampier	3.00
PC17	Lorenzen Wright	1.00
PC18	Kobe Bryant	25.00
PC19	Shaquille O'Neal	12.00
PC20	Alonzo Mourning	3.00
PC21	Ray Allen	8.00
PC22	Kevin Garnett	15.00
PC23	Stephon Marbury	16.00
PC24	Kerry Kittles	6.00
PC25	Walter McCarty	2.00
PC26	John Wallace	4.00
PC27	Anfernee Hardaway	15.00
PC28	Allen Iverson	20.00
PC29	Jerry Stackhouse	5.00
PC30	Steve Nash	1.00
PC31	Jermaine O'Neal	4.00
PC32	Brian Grant	1.00
PC33	Mitch Richmond	2.00
PC34	David Robinson	4.00
PC35	Shawn Kemp	8.00
PC36	Marcus Camby	12.00
PC37	Damon Stoudamire	8.00
PC38	John Stockton	3.00
PC39	Shareef Abdur-Rahim	12.00
PC40	Juwan Howard	5.00

1996-97 SP Inside Info

The 17-card insert set, seeded in each box, features a mini pull-out card within the standard-size card. The card fronts feature a Light F/X action shot with the mini pull-out card also having Light F/X treatment. The cards are numbered with the "IN" prefix and a gold version was inserted every 720 packs.

		MT
Complete Set (17):		250.00
Common Player:		4.00
IN1	Charles Barkley	8.00
IN2	Kevin Garnett	25.00
IN3	Anfernee Hardaway	30.00
IN4	Grant Hill	30.00
IN5	Allen Iverson	30.00
IN6	Jason Kidd	6.00
IN7	Shawn Kemp	15.00
IN8	Antonio McDyess	4.00
IN9	Dikembe Mutombo	4.00
IN10	Shaquille O'Neal	25.00
IN11	Hakeem Olajuwon	10.00
IN12	Dennis Rodman	25.00
IN13	Jerry Stackhouse	8.00
IN14	John Stockton	6.00
IN15	Damon Stoudamire	12.00
IN16	Chris Webber	10.00
25K	Michael Jordan	60.00

1997 SPx

The 50-card set, released in June of 1997, features die-cut cards in the shape of an "x" along the horizontal right side. The cards have the team colors of the player featured with a holoview headshot of the player and a Light F/X action shot along the left side. The player's number and position are located in the lower right corner with the SPx logo in the upper right corner. The horizontal card backs contain a color shot in the right half with statistics and career highlights on the left. A gold parallel of each card was inserted every nine packs. Inserts to the set are Holoview Heroes, NBA PROmotion and autographed NBA PROmotion parallels.

		MT
Complete Set (50):		110.00
Common Player:		.75
Wax Box:		100.00
1	Mookie Blaylock	.75
2	Antoine Walker	6.00
3	Eric Williams	.75
4	Tony Delk	.75
5	Michael Jordan	16.00
6	Dennis Rodman	6.00
7	Vitaly Potapenko	.75
8	Bob Sura	.75
9	Jamal Mashburn	.75
10	Samaki Walker	.75
11	Antonio McDyess	1.50
12	Joe Dumars	.75
13	Grant Hill	8.00
14	Joe Smith	2.50
15	Latrell Sprewell	1.50
16	Charles Barkley	2.00
17	Hakeem Olajuwon	3.00
18	Erick Dampier	.75
19	Reggie Miller	1.50
20	Brent Barry	.75
21	Lorenzen Wright	.75
22	Kobe Bryant	10.00
23	Eddie Jones	3.00
24	Shaquille O'Neal	5.00
25	Alonzo Mourning	1.50
26	Kurt Thomas	.75
27	Vin Baker	1.50
28	Glenn Robinson	1.50
29	Kevin Garnett	8.00
30	Stephon Marbury	8.00
31	Kerry Kittles	4.00
32	Patrick Ewing	1.50
33	John Wallace	2.00
34	Anfernee Hardaway	8.00
35	Allen Iverson	12.00
36	Jerry Stackhouse	2.50
37	Kevin Johnson	.75
38	Steve Nash	.75
39	Jermaine O'Neal	3.00
40	Mitch Richmond	1.50
41	David Robinson	2.00
42	Shawn Kemp	4.00
43	Gary Payton	2.00
44	Marcus Camby	6.00
45	Damon Stoudamire	4.00
46	Karl Malone	1.50
47	John Stockton	1.50
48	Shareef Abdur-Rahim	7.00
49	Bryant Reeves	.75
50	Juwan Howard	1.50

1997 SPx Gold

Gold versions of all 50 cards in the SPx set were produced featuring gold foil around the border. One per nine packs contained a Gold version.

	MT
Gold Cards:	2x-3x

1997 SPx Holoview Heroes

Inserted every 75 packs, the set features 20 of the top players in the league with a die-cut Holoview card. The left half of the vertical card features the Holoview action photo with the right side having a color action shot. "Holoview Heroes" is printed in a black stripe separating the two. The vertical backs have another color action shot with highlight text found on the left. The cards are numbered with the "H" prefix.

		MT
Complete Set (20):		600.00
Common Player:		10.00
H1	Michael Jordan	120.00
H2	Grant Hill	60.00
H3	Reggie Miller	10.00
H4	Joe Smith	18.00
H5	Kevin Garnett	60.00
H6	Mitch Richmond	10.00
H7	Allen Iverson	70.00
H8	Patrick Ewing	10.00
H9	Hakeem Olajuwon	20.00
H10	David Robinson	15.00
H11	Anfernee Hardaway	60.00
H12	Juwan Howard	10.00
H13	Gary Payton	15.00
H14	Dennis Rodman	45.00
H15	Shaquille O'Neal	40.00
H16	Charles Barkley	15.00
H17	Damon Stoudamire	30.00
H18	Shawn Kemp	30.00
H19	Glenn Robinson	10.00
H20	John Stockton	10.00

1997 SPx NBA Pro-Motion

The five-card insert set, seeded every 430 packs, features the same die-cut design as the base set with a double Holoview image of the player. The player's team name appears in the lower right corner with the player's number and position just to the left. Autographed versions of the cards were limited to 500 each.

		MT
Complete Set (4):		300.00
Common Player:		20.00
1	Michael Jordan	150.00
2	Damon Stoudamire	20.00
3	Anfernee Hardaway	75.00
4	Shawn Kemp	50.00

1996-97 Upper Deck UD3

The 60-card, standard-size set was issued in May of 1997 in three-card packs with a retail of $3.99. The inaugural edition of the retail-only release was packaged first in a foil wrapper and then in a matchbox-like cardboard container. The main set was broken into three 20-card sub-sets: Hardwood Prospects, NBA Star-Focus and Aerial Artists. Inserts in the set include the autographed Court Commemoratives, The Winning Edge and Super Star Spotlight.

		MT
Complete Set (60):		50.00
Common Player:		.25
Wax Box:		85.00
1	Kerry Kittles	1.25
2	Stephon Marbury	3.00
3	Jermaine O'Neal	1.00
4	Shareef Abdur-Rahim	2.50
5	Ray Allen	1.75
6	Antoine Walker	2.00
7	Erick Dampier	.25
8	Walter McCarty	.25
9	Todd Fuller	.25
10	Tony Delk	.25
11	Marcus Camby	2.50
12	John Wallace	.25
13	Vitaly Potapenko	.25
14	Allen Iverson	4.00
15	Steve Nash	.25
16	Derek Fisher	.25
17	Samaki Walker	.25
18	Roy Rogers	.25
19	Kobe Bryant	5.00
20	Lorenzen Wright	.25
21	Kevin Garnett	3.00
22	Hakeem Olajuwon	1.50
23	Michael Jordan	8.00
24	John Stockton	.25
25	Terrell Brandon	.25
26	Damon Stoudamire	1.50
27	Charles Barkley	1.00
28	Dikembe Mutombo	.25
29	Gary Payton	1.00
30	Patrick Ewing	.25
31	Dennis Rodman	3.00
32	Joe Smith	1.00
33	Grant Hill	4.00
34	Shaquille O'Neal	4.00
35	Kevin Johnson	.25
36	David Robinson	1.00
37	Juwan Howard	1.00
38	Mitch Richmond	.25
39	Alonzo Mourning	.25
40	Reggie Miller	.25
41	Shawn Kemp	2.00
42	Scottie Pippen	2.00
43	Kobe Bryant	5.00
44	Anfernee Hardaway	4.00
45	Brent Barry	.25
46	Glenn Robinson	.25
47	Karl Malone	.25
48	Chris Webber	1.00
49	Danny Manning	.25
50	Antonio McDyess	.25
51	Dominique Wilkins	.25
52	Vin Baker	.25
53	Isaiah Rider	.25
54	Eddie Jones	1.00
55	Glen Rice	.25
56	Larry Johnson	.25
57	Latrell Sprewell	.25
58	Sean Elliott	.25
59	Clyde Drexler	.25
60	Jerry Stackhouse	1.00

1996-97 Upper Deck UD3 Court Commemorative Autographs

The four-card inset set, seeded every 1,500 packs of UD3 Basketball, featured signed cards of Anfernee Hardaway, Shawn Kemp, Damon Stoudamire and Michael Jordan.

		MT
Complete Set (4):		2750.00
Common Player:		150.00
C1	Michael Jordan	2500.
C2	Damon Stoudamire	150.00
C3	Anfernee Hardaway	400.00
C4	Shawn Kemp	250.00

1996-97 Upper Deck UD3 SuperStar Spotlight

The 10-card insert set utilizes a special cel-chrome technology and was found every 144 packs. The set logo appears in the upper right corner with the circular cel-chrome in the middle. "Superstar" is printed in a blue stripe above the circle with "Spotlight" below in a blue stripe.

		MT
Complete Set (10):		600.00
Common Player:		15.00
S1	Shaquille O'Neal	50.00
S2	Alonzo Mourning	15.00
S3	Anfernee Hardaway	75.00
S4	Karl Malone	15.00
S5	Michael Jordan	150.00
S6	Hakeem Olajuwon	30.00
S7	Shawn Kemp	40.00
S8	Allen Iverson	75.00
S9	Dennis Rodman	50.00
S10	Charles Barkley	25.00

1996-97 Upper Deck UD3 Winning Edge

The 20-card insert set features Light F/X and highlights the characteristics that make the top players some of the best ever. "Winning" is featured prominently in red foil along the top border with a player close-up in the right corner in a small circle. The cards were inserted every 11 packs.

		MT
Complete Set (20):		120.00
Common Player:		2.00
W1	Michael Jordan	40.00
W2	Charles Barkley	5.00
W3	Reggie Miller	2.00
W4	Grant Hill	20.00
W5	Larry Johnson	2.00
W6	Hakeem Olajuwon	8.00
W7	Anfernee Hardaway	20.00

W8	Shaquille O'Neal	15.00
W9	Vin Baker	2.00
W10	Kevin Garnett	15.00
W11	Juwan Howard	6.00
W12	John Stockton	2.00
W13	Mookie Blaylock	2.00
W14	Shawn Kemp	10.00
W15	David Robinson	5.00
W16	Kevin Johnson	2.00
W17	Joe Dumars	2.00
W18	Marcus Camby	12.00
W19	Clyde Drexler	4.00
W20	Chris Webber	6.00

1997-98 Fleer

Fleer's 1997-98 Series I release included 200 cards all printed on matte finish. The fronts have full-bleed photos with the player's name, team and position printed in gold foil across the bottom and the Fleer logo in the upper right corner. Backs are white with a color photo at the top and statistics filling up the remainder. Inserts in Series I include: Fleer NBA Million Dollar Moments, Key Ingredients, Rookie Rewind, Flair Hardwood Legends, Decade of Excellence, Franchise Futures and Game Breakers, as well as two parallel sets called Tiffany Collection and Crystal Collection.

		MT
Complete Set (200):		20.00
Common Player:		.05
Wax Box:		45.00
1	Anfernee Hardaway	1.25
2	Mitch Richmond	.15
3	Allen Iverson	1.25
4	Chris Webber	.30
5	Sasha Danilovic	.05
6	Avery Johnson	.05
7	Kenny Anderson	.05
8	Antoine Walker	.50
9	Nick Van Exel	.10
10	Mookie Blaylock	.05
11	Wesley Person	.05
12	Vlade Divac	.05
13	Glenn Robinson	.15
14	Chris Mills	.05
15	Latrell Sprewell	.20
16	Jayson Williams	.05
17	Travis Best	.05
18	Charlie Ward	.05
19	Theo Ratliff	.05
20	Gary Payton	.20
21	Marcus Camby	.50
22	Clyde Drexler	.20
23	Michael Jordan	3.00
24	Antonio McDyess	.15
25	Stephon Marbury	1.00
26	Isaac Austin	.05
27	Shareef Abdur-Rahim	.75
28	Malik Sealy	.05
29	Arvydas Sabonis	.05
30	Kerry Kittles	.30
31	Reggie Miller	.20
32	Karl Malone	.25
33	Grant Hill	1.50
34	Hakeem Olajuwon	.50
35	Danny Ferry	.05
36	Dominique Wilkins	.05
37	Armon Gilliam	.05
38	Danny Manning	.05
39	Larry Johnson	.10
40	Dino Radja	.05

41	Jason Caffey	.05
42	Jerry Stackhouse	.30
43	Alonzo Mourning	.20
44	Shawn Bradley	.05
45	Bo Outlaw	.05
46	Bryon Russell	.05
47	Doug West	.05
48	Lawrence Moten	.05
49	Dale Ellis	.05
50	Kobe Bryant	1.50
51	Carlos Rogers	.05
52	Todd Fuller	.05
53	Tyus Edney	.05
54	Horace Grant	.05
55	Dikembe Mutombo	.05
56	Jim McIlvaine	.05
57	Harvey Grant	.05
58	Dean Garrett	.05
59	Samaki Walker	.05
60	Johnny Newman	.05
61	Antonio Davis	.05
62	Jamal Mashburn	.10
63	Muggsy Bogues	.05
64	Rod Strickland	.05
65	Craig Ehlo	.05
66	Rex Walters	.05
67	Bob Sura	.05
68	Travis Knight	.05
69	Toni Kukoc	.05
70	Antoine Carr	.05
71	Mario Elie	.05
72	Popeye Jones	.05
73	David Wesley	.05
74	John Wallace	.10
75	Calbert Cheaney	.05
76	Grant Long	.05
77	Will Perdue	.05
78	Rasheed Wallace	.05
79	Chris Gatling	.05
80	Corliss Williamson	.05
81	B.J. Armstrong	.05
82	Brian Shaw	.05
83	Darrick Martin	.05
84	Vinny Del Negro	.05
85	Tony Delk	.05
86	Greg Anthony	.05
87	Mark Davis	.05
88	Anthony Goldwire	.05
89	Rex Chapman	.05
90	Stojko Vrankovic	.05
91	Dennis Rodman	.75
92	Detlef Schrempf	.05
93	Henry James	.05
94	Tracy Murray	.05
95	Voshon Lenard	.05
96	Sharone Wright	.05
97	Ed O'Bannon	.05
98	Gerald Wilkins	.05
99	Kevin Willis	.05
100	Shaquille O'Neal	1.00
101	Jim Jackson	.10
102	Mark Price	.05
103	Patrick Ewing	.20
104	Lorenzen Wright	.05
105	Tyrone Hill	.05
106	Ray Allen	.30
107	Jermaine O'Neal	.20
108	Anthony Mason	.05
109	Mahmoud Abdul-Rauf	.05
110	Terry Mills	.05
111	Gheorghe Muresan	.05
112	Mark Jackson	.05
113	Greg Ostertag	.05
114	Kevin Johnson	.05
115	Anthony Peeler	.05
116	Rony Seikaly	.05
117	Keith Askins	.05
118	Todd Day	.05
119	Chris Childs	.05
120	Chris Carr	.05
121	Erick Strickland	.05
122	Elden Campbell	.05
123	Elliott Perry	.05
124	Pooh Richardson	.05
125	Juwan Howard	.25
126	Ervin Johnson	.05
127	Eric Montross	.05
128	Otis Thorpe	.05
129	Hersey Hawkins	.05
130	Bimbo Coles	.05
131	Olden Polynice	.05
132	Christian Laettner	.05
133	Sean Elliott	.05
134	Othella Harrington	.05
135	Erick Dampier	.05
136	Vitaly Potapenko	.05
137	Doug Christie	.05
138	Luc Longley	.05
139	Clarence Weatherspoon	.05
140	Gary Trent	.05
141	Shandon Anderson	.05

142	Sam Perkins	.05
143	Derek Harper	.05
144	Robert Horry	.05
145	Roy Rogers	.05
146	John Starks	.05
147	Tyrone Corbin	.05
148	Andrew Lang	.05
149	Derek Strong	.05
150	Joe Smith	.30
151	Ron Harper	.05
152	Sam Cassell	.05
153	Brent Barry	.05
154	LaPhonso Ellis	.05
155	Matt Geiger	.05
156	Steve Nash	.05
157	Michael Smith	.05
158	Eric Williams	.05
159	Tom Gugliotta	.05
160	Monty Williams	.05
161	Lindsey Hunter	.05
162	Oliver Miller	.05
163	Brent Price	.05
164	Derrick McKey	.05
165	Robert Pack	.05
166	Derrick Coleman	.05
167	Isaiah Rider	.05
168	Dan Majerle	.05
169	Jeff Hornacek	.05
170	Terrell Brandon	.05
171	Nate McMillan	.05
172	Cedric Ceballos	.05
173	Derek Fisher	.05
174	Rodney Rogers	.05
175	Blue Edwards	.05
176	Brooks Thompson	.05
177	Sherman Douglas	.05
178	Sam Mitchell	.05
179	Charles Oakley	.05
180	Greg Minor	.05
181	Chris Mullin	.05
182	P.J. Brown	.05
183	Stacey Augmon	.05
184	Don MacLean	.05
185	Aaron McKie	.05
186	Dale Davis	.05
187	Vernon Maxwell	.05
188	Dell Curry	.05
189	Kendall Gill	.05
190	Billy Owens	.05
191	Steve Kerr	.05
192	Matt Maloney	.10
193	Dennis Scott	.05
194	A.C. Green	.05
195	George McCloud	.05
196	Walt Williams	.05
197	Eldridge Recasner	.05
198	Checklist	.05
199	Checklist	.05
200	Checklist	.05

1997-98 Fleer Crystal

Crystal Collection paralleled the regular-issue Fleer set, and was inserted every two hobby packs. Crystal Collection contains silver foil printing and a small logo that reads "Traditions Crystal" in the upper right corner.

	MT
Complete Set (200):	120.00
Crystal Cards:	3x-6x

1997-98 Fleer Tiffany

This parallel set of Fleer was inserted at a rate of one per 20 hobby packs and contains each regular-issue card printed in holographic silver foil. The cards are identified by a Traditions Tiffany logo in the upper right corner.

	MT
Complete Set (200):	1000.00
Tiffany Cards:	25x-50x

1997-98 Fleer Decade of Excellence

This 10-card insert set features designs from the 1987-88 Fleer set and includes players that have been active for 10 years in the NBA. Decade of Excellence inserts were found in one per 36 hobby packs. Rare Traditions versions of these also exist with a special foil treatment.

		MT
Complete Set (12):		100.00
Common Player:		3.00
1	Charles Barkley	12.00
2	Clyde Drexler	8.00
3	Patrick Ewing	6.00
4	Kevin Johnson	3.00
5	Michael Jordan	50.00
6	Karl Malone	8.00
7	Reggie Miller	6.00
8	Hakeem Olajuwon	15.00
9	Scottie Pippen	25.00
10	Dennis Rodman	25.00
11	John Stockton	8.00
12	Dominique Wilkins	3.00

1997-98 Fleer Decade of Excellence Rare Traditions

Decade of Excellence inserts arrived in two different versions, regular and Rare Traditions. Rare Traditions versions featured a special foil treatment and were inserted every 360 hobby packs.

	MT
Complete Set (12):	300.00
Rare Tradition Cards:	1.5x-3x

1997-98 Fleer Flair Hardwood Leaders

Hardwood Leaders features one player from each of the 29 teams on a Flair-type card. The top and bottom of the card, as well as the border, give the appearance of wood grain, while the player's image is printed over a cloud background. The horizontal card back featured another shot of the player with text printed over the player's team logo and the border in a simulated wood grain style.

		MT
Complete Set (29):		55.00
Common Player:		.75
1	Christian Laettner	.75
2	Antoine Walker	4.00
3	Glen Rice	1.50
4	Michael Jordan	15.00
5	Terrell Brandon	.75
6	Michael Finley	1.50
7	Antonio McDyess	1.50
8	Grant Hill	8.00
9	Latrell Sprewell	2.00
10	Hakeem Olajuwon	3.00
11	Reggie Miller	1.50
12	Loy Vaught	.75
13	Shaquille O'Neal	6.00
14	Alonzo Mourning	1.50
15	Vin Baker	1.50
16	Kevin Garnett	8.00
17	Kerry Kittles	2.00
18	Patrick Ewing	1.50
19	Anfernee Hardaway	8.00
20	Jerry Stackhouse	2.00
21	Jason Kidd	1.50
22	Kenny Anderson	.75
23	Mitch Richmond	1.50
24	David Robinson	2.00
25	Shawn Kemp	4.00
26	Damon Stoudamire	2.50
27	Karl Malone	1.50
28	Shareef Abdur-Rahim	5.00
29	Chris Webber	2.00

1997-98 Fleer Franchise Futures

Franchise Futures was a 10-card insert that was found exclusively in retail packs at a rate of one per 36. The insert contained players who had less than three years of NBA experience and appeared to be the future of their teams.

		MT
Complete Set (10):		100.00
Common Player:		3.00
1	Shareef Abdur-Rahim	10.00
2	Ray Allen	3.00
3	Kobe Bryant	20.00
4	Kevin Garnett	20.00
5	Grant Hill	20.00
6	Juwan Howard	3.00
7	Allen Iverson	20.00
8	Kerry Kittles	3.00
9	Joe Smith	3.00
10	Damon Stoudamire	5.00

1997-98 Fleer Game Breakers

Inserted at one per 288 packs of Series I, Game Breakers included some of the NBA's most potent duos.

		MT
Complete Set (12):		600.00
Common Player:		15.00
1	Michael Jordan, Dennis Rodman	150.00
2	Joe Dumars, Grant Hill	80.00
3	Joe Smith, Latrell Sprewell	15.00
4	Charles Barkley, Hakeem Olajuwon	30.00
5	Eddie Jones, Shaquille O'Neal	60.00
6	Kevin Garnett, Stephon Marbury	80.00
7	Nick Anderson, Anfernee Hardaway	70.00
8	Allen Iverson, Jerry Stackhouse	60.00
9	Shawn Kemp, Gary Payton	45.00
10	Marcus Camby, Damon Stoudamire	40.00
11	Karl Malone, John Stockton	15.00
12	Juwan Howard, Chris Webber	25.00

1997-98 Fleer Key Ingredients

This 15-card insert featured players who are the "key ingredients" to their NBA teams. These inserts were found every two retail packs of Series I.

		MT
Complete Set (15):		10.00
Common Player:		.25
Gold Cards:		4x-8x

1	Charles Barkley	.50
2	Marcus Camby	1.00
3	Anfernee Hardaway	1.75
4	Juwan Howard	.50
5	Shawn Kemp	1.00
6	Karl Malone	.50
7	Stephon Marbury	1.50
8	Alonzo Mourning	.25
9	Shaquille O'Neal	1.50
10	Scottie Pippen	1.00
11	Mitch Richmond	.25
12	David Robinson	.50
13	Joe Smith	.50
14	Jerry Stackhouse	.50
15	Antoine Walker	1.00

1997-98 Fleer Rookie Rewind

This 10-card insert was inserted every four packs of Series I and contained the top rookies of the 1996 NBA Draft. The cards featured a color shot of the player, with the words "Rookie Rewind" in silver foil in a circular fashion.

		MT
Complete Set (10):		15.00
Common Player:		.50
1	Shareef Abdur-Rahim	2.50
2	Ray Allen	1.00
3	Kobe Bryant	5.00
4	Marcus Camby	2.00
5	Allen Iverson	4.00
6	Kerry Kittles	1.00
7	Matt Maloney	1.00
8	Stephon Marbury	3.00
9	Roy Rogers	.50
10	Antoine Walker	2.00

1997-98 Hoops

Hoops Series I had 165 cards, including two checklists in 1997-98. This release marked the return of Autographics to basketball for the second year, as well as Hoops move down to 99 cents versus its previous $1.29 suggested retail price. The cards featured the player over a water color-like background of team colors and a large team logo inside a solid white border. Backs captured another large shot of the player along with statistics on a white card. Inserts in Series I included: Talkin' Hoops, Dish N Swish, Chill with Hill, Frequent Flyer Club, Rookie Headliners, Autographics and Hooperstars.

		MT
Complete Set (165):		14.00
Common Player:		.05
Comp. Chill with Hill (10):		20.00
Chill with Hill Cards:		2.00
Wax Box:		30.00
1	Michael Jordan (league leader scoring)	1.50
2	Dennis Rodman (league leader rebounding)	.50
3	Mark Jackson (league leader assists)	.05
4	Shawn Bradley (league leader blocked shots)	.05
5	Glen Rice (league leader 3-pt shooting)	.05
6	Mookie Blaylock (league leader steals)	.05
7	Gheorghe Muresan (league leader FG%)	.05
8	Mark Price (league leader FT%)	.05
9	Tyrone Corbin	.05
10	Christian Laettner	.10
11	Priest Lauderdale	.05
12	Dikembe Mutombo	.10
13	Steve Smith	.05
14	Todd Day	.05
15	Rick Fox	.05
16	Brett Szabo	.05
17	Antoine Walker	.50
18	David Wesley	.05
19	Muggsy Bogues	.05
20	Dell Curry	.05
21	Tony Delk	.05
22	Anthony Mason	.05
23	Glen Rice	.15
24	Malik Rose	.05
25	Steve Kerr	.05
26	Toni Kukoc	.10
27	Luc Longley	.05
28	Robert Parish	.05
29	Scottie Pippen	.75
30	Dennis Rodman	1.00
31	Terrell Brandon	.10
32	Danny Ferry	.05
33	Tyrone Hill	.05
34	Bobby Phills	.05
35	Vitaly Potapenko	.05
36	Shawn Bradley	.05
37	Sasha Danilovic	.05
38	Derek Harper	.05
39	Martin Muursepp	.05
40	Robert Pack	.05
41	Khalid Reeves	.05
42	Vincent Askew	.05
43	Dale Ellis	.05
44	LaPhonso Ellis	.05
45	Ervin Johnson	.05
46	Antonio McDyess	.25
47	Joe Dumars	.05
48	Grant Hill	1.50
49	Lindsey Hunter	.05
50	Aaron McKie	.05
51	Theo Ratliff	.05
52	Scott Burrell	.05
53	Todd Fuller	.05
54	Chris Mullin	.05
55	Mark Price	.05
56	Joe Smith	.30
57	Latrell Sprewell	.20
58	Clyde Drexler	.25
59	Mario Elie	.05
60	Othella Harrington	.05
61	Matt Maloney	.15
62	Hakeem Olajuwon	.50
63	Kevin Willis	.05
64	Travis Best	.05
65	Antonio Davis	.05
66	Dale Davis	.05
67	Erick Dampier	.10
68	Mark Jackson	.05
69	Reggie Miller	.20
70	Brent Barry	.05
71	Darrick Martin	.05
72	Charles Outlaw	.05
73	Loy Vaught	.05
74	Lorenzen Wright	.05
75	Kobe Bryant	1.25
76	Derek Fisher	.05
77	Robert Horry	.05
78	Eddie Jones	.30
79	Travis Knight	.05

80	George McCloud	.05
81	Shaquille O'Neal	1.00
82	P.J. Brown	.05
83	Tim Hardaway	.10
84	Voshon Lenard	.05
85	Alonzo Mourning	.15
86	Jamal Mashburn	.05
87	Ray Allen	.25
88	Vin Baker	.20
89	Sherman Douglas	.05
90	Armon Gilliam	.05
91	Glenn Robinson	.20
92	Kevin Garnett	1.25
93	Dean Garrett	.05
94	Tom Gugliotta	.05
95	Stephon Marbury	.75
96	Stojko Vrankovic	.05
97	Chris Gatling	.05
98	Kendall Gill	.05
99	Jim Jackson	.10
100	Kerry Kittles	.25
101	Eric Montross	.05
102	Chris Childs	.05
103	Patrick Ewing	.20
104	Allan Houston	.05
105	Larry Johnson	.05
106	John Starks	.05
107	John Wallace	.15
108	Nick Anderson	.05
109	Horace Grant	.05
110	Anfernee Hardaway	1.25
111	Derek Strong	.05
112	Rony Seikaly	.05
113	Derrick Coleman	.05
114	Allen Iverson	1.00
115	Don MacLean	.05
116	Jerry Stackhouse	.15
117	Rex Walters	.05
118	Cedric Ceballos	.05
119	Kevin Johnson	.10
120	Jason Kidd	.10
121	Steve Nash	.05
122	Wesley Person	.05
123	Kenny Anderson	.05
124	Jermaine O'Neal	.20
125	Isaiah Rider	.05
126	Arvydas Sabonis	.05
127	Gary Trent	.05
128	Tyus Edney	.05
129	Brian Grant	.05
130	Olden Polynice	.05
131	Mitch Richmond	.15
132	Corliss Williamson	.05
133	Vinny Del Negro	.05
134	Sean Elliott	.05
135	Avery Johnson	.05
136	Will Perdue	.05
137	Dominique Wilkins	.05
138	Craig Ehlo	.05
139	Hersey Hawkins	.05
140	Shawn Kemp	.75
141	Jim McIlvaine	.05
142	Sam Perkins	.05
143	Detlef Schrempf	.05
144	Marcus Camby	.50
145	Doug Christie	.05
146	Popeye Jones	.05
147	Damon Stoudamire	.50
148	Walt Williams	.05
149	Jeff Hornacek	.05
150	Karl Malone	.25
151	Greg Ostertag	.05
152	Bryon Russell	.05
153	John Stockton	.25
154	Shareef Abdur-Rahim	.75
155	Greg Anthony	.05
156	Anthony Peeler	.05
157	Bryant Reeves	.05
158	Roy Rogers	.05
159	Calbert Cheaney	.05
160	Juwan Howard	.30
161	Gheorghe Muresan	.05
162	Rod Strickland	.05
163	Chris Webber	.30
164	Checklist	.05
165	Checklist	.05

1997-98 Hoops
Frequent Flyer Club

Frequent Flyer inserts were seeded every 36 hobby packs in Hoops Series I. This 20-card insert was printed on a horizontal, credit card-type design with the player's image on the left and a Hoops Airlines logo on the right side with the words "Frequent Flyer"

across the bottom in gold foil. A rarer Upgrade version, which is printed on plastic is also available in one per 360 hobby packs.

		MT
Complete Set (20):		150.00
Common Player:		2.00
FF1	Christian Laettner	2.00
FF2	Antoine Walker	10.00
FF3	Glen Rice	2.00
FF4	Michael Jordan	40.00
FF5	Dennis Rodman	15.00
FF6	Grant Hill	20.00
FF7	Latrell Sprewell	2.00
FF8	Charles Barkley	6.00
FF9	Kobe Bryant	20.00
FF10	Shaquille O'Neal	15.00
FF11	Ray Allen	5.00
FF12	Kevin Garnett	20.00
FF13	Kerry Kittles	5.00
FF14	Anfernee Hardaway	15.00
FF15	Jerry Stackhouse	4.00
FF16	Cedric Ceballos	2.00
FF17	Shawn Kemp	10.00
FF18	Marcus Camby	10.00
FF19	Juwan Howard	6.00
FF20	Chris Webber	6.00

1997-98 Hoops
Frequent Flyer Club Upgrade

Frequent Flyer Upgrades parallel the regular Frequent Flyer Club insert, but are printed on plastic instead of cardboard. The cards are also identified by a large "Upgrade" stamp across the bottom right side. Upgrade versions are seeded one per 360 hobby packs.

	MT
Complete Set (20):	600.00
Upgrade Cards:	2x-4x

1997-98 Hoops HOOPerstars

This 10-card insert was seeded one per 288 packs of Hoops Series I, and features the player's name and the words "HOOPerstars" both printed in holographic silver foil on a die-cut design.

		MT
Complete Set (10):		300.00
Common Player:		6.00
H1	Michael Jordan	100.00
H2	Grant Hill	50.00
H3	Shaquille O'Neal	30.00
H4	Ray Allen	6.00
H5	Stephon Marbury	40.00
H6	Anfernee Hardaway	40.00
H7	Allen Iverson	50.00
H8	Shawn Kemp	25.00
H9	Marcus Camby	25.00
H10	Shareef Abdur-Rahim	25.00

1997-98 Hoops
Rookie Headliners

Rookie Headliners featured 10 top rookies from the 1996-97 season with a made-up newspaper background with that player dominating the headlines. This insert was found in packs of Hoops I at a one per 48 rate.

		MT
Complete Set (10):		100.00
Common Player:		1.50
RH1	Antoine Walker	15.00
RH2	Matt Maloney	1.50
RH3	Kobe Bryant	30.00
RH4	Ray Allen	7.50
RH5	Stephon Marbury	25.00
RH6	Kerry Kittles	7.50
RH7	John Wallace	1.50
RH8	Allen Iverson	30.00
RH9	Marcus Camby	15.00
RH10	Shareef Abdur-Rahim	15.00

1997-98 Hoops
Talkin' Hoops

Each pack of Hoops I contained one of 30 different Talkin' Hoops inserts featuring ex-NBA star Bill Walton. The cards were printed on silver foilboard, with the words "Talkin' Hoops" running up the left side in a black box and Bill Walton's close-up in the lower right corner.

		MT
Complete Set (30):		10.00
Common Player:		.10
TH1	Christian Laettner	.20
TH2	Antoine Walker	1.00
TH3	Glen Rice	.20
TH4	Dennis Rodman	2.00
TH5	Scottie Pippen	1.50
TH6	Terrell Brandon	.20
TH7	Michael Finley	.10
TH8	Grant Hill	3.00
TH9	Joe Smith	.30
TH10	Charles Barkley	.40
TH11	Hakeem Olajuwon	.75
TH12	Reggie Miller	.30
TH13	Loy Vaught	.10
TH14	Shaquille O'Neal	2.00
TH15	Kobe Bryant	3.00
TH16	Kevin Garnett	2.00
TH17	Tom Gugliotta	.10
TH18	Kerry Kittles	.50
TH19	John Wallace	.20
TH20	Patrick Ewing	.20
TH21	Jerry Stackhouse	.50
TH22	David Robinson	.50
TH23	Gary Payton	.50
TH24	Shawn Kemp	1.50
TH25	Damon Stoudamire	.75
TH26	John Stockton	.30
TH27	Karl Malone	.30
TH28	Shareef Abdur-Rahim	1.50
TH29	Juwan Howard	.50
TH30	Chris Webber	.75

1997 Press Pass

Press Pass Draft Picks included 40 players who were eligible for the 1997 NBA Draft, four multiple player cards and one checklist card. The cards featured color action shots with a gold foil strip through the bottom with the player's first name above the strip and last name under the strip, and a Press Pass logo in the lower right corner. Inserts included: Autographs, Jersey Cards, Lotto, One on One, All-American, In Your Face, Not Burners and two parallel sets - In the Zone, Torquers.

		MT
Complete Set (45):		15.00
Common Player:		.10
Wax Box:		65.00
1	Tim Duncan	3.00
2	Ron Mercer	1.00
3	Keith Van Horn	2.25
4	Tony Battie	1.25
5	Olivier Saint-Jean	.50
6	Tim Thomas	1.00
7	Adonal Foyle	.75
8	Tracy McGrady	1.75
9	Antonio Daniels	1.00
10	Kelvin Cato	.50
11	Danny Fortson	.75
12	Chauncey Billups	1.00
13	Brevin Knight	.50
14	Jacque Vaughn	.40
15	James Collins	.10
16	Johnny Taylor	.40
17	Derek Anderson	1.00
18	Austin Croshere	.75
19	Reggie Freeman	.10
20	Maurice Taylor	.10
21	Shea Seals	.10

22	Anthony Parker	.10
23	John Thomas	.40
24	Kebu Stewart	.30
25	Dedric Willoughby	.10
26	Serge Zwikker	.30
27	Paul Grant	.10
28	Victor Page	.10
29	Bubba Wells	.10
30	Ed Gray	.40
31	Charles O'Bannon	.20
32	Bobby Jackson	.40
33	Keith Booth	.20
34	Eddie Elisma	.10
35	Scot Pollard	.20
36	Harold Deane	.10
37	Jeff Capel	.20
38	Kiwane Garris	.20
39	Charles Smith	.10
40	Alvin Sims	.10
41	Serge Zwikker, Tim Duncan, Eddie Elisma	1.00
42	Austin Croshere, Tim Thomas	.10
43	Tony Battie, Jacque Vaughn, Chauncey Billups	.10
44	Ron Mercer, Derek Anderson	.10
45	Checklist Tim Duncan	1.00

1997 Press Pass Autographs

The 29-card, standard-size set was inserted every 18 packs of Draft Pick. The card fronts contain the player's autograph while the backs inform the collectors of his/her pull. The cards are unnumbered.

	MT
Complete Set (29):	450.00
Common Player:	7.00
Tim Duncan	100.00
Keith Van Horn	60.00
Chauncey Billups	35.00
Antonio Daniels	35.00
Tony Battie	30.00
Tim Thomas	30.00
Adonal Foyle	12.00
Tracy McGrady	40.00
Danny Fortson	20.00
Olivier Saint-Jean	20.00
Austin Croshere	20.00
Derek Anderson	25.00
Kelvin Cato	20.00
Brevin Knight	20.00
Johnny Taylor	7.00
Chris Anstey	7.00
Scot Pollard	7.00
Paul Grant	7.00
Anthony Parker	7.00
Bobby Jackson	30.00
John Thomas	7.00
Charles Smith	7.00
Jacque Vaughn	20.00
Serge Zwikker	7.00
Charles O'Bannon	15.00
Bubba Wells	7.00
Kebu Stewart	15.00
James Collins	7.00
Eddie Elisma	7.00

1997 Press Pass Net Burners

This 36-card parallel set featured top players from the regular-issue set on a horizontal, die-cut card. Net Burners carried an "NB" prefix on the card number and were inserted into each pack of Press Pass.

	MT
Complete Set (36):	30.00
Common Player:	.20
NB1 Tim Duncan	6.00
NB2 Ron Mercer	2.00
NB3 Keith Van Horn	4.50
NB4 Tony Battie	2.50
NB5 Scot Pollard	.40
NB6 Tim Thomas	2.00
NB7 Adonal Foyle	1.50
NB8 Tracy McGrady	3.50
NB9 Antonio Daniels	2.00
NB10 Kelvin Cato	1.00
NB11 Danny Fortson	1.50
NB12 Chauncey Billups	2.00
NB13 Brevin Knight	1.00
NB14 Jacque Vaughn	.75
NB15 James Collins	.20
NB16 Alvin Sims	.20
NB17 Derek Anderson	2.00
NB18 Austin Croshere	1.50
NB19 Reggie Freeman	.20
NB20 Maurice Taylor	.20
NB21 Shea Seals	.20
NB22 Anthony Parker	.20
NB23 Johnny Taylor	.75
NB24 Kebu Stewart	.50
NB25 Dedric Willoughby	.20
NB26 Serge Zwikker	.50
NB27 Olivier Saint-Jean	1.00
NB28 Victor Page	.20
NB29 Bubba Wells	.20
NB30 Ed Gray	.75
NB31 Charles O'Bannon	.40
NB32 Bobby Jackson	.75
NB33 Eddie Elisma	.20
NB34 Kiwane Garris	.40
NB35 Keith Booth	.40
NB36 Checklist Tim Duncan	2.00

1997 Press Pass Red Zone

Red Zone was a 45-card parallel set that was inserted one per hobby pack. These cards contain a red foil stamp across the bottom instead of the gold foil found on regular-issue cards. There is also a retail-only Torquers parallel set that features blue foil and seeded one per pack.

	MT
Complete Set (45):	30.00
Red Zone Cards:	2x

1997 Press Pass All-American

This 12-card set includes 1997 rookies printed on NitroKrome technology. The player is featured on the right half of the card, with a basketball in the lower left corner containing the

insert name. These cards were included in one per 12 packs and numbered with an "A" prefix.

	MT
Complete Set (12):	80.00
Common Player:	2.00
A1 Tim Duncan	20.00
A2 Keith Van Horn	15.00
A3 Ron Mercer	7.00
A4 Tracy McGrady	12.00
A5 Danny Fortson	5.00
A6 Brevin Knight	3.50
A7 Tony Battie	8.00
A8 Jacque Vaughn	3.00
A9 Chauncey Billups	7.00
A10 Bobby Jackson	3.00
A11 Adonal Foyle	5.00
A12 Shea Seals	2.00

1997 Press Pass Jersey Card

This five-card set had three cards (JC1, JC4 and a bonus Chauncey Billups card) in Press Pass Draft Picks and two additional cards in Double Threats, which was released later in the year. Fronts feature a wood basketball court frame with the player pictured in an oval and the piece of game-worn jersey included near the bottom of the oval. Seeded one per 612 packs, this insert contains a white box in the bottom left corner for individual numbering.

	MT
Complete Set (3):	300.00
Common Player:	80.00
JC1 Tim Duncan	150.00
JC4 Jacque Vaughn	80.00
Bonus Chauncey Billups	100.00

1997 Press Pass In Your Face

In Your Face was a hobby exclusive, nine-card set that was seeded one per 36 hobby packs. The cards were printed on clear acetate, with a shot from the sky of a player jumping off a wood basketball floor going toward the rim. The player's name is

printed in a rounded shadow from the top left corner to the bottom right, with the insert name in gold foil in the lower left. These were numbered with an "IYF" prefix.

	MT
Complete Set (9):	100.00
Common Player:	7.00
IYF1 Ron Mercer	12.00
IYF2 Danny Fortson	9.00
IYF3 Chauncey Billups	12.00
IYF4 Maurice Taylor	7.00
IYF5 Keith Van Horn	25.00
IYF6 Bobby Jackson	7.00
IYF7 Tony Battie	15.00
IYF8 Tim Duncan	35.00
IYF9 Kelvin Cato	7.00

1997 Press Pass Lotto

Lotto was a six-card progressive insert that contained the top six picks in the 1997 NBA Draft. The cards are printed on silver foil with the player's last name across the top and insert name included in the lower left corner. The back pictures all six players in the set and is numbered with an "L" prefix. Card #1 was seeded one per 720; #2 seeded one per 360; #3 seeded one per 180; #4 seeded one per 90; #5 seeded one per 45; and #6 seeded one per 36.

	MT
Complete Set (7):	250.00
Common Player:	15.00
L1 Tim Duncan	125.00
L2 Ron Mercer	60.00
L3 Keith Van Horn	45.00
L4 Tony Battie	30.00
L5 Adonal Foyle	15.00
L6 Tim Thomas	15.00
Bonus Chauncey Billups	60.00

1997 Press Pass One on One

One on One consisted of nine cards featuring two of the year's best rookies going head to head on silver foil board. Cards are split down the middle with the words "One on One" in yellow letters, with one player on the right and one on the left. These cards carry no letter prefix and are inserted one per 18 packs.

		MT
Complete Set (9):		90.00
Common Player:		5.00
1	Tim Duncan, Tony Battie	20.00
2	Danny Fortson, Tim Duncan	20.00
3	Ron Mercer, Tracy McGrady	12.00
4	Keith Van Horn, Tim Thomas	15.00
5	Antonio Daniels, Chauncey Billups	10.00
6	Adonal Foyle, Kelvin Cato	7.00
7	Derek Anderson, Ron Mercer	10.00
8	Jacque Vaughn, Brevin Knight	5.00
9	Austin Croshere, Maurice Taylor	5.00

1997 Score Board Basketball Rookies

This 100-card set, included 60 regular cards, 10 All- Americans, 15 1996-97 All-Rookie Team and 11 Back in the Day and four checklists. The set features 1997 NBA Draft members in their college uniforms, as well as a select number of pros in a mix of college uniforms and air-brushed pro uniforms. Card fronts feature a full bleed photo with a faded, black and white background. A large black strip across the bottom contains the player's school, position and a Score Board logo in it, with the player's name above the black part in white letters. Inserts include a parallel Dean's List, Rookie #1 Die-Cuts, Varsity Club and Game Wear.

		MT
Complete Set (100):		10.00
Common Player:		.05
1	Tim Duncan	2.00
2	Ron Mercer	.75
3	Marc Jackson	.05
4	Tunji Awojobi	.05
5	Reggie Freeman	.05
6	John Thomas	.05
7	Scot Pollard	.10
8	Brevin Knight	.50
9	Keith Booth	.05
10	Reggie Welch	.05
11	Alvin Sims	.05
12	Victor Page	.05
13	Jason Lawson	.05
14	Paul Grant	.05
15	Kiwane Garris	.30
16	Eddie Elisma	.05
17	Antonio Daniels	.50
18	James Collins	.05
19	Kelvin Cato	.50
20	Peter Aluma	.05
21	Derek Anderson	.30
22	Lorenzo Coleman	.05
23	Austin Croshere	.50
24	Harold Deane	.05
25	Nate Erdmann	.05
26	Adonal Foyle	.50
27	Tony Gonzalez	.10
28	Ed Gray	.05
29	Quincy Lee	.05
30	Charles O'Bannon	.50
31	Shea Seals	.10
32	Keith Van Horn	1.25
33	Tony Battie	.75
34	Bobby Jackson	.30
35	Anthony Parker	.05
36	Kebu Stewart	.30
37	Chris Anstey	.05
38	Jacque Vaughn	.50
39	DeJuan Wheat	.05
40	Anthony Johnson	.05
41	Danny Fortson	.50
42	Mark Sanford	.05
43	Jerald Honeycutt	.05
44	Olivier Saint-Jean	.40
45	Chauncey Billups	.75
46	Isaac Fontaine	.05
47	Otis Hill	.05
48	Tracy McGrady	1.00
49	Johnny Taylor	.05
50	God Shammgod	.30
51	Dedric Willoughby	.05
52	Tim Thomas	.50
53	Alvin Williams	.05
54	Gordon Malone	.05
55	Serge Zwikker	.10
56	Charles Smith	.05
57	Tim Duncan	1.00
58	Ron Mercer	.30
59	Keith Van Horn	.50
60	Tim Thomas	.30
61	Checklist Tim Duncan	1.00
62	Tim Duncan	1.00
63	Ron Mercer	.30
64	Keith Van Horn	.50
65	Tony Battie	.30
66	Tracy McGrady	.50
67	Danny Fortson	.25
68	Brevin Knight	.25
69	DeJuan Wheat	.05
70	Adonal Foyle	.25
71	Jacque Vaughn	.25
72	Checklist Tim Duncan	1.00
73	Allen Iverson	.40
74	Marcus Camby	.25
75	Shareef Abdur-Rahim	.25
76	Stephon Marbury	.30
77	Ray Allen	.10
78	Antoine Walker	.20
79	Lorenzen Wright	.05
80	Kerry Kittles	.10
81	Erick Dampier	.05
82	Vitaly Potapenko	.05
83	Kobe Bryant	.40
84	Tony Delk	.05
85	John Wallace	.10
86	Walter McCarty	.05
87	Roy Rogers	.05
88	Checklist Allen Iverson	.40
89	Rasheed Wallace	.05
90	Damon Stoudamire	.20
91	Joe Smith	.10
92	Glenn Robinson	.05
93	Scottie Pippen	.20
94	Ed O'Bannon	.05
95	Antonio McDyess	.05
96	Alonzo Mourning	.05
97	Clyde Drexler	.10
98	Dikembe Mutombo	.05
99	Hakeem Olajuwon	.10
100	Checklist Scottie Pippen	.10

1997 Score Board BK Rookies Dean's List

This 100-card parallel set was seeded one per five packs and includes each card in the regular-issue set. Dean's List inserts are identified by a large silver foil area at the bottom of the card, with the words "Dean's List" in it. The cards carry no special prefix on the card number.

	MT
Complete Set (100):	40.00
Dean's List Cards:	2x-4x

1997 Score Board Basketball Rookies #1 Die-Cuts

Rookie #1 Die-Cuts featured 1997 lottery picks as well as established stars on silver foil board die-cut in the shape of a number one. This 20-card insert was inserted one per 36 packs.

		MT
Complete Set (20):		250.00
Common Player:		3.00
DC1	Tim Duncan	35.00
DC2	Tony Battie	15.00
DC3	Ron Mercer	15.00
DC4	Keith Van Horn	25.00
DC5	Antonio Daniels	10.00
DC6	Tim Thomas	10.00
DC7	Adonal Foyle	10.00
DC8	Derek Anderson	3.00
DC9	Chauncey Billups	15.00
DC10	Tracy McGrady	20.00
DC11	Danny Fortson	10.00
DC12	Brevin Knight	10.00
DC13	Jacque Vaughn	10.00
DC14	Austin Croshere	10.00
DC15	Stephon Marbury	15.00
DC16	Kobe Bryant	20.00
DC17	Clyde Drexler	3.00
DC18	Scottie Pippen	8.00
DC19	Allen Iverson	20.00
DC20	Alonzo Mourning	3.00

1997 Score Board Basketball Rookies Varsity Club

Varsity Club features 20 players selected in the 1997 NBA Draft on a horizontal, basketball and wood grain background. A shot of the player is on the right side, with a large holographic, pennant design on the left side. This 20-card insert was found every 18 packs of 1997 Basketball Rookies and is numbered VC1-VC20.

		MT
Complete Set (20):		150.00
Common Player:		2.00
VC1	Tim Duncan	25.00
VC2	Ron Mercer	10.00
VC3	Keith Van Horn	20.00
VC4	Tim Thomas	7.00
VC5	Adonal Foyle	7.00
VC6	Tony Battie	10.00
VC7	Antonio Daniels	7.00
VC8	Kelvin Cato	7.00
VC9	Charles O'Bannon	7.00
VC10	Brevin Knight	7.00
VC11	Danny Fortson	7.00
VC12	Derek Anderson	2.00
VC13	Austin Croshere	7.00
VC14	Tracy McGrady	15.00
VC15	Jacque Vaughn	7.00
VC16	God Shammgod	5.00
VC17	DeJuan Wheat	2.00
VC18	Danya Abrams	2.00
VC19	Reggie Freeman	2.00
VC20	Tony Gonzalez	2.00

1997-98 SkyBox Z-Force

This 110-card set included 108 player cards and two checklists in Series I. Fronts featured the player over an artsy, spiral background, with the player's name running down the right side in foil. The player's team, uniform number, position and the Z-Force logo run across the bottom. The back is white with another shot of the player, statistics and the card number in the lower right corner. Inserts in Series I include: Boss, Super Boss, Limited Access, Fast Track, Total Impact, Rave Reviews, Autographics and the parallel Raves.

	MT
Complete Set (110):	16.00
Common Player:	.10
1	Anfernee Hardaway	1.50
2	Mitch Richmond	.20
3	Stephon Marbury	1.25
4	Charles Barkley	.40
5	Juwan Howard	.30
6	Avery Johnson	.10
7	Rex Chapman	.10
8	Antoine Walker	.75
9	Nick Van Exel	.20
10	Tim Hardaway	.10
11	Clarence Weatherspoon	.10
12	John Stockton	.30
13	Glenn Robinson	.30
14	Anthony Mason	.10
15	Latrell Sprewell	.20
16	Kendall Gill	.10
17	Terry Mills	.10
18	Mookie Blaylock	.10
19	Michael Finley	.10
20	Gary Payton	.30
21	Kevin Garnett	1.75
22	Clyde Drexler	.30
23	Michael Jordan	3.50
24	Antonio McDyess	.30
25	Nick Anderson	.10
26	Patrick Ewing	.30
27	Anthony Peeler	.10
28	Doug Christie	.10
29	Bobby Phills	.10
30	Kerry Kittles	.40
31	Reggie Miller	.20
32	Karl Malone	.30
33	Grant Hill	1.75
34	Shaquille O'Neal	1.25
35	Loy Vaught	.10
36	Kenny Anderson	.10
37	Wesley Person	.10
38	Jamal Mashburn	.10
39	Christian Laettner	.10
40	Shawn Kemp	.75
41	Glen Rice	.20
42	Vin Baker	.30
43	David Wesley	.10
44	Derrick Coleman	.10
45	Rik Smits	.10
46	Dale Ellis	.10
47	Rod Strickland	.10
48	Mark Price	.10
49	Toni Kukoc	.10
50	David Robinson	.40
51	John Wallace	.20
52	Samaki Walker	.10
53	Shareef Abdur-Rahim	1.00
54	Rodney Rogers	.10
55	Dikembe Mutombo	.10
56	Rony Seikaly	.10
57	Matt Maloney	.20
58	Chris Webber	.50
59	Robert Horry	.10
60	Rasheed Wallace	.10
61	Jeff Hornacek	.10
62	Walt Williams	.10
63	Detlef Schrempf	.10
64	Dan Majerle	.10
65	Dell Curry	.10
66	Scottie Pippen	.75
67	Greg Anthony	.10
68	Mahmoud Abdul-Rauf	.10
69	Cedric Ceballos	.10
70	Terrell Brandon	.10
71	Arvydas Sabonis	.10
72	Dino Radja	.10
73	Jim Jackson	.10
74	Joe Dumars	.10
75	Joe Smith	.30
76	Shawn Bradley	.10
77	Gheorghe Muresan	.10
78	Dale Davis	.10
79	Bryant Stith	.10
80	Lorenzen Wright	.10
81	Chris Childs	.10
82	Bryon Russell	.10
83	Steve Smith	.10
84	Jerry Stackhouse	.30
85	Hersey Hawkins	.10
86	Ray Allen	.40
87	Dominique Wilkins	.10
88	Kobe Bryant	1.75
89	Tom Gugliotta	.10
90	Dennis Scott	.10
91	Dennis Rodman	1.00
92	Bryant Reeves	.10
93	Vlade Divac	.10
94	Jason Kidd	.20
95	Mario Elie	.10
96	Lindsey Hunter	.10
97	Olden Polynice	.10
98	Allan Houston	.10
99	Alonzo Mourning	.20
100	Allen Iverson	1.75
101	LaPhonso Ellis	.10
102	Bob Sura	.10
103	Chris Mullin	.10
104	Sam Cassell	.10
105	Eric Williams	.10
106	Antonio Davis	.10
107	Marcus Camby	.75
108	Isaiah Rider	.10
109	Checklist	.10
110	Checklist	.10

1997-98 SkyBox Z-Force Raves

This 108-card parallel set (110 minus the two checklists) included prismatic silver foil on the front, and individual numbering to 399 on the back. No odds for Rave inserts were given, but it is estimated that they are seeded one per 60-80 packs.

	MT
Rave Cards:	50x-100x

1997-98 SkyBox Z-Force Boss

This 20-card insert was seeded one per six packs of Z-Force Series I. The cards feature an embossed player image on the front over a wood basketball floor-like background, with the insert name printed in red letters up the right side and a large "Z" in black and yellow in the lower right corner. Boss inserts were numbered "x of 20/B". There are also Super Boss parallels with a foil finish that were inserted every 36 packs and numbered "x of 20/SB".

		MT
Complete Set (20):		50.00
Common Player:		.50
1	Shareef Abdur-Rahim	4.00
2	Ray Allen	.50
3	Kobe Bryant	6.00
4	Marcus Camby	2.00
5	Kevin Garnett	6.00
6	Anfernee Hardaway	5.00
7	Grant Hill	6.00
8	Allen Iverson	6.00
9	Eddie Jones	1.50
10	Michael Jordan	12.00
11	Shawn Kemp	3.00
12	Kerry Kittles	.50
13	Stephon Marbury	5.00
14	Shaquille O'Neal	4.00
15	Hakeem Olajuwon	2.00
16	Scottie Pippen	3.00
17	Dennis Rodman	4.00
18	Joe Smith	.50
19	Damon Stoudamire	.50
20	Antoine Walker	3.00

1997-98 SkyBox Z-Force Super Boss

This 20-card insert parallels the Boss insert, but is inserted every 36 packs. Super Boss inserts are identified by a gold foil finish over the entire card front and an "SB" notation on the back following the card number.

	MT
Complete Set (20):	200.00
Super Boss Cards:	2x-4x

1997-98 SkyBox Z-Force Fast Track

Fast Track highlighted 12 players who are quickly approaching super stardom. Fronts are yellow with large black felt letters "Fast" on the top and "Track" across the bottom, with the team name in a black strip across the bottom in white letters. Fast Track inserts were seeded one per 24 packs, and numbered "x of 12/FT".

		MT
Complete Set (12):		70.00
Common Player:		3.00
1	Ray Allen	3.00
2	Kobe Bryant	20.00
3	Marcus Camby	8.00
4	Juwan Howard	6.00
5	Eddie Jones	6.00
6	Kerry Kittles	3.00
7	Antonio McDyess	3.00
8	Joe Smith	6.00
9	Jerry Stackhouse	6.00
10	Damon Stoudamire	6.00
11	Antoine Walker	10.00
12	Chris Webber	8.00

1997-98 SkyBox Z-Force Limited Access

Each card takes an in-depth statistical analysis of ten players on a bi-fold card. They were available exclusively in retail packs at a rate of 1:18.

		MT
Complete Set (10):		50.00
Common Player:		2.00
1	Shareef Abdur-Rahim	6.00
2	Ray Allen	2.00
3	Charles Barkley	3.00
4	Anfernee Hardaway	8.00
5	Juwan Howard	2.00
6	Michael Jordan	20.00
7	Stephon Marbury	8.00
8	Shaquille O'Neal	6.00
9	Dennis Rodman	6.00
10	Antoine Walker	6.00

1997-98 SkyBox Z-Force Rave Reviews

Rave Reviews showcased 12 of the top players in the NBA on gold prismatic foil with black around the edges. Inserted at a rate of one per 288 packs, these cards contained the insert name and player's name in silver foil across the middle of the card. Backs were mostly black with white lettering.

		MT
Complete Set (12):		625.00
Common Player:		25.00
1	Shareef Abdur-Rahim	50.00
2	Kevin Garnett	75.00
3	Anfernee Hardaway	60.00
4	Grant Hill	75.00
5	Allen Iverson	75.00
6	Michael Jordan	150.00
7	Shawn Kemp	40.00
8	Stephon Marbury	60.00
9	Shaquille O'Neal	50.00
10	Hakeem Olajuwon	25.00
11	Scottie Pippen	40.00
12	Dennis Rodman	50.00

1997-98 SkyBox Z-Force Total Impact

This 12-card set featured the player over a glittery background with silver highlights. The insert name runs up the left side, with the player's name in the top left corner. Inserted at a one per 48 rate, the cards were numbered "x of 12/TI".

		MT
Complete Set (12):		150.00
Common Player:		4.00
1	Kobe Bryant	30.00
2	Marcus Camby	10.00
3	Kevin Garnett	30.00
4	Grant Hill	30.00
5	Allen Iverson	30.00
6	Eddie Jones	6.00
7	Shawn Kemp	15.00
8	Kerry Kittles	4.00
9	Hakeem Olajuwon	10.00
10	Scottie Pippen	15.00
11	Joe Smith	4.00
12	Chris Webber	8.00

1997-98 Topps

Topps 1997-98 Series I consisted of 110 cards with white border. The featured player's image was glossy, with the rest of the background slightly dulled, with two color strips up the left side and one color strip across the bottom with the player's name in gold foil stamped in it. Inserts in Series I included: Minted in Springfield parallel cards, Autographs, Rock Stars, Fantastic 15, Topps 40, Rookie Redemption, Season's Best and Bound for Glory.

		MT
Complete Set (110):		12.00
Common Player:		.05
Wax Box:		45.00
1	Scottie Pippen	.75
2	Nate McMillan	.05
3	Byron Scott	.05
4	Mark Davis	.05
5	Rod Strickland	.05
6	Brian Grant	.05
7	Damon Stoudamire	.50
8	John Stockton	.20
9	Grant Long	.05
10	Darrell Armstrong	.05
11	Anthony Mason	.05
12	Travis Best	.05
13	Stephon Marbury	.75
14	Jamal Mashburn	.10
15	Detlef Schrempf	.05
16	Terrell Brandon	.10
17	Charles Barkley	.30
18	Vin Baker	.20
19	Gary Trent	.05
20	Vinny Del Negro	.05
21	Todd Day	.05
22	Malik Sealy	.05
23	Wesley Person	.05
24	Reggie Miller	.20
25	Dan Majerle	.05
26	Todd Fuller	.05
27	Juwan Howard	.30
28	Clarence Weatherspoon	.05
29	Grant Hill	1.50
30	John Williams	.05
31	Ken Norman	.05
32	Patrick Ewing	.20
33	Bryon Russell	.05
34	Tony Smith	.05
35	Andrew Lang	.05
36	Rony Seikaly	.05
37	Billy Owens	.05
38	Dino Radja	.05
39	Chris Gatling	.05
40	Dale Davis	.05
41	Arvydas Sabonis	.05
42	Chris Mills	.05
43	A.C. Green	.05
44	Tyrone Hill	.05
45	Tracy Murray	.05
46	David Robinson	.40
47	Lee Mayberry	.05
48	Jayson Williams	.05
49	Jason Kidd	.25
50	Bryant Stith	.05
51	Latrell Sprewell	.20
52	Brent Barry	.05
53	Henry James	.05
54	Allen Iverson	1.00
55	Shandon Anderson	.05
56	Mitch Richmond	.15
57	Allan Houston	.05
58	Ron Harper	.05
59	Gheorghe Muresan	.05
60	Vincent Askew	.05
61	Ray Allen	.25
62	Kenny Anderson	.10
63	Dikembe Mutombo	.10
64	Sam Perkins	.05
65	Walt Williams	.05
66	Chris Carr	.05
67	Vlade Divac	.05
68	LaPhonso Ellis	.05
69	B.J. Armstrong	.05
70	Jim Jackson	.10
71	Clyde Drexler	.20
72	Lindsey Hunter	.05
73	Sasha Danilovic	.05
74	Elden Campbell	.05
75	Robert Pack	.05
76	Dennis Scott	.05
77	Will Perdue	.05
78	Anthony Peeler	.05
79	Steve Smith	.05
80	Steve Kerr	.05
81	Buck Williams	.05
82	Terry Mills	.05
83	Michael Smith	.05
84	Adam Keefe	.05
85	Kevin Willis	.05
86	David Wesley	.05
87	Muggsy Bogues	.05
88	Bimbo Coles	.05
89	Tom Gugliotta	.05
90	Jermaine O'Neal	.20
91	Cedric Ceballos	.10
92	Shawn Kemp	.75
93	Horace Grant	.05
94	Shareef Abdur-Rahim	.60
95	Robert Horry	.05
96	Vitaly Potapenko	.05
97	Pooh Richardson	.05
98	Doug Christie	.05
99	Voshon Lenard	.05
100	Dominique Wilkins	.10
101	Alonzo Mourning	.15
102	Sam Cassell	.05
103	Sherman Douglas	.05
104	Shawn Bradley	.05
105	Mark Jackson	.05
106	Dennis Rodman	.75
107	Charles Oakley	.05
108	Matt Maloney	.15
109	Shaquille O'Neal	1.00
110	Checklist	.05

1997-98 Topps Mint

This 110-card parallel set was gold foil stamped at the Basketball Hall of Fame in Springfield, Mass., and inserted one per six packs. Minted in Springfield inserts were identical to the base cards, except for a gold foil Basketball Hall of Fame stamp in the lower left corner.

	MT
Minted Cards:	4x-8x

1997-98 Topps Autographs

Eight NBA superstars, including Hakeem Olajuwon, Glenn Robinson and Juwan Howard, signed cards for hobby packs of Topps Series I. These cards can be found every 212 hobby packs.

		MT
Complete Set (8):		300.00
Common Player:		15.00
1	John Starks	20.00
2	Juwan Howard	60.00
3	Mitch Richmond	30.00
4	Hakeem Olajuwon	100.00
5	Glenn Robinson	40.00
6	Steve Smith	15.00
7	Antoine Walker	80.00
8	Clyde Drexler	60.00

1997-98 Topps Bound for Glory

Bound for Glory featured 15 top stars on a holographic foil card and inserted one per 36 Series I hobby packs. The card numbers carried a "BG" prefix and displayed the insert name across the top with large pillars in the background.

		MT
Complete Set (15):		100.00
Common Player:		1.50
BG1	Robert Parish	1.50
BG2	Grant Hill	25.00
BG3	Chris Mullin	1.50
BG4	Hakeem Olajuwon	7.00
BG5	Dennis Rodman	15.00
BG6	Patrick Ewing	3.00
BG7	Karl Malone	3.00
BG8	Charles Barkley	5.00
BG9	David Robinson	5.00
BG10	Michael Jordan	40.00
BG11	Dominique Wilkins	1.50
BG12	Shaquille O'Neal	15.00
BG13	Clyde Drexler	4.00
BG14	John Stockton	3.00
BG15	Scottie Pippen	10.00

1997-98 Topps Draft Redemption

Topps gave collectors the chance to score the first Topps cards of the 1997 NBA Draft Picks with the inclusion of 29 Rookie Redemption cards. Every redemption card has a number corresponding to each draft position of the first round, and could be exchanged for a special card of that player taken in that draft position once he signed his NBA contract. They were seeded every 12 hobby and 18 retail packs.

		MT
Complete Set (29):		100.00
Common Player:		1.50
1	Tim Duncan	20.00
2	Keith Van Horn	15.00
3	Chauncey Billups	10.00
4	Antonio Daniels	10.00
5	Tony Battie	10.00
6	Ron Mercer	10.00
7	Tim Thomas	6.00
8	Adonal Foyle	4.00
9	Tracy McGrady	10.00
10	Danny Fortson	6.00
11	Tariq Abdul-Wahad	1.50
12	Austin Croshere	3.00
13	Derek Anderson	6.00
14	Maurice Taylor	1.50
15	Kelvin Cato	3.00
16	Brevin Knight	6.00
17	Johnny Taylor	1.50
18	Chris Anstey	1.50
19	Scot Pollard	1.50
20	Paul Grant	1.50
21	Anthony Parker	1.50
22	Ed Gray	1.50
23	Bobby Jackson	8.00
24	Rodrick Rhodes	4.00
25	John Thomas	1.50
26	Charles Smith	1.50
27	Jacque Vaughn	3.00
28	Keith Booth	1.50
29	Serge Zwikker	1.50

1997-98 Topps Fantastic 15

This insert was seeded every 36 Series I retail packs and contains an "F" prefix on the card number. The insert name is printed in large letters across the top, with multi-colored holographic foil in the background.

		MT
Complete Set (15):		100.00
Common Player:		2.00
F1	Antoine Walker	10.00

		MT
F2	Damon Stoudamire	5.00
F3	Brent Barry	2.00
F4	Michael Finley	2.00
F5	Ray Allen	3.00
F6	Allen Iverson	20.00
F7	Stephon Marbury	15.00
F8	Kerry Kittles	4.00
F9	John Wallace	2.00
F10	Kevin Garnett	20.00
F11	Jerry Stackhouse	4.00
F12	Kobe Bryant	20.00
F13	Marcus Camby	8.00
F14	Joe Smith	4.00
F15	Shareef Abdur-Rahim	10.00

1997-98 Topps Rock Stars

This 20-card, die-cut and borderless insert featured 20 stars and was inserted every 36 Series I packs. The cards utilize Finest technology and are die-cut around rocks across the top of the card. The card numbers carry an "RS" prefix. There are also Refractor versions of Rock Stars inserts available.

		MT
Complete Set (20):		150.00
Common Player:		2.00
RS1	Dikembe Mutombo	2.00
RS2	Tom Gugliotta	2.00
RS3	Jerry Stackhouse	6.00
RS4	Shawn Kemp	12.00
RS5	Gary Payton	5.00
RS6	Damon Stoudamire	8.00
RS7	Karl Malone	4.00
RS8	Juwan Howard	5.00
RS9	Chris Webber	6.00
RS10	Michael Jordan	50.00
RS11	Scottie Pippen	12.00
RS12	Dennis Rodman	15.00
RS13	Grant Hill	30.00
RS14	Charles Barkley	6.00
RS15	Hakeem Olajuwon	10.00
RS16	Shaquille O'Neal	18.00
RS17	Tim Hardaway	2.00
RS18	Alonzo Mourning	4.00
RS19	Kevin Garnett	25.00
RS20	Anfernee Hardaway	25.00

1997-98 Topps Rock Stars Refractors

This insert ran parallel to the Finest Rock Stars set, but was printed using Finest technology. These parallel versions were seeded one per 144 Series I packs.

	MT
Refractors:	2x-4x

1997-98 Topps Season's Best

Season's Best is a 30-card insert that showcases 25 stars who dominated statistical categories, and five rookies. These cards were printed on borderless prismatic foilboard and inserted one per 16 Series I packs. There are six different subsets, including Key Masters, Power Core, Shooting Stars, Frontcourt Finesse, Pressure Points and Hot Shots.

		MT
Complete Set (30):		100.00
Common Player:		1.50
SB1	Gary Payton	4.00
SB2	Kevin Johnson	1.50
SB3	Tim Hardaway	1.50
SB4	John Stockton	4.00
SB5	Damon Stoudamire	5.00
SB6	Michael Jordan	30.00
SB7	Mitch Richmond	4.00
SB8	Latrell Sprewell	4.00
SB9	Reggie Miller	4.00
SB10	Clyde Drexler	4.00
SB11	Grant Hill	20.00
SB12	Scottie Pippen	8.00
SB13	Kendall Gill	1.50
SB14	Glen Rice	3.00
SB15	LaPhonso Ellis	1.50
SB16	Karl Malone	4.00
SB17	Charles Barkley	5.00
SB18	Vin Baker	4.00
SB19	Chris Webber	5.00
SB20	Tom Gugliotta	1.50
SB21	Shaquille O'Neal	12.00
SB22	Patrick Ewing	4.00
SB23	Hakeem Olajuwon	6.00
SB24	Alonzo Mourning	3.00
SB25	Dikembe Mutombo	1.50
SB26	Allen Iverson	15.00
SB27	Antoine Walker	7.00
SB28	Shareef Abdur-Rahim	8.00
SB29	Stephon Marbury	12.00
SB30	Kerry Kittles	4.00

1997-98 Topps 40

This insert includes selections from NBA players, writers and coaches to come up with the top 40 players in the NBA. Series I has 20 cards, with the other 20 found in Series II, both with insertion rates of one per 12 packs and numbered "T40-x". The cards are printed on reflective, foil-stamped mirrorboard cards, with a large number 40 across the bottom.

		MT
Complete Set (20):		35.00
Common Player:		.50
1	Glen Rice	1.00
2	Patrick Ewing	1.50
3	Terrell Brandon	.50
4	Jerry Stackhouse	2.00
5	Michael Jordan	15.00
6	Christian Laettner	.50
7	Latrell Sprewell	1.50
8	Reggie Miller	1.00
9	Gary Payton	1.50
10	Detlef Schrempf	.50
11	Kevin Garnett	8.00
12	Eddie Jones	2.50
13	Clyde Drexler	1.50
14	Anfernee Hardaway	8.00
15	Chris Webber	2.50
16	Jayson Williams	.50
17	Joe Smith	2.00
18	Karl Malone	1.50
19	Tim Hardaway	.50
20	Vin Baker	1.00

1997 The Year in Football Cards

When is enough too much?

That's the question being currently asked in the hobby as the football card market reaches a point of diminished return. The flood of new releases has confused dealers and collectors, and the end result is a flat market during a time when the National Football League is red-hot.

What's the main reason for the down market during a hot season? Too many products. For convenience sake, we focused on a one year span from Oct. 1, 1996, through Oct. 1, 1997. The numbers we found were mind-boggling.

During that period, 60 football products were released – which averages out to five sets per month.

Better yet, if one breaks down the 60 sets over a 16-game season, it averages about 3.75 sets per week. That's a better clip than the Chicago Bears offense's per play average in 1997.

Obviously, those 60 sets are too much. On one hand, it gives collectors a variety to choose from – you know, like peanut butter, we can choose the fat-free, regular, chunky or extra chunky varieties of over a dozen brands on the market.

However, on the other side of the coin, 60 sets adds up to plenty of confusion for the collector. The set collector who was so prevalent five years ago has gone the way of the dinosaur. Now, collectors are more specialized, focusing on a certain team or player.

This recent flood has hurt what had become the most promising area of the hobby. Remember, in 1995 football card sales jumped 35 percent from the previous year and everything looked rosy. But even then the football card market was busting at the seams.

Consider this: In 1988 there was only one football card set, Topps. The next year the market took off and there were five different releases. The number of releases grew to nine in 1990, 14 in 1991, 17 in 1992, 21 in 1993 and 26 in 1994 before making the big jump in 1995 to 39.

Then, in 1996, things got out of hand as the number of releases reached 64. This brings up the obvious question: When is enough too much?

We believe the football card market has reached that point and it's time to end the deluge before it's too late. NFL Properties

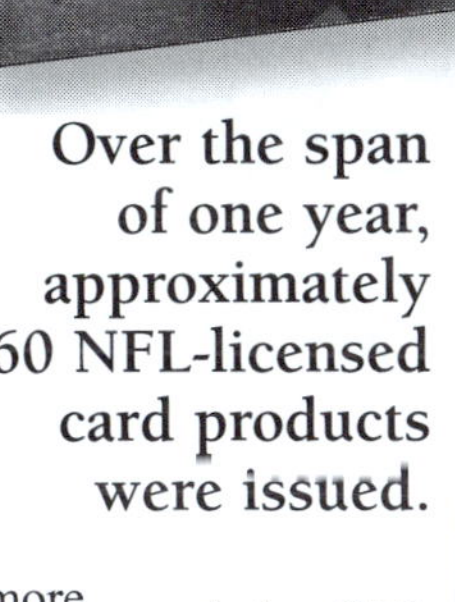

Over the span of one year, approximately 60 NFL-licensed card products were issued.

and the NFL Players Association needs to limit the number of releases each of its licensees produces every year and do it now. Let the game – along with superstars such as Steve Young, Emmitt Smith and Brett Favre – drive the market to new heights. More releases will just suffocate what should be the most promising area of our industry.

If you're already gasping from lack of oxygen, take a look at this. There were approximately 360 football card insert sets that were produced over our surveyed time of one year. If we subtract the holidays from the calendar, there's one insert set for every day of the year.

Just think, some enterprising collector could actually make some cash by producing one of those Far Side-type desktop calendars that features a photo of an insert card on each page.

Imagine the joy when you rip off the title page to show SkyBox Autographics featured on the Jan. 1 page. The Jan. 2 page showcases a photo of a Topps Finest Mystery insert. Oooo, now you're talking.

Of those 360 chase sets, four of them stand out as the hottest of the time span. Collector's Edge picks up three honors with its Game Balls, Super Bowl Game Balls and Excalibur Game Gear. Pinnacle won over collectors with its Select Certified Mirror Golds.

Inserted at a rate of one per 72 packs in 1996 Collector's Edge Advantage, the 36-card Game Balls set started out at $1,000, with the Favre, Smith and Dan Marino cards selling for $75 each. They have since reached the $150 mark.

The 36-card Super Bowl Game Balls chase set was also seeded in 1996 Edge Advantage packs, but at a tougher rate of 1:164. The set debuted in the price guides at $1,600 and is now in the $2,200 range. The Smith and Marino cards started out at $225 each and are currently up to $325 each.

Edge took the game-used concept one step further with its 1997 Excalibur product when it introduced the Game Gear cards that featured a piece of the player's helmet embedded into the card.

Inserted at a 1:60 ratio, the 25 card

set opened at $750 and now lists for $900. Favre's card is sitting at $100, while Smith's and Marino's are at $90 apiece.

As for the Select Certified Mirror Golds, this was the first year that Pinnacle limited these to 35 of each. The odds were listed at 1:300 packs. The top players from this set include Favre, Smith and Marino at $1,500 each.

Looking at the new products which were released between our Oct. 1, 1996, and Oct. 1, 1997 window, the list shows 17 sets that made their debut. Some of them replaced products from the previous year.

Included in that new product list are: Score Board NFL Lasers, Donruss, Ultra Sensations, Leaf, Motion Vision, Pacific Invincible, Pacific Litho-Cel, Pinnacle Mint, Playoff Illusions, SkyBox Impact Rookies, SkyBox SkyMotion, Topps Chrome, Topps Laser, Goudey, Pacific Philadelphia, Playoff First and 10, Topps Stars and Upper Deck Black Diamond.

Old products which were not released during our window include: Upper Deck Silver (replaced by Black Diamond), Topps Gilt Edge (replaced by Topps Stars), Playoff Prime (replaced by First and 10), Sportflix, Upper Deck SP Championship and Pacific Prisms.

The winner of the hot product from our surveyed time span was the 1996 Motion Vision Series 1.0. Its packs debuted at $5, with boxes at $100 during the first couple of weeks after its release.

The prices jumped to $10 a pack and $220 per box. There's no doubt that technology made this product hot among collectors.

Unfortunately, Series 2.0 didn't have the same impact on collectors, because nothing was new that collectors hadn't seen in the first series.

Favre takes the cake for the player's card who jumped extensively in price over the past year. His 1991 Stadium Club No. 94 rookie card skyrocketed from $35 to $70, while his 1992

Stadium Club III card No. 683 leaped from $35 to $90.

Other regular issue single cards to keep an eye on are Barry Sanders' 1989 Score No. 257 ($65), Drew Bledsoe's 1993 Upper Deck SP No. 9 ($75) and Mark Brunell's 1993 SP No. 91 ($40).

Even though Jerry Rice missed most of the 1997 season, his 1986 Topps No. 161 rookie card is still sitting at $120. His popularity never slipped, as his card was listed at the same value the day of his injury as it is today.

Also keep a lookout for John Elway's 1984 Topps No. 63 ($50), Jerome Bettis' 1993 Upper Deck SP No. 6 ($20), Dan Marino's 1984 Topps No. 123 ($130) and Adrian Murrell's 1993 SP No. 196.

Bettis had another 1,000-yard rushing season in 1997 and collectors are buying up his rookie

> There were approximately 360 football card insert sets that were produced over our surveyed time of one year. If we subtract the holidays from the calendar, there's one insert set for every day of the year.

while it's still affordable.

As for Murrell, what a difference a year makes. Last year, collectors could have found this card in some dealers' common boxes, but not anymore. This single has jumped $11 in the past year to $14.

A technology which has really caught on with collectors over the past year was Upper Deck's Game Jersey chase set, which featured a piece of game-used jersey.

Debuting in the 1996 Upper Deck set, Game Jerseys continue to captured the collectors' eyes one year later, as they remained hot through 1997.

Collectors who wanted this set could expect to shell out $3,500.

Collectors who focus on the top cards from the set could also expect to break the bank. The 1996 Joe Montana Game Jersey No. GJ3 has been on the rise since its release and has skyrocketed to $550.

Marino's 1996 Game Jersey card also was popular with collectors in 1997. The odds of pulling a Marino or a Rice Game Jersey card were much better, because both had two different cards inserted into packs. Marino's cards are a bit pricey at $575.

Rice's 1996 Game Jersey cards, on the other hand, are priced at $350 apiece.

Other 1996 Upper Deck Game Jersey cards to watch for are Barry Sanders ($375), Mark Brunell and Steve Young (both at $300) and Marshall Faulk at $200.

Pinnacle had a winner on its hands with its 1996 Laser View Inscriptions chase set, which was inserted one per 20 packs.

The 25 card insert set featured autographs of the NFL Quarterback Club. It carries a price tag of $1,450.

The two hottest Inscriptions cards featured signatures from Rice and Favre.

The NFL's all-time greatest receiver signed only 900 of his Inscriptions cards. The future Hall of Famer was the card to get from this chase set.

Collectors who wanted to pick up this card had to open up their pocketbooks, as it was valued at $350.

Favre's Laser View Inscriptions card also opened a few eyes. The two-time MVP autographed 4,850 cards. Individual cards were valued at $125 each. Steve Young signed 1,950 Inscriptions cards and each is priced at $125, while Barry Sanders autographed 2,900 and each is valued at $120.

All of this could make 1997-98 another interesting era in the hobby.

TOP TEN

INSERT SINGLES

THE FOLLOWING LIST OF CARDS HAVE GENERATED THE MOST DEMAND WITHIN THE HOBBY OVER THE LAST YEAR. THE RANKINGS ARE DETERMINED BY COLLECTORS AND DEALERS FROM THE HOBBY.

No. 1 — BRETT FAVRE
'97 Upper Deck Game Jersey #GM4
The Game Jersey set is on the rise, and it's just a matter of time before both Favre cards in this set also move up. Collectors are having a difficult time trying to find this single at shops or shows. If you're lucky enough to find one, expect to pay $600.

taking a look back...

No. 2 — BRETT FAVRE
'97 SkyBox Autographics Century Mark
You can only find this card in SkyBox Premium packs. This Favre Century Mark is numbered to 100 and sells for between $500 and $600.

No. 3 — JOE MONTANA
'96 Upper Deck Game Jersey #GJ3
Last year's Game Jerseys are just as popular as this year's. Joe Montana's single has been on the rise since its release a year ago and it's up to $550.

No. 4 — DAN MARINO
'96 Upper Deck Game Jersey #GJ1
Your odds of pulling a Marino or a Rice out of a pack are better than finding others, as both have two cards. Marino is still one of the top sellers, at $575.

No. 5 — BRETT FAVRE
'97 Finest II Rare Refractor #340
There are plenty of Favre cards to choose from, but collectors are always chasing the newest Refractors. This Finest II is one of the best at $400.

No. 6 — BRETT FAVRE
'97 Studio Stained Glass #9
The Favre Stained Glass card can only be found in Studio and is numbered to 1,000. Favre is one of 24 cards in the set and has been selling for $125 to $150.

No. 7 — TERRELL DAVIS
'97 SkyBox Autographics
Terrell Davis is having an MVP season, and many of his inserts are becoming tougher to find. This Autographics insert is one of his best in '97 and is selling for $150.

1995 UPPER DECK PREDICTOR DREW BLEDSOE #HP1

This was the second year Upper Deck released its Predictor insert and if your player finished 1st or 2nd in the category on the front, then you won. Winners could send in their card, along with $3, for a super foil-enhanced Predictor Trade Set.

No. 8 — BRETT FAVRE
'97 E-X2000 A Cut Above #2
You can find a Cut Above card in every 288 packs. Favre is one of 10 players in the set, which is why it's difficult to find this $120 card.

No. 9 — BRETT FAVRE
'97 Pacific Cramer's Choice #6
Cramer's Choice cards have always been a big hit with collectors since their first release three years ago. Favre has had two cards, and this '97 is one of the best, at $250.

No. 10 — BRETT FAVRE
'97 SkyBox Premium Player #6
Favre is the top card chased in most insert sets, including this one. The Premium Players are found 1:192 packs, and Favre is at the top at $120.

TOP TEN

INSERT SETS

THE FOLLOWING LIST OF SETS HAVE GENERATED THE MOST DEMAND WITHIN THE HOBBY OVER THE LAST YEAR. THE RANKINGS ARE DETERMINED BY COLLECTORS AND DEALERS FROM THE HOBBY.

No. 1 — 1997 UPPER DECK GAME JERSEYS
We've hinted all along that we thought this set was a bargain at $2,500, and we were right. Cards of Favre, Davis, Elway and Aikman have vaulted the price of this set by $300 this month to $2,800.

taking a look back...

No. 2 — 1996 UPPER DECK GAME JERSEYS
Interest in the Montana and now Barry Sanders cards has this set locked in at No. 2. This was the first Game Jersey set out and is strong at $3,500.

No. 3 — 1997 SKYBOX AUTOGRAPHICS
This is the first year for Autographics in football, and it's causing a stir. Favre, Davis and Stewart can be found throughout various SkyBox products.

No. 4 — 1997 TOPPS GALLERY PLAYERS PRIVATE ISSUE
The cards aren't hard to find and are a hit with collectors. They have doubled in price, now at 20x-40x the base card.

1996 SP HOLOVIEW

This was the third year Upper Deck released this insert and it was well received. The '96 cards were inserted in SP packs at a rate of 1:7 packs, up from the normal 1:5 packs two years earlier, and the set size also went from 40 cards to 48. The set remains popular today and retails for $250.

No. 5 — 1997 E-X2000 A CUT ABOVE
This set is full of star players, including Favre, Rice and George. The cards are inserted 1:288 packs, and the 10-card set is listed for $600.

No. 6 — 1997 FINEST II COMMON REFRACTORS
This insert, which can be found 1:12 packs, is loaded with stars and rookies. The 100-card set lists for $850.

No. 7 — 1997 STUDIO STAINED GLASS
The large size of these cards make this set great. Cards, with a stained glass background, are numbered to 1,000. The 24-card set lists for $800.

No. 8 — 1997 SKYBOX PREMIUM PLAYERS
This insert set can be found in SkyBox packs at a rate of 1:192. Favre, Martin, Bledsoe and George are just a few in this $800, 15-card set.

No. 9 — 1997 E-X2000 FLEET OF FOOT
Many collectors like this insert because it isn't that difficult to pull from packs at 1:20. Many of the top players are in this 20-card set, which lists for $220.

No. 10 — 1997 STUDIO RED ZONE MASTERPIECES
This insert is much easier to find than some of the others in Studio. Each card is numbered to 3,500 and the 24-card set sells for $200-$250.

TOP TEN

REGULAR-ISSUE SINGLES

THE FOLLOWING LIST OF CARDS HAVE GENERATED THE MOST DEMAND WITHIN THE HOBBY OVER THE LAST YEAR. THE RANKINGS ARE DETERMINED BY COLLECTORS AND DEALERS FROM THE HOBBY.

No. 1 — BRETT FAVRE
'92 Stadium Club III #683
We initially said it would take another MVP Award for this card to break $100, but so far, that's not the case. It's hard to believe that this Favre could get any hotter, but collectors are paying whatever it takes to get this for their collection. It continues to climb, currently booking at $100.

No. 2 — BARRY SANDERS
'89 Score #257
This card is just as popular as our No.1 selection. The Lions might not make the playoffs, but don't tell collectors it's Barry's fault. His rookie just gets hotter at $65.

No. 3 — BRETT FAVRE
'91 Stadium Club #94
Favre is the top player chased in the football market today. Marino and Smith's cards are priced high, but collectors say Favre is No.1. This rookie card holds at $70.

No. 4 — DREW BLEDSOE
'93 Upper Deck SP #9
Many forget how young Bledsoe is for the numbers he has put up. Smart collectors are picking up this card now for $75.

No. 5 — MARK BRUNELL
'93 SP #91
Less than a year ago, you could have found this for under $5. Now collectors are struggling to find it for $40. If Brunell can get to the Super Bowl, look for another jump.

No. 6 — JERRY RICE
'86 Topps #161
Rice may have missed most of the season due to injury, but his rookie card hasn't slipped on our list at all. It was listed at $120 the day of his injury and is still at that price today.

No. 7 — JOHN ELWAY
'84 Topps #63
This card may be the Scottie Pippen rookie of the football card market. For everything Elway has accomplished, you can still find this 13-year old card for $50.

No. 8 — JEROME BETTIS
'93 Upper Deck SP #6
Bettis had another 1,000-yard rushing season and is headed toward another Pro Bowl. That's why many collectors are buying up this rookie card for only $20.

No. 9 — DAN MARINO
'84 Topps #123
Many collectors are trying their luck at pulling this card from a wax pack that will run you $15. You can buy almost nine packs and chase it, or buy the single for $130.

No. 10 — ADRIAN MURRELL
'93 SP #196
What a difference a year makes. Last year, you could have found this card in some dealers' common boxes, but not anymore. This single has jumped $11 in the last year to $14.

TOP TEN

REGULAR-ISSUE SETS

THE FOLLOWING LIST OF SETS HAVE GENERATED THE MOST DEMAND WITHIN THE HOBBY OVER THE LAST YEAR. THE RANKINGS ARE DETERMINED BY COLLECTORS AND DEALERS FROM THE HOBBY.

No. 1 — 1992 STADIUM CLUB III
This is by far the best set out of the great run of 1992 football card releases. Many collectors passed on this set when it was first released, because it was either too hard to find, or it cost too much to complete at $5 or $6 a pack. Now, packs will run you $15 and boxes $450. The Favre single has gone up another $10 this month to $100, and the 100-card set is up $15 to $125.

No. 2 — 1993 SP
Collectors are once again chasing top rookie cards of key players, and SP is loaded with key rookies. Bledsoe, Brunell, Bettis and Murrell are all included in this 270-card set, which lists for $170.

No. 3 — 1997 E-X2000
This is a product that many like for the base set and not just the inserts. Two-card packs sell for $4, with boxes moving at $80. Top inserts include A Cut Above and Fleet of Foot.

No. 4 — 1996 MOVI MOTIONVISION
Many feel this is still the best product MotionVision has put out. Packs are at $10, with 25-count boxes at $200. Marino and Smith can be found in this $120 set.

No. 5 — 1997 FINEST II
Finest II is loaded with Refractors, while many of the top rookies can be found in the Common or Bronze set. Packs are at $5, with boxes at $100. The complete 175-card set is priced at $900.

No. 6 — 1997 TOPPS GALLERY
This product has some of the best photography around. Packs are at $3 and boxes at $70 as the inserts and base set look great. The Private Issue cards are the top insert.

No. 7 — 1991 STADIUM CLUB
The Favre card drives this product. Collectors used to buy this for the Smith and Sanders cards, but now they're spending $3 a pack in search of the Favre rookie.

No. 8 — 1997 STUDIO
Studio is the first product with every card measuring 8x10. You receive two cards for $5 a pack. The top two inserts are the Stained Glass (# to 1,000) and the Gold Portrait Proofs (# to 1,000).

No. 9 — 1997 MOVI MOTIONVISION 1.1
They expanded this year's set to 20 cards and all of the top players are in this $160 set. Packs are selling for $6, with 25-count boxes moving at $135.

No. 10 — 1997 SKYBOX
This year's product is much sharper, with a thicker stock. Eight-card packs are selling for $2.75, with boxes moving at $60. The 250-card set includes all of this year's rookies and lists for $35.

1996 Bowman's Best

Bowman's Best contained 135 key veterans on gold designs and 45 1996 NFL draft picks on silver designed cards. All 180 cards are also found in a parallel Refractors and Atomic Refractors insert. The cards show the player in front of a fake field with yard markers running down the length of the card. The player's name and team logo are near the bottom. Bowman's Best had three inserts - Mirror Images, Best Bets and Best Cuts.

		MT
Complete Set (180):		110.00
Common Player:		.25
Wax Box:		110.00
1	Emmitt Smith	8.00
2	Kordell Stewart	4.00
3	Mark Chmura	.25
4	Sean Dawkins	.25
5	Steve Young	3.00
6	Tamarick Vanover	2.00
7	Scott Mitchell	.25
8	Aaron Hayden	.25
9	William Thomas	.25
10	Dan Marino	8.00
11	Curtis Conway	.25
12	Steve Atwater	.25
13	Derrick Brooks	.25
14	Rick Mirer	.25
15	Mark Brunell	3.00
16	Garrison Hearst	.25
17	Eric Turner	.25
18	Mark Carrier	.25
19	Darnay Scott	.25
20	Steve McNair	4.00
21	Jim Everett	.25
22	Wayne Chrebet	.25
23	Ben Coates	.25
24	Harvey Williams	.25
25	Michael Westbrook	.50
26	Kevin Carter	.25
27	Dave Brown	.25
28	Jake Reed	.25
29	Thurman Thomas	.50
30	Jeff George	.25
31	Carnell Lake	.25
32	J.J. Stokes	.50
33	Jay Novacek	.25
34	Brett Perriman	.25
35	Robert Brooks	.25
36	Neil Smith	.25
37	Chris Zorich	.25
38	Michael Barrow	.25
39	Quentin Coryatt	.25
40	Kerry Collins	1.00
41	Aeneas Williams	.25
42	James Stewart	.25
43	Warren Moon	.25
44	Willie McGinest	.25
45	Rodney Hampton	.25
46	Jeff Hostetler	.25
47	Darrell Green	.25
48	Warren Sapp	.25
49	Troy Drayton	.25
50	Junior Seau	.25
51	Mike Mamula	.25
52	Antonio Langham	.25
53	Eric Metcalf	.25
54	Adrian Murrell	.25
55	Joey Galloway	2.00
56	Anthony Miller	.25
57	Carl Pickens	.25
58	Bruce Smith	.25
59	Merton Hanks	.25
60	Troy Aikman	4.00
61	Erik Kramer	.25
62	Tyrone Poole	.25
63	Michael Jackson	.25
64	Rob Moore	.25
65	Marcus Allen	.25
66	Orlando Thomas	.25
67	David Meggett	.25
68	Trent Dilfer	.25
69	Herman Moore	.75
70	Brett Favre	8.00
71	Blaine Bishop	.25
72	Eric Allen	.25
73	Bernie Parmalee	.25
74	Kyle Brady	.25
75	Terry McDaniel	.25
76	Rodney Peete	.25
77	Yancey Thigpen	.25
78	Stan Humphries	.25
79	Craig Heyward	.25
80	Rashaan Salaam	.75
81	Shannon Sharpe	.25
82	Jim Harbaugh	.25
83	Vinnie Clark	.25
84	Steve Bono	.25
85	Drew Bledsoe	4.00
86	Ken Norton	.25
87	Brian Mitchell	.25
88	Hardy Nickerson	.25
89	Todd Lyght	.25
90	Barry Sanders	4.00
91	Robert Blackmon	.25
92	Larry Centers	.25
93	Jim Kelly	.25
94	Lamar Lathon	.25
95	Cris Carter	.25
96	Hugh Douglas	.25
97	Michael Strahan	.25
98	Lee Woodall	.25
99	Michael Irvin	.25
100	Marshall Faulk	1.00
101	Terance Mathis	.25
102	Eric Zeier	.25
103	Marty Carter	.25
104	Steve Tovar	.25
105	Isaac Bruce	1.50
106	Tony Martin	.25
107	Dale Carter	.25
108	Terry Kirby	.25
109	Tyrone Hughes	.25
110	Bryce Paup	.25
111	Errict Rhett	.75
112	Ricky Watters	.50
113	Chris Chandler	.25
114	Edgar Bennett	.25
115	John Elway	3.00
116	Sam Mills	.25
117	Seth Joyner	.25
118	Jeff Lageman	.25
119	Chris Calloway	.25
120	Curtis Martin	6.00
121	Ken Harvey	.25
122	Eugene Daniel	.25
123	Tim Brown	.25
124	Mo Lewis	.25
125	Jeff Blake	.75
126	Jessie Tuggle	.25
127	Vinny Testaverde	.25
128	Chris Warren	.25
129	Terrell Davis	4.00
130	Greg Lloyd	.25
131	Deion Sanders	3.00
132	Derrick Thomas	.25
133	Darryll Lewis	.25
134	Reggie White	.50
135	Jerry Rice	4.00
136	*Tony Banks*	4.00
137	*Derrick Mayes*	.25
138	*Leeland McElroy*	2.00
139	*Bryan Still*	.25
140	*Tim Biakabutuka*	2.50
141	*Rickey Dudley*	2.00
142	*Troy James*	.25
143	*Lawyer Milloy*	.25
144	*Mike Ulufale*	.25
145	*Bobby Engram*	2.50
146	*Willie Anderson*	.25
147	*Terrell Owens*	6.00
148	*Jonathan Ogden*	.25
149	*Darrius Johnson*	.25
150	*Kevin Hardy*	1.00
151	*Simeon Rice*	1.00
152	*Alex Molden*	.25
153	*Cedric Jones*	.25
154	*Duane Clemons*	.25
155	*Karim Abdul-Jabbar*	6.00
156	*Dedric Mathis*	.25
157	*John Michels*	.25
158	*Winslow Oliver*	.25
159	*Stepfret Williams*	.25
160	*Eddie Kennison*	4.00
161	*Marcus Coleman*	.25
162	*Tedy Bruschi*	.25
163	*Detron Smith*	.25
164	*Ray Lewis*	.25
165	*Marvin Harrison*	5.00
166	*Je'Rod Cherry*	.25
167	*Jerris McPhail*	.25
168	*Eric Moulds*	1.50
169	*Walt Harris*	.25
170	*Eddie George*	15.00
171	*Jermaine Lewis*	.25
172	*Jeff Lewis*	.25
173	*Ray Mickens*	.25
174	*Amani Toomer*	.25
175	*Zach Thomas*	4.00
176	*Lawrence Phillips*	5.00
177	*John Mobley*	.25
178	*Anthony Dorsett Jr.*	.25
179	*DeRon Jenkins*	.25
180	*Keyshawn Johnson*	5.00

1996 Bowman's Best Refractors

All 180 cards in Bowman's Best Football had parallel Refractor versions, inserted every 12 packs. The fronts feature a refractive foil, while the backs contain the word "Refractor" within the white card number box.

	MT
Refractors:	5x-10x

1996 Bowman's Best Atomic Refractors

All 180 cards in Bowman's Best Football also had Atomic Refractor parallel versions, inserted every 48 packs. Atomic Refractors featured a prismatic refractive foil on the card fronts and the words "Atomic Refractor" on the back within the white card number box.

	MT
Atomic Refractors:	15x-30x

1996 Bowman's Best Best Bets

Bowman's Best Bets highlighted nine top rookies on a borderless design with "screws" in all four corners as if the card was in a screw-down holder. Regular versions are seeded every 12 packs, Refractors are found every 48 packs with Atomic Refractors every 96 packs.

		MT
Complete Set (9):		45.00
Common Player:		2.00
Refractors:		2x
Atomic Refractors:		4x
1	Keyshawn Johnson	10.00
2	Lawrence Phillips	10.00
3	Tim Biakabutuka	5.00
4	Eddie George	20.00
5	John Mobley	2.00
6	Eddie Kennison	6.00
7	Marvin Harrison	10.00
8	Amani Toomer	2.00
9	Bobby Engram	4.00

1996 Bowman's Best Best Cuts

Bowman's Best Cuts displays 15 of the top players in the NFL on die-cut chromium cards. The player's name runs along the right side, with the majority of the die-cutting on that side. Regular versions are found every 24 packs, Refractors are seeded every 48 packs and Atomic Refractor versions are found every 96 packs.

		MT
Complete Set (15):		250.00
Common Player:		5.00
Refractors:		2x
Atomic Refractors:		4x
1	Dan Marino	40.00
2	Emmitt Smith	40.00
3	Rashaan Salaam	5.00
4	Herman Moore	5.00
5	Brett Favre	40.00
6	Marshall Faulk	10.00
7	John Elway	12.00
8	Curtis Martin	25.00
9	Deion Sanders	12.00
10	Jerry Rice	20.00
11	Terrell Davis	20.00
12	Kerry Collins	20.00
13	Steve Young	15.00
14	Troy Aikman	20.00
15	Barry Sanders	20.00

1996 Bowman's Best Mirror Images

Bowman's Best Mirror Images was a nine-card insert that featured four players per card, with two on each side. Regular versions are seeded every 48 packs, Refractors are found every 96 packs and Atomic Refractors are seeded every 192 packs. Card No. 7 has Jerry Rice on the front with Isaac Bruce with him, but lists running backs as their position. This card was an uncorrected error.

		MT
Complete Set (9):		175.00
Common Player:		12.00
Refractors:		2x
Atomic Refractors:		4x
1	Steve Young, Kerry Collins Dan Marino, Mark Brunell	40.00
2	Brett Favre, Elvis Grbac John Elway, Drew Bledsoe	40.00
3	Troy Aikman, Gus Frerotte Jim Harbaugh, Jeff Blake	20.00
4	Emmitt Smith, Errict Rhett Chris Warren, Curtis Martin	40.00
5	Barry Sanders, Rashaan Salaam Thurman Thomas, Terrell Davis	25.00
6	Rodney Hampton, Lawrence Phillips Marcus Allen, Marshall Faulk	12.00
7	Jerry Rice, Isaac Bruce Tim Brown, Joey Galloway	20.00
8	Cris Carter, Curtis Conway Carl Pickens, Keyshawn Johnson	12.00
9	Robert Brooks, Michael Westbrook Anthony Miller, O.J. McDuffie	12.00

1996 Collector's Edge Advantage

Collector's Edge's 1996 Advantage set includes 150 cards, including 25 cards of rookies in their NFL uniforms. Each card front and back is gold foil stamped and embossed, with the rookies cards featuring extra foil stamping. The base set is also paralleled by Perfect Play holofoil inserts; these cards, seeded one per every two packs, use prism art technology. Five other insert sets were also produced - Role Models, Edge Video, Crystal Cuts, Game Ball and Super Bowl Game Ball. Portions of the proceeds made from the sale of this product were to be donated to the Pop Warner Football program.

	MT
Complete Set (150):	25.00
Common Player:	.10
Wax Box:	55.00

1	Drew Bledsoe	1.00
2	Chris Warren	.10
3	*Eddie George*	3.50
4	Barry Sanders	1.25
5	Scott Mitchell	.10
6	Carl Pickens	.10
7	Tim Brown	.10
8	John Elway	.75
9	Michael Westbrook	.20
10	Cris Carter	.10
11	Troy Aikman	1.25
12	Ben Coates	.10
13	Brett Favre	2.50
14	Marshall Faulk	.40
15	Steve Young	1.00
16	Terrell Davis	2.00
17	*Keyshawn Johnson*	1.50
18	Mario Bates	.10
19	Steve McNair	.75
20	Kerry Collins	1.25
21	Natrone Means	.10
22	Kordell Stewart	1.25
23	Jeff George	.10
24	Rick Mirer	.10
25	Herman Moore	.20
26	Rodney Peete	.10
27	Isaac Bruce	.50
28	Errict Rhett	.20
29	Jerry Rice	1.25
30	Rashaan Salaam	.50
31	Eric Metcalf	.10
32	Jim Kelly	.20
33	Jerome Bettis	.20
34	Deion Sanders	.75
35	J.J. Stokes	.20
36	Neil O'Donnell	.10
37	Marcus Allen	.20
38	Thurman Thomas	.20
39	Dan Marino	2.50
40	*Rickey Dudley*	.75
41	Napoleon Kaufman	.10
42	Kyle Brady	.10
43	Emmitt Smith	2.50
44	Tyrone Wheatley	.10
45	Jeff Blake	.20
46	Reggie White	.20
47	Joey Galloway	1.00
48	Antonio Langham	.10
49	Craig Heyward	.10
50	Curtis Martin	1.75
51	*Karim Abdul-Jabbar*	2.25
52	Antonio Freeman	.10
53	Ki-Jana Carter	.20
54	Willie Davis	.10
55	Jim Everett	.10
56	Gus Frerotte	.10
57	Daryl Gardener	.10
58	Charles Haley	.10
59	Michael Irvin	.20
60	Keith Jackson	.10
61	Cortez Kennedy	.10
62	Greg Lloyd	.10
63	Tony Martin	.10
64	Ken Norton Jr.	.10
65	Leslie O'Neal	.10
66	Bryce Paup	.10
67	Jake Reed	.10
68	Frank Sanders	.10
69	Vinny Testaverde	.10
70	Regan Upshaw	.10
71	Tamarick Vanover	.50
72	Walt Harris	.10
73	John Randle	.10
74	Ricky Watters	.20
75	Terry Allen	.10
76	Edgar Bennett	.10
77	Larry Centers	.10
78	Chris Penn	.10
79	*Bobby Engram*	.75
80	Irving Fryar	.10
81	Charlie Garner	.10
82	Rodney Hampton	.10
83	Michael Jackson	.10
84	O.J. McDuffie	.10
85	Shannon Sharpe	.10
86	Aaron Hayden	.10
87	*Mushin Muhammad*	1.00
88	Rodney Woodson	.10
89	Levon Kirkland	.10
90	Chad Brown	.10
91	Junior Seau	.10
92	Terry Kirby	.10
93	*Zach Thomas*	1.00
94	Harvey Williams	.10
95	Robert Brooks	.10
96	Darrell Green	.10
97	Chester McGlockton	.10
98	Neil Smith	.10
99	Eric Swann	.10
100	*Mike Alstott*	.75
101	*Tim Biakabutuka*	1.00
102	Mark Brunell	1.00
103	Chris Doleman	.10
104	Sean Gilbert	.10
105	Jim Harbaugh	.10
106	Chris T. Jones	.10
107	Tyrone Hughes	.10
108	*Amani Toomer*	.40
109	Larry Brown	.10
110	Kevin Greene	.10
111	John Mobley	.10
112	*Danny Kanell*	.40
113	*Kevin Hardy*	.40
114	Brett Perriman	.10
115	*Simeon Rice*	.40
116	Chris Sanders	.10
117	Dave Brown	.10
118	Bryan Cox	.10
119	Yancey Thigpen	.10
120	Terance Mathis	.10
121	Warren Moon	.10
122	Derrick Thomas	.10
123	Trent Dilfer	.10
124	*Terry Glenn*	2.50
125	Jeff Hostetler	.10
126	*Leeland McElroy*	.50
127	Hardy Nickerson	.10
128	Steve Bono	.10
129	Stanley Pritchett	.10
130	Dana Stubblefield	.10
131	Andre Coleman	.10
132	Anthony Miller	.10
133	Stan Humphries	.10
134	Robert Smith	.10
135	Curtis Conway	.10
136	Derrick Holmes	.10
137	Pat Swilling	.10
138	Andre Rison	.10
139	Erik Kramer	.10
140	Jason Dunn	.10
141	Torrance Small	.10
142	Cedric Jones	.10
143	Derek Loville	.10
144	Brian Mitchell	.10
145	*Eric Moulds*	.75
146	James Stewart	.10
147	Bruce Smith	.10
148	Keenan McCardell	.10
149	Warren Sapp	.10
150	*Marvin Harrison*	1.25

1996 Collector's Edge Advantage Perfect Play Holofoil

Perfect Play Holofoil cards put a prismatic finish on all 150 cards in the Advantage set. These parallel cards were inserted every two packs.

	MT
Complete Set (150):	150.00
Holofoil Cards:	3x-6x

1996 Collector's Edge Advantage Crystal Cuts

These 1996 Collector's Edge Advantage die-cut inserts are printed on clear plastic stock. The cards, dual numbered up to 5,000, were seeded one per every eight packs. The card front has a color photo on it, with a background which makes the card look like a filmstrip. The player's name, position, number and team name are in gold foil and form a circle at the bottom of the card. The Collector's Edge logo is stamped in gold foil in the middle.

		MT
Complete Set (25):		125.00
Common Player:		2.50
1	Barry Sanders	7.00
2	Eddie George	12.00
3	Curtis Martin	12.00
4	J.J. Stokes	5.00
5	Kyle Brady	2.50
6	Chris Warren	2.50
7	Jerry Rice	7.00
8	Ben Coates	2.50
9	Terrell Davis	8.00
10	Marcus Allen	2.50
11	John Elway	6.00
12	Joey Galloway	5.00
13	Dan Marino	14.00
14	Napoleon Kaufman	2.50
15	Emmitt Smith	14.00
16	Eric Metcalf	2.50
17	Kerry Collins	7.00
18	Troy Aikman	7.00
19	Rickey Dudley	3.00
20	Steve McNair	6.00
21	Steve Young	6.00
22	Isaac Bruce	4.00
23	Kordell Stewart	7.00
24	LeShon Johnson	2.50
25	Scott Mitchell	2.50

1996 Collector's Edge Advantage Edge Video

These 1996 Collector's Edge Advantage inserts depict real game action with an overlaid photograph. The card front has a stand-out player shot with a state-of-the-art "Edge Video" background showing actual in-motion footage. The cards, each limited to 1,200, were seeded one per every 36 packs.

		MT
Complete Set (25):		200.00
Common Player:		4.00
1	Brett Favre	35.00
2	Keyshawn Johnson	10.00
3	Deion Sanders	10.00
4	Marcus Allen	4.00
5	Rashaan Salaam	8.00
6	Thurman Thomas	4.00
7	Emmitt Smith	35.00
8	Isaac Bruce	6.00
9	Michael Westbrook	4.00
10	Cris Carter	4.00
11	Marshall Faulk	6.00
12	Jerry Rice	17.00
13	Tim Brown	4.00
14	Steve Young	12.00
15	Eric Metcalf	4.00
16	Chris Warren	4.00
17	Drew Bledsoe	17.00
18	Barry Sanders	17.00
19	Herman Moore	6.00
20	Rodney Peete	4.00
21	Troy Aikman	17.00
22	Jerome Bettis	4.00
23	Errict Rhett	6.00
24	Dan Marino	35.00
25	Natrone Means	4.00

1996 Collector's Edge Advantage Game Ball

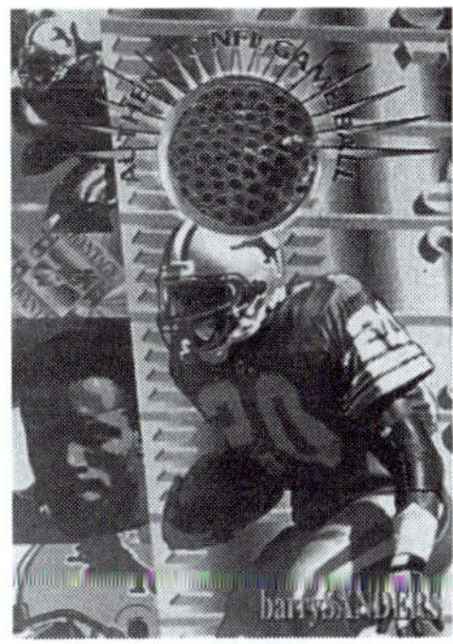

These 1996 Collector's Edge Advantage inserts feature a medallion cut from an authentic game-used NFL football, with highlights of the game in which the ball was used. The card front has a color photo on it, plus foil stamping. The background of the card has a football field, with smaller color photos along the left side. Each card back contains a statement of authentication for the ball and game in which it was used. The cards are limited to 400 individually dual-numbered cards, seeded one per every 72 packs.

		MT
Complete Set (36):		1600.00
Common Player:		25.00
1	Kordell Stewart	75.00
2	Emmitt Smith	150.00
3	Brett Favre	150.00
4	Steve Young	50.00
5	Barry Sanders	70.00
6	John Elway	40.00
7	Drew Bledsoe	60.00
8	Dan Marino	150.00
9	Keyshawn Johnson	40.00
10	Eddie George	85.00
11	Kevin Hardy	25.00
12	Terry Glenn	75.00
13	Michael Westbrook	25.00
14	Joey Galloway	50.00
15	John Mobley	25.00
16	Curtis Martin	80.00
17	Rashaan Salaam	25.00
18	J.J. Stokes	25.00
19	Kerry Collins	60.00
20	Deion Sanders	50.00
21	Shannon Sharpe	25.00
22	Terry Allen	25.00
23	Rickey Watters	25.00
24	Marshall Faulk	40.00
25	Tim Biakabutaka	30.00
26	Troy Aikman	60.00
27	Jerry Rice	60.00
28	Chris Warren	25.00
29	Jeff Blake	25.00
30	Carl Pickens	25.00
31	Isaac Bruce	35.00
32	Terrell Davis	80.00
33	Mark Brunell	75.00
34	Karim Abdul-Jabbar	50.00
35	Herman Moore	25.00
36	Cris Carter	25.00

1996 Collector's Edge Advantage Role Models

These 1996 Collector's Edge Advantage inserts were seeded one per every 12 packs. Each card front has an action shot on it, on a die-cut, embossed metallized card. A smaller photo is in the background of the card front, which has the Collector's Edge logo stamped in gold foil. The cards were seeded one per every 12 packs.

		MT
Complete Set (12):		60.00
Common Player:		2.50
1	John Elway	7.00
2	Dan Marino	16.00
3	Jerry Rice	8.00
4	Emmitt Smith	16.00
5	Chris Warren	2.50
6	Tim Brown	2.50
7	Jeff George	6.00
8	Tyrone Wheatley	2.50
9	Steve Bono	2.50
10	Kerry Collins	8.00
11	Jerome Bettis	5.00
12	Steve Beuerlein	2.50

1996 Collector's Edge Advantage Super Bowl Game Ball

Collector's Edge obtained several footballs from the Super Bowl to create these 1996 inserts. Each card has a medallion cut from an authentic NFL Super Bowl game-used ball, with highlights of the game in which the ball was used. The 36 cards were limited to 200 individually-numbered cards each, with odds of one per every 164 packs.

		MT
Complete Set (36):		2200.00
Common Player:		30.00
1	Emmitt Smith	325.00
2	Troy Aikman	100.00
3	Michael Irvin	50.00
4	Deion Sanders	130.00
5	John Elway	160.00
6	Dan Marino	325.00
7	Marcus Allen	80.00
8	Kordell Stewart	180.00
9	Steve Young	130.00
10	Ricky Watters	50.00
11	Jerry Rice	180.00
12	Jim Kelly	80.00
13	Thurman Thomas	50.00
14	Bruce Smith	30.00
15	Stan Humphries	30.00
16	Junior Seau	50.00
17	Natrone Means	30.00
18	Neil O'Donnell	30.00
19	Rod Woodson	30.00
20	Andre Reed	30.00
21	Jeff Hostetler	30.00
22	Dave Meggett	30.00
23	Greg Lloyd	30.00
24	Kevin Green	30.00
25	Yancey Thigpen	30.00
26	Charles Haley	30.00
27	Bam Morris	30.00
28	Alvin Harper	30.00
29	Ken Norton Jr.	30.00
30	William Floyd	30.00
31	Leslie O'Neal	30.00
32	Jay Novacek	30.00
33	Irvin Fryar	30.00
34	Leon Lett	30.00
35	Tony Martin	30.00
36	Mark Collins	30.00

1996 Donruss

This 250-card set marks the debut of Donruss football cards. The base brand includes 10 Rated Rookies, a subset made popular in the Donruss baseball sets. Each card front has a full-bleed color action photo, with a banner at the top in the team's primary color containing the player's name. The Donruss logo is stamped in silver in the upper left corner. A football, using team colors, is at the bottom of the card, with the position along the top and the team name below. A star in the middle of the football contains a team logo. The horizontal back has the player's position in the upper left corner, with the player's name running in a team-colored banner along the top. Career totals and stats from 1995 are below this information, followed by a brief recap of the player's accomplishments underneath. The background is a team logo. The right side of the card has a number in the upper corner, with a photograph below. Biographical information is in a stripe along the bottom. There were 240 of the cards also produced as a parallel Press Proof set. Each card, numbered 1 of 2,000, has a helmet die-cut in it. The Donruss logo is stamped at the top in gold foil, which is also used for the words "First 2,000 Printed" and "Press Proof" toward the bottom. Insert sets include Hit List, Stop Action, What If?, Will to Win and Silver and Gold Elite cards.

		MT
Complete Set (240):		20.00
Common Player:		.05
Wax Box:		30.00
1	Barry Sanders	1.00
2	Flipper Anderson	.05
3	Ben Coates	.05
4	Rob Johnson	.05
5	Rodney Hampton	.05
6	Desmond Howard	.05
7	Craig Heyward	.05
8	Alvin Harper	.05
9	Todd Collins	.05
10	Ken Norton Jr.	.05
11	Stan Humphries	.05
12	Aeneas Williams	.05
13	Jeff Hostetler	.05
14	Frank Sanders	.05
15	J.J. Birden	.05
16	Bryce Paup	.05
17	Bill Brooks	.05
18	Kevin Williams	.05
19	Boomer Esiason	.05
20	O.J. McDuffie	.05
21	Eric Swann	.05
22	Neil Smith	.05
23	Charlie Garner	.05
24	Greg Lloyd	.05
25	Willie Jackson	.05
26	Shawn Jefferson	.05
27	Rodney Peete	.05
28	Michael Westbrook	.50
29	J.J. Stokes	.50
30	Troy Aikman	1.00
31	Sean Dawkins	.05
32	Larry Centers	.05
33	Herschel Walker	.05
34	Stoney Case	.05
35	Kevin Greene	.05
36	Quinn Early	.05
37	Fred Barnett	.05
38	Andre Coleman	.05
39	Mark Chmura	.25
40	Adrian Murrell	.05
41	Roosevelt Potts	.05
42	Jay Novacek	.05
43	Derrick Alexander	.05
44	Ken Dilger	.05
45	Rob Moore	.05
46	Cris Carter	.05
47	Jeff Blake	.50
48	Derek Loville	.05
49	Tyrone Wheatley	.05
50	Terrell Fletcher	.05
51	Sherman Williams	.05
52	Justin Armour	.05
53	Kordell Stewart	1.00
54	Tim Brown	.05
55	Kevin Carter	.05
56	Andre Rison	.05
57	James Stewart	.05
58	Brent Jones	.05
59	Erik Kramer	.05
60	Floyd Turner	.05
61	Ricky Watters	.05
62	Hardy Nickerson	.05
63	Aaron Craver	.05
64	Dave Krieg	.05
65	Warren Moon	.05
66	Wayne Chrebet	.05
67	Napoleon Kaufman	.10
68	Terance Mathis	.05
69	Chad May	.05
70	Andre Reed	.05
71	Reggie White	.10
72	Brett Favre	2.00
73	Chris Zorich	.05
74	Kerry Collins	1.00
75	Herman Moore	.30
76	Yancey Thigpen	.50
77	Glenn Foley	.05
78	Quentin Coryatt	.05
79	Terry Kirby	.05
80	Edgar Bennett	.05
81	Mark Brunell	.75
82	Heath Shuler	.05
83	Gus Frerotte	.05
84	Deion Sanders	.50
85	Calvin Williams	.05
86	Junior Seau	.10
87	Jim Kelly	.10
88	Daryl Johnston	.05
89	Irving Fryar	.05
90	Brian Blades	.05
91	Willie Davis	.05
92	Jerome Bettis	.10
93	Marcus Allen	.10
94	Jeff Graham	.05
95	Rick Mirer	.05
96	Harvey Williams	.05
97	Steve Atwater	.05
98	Carl Pickens	.10
99	Darick Holmes	.05
100	Bruce Smith	.05
101	Vinny Testaverde	.05
102	Thurman Thomas	.10
103	Drew Bledsoe	.75
104	Bernie Parmalee	.05
105	Greg Hill	.05
106	Steve McNair	.50
107	Andre Hastings	.05
108	Eric Metcalf	.05
109	Kimble Anders	.05
110	Steve Tasker	.05
111	Mark Carrier	.05
112	Jerry Rice	1.00
113	Joey Galloway	.75
114	Robert Smith	.05
115	Hugh Douglas	.05
116	Willie McGinest	.05
117	Terrell Davis	.75
118	Cortez Kennedy	.05
119	Marshall Faulk	.50
120	Michael Haynes	.05
121	Isaac Bruce	.50
122	Brian Mitchell	.05
123	Bryan Cox	.05
124	Tamarick Vanover	.50
125	William Floyd	.05
126	Chris Chandler	.05
127	Carnell Lake	.05

128	Aaron Bailey	.05
129	Darnay Scott	.20
130	Darren Woodson	.05
131	Ernie Mills	.05
132	Charles Haley	.05
133	Rocket Ismail	.05
134	Bert Emanuel	.05
135	Lake Dawson	.05
136	Jake Reed	.05
137	Dave Brown	.05
138	Steve Bono	.05
139	Terry Allen	.05
140	Errict Rhett	.20
141	Rod Woodson	.05
142	Charles Johnson	.05
143	Emmitt Smith	2.00
144	Ki-Jana Carter	.40
145	Garrison Hearst	.05
146	Rashaan Salaam	.50
147	Tony Boselli	.05
148	Derrick Thomas	.05
149	Mark Seay	.05
150	Derrick Alexander	.05
151	Christian Fauria	.05
152	Aaron Hayden	.05
153	Chris Warren	.10
154	Dave Meggett	.05
155	Jeff George	.10
156	Jackie Harris	.05
157	Michael Irvin	.10
158	Scott Mitchell	.05
159	Trent Dilfer	.05
160	Kyle Brady	.05
161	Dan Marino	2.00
162	Curtis Martin	1.50
163	Mario Bates	.05
164	Erric Pegram	.05
165	Eric Zeier	.05
166	Rodney Thomas	.05
167	Neil O'Donnell	.05
168	Warren Sapp	.05
169	Jim Harbaugh	.10
170	Henry Ellard	.05
171	Anthony Miller	.05
172	Derrick Moore	.05
173	John Elway	.50
174	Vincent Brisby	.05
175	Antonio Freeman	.05
176	Chris Sanders	.30
177	Steve Young	.75
178	Shannon Sharpe	.05
179	Brett Perriman	.05
180	Orlando Thomas	.05
181	Eric Bjornson	.05
182	Natrone Means	.05
183	Jim Everett	.05
184	Curtis Conway	.05
185	Robert Brooks	.10
186	Tony Martin	.05
187	Mark Carrier	.05
188	LeShon Johnson	.05
189	Bernie Kosar	.05
190	Ray Zellars	.05
191	Steve Walsh	.05
192	Craig Erickson	.05
193	Tommy Maddox	.05
194	Leslie O'Neal	.05
195	Harold Green	.05
196	Steve Beuerlein	.05
197	Ron Moore	.05
198	Leslie Shepherd	.05
199	Leroy Hoard	.05
200	Michael Jackson	.05
201	Will Moore	.05
202	Ricky Ervins	.05
203	Keith Jennings	.05
204	Eric Green	.05
205	Mark Rypien	.05
206	Torrance Small	.05
207	Sean Gilbert	.05
208	*Mike Alstott*	.50
209	Willie Anderson	.05
210	Alex Molden	.05
211	Jonathan Ogden	.05
212	Stepfret Williams	.05
213	Jeff Lewis	.05
214	Regan Upshaw	.05
215	Daryl Gardener	.05
216	*Danny Kanell*	.20
217	John Mobley	.05
218	Reggie Brown	.05
219	*Mushin Muhammad*	.60
220	*Kevin Hardy*	.25
221	*Stanley Pritchett*	.40
222	Cedric Jones	.05
223	Marco Battaglia	.05
224	Duane Clemons	.05
225	Jerald Moore	.05
226	*Simeon Rice*	.30
227	Chris Darkins	.10
228	*Bobby Hoying*	.30

229	*Stephen Davis*	.40
230	*Walt Harris*	.30
231	Jermain Mayberry	.05
232	Tony Brackens	.05
233	*Eric Moulds*	1.00
234	*Alex Van Dyke*	.50
235	*Marvin Harrison*	1.75
236	*Rickey Dudley*	.50
237	*Terrell Owens*	1.50
238	Checklist Jerry Rice CL	.25
239	Checklist Dan Marino CL	.30
240	Checklist	.05

1996 Donruss Press Proofs

Press Proofs paralleled the 240-card regular-issue set, and included the words "Press Proof" in gold foil on the front of the card, along with a die-cut. Each Gold Press Proof was numbered 1 of 2,000.

	MT
Complete Set (240):	600.00
Press Proof Cards:	12x-24x

1996 Donruss Elite

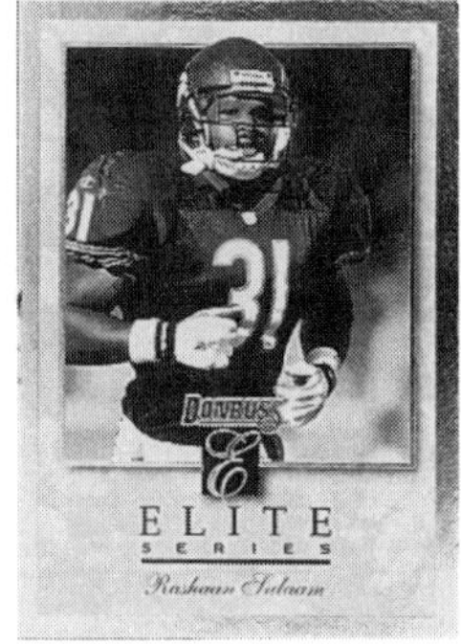

Donruss' initial football set continues the legacy of an Elite insert set, which debuted in the company's baseball line in 1991. Ten of the NFL's premiere running backs are featured on two versions of the foil-enhanced card - Silver Elite and Gold Elite. The Silver cards are limited to 10,000 each; the Gold ones are sequentially numbered to 2,000. The card front uses the corresponding color for the foiled borders around the picture, plus the Donruss and Elite logos. The card back uses the appropriate color for the background, which has a scripted Elite "E" and a short player profile on the left side. The right side has a color photo with a team logo underneath. The card number, one of twenty, etc., is along the top of the card.

	MT
Complete Set (20):	300.00
Common Player:	4.00
1 Emmitt Smith	40.00
2 Barry Sanders	20.00
3 Marshall Faulk	15.00

4	Curtis Martin	30.00
5	Junior Seau	4.00
6	Troy Aikman	20.00
7	Steve Young	15.00
8	Dan Marino	40.00
9	Brett Favre	40.00
10	John Elway	10.00
11	Kerry Collins	20.00
12	Drew Bledsoe	20.00
13	Jerry Rice	20.00
14	Keyshawn Johnson	20.00
15	Deion Sanders	12.00
16	Isaac Bruce	10.00
17	Rashaan Salaam	4.00
18	Tim Biakabutuka	15.00
19	Lawrence Phillips	15.00
20	Robert Brooks	4.00

1996 Donruss Elite Gold

Donruss Elite Golds run parallel with the Elite Silvers, but are numbered up to 2,000. In this insert, the silver foil is replaced by gold foil.

	MT
Complete Set (20):	900.00
Gold Cards:	3x

1996 Donruss Hit List

These 1996 Donruss insert cards feature the NFL's most physical players on cards which use silver holographic foil and die-cutting for the design. The front has a color photo, with a holographic background. "Hit List" is written at the top of the card; Donruss and the player's team name are below the photo. The sides of the card are die cut, with foiled rivets in them. The card back has a color photo on it, with most of it, except for the player's face, ghosted as the background. The player's face is in full color, highlighted by a sunburst around it. There's a paragraph below which details a moment when the player survived, or delivered, a devastating hit. A serial number appears in a white rectangle along the bottom. The card number, 1 of 20, etc., is in the upper right corner.

	MT
Complete Set (20):	180.00
Common Player:	3.00
1 Bruce Smith	3.00
2 Barry Sanders	10.00
3 Kevin Hardy	3.00
4 Greg Lloyd	3.00
5 Brett Favre	25.00
6 Emmitt Smith	25.00
7 Kerry Collins	10.00
8 Ken Norton Jr.	3.00
9 Steve Atwater	3.00
10 Curtis Martin	15.00
11 Chris Warren	3.00
12 Steve Young	10.00
13 Marshall Faulk	5.00
14 Junior Seau	3.00
15 Lawrence Phillips	12.00
16 Troy Aikman	12.00
17 Jerry Rice	12.00

18	Dan Marino	25.00
19	Reggie White	3.00
20	John Elway	8.00

1996 Donruss Rated Rookies

In a concept first made popular with its baseball line, Donruss has issued this 10-card insert set honoring 10 of the top NFL newcomers.

	MT
Complete Set (10):	40.00
Common Player:	2.00
1 Keyshawn Johnson	5.00
2 Terry Glenn	7.00
3 Tim Biakabutuka	4.00
4 Bobby Engram	2.00
5 Leeland McElroy	2.00
6 Eddie George	8.00
7 Lawrence Phillips	4.00
8 Derrick Mayes	2.00
9 Karim Abdul-Jabbar	5.00
10 Eddie Kennison	4.00

1996 Donruss Stop Action

1996 Donruss football magazine packs have these Stop Action inserts, which feature some of the best action photos in the sport. Each shot is enhanced by holographic foil and die-cutting. Each card is serial numbered to 5,000.

	MT
Complete Set (10):	275.00
Common Player:	10.00
1 Deion Sanders	17.00
2 Troy Aikman	25.00
3 Brett Favre	50.00
4 Steve Young	20.00
5 Joey Galloway	10.00
6 Dan Marino	50.00
7 Jerry Rice	25.00
8 Emmitt Smith	50.00
9 Isaac Bruce	10.00
10 Barry Sanders	25.00

1996 Donruss What If?

These 1996 Donruss inserts go back in time to chronicle the NFL's top talents with a post-dated rookie card.

Each card uses rookie photography, with a design that fits the era that the player entered the league. Each card also has a sequential serial number. Cards were in hobby packs only.

		MT
Complete Set (10):		200.00
Common Player:		10.00
1	Troy Aikman	25.00
2	Jerry Rice	25.00
3	Barry Sanders	25.00
4	Drew Bledsoe	15.00
5	Deion Sanders	10.00
6	Brett Favre	40.00
7	Dan Marino	40.00
8	Steve Young	15.00
9	Emmitt Smith	40.00
10	John Elway	12.00

1996 Donruss Will to Win

These inserts are exclusive to 1996 Donruss retail packs only. The cards, having sequential numbering to 5,000, are one of the scarcest inserts in the product. They feature some of the NFL's grittiest competitors.

		MT
Complete Set (10):		170.00
Common Player:		7.00
1	Emmitt Smith	30.00
2	Brett Favre	30.00
3	Curtis Martin	25.00
4	Jerry Rice	17.00
5	Barry Sanders	17.00
6	Errict Rhett	7.00
7	Troy Aikman	17.00
8	Dan Marino	30.00
9	Steve Young	15.00
10	John Elway	15.00

1996 Metal

Fleer's 1996 Metal set has an all-new look for 1996 - metalized foil engraved by hand on each card front, meaning no two player cards are alike. The basic set includes 123 regular cards, 25 rookies and two checklists. The card front has a full-bleed color photograph, with the player's name "tearing through" the lower right-hand corner of the card. The back has another photo, a close-cropped head-

shot bursting through the card, 1995 and career statistics, and biographical information. An extra-rare parallel set - Precious Metal - was also produced. These cards, seeded one per box, feature an all-silver front and were limited to less than 550 each. They are numbered on the back using a PM prefix. There were five other insert sets included in packs - Goldfingers, Goldflingers, Platinum Portraits, Molten Metal and Freshly Forged.

		MT
Complete Set (150):		30.00
Common Player:		.10
Wax Box:		50.00
1	Garrison Hearst	.10
2	Rob Moore	.10
3	Frank Sanders	.10
4	Eric Swann	.10
5	Jeff George	.20
6	Craig Heyward	.10
7	Terance Mathis	.10
8	Eric Metcalf	.10
9	Derrick Alexander	.10
10	Andre Rison	.10
11	Vinny Testaverde	.10
12	Eric Turner	.10
13	Jim Kelly	.10
14	Bryce Paup	.10
15	Bruce Smith	.10
16	Thurman Thomas	.20
17	Bob Christian	.10
18	Kerry Collins	1.50
19	Lamar Lathon	.10
20	Tyrone Poole	.10
21	Curtis Conway	.10
22	Bryan Cox	.10
23	Erik Kramer	.10
24	Rashaan Salaam	.50
25	Jeff Blake	1.00
26	Ki-Jana Carter	.50
27	Carl Pickens	.20
28	Darnay Scott	.30
29	Troy Aikman	1.50
30	Michael Irvin	.20
31	Daryl Johnston	.10
32	Deion Sanders	.75
33	Emmitt Smith	3.00
34	Terrell Davis	1.25
35	John Elway	.75
36	Anthony Miller	.10
37	Shannon Sharpe	.10
38	Scott Mitchell	.10
39	Herman Moore	.75
40	Brett Perriman	.10
41	Barry Sanders	1.50
42	Edgar Bennett	.10
43	Robert Brooks	.20
44	Mark Chmura	.30
45	Brett Favre	3.00
46	Reggie White	.20
47	Mel Gray	.10
48	Steve McNair	1.00
49	Chris Sanders	.30
50	Rodney Thomas	.20
51	Quentin Coryatt	.10
52	Sean Dawkins	.10
53	Ken Dilger	.10
54	Marshall Faulk	.75
55	Jim Harbaugh	.20
56	Tony Boselli	.10
57	Mark Brunell	1.00
58	Natrone Means	.20
59	James Stewart	.10
60	Marcus Allen	.20
61	Steve Bono	.20
62	Neil Smith	.10
63	Tamarick Vanover	1.00
64	Eric Green	.10
65	Terry Kirby	.10
66	Dan Marino	3.00
67	O.J. McDuffie	.10
68	Cris Carter	.10
69	Qadry Ismail	.10
70	Warren Moon	.10
71	Jake Reed	.10
72	Drew Bledsoe	1.25
73	Ben Coates	.10
74	Curtis Martin	2.50
75	David Meggett	.10
76	Mario Bates	.10
77	Jim Everett	.10
78	Michael Haynes	.10
79	Tyrone Hughes	.10
80	Dave Brown	.10
81	Rodney Hampton	.10
82	Thomas Lewis	.10

83	Tyrone Wheatley	.10
84	Kyle Brady	.10
85	Hugh Douglas	.10
86	Adrian Murrell	.10
87	Neil O'Donnell	.10
88	Tim Brown	.10
89	Jeff Hostetler	.10
90	Napoleon Kaufman	.30
91	Harvey Williams	.10
92	Charlie Garner	.10
93	Rodney Peete	.10
94	Ricky Watters	.10
95	Calvin Williams	.10
96	Jerome Bettis	.20
97	Greg Lloyd	.10
98	Kordell Stewart	1.00
99	Yancey Thigpen	.30
100	Rod Woodson	.10
101	Isaac Bruce	1.00
102	Kevin Carter	.10
103	Steve Walsh	.10
104	Aaron Hayden	.10
105	Stan Humphries	.10
106	Junior Seau	.10
107	William Floyd	.10
108	Brent Jones	.10
109	Jerry Rice	1.50
110	J.J. Stokes	.20
111	Steve Young	1.00
112	Brian Blades	.10
113	Joey Galloway	1.00
114	Rick Mirer	.10
115	Chris Warren	.20
116	Trent Dilfer	.10
117	Alvin Harper	.10
118	Hardy Nickerson	.10
119	Errict Rhett	.30
120	Terry Allen	.10
121	Brian Mitchell	.10
122	Heath Shuler	.10
123	Michael Westbrook	.20
124	*Karim Abdul-Jabbar*	2.50
125	*Tim Biakabutuka*	1.25
126	*Duane Clemons*	.10
127	*Stephen Davis*	.20
128	*Rickey Dudley*	.30
129	*Bobby Engram*	1.25
130	*Daryl Gardener*	.10
131	*Eddie George*	4.00
132	*Terry Glenn*	3.00
133	*Kevin Hardy*	.20
134	*Walt Harris*	.20
135	*Marvin Harrison*	2.00
136	*Keyshawn Johnson*	2.00
137	*Cedric Jones*	.10
138	*Eddie Kennison*	1.25
139	*Sam Manuel,Sean Manuel*	.10
140	*Leeland McElroy*	.30
141	*Ray Mickens*	.10
142	*Jonathan Ogden*	.10
143	*Lawrence Phillips*	.75
144	*Kavika Pittman*	.10
145	*Simeon Rice*	.20
146	*Regan Upshaw*	.10
147	*Alex Van Dyke*	.20
148	*Stepfret Williams*	.10
149	Checklist	.10
150	Checklist	.10

1996 Metal Precious Metal

One Precious Metals parallel card was found in each box of Metal Football in 1996. The set included each card in the regular-issue set (minus the two checklists), but featured all-silver fronts and the letters "PM" preceding the card number on the back.

	MT
Complete Set (148):	800.00
Precious Metal Cards:	15x-30x

1996 Metal Freshly Forged

These 1996 Fleer Metal inserts highlight second-year NFL standouts and flashy rookies. The cards, seeded one per every 30 hobby packs only, are acrylic. The card front has a color action photo on it, with an NFL logo and line drawing of the photo as the background. The Fleer Metal logo is in an upper corner. The player's name

and "Freshly Forged" are stamped in gold foil along the bottom. The card back shows the entire NFL logo, with a description of the player's skills inside. A card number, 1 of 10, etc., is also on the back.

		MT
Complete Set (10):		125.00
Common Player:		4.00
1	Tim Biakabutuka	12.00
2	Jeff Blake	10.00
3	Ki-Jana Carter	4.00
4	Eddie George	25.00
5	Terry Glenn	20.00
6	Keyshawn Johnson	12.00
7	Curtis Martin	20.00
8	Leeland McElroy	8.00
9	Lawrence Phillips	12.00
10	Kordell Stewart	18.00

1996 Metal Goldfingers

These 24-karat etched gold foil-stamped inserts feature some of the NFL's top-flight receivers. Each card front has a color action photo against a metallic background with an image of a gold hand. The Fleer logo is in the upper left corner. The player's name and "Gold Fingers" are in gold foil in an arch at the bottom. The card back, numbered 1 of 10, etc., has a color photo on one side, with the player's name in the upper left corner. A brief player profile is below. Cards were seeded one per every eight packs.

		MT
Complete Set (12):		40.00
Common Player:		2.00
1	Isaac Bruce	5.00
2	Joey Galloway	7.00
3	Michael Irvin	3.00
4	Herman Moore	4.00
5	Carl Pickens	2.00
6	Jerry Rice	10.00
7	Chris Sanders	3.00
8	Frank Sanders	2.00
9	J.J. Stokes	4.00
10	Yancey Thigpen	4.00
11	Tamarick Vanover	6.00
12	Michael Westbrook	4.00

1996 Metal Goldflingers

Twelve of the top quarterbacks in football were included in the Goldflingers insert, not to be confused with Goldfingers, which were both out of Metal. Goldflingers was a retail exclusive insert found every 12 packs.

		MT
Complete Set (12):		50.00
Common Player:		2.00
1	Troy Aikman	7.00
2	Steve Bono	2.00
3	Kerry Collins	7.00
4	Trent Dilfer	2.00
5	Brett Favre	14.00
6	Gus Frerotte	2.00
7	Stan Humphries	2.00
8	Dan Marino	14.00
9	Steve McNair	5.00
10	Scott Mitchell	2.00
11	Steve Young	5.00
12	Eric Zeier	2.00

1996 Metal Molten Metal

Featuring 10 red-hot superstars, these 1996 Fleer inserts use foil embossing on the front. The Fleer Metal logo is in an upper corner; Molten Metal, in gold foil, is in the lower left corner. The player's name is in gold foil, too, along the right side of the card. The card back, numbered 1 of 10, etc., has a photo on one side. The other side has a white rectangle which includes a brief player profile. The player's name is above the box. These cards were the scarcest of the Fleer Metal inserts; they were seeded one per every 120 packs.

		MT
Complete Set (10):		250.00
Common Player:		10.00
1	Troy Aikman	25.00
2	Ki-Jana Carter	10.00
3	Kerry Collins	25.00
4	Terrell Davis	35.00
5	Marshall Faulk	15.00
6	Brett Favre	50.00
7	Keyshawn Johnson	15.00
8	Curtis Martin	35.00
9	Deion Sanders	15.00
10	Emmitt Smith	50.00

1996 Metal Platinum Portraits

This 1996 Fleer Metal set uses the serillusion process to profile 10 NFL stars. The front shows a closeup head shot of the player, using a silvery embossed effect to create depth. The Fleer Metal logo is in the upper left corner; "Platinum Portraits" is written along the right side of the card. The player's name is along the bottom. The horizontal card back shows an image of the photo from the front as a background, with a brief writeup over it. One side of the card has a color action photo on it. The card number, 1 of 12, etc., is in the upper left corner, with the player's name next to it.

		MT
Complete Set (10):		100.00
Common Player:		5.00
1	Isaac Bruce	12.00
2	Terrell Davis	16.00
3	John Elway	12.00
4	Joey Galloway	16.00
5	Steve McNair	15.00
6	Errict Rhett	10.00
7	Rashaan Salaam	10.00
8	Barry Sanders	20.00
9	Chris Warren	5.00
10	Steve Young	18.00

1996 Ultra Sensations

Ultra Sensations was a Series II product, but didn't resemble the Series I release. Instead it went a new direction with 100 cards that appeared in five different versions. Forty percent of the print run had gold borders, 30 percent blue, 20 percent marbleized gold, nine percent pewter and one percent holographic gold foil. The only differentiation between any of the versions was a thick border around the entire card. Ultra Sensations included two inserts: Creative Chaos and Random Rookies.

		MT
Complete Gold Set (100):		20.00
Common Player:		.10
Blue Cards:		1.5x
Marbleized Gold Cards:		2x
Pewter Cards:		4x
Holographic Gold Cards:		15x
Wax Box:		50.00
1	*Leeland McElroy*	.30
2	Frank Sanders	.10
3	Eric Swann	.10
4	Jeff George	.10
5	Terrance Mathis	.10
6	Eric Metcalf	.10
7	Michael Jackson	.10
8	Eric Turner	.10
9	Jim Kelly	.10
10	Bryce Paup	.10
11	Bruce Smith	.10
12	Thurman Thomas	.20
13	*Tim Biakabutuka*	1.00
14	Kerry Collins	1.25
15	*Muhsin Muhammad*	1.00
16	Winslow Oliver	.10
17	Curtis Conway	.10
18	Bryan Cox	.10
19	*Bobby Engram*	1.00
20	Erik Kramer	.10
21	Rashaan Salaam	.30
22	Jeff Blake	.30
23	Ki-Jana Carter	.20
24	Carl Pickens	.10
25	Troy Aikman	1.25
26	Michael Irvin	.20
27	Daryl Johnston	.10
28	Deion Sanders	.75
29	Emmitt Smith	2.50
30	Terrell Davis	1.75
31	John Elway	1.00
32	Anthony Miller	.10
33	John Mobley	.10
34	Scott Mitchell	.10
35	Herman Moore	.20
36	Barry Sanders	1.25
37	Edgar Bennett	.10
38	Robert Brooks	.10
39	Brett Favre	2.50
40	Reggie White	.20
41	*Eddie George*	3.00
42	Steve McNair	.75
43	Chris Sanders	.10
44	Quentin Coryatt	.10
45	Marshall Faulk	.30
46	Jim Harbaugh	.10
47	*Marvin Harrison*	1.75
48	Mark Brunell	1.00
49	Natrone Means	.10
50	Andre Rison	.10
51	Marcus Allen	.20
52	Steve Bono	.10
53	Greg Hill	.10
54	Tamarick Vanover	.30
55	*Karim Abdul-Jabbar*	2.50
56	Dan Marino	2.50
57	O.J. McDuffie	.10
58	*Zach Thomas*	1.00
59	Cris Carter	.10
60	Warren Moon	.10
61	Jake Reed	.10
62	Drew Bledsoe	1.25
63	Ben Coates	.10
64	*Terry Glenn*	3.00
65	Curtis Martin	2.00
66	Mario Bates	.10
67	Michael Haynes	.10
68	Dave Brown	.10
69	Rodney Hampton	.10
70	Amani Toomer	.10
71	Tyrone Wheatley	.10
72	*Keyshawn Johnson*	1.75
73	Neil O'Donnell	.10
74	Tim Brown	.10
75	*Rickey Dudley*	.30
76	Napoleon Kaufman	.10
77	Chester McGlockton	.10
78	Charlie Garner	.10
79	Chris T. Jones	.10
80	Ricky Watters	.20
81	Jerome Bettis	.20
82	Kordell Stewart	1.25
83	Rod Woodson	.10
84	Aaron Hayden	.10
85	Stan Humphries	.10
86	Junior Seau	.10
87	*Tony Banks*	1.00
88	Isaac Bruce	.50
89	*Lawrence Phillips*	.50
90	Derek Loville	.10
91	Jerry Rice	1.25
92	J.J. Stokes	.40
93	Steve Young	1.00
94	Joey Galloway	1.00
95	Rick Mirer	.10
96	Chris Warren	.10
97	Trent Dilfer	.10
98	Errict Rhett	.30
99	Terry Allen	.10
100	Michael Westbrook	.20

1996 Ultra Sensations Creative Chaos

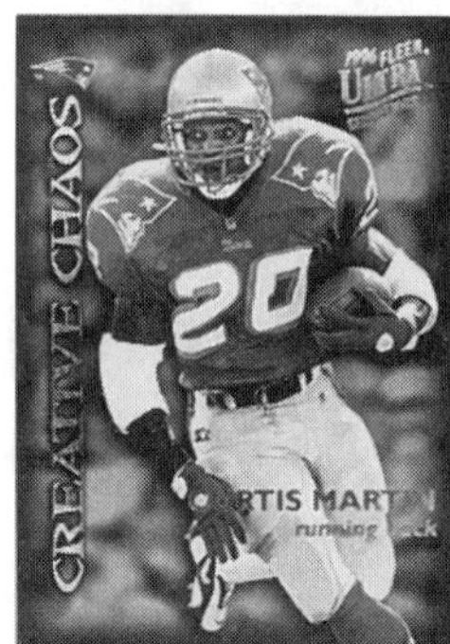

Creative Chaos featured 10 players on double-sided cards that matched each player, resulting in 100 total cards. These inserts were included in every 12 packs.

		MT
Complete Set (100):		600.00
Common Player:		4.00
1	Emmitt Smith, Emmitt Smith	20.00
1	Emmitt Smith, Brett Favre	18.00
1	Emmitt Smith, Curtis Martin	16.00
1	Emmitt Smith, Chris Warren	12.00
1	Emmitt Smith, Deion Sanders	13.00
1	Emmitt Smith, Steve Young	14.00
1	Emmitt Smith, Jerry Rice	15.00
1	Emmitt Smith, Terrell Davis	15.00
1	Emmitt Smith, Carl Pickens	12.00
1	Emmitt Smith, Marshall Faulk	13.00
2	Brett Favre, Emmitt Smith	18.00
2	Brett Favre, Brett Favre	16.00
2	Brett Favre, Curtis Martin	14.00
2	Brett Favre, Chris Warren	10.00
2	Brett Favre, Deion Sanders	11.00
2	Brett Favre, Steve Young	12.00
2	Brett Favre, Jerry Rice	13.00
2	Brett Favre, Terrell Davis	13.00
2	Brett Favre, Carl Pickens	10.00
2	Brett Favre, Marshall Faulk	11.00
3	Curtis Martin, Emmitt Smith	16.00
3	Curtis Martin, Brett Favre	14.00
3	Curtis Martin, Curtis Martin	12.00
3	Curtis Martin, Chris Warren	8.00
3	Curtis Martin, Deion Sanders	9.00
3	Curtis Martin, Steve Young	10.00
3	Curtis Martin, Jerry Rice	11.00
3	Curtis Martin, Terrell Davis	11.00
3	Curtis Martin, Carl Pickens	8.00
3	Curtis Martin, Marshall Faulk	9.00
4	Chris Warren, Emmitt Smith	12.00
4	Chris Warren, Brett Favre	10.00
4	Chris Warren, Curtis Martin	8.00
4	Chris Warren, Chris Warren	4.00
4	Chris Warren, Deion Sanders	4.00
4	Chris Warren, Steve Young	4.00
4	Chris Warren, Jerry Rice	8.00
4	Chris Warren, Terrell Davis	8.00
4	Chris Warren, Carl Pickens	4.00
4	Chris Warren, Marshall Faulk	4.00
5	Deion Sanders, Emmitt Smith	13.00
5	Deion Sanders, Brett Favre	11.00
5	Deion Sanders, Curtis Martin	9.00
5	Deion Sanders, Chris Warren	4.00
5	Deion Sanders, Deion Sanders	8.00

#	Player	Price
5	Deion Sanders, Steve Young	8.00
5	Deion Sanders, Jerry Rice	8.00
5	Deion Sanders, Terrell Davis	8.00
5	Deion Sanders, Carl Pickens	4.00
5	Deion Sanders, Marshall Faulk	4.00
6	Steve Young, Emmitt Smith	14.00
6	Steve Young, Brett Favre	12.00
6	Steve Young, Curtis Martin	10.00
6	Steve Young, Chris Warren	4.00
6	Steve Young, Deion Sanders	4.00
6	Steve Young, Steve Young	4.00
6	Steve Young, Jerry Rice	8.00
6	Steve Young, Terrell Davis	9.00
6	Steve Young, Carl Pickens	4.00
6	Steve Young, Marshall Faulk	4.00
7	Jerry Rice, Emmitt Smith	15.00
7	Jerry Rice, Brett Favre	13.00
7	Jerry Rice, Curtis Martin	11.00
7	Jerry Rice, Chris Warren	8.00
7	Jerry Rice, Deion Sanders	8.00
7	Jerry Rice, Steve Young	8.00
7	Jerry Rice, Jerry Rice	10.00
7	Jerry Rice, Terrell Davis	10.00
7	Jerry Rice, Carl Pickens	8.00
7	Jerry Rice, Marshall Faulk	8.00
8	Terrell Davis, Emmitt Smith	15.00
8	Terrell Davis, Brett Favre	13.00
8	Terrell Davis, Curtis Martin	11.00
8	Terrell Davis, Chris Warren	8.00
8	Terrell Davis, Deion Sanders	8.00
8	Terrell Davis, Steve Young	9.00
8	Terrell Davis, Jerry Rice	10.00
8	Terrell Davis, Terrell Davis	10.00
8	Terrell Davis, Carl Pickens	8.00
8	Terrell Davis, Marshall Faulk	8.00
9	Carl Pickens, Emmitt Smith	12.00
9	Carl Pickens, Brett Favre	10.00
9	Carl Pickens, Curtis Martin	8.00
9	Carl Pickens, Chris Warren	4.00
9	Carl Pickens, Deion Sanders	4.00
9	Carl Pickens, Steve Young	4.00
9	Carl Pickens, Jerry Rice	8.00
9	Carl Pickens, Terrell Davis	8.00
9	Carl Pickens, Carl Pickens	4.00
9	Carl Pickens, Marshall Faulk	4.00
10	Marshall Faulk, Emmitt Smith	13.00
10	Marshall Faulk, Brett Favre	11.00
10	Marshall Faulk, Curtis Martin	9.00
10	Marshall Faulk, Chris Warren	4.00
10	Marshall Faulk, Deion Sanders	4.00
10	Marshall Faulk, Steve Young	4.00
10	Marshall Faulk, Jerry Rice	8.00
10	Marshall Faulk, Terrell Davis	8.00
10	Marshall Faulk, Carl Pickens	4.00
10	Marshall Faulk, Marshall Faulk	4.00

1996 Ultra Sensations Random Rookies

Random Rookies arrived with 80 percent of the print run in silver foil and 20 percent in gold foil. The set includ-ed 10 cards, with the first five in hobby and the second five in retail packs. Random Rookies were seeded one every 48 packs.

		MT
Complete Set (10):		60.00
Common Player:		2.00
Gold Cards:		2x-3x
1	Keyshawn Johnson	10.00
2	Eddie George	25.00
3	Leeland McElroy	4.00
4	Eric Moulds	2.00
5	Lawrence Phillips	8.00
6	Marvin Harrison	10.00
7	Tim Biakabutuka	8.00
8	Terry Glenn	20.00
9	Rickey Dudley	6.00
10	Tony Banks	8.00

1996 Leaf

Leaf Football contained 190 cards in the regular-issue set, plus 10 Gold Leaf Rookies that were numbered like inserts, but considered part of the reg-ular-issue set. Leaf arrived for the first time since 1949, and was packaged in 10-card packs. The 190 players from the base set were also available in factory sets receiving special foil treat-ment and limited to 1,996 sets. The factory sets also included one of 25 different autographed future stars. In-serts found in Leaf Football included: 190-card Press Proof parallel set, Sta-tistical Standouts, Grass Roots, Gold Leaf Stars, American All-Stars and Shirt Off My Back. Cards from regular packs had the bottom strip of the card in the player's team colors, with no foil, while pre- priced packs featured red foil and Collector's Edition cards had gold foil.

		MT
Complete Set (190):		20.00
Common Player:		.10
Wax Box:		45.00
1	Troy Aikman	1.50
2	Ricky Watters	.20
3	Robert Brooks	.10
4	Ki-Jana Carter	.20
5	Drew Bledsoe	1.25
6	Eric Swann	.10
7	Hardy Nickerson	.10
8	Tony Martin	.10
9	Garrison Hearst	.10
10	Bernie Parmalee	.10
11	Neil Smith	.10
12	Aaron Craver	.10
13	Rashaan Salaam	.20
14	Greg Hill	.10
15	Charlie Garner	.10
16	Kimble Anders	.10
17	Steve McNair	1.00
18	Neil O'Donnell	.10
19	Greg Lloyd	.10
20	Warren Moon	.10
21	Bernie Kosar	.10
22	Derrick Thomas	.10
23	Andre Hastings	.10
24	Wayne Chrebet	.10
25	Mark Seay	.10
26	Eric Metcalf	.10
27	Shawn Jefferson	.10
28	Napoleon Kaufman	.10
29	Steve Walsh	.10
30	Derrick Alexander	.10
31	Rodney Peete	.10
32	Terance Mathis	.10
33	Michael Westbrook	.20
34	Kevin Carter	.10
35	Aaron Hayden	.10
36	J.J. Stokes	.20
37	Andre Reed	.10
38	Chris Warren	.20
39	Jerry Rice	1.50
40	Ben Coates	.10
41	Reggie White	.20
42	Joey Galloway	1.25
43	Sean Dawkins	.10
44	Brett Favre	3.00
45	Jeff George	.10
46	Robert Smith	.10
47	Ken Dilger	.10
48	Larry Centers	.10
49	Jackie Harris	.10
50	Hugh Douglas	.10
51	Herschel Walker	.10
52	Kerry Collins	1.50
53	Michael Irvin	.20
54	Willie McGinest	.10
55	Herman Moore	.20
56	Leroy Hoard	.10
57	Scott Mitchell	.10
58	Terrell Davis	1.50
59	Kevin Greene	.10
60	Yancey Thigpen	.20
61	Kevin Smith	.10
62	Trent Dilfer	.10
63	Cortez Kennedy	.10
64	Carnell Lake	.10
65	Quinn Early	.10
66	Kyle Brady	.10
67	Marshall Faulk	.30
68	Fred Barnett	.10
69	Quentin Coryatt	.10
70	Dan Marino	3.00
71	Junior Seau	.10
72	Andre Coleman	.10
73	Terry Kirby	.10
74	Curtis Martin	2.00
75	Isaac Bruce	.75
76	Mark Chmura	.10
77	Edgar Bennett	.10
78	Mario Bates	.10
79	Eric Zeier	.10
80	Adrian Murrell	.10
81	Mark Brunell	1.00
82	Mark Rypien	.10
83	Erric Pegram	.10
84	Bryan Cox	.10
85	Heath Shuler	.10
86	Lake Dawson	.10
87	O.J. McDuffie	.10
88	Emmitt Smith	3.00
89	Jim Harbaugh	.10
90	Aaron Bailey	.10
91	Jim Kelly	.20
92	Rodney Hampton	.10
93	Cris Carter	.10
94	Henry Ellard	.10
95	Darnay Scott	.20
96	Daryl Johnston	.10
97	Tamarick Vanover	.20
98	Jeff Blake	.75
99	Anthony Miller	.10
100	Darren Woodson	.10
101	Irving Fryar	.10
102	Craig Heyward	.10
103	Derek Loville	.10
104	Ernie Mills	.10
105	Brian Blades	.10
106	Gus Frerotte	.10
107	Alvin Harper	.10
108	Tyrone Wheatley	.10
109	John Elway	1.00
110	Charles Haley	.10
111	Terrell Fletcher	.10
112	Vincent Brisby	.10
113	Jerome Bettis	.20
114	Barry Sanders	1.50
115	Ken Norton Jr.	.10
116	Sherman Williams	.10
117	Antonio Freeman	.10
118	Bert Emanuel	.10
119	Marcus Allen	.20
120	Stan Humphries	.10
121	Chris Sanders	.10
122	Jeff Graham	.10
123	Jay Novacek	.10
124	Aeneas Williams	.10
125	Kordell Stewart	1.25
126	Steve Young	1.00
127	Jake Reed	.10
128	Rick Mirer	.10
129	Jeff Hostetler	.10
130	Tim Brown	.10
131	Shannon Sharpe	.10
132	Dave Brown	.10
133	Harvey Williams	.10
134	Rodney Thomas	.10
135	Frank Sanders	.10
136	Brett Perriman	.10
137	Steve Bono	.10
138	Steve Atwater	.10
139	Andre Rison	.10
140	Orlando Thomas	.10
141	Terry Allen	.10
142	Carl Pickens	.20
143	William Floyd	.20
144	Bryce Paup	.10
145	James Stewart	.10
146	Eric Bjornson	.10
147	Errict Rhett	.20
148	Darick Holmes	.10
149	Bill Brooks	.10
150	Brent Jones	.10
151	Natrone Means	.10
152	Rod Woodson	.10
153	Bruce Smith	.10
154	Deion Sanders	.75
155	Kevin Williams	.10
156	Erik Kramer	.10
157	Jim Everett	.10
158	Vinny Testaverde	.10
159	Boomer Esiason	.10
160	Floyd Turner	.10
161	Curtis Conway	.20
162	Thurman Thomas	.20
163	Tony Brackens	.10
164	Stepfret Williams	.10
165	Alex Van Dyke	.75
166	Cedric Jones	.10
167	Stanley Pritchett	.10
168	Willie Anderson	.10
169	Regan Upshaw	.10
170	Daryl Gardener	.10
171	Alex Molden	.10
172	John Mobley	.10
173	Danny Kanell	.30
174	Marco Battaglia	.10
175	Simeon Rice	.10
176	*Tony Banks*	2.00
177	Stephen Davis	.10
178	Walt Harris	.30
179	Amani Toomer	.30
180	Derrick Mayes	.60
181	Jeff Lewis	.10
182	Chris Darkins	.10
183	Rickey Dudley	.75
184	Jonathan Ogden	.10
185	Mike Alstott	.75
186	Eric Moulds	.75
187	Karim Abdul-Jabbar	2.50
188	Checklist	.10
189	Checklist	.10
190	Checklist	.10

1996 Leaf Press Proofs

The first 190 cards in 1996 Leaf Football were die-cut and printed in gold foil to form this Press Proofs par-allel set. Each Press Proof insert carred a 1 of 2,000 produced number.

		MT
Complete Set (190):		600.00
Press Proof Cards:		15x-30x

1996 Leaf American All-Stars

American All-Stars showcased 20 NFL players who were All-America se-lections in college. The cards were printed on a simulated sail cloth card stock that attempts to have the look and feel of an American flag. Ameri-can All-Stars arrived in regular and Gold Team versions, with 5,000 regu-lar sets and 1,000 Gold Team sets.

		MT
Complete Set (20):		300.00
Common Player:		4.00
1	Emmitt Smith	40.00
2	Drew Bledsoe	15.00

3	Jerry Rice	20.00
4	Kerry Collins	20.00
5	Eddie George	25.00
6	Keyshawn Johnson	15.00
7	Lawrence Phillips	15.00
8	Rashaan Salaam	4.00
9	Deion Sanders	10.00
10	Marshall Faulk	15.00
11	Steve Young	15.00
12	Ki-Jana Carter	4.00
13	Curtis Martin	30.00
14	Joey Galloway	18.00
15	Troy Aikman	20.00
16	Barry Sanders	20.00
17	Dan Marino	40.00
18	John Elway	15.00
19	Steve McNair	4.00
20	Tim Biakabutuka	12.00

1996 Leaf American All-Stars Gold

American All-Stars Gold featured the same 20 cards found in the All-Stars Silver set, but with upgraded cloth stock and gold enhancements. Gold versions are sequentially numbered up to 1,000.

	MT
Complete Set (20):	900.00
Gold Cards:	2x-3x

1996 Leaf Collector's Edition Autographs

This 12-card autographed set was found one per Collector's Edition factory sets from Leaf. The autographed cards all carry the words "Authentic Signature" on the front. Autographs of Leeland McElroy, Marvin Harrison, Lawrence Phillips, Bobby Engram and Eddie Kennison were printed on Gold Leaf Rookies inserts. Autographs of Tony Banks and Karim Abdul-Jabbar were on rookie subset cards, while the remaining autographs were found on regular-issue cards.

	MT
Complete Set (12):	225.00
Common Player:	10.00
Karim Abdul-Jabbar	30.00
Tony Banks	15.00
Isaac Bruce	15.00
Terrell Davis	50.00
Bobby Engram	10.00
Joey Galloway	20.00
Marvin Harrison	20.00
Eddie Kennison	20.00
Leeland McElroy	10.00
Lawrence Phillips	10.00
Rashaan Salaam	15.00
Tamarick Vanover	10.00

1996 Leaf Gold Leaf Rookies

Gold Leaf Rookies were numbered as an insert set, but are actually considered part of the base set. It features 10 rookies on a distinctly different design than base cards.

		MT
Complete Set (10):		40.00
Common Player:		3.00
1	Leeland McElroy	3.00
2	Marvin Harrison	6.00
3	Lawrence Phillips	4.00
4	Bobby Engram	3.00
5	Kevin Hardy	3.00
6	Keyshawn Johnson	5.00
7	Eddie Kennison	5.00
8	Tim Biakabutuka	4.00
9	Eddie George	12.00
10	Terry Glenn	8.00

1996 Leaf Gold Leaf Stars

Fifteen of the top players in the NFL were included in Gold Leaf Stars. These were found in retail packs only and contain a 22kt. gold logo.

		MT
Complete Set (15):		550.00
Common Player:		10.00
1	Drew Bledsoe	30.00
2	Jerry Rice	40.00
3	Emmitt Smith	80.00
4	Dan Marino	80.00
5	Isaac Bruce	20.00
6	Kerry Collins	30.00
7	Barry Sanders	40.00
8	Keyshawn Johnson	40.00
9	Errict Rhett	10.00
10	Joey Galloway	20.00
11	Brett Favre	80.00
12	Curtis Martin	60.00
13	Steve Young	30.00
14	Troy Aikman	40.00
15	John Elway	20.00

1996 Leaf Grass Roots

Printed on a card stock that simulates artificial turf, Grass Roots highlighted 20 running backs that perform the best on artificial turf. This insert was limited to 5,000 sets produced.

		MT
Complete Set (20):		250.00
Common Player:		4.00
1	Thurman Thomas	8.00
2	Eddie George	25.00
3	Rodney Hampton	4.00
4	Rashaan Salaam	8.00
5	Natrone Means	4.00
6	Errict Rhett	8.00
7	Leeland McElroy	4.00
8	Emmitt Smith	40.00
9	Marshall Faulk	8.00
10	Ricky Watters	4.00
11	Chris Warren	4.00
12	Tim Biakabutuka	8.00
13	Barry Sanders	20.00
14	Karim Abdul-Jabbar	20.00
15	Darick Holmes	4.00
16	Terrell Davis	20.00
17	Lawrence Phillips	8.00
18	Ki-Jana Carter	8.00
19	Curtis Martin	30.00
20	Kordell Stewart	20.00

1996 Leaf Shirt Off My Back

Shirt Off My Back inserts were found only in special pre-priced retail packs. The cards were printed on stock that simulates jersey material and includes 10 of the top quarterbacks. Shirt Off My Back was limited to 2,500 sets.

		MT
Complete Set (10):		250.00
Common Player:		8.00
1	Steve Young	30.00
2	Jeff Blake	10.00
3	Drew Bledsoe	30.00
4	Kordell Stewart	30.00
5	Troy Aikman	30.00
6	Steve McNair	8.00
7	John Elway	20.00

8	Dan Marino	60.00
9	Kerry Collins	30.00
10	Brett Favre	60.00

1996 Leaf Statisical Standouts

Printed on simulated leather and inserted only in hobby packs, Statistical Standouts includes 15 top players. These cards have the feel of leather and are individually numbered to 2,500.

		MT
Complete Set (15):		425.00
Common Player:		10.00
1	John Elway	30.00
2	Jerry Rice	40.00
3	Reggie White	10.00
4	Drew Bledsoe	30.00
5	Chris Warren	10.00
6	Bruce Smith	10.00
7	Barry Sanders	40.00
8	Greg Lloyd	10.00
9	Emmitt Smith	80.00
10	Dan Marino	80.00
11	Steve Young	30.00
12	Steve Atwater	10.00
13	Isaac Bruce	20.00
14	Deion Sanders	20.00
15	Brett Favre	80.00

1996 Motion Vision

Motion Vision debuted in 1996 with two, 12-card series. The first was called Motion Vision, the second carried a 2.0 suffix. This product arrived in one card "packs" that actually resembled a compact disk case, with the cards inside a poly-sleeve. Motion Vision used Kodak technology to simulate actual game footage with tremendous clarity. The cards carried a Movi Motion Vision logo in the upper left-hand corner and the card number in the upper right-hand corner. The bottom of the card has the player's name, with nothing on the back. The card is best viewed by holding the plastic card up to light and rotating it to see game action. Motion Vision also had a 10-card Limited Digital Replay insert that was differentiated by having 25,000 produced.

		MT
Complete Set (24):		240.00
Comp. Series 1 (12):		120.00
Comp. Series 2 (12):		120.00
Series 1 Wax Box:		200.00
Series 2 Wax Box:		160.00
1	Troy Aikman	10.00
2	Dan Marino	20.00
3	Steve Young	10.00
4	Emmitt Smith	20.00
5	Drew Bledsoe	12.00
6	Kordell Stewart	10.00
7	Jerry Rice	10.00
8	Warren Moon	5.00
9	Junior Seau	5.00
10	Barry Sanders	10.00

11	Jim Harbaugh	5.00
12	John Elway	10.00
13	Brett Favre	20.00
14	Brett Favre	20.00
15	Troy Aikman	10.00
16	Emmitt Smith	20.00
17	Dan Marino	20.00
18	Kordell Stewart	10.00
19	John Elway	10.00
20	Kerry Collins	10.00
21	Jim Kelly	4.00
22	Drew Bledsoe	12.00
23	Mark Brunell	10.00
24	Jerry Rice	10.00

1996 Motion Vision Limited Digital Replays

Limited Digital Replays were the only insert set in 1996 Motion Vision. The first six cards were inserted every 25 packs of Series I, with only 2,500 sets produced, while the last four were found in Series 2.0 at a rate of one per 22 packs, with 3,500 sets produced. LDRs are distinguished by having a card back that features another shot of the player and statistics (regular-issue cards have no backs). LDR fronts also carry no logos on the front and instead of a phrase at the bottom describing the play, LDRs have only the player's name. Cards are numbered LDR1-LDR10.

	MT
Complete Set (10):	400.00
Comp. Series 1 (6):	200.00
Comp. Series 2 (4):	200.00
LDR1Troy Aikman	30.00
LDR2Dan Marino	60.00
LDR3Steve Young	25.00
LDR4Emmitt Smith	60.00
LDR5Drew Bledsoe	30.00
LDR6Kordell Stewart	25.00
LDR7Brett Favre	60.00
LDR8Brett Favre	60.00
LDR9Emmitt Smith	60.00
LDR10Kerry Collins	30.00

1996 Motion Vision LDR Autographs

Limted Digital Replays Autographs consisted of four players who signed their LDR insert in 1996 Motion Vision. Drew Bledsoe, Kordell Stewart and Steve Young were inserted in Series I, while Troy Aikman and the remaining Steve Young cards were in Series 2.0. Fronts of these were the same, with the autograph on the back along with a seal to prove its autheticity.

	MT
Complete Set (4):	1000.00
Common Player:	250.00
LDR1Troy Aikman AUTO	300.00
LDR3Steve Young AUTO	250.00
LDR5Drew Bledsoe AUTO	300.00
LDR6Kordell Stewart AUTO	275.00

1996 Pacific

Pacific's 1996 Crown Collection set includes 450 cards (no subsets), each of which has gold-foiled etching along the bottom for the player's name, team helmet and a gridiron. The Pacific logo is also stamped in gold on the front, which features a full-bleed color action photo. The horizontal back has a color closeup shot on one side, with the player's name and position in team colors on the opposite side in the top corner. Underneath is biographical information and a career recap. The card number and a Pacific logo are in the lower right corner. Two parallel versions of the regular set were also made - Scorching Red Foil (nine in every 37 retail packs) and Electric Blue Foil (nine in every 37 hobby packs). There are six insert sets - Card-Supials, Cramer's Choice Awards, Bomb Squad, Gold Crown Die-Cuts, Gems of the Crown and The Zone.

		MT
Complete Set (450):		40.00
Common Player:		.05
Wax Box:		48.00
1	Jeff Feagles	.05
2	Rob Moore	.05
3	Clyde Simmons	.05
4	Mike Buck	.05
5	Aeneas Williams	.05
6	*Simeon Rice*	.25
7	Garrison Hearst	.10
8	Eric Swann	.05
9	Dave Krieg	.05
10	*Leeland McElroy*	.75
11	Oscar McBride	.05
12	Frank Sanders	.05
13	Larry Centers	.05
14	Seth Joyner	.05
15	Stevie Anderson	.05
16	Craig Heyward	.05
17	Devin Bush	.05
18	Eric Metcalf	.05
19	Jeff George	.10
20	Richard Huntley	.05
21	*Jamal Anderson*	2.00
22	Bert Emanuel	.05
23	Terance Mathis	.05
24	Roman Fortin	.05
25	Jessie Tuggle	.05
26	Morten Andersen	.05
27	Chris Doleman	.05
28	D.J. Johnson	.05
29	Kevin Ross	.05
30	Michael Jackson	.05
31	Eric Zeier	.05
32	Jonathan Ogden	.05
33	Eric Turner	.05
34	Andre Rison	.05
35	Lorenzo White	.05
36	Earnest Byner	.05
37	Derrick Alexander	.05
38	Brian Kinchen	.05
39	Anthony Pleasant	.05
40	Vinny Testaverde	.05
41	Pepper Johnson	.05
42	Frank Hartley	.05
43	Craig Powell	.05
44	Leroy Hoard	.05
45	Kent Hull	.05
46	Bryce Paup	.05
47	Andre Reed	.05
48	Darick Holmes	.05

49	Russell Copeland	.05
50	Jerry Ostroski	.05
51	Chris Green	.05
52	*Eric Moulds*	.75
53	Justin Armour	.05
54	Jim Kelly	.10
55	Cornelius Bennett	.05
56	Steve Tasker	.05
57	Thurman Thomas	.10
58	Bruce Smith	.05
59	Todd Collins	.05
60	Shawn King	.05
61	Don Beebe	.05
62	John Kasay	.05
63	Tim McKyer	.05
64	Darion Conner	.05
65	Pete Metzelaars	.05
66	Derrick Moore	.05
67	Blake Brockermeyer	.05
68	*Tim Biakabutuka*	1.00
69	Sam Mills	.05
70	Vince Workman	.05
71	Kerry Collins	.75
72	Carlton Bailey	.05
73	Mark Carrier	.05
74	Donnell Woolford	.05
75	*Walt Harris*	.25
76	John Thierry	.05
77	Al Fontenot	.05
78	Lewis Tillman	.05
79	Curtis Conway	.10
80	Chris Zorich	.05
81	Mark Carrier	.05
82	*Bobby Engram*	1.00
83	Alonzo Spellman	.05
84	Rashaan Salaam	.50
85	Michael Timpson	.05
86	Nate Lewis	.05
87	James Williams	.05
88	Jeff Graham	.05
89	Erik Kramer	.05
90	Willie Anderson	.05
91	Tony McGee	.05
92	Marco Battaglia	.05
93	Dan Wilkinson	.05
94	John Walsh	.05
95	Eric Bieniemy	.05
96	Ricardo McDonald	.05
97	Carl Pickens	.10
98	Kevin Sargent	.05
99	David Dunn	.05
100	Jeff Blake	.50
101	Harold Green	.05
102	James Francis	.05
103	John Copeland	.05
104	Darnay Scott	.05
105	Darren Woodson	.05
106	Jay Novacek	.05
107	Charles Haley	.05
108	Mark Tuinei	.05
109	Michael Irvin	.10
110	Troy Aikman	.75
111	Chris Boniol	.05
112	Sherman Williams	.05
113	Deion Sanders	.50
114	Emmitt Smith	2.00
115	Eric Bjornson	.05
116	Nate Newton	.05
117	Larry Allen	.05
118	Kevin Williams	.05
119	Leon Lett	.05
120	John Mobley	.05
121	Anthony Miller	.05
122	Brian Habib	.05
123	Aaron Craver	.05
124	Glyn Milburn	.05
125	Shannon Sharpe	.05
126	Steve Atwater	.05
127	Jason Elam	.05
128	John Elway	.35
129	Reggie Rivers	.05
130	Mike Pritchard	.05
131	Vance Johnson	.05
132	Terrell Davis	1.25
133	Tyrone Braxton	.05
134	Ed McCaffrey	.05
135	Brett Perriman	.05
136	Chris Spielman	.05
137	Luther Elliss	.05
138	Johnnie Morton	.05
139	Zefross Moss	.05
140	Barry Sanders	.75
141	Lomas Brown	.05
142	Cory Schlesinger	.05
143	Jason Hanson	.05
144	Kevin Glover	.05
145	Ron Rivers	.05
146	Aubrey Matthews	.05
147	Reggie Brown	.05
148	Herman Moore	.30
149	Scott Mitchell	.05

150	Brett Favre	2.00
151	Sean Jones	.05
152	Leroy Butler	.05
153	Mark Chmura	.20
154	*Derrick Mayes*	.50
155	Mark Ingram	.05
156	Antonio Freeman	.05
157	*Chris Darkins*	.25
158	Robert Brooks	.10
159	William Henderson	.05
160	George Koonce	.05
161	Craig Newsome	.05
162	Darius Holland	.05
163	George Teague	.05
164	Edgar Bennett	.05
165	Reggie White	.10
166	Michael Barrow	.05
167	Mel Gray	.05
168	Anthony Dorsett Jr.	.05
169	Roderick Lewis	.05
170	Henry Ford	.05
171	Mark Stepnoski	.05
172	Chris Sanders	.05
173	Anthony Cook	.05
174	Eddie Robinson	.05
175	Steve McNair	.50
176	Haywood Jeffires	.05
177	*Eddie George*	3.50
178	Marion Butts	.05
179	Malcolm Seabron	.05
180	Rodney Thomas	.05
181	Ken Dilger	.05
182	Zack Crockett	.05
183	Tony Bennett	.05
184	Quentin Coryatt	.05
185	Marshall Faulk	.50
186	Sean Dawkins	.05
187	Jim Harbaugh	.05
188	Eugene Daniel	.05
189	Roosevelt Potts	.05
190	Lamont Warren	.05
191	Will Wolford	.05
192	Tony Siragusa	.05
193	Aaron Bailey	.05
194	Trev Alberts	.05
195	*Kevin Hardy*	.10
196	Greg Spann	.05
197	Steve Beuerlein	.05
198	Steve Taneyhill	.05
199	Vaughn Dunbar	.05
200	Mark Brunell	.75
201	Bernard Carter	.05
202	James Stewart	.05
203	Tony Boselli	.05
204	Chris Doering	.05
205	Willie Jackson	.05
206	*Tony Brackens*	.30
207	Ernest Givins	.05
208	Le'Shai Maston	.05
209	Pete Mitchell	.05
210	Desmond Howard	.05
211	Vinnie Clark	.05
212	Jeff Lageman	.05
213	Derrick Walker	.05
214	Dan Saleaumua	.05
215	Derrick Thomas	.05
216	Neil Smith	.05
217	Willie Davis	.05
218	Mark Collins	.05
219	Lake Dawson	.05
220	Greg Hill	.05
221	Anthony Davis	.05
222	Kimble Anders	.05
223	Webster Slaughter	.05
224	Tamarick Vanover	.50
225	Marcus Allen	.10
226	Steve Bono	.10
227	Will Shields	.05
228	*Karim Abdul-Jabbar*	2.00
229	Tim Bowens	.05
230	Keith Sims	.05
231	Terry Kirby	.05
232	Gene Atkins	.05
233	Dan Marino	2.00
234	Richmond Webb	.05
235	Gary Clark	.05
236	O.J. McDuffie	.05
237	Marco Coleman	.05
238	Bernie Parmalee	.05
239	Randal Hill	.05
240	Bryan Cox	.05
241	Irving Fryar	.05
242	Derrick Alexander	.05
243	Qadry Ismail	.05
244	Warren Moon	.05
245	Cris Carter	.05
246	Chad May	.05
247	Robert Smith	.05
248	Fuad Reveiz	.05
249	Orlando Thomas	.05
250	Chris Hinton	.05

251	Jack Del Rio	.05
252	Moe Williams	.05
253	Roy Barker	.05
254	Jake Reed	.05
255	Adrian Cooper	.05
256	Curtis Martin	1.50
257	Ben Coates	.05
258	Drew Bledsoe	.75
259	Maurice Hurst	.05
260	Troy Brown	.05
261	Bruce Armstrong	.05
262	Myron Guyton	.05
263	Dave Meggett	.05
264	*Terry Glenn*	2.50
265	Chris Slade	.05
266	Vincent Brisby	.05
267	Willie McGinest	.05
268	Vincent Brown	.05
269	Will Moore	.05
270	Jay Barker	.05
271	Ray Zellars	.05
272	Derek Brown	.05
273	William Roaf	.05
274	Quinn Early	.05
275	Michael Haynes	.05
276	Rufus Porter	.05
277	Renaldo Turnbull	.05
278	Wayne Martin	.05
279	Tyrone Hughes	.05
280	Irv Smith	.05
281	Eric Allen	.05
282	Mark Fields	.05
283	Mario Bates	.05
284	Jim Everett	.05
285	Vince Buck	.05
286	Alex Molden	.05
287	Tyrone Wheatley	.05
288	Chris Calloway	.05
289	Jessie Armstead	.05
290	Arthur Marshall	.05
291	Aaron Pierce	.05
292	Dave Brown	.05
293	Rodney Hampton	.05
294	John Elliott	.05
295	Mike Sherrard	.05
296	Howard Cross	.05
297	Michael Brooks	.05
298	Herschel Walker	.05
299	*Danny Kanell*	.25
300	Keith Elias	.05
301	Bobby Houston	.05
302	Dexter Carter	.05
303	Tony Casillas	.05
304	Kyle Brady	.05
305	Glenn Foley	.05
306	Ron Moore	.05
307	Ryan Yarborough	.05
308	Aaron Glenn	.05
309	Adrian Murrell	.05
310	Boomer Esiason	.05
311	Kyle Clifton	.05
312	Wayne Chrebet	.05
313	Erik Howard	.05
314	*Keyshawn Johnson*	1.75
315	Marvin Washington	.05
316	Johnny Mitchell	.05
317	*Alex Van Dyke*	.50
318	Billy Joe Hobert	.05
319	Andrew Glover	.05
320	Vince Evans	.05
321	Chester McGlockton	.05
322	Pat Swilling	.05
323	Raghib Ismail	.05
324	Eddie Anderson	.05
325	*Rickey Dudley*	.50
326	Steve Wisniewski	.05
327	Harvey Williams	.05
328	Napoleon Kaufman	.05
329	Tim Brown	.10
330	Jeff Hostetler	.05
331	Anthony Smith	.05
332	Terry McDaniel	.05
333	Charlie Garner	.05
334	Ricky Watters	.05
335	Brian Dawkins	.05
336	Randall Cunningham	.05
337	Gary Anderson	.05
338	Calvin Williams	.05
339	Chris T. Jones	.05
340	*Bobby Hoying*	.20
341	William Fuller	.05
342	William Thomas	.05
343	Mike Mamula	.05
344	Fred Barnett	.05
345	Rodney Peete	.05
346	Mark McMillian	.05
347	Bobby Taylor	.05
348	Yancey Thigpen	.35
349	Neil O'Donnell	.05
350	Rod Woodson	.05
351	Kordell Stewart	.75

352	Dermontti Dawson	.05
353	Norm Johnson	.05
354	Ernie Mills	.05
355	Bam Morris	.05
356	Mark Bruener	.05
357	Kevin Greene	.05
358	Greg Lloyd	.05
359	Andre Hastings	.05
360	Erric Pegram	.05
361	Carnell Lake	.05
362	Dwayne Harper	.05
363	Ronnie Harmon	.05
364	Leslie O'Neal	.05
365	John Carney	.05
366	Stan Humphries	.05
367	Brian Roche	.05
368	Terrell Fletcher	.05
369	Shaun Gayle	.05
370	Alfred Pupunu	.05
371	Shawn Jefferson	.05
372	Junior Seau	.05
373	Mark Seay	.05
374	Aaron Hayden	.05
375	Tony Martin	.05
376	Steve Young	.75
377	J.J. Stokes	.50
378	Jerry Rice	.75
379	Derek Loville	.05
380	Lee Woodall	.05
381	*Terrell Owens*	1.00
382	Elvis Grbac	.05
383	Ricky Ervins	.05
384	Eric Davis	.05
385	Dana Stubblefield	.05
386	Gary Plummer	.05
387	Tim McDonald	.05
388	William Floyd	.05
389	Ken Norton Jr.	.05
390	Merton Hanks	.05
391	Bart Oates	.05
392	Brent Jones	.05
393	Steve Broussard	.05
394	Robert Blackmon	.05
395	Rick Tuten	.05
396	Pete Kendall	.05
397	John Friesz	.05
398	Terry Wooden	.05
399	Rick Mirer	.05
400	Chris Warren	.10
401	Joey Galloway	.50
402	Howard Ballard	.05
403	Jason Kyle	.05
404	Kevin Mawae	.05
405	Mack Strong	.05
406	Reggie Brown	.05
407	Cortez Kennedy	.05
408	Sean Gilbert	.05
409	J.T. Thomas	.05
410	Shane Conlan	.05
411	Johnny Bailey	.05
412	Mark Rypien	.05
413	Leonard Russell	.05
414	Troy Drayton	.05
415	Jerome Bettis	.05
416	Jessie Hester	.05
417	Isaac Bruce	.50
418	Roman Phifer	.05
419	Todd Kinchen	.05
420	Alexander Wright	.05
421	Marcus Jones	.05
422	Horace Copeland	.05
423	Eric Curry	.05
424	Courtney Hawkins	.05
425	Alvin Harper	.05
426	Derrick Brooks	.05
427	Errict Rhett	.25
428	Trent Dilfer	.05
429	Hardy Nickerson	.05
430	Brad Culpepper	.05
431	Warren Sapp	.05
432	Reggie Roby	.05
433	Santana Dotson	.05
434	Jerry Ellison	.05
435	Lawrence Dawsey	.05
436	Heath Shuler	.05
437	Stanley Richard	.05
438	Rod Stephens	.05
439	*Stephen Davis*	.25
440	Terry Allen	.05
441	Michael Westbrook	.40
442	Ken Harvey	.05
443	Coleman Bell	.05
444	Marvcus Patton	.05
445	Gus Frerotte	.05
446	Leslie Shepherd	.05
447	Tom Carter	.05
448	Brian Mitchell	.05
449	Darrell Green	.05
450	Tony Woods	.05

1996 Pacific Blue/Red/Silver

Pacific Crown Collection Football was offered in three different parallel versions - blue, red and silver. Electric Blue versions of the 450-card set were available in hobby packs, with Scorching Red versions in retail, both seeded nine per 37 packs. There was also a Silver version available in special retail packs, with roughly the same production as the Red and Blue set. The only differences in these cards from the base cards is the color of the foil stamping.

	MT
Complete Blue Set (450):	300.00
Blue Cards:	4x-8x
Complete Red Set (450):	300.00
Red Cards:	4x-8x
Complete Silver Set (450):	300.00
Silver Cards:	4x-8x

1996 Pacific Bomb Squad

The NFL's finest quarterback/receiver combinations are spotlighted on these 1996 Pacific inserts. The cards, seeded one per every 73 packs, feature a player on each side against a background of team-colored swirls. The Pacific logo is in the upper left corner; the player's name and position run down the right side of the card. One side has a card number, which uses a "BS" prefix.

		MT
Complete Set (10):		200.00
Common Player:		10.00
1	Jeff Blake, Carl Pickens	10.00
2	John Elway, Anthony Miller	16.00
3	Scott Mitchell, Herman Moore	10.00
4	Troy Aikman, Jay Novacek	25.00
5	Brett Favre, Robert Brooks	45.00
6	Steve McNair, Chris Sanders	15.00
7	Dan Marino, Irving Fryar	45.00
8	Drew Bledsoe, Terry Glenn	35.00
9	Kordell Stewart, Kordell Stewart	20.00
10	Steve Young, Jerry Rice	25.00

1996 Pacific Card-Supials

This 36-card Pacific insert set features cards with flashy gold embossing on the front for the Pacific logo, player's name and outline of the letters in the player's position and team name. The back has a little cut in the card, creating a pouch for another mini (1-1/4" x 1-3/4") card of the player - a marsupial. Hence, the name Card-Supials. The card back of the regular card is black-and-white; the mini card, when placed in the pouch, fills in the area with color. The bottom of the card has a brief paragraph about the play-

er, plus a card number (1 of 36, etc.). The mini card's back has the player's name and position along the side. A closeup shot and player profile complete the back. The card is numbered 1a of 36, etc. Cards were seeded one per every 37 packs, but the minis were not always matched up with the larger card.

		MT
Complete Set (72):		500.00
Comp. Large Set (36):		300.00
Comp. Small Set (36):		200.00
Common Large:		4.00
Small Cards:		Half Price
1	Garrison Hearst	4.00
2	Jeff George	4.00
3	Eric Zeier	4.00
4	Jim Kelly	4.00
5	Kerry Collins	20.00
6	Rashaan Salaam	6.00
7	Jeff Blake	6.00
8	Troy Aikman	20.00
9	Emmitt Smith	40.00
10	Terrell Davis	20.00
11	John Elway	10.00
12	Deion Sanders	12.00
13	Barry Sanders	20.00
14	Brett Favre	40.00
15	Steve McNair	10.00
16	Marshall Faulk	6.00
17	Mark Brunell	15.00
18	Tamarick Vanover	6.00
19	Dan Marino	40.00
20	Cris Carter	4.00
21	Keyshawn Johnson	6.00
22	Rodney Hampton	4.00
23	Curtis Martin	25.00
24	Drew Bledsoe	20.00
25	Mario Bates	4.00
26	Napoleon Kaufman	4.00
27	Ricky Watters	4.00
28	Kordell Stewart	20.00
29	Junior Seau	4.00
30	Steve Young	18.00
31	Jerry Rice	20.00
32	Isaac Bruce	8.00
33	Joey Galloway	15.00
34	Chris Warren	4.00
35	Errict Rhett	6.00
36	Michael Westbrook	6.00

1996 Pacific Cramer's Choice Awards

Cramer's Choice Awards return as an insert for Pacific's 1996 football line. The die-cut cards, which showcase some of the NFL's most amazing athletes, have a silver background for the card, which is shaped like a trophy. The cards are the rarest in this product line; they are seeded one per every 721 packs. The back has comments about the player by Michael Cramer, CEO and president of Pacific, who made the selections.

		MT
Complete Set (10):		1200.00
Common Player:		40.00
1	Emmitt Smith	200.00
2	John Elway	100.00
3	Barry Sanders	125.00
4	Brett Favre	200.00
5	Reggie White	40.00
6	Dan Marino	200.00
7	Curtis Martin	150.00
8	Keyshawn Johnson	60.00
9	Kordell Stewart	100.00
10	Jerry Rice	125.00

1996 Pacific Gems of the Crown

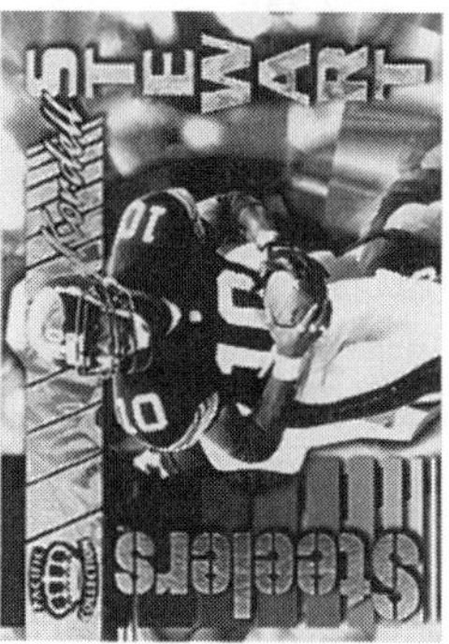

These 1996 Pacific inserts, numbered 19-36, were seeded one per every 37 packs. (Cards 1-18 were inserts in 1996 Dynagon Prism packs.) The horizontal card front has a color photo in the middle, with an outline around it. The team name is stamped in gold along the left side; the player's last name is stamped in gold along the right. A gold-foiled panel along the top has the Pacific logo and the player's first name in the upper right corner.

		MT
Complete Set (18):		130.00
Common Player:		3.00
19	Garrison Hearst	3.00
20	Jeff Blake	8.00
21	Troy Aikman	12.00
22	Deion Sanders	10.00
23	Brett Favre	20.00
24	Robert Smith	3.00
25	Mario Bates	3.00
26	Napoleon Kaufman	3.00
27	Kordell Stewart	12.00
28	Jim Kelly	3.00
29	Jim Harbaugh	3.00
30	Tamarick Vanover	10.00
31	Dan Marino	20.00
32	Warren Moon	3.00
33	Curtis Martin	18.00
34	Rodney Hampton	3.00
35	Ricky Watters	3.00
36	Joey Galloway	10.00

1996 Pacific Gold Crown Die-Cuts

These 1996 Pacific inserts were seeded one per every 37 packs. Each card features a full-bleed color action photo on the front, with a die-cut gold foiled crown at the top. The player's name is at the bottom in foil, too, next to a team helmet. The card back has the crown image at the top. The player's name runs across the middle, with a closeup shot of the player in a diamond on one side and brief player profile on the other. A card number, using a "GC" prefix, is in the lower left corner.

		MT
Complete Set (20):		350.00
Common Player:		7.00
1	Emmitt Smith	40.00
2	Troy Aikman	20.00
3	Barry Sanders	20.00
4	Kerry Collins	25.00
5	Jeff Blake	15.00
6	John Elway	15.00
7	Terrell Davis	20.00
8	Deion Sanders	15.00
9	Brett Favre	40.00
10	Dan Marino	40.00
11	Eddie George	25.00
12	Curtis Martin	25.00
13	Drew Bledsoe	20.00
14	Keyshawn Johnson	15.00
15	Napoleon Kaufman	7.00
16	Kordell Stewart	20.00
17	Steve Young	15.00
18	Jerry Rice	20.00
19	Joey Galloway	20.00
20	Chris Warren	7.00

1996 Pacific Power Corps

Power Corps was a 20-card insert that was only available in special retail packs on Pacific Crown Collection in 1996. The cards contained the words "Power Corps" running down the left side, with the player's name running down the right side. The cards were numbered PC1-PC20. There were also foil parallel versions of card numbers 1, 11, 14, 17 and 19.

		MT
Complete Set (20):		90.00
Common Player:		2.50
1	Troy Aikman	6.00
2	Jeff Blake	2.50
3	Drew Bledsoe	6.00
4	Kerry Collins	6.00
5	Terrell Davis	8.00
6	John Elway	4.00
7	Marshall Faulk	3.00
8	Brett Favre	12.00
9	Joey Galloway	2.50
10	Garrison Hearst	2.50
11	Dan Marino	12.00
12	Curtis Martin	8.00
13	Steve McNair	6.00
14	Jerry Rice	6.00
15	Rashaan Salaam	4.00
16	Barry Sanders	6.00
17	Emmitt Smith	12.00
18	Kordell Stewart	6.00
19	Chris Warren	2.50
20	Steve Young	4.00

1996 Pacific The Zone

Only the NFL's most productive players who found the end zone on a regular basis in 1995 are featured on these die-cut inserts. The cards were

seeded one per every 145 packs. Each card front has a die-cut goal post, with the player photo between the posts. The player's name is in gold foil on the cross bar. His team's name is on the post. Pacific and the logo are in gold foil on the bottom of the card, which has a grassy background. The card back has a closeup shot of the player, his name and a team logo between the posts. His position and city name are on the cross bar. The bottom of the card has a grassy background with a recap of some of the player's accomplishments. The card number is also at the bottom, using a "Z" prefix.

		MT
Complete Set (20):		700.00
Common Player:		10.00
1	Jim Kelly	10.00
2	Rashaan Salaam	20.00
3	Carl Pickens	10.00
4	Jeff Blake	20.00
5	Kerry Collins	40.00
6	Emmitt Smith	100.00
7	Troy Aikman	45.00
8	John Elway	30.00
9	Barry Sanders	45.00
10	Herman Moore	10.00
11	Scott Mitchell	10.00
12	Brett Favre	100.00
13	Robert Brooks	10.00
14	Marshall Faulk	30.00
15	Dan Marino	100.00
16	Drew Bledsoe	50.00
17	Curtis Martin	50.00
18	Steve Young	45.00
19	Jerry Rice	45.00
20	Chris Warren	10.00

1996 Pacific Crown Royale

Pacific's 1996 Crown Royale release features a 144-card, regular-size cards that are highlighted by etched, die-cut cards. Each horizontal card is topped with a die-cut gold crown and the front has the player's name, position and team logo. Two parallel versions are available: Royale Blue (hobby) and Royale Silver (retail). Also, five insert sets were inserted: Cramer's Choice Awards, Field Force Etch-Tech, Pro Bowl Die-

Cut, Triple Crown Die-Cut and NFL Regime. The 144-card base set was sold in five-card packs and each regular card back was listed by the "CR" prefix.

		MT
Complete Set (144):		160.00
Common Player:		.50
Wax Box:		110.00
1	Dan Marino	10.00
2	Frank Sanders	.50
3	*Bobby Engram*	5.00
4	Cornelius Bennett	.50
5	Steve Bono	.50
6	Aaron Hayden	.50
7	Leroy Hoard	.50
8	Brett Perriman	.50
9	Irv Smith	.50
10	Jim Kelly	1.00
11	Rodney Thomas	.50
12	Eric Bieniemy	.50
13	Darnay Scott	1.00
14	Ki-Jana Carter	2.00
15	Kerry Collins	6.00
16	Shannon Sharpe	.50
17	Michael Westbrook	2.00
18	Steve McNair	5.00
19	*Tony Banks*	6.00
20	Rashaan Salaam	2.00
21	Terrell Fletcher	.50
22	Michael Timpson	.50
23	*Bobby Hoying*	2.00
24	Quinn Early	.50
25	Warren Moon	1.00
26	Tommy Vardell	.50
27	*Marvin Harrison*	5.00
28	Lake Dawson	.50
29	*Karim Abdul-Jabbar*	8.00
30	Chris Warren	2.00
31	Heath Shuler	1.00
32	Bert Emanuel	.50
33	Howard Griffith	.50
34	*Alex Van Dyke*	2.00
35	Isaac Bruce	4.00
36	Mark Brunell	5.00
37	Winslow Oliver	.50
38	O.J. McDuffie	.50
39	*Terrell Owens*	8.00
40	Jerry Rice	5.00
41	Henry Ellard	.50
42	Chris Sanders	.50
43	Craig Heyward	.50
44	*Eddie Kennison*	5.00
45	Terrell Davis	8.00
46	Rodney Hampton	.50
47	Bryan Still	.50
48	Tim Brown	.50
49	*Keyshawn Johnson*	7.00
50	Barry Sanders	5.00
51	Terry Allen	1.00
52	Sean Dawkins	.50
53	Bryce Paup	.50
54	Brett Favre	10.00
55	Deion Sanders	3.00
56	*Kevin Hardy*	2.00
57	Kevin Williams	.50
58	Jeff George	.50
59	*Tim Biakabutuka*	5.00
60	Drew Bledsoe	5.00
61	Michael Jackson	.50
62	James Stewart	.50
63	Mario Bates	.50
64	Daryl Johnston	.50
65	Herman Moore	2.00
66	Ben Coates	.50
67	*Terry Glenn*	10.00
68	Robert Smith	.50
69	Irving Fryar	.50
70	Napoleon Kaufman	.50
71	*Rickey Dudley*	3.00
72	Bernie Parmalee	.50
73	Kyle Brady	.50
74	Neil O'Donnell	.50
75	*Lawrence Phillips*	4.00
76	Hardy Nickerson	.50
77	John Elway	4.00
78	Pete Mitchell	.50
79	Jason Dunn	.50
80	Reggie White	1.00
81	J.J. Stokes	2.00
82	Jake Reed	.50
83	Yancey Thigpen	.50
84	Jonathan Ogden	.50
85	Larry Centers	.50
86	Scott Mitchell	.50
87	Eric Zeier	.50
88	Anthony Miller	.50
89	Brian Blades	.50
90	Cris Carter	.50
91	Kordell Stewart	5.00
92	Charles Way	.50
93	Jeff Hostetler	.50
94	*Brad Johnson*	3.00
95	Marcus Allen	1.00
96	Errict Rhett	2.00
97	Stan Humphries	.50
98	Michael Haynes	.50
99	Curtis Martin	8.00
100	Troy Aikman	5.00
101	Earnest Byner	.50
102	Vincent Brisby	.50
103	Zack Crockett	.50
104	Haywood Jeffires	.50
105	Joey Galloway	4.00
106	Carl Pickens	1.00
107	*Leeland McElroy*	3.00
108	Adrian Murrell	.50
109	Joe Horn	.50
110	Steve Young	4.00
111	Andre Rison	.50
112	Jim Everett	.50
113	*Jamie Asher*	2.00
114	Steve Walsh	.50
115	Robert Brooks	1.00
116	*Eric Moulds*	3.00
117	Edgar Bennett	.50
118	Greg Lloyd	.50
119	Jerris McPhail	.50
120	Marshall Faulk	3.00
121	Dave Brown	.50
122	Harvey Williams	.50
123	Trent Dilfer	1.00
124	*Eddie George*	14.00
125	Jeff Blake	2.00
126	Mark Chmura	.50
127	Boomer Esiason	.50
128	Jim Harbaugh	.50
129	Bryan Cox	.50
130	Ricky Watters	1.00
131	*Amani Toomer*	2.00
132	Jim Miller	.50
133	Cortez Kennedy	.50
134	Courtney Hawkins	.50
135	Junior Seau	.50
136	Tamarick Vanover	2.00
137	Jerome Bettis	1.00
138	Chris Calloway	.50
139	Rick Mirer	.50
140	Thurman Thomas	1.00
141	Sheddrick Wilson	.50
142	Charlie Garner	.50
143	Erik Kramer	.50
144	Emmitt Smith	10.00

1996 Pacific Crown Royale Blue/Silver

Each card in the 144-card 1996 Crown Royale set were reprinted in two different versions. Hobby packs had Royale Blue parallels, while retail packs had Royale Silver parallels, with both seeded four per 25 packs. These parallel sets are distinguished only by the color of the foil stamping.

		MT
Complete Blue Set (144):		700.00
Blue Cards:		2x-4x
Complete Silver Set (144):		1000.00
Silver Cards:		3x-6x

1996 Pacific Crown Royale Cramer's Choice Awards

The large-sized set (5-1/2" x 4") was offered as part of a redemption offer in the Crown Royale set. Redemption cards, inserted every 385 packs, enabled collectors to obtain the 10-card, die-cut set. The cards are cut into the shape of a pyramid and the players honored were chosen by Pacific President and CEO Michael Cramer. The card backs are each listed with the "CC" prefix.

		MT
Complete Set (10):		800.00
Common Player:		50.00
1	John Elway	80.00

2	Brett Favre	125.00
3	Keyshawn Johnson	50.00
4	Dan Marino	125.00
5	Curtis Martin	100.00
6	Jerry Rice	85.00
7	Barry Sanders	85.00
8	Emmitt Smith	125.00
9	Kordell Stewart	75.00
10	Reggie White	50.00

1996 Pacific Crown Royale Field Force

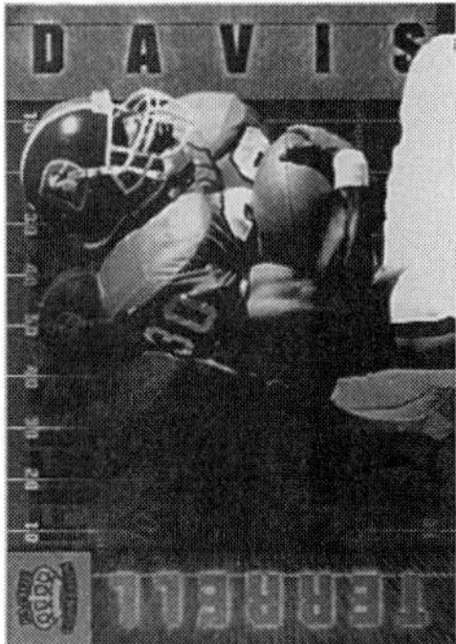

The 20-card, regular-sized set was inserted in 1996 packs of Crown Royale. Inserted every 49 packs, the horizontal cards employ etch-tech design and feature the player's name written on the side margins in foil etching of the player's team colors. The card backs contain a headshot of the player and are numbered with the "FF" prefix.

		MT
Complete Set (20):		900.00
Common Player:		15.00
1	Troy Aikman	60.00
2	Karim Abdul-Jabbar	45.00
3	Jeff Blake	25.00
4	Drew Bledsoe	60.00
5	Lawrence Phillips	35.00
6	Kerry Collins	65.00
7	Terrell Davis	65.00
8	John Elway	40.00
9	Brett Favre	100.00
10	Eddie George	60.00
11	Dan Marino	100.00
12	Curtis Martin	80.00
13	Jerry Rice	65.00
14	Rashaan Salaam	15.00
15	Barry Sanders	65.00
16	Deion Sanders	50.00
17	Emmitt Smith	100.00
18	Kordell Stewart	65.00
19	Chris Warren	15.00
20	Steve Young	50.00

1996 Pacific Crown Royale NFL Regime

The 110-card, regular-sized set was included in each of the 1996 Crown Royale five-card packs. The card fronts feature a gray border with the player's name on top in red lettering and a white globe centered on a red ribbon which reads "NFL Regime." The card backs contain a headshot of the player and the prefix "NR."

		MT
Complete Set (110):		25.00
Common Player:		.20
1	Steve Young	1.00
2	Jamir Miller	.20
3	Tyrone Brown	.20
4	Chris Shelling	.20
5	Warren Moon	.20
6	Shane Bonham	.20
7	Gary Brown	.20
8	Chris Chandler	.20
9	Bradford Banta	.20
10	John Elway	.75
11	Tom McManus	.20
12	Alfred Jackson	.20
13	Jay Barker	.20
14	Kirk Botkin	.20
15	Jim Kelly	.20
16	Lou Benfatti	.20
17	Billy Joe Hobert	.20
18	John Jackson	.20
19	Torin Dorn	.20
20	Drew Bledsoe	1.00
21	Gale Gilbert	.20
22	James Atkins	.20
23	John Lynch	.20
24	James Jenkins	.20
25	Kerry Collins	1.25
26	Eric Swann	.20
27	Dan Stryzinski	.20
28	Mike Groh	.20
29	Tim Tindale	.20
30	Kordell Stewart	1.25
31	Frank Garcia	.20
32	Mill Coleman	.20
33	Bracey Walker	.20
34	Ryan McNeil	.20
35	Rodney Hampton	.20
36	John Mobley	.20
37	Derek Russell	.20
38	Jeff George	.20
39	Steve Morrison	.20
40	Rashaan Salaam	.40
41	Ryan Christopherson	.20
42	Darren Anderson	.20
43	Ronnie Williams	.20
44	Scottie Graham	.20
45	Thurman Thomas	.40
46	Corwin Brown	.20
47	Lee DeRamus	.20
48	Ray Agnew	.20
49	Erik Howard	.20
50	Emmitt Smith	2.50
51	Dan Land	.20
52	Vinny Testaverde	.20
53	Myron Bell	.20
54	Keith Lyle	.20
55	Aaron Hayden	.20
56	Jeff Brohm	.20
57	Ronnie Harris	.20
58	Trent Dilfer	.20
59	Browning Nagle	.20
60	Jeff Blake	.75
61	Rich Owens	.20
62	Anthony Edwards	.20
63	Orlando Brown	.20
64	Matthew Campbell	.20
65	Ricky Watters	.40
66	Travis Hannah	.20
67	Melvin Tuten	.20
68	Aaron Taylor	.20
69	Dale Hellestrae	.20
70	Marshall Faulk	1.00
71	Gary Anderson	.20
72	David Williams	.20
73	Jim Harbaugh	.20
74	Ray Hall	.20
75	Dan Marino	2.50
76	Chris Mims	.20
77	Matt Blundin	.20
78	Roy Barker	.20
79	John Burke	.20
80	Troy Aikman	1.25
81	Ed King	.20
82	Stan White	.20
83	Vance Joseph	.20
84	David Klingler	.20
85	Terrell Davis	1.00
86	Bobby Hoying	.20
87	Lethon Flowers	.20
88	Dwayne White	.20
89	Vaughn Parker	.20
90	Jerry Rice	1.25
91	Casey Weldon	.20
92	Rick Mirer	.20
93	Jim Pyne	.20
94	Matt Turk	.20
95	Marcus Allen	.20
96	Rob Moore	.20
97	Ruben Brown	.20
98	Zach Thomas	.20
99	Carwell Gardner	.20
100	Barry Sanders	1.25
101	Ben Coleman	.20
102	Steve Rhem	.20
103	Everett McIver	.20
104	Cole Ford	.20
105	Dave Krieg	.20
106	Anthony Parker	.20
107	Michael Brandon	.20
108	Michael McCrary	.20
109	Chad Fann	.20
110	Brett Favre	2.50

1996 Pacific Crown Royale Pro Bowl Die-Cut

The 20-card, regular-sized, die-cut cards were inserted every 25 packs of Crown Royale. Each player is pictured in his Pro Bowl jersey and is backdropped with a die-cut palm tree and pineapple. The card backs feature an exploding volcano and a headshot of the player and are numbered with the "PB" prefix.

		MT
Complete Set (20):		550.00
Common Player:		10.00
1	Jeff Blake	12.00
2	Mark Chmura	10.00
3	Marshall Faulk	12.00
4	Brett Favre	100.00
5	Charles Haley	10.00
6	Merton Hanks	10.00
7	Greg Lloyd	10.00
8	Dan Marino	100.00
9	Curtis Martin	70.00
10	Anthony Miller	10.00
11	Herman Moore	12.00
12	Bryce Paup	10.00
13	Jerry Rice	50.00
14	Barry Sanders	50.00
15	Junior Seau	10.00
16	Emmitt Smith	100.00
17	Yancey Thigpen	10.00
18	Chris Warren	10.00
19	Ricky Watters	10.00
20	Steve Young	35.00

1996 Pacific Crown Royale Triple Crown Die-Cut

The 10-card, regular-sized, die-cut set honors 10 players who led the league in at least three different categories. Inserted every 73 packs in 1996 Crown Royale, the cards feature a similar die-cut crown design with gold foil as the base cards in Crown Royale. The card backs are labeled with the "TC" prefix and are individually numbered.

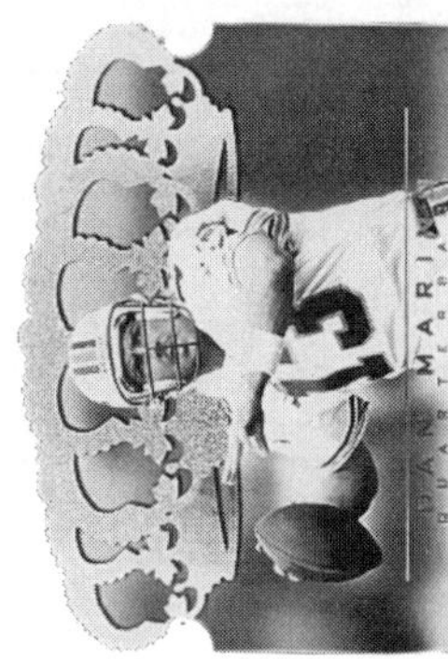

		MT
Complete Set (10):		600.00
Common Player:		20.00
1	Troy Aikman	60.00
2	John Elway	40.00
3	Brett Favre	90.00
4	Keyshawn Johnson	20.00
5	Dan Marino	90.00
6	Curtis Martin	80.00
7	Jerry Rice	60.00
8	Barry Sanders	60.00
9	Emmitt Smith	90.00
10	Steve Young	40.00

1996 Pacific Invincible

Pacific's 1996 Invincible Football (Prism II) has 150 cards in the set. Each is paralleled in four different versions. The regular card front has a color or action photo in the middle, with a gold-foiled sunburst design as a background pattern. The Pacific logo is in the upper left corner; the player's team logo is in a team color-coordinated banner at the bottom. The lower left corner has a small oval with a plastic piece inside featuring the player's mug shot. His name is in gold foil above the photo; his position is below. The back side has a rectangle at the top, with a color photo inside it. The Pacific logo is in the upper left corner. The player's name is below the photo, with a recap of his career comprising most of the back side. The plastic mug shot is reversed on the front and is in the lower left corner. The card number (using an "I" prefix) is at the bottom of the card. The regular cards have four parallel versions. Hobby packs have a bronze parallel (four per 25 packs), while retail packs have a silver parallel (four per 25 packs). Then a platinum (one per 25) and a gold parallel set are found in both hobby and retail packs. There are also four insert sets - Kick-Starters Die-Cuts, Pro Bowl Stars, Smash Mouth, and a 10-card Chris Warren set.

		MT
Complete Set (150):		175.00
Common Player:		1.00
Wax Box:		60.00
1	Larry Centers	1.00

2	Garrison Hearst	1.00
3	Seth Joyner	1.00
4	*Simeon Rice*	2.00
5	Eric Swann	1.00
6	Bert Emanuel	1.00
7	Jeff George	1.00
8	Craig Heyward	1.00
9	Terance Mathis	1.00
10	Eric Metcalf	1.00
11	Derrick Alexander	1.00
12	Leroy Hoard	1.00
13	Andre Rison	1.00
14	Tommy Vardell	1.00
15	Eric Zeier	1.00
16	Jim Kelly	2.00
17	*Eric Moulds*	5.00
18	Bryce Paup	1.00
19	Bruce Smith	1.00
20	Thurman Thomas	2.00
21	*Tim Biakabutuka*	5.00
22	Blake Brockermeyer	1.00
23	Kerry Collins	8.00
24	Howard Griffith	1.00
25	Lamar Lathon	1.00
26	Mark Carrier	1.00
27	Curtis Conway	1.00
28	Erik Kramer	1.00
29	Rashaan Salaam	2.00
30	Alonzo Spellman	1.00
31	Jeff Blake BR	4.00
32	Harold Green	1.00
33	Carl Pickens	2.00
34	Darnay Scott	2.00
35	Dan Wilkinson	1.00
36	Troy Aikman	6.00
37	Jay Novacek	1.00
38	Deion Sanders	5.00
39	Emmitt Smith	12.00
40	Kevin Williams	1.00
41	Terrell Davis	8.00
42	John Elway	4.00
43	Anthony Miller	1.00
44	Michael Dean Perry	1.00
45	Shannon Sharpe	1.00
46	Scott Mitchell	1.00
47	Herman Moore	2.00
48	Brett Perriman	1.00
49	Barry Sanders	6.00
50	Chris Spielman	1.00
51	Edgar Bennett	1.00
52	Robert Brooks	1.00
53	Brett Favre	12.00
54	*Derrick Mayes*	3.00
55	Reggie White	2.00
56	*Eddie George*	12.00
57	Haywood Jeffires	1.00
58	Steve McNair	5.00
59	Chris Sanders	2.00
60	Rodney Thomas	2.00
61	Tony Bennett	1.00
62	Quentin Coryatt	1.00
63	Ken Dilger	1.00
64	Marshall Faulk	4.00
65	Jim Harbaugh	1.00
66	Tony Boselli	1.00
67	Mark Brunell	5.00
68	Kevin Hardy	1.00
69	Desmond Howard	1.00
70	James Stewart	1.00
71	Marcus Allen	2.00
72	Steve Bono	1.00
73	Neil Smith	1.00
74	Derrick Thomas	1.00
75	Tamarick Vanover	4.00
76	*Karim Abdul-Jabbar*	8.00
77	Irving Fryar	1.00
78	Eric Green	1.00
79	Dan Marino	12.00
80	Bernie Parmalee	1.00
81	Cris Carter	1.00
82	Warren Moon	1.00
83	Jake Reed	1.00
84	Robert Smith	1.00
85	Moe Williams	1.00
86	Drew Bledsoe	6.00
87	Ben Coates	1.00
88	*Terry Glenn*	10.00
89	Curtis Martin	12.00
90	Dave Meggett	1.00
91	Mario Bates	1.00
92	Jim Everett	1.00
93	Michael Haynes	1.00
94	Torrance Small	1.00
95	Ray Zellars	1.00
96	Kyle Brady	1.00
97	Wayne Chrebet	1.00
98	*Keyshawn Johnson*	6.00
99	Adrian Murrell	1.00
100	*Alex Van Dyke*	3.00
101	Michael Brooks	1.00
102	Dave Brown	1.00
103	Chris Calloway	1.00
104	Rodney Hampton	1.00
105	*Amani Toomer*	3.00
106	Tyrone Wheatley	1.00
107	Tim Brown	1.00
108	*Rickey Dudley*	3.00
109	Billy Joe Hobert	1.00
110	Raghib Ismail	1.00
111	Napoleon Kaufman	1.00
112	Harvey Williams	1.00
113	Charlie Garner	1.00
114	*Bobby Hoying*	2.00
115	Rodney Peete	1.00
116	Ricky Watters	2.00
117	Greg Lloyd	1.00
118	Erric Pegram	1.00
119	Kordell Stewart	7.00
120	Yancey Thigpen	2.00
121	Jon Witman	1.00
122	Aaron Hayden	1.00
123	Stan Humphries	1.00
124	Tony Martin	1.00
125	Leslie O'Neal	1.00
126	Junior Seau	1.00
127	Jerome Bettis	2.00
128	Isaac Bruce	4.00
129	Ernie Conwell	1.00
130	*Lawrence Phillips*	4.00
131	William Floyd	1.00
132	*Terrell Owens*	8.00
133	Jerry Rice	7.00
134	J.J. Stokes	2.00
135	Steve Young	6.00
136	Brian Blades	1.00
137	Christian Fauria	1.00
138	Joey Galloway	6.00
139	Rick Mirer	1.00
140	Chris Warren	2.00
141	Horace Copeland	1.00
142	Trent Dilfer	1.00
143	Alvin Harper	1.00
144	Dave Moore	1.00
145	Errict Rhett	2.00
146	Terry Allen	1.00
147	Gus Frerotte	1.00
148	Brian Mitchell	1.00
149	Heath Shuler	1.00
150	Michael Westbrook	2.00

1996 Pacific Invincible Bronze/Silver/Platinum

Pacific's 150-card Invincible set was paralleled in a total of four different versions. Hobby packs contained Bronze parallels, while retail packs had Silver versions of the base set, with both seeded four per 25 packs. In addition, Invincible Platinums (1:25) and Golds were available in both types of packs at a reduced rate. Each version is distinguished by the color foil used.

	MT
Complete Bronze Set (149):	1000.00
Bronze Cards:	3x-6x
Complete Silver Set (149):	1000.00
Silver Cards:	3x-6x
Complete Platinum Set (149):	2000.00
Platinum Cards:	6x-12x

1996 Pacific Invincible Chris Warren

This 10-card set is entirely devoted to Seattle Seahawks running back Chris Warren. Each card features a different action shot of Warren, with cards found every 10 packs.

		MT
Complete Set (10):		10.00
Common Warren:		1.00
1	Chris Warren	1.00
2	Chris Warren	1.00
3	Chris Warren	1.00
4	Chris Warren	1.00
5	Chris Warren	1.00
6	Chris Warren	1.00
7	Chris Warren	1.00
8	Chris Warren	1.00
9	Chris Warren	1.00
10	Chris Warren	1.00

1996 Pacific Invincible Kick-Starters

These 1996 Pacific Invincible inserts are the most limited; they are seeded one per every 49 packs. The cards are die-cut into a gold-foiled football with a color action photo on it. The player's name is written along the left side of the card against a grassy background. The Pacific logo is in the upper left corner. The card back has a color action photo on the football part of the card; the right side has the player's name and a recap of a time when the player jump-started his team. The card is numbered using a "KS" prefix.

		MT
Complete Set (20):		500.00
Common Player:		15.00
1	Jeff Blake	18.00
2	Tim Brown	15.00
3	Kerry Collins	40.00
4	John Elway	30.00
5	Marshall Faulk	10.00
6	Brett Favre	75.00
7	Keyshawn Johnson	25.00
8	Dan Marino	75.00
9	Curtis Martin	50.00
10	Steve McNair	25.00
11	Errict Rhett	18.00
12	Jerry Rice	40.00
13	Rashaan Salaam	15.00
14	Barry Sanders	40.00
15	Deion Sanders	30.00
16	Emmitt Smith	75.00
17	Kordell Stewart	40.00
18	Tamarick Vanover	18.00
19	Chris Warren	15.00
20	Ricky Watters	15.00

1996 Pacific Invincible Pro Bowl

Every 25th pack of 1996 Pacific Invincible has one of these insert cards devoted to participants in the previous Pro Bowl game. Each card front shows the player in his Pro Bowl uniform against a colorful metallic background which incorporates the Pacific logo into the pattern. The player's name is written along the bottom. The horizontal back, numbered using a "PB" prefix, has a closeup shot of the player in his uniform, along with a Pro Bowl logo and a recap of some of his accomplishments as a Pro Bowler.

		MT
Complete Set (20):		175.00
Common Player:		4.00
1	Jeff Blake	6.00
2	Steve Bono	4.00
3	Tim Brown	4.00
4	Cris Carter	4.00
5	Ben Coates	4.00
6	Brett Favre	30.00
7	Jim Harbaugh	4.00
8	Curtis Martin	25.00
9	Warren Moon	4.00
10	Herman Moore	8.00
11	Carl Pickens	4.00
12	Jerry Rice	18.00
13	Barry Sanders	18.00
14	Shannon Sharpe	4.00
15	Emmitt Smith	30.00
16	Yancey Thigpen	7.00
17	Chris Warren	4.00
18	Ricky Watters	4.00
19	Reggie White	4.00
20	Steve Young	14.00

1996 Pacific Invincible Smash-Mouth

Some of the NFL's most intense players and hardest hitters are featured on these 1996 Pacific Invincible inserts. The cards, numbered on the back using an "SM" prefix, were seeded two per pack. Each card front shows a player busting through a hole against a football field background. The Pacific logo is in the upper right corner; the player's name is along the bottom. The back has a square in the upper right corner which has a mug shot inside. A summary of some of his accomplishments is given below the photo. The player's name, team name and position are written along the left side of the card, below the Pacific logo.

		MT
Complete Set (180):		30.00
Common Player:		.20
1	Marcus Dowdell	.20
2	Karl Dunbar	.20

No.	Player	Price
3	Eric England	.20
4	Garrison Hearst	.20
5	Bryan Reeves	.20
6	Simeon Rice	.20
7	Jeff George	.20
8	Bobby Hebert	.20
9	Craig Heyward	.20
10	Dave Richard	.20
11	Elbert Shelley	.20
12	Lonnie Johnson	.20
13	Jim Kelly	.20
14	Corbin Lacina	.20
15	Bryce Paup	.20
16	Sam Rogers	.20
17	Bruce Smith	.20
18	Thurman Thomas	.40
19	Carl Banks	.20
20	Dan Footman	.20
21	Louis Riddick	.20
22	Matt Stover	.20
23	Tommy Barnhardt	.20
24	Kerry Collins	1.50
25	Mark Dennis	.20
26	Matt Elliott	.20
27	Eric Guliford	.20
28	Lamar Lathon	.20
29	Joe Cain	.20
30	Marty Carter	.20
31	Robert Green	.20
32	Erik Kramer	.20
33	Todd Perry	.20
34	Rashaan Salaam	.40
35	Alonzo Spellman	.20
36	Jeff Blake	.75
37	Andre Collins	.20
38	Todd Kelly	.20
39	Carl Pickens	.20
40	Kevin Sargent	.20
41	Troy Aikman	1.25
42	Charles Haley	.20
43	Daryl Johnston	.20
44	Nate Newton	.20
45	Deion Sanders	.75
46	Emmitt Smith	3.00
47	Steve Atwater	.20
48	Terrell Davis	1.00
49	John Elway	.75
50	Michael Dean Perry	.20
51	Shannon Sharpe	.20
52	Dave Wyman	.20
53	Bennie Blades	.20
54	Kevin Glover	.20
55	Herman Moore	.50
56	Robert Porcher	.20
57	Barry Sanders	1.25
58	Henry Thomas	.20
59	Edgar Bennett	.20
60	Robert Brooks	.20
61	Brett Favre	3.00
62	Harry Galbreath	.20
63	Sean Jones	.20
64	Reggie White	.40
65	Blaine Bishop	.20
66	Chuck Cecil	.20
67	Cris Dishman	.20
68	Steve McNair	.75
69	Rodney Thomas	.20
70	Jason Belser	.20
71	Ray Buchanan	.20
72	Quentin Coryatt	.20
73	Marshall Faulk	1.00
74	Jim Harbaugh	.20
75	Devon McDonald	.20
76	Tony Boselli	.20
77	Tony Brackens	.20
78	Mark Brunell	.75
79	Don Davey	.20
80	Rich Griffith	.20
81	Kevin Hardy	.20
82	Mickey Washington	.20
83	Louis Aguiar	.20
84	Dan Saleaumua	.20
85	Will Shields	.20
86	Neil Smith	.20
87	Derrick Thomas	.20
88	Tamarick Vanover	.75
89	Gene Atkins	.20
90	Bryan Cox	.20
91	Steve Emtman	.20
92	Chris Gray	.20
93	Dan Marino	3.00
94	Derrick Alexander	.20
95	Cris Carter	.20
96	Jeff Christy	.20
97	Robert Smith	.20
98	Korey Stringer	.20
99	Orlando Thomas	.20
100	Esera Tuaolo	.20
101	Drew Bledsoe	1.00
102	Eddie Cade	.20
103	Mike Jones	.20
104	Curtis Martin	2.00
105	Willie McGinest	.20
106	Chris Slade	.20
107	Eric Allen	.20
108	Mario Bates	.20
109	Jim Dombrowski	.20
110	Wayne Martin	.20
111	William Roaf	.20
112	Irv Smith	.20
113	Michael Brooks	.20
114	Stacey Dillard	.20
115	Rodney Hampton	.20
116	Doug Riesenberg	.20
117	Coleman Rudolph	.20
118	Tyrone Wheatley	.20
119	Kyle Brady	.20
120	Roger Duffy	.20
121	Keyshawn Johnson	1.00
122	Gary Jones	.20
123	Eddie Anderson	.20
124	Rickey Dudley	.40
125	Napoleon Kaufman	.20
126	Greg Skrepenak	.20
127	Pat Swilling	.20
128	Steve Wisniewski	.20
129	William Fuller	.20
130	Kurt Gouvela	.20
131	Andy Harmon	.20
132	Mike Mamula	.20
133	Guy McIntyre	.20
134	Ricky Watters	.20
135	Kevin Greene	.20
136	Bill Johnson	.20
137	Carnell Lake	.20
138	Greg Lloyd	.20
139	Erric Pegram	.20
140	Leon Searcy	.20
141	Shane Conlan	.20
142	Troy Drayton	.20
143	Wayne Gandy	.20
144	Sean Gilbert	.20
145	Carlos Jenkins	.20
146	Lawrence Phillips	1.00
147	Aaron Hayden	.20
148	Stan Humphries	.20
149	Leslie O'Neal	.20
150	Bo Orlando	.20
151	Junior Seau	.20
152	Harry Swayne	.20
153	Harris Barton	.20
154	Merton Hanks	.20
155	Rod Milstead	.20
156	Ken Norton Jr.	.20
157	Gary Plummer	.20
158	Jerry Rice	1.50
159	Steve Wallace	.20
160	Steve Young	1.00
161	James Atkins	.20
162	Brian Blades	.20
163	Matt Joyce	.20
164	Cortez Kennedy	.20
165	Kevin Mawae	.20
166	Winston Moss	.20
167	Chris Warren	.40
168	Derrick Brooks	.20
169	Trent Dilfer	.20
170	Santana Dotson	.20
171	Alvin Harper	.20
172	Hardy Nickerson	.20
173	Errict Rhett	.40
174	Warren Sapp	.20
175	Terry Allen	.20
176	John Gesek	.20
177	Ken Harvey	.20
178	Tre Johnson	.20
179	Rod Stephens	.20
180	Michael Westbrook	.40

1996 Pacific Litho-Cel

The 100-card, regular-sized set actually is two 100-card sets, with Cel and Litho versions. The Cel cards feature a clear oval center with a blue color image. The Litho cards are the same card fronts, but with a red color, non-clear oval center image. When the Cel card is placed over the Litho card, a 3-D effect makes the center oval image appear in full color. The card backs of the Cel cards are numbered with the "Cel" prefix while the Litho cards feature the same corresponding number with a "Litho" prefix. Litho-Cel came in three-card packs and included Moments In Time, Feature Performers, Game Time, Litho-Proof and Certified Litho-Proof inserts, as well as parallel silver foil (3:25) and Blue-Platinum (retail 3:25) versions. Pacific Litho-Cel was available in three-card packs which contained one Cel card, one Litho card and one Game Time card or other insert card.

	MT
Complete Set (100):	175.00
Common Player:	.75
Wax Box:	70.00

Prices are for both Litho and Cel cards together.

No.	Player	Price
1	Kent Graham	.75
2	LeShon Johnson	.75
3	*Leeland McElroy*	3.00
4	Frank Sanders	.75
5	*Jamal Anderson*	3.00
6	Cornelius Bennett	.75
7	Bobby Hebert	.75
8	Earnest Byner	.75
9	Michael Jackson	.75
10	Vinny Testaverde	.75
11	Jim Kelly	.75
12	Andre Reed	.75
13	Bruce Smith	.75
14	Thurman Thomas	1.50
15	Kerry Collins	7.00
16	Lamar Lathon	.75
17	Kevin Greene	.75
18	*Bobby Engram*	3.00
19	Erik Kramer	.75
20	Rashaan Salaam	3.00
21	Jeff Blake	3.00
22	Garrison Hearst	.75
23	Carl Pickens	.75
24	Darnay Scott	.75
25	Troy Aikman	7.00
26	Eric Bjornson	.75
27	Deion Sanders	5.00
28	Emmitt Smith	14.00
29	Terrell Davis	8.00
30	John Elway	5.00
31	Anthony Miller	.75
32	John Mobley	.75
33	Scott Mitchell	.75
34	Herman Moore	1.50
35	Brett Perriman	.75
36	Barry Sanders	7.00
37	Edgar Bennett	.75
38	Robert Brooks	.75
39	Brett Favre	14.00
40	Reggie White	1.50
41	Chris Chandler	.75
42	*Eddie George*	15.00
43	Steve McNair	4.00
44	Chris Sanders	.75
45	Ken Dilger	.75
46	Marshall Faulk	4.00
47	Jim Harbaugh	.75
48	Mark Brunell	5.00
49	Keenan McCardell	.75
50	James Stewart	.75
51	Marcus Allen	1.50
52	Steve Bono	.75
53	Greg Hill	.75
54	Tamarick Vanover	3.00
55	*Karim Abdul-Jabbar*	8.00
56	Dan Marino	14.00
57	*Zach Thomas*	4.00
58	Cris Carter	.75
59	Warren Moon	.75
60	Robert Smith	.75
61	Drew Bledsoe	6.00
62	*Terry Glenn*	12.00
63	Curtis Martin	10.00
64	Mario Bates	.75
65	Jim Everett	.75
66	Haywood Jeffires	.75
67	Dave Brown	.75
68	Rodney Hampton	.75
69	*Amani Toomer*	1.50
70	Adrian Murrell	.75
71	Neil O'Donnell	.75
72	*Alex Van Dyke*	3.00
73	Tim Brown	.75
74	Jeff Hostetler	.75
75	Napoleon Kaufman	.75
76	Irving Fryar	.75
77	Chris T. Jones	.75
78	Ricky Watters	1.50
79	Jerome Bettis	1.50
80	Kordell Stewart	7.00
81	*Tony Banks*	4.00
82	*Eddie Kennison*	5.00
83	*Lawrence Phillips*	3.00
84	Stan Humphries	.75
85	Tony Martin	.75
86	Leonard Russell	.75
87	Junior Seau	.75
88	Jerry Rice	7.00
89	J.J. Stokes	1.50
90	Tommy Vardell	.75
91	Steve Young	5.00
92	Joey Galloway	5.00
93	Rick Mirer	.75
94	Chris Warren	.75
95	Mike Alstott	2.00
96	Trent Dilfer	.75
97	Nilo Silvan	.75
98	Terry Allen	.75
99	Gus Frerotte	.75
100	Michael Westbrook	1.50

1996 Pacific Litho-Cel Bronze/Silver

Each card in the 100-card Litho-Cel set was reprinted in two different foil versions. Silver foil parallels were found in three per 25 hobby packs, while bronze versions were found in three per 25 retail packs. The only difference between these parallels and the regular-issue cards is the color of the foil stamping.

	MT
Complete Bronze Set (100):	700.00
Bronze Cards:	2x-4x
Complete Silver Set (100):	700.00
Silver Cards:	2x-4x

1996 Pacific Litho-Cel Litho-Proof

The 36-card, regular-sized set was inserted in every 97 packs of 1996 Lith-Cel. The card fronts feature the same color photo and design as the basic Litho-Cel set, without the clear blue cel imaging. Also differentiating between the two sets is a gray seal in the lower left section of the card front which reads, "1996 Pacific Litho Cards - Litho-Proof." The cards are sequentially numbered as "x of 360" and are listed with a "Litho-Proof" prefix. A parallel version, Certified Litho-Proof, features a second seal "Pacific Collection" and is inserted every 481 packs.

		MT
	Complete Set (36):	1600.00
	Common Player:	15.00
1	Jim Kelly	15.00
2	Kerry Collins	80.00
3	Rashaan Salaam	30.00
4	Jeff Blake	30.00
5	Carl Pickens	15.00
6	Troy Aikman	80.00
7	Deion Sanders	70.00
8	Emmitt Smith	160.00
9	Terrell Davis	100.00
10	John Elway	70.00
11	Herman Moore	30.00
12	Barry Sanders	80.00
13	Robert Brooks	15.00
14	Brett Favre	160.00
15	Reggie White	15.00
16	Eddie George	90.00
17	Marshall Faulk	50.00
18	Jim Harbaugh	15.00
19	Mark Brunell	70.00
20	Marcus Allen	15.00
21	Steve Bono	15.00
22	Karim Abdul-Jabbar	70.00
23	Dan Marino	160.00
24	Warren Moon	15.00
25	Drew Bledsoe	80.00
26	Curtis Martin	100.00
27	Amani Toomer	15.00
28	Tim Brown	15.00
29	Napoleon Kaufman	15.00
30	Ricky Watters	15.00
31	Jerome Bettis	15.00
32	Kordell Stewart	80.00
33	Jerry Rice	80.00
34	Steve Young	70.00
35	Joey Galloway	70.00
36	Terry Allen	15.00

1996 Pacific Litho-Cel Certified Litho-Proofs

Certified Litho Proofs are similar to the regular Litho Proof inserts, but contain a large Pacific Crown Collection logo over top of the Litho Proof logo in the bottom left corner. Certified Litho Proofs were inserted at a rate of one per 481 packs.

	MT
Complete Set (36):	6000.00
Certified Litho-Proofs:	2x-4x

1996 Pacific Litho-Cel Feature Performers

The 20-card, regular-sized inserts were included in every 25 packs of Litho-Cel. The card fronts feature the player over gold foil with his respective team helmet outlined on the bottom half of the card. The player's name is written in the player's team color down the right side while the backs are numbered with the "FP" prefix.

		MT
	Complete Set (20):	300.00
	Common Player:	7.00
1	Jim Kelly	7.00
2	Troy Aikman	20.00
3	Deion Sanders	15.00
4	Emmitt Smith	40.00

5	Terrell Davis	30.00
6	John Elway	20.00
7	Herman Moore	10.00
8	Barry Sanders	20.00
9	Robert Brooks	7.00
10	Brett Favre	40.00
11	Eddie George	25.00
12	Jim Harbaugh	7.00
13	Marcus Allen	7.00
14	Karim Abdul-Jabbar	15.00
15	Dan Marino	40.00
16	Joey Galloway	15.00
17	Curtis Martin	30.00
18	Jerome Bettis	10.00
19	Jerry Rice	20.00
20	Steve Young	15.00

1990 Pacific Litho-Cel Game Time

The 96-card, regular-sized set was inserted in each pack of Litho-Cel. The card fronts feature the player centered in an array of statistical cut-out boxes and the player's name is written in a curved pattern over the position on the bottom. The card backs feature headshots of the players in the lower lefthand corner, framed in a stop watch. The cards are numbered with the "GT" prefix.

		MT
	Complete Set (96):	25.00
	Common Player:	.20
1	Eddie George	2.00
2	Larry Bowie	.20
3	Jarius Hayes	.20
4	Jamal Anderson	.75
5	Earnest Hunter	.20
6	Darick Holmes	.20
7	Kerry Collins	1.50
8	Raymont Harris	.20
9	Jeff Blake	.75
10	Troy Aikman	1.50
11	Terrell Davis	1.50
12	Kevin Glover	.20
13	Brett Favre	3.00
14	Al Del Greco	.20
15	Marshall Faulk	1.00
16	Bryan Barker	.20
17	Rich Gannon	.20
18	Dwight Hollier	.20
19	Dixon Edwards	.20
20	Drew Bledsoe	1.00
21	Paul Green	.20
22	Lawrence Dawsey	.20
23	Ron Carpenter	.20
24	Joe Aska	.20
25	Joe Panos	.20
26	Norm Johnson	.20
27	Tony Banks	1.00
28	Darren Bennett	.20
29	Steve Israel	.20
30	Mike Barber	.20
31	Dexter Nottage	.20
32	Kwamie Lassiter	.20
33	Travis Hall	.20
34	Greg Montgomery	.20
35	Jim Kelly	.20
36	Matt Elliott	.20
37	Jack Jackson	.20
38	Ki-Jana Carter	.40
39	Deion Sanders	1.00
40	Jason Elam	.20
41	Johnnie Morton	.20
42	Darius Holland	.20
43	Sheddrick Wilson	.20

44	Derrick Frazier	.20
45	Travis Davis	.20
46	Pellom McDaniels	.20
47	Dan Marino	3.00
48	Ben Hanks	.20
49	Tedy Bruschi	.20
50	Tom Hodson	.20
51	Amani Toomer	.50
52	Brian Hansen	.20
53	Paul Butcher	.20
54	Kevin Turner	.20
55	Darren Perry	.20
56	Mike Gruttadauria	.20
57	Charlie Jones	.20
58	Iheanyi Uwaezuoke	.20
59	Glenn Montgomery	.20
60	Mike Alstott	.75
61	Joe Patton	.20
62	Leeland McElroy	.75
63	Robbie Tobeck	.20
64	Vinny Testaverde	.20
65	Chris Spielman	.20
66	Anthony Johnson	.20
67	Todd Sauerbrun	.20
68	Jeff Hill	.20
69	Emmitt Smith	3.00
70	John Elway	1.00
71	Barry Sanders	1.50
72	Brian Williams	.20
73	Chris Gardocki	.20
74	Jimmy Smith	.20
75	Ricky Siglar	.20
76	Tim Ruddy	.20
77	Moe Williams	.20
78	Willie Clay	.20
79	Henry Lusk	.20
80	Brian Williams	.20
81	Ronald Moore	.20
82	Trey Junkin	.20
83	James Willis	.20
84	Joel Steed	.20
85	Jamie Martin	.20
86	Shawn Lee	.20
87	Steve Young	1.00
88	Barrett Robbins	.20
89	Charles Dimry	.20
90	Darryl Pounds	.20
91	Herschel Walker	.20
92	Bill Romanowski	.20
93	David Tate	.20
94	Marrio Grier	.20
95	Rodney Young	.20
96	Lamar Smith	.20

1996 Pacific Litho-Cel Moments in Time

The 20-card, regular-sized, die-cut set was inserted every 49 packs of Litho-Cel. The horizontal cards are die-cut in the shape of a scoreboard and feature red-foil printing. The score of a particular game, along with the player's statistics for that game are included on the card front in scoreboard script, while the card back describes the player's performance with a highlight. The cards are numbered with the "MT" prefix.

		MT
	Complete Set (20):	500.00
	Common Player:	8.00
1	Jim Kelly	8.00
2	Kerry Collins	50.00
3	Rashann Salaam	20.00
4	Troy Aikman	50.00
5	Deion Sanders	30.00

6	Emmitt Smith	100.00
7	Terrell Davis	50.00
8	John Elway	30.00
9	Barry Sanders	50.00
10	Robert Brooks	8.00
11	Brett Favre	100.00
12	Marshall Faulk	20.00
13	Jim Harbaugh	8.00
14	Steve Bono	8.00
15	Dan Marino	100.00
16	Drew Bledsoe	50.00
17	Curtis Martin	60.00
18	Jerry Rice	50.00
19	Steve Young	40.00
20	Terry Allen	8.00

1996 Pinnacle

Pinnacle's 1996 football set includes 200 cards in the regular set, including 30 Rookies, six Bid For Six subset cards, five checklists and a Brett Favre Cheesehead card. The set is paralleled twice in normal packs - Trophy Collection (one in five packs, these cards use all-foil Dufex) and Artist's Proof (one in 47 packs, these have a holographic gold foil stamp). These parallel cards are labeled accordingly on them. Each regular card has a full-bleed color action photo on the front, with a Pinnacle logo in an upper corner. The player's name is in a gold-foiled triangle at the bottom. The card back has logo in an upper corner, with the card number in white in a black square. The upper half of the card has a photo; the lower half has a brief profile, stats, biographical information, the player's name and team logo, and his position. Insert sets include Black 'N Blue, Double Disguise, On the Line, Team Pinnacle and 321 Die-Cut Jersey cards. Pinnacle also offers hobby-exclusive packs called premium stock, which contain 25 cards and carry a suggested retail price of $6.99. In these packs each common card in the set is printed on a super-premium, 24-point card stock featuring silver foil stamping. Premium stock packs also have five inserts - Trophy Collection, Artist's Proofs, Team Pinnacle, Double Disguise and an exclusive rainbow holographic foil version of 321.

		MT
	Complete Set (200):	25.00
	Common Player:	.10
	Wax Box:	50.00
1	Emmitt Smith	2.50
2	Robert Brooks	.20
3	Joey Galloway	.75
4	Dan Marino	2.50
5	Frank Sanders	.20
6	Cris Carter	.10
7	Jeff Blake	.75
8	Steve McNair	.75
9	Tamarick Vanover	.75
10	Andre Reed	.10
11	Junior Seau	.10
12	Alvin Harper	.10

#	Player	MT
13	Trent Dilfer	.10
14	Kordell Stewart	1.00
15	Kyle Brady	.10
16	Charles Haley	.10
17	Greg Lloyd	.10
18	Mario Bates	.10
19	Shannon Sharpe	.10
20	Scott Mitchell	.10
21	Craig Heyward	.10
22	Marcus Allen	.10
23	Curtis Martin	1.75
24	Drew Bledsoe	1.00
25	Jerry Rice	1.00
26	Charlie Garner	.10
27	Michael Irvin	.10
28	Curtis Conway	.10
29	Terrell Davis	1.25
30	Jeff Hostetler	.10
31	Neil O'Donnell	.10
32	Errict Rhett	.50
33	Stan Humphries	.10
34	Jeff Graham	.10
35	Floyd Turner	.10
36	Vincent Brisby	.10
37	Steve Young	1.00
38	Carl Pickens	.10
39	Terance Mathis	.10
40	Brett Favre	2.50
41	Ki-Jana Carter	.40
42	Jim Everett	.10
43	Marshall Faulk	.75
44	William Floyd	.10
45	Deion Sanders	.50
46	Garrison Hearst	.10
47	Chris Sanders	.10
48	Isaac Bruce	.75
49	Natrone Means	.10
50	Troy Aikman	1.25
51	Ben Coates	.10
52	Tony Martin	.10
53	Rod Woodson	.10
54	Edgar Bennett	.10
55	Eric Zeier	.10
56	Steve Bono	.10
57	Tim Brown	.10
58	Kevin Williams	.10
59	Erik Kramer	.10
60	Jim Kelly	.10
61	Larry Centers	.10
62	Terrell Fletcher	.10
63	Michael Westbrook	.20
64	Kerry Collins	1.25
65	Jay Novacek	.10
66	J.J. Stokes	.20
67	John Elway	.50
68	Jim Harbaugh	.10
69	Aeneas Williams	.10
70	Tyrone Wheatley	.10
71	Chris Warren	.20
72	Rodney Thomas	.10
73	Jeff George	.10
74	Rick Mirer	.10
75	Yancey Thigpen	.50
76	Herman Moore	.50
77	Gus Frerotte	.10
78	Anthony Miller	.10
79	Ricky Watters	.10
80	Sherman Williams	.10
81	Hardy Nickerson	.10
82	Henry Ellard	.10
83	Aaron Craver	.10
84	Rodney Peete	.10
85	Eric Metcalf	.10
86	Brian Blades	.10
87	Rob Moore	.10
88	Kimble Anders	.10
89	Harvey Williams	.10
90	Thurman Thomas	.20
91	Dave Brown	.10
92	Terry Allen	.10
93	Ken Norton	.10
94	Reggie White	.20
95	Mark Chmura	.20
96	Bert Emanuel	.10
97	Brett Perriman	.10
98	Antonio Freeman	.10
99	Brian Mitchell	.10
100	Orlando Thomas	.10
101	Aaron Hayden	.10
102	Quinn Early	.10
103	Lovell Pinkney	.10
104	Napoleon Kaufman	.20
105	Daryl Johnston	.10
106	Steve Tasker	.10
107	Brent Jones	.10
108	Mark Brunell	.75
109	Leslie O'Neal	.10
110	Irving Fryar	.10
111	Jim Miller	.10
112	Sean Dawkins	.10
113	Boomer Esiason	.10
114	Heath Shuler	.10
115	Bruce Smith	.10
116	Russell Maryland	.10
117	Jake Reed	.10
118	O.J. McDuffie	.10
119	Erik Williams	.10
120	Willie McGinest	.10
121	Terry Kirby	.10
122	Fred Barnett	.10
123	Andre Hastings	.10
124	Dale Hellestrae	.10
125	Darren Woodson	.10
126	Steve Atwater	.10
127	Quentin Coryatt	.10
128	Derrick Thomas	.10
129	Nate Newton	.10
130	Kevin Greene	.10
131	Barry Sanders	1.25
132	Warren Moon	.10
133	Rashaan Salaam	.50
134	Rodney Hampton	.10
135	James Stewart	.10
136	Erric Pegram	.10
137	Bryan Cox	.10
138	Adrian Murrell	.10
139	Robert Smith	.10
140	Bernie Parmalee	.10
141	Bryce Paup	.10
142	Darick Holmes	.10
143	Hugh Douglas	.10
144	Ken Dilger	.10
145	Derek Loville	.10
146	Horace Copeland	.10
147	Wayne Chrebet	.10
148	Andre Coleman	.10
149	Greg Hill	.10
150	Eric Swann	.10
151	Tyrone Hughes	.10
152	Ernie Mills	.10
153	*Terry Glenn*	3.00
154	*Cedric Jones*	.10
155	*Leeland McElroy*	.30
156	*Bobby Engram*	1.00
157	*Willie Anderson*	.10
158	*Mike Alstott*	.50
159	*Alex Van Dyke*	.20
160	*Jeff Lewis*	.10
161	*Keyshawn Johnson*	2.00
162	*Regan Upshaw*	.10
163	*Eric Moulds*	1.00
164	*Tim Biakabutuka*	1.00
165	*Kevin Hardy*	.20
166	*Marvin Harrison*	1.50
167	*Karim Abdul-Jabbar*	2.50
168	*Tony Brackens*	.30
169	*Stepfret Williams*	.10
170	*Eddie George*	4.00
171	*Lawrence Phillips*	.50
172	*Danny Kanell*	.40
173	*Derrick Mayes*	1.00
174	*Daryl Gardener*	.10
175	*Jonathan Ogden*	.10
176	*Alex Molden*	.10
177	*Chris Darkins*	.20
178	*Stephen Davis*	.40
179	*Rickey Dudley*	.30
180	*Eddie Kennison*	1.25
181	*Simeon Rice*	.40
182	*Bobby Hoying*	.20
183	Troy Aikman	.50
184	Emmitt Smith	1.00
185	Michael Irvin	.10
186	Deion Sanders	.25
187	Daryl Johnston	.10
188	Jay Novacek	.10
189	Steve Young	.40
190	Jerry Rice	.50
191	J.J. Stokes	.10
192	Ken Norton	.10
193	William Floyd	.10
194	Brent Jones	.10
195	Dan Marino CL	.40
196	Brett Favre CL	.30
197	Emmitt Smith CL	.40
198	Barry Sanders CL	.30
199	Checklist Emmitt Smith, Dan Marino, Brett Favre, Barry Sanders CL	.30
200	Brett Favre Cheese	2.50

1996 Pinnacle Trophy Collection

Trophy Collection features all 200 cards from 1996 Pinnacle, reprinted in Dufex foil fronts and a stamp on the back that reads "Trophy Collection."

Regular packs had Trophy Collection cards every five packs, while Premium Stock packs contained them every two packs. There is no difference between regular and Premium Stock cards in Trophy Collection.

	MT
Complete Trophy Set (200):	500.00
Trophy Cards:	10x-20x

1996 Pinnacle Foils

Pinnacle Foils were available only in All-Foil packs, which were available in retail locations. These Foils were the "regular-issue" cards of All-Foil packs that also included Black and Blue inserts.

	MT
Complete Set (200):	35.00
Foil Cards:	1.5x

1996 Pinnacle Artist's Proofs

This 200-card parallel set features each card in 1996 Pinnacle Football, but includes a holographic Artist's Proof logo on the front, as well as a logo on the back. Artist's Proofs were included in every 48 hobby and retail packs. Regular Artist's Proofs contained gold foil at the bottom of the card in contrast to Premium Stock Artist's Proofs that included silver foil and are included in a separate entry.

	MT
Complete Set (200):	1500.00
Artist's Proof Cards:	25x-50x

1996 Pinnacle Premium Stock

Pinnacle Premium Stock was issued as a hobby exclusive product that was offered in addition to regular Pinnacle Football. The base cards were different in that they had silver foil at the bottom instead of gold foil. Packs of Premium Stock contained 25 cards, and included Artist's Proofs, Trophy Collection, Team Pinnacle, Die-Cut Jerseys and Double Disguise inserts. Only the Artist's Proofs and Die-Cut Jerseys are different than regular-issue inserts.

	MT
Complete Set (200):	50.00
Premium Stock Cards:	2x

1996 Pinnacle Premium Stock Artist's Proofs

Each card in the 200-card Premium Stock set was featured in the parallel Artist's Proof insert. This means that the Premium Stock Artist's Proofs feature silver foil on the fronts instead of gold foil on the regular-issue Artist's Proofs. Premium Stock Artist's Proofs were inserted every 12 packs.

	MT
Complete Set (200):	1500.00
PS Artist's Proofs:	25x-50x

1996 Pinnacle Black 'N Blue

Twenty-five of the NFL's most rugged players show the hard-nosed, aggressive play which has earned them a spot in this set. The cards were seeded one per every 33 magazine packs. Each card front has two photos on it.

#	Player	MT
	Complete Set (25):	275.00
	Common Player:	5.00
1	Steve Young	15.00
2	Troy Aikman	20.00
3	Dan Marino	40.00
4	Michael Irvin	5.00
5	Jerry Rice	20.00
6	Emmitt Smith	40.00
7	Brett Favre	40.00
8	Drew Bledsoe	20.00
9	John Elway	15.00
10	Barry Sanders	20.00
11	Cris Carter	5.00
12	Jeff Blake	8.00
13	Chris Warren	5.00
14	Kerry Collins	20.00
15	Natrone Means	5.00
16	Herman Moore	5.00
17	Steve McNair	10.00
18	Ricky Watters	5.00
19	Tamarick Vanover	10.00
20	Deion Sanders	15.00
21	Terrell Davis	20.00
22	Rodney Thomas	5.00
23	Rashaan Salaam	8.00
24	Darick Holmes	5.00
25	Eric Zeier	5.00

1996 Pinnacle Die-Cut Jerseys

The best and youngest players in the NFL - those with three or less years of experience - are featured on these die-cut Pinnacle insert cards. The cards are hobby-exclusive; they were seeded one per every 23 hobby packs. The card front has a color action shot against a die-cut version of his jersey. "3-2-1" is included as a tag in the jersey's collar. The Pinnacle logo and player's name are stamped in gold foil along the bottom of the card. The back of the card uses the back of the player's jersey as a background. A second photo appears, along with a team logo, a brief summary of one of his accomplishments, and a card number (1 of 20, etc.).

		MT
Complete Set (20):		160.00
Common Player:		4.00
1	Errict Rhett	6.00
2	Marshall Faulk	8.00
3	Isaac Bruce	8.00
4	William Floyd	4.00
5	Heath Shuler	4.00
6	Kerry Collins	15.00
7	Kordell Stewart	14.00
8	Rashaan Salaam	6.00
9	Terrell Davis	18.00
10	Rodney Thomas	4.00
11	Curtis Martin	20.00
12	Steve McNair	10.00
13	J.J. Stokes	8.00
14	Joey Galloway	10.00
15	Michael Westbrook	6.00
16	Keyshawn Johnson	10.00
17	Lawrence Phillips	10.00
18	Terry Glenn	18.00
19	Tim Biakabutuka	8.00
20	Eddie George	20.00

1996 Pinnacle Premium Stock Die-Cut Jerseys

Premium Stock packs included a unique version of the Die-cut Jerseys that featured the fronts in prismatic foil. These versions of Die-Cut Jerseys were inserted every six packs and only included in Premium Stock.

	MT
Complete Set (20):	320.00
PS Die-Cut Jerseys:	2x

1996 Pinnacle Double Disguise

These 1996 Pinnacle inserts showcase five players in 20 different combinations. The cards are printed on plastic and are covered with an opaque plastic protector which is meant to be peeled off. Each side features combinations of Emmitt Smith,

Dan Marino, Brett Favre, Kerry Collins and Steve Young matched up. The card's background shows the length of a football field as seen through a fisheye lens. The front side uses gold-foil stamping for the Pinnacle logo, player's name and set name. These are not in foil on the opposite side, which has a card number (1 of 20, etc.). The cards were seeded one per every 18 packs.

		MT
Complete Set (20):		150.00
Common Player:		4.00
1	Emmitt Smith, Emmitt Smith	15.00
2	Emmitt Smith, Dan Marino	15.00
3	Emmitt Smith, Brett Favre	12.00
4	Emmitt Smith, Steve Young	10.00
5	Dan Marino, Dan Marino	12.00
6	Dan Marino, Emmitt Smith	15.00
7	Dan Marino, Kerry Collins	10.00
8	Dan Marino, Steve Young	10.00
9	Kerry Collins, Kerry Collins	4.00
10	Kerry Collins, Dan Marino	10.00
11	Kerry Collins, Brett Favre	10.00
12	Kerry Collins, Steve Young	4.00
13	Brett Favre, Brett Favre	10.00
14	Brett Favre, Kerry Collins	10.00
15	Brett Favre, Dan Marino	10.00
16	Brett Favre, Emmitt Smith	12.00
17	Steve Young, Steve Young	4.00
18	Steve Young, Brett Favre	8.00
19	Steve Young, Emmitt Smith	10.00
20	Steve Young, Kerry Collins	4.00

1996 Pinnacle On the Line

The NFL's top pass catchers are featured on these 1996 Pinnacle inserts. The cards, seeded one per every 23 retail packs, use Dufex for the design. The card front has a full-bleed color action photo on it, with the player's name at the bottom near a grid which says "On the Line." The Pinnacle logo is in an upper corner.

		MT
Complete Set (15):		80.00
Common Player:		3.00
1	Michael Irvin	3.00
2	Robert Brooks	3.00
3	Herman Moore	6.00
4	Cris Carter	3.00
5	Chris Sanders	3.00
6	Jerry Rice	20.00
7	Michael Westbrook	3.00
8	Carl Pickens	3.00
9	Bobby Engram	10.00
10	Alex Van Dyke	3.00
11	Keyshawn Johnson	12.00
12	Terry Glenn	18.00
13	Eric Moulds	8.00
14	Marvin Harrison	13.00
15	Eddie Kennison	10.00

1996 Pinnacle Team Pinnacle

These 1996 Pinnacle inserts feature the best AFC player at each position on a card that is complemented by

the top NFC position player on the flip side. The cards were seeded one per every 90 packs for both hobby and retail packs. The design shows a pin-stripe-framed color action photo against a football background. The player's name, position and Team Pinnacle are written in a rectangle at the bottom. The card is numbered 1 of 20, etc.

		MT
Complete Set (10):		300.00
Common Player:		20.00
1	Troy Aikman, Drew Bledsoe	40.00
2	Steve Young, Jeff Blake	25.00
3	Brett Favre, John Elway	50.00
4	Kerry Collins, Dan Marino	60.00
5	Emmitt Smith, Curtis Martin	60.00
6	Barry Sanders, Chris Warren	35.00
7	Errict Rhett, Marshall Faulk	20.00
8	Jerry Rice, Carl Pickens	35.00
9	Michael Irvin, Joey Galloway	20.00
10	Isaac Bruce, Kordell Stewart	25.00

1996 Pinnacle Mint Cards

The 30-card, regular-sized set comes in three-card packs and contains two coin cards and one regular-issue card. The die-cut coin cards feature a closeup player shot and an action shot on the front with the same action shot in black and white on the back. The cards have a circular cutout in the upper right quadrant where the included brass, nickel- silver or gold coins fit. The regular-issue cards feature a foil team emblem (where the hole is on the coin cards) in brass (common), silver (1:20) or gold (1:48). Each of the 30 players represented in the set are members of the Quarterback Club.

		MT
Complete Die-Cut (30):		18.00
Common Player:		.20
Bronze Cards:		2x
Silver Cards:		4x-8x
Gold Cards:		10x-20x
Wax Box:		50.00
1	Troy Aikman	1.50

		MT
2	John Elway	.75
3	Jim Kelly	.40
4	Dan Marino	3.00
5	Warren Moon	.20
6	Steve Young	1.50
7	Jerry Rice	1.50
8	Boomer Esiason	.20
9	Jim Everett	.20
10	Brett Favre	3.00
11	Jim Harbaugh	.40
12	Jeff Hostetler	.20
13	Neil O'Donnell	.20
14	Drew Bledsoe	1.50
15	Rick Mirer	.20
16	Emmitt Smith	3.00
17	Barry Sanders	1.50
18	Junior Seau	.20
19	Dave Brown	.20
20	Heath Shuler	.20
21	Jeff Blake	.75
22	Kerry Collins	1.00
23	Scott Mitchell	.20
24	Kordell Stewart	1.50
25	Jeff George	.20
26	Mark Brunell	1.00
27	Erik Kramer	.20
28	Bernie Kosar	.20
29	Frank Reich	.20
30	Randall Cunningham	.20

1996 Pinnacle Mint Coins

The 30-piece set was included twice in every three-pack of Pinnacle Mint Collection football. Two variations of the common brass coin were available: nickel-silver (1:20) and 24 kt. gold (1:48). Solid silver coins were also inserted every 2,300 packs and one redemption card was available for an all-gold coin with the odds being one in 47,200. The coin face has the image of the player's face with his name, team and uniform number. The coin backs feature the Quarterback Club logo, as each of the 30 players represented in the set are members.

		MT
Complete Brass (30):		50.00
Common Brass Coin:		.75
Nickel Coins:		2x-4x
Gold Plated Coins:		4x-8x
1	Troy Aikman	4.00
2	John Elway	3.00
3	Jim Kelly	1.50
4	Dan Marino	8.00
5	Warren Moon	.75
6	Steve Young	3.00
7	Jerry Rice	4.00
8	Boomer Esiason	.75
9	Jim Everett	.75
10	Brett Favre	8.00
11	Jim Harbaugh	.75
12	Jeff Hostetler	.75
13	Neil O'Donnell	.75
14	Drew Bledsoe	4.00
15	Rick Mirer	.75
16	Emmitt Smith	8.00
17	Barry Sanders	4.00
18	Junior Seau	1.50
19	Dave Brown	.75
20	Heath Shuler	.75
21	Jeff Blake	1.50
22	Kerry Collins	4.00
23	Scott Mitchell	.75
24	Kordell Stewart	4.00
25	Jeff George	.75
26	Mark Brunell	3.00
27	Erik Kramer	.75
28	Bernie Kosar	.75
29	Frank Reich	.75
30	Randall Cunningham	.75

1996 Select Certified

The 125-card, regular-sized set was available in six-card packs. The card fronts feature a full mirror background with the color player action shot. The player's name is printed down the right border with in-depth statistics printed on the horizontal card back. Parallel versions of the base set are available in Certified Red (1:5) and Certified Blue (1:50). Mirror Red (1:100), Mirror Blue (1:200) and Mirror Gold (1:300) parallel inserts were also issued. Artist's Proof (1:18), Gold Team (1:38) and Thumbs Up (1:41) were the other inserts and each card was also available in Premium Stock, nine-card packs.

		MT
Complete Set (125):		50.00
Common Player:		.20
Wax Box:		150.00
1	Isaac Bruce	1.00
2	Rick Mirer	.20
3	Jake Reed	.20
4	Reggie White	.40
5	Harvey Williams	.20
6	Jim Everett	.20
7	Tony Martin	.20
8	Craig Heyward	.20
9	Tamarick Vanover	1.25
10	Hugh Douglas	.20
11	Erik Kramer	.20
12	Charlie Garner	.20
13	Erric Pegram	.20
14	Scott Mitchell	.20
15	Michael Westbrook	.75
16	Robert Smith	.20
17	Kerry Collins	3.00
18	Derek Loville	.20
19	Jeff Blake	.75
20	Terry Kirby	.20
21	Bruce Smith	.20
22	Stan Humphries	.20
23	Rodney Thomas	.20
24	Wayne Chrebet	.20
25	Napoleon Kaufman	.20
26	Marshall Faulk	1.00
27	Emmitt Smith	5.00
28	Natrone Means	.20
29	Neil O'Donnell	.20
30	Warren Moon	.40
31	Junior Seau	.40
32	Chris Sanders	.20
33	Barry Sanders	2.50
34	Jeff Graham	.20
35	Kordell Stewart	2.50
36	Jim Harbaugh	.20
37	Chris Warren	.20
38	Cris Carter	.20
39	J.J. Stokes	.75
40	Tyrone Wheatley	.40
41	Terrell Davis	3.00
42	Mark Brunell	1.50
43	Steve Young	2.00
44	Rodney Hampton	.20
45	Drew Bledsoe	2.00
46	Larry Centers	.20
47	Ken Norton Jr.	.20
48	Deion Sanders	2.00
49	Alvin Harper	.20
50	Trent Dilfer	.40
51	Steve McNair	2.00
52	Robert Brooks	.20
53	Edgar Bennett	.20
54	Troy Aikman	2.50
55	Dan Marino	5.00
56	Steve Bono	.20
57	Marcus Allen	.40
58	Rodney Peete	.20
59	Ben Coates	.20
60	Yancey Thigpen	.40
61	Tim Brown	.20
62	Jerry Rice	2.50
63	Quinn Early	.20
64	Ricky Watters	.40
65	Thurman Thomas	.40
66	Greg Lloyd	.20
67	Eric Metcalf	.20
68	Jeff George	.20
69	John Elway	2.00
70	Frank Sanders	.20
71	Curtis Conway	.20
72	Greg Hill	.20
73	Darick Holmes	.20
74	Herman Moore	.40
75	Carl Pickens	.20
76	Eric Zeier	.20
77	Curtis Martin	3.50
78	Rashaan Salaam	1.00
79	Joey Galloway	1.50
80	Jeff Hostetler	.20
81	Jim Kelly	.40
82	Dave Brown	.20
83	Errict Rhett	.75
84	Michael Irvin	.40
85	Brett Favre	5.00
86	Cedric Jones	.20
87	Jeff Lewis	.20
88	*Alex Van Dyke*	.40
89	*Regan Upshaw*	.20
90	*Karim Abdul-Jabbar*	5.00
91	*Marvin Harrison*	3.00
92	*Stephen Davis*	.50
93	*Terry Glenn*	6.00
94	*Kevin Hardy*	.40
95	*Derrick Mayes*	.40
96	*Willie Anderson*	.20
97	*Lawrence Phillips*	1.00
98	*Bobby Hoying*	.40
99	*Amani Toomer*	.40
100	*Eddie George*	12.00
101	*Stepfret Williams*	.20
102	*Eric Moulds*	1.50
103	*Simeon Rice*	.40
104	*Mike Alstott*	2.00
105	*Keyshawn Johnson*	3.50
106	*Daryl Gardener*	.20
107	*Tony Banks*	4.00
108	*Bobby Engram*	1.50
109	*Jonathan Ogden*	.40
110	*Eddie Kennison*	3.00
111	*Danny Kanell*	.40
112	*Tony Brackens*	.40
113	*Tim Biakabutuka*	2.00
114	*Leeland McElroy*	1.00
115	*Rickey Dudley*	1.00
116	Troy Aikman	1.00
117	Brett Favre	2.00
118	Drew Bledsoe	1.00
119	Steve Young	1.00
120	Kerry Collins	1.00
121	John Elway	1.00
122	Dan Marino	2.50
123	Kordell Stewart	1.25
124	Jeff Blake	.40
125	Jim Harbaugh	.20

1996 Select Certified Red

Certified Red parallel cards were a parallel set to the 125-card Select Certified set in 1996. They were inserted every five packs and feature a full red background.

	MT
Complete Set (125):	300.00
Certified Red Cards:	3x-6x

1996 Select Certified Blue

This 125-card set paralleled the 1996 Select Certified set, but pictured each card on a full blue background. Certified Blue inserts were seeded every 50 packs.

	MT
Complete Set (125):	2500.00
Certified Blue Cards:	25x-50x

1996 Select Certified Artist's Proofs

This 125-card set paralleled the 1996 Select Certified set, but includes a holographic Artist's Proof stamp on the front of the card. Artist's Proofs were seeded every 18 packs.

	MT
Complete Set (125):	1200.00
Artist's Proof Cards:	12x-24x

1996 Select Certified Mirror Red

Mirror Red included all 125 cards in 1996 Select Certified, but featured roughly three-fourths of the background in red, with the remaining portion unchanged from regular-issue cards. The entire front then has a mirror effect. Mirror Red inserts were seeded every 100 packs.

	MT
Mirror Red Cards:	40x-80x

1996 Select Certified Mirror Blue

This 125-card set featured a mostly blue background, with the rest still having the regular-issue background color, then a mirror background over the entire front. Mirror Blues parallel the regular-issue set and are seeded every 200 packs.

	MT
Mirror Blue Cards:	75x-150x

1996 Select Certified Mirror Gold

Mirror Golds parallel the 125-card base set and feature most of the background in gold, with the remaining portion in regular-issue card color. The entire front is put through a mirror process that gives it a holographic appearance. Mirror Gold inserts are found every 300 packs.

	MT
Mirror Gold Cards:	150x-300x

1996 Select Certified Gold Team

The Gold Team is an 18-card, regular-sized insert set that was found every 38 packs of 1996 Select Certified. The card fronts feature a full gold action shot while the backs, also in complete gold, are individually numbered as "x of 18."

		MT
Complete Set (18):		500.00
Common Player:		8.00
1	Emmitt Smith	60.00
2	Barry Sanders	30.00
3	Dan Marino	60.00
4	Steve Young	25.00
5	Troy Aikman	30.00
6	Jerry Rice	30.00
7	Rashaan Salaam	8.00
8	Marshall Faulk	15.00
9	Drew Bledsoe	30.00
10	Steve McNair	15.00
11	Brett Favre	60.00
12	Terrell Davis	30.00
13	Kordell Stewart	30.00
14	Keyshawn Johnson	15.00
15	Kerry Collins	30.00
16	Curtis Martin	45.00
17	Isaac Bruce	15.00
18	Terry Glenn	25.00

1996 Select Certified Thumbs Up

The 24-card, regular-sized set was inserted every 41 packs of Select Certified. The silver card fronts feature an actual thumbprint of the Quarterback Club member pictured. The card backs include another photo and the player's "Thumbs Up moment" and are individually numbered as "x of 24."

		MT
Complete Set (24):		450.00
Common Player:		8.00
1	Steve Young	30.00
2	Jeff Blake	15.00
3	Dan Marino	60.00
4	Kerry Collins	30.00
5	John Elway	25.00
6	Neil O'Donnell	8.00
7	Brett Favre	60.00
8	Scott Mitchell	8.00
9	Troy Aikman	30.00
10	Jim Harbaugh	8.00
11	Drew Bledsoe	30.00
12	Jeff Hostetler	8.00
13	Marvin Harrison	15.00
14	Tim Biakabutuka	8.00
15	Eddie George	35.00
16	Tony Brackens	8.00
17	Karim Abdul-Jabbar	20.00
18	Daryl Gardener	8.00
19	Alex Van Dyke	8.00
20	Terry Glenn	30.00
21	Eric Moulds	8.00
22	Eddie Kennison	12.00
23	Regan Upshaw	8.00
24	Mike Alstott	10.00

1996 Select Certified Premium Stock

Premium Stock was an enhanced version of Select Certified that was available to the hobby only in jumbo nine-card packs. Premium Stock treated the base cards and the Mirror Red inserts with a micro-etching process, while all other inserts are the same. Packs of Premium Stock contained all of the inserts, but at easier insertion rates than regular packs. The odds on Premium Stock were: Certified Red (1:3), Certified Blue (1:33), Mirror Red (1:66), Mirror Blue (1:133), Mirror Gold (1:199), Artist's Proof (1:12), Gold Team (1:25) and Thumbs Up (1:27).

	MT
Complete Set (125):	100.00
Premium Stock Cards:	2x

1996 Select Certified Premium Stock Etched Mirror Red

Premium Stock Etched Mirror Red inserts paralleled the 125-card Select Certified set, but were available only in Premium Stock packs at a rate of one per 66 packs. This was the only insert that was changed in Premium Stock versus the regular-issue packs. The fronts of these cards have etched foil similar to the base set for Premium Stock.

	MT
Etched Mirror Red Cards:	150x-300x

1996 Summit

The 200-card, regular-sized set came in seven-card packs and included three subsets: Rookies (35), Quarterhorses (15) and Checklists (4). The card fronts feature the player's name and team helmet in gold foil. The card backs include a headshot of the player with three statistical categories and the card number in the upper left corner. A parallel insert set, Ground Zero, is inserted every six packs and features prismatic foil renditions of the base set. Artist's Proofs, another 200-card parallel set, add special holographic foil stamps to the base set and are inserted every 35 packs. Other insert sets in Summit are Turf Team, Inspirations, 3rd & Long and its parallel insert set - 3rd & Long Mirage.

	MT
Complete Set (200):	35.00
Common Player:	.10
Wax Box:	50.00
1 Troy Aikman	1.25
2 Marshall Faulk	.50
3 Bruce Smith	.10
4 Jerome Bettis	.20
5 Bryan Cox	.10
6 Robert Brooks	.20
7 Dan Marino	2.50
8 Irving Fryar	.10
9 Jerry Rice	1.25
10 Ki-Jana Carter	.20
11 Herman Moore	.30
12 Derrick Thomas	.10
13 Curtis Martin	1.75
14 Jeff Hostetler	.10
15 Errict Rhett	.30
16 Emmitt Smith	2.50
17 Aaron Craver	.10
18 Kyle Brady	.10
19 Tony Martin	.10
20 Vinny Testaverde	.10
21 Charles Haley	.10
22 Rodney Thomas	.10
23 Jim Everett	.10
24 Brian Blades	.10
25 Frank Sanders	.10
26 Bryce Paup	.10
27 Anthony Miller	.10
28 Ken Dilger	.10
29 Orlando Thomas	.10
30 Rodney Hampton	.10
31 Ken Norton Jr.	.10
32 Darren Woodson	.10
33 Antonio Freeman	.10
34 Steve Bono	.10
35 Ben Coates	.10
36 Jeff George	.10
37 Curtis Conway	.10
38 Steve Atwater	.10
39 Fred Barnett	.10
40 Joey Galloway	1.25
41 Jim Kelly	.20
42 Michael Irvin	.20
43 Steve Tasker	.10
44 Warren Moon	.10
45 Hugh Douglas	.10
46 Steve Walsh	.10
47 Kerry Collins	1.25
48 Barry Sanders	1.25
49 Steve Young	.75
50 Jim Harbaugh	.10
51 Tyrone Wheatley	.10
52 Boomer Esiason	.10
53 Deion Sanders	.75
54 Steve McNair	1.00
55 Willie McGinest	.10
56 Adrian Murrell	.10
57 Thurman Thomas	.20
58 John Elway	.75
59 William Floyd	.10
60 Eric Zeier	.10
61 Dave Krieg	.10
62 Eric Bjornson	.10
63 Brett Favre	2.50
64 Derrick Alexander	.10
65 Charlie Garner	.10
66 Stan Humphries	.10
67 Bert Emanuel	.10
68 Scott Mitchell	.10
69 Quentin Coryatt	.10
70 Eric Green	.10
71 Jeff Graham	.10
72 Ernie Mills	.10
73 Trent Dilfer	.20
74 Sherman Williams	.10
75 Tamarick Vanover	.50
76 Drew Bledsoe	1.25
77 Jay Novacek	.10
78 Edgar Bennett	.10
79 Tim Brown	.10
80 Greg Lloyd	.10
81 Derrick Holmes	.10
82 Carl Pickens	.10
83 Flipper Anderson	.10
84 Bernie Kosar	.10
85 Dave Brown	.10
86 Calvin Williams	.10
87 Michael Westbrook	.20
88 Kevin Williams	.10
89 Chris Sanders	.10
90 Robert Smith	.10
91 Cris Carter	.10
92 Gus Frerotte	.10
93 Larry Centers	.10
94 Eric Metcalf	.10
95 Isaac Bruce	.50
96 Kordell Stewart	1.50
97 Ricky Watters	.20
98 Terrell Fletcher	.10
99 Bernie Parmalee	.10
100 Harvey Williams	.10
101 Hardy Nickerson	.10
102 Jeff Blake	.50
103 Terry Allen	.10
104 Yancey Thigpen	.30
105 Greg Hill	.10
106 Chris Warren	.20
107 Terrell Davis	1.50
108 Mark Brunell	1.00
109 Alvin Harper	.10
110 Marcus Allen	.20
111 Garrison Hearst	.10
112 Derek Loville	.10
113 Craig Heyward	.10
114 Kimble Anders	.10
115 O.J. McDuffie	.10
116 Junior Seau	.20
117 Terry Kirby	.10
118 Erric Pegram	.10
119 Rick Mirer	.10
120 Erik Kramer	.10
121 Brett Perriman	.10
122 Shawn Jefferson	.10
123 J.J. Stokes	.20
124 Kevin Greene	.10
125 Daryl Johnston	.10
126 Mark Chmura	.10
127 James Stewart	.10
128 Mario Bates	.10
129 Rodney Peete	.10
130 Quinn Early	.10
131 Shannon Sharpe	.10
132 Neil Smith	.10
133 Herschel Walker	.10
134 Aaron Bailey	.10
135 Rashaan Salaam	.40
136 Kevin Smith	.10
137 Sean Dawkins	.10
138 Jake Reed	.10
139 Neil O'Donnell	.10
140 Reggie White	.20
141 Vincent Brisby	.10
142 Napoleon Kaufman	.10
143 Brent Jones	.10
144 Mark Seay	.10
145 Heath Shuler	.10
146 Wayne Chrebet	.10
147 *Leeland McElroy*	.30
148 *Tim Biakabutuka*	1.00
149 *John Mobley*	.10
150 *Tony Brackens*	.20
151 *Danny Kanell*	.20
152 *Eddie Kennison*	1.25
153 *Jonathan Ogden*	.20
154 *Bobby Engram*	.75
155 *Chris Darkins*	.10
156 *Daryl Gardener*	.10
157 *Keyshawn Johnson*	2.00
158 *Mike Alstott*	1.00
159 *Simeon Rice*	.20
160 *Eric Moulds*	.75
161 *Stepfret Williams*	.10
162 *Eddie George*	4.00
163 *Duane Clemons*	.10
164 *Amani Toomer*	.20
165 *Rickey Dudley*	.30
166 *Bobby Hoying*	.20
167 *Lawrence Phillips*	.75
168 *Willie Anderson*	.10
169 *Derrick Mayes*	.75
170 *Kevin Hardy*	.20
171 *Terry Glenn*	3.00
172 *Stephen Davis*	.20
173 *Walt Harris*	.20
174 *Marvin Harrison*	1.50
175 *Karim Abdul-Jabbar*	2.50
176 *Alex Molden*	.10
177 *Regan Upshaw*	.10
178 *Jerald Moore*	.10
179 *Alex Van Dyke*	.20
180 *Jeff Lewis*	.10
181 *Cedric Jones*	.10
182 *Jim Kelly*	.10
183 *Troy Aikman*	.50
184 Jim Harbaugh	.10
185 Neil O'Donnell	.10
186 Steve Young	.30
187 Kerry Collins	.75
188 Scott Mitchell	.10
189 Drew Bledsoe	.50
190 Kordell Stewart	.75
191 Erik Kramer	.10
192 Brett Favre	1.00
193 Warren Moon	.10
194 Jeff Blake	.25
195 Mark Brunell	.50
196 John Elway	.25
197 Checklist Emmitt Smith	.30
198 Checklist Dan Marino	.30
199 Checklist Brett Favre	.30
200 Checklist Jim Harbaugh	.10

1996 Summit Ground Zero

Ground Zero is a 200-card prismatic foil rendition of the regular-issue set. These parallel cards are inserted every six packs.

	MT
Complete Set (200):	400.00
Ground Zero Cards:	6x-12x

1996 Summit Artist's Proofs

Artist's Proofs add a holographic Artist's Proof stamp to all 200 cards in the regular-issue set. These parallel cards are inserted at a rate of one per 35 packs.

	MT
Complete Set (200):	1400.00
Artist's Proof Cards:	20x-40x

1996 Summit Premium Stock

Premium Stock was available in hobby stores and was an upgraded version of Summit Football. In 13-card packs of Premium Stock, the regular-issue set was reprinted in a rainbow holographic foil version. In addition, Turf Team inserts also received special prismatic foil treatment. Other inserts were the same as the regular-issue product.

	MT
Complete Set (200):	50.00
Premium Stock Cards:	1.5x

1996 Summit Hit The Hole

The 16-card, regular-sized set, limited to a production run of 1,000, was randomly inserted in five-card retail packs of 1996 Pinnacle Summit. The set features 16 top offensive players on all-foil printing.

	MT
Complete Set (16):	400.00
Common Player:	10.00
1 Rashaan Salaam	10.00
2 Marshall Faulk	20.00
3 Ricky Watters	10.00
4 Leeland McElroy	10.00
5 Emmitt Smith	70.00
6 Eddie George	50.00
7 Curtis Martin	50.00

8	Lawrence Phillips	25.00
9	Darick Holmes	10.00
10	Barry Sanders	40.00
11	Karim Abdul-Jabbar	35.00
12	Errict Rhett	20.00
13	Terrell Davis	40.00
14	Chris Warren	10.00
15	Rodney Thomas	10.00
16	Tim Biakabutuka	20.00

1996 Summit Inspirations

The 18-card, regular-sized set was inserted in every 17 packs of Summit football. The cards feature foil printing and the production run was limited to 8,000.

		MT
Complete Set (18):		140.00
Common Player:		3.00
1	Jim Harbaugh	3.00
2	Alex Van Dyke	5.00
3	Mike Alstott	5.00
4	Jonathan Ogden	3.00
5	Brett Favre	30.00
6	Tony Brackens	3.00
7	Drew Bledsoe	15.00
8	Danny Kanell	3.00
9	Eric Moulds	5.00
10	John Elway	12.00
11	Eddie George	25.00
12	Karim Abdul-Jabbar	18.00
13	Tim Biakabutuka	10.00
14	Jeff Lewis	3.00
15	Terry Glenn	25.00
16	Jeff Blake	7.00
17	Kevin Hardy	3.00
18	Bobby Engram	7.00

1996 Summit Turf Team

The 16-card, regular-sized set, inserted in hobby packs of Summit football, features spot-embossed technology and is limited to a production run of 4,000.

		MT
Complete Set (16):		350.00
Common Player:		6.00
1	Emmitt Smith	50.00
2	Brett Favre	50.00
3	Curtis Martin	40.00
4	Steve Young	20.00
5	Kerry Collins	25.00
6	Barry Sanders	25.00
7	Dan Marino	50.00
8	Isaac Bruce	12.00
9	Troy Aikman	25.00
10	Marshall Faulk	18.00
11	Joey Galloway	20.00
12	Jeff Blake	6.00
13	Drew Bledsoe	25.00
14	John Elway	20.00
15	Jerry Rice	25.00
16	Michael Irvin	6.00

1996 Summit Third and Long

The 18-card, regular-sized set was inserted in hobby, retail and magazine packs and was limited to a production run of 2,000. The cards are printed on rainbow holographic foil with sequential numbering. An 18-card parallel inserts set, Mirage, features a floating football hologram behind the player's image. Mirage is limited to 600 sets.

		MT
Complete Set (18):		650.00
Common Player:		10.00
Mirage Cards:		2x
1	Michael Irvin	10.00
2	Dan Marino	80.00
3	Keyshawn Johnson	30.00
4	Chris Warren	10.00
5	Rashaan Salaam	10.00
6	Brett Favre	80.00

7	Terry Glenn	45.00
8	Steve Young	30.00
9	Kerry Collins	40.00
10	Emmitt Smith	80.00
11	Marvin Harrison	25.00
12	Jerry Rice	40.00
13	John Elway	30.00
14	Drew Bledsoe	40.00
15	Eddie Kennison	15.00
16	Troy Aikman	40.00
17	Barry Sanders	40.00
18	Terrell Davis	50.00

1996 Playoff Contenders Leather

This 100-card base set lives up to its name, with a leather card front. The player's name, which can be printed in green, purple or red, is printed inside a black oval along the left side of the card. The Playoff Contenders' and Genuine Leather logos appear on the front. If the player's name is printed in green foil, it is a "Scarce" card, which was most frequently inserted. Purple foil is a "Rare" card, seeded one per 11 packs Red foil is "Ultra Rare," and seeded one per 22 packs. The card backs include a full-bleed photo of the player. The card number is printed in the upper right.

		MT
Complete Set (100):		1200.00
Common Player:		.75
Wax Box:		80.00
1	Brett Favre R	100.00
2	Steve Young P	20.00
3	Herman Moore P	5.00
4	Jim Harbaugh P	3.00
5	Curtis Martin R	60.00
6	Junior Seau	.75
7	John Elway R	45.00
8	Troy Aikman R	50.00
9	Terry Allen	.75
10	Kordell Stewart R	50.00
11	Drew Bledsoe R	50.00
12	Jim Kelly R	15.00
13	Dan Marino R	100.00
14	Andre Rison	.75
15	Jeff Hostetler	.75
16	Scott Mitchell	.75
17	Carl Pickens	.75
18	Larry Centers R	5.00
19	Craig Heyward	.75
20	Barry Sanders R	50.00
21	Deion Sanders P	15.00
22	Emmitt Smith R	100.00
23	Rashaan Salaam P	9.00
24	Mario Bates	.75
25	Lawrence Phillips R	25.00
26	Napoleon Kaufman P	7.00
27	Rodney Hampton	.75
28	Marshall Faulk R	20.00
29	Trent Dilfer	.75
30	Leeland McElroy	3.00
31	Marcus Allen	2.00
32	Ricky Watters R	15.00
33	Karim Abdul-Jabbar R	40.00
34	Herschel Walker	.75
35	Thurman Thomas	2.00
36	Jerome Bettis	2.00
37	Gus Frerotte P	3.00
38	Neil O'Donnell P	3.00
39	Rick Mirer	.75
40	Mike Alstott P	15.00

41	Vinny Testaverde P	3.00
42	Derek Loville	.75
43	Ben Coates	.75
44	Steve McNair	6.00
45	Bobby Engram	2.00
46	Yancey Thigpen	.75
47	Lake Dawson	.75
48	Terrell Davis	10.00
49	Kerry Collins P	30.00
50	Eric Metcalf	.75
51	Stanley Pritchett P	3.00
52	Robert Brooks	.75
53	Isaac Bruce R	30.00
54	Tim Brown	.75
55	Edgar Bennett	.75
56	Warren Moon	.75
57	Jerry Rice R	50.00
58	Michael Westbrook	2.00
59	Keyshawn Johnson R	30.00
60	Steve Bono	.75
61	Derrick Mayes	2.00
62	Erik Kramer	.75
63	Rodney Peete	.75
64	Eddie Kennison P	15.00
65	Derrick Thomas	.75
66	Joey Galloway P	15.00
67	Amani Toomer	2.00
68	Reggie White P	7.00
69	Heath Shuler R	7.00
70	Dave Brown R	7.00
71	Tony Banks	6.00
72	Chris Warren R	7.00
73	J.J. Stokes R	8.00
74	Rickey Dudley	3.00
75	Stan Humphries	.75
76	Jason Dunn	.75
77	Tyrone Wheatley P	3.00
78	Jim Everett R	7.00
79	Cris Carter P	3.00
80	Alex Van Dyke	2.00
81	O.J. McDuffie	.75
82	Mark Chmura	.75
83	Terry Glenn	10.00
84	Boomer Esiason	.75
85	Bruce Smith	.75
86	Curtis Conway P	3.00
87	Ki-Jana Carter	2.00
88	Tamarick Vanover	2.00
89	Michael Jackson	.75
90	Mark Brunell P	20.00
91	Tim Biakabutuka P	12.00
92	Anthony Miller P	3.00
93	Marvin Harrison P	15.00
94	Jeff George R	7.00
95	Jeff Blake P	12.00
96	Eddie George R	50.00
97	Eric Moulds	2.00
98	Mike Tomczak P	3.00
99	Chris Sanders P	3.00
100	Chris Chandler	.75

1996 Playoff Contenders Pennants

This 100-card pennant-shaped base set includes a photo of the player, with the Playoff Pennants 1996 logo at the top. The player's name is printed in silver foil, also at the top. The felt-like material is coordinated with the player's team color. Three levels of this base set exist. If the "Pennants" logo is green it is a "Scarce" card, which was most frequently inserted card. If it is purple, it is "Rare" and inserted one per eight packs. If it is red, it is "Ultra Rare" and

inserted one per 16 packs. Card backs also have the felt-like surface, with the player's name in a colored bar in the middle.

		MT
Complete Set (100):		800.00
Common Player:		1.00
1	Brett Favre R	90.00
2	Steve Young R	40.00
3	Herman Moore R	10.00
4	Jim Harbaugh R	6.00
5	Curtis Martin R	40.00
6	Junior Seau	1.00
7	John Elway R	35.00
8	Troy Aikman P	20.00
9	Terry Allen	1.00
10	Kordell Stewart R	40.00
11	Drew Bledsoe	10.00
12	Jim Kelly P	6.00
13	Dan Marino P	40.00
14	Andre Rison	1.00
15	Jeff Hostetler	1.00
16	Scott Mitchell	1.00
17	Carl Pickens R	6.00
18	Larry Centers P	3.00
19	Craig Heyward	1.00
20	Barry Sanders P	18.00
21	Deion Sanders R	20.00
22	Emmitt Smith R	90.00
23	Rashaan Salaam R	15.00
24	Mario Bates	1.00
25	Lawrence Phillips	5.00
26	Napoleon Kaufman	1.00
27	Rodney Hampton	1.00
28	Marshall Faulk P	10.00
29	Trent Dilfer	1.00
30	Leeland McElroy P	10.00
31	Marcus Allen P	6.00
32	Ricky Watters	2.00
33	Karim Abdul-Jabbar	10.00
34	Herschel Walker P	3.00
35	Thurman Thomas R	15.00
36	Jerome Bettis P	6.00
37	Gus Frerotte	1.00
38	Neil O'Donnell	1.00
39	Rick Mirer	1.00
40	Mike Alstott R	20.00
41	Vinny Testaverde R	6.00
42	Derek Loville	1.00
43	Ben Coates	1.00
44	Steve McNair R	25.00
45	Bobby Engram P	6.00
46	Yancey Thigpen	1.00
47	Lake Dawson	1.00
48	Terrell Davis P	18.00
49	Kerry Collins R	40.00
50	Eric Metcalf	1.00
51	Stanley Pritchett R	6.00
52	Robert Brooks R	6.00
53	Isaac Bruce	3.00
54	Tim Brown	1.00
55	Edgar Bennett P	3.00
56	Warren Moon	1.00
57	Jerry Rice R	40.00
58	Michael Westbrook	2.00
59	Keyshawn Johnson	5.00
60	Steve Bono R	6.00
61	Derrick Mayes P	6.00
62	Erik Kramer P	3.00
63	Rodney Peete	1.00
64	Eddie Kennison	6.00
65	Derrick Thomas	1.00
66	Joey Galloway R	15.00
67	Amani Toomer P	6.00
68	Reggie White	2.00
69	Heath Shuler	1.00
70	Dave Brown	1.00
71	Tony Banks P	8.00
72	Chris Warren	1.00
73	J.J. Stokes	2.00
74	Rickey Dudley P	7.00
75	Stan Humphries	1.00
76	Jason Dunn P	3.00
77	Tyrone Wheatley	1.00
78	Jim Everett	1.00
79	Cris Carter P	3.00
80	Alex Van Dyke P	6.00
81	O.J. McDuffie	1.00
82	Mark Chmura P	3.00
83	Terry Glenn P	20.00
84	Boomer Esiason R	6.00
85	Bruce Smith	1.00
86	Curtis Conway	1.00
87	Ki-Jana Carter	2.00
88	Tamarick Vanover	2.00
89	Michael Jackson	1.00
90	Mark Brunell	10.00
91	Tim Biakabutuka R	25.00
92	Anthony Miller	1.00
93	Marvin Harrison R	20.00

#	Player	MT
94	Jeff George P	3.00
95	Jeff Blake R	18.00
96	Eddie George	12.00
97	Eric Moulds P	6.00
98	Mike Tomczak	1.00
99	Chris Sanders	1.00
100	Chris Chandler	1.00

1996 Playoff Contenders Open Field

These mini-cards, which measure 3-1/8" x 2-1/4", were part of the Contenders base set. A color photo of the player is showcased, with a holographic background of a football field. The Open Field logo also is included in the hologram. Three levels of this base set exist. The "Scarce" cards, which have the player's name in a green oval, are the most frequently inserted. The "Rare" cards have the oval in purple and were inserted one per five packs. The "Ultra Rare" cards have the oval in red and are seeded one per nine packs. Card backs have a photo on the left, with a "Playoff The Wall Fact" on the right.

		MT
Complete Set (100):		400.00
Common Player:		.75
1	Brett Favre P	20.00
2	Steve Young R	15.00
3	Herman Moore P	4.00
4	Jim Harbaugh	.75
5	Curtis Martin P	15.00
6	Junior Seau P	2.00
7	John Elway P	10.00
8	Troy Aikman R	18.00
9	Terry Allen	.75
10	Kordell Stewart P	12.00
11	Drew Bledsoe	6.00
12	Jim Kelly	2.00
13	Dan Marino R	35.00
14	Andre Rison P	2.00
15	Jeff Hostetler	.75
16	Scott Mitchell R	3.00
17	Carl Pickens	.75
18	Larry Centers	.75
19	Craig Heyward R	3.00
20	Barry Sanders R	18.00
21	Deion Sanders P	8.00
22	Emmitt Smith P	20.00
23	Rashaan Salaam R	7.00
24	Mario Bates P	2.00
25	Lawrence Phillips P	10.00
26	Napoleon Kaufman	.75
27	Rodney Hampton	.75
28	Marshall Faulk R	10.00
29	Trent Dilfer	.75
30	Leeland McElroy R	8.00
31	Marcus Allen	2.00
32	Ricky Watters P	4.00
33	Karim Abdul-Jabbar P	15.00
34	Herschel Walker R	3.00
35	Thurman Thomas	2.00
36	Jerome Bettis	2.00
37	Gus Frerotte R	3.00
38	Neil O'Donnell	.75
39	Rick Mirer	.75
40	Mike Alstott	3.00
41	Vinny Testaverde	.75
42	Derek Loville	.75
43	Ben Coates	.75
44	Steve McNair	3.00
45	Bobby Engram R	6.00
46	Yancey Thigpen	.75
47	Lake Dawson P	2.00
48	Terrell Davis	6.00
49	Kerry Collins P	15.00
50	Eric Metcalf	.75
51	Stanley Pritchett	.75
52	Robert Brooks P	2.00
53	Isaac Bruce P	7.00
54	Tim Brown P	2.00
55	Edgar Bennett	.75
56	Warren Moon P	2.00
57	Jerry Rice P	15.00
58	Michael Westbrook	2.00
59	Keyshawn Johnson P	8.00
60	Steve Bono	.75
61	Derrick Mayes R	6.00
62	Erik Kramer	.75
63	Rodney Peete	.75
64	Eddie Kennison	4.00
65	Derrick Thomas	.75
66	Joey Galloway R	10.00
67	Amani Toomer R	6.00
68	Reggie White R	6.00
69	Heath Shuler P	2.00
70	Dave Brown	.75
71	Tony Banks R	8.00
72	Chris Warren	.75
73	J.J. Stokes	2.00
74	Rickey Dudley R	8.00
75	Stan Humphries	.75
76	Jason Dunn R	3.00
77	Tyrone Wheatley	.75
78	Jim Everett	.75
79	Cris Carter	.75
80	Alex Van Dyke R	6.00
81	O.J. McDuffie P	2.00
82	Mark Chmura	.75
83	Terry Glenn R	25.00
84	Boomer Esiason	.75
85	Bruce Smith	.75
86	Curtis Conway	.75
87	Ki-Jana Carter R	6.00
88	Tamarick Vanover P	4.00
89	Michael Jackson R	3.00
90	Mark Brunell	6.00
91	Tim Biakabutuka	4.00
92	Anthony Miller	.75
93	Marvin Harrison	4.00
94	Jeff George	.75
95	Jeff Blake	4.00
96	Eddie George P	20.00
97	Eric Moulds R	6.00
98	Mike Tomczak R	3.00
99	Chris Sanders	.75
100	Chris Chandler	.75

1996 Playoff Contenders Leather Accents

The difference between Genuine Leather and Genuine Leather Accents parallel set is Accents has the Genuine Leather and Playoff Contenders' logo and name oval in teal foil. Different scarcities also exist with the green, purple and red foils on the player's names. The card backs have a full-bleed photo, with the card number in the upper right. "Accent" is printed in teal foil in the lower center on the card back. One card was seeded per 216 packs.

		MT
Common Player:		25.00
1	Brett Favre	600.00
2	Steve Young	200.00
3	Herman Moore	50.00
4	Jim Harbaugh	25.00
5	Curtis Martin	350.00
6	Junior Seau	50.00
7	John Elway	200.00
8	Troy Aikman	300.00
9	Terry Allen	25.00
10	Kordell Stewart	250.00
11	Drew Bledsoe	300.00
12	Jim Kelly	50.00
13	Dan Marino	600.00
14	Andre Rison	25.00
15	Jeff Hostetler	25.00
16	Scott Mitchell	25.00
17	Carl Pickens	50.00
18	Larry Centers	25.00
19	Craig Heyward	25.00
20	Barry Sanders	300.00
21	Deion Sanders	200.00
22	Emmitt Smith	600.00
23	Rashaan Salaam	100.00
24	Mario Bates	25.00
25	Lawrence Phillips	125.00
26	Napoleon Kaufman	25.00
27	Rodney Hampton	25.00
28	Marshall Faulk	150.00
29	Trent Dilfer	50.00
30	Leeland McElroy	75.00
31	Marcus Allen	50.00
32	Ricky Watters	50.00
33	Karim Abdul-Jabbar	200.00
34	Herschel Walker	25.00
35	Thurman Thomas	50.00
36	Jerome Bettis	75.00
37	Gus Frerotte	25.00
38	Neil O'Donnell	25.00
39	Rick Mirer	25.00
40	Mike Alstott	75.00
41	Vinny Testaverde	25.00
42	Derek Loville	25.00
43	Ben Coates	25.00
44	Steve McNair	200.00
45	Bobby Engram	75.00
46	Yancey Thigpen	25.00
47	Lake Dawson	25.00
48	Terrell Davis	350.00
49	Kerry Collins	300.00
50	Eric Metcalf	25.00
51	Stanley Pritchett	50.00
52	Robert Brooks	50.00
53	Isaac Bruce	100.00
54	Tim Brown	25.00
55	Edgar Bennett	25.00
56	Warren Moon	50.00
57	Jerry Rice	300.00
58	Michael Westbrook	50.00
59	Keyshawn Johnson	150.00
60	Steve Bono	25.00
61	Derrick Mayes	50.00
62	Erik Kramer	25.00
63	Rodney Peete	25.00
64	Eddie Kennison	75.00
65	Derrick Thomas	25.00
66	Joey Galloway	150.00
67	Amani Toomer	50.00
68	Reggie White	75.00
69	Heath Shuler	50.00
70	Dave Brown	25.00
71	Tony Banks	75.00
72	Chris Warren	25.00
73	J.J. Stokes	50.00
74	Rickey Dudley	75.00
75	Stan Humphries	25.00
76	Jason Dunn	50.00
77	Tyrone Wheatley	50.00
78	Jim Everett	25.00
79	Cris Carter	25.00
80	Alex Van Dyke	50.00
81	O.J. McDuffie	25.00
82	Mark Chmura	25.00
83	Terry Glenn	300.00
84	Boomer Esiason	25.00
85	Bruce Smith	25.00
86	Curtis Conway	50.00
87	Ki-Jana Carter	50.00
88	Tamarick Vanover	75.00
89	Michael Jackson	25.00
90	Mark Brunell	250.00
91	Tim Biakabutuka	100.00
92	Anthony Miller	25.00
93	Marvin Harrison	150.00
94	Jeff George	25.00
95	Jeff Blake	75.00
96	Eddie George	300.00
97	Eric Moulds	50.00
98	Mike Tomczak	25.00
99	Chris Sanders	25.00
100	Chris Chandler	25.00

1996 Playoff Contenders Air Command

This insert set features a photograph of the player showcased over a hologram background comprised of jets and clouds. The Playoff Air Command '96 logo appears in the upper left. The player's name is printed in gold foil in the lower left. The card back has a silver and blue etched-foil background and a color photo of the player. The Playoff Contenders logo is in the upper left, with the card number, prefixed by "AC," in the upper right. Each card measures 3-1/8" x 2-1/4". The cards were inserted one per 96 packs.

		MT
Complete Set (8):		250.00
Common Player:		15.00
1	Dan Marino	90.00
2	Brett Favre	90.00
3	Troy Aikman	50.00
4	Mike Tomczak	15.00
5	John Elway	40.00
6	Jeff George	15.00
7	Chris Chandler	15.00
8	Steve Bono	15.00

1996 Playoff Contenders Ground Hogs

This insert set, which was seeded one per 44 packs, featured a leather front. A rainbow foil "swoosh" follows behind the player. The Ground Hogs logo appears in one of the lower corners. The player's name is in gold foil at the top of the card. The card back has the Playoff Contenders' logo in the upper left and the card number, prefixed by "GH," in the upper right. A color photo of the player is featured on the back, with the running back in focus and the background blurry.

		MT
Complete Set (8):		400.00
Common Player:		20.00
1	Emmitt Smith	120.00
2	Barry Sanders	70.00
3	Marshall Faulk	30.00
4	Curtis Martin	80.00
5	Chris Warren	20.00
6	Ricky Watters	20.00
7	Thurman Thomas	20.00
8	Terrell Davis	70.00

1996 Playoff Contenders Honors

A continuation from Prime, this insert set had a new design that featured the Playoff Honors' logo and player's name in teal foil on the front of the card. The holographic background includes the various achievements of the player. The card back has a full-bleed photo of the player. The card numbers, prefixed by a "PH," are in the upper right. One card was seeded per 7,200 packs.

	MT
Complete Set (3):	600.00
Common Player:	100.00
4 Dan Marino	500.00
5 Deion Sanders	175.00
6 Marcus Allen	100.00

1996 Playoff Contenders Pennant Flyers

This pennant-shaped insert set in-cludes a felt-like surface on the right, with the player's last name embossed on the left in a gold-foil bar along the left border. The Playoff Pennant Flyer logo is pictured on the front, with "1996" embossed in a gold-foil oval. The player's team's main color is used for the felt on the front and back. The card backs include the player's full name embossed in the gold-foil band, team logo inside a circle and a gold-foil embossed Playoff Contenders' logo. These were seeded one per 48 packs. The card numbers are prefixed with "PF."

	MT
Complete Set (8):	175.00
Common Player:	10.00
1 Jerry Rice	60.00
2 Joey Galloway	25.00
3 Isaac Bruce	20.00
4 Herman Moore	15.00
5 Carl Pickens	10.00
6 Yancey Thigpen	10.00
7 Deion Sanders	40.00
8 Robert Brooks	10.00

1996 Playoff Illusions

The 120-card set's base cards are printed in different color schemes and graphics. The set features six different designs, each representing the six NFL divisions, as well as two levels of insertions. Cards Nos. 1-63 appeared in approximately 3.5 cards per pack, while card Nos. 64-120 were found approximately one card per pack.

	MT
Complete Set (120):	125.00
Common Player (1-63):	.25
Common Player (64-120):	.50
Wax Box:	70.00
1 Troy Aikman	2.00
2 Larry Centers	.25
3 Terance Mathis	.25
4 Calvin Williams	.25
5 Jim Kelly	.25
6 *Tim Biakabutuka*	1.00
7 Rashaan Salaam	.75
8 Ki-Jana Carter	.50
9 Anthony Miller	.25
10 Deion Sanders	1.25
11 Scott Mitchell	.25
12 Robert Brooks	.25
13 Willie Davis	.25
14 Zack Crockett	.25
15 James Stewart	.25
16 Tamarick Vanover	.75
17 Stanley Pritchett	.25
18 Warren Moon	.25
19 Shawn Jefferson	.25
20 Shannon Sharpe	.25
21 Jim Everett	.25
22 Dave Brown	.25
23 Adrian Murrell	.25
24 *Rickey Dudley*	.75
25 Chris T. Jones	.25
26 Andre Hastings	.25
27 Stan Humphries	.25
28 Steve Young	1.50
29 Joey Galloway	1.50
30 Jim Harbaugh	.25
31 *Eddie Kennison*	2.00
32 *Mike Alstott*	1.00
33 Michael Westbrook	.50
34 *Leeland McElroy*	.75
35 Erik Kramer	.25
36 Mark Chmura	.25
37 Cris Carter	.25
38 Ben Coates	.25
39 Wayne Chrebet	.25
40 Jerome Bettis	.50
41 Tim Brown	.25
42 Jason Dunn	.25
43 William Henderson	.25
44 Rick Mirer	.25
45 J.J. Stokes	.50
46 Rodney Peete	.25
47 Neil O'Donnell	.25
48 Tyrone Wheatley	.25
49 *Terry Glenn*	3.50
50 Junior Seau	.25
51 Jake Reed	.25
52 O.J. McDuffie	.25
53 Steve Bono	.25
54 Steve McNair	2.00
55 Antonio Freeman	.50
56 Johnnie Morton	.25
57 Eric Metcalf	.25
58 Andre Reed	.25
59 *Bobby Engram*	1.00
60 Gus Frerotte	.25
61 Jeff Blake	.75
62 Erric Pegram	.25
63 Jeff Hostetler	.25
64 Edgar Bennett	.50
65 *Eddie George*	7.00
66 *Marvin Harrison*	4.00
67 LeShon Johnson	.50
68 *Jamal Anderson*	3.00
69 Thurman Thomas	1.00
70 Barry Sanders	5.00
71 *Muhsin Muhammad*	2.50
72 Robert Green	.50
73 Garrison Hearst	.50
74 John Elway	4.00
75 Herman Moore	1.00
76 Chris Chandler	.50
77 Marshall Faulk	1.50
78 Mark Brunell	4.00
79 *Tony Banks*	4.00
80 Terrell Davis	6.00
81 Marcus Allen	1.00
82 Dan Marino	10.00
83 Robert Smith	.50
84 Curtis Martin	7.00
85 *Amani Toomer*	1.00
86 Napoleon Kaufman	.50
87 Ricky Watters	1.00
88 Kordell Stewart	5.00
89 *Keyshawn Johnson*	4.00
90 Emmitt Smith	10.00
91 Chris Warren	.50
92 Isaac Bruce	2.00
93 Terry Allen	.50
94 Trent Dilfer	.50
95 Vinny Testaverde	.50
96 Bruce Smith	.50
97 Kerry Collins	5.00
98 Curtis Conway	.50
99 *Karim Abdul-Jabbar*	5.00
100 Brett Favre	10.00
101 Carl Pickens	.50
102 Brett Perriman	.50
103 Keith Jackson	.50
104 Drew Bledsoe	5.00
105 Rodney Hampton	.50
106 Ray Zellars	.50
107 Jeff Graham	.50
108 Irving Fryar	.50
109 *Lawrence Phillips*	3.00
110 Jerry Rice	5.00
111 Mike Tomczak	.50
112 Tony Martin	.50
113 Brian Blades	.50
114 Bill Brooks	.50
115 Rob Moore	.50
116 Quinn Early	.50
117 Darnay Scott	.50
118 Ken Dilger	.50
119 Derek Loville	.50
120 Reggie White	1.00

1996 Playoff Illusions Spectralusion Elite

This 120-card parallel set utilizes Illlusion printing technology and silver holographic foil background. It is one of four different parallel sets associat-ed with the Illusion product, and is the easiest to get with a one per five packs insertion rate.

	MT
Complete Set (120):	300.00
Common Player:	1.00
1 Troy Aikman	10.00
2 Larry Centers	1.00
3 Terance Mathis	1.00
4 Calvin Williams	1.00
5 Jim Kelly	2.00
6 Tim Biakabutuka	4.00
7 Rashaan Salaam	2.00
8 Ki-Jana Carter	2.00
9 Anthony Miller	1.00
10 Deion Sanders	7.00
11 Scott Mitchell	1.00
12 Robert Brooks	1.00
13 Willie Davis	1.00
14 Zack Crockett	1.00
15 James Stewart	1.00
16 Tamarick Vanover	5.00
17 Stanley Pritchett	1.00
18 Warren Moon	1.00
19 Shawn Jefferson	1.00
20 Shannon Sharpe	1.00
21 Jim Everett	1.00
22 Dave Brown	1.00
23 Adrian Murrell	1.00
24 Rickey Dudley	4.00
25 Chris T. Jones	1.00
26 Andre Hastings	1.00
27 Stan Humphries	1.00
28 Steve Young	8.00
29 Joey Galloway	7.00
30 Jim Harbaugh	1.00
31 Eddie Kennison	6.00
32 Mike Alstott	4.00
33 Michael Westbrook	2.00
34 Leeland McElroy	2.00
35 Erik Kramer	1.00
36 Mark Chmura	1.00
37 Cris Carter	1.00
38 Ben Coates	1.00
39 Wayne Chrebet	1.00
40 Jerome Bettis	2.00
41 Tim Brown	1.00
42 Jason Dunn	1.00
43 William Henderson	1.00
44 Rick Mirer	1.00
45 J.J. Stokes	2.00
46 Rodney Peete	1.00
47 Neil O'Donnell	1.00
48 Tyrone Wheatley	1.00
49 Terry Glenn	12.00
50 Junior Seau	1.00
51 Jake Reed	1.00
52 O.J. McDuffie	1.00
53 Steve Bono	1.00
54 Steve McNair	5.00
55 Antonio Freeman	1.00
56 Johnnie Morton	1.00
57 Eric Metcalf	1.00
58 Andre Reed	1.00

	MT
59 Bobby Engram	4.00
60 Gus Frerotte	1.00
61 Jeff Blake	4.00
62 Erric Pegram	1.00
63 Jeff Hostetler	1.00
64 Edgar Bennett	1.00
65 Eddie George	12.00
66 Marvin Harrison	8.00
67 LeShon Johnson	1.00
68 Jamal Anderson	4.00
69 Thurman Thomas	2.00
70 Barry Sanders	10.00
71 Muhsin Muhammad	2.00
72 Robert Green	1.00
73 Garrison Hearst	1.00
74 John Elway	7.00
75 Herman Moore	3.00
76 Chris Chandler	1.00
77 Marshall Faulk	4.00
78 Mark Brunell	6.00
79 Tony Banks	5.00
80 Terrell Davis	10.00
81 Marcus Allen	2.00
82 Dan Marino	20.00
83 Robert Smith	1.00
84 Curtis Martin	12.00
85 Amani Toomer	3.00
86 Napoleon Kaufman	1.00
87 Ricky Watters	2.00
88 Kordell Stewart	10.00
89 Keyshawn Johnson	8.00
90 Emmitt Smith	20.00
91 Chris Warren	1.00
92 Isaac Bruce	5.00
93 Terry Allen	1.00
94 Trent Dilfer	1.00
95 Vinny Testaverde	1.00
96 Bruce Smith	1.00
97 Kerry Collins	10.00
98 Curtis Conway	1.00
99 Karim Abdul-Jabbar	10.00
100 Brett Favre	20.00
101 Carl Pickens	1.00
102 Brett Perriman	1.00
103 Keith Jackson	1.00
104 Drew Bledsoe	10.00
105 Rodney Hampton	1.00
106 Ray Zellars	1.00
107 Jeff Graham	1.00
108 Irving Fryar	1.00
109 Lawrence Phillips	7.00
110 Jerry Rice	10.00
111 Mike Tomczak	1.00
112 Tony Martin	1.00
113 Brian Blades	1.00
114 Bill Brooks	1.00
115 Rob Moore	1.00
116 Quinn Early	1.00
117 Darnay Scott	1.00
118 Ken Dilger	1.00
119 Derek Loville	1.00
120 Reggie White	2.00

1996 Playoff Illusions Spectralusion Dominion

Spectralusion Dominion was a 120-card parallel set that utilized Illu-sion printing technology and a gold holographic foil background. These parallel cards were inserted every 192 packs.

	MT
Spec. Dominion Cards:	10x-20x

1996 Playoff Illusions XXXI

XXXI reprints all 120 cards in the base set in a die-cut, parallel that features the roman numerals XXXI across the top of the card. This parallel set is inserted at a rate of one per 12 packs. These cards are also featured in a more difficult gold holographic parallel called Spectralusion Dominion.

	MT
Complete XXXI Set (120):	600.00
XXXI Cards:	2x

1996 Playoff Illusions XXXI Spectralusion Dominion

XXXI Spectralusion Dominion reprints the die-cut XXXI cards and adds a gold holographic background. These parallel cards are found in every 96 packs.

	MT
XXXI Spec. Dominion:	6x-12x

1996 Playoff Illusions Optical Illusions

This 18-card chase set, found one per 96 packs, featured Troy Aikman handing off to Barry Sanders and Brett Favre passing to Jerry Rice.

		MT
Complete Set (18):		800.00
Common Player:		15.00
1	Brett Favre, Jerry Rice	150.00
2	Troy Aikman, Barry Sanders	100.00
3	Dan Marino, Emmitt Smith	175.00
4	Warren Moon, Carl Pickens	15.00
5	John Elway, Herman Moore	60.00
6	Steve Young, Anthony Miller	60.00
7	Jim Harbaugh, Terrell Davis	60.00
8	Kordell Stewart, Kordell Stewart	70.00
9	Deion Sanders, Deion Sanders	50.00
10	Kerry Collins, Curtis Martin	90.00
11	Scott Mitchell, Robert Brooks	15.00
12	Jeff Blake, Tony Martin	25.00
13	Mark Brunell, Marshall Faulk	50.00
14	Drew Bledsoe, Jerome Bettis	70.00
15	Gus Frerotte, Karim Abdul-Jabbar	40.00
16	Steve Bono, Ricky Watters	15.00
17	Chris Chandler, Terry Allen	15.00
18	Tony Banks, Keyshawn Johnson	40.00

1996 Pro Line II Intense

Pro Line II Intense features 100 cards, a parallel set and four insert sets. Each regular card has a full-bleed color photo on the front, with the Intense logo at the top. The player's name and position are in a bar along the bottom, flanked by a team helmet in the lower left corner. The back has a card number and the player's name at the top, with a photo on one side and statistics on the other. A box with biographical information is in the lower left corner. There were also parallel Double Intensity cards made; they were seeded one per every five packs and are stamped in bronze on the front. Three other insert sets were also made - Determined and $3 and $5 Sprint Foncards. There's an average of $11 in phone time in every box.

		MT
Complete Set (100):		20.00
Common Player:		.05
Wax Box:		30.00
1	Kerry Collins	1.25
2	Jeff George	.05
3	Mark Brunell	1.00
4	Steve McNair	.75
5	Rick Mirer	.05
6	Dave Brown	.05
7	Rashaan Salaam	.50
8	Marshall Faulk	.50
9	Erric Pegram	.05
10	Cris Carter	.05
11	Eric Allen	.05
12	Jim Kelly	.05
13	Jeff Blake	.50
14	Stan Humphries	.05
15	Scott Mitchell	.05
16	Jeff Hostetler	.05
17	Rodney Peete	.05
18	Warren Moon	.05
19	Errict Rhett	.40
20	Terrell Davis	2.00
21	J.J. Stokes	.10
22	Marco Coleman	.05
23	Heath Shuler	.05
24	Duane Clemons	.05
25	*Amani Toomer*	.10
26	Leslie O'Neal	.05
27	Tamarick Vanover	.50
28	Steve Bono	.05
29	Jim Everett	.05
30	Erik Kramer	.05
31	Trent Dilfer	.10
32	Jim Harbaugh	.05
33	Vinny Testaverde	.05
34	Rodney Hampton	.05
35	Chris Warren	.10
36	Curtis Martin	2.00
37	*Eddie Kennison*	.50
38	Herman Moore	.40
39	Terance Mathis	.05
40	Carl Pickens	.05
41	Isaac Bruce	.50
42	Reggie White	.10
43	Junior Seau	.05
44	Bryce Paup	.05
45	Deion Sanders	.50
46	Thurman Thomas	.10
47	Gus Frerotte	.05
48	Jerome Bettis	.10
49	Michael Irvin	.10
50	Wayne Chrebet	.05
51	*Bobby Engram*	.75
52	Marcus Jones	.05
53	Daryl Gardener	.05
54	*Alex Van Dyke*	.10
55	Cedric Jones	.05
56	Regan Upshaw	.05
57	*Jason Dunn*	.30
58	Mark Chmura	.25
59	Ray Lewis	.05
60	*Rickey Dudley*	.20
61	*Leeland McElroy*	.20
62	Derrick Thomas	.05
63	*Bobby Hoying*	.15
64	Robert Brooks	.05
65	Tim Brown	.05
66	Michael Westbrook	.40
67	Jim Miller	.05
68	Aaron Hayden	.05
69	Marcus Allen	.05
70	Troy Aikman	1.00
71	Steve Young	.75
72	Neil O'Donnell	.05
73	Drew Bledsoe	.75
74	Emmitt Smith	2.00
75	Ki-Jana Carter	.30
76	Irving Fryar	.05
77	*Joey Galloway*	.75
78	Russell Maryland	.05
79	Kordell Stewart	1.00
80	Barry Sanders	1.00
81	Bryan Cox	.05
82	*Keyshawn Johnson*	1.50
83	*Karim Abdul-Jabbar*	1.75
84	*Kevin Hardy*	.30
85	Rodney Thomas	.05
86	John Elway	.50
87	Dan Marino	2.00
88	Brett Favre	2.00
89	John Mobley	.05
90	Jonathan Ogden	.05
91	*Eddie George*	2.50
92	*Simeon Rice*	.25
93	*Tim Biakabutuka*	1.00
94	*Terry Glenn*	1.75
95	*Marvin Harrison*	1.00
96	*Lawrence Phillips*	.50
97	Natrone Means	.10
98	Jerry Rice	.75
99	Ricky Watters	.10
100	Checklist	.05

1996 Pro Line II Intense Double Intensity

Pro Line II Intense Double Intensity was a 100-card parallel set that included the words "Double Intensity" on the front in foil. These parallel cards were inserted at a rate of one per five packs.

	MT
Complete Set (100):	160.00
Double Intensity Cards:	4x-8x

1996 Pro Line II Intense Determined

These 1996 Pro Line II inserts offer an in-depth view of the look and determination of 20 of the NFL's fiercest competitors. Each card front has an action photo of the player against a metallic ghosted close-up image of him as the background. The Pro Line II logo is at the top of the card; the player's name and position are in a bar at the bottom, above the word "Determined." The card back, numbered 1 of 20, etc., has a full-bleed color action photo on it, with an oval toward the bottom which recaps some of the player's achievements.

		MT
Complete Set (20):		250.00
Common Player:		4.00
1	Kerry Collins	15.00
2	Troy Aikman	15.00
3	Herman Moore	6.00
4	Mark Brunell	15.00
5	Dan Marino	30.00
6	Kordell Stewart	15.00
7	Junior Seau	4.00
8	Steve Young	12.00
9	John Elway	12.00
10	Emmitt Smith	30.00
11	Steve McNair	10.00
12	Drew Bledsoe	15.00
13	Joey Galloway	12.00
14	Deion Sanders	10.00
15	Kevin Hardy	4.00
16	Keyshawn Johnson	12.00
17	Marvin Harrison	10.00
18	Tim Biakabutuka	8.00
19	Eddie George	25.00
20	Terry Glenn	20.00

1996 Pro Line Memorabilia

Pro Line Memorabilia was the third installment of Pro Line Football in 1996. The same 100 players from Intense were used, but with different designs. Memorabilia included one autographed memorabilia redemption cards, two autographed cards, with one of a 1996 NFL first-round pick, as well as two inserts - Down the Stretch and Producers.

		MT
Complete Set (100):		25.00
Common Player:		.10
Wax Box:		100.00
1	Kerry Collins	1.50
2	Jeff George	.10
3	Mark Brunell	1.50
4	Steve McNair	1.00
5	Rick Mirer	.20
6	Dave Brown	.10
7	Rashaan Salaam	.30
8	Marshall Faulk	.30
9	Erric Pegram	.10
10	Cris Carter	.10
11	Eric Allen	.10
12	Jim Kelly	.20
13	Jeff Blake	.30
14	Stan Humphries	.10
15	Scott Mitchell	.10
16	Jeff Hostetler	.10
17	Rodney Peete	.10
18	Warren Moon	.20
19	Errict Rhett	.30
20	Terrell Davis	1.75
21	J.J. Stokes	.20
22	Marco Coleman	.10
23	Heath Shuler	.20
24	Duane Clemons	.10
25	Amani Toomer	.20
26	Leslie O'Neal	.10
27	Tamarick Vanover	.20
28	Steve Bono	.10
29	Jim Everett	.10
30	Erik Kramer	.10
31	Trent Dilfer	.20
32	Jim Harbaugh	.10
33	Vinny Testaverde	.10
34	Rodney Hampton	.10
35	Chris Warren	.10
36	Curtis Martin	1.75
37	Eddie Kennison	1.50
38	Herman Moore	.30

		MT
39	Terance Mathis	.10
40	Carl Pickens	.20
41	Isaac Bruce	.30
42	Reggie White	.20
43	Junior Seau	.20
44	Bryce Paup	.10
45	Deion Sanders	.75
46	Thurman Thomas	.20
47	Gus Frerotte	.10
48	Tony Mandarich	.10
49	Michael Irvin	.20
50	Wayne Chrebet	.10
51	Bobby Engram	1.00
52	Marcus Jones	.10
53	Daryl Gardener	.10
54	Alex Van Dyke	.20
55	Andre Rison	.10
56	Regan Upshaw	.10
57	Jason Dunn	.10
58	Mark Chmura	.20
59	Ray Lewis	.10
60	Rickey Dudley	.30
61	Leeland McElroy	.20
62	Derrick Thomas	.10
63	Bobby Hoying	.20
64	Robert Brooks	.20
65	Tim Brown	.20
66	Michael Westbrook	.20
67	Jim Miller	.10
68	Aaron Hayden	.10
69	Marcus Allen	.20
70	Troy Aikman	1.50
71	Steve Young	1.00
72	Neil O'Donnell	.10
73	Drew Bledsoe	1.50
74	Emmitt Smith	3.00
75	Ki-Jana Carter	.20
76	Irving Fryar	.10
77	Joey Galloway	.50
78	Russell Maryland	.10
79	Kordell Stewart	1.50
80	Barry Sanders	1.50
81	Bryan Cox	.10
82	Keyshawn Johnson	1.50
83	Karim Abdul-Jabbar	2.00
84	Kevin Hardy	.20
85	Rodney Thomas	.10
86	John Elway	1.00
87	Dan Marino	3.00
88	Brett Favre	3.00
89	Eric Metcalf	.10
90	Jonathan Ogden	.20
91	Eddie George	3.00
92	Simeon Rice	.20
93	Tim Biakabutuka	.30
94	Terry Glenn	2.50
95	Marvin Harrison	1.50
96	Lawrence Phillips	.30
97	Natrone Means	.20
98	Jerry Rice	1.50
99	Ricky Watters	.20
100	Checklist Emmitt Smith	.50

1996 Pro Line Memorabilia Stretch Drive

Stretch Drive featured 30 top players on a foil background, with cards numbered DS1-DS30. Regular versions were inserted every three packs, while Signature Series versions, which had facsimile signatures, were inserted every 25 packs.

		MT
Complete Set (30):		150.00
Common Player:		2.50
1	Jim Kelly	5.00

		MT
2	Kerry Collins	10.00
3	Rashaan Salaam	5.00
4	Jeff Blake	5.00
5	Deion Sanders	6.00
6	Troy Aikman	10.00
7	Emmitt Smith	18.00
8	John Elway	8.00
9	Terrell Davis	12.00
10	Barry Sanders	10.00
11	Herman Moore	5.00
12	Brett Favre	18.00
13	Steve McNair	8.00
14	Eddie George	12.00
15	Marshall Faulk	5.00
16	Marvin Harrison	6.00
17	Dan Marino	18.00
18	Curtis Martin	12.00
19	Drew Bledsoe	10.00
20	Terry Glenn	10.00
21	Neil O'Donnell	2.50
22	Keyshawn Johnson	6.00
23	Ricky Watters	5.00
24	Kordell Stewart	10.00
25	J.J. Stokes	2.50
26	Steve Young	8.00
27	Joey Galloway	6.00
28	Lawrence Phillips	5.00
29	Isaac Bruce	5.00
30	Errict Rhett	5.00

1996 Pro Line Memorabilia Producers

Producers was a 10-card insert found in every six packs of Memorabilia. Cards in this insert were numbered P1-P10. There are also Signature Series Producers, which have facsimile signatures, inserted every 100 packs.

		MT
Complete Set (10):		50.00
Common Player:		1.00
Silver Signatures:		2x-4x
1	Keyshawn Johnson	3.00
2	Barry Sanders	5.00
3	Eddie George	8.00
4	Emmitt Smith	10.00
5	Jerry Rice	5.00
6	Brett Favre	10.00
7	Marshall Faulk	1.00
8	Dan Marino	10.00
9	Deion Sanders	4.00
10	Ricky Watters	1.00

1996 Score Board NFL Lasers

This 100-card set features some of the NFL's top stars, including seven who have autographed special inserts. The regular card front has a color action photo on it against a metallic background. The left frame of the card is green; the upper right and lower right corners are gold, with NFL Lasers and the player's team name in them. The player's name and position are above the bottom frame. The card back has a card number and the player's name at the top, with biographical information below. The right border has the player's name at the top, with his team name running horizontally toward the bottom. 1995 and career stats are along the bottom. A photo completes the back. The autographed cards, available at a rate of two per case, come in two versions - regular (400 each, one per 150 packs), and die-cuts (100 each, one per 930 packs). The other inserts are Laser Images and Sunday's Heroes.

		MT
Complete Set (100):		30.00
Common Player:		.10
Wax Box:		80.00
1	Brett Favre	2.50
2	Chris Warren	.10
3	J.J. Stokes	.25
4	Barry Sanders	1.25
5	Ben Coates	.10
6	Bryan Cox	.10
7	Carl Pickens	.10
8	Cris Carter	.10
9	Curtis Martin	2.00
10	Dan Marino	2.50
11	Dave Brown	.10
12	Drew Bledsoe	1.00
13	Edgar Bennett	.10
14	Herman Moore	.30
15	Jeff Blake	.30
16	Jerry Rice	1.25
17	Jim Kelly	.20
18	John Elway	.75
19	Junior Seau	.10
20	Kerry Collins	1.25
21	Kordell Stewart	1.00
22	Leonard Russell	.10
23	Mark Brunell	.50
24	Marshall Faulk	.30
25	Mike Tomczak	.10
26	Reggie White	.20
27	Ricky Watters	.20
28	Rod Woodson	.10
29	Rodney Peete	.10
30	Stan Humphries	.10
31	Steve McNair	.75
32	Terry Allen	.10
33	Thurman Thomas	.20
34	Troy Aikman	1.25
35	Vinny Testaverde	.10
36	Chris T. Jones	.10
37	Deion Sanders	.75
38	Eric Metcalf	.10
39	Erik Kramer	.10
40	Emmitt Smith	2.50
41	Gus Frerotte	.10
42	Jeff George	.10
43	Jerome Bettis	.20
44	Jim Harbaugh	.10
45	Isaac Bruce	.50
46	Jeff Hostetler	.10
47	Ki-Jana Carter	.20
48	Marcus Allen	.20
49	Neil O'Donnell	.10
50	Rashaan Salaam	.40
51	Robert Brooks	.10
52	Steve Bono	.10
53	Scott Mitchell	.10
54	Terrell Davis	1.50
55	Tim Brown	.10
56	Troy Vincent	.10
57	Warren Moon	.10
58	Tony Martin	.10
59	Rodney Hampton	.10
60	Steve Young	1.00
61	Rick Mirer	.10
62	Mark Chmura	.10
63	Larry Centers	.10
64	Ken Dilger	.10
65	Joey Galloway	1.00
66	Jim Everett	.10
67	Chris Chandler	.10
68	James Stewart	.10

		MT
69	Robert Smith	.10
70	Tamarick Vanover	.50
71	Wayne Chrebet	.10
72	*Keyshawn Johnson*	1.00
73	*Kevin Hardy*	.20
74	*Lawrence Phillips*	.50
75	*Jonathan Ogden*	.20
76	*Terry Glenn*	3.00
77	*Tim Biakabutuka*	1.00
78	*Eddie George*	4.00
79	*Eric Moulds*	1.00
80	*John Mobley*	.10
81	*Amani Toomer*	.20
82	*Marvin Harrison*	1.50
83	*Leeland McElroy*	.30
84	*Rickey Dudley*	.30
85	*Tony Banks*	1.00
86	*Zach Thomas*	1.00
87	*Alex Molden*	.10
88	*Daryl Gardener*	.10
89	*Jamal Anderson*	1.50
90	*Karim Abdul-Jabbar*	2.50
91	*Simeon Rice*	.20
92	*Walt Harris*	.20
93	*Bobby Engram*	.75
94	Kevin Williams	.10
95	Sean Gilbert	.10
96	Kevin Greene	.10
97	Regan Upshaw	.10
98	Marcus Jones	.10
99	Ray Lewis	.10
100	Checklist	.10

1996 Score Board NFL Lasers Autographs

Seven players have autographed these 1996 Score Board inserts - Emmitt Smith, Troy Aikman, Keyshawn Johnson, Marshall Faulk, Drew Bledsoe, Steve Young and Kordell Stewart. The cards were available at a rate of two per case, in two different versions. Regular versions (400 each) were seeded one per every 150 packs. Die-cut versions (100 each) were seeded one per every 930 packs.

	MT
Complete Set (7):	850.00
Troy Aikman	150.00
Steve Young	120.00
Kordell Stewart	150.00
Keyshawn Johnson	100.00
Emmitt Smith	250.00
Marshall Faulk	100.00
Drew Bledsoe	150.00

1996 Score Board NFL Lasers Die-Cut Autographs

Also included in packs of NFL Lasers were die-cut versions of each of the seven players. Die-cut versions listed no odds, but were limited to only 100 of each.

	MT
Complete Set (7):	1700.00
Troy Aikman	300.00
Steve Young	240.00
Kordell Stewart	300.00
Keyshawn Johnson	200.00
Emmitt Smith	500.00
Marshall Faulk	200.00
Drew Bledsoe	300.00

1996 Score Board NFL Lasers Laser Images

These cards are seeded one per every 30 packs of 1996 Score Board NFL Lasers. The card front has a color action photo of the player, with a ghosted black laser image of the player in the background, which is metallic. The card has gold foil stamped around three sides as a border; the player's name is also in gold foil on the right side. The Laser Images logo is also on the front. The card back has a color photo of the laser image from the front, with a column down the left side which has a recap of the player's accomplishments and a team logo at the bottom. The card number, using an I prefix, is in the upper left corner. The player's name is in a rectangle in the upper right corner. His last name is in scripted letter along the left side of the card.

	MT
Complete Set (30):	250.00
Common Player:	3.00
I1 Steve Bono	3.00
I2 Kerry Collins	20.00
I3 Tim Biakabutuka	6.00
I4 Rashaan Salaam	3.00
I5 Jeff Blake	6.00
I6 Emmitt Smith	30.00
I7 Troy Aikman	20.00
I8 Deion Sanders	12.00
I9 John Elway	12.00
I10 Herman Moore	3.00
I11 Brett Favre	30.00
I12 Eddie George	20.00
I13 Marvin Harrison	12.00
I14 Mark Brunell	12.00
I15 Dan Marino	30.00
I16 Karim Abdul-Jabbar	15.00
I17 Cris Carter	3.00
I18 Drew Bledsoe	15.00
I19 Curtis Martin	20.00
I20 Keyshawn Johnson	10.00
I21 Chris T. Jones	3.00
I22 Kordell Stewart	15.00
I23 Junior Seau	3.00
I24 Steve Young	15.00
I25 Jerry Rice	20.00
I26 Joey Galloway	12.00
I27 Lawrence Phillips	12.00
I28 Jonathan Ogden	3.00
I29 Jim Harbaugh	3.00
I30 Neil O'Donnell	3.00

1996 Score Board NFL Lasers Sunday's Heroes

These cards, numbered using an "S" prefix, capture 25 stars on a thicker, embossed surface. Cards were

seeded one per every 22 packs of 1996 Score Board NFL Lasers product.

	MT
Complete Set (25):	450.00
Common Player:	8.00
S1 Tim Brown	8.00
S2 Kerry Collins	30.00
S3 Tim Biakabutuka	15.00
S4 Rashaan Salaam	12.00
S5 Jeff Blake	15.00
S6 Ki-Jana Carter	12.00
S7 Emmitt Smith	50.00
S8 Troy Aikman	30.00
S9 Deion Sanders	20.00
S10 Terrell Davis	30.00
S11 Barry Sanders	30.00
S12 Brett Favre	50.00
S13 Reggie White	12.00
S14 Marshall Faulk	20.00
S15 Mark Brunell	20.00
S16 Kevin Hardy	8.00
S17 Dan Marino	50.00
S18 Drew Bledsoe	25.00
S19 Curtis Martin	40.00
S20 Keyshawn Johnson	20.00
S21 Kordell Stewart	25.00
S22 Steve Young	25.00
S23 Jerry Rice	30.00
S24 Chris Warren	8.00
S25 Karim Abdul-Jabbar	30.00

1996 SkyBox

SkyBox Premium was a 250-card set that marked the fifth anniversary of the product. The regular-issue set includes 178 regular player cards, 50 rookies (179-228), 10 Prime Time Rookie Retrospectives (229-238), which are quad cards, 10 Panorama (239-248) and two checklists (249-250). SkyBox Premium was issued in 10-card packs and contains the final two cards in the Brett Favre MVP Series (cards 1, 2, 3 were in Impact), side B of the Favre Lenticular Exchange card, six SkyBox spokesperson autographs and a Rubies parallel set (1-147). Inserts include: V, Next Big Thing, Thunder and Lightning, Close-Ups, Prime Time Rookies.

	MT
Complete Set (250):	25.00
Common Player:	.10
Wax Box:	50.00
1 Larry Centers	.10
2 Boomer Esiason	.10
3 Garrison Hearst	.10
4 Rob Moore	.10
5 Frank Sanders	.20
6 Eric Swann	.10
7 Bert Emanuel	.10
8 Jeff George	.10
9 Craig Heyward	.10
10 Terance Mathis	.10
11 Eric Metcalf	.10
12 Derrick Alexander	.10
13 Leroy Hoard	.10
14 Michael Jackson	.10
15 Vinny Testaverde	.10
16 Eric Turner	.10
17 Darick Holmes	.40
18 Jim Kelly	.20
19 Bryce Paup	.10
20 Andre Reed	.10
21 Bruce Smith	.10
22 Thurman Thomas	.20
23 Tim Tindale	.10
24 Mark Carrier	.10
25 Kerry Collins	1.50
26 Willie Green	.10
27 Lamar Lathon	.10
28 Tyrone Poole	.10
29 Curtis Conway	.10
30 Bryan Cox	.10
31 Erik Kramer	.10
32 Nate Lewis	.10
33 Rashaan Salaam	.75
34 Alonzo Spellman	.10
35 Michael Timpson	.10
36 Jeff Blake	.75
37 Ki-Jana Carter	.20
38 David Dunn	.10
39 Carl Pickens	.10
40 Darnay Scott	.10
41 Troy Aikman	1.50
42 Charles Haley	.10
43 Michael Irvin	.10
44 Daryl Johnston	.10
45 Jay Novacek	.10
46 Deion Sanders	1.00
47 Emmitt Smith	2.50
48 Kevin Williams	.10
49 Steve Atwater	.10
50 Terrell Davis	1.25
51 John Elway	.75
52 Anthony Miller	.10
53 Shannon Sharpe	.10
54 Mike Sherrard	.10
55 Scott Mitchell	.10
56 Herman Moore	.50
57 Johnnie Morton	.10
58 Brett Perriman	.10
59 Barry Sanders	1.50
60 Edgar Bennett	.10
61 Robert Brooks	.10
62 Mark Chmura	.25
63 Brett Favre	2.50
64 Antonio Freeman	.10
65 Keith Jackson	.10
66 Reggie White	.20
67 Chris Chandler	.10
68 Mel Gray	.10
69 Steve McNair	1.00
70 Chris Sanders	.40
71 Rodney Thomas	.30
72 Quentin Coryatt	.10
73 Sean Dawkins	.10
74 Ken Dilger	.10
75 Marshall Faulk	.75
76 Jim Harbaugh	.10
77 Lamont Warren	.10
78 Tony Boselli	.10
79 Mark Brunell	1.00
80 Willie Jackson	.10
81 Natrone Means	.10
82 James Stewart	.10
83 Marcus Allen	.10
84 Kimble Anders	.10
85 Steve Bono	.10
86 Lake Dawson	.10
87 Neil Smith	.10
88 Derrick Thomas	.10
89 Tamarick Vanover	.75
90 Fred Barnett	.10
91 Terry Kirby	.10
92 Dan Marino	2.50
93 O.J. McDuffie	.10
94 Bernie Parmalee	.10
95 Richmond Webb	.10
96 Cris Carter	.10
97 Qadry Ismail	.10
98 Scottie Graham	.10
99 Warren Moon	.10
100 Jake Reed	.10
101 Robert Smith	.10
102 Drew Bledsoe	1.25
103 Vincent Brisby	.10
104 Ben Coates	.10
105 Curtis Martin	2.00
106 David Meggett	.10
107 Chris Slade	.10
108 Mario Bates	.10
109 Jim Everett	.10
110 Michael Haynes	.10
111 Tyrone Hughes	.10
112 Renaldo Turnbull	.10
113 Dave Brown	.10
114 Chris Calloway	.10
115 Rodney Hampton	.10
116 Thomas Lewis	.10
117 Tyrone Wheatley	.10
118 Kyle Brady	.10
119 Hugh Douglas	.10
120 Aaron Glenn	.10
121 Jeff Graham	.10
122 Adrian Murrell	.10
123 Neil O'Donnell	.10
124 Tim Brown	.10
125 Nolan Harrison	.10
126 Billy Joe Hobert	.10
127 Jeff Hostetler	.10
128 Napoleon Kaufman	.30
129 Chester McGlockton	.10
130 Harvey Williams	.10
131 Charlie Garner	.10
132 Andy Harmon	.10
133 Chris T. Jones	.10
134 Mike Mamula	.10
135 Rodney Peete	.10
136 Bobby Taylor	.10
137 Ricky Watters	.10
138 Jerome Bettis	.20
139 Greg Lloyd	.10
140 Jim Miller	.10
141 Ernie Mills	.10
142 Kordell Stewart	1.25
143 Yancey Thigpen	.30
144 Rod Woodson	.10
145 Andre Coleman	.10
146 Terrell Fletcher	.10
147 *Aaron Hayden*	.30
148 Stan Humphries	.10
149 Junior Seau	.10
150 Isaac Bruce	.75
151 Kevin Carter	.10
152 Todd Kinchen	.10
153 Leslie O'Neal	.10
154 Mark Rypien	.10
155 William Floyd	.10
156 Merton Hanks	.10
157 Brent Jones	.10
158 Derek Loville	.10
159 Ken Norton	.10
160 Jerry Rice	1.50
161 J.J. Stokes	.75
162 Steve Young	1.00
163 Brian Blades	.10
164 Christian Fauria	.10
165 Joey Galloway	1.00
166 Rick Mirer	.10
167 Chris Warren	.20
168 Trent Dilfer	.10
169 Alvin Harper	.10
170 Jackie Harris	.10
171 Hardy Nickerson	.10
172 Errict Rhett	.50
173 Terry Allen	.10
174 Henry Ellard	.10
175 Gus Frerotte	.10
176 Brian Mitchell	.10
177 Heath Shuler	.10
178 Michael Westbrook	.75
179 *Karim Abdul-Jabbar*	3.00
180 *Mike Alstott*	.75
181 *Willie Anderson*	.10
182 *Marco Battaglia*	.10
183 *Tim Biakabutuka*	1.00
184 *Tony Brackens*	.10
185 *Duane Clemons*	.10
186 *Marcus Coleman*	.10
187 *Ernie Conwell*	.10
188 *Chris Darkins*	.10
189 *Stephen Davis*	.30
190 *Brian Dawkins*	.10
191 *Rickey Dudley*	.30
192 *Jason Dunn*	.30
193 *Bobby Engram*	1.00
194 *Daryl Gardener*	.10
195 *Eddie George*	4.00
196 *Terry Glenn*	3.00
197 *Kevin Hardy*	.50
198 *Walt Harris*	.20
199 *Marvin Harrison*	2.00
200 *Bobby Hoying*	.40
201 *Isreal Ifeanyi*	.10
202 *DeRon Jenkins*	.10
203 *Keyshawn Johnson*	2.00
204 *Lance Johnstone*	.10
205 *Cedric Jones*	.30
206 *Marcus Jones*	.10
207 *Eddie Kennison*	1.25
208 *Jevon Langford*	.10
209 *Dedric Mathis*	.10
210 *Jermaine Mayberry*	.10
211 *Leeland McElroy*	.30
212 *Johnny McWilliams*	.10
213 *Ray Mickens*	.10
214 *John Mobley*	.25
215 *Jerald Moore*	.25
216 *Eric Moulds*	1.50
217 *Mushin Muhammad*	.75
218 *Jonathan Ogden*	.20
219 *Lawrence Phillips*	.50
220 *Kavika Pittman*	.10
221 *Stanley Pritchett*	.50

222	*Simeon Rice*	.30
223	*Detron Smith*	.10
224	*Bryan Still*	.50
225	*Amani Toomer*	.50
226	*Regan Upshaw*	.10
227	*Alex Van Dyke*	.20
228	*Stepfret Williams*	.10
229	Primetime Rookie Retros	.10
230	Primetime Rookie Retros	.10
231	Primetime Rookie Retros	.10
232	Primetime Rookie Retros	.10
233	Primetime Rookie Retros	.10
234	Primetime Rookie Retros	.10
235	Primetime Rookie Retros	.10
236	Primetime Rookie Retros	.10
237	Primetime Rookie Retros	.10
238	Primetime Rookie Retros	.10
239	Panorama (AFC Championship)	.10
240	Panorama (Bucs vs. Packers)	.10
241	Panorama (Falcons vs. Bills)	.10
242	Panorama (Cardinals vs. Chargers	.10
243	Panorama (Giants vs. Packers)	.10
244	Panorama (Saints vs. 49ers)	.10
245	Panorama (Redskins vs. Cardinals)	.10
246	Panorama (AFC Wild Card)	.10
247	Panorama (NFC Championship)	.10
248	Panorama (Packers vs. Browns)	.10
249	Checklist	.10
250	Checklist	.10

1996 SkyBox Rubies

Rubies was a 248-card parallel set (250 minus checklists) that were inserted into hobby boxes under the packs. Rubies awarded collectors that purchased sealed boxes since the person who opened the box would pull a Rubies insert. Rubies are distinguished by ruby foil in place of the gold foil found on common cards.

	MT
Complete Set (228):	1800.00
Rubies:	20x-40x

1996 SkyBox Autographs

The six spokesman for Fleer/Sky-Box signed cards to be inserted into packs of Premium at a rate of one per 450. Highlighted by Brett Favre, the set also includes Trent Dilfer, Daryl Johnston, Eric Turner, Dave Meggett and William Floyd.

	MT
Complete Set (6):	350.00
Common Player:	20.00
Trent Dilfer	40.00
Brett Favre	250.00
William Floyd	20.00
Daryl Johnston	20.00
Dave Meggett	20.00
Eric Turner	20.00

1996 SkyBox Brett Favre MVP

Brett Favre MVP Series was a five-card insert devoted to SkyBox spokesman and NFL MVP Brett Favre. Cards 1-3A were found in Impact, with a one per 480 insert rate, while cards 3B-5 were in packs of Premium, with a one per 240 insertion rate. Each card showed off a different technology, with No. 1 printed on foil, No. 2 printed on acrylic, No. 3 utilizing lenticular technology, No. 4 was die-

cut and No. 5 was printed on leather. Card No. 3 required collectors to obtain sides A and B, from Impact and Premium, respectively, to redeem it for the actual lenticular card.

		MT
Complete Set (6):		180.00
Common Player:		20.00
1	Brett Favre Foil	40.00
2	Brett Favre Acrylic	40.00
3a	Brett Favre Exch.A	30.00
3b	Brett Favre Exch.B	40.00
3c	Brett Favre Prize	60.00
4	Brett Favre Die-Cut	30.00
5	Brett Favre Leather	30.00

1996 SkyBox Close-Ups

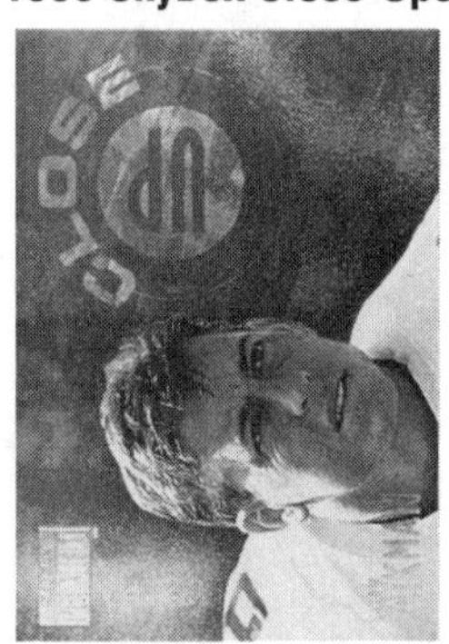

Ten NFL stars are featured in close-up shots in this retail exclusive insert, which was found every 30 packs.

		MT
Complete Set (10):		175.00
Common Player:		7.00
1	Troy Aikman	25.00
2	Drew Bledsoe	25.00
3	Isaac Bruce	12.00
4	Terrell Davis	30.00
5	John Elway	20.00
6	Barry Sanders	25.00
7	Emmitt Smith	50.00
8	Kordell Stewart	20.00
9	Tamarick Vanover	7.00
10	Ricky Watters	7.00

1996 SkyBox Next Big Thing

Next Big Thing showcases 15 young players that are expected to produce big things through their careers. Inserted at a one per 40 rate, these inserts feature a multi-colored foil background with the words "Next Big Thing" in bold.

		MT
Complete Set (15):		120.00
Common Player:		4.00
1	Mark Brunell	10.00
2	Rickey Dudley	8.00
3	Bobby Engram	8.00
4	Antonio Freeman	4.00
5	Eddie George	30.00
6	Terry Glenn	25.00
7	Marvin Harrison	12.00
8	Keyshawn Johnson	18.00
9	Napoleon Kaufman	4.00
10	Steve McNair	10.00
11	Alex Molden	4.00
12	Frank Sanders	4.00
13	Kordell Stewart	15.00
14	Amani Toomer	4.00
15	Alex Van Dyke	4.00

1996 SkyBox Prime-Time Rookies

Prime Time Rookies returned to Premium as a hobby- only insert that showcased the top rookies from the 1996 NFL Draft. These inserts were found every 96 packs.

		MT
Complete Set (10):		170.00
Common Player:		12.00
1	Tim Biakabutuka	20.00
2	Rickey Dudley	12.00
3	Bobby Engram	14.00
4	Eddie George	40.00
5	Terry Glenn	35.00
6	Marvin Harrison	20.00
7	Keyshawn Johnson	25.00
8	Leeland McElroy	12.00
9	Eric Moulds	12.00
10	Lawrence Phillips	25.00

1996 SkyBox Thunder and Lightning

Thunder and Lightning was made up of 20 players featured on 10 different cards (numbered 1-10 a & b) who

make lethal 1-2 combinations. Each card is actually a card- within-a-card where the "lightning" player is inserted into the "thunder" card. Thunder and Lightning inserts were found every 72 packs.

		MT
Complete Set (10):		200.00
Common Player:		8.00
1	Emmitt Smith, Troy Aikman	50.00
2	Barry Sanders, Scott Mitchell	25.00
3	Marshall Faulk, Jim Harbaugh	20.00
4	Dan Marino, O.J. McDuffie	40.00
5	Jerry Rice, Steve Young	30.00
6	Jeff Blake, Carl Pickens	8.00
7	Brett Favre, Edgar Bennett	40.00
8	Curtis Martin, Drew Bledsoe	30.00
9	Errict Rhett, Trent Dilfer	8.00
10	Rick Mirer, Chris Warren	8.00

1996 SkyBox V

Ten players who changed the game over the last five years are featured in V, which was seeded every 18 packs. This insert celebrates Sky-Box's fifth anniversary with die-cut, V-shaped designs.

		MT
Complete Set (10):		40.00
Common Player:		1.50
1	Ki-Jana Carter	4.00
2	Kerry Collins	10.00
3	Trent Dilfer	1.50
4	Joey Galloway	8.00
5	Herman Moore	4.00
6	Errict Rhett	4.00
7	Rashaan Salaam	5.00
8	Deion Sanders	8.00
9	Thurman Thomas	1.50
10	Reggie White	1.50

1996 SkyBox Impact Rookies

Although released in early 1997, Impact Rookies is generally considered a 1996 product due to its focus on 1996 rookies. The set consists of 150 cards, including 70 1996 rookies, 50 All-Time Impact Rookies, 20 Rookie Sleepers and 10 Rookie Record Holders. Ten-card packs had the following inserts: 1996 All-Rookie Team, Draft Board, Rookie Rewind, 1997 NFL Draft Exchange and 1996 Rookies. In addition, autographed versions of Karim Abdul-Jabbar, Rickey Dudley, Marvin Harrison, Lawrence Phillips, Eddie Kennison and Amani Toomer 1996 Rookies inserts were available through a case topper redemption offer. One redemption card was included in six-box cases, with two per 12-box case and three per 20-box case.

		MT
Complete Set (150):		12.00
Common Player:		.05
1	Leeland McElroy	.30
2	Johnny McWilliams	.05
3	Simeon Rice	.20
4	DeRon Jenkins	.05
5	Jermaine Lewis	.05
6	Ray Lewis	.05
7	Jonathan Ogden	.10
8	Eric Moulds	.30
9	Tim Biakabutuka	.40
10	Muhsin Muhammad	.10
11	Winslow Oliver	.05
12	Bobby Engram	.30
13	Walt Harris	.10
14	Willie Anderson	.05
15	Marco Battaglia	.05
16	Jevon Langford	.05
17	Kavika Pittman	.05
18	Stepfret Williams	.05
19	Tory James	.05
20	Jeff Lewis	.05
21	John Mobley	.05
22	Detron Smith	.05
23	Derrick Mayes	.30
24	Eddie George	2.00
25	Marvin Harrison	.75
26	Dedric Mathis	.05
27	Tony Brackens	.05
28	Kevin Hardy	.20
29	Jerome Woods	.05
30	Karim Abdul-Jabbar	1.00
31	Daryl Gardener	.05
32	Jerris McPhail	.05
33	Stanley Pritchett	.05
34	Zach Thomas	.50
35	Duane Clemons	.05
36	Moe Williams	.05
37	Tedy Bruschi	.05
38	Terry Glenn	1.50
39	Alex Molden	.05
40	Rickey Whittle	.05
41	Cedric Jones	.05
42	Danny Kanell	.20
43	Amani Toomer	.20
44	Marcus Coleman	.05
45	Keyshawn Johnson	.75
46	Ray Mickens	.05
47	Alex Van Dyke	.20
48	Rickey Dudley	.25
49	Lance Johnstone	.05
50	Brian Dawkins	.05
51	Jason Dunn	.05
52	Ray Farmer	.05
53	Bobby Hoying	.05
54	Jermaine Mayberry	.05
55	Steven Conley	.05
56	Bryan Still	.05
57	Tony Banks	.50
58	Ernie Conwell	.05
59	Eddie Kennison	.50
60	Jerald Moore	.05
61	Lawrence Phillips	.75
62	Isreal Ifeanyi	.05
63	Terrell Owens	1.00
64	Pete Kendall	.05
65	Mike Alstott	.25
66	Marcus Jones	.05
67	Nilo Silvan	.05
68	Regan Upshaw	.05
69	Stephen Davis	.20
70	Andre Johnson	.05
71	Troy Aikman	.40
72	Terry Allen	.05
73	Edgar Bennett	.05
74	Jerome Bettis	.10
75	Drew Bledsoe	.40
76	Tim Brown	.05
77	Mark Brunell	.25
78	Cris Carter	.05
79	Kerry Collins	.40
80	Terrell Davis	.50
81	John Elway	.30
82	Marshall Faulk	.10
83	Brett Favre	.75
84	Joey Galloway	.25
85	Rodney Hampton	.05
86	Jim Harbaugh	.05
87	Michael Irvin	.05
88	Chris T. Jones	.05
89	Napoleon Kaufman	.05
90	Jim Kelly	.05
91	Dan Marino	.75
92	Curtis Martin	.50
93	Terance Mathis	.05
94	Steve McNair	.20
95	Anthony Miller	.05
96	Scott Mitchell	.05
97	Herman Moore	.10
98	Brett Perriman	.05
99	Carl Pickens	.05
100	Jerry Rice	.40
101	Andre Rison	.05
102	Rashaan Salaam	.10
103	Barry Sanders	.40
104	Chris Sanders	.05
105	Deion Sanders	.30
106	Frank Sanders	.05
107	Bruce Smith	.05
108	Emmitt Smith	.75
109	Robert Smith	.05
110	Kordell Stewart	.30
111	J.J. Stokes	.05
112	Yancey Thigpen	.05
113	Thurman Thomas	.05
114	Eric Turner	.05
115	Tamarick Vanover	.15
116	Chris Warren	.05
117	Ricky Watters	.10
118	Michael Westbrook	.05
119	Reggie White	.10
120	Steve Young	.30
121	Jeff Blake	.10
122	Robert Brooks	.05
123	Isaac Bruce	.15
124	Mark Chmura	.05
125	Wayne Chrebet	.05
126	Ben Coates	.05
127	Ken Dilger	.05
128	Bert Emanuel	.05
129	Gus Frerotte	.05
130	Kevin Greene	.05
131	Erik Kramer	.05
132	Greg Lloyd	.05
133	Tony Martin	.05
134	Brian Mitchell	.05
135	Bryce Paup	.05
136	Jake Reed	.05
137	Errict Rhett	.15
138	Yancey Thigpen	.05
139	Tamarick Vanover	.15
140	Chris Warren	.05
141	Marcus Allen	.05
142	Jerome Bettis	.10
143	Tim Brown	.05
144	Mark Carrier	.05
145	Marshall Faulk	.10
146	Tyrone Hughes	.05
147	Dan Marino	.75
148	Curtis Martin	.50
149	Barry Sanders	.40
150	Orlando Thomas	.05

1996 SkyBox Impact Rookies All-Rookie Team

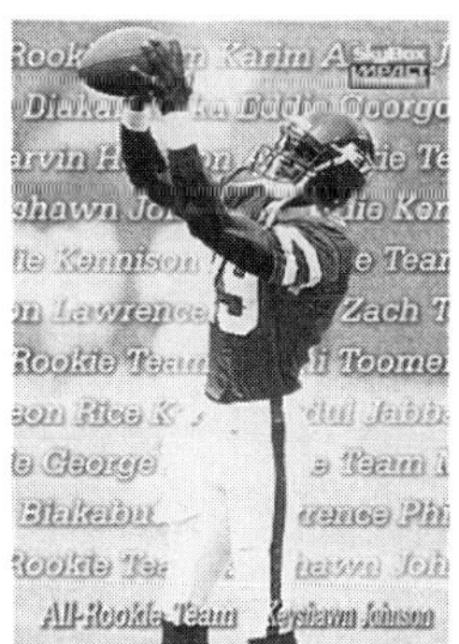

This 10-card insert includes some of the top rookies from the 1996 season. The fronts feature an embossed image of the player on a matte finish, with the words All-Rookie Team and the names of different members of the team printed in the background in white, embossed letters. All-Rookie Team inserts are numbered "x of 10" and inserted every six packs.

		MT
Complete Set (10):		20.00
Common Player:		1.00
1	Karim Abdul-Jabbar	4.00
2	Tim Biakabutuka	2.00
3	Eddie George	6.00
4	Marvin Harrison	3.00
5	Keyshawn Johnson	3.00
6	Eddie Kennison	2.00
7	Lawrence Phillips	3.00
8	Zach Thomas	2.00
9	Amani Toomer	1.00
10	Simeon Rice	1.00

1996 SkyBox Impact Rookies 1996 Rookies

This insert showcased the top rookies of 1996 on cards that were individually numbered to 1,996. The 10 offensive stars included in this insert are found every 144 packs. Autographed versions of Abdul-Jabbar, Dudley, Harrison, Phillips, Kennison and Toomer were available as case toppers.

		MT
Complete Set (10):		200.00
Common Player:		8.00
1	Karim Abdul-Jabbar	30.00
2	Tim Biakabutuka	8.00
3	Rickey Dudley	8.00
4	Eddie George	45.00
5	Terry Glenn	35.00
6	Marvin Harrison	25.00
7	Keyshawn Johnson	25.00
8	Eddie Kennison	15.00
9	Lawrence Phillips	20.00
10	Amani Toomer	8.00

1996 SkyBox Impact Rookies Draft Board

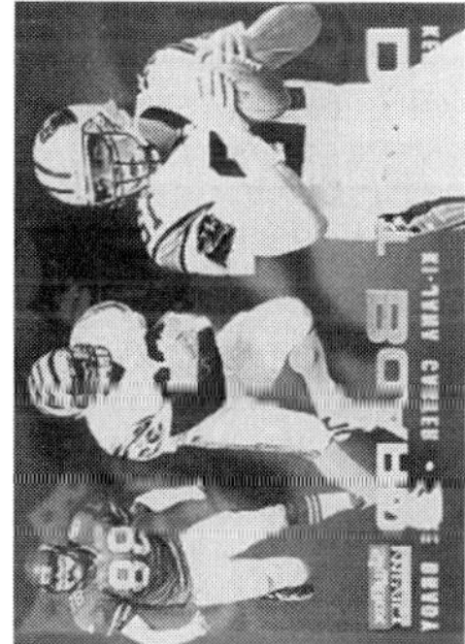

Draft Board has 20 cards that feature multiple players on the front in a horizontal format against a maroon background. The back explains the tie between the players - whether they were all late round picks or attended the same college - and is numbered "x of 20." Draft Board inserts are found every 24 packs.

		MT
Complete Set (20):		170.00
Common Player:		4.00
1	Terry Glenn, Rickey Dudley, Bobby Hoying	12.00
2	Simeon Rice, Kevin Hardy	4.00
3	Emmitt Smith, Errict Rhett	30.00
4	Deion Sanders, Corey Sawyer, Derrick Brooks	10.00
5	Terry Allen, Marcus Allen	4.00
6	John Mobley, Andre Reed	4.00
7	Drew Bledsoe, Rick Mirer, Mark Brunell	14.00
8	John Elway, Jim Kelly, Dan Marino	30.00
9	Carl Pickens, Anthony Miller	4.00
10	Antonio Freeman, Robert Brooks, Chris T. Jones	4.00
11	Jerome Bettis, Ricky Watters, Tim Brown	4.00
12	Jerry Rice, Herman Moore, Michael Irvin	15.00
13	Terrell Davis, Rodney Hampton, Garrison Hearst	15.00
14	Kerry Collins, Ki-Jana Carter, Kyle Brady	15.00
15	Barry Sanders, Thurman Thomas	15.00
16	Jermaine Lewis, Jeff Lewis, Ray Lewis	4.00
17	Steve Young, Troy Aikman	15.00
18	Curtis Martin, Chris Warren, Jamal Anderson	20.00
19	Kordell Stewart, Rashaan Salaam, Michael Westbrook	8.00
20	Tony Banks, Muhsin Muhammad	6.00

1996 SkyBox Impact Rookies Rookie Rewind

Rookie Rewind looks back on past drafts to reflect their rise to stardom. Ten different players are featured over a swirl background with the words "Rookie Rewind" in gold foil across the bottom. Rookie Rewind inserts were found only in hobby packs and carried an insertion rate of one per 120.

		MT
Complete Set (10):		50.00
Common Player:		1.50
1	Jamal Anderson	3.00
2	Jeff Blake	3.00
3	Robert Brooks	1.50
4	Mark Brunell	8.00
5	Brett Favre	18.00
6	Aaron Hayden	1.50
7	Derek Loville	1.50
8	Emmitt Smith	18.00
9	Robert Smith	1.50
10	Tamarick Vanover	3.00

1996 SkyBox SkyMotion

SkyBox's 1996 SkyMotion set features the video work of NFL films to reproduce 3.5 seconds of game action on each card. No special lights or glasses are needed to get the full effect of the card; all it takes is a flick of the wrist. The cards provide the whole picture of how the play unfolds. The cards are laminated onto paper, enabling SkyBox to print stats and other information on the back for the first time. (Previous cards were plastic, printed on one side only). In addition, there's a Replay parallel set of all 60 cards; these cards feature rounded edges with special foil stamping on the card back. One Replay card is included in each box. Two other insert sets were also made - Big Bang and Team Galaxy.

		MT
Complete Set (60):		150.00
Common Player:		1.50
Wax Box:		75.00
1	Troy Aikman	10.00
2	Marcus Allen	3.00
3	Jeff Blake	5.00
4	Drew Bledsoe	10.00
5	Tim Brown	1.50
6	Isaac Bruce	6.00
7	Mark Brunell	7.00
8	Cris Carter	1.50
9	Kerry Collins	10.00
10	Ben Coates	1.50
11	Curtis Conway	1.50
12	Terrell Davis	10.00
13	Trent Dilfer	1.50
14	Hugh Douglas	1.50
15	John Elway	6.00
16	Marshall Faulk	5.00
17	Brett Favre	15.00
18	William Floyd	1.50
19	Joey Galloway	7.00
20	Jeff George	1.50
21	Rodney Hampton	1.50
22	Jim Harbaugh	1.50
23	*Aaron Hayden*	3.00
24	Jeff Hostetler	1.50
25	Tyrone Hughes	1.50
26	Michael Irvin	3.00
27	Daryl Johnston	1.50
28	Jim Kelly	1.50
29	Greg Lloyd	1.50
30	Dan Marino	15.00
31	Curtis Martin	12.00
32	Chester McGlockton	1.50
33	Steve McNair	6.00
34	Eric Metcalf	1.50
35	Scott Mitchell	1.50
36	Herman Moore	4.00
37	Bryce Paup	1.50
38	Carl Pickens	1.50
39	Errict Rhett	4.00
40	Jerry Rice	10.00
41	Rashaan Salaam	4.00
42	Barry Sanders	10.00
43	Chris Sanders	1.50
44	Deion Sanders	6.00
45	Junior Seau	1.50
46	Heath Shuler	1.50
47	Bruce Smith	1.50
48	Emmitt Smith	15.00
49	Kordell Stewart	8.00
50	Eric Swann	1.50
51	Derrick Thomas	1.50
52	Thurman Thomas	1.50
53	Eric Turner	1.50
54	Tamarick Vanover	6.00
55	Chris Warren	3.00
56	Ricky Watters	1.50
57	Michael Westbrook	4.00
58	Reggie White	3.00
59	Rod Woodson	1.50
60	Steve Young	7.00

1996 SkyBox SkyMotion Gold

Actually called Replay, but referred to in the hobby as Golds, this 60-card parallel set featured rounded edges and special foil stamping on the card back to differentiate it from regular-issue cards. Gold parallels were inserted as a box topper into every other hobby box as a reward to box purchasers.

		MT
Complete Set (60):		1000.00
Gold Cards:		4x-8x

1996 SkyBox SkyMotion Big Bang

These 1996 SkyBox SkyMotion inserts have 10 top rookies against a background of exploding fireworks. The cards, using lenticular printing, were seeded one per every nine packs.

		MT
Complete Set (10):		100.00
Common Player:		4.00
	Tim Biakabutuka	10.00
	Rickey Dudley	8.00
	Eddie George	25.00
	Terry Glenn	20.00
	Kevin Hardy	4.00
	Marvin Harrison	15.00
	Keyshawn Johnson	15.00
	Leeland McElroy	8.00
	Lawrence Phillips	15.00
	Simeon Rice	4.00

1996 SkyBox SkyMotion Team Galaxy

These 1996 SkyBox SkyMotion inserts showcase five of the NFL's top stars against a backdrop of planets and footballs. The cards, printed using lenticular printing, were seeded one per every 35 packs.

		MT
Complete Set (5):		150.00
Common Player:		20.00
1	Karim Abdul-Jabbar	20.00
2	Brett Favre	50.00
3	Curtis Martin	40.00
4	Jerry Rice	35.00
5	Emmitt Smith	50.00

1996 Topps Chrome

Chrome Football includes 165 of the best cards from Topps Football and adds its chromium finish. Among the cards in Chrome are Draft Picks, 1000 Yard Club and 3000 Yard Club subsets. Four-card packs included Tide Turners and 40th Anniversary inserts, as well as Refractor versions of the entire set and all inserts.

		MT
Complete Set (165):		80.00
Common Player:		.20
Wax Box:		70.00
1	Troy Aikman	2.50
2	Kevin Greene	.20
3	Robert Brooks	.20
4	Junior Seau	.20
5	Brett Perriman	.20
6	Cortez Kennedy	.20
7	Orlando Thomas	.20
8	Anthony Miller	.20
9	Jeff Blake	1.00
10	Trent Dilfer	.20
11	Heath Shuler	.20
12	Michael Jackson	.20
13	Merton Hanks	.20
14	Dale Carter	.20
15	Eric Metcalf	.20
16	Barry Sanders	2.50
17	Joey Galloway	1.75
18	Bryan Cox	.20
19	Harvey Williams	.20
20	Terrell Davis	3.00
21	Darnay Scott	.20
22	Kerry Collins	2.50
23	Warren Sapp	.20
24	Michael Westbrook	.50
25	Mark Brunell	1.50
26	Craig Heyward	.20
27	Eric Allen	.20
28	Dana Stubblefield	.20
29	Steve Bono	.20
30	Larry Brown	.20
31	Warren Moon	.20
32	Jim Kelly	.20
33	Terry McDaniel	.20
34	Dan Wilkinson	.20
35	Dave Brown	.20
36	Todd Lyght	.20
37	Aeneas Williams	.20
38	Shannon Sharpe	.20
39	Errict Rhett	.50
40	Yancey Thigpen	.40
41	J.J. Stokes	.50
42	Marshall Faulk	.75
43	Chester McGlockton	.20
44	Darryll Lewis	.20
45	Drew Bledsoe	2.50
46	Tyrone Wheatley	.20
47	Herman Moore	.50
48	Darren Woodson	.20
49	Ricky Watters	.20
50	Emmitt Smith	2.50
51	Barry Sanders	1.25
52	Curtis Martin	1.75
53	Chris Warren	.20
54	Errict Rhett	.20
55	Rodney Hampton	.20
56	Terrell Davis	1.25
57	Marshall Faulk	.20
58	Rashaan Salaam	.20
59	Curtis Conway	.20
60	Isaac Bruce	1.00
61	Thurman Thomas	.20
62	Terry Allen	.20
63	Lamar Lathon	.20
64	Mark Chmura	.20
65	Chris Warren	.20
66	Jessie Tuggle	.20
67	Erik Kramer	.20
68	Tim Brown	.20
69	Derrick Thomas	.20
70	Willie McGinest	.20
71	Frank Sanders	.20
72	Bernie Parmalee	.20
73	Kordell Stewart	3.00
74	Brent Jones	.20
75	Edgar Bennett	.20
76	Rashaan Salaam	1.00
77	Carl Pickens	.20
78	Terance Mathis	.20
79	Deion Sanders	2.00
80	Glyn Milburn	.20
81	Lee Woodall	.20
82	Neil Smith	.20
83	Stan Humphries	.20
84	Rick Mirer	.20
85	Troy Vincent	.20
86	Sam Mills	.20
87	Brian Mitchell	.20
88	Hardy Nickerson	.20
89	Tamarick Vanover	1.50
90	Steve McNair	3.00
91	Jerry Rice	1.25
92	Isaac Bruce	.40
93	Herman Moore	.20
94	Cris Carter	.20
95	Tim Brown	.20
96	Carl Pickens	.20
97	Joey Galloway	.75
98	Jerry Rice	2.50
99	Cris Carter	.20
100	Curtis Martin	3.50
101	Scott Mitchell	.20
102	Ken Harvey	.20
103	Rodney Hampton	.20
104	Reggie White	.40
105	Eddie Robinson	.20
106	Greg Lloyd	.20
107	Phillippi Sparks	.20
108	Emmitt Smith	5.00
109	Tom Carter	.20
110	Jim Everett	.20
111	James Stewart	.20
112	Kyle Brady	.20
113	Irving Fryar	.20
114	Vinny Testaverde	.20
115	John Elway	1.75
116	Chris Spielman	.20
117	Mike Mamula	.20
118	Jim Harbaugh	.20
119	Ken Norton	.20
120	Bruce Smith	.20
121	Daryl Johnston	.20
122	Blaine Bishop	.20
123	Jeff George	.20
124	Jeff Hostetler	.20
125	Jerome Bettis	.40
126	Jay Novacek	.20
127	Bryce Paup	.20
128	Neil O'Donnell	.20
129	Marcus Allen	.20
130	Steve Young	1.75
131	Brett Favre	2.25
132	Scott Mitchell	.20
133	John Elway	.75
134	Jeff Blake	.40
135	Dan Marino	2.50
136	Drew Bledsoe	1.25
137	Troy Aikman	1.25
138	Steve Young	.75
139	Jim Kelly	.20
140	Jeff Graham	.20
141	Hugh Douglas	.20
142	Dan Marino	5.00
143	Darrell Green	.20
144	Eric Zeier	.20
145	Brett Favre	5.00
146	Carnell Lake	.20
147	Ben Coates	.20
148	Tony Martin	.20
149	Michael Irvin	.20
150	*Lawrence Phillips*	1.00
151	*Alex Van Dyke*	.40
152	*Kevin Hardy*	.20
153	*Rickey Dudley*	.50
154	*Eric Moulds*	1.50
155	*Simeon Rice*	.40
156	*Marvin Harrison*	3.00
157	*Tim Biakabutuka*	1.75
158	*Duane Clemons*	.20
159	*Keyshawn Johnson*	3.00
160	*John Mobley*	.20
161	*Leeland McElroy*	.50
162	*Eddie George*	10.00
163	*Jonathan Ogden*	.20
164	*Eddie Kennison*	2.50
165	Checklist	.20

1996 Topps Chrome Refractors

Refractors paralleled the entire 165-card set in Chrome, and carried an insertion rate of one per 12 packs.

	MT
Complete Set (165):	1400.00
Refractors:	8x-16x

1996 Topps Chrome 40th Anniversary

Originally found in Topps, this 40-card insert was printed with a Chrome finish and inserted every eight packs. 40th Anniversary insert celebrated 40 years of Topps football with today's players in classic poses and original card designs from 1955 to 1995.

		MT
Complete Set (40):		125.00
Common Player:		2.00
1	Jim Harbaugh (1956)	2.00
2	Greg Lloyd (1957)	2.00
3	Barry Sanders (1958)	10.00
4	Merton Hanks (1959)	2.00
5	Herman Moore (1960)	2.00
6	Tim Brown (1961)	2.00
7	Brett Favre (1962)	20.00
8	Cris Carter (1963)	2.00
9	Curtis Martin (1964)	15.00
10	Bryce Paup (1965)	2.00
11	Steve Bono (1966)	2.00

12	Blaine Bishop (1967)	2.00
13	Emmitt Smith (1968)	20.00
14	Carnell Lake (1969)	2.00
15	Marshall Faulk (1970)	4.00
16	Bam Morris (1971)	2.00
17	Shannon Sharpe (1972)	2.00
18	Steve Young (1973)	8.00
19	Jeff George (1974)	2.00
20	Junior Seau (1975)	2.00
21	Chris Warren (1976)	2.00
22	Heath Shuler (1977)	2.00
23	Jeff Blake (1978)	5.00
24	Reggie White (1979)	2.00
25	Jeff Hostetler (1980)	2.00
26	Errict Rhett (1981)	2.00
27	Rodney Hampton (1982)	2.00
28	Jerry Rice (1983)	10.00
29	Jim Everett (1984)	2.00
30	Isaac Bruce (1985)	5.00
31	Dan Marino (1986)	20.00
32	Marcus Allen (1987)	2.00
33	Erik Kramer (1988)	2.00
34	John Elway (1989)	7.00
35	Ricky Watters (1990)	2.00
36	Troy Aikman (1991)	10.00
37	Drew Bledsoe (1992)	10.00
38	Scott Mitchell (1993)	2.00
39	Rashaan Salaam (1994)	4.00
40	Kerry Collins (1995)	10.00

1996 Topps Chrome 40th Anniversary Refractors

Each card in Chrome's 40th Anniversary insert was also printed in a Refractor version. Refractors of this insert are found every 24 packs.

	MT
Complete Set (40):	375.00
Refractors:	2x-3x

1996 Topps40 Chrome Tide Turners

Tide Turners was a 10-card insert that was exclusively produced for Chromo. It featured top playmakers in the NFL and was inserted every 12 packs.

		MT
Complete Set (15):		70.00
Common Player:		1.50
1	Rashaan Salaam	3.00
2	Warren Moon	1.50
3	Marshall Faulk	4.00
4	Jeff Blake	3.00
5	Curtis Martin	10.00
6	Eric Metcalf	1.50
7	Errict Rhett	3.00
8	Scott Mitchell	1.50
9	Ricky Watters	3.00
10	Jerry Rice	8.00
11	Emmitt Smith	15.00
12	Erik Kramer	1.50
13	Jim Harbaugh	1.50
14	Barry Sanders	8.00
15	John Elway	6.00

1996 Topps Chrome Tide Turners Refractors

This 10-card set is a parallel to the regular Tide Turners inserts. It includes Topps' popular Refractor finish and was inserted every 48 packs.

	MT
Complete Set (15):	280.00
Refractors:	4x-6x

1996 Finest II

Topps' 1996 Finest football has 350 cards, split into five different subsets - 113 Destroyers, 43 Future, 34 Freshman, 115 Playmakers and 52 Sterling cards. Cards are numbered within the regular issue set from 1-359, and also within the subset, using a D, F, P or S prefix. Within the regular issue set there are three types of cards. There are 220 common cards, 91 uncommon cards (one per every four packs) 47 rare cards (one per every 24 packs). Commons have a bronze border, uncommons have a silver border, and rares have a gold border. Refractors of every card were also made. Commons are seeded one per every 12 packs, uncommons are one per every 48, and rares are one every 288. Fewer than 150 Refractor sets were produced.

		MT
Comp. Bronze Ser.2 (110):		50.00
Common Bronze Player:		.25
Comp. Silver Ser.2 (36):		150.00
Common Silver Player:		2.00
Comp. Gold Ser.2 (22):		500.00
Common Gold Player:		15.00
Wax Box Series 2:		110.00
192	Gus Frerotte	.25
193	Michael Irvin G	20.00
194	Brett Maxie	.25
195	Harvey Williams S	2.00
196	Warren Moon G	20.00
197	Jeff George S	2.00
198	*Eddie Kennison*	4.00
199	Ricky Watters S	4.00
200	Steve Young G	35.00
201	Marcus Jones	.25
202	Terry Allen	.50
203	Leroy Hoard	.25
204	Steve Bono S	2.00
205	Reggie White	.50
206	Larry Centers	.25
207	*Alex Van Dyke G*	25.00
208	Vincent Brisby	.25
209	Michael Timpson	.25
210	Jeff Blake S	6.00
211	John Mobley	.25
212	Clay Matthews	.25
213	Shannon Sharpe	.25
214	Tony Bennett	.25
215	Phillippi Sparks S	2.00
216	Mickey Washington	.25
217	Fred Barnett	.25
218	Michael Haynes	.25
219	Stan Humphries	.25
220	Cris Carter G	15.00
221	Winston Moss	.25
222	*Tim Biakabutuka*	4.00
223	*Leeland McElroy*	3.00

		MT
224	Vinnie Clark	.25
225	*Keyshawn Johnson*	6.00
226	William Floyd S	4.00
227	Troy Drayton S	2.00
228	Tony Woods	.25
229	Rodney Hampton S	2.00
230	John Elway G	40.00
231	Anthony Pleasant	.25
232	Jeff George	.25
233	Curtis Conway	.50
234	Charles Haley G	15.00
235	Jeff Lewis	.25
236	Edgar Bennett	.25
237	Regan Upshaw	.25
238	William Fuller	.25
239	Duane Clemons S	2.00
240	Jim Kelly G	20.00
241	Willie Anderson	.25
242	Derrick Thomas	.25
243	*Marvin Harrison*	4.00
244	Darion Conner	.25
245	Antonio Langham	.25
246	Rodney Peete	.25
247	Tim McDonald	.25
248	Robert Jones	.25
249	Curtis Conway S	4.00
250	Rodney Hampton G	15.00
251	Mark Carrier	.25
252	Steve Grant	.25
253	John Mobley S	2.00
254	Jeff Hostetler	.25
255	Darrell Green	.25
256	Errict Rhett G	30.00
257	*Alex Molden G*	15.00
258	Chris Slade S	2.00
259	Derrick Thomas S	2.00
260	*Kevin Hardy G*	25.00
261	Eric Swann	.25
262	Eric Metcalf S	2.00
263	Irv Smith	.25
264	Tim McKyer	.25
265	Emmitt Smith S	30.00
266	Sean Jones	.25
267	Bryant Young G	15.00
268	Jeff Blake G	30.00
269	Jeff Hostetler S	2.00
270	*Keyshawn Johnson G*	40.00
271	Yancey Thigpen	1.00
272	Thurman Thomas S	4.00
273	Quentin Coryatt	.25
274	Hardy Nickerson	.25
275	Ricardo McDonald	.25
276	Steve Atwater S	2.00
277	Robert Blackmon	.25
278	Junior Seau G	20.00
279	Alonzo Spellman	.25
280	Isaac Bruce S	8.00
281	*Rickey Dudley*	2.00
282	Joe Cain	.25
283	Neil O'Donnell S	2.00
284	John Randle	.25
285	Terry Kirby G	15.00
286	Vinny Testaverde	.25
287	Jim Kelly S	4.00
288	*Lawrence Phillips S*	15.00
289	Henry Jones	.25
290	*Simeon Rice*	1.50
291	Terance Mathis S	2.00
292	Errict Rhett S	6.00
293	Hugh Douglas G	15.00
294	Santo Stephens S	2.00
295	Leslie O'Neal	.25
296	Reggie White G	20.00
297	Greg Hill	.25
298	Elvis Grbac G	15.00
299	*Walt Harris S*	4.00
300	Emmitt Smith G	90.00
301	Eric Metcalf	.25
302	Jamir Miller S	2.00
303	Jerome Woods S	.25
304	Ben Coates S	2.00
305	Marcus Allen S	4.00
306	Anthony Smith	.25
307	Darren Perry	.25
308	*Jonathan Ogden S*	6.00
309	Ricky Watters G	20.00
310	John Elway S	12.00
311	James Hasty	.25
312	Cris Carter	.50
313	Irving Fryar S	2.00
314	*Lawrence Phillips*	3.00
315	Junior Seau S	4.00
316	*Alex Molden S*	2.00
317	Aeneas Williams	.25
318	Eric Hill	.25
319	*Kevin Hardy*	1.50
320	Steve Young S	12.00
321	Chris Chandler	.25
322	Raghib Ismail	.25
323	Anthony Parker	.25
324	John Thierry	.25

		MT
325	Michael Barrow	.25
326	Henry Ford	.25
327	Aaron Hayden	.25
328	Terance Mathis	.25
329	Kirk Pointer	.25
330	*Ray Mickens*	.75
331	Jermaine Mayberry	.25
332	Mario Bates	.25
333	Carlton Gray	.25
334	Derek Loville	.25
335	*Mike Alstott*	2.00
336	Eric Guliford	.25
337	Marvcus Patton	.25
338	*Terrell Owens*	7.00
339	Lance Johnstone	.25
340	Lake Dawson	.25
341	Winslow Oliver	.25
342	Adrian Murrell	.25
343	Jason Belser	.25
344	Brian Dawkins	.25
345	Reggie Brown	.25
346	Shaun Gayle	.25
347	*Tony Brackens*	1.00
348	Thomas Lewis	.25
349	Kelvin Pritchett	.25
350	*Bobby Engram*	2.00
351	Moe Williams	.25
352	Thomas Smith	.25
353	Dexter Carter	.25
354	Qadry Ismail	.25
355	Marco Battaglia	.25
356	Levon Kirkland	.25
357	Eric Allen	.25
358	*Bobby Hoying*	1.00
359	Checklist	.25

1996 Finest II Refractors

Each card in Topps' 1996 Finest set has a Refractor card made for it, as labeled on the back. Commons are seeded one per every 12 packs, uncommons are one every 48, and rares are one every 288 packs. Fewer than 150 rare Refractor sets were produced.

		MT
Comp. Bronze Ser.2 (110):		600.00
Common Bronze Player:		3.00
Comp. Silver Ser.2 (36):		1000.00
Common Silver Player:		12.00
Comp. Gold Ser.2 (22):		2000.00
Common Gold Player:		25.00
192	Gus Frerotte	3.00
193	Michael Irvin G	50.00
194	Brett Maxie	3.00
195	Harvey Williams S	12.00
196	Warren Moon G	50.00
197	Jeff George S	12.00
198	Eddie Kennison	25.00
199	Ricky Watters S	24.00
200	Steve Young G	200.00
201	Marcus Jones	3.00
202	Terry Allen	6.00
203	Leroy Hoard	3.00
204	Steve Bono S	12.00
205	Reggie White	6.00
206	Larry Centers	3.00
207	Alex Van Dyke G	75.00
208	Vincent Brisby	3.00
209	Michael Timpson	3.00
210	Jeff Blake S	50.00
211	John Mobley	3.00
212	Clay Matthews	3.00
213	Shannon Sharpe	3.00
214	Tony Bennett	3.00
215	Phillippi Sparks S	12.00
216	Mickey Washington	3.00
217	Fred Barnett	3.00
218	Michael Haynes	3.00
219	Stan Humphries	3.00
220	Cris Carter G	25.00
221	Winston Moss	3.00
222	Tim Biakabutuka	20.00
223	Leeland McElroy	20.00
224	Vinnie Clark	3.00
225	Keyshawn Johnson	40.00
226	William Floyd S	24.00
227	Troy Drayton S	12.00
228	Tony Woods	3.00
229	Rodney Hampton S	12.00
230	John Elway G	200.00
231	Anthony Pleasant	3.00
232	Jeff George	3.00
233	Curtis Conway	6.00
234	Charles Haley G	25.00
235	Jeff Lewis	3.00
236	Edgar Bennett	3.00

237	Regan Upshaw	3.00
238	William Fuller	3.00
239	Duane Clemons S	12.00
240	Jim Kelly G	80.00
241	Willie Anderson	3.00
242	Derrick Thomas	3.00
243	Marvin Harrison	30.00
244	Darion Conner	3.00
245	Antonio Langham	3.00
246	Rodney Peete	3.00
247	Tim McDonald	3.00
248	Robert Jones	3.00
249	Curtis Conway S	24.00
250	Rodney Hampton G	25.00
251	Mark Carrier	3.00
252	Steve Grant	3.00
253	John Mobley S	12.00
254	Jeff Hostetler	3.00
255	Darrell Green	3.00
256	Errict Rhett G	75.00
257	Alex Molden G	25.00
258	Chris Slade S	12.00
259	Derrick Thomas S	12.00
260	Kevin Hardy G	75.00
261	Eric Swann	3.00
262	Eric Metcalf S	12.00
263	Irv Smith	3.00
264	Tim McKyer	3.00
265	Emmitt Smith S	200.00
266	Sean Jones	3.00
267	Bryant Young G	25.00
268	Jeff Blake G	75.00
269	Jeff Hostetler S	12.00
270	Keyshawn Johnson G	150.00
271	Yancey Thigpen	12.00
272	Thurman Thomas S	24.00
273	Quentin Coryatt	3.00
274	Hardy Nickerson	3.00
275	Ricardo McDonald	3.00
276	Steve Atwater S	12.00
277	Robert Blackmon	3.00
278	Junior Seau G	50.00
279	Alonzo Spellman	3.00
280	Isaac Bruce S	50.00
281	Rickey Dudley	15.00
282	Joe Cain	3.00
283	Neil O'Donnell S	12.00
284	John Randle	3.00
285	Terry Kirby G	25.00
286	Vinny Testaverde	3.00
287	Jim Kelly S	24.00
288	Lawrence Phillips S	70.00
289	Henry Jones	3.00
290	Simeon Rice	3.00
291	Terance Mathis S	12.00
292	Errict Rhett S	60.00
293	Hugh Douglas G	25.00
294	Santo Stephens S	12.00
295	Leslie O'Neal	3.00
296	Reggie White G	80.00
297	Greg Hill	3.00
298	Elvis Grbac G	60.00
299	Walt Harris S	24.00
300	Emmitt Smith G	600.00
301	Eric Metcalf	3.00
302	Jamir Miller S	12.00
303	Jerome Woods	3.00
304	Ben Coates S	12.00
305	Marcus Allen S	24.00
306	Anthony Smith	3.00
307	Darren Perry	3.00
308	Jonathan Ogden S	35.00
309	Ricky Watters G	50.00
310	John Elway S	85.00
311	James Hasty	3.00
312	Cris Carter	6.00
313	Irving Fryar S	12.00
314	Lawrence Phillips	35.00
315	Junior Seau S	24.00
316	Alex Molden S	12.00
317	Aeneas Williams	3.00
318	Eric Hill	3.00
319	Kevin Hardy	12.00
320	Steve Young S	85.00
321	Chris Chandler	3.00
322	Raghib Ismail	3.00
323	Anthony Parker	3.00
324	John Thierry	3.00
325	Michael Barrow	3.00
326	Henry Ford	3.00
327	Aaron Hayden	3.00
328	Terance Mathis	3.00
329	Kirk Pointer	3.00
330	Ray Mickens	7.50
331	Jermaine Mayberry	3.00
332	Mario Bates	3.00
333	Carlton Gray	3.00
334	Derek Loville	3.00
335	Mike Alstott	20.00
336	Eric Guliford	3.00
337	Marvcus Patton	3.00
338	Terrell Owens	35.00
339	Lance Johnstone	3.00
340	Lake Dawson	3.00
341	Winslow Oliver	3.00
342	Adrian Murrell	3.00
343	Jason Belser	3.00
344	Brian Dawkins	3.00
345	Reggie Brown	3.00
346	Shaun Gayle	3.00
347	Tony Brackens	3.00
348	Thomas Lewis	3.00
349	Kelvin Pritchett	3.00
350	Bobby Engram	20.00
351	Moe Williams	3.00
352	Thomas Smith	3.00
353	Dexter Carter	3.00
354	Qadry Ismail	3.00
355	Marco Battaglia	3.00
356	Levon Kirkland	3.00
357	Eric Allen	3.00
358	Bobby Hoying	3.00
359	Checklist	3.00

1996 Topps Laser

After its debut in baseball, Topps Laser Football arrived in four-card packs with 128 cards in the regular-issue set. Laser featured surgically precise cutting across the entire card surface, with silver stamped AFC cards and gold stamped NFC cards. Laser was released in a single series and included three insert sets, called Bright Spots, 1996 Draft Picks and Stadium Stars.

		MT
Complete Set (128):		70.00
Common Player:		.25
Wax Box:		100.00
1	Marshall Faulk	.50
2	Alonzo Spellman	.25
3	Frank Sanders	.25
4	Anthony Pleasant	.25
5	Scott Mitchell	.25
6	Robert Brooks	.50
7	Robert Jones	.25
8	Phillippi Sparks	.25
9	Rodney Peete	.25
10	Kordell Stewart	3.00
11	Ken Norton	.25
12	Brian Mitchell	.25
13	Ben Coates	.25
14	Quinn Early	.25
15	Emmitt Smith	6.00
16	Steve Bono	.25
17	Anthony Miller	.25
18	Mel Gray	.25
19	Neil O'Donnell	.25
20	Tim Brown	.50
21	Terrell Fletcher	.25
22	John Randle	.25
23	Fred Barnett	.25
24	Craig Heyward	.25
25	Ki-Jana Carter	.50
26	Eric Allen	.25
27	Warren Sapp	.25
28	Terry Wooden	.25
29	Darion Conner	.25
30	Mark Brunell	2.00
31	Vinny Testaverde	.25
32	Chris Calloway	.25
33	Steve Walsh	.25
34	Ken Dilger	.25
35	Bryan Cox	.25
36	Rob Moore	.25
37	Henry Thomas	.25
38	Henry Ellard	.25
39	Mark Chmura	.25
40	Jerry Rice	3.00
41	Michael Irvin	.50
42	Willie McGinest	.25
43	Steve McNair	3.00
44	Tamarick Vanover	2.00
45	Cris Carter	.25
46	Levon Kirkland	.25
47	Terry McDaniel	.25
48	Jessie Tuggle	.25
49	O.J. McDuffie	.25
50	Bruce Smith	.25
51	Tyrone Hughes	.25
52	Tony Martin	.25
53	Hardy Nickerson	.25
54	Garrison Hearst	.25
55	Sam Mills	.25
56	Mark Carrier	.25
57	Quentin Coryatt	.25
58	Neil Smith	.25
59	Michael Westbrook	2.00
60	Greg Lloyd	.25
61	Jeff Hostetler	.25
62	Wayne Chrebet	.25
63	Herschel Walker	.25
64	Pepper Johnson	.25
65	John Elway	3.00
66	Reggie White	.50
67	James Stewart	.25
68	Bernie Parmalee	.25
69	Robert Smith	.25
70	Drew Bledsoe	3.00
71	Marvcus Patton	.25
72	Stan Humphries	.25
73	Darnay Scott	.50
74	Jim Kelly	.50
75	Terance Mathis	.25
76	Erik Kramer	.25
77	Marcus Allen	.50
78	Ernie Mills	.25
79	Harvey Williams	.25
80	Brett Favre	6.00
81	Seth Joyner	.25
82	Tyrone Poole	.25
83	Troy Aikman	3.00
84	Warren Moon	.50
85	Isaac Bruce	1.00
86	Errict Rhett	.50
87	Rick Mirer	.25
88	Anthony Smith	.25
89	Bert Emanuel	.25
90	Junior Seau	.50
91	Terry Allen	.25
92	Brent Jones	.25
93	Adrian Murrell	.25
94	Dave Brown	.25
95	Bryce Paup	.25
96	Jim Everett	.25
97	Brian Washington	.25
98	Jim Harbaugh	.25
99	Shannon Sharpe	.25
100	Dan Marino	6.00
101	Curtis Martin	4.00
102	Ricky Watters	.50
103	Yancey Thigpen	.50
104	Trent Dilfer	.50
105	Joey Galloway	3.00
106	Edgar Bennett	.25
107	Willie Jackson	.25
108	Mark Collins	.25
109	Rashaan Salaam	.50
110	Eric Metcalf	.25
111	Terrell Davis	4.00
112	Darryll Lewis	.25
113	Ken Harvey	.25
114	Rob Fredrickson	.25
115	Rodney Hampton	.25
116	Chris Slade	.25
117	Jeff George	.25
118	Lamar Lathon	.25
119	Curtis Conway	.25
120	Barry Sanders	3.00
121	Eric Zeier	.25
122	Jeff Blake	2.00
123	Derrick Thomas	.25
124	Tyrone Wheatley	.25
125	Steve Young	3.00
126	Napoleon Kaufman	.25
127	David Meggett	.25
128	Kerry Collins	3.00

1996 Topps Laser Bright Spots

Bright Spots included 16 top young players on full-bleed, double-diffraction foil-stamped cards. Bright Spots were seeded every 24 packs of Laser.

		MT
Complete Set (16):		175.00
Common Player:		6.00
1	Curtis Martin	30.00
2	Tom Carter	6.00
3	Dave Brown	6.00
4	Wayne Chrebet	6.00
5	Rashaan Salaam	10.00
6	Mark Brunell	15.00
7	Elvis Grbac	6.00
8	Errict Rhett	6.00
9	Isaac Bruce	10.00
10	Kerry Collins	25.00
11	Mario Bates	6.00
12	Joey Galloway	20.00
13	Napoleon Kaufman	6.00
14	Tamarick Vanover	6.00
15	Marshall Faulk	8.00
16	Terrell Davis	30.00

1996 Topps Laser Draft Picks

Sixteen different 1996 draft picks can be found in this insert. Draft Picks inserts are laser cut with double-diffraction foil and inserted every 12 packs.

		MT
Complete Set (16):		90.00
Common Player:		5.00
1	Keyshawn Johnson	16.00
2	Lawrence Phillips	10.00
3	Bobby Hoying	5.00
4	Marco Battaglia	5.00
5	Kevin Hardy	5.00
6	Jerome Woods	5.00
7	Ray Mickens	5.00
8	John Mobley	5.00
9	Marvin Harrison	15.00
10	Walt Harris	5.00
11	Duane Clemons	5.00
12	Regan Upshaw	5.00
13	Brian Dawkins	5.00
14	Bobby Engram	10.00
15	Eddie Kennison	15.00
16	Jeff Lewis	5.00

1996 Topps Laser Stadium Stars

Stadium Stars included 16 of the top players in the NFL on cards that have a laser-sculpted cover that reveals a full-bleed card of the player underneath. These book-like inserts are seeded every 48 packs.

		MT
Complete Set (16):		350.00
Common Player:		10.00
1	Barry Sanders	50.00
2	Jim Harbaugh	10.00
3	Tim Brown	10.00
4	Jim Everett	10.00
5	Brett Favre	80.00
6	Junior Seau	10.00
7	Greg Lloyd	10.00
8	Cris Carter	10.00
9	Emmitt Smith	80.00
10	Dan Marino	80.00
11	Jeff Blake	20.00
12	Darrell Green	10.00
13	John Elway	30.00
14	Marcus Allen	10.00
15	Steve Young	35.00
16	Drew Bledsoe	50.00

1996 Stadium Club II

Topps' 1996 Stadium Club football has 180 cards in its initial series. Insert sets include Contact Prints, Dot Matrix Parallel, Pro Bowl Embossed, Laser Sites, Cut Backs, and three versions of Extreme Player cards (bronze, silver and gold). Series II also has 180 cards in it, featuring 45 of the league's top rookies and traded players in their new uniforms. All regular cards in both series have etched gold foil and are UV coated. Series II inserts include Photo Gallery, New Age, TSC Matrix Parallel, NFL Playoff Box, Fusion Laser Cut (hobby exclusive) and Brace Yourself (retail only). Interactive game cards (Sunday Night Box, in Series I, and NFL Playoff Box, in Series II) were seeded in packs (one in 12 and 1 in 24 packs, respectively). Those who find the cards were eligible to win prizes based on the final scores of selected games.

		MT
Complete Series 2 (180):		40.00
Common Player:		.10
Wax Box Series 2:		50.00
181	Joey Galloway	1.00
182	Dwayne Harper	.10
183	Antonio Langham	.10
184	Chris Zorich	.10
185	Willie McGinest	.10
186	Wayne Chrebet	.10
187	Dermontti Dawson	.10
188	Charlie Garner	.10
189	Quentin Coryatt	.10
190	Rodney Hampton	.10
191	Kelvin Pritchett	.10
192	Willie Green	.10
193	Garrison Hearst	.10
194	Tracy Scroggins	.10
195	Raghib Ismail	.10
196	Michael Westbrook	.30
197	Troy Drayton	.10
198	Rob Fredrickson	.10
199	Sean Lumpkin	.10
200	John Elway	.75
201	Bernie Parmalee	.10
202	Chris Chandler	.10
203	Lake Dawson	.10
204	Orlando Thomas	.10
205	Carl Pickens	.20
206	Kurt Schulz	.10
207	Clay Matthews	.10
208	Winston Moss	.10
209	Sean Dawkins	.10
210	Emmitt Smith	2.50
211	Mark Carrier	.10
212	Clyde Simmons	.10
213	Derrick Brooks	.10
214	William Floyd	.20
215	Aaron Hayden	.10
216	Brian DeMarco	.10
217	Ben Coates	.10
218	Renaldo Turnbull	.10
219	Adrian Murrell	.10
220	Marcus Allen	.20
221	Brett Maxie	.10
222	Trev Alberts	.10
223	Darren Woodson	.10
224	Brian Mitchell	.10
225	Michael Haynes	.10
226	Sean Jones	.10
227	Eric Zeier	.10
228	Herman Moore	.30
229	Shane Conlan	.10
230	Chris Warren	.20
231	Dana Stubblefield	.10
232	Andre Coleman	.10
233	Kordell Stewart	1.25
234	Ray Crockett	.10
235	Craig Heyward	.10
236	Mike Fox	.10
237	Derek Brown	.10
238	Thomas Lewis	.10
239	Hugh Douglas	.10
240	Tom Carter	.10
241	Toby Wright	.10
242	Jason Belser	.10
243	Rodney Peete	.10
244	Napoleon Kaufman	.10
245	Merton Hanks	.10
246	Harry Colon	.10
247	Greg Hill	.10
248	Vincent Brisby	.10
249	Eric Hill	.10
250	Brett Favre	2.50
251	Leroy Hoard	.10
252	Eric Guliford	.10
253	Stanley Richard	.10
254	Carlos Jenkins	.10
255	D'Marco Farr	.10
256	Carlton Gray	.10
257	Derek Loville	.10
258	Ray Buchanan	.10
259	Jake Reed	.10
260	Dan Marino	2.50
261	Brad Baxter	.10
262	Pat Swilling	.10
263	Andy Harmon	.10
264	Harold Green	.10
265	Shannon Sharpe	.10
266	Erik Kramer	.10
267	Lamar Lathon	.10
268	Stevon Moore	.10
269	Tony Martin	.10
270	Bruce Smith	.10
271	James Washington	.10
272	Tyrone Poole	.10
273	Eric Swann	.10
274	Dexter Carter	.10
275	Greg Lloyd	.10
276	Michael Zordich	.10
277	Steve Wisniewski	.10
278	Chris Calloway	.10
279	Irv Smith	.10
280	Steve Young	1.00
281	James Stewart	.10
282	Blaine Bishop	.10
283	Rob Moore	.10
284	Eric Metcalf	.10
285	Kerry Collins	1.50
286	Dan Wilkinson	.10
287	Curtis Conway	.10
288	Jay Novacek	.10
289	Henry Ellard	.10
290	Curtis Martin	2.00
291	Brett Perriman	.10
292	Jeff Lageman	.10
293	Trent Dilfer	.10
294	Cortez Kennedy	.10
295	Jeff Hostetler	.10
296	Mark Fields	.10
297	Qadry Ismail	.10
298	Steve Bono	.10
299	Tony Tolbert	.10
300	Jerry Rice	1.25
301	Marvcus Patton	.10
302	Robert Brooks	.20
303	Terry Ray	.10
304	John Thierry	.10
305	Errict Rhett	.30
306	Ricardo McDonald	.10
307	Antonio London	.10
308	Lonnie Johnson	.10
309	Mark Collins	.10
310	Marshall Faulk	.50
311	Anthony Pleasant	.10
312	Howard Griffith	.10
313	Roosevelt Potts	.10
314	Jim Flanigan	.10
315	'Omar Ellison	.10
316	Boomer Esiason	.10
317	Leslie O'Neal	.10
318	Jerome Bettis	.20
319	Larry Brown	.10
320	Neil O'Donnell	.10
321	Andre Rison	.10
322	Cornelius Bennett	.10
323	Quinn Early	.10
324	Bryan Cox	.10
325	Irving Fryar	.10
326	Eddie Robinson	.10
327	Chris Doleman	.10
328	Sean Gilbert	.10
329	Steve Walsh	.10
330	Kevin Greene	.10
331	Chris Spielman	.10
332	Jeff Graham	.10
333	*Anthony Dorsett Jr.*	.10
334	*Amani Toomer*	.50
335	*Walt Harris*	.20
336	*Ray Mickens*	.10
337	*Danny Kanell*	.50
338	*Daryl Gardener*	.10
339	*Jonathan Ogden*	.10
340	*Eddie George*	5.00
341	*Jeff Lewis*	.10
342	*Terrell Owens*	3.00
343	*Brian Dawkins*	.10
344	Tim Biakabutuka	.75
345	Marvin Harrison	1.00
346	*Lawyer Milloy*	.10
347	Eric Moulds	.20
348	Alex Van Dyke	.20
349	*John Mobley*	.10
350	*Kevin Hardy*	.10
351	*Ray Lewis*	.10
352	Lawrence Phillips	.30
353	*Stepfret Williams*	.10
354	*Bobby Engram*	1.00
355	*Leeland McElroy*	.30
356	*Marco Battaglia*	.10
357	Rickey Dudley	.20
358	*Bobby Hoying*	.20
359	*Cedric Jones*	.10
360	Keyshawn Johnson	1.00

1996 Stadium Club II Dot Matrix

Ninety of the cards from Topps' 1996 Stadium Club set have been duplicated for a parallel insert set. Forty-five cards from Series I have been selected, using dot matrix foil for the design. There were also 45 Series II cards chosen; these cards also have holographic foil in the design. Cards were seeded one per every 12 packs in the corresponding series. The TSC logo is on the card front.

		MT
Common Player:		1.00
181	Joey Galloway	10.00
182	Chris Zorich	1.00
185	Willie McGinest	1.00
186	Wayne Chrebet	1.00
190	Rodney Hampton	1.00
196	Michael Westbrook	5.00
200	John Elway	10.00
204	Orlando Thomas	1.00
205	Carl Pickens	2.00
210	Emmitt Smith	25.00
213	Derrick Brooks	1.00
217	Ben Coates	1.00
220	Marcus Allen	2.00
224	Brian Mitchell	1.00
227	Eric Zeier	1.00
228	Herman Moore	4.00
230	Chris Warren	2.00
233	Kordell Stewart	12.00
235	Craig Heyward	1.00
239	Hugh Douglas	1.00
240	Tom Carter	1.00
243	Rodney Peete	1.00
244	Napoleon Kaufman	1.00
250	Brett Favre	25.00
260	Dan Marino	25.00
265	Shannon Sharpe	1.00
266	Erik Kramer	1.00
267	Lamar Lathon	1.00
270	Bruce Smith	1.00
275	Greg Lloyd	1.00
280	Steve Young	10.00
282	Blaine Bishop	1.00
284	Eric Metcalf	1.00
285	Kerry Collins	15.00
286	Dan Wilkinson	1.00
287	Curtis Conway	1.00
288	Jay Novacek	1.00
290	Curtis Martin	20.00
293	Trent Dilfer	1.00
295	Jeff Hostetler	1.00
298	Steve Bono	1.00
300	Jerry Rice	12.00
302	Robert Brooks	2.00
305	Errict Rhett	3.00
310	Marshall Faulk	5.00

1996 Stadium Club II Match Proofs

Match Proofs are a parallel set that runs through all 270 cards from Series I and II. This parallel set features identical fronts, but has different backs than regular-issue cards. Production of Match Proofs was limited to only 100 sets.

	MT
Match Proof Cards:	100x

1996 Stadium Club II Brace Yourself

These cards are Stadium Club's retail-only inserts in Series II. Each card features a gridiron great on an embossed, holographic foil card. The front has a photo in the middle, with a bull's-eye as the background. The TSC logo is in the upper right corner; the player's name is in the lower left corner. "Brace Yourself" is written along the right side. The card back repeats the bull's-eye pattern as the background, with the player's name, team name, position and card number (using a "BY" prefix) toward the top. The middle of the card comments about the player's talents. Cards were seeded one per every 24 packs.

		MT
Complete Set (10):		125.00
Common Player:		3.00
1	Dan Marino	30.00
2	Marshall Faulk	10.00
3	Greg Lloyd	3.00
4	Steve Young	20.00
5	Emmitt Smith	30.00
6	Junior Seau	3.00
7	Chris Warren	3.00
8	Jerry Rice	20.00
9	Troy Aikman	20.00
10	Barry Sanders	20.00

1996 Stadium Club II Fusion

These cards were found exclusively in 1996 Topps Stadium Club Series II packs, one per every 24 packs. Cards, which are laser cut along one side, are intended to be "fused" together to match up a pair of teammates, forming a larger image. Eight different dynamic duos are spotlighted in this set.

		MT
Complete Set (16):		135.00
Common Player:		4.00
1A	Steve Young	16.00
1B	Jerry Rice	20.00
2A	Drew Bledsoe	20.00
2B	Curtis Martin	25.00
3A	Trent Dilfer	4.00
3B	Errict Rhett	8.00
4A	Jeff Hostetler	4.00
4B	Tim Brown	4.00
5A	Brett Favre	30.00
5B	Robert Brooks	4.00
6A	Jim Harbaugh	4.00
6B	Marshall Faulk	10.00
7A	Erik Kramer	4.00
7B	Rashaan Salaam	8.00
8A	Scott Mitchell	4.00
8B	Barry Sanders	20.00

1996 Stadium Club II New Age

These cards were seeded one per every 24 packs of 1996 Topps Stadium Club Series II product. Twenty 1996 NFL draft picks and first-year rookies are spotlighted on the cards, which use etched dot matrix technology for the front. The front also has a color photo in the middle, with a frame around it. A team logo is in the upper left corner of the frame. A TSC logo is at the top of the card; the player's name is along the bottom. The card back has a rectangle in the middle which has the player's name, team name and position toward the top, just below a card number (which uses an "NA" prefix). Inside the rectangle is a recap of the player's collegiate accomplishments. "New Age" is at the top of the card.

		MT
Complete Set (20):		100.00
Common Player:		3.00
1	Alex Van Dyke	5.00
2	Lawrence Phillips	10.00
3	Tim Biakabutuka	10.00
4	Reggie Brown	3.00
5	Duane Clemons	3.00
6	Marco Battaglia	3.00
7	Cedric Jones	3.00
8	Jerome Woods	3.00
9	Eric Moulds	10.00
10	Kevin Hardy	3.00
11	Rickey Dudley	5.00
12	Regan Upshaw	3.00
13	Eddie Kennison	15.00
14	Jonathan Ogden	3.00
15	John Mobley	3.00
16	Mike Alstott	10.00
17	Alex Molden	3.00
18	Marvin Harrison	15.00
19	Simeon Rice	3.00
20	Keyshawn Johnson	15.00

1996 Stadium Club II Photo Gallery

These cards were seeded one per every 18 packs of 1996 Topps Stadium Club Series II product. Each card features a customized design that compliments the outstanding photography, and is printed on smooth cast-coated stock with an exclusive Topps high gloss laminate. The Photo Gallery logo, player's name, opponent, and game date from when the picture was taken are stamped in red, blue or silver foil on the front. The card back has the player's team name and position listed at the top, with the player's name below. The date of the game is under his name, with a recap of the game below, on one side. A color photo is on the other side. The card number, using a "PG" prefix, is in the lower left corner.

		MT
Complete Set (21):		150.00
Common Player:		2.00
1	Emmitt Smith	25.00
2	Jeff Blake	5.00
3	Junior Seau	2.00
4	Robert Brooks	2.00
5	Barry Sanders	13.00
6	Drew Bledsoe	13.00
7	Joey Galloway	10.00
8	Marshall Faulk	8.00
9	Mark Brunell	10.00
10	Jerry Rice	13.00
11	Rashaan Salaam	6.00
12	Troy Aikman	13.00
13	Steve Young	10.00
14	Tim Brown	2.00
15	Brett Favre	25.00
16	Kerry Collins	13.00
17	John Elway	10.00
18	Curtis Martin	18.00
19	Deion Sanders	10.00
20	Dan Marino	25.00
21	Chris Warren	2.00

1996 SP

The 188-card, regular-sized set was issued in eight-card packs and included the subset, Premiere Prospects. The release included a five-card SPx Force preview along with an autographed parallel version. Other inserts were: Focus On The Future, Explosive, Holoview and F/X Holoview. The base set cards include an action shot with a player headshot inset along the right border. The player's name appears on the top border with team nickname and position along the bottom.

		MT
Complete Set (188):		60.00
Common Player:		.20
Wax Box:		125.00
1	*Keyshawn Johnson*	4.00
2	*Kevin Hardy*	.75
3	*Simeon Rice*	.75
4	*Jonathan Ogden*	.20
5	*Eddie George*	12.00
6	*Terry Glenn*	8.00
7	*Terrell Owens*	5.00
8	*Tim Biakabutuka*	2.00
9	*Lawrence Phillips*	2.00
10	*Alex Molden*	.20
11	*Regan Upshaw*	.20
12	*Rickey Dudley*	1.50
13	*Duane Clemons*	.20
14	*John Mobley*	.20
15	*Eddie Kennison*	3.00
16	*Karim Abdul-Jabbar*	6.00
17	*Eric Moulds*	2.00
18	*Marvin Harrison*	4.00
19	*Stepfret Williams*	.20
20	*Stephen Davis*	.20
21	Deion Sanders	1.50
22	Emmitt Smith	5.00
23	Troy Aikman	2.50
24	Michael Irvin	.40
25	Herschel Walker	.20
26	Kavika Pittman	.20
27	Andre Hastings	.20
28	Jerome Bettis	.40
29	Mike Tomczak	.20
30	Kordell Stewart	2.00
31	Charles Johnson	.20
32	Greg Lloyd	.20
33	Brett Favre	5.00
34	Mark Chmura	.20
35	Edgar Bennett	.20
36	Robert Brooks	.20
37	Craig Newsome	.20
38	Reggie White	.40
39	Marshall Faulk	1.50
40	Jim Harbaugh	.20
41	Sean Dawkins	.20
42	Quentin Coryatt	.20
43	Ray Buchanan	.20
44	Ken Dilger	.20
45	Jerry Rice	2.50
46	J.J. Stokes	.40
47	Steve Young	2.00
48	Derek Loville	.20
49	Terry Kirby	.20
50	Ken Norton	.20
51	Tamarick Vanover	1.00
52	Steve Bono	.20
53	Marcus Allen	.40
54	Neil Smith	.20
55	Derrick Thomas	.20
56	Dale Carter	.20
57	Terance Mathis	.20
58	Eric Metcalf	.20
59	*Jamal Anderson*	2.00
60	Bert Emanuel	.20
61	Craig Heyward	.20
62	Cornelius Bennett	.20
63	Tony Martin	.20
64	Stan Humphries	.20
65	Andre Coleman	.20
66	Junior Seau	.20
67	Terrell Fletcher	.20
68	John Carney	.20
69	Charlie Jones	.20
70	Ricky Watters	.40
71	Charlie Garner	.20
72	*Bobby Hoying*	.75
73	Jason Dunn	.20
74	Bobby Taylor	.20
75	Irving Fryar	.20
76	Jim Kelly	.20
77	Thurman Thomas	.40
78	Darick Holmes	.20
79	Bryce Paup	.20
80	Bruce Smith	.20
81	Andre Reed	.20
82	Glyn Milburn	.20
83	Brett Perriman	.20
84	Herman Moore	.75
85	Scott Mitchell	.20
86	Barry Sanders	2.50
87	Johnnie Morton	.20
88	Dan Marino	5.00
89	O.J. McDuffie	.20
90	Stanley Pritchett	.20
91	*Zach Thomas*	2.50
92	Daryl Gardner	.20
93	Rashaan Salaam	.75
94	Erik Kramer	.20
95	Curtis Conway	.20
96	*Bobby Engram*	2.00
97	Walt Harris	.20
98	Bryan Cox	.20
99	John Elway	2.00
100	Terrell Davis	2.50
101	Anthony Miller	.20
102	Shannon Sharpe	.20
103	Steve Atwater	.20
104	Jeff Lewis	.20
105	Joey Galloway	1.50
106	Chris Warren	.20
107	Rick Mirer	.20
108	Cortez Kennedy	.20
109	Michael Sinclair	.20
110	John Friesz	.20
111	Warren Moon	.20
112	Cris Carter	.20
113	Jake Reed	.20
114	Robert Smith	.20
115	John Randle	.20
116	Orlanda Thomas	.20
117	Jeff Hostetler	.20
118	Tim Brown	.20
119	Joe Aska	.20
120	Napoleon Kaufman	.20
121	Terry McDaniel	.20
122	Harvey Williams	.20
123	Trent Dilfer	.20
124	Reggie Brooks	.20
125	Alvin Harper	.20
126	*Mike Alstott*	2.50
127	Hardy Nickerson	.20
128	Mario Bates	.20
129	Jim Everett	.20
130	Tyrone Hughes	.20
131	Michael Haynes	.20
132	Eric Allen	.20
133	Isaac Bruce	1.50
134	Kevin Carter	.20
135	Leslie O'Neal	.20
136	*Tony Banks*	4.00
137	Chris Chandler	.20
138	Steve McNair	2.00
139	Chris Sanders	.20
140	Ronnie Harmon	.20
141	Willie Davis	.20
142	Michael Westbrook	.40
143	Terry Allen	.20
144	Brian Mitchell	.20
145	Henry Ellard	.20
146	Gus Frerotte	.20
147	Kerry Collins	2.50
148	Sam Mills	.20
149	Wesley Walls	.20
150	Kevin Greene	.20
151	*Mushin Muhammad*	1.50
152	Winslow Oliver	.20
153	Jeff Blake	.50
154	Carl Pickens	.20
155	Darnay Scott	.20
156	Garrison Hearst	.20
157	Marco Battaglia	.20
158	Drew Bledsoe	2.00
159	Curtis Martin	4.00
160	Shawn Jefferson	.20

		MT
161	Ben Coates	.20
162	Lawyer Milloy	.20
163	Tyrone Wheatley	.20
164	Rodney Hampton	.20
165	Chris Calloway	.20
166	Dave Brown	.20
167	*Amani Toomer*	.40
168	Vinny Testaverde	.20
169	Michael Jackson	.20
170	Eric Turner	.20
171	DeRon Jenkins	.20
172	Jermaine Lewis	.20
173	Frank Sanders	.20
174	Rob Moore	.20
175	Kent Graham	.50
176	*Leeland McElroy*	1.50
177	Larry Centers	.20
178	Eric Swann	.20
179	Mark Brunell	1.50
180	Willie Jackson	.20
181	James O. Stewart	.20
182	Natrone Means	.20
183	*Tony Brackens*	.75
184	Adrian Murrell	.20
185	Neil O'Donnell	.20
186	Hugh Douglas	.20
187	Jeff Graham	.20
188	*Alex Van Dyke*	.40

1996 SP Explosive

The 20-card, regular-sized, die-cut set was inserted every 360 packs of 1996 Upper Deck SP football. The die-cut cards are in the shape of an "X" and feature a circular headshot of the player over a black and white background. The player's first name appears in the lower left corner in lowercase letters with the last name in the right corner, also in lowercase. The cards backs are numbered with the "X" prefix.

		MT
Complete Set (20):		1700.00
Common Player:		25.00
X1	Emmitt Smith	250.00
X2	Jerry Rice	125.00
X3	Rashaan Salaam	25.00
X4	Brett Favre	250.00
X5	Tim Brown	25.00
X6	Tim Biakabutuka	75.00
X7	John Elway	100.00
X8	Steve Young	100.00
X9	Napoleon Kaufman	25.00
X10	Troy Aikman	125.00
X11	Drew Bledsoe	125.00
X12	Carl Pickens	25.00
X13	Dan Marino	250.00
X14	Eddie George	150.00
X15	Joey Galloway	75.00
X16	Deion Sanders	75.00
X17	Curtis Martin	150.00
X18	Marshall Faulk	60.00
X19	Keyshawn Johnson	75.00
X20	Barry Sanders	125.00

1996 SP Focus on the Future

The 30-card, regular-sized, die-cut set was inserted every 30 packs of SP football. The card fronts feature a color player shot over a gold background with a slide film-type addition on the right side. The cel contains a color headshot of the player with the photographer listed along the right border. The card backs are numbered with the "F" prefix.

		MT
Complete Set (30):		300.00
Common Player:		6.00
F1	Leeland McElroy	6.00
F2	Frank Sanders	6.00
F3	Darick Holmes	6.00
F4	Eric Moulds	10.00
F5	Kerry Collins	35.00
F6	Tim Biakabutuka	15.00
F7	Ki-Jana Carter	6.00
F8	Jeff Blake	10.00
F9	John Mobley	6.00
F10	Johnnie Morton	6.00
F11	Eddie George	40.00
F12	Steve McNair	20.00
F13	Marshall Faulk	8.00
F14	Kevin Hardy	6.00
F15	Greg Hill	6.00
F16	Tamarick Vanover	8.00
F17	Karim Abdul-Jabbar	30.00
F18	Drew Bledsoe	30.00
F19	Curtis Martin	40.00
F20	Danny Kanell	6.00
F21	Keyshawn Johnson	20.00
F22	Napoleon Kaufman	6.00
F23	Rickey Dudley	8.00
F24	Kordell Stewart	30.00
F25	Lawrence Phillips	15.00
F26	Isaac Bruce	15.00
F27	J.J. Stokes	6.00
F28	Joey Galloway	25.00
F29	Errict Rhett	8.00
F30	Mike Alstott	8.00

1996 SP Holoview

The 48-card, regular-sized set was inserted every seven packs of SP football. The card fronts feature a color player shot over a over a Holoview image headshot and multiple team logo. The player's name, position and team nickname appears in the upper right quadrant. A 48-card, die-cut parallel version was inserted every 75 packs. The cards also featured the same Holoview image but had a gold top border instead of a team-color top border.

		MT
Complete Set (48):		250.00
Common Player:		2.00
1	Jerry Rice	12.00
2	Herman Moore	4.00
3	Kerry Collins	12.00
4	Brett Favre	25.00
5	Junior Seau	2.00
6	Troy Aikman	12.00
7	John Elway	8.00
8	Steve Young	8.00
9	Reggie White	4.00
10	Kordell Stewart	12.00
11	Drew Bledsoe	12.00
12	Jeff Blake	4.00
13	Dan Marino	25.00
14	Curtis Martin	15.00
15	Marshall Faulk	6.00
16	Greg Lloyd	2.00
17	Cris Carter	2.00
18	Isaac Bruce	0.00
19	Joey Galloway	8.00
20	Barry Sanders	12.00
21	Emmitt Smith	25.00
22	Edgar Bennett	2.00
23	Rashaan Salaam	4.00
24	Steve McNair	8.00
25	Tamarick Vanover	4.00
26	Deion Sanders	6.00
27	Keyshawn Johnson	6.00
28	Kevin Hardy	2.00
29	Simeon Rice	2.00
30	Lawrence Phillips	6.00
31	Tim Biakabutuka	6.00
32	Terry Glenn	12.00
33	Rickey Dudley	4.00
34	Regan Upshaw	2.00
35	Eddie George	15.00
36	John Mobley	2.00
37	Eddie Kennison	8.00
38	Marvin Harrison	8.00
39	Leeland McElroy	4.00
40	Eric Moulds	4.00
41	Alex Van Dyke	4.00
42	Mike Alstott	5.00
43	Jeff Lewis	2.00
44	Bobby Engram	4.00
45	Derrick Mayes	2.00
46	Karim Abdul-Jabbar	10.00
47	Stepfret Williams	2.00
48	Stephen Davis	2.00

1996 SP Holoview Die-Cuts

Holoview Die-Cuts are a parallel set to the Holoview Collection, and seeded one per 74 packs. The 48 regular Holoviews are double die-cut on the top and bottom, and have gold foil added to them.

	MT
Complete Set (48):	1000.00
Holoview Die-Cuts:	2x-4x

1996 SP SPx Force

The five-card, regular-sized, die-cut set was inserted every 950 packs of 1996 SP football. Each card contained four Holoview images of top players at quarterback, running back, wide receiver and rookies. The fifth card features Holoviews of the top four at each position (and rookies) and will have an autographed parallel version (1:8,820).

		MT
Complete Set (4):		600.00
Common Player:		100.00
Set price does not include Autographs.		
1	Keyshawn Johnson, Lawrence Phillips, Terry Glenn, Tim Biakabutuka	100.00
2	Barry Sanders, Emmitt Smith, Marshall Faulk, Curtis Martin	225.00
3	Dan Marino, Brett Favre, Drew Bledsoe, Troy Aikman	250.00
4	Jerry Rice, Herman Moore, Carl Pickens, Isaac Bruce	125.00
5A	Keyshawn Johnson AUTO	350.00
5B	Dan Marino AUTO	1000.
5C	Jerry Rice AUTO	1000.
5D	Barry Sanders AUTO	1000.

1996 Collector's Choice Update

The 200-card, regular-sized set was issued as an update to the 375-card Collector's choice set in 1996. The Update set included a 60-card rookies subset and 30 Franchise Play Makers subset. The base card fronts included the player's team colors along the left border with the player's position and team helmet. Inserts included were Play Action Stickums, Play Action Stickums Base Cards, Record-Breaking Trio, You Make The Play and Meet The Stars Trivia Game Cards.

		MT
Complete Set (200):		15.00
Common Player:		.05
Wax Box:		00.00
1	*Zack Thomas*	.75
2	Simeon Rice	.10
3	Jonathan Ogden	.05
4	Eric Moulds	.20
5	Tim Biakabutuka	.20
6	Walt Harris	.10
7	Willie Anderson	.05
8	Rickey Whittle	.05
9	John Mobley	.05
10	Reggie Brown	.05
11	John Michels	.05
12	Eddie George	1.00
13	Marvin Harrison	.50
14	Kevin Hardy	.10
15	Kavika Pittman	.05
16	Daryl Gardener	.05
17	Duane Clemons	.05
18	Terry Glenn	.75
19	Alex Molden	.05
20	Cedric Jones	.05
21	Keyshawn Johnson	.60
22	Rickey Dudley	.20
23	Jason Dunn	.05
24	Jermain Stephens	.05
25	Lawrence Phillips	.60
26	Bryan Still	.05
27	Isreal Ifeanyi	.05
28	Pete Kendall	.05
29	Regan Upshaw	.05
30	Andre Johnson	.05
31	Leeland McElroy	.20

32	Ray Lewis	.05
33	Sean Moran	.05
34	*Mushin Muhammad*	.50
35	Bobby Engram	.20
36	Marco Battaglia	.05
37	Stepfret Williams	.05
38	Jeff Lewis	.05
39	Derrick Mayes	.05
40	Reggie Tongue	.05
41	Tory James	.05
42	*Tony Banks*	.75
43	Tedy Bruschi	.05
44	Mike Alstott	.20
45	Anthony Dorsett Jr.	.05
46	*Tony Brackens*	.30
47	Bryant Mix	.05
48	Karim Abdul-Jabbar	.75
49	Moe Williams	.05
50	Lawyer Milloy	.05
51	Je'Rod Cherry	.05
52	*Amani Toomer*	.30
53	Alex Van Dyke	.20
54	Lance Johnstone	.05
55	Bobby Hoying	.05
56	John Wittman	.05
57	*Eddie Kennison*	.75
58	Brian Roche	.05
59	*Terrell Owens*	1.00
60	Stephen Davis	.05
61	Jeff George	.05
62	Darick Holmes	.05
63	Kerry Collins	.40
64	Rashaan Salaam	.05
65	Jeff Blake	.20
66	Emmitt Smith	.75
67	Troy Aikman	.40
68	John Elway	.30
69	Terrell Davis	.50
70	Barry Sanders	.40
71	Herman Moore	.05
72	Brett Favre	.75
73	Robert Brooks	.05
74	Steve McNair	.20
75	Marshall Faulk	.20
76	Marcus Allen	.05
77	Dan Marino	.75
78	Warren Moon	.05
79	Drew Bledsoe	.40
80	Curtis Martin	.50
81	Mario Bates	.05
82	Tim Brown	.05
83	Charlie Garner	.05
84	Kordell Stewart	.40
85	Isaac Bruce	.20
86	Tony Martin	.05
87	Jerry Rice	.40
88	J.J. Stokes	.05
89	Joey Galloway	.20
90	Errict Rhett	.15
91	Mike Pritchard	.05
92	Jerome Bettis	.10
93	Winslow Oliver	.05
94	David Klingler	.05
95	Lawrence Dawsey	.05
96	Charlie Jones	.05
97	Dave Krieg	.05
98	Chris Spielman	.05
99	Stanley Pritchett	.05
100	Sean Gilbert	.05
101	Tommy Vardell	.05
102	DeRon Jenkins	.05
103	Larry Bowie	.05
104	Kyle Wachholz	.05
105	Brady Smith	.05
106	Steve Walsh	.05
107	Wesley Walls	.05
108	Kevin Ross	.05
109	Willie Clay	.05
110	Olanda Truitt	.05
111	Calvin Williams	.05
112	Chris Doleman	.05
113	Irving Fryar	.05
114	Jimmy Spencer	.05
115	Reggie Barlow	.05
116	Reggie Brown	.05
117	Dixon Edwards	.05
118	Haywood Jeffires	.05
119	Santana Dotson	.05
120	Herschel Walker	.05
121	Darryl Williams	.05
122	Bryan Cox	.05
123	Lamar Thomas	.05
124	Hendrick Lusk	.05
125	Jahine Arnold	.05
126	Boomer Esiason	.05
127	Willie Davis	.05
128	Pete Stoyanovich	.05
129	Bill Romanowski	.05
130	Tim McKyer	.05
131	Patrick Sapp	.05
132	Natrone Means	.05

133	Quinn Early	.05
134	Leslie O'Neal	.05
135	Mark Seay	.05
136	Pete Metzelaars	.05
137	Jay Leuwenberg	.05
138	Buster Owens	.05
139	Todd McNair	.05
140	Eugene Robinson	.05
141	Sean Salisbury	.05
142	Eugene Robinson	.05
143	Jerris McPhail	.05
144	Ray Farmer	.05
145	Garrison Hearst	.05
146	Leonard Russell	.05
147	Ray Barker	.05
148	Larry Brown	.05
159	Webster Slaughter	.05
150	Roman Oben	.05
151	LeShon Johnson	.05
152	Patrick Bates	.05
153	Iheanyi Uwaezuoke	.05
154	Scott Slutzker	.05
155	John Jurkovic	.05
156	Brian Milne	.05
157	Mike Sherrard	.05
158	Neil O'Donnell	.05
159	Roger Harper	.05
160	Desmond Howard	.05
161	Alfred Williams	.05
162	Ronnie Harmon	.05
163	Sammie Burroughs	.05
164	Keenan McCardell	.05
165	Shane Dronett	.05
166	Jeff Graham	.05
167	Bill Brooks	.05
168	Shawn Jefferson	.05
169	Detron Smith	.05
170	Danny Kanell	.05
171	Jevon Langford	.05
172	Russell Maryland	.05
173	Scott Milanovich	.05
174	Eric Davis	.05
175	Ernie Conwell	.05
176	Kurt Gouveia	.05
177	Andre Rison	.05
178	Harold Green	.05
179	Frank Reich	.05
180	Glyn Milburn	.05
181	Nilo Silvan	.05
182	Cornelius Bennett	.05
183	Freddie Solomon	.05
184	Pat Terrell	.05
185	Miles Mecik	.05
186	Bo Orlando	.05
187	Kelvin Martin	.05
188	Todd Kinchen	.05
189	Reggie Brooks	.05
190	Steve Beuerlein	.05
191	Marco Coleman	.05
192	Johnnie Johnson	.05
193	Dedric Mathis	.05
194	Leon Searcy	.05
195	Kevin Greene	.05
196	Daniel Stubbs	.05
197	Ray Mickens	.05
198	Devin Wyman	.05
199	Lorenzo Lynch	.05
200	Checklist	.20

1996 Collector's Choice Update Record Breaking Trio

The four-card, regular-sized, die-cut set was inserted every 100 packs of Collector's Choice 1996 Update. The cards feature Joe Montana, Dan Marino, Jerry Rice and a fourth card including all three.

	MT
Complete Set (4):	60.00
Common Player:	10.00
RS1 Joe Montana	10.00
RS2 Dan Marino	25.00
RS3 Jerry Rice	15.00
RS4 Joe Montana, Dan Marino, Jerry Rice	10.00

1996 Collector's Choice Update Stick-Ums

The 30-card Stick-Ums set was inserted every four packs of Collector's Choice 1996 Update. The regular-sized set came with peel-off stickers of the player, team helmet and name. Thirty base cards were also inserted every four packs. The base cards feature a white outline of the corresponding player and contain clues as to which player's sticker goes with which base card.

	MT
Complete Set (30):	15.00
Common Player:	.25
S1 Jeff George	.25
S2 Darren Bennett	.25
S3 Marcus Allen	.50
S4 Brett Favre	2.00
S5 Carl Pickens	.25
S6 Troy Aikman	1.00
S7 John Elway	.75
S8 Steve Young	.75
S9 Norm Johnson	.25
S10 Kordell Stewart	1.00
S11 Drew Bledsoe	1.00
S12 Jim Kelly	.50
S13 Dan Marino	2.00
S14 Joey Galloway	.50
S15 Lawrence Phillips	.50
S16 Reggie White	.50
S17 Kevin Hardy	.25
S18 Isaac Bruce	.75
S19 Keyshawn Johnson	.75
S20 Barry Sanders	1.00
S21 Deion Sanders	.75
S22 Emmitt Smith	2.00
S23 Chris Warren	.25
S24 Tim Biakabutuka	.50
S25 Terry Glenn	1.00
S26 Marshall Faulk	.50
S27 Tamarick Vanover	.25
S28 Curtis Martin	1.50
S29 Terrell Davis	1.50
S30 Jerry Rice	1.00

1996 Collector's Choice Update Stick-Ums Mystery Base

Each Stick-Ums card in Collector's Choice Update has a corresponding Mystery Base card. It is printed on cardboard stock like regular-issue cards and have a background of an action shot, with a white space where the player is supposed to be. The sticker is supposed to be used with the Mystery Base base to complete the football action scene. One

Mystery Base card is included in every four packs of Collector's Choice Update.

	MT
Complete Set (30):	7.50
Mystery Base Cards:	.5x

1996 Collector's Choice Update You Make The Play

You Make the Play is an interactive card deck that allow collectors to play a football game through cards. The deck contains 90 cards and is found at a rate of one per pack.

	MT
Complete Set (90):	20.00
Common Player:	.10
1 Norm Johnson	.10
2 Jerry Rice	1.00
3 Dan Marino	2.00
4 Marshall Faulk	.30
5 Neil Smith	.10
6 Herman Moore	.20
7 Brett Favre	2.00
8 Curtis Martin	1.50
9 Reggie White	.20
10 Cris Carter	.10
11 Rick Tuten	.10
12 Steve Young	.75
13 Barry Sanders	1.00
14 Deion Sanders	.50
15 Isaac Bruce	.30
16 Troy Aikman	1.00
17 Emmitt Smith	2.00
18 Junior Seau	.10
19 Joey Galloway	.30
20 Drew Bledsoe	1.00
21 Jason Elam	.10
22 Edgar Bennett	.10
23 Greg Lloyd	.10
24 Tamarick Vanover	.20
25 John Elway	.75
26 Larry Centers	.10
27 Derrick Thomas	.10
28 Michael Irvin	.20
29 Jeff George	.10
30 Thurman Thomas	.20
31 Darren Bennett	.10
32 Ken Norton	.10
33 Carl Pickens	.10
34 Jeff Blake	.20
35 Craig Heyward	.10
36 Aeneas Williams	.10
37 Terance Mathis	.10
38 Jim Kelly	.20
39 Marcus Allen	.20
40 Tim McDonald	.10

#	Player	Price
41	Jason Hanson	.10
42	Scott Mitchell	.10
43	Tim Brown	.10
44	Kordell Stewart	1.00
45	Eric Metcalf	.10
46	Norm Johnson	.10
47	Jerry Rice	1.00
48	Dan Marino	2.00
49	Marshall Faulk	.30
50	Neil Smith	.10
51	Herman Moore	.30
52	Brett Favre	2.00
53	Curtis Martin	1.50
54	Reggie White	.20
55	Cris Carter	.10
56	Rick Tuten	.10
57	Steve Young	.75
58	Barry Sanders	1.00
59	Deion Sanders	.50
60	Isaac Bruce	.30
61	Troy Aikman	1.00
62	Emmitt Smith	2.00
63	Junior Seau	.20
64	Joey Galloway	.30
65	Drew Bledsoe	1.00
66	Jason Elam	.10
67	Edgar Bennett	.10
68	Greg Lloyd	.10
69	Tamarick Vanover	.20
70	John Elway	.75
71	Larry Centers	.10
72	Derrick Thomas	.10
73	Michael Irvin	.20
74	Jeff George	.10
75	Thurman Thomas	.20
76	Darren Bennett	.10
77	Ken Norton	.10
78	Carl Pickens	.10
79	Jeff Blake	.20
80	Craig Heyward	.10
81	Aeneas Williams	.10
82	Terance Mathis	.10
83	Jim Kelly	.20
84	Marcus Allen	.20
85	Tim McDonald	.10
86	Jason Hanson	.10
87	Scott Mitchell	.10
88	Tim Brown	.10
89	Kordell Stewart	1.00
90	Eric Metcalf	.10

1997 Action Packed

The 125-card set features a brown football pebble grain at the bottom of the card front. The player's photo is printed at the top, with the player embossed. The Pinnacle Action Packed logo is at the bottom center, with the player's name printed directly below. The card backs have a player photo with a ghosted photo in the background. The player's bio is listed along the upper right border. The player's name, position and stats are printed at the bottom left. The First Impressions silver-foil parallel of the base set was inserted 1:15 packs, while the Gold Impressions parallel set, which includes gold foil, was seeded 1:44 packs. A 15-card Down 'N' Dirty subset was included as part of the base set.

	MT
Complete Set (125):	40.00
Common Player:	.10
First Impressions:	6x-12x
Gold Impressions:	5x-30x
Wax Box:	60.00
1 Jerry Rice	2.00
2 Troy Aikman	2.00

#	Player	Price
3	Ricky Watters	.20
4	Dan Marino	4.00
5	Emmitt Smith	4.00
6	Warren Moon	.20
7	Rashaan Salaam	.50
8	Drew Bledsoe	2.00
9	Eddie George	2.00
10	John Elway	1.25
11	Robert Brooks	.10
12	Scott Mitchell	.10
13	Isaac Bruce	.50
14	Marshall Faulk	.75
15	Steve Bono	.10
16	Barry Sanders	2.00
17	Brett Favre	4.00
18	Curtis Martin	3.00
19	Keyshawn Johnson	.75
20	Dave Brown	.10
21	Frank Sanders	.10
22	Gus Frerotte	.10
23	Eric Metcalf	.10
24	Thurman Thomas	.20
25	Steve Young	1.25
26	Alvin Harper	.10
27	Mark Brunell	2.00
28	Kordell Stewart	2.00
29	Terry Glenn	1.50
30	Junior Seau	.20
31	Karim Abdul-Jabbar	1.25
32	Jeff Hostetler	.10
33	Rodney Hampton	.10
34	Irving Fryar	.10
35	Cris Carter	.10
36	James Stewart	.10
37	Marcus Allen	.20
38	Napoleon Kaufman	.20
39	Shannon Sharpe	.20
40	LeShon Johnson	.10
41	Tony Banks	.50
42	Lawrence Phillips	.20
43	Kerry Collins	2.00
44	Curtis Conway	.10
45	Jim Harbaugh	.10
46	Garrison Hearst	.10
47	Trent Dilfer	.20
48	Terance Mathis	.10
49	Jerome Bettis	.30
50	Chris Sanders	.10
51	Deion Sanders	1.00
52	Herman Moore	.30
53	Elvis Grbac	.10
54	O.J. McDuffie	.10
55	Ben Coates	.10
56	Jim Kelly	.20
57	J.J. Stokes	.10
58	Terrell Davis	3.00
59	Stan Humphries	.10
60	Carl Pickens	.20
61	Neil O'Donnell	.10
62	Edgar Bennett	.10
63	Yancey Thigpen	.10
64	Bert Emanuel	.10
65	Amani Toomer	.10
66	Jeff Blake	.20
67	Eddie Kennison	.75
68	Jason Dunn	.10
69	Rob Moore	.10
70	Andre Rison	.10
71	Vinny Testaverde	.10
72	Henry Ellard	.10
73	Dale Carter	.10
74	Tony Martin	.10
75	Jim Everett	.10
76	Joey Galloway	.50
77	Mike Alstott	.20
78	Kevin Hardy	.10
79	Jake Reed	.10
80	Tim Brown	.10
81	Sean Dawkins	.10
82	Bobby Engram	.10
83	Michael Irvin	.20
84	Rickey Dudley	.20
85	Chris Chandler	.10
86	Keith Jackson	.10
87	Muhsin Muhammad	.20
88	Tamarick Vanover	.20
89	Chris Warren	.10
90	Johnnie Morton	.10
91	Terry Allen	.20
92	Stanley Pritchett	.10
93	Charles Johnson	.10
94	Chris T. Jones	.10
95	Winslow Oliver	.10
96	Anthony Miller	.10
97	Tyrone Wheatley	.10
98	Robert Smith	.10
99	Eric Moulds	.10
100	Hardy Nickerson	.10
101	Derrick Alexander	.10
102	Michael Haynes	.10
103	Jamal Anderson	.20

#	Player	Price
104	Marvin Harrison	.75
105	Antonio Freeman	.20
106	Dorsey Levens	.20
107	Natrone Means	.20
108	Keenan McCardell	.10
109	Mark Chmura	.10
110	Darren Woodson	.10
111	Brett Favre	2.00
112	Emmitt Smith	2.00
113	Junior Seau	.10
114	Jerry Rice	1.00
115	Barry Sanders	1.00
116	Bruce Smith	.10
117	Troy Aikman	1.00
118	Bryan Cox	.10
119	Zach Thomas	.30
120	Reggie White	.10
121	Ben Coates	.10
122	Jerome Bettis	.10
123	Michael Irvin	.10
124	Quentin Coryatt	.10
125	Checklist	.10

1997 Action Packed Crash Course

Inserted 1:23 packs, the 18-card set includes the Crash Course logo at the bottom center. The Action Packed logo is in the upper right. The player's name is printed vertically along the upper right side.

	MT
Complete Set (18):	200.00
Common Player:	5.00
1 Dan Marino	35.00
2 Troy Aikman	20.00
3 Barry Sanders	20.00
4 Emmitt Smith	35.00
5 Brett Favre	40.00
6 John Elway	15.00
7 Keyshawn Johnson	10.00
8 Jim Harbaugh	5.00
9 Kerry Collins	20.00
10 Karim Abdul-Jabbar	15.00
11 Eddie Kennison	10.00
12 Curtis Martin	20.00
13 Tony Banks	10.00
14 Dorsey Levens	5.00
15 Jerome Bettis	10.00
16 Drew Bledsoe	20.00
17 Marvin Harrison	10.00
18 Jerry Rice	20.00

1997 Action Packed Studs

Numbered as one of 1,500 sets, the nine-card chase set was inserted 1:167 packs. The cards include a real diamond chip in the ears of the player on the card front.

	MT
Complete Set (9):	800.00
Common Player:	35.00
1 Deion Sanders	60.00
2 Barry Sanders	110.00
3 Eddie George	130.00
4 Jerry Rice	110.00

#	Player	Price
5	Kordell Stewart	80.00
6	Emmitt Smith	225.00
7	Terrell Davis	100.00
8	Keyshawn Johnson	35.00
9	Robert Smith	35.00

1997 Action Packed 24K Team

The 15-card chase set was inserted 1:71 packs. The top of the card front has a gold banner, which includes "24KT Gold." The player's name is printed directly below the banner. The player's photo is superimposed over a gold background and silver rays. The Action Packed logo is printed at the bottom center.

	MT
Complete Set (15):	550.00
Common Player:	15.00
1 Brett Favre	90.00
2 Steve Young	35.00
3 Terrell Davis	45.00
4 Barry Sanders	45.00
5 Isaac Bruce	25.00
6 Deion Sanders	30.00
7 Dan Marino	80.00
8 Jim Harbaugh	15.00
9 Jerry Rice	45.00
10 John Elway	35.00
11 Herman Moore	15.00
12 Troy Aikman	45.00
13 Emmitt Smith	80.00
14 Drew Bledsoe	45.00
15 Eddie George	50.00

1997 Collector's Edge Excalibur

The 150-card base set appears in two versions. The base set includes a space-motif Excalibur dragon in the top corner, with the tail filling the bottom right of the card. The premium parallel set featured a gold-foil stamped dragon. The backs have the player's headshot on the left over an outer space background. An Excalibur medallion is pictured in the upper right, along with the card number, player's name and bio. His stats appear in six sword blades near the bottom of the card back.

	MT
Complete Set (150):	30.00
Common Player:	.10
Wax Box:	85.00
1 Larry Centers	.10
2 Leeland McElroy	.20
3 Simeon Rice	.10
4 Eric Swann	.10
5 Jamal Anderson	.30
6 Bert Emanuel	.10
7 Eric Metcalf	.10
8 Ray Lewis	.10

		MT
9	Derrick Alexander	.10
10	Michael Jackson	.10
11	Vinny Testaverde	.10
12	Todd Collins	.20
13	Jim Kelly	.20
14	Eric Moulds	.10
15	Andre Reed	.10
16	Bruce Smith	.10
17	Thurman Thomas	.20
18	Tim Biakabutuka	.20
19	Kerry Collins	1.25
20	Kevin Greene	.10
21	Anthony Johnson	.10
22	Lamar Lathon	.10
23	Muhsin Muhammad	.10
24	Curtis Conway	.20
25	Bryan Cox	.10
26	Walt Harris	.10
27	Erik Kramer	.10
28	Rick Mirer	.10
29	Rashaan Salaam	.20
30	Jeff Blake	.30
31	Ki-Jana Carter	.20
32	Carl Pickens	.20
33	Troy Aikman	1.50
34	Michael Irvin	.20
35	Daryl Johnston	.10
36	Emmitt Smith	2.50
37	Broderick Thomas	.10
38	Terrell Davis	1.50
39	John Elway	1.00
40	Anthony Miller	.10
41	John Mobley	.10
42	Shannon Sharpe	.10
43	Neil Smith	.10
44	Scott Mitchell	.10
45	Herman Moore	.30
46	Brett Perriman	.10
47	Barry Sanders	1.50
48	Edgar Bennett	.10
49	Robert Brooks	.20
50	Brett Favre	3.00
51	Antonio Freeman	.30
52	Dorsey Levens	.20
53	Reggie White	.20
54	Eddie George	1.75
55	Darryll Lewis	.10
56	Steve McNair	1.25
57	Chris Sanders	.10
58	Marshall Faulk	.20
59	Jim Harbaugh	.10
60	Marvin Harrison	.75
61	Jimmy Smith	.10
62	Tony Brackens	.10
63	Mark Brunell	1.50
64	Kevin Hardy	.10
65	Keenan McCardell	.10
66	Natrone Means	.20
67	Marcus Allen	.20
68	Elvis Grbac	.10
69	Derrick Thomas	.10
70	Tamarick Vanover	.10
71	Karim Abdul-Jabbar	1.25
72	Terrell Buckley	.10
73	Irving Fryar	.10
74	Dan Marino	2.50
75	O.J. McDuffie	.10
76	Zach Thomas	.50
77	Terry Kirby	.10
78	Cris Carter	.20
79	Brad Johnson	.10
80	John Randle	.10
81	Jake Reed	.10
82	Robert Smith	.10
83	Drew Bledsoe	1.50
84	Ben Coates	.10
85	Terry Glenn	1.50
86	Ty Law	.10
87	Curtis Martin	1.50
88	Willie McGinest	.10
89	Mario Bates	.10
90	Jim Everett	.10
91	Wayne Martin	.10
92	Heath Shuler	.10
93	Torrance Small	.10
94	Ray Zellars	.10
95	Dave Brown	.10
96	Jason Sehorn	.10
97	Amani Toomer	.10
98	Tyrone Wheatley	.10
99	Hugh Douglas	.10
100	Aaron Glenn	.10
101	Jeff Graham	.10
102	Keyshawn Johnson	.75
103	Adrian Murrell	.10
104	Neil O'Donnell	.10
105	Tim Brown	.10
106	Jeff George	.10
107	Jeff Hostetler	.10
108	Napoleon Kaufman	.20
109	Chester McGlockton	.10
110	Fred Barnett	.10
111	Ty Detmer	.10
112	Chris T. Jones	.10
113	Ricky Watters	.20
114	Bobby Engram	.10
115	Jerome Bettis	.20
116	Charles Johnson	.10
117	Greg Lloyd	.10
118	Kordell Stewart	1.50
119	Yancey Thigpen	.10
120	Rod Woodson	.10
121	Stan Humphries	.10
122	Tony Martin	.10
123	Leonard Russell	.10
124	Junior Seau	.10
125	Chad Brown	.10
126	John Friesz	.10
127	Joey Galloway	.40
128	Cortez Kennedy	.10
129	Warren Moon	.10
130	Chris Warren	.10
131	Garrison Hearst	.10
132	Terrell Owens	1.00
133	Jerry Rice	1.50
134	Dana Stubblefield	.10
135	Bryant Young	.10
136	Steve Young	1.00
137	Tony Banks	.75
138	Isaac Bruce	.30
139	Eddie Kennison	.75
140	Keith Lyle	.10
141	Lawrence Phillips	.20
142	Mike Alstott	.20
143	Hardy Nickerson	.10
144	Errict Rhett	.20
145	Warren Sapp	.10
146	Gus Frerotte	.10
147	Sean Gilbert	.10
148	Ken Harvey	.10
149	Terry Allen	.10
150	Michael Westbrook	.20

1997 Collector's Edge Excalibur Castle Cards

The 25 acetate cards are die-cut at the top and on the left in a castle design. The top and left side of the cards also feature a rock-style background, with the player's photo on the right side of the card. The player's last name is printed inside a marble-style rectangle in the lower right of the fronts. The backs have the card number in the upper left, with the bricks at the top and bottom. The player's headshot is in the left-center of the backs, with the team's logo, player's name and bio printed to the right of the photo. The background is made up of red and orange. The card's individual number is printed in the bottom right. Edge produced 750 of each card.

		MT
	Complete Set (25):	120.00
	Common Player:	2.50
1	Jeff Blake	5.00
2	Mark Brunell	12.00
3	Bobby Engram	2.50
4	Joey Galloway	6.00
5	Eddie Kennison	6.00
6	Terrell Davis	12.00
7	Joey Galloway	2.50
8	Hardy Nickerson	2.50
9	Errict Rhett	2.50
10	Emmitt Smith	20.00
11	Kordell Stewart	12.00
12	Steve Young	8.00
13	Marcus Allen	2.50
14	Edgar Bennett	2.50
15	Robert Brooks	2.50
16	Kerry Collins	10.00
17	Todd Collins	2.50
18	Brett Favre	25.00
19	Gus Frerotte	2.50
20	Elvis Grbac	2.50
21	Jeff Hostetler	2.50
22	Tony Martin	2.50
23	Terrell Owens	8.00
24	Dorsey Levens	2.50
25	Thurman Thomas	2.50

1997 Collector's Edge Excalibur Crusaders

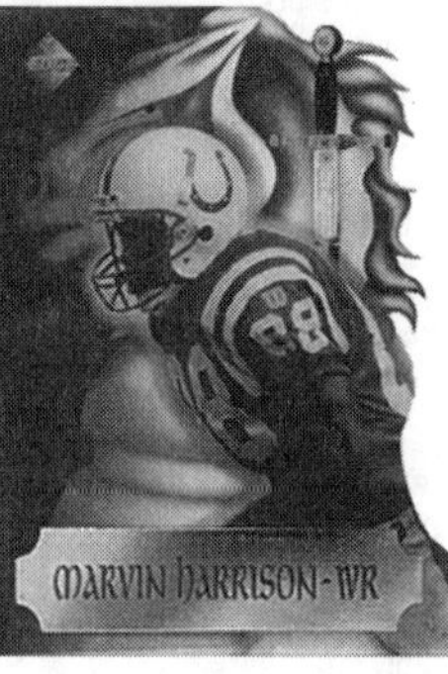

The 25 acetate die-cut cards have the player's photo superimposed over a chess piece background on the front. The Edge logo is printed in the upper left, with an Excalibur sword printed in the background on the right side. The player's name is printed inside a gold-foil "plaque" at the bottom of the front. The chess piece is printed in purple in the background. The backs are a reverse of the front, with the card number inside a diamond in the upper right. The card's individual number is printed at the bottom center. Edge produced 750 of each card.

		MT
	Complete Set (25):	250.00
	Common Player:	5.00
1	Brett Favre	50.00
2	Mark Brunell	25.00
3	Jim Kelly	10.00
4	Michael Westbrook	5.00
5	Emmitt Smith	40.00
6	Marshall Faulk	10.00
7	Kerry Collins	20.00
8	Jeff Hostetler	5.00
9	Rashaan Salaam	5.00
10	Garrison Hearst	5.00
11	Tamarick Vanover	5.00
12	Rodney Hampton	5.00
13	Leeland McElroy	5.00
14	Tony Banks	15.00
15	Deion Sanders	15.00
16	Errict Rhett	5.00
17	Thurman Thomas	10.00
18	Chris Warren	5.00
19	Andre Reed	5.00
20	Napoleon Kaufman	10.00
21	Terry Allen	5.00
22	Carl Pickens	5.00
23	Marvin Harrison	10.00
24	Lawrence Phillips	5.00
25	Troy Aikman	25.00

1997 Collector's Edge Excalibur Game Gear

The 19 Game Gear chase cards are hard to miss, as they are as thick as six base cards. The fronts include a photo of the player along with a circular piece of the player's game-used helmet. Edge produced 500 of each card, which were inserted one per 60 packs. Autographed Game Gear cards were inserted one per 350 packs.

		MT
	Complete Set (25):	900.00
	Common Player:	12.00
1	Brett Favre	100.00
2	Mark Brunell	50.00
3	Barry Sanders	50.00
4	John Elway	40.00
5	Emmitt Smith	90.00
6	Drew Bledsoe	50.00
7	Troy Aikman	50.00
8	Dan Marino	90.00
9	Eddie George	60.00
10	Terry Glenn	50.00
11	Keyshawn Johnson	20.00
12	Terrell Davis	50.00
13	Curtis Martin	50.00
14	Steve McNair	40.00
15	Muhsin Muhammad	12.00
16	Antonio Freeman	20.00
17	Ricky Watters	12.00
18	Jerome Bettis	12.00
19	Herman Moore	12.00
20	Isaac Bruce	20.00
21	Deion Sanders	25.00
22	Cris Carter	12.00
23	Tim Biakabutuka	12.00
24	Karim Abdul-Jabbar	35.00
25	Mike Alstott	12.00

1997 Collector's Edge Excalibur Gridiron Wizards

Similar to the Gridiron Sorcerers, this 25-card set included the top players from the 1997 draft. Like the Sorcerers cards, the Wizard cards were inserted one per 20 packs. The only difference being the Wizard cards were seeded in super premium boxes and the Sorcerers cards were inserted in premium packs.

		MT
	Complete Set (25):	120.00
	Common Player:	2.50
1	Orlando Pace	4.00
2	Peter Boulware	2.50
3	Darrell Russell	2.50
4	Shawn Springs	5.00
5	Yatil Green	8.00
6	Jim Druckenmiller	15.00
7	Bryant Westbrook	2.50
8	Dwayne Rudd	2.50
9	David LaFleur	5.00
10	Rae Carruth	8.00
11	Corey Dillon	8.00
12	Antowain Smith	8.00
13	Tiki Barber	12.00
14	Marcus Harris	2.50
15	Warrick Dunn	20.00
16	Chris Canty	2.50
17	Tony Gonzalez	6.00
18	Danny Wuerffel	15.00
19	Ike Hilliard	10.00
20	James Farrior	2.50
21	Reidel Anthony	12.00
22	Jake Plummer	2.50
23	Troy Davis	12.00
24	Pat Barnes	2.50
25	Darnell Autry	6.00

1997 Collector's Edge Excalibur Marauders

The 25-card set featured 50 players, as two appeared on each double-front cards. The player's photo is superimposed over a blue lenticular background, which featured vertical black lines moving from side-to-side. The team's logo appears in the upper left inside a shield, while the team name and his position are printed in gold foil in the upper right. The player's last name is printed inside a gold-foil stripe in the upper right. The appropriate logos appear in the lower left, while "Marauders" and the card number are printed in the lower right in dark blue. The cards were inserted in one of 20 super premium packs.

		MT
Complete Set (25):		175.00
Common Player:		3.00
1	Antonio Freeman, Tony Banks	8.00
2	Heath Shuler, Tim Biakabutuka	3.00
3	Brett Favre, Eddie Kennison	25.00
4	Marcus Allen, Todd Collins	3.00
5	Dan Marino, Shannon Sharpe	20.00
6	Desmond Howard, Napoleon Kaufman	3.00
7	Dorsey Levens, Muhsin Muhammad	3.00
8	Drew Bledsoe, Mike Alstott	12.00
9	Emmitt Smith, Michael Westbrook	20.00
10	Heath Shuler, Marvin Harrison	6.00
11	Jeff Blake, Marshall Faulk	3.00
12	Jeff George, Lawrence Phillips	3.00
13	Tony Martin, Edgar Bennett	3.00
14	Jerry Rice, Karim Abdul-Jabbar	12.00
15	Jim Harbaugh, Terrell Owens	10.00
16	John Elway, Isaac Bruce	10.00
17	Dave Brown, Eric Metcalf	3.00
18	Junior Seau, Eddie Kennison	6.00
19	Mark Brunell, Eddie George	15.00
20	Cris Carter, Deion Sanders	6.00
21	Steve Young, Eric Moulds	8.00
22	Ben Coates, Chris Warren	3.00
23	Robert Brooks, Carl Pickens	3.00
24	Tim Brown, Bobby Engram	3.00
25	Troy Aikman, Ben Coates	12.00

1997 Collector's Edge Excalibur Over Lords

The 25-card set, which is printed on acetate, features a die-cut design in the shape of a dragon. The player's photo is superimposed over a orange and red dragon in the background on the front. The player's last name is printed in large capital letters at the bottom, with his first name printed in white in small letters. The team's logo is printed to the left of the player's name on the front. The backs have the player's headshot in the left center, with the team logo, his name and bio to the right of the photo. The top and bottom of the back have a brick design. The card's individual number appears at the bottom right. Edge produced 750 of each card.

		MT
Complete Set (25):		120.00
Common Player:		2.50
1	Jeff Blake	5.00
2	Mark Brunell	12.00
3	Bobby Engram	2.50
4	Joey Galloway	6.00
5	Eddie Kennison	6.00
6	Terrell Davis	12.00
7	Joey Galloway	2.50
8	Hardy Nickerson	2.50
9	Errict Rhett	2.50
10	Emmitt Smith	20.00
11	Kordell Stewart	12.00
12	Steve Young	8.00
13	Marcus Allen	2.50
14	Edgar Bennett	2.50
15	Robert Brooks	2.50
16	Kerry Collins	10.00
17	Todd Collins	2.50
18	Brett Favre	25.00
19	Gus Frerotte	2.50
20	Elvis Grbac	2.50
21	Jeff Hostetler	2.50
22	Tony Martin	2.50
23	Terrell Owens	8.00
24	Dorsey Levens	2.50
25	Thurman Thomas	2.50

1997 Collector's Edge Excalibur 22k Knights

The 25-card set includes a player photo superimposed over a foil background on the card front. The player's name is printed in gold foil at the top, while the "Excalibur 22k" logo is printed at the bottom center. The backs have the player's name printed vertically along the left border of the card. The player's head shot appears in the center, with his bio in the lower right. Edge produced 2,000 of each card. The cards were inserted 1:20 packs. A 22k Black Magnum Knights parallel version, which includes a prism logo

printed above the Excalibur 22k logo on the card front, was inserted 1:75 packs in super premium boxes.

		MT
Complete Set (25):		175.00
Common Player:		2.50
Magnum Cards:		2x-3x
1	Troy Aikman	10.00
2	John Elway	8.00
3	Brett Favre	25.00
4	Dan Marino	20.00
5	Barry Sanders	10.00
6	Emmitt Smith	20.00
7	Mark Brunell	10.00
8	Jerry Rice	10.00
9	Terrell Davis	10.00
10	Natrone Means	2.50
11	Joey Galloway	2.50
12	Keyshawn Johnson	2.50
13	Curtis Martin	10.00
14	Herman Moore	2.50
15	Eddie George	12.00
16	Terry Glenn	10.00
17	Steve McNair	8.00
18	Marshall Faulk	2.50
19	Ricky Watters	2.50
20	Karim Abdul-Jabbar	8.00
21	Gus Frerotte	2.50
22	Terry Allen	2.50
23	Andre Reed	2.50
24	Jerome Bettis	2.50
25	Tim Brown	2.50

1997 Collector's Edge Masters

The 270 standard-sized cards include 240 player cards and 30 team flag cards. The fronts have a player photo superimposed over a background of etched foil that is in a "burst" design. The player's last name is printed in gold at the top center, while the Edge Masters' logo is located at the bottom center and printed in gold. The card backs have the player's headshot in the upper left, with the card number in the upper right. The player's name and bio runs vertically along the right side of the back. The stats are printed horizontally inside stripes along the left side of the back. All of the information is printed over a teal ghosted image of a Wilson football.

		MT
Complete Set (270):		25.00
Common Player:		.05
Wax Box:		70.00
1	Arizona Cardinals	.05
2	Larry Centers	.05
3	Rob Moore	.05
4	Frank Sanders	.05
5	Eric Swann	.05
6	Atlanta Falcons	.05
7	Morten Andersen	.05
8	Bert Emanuel	.05
9	Jeff George	.05
10	Craig Heyward	.05
11	Terance Mathis	.05
12	Clay Matthews	.05
13	Eric Metcalf	.05
14	Baltimore Ravens	.05
15	Rob Burnett	.05
16	Leroy Hoard	.05
17	Earnest Hunter	.05
18	Michael Jackson	.05
19	Stevon Moore	.05
20	Anthony Pleasant	.05
21	Vinny Testaverde	.05
22	Eric Zeier	.05
23	Buffalo Bills	.05
24	Todd Collins	.05
25	Russell Copeland	.05
26	Quinn Early	.05
27	Jim Kelly	.10
28	Bryce Paup	.05
29	Andre Reed	.05
30	Bruce Smith	.05
31	Carolina Panthers	.05
32	Steve Beuerlein	.05
33	Mark Carrier	.05
34	Kerry Collins	1.00
35	Willie Green	.05
36	Kevin Greene	.05
37	Eric Guliford	.05
38	Brett Maxie	.05
39	Tim McKyer	.05
40	Derrick Moore	.05
41	Chicago Bears	.05
42	Curtis Conway	.05
43	Bryan Cox	.05
44	Jim Flanigan	.05
45	Robert Green	.05
46	Erik Kramer	.05
47	Dave Krieg	.05
48	Rashaan Salaam	.10
49	Alonzo Spellman	.05
50	Donnell Woolford	.05
51	Chris Zorich	.05
52	Cincinnati Bengals	.05
53	Eric Bieniemy	.05
54	Jeff Blake	.20
55	Ki-Jana Carter	.05
56	John Copeland	.05
57	Garrison Hearst	.05
58	Tony McGee	.05
59	Carl Pickens	.05
60	Darnay Scott	.05
61	Bracey Walker	.05
62	Dan Wilkinson	.05
63	Dallas Cowboys	.05
64	Troy Aikman	1.00
65	Bill Bates	.05
66	Shante Carver	.05
67	Michael Irvin	.10
68	Daryl Johnston	.05
69	Jay Novacek	.05
70	Deion Sanders	.50
71	Emmitt Smith	2.00
72	Herschel Walker	.05
73	Sherman Williams	.05
74	Denver Broncos	.05
75	Terrell Davis	1.50
76	John Elway	.75
77	Ed McCaffrey	.05
78	Anthony Miller	.05
79	Michael Dean Perry	.05
80	Shannon Sharpe	.05
81	Mike Sherrard	.05
82	Detroit Lions	.05
83	Scott Mitchell	.05
84	Glyn Milburn	.05
85	Herman Moore	.20
86	Johnnie Morton	.05
87	Brett Perriman	.05
88	Barry Sanders	1.00
89	Tracy Scroggins	.05
90	Green Bay Packers	.05
91	Edgar Bennett	.05
92	Robert Brooks	.05
93	Santana Dotson	.05
94	Brett Favre	2.00
95	Dorsey Levens	.10
96	Craig Newsome	.05
97	Wayne Simmons	.05
98	Reggie White	.10
99	Houston Oilers	.05
100	Chris Chandler	.05
101	Anthony Cook	.05
102	Willie Davis	.05
103	Mel Gray	.05
104	Ronnie Harmon	.05
105	Darryll Lewis	.05
106	Steve McNair	1.00
107	Todd McNair	.05
108	Rodney Thomas	.05
109	Indianapolis Colts	.05
110	Trev Alberts	.05
111	Tony Bennett	.05
112	Quentin Coryatt	.05
113	Sean Dawkins	.05
114	Ken Dilger	.05
115	Marshall Faulk	.25
116	Jim Harbaugh	.05
117	Ronald Humphrey	.05
118	Floyd Turner	.05

119	Jacksonville Jaguars	.05
120	Tony Boselli	.05
121	Mark Brunell	1.00
122	Willie Jackson	.05
123	Jeff Lageman	.05
124	Natrone Means	.05
125	Andre Rison	.05
126	James Stewart	.05
127	Cedric Tillman	.05
128	Kansas City Chiefs	.05
129	Marcus Allen	.10
130	Kimble Anders	.05
131	Steve Bono	.05
132	Dale Carter	.05
133	Lake Dawson	.05
134	Dan Salesaumua	.05
135	Neil Smith	.05
136	Derrick Thomas	.05
137	Tamarick Vanover	.15
138	Miami Dolphins	.05
139	Fred Barnett	.05
140	Steve Emtman	.05
141	Eric Green	.05
142	Dan Marino	2.00
143	O.J. McDuffie	.05
144	Bernie Parmalee	.05
145	Minnesota Vikings	.05
146	Cris Carter	.05
147	Jack Del Rio	.05
148	Qadry Ismail	.05
149	Amp Lee	.05
150	Warren Moon	.05
151	John Randle	.05
152	Jake Reed	.05
153	Robert Smith	.05
154	New England Patriots	.05
155	Drew Bledsoe	1.00
156	Vincent Brisby	.05
157	Willie Clay	.05
158	Ben Coates	.05
159	Curtis Martin	1.50
160	Dave Meggett	.05
161	Will Moore	.05
162	Chris Slade	.05
163	New Orleans Saints	.05
164	Mario Bates	.05
165	Jim Everett	.05
166	Michael Haynes	.05
167	Tyrone Hughes	.05
168	Haywood Jeffires	.05
169	Wayne Martin	.05
170	Renaldo Turnbull	.05
171	New York Giants	.05
172	Dave Brown	.05
173	Chris Calloway	.05
174	Rodney Hampton	.05
175	Michael Strahan	.05
176	Tyrone Wheatley	.05
177	New York Jets	.05
178	Kyle Brady	.05
179	Wayne Chrebet	.05
180	Hugh Douglas	.05
181	Jeff Graham	.05
182	Adrian Murrell	.05
183	Neil O'Donnell	.05
184	Oakland Raiders	.05
185	Tim Brown	.05
186	Aundray Bruce	.05
187	Andrew Glover	.05
188	Jeff Hostetler	.05
189	Napoleon Kaufman	.05
190	Terry McDaniel	.05
191	Chester McGlockton	.05
192	Pat Swilling	.05
193	Harvey Williams	.05
194	Philadelphia Eagles	.05
195	Randall Cunningham	.05
196	Irving Fryar	.05
197	William Fuller	.05
198	Charlie Garner	.05
199	Andy Harmon	.05
200	Rodney Peete	.05
201	Mark Seay	.05
202	Troy Vincent	.05
203	Ricky Watters	.10
204	Calvin Williams	.05
205	Pittsburgh Steelers	.05
206	Jerome Bettis	.10
207	Chad Brown	.05
208	Greg Lloyd	.05
209	Bam Morris	.05
210	Erric Pegram	.05
211	Kordell Stewart	1.00
212	Yancey Thigpen	.05
213	Rod Woodson	.05
214	San Diego Chargers	.05
215	Darren Bennett	.05
216	Marco Coleman	.05
217	Stan Humphries	.05
218	Tony Martin	.05
219	Junior Seau	.05

220	San Francisco 49ers	.05
221	Chris Doleman	.05
222	William Floyd	.05
223	Merton Hanks	.05
224	Brent Jones	.05
225	Terry Kirby	.05
226	Derek Loville	.05
227	Ken Norton Jr.	.05
228	Gary Plummer	.05
229	Jerry Rice	1.00
230	J.J. Stokes	.10
231	Dana Stubblefield	.05
232	John Taylor	.05
233	Bryant Young	.05
234	Steve Young	.75
235	Seattle Seahawks	.05
236	Brian Blades	.05
237	Joey Galloway	.30
238	Carlton Gray	.05
239	Cortez Kennedy	.05
240	Rick Mirer	.05
241	Chris Warren	.05
242	St. Louis Rams	.05
243	Isaac Bruce	.20
244	Troy Drayton	.05
245	D'Marco Farr	.05
246	Harold Green	.05
247	Chris Miller	.05
248	Leslie O'Neal	.05
249	Roman Phifer	.05
250	Tampa Bay Buccaneers	.05
251	Trent Dilfer	.10
252	Alvin Harper	.05
253	Jackie Harris	.05
254	John Lynch	.05
255	Hardy Nickerson	.05
256	Errict Rhett	.20
257	Warren Sapp	.05
258	Todd Scott	.05
259	Charles Wilson	.05
260	Washington Redskins	.05
261	Terry Allen	.05
262	Bill Brooks	.05
263	Henry Ellard	.05
264	Gus Frerotte	.05
265	Sean Gilbert	.05
266	Ken Harvey	.05
267	Brian Mitchell	.05
268	Heath Shuler	.05
269	James Washington	.05
270	Michael Westbrook	.10

1997 Collector's Edge Masters Crucibles

Inserted one per six hobby packs, the chase set includes a color photo of the player on the right. The left side of the front is printed in holographic foil, with a "rolled over" effect in the center. The player's name and position are in the upper left, while the team logo is in the center left and the team name printed directly underneath. "Crucibles" is printed in large capital letters along the bottom front, with "1997 NFL Draft" printed in red over "Crucibles." The backs have the player's write-up along the left and right, with his name, team helmet and bio printed in the center over a ghosted gray background. The card's serial number is printed in the lower right. Edge produced 3,000 of each card in the chase set.

		MT
Complete Set (25):		75.00
Common Player:		1.50
1	Jake Plummer	3.00
2	Byron Harnspard	4.00
3	Peter Boulware	1.50
4	Jay Graham	1.50
5	Antowain Smith	5.00
6	Rae Carruth	4.00
7	Darnell Autry	3.00
8	Corey Dillion	5.00
9	Bryant Westbrook	3.00
10	Joey Kent	3.00
11	Kevin Lockett	3.00
12	Pat Barnes	3.00
13	Tony Gonzalez	3.00
14	Yatil Green	5.00
15	Danny Wuerffel	6.00
16	Troy Davis	6.00
17	Tiki Barber	6.00
18	Ike Hilliard	6.00
19	Darrell Russell	1.50
20	Leon Johnson	1.50
21	Jim Druckenmiller	7.00
22	Shawn Springs	3.00
23	Orlando Pace	3.00
24	Warrick Dunn	10.00
25	Reidel Anthony	6.00

1997 Collector's Edge Masters Night Games

Inserted one per 20 packs, the 25-card chase set features a color photo of the player superimposed over a black and brown computer-generated background. The player's name is printed in gold foil at the top, while the Night Games' logo is printed at the bottom center. The backs have the player's name running vertically along the left. The player's bio runs vertically along the right border. The card number is in the upper right. A color photo of the player is located at the bottom center printed over a colored ghosted image of the player. The card's serial number is printed in the lower right. Edge produced 1,500 of each card in the chase set. A Prism parallel set was inserted 1:60 packs. Edge produced 250 of each Prism card.

		MT
Complete Set (25):		175.00
Common Player:		2.00
1	Terry Glenn	8.00
2	Eddie George	10.00
3	Ricky Watters	2.00
4	Barry Sanders	10.00
5	Curtis Martin	15.00
6	Brett Favre	20.00
7	Emmitt Smith	20.00
8	John Elway	8.00
9	Keyshawn Johnson	4.00
10	Kordell Stewart	8.00
11	Drew Bledsoe	10.00
12	Kerry Collins	10.00
13	Terrell Davis	15.00
14	Karim Abdul-Jabbar	7.00
15	Jerome Bettis	2.00
16	Antonio Freeman	2.00
17	Dorsey Levens	2.00
18	Herman Moore	2.00
19	Jerry Rice	10.00
20	Mark Brunell	10.00
21	Mike Alstott	2.00

22	Napoleon Kaufman	2.00
23	Terry Allen	2.00
24	Tony Banks	2.00
25	Vinny Testaverde	2.00

1997 Collector's Edge Masters '96 Rookies

Inserted in retail packs, this chase set included a color photo of the player in the top center of the front. The photo is surrounded by holographic foil, with the Rookie Year '96 logo printed in the upper right. Printed at the bottom of the front is "'96 Rookies." The player's name is printed in yellow at the top center of the card. The backs have the player's name printed in yellow in the top center, followed by the team logo, his bio and stats. The card number is printed in the upper right. Each card is serial numbered, which is located along the left of the back. All the information on the back is printed over a ghosted image of a football player. Overall, 2,000 of each card was produced by Edge.

		MT
Complete Set (25):		45.00
Common Player:		1.00
1	Simeon Rice	1.00
2	Jonathan Ogden	1.00
3	Eric Moulds	2.00
4	Tim Biakabutuka	3.00
5	Walt Harris	1.00
6	John Mobley	1.00
7	Reggie Brown	1.00
8	Derrick Mayes	1.00
9	Eddie George	10.00
10	Marvin Harrison	4.00
11	Kevin Hardy	1.00
12	Jerome Woods	1.00
13	Karim Abdul-Jabbar	7.00
14	Duane Clemons	1.00
15	Terry Glenn	8.00
16	Rickey Whittle	1.00
17	Amani Toomer	1.00
18	Keyshawn Johnson	5.00
19	Rickey Dudley	1.00
20	Bobby Hoying	1.00
21	Eddie Kennison	4.00
22	Bryan Still	1.00
23	Terrell Owens	6.00
24	Reggie Brown	1.00
25	Mike Alstott	2.00

1997 Collector's Edge Masters Nitro-Hobby

This chase set was split between hobby and retail packs. The fronts resemble the base cards with a player photo superimposed over an etched-foil background. The player's name is printed in gold at the top, while a gold-foil burst is printed at bottom of the card and includes the Nitro logo and the player's outstanding stat. The backs are identical to the base cards.

	MT
Complete Set (18):	20.00
Common Player:	.75
2 Larry Centers	.75
24 Todd Collins	.75
34 Kerry Collins	2.50
59 Carl Pickens	.75
71 Emmitt Smith	5.00
76 John Elway	1.50
88 Barry Sanders	2.50
116 Jim Harbaugh	.75
121 Mark Brunell	2.50
137 Tamarick Vanover	.75
159 Curtis Martin	3.50
189 Napoleon Kaufman	.75
206 Jerome Bettis	1.00
211 Kordell Stewart	2.00
229 Jerry Rice	2.50
237 Joey Galloway	1.50
243 Isaac Bruce	1.25
264 Gus Frerotte	.75

1997 Collector's Edge Masters Nitro-Retail

This chase set was split between hobby and retail packs. The fronts are identical to the base cards, except for a gold-foil "burst" at the bottom of the card front. The Nitro logo and an outstanding player stats are printed inside the burst. The backs are identical to the base cards.

	MT
Complete Set (18):	20.00
Common Player:	.75
18 Michael Jackson	.75
30 Bruce Smith	.75
36 Kevin Green	.75
64 Troy Aikman	2.50
75 Terrell Davis	3.50
85 Herman Moore	1.25
94 Brett Favre	5.00
98 Reggie White	1.00
106 Steve McNair	2.50
126 Derrick Thomas	.75
142 Dan Marino	5.00
155 Drew Bledsoe	2.50
167 Tyrone Huges	.75
200 Ricky Watters	.75
207 Chad Brown	.75
218 Tony Martin	.75
234 Steve Young	1.50
261 Terry Allen	.75

1997 Collector's Edge Masters Playoff Game Ball

Inserted one per 72 packs, the 19-card set features two player photos on the front. The horizontal cards have a gold-foil background at the top, with the NFC or AFC logo in the top center. The two teams which matched up in the playoff game are printed in black over the logo. A piece of a game-used ball from the contest is embedded into the card in the bottom center. The bottom half of the card front has a Wilson football background. The player's names are printed over their respective photos in the lower corners of the front. The backs have a photo of each of the players, their names, game summary, score and date. All of the information is printed over a football background. Edge produced 250 of each of the cards in the chase set.

	MT
Complete Set (19):	1000.00
Common Player:	15.00
1 Natrone Means, Thurman Thomas	15.00
2 Tony Boselli, Bruce Smith	15.00
3 Jerome Bettis, Marshall Faulk	15.00
4 Kordell Stewart, Jim Harbaugh	35.00
5 Natrone Means, Terrell Davis	50.00
6 Mark Brunell, John Elway	80.00
7 Curtis Martin, Jerome Bettis	50.00
8 Drew Bledsoe, Mark Brunell	100.00
9 Terry Glenn, Keenan McCardell	45.00
10 Troy Aikman, Brad Johnson	40.00
11 Steve Young, Ty Detmer	15.00
12 Jerry Rice, Irving Fryer	60.00
13 Dorsey Levens, Terry Kirby	15.00
14 Brett Favre, Steve Young	110.00
15 Andre Rison, Jerry Rice	60.00
16 Reggie White, Ken Norton Jr.	15.00
17 Kerry Collins, Troy Aikman	70.00
18 Kerry Collins, Brett Favre	120.00
19 Kevin Green, Reggie White	15.00

1997 Collector's Edge Masters Radical Rivals

The 12-card set features two players on each card, one on each side. A player photo is superimposed over a background of the two players' teams' helmets. The player's name and team are printed at the top in gold, while "Radical Rivals" and the card number are printed vertically along the left. The card's serial number is printed along the left border on one side of the card. Edge produced 1,000 of each card. The cards were inserted one per 30 hobby packs.

	MT
Complete Set (12):	130.00
Common Player:	2.00
1 Emmitt Smith, Eddie George	25.00
2 Brett Favre, Kerry Collins	25.00
3 Jerry Rice, Antonio Freeman	12.00
4 Ricky Watters, Napoleon Kaufman	2.00
5 Herman Moore, Keyshawn Johnson	6.00
6 Dan Marino, John Elway	25.00
7 Jerome Bettis, Karim Abdul-Jabbar	10.00
8 Isaac Bruce, Carl Pickens	2.00
9 Barry Sanders, Terry Allen	12.00
10 Terry Glenn, Joey Galloway	10.00
11 Mark Brunell, Steve Young	12.00
12 Terrell Davis, Curtis Martin	18.00

1997 Collector's Edge Masters Ripped

This retail-only chase set continues where the 1996 Ripped set left off, beginning with No. 19. The card fronts have the "Ripped" logo in the upper left, with the player's name printed vertically in black along the lower left border. A color photo of the player is superimposed over a background of red and blue prism-effect foil. The Edge logo is in the lower right of the front. The backs have the card number in gold in the upper right, with a quote about the player from Dick Butkus printed at the top. The player's head shot is printed in the right center, with the team's helmet and player's name, team, position and number printed to the left.

	MT
Complete Set (18):	150.00
Common Player:	3.00
19 Troy Aikman	15.00
20 Drew Bledsoe	15.00
21 Tim Brown	3.00
22 Mark Brunell	15.00
23 Cris Carter	3.00
24 Kerry Collins	15.00
25 Barry Sanders	15.00
26 Michael Irvin	3.00
27 Jeff Hostetler	3.00
28 Curtis Martin	20.00
29 Carl Pickens	3.00
30 Marshall Faulk	6.00
31 Rashaan Salaam	6.00
32 Deion Sanders	8.00
33 Emmitt Smith	30.00
34 Kordell Stewart	10.00
35 Ricky Watters	3.00
36 Steve Young	10.00

1997 Collector's Edge Masters Super Bowl XXXI Game Ball

Included with each card in this chase set was a circular piece of a game-used football from Super Bowl XXXI. Featured on the fronts are photos of one New England player and one Green Bay player (one on each side of the front). The Super Bowl XXXI logo appears in the top center in gold foil. The football piece is embedded in the card in the lower center of the front. The player's names are printed in the bottom corners. The Superdome is printed in the background of the lower part of the front. The backs have the player photos over the Super Bowl logo on the left. On the right over a gold foil are the player's names, game score, date, game summary and team logos. Edge produced 250 of each card. One card was inserted per 350 packs.

	MT
Complete Set (6):	475.00
Common Player:	30.00
1 Brett Favre, Drew Bledsoe	300.00
2 Dorsey Levens, Curtis Martin	125.00
3 Desmond Howard, Dave Meggett	30.00
4 Antonio Freeman, Terry Glenn	100.00
5 Keith Jackson, Ben Coates	30.00
6 Reggie White, Willie McGinest	30.00

1997 Donruss

The 230-card set features a full-bleed photo on the front. The Donruss logo is in the upper left. The team name is printed vertically in the lower left, while the team logo and player position are in the lower left corner. The player's name is to the right of the team logo. The base set is paralleled with a Press Proofs set, which are numbered "1 of 1,500," and Press Proofs - First 500, which are numbered "1 of 500" and die-cut with gold foil.

	MT
Complete Set (230):	20.00
Common Player:	.05
Silvers:	15x-30x
Golds:	25x-50x
Wax Box:	45.00
1 Dan Marino	1.50
2 Brett Favre	1.75
3 Emmitt Smith	1.50
4 Eddie George	1.25
5 Karim Abdul-Jabbar	.50
6 Terrell Davis	1.00
7 Curtis Martin	1.00
8 Drew Bledsoe	.75
9 Jerry Rice	.75
10 Troy Aikman	.75
11 Barry Sanders	.75
12 Mark Brunell	.75
13 Kerry Collins	.75
14 Steve Young	.50
15 Kordell Stewart	.75
16 Eddie Kennison	.40
17 Terry Glenn	.75
18 John Elway	.50
19 Joey Galloway	.30
20 Deion Sanders	.40
21 Keyshawn Johnson	.40
22 Lawrence Phillips	.10
23 Ricky Watters	.10
24 Marvin Harrison	.40
25 Bobby Engram	.10
26 Marshall Faulk	.10
27 Carl Pickens	.10
28 Isaac Bruce	.15
29 Herman Moore	.15
30 Jerome Bettis	.10
31 Rashaan Salaam	.10
32 Errict Rhett	.10
33 Tim Biakabutuka	.10
34 Robert Brooks	.10
35 Antonio Freeman	.00
36 Steve McNair	.50
37 Jeff Blake	.10
38 Tony Banks	.30
39 Terrell Owens	.50
40 Eric Moulds	.05
41 Leeland McElroy	.10
42 Chris Sanders	.05
43 Thurman Thomas	.10
44 Bruce Smith	.05
45 Reggie White	.10
46 Chris Warren	.05
47 J.J. Stokes	.05
48 Ben Coates	.05
49 Tim Brown	.05
50 Marcus Allen	.10
51 Michael Irvin	.10
52 William Floyd	.05
53 Ken Dilger	.05
54 Bobby Taylor	.05
55 Keenan McCardell	.05

#	Player	Price
56	Raymont Harris	.05
57	Keith Byars	.05
58	O.J. McDuffie	.05
59	Robert Smith	.05
60	Bert Emanuel	.05
61	Rick Mirer	.05
62	Vinny Testaverde	.05
63	Kyle Brady	.05
64	Mark Bruener	.05
65	Neil O'Donnell	.05
66	Anthony Johnson	.05
67	Ken Norton	.05
68	Warren Sapp	.05
69	Amani Toomer	.05
70	Simeon Rice	.05
71	Kevin Hardy	.05
72	Junior Seau	.05
73	Neil Smith	.05
74	LeShon Johnson	.05
75	Quinn Early	.05
76	Andre Reed	.05
77	Jake Reed	.05
78	Elvis Grbac	.05
79	Tyrone Wheatley	.05
80	Adrian Murrell	.05
81	Fred Barnett	.05
82	Darrell Green	.05
83	Stan Humphries	.05
84	Troy Drayton	.05
85	Steve Atwater	.05
86	Quentin Coryatt	.05
87	Dan Wilkinson	.05
88	Scott Mitchell	.05
89	Willie McGinest	.05
90	Kevin Smith	.05
91	Gus Frerotte	.05
92	Bam Morris	.05
93	Darick Holmes	.05
94	Zach Thomas	.20
95	Tom Carter	.05
96	Cortez Kennedy	.05
97	Kevin Williams	.05
98	Michael Haynes	.05
99	Lamont Warren	.05
100	Jeff Graham	.05
101	Alex Van Dyke	.05
102	Jim Everett	.05
103	Chris Chandler	.05
104	Qadry Ismail	.05
105	Ray Zellars	.05
106	Chris T. Jones	.05
107	Charlie Garner	.05
108	Bobby Hoying	.05
109	Mark Chmura	.05
110	Cris Carter	.05
111	Darnay Scott	.05
112	Anthony Miller	.05
113	Desmond Howard	.05
114	Terance Mathis	.05
115	Rodney Hampton	.05
116	Napoleon Kaufman	.05
117	Jim Harbaugh	.05
118	Shannon Sharpe	.05
119	Irving Fryar	.05
120	Garrison Hearst	.05
121	Terry Allen	.05
122	Larry Centers	.05
123	Sean Dawkins	.05
124	Jeff George	.05
125	Tony Martin	.05
126	Mike Alstott	.10
127	Rickey Dudley	.05
128	Kevin Carter	.05
129	Derrick Alexander	.05
130	Greg Lloyd	.05
131	Bryce Paup	.05
132	Derrick Thomas	.05
133	Greg Hill	.05
134	Jamal Anderson	.05
135	Curtis Conway	.05
136	Frank Sanders	.05
137	Brett Perriman	.05
138	Edgar Bennett	.05
139	Wayne Chrebet	.05
140	Natrone Means	.05
141	Eric Metcalf	.05
142	Trent Dilfer	.05
143	Terry Kirby	.05
144	Johnnie Morton	.05
145	Dale Carter	.05
146	Michael Westbrook	.05
147	Stanley Pritchett	.05
148	Todd Collins	.05
149	Tamarick Vanover	.05
150	Kevin Greene	.05
151	Lamar Lathon	.05
152	Muhsin Muhammad	.05
153	Dorsey Levens	.10
154	Rod Woodson	.05
155	Brent Jones	.05
156	Michael Jackson	.05

#	Player	Price
157	Shawn Jefferson	.05
158	Kimble Anders	.05
159	Sean Gilbert	.05
160	Carnell Lake	.05
161	Darren Woodson	.05
162	Dave Meggett	.05
163	Henry Ellard	.05
164	Eric Swann	.05
165	Tony Boselli	.05
166	Daryl Johnston	.05
167	Willie Jackson	.05
168	Wesley Walls	.05
169	Mario Bates	.05
170	Lake Dawson	.05
171	Mike Mamula	.05
172	Ed McCaffrey	.05
173	Tony Brackens	.05
174	Craig Heyward	.05
175	Harvey Williams	.05
176	Dave Brown	.05
177	Aaron Glenn	.05
178	Jeff Hostetler	.05
179	Alvin Harper	.05
180	Ty Detmer	.05
181	James Jett	.05
182	James Stewart	.05
183	Warren Moon	.05
184	Herschel Walker	.05
185	Ki-Jana Carter	.05
186	Leslie O'Neal	.05
187	Danny Kanell	.05
188	Eric Bjornson	.05
189	Alex Molden	.05
190	Bryant Young	.05
191	Merton Hanks	.05
192	Heath Shuler	.05
193	Brian Blades	.05
194	Steve Bono	.05
195	Wayne Simmons	.05
196	*Warrick Dunn*	2.50
197	*Peter Boulware*	.10
198	*David LaFleur*	.50
199	*Shawn Springs*	.40
200	*Reidel Anthony*	1.00
201	*Jim Druckenmiller*	1.50
202	*Orlando Pace*	.40
203	*Yatil Green*	.75
204	*Bryant Westbrook*	.10
205	*Tiki Barber*	1.00
206	*James Farrior*	.10
207	*Rae Carruth*	.75
208	*Danny Wuerffel*	1.25
209	*Corey Dillon*	.60
210	*Ike Hilliard*	1.00
211	*Tony Gonzalez*	.50
212	*Antowain Smith*	1.00
213	*Pat Barnes*	.50
214	*Troy Davis*	1.00
215	*Byron Hanspard*	.60
216	*Joey Kent*	.40
217	*Jake Plummer*	.50
218	*Kenny Holmes*	.10
219	*Darnell Autry*	.40
220	*Darrell Russell*	.10
221	*Walter Jones*	.10
222	*Dwayne Rudd*	.10
223	*Tom Knight*	.10
224	*Kevin Lockett*	.20
225	*Will Blackwell*	.20
226	Checklist Dan Marino	.75
227	Checklist Brett Favre	1.00
228	Checklist Emmitt Smith	.75
229	Checklist Barry Sanders	.30
230	Checklist Jerry Rice	.30

#	Player	Price
10	Jerry Rice	25.00
11	Steve McNair	20.00
12	Kerry Collins	20.00
13	John Elway	18.00
14	Eddie George	25.00
15	Karim Abdul-Jabbar	15.00
16	Kordell Stewart	25.00
17	Jerome Bettis	6.00
18	Terry Glenn	20.00
19	Errict Rhett	6.00
20	Carl Pickens	6.00

1997 Donruss Legends of the Fall

The 10-card chase set is numbered to 10,000 and features artwork from artist Dan Gardiner. The first 500 of the cards were printed directly on actual canvas.

		MT
Complete Set (10):		125.00
Common Player:		5.00
Canvas Cards:		3x-6x
1	Troy Aikman	16.00
2	Barry Sanders	16.00
3	John Elway	10.00
4	Dan Marino	30.00
5	Emmitt Smith	30.00
6	Jerry Rice	16.00
7	Deion Sanders	10.00
8	Brett Favre	35.00
9	Marcus Allen	5.00
10	Steve Young	10.00

1997 Donruss Passing Grade

The 16-card hobby-exclusive set is styled like a report card. The die-cut insert showcases the talents of the top quarterbacks. It utilizes a card-within-a-card design with red-foil stamping. Each football shaped, die-cut card came in its own envelope. The cards are numbered to 3,000.

		MT
Complete Set (16):		225.00
Common Player:		5.00
1	Steve Young	12.00

1997 Donruss Elite

The 20-card chase set is featured on Silver and Gold foil cards. The Silver Elite is numbered to 5,000, while the Gold version was produced in an edition of 2,000 sets.

		MT
Complete Set (20):		400.00
Common Player:		6.00
Gold Cards:		2x
1	Emmitt Smith	45.00
2	Dan Marino	45.00
3	Brett Favre	50.00
4	Curtis Martin	25.00
5	Terrell Davis	25.00
6	Barry Sanders	25.00
7	Drew Bledsoe	25.00
8	Mark Brunell	25.00
9	Troy Aikman	25.00

#	Player	Price
2	Drew Bledsoe	20.00
3	Mark Brunell	20.00
4	Kerry Collins	20.00
5	Steve McNair	15.00
6	John Elway	12.00
7	Ty Detmer	5.00
8	Jeff Blake	5.00
9	Dan Marino	40.00
10	Kordell Stewart	20.00
11	Tony Banks	10.00
12	Brett Favre	45.00
13	Gus Frerotte	5.00
14	Troy Aikman	20.00
15	Jeff George	5.00
16	Brad Johnson	5.00

1997 Donruss Rated Rookies

The 10-card chase set features a rookie player, with the Rated Rookies logo in the lower left corner. The set was paralleled by a Medalist micro-etched, all foil set with gold-foil holographic stamping.

		MT
Complete Set (10):		45.00
Common Player:		3.00
Medalist Cards:		5x-10x
1	Ike Hilliard	6.00
2	Warrick Dunn	12.00
3	Yatil Green	5.00
4	Jim Druckenmiller	8.00
5	Rae Carruth	4.00
6	Antowain Smith	6.00
7	Tiki Barber	6.00
8	Byron Hanspard	3.00
9	Reidel Anthony	6.00
10	Jake Plummer	3.00

1997 Donruss Zoning Commission

The 20-card retail-exclusive set is printed on a micro-etched, holographic foil card stock, with gold-foil stamping. The cards are numbered to 5,000.

		MT
Complete Set (20):		200.00
Common Player:		5.00
1	Brett Favre	40.00
2	Jerry Rice	20.00
3	Jerome Bettis	5.00
4	Troy Aikman	20.00
5	Drew Bledsoe	20.00
6	Natrone Means	5.00
7	Steve Young	15.00
8	John Elway	15.00
9	Barry Sanders	20.00
10	Emmitt Smith	35.00
11	Curtis Martin	20.00
12	Terry Allen	5.00
13	Dan Marino	35.00
14	Mark Brunell	20.00
15	Terry Glenn	10.00
16	Herman Moore	5.00
17	Ricky Watters	5.00
18	Terrell Davis	20.00
19	Isaac Bruce	5.00
20	Curtis Conway	5.00

1997 Fleer

The 450-card set includes 415 player cards, five checklists and 30 Something Special subset cards. The matte-finish cards have full-bleed photos on the front, with his last name in large block letters at the bottom. His first name is printed in small letters above, while his team and position appear directly below the player's last name. The backs have the name in the upper left, with the card number in the upper right. Rounding out the backs are a player head shot, team name and logo, highlights, bio and career stats. Two parallels are randomly seeded in hobby packs. Crystal Collection cards were seeded 1:2, while Tiffany Collection cards were 1:20.

		MT
Complete Set (450):		35.00
Common Player:		.05
Crystal Collection:		2x-4x
Tiffany Collection:		25x-50x
Wax Box:		45.00
1	Mark Brunell	1.00
2	Andre Reed	.05
3	Darrell Green	.05
4	Mario Bates	.05
5	Eddie George	1.50
6	Crie Carter	.05
7	Terrell Owens	1.00
8	Bill Romanowski	.05
9	Isaac Bruce	.20
10	Eric Curry	.05
11	Danny Kanell	.05
12	Ki-Jana Carter	.10
13	Antonio Freeman	.30
14	Ricky Watters	.10
15	Ty Law	.05
16	Alonzo Spellman	.05
17	Kordell Stewart	.75
18	Jerry Rice	1.00
19	Derrick Alexander	.05
20	Barry Sanders	1.00
21	Keyshawn Johnson	.75
22	Emmitt Smith	2.00
23	Ricky Proehl	.05
24	Daryl Gardner	.05
25	Dan Saleaumua	.05
26	Kevin Greene	.05
27	Junior Seau	.10
28	Randall McDaniel	.05
29	Marshall Faulk	.25
30	Lorenzo Lynch	.05
31	Terance Mathis	.05
32	Warren Sapp	.05
33	Chris Sanders	.05
34	Tom Carter	.05
35	Aeneas Williams	.05
36	Lawrence Phillips	.10
37	John Elway	.75
38	Stanley Richard	.05
39	Darryl Williams	.05
40	Phillippi Sparks	.05
41	Tedy Bruschi	.05
42	Merton Hanks	.05
43	Ray Lewis	.05
44	Erik Williams	.05
45	Jason Gildon	.05
46	George Koonce	.05
47	Louis Oliver	.05
48	Muhsin Muhammad	.30
49	Daryl Hobbs	.05
50	Terry Glenn	1.25
51	Marvin Harrison	.75
52	Brian Dawkins	.05
53	Dale Carter	.05
54	Alex Molden	.05
55	Raymont Harris	.05
56	Jeff Burris	.05
57	Don Beebe	.05
58	Jamir Miller	.05
59	Carl Pickens	.10
60	Antonio London	.05
61	Courtney Hall	.05
62	Derrick Brooks	.05
63	Chris Boniol	.05
64	Jeff Lageman	.05
65	Roy Barker	.05
66	Devin Bush	.05
67	Aaron Glenn	.05
68	Wayne Simmons	.05
69	Steve Atwater	.05
70	Jimmie Jones	.05
71	Mark Carrier	.05
72	Chris Chandler	.05
73	Andy Harmon	.05
74	John Friesz	.05
75	Karim Abdul-Jabbar	1.00
76	Levon Kirkland	.05
77	Torrance Small	.05
78	Harvey Williams	.05
79	Chris Calloway	.05
80	Vinny Testaverde	.05
81	Bryant Young	.05
82	Ray Buchanan	.05
83	Robert Smith	.05
84	Robert Brooks	.10
85	Ray Crockett	.05
86	Bennie Blades	.05
87	Mark Carrier	.05
88	Mike Tomczak	.05
89	Darick Holmes	.05
90	Drew Bledsoe	1.00
91	Darren Woodson	.05
92	Dan Wilkinson	.05
93	Charles Way	.05
94	Ray Farmer	.05
95	Marcus Allen	.10
96	Marco Coleman	.05
97	Zach Thomas	.30
98	Wesley Walls	.05
99	Frank Wycheck	.05
100	Troy Aikman	1.00
101	Clyde Simmons	.05
102	Courtney Hawkins	.05
103	Chuck Smith	.05
104	Neil O'Donnell	.05
105	Kevin Carter	.05
106	Chris Slade	.05
107	Jessie Armstead	.05
108	Sean Dawkins	.05
109	Robert Blackmon	.05
110	Kevin Smith	.05
111	Lonnie Johnson	.05
112	Craig Newsome	.05
113	Jonathan Ogden	.05
114	Chris Zorich	.05
115	Tim Brown	.05
116	Fred Barnett	.05
117	Michael Haynes	.05
118	Eric Hill	.05
119	Ronnie Harmon	.05
120	Sean Gilbert	.05
121	Derrick Alexander	.05
122	Derrick Thomas	.10
123	Tyrone Wheatley	.10
124	Cortez Kennedy	.05
125	Jeff George	.05
126	Chad Cota	.05
127	Gary Zimmerman	.05
128	Johnnie Morton	.05
129	Chad Brown	.05
130	Marvcus Patton	.05
131	James Stewart	.05
132	Terry Kirby	.05
133	Chris Mims	.05
134	William Thomas	.05
135	Steve Tasker	.05
136	Jason Belser	.05
137	Bryan Cox	.05
138	Jessie Tuggle	.05
139	Ashley Ambrose	.05
140	Mark Chmura	.05
141	Jeff Hostetler	.05
142	Rich Owens	.05
143	Willie Davis	.05
144	Hardy Nickerson	.05
145	Curtis Martin	1.25
146	Ken Norton	.05
147	Victor Green	.05
148	Anthony Miller	.05
149	John Kasay	.05
150	O.J. McDuffie	.05
151	Darren Perry	.05
152	Luther Elliss	.05
153	Greg Hill	.05
154	John Randle	.05
155	Stephen Grant	.05
156	Leon Lett	.05
157	Darrien Gordon	.05
158	Ray Zellars	.05
159	Michael Jackson	.05
160	Leslie O'Neal	.05
161	Bruce Smith	.05
162	Santana Dotson	.05
163	Bobby Hebert	.05
164	Keith Hamilton	.05
165	Tony Boselli	.05
166	Alfred Williams	.05
167	Ty Detmer	.05
168	Chester McGlockton	.05
169	William Floyd	.05
170	Bruce Matthews	.05
171	Simeon Rice	.05
172	Scott Mitchell	.05
173	Ricardo McDonald	.05
174	Tyrone Poole	.05
175	Greg Lloyd	.05
176	Bruce Armstrong	.05
177	Erik Kramer	.05
178	Kimble Anders	.05
179	Lamar Smith	.05
180	Tony Tolbert	.05
181	Joe Aska	.05
182	Eric Allen	.05
183	Eric Turner	.05
184	Brad Johnson	.05
185	Tony Martin	.05
186	Mike Mamula	.05
187	Irving Spikes	.05
188	Keith Jackson	.05
189	Carlton Bailey	.05
190	Tyrone Braxton	.05
191	Chad Bratzke	.05
192	Adrian Murrell	.05
193	Roman Phifer	.05
194	Todd Collins	.05
195	Chris Warren	.05
196	Kevin Hardy	.05
197	Rick Mirer	.10
198	Cornelius Bennett	.05
199	Jimmy Hitchcock	.05
200	Michael Irvin	.10
201	Quentin Coryatt	.05
202	Reggie White	.10
203	Larry Centers	.05
204	Rodney Thomas	.05
205	Dana Stubblefield	.05
206	Rod Woodson	.05
207	Rhett Hall	.05
208	Steve Tovar	.05
209	Michael Westbrook	.10
210	Steve Wisniewski	.05
211	Carlester Crumpler	.05
212	Elvis Grbac	.10
213	Tim Bowens	.05
214	Kevin Porcher	.05
215	John Carney	.05
216	Anthony Newman	.05
217	Ernest Byner	.05
218	DeWayne Washington	.05
219	Willie Green	.05
220	Terry Allen	.10
221	William Fuller	.05
222	Al Del Greco	.05
223	Trent Dilfer	.10
224	Michael Dean Perry	.05
225	Larry Allen	.05
226	Mark Bruener	.05
227	Clay Matthews	.05
228	Ruben Brown	.05
229	Edgar Bennett	.05
230	Neil Smith	.05
231	Ken Harvey	.05
232	Kyle Brady	.05
233	Corey Miller	.05
234	Tony Siragusa	.05
235	Todd Sauerbrun	.05
236	Daniel Stubbs	.05
237	Robb Thomas	.05
238	Jimmy Smith	.05
239	Marquez Pope	.05
240	Tim Biakabutuka	.10
241	Jamie Asher	.05
242	Steve McNair	.75
243	Harold Green	.05
244	Frank Sanders	.05
245	Joe Johnson	.05
246	Eric Bieniemy	.05
247	Kevin Turner	.05
248	Rickey Dudley	.10
249	Orlando Thomas	.05
250	Dan Marino	2.00
251	Deion Sanders	.50
252	Dan Williams	.05
253	Sam Gash	.05
254	Lonnie Marts	.05
255	Mo Lewis	.05
256	Charles Johnson	.05
257	Chris Jacke	.05
258	Keenan McCardell	.05
259	Donnell Woolford	.05
260	Terrance Shaw	.05
261	Jason Dunn	.05
262	Willie McGinest	.05
263	Ken Dilger	.05
264	Keith Lyle	.05
265	Antonio Langham	.05
266	Carlton Gray	.05
267	LeShon Johnson	.05
268	Thurman Thomas	.10
269	Jesse Campbell	.05
270	Carnell Lake	.05
271	Cris Dishman	.05
272	Kevin Williams	.05
273	Troy Brown	.05
274	William Roaf	.05
275	Terrell Davis	1.25
276	Herman Moore	.90
277	Walt Harris	.05
278	Mark Collins	.05
279	Bert Emanuel	.05
280	Qadry Ismail	.05
281	Phil Hansen	.05
282	Steve Young	.75
283	Michael Sinclair	.05
284	Jeff Graham	.05
285	Sam Mills	.05
286	Terry McDaniel	.05
287	Eugene Robinson	.05
288	Tony Bennett	.05
289	Daryl Johnston	.05
290	Eric Swann	.05
291	Bam Morris	.05
292	Thomas Lewis	.05
293	Terrell Fletcher	.05
294	Gus Frerotte	.05
295	Stanley Pritchett	.05
296	Mike Alstott	.10
297	Will Shields	.05
298	Errict Rhett	.10
299	Garrison Hearst	.05
300	Kerry Collins	1.00
301	Darryll Lewis	.05
302	Chris T. Jones	.05
303	Yancey Thigpen	.05
304	Jackie Harris	.05
305	Steve Christie	.05
306	Gilbert Brown	.05
307	Terry Wooden	.05
308	Pete Mitchell	.05
309	Tim McDonald	.05
310	Jake Reed	.05
311	Ed McCaffrey	.05
312	Chris Doleman	.05
313	Eric Metcalf	.05
314	Ricky Reynolds	.05
315	David Sloan	.05
316	Marvin Washington	.05
317	Herschel Walker	.05
318	Michael Timpson	.05
319	Blaine Bishop	.05
320	Irv Smith	.05
321	Seth Joyner	.05
322	Terrell Buckley	.05
323	Michael Strahan	.05
324	Sam Adams	.05
325	Leslie Shepherd	.05
326	James Jett	.05
327	Anthony Pleasant	.05
328	Lee Woodall	.05
329	Shannon Sharpe	.05
330	Jamal Anderson	.20
331	Andre Hastings	.05
332	Troy Vincent	.05
333	Sean LaChapelle	.05
334	Winslow Oliver	.05
335	Sean Jones	.05
336	Darnay Scott	.05
337	Todd Lyght	.05
338	Leonard Russell	.05
339	Nate Newton	.05
340	Zack Crockett	.05
341	Amp Lee	.05
342	Bobby Engram	.05
343	Mike Hollis	.05
344	Rodney Hampton	.05
345	Mel Gray	.05
346	Van Malone	.05
347	Aaron Craver	.05
348	Jim Everett	.05
349	Trace Armstrong	.05
350	Pat Swilling	.05
351	Brent Jones	.05
352	Chris Spielman	.05
353	Brett Perriman	.05
354	Brian Kinchen	.05
355	Joey Galloway	.30
356	Henry Ellard	.05

357	Ben Coates	.05
358	Dorsey Levens	.20
359	Charlie Garner	.05
360	Erric Pegram	.05
361	Anthony Johnson	.05
362	Rashaan Salaam	.10
363	Jeff Blake	.20
364	Kent Graham	.05
365	Broderick Thomas	.05
366	Richmond Webb	.05
367	Alfred Pupunu	.05
368	Mark Stepnoski	.05
369	David Dunn	.05
370	Bobby Houston	.05
371	Anthony Parker	.05
372	Quinn Early	.05
373	LeRoy Butler	.05
374	Kurt Gouveia	.05
375	Greg Biekert	.05
376	Jim Harbaugh	.05
377	Eric Bjornson	.05
378	Craig Heyward	.05
379	Steve Bono	.05
380	Tony Banks	.30
381	John Mobley	.05
382	Irving Fryar	.05
383	Dermontti Dawson	.05
384	Eric Davis	.05
385	Natrone Means	.10
386	Jason Sehorn	.05
387	Michael McCrary	.05
388	Corwin Brown	.05
389	Kevin Glover	.05
390	Jerris McPhail	.05
391	Bobby Taylor	.05
392	Tony McGee	.05
393	Curtis Conway	.05
394	Napoleon Kaufman	.05
395	Brian Blades	.05
396	Richard Dent	.05
397	Dave Brown	.05
398	Stan Humphries	.05
399	Stevon Moore	.05
400	Brett Favre	2.00
401	Jerome Bettis	.10
402	Darrin Smith	.05
403	Chris Penn	.05
404	Rob Moore	.05
405	Michael Barrow	.05
406	Tony Brackens	.05
407	Wayne Martin	.05
408	Warren Moon	.05
409	Jason Elam	.05
410	J.J. Birden	.05
411	Hugh Douglas	.05
412	Lamar Lathon	.05
413	John Kidd	.05
414	Bryce Paup	.05
415	Shawn Jefferson	.05
416	Leeland McElroy	.10
417	Elbert Shelley	.05
418	Jermaine Lewis	.05
419	Eric Moulds	.10
420	Michael Bates	.05
421	John Mangum	.05
422	Corey Sawyer	.05
423	Jim Schwantz	.05
424	Rod Smith	.05
425	Glyn Milburn	.05
426	Desmond Howard	.10
427	John Henry Mills	.05
428	Cary Blanchard	.05
429	Chris Hudson	.05
430	Tamarick Vanover	.10
431	Kirby Dar Dar	.05
432	David Palmer	.05
433	Dave Meggett	.05
434	Tyrone Hughes	.05
435	Amani Toomer	.10
436	Wayne Chrebet	.05
437	Carl Kidd	.05
438	Derrick Witherspoon	.05
439	Jahine Arnold	.05
440	Andre Coleman	.05
441	Jeff Wilkins	.05
442	Jay Bellamy	.05
443	Eddie Kennison	.50
444	Nilo Silvan	.05
445	Brian Mitchell	.05
446	Checklist	.05
447	Checklist	.05
448	Checklist	.05
449	Checklist	.05
450	Checklist	.05

1997 Fleer All-Pro

This 24-card set was inserted 1:36 retail packs. All-Pros from the previous season were commemorated.

		MT
	Complete Set (24):	160.00
	Common Player:	2.00
1	Troy Aikman	15.00
2	Larry Allen	2.00
3	Drew Bledsoe	15.00
4	Terrell Davis	18.00
5	Dermontti Dawson	2.00
6	John Elway	12.00
7	Brett Favre	30.00
8	Herman Moore	4.00
9	Jerry Rice	15.00
10	Barry Sanders	15.00
11	Shannon Sharpe	2.00
12	Erik Williams	2.00
13	Ashley Ambrose	2.00
14	Chad Brown	2.00
15	LeRoy Butler	2.00
16	Kevin Greene	2.00
17	Sam Mills	2.00
18	John Randle	2.00
19	Deion Sanders	8.00
20	Junior Seau	4.00
21	Bruce Smith	2.00
22	Alfred Williams	2.00
23	Darren Woodson	2.00
24	Bryant Young	2.00

1997 Fleer Decade of Excellence

Inserted 1:36 hobby packs, this 12-card set featured photography from 10 years prior. Ten percent of the cards were printed with holographic foil and were inserted 1:360 hobby packs.

		MT
	Complete Set (12):	70.00
	Common Player:	3.00
1	Marcus Allen	6.00
2	Cris Carter	3.00
3	John Elway	10.00
4	Irving Fryar	3.00
5	Darrell Green	3.00
6	Dan Marino	25.00
7	Jerry Rice	15.00
8	Bruce Smith	3.00
9	Herschel Walker	3.00
10	Reggie White	6.00
11	Rod Woodson	3.00
12	Steve Young	10.00

1997 Fleer Game Breakers

Inserted 1:2 retail packs, this 20-card set showcased players who have the ability to break a game open. A Game Breakers Supreme parallel was inserted 1:18 of all pack types.

		MT
	Complete Set (20):	20.00
	Common Player:	.30
	Supreme Cards:	2x-4x
1	Troy Aikman	2.50
2	Jerome Bettis	.60
3	Drew Bledsoe	2.50
4	Isaac Bruce	.75
5	Mark Brunell	2.50
6	Kerry Collins	2.00
7	Terrell Davis	2.50
8	Marshall Faulk	.30
9	Antonio Freeman	.60
10	Joey Galloway	1.00
11	Terry Glenn	2.50
12	Desmond Howard	.30
13	Keyshawn Johnson	1.00
14	Eddie Kennison	1.00
15	Curtis Martin	2.50
16	Herman Moore	.30
17	Lawrence Phillips	.60
18	Barry Sanders	2.50
19	Shannon Sharpe	.30
20	Emmitt Smith	5.00

1997 Fleer Million Dollar Moments

The 50-card set was part of a season-long multi-sport promotion which was available in all 1997 packs of Fleer, Fleer Ultra and Flair Showcase football products released after June 1997. Each pack contained one of 50 different Million Dollar Moments cards. The fronts of the cards had the Million Dollar Moments logo in the upper left. The player's name, date of his highlight and highlight are included at the bottom front. The backs include the contest details. Cards numbered 1-45 are common, while 46-50 are difficult to find. Those who collected cards 1-45 plus any one of 46-49 won up to a $1,000 shopping spree. The grand prize of $1 million was awarded to the collector of all 50 cards. To reward collectors who complete the "common" 45-card set, Fleer offered the opportunity to redeem the 45-card set (with $5.99 for shipping) for a complete parallel 50-card set.

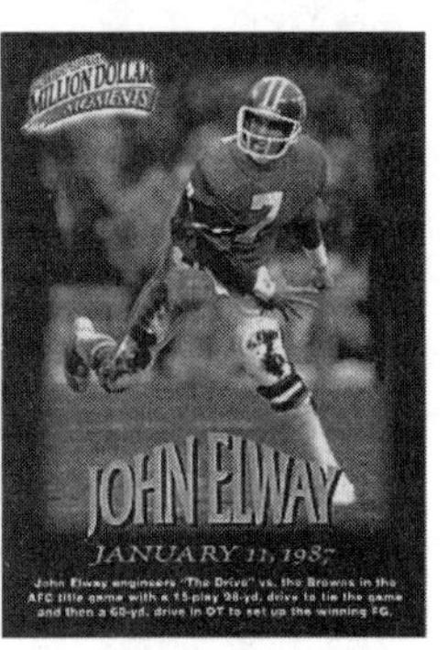

		MT
	Complete Set (45):	5.00
	Common Player:	.05
1	Checklist	.05
2	Troy Aikman	.50
3	Sid Luckman	.10
4	Barry Sanders	.50
5	Tom Fears	.05
6	Reggie White	.10
7	Lou Groza	.05
8	John Elway	.35
9	Raymond Berry	.05
10	Marcus Allen	.10
11	Paul Hornung	.10
12	Herschel Walker	.05
13	Norm Van Brocklin	.05
14	Bruce Smith	.05
15	Billy Wade	.05
16	Andre Reed	.05
17	Gale Sayers	.10
18	Terrell Davis	.50
19	Jim Bakken	.05
20	Marshall Faulk	.10
21	Tom Dempsey	.05
22	Dan Marino	1.00
23	Garo Yepremian	.05
24	Jerry Rice	.50
25	Herman Edwards	.05
26	Derrick Thomas	.05
27	Kellen Winslow	.05
28	Steve Young	.35
29	Tony Dorsett	.10
30	Desmond Howard	.05
31	Roger Craig	.05
32	Drew Bledsoe	.50
33	Doug Williams	.05
34	Jerome Bettis	.10
35	Bobby Layne	.05
36	Junior Seau	.10
37	Roman Gabriel	.05
38	Cris Carter	.10
39	Drew Pearson	.05
40	Warren Moon	.05
41	Wesley Walker	.05
42	Ricky Watters	.10
43	Carl Eller	.05
44	Kordell Stewart	.50
45	John Mackey	.05
46	Thurman Thomas	—
47	Ken Stabler	—
48	Emmitt Smith	—
49	Jim Brown	—
50	Eddie George	—

1997 Fleer Prospects

The 10-card set was inserted 1:6 packs. It featured the top prospects from the 1997 NFL Draft.

		MT
	Complete Set (10):	20.00
	Common Player:	.75
1	Peter Boulware	.75
2	Rae Carruth	3.00
3	Jim Druckenmiller	5.00
4	Warrick Dunn	7.00
5	Tony Gonzalez	1.50
6	Yatil Green	4.00
7	Ike Hilliard	4.00
8	Orlando Pace	1.50
9	Darrell Russell	.75
10	Shawn Springs	1.50

1997 Fleer Rookie Sensations

Inserted 1:4 packs, the 20-card set focused on rookies who had positive impacts on their team in 1996.

		MT
	Complete Set (20):	25.00
	Common Player:	.50
1	Karim Abdul-Jabbar	3.00
2	Mike Alstott	1.00
3	Tony Banks	2.00
4	Tony Brackens	.50
5	Rickey Dudley	.50
6	Bobby Engram	.50
7	Eddie George	7.00
8	Terry Glenn	4.00
9	Kevin Hardy	.50
10	Marvin Harrison	2.00
11	Keyshawn Johnson	2.00
12	Eddie Kennison	2.00
13	Jermaine Lewis	.50
14	Ray Lewis	.50
15	John Mobley	.50
16	Eric Moulds	.50
17	Jonathan Ogden	.50
18	Lawrence Phillips	1.00
19	Simeon Rice	.50
20	Zach Thomas	1.50

1997 Fleer Thrill Seekers

Inserted 1:288 packs, the 12-card set looks at players known for making the big play.

		MT
Complete Set (12):		500.00
Common Player:		15.00
1	Karim Abdul-Jabbar	40.00
2	Jerome Bettis	15.00
3	Terrell Davis	50.00
4	John Elway	35.00
5	Brett Favre	90.00
6	Eddie George	65.00
7	Terry Glenn	50.00
8	Keyshawn Johnson	30.00
9	Dan Marino	80.00
10	Curtis Martin	50.00
11	Deion Sanders	20.00
12	Emmitt Smith	80.00

1997 Fleer Goudey

Goudey included 150 cards that adopted the old-time look of the Goudey brand from the 1930s. The cards measure 2-3/8" x 2-7/8", with player pictures appearing as illustrations. Backs include a player synopsis "old-time" text. Also included in the regular-issue set were cards of Chuck Bednarik and Y.A. Tittle, as well as two checklists and a History of Goudey card. Insert sets found in Goudey were: Gridiron Greats (parallel set), Heads Up, Concrete Chuck Bednarik Says, Y.A. Tittle Says and Pigskin 2000.

		MT
Complete Set (150):		18.00
Common Player:		.05
Goudy Greats		
Complete Set (147):		100.00
Goudy Greats Cards:		3x-6x
Wax Box:		50.00
1	Michael Jackson	.05
2	Ray Lewis	.05
3	Vinny Testaverde	.05
4	Eric Turner	.05
5	Jim Kelly	.10
6	Bryce Paup	.05
7	Andre Reed	.05
8	Bruce Smith	.05
9	Thurman Thomas	.10
10	Jeff Blake	.10
11	Ki-Jana Carter	.10
12	Carl Pickens	.05
13	Darnay Scott	.05
14	Terrell Davis	1.25
15	John Elway	.75
16	Anthony Miller	.05
17	John Mobley	.05
18	Shannon Sharpe	.05
19	Chris Chandler	.05
20	Eddie George	1.50
21	Steve McNair	.50
22	Chris Sanders	.05
23	Quentin Coryatt	.05
24	Sean Dawkins	.05
25	Ken Dilger	.05
26	Marshall Faulk	.30
27	Jim Harbaugh	.05
28	Marvin Harrison	.75
29	Tony Brackens	.05
30	Mark Brunell	1.00
31	Kevin Hardy	.10
32	Keenan McCardell	.05
33	James Stewart	.05
34	Marcus Allen	.10
35	Steve Bono	.05
36	Dale Carter	.05
37	Neil Smith	.05
38	Derrick Thomas	.05
39	Tamarick Vanover	.10
40	Karim Abdul-Jabbar	1.00
41	Dan Marino	2.00
42	O.J. McDuffie	.05
43	Stanley Pritchett	.05
44	Zach Thomas	.50
45	Drew Bledsoe	1.00
46	Ben Coates	.05
47	Terry Glenn	1.50
48	Shawn Jefferson	.05
49	Curtis Martin	1.50
50	David Meggett	.05
51	Hugh Douglas	.05
52	Keyshawn Johnson	.75
53	Adrian Murrell	.05
54	Tim Brown	.05
55	Rickey Dudley	.10
56	Jeff Hostetler	.05
57	Napoleon Kaufman	.05
58	Chester McGlockton	.05
59	Jerome Bettis	.10
60	Andre Hastings	.05
61	Greg Lloyd	.05
62	Kordell Stewart	1.00
63	Yancey Thigpen	.05
64	Rod Woodson	.05
65	Andre Coleman	.05
66	Stan Humphries	.05
67	Tony Martin	.05
68	Leonard Russell	.05
69	Junior Seau	.05
70	Brian Blades	.05
71	Joey Galloway	.50
72	Chris Warren	.05
73	Larry Centers	.05
74	Leeland McElroy	.10
75	Simeon Rice	.10
76	Frank Sanders	.05
77	Eric Swann	.05
78	Jamal Anderson	.40
79	Bert Emanuel	.05
80	Terance Mathis	.05
81	Eric Metcalf	.05
82	Tim Biakabutuka	.40
83	Kerry Collins	1.00
84	Kevin Greene	.05
85	Muhsin Muhammad	.10
86	Wesley Walls	.05
87	Curtis Conway	.05
88	Bryan Cox	.05
89	Walt Harris	.05
90	Erik Kramer	.05
91	Rashaan Salaam	.10
92	Troy Aikman	1.00
93	Michael Irvin	.10
94	Daryl Johnston	.05
95	Leon Lett	.05
96	Deion Sanders	.50
97	Emmitt Smith	2.00
98	Scott Mitchell	.05
99	Herman Moore	.10
100	Johnnie Morton	.05
101	Brett Perriman	.05
102	Barry Sanders	1.00
103	Edgar Bennett	.05
104	Robert Brooks	.05
105	Brett Favre	2.00
106	Antonio Freeman	.05
107	Keith Jackson	.05
108	Reggie White	.10
109	Cris Carter	.05
110	Warren Moon	.10
111	John Randle	.05
112	Jake Reed	.05
113	Robert Smith	.05
114	Jim Everett	.05
115	Michael Haynes	.05
116	Alex Molden	.05
117	Ray Zellars	.05
118	Chris Calloway	.05
119	Rodney Hampton	.05
120	Phillippi Sparks	.05
121	Amani Toomer	.10
122	Ty Detmer	.05
123	Jason Dunn	.05
124	Irving Fryar	.05
125	Chris T. Jones	.05
126	Ricky Watters	.10
127	Tony Banks	.75
128	Isaac Bruce	.25
129	Eddie Kennison	.75
130	Lawrence Phillips	.10
131	Merton Hanks	.05
132	Terry Kirby	.05
133	Ken Norton	.05
134	Jerry Rice	1.00
135	J.J. Stokes	.10
136	Steve Young	.75
137	Alvin Harper	.05
138	Jackie Harris	.05
139	Hardy Nickerson	.05
140	Errict Rhett	.20
141	Terry Allen	.05
142	Henry Ellard	.05
143	Gus Frerotte	.05
144	Brian Mitchell	.05
145	Michael Westbrook	.10
146	Chuck Bednarik	.10
147	Y.A. Tittle	.10
148	Checklist	.05
149	Checklist	.05
150	Checklist	.05

1997 Fleer Goudey Heads Up

Heads Up contained 20 players in a cartoon format, with the player's head larger and in color, compared to the small black and white body. The player's last name runs up the left side in white letters. Heads Up cards were found in every 30 hobby packs and every 36 retail packs.

		MT
Complete Set (20):		150.00
Common Player:		3.00
1	Troy Aikman	15.00
2	Marcus Allen	3.00
3	Tim Biakabutuka	6.00
4	Robert Brooks	3.00
5	Isaac Bruce	8.00
6	Kerry Collins	15.00
7	Terrell Davis	18.00
8	Brett Favre	30.00
9	Terry Glenn	15.00
10	Rodney Hampton	3.00
11	Michael Irvin	6.00
12	Chris T. Jones	3.00
13	Carl Pickens	3.00
14	Barry Sanders	15.00
15	Kordell Stewart	15.00
16	Thurman Thomas	3.00
17	Tamarick Vanover	8.00
18	Chris Warren	3.00
19	Ricky Watters	3.00
20	Steve Young	10.00

1997 Fleer Goudey Pigskin 2000

Pigskin 2000 was a 15-card foil-etched insert that highlighted some of the NFL's elite. The insert name and player's name are included in gold foil along the left side, with the Fleer Goudey logo in the top left corner. Pigskin 2000 cards are found every 360 hobby packs.

		MT
Complete Set (15):		400.00
Common Player:		10.00
1	Karim Abdul-Jabbar	40.00
2	Jeff Blake	10.00
3	Drew Bledsoe	40.00
4	Robert Brooks	10.00
5	Terrell Davis	40.00
6	Marshall Faulk	20.00
7	Joey Galloway	10.00
8	Eddie George	40.00
9	Terry Glenn	35.00
10	Keyshawn Johnson	20.00
11	Chris T. Jones	10.00
12	Curtis Martin	40.00
13	Steve McNair	25.00
14	Lawrence Phillips	10.00
15	Kordell Stewart	30.00

1997 Fleer Goudey Tittle Says

Y.A. Tittle Says shows 20 of the top offensive stars, with Tittle providing insight on each card back. Each card has a color photo of the player over a color background with the insert's name scattered across it. They were found every 72 hobby and every 85 retail packs.

		MT
Complete Set (20):		225.00
Common Player:		5.00
1	Karim Abdul-Jabbar	15.00
2	Jerome Bettis	5.00
3	Tim Brown	5.00
4	Isaac Bruce	8.00
5	Cris Carter	5.00
6	Curtis Conway	5.00
7	John Elway	12.00
8	Marshall Faulk	10.00
9	Brett Favre	30.00
10	Joey Galloway	5.00
11	Eddie George	25.00
12	Keyshawn Johnson	12.00
13	Dan Marino	30.00
14	Curtis Martin	25.00
15	Herman Moore	5.00
16	Jerry Rice	15.00
17	Barry Sanders	15.00
18	Emmitt Smith	30.00
19	Thurman Thomas	5.00
20	Ricky Watters	5.00

1997 Fleer Goudey Bednarik Says

This insert highlighted 15 of the top defensive players in the league, with Bednarik's assessment of each player on the card back. Cards in this insert are identified by a large solid block pattern in the back featuring the team's colors, with a black strip near the bottom with the words "Concrete Chuck Bednarik" in it. These inserts were found every 60 hobby packs and every 72 retail packs.

		MT
Complete Set (15):		100.00
Common Player:		3.00
1	Kevin Greene	3.00
2	Ray Lewis	3.00
3	Greg Lloyd	3.00
4	Chester McGlockton	3.00
5	Hardy Nickerson	3.00
6	Bryce Paup	3.00
7	Simeon Rice	3.00
8	Deion Sanders	14.00
9	Junior Seau	3.00
10	Bruce Smith	3.00
11	Derrick Thomas	3.00
12	Zach Thomas	12.00
13	Eric Turner	3.00
14	Reggie White	10.00
15	Rod Woodson	3.00

1997 Metal

The 200-card set contains 173 player cards, two checklists and 25 rookies. Each card featured all etched foil. The players are presented in original Marvel comic illustrations on full-bleed backgrounds, with the player's name, team, position and Metal Universe logo located near the bottom of the card. Card backs contain another player photo and stats.

		MT
Complete Set (200):		30.00
Common Player:		.10
Wax Box:		55.00
1	Terry Glenn	1.00
2	Terry Kirby	.10
3	Thomas Lewis	.10
4	Tim Biakabutuka	.20
5	Tim Brown	.10
6	Todd Collins	.10
7	Tony Banks	.40
8	Tony Brackens	.10
9	Tony Martin	.10
10	Trent Dilfer	.20
11	Troy Aikman	1.00
12	Ty Detmer	.10
13	Tyrone Wheatley	.10
14	Vinny Testaverde	.10
15	Wayne Chrebet	.10
16	Wesley Walls	.10
17	William Floyd	.10
18	Willie McGinest	.10
19	Yancey Thigpen	.10
20	Zach Thomas	.30
21	Terry Allen	.10
22	Terrell Owens	.50
23	Terrell Davis	1.25
24	Terance Mathis	.10
25	Ted Johnson	.10
26	Tamarick Vanover	.20
27	Steve Young	.75
28	Steve McNair	.75
29	Stan Humphries	.10
30	Simeon Rice	.10
31	Shannon Sharpe	.10
32	Sean Jones	.10
33	Scott Mitchell	.10
34	Sam Mills	.10
35	Rodney Hampton	.10
36	Rod Woodson	.10
37	Robert Smith	.10
38	Rob Moore	.10
39	Ricky Watters	.20
40	Rickey Dudley	.10
41	Rick Mirer	.10
42	Reggie White	.20
43	Ray Zellars	.10
44	Ray Lewis	.10
45	Rashaan Salaam	.20
46	Quentin Coryatt	.10
47	Qadry Ismail	.10
48	O.J. McDuffie	.10
49	Nilo Silvan	.10
50	Neil Smith	.10
51	Neil O'Donnell	.10
52	Natrone Means	.20
53	Napoleon Kaufman	.10
54	Mike Tomczak	.10
55	Mike Alstott	.20
56	Michael Westbrook	.10
57	Michael Jackson	.10
58	Michael Irvin	.20
59	Michael Haynes	.10
60	Michael Bates	.10
61	Mel Gray	.10
62	Marvin Harrison	.50
63	Marshall Faulk	.30
64	Mark Brunell	1.00
65	Mario Bates	.10
66	Marcus Allen	.20
67	Lorenzo Neal	.10
68	Levon Kirkland	.10
69	Leonard Russell	.10
70	Leeland McElroy	.10
71	Lawyer Milloy	.10
72	Lawrence Phillips	.20
73	Larry Centers	.10
74	Lamar Lathon	.10
75	Kordell Stewart	.75
76	Kimble Anders	.10
77	Ki-Jana Carter	.10
78	Keyshawn Johnson	.50
79	Kevin Turner	.10
80	Jermaine Lewis	.10
81	Jerome Bettis	.20
82	Jerris McPhail	.10
83	Joey Galloway	.40
84	Jerry Rice	1.00
85	Jim Everett	.10
86	Jimmy Smith	.10
87	Jim Harbaugh	.10
88	John Elway	.75
89	John Friez	.10
90	John Mobley	.10
91	Johnnie Morton	.10
92	Junior Seau	.10
93	Karim Abdul-Jabbar	.75
94	Keenan McCardell	.10
95	Ken Dilger	.10
96	Ken Norton	.10
97	Kent Graham	.10
98	Kerry Collins	1.00
99	Kevin Greene	.10
100	Kevin Hardy	.10
101	Jeff Lewis	.10
102	Jeff George	.10
103	Jeff Graham	.10
104	Jeff Blake	.30
105	Jason Sehorn	.10
106	Jason Dunn	.10
107	Jamie Asher	.10
108	Jamal Anderson	.30
109	Jake Reed	.10
110	Isaac Bruce	.30
111	Irving Fryar	.10
112	Iheanyi Uwaezuoke	.10
113	Hugh Douglas	.10
114	Herman Moore	.20
115	Harvey Williams	.10
116	Hardy Nickerson	.10
117	Gus Frerotte	.10
118	Greg Hill	.10
119	Glyn Milburn	.10
120	Frank Wycheck	.10
121	Frank Sanders	.10
122	Errict Rhett	.20
123	Erik Kramer	.10
124	Eric Moulds	.10
125	Eric Metcalf	.10
126	Emmitt Smith	2.00
127	Edgar Bennett	.10
128	Eddie Kennison	.50
129	Eddie George	1.50
130	Drew Bledsoe	1.00
131	Dorsey Levens	.20
132	Desmond Howard	.10
133	Derrick Thomas	.10
134	Derrick Alexander	.10
135	Deion Sanders	.50
136	Dave Brown	.10
137	Daryl Johnston	.10
138	Darnay Scott	.10
139	Darick Holmes	.10
140	Dan Marino	2.00
141	Curtis Martin	1.25
142	Curtis Conway	.10
143	Cris Carter	.10
144	Chris Warren	.10
145	Chris T. Jones	.10
146	Chris Slade	.10
147	Chris Sanders	.10
148	Chester McGlockton	.10
149	Charlie Jones	.10
150	Charles Way	.10
151	Carl Pickens	.10
152	Bryan Still	.10
153	Bruce Smith	.10
154	Brian Mitchell	.10
155	Brett Perriman	.10
156	Brett Favre	2.50
157	Brad Johnson	.10
158	Thurman Thomas	.20
159	Bobby Engram	.10
160	Bert Emanuel	.10
161	Ben Coates	.10
162	Barry Sanders	1.00
163	Bam Morris	.10
164	Ashley Ambrose	.10
165	Antonio Freeman	.30
166	Anthony Miller	.10
167	Anthony Johnson	.10
168	Andre Rison	.10
169	Andre Reed	.10
170	Alex Molden	.10
171	Aeneas Williams	.10
172	Adrian Murrell	.10
173	Aaron Hayden	.10
174	*Darnell Autry*	.75
175	*Orlando Pace*	.75
176	*Darrell Russell*	.10
177	*Peter Boulware*	.10
178	*Shawn Springs*	1.00
179	*Bryant Westbrook*	.10
180	*Dwayne Rudd*	.10
181	*Rae Carruth*	1.00
182	*Troy Davis*	2.00
183	*Antowain Smith*	1.75
184	*James Farrior*	.10
185	*Walter Jones*	.10
186	*Sam Madison*	.10
187	*Tom Knight*	.10
188	*Reidel Anthony*	2.00
189	*Warrick Dunn*	4.00
190	*Reinard Wilson*	.10
191	*Tyrus McCloud*	.10
192	*Michael Booker*	.10
193	*Tony Gonzalez*	.75
194	*Pat Barnes*	1.00
195	*Tiki Barber*	1.50
196	*Sedrick Shaw*	.75
197	*Corey Dillon*	1.50
198	*Danny Wuerffel*	2.50
199	Checklist	.10
200	Checklist	.10

1997 Metal Precious Metal Gems

The 198-card parallel of the base set, not including the two checklists, was randomly seeded in packs. Sky-Box produced 150 serial numbered sets. The first 15 cards of the print run were printed with green foil.

	MT
Precious Metal Stars:	40x-80x
Precious Metal Rookies:	20x-40x

1997 Metal Autographics Previews

Inserted 1:500 packs, auto-graphed cards of 10 of the 75 NFL players appearing in the debut of the Autographics program are found here.

	MT
Complete Set (12):	800.00
Common Player:	25.00
Karim Abdul-Jabbar	100.00
Mike Alstott	50.00

Darnell Autry	40.00
Rae Carruth	60.00
Ty Detmer	25.00
Eddie Kennison	75.00
Brian Manning	25.00
Ed McCaffrey	25.00
Jerry Rice	350.00
Shannon Sharpe	40.00
Mike Vrabel	25.00
Chris Warren	25.00

1997 Metal Body Shop

Inserted 1:96 packs, the 15-card set mixes photography and technology. Drew Bledsoe's arm and Jamal Anderson's legs turn bionic on these cards.

	MT
Complete Set (15):	220.00
Common Player:	10.00
Minor Stars:	20.00
BS1 Zach Thomas	20.00
BS2 Steve Young	25.00
BS3 Steve McNair	35.00
BS4 Simeon Rice	10.00
BS5 Shannon Sharpe	10.00
BS6 Napoleon Kaufman	10.00
BS7 Mike Alstott	10.00
BS8 Michael Westbrook	10.00
BS9 Kordell Stewart	35.00
BS10 Kevin Hardy	10.00
BS11 Kerry Collins	35.00
BS12 Junior Seau	10.00
BS13 Jamal Anderson	10.00
BS14 Drew Bledsoe	35.00
BS15 Deion Sanders	25.00

1997 Metal Gold Universe

The 10-card set was inserted 1:120 retail packs. The players are il-lustrated in space on the card fronts.

	MT
Complete Set (10):	200.00
Common Player:	10.00
GU1 Dan Marino	75.00
GU2 Deion Sanders	25.00
GU3 Drew Bledsoe	40.00
GU4 Isaac Bruce	15.00
GU5 Joey Galloway	15.00
GU6 Karim Abdul-Jabbar	25.00
GU7 Lawrence Phillips	10.00
GU8 Marshall Faulk	15.00
GU9 Marvin Harrison	15.00
GU10 Steve Young	25.00

1997 Metal Iron Rookies

Inserted 1:24 packs, the 15-card set features the top players who were chosen in the 1997 NFL Draft.

	MT
Complete Set (15):	70.00
Common Player:	2.50
IC1 Darnell Autry	6.00
IC2 Orlando Pace	5.00
IC3 Peter Boulware	2.50
IC4 Shawn Springs	5.00
IC5 Bryant Westbrook	2.50
IC6 Rae Carruth	8.00

IC7	Troy Davis	12.00
IC8	Antowain Smith	10.00
IC9	James Farrior	2.50
IC10	Dwayne Rudd	2.50
IC11	Darrell Russell	2.50
IC12	Warrick Dunn	20.00
IC13	Sedrick Shaw	5.00
IC14	Danny Wuerffel	18.00
IC15	Sam Madison	2.50

1997 Metal Marvel Metal

Inserted 1:6 packs, the 20-card set compares the players with Marvel Superheroes. For example, Isaac Bruce is pictured with Spider-man.

	MT
Complete Set (20):	40.00
Common Player:	1.00
MM1 Barry Sanders	5.00
MM2 Bruce Smith	1.00
MM3 Desmond Howard	1.00
MM4 Eddie George	6.00
MM5 Eddie Kennison	2.50
MM6 Jerry Rice	5.00
MM7 Joey Galloway	2.00
MM8 John Elway	3.00
MM9 Karim Abdul-Jabbar	3.00
MM10 Kerry Collins	4.00
MM11 Kevin Hardy	1.00
MM12 Kordell Stewart	4.00
MM13 Mark Brunell	5.00
MM14 Marshall Faulk	2.00
MM15 Michael Westbrook	1.00
MM16 Simeon Rice	1.00
MM17 Steve McNair	4.00
MM18 Terry Glenn	5.00
MM19 Tony Brackens	1.00
MM20 Tony Martin	1.00

1997 Metal Platinum Portraits

Inserted 1:288 packs, the 10-card set features the players on the card fronts with an etched-foil look. This was the third year for the chase set.

	MT
Complete Set (10):	450.00
Common Player:	20.00
PP1 Troy Aikman	45.00
PP2 Terrell Davis	45.00
PP3 Marvin Harrison	20.00
PP4 Keyshawn Johnson	20.00
PP5 Jerry Rice	45.00
PP6 Emmitt Smith	80.00
PP7 Dan Marino	80.00
PP8 Curtis Martin	45.00
PP9 Brett Favre	90.00
PP10 Barry Sanders	45.00

1997 Metal Titanium

Inserted 1:72 hobby packs, the 20-card set featured a titanium background on die-cut cards.

	MT
Complete Set (20):	400.00
Common Player:	7.00
TT1 Barry Sanders	30.00
TT2 Brett Favre	60.00
TT3 Curtis Martin	30.00
TT4 Eddie George	35.00
TT5 Eddie Kennison	14.00
TT6 Emmitt Smith	50.00
TT7 Herman Moore	14.00
TT8 Isaac Bruce	14.00
TT9 Jerry Rice	30.00
TT10 John Elway	25.00
TT11 Keyshawn Johnson	7.00
TT12 Lawrence Phillips	7.00
TT13 Mark Brunell	30.00
TT14 Mike Alstott	7.00
TT15 Steve McNair	25.00
TT16 Steve Young	25.00
TT17 Terrell Davis	30.00
TT18 Terry Glenn	25.00
TT19 Tony Banks	14.00
TT20 Troy Aikman	30.00

1997 Ultra

The 200-card set featured 198 cards and two checklists. The fronts showcase a full-bleed photo with the Ultra logo in the upper left. The player's name is written in script at the bottom center, while the team and his position are printed beneath the name. The backs include two photos, with his name, bio and stats beginning in the center and continuing to the bottom. The Gold Medallion parallel cards were inserted one per pack, while the Platinum Medallion parallel cards were exclusive in hobby packs and found 1:100 packs.

	MT
Complete Set (200):	30.00
Common Player:	.10
Gold Cards:	2x-4x
Platinum Stars:	40x-80x
Platinum Rookies:	20x-40x
Wax Box:	55.00
1 Brett Favre	2.50
2 Ricky Watters	.20
3 Dan Marino	2.00
4 Bryan Still	.10
5 Chester McGlockton	.10
6 Tim Biakabutuka	.20
7 Dave Brown	.10
8 Mike Alstott	.20
9 O.J. McDuffie	.10
10 Mark Brunell	1.25
11 Michael Bates	.10
12 Tyrone Wheatley	.10
13 Eddie George	1.50
14 Kevin Greene	.10
15 Jerris McPhail	.10
16 Harvey Williams	.10
17 Eric Swann	.10
18 Carl Pickens	.10
19 Darrell Davis	.10
20 Charles Way	.10
21 Jamie Asher	.10
22 Qadry Ismail	.10
23 Lawrence Phillips	.20
24 John Friez	.10
25 Dorsey Levens	.20
26 Willie McGinest	.10
27 Chris T. Jones	.10
28 Cortez Kennedy	.10
29 Raymont Harris	.10
30 William Roaf	.10
31 Ted Johnson	.10
32 Tony Martin	.10
33 Jim Everett	.10
34 Ray Zellars	.10
35 Derrick Alexander	.10
36 Leonard Russell	.10
37 William Thomas	.10
38 Karim Abdul-Jabbar	1.00
39 Kevin Turner	.10
40 Robert Brooks	.10
41 Kent Graham	.10
42 Tony Brackens	.10
43 Rodney Hampton	.10
44 Drew Bledsoe	1.25
45 Barry Sanders	1.25
46 Tim Brown	.10
47 Reggie White	.20
48 Terry Allen	.10
49 Jim Harbaugh	.10
50 John Elway	.75
51 William Floyd	.10
52 Michael Jackson	.10
53 Larry Centers	.10
54 Emmitt Smith	2.00
55 Bruce Smith	.10
56 Terrell Owens	.50
57 Deion Sanders	.50
58 Neil O'Donnell	.10
59 Kordell Stewart	1.00
60 Bobby Engram	.10
61 Keenan McCardell	.10
62 Ben Coates	.10
63 Curtis Martin	1.75
64 Hugh Douglas	.10
65 Eric Moulds	.20
66 Derrick Thomas	.20
67 Dan Morris	.10
68 Bryan Cox	.10
69 Rob Moore	.10
70 Michael Haynes	.10
71 Brian Mitchell	.10
72 Alex Molden	.10
73 Steve Young	.75
74 Andre Reed	.10
75 Michael Westbrook	.20
76 Eric Metcalf	.10
77 Tony Banks	.30
78 Ken Dilger	.10
79 John Henry Mills	.10
80 Ashley Ambrose	.10
81 Jason Dunn	.10
82 Trent Dilfer	.20
83 Wayne Chrebet	.10
84 Ty Detmer	.10
85 Aeneas Williams	.10
86 Frank Wycheck	.10
87 Jessie Tuggle	.10
88 Steve McNair	1.00
89 Chris Slade	.10
90 Anthony Johnson	.10
91 Simeon Rice	.10
92 Mike Tomczak	.10
93 Sean Jones	.10
94 Wesley Walls	.10
95 Thurman Thomas	.20
96 Scott Mitchell	.10
97 Desmond Howard	.10
98 Chris Warren	.10
99 Glyn Milburn (RB)	.10
100 Vinny Testaverde	.10
101 James Stewart	.10
102 Iheanyi Uwaezuoke	.10
103 Stan Humphries	.10
104 Terance Mathis	.10
105 Thomas Lewis	.10
106 Eddie Kennison	.40
107 Rashaan Salaam	.20
108 Curtis Conway	.10
109 Chris Sanders	.10
110 Marcus Allen	.20
111 Gilbert Brown	.10
112 Jason Sehorn	.10
113 Zach Thomas	.20
114 Bobby Hebert	.10
115 Herman Moore	.20
116 Ray Lewis	.10
117 Darnay Scott	.10
118 Jamal Anderson	.20
119 Keyshawn Johnson	.40
120 Adrian Murrell	.10
121 Sam Mills	.10
122 Irving Fryar	.10
123 Ki-Jana Carter	.10
124 Gus Frerotte	.10
125 Terry Glenn	1.25
126 Quentin Coryatt	.10
127 Robert Smith	.10
128 Jeff Blake	.20
129 Natrone Means	.20
130 Isaac Bruce	.30
131 Lamar Lathon	.10
132 Johnnie Morton	.10
133 Jerry Rice	1.25
134 Errict Rhett	.20
135 Junior Seau	.20
136 Joey Galloway	.40
137 Napoleon Kaufman	.10
138 Troy Aikman	1.25
139 Kevin Hardy	.10
140 Jimmy Smith	.10
141 Edgar Bennett	.10
142 Hardy Nickerson	.10
143 Greg Lloyd	.10
144 Dale Carter (WR)	.10
145 Jake Reed	.10
146 Cris Carter	.10
147 Todd Collins	.10
148 Mel Gray	.10
149 Lawyer Milloy	.10
150 Kimble Anders	.10
151 Darick Holmes	.10
152 Bert Emanuel	.10
153 Marshall Faulk	.20
154 Frank Sanders	.10
155 Leeland McElroy	.20
156 Rickey Dudley	.20
157 Tamarick Vanover	.20
158 Kerry Collins	1.25
159 Jeff Graham	.10
160 Jerome Bettis	.20
161 Greg Hill	.10
162 John Mobley	.10
163 Michael Irvin	.20
164 Marvin Harrison	.10
165 Jim Schwantz	.10
166 Jermaine Lewis	.10
167 Levon Kirkland	.10
168 Nilo Silvan	.10
169 Ken Norton	.10
170 Yancey Thigpen	.10
171 Antonio Freeman	.20
172 Terry Kirby	.10
173 Brad Johnson	.10
174 *Reidel Anthony*	1.75
175 *Tiki Barber*	1.50
176 *Pat Barnes*	1.00
177 *Michael Booker*	.20
178 *Peter Boulware*	.20
179 *Rae Carruth*	1.50
180 *Troy Davis*	1.50
181 *Corey Dillon*	1.00
182 *Jim Druckenmiller*	3.00
183 *Warrick Dunn*	3.50
184 *James Farrior*	.20
185 *Yatil Green*	1.50
186 *Walter Jones*	.20
187 *Tom Knight*	.20
188 *Sam Madison*	.20
189 *Tyrus McCloud*	.20
190 *Orlando Pace*	1.00
191 *Jake Plummer*	1.50
192 *Dwayne Rudd*	.20
193 *Darrell Russell*	.20
194 *Sedrick Shaw*	.75
195 *Shawn Springs*	1.00

196	*Bryant Westbrook*	.50
197	*Danny Wuerffel*	2.50
198	*Reinard Wilson*	.20
199	Checklist	.10
200	Checklist	.10

1997 Ultra Blitzkrieg

Inserted 1:6 packs, the 18-card set featured "Blitzkrieg" printed along the left border of the card. The player's photo is superimposed over a multiple-photo background. The player's name is printed vertically along the upper right border. The Ultra logo is in the lower right. The backs have the player's photo on the left, with his name in the upper right. His highlights appear to the right of the photo. The card number, which is labeled "of 18," is printed in the lower right. The Ultra Blitzkrieg die-cut parallel set was inserted 1:36 packs. The die-cut was featured only on the left border.

		MT
Complete Set (18):		90.00
Common Player:		2.00
Die-Cut Cards:		2x-3x
1	Eddie George	8.00
2	Terry Glenn	6.00
3	Karim Abdul-Jabbar	5.00
4	Emmitt Smith	12.00
5	Dan Marino	12.00
6	Brett Favre	15.00
7	Keyshawn Johnson	2.00
8	Curtis Martin	8.00
9	Marvin Harrison	4.00
10	Barry Sanders	8.00
11	Jerry Rice	8.00
12	Terrell Davis	8.00
13	Troy Aikman	8.00
14	Drew Bledsoe	8.00
15	John Elway	6.00
16	Kordell Stewart	8.00
17	Kerry Collins	8.00
18	Steve Young	6.00

1997 Ultra Play of the Game

The 10-card set was inserted 1:8 packs. The card front features a player photo superimposed over a brown background and two additional ghosted player photos. The Play of the

---

Game logo and the player's name are printed at the bottom center. The backs, which are numbered "of 10," have the player's name and team in the upper left. The player's photo is on the right, with his highlights printed to the left of the photo.

		MT
Complete Set (10):		30.00
Common Player:		1.00
1	Deion Sanders	3.00
2	Jerry Rice	7.00
3	Michael Westbrook	1.00
4	Steve McNair	5.00
5	Marshall Faulk	2.00
6	Terrell Davis	7.00
7	Mark Brunell	7.00
8	Isaac Bruce	2.00
9	Tony Banks	4.00
10	Jamal Anderson	1.00

1997 Ultra Rookies

The 12-card set was inserted 1:4 packs. The player is featured in his college photo on the front and superimposed over a purple and blue background. "Rookies" is printed in green at the bottom, with his name in silver foil in the lower right. The backs, which are numbered "of 12," features "Rookies" in the upper left and his highlights below. His photo and name are printed along the right side. The Ultra Rookies parallel version was seeded 1:18 packs. The parallel cards feature a sculpted-embossed player image over a matte finish background.

		MT
Complete Set (12):		20.00
Common Player:		.75
Gold Embossed:		2x-3x
1	Darnell Autry	2.00
2	Orlando Pace	1.50
3	Peter Boulware	.75
4	Shawn Springs	1.50
5	Bryant Westbrook	.75
6	Rae Carruth	2.00
7	Jim Druckenmiller	6.00
8	Yatil Green	2.50
9	James Farrior	.75
10	Dwayne Rudd	.75
11	Darrell Russell	.75
12	Warrick Dunn	8.00

1997 Ultra Starring Role

The 10-card set was inserted 1:288 packs. The acrylic die-cut cards feature a silver-foil stamp on the front.

		MT
Complete Set (10):		500.00
Common Player:		20.00
1	Emmitt Smith	90.00
2	Barry Sanders	50.00
3	Curtis Martin	50.00
4	Dan Marino	90.00
5	Keyshawn Johnson	20.00
6	Marvin Harrison	30.00
7	Terry Glenn	50.00
8	Eddie George	70.00
9	Brett Favre	100.00
10	Karim Abdul-Jabbar	50.00

1997 Ultra Sunday School

Inserted 1:8 packs, the 10-card chase set features a player photo superimposed over a black background on the left side of the card. Also included in the background is a play diagramed in silver foil. The player's name is printed in silver foil in the lower left, while the Sunday School logo is printed vertically along the right border. The backs, numbered "of 10," have the player's photo on the left side, with his name, highlights and card number to the right of it.

		MT
Complete Set (10):		40.00
Common Player:		1.00
1	Marvin Harrison	3.00
2	Barry Sanders	7.00
3	Troy Aikman	7.00
4	Drew Bledsoe	7.00
5	John Elway	5.00
6	Kordell Stewart	6.00
7	Kerry Collins	6.00
8	Steve Young	5.00
9	Deion Sanders	4.00
10	Joey Galloway	1.00

1997 Ultra Talent Show

Inserted 1:4 packs, this 10-card set features the player photo superimposed over a multicolored background. The Talent Show logo appears in gold in the lower left, with the player's name in the lower right.

The back, numbered "of 10," features a full-bleed photo of the player. Printed along the left border inside a box is the player's name, his highlights and card number.

		MT
Complete Set (10):		12.00
Common Player:		.75
1	Joey Galloway	2.00
2	Steve McNair	3.00
3	Marshall Faulk	1.00
4	Isaac Bruce	1.50
5	Michael Westbrook	.75
6	Zach Thomas	1.25
7	Jamal Anderson	.75
8	Mike Alstott	.75
9	Mark Brunell	4.00
10	Eddie Kennison	2.50

1997 Pacific Crown

The 450-card set showcases a full-bleed photo on the front, with the Pacific Crown Collection logo in the upper left. The team's helmet is in color in the lower left and reproduced in gold foil towards the bottom center. The player's name is printed in capital gold-foil letters in the lower right of the front. A Copper parallel was inserted 1:1 hobby packs, while a Silver parallel was seeded 1:1 retail packs. A Platinum Blue hobby and retail parallel was included in 1:73 packs. Red-foil parallels were found one per Treat Entertainment U.S. retail pack.

		MT
Complete Set (450):		40.00
Common Player:		.05
Copper/Silver Cards:		3x-6x
Blue Cards:		50x-100x
Wax Box:		50.00
1	Lomas Brown	.05
2	Pat Carter	.05
3	Larry Centers	.05
4	Matt Darby	.05
5	Marcus Dowdell	.05
6	Aaron Graham	.05
7	Kent Graham	.10
8	LeShon Johnson	.05
9	Seth Joyner	.05
10	Leeland McElroy	.10
11	Rob Moore	.05
12	Simeon Rice	.05
13	Eric Swann	.05
14	Aeneas Williams	.05
15	Morten Andersen	.05
16	Jamal Anderson	.20
17	Lester Archambeau	.05
18	Cornelius Bennett	.05
19	J.J. Birden	.05
20	Antone Davis	.05
21	Bert Emanuel	.05
22	Travis Hall	.05
23	Bobby Hebert	.05
24	Craig Heyward	.05
25	Terance Mathis	.05
26	Tim McKyer	.05
27	Eric Metcalf	.05
28	Jessie Tuggle	.05
29	Derrick Alexander	.05
30	Orlando Brown	.05
31	Rob Burnett	.05
32	Earnest Byner	.05
33	Ray Ethridge	.05

No.	Player	Value
34	Steve Everett	.05
35	Carwell Gardner	.05
36	Michael Jackson	.05
37	Jamal Lewis	.05
38	Stevon Moore	.05
39	Bam Morris	.05
40	Jonathan Ogden	.05
41	Vinny Testaverde	.10
42	Todd Collins	.10
43	Russell Copeland	.05
44	Quinn Early	.05
45	John Fina	.05
46	Phil Hansen	.05
47	Eric Moulds	.15
48	Bryce Paup	.05
49	Andre Reed	.05
50	Kurt Schulz	.05
51	Bruce Smith	.05
52	Chris Spielman	.05
53	Steve Tasker	.05
54	Thurman Thomas	.10
55	Carlton Bailey	.05
56	Michael Bates	.05
57	Blake Brockermeyer	.05
58	Mark Carrier	.05
59	Kerry Collins	1.00
60	Eric Davis	.05
61	Kevin Greene	.05
62	Raghib Ismail	.05
63	Anthony Johnson	.05
64	Shawn King	.05
65	Greg Kragen	.05
66	Sam Mills	.05
67	Tyrone Poole	.05
68	Wesley Walls	.05
69	Mark Carrier	.05
70	Curtis Conway	.10
71	Bobby Engram	.10
72	Jim Flanigan	.05
73	Al Fontenot	.05
74	Raymont Harris	.05
75	Walt Harris	.05
76	Andy Heck	.05
77	Dave Krieg	.05
78	Rashaan Salaam	.10
79	Vinson Smith	.05
80	Alonzo Spellman	.05
81	Michael Timpson	.05
82	James Williams	.05
83	Ashley Ambrose	.05
84	Eric Bieniemy	.05
85	Jeff Blake	.15
86	Ki-Jana Carter	.10
87	John Copeland	.05
88	David Dunn	.05
89	Jeff Hill	.05
90	Ricardo McDonald	.05
91	Tony McGee	.05
92	Greg Myers	.05
93	Carl Pickens	.10
94	Corey Sawyer	.05
95	Darnay Scott	.05
96	Dan Wilkinson	.05
97	Troy Aikman	1.00
98	Larry Allen	.05
99	Eric Bjornson	.05
100	Ray Donaldson	.05
101	Michael Irvin	.10
102	Daryl Johnston	.05
103	Nate Newton	.05
104	Deion Sanders	.40
105	Jim Schwantz	.05
106	Emmitt Smith	1.75
107	Broderick Thomas	.05
108	Tony Tolbert	.05
109	Erik Williams	.05
110	Sherman Williams	.05
111	Darren Woodson	.05
112	Steve Atwater	.05
113	Aaron Craver	.05
114	Ray Crockett	.05
115	Terrell Davis	1.25
116	Jason Elam	.05
117	John Elway	.60
118	Todd Kinchen	.05
119	Ed McCaffrey	.05
120	Anthony Miller	.05
121	John Mobley	.05
122	Michael Dean Perry	.05
123	Reggie Rivers	.05
124	Shannon Sharpe	.05
125	Alfred Williams	.05
126	Reggie Brown	.05
127	Luther Elliss	.05
128	Kevin Glover	.05
129	Jason Hanson	.05
130	Pepper Johnson	.05
131	Glyn Milburn	.05
132	Scott Mitchell	.05
133	Herman Moore	.15
134	Johnnie Morton	.05
135	Brett Perriman	.05
136	Robert Porcher	.05
137	Ron Rivers	.05
138	Barry Sanders	1.00
139	Henry Thomas	.05
140	Don Beebe	.05
141	Edgar Bennett	.05
142	Robert Brooks	.05
143	LeRoy Butler	.05
144	Mark Chmura	.05
145	Brett Favre	2.00
146	Antonio Freeman	.25
147	Chris Jacke	.05
148	Travis Jervey	.05
149	Sean Jones	.05
150	Dorsey Levens	.10
151	John Michels	.05
152	Craig Newsome	.05
153	Eugene Robinson	.05
154	Reggie White	.10
155	Michael Barrow	.05
156	Blaine Bishop	.05
157	Chris Chandler	.05
158	Anthony Cook	.05
159	Malcolm Floyd	.05
160	Eddie George	1.25
161	Roderick Lewis	.05
162	Steve McNair	.75
163	John Henry Mills	.05
164	Derek Russell	.05
165	Chris Sanders	.05
166	Mark Stepnoski	.05
167	Frank Wycheck	.05
168	Robert Young	.05
169	Trev Alberts	.05
170	Aaron Bailey	.05
171	Tony Bennett	.05
172	Ray Buchanan	.05
173	Quentin Coryatt	.05
174	Eugene Daniel	.05
175	Sean Dawkins	.05
176	Ken Dilger	.05
177	Marshall Faulk	.10
178	Jim Harbaugh	.05
179	Marvin Harrison	.40
180	Paul Justin	.05
181	Lamont Warren	.05
182	Bernard Whittingham	.05
183	Tony Bosselli	.05
184	Tony Brackens	.05
185	Mark Brunell	.75
186	Brian DeMarco	.05
187	Greg Griffith	.05
188	Kevin Hardy	.05
189	Willie Jackson	.05
190	Jeff Lageman	.05
191	Keenan McCardell	.10
192	Natrone Means	.10
193	Pete Mitchell	.05
194	Joel Smeenge	.05
195	Jimmy Smith	.10
196	James Stewart	.10
197	Marcus Allen	.10
198	John Art	.05
199	Kimble Anders	.05
200	Steve Bono	.10
201	Vaughn Booker	.05
202	Dale Carter	.05
203	Mark Collins	.05
204	Greg Hill	.05
205	Joe Horn	.05
206	Dan Saleaumua	.05
207	Will Shields	.05
208	Neil Smith	.05
209	Derrick Thomas	.10
210	Tamarick Vanover	.10
211	Karim Abdul-Jabbar	.75
212	Fred Barnett	.05
213	Tim Bowens	.05
214	Kirby Dar Dar	.05
215	Troy Drayton	.05
216	Craig Erickson	.05
217	Daryl Gardener	.05
218	Randal Hill	.05
219	Dan Marino	1.75
220	O.J. McDuffie	.05
221	Bernie Parmalee	.05
222	Stanley Pritchett	.05
223	Daniel Stubbs	.05
224	Zach Thomas	.20
225	Derrick Alexander	.05
226	Cris Carter	.10
227	Jeff Christy	.05
228	Qadry Ismail	.05
229	Brad Johnson	.05
230	Andrew Jordan	.05
231	Randall McDaniel	.05
232	David Palmer	.05
233	John Randle	.05
234	Jake Reed	.05
235	Scott Sisson	.05
236	Korey Stringer	.05
237	Darryl Talley	.05
238	Orlando Thomas	.05
239	Bruce Armstrong	.05
240	Drew Bledsoe	1.00
241	Willie Clay	.05
242	Ben Coates	.05
243	Frank Collins	.05
244	Terry Glenn	1.00
245	Jerome Henderson	.05
246	Shawn Jefferson	.05
247	Dietrich Jells	.05
248	Ty Law	.05
249	Curtis Martin	1.25
250	Willie McGinest	.05
251	David Meggett	.05
252	Lawyer Milloy	.05
253	Chris Slade	.05
254	Je'Rod Cherry	.05
255	Jim Everett	.05
256	Mark Fields	.05
257	Michael Haynes	.05
258	Tyrone Hughes	.05
259	Haywood Jeffires	.05
260	Wayne Martin	.05
261	Mark McMillian	.05
262	Rufus Porter	.05
263	William Roaf	.05
264	Torrance Small	.05
265	Renaldo Turnbull	.05
266	Ray Zellars	.05
267	Jessie Armstead	.05
268	Chad Bratzke	.05
269	Dave Brown	.05
270	Chris Calloway	.05
271	Howard Cross	.05
272	Lawrence Dawsey	.05
273	Rodney Hampton	.05
274	Danny Kanell	.05
275	Arthur Marshall	.05
276	Aaron Pierce	.05
277	Phillippi Sparks	.05
278	Amani Toomer	.05
279	Charles Way	.05
280	Richie Anderson	.05
281	Fred Baxter	.05
282	Wayne Chrebet	.05
283	Kyle Clifton	.05
284	John Elliott	.05
285	Aaron Glenn	.05
286	Jeff Graham	.05
287	Bobby Hamilton	.05
288	Keyshawn Johnson	.40
289	Adrian Murrell	.05
290	Neil O'Donnell	.05
291	Webster Slaughter	.05
292	Alex Van Dyke	.05
293	Marvin Washington	.05
294	Joe Aska	.05
295	Jerry Ball	.05
296	Tim Brown	.10
297	Rickey Dudley	.10
298	Pat Harlow	.05
299	Nolan Harrison	.05
300	Billy Joe Hobert	.05
301	James Jett	.05
302	Napoleon Kaufman	.10
303	Lincoln Kennedy	.05
304	Albert Lewis	.05
305	Chester McGlockton	.05
306	Pat Swilling	.05
307	Steve Wisniewski	.05
308	Darion Conner	.05
309	Ty Detmer	.05
310	Jason Dunn	.05
311	Irving Fryar	.05
312	Jeff Fuller	.05
313	William Fuller	.05
314	Charlie Garner	.05
315	Bobby Hoying	.05
316	Tom Hutton	.05
317	Chris T. Jones	.05
318	Mike Mamula	.05
319	Mark Seay	.05
320	Bobby Taylor	.05
321	Ricky Watters	.10
322	Jahine Arnold	.05
323	Jerome Bettis	.10
324	Chad Brown	.05
325	Mark Bruener	.05
326	Andre Hastings	.05
327	Norm Johnson	.05
328	Levon Kirkland	.05
329	Carnell Lake	.05
330	Greg Lloyd	.05
331	Ernie Mills	.05
332	Orpheus Roye	.05
333	Kordell Stewart	.75
334	Yancey Thigpen	.05
335	Mike Tomczak	.05
336	Rod Woodson	.05
337	Tony Banks	.25
338	Bern Brostek	.05
339	Isaac Bruce	.15
340	Ernie Conwell	.05
341	Keith Crawford	.05
342	Wayne Gandy	.05
343	Harold Green	.05
344	Carlos Jenkins	.05
345	Jimmie Jones	.05
346	Eddie Kennison	.40
347	Todd Lyght	.05
348	Leslie O'Neal	.05
349	Lawrence Phillips	.10
350	Greg Robinson	.05
351	Darren Bennett	.05
352	Lewis Bush	.05
353	Eric Castle	.05
354	Terrell Fletcher	.05
355	Darrien Gordon	.05
356	Kurt Gouveia	.05
357	Aaron Hayden	.05
358	Stan Humphries	.05
359	Tony Martin	.05
360	Vaughn Parker	.05
361	Brian Roche	.05
362	Leonard Russell	.05
363	Junior Seau	.10
364	Roy Barker	.05
365	Harris Barton	.05
366	Dexter Carter	.05
367	Chris Doleman	.05
368	Tyronne Drakeford	.05
369	Elvis Grbac	.05
370	Derek Loville	.05
371	Tim McDonald	.05
372	Ken Norton	.05
373	Terrell Owens	.50
374	Gary Plummer	.05
375	Jerry Rice	1.00
376	Dana Stubblefield	.05
377	Lee Woodall	.05
378	Steve Young	.60
379	Robert Blackman	.05
380	Brian Blades	.05
381	Carlester Crumpler	.05
382	Christian Fauria	.05
383	John Friesz	.05
384	Joey Galloway	.25
385	Derrick Graham	.05
386	Cortez Kennedy	.05
387	Warren Moon	.10
388	Winston Moss	.05
389	Mike Pritchard	.05
390	Michael Sinclair	.05
391	Lamar Smith	.05
392	Chris Warren	.05
393	Chidi Ahanotu	.05
394	Mike Alstott	.15
395	Reggie Brooks	.05
396	Trent Dilfer	.10
397	Jerry Ellison	.05
398	Paul Gruber	.05
399	Alvin Harper	.05
400	Courtney Hawkins	.05
401	Dave Moore	.05
402	Errict Rhett	.10
403	Warren Sapp	.05
404	Nilo Silvan	.05
405	Regan Upshaw	.05
406	Casey Weldon	.05
407	Terry Allen	.05
408	Jamie Asher	.05
409	Bill Brooks	.05
410	Tom Carter	.05
411	Henry Ellard	.05
412	Gus Frerotte	.05
413	Darrell Green	.05
414	Ken Harvey	.05
415	Tre' Johnson	.05
416	Brian Mitchell	.05
417	Rich Owens	.05
418	Heath Shuler	.10
419	Michael Westbrook	.05
420	Tony Woods	.10
421	Reidel Anthony	1.50
422	Darnell Autry	.50
423	Tiki Barber	1.00
424	Pat Barnes	.75
425	Terry Battle	.10
426	Will Blackwell	.30
427	Peter Boulware	.10
428	Rae Carruth	1.00
429	Troy Davis	1.50
430	Jim Druckenmiller	2.00
431	Warrick Dunn	2.50
432	Marc Edwards	.10
433	James Farrior	.10
434	Yatil Green	1.25
435	Byron Hanspard	1.00
436	Ike Hilliard	1.50
437	David LaFleur	.50

438	*Kevin Lockett*	.25
439	*Sam Madison*	.10
440	*Brian Manning*	.10
441	*Orlando Pace*	.50
442	*Jake Plummer*	.75
443	*Chad Scott*	.10
444	*Sedrick Shaw*	.75
445	*Antowain Smith*	1.00
446	*Shawn Springs*	.75
447	*Ross Verba*	.20
448	*Bryant Webster*	.10
449	*Renaldo Wynn*	.10
450	*Jimmy Johnson*	.30

1997 Pacific Crown
Big Number Die-Cuts

Inserted 1:37 packs, the 20-card die-cut set features the player's last name and jersey number on the front of the card. The backs have the player's name at the top, with the Pacific Crown logo in the upper right. A player photo is in the center, with his highlights located inside a box near the bottom.

		MT
Complete Set (20):		325.00
Common Player:		4.00
1	Jamal Anderson	4.00
2	Kerry Collins	20.00
3	Troy Aikman	20.00
4	Emmitt Smith	35.00
5	Terrell Davis	20.00
6	John Elway	15.00
7	Barry Sanders	20.00
8	Brett Favre	40.00
9	Eddie George	25.00
10	Mark Brunell	20.00
11	Marcus Allen	4.00
12	Karim Abdul-Jabbar	15.00
13	Dan Marino	35.00
14	Drew Bledsoe	20.00
15	Curtis Martin	20.00
16	Napoleon Kaufman	4.00
17	Jerome Bettis	4.00
18	Eddie Kennison	8.00
19	Jerry Rice	20.00
20	Steve Young	15.00

1997 Pacific Crown
Mark Brunell

The four-card set was split between Crown Collection and Invincible. Card Nos. 1-2 were seeded 1:72 packs of Crown, while Nos. 3-4 were inserted 1:72 in Invincible packs.

	MT
Complete Set (4):	40.00
Common Player:	10.00

1997 Pacific Crown
Card Supials

Inserted 1:37 packs, the 36-card set features a player photo superimposed on the front, with a gold-foil version of the same photo printed along

the right side of the front. The Crown logo is in the upper left, while the player's first name is in the upper right. His last name is printed vertically along the left edge of the front. The backs include a slot where a miniature die-cut card of the player can be inserted. The mini card includes a photo inside a die-cut football, which is sitting on a tee. The team's logo is in the lower right of the mini-card front.

		MT
Complete Set (72):		525.00
Complete Large Set (36):		350.00
Complete Small Set (36):		175.00
Common Large Player:		3.00
Common Small Player:		Half Price
1	Todd Collins	3.00
2	Kerry Collins	15.00
3	Wesley Walls	3.00
4	Jeff Blake	6.00
5	Troy Aikman	15.00
6	Emmitt Smith	25.00
7	Terrell Davis	20.00
8	John Elway	10.00
9	Herman Moore	3.00
10	Barry Sanders	15.00
11	Brett Favre	30.00
12	Dorsey Levens	3.00
13	Eddie George	20.00
14	Steve McNair	12.00
15	Marshall Faulk	3.00
16	Mark Brunell	15.00
17	Natrone Means	3.00
18	Marcus Allen	3.00
19	Karim Abdul-Jabbar	12.00
20	Dan Marino	25.00
21	Brad Johnson	3.00
22	Drew Bledsoe	15.00
23	Terry Glenn	15.00
24	Curtis Martin	15.00
25	Napoleon Kaufman	3.00
26	Ricky Watters	3.00
27	Jerome Bettis	3.00
28	Kordell Stewart	15.00
29	Tony Banks	6.00
30	Isaac Bruce	6.00
31	Eddie Kennison	8.00
32	Jerry Rice	15.00
33	Steve Young	10.00
34	Joey Galloway	8.00
35	Chris Warren	3.00
36	Gus Frerotte	3.00

1997 Pacific Crown
Cramer's Choice

Inserted 1:721 packs, the 10-card set showcases a player photo superimposed over a pyramid die-cut background. "1997 Cramer's Choice Awards" and the Crown logo are printed at the top of the award, while the gold base of the award includes the Crown logo, player's name and position.

		MT
Complete Set (10):		1250.00
Common Player:		40.00
1	Kevin Greene	40.00
2	Emmitt Smith	225.00
3	Terrell Davis	125.00
4	John Elway	100.00
5	Barry Sanders	125.00

		MT
6	Brett Favre	250.00
7	Eddie George	150.00
8	Mark Brunell	125.00
9	Terry Glenn	100.00
10	Jerry Rice	125.00

1997 Pacific Crown
Gold Crown Die-Cut

The 36-card set was inserted 1:37 packs. The top of the cards feature a die-cut gold crown at the top. The player's photo is superimposed over the crown. The bottom of the card front has three gold-foil stripes, with the player's name printed in the center of the middle stripe. A circle at the bottom center features the team logo inside a shield. Eight sun rays are printed diagonally at the bottom of the front.

		MT
Complete Set (36):		500.00
Common Player:		5.00
1	Larry Centers	5.00
2	Vinny Testaverde	5.00
3	Kerry Collins	20.00
4	Kevin Green	5.00
5	Anthony Johnson	5.00
6	Jeff Blake	10.00
7	Troy Aikman	20.00
8	Emmitt Smith	40.00
9	Terrell Davis	25.00
10	John Elway	15.00
11	Barry Sanders	20.00
12	Brett Favre	45.00
13	Antonio Freeman	10.00
14	Eddie George	30.00
15	Marshall Faulk	10.00
16	Mark Brunell	20.00
17	Jimmy Smith	5.00
18	Marcus Allen	5.00
19	Karim Abdul-Jabbar	15.00
20	Dan Marino	40.00
21	Brad Johnson	5.00
22	Drew Bledsoe	20.00
23	Terry Glenn	20.00
24	Curtis Martin	25.00
25	Adrian Murrell	5.00
26	Tim Brown	5.00
27	Jerome Bettis	10.00
28	Kordell Stewart	20.00
29	Tony Banks	10.00
30	Terrell Owens	10.00
31	Jerry Rice	20.00
32	Steve Young	15.00
33	Chris Warren	5.00
34	Terry Allen	5.00
35	Gus Frerotte	5.00
36	Jim Druckenmiller	20.00

1997 Pacific Crown
Team Checklists

The 30-card set is inserted 1:37 packs. The fronts feature an action shot of a player on the left side, with his name printed in gold across his body, while the team's two other stars have each of their head shot printed on football-shaped acetate pieces on the right. Their names appear above the

top football and below the bottom football. The team's name and the word "checklist" are repeated many times beginning on the left border and continuing to a thin area on the right side.

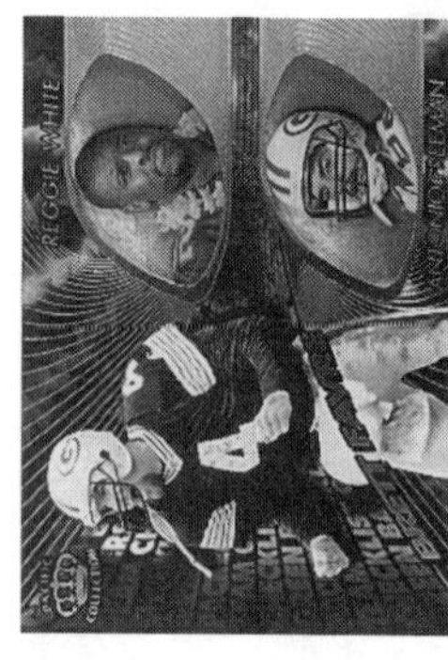

		MT
Complete Set (30):		325.00
Common Player:		6.00
1	Arizona Cardinals	6.00
2	Atlanta Falcons	6.00
3	Baltimore Ravens	6.00
4	Buffalo Bills	12.00
5	Carolina Panthers	18.00
6	Chicago Bears	6.00
7	Cincinnati Bengals	12.00
8	Dallas Cowboys	40.00
9	Denver Broncos	18.00
10	Detroit Lions	18.00
11	Green Bay Packers	45.00
12	Houston Oilers	25.00
13	Indianapolis Colts	6.00
14	Jacksonville Jaguars	18.00
15	Kansas City Chiefs	6.00
16	Miami Dolphins	40.00
17	Minnesota Vikings	6.00
18	New England Patriots	25.00
19	New Orleans Saints	6.00
20	New York Giants	6.00
21	New York Jets	6.00
22	Oakland Raiders	6.00
23	Philadelphia Eagles	6.00
24	Pittsburgh Steelers	18.00
25	St. Louis Rams	12.00
26	San Diego Chargers	6.00
27	San Francisco 49ers	25.00
28	Seattle Seahawks	6.00
29	Tampa Bay Buccaneers	6.00
30	Washington Redskins	6.00

1997 Pacific Crown
The Zone Die-Cuts

Inserted 1:73 packs, the 20-card set is die-cut in the shape of a goal post. The front has a photo of the player inside the uprights, while his name and position are printed at the base of the goal post.

		MT
Complete Set (20):		450.00
Common Player:		6.00
1	Kerry Collins	25.00
2	Jeff Blake	12.00
3	Emmitt Smith	50.00
4	Terrell Davis	25.00
5	John Elway	20.00

6	Barry Sanders	25.00
7	Brett Favre	55.00
8	Mark Brunell	25.00
9	Karim Abdul-Jabbar	18.00
10	Dan Marino	50.00
11	Drew Bledsoe	25.00
12	Terry Glenn	25.00
13	Curtis Martin	25.00
14	Napoleon Kaufman	6.00
15	Jerome Bettis	12.00
16	Eddie Kennison	12.00
17	Tony Martin	6.00
18	Jerry Rice	25.00
19	Steve Young	20.00
20	Terry Allen	6.00

1997 Pacific Dynagon

The 1997 Pacific Dynagon prism set consists of 144 regular-sized cards. The card fronts feature a gold-foil helmet background with the player's image outlined on top. The background also has the player's team colors with the player's name printed down the right side. The card backs include a head shot in the upper right-hand corner and a brief career highlight. Included with Dynagon Prism football are Tandems, Careers, Player Of The Week, Royal Connections and Best Kept Secrets insert sets. Each pack of Dynagon Prism contains three cards: one base card, one Best Kept Secrets card and one other insert card. A Silver parallel was available in retail packs (2:37), while a Copper parallel was included in 2:37 hobby packs. Red-foil parallels were found in 4:21 Treat Entertainment U.S. retail packs.

		MT
Complete Set (144):		120.00
Common Player:		.50
Wax Box:		75.00
1	Larry Centers	.50
2	Kent Graham	.50
3	Leeland McElroy	1.00
4	Frank Sanders	.50
5	Jamal Anderson	1.00
6	Bert Emanuel	.50
7	Bobby Hebert	.50
8	Terance Mathis	.50
9	Eric Metcalf	.50
10	Derrick Alexander	.50
11	Earnest Byner	.50
12	Michael Jackson	.50
13	Vinny Testaverde	.50
14	Quinn Early	.50
15	Jim Kelly	.50
16	Eric Moulds	2.00
17	Andre Reed	.50
18	Bruce Smith	.50
19	Thurman Thomas	1.00
20	Tshimanga Biakabutuka	2.00
21	Mark Carrier	.50
22	Kerry Collins	5.00
23	Kevin Greene	.50
24	Anthony Johnson	.50
25	Wesley Walls	.50
26	Curtis Conway	.50
27	Bobby Engram	1.00
28	Raymont Harris	.50
29	Dave Krieg	.50
30	Rashaan Salaam	1.00
31	Jeff Blake	1.00
32	Ki-Jana Carter	.50

33	Garrison Hearst	.50
34	Carl Pickens	.50
35	Darnay Scott	.50
36	Troy Aikman	5.00
37	Chris Boniol	.50
38	Michael Irvin	1.00
39	Deion Sanders	3.00
40	Emmitt Smith	10.00
41	Herschel Walker	.50
42	Terrell Davis	7.00
43	John Elway	4.00
44	Ed McCaffrey	.50
45	Shannon Sharpe	.50
46	Alfred Williams	.50
47	Scott Mitchell	.50
48	Herman Moore	1.00
49	Brett Perriman	.50
50	Barry Sanders	5.00
51	Edgar Bennett	.50
52	Robert Brooks	.50
53	Mark Chmura	.50
54	Brett Favre	10.00
55	Antonio Freeman	1.50
56	Desmond Howard	.50
57	Reggie White	1.00
58	Chris Chandler	.50
59	Eddie George	7.00
60	James McKeehan	.50
61	Steve McNair	3.50
62	Chris Sanders	.50
63	Sean Dawkins	.50
64	Ken Dilger	.50
65	Marshall Faulk	2.00
66	Jim Harbaugh	.50
67	Marvin Harrison	2.50
68	Tony Boselli	.50
69	Mark Brunell	5.00
70	Keenan McCardell	.50
71	Natrone Means	1.00
72	Jimmy Smith	.50
73	Marcus Allen	1.00
74	Kimble Anders	.50
75	Dale Carter	.50
76	Greg Hill	.50
77	Derrick Thomas	.50
78	Tamarick Vanover	1.00
79	Karim Abdul-Jabbar	4.00
80	Dan Marino	10.00
81	O.J. McDuffie	.50
82	Jerris McPhail	.50
83	Zach Thomas	1.50
84	Cris Carter	.50
85	Brad Johnson	.50
86	Jake Reed	.50
87	Robert Smith	.50
88	Drew Bledsoe	5.00
89	Ben Coates	.50
90	Terry Glenn	5.00
91	Curtis Martin	8.00
92	Willie McGinest	.50
93	Jim Everett	.50
94	Michael Haynes	.50
95	Haywood Jeffires	.50
96	Ray Zellars	.50
97	Dave Brown	.50
98	Rodney Hampton	.50
99	Danny Kanell	.50
100	Thomas Lewis	.50
101	Wayne Chrebet	.50
102	Keyshawn Johnson	2.50
103	Adrian Murrell	.50
104	Neil O'Donnell	.50
105	Tim Brown	.50
106	Rickey Dudley	1.00
107	Jeff Hostetler	.50
108	Napoleon Kaufman	.50
109	Ty Detmer	.50
110	Jason Dunn	.50
111	Irving Fryar	.50
112	Chris T. Jones	.50
113	Ricky Watters	.50
114	Jerome Bettis	1.00
115	Chad Brown	.50
116	Kordell Stewart	4.00
117	Mike Tomczak	.50
118	Rod Woodson	.50
119	Tony Banks	1.50
120	Isaac Bruce	1.50
121	Eddie Kennison	2.50
122	Lawrence Phillips	1.00
123	Terrell Fletcher	.50
124	Stan Humphries	.50
125	Tony Martin	.50
126	Junior Seau	.50
127	Elvis Grbac	.50
128	Terrell Owens	3.00
129	Ted Popson	.50
130	Jerry Rice	5.00
131	Steve Young	4.00
132	John Friesz	.50
133	Joey Galloway	2.00

134	Michael McCrary	.50
135	Lamar Smith	.50
136	Chris Warren	.50
137	Mike Alstott	1.00
138	Trent Dilfer	.50
139	Courtney Hawkins	.50
140	Errict Rhett	1.00
141	Terry Allen	.50
142	Henry Ellard	.50
143	Gus Frerotte	.50
144	Leslie Shepherd	.50

1997 Pacific Dynagon Careers

The 10-card, regular-sized cards were inserted every 360 packs in Dynagon Prism. The card fronts feature gold foil in an outline of a football. The player's name is printed down the right side in blue and the player's image is outlined over a crescent-shaped swirl of the player's statistics. The card backs feature a circular photo of the player with several career highlights and are numbered 1-10.

		MT
Complete Set (10):		450.00
Common Player:		30.00
1	Jim Kelly	30.00
2	Emmitt Smith	100.00
3	John Elway	40.00
4	Barry Sanders	50.00
5	Brett Favre	100.00
6	Reggie White	30.00
7	Dan Marino	100.00
8	Drew Bledsoe	50.00
9	Jerry Rice	50.00
10	Steve Young	40.00

1997 Pacific Dynagon Player of the Week

The 20-card, regular-sized set was inserted every 37 packs of Dynagon Prism. The card fronts feature an action shot centered in a diamond. The player's first name is printed on the upper right section of the diamond while the last name appears on the lower left section. The player's team helmet is located in the upper right part of the horizontal card front, centered in a

diamond. The card backs feature another shot of the player, again centered in a diamond. The card number corresponds with the week the player excelled during the 1996 season and was voted by visitors to Pacific's website as the Player Of The Week.

		MT
Complete Set (20):		250.00
Common Player:		5.00
1	Karim Abdul-Jabbar	10.00
2	Eddie George	15.00
3	Curtis Martin	20.00
4	Mark Brunell	15.00
5	John Elway	10.00
6	Drew Bledsoe	15.00
7	Emmitt Smith	30.00
8	Terrell Davis	20.00
9	Troy Aikman	15.00
10	Jerry Rice	15.00
11	Dan Marino	30.00
12	Barry Sanders	15.00
13	Brett Favre	30.00
14	Steve Young	10.00
15	Kerry Collins	15.00
16	Eddie Kennison	5.00
17	Terry Allen	5.00
18	Brett Favre	30.00
19	Desmond Howard	5.00
20	Mark Brunell	15.00

1997 Pacific Dynagon Royal Connections

Royal Connections, inserted every 73 packs of 1997 Dynagon Prism, is actually a 30-card, regular-sized, die-cut set that can be fitted with its counterpart to form 15 3-1/2" x 4-1/4" cards. The cards are numbered to 15 with A and B versions. The A versions feature quarterbacks and the right edge of the card is die-cut in the shape of a football with laces. The B versions highlight a wide receiver from a corresponding team and the left side is die-cut to allow the A version to fit with it to form a single card.

		MT
Complete Set (30):		650.00
Common Player:		8.00
1a	Kent Graham	8.00
1b	Larry Centers	8.00
2a	Jim Kelly	8.00
2b	Andre Reed	8.00
3a	Kerry Collins	50.00
3b	Wesley Walls	8.00
4a	Jeff Blake	15.00
4b	Carl Pickens	8.00
5a	Troy Aikman	50.00
5b	Michael Irvin	8.00
6a	John Elway	35.00
6b	Shannon Sharpe	8.00
7a	Brett Favre	100.00
7b	Antonio Freeman	15.00
8a	Mark Brunell	50.00
8b	Keenan McCardell	8.00
9a	Dan Marino	100.00
9b	O.J. McDuffie	8.00
10a	Brad Johnson	8.00
10b	Jake Reed	8.00
11a	Drew Bledsoe	50.00
11b	Terry Glenn	35.00
12a	Ty Detmer	8.00

		MT
12b	Irving Fryar	8.00
13a	Kordell Stewart	40.00
13b	Charles Johnson	8.00
14a	Tony Banks	15.00
14b	Isaac Bruce	20.00
15a	Steve Young	35.00
15b	Jerry Rice	50.00

1997 Pacific Dynagon Tandems

Inserted 1:37 packs, the 72 double-fronted cards feature the same 144 players from the base set, with one player on each side. Foiled in emerald, the cards have the numbers printed in the upper right.

		MT
Complete Set (72):		1300.00
Common Player:		10.00
1	Jerome Bettis, Eddie George	50.00
2	Jamal Anderson, Eric Moulds	20.00
3	Kerry Collins, Kordell Stewart	80.00
4	Jeff Blake, Ty Detmer	20.00
5	Michael Irvin, Tim Brown	20.00
6	Deion Sanders, Ray Zellars	40.00
7	Emmitt Smith, Steve Young	150.00
8	Terrell Davis, Barry Sanders	90.00
9	John Elway, Dan Marino	150.00
10	Robert Brooks, Eddie Kennison	20.00
11	Mark Chmura, Shannon Sharpe	10.00
12	Brett Favre, Mark Brunell	150.00
13	Antonio Freeman, Isaac Bruce	30.00
14	Desmond Howard, Natrone Means	20.00
15	Reggie White, Keyshawn Johnson	30.00
16	Edgar Bennett, Chris Sanders	10.00
17	Terry Glenn, Jerry Rice	80.00
18	Steve McNair, Karim Abdul-Jabbar	45.00
19	Marshall Faulk, Tamarick Vanover	20.00
20	Gus Frerotte, Brad Johnson	10.00
21	Jim Kelly, Tim Biakabutuka	20.00
22	Lawrence Phillips, Ben Coates	20.00
23	Napoleon Kaufman, Terrell Owens	25.00
24	Elvis Grbac, Junior Seau	10.00
25	Drew Bledsoe, Tony Banks	75.00
26	Curtis Martin, Troy Aikman	90.00
27	Curtis Conway, Brett Perriman	10.00
28	Bobby Engram, Larry Centers	10.00
29	Raymont Harris, Eric Metcalf	10.00
30	Dave Krieg, Derrick Alexander	10.00
31	Rashaan Salaam, Leeland McElroy	10.00
32	Ki-Jana Carter, Herman Moore	20.00
33	Garrison Hearst, Earnest Byner	10.00
34	Carl Pickens, Frank Sanders	10.00
35	Darnay Scott, Michael Jackson	10.00
36	Chris Boniol, Kent Graham	10.00
37	Herschel Walker, Thurman Thomas	10.00
38	Ed McCaffrey, Quinn Early	10.00
39	Alfred Williams, Mike Alstott	10.00
40	Scott Mitchell, Mark Carrier	10.00
41	Bert Emanuel, Henry Ellard	10.00
42	Bobby Hebert, Trent Dilfer	10.00
43	Terance Mathis, Andre Reed	10.00
44	Vinny Testaverde, Chris Warren	10.00
45	Bruce Smith, Kevin Greene	10.00
46	Anthony Johnson, Terry Allen	10.00
47	Wesley Walls, Errict Rhett	10.00
48	John Friesz, Jeff Hostetler	10.00
49	Joey Galloway, Leslie Shepherd	20.00
50	Michael McCrary, Chris T. Jones	10.00
51	Lamar Smith, Courtney Hawkins	10.00
52	Rickey Dudley, Jason Dunn	10.00
53	Irving Fryar, Tony Martin	10.00
54	Ted Popson, Ricky Watters	10.00
55	Chad Brown, Zach Thomas	20.00
56	Mike Tomczak, Stan Humphries	10.00
57	Rod Woodson, Willie McGinnest	10.00
58	Terrell Fletcher, Jerris McPhail	10.00
59	O.J. McDuffie, Cris Carter	10.00
60	Jake Reed, Marcus Allen	10.00
61	Robert Smith, Greg Hill	10.00
62	Jim Everett, Dave Brown	10.00
63	Michael Haynes, James McKeehan	10.00
64	Haywood Jeffires, Sean Dawkins	10.00
65	Rodney Hampton, Adrian Murrell	10.00
66	Danny Kanell, Marvin Harrison	20.00
67	Thomas Lewis, Dale Carter	10.00
68	Wayne Chrebet, Ken Dilger	10.00
69	Neil O'Donnell, Chris Chandler	10.00
70	Jim Harbaugh, Jimmy Smith	10.00
71	Derrick Thomas, Tony Boselli	10.00
72	Keenan McCardell, Kimble Anders	10.00

1997 Pacific Invincible

The 150-card set features a player action photo superimposed over a multicolored and gold-foiled background. At the bottom center of the card front is a player head shot printed on acetate. The player's name is printed in gold foil inside a black banner beneath the shield. The Pacific Invincible logo is located in the upper left. The base set is paralleled in Copper foil in hobby packs (2:37), Silver parallel in retail (2:37) and Platinum Blue (1:73). Red-foil parallel was seeded 4:37 in Treat Entertainment U.S. retail packs.

		MT
Complete Set (150):		150.00
Common Player:		.75
Copper Cards:		4x-8x
Silver Cards:		4x-8x
Blue Cards:		10x-20x
Wax Box:		80.00
1	Larry Centers	.75
2	Kent Graham	.75
3	LeShon Johnson	.75
4	Leeland McElroy	1.50
5	*Jake Plummer*	2.50
6	Frank Sanders	.75
7	Morten Andersen	.75
8	Jamal Anderson	1.50
9	Bert Emanuel	.75
10	Bobby Hebert	.75
11	Roell Preston	.75
12	Derrick Alexander	.75
13	Michael Jackson	.75
14	Bam Morris	.75
15	Vinny Testaverde	.75
16	Todd Collins	1.50
17	Andre Reed	.75
18	*Antowain Smith*	5.00
19	Steve Tasker	.75
20	Thurman Thomas	1.50
21	Tim Biakabutuka	1.50
22	*Rae Carruth*	4.00
23	Kerry Collins	5.00
24	Kevin Greene	.75
25	Anthony Johnson	.75
26	Wesley Walls	.75
27	*Darnell Autry*	2.00
28	Curtis Conway	.75
29	Raymont Harris	.75
30	Rashaan Salaam	1.50
31	Jeff Blake	1.50
32	Ki-Jana Carter	1.50
33	David Dunn	.75
34	Carl Pickens	.75
35	Darnay Scott	.75
36	Troy Aikman	5.00
37	Michael Irvin	1.50
38	Deion Sanders	3.00
39	Emmitt Smith	10.00
40	Herschel Walker	.75
41	Kevin Williams	.75
42	Steve Atwater	.75
43	Terrell Davis	5.00
44	John Elway	4.00
45	Ed McCaffrey	.75
46	Shannon Sharpe	.75
47	Scott Mitchell	.75
48	Herman Moore	1.50
49	Brett Perriman	.75
50	Barry Sanders	5.00
51	Edgar Bennett	.75
52	Robert Brooks	.75
53	Brett Favre	12.00
54	Antonio Freeman	2.00
55	Dorsey Levens	.75
56	Reggie White	1.50
57	Eddie George	7.00
58	Steve McNair	4.00
59	Chris Sanders	.75
60	Sean Dawkins	.75
61	Marshall Faulk	1.50
62	Jim Harbaugh	.75
63	Marvin Harrison	2.50
64	Brian Stablein	.75
65	Mark Brunell	4.00
66	Keenan McCardell	.75
67	Natrone Means	1.50
68	Pete Mitchell	.75
69	Jimmy Smith	.75
70	Marcus Allen	1.50
71	Kimble Anders	.75
72	Greg Hill	.75
73	Kevin Lockett	.75
74	Derrick Thomas	.75
75	Tamarick Vanover	.75
76	Karim Abdul-Jabbar	3.50
77	*Yatil Green*	3.00
78	Randal Hill	.75
79	Dan Marino	10.00
80	Stanley Pritchett	.75
81	Irving Spikes	.75
82	Cris Carter	.75
83	Brad Johnson	.75
84	Robert Smith	.75
85	Darryl Talley	.75
86	Drew Bledsoe	5.00
87	Ben Coates	.75
88	Terry Glenn	5.00
89	Curtis Martin	5.00
90	*Sedrick Shaw*	2.00
91	Mario Bates	.75
92	*Troy Davis*	4.00
93	Jim Everett	.75
94	Michael Haynes	.75
95	*Tiki Barber*	5.00
96	Dave Brown	.75
97	Rodney Hampton	.75
98	*Ike Hilliard*	4.00
99	Danny Kanell	.75
100	Wayne Chrebet	.75
101	Keyshawn Johnson	2.50
102	Adrian Murrell	.75
103	Neil O'Donnell	.75
104	Alex Van Dyke	.75
105	Joe Aska	.75
106	Tim Brown	.75
107	Rickey Dudley	.75
108	Napoleon Kaufman	1.50
109	Carl Kidd	.75
110	Ty Detmer	.75
111	Jason Dunn	.75
112	Irving Fryar	.75
113	Bobby Hoying	.75
114	Ricky Watters	1.50
115	Jerome Bettis	1.50
116	Charles Johnson	.75
117	Greg Lloyd	.75
118	Kordell Stewart	4.00
119	Rod Woodson	.75
120	Tony Banks	2.50
121	Isaac Bruce	1.50
122	Eddie Kennison	2.50
123	Lawrence Phillips	1.50
124	Stan Humphries	.75
125	Tony Martin	.75
126	*Corey Dillon*	3.00
127	Leonard Russell	.75
128	Junior Seau	1.50
129	*Jim Druckenmiller*	6.00
130	Marc Edwards	.75
131	Ken Norton Jr.	.75
132	Terrell Owens	3.50
133	Jerry Rice	5.00
134	Iheanyi Uwaezuoke	.75
135	Steve Young	4.00
136	John Friesz	.75
137	Joey Galloway	2.00
138	Warren Moon	.75
139	Todd Peterson	.75
140	Chris Warren	.75
141	Mike Alstott	.75
142	*Reidel Anthony*	5.00
143	Trent Dilfer	1.50
144	*Warrick Dunn*	10.00
145	Errict Rhett	1.50
146	Terry Allen	.75
147	Henry Ellard	.75
148	Gus Frerotte	.75
149	Brian Mitchell	.75
150	Leslie Shepherd	.75

1997 Pacific Invincible Canton, Ohio

The 10-card Canton, Ohio, chase set was inserted 1:361 packs. The player's photo is superimposed over a crown and multicolored background. The player is standing on an oval, while his name is printed directly beneath it. The chase set's name is printed at the top, with the Invincible logo at the top center.

		MT
Complete Set (10):		500.00
Common Player:		30.00
1	Troy Aikman	50.00
2	Emmitt Smith	100.00
3	John Elway	40.00
4	Barry Sanders	50.00
5	Brett Favre	100.00
6	Reggie White	30.00
7	Marcus Allen	30.00
8	Dan Marino	100.00
9	Jerry Rice	50.00
10	Steve Young	40.00

1997 Pacific Invincible Moments in Time

The 20-card Moments in Time was inserted 1:73 packs. The die-cut cards have a scoreboard-like front, with a player photo on the left. His name is printed beneath his team's and opponent's helmets. The date of the game, his yards and stats, along with the score of the game are printed on the front.

		MT
Complete Set (20):		800.00
Common Player:		20.00
1	Kerry Collins	50.00
2	Troy Aikman	50.00
3	Emmitt Smith	100.00
4	Terrell Davis	50.00
5	John Elway	35.00
6	Barry Sanders	50.00
7	Brett Favre	100.00
8	Reggie White	20.00
9	Eddie George	50.00
10	Mark Brunell	50.00
11	Marcus Allen	20.00
12	Karim Abdul-Jabbar	35.00
13	Dan Marino	100.00
14	Drew Bledsoe	50.00
15	Terry Glenn	50.00
16	Curtis Martin	50.00
17	Jerome Bettis	20.00
18	Eddie Kennison	20.00
19	Jerry Rice	50.00
20	Steve Young	35.00

1997 Pacific Invincible Pop Cards

The 10-card set was inserted 2:37 packs. The front of the card included a player photo, which was surrounded by gold-foil squares. The player's name and position are printed at the bottom center. The Pop Card redemption program worked like this. Remove the Pop Card piece from the card back to reveal a player photo and create a new card. If a collector collected all four pieces of a given player's card, the pieces could be sent to Pacific to receive a limited edition gold-foil card of that same player. Details are provided on the backs of each card.

		MT
Complete Set (10):		50.00
Common Player:		3.00
1	Kerry Collins	6.00
2	Troy Aikman	6.00
3	Emmitt Smith	12.00
4	John Elway	3.00
5	Barry Sanders	6.00
6	Brett Favre	12.00
7	Mark Brunell	6.00

8	Dan Marino	12.00
9	Drew Bledsoe	6.00
10	Jerry Rice	6.00

1997 Pacific Invincible Smash Mouth

This 220-card bonus set was inserted one or two per pack. The cards features a player photo on the front inside an oval, surrounded by a metal-diamond-type border. The team's logo is in the lower left, while the player's position is in the lower right. The player's name runs along the bottom of the front. In addition, a Smash Mouth X-tra 59-card set was also inserted one or two cards per pack. The card fronts include a large photo on the left, with the player's name printed in a stencil font vertically along the right border. The backs include a photo in the upper right corner.

		MT
Complete Set (220):		20.00
Common Player:		.10
1	Don Majkowski	.10
2	Leo Araguz	.10
3	John Carney	.10
4	Brett Favre	2.25
5	Cole Ford	.10
6	Marty Carter	.10
7	John Elway	.75
8	Mark Brunell	1.00
9	Rodney Peete	.10
10	Jeff Feagles	.10
11	Drew Bledsoe	1.00
12	Kerry Collins	.75
13	Dan Marino	2.00
14	Torrian Gray	.10
15	Reidel Anthony	.75
16	Jim Druckenmiller	1.00
17	Jim Everett	.10
18	Pat Barnes	.20
19	Ike Hilliard	.50
20	Barry Sanders	1.00
21	Terry Allen	.20
22	Emmitt Smith	2.00
23	Antowain Smith	.75
24	Robert Griffith	.10
25	Mickey Washington	.10
26	Napoleon Kaufman	.30
27	Eddie George	1.50
28	Curtis Martin	1.00
29	Anthony Lynn	.10
30	Terrell Davis	1.00
31	Steve Broussard	.10
32	Ricky Watters	.20
33	Karim Abdul-Jabbar	.50
34	Thurman Thomas	.20
35	Ross Verba	.10
36	Jerome Bettis	.20
37	Chad Cota	.10
38	Antonio Langham	.10
39	Brett Maxie	.10
40	James Hasty	.10
41	Conrad Hamilton	.10
42	Chris Warren	.10
43	George Jones	.10
44	Byron Hanspard	.50
45	Henri Crockett	.10
46	Brent Alexander	.10
47	John Lynch	.10
48	Renaldo Wynn	.10
49	Jared Tomich	.10
50	James Francis	.10

51	Brian Williams	.10
52	Kevin Mawae	.10
53	Marvcus Patton	.10
54	Mike Barber	.10
55	Robert Jones	.10
56	Ernest Dixon	.10
57	Mo Lewis	.10
58	Peter Boulware	.10
59	Wayne Simmons	.10
60	Anthony Redmon	.10
61	Tim Ruddy	.10
62	Victor Green	.10
63	Kirk Lowdermilk	.10
64	John Jurkovic	.10
65	John Jackson	.10
66	Kevin Gogan	.10
67	Adam Schrieber	.10
68	Mike Morris	.10
69	Albert Connell	.10
70	Tony Mayberry	.10
71	Mark Tuinei	.10
72	Harry Swayne	.10
73	Todd Steussie	.10
74	Glenn Parker	.10
75	D'Marco Farr	.10
76	Ed Simmons	.10
77	Tarik Glenn	.10
78	Rick Hamilton	.10
79	Dave Szott	.10
80	Jerry Rice	1.00
81	Tim Brown	.20
82	Charlie Jones	.10
83	Jerry Wunsch	.10
84	Lonnie Johnson	.10
85	Reggie Johnson	.10
86	Willie Davis	.10
87	Greg Clark	.10
88	Deems May	.10
89	J.J. Birden	.10
90	Chuck Smith	.10
91	Coleman Rudolph	.10
92	Leon Johnson	.10
93	Trace Armstrong	.10
94	John Thierry	.10
95	Dean Wells	.10
96	Mike Jones	.10
97	Mike Lodish	.10
98	Tony Siragusa	.10
99	Daved Benefield	.10
100	Michael Bankston	.10
101	Jamal Anderson	.20
102	Greg Montgomery	.10
103	Mark Maddox	.10
104	Matt Elliott	.10
105	Joe Cain	.10
106	Jeff Blake	.20
107	Troy Aikman	1.00
108	Brian Habib	.10
109	Pete Chryplewicz	.10
110	Earl Dotson	.10
111	Joe Bowden	.10
112	Marshall Faulk	.20
113	Reggie Barlow	.10
114	Marcus Allen	.20
115	Jeff Buckey	.10
116	Mitch Berger	.10
117	Corwin Brown	.10
118	Troy Davis	.50
119	Rodney Hampton	.10
120	Tom Knight	.10
121	Michael Booker	.10
122	Matt Stover	.10
123	Mark Pike	.10
124	Robin Stark	.10
125	Todd Sauerbrun	.10
126	Corey Dillon	.50
127	Tyji Armstrong	.10
128	Vaughn Hebron	.10
129	Antonio London	.10
130	Santana Dotson	.10
131	Oris Dishman	.10
132	Stephen Grant	.10
133	Mike Hollis	.10
134	Martin Bayless	.10
135	Sam Madison	.10
136	Esera Tuaolo	.10
137	Hason Graham	.10
138	Jim Dombrowski	.10
139	Bernard Holsey	.10
140	Kyle Brady	.10
141	David Klingler	.10
142	Don Griffin	.10
143	Bernard Dafney	.10
144	Derrick Harris	.10
145	Charles Johnson	.10
146	Dedrick Dodge	.10
147	Antonio Edwards	.10
148	Jorge Diaz	.10
149	Marc Logan	.10
150	Lou D'Agostino	.10
151	Lance Johnstone	.10

152	Ray Farmer	.10
153	Brenston Buckner	.10
154	Tony Banks	.50
155	'OMar Ellison	.10
156	Derrick Deese	.10
157	Howard Ballard	.10
158	Ronde Barber	.10
159	Gus Frerotte	.10
160	Leeland McElroy	.10
161	Devin Bush	.10
162	Eddie Sutter	.10
163	Sam Rogers	.10
164	Carl Simpson	.10
165	Lee Johnson	.10
166	Tony Casillas	.10
167	Randy Hilliard	.10
168	Ryan McNeil	.10
169	William Henderson	.10
170	Irv Eatman	.10
171	Derwin Gray	.10
172	Rob Johnson	.10
173	Derrick Walker	.10
174	Chris Singleton	.10
175	Chris Walsh	.10
176	Marty Moore	.10
177	Paul Green	.10
178	Brian Williams	.10
179	Robert Farmer	.10
180	Derrick Witherspoon	.10
181	Jim Miller	.10
182	James Harris	.10
183	Shannon Mitchell	.10
184	Steve Young	.75
185	Ronnie Harris	.10
186	Trent Dilfer	.25
187	Joe Patton	.10
188	Jake Plummer	.30
189	Ron George	.10
190	Vinny Testaverde	.10
191	Ryan Wetnight	.10
192	Steve Tovar	.10
193	Godfrey Myles	.10
194	Rod Smith	.10
195	Zefross Moss	.10
196	Jerald Sowell	.10
197	Jason Layman	.10
198	Ray McElroy	.10
199	Tom McManus	.10
200	Shawn Wooden	.10
201	Tony Johnson	.10
202	James Farrior	.10
203	Marc Woodard	.10
204	Chad Scott	.10
205	Dwayne White	.10
206	Warrick Dunn	2.00
207	Joe Wolf	.10
208	Dedric Ward	.10
209	Bennie Thompson	.10
210	Bracey Walker	.10
211	Tracy Scroggins	.10
212	Derrick Mason	.10
213	Ed King	.10
214	Harry Galbreath	.10
215	Joel Steed	.10
216	Jackie Harris	.10
217	Craig Sauer	.10
218	Reinard Wilson	.10
219	Barron Wortham	.10
220	Errict Rhett	.10

1997 Pacific Invincible Smash Mouth X-tra

		MT
Complete Set (59):		15.00
Common Player:		.10
1	Steve Young	.75
2	Jeff Blake	.20
3	Troy Aikman	1.00
4	Brett Favre	2.25
5	Gus Frerotte	.10
6	Tony Banks	.50
7	John Elway	.75
8	Mark Brunell	1.00
9	Rodney Peete	.10
10	Trent Dilfer	.30
11	Drew Bledsoe	1.00
12	Kerry Collins	.75
13	Dan Marino	2.00
14	Vinny Testaverde	.10
15	Reidel Anthony	.75
16	Jim Druckenmiller	1.00
17	Jim Everett	.10
18	Pat Barnes	.30
19	Ike Hilliard	.50
20	Barry Sanders	1.00
21	Terry Allen	.20
22	Emmitt Smith	2.00

23	Antowain Smith	.75
24	Jake Plummer	.30
25	Vaughn Hebron	.10
26	Napoleon Kaufman	.25
27	Eddie George	1.50
28	Curtis Martin	1.00
29	Rodney Hampton	.10
30	Terrell Davis	1.00
31	Marshall Faulk	.20
32	Ricky Watters	.20
33	Karim Abdul-Jabbar	.50
34	Thurman Thomas	.20
35	Troy Davis	.50
36	Jerome Bettis	.20
37	Warrick Dunn	2.00
38	Leeland McElroy	.10
39	William Henderson	.10
40	Jamal Anderson	.20
41	Errict Rhett	.10
42	Chris Warren	.10
43	George Jones	.10
44	Byron Hanspard	.50
45	Jerald Sowell	.10
46	Marcus Allen	.20
47	Kirk Lowdermilk	.10
48	Brian Habib	.10
49	Derrick Mason	.10
50	Jerry Rice	1.00
51	Albert Connell	.10
52	Kyle Brady	.10
53	Tim Brown	.20
54	Charles Johnson	.10
55	Jackie Harris	.10
56	Lonnie Johnson	.10
57	Deems May	.10
58	Peter Boulware	.10
59	Wayne Simmons	.10

1997 Pacific Philadelphia

The 330-card set features a white border on the front of the cards, surrounding the player photo. The Philadelphia logo is in the upper left. The bottom left of the photo includes the player's name, team and position. The team's logo is printed in the lower right. The backs included the player's name inside a stripe at the top left, with the card number inside a circle in the upper right. The player's bio, highlights and stats round out the back. Two football player images are printed in the background of the highlights and stats. Red-foil parallels were included one per Treat Entertainment U.S. retail pack.

		MT
Complete Set (330):		30.00
Common Player:		.05
Wax Box:		45.00
1	Kevin Butler	.05
2	Larry Centers	.05
3	Kent Graham	.05
4	Leeland McElroy	.10
5	Ronald McKinnon	.05
6	Johnny McWilliams	.05
7	Brad Ottis	.05
8	Frank Sanders	.05
9	Rob Selby	.05
10	Cedric Smith	.05
11	Joe Staysniak	.05
12	Cornelius Bennett	.05
13	David Brandon	.05
14	Tyrone Brown	.05
15	John Burrough	.05

16	Browning Nagle	.05
17	Dan Owens	.05
18	Anthony Phillips	.05
19	Roell Preston	.05
20	Darnell Walker	.05
21	Bob Whitfield	.05
22	Mike Zandofsky	.05
23	Vashone Adams	.05
24	Derrick Alexander	.05
25	Harold Bishop	.05
26	Jeff Blackshear	.05
27	Donny Brady	.05
28	Mike Frederick	.05
29	Tim Goad	.05
30	DeRon Jenkins	.05
31	Ray Lewis	.05
32	Rick Lyle	.05
33	Bam Morris	.05
34	Chris Brantley	.05
35	Jeff Burris	.05
36	Todd Collins	.10
37	Rob Coons	.05
38	Corbin Lacina	.05
39	Emanuel Martin	.05
40	Marlo Perry	.05
41	Sahwn Price	.05
42	Thomas Smith	.05
43	Matt Stevens	.05
44	Thurman Thomas	.15
45	Jay Barker	.05
46	Tshimanga Biakabutuka	.10
47	Kerry Collins	1.50
48	Matt Elliott	.05
49	Howard Griffith	.05
50	Anthony Johnson	.05
51	John Kasay	.05
52	Muhsin Muhammad	.40
53	Winslow Oliver	.05
54	Walter Rasby	.05
55	Gerald Williams	.05
56	Mark Butterfield	.05
57	Bryan Cox	.05
58	Mike Faulkerson	.05
59	Paul Grasmanis	.05
60	Robert Green	.05
61	Jack Jackson	.05
62	Bob Neely	.05
63	Todd Perry	.05
64	Evan Pilgrim	.05
65	Octus Polk	.05
66	Rashaan Salaam	.10
67	Willie Anderson	.05
68	Jeff Blake	.20
69	Scott Brumfield	.05
70	Jeff Cothran	.05
71	Gerald Dixon	.05
72	Garrison Hearst	.05
73	James Hundon	.05
74	Brian Milne	.05
75	Troy Sadowski	.05
76	Tom Tumulty	.05
77	Kimo Von Oelhoffen	.05
78	Troy Aikman	1.50
79	Dale Hellestrae	.05
80	Roger Harper	.05
81	Michael Irvin	.10
82	John Jett	.05
83	Kelvin Martin	.05
84	Deion Sanders	.75
85	Darrin Smith	.05
86	Emmitt Smith	3.00
87	Herschel Walker	.05
88	Charlie Williams	.05
89	Glenn Cadrez	.05
90	Dwayne Carswell	.05
91	Terrell Davis	1.75
92	David Diaz-infante	.05
93	John Elway	1.00
94	Harold Hasselbach	.05
95	Tory James	.05
96	Bill Musgrave	.05
97	Ralph Tamm	.05
98	Maa Tunavasa	.05
99	Gary Zimmerman	.05
100	Shane Bonham	.05
101	Stephen Boyd	.05
102	Jeff Hartings	.05
103	Hessley Hempstead	.05
104	Scott Kowalkowski	.05
105	Herman Moore	.20
106	Barry Sanders	1.50
107	Tony Semple	.05
108	Ryan Stewart	.05
109	Mike Wells	.05
110	Richard Woodley	.05
111	Brett Favre	3.00
112	Bernardo Harris	.05
113	Keith McKenzie	.05
114	Terry Mickens	.05
115	Doug Pederson	.05
116	Jeff Thomason	.05

117	Adam Timmerman	.05
118	Reggie White	.20
119	Bruce Wilkerson	.05
120	Gabe Wilkens	.05
121	Tyrone Williams	.05
122	Al Del Greco	.05
123	Anthony Dorsett	.05
124	Josh Evans	.05
125	Eddie George	2.00
126	Lemanski Hall	.05
127	Ronnie Harmon	.05
128	Steve McNair	1.00
129	Michael Roan	.05
130	Marcus Robertson	.05
131	Jon Runyan	.05
132	Chris Sanders	.05
133	Kerwin Bell	.05
134	Marshall Faulk	.30
135	Clif Groce	.05
136	Jim Harbaugh	.05
137	Marvin Harrison	1.00
138	Eric Mahlum	.05
139	Tony Mandarich	.05
140	Dedric Mathis	.05
141	Marcus Pollard	.05
142	Scott Slutzker	.05
143	Mark Stock	.05
144	Bucky Brooks	.05
145	Mark Brunell	1.50
146	Kendricke Bullard	.05
147	Randy Jordan	.05
148	Jeff Kopp	.05
149	Le'Shai Maston	.05
150	Keenan McCardell	.05
151	Clyde Simmons	.05
152	Jimmy Smith	.05
153	Rich Tylski	.05
154	Dave Widell	.05
155	Marcus Allen	.10
156	Keith Cash	.05
157	Donnie Edwards	.05
158	Trezelle Jenkins	.05
159	Sean LaChapelle	.05
160	Greg Manusky	.05
161	Steve Matthews	.05
162	Pellom McDaniels	.05
163	Chris Penn	.05
164	Danny Villa	.05
165	Jerome Woods	.05
166	Karim Abdul-Jabbar	1.25
167	John Bock	.05
168	O.J. Brigance	.05
169	Norman Hand	.05
170	Anthony Harris	.05
171	Larry Izzo	.05
172	Charles Jordan	.05
173	Dan Marino	3.00
174	Everett McIver	.05
175	Joe Nedney	.05
176	Robert Wilson	.05
177	David Dixon	.05
178	Charlie Evans	.05
179	Hunter Goodwin	.05
180	Ben Hanks	.05
181	Warren Moon	.10
182	Harold Morrow	.05
183	Fernando Smith	.05
184	Robert Smith	.10
185	Sean Vanhorse	.05
186	Jay Walker	.05
187	DeWayne Washington	.05
188	Moe Williams	.05
189	Mike Bartrum	.05
190	Drew Bledsoe	1.50
191	Troy Brown	.05
192	Chad Eaton	.05
193	Sam Gash	.05
194	Mike Gisler	.05
195	Curtis Martin	1.75
196	Dave Richards	.05
197	Todd Rucci	.05
198	Chris Sullivan	.05
199	Adam Vinatieri	.05
200	Doug Brien	.05
201	Derek Brown	.05
202	Lee DeRamus	.05
203	Jim Everett	.05
204	Mercury Hayes	.05
205	Joe Johnson	.05
206	Henry Lusk	.05
207	Andy McCollum	.05
208	Alex Molden	.05
209	Ray Zellars	.05
210	Marcus Buckley	.05
211	Doug Coleman	.05
212	Percy Ellsworth	.05
213	Rodney Hampton	.05
214	Brian Saxton	.05
215	Jason Sehorn	.05
216	Stan White	.05
217	Corey Widmer	.05

218	Rodney Young	.05
219	Rob Zatechka	.05
220	Henry Bailey	.05
221	Chad Cascadden	.05
222	Wayne Chrebet	.05
223	Tyrone Davis	.05
224	Kwame Ellis	.05
225	Glenn Foley	.05
226	Erik Howard	.05
227	Gary Jones	.05
228	Adrian Murrell	.05
229	Marc Spindler	.05
230	Lonnie Young	.05
231	Eric Zomalt	.05
232	Tim Brown	.10
233	Aundray Bruce	.05
234	Darren Carrington	.05
235	Rick Cunningham	.05
236	Rob Homberg	.05
237	Jeff Hostetler	.05
238	Lorenzo Lynch	.05
239	Barrett Robbins	.05
240	Dan Turk	.05
241	Harvey Williams	.05
242	Brian Dawkins	.05
243	Ty Detmer	.05
244	Troy Drake	.05
245	Rhett Hall	.05
246	Joe Panos	.05
247	Johnny Thomas	.05
248	Kevin Turner	.05
249	Ricky Watters	.10
250	Derrick Whiterspoon	.05
251	Sylvester Wright	.05
252	Jerome Bettis	.20
253	Carlos Emmons	.05
254	Jason Gildon	.05
255	Jonathan Hayes	.05
256	Kevin Henry	.05
257	Jerry Olsavsky	.05
258	Erric Pegram	.05
259	Brenden Stai	.05
260	Justin Strzelczyk	.05
261	Mike Tomczak	.05
262	Tony Banks	.50
263	Hayward Clay	.05
264	Percell Gaskins	.05
265	Eddie Kennison	.05
266	Aaron Laing	.05
267	Keith Lyle	.05
268	Jamie Martin	.05
269	Lawrence Phillips	.10
270	Zach Wiegert	.05
271	Toby Wright	.05
272	Darren Bennett	.05
273	Tony Berti	.05
274	Freddie Bradley	.05
275	Joe Cocozzo	.05
276	Andre Coleman	.05
277	Marco Coleman	.05
278	Rodney Harrison	.05
279	David Hendrix	.05
280	Leonard Russell	.05
281	Sean Salisbury	.05
282	Dennis Brown	.05
283	Chris Dalman	.05
284	Brent Jones	.05
285	Sean Manuel	.05
286	Marquez Pope	.05
287	Jerry Rice	1.50
288	Kirk Scrafford	.05
289	Iheanyi Uwaezuoke	.05
290	Tommy Vardell	.05
291	Steve Young	1.00
292	James Atkins	.05
293	T.J. Cunningham	.05
294	Stan Gelbaugh	.05
295	James Logan	.05
296	James McKnight	.05
297	Rick Mirer	.10
298	Todd Peterson	.05
299	Fred Thomas	.05
300	Rick Tuten	.05
301	Chris Warren	.05
302	Donnie Abraham	.05
303	Trent Dilfer	.10
304	Kenneth Gant	.05
305	Jeff Gooch	.05
306	Courtney Hawkins	.05
307	Tyoka Jackson	.05
308	Melvin Johnson	.05
309	Lonnie Marts	.05
310	Hardy Nickerson	.05
311	Errict Rhett	.20
312	Terry Allen	.10
313	Flipper Anderson	.05
314	William Bell	.05
315	Scott Blanton	.05
316	Leomont Evans	.05
317	Gus Frerotte	.05
318	Darryl Morrison	.05

319	Matt Turk	.05
320	Jeff Uhlenhake	.05
321	Bryan Walker	.05
322	Mark Brunell (1996 Statistical Leaders)	.75
323	Barry Sanders (1996 Statistical Leaders)	.75
324	Isaac Bruce (1996 Statistical Leaders)	.05
325	Terry Allen (1996 Statistical Leaders)	.05
326	Steve Young (1996 Statistical Leaders)	.50
327	Jerry Rice (1996 Statistical Leaders)	.75
328	Ricky Watters (1996 Statistical Leaders)	.05
329	Kevin Greene (1996 Statistical Leaders)	.05
330	Brett Favre (1996 Statistical Leaders)	1.50

1997 Pacific Philadelphia Gold

The 200-card set was a bonus in packs of the product. Each pack contained two Philadelphia Gold cards and either one insert card or an additional Philadelphia Gold card per pack. The card fronts showcased a full-bleed photo, with the Philadelphia logo in the upper left. The player's name is printed in gold foil over a gold-foil "spiral background" at the bottom left of the card. The team's logo is printed inside a banner over a football in the lower right. The backs have the player's name, position and highlights along the left, with a photo on the right. The card number is printed inside a circle in the lower right. A Hobby parallel version was printed with copper foil and inserted 2:37 packs. A Retail parallel version was produced with silver foil and inserted 2:37 packs.

		MT
Complete Set (200):		10.00
Common Player:		.15
Copper Cards:		2x-4x
Silver Cards:		3x-6x
1	Ryan Christopherson	.15
2	James Dexter	.15
3	Boomer Esiason	.15
4	Jarius Hayes	.15
5	Eric Hill	.15
6	Trey Junkin	.15
7	Kwamie Lassiter	.15
8	Patrick Bates	.15
9	Brad Edwards	.15
10	Roman Fortin	.15
11	Harper LeBel	.15
12	Lorenzo Styles	.15
13	Robbie Tobeck	.15
14	Mike Caldwell	.15
15	Eric Green	.15
16	Brian Kinchen	.15
17	Eric Turner	.15
18	Jerrol Williams	.15
19	Eric Zeier	.15
20	Darick Holmes	.30
21	Ken Irvin	.15
22	Jerry Ostroski	.15
23	Andre Reed	.15
24	Steve Tasker	.15
25	Thurman Thomas	.30
26	Steve Beuerlein	.15
27	Kerry Collins	2.00
28	Eric Davis	.15
29	Norberto Garrido	.15
30	Lamar Lathon	.15
31	Andre Royal	.15
32	Tony Carter	.15
33	Jerry Fontenot	.15
34	Raymont Harris	.30
35	Anthony Marshall	.15
36	Barry Minter	.15
37	Steve Stenstrom	.15
38	Donnell Woolford	.15
39	Ken Blackman	.15
40	Jeff Blake	.50
41	Carl Pickens	.30
42	Artie Smith	.15
43	Ramondo Stallings	.15
44	Melvin Tuten	.15
45	Joe Walter	.15
46	Troy Aikman	2.00
47	Billy Davis	.15
48	Chad Hennings	.15
49	Emmitt Smith	4.00
50	George Teague	.15
51	Kevin Williams	.15
52	Terrell Davis	2.50
53	John Elway	1.25
54	Tom Nalen	.15
55	Bill Romanowski	.15
56	Rod Smith	.15
57	Dan Williams	.15
58	Mike Compton	.15
59	Eric Lynch	.15
60	Aubrey Matthews	.15
61	Pete Metzelaars	.15
62	Herman Moore	.30
63	Barry Sanders	2.00
64	Keith Washington	.15
65	Edgar Bennett	.15
66	Brett Favre	4.00
67	Lamont Hollinquest	.15
68	Keith Jackson	.15
69	Derrick Mayes	.15
60	Andre Rison	.15
71	Eddie George	2.50
72	Mel Gray	.15
73	Darryll Lewis	.15
74	John Henry Mills	.15
75	Rodney Thomas	.15
76	Gary Walker	.15
77	Troy Auzenne	.15
78	Sammie Burroughs	.15
79	Jim Harbaugh	.15
80	Tony McCoy	.15
81	Brian Stablein	.15
82	Kipp Vickers	.15
83	Aaron Beasley	.15
84	Mark Brunell	2.00
85	Don Davey	.15
86	Chris Hudson	.15
87	Greg Huntington	.15
88	Ernie Logan	.15
89	Donnell Bennett	.15
90	Anthony Davis	.15
91	Tim Grunhard	.15
92	Danan Hughes	.15
93	Tony Richardson	.15
94	Tracy Simien	.15
95	Karim Abdul-Jabbar	1.50
96	Dwight Hollier	.15
97	John Kidd	.15
98	Dan Marino	4.00
99	Jerris McPhail	.15
100	Irving Spikes	.15
101	Richmond Webb	.15
102	Jeff Brady	.15
103	Richard Brown	.15
104	Corey Fuller	.15
105	John Gerak	.15
106	Scottie Graham	.15
107	Amp Lee	.15
108	Drew Bledsoe	2.00
109	Tedy Bruschi	.15
110	Todd Collins	.15
111	Bob Kratch	.15
112	Curtis Martin	2.50
113	David Meggett	.15
114	Tom Tupa	.15
115	Eric Allen	.15
116	Mario Bates	.15
117	Clarence Jones	.15
118	Sean Lumpkin	.15
119	Doug Nussmeier	.15
120	Irv Smith	.15
121	Winfred Tubbs	.15
122	Willie Beamon	.15
123	Greg Bishop	.15
124	Dave Brown	.15
125	Gary Downs	.15
126	Thomas Lewis	.15
127	Michael Strahan	.15
128	Tyrone Wheatley	.15
129	Matt Brock	.15
130	Mike Chalenski	.15
131	Roger Duffy	.15
132	John Hudson	.15
133	Frank Reich	.15
134	David Williams	.15
135	Greg Biekert	.15
136	Mike Jones	.15
137	Napoleon Kaufman	.15
138	Carl Kidd	.15
139	Terry McDaniel	.15
140	Mike Morton	.15
141	Orlanda Truitt	.15
142	Gary Anderson	.15
143	Richard Cooper	.15
144	Jimmie Johnson	.15
145	Joe Kelly	.15
146	William Thomas	.15
147	Ricky Watters	.30
148	Ed West	.15
149	Michael Zordich	.15
150	Jerome Bettis	.50
151	Dermontti Dawson	.15
152	Lethon Flowers	.15
153	Charles Johnson	.15
154	Darren Perry	.15
155	Kordell Stewart	2.00
156	Will Wolford	.15
157	Isaac Bruce	.75
158	Kevin Carter	.15
159	Torin Dorn	.15
160	Leo Goeas	.15
161	Gerald McBurrows	.15
162	Chuck Osborne	.15
163	J.T. Thomas	.15
164	Dwayne Gordon	.15
165	Stan Humphries	.15
166	Shawn Lee	.15
167	Chris Mims	.15
168	John Parrella	.15
169	Junior Seau	.15
170	Bryan Still	.15
171	Curtis Buckley	.15
172	William Floyd	.15
173	Merton Hanks	.15
174	Terry Kirby	.15
175	Jerry Rice	2.00
176	J.J. Stokes	.15
177	Jeff Wilkins	.15
178	Bryant Young	.15
179	Sam Adams	.15
180	John Friesz	.15
181	Joey Galloway	.75
182	Pete Kendall	.15
183	Jason Kyle	.15
184	Darryl Williams	.15
185	Ronnie Williams	.15
186	Mike Alstott	.30
187	Trent Dilfer	.30
188	Tyrone Legette	.15
189	Martin Mayhew	.15
190	Jason Odom	.15
191	Warren Sapp	.15
192	Karl Williams	.15
193	Terry Allen	.15
194	Romeo Bandison	.15
195	Alcides Catanho	.15
196	Gus Frerotte	.15
197	William Gaines	.15
198	Ken Harvey	.15
199	Trevor Matich	.15
200	Scott Turner	.15

1997 Pacific Philadelphia Heart of the Game

The 20-card set was inserted 1:73 packs. The fronts showcased a full-bleed photo, with the Philadelphia logo in the upper left corner. The player's name is printed in large gold-foil letters at the bottom of the front. In the bottom center of the name is an oval globe. A red heartbeat runs from the lower left to the lower right, with the date of a key game printed in red in the center.

		MT
Complete Set (20):		275.00
Common Player:		6.00
1	Thurman Thomas	6.00
2	Kerry Collins	20.00
3	Troy Aikman	20.00
4	Emmitt Smith	40.00
5	Terrell Davis	20.00
6	John Elway	15.00
7	Barry Sanders	20.00
8	Brett Favre	45.00
9	Antonio Freeman	12.00
10	Marshall Faulk	12.00
11	Mark Brunell	20.00
12	Marcus Allen	6.00
13	Dan Marino	40.00
14	Drew Bledsoe	20.00
15	Curtis Martin	20.00
16	Napoleon Kaufman	6.00
17	Jerome Bettis	12.00
18	Isaac Bruce	12.00
19	Jerry Rice	20.00
20	Steve Young	15.00

1997 Pacific Philadelphia Milestones

The 20-card set was inserted 1:37 packs. The fronts feature a red-orange border, with a player photo superimposed over a helmet and gold-foil Milestones banner that runs from the upper right to the lower left. The player's milestone is printed in the center of the banner, with his name in the lower left of the banner. The Philadelphia logo is located in the lower right.

		MT
Complete Set (20):		200.00
Common Player:		4.00
1	Simeon Rice	4.00
2	Thurman Thomas	4.00
3	Troy Aikman	15.00
4	Emmitt Smith	30.00
5	Terrell Davis	15.00
6	John Elway	12.00
7	Brett Favre	35.00
8	Desmond Howard	4.00
9	Reggie White	8.00
10	Mark Brunell	15.00
11	Marcus Allen	4.00
12	Karim Abdul-Jabbar	12.00
13	Dan Marino	30.00
14	Drew Bledsoe	15.00
15	Terry Glenn	15.00
16	Curtis Martin	15.00
17	Tony Banks	8.00
18	Jerry Rice	15.00
19	Steve Young	12.00
20	Terry Allen	4.00

1997 Pacific Philadelphia Photoengravings

Inserted 2:37 packs, the 36-card set has the look and feel of playing cards. The rounded-bordered cards have a player photo in the center of the card surrounded by a brown border and background. The player's name is printed in black at the bottom center. The Philadelphia logo is located in the upper left of the card front.

		MT
Complete Set (36):		225.00
Common Player:		3.00
1	Thurman Thomas	6.00
2	Kerry Collins	12.00
3	Jeff Blake	6.00
4	Troy Aikman	12.00
5	Deion Sanders	7.00
6	Emmitt Smith	25.00
7	Terrell Davis	15.00
8	John Elway	10.00
9	Herman Moore	6.00
10	Barry Sanders	12.00
11	Brett Favre	30.00
12	Desmond Howard	3.00
13	Dorsey Levens	3.00
14	Eddie George	15.00
15	Marshall Faulk	6.00
16	Jim Harbaugh	3.00
17	Marvin Harrison	6.00
18	Mark Brunell	12.00
19	Keenan McCardell	3.00
20	Karim Abdul-Jabbar	10.00
21	Dan Marino	25.00
22	Brad Johnson	3.00
23	Drew Bledsoe	12.00
24	Terry Glenn	12.00
25	Curtis Martin	12.00
26	Keyshawn Johnson	6.00
27	Tim Brown	3.00
28	Napoleon Kaufman	3.00
29	Ricky Watters	3.00
30	Jerome Bettis	6.00
31	Kordell Stewart	12.00
32	Eddie Kennison	6.00
33	Jerry Rice	12.00
34	Steve Young	10.00
35	Chris Warren	3.00
36	Terry Allen	3.00

1997 Zenith

The 150-card, regular-sized set included Season Highlights (15) and Awesome Foursome (1) and Rookies (35) subsets and was available in six-card packs. The base cards feature the player's image over a gold foil circle. The player's name is also printed in gold foil on the card face bottom. The card backs feature another photo with in-depth statistical information. Insert sets include the Rookie Rising, V2, Z Team, Gold Mirror Mylar Z Team and the base-set parallel Artist's Proof.

		MT
Complete Set (150):		50.00
Common Player:		.15
Wax Box:		90.00
1	Brett Favre	4.00
2	Jerry Rice	2.00
3	Shannon Sharpe	.15
4	Dan Marino	4.00
5	James Stewart	.15
6	Warren Moon	.15
7	Emmitt Smith	4.00
8	Kordell Stewart	2.00
9	Kerry Collins	2.00
10	Ricky Watters	.15
11	Gus Frerotte	.15
12	Barry Sanders	2.00
13	Joey Galloway	.75
14	Marshall Faulk	1.00
15	Todd Collins	.15
16	Steve McNair	1.00
17	Tyrone Wheatley	.15
18	Isaac Bruce	.50
19	Troy Aikman	2.00
20	Larry Centers	.15
21	Alvin Harper	.15
22	Rashaan Salaam	.15
23	Eric Metcalf	.15
24	Jim Everett	.15
25	Ken Dilger	.15
26	Curtis Martin	3.00
27	Neil O'Donnell	.15
28	Thurman Thomas	.15
29	Andre Rison	.15
30	Steve Bono	.15
31	Garrison Hearst	.15
32	Junior Seau	.15
33	Napoleon Kaufman	.15
34	Jerome Bettis	.15
35	Frank Wycheck	.15
36	Lamar Smith	.15
37	Derrick Alexander	.15
38	Steve Young	1.50
39	Cris Carter	.15
40	O.J. McDuffie	.15
41	Deion Sanders	1.25
42	Robert Brooks	.15
43	Jeff Blake	.50
44	Marcus Allen	.15
45	Herman Moore	.15
46	Ray Zellars	.15
47	Tim Brown	.15
48	John Elway	1.50
49	Charles Johnson	.15
50	Rodney Peete	.15
51	Curtis Conway	.15
52	Kevin Greene	.15
53	Andre Reed	.15
54	Mark Brunell	2.00
55	Tony Martin	.15
56	Elvis Grbac	.15
57	Wayne Chrebet	.15
58	Vinny Testaverde	.15
59	Terry Allen	.15
60	Dave Brown	.15
61	LaShon Johnson	.15
62	Trent Dilfer	.15
63	Chris Warren	.15
64	Chris Sanders	.15
65	Kevin Carter	.15
66	Jim Harbaugh	.15
67	Terance Mathis	.15
68	Ben Coates	.15
69	Robert Smith	.15
70	Drew Bledsoe	2.00
71	Henry Ellard	.15
72	Scott Mitchell	.15
73	Andre Hastings	.15
74	Rodney Hampton	.15
75	Michael Jackson	.15
76	Jeff Hostetler	.15
77	Reggie White	.15
78	Kent Graham	.15
79	Adrian Murrell	.15
80	Carl Pickens	.15
81	Erik Kramer	.15
82	Terrell Davis	2.50
83	Sean Dawkins	.15
84	Jamal Anderson	.50
85	Stan Humphries	.15
86	Chris T. Jones	.15
87	Hardy Nickerson	.15
88	Anthony Johnson	.15
89	Michael Haynes	.15
90	Irving Spikes	.15
91	Bruce Smith	.15
92	Keenan McCardell	.15
93	Chris Chandler	.15
94	Tamarick Vanover	.15
95	Cortez Kennedy	.15
96	Roman Phifer	.15
97	Michael Irvin	.15
98	Tim Biakabutuka	1.00
99	Stepfret Williams	.15
100	Eddie George	3.00
101	Karim Abdul-Jabbar	1.75
102	Amani Toomer	.15
103	Tony Banks	1.00
104	Regan Upshaw	.15
105	Leeland McElroy	.15
106	Jason Dunn	.15
107	Keyshawn Johnson	1.00
108	Winslow Oliver	.15
109	Walt Harris	.15
110	Stanley Pritchett	.15
111	Eddie Kennison	1.25
112	Terrell Owens	1.75
113	Duane Clemons	.15
114	John Mobley	.15
115	Simeon Rice	.15
116	Ernie Conwell	.15
117	Eric Moulds	.30
118	Marvin Harrison	1.25
119	Rickey Dudley	.30
120	Mike Alstott	.30
121	Terry Glenn	2.50
122	Brian Dawkins	.15
123	Kevin Hardy	.15
124	Bobby Engram	1.00
125	Alex Van Dyke	.15
126	Zach Thomas	.75
127	Bryan Still	.15
128	Detron Smith	.15
129	Jerome Woods	.15
130	Muhsin Muhammad	.50
131	Lawrence Phillips	1.00
132	Alex Molden	.15
133	Steve Young	.75
134	Troy Aikman	1.00
135	Junior Seau	.15
136	John Elway	.75
137	Dan Marino	2.00
138	Lawrence Phillips	.15
139	Brett Favre	2.00
140	Jerry Rice	1.00
141	Kerry Collins	1.00
142	Barry Sanders	1.00
143	Mark Brunell	1.00
144	Drew Bledsoe	1.00
145	Eddie Kennison	.50
146	Marvin Harrison	.50
147	Emmitt Smith	2.00
148	Eddie George, Terry Glenn, Rickey Dudley, Bobby Hoying	2.00
149	Emmitt Smith	2.00
150	Dan Marino	2.00

1997 Zenith Artist's Proofs

Artist's Proofs paralled all 150 cards in the regular-issue set. The cards are distinguished by a holographic foil Artist's Proof stamp, and are inserted every 47 packs.

	MT
Complete Set (150):	1500.00
Artist's Proof Cards:	15x-30x

1997 Zenith Rookie Rising

The 24-card, regular-sized set was inserted every 23 packs of Pinnacle Zenith. The cards are individually numbered as "x of 24" and feature the rookie on the card face in Dufex printing over a common stadium. The horizontal cards have "Rookie Rising" printed in gold script on the front with the player's name written in script in the upper left corner. The backs feature a player shot over a football.

		MT
Complete Set (24):		160.00
Common Player:		3.00
1	Eddie Kennison	8.00
2	Marvin Harrison	8.00
3	Keyshawn Johnson	8.00
4	Leeland McElroy	3.00
5	Terrell Owens	12.00
6	Terry Glenn	18.00
7	Bobby Engram	3.00
8	Karim Abdul-Jabbar	15.00
9	Lawrence Phillips	3.00
10	Amani Toomer	3.00
11	Eric Moulds	3.00
12	Jason Dunn	3.00
13	Stanley Pritchett	3.00
14	Eddie George	20.00
15	Muhsin Muhammad	8.00
16	Rickey Dudley	3.00
17	Tony Banks	8.00
18	Bryan Still	3.00
19	Tim Biakabutuka	3.00
20	Simeon Rice	3.00
21	Zach Thomas	8.00
22	Kevin Hardy	3.00
23	Jerris McPhail	3.00
24	Mike Alstott	6.00

1997 Zenith V2

The 18-card, regular-sized set features full-motion lenticular printing along with a conventional player photo. Inserted every 23 packs, the die-cut cards have "V2" printed underneath a motion picture with the player's name and team on the top and bottom of the horizontal card, respectively. The card backs are numbered with the "V" prefix and contain 1996 statistics and a brief highlight.

		MT
Complete Set (18):		350.00
Common Player:		6.00
1	Troy Aikman	25.00
2	John Elway	20.00
3	Jim Harbaugh	6.00
4	Barry Sanders	25.00
5	Deion Sanders	12.00
6	Drew Bledsoe	25.00
7	Dan Marino	45.00
8	Terrell Davis	30.00
9	Isaac Bruce	10.00
10	Jerome Bettis	6.00
11	Emmitt Smith	45.00
12	Brett Favre	50.00
13	Steve Young	15.00
14	Mark Brunell	25.00
15	Joey Galloway	6.00
16	Kordell Stewart	20.00
17	Jerry Rice	25.00
18	Curtis Martin	30.00

1997 Zenith Z-Team

The 18-card, regular-sized set was inserted every 71 packs of Pinnacle Zenith while the parallel Gold Mirror Mylar Z Team set was found every 191 packs. The standard Z Team cards feature the player's image on a horizontal card with a "Z" printed on the left side over a large football backdrop. The card backs are numbered with the "Z" prefix and feature another player shot over a large football. A large black "Z" with a highlight text insert is on the left side. The Gold Mirror Mylar Z Team inserts are distinguishable by the reflective gold background on the card fronts. The card backs are essentially the same, with the exception of the words "Mirror Gold" printed along the left border.

		MT
Complete Set (18):		650.00
Common Player:		15.00
1	Emmitt Smith	80.00
2	Dan Marino	80.00
3	Jerry Rice	40.00
4	John Elway	30.00
5	Curtis Martin	50.00
6	Deion Sanders	25.00
7	Tony Banks	15.00
8	Jim Harbaugh	15.00
9	Joey Galloway	15.00
10	Troy Aikman	40.00
11	Brett Favre	80.00
12	Keyshawn Johnson	25.00
13	Eddie George	50.00
14	Barry Sanders	40.00
15	Kordell Stewart	40.00
16	Steve Young	30.00
17	Terrell Davis	50.00
18	Drew Bledsoe	40.00

1997 Zenith Z-Team Mirror Golds

7-Team Mirror Golds feature all 18 cards in the regular Z-Team set, but these inserts feature a Mirror Gold finish, and are inserted every 191 packs.

	MT
Complete Set (18):	1600.00
Mirror Golds:	2x-3x

1997 Playoff Absolute

The 200-card set showcases an action shot of the player with a map of his hometown serving as the background on the card front. Named "Absolute Beginnings," the backs include the player's bio at the top left and the card number in the upper right inside a shape of an NFL shield. A headshot of the player is featured in the left center, while his name, number, position and team, along with interesting facts regarding the player's hometown and his pre-collegiate years are included to the right of the photo. His 1996 and total stats are printed along the bottom. The base set has three levels of color coded insertion ratios: Green (card Nos. 1-100, 3.5 per pack), Blue (Nos. 101-150, 1 per pack) and Red (Nos. 151-200, 1 per every 2 packs). The backs for each colored card are identical. The cards are standard size.

		MT
Complete Set (200):		170.00
Comp. Green Set (100):		20.00
Comp. Blue Set (50):		40.00
Comp. Red Set (50):		110.00
Common Green Player (1-100):		.10
Common Blue Player (101-150):		.40
Common Red Player (151-200):		1.00
Wax Box:		80.00
1	Marcus Allen	.20
2	Eric Bieniemy	.10
3	Jason Dunn	.10
4	Jim Harbaugh	.20
5	Michael Westbrook	.20
6	*Tiki Barber*	1.50
7	Frank Reich	.10
8	Irving Fryar	.10
9	Courtney Hawkins	.10
10	Eric Zeier	.10
11	Kent Graham	.10
12	Trent Dilfer	.20
13	Neil O'Donnell	.10
14	*Reidel Anthony*	2.00
15	Jeff Hostetler	.10
16	Lawrence Phillips	.20
17	Dave Brown	.10
18	Mike Tomczak	.10
19	Jake Reed	.10
20	Anthony Miller	.10
21	Eric Metcalf	.10
22	*Sedrick Shaw*	.75
23	Anthony Johnson	.10
24	Mario Bates	.10
25	Dorsey Levens	.30
26	Stan Humphries	.10
27	Ben Coates	.10
28	Tyrone Wheatley	.10
29	Adrian Murrell	.10
30	William Henderson	.10
31	*Warrick Dunn*	4.00
32	LeShon Johnson	.10
33	James Stewart	.10
34	Edgar Bennett	.10
35	Raymont Harris	.10
36	Leroy Butler	.10
37	Darren Woodson	.10
38	*Darnell Autry*	1.00
39	Johnnie Morton	.10
40	William Floyd	.10
41	Terrell Fletcher	.10
42	Leonard Russell	.10
43	Henry Ellard	.10
44	Terrell Owens	.75
45	John Friesz	.10
46	*Antowain Smith*	1.50
47	Charles Johnson	.10
48	Rickey Dudley	.10
49	Lake Dawson	.10
50	Bert Emanuel	.10
51	Zach Thomas	.30
52	Ernest Byner	.10
53	*Yatil Green*	1.50
54	Chris Spielman	.10
55	Muhsin Muhammad	.30
56	Bobby Engram	.20
57	Eric Bjornson	.10
58	Willie Green	.10
59	Derrick Mayes	.10
60	Chris Sanders	.10
61	Jimmy Smith	.10
62	*Tony Gonzalez*	.75
63	Rich Gannon	.10
64	Stanley Pritchett	.10
65	Brad Johnson	.10
66	Rodney Peete	.10
67	Sam Gash	.10
68	Chris Calloway	.10
69	Chris T. Jones	.10
70	*Will Blackwell*	.50
71	Mark Bruener	.10
72	Terry Kirby	.10
73	Brian Blades	.10
74	Craig Heyward	.10
75	Jamie Asher	.10
76	Terance Mathis	.10
77	*Troy Davis*	1.50
78	Bruce Smith	.10
79	Simeon Rice	.10
80	Fred Barnett	.10
81	Tim Brown	.20
82	James Jett	.10
83	Mark Carrier	.10
84	Shawn Jefferson	.10
85	Ken Dilger	.10
86	*Rae Carruth*	1.00
87	Keenan McCardell	.10
88	Michael Irvin	.20
89	Mark Chmura	.20
90	Derrick Alexander	.10
91	Andre Reed	.10
92	Ed McCaffrey	.10
93	Erik Kramer	.10
94	Albert Connell	.10
95	Frank Wycheck	.10
96	Zach Crockett	.10
97	Jim Everett	.10
98	Michael Haynes	.10
99	Jeff Graham	.10
100	Brent Jones	.10
101	Troy Aikman	3.50
102	*Byron Hanspard*	2.50
103	Robert Brooks	.75
104	Karim Abdul-Jabbar	2.50
105	Drew Bledsoe	3.50
106	Napoleon Kaufman	.40
107	Steve Young	2.50
108	Leeland McElroy	.40
109	Jamal Anderson	1.50
110	*David LaFleur*	1.75
111	Vinny Testaverde	.40
112	Eric Moulds	.75
113	Tim Biakabutuka	.75
114	Rick Mirer	.75
115	Jeff Blake	.75
116	Jim Schwantz	.40
117	Herman Moore	1.00
118	*Ike Hilliard*	4.00
119	Reggie White	.75
120	Steve McNair	2.00
121	Marshall Faulk	1.25
122	Natrone Means	.75
123	Greg Hill	.40
124	O.J. McDuffie	.40
125	Robert Smith	.40
126	*Bryant Westbrook*	1.25
127	Ray Zellars	.40
128	Rodney Hampton	.40
129	Wayne Chrebet	.40
130	Desmond Howard	.75
131	Ty Detmer	.75
132	Erric Pegram	.40
133	Yancey Thigpen	.40
134	*Danny Wuerffel*	6.00
135	Charlie Jones	.40
136	Chris Warren	.75
137	Isaac Bruce	1.25
138	Errict Rhett	1.00
139	Gus Frerotte	.40
140	Frank Sanders	.40
141	Todd Collins	.40
142	*Jake Plummer*	1.75
143	Darnay Scott	.75
144	Rashaan Salaam	.75
145	Terrell Davis	4.00
146	Scott Mitchell	.40
147	Junior Seau	.75
148	Warren Moon	.40
149	Wesley Walls	.40
150	Daryl Johnston	.40
151	Brett Favre	14.00
152	Emmitt Smith	12.00
153	Dan Marino	12.00
154	Larry Centers	1.00
155	Michael Jackson	1.00
156	Kerry Collins	6.00
157	Curtis Conway	2.00
158	Peter Boulware	1.00
159	Carl Pickens	2.00
160	Shannon Sharpe	2.00
161	Brett Perriman	1.00
162	Eddie George	8.00
163	Mark Brunell	6.00
164	Tamarick Vanover	2.00
165	Cris Carter	1.00
166	*Corey Dillon*	4.00
167	Curtis Martin	7.00
168	Amani Toomer	1.00
169	Jeff George	1.00
170	Kordell Stewart	6.00
171	Garrison Hearst	1.00
172	Tony Banks	3.00
173	Mike Alstott	2.00
174	*Jim Druckenmiller*	10.00
175	Chris Chandler	1.00
176	Bam Morris	1.00
177	Billy Joe Hobert	1.00
178	Ernie Mills	1.00
179	Ki-Jana Carter	1.00
180	Deion Sanders	4.00
181	Ricky Watters	2.00
182	*Shawn Springs*	3.00
183	Barry Sanders	6.00
184	Antonio Freeman	3.00
185	Marvin Harrison	3.00
186	Elvis Grbac	1.00
187	Terry Glenn	5.00
188	Willie Roaf	1.00
189	Keyshawn Johnson	3.00
190	*Orlando Pace*	3.00
191	Jerome Bettis	2.00
192	Tony Martin	1.00
193	Jerry Rice	6.00
194	Joey Galloway	2.00
195	Terry Allen	2.00
196	Eddie Kennison	3.00
197	Thurman Thomas	2.00
198	Darrell Russell	1.00
199	Rob Moore	1.00
200	John Elway	5.00

1997 Playoff Absolute Chip Shots

Inserted one per pack, the Chip Shots resembled poker chips. The chips, which measure approximately 1-1/2" in diameter, were available in assorted colors. The plastic tokens were a 200-player parallel of the base set.

		MT
Complete Set (200):		220.00
Common Player:		.40
1	Marcus Allen	.75
2	Eric Bieniemy	.40
3	Jason Dunn	.40
4	Jim Harbaugh	.40
5	Michael Westbrook	.40
6	Tiki Barber	2.00
7	Frank Reich	.40
8	Irving Fryar	.40
9	Courtney Hawkins	.40
10	Eric Zeier	.40
11	Kent Graham	.40
12	Trent Dilfer	.75
13	Neil O'Donnell	.40
14	Reidel Anthony	4.00
15	Jeff Hostetler	.40
16	Lawrence Phillips	.75
17	Dave Brown	.40
18	Mike Tomczak	.40
19	Jake Reed	.40
20	Anthony Miller	.40
21	Eric Metcalf	.40
22	Sedrick Shaw	1.00
23	Anthony Johnson	.40
24	Mario Bates	.40
25	Dorsey Levens	1.00
26	Stan Humphries	.40
27	Ben Coates	.40
28	Tyrone Wheatley	.40
29	Adrian Murrell	.40
30	William Henderson	.40
31	Warrick Dunn	8.00
32	LeShon Johnson	.40
33	James Stewart	.40
34	Edgar Bennett	.40
35	Raymont Harris	.40
36	Leroy Butler	.40

#	Player	MT
37	Darren Woodson	.40
38	Darnell Autry	2.00
39	Johnnie Morton	.40
40	William Floyd	.40
41	Terrell Fletcher	.40
42	Leonard Russell	.40
43	Henry Ellard	.40
44	Terrell Owens	4.00
45	John Friesz	.40
46	Antowain Smith	2.00
47	Charles Johnson	.40
48	Rickey Dudley	.40
49	Lake Dawson	.40
50	Bert Emanuel	.40
51	Zach Thomas	1.00
52	Ernest Byner	.40
53	Yatil Green	3.00
54	Chris Spielman	.40
55	Muhsin Muhammad	.75
56	Bobby Engram	.75
57	Eric Bjornson	.40
58	Willie Green	.40
59	Derrick Mayes	.40
60	Chris Sanders	.40
61	Jimmy Smith	.40
62	Tony Gonzalez	1.00
63	Rich Gannon	.40
64	Stanley Pritchett	.40
65	Brad Johnson	.75
66	Rodney Peete	.40
67	Sam Gash	.40
68	Chris Calloway	.40
69	Chris T. Jones	.40
70	Will Blackwell	.75
71	Mark Bruener	.40
72	Terry Kirby	.40
73	Brian Blades	.40
74	Craig Heyward	.40
75	Jamie Asher	.40
76	Terance Mathis	.40
77	Troy Davis	3.00
78	Bruce Smith	.40
79	Simeon Rice	.40
80	Fred Barnett	.40
81	Tim Brown	.40
82	James Jett	.40
83	Mark Carrier	.40
84	Shawn Jefferson	.40
85	Ken Dilger	.40
86	Rae Carruth	2.00
87	Keenan McCardell	.75
88	Michael Irvin	.75
89	Mark Chmura	.40
90	Derrick Alexander	.40
91	Andre Reed	.40
92	Ed McCaffrey	.40
93	Erik Kramer	.40
94	Albert Connell	.40
95	Frank Wycheck	.40
96	Zach Crockett	.40
97	Jim Everett	.40
98	Michael Haynes	.40
99	Jeff Graham	.40
100	Brent Jones	.40
101	Troy Aikman	7.00
102	Byron Hanspard	2.00
103	Robert Brooks	.75
104	Karim Abdul-Jabbar	4.00
105	Drew Bledsoe	7.00
106	Napoleon Kaufman	.75
107	Steve Young	4.00
108	Leeland McElroy	.40
109	Jamal Anderson	1.00
110	David LaFleur	1.50
111	Vinny Testaverde	.40
112	Eric Moulds	.75
113	Tim Biakabutuka	.75
114	Rick Mirer	.40
115	Jeff Blake	1.00
116	Jim Schwantz	.40
117	Herman Moore	1.00
118	Ike Hilliard	4.00
119	Reggie White	.75
120	Steve McNair	4.00
121	Marshall Faulk	1.00
122	Natrone Means	.75
123	Greg Hill	.40
124	O.J. McDuffie	.40
125	Robert Smith	.40
126	Bryant Westbrook	1.00
127	Ray Zellars	.40
128	Rodney Hampton	.40
129	Wayne Chrebet	.40
130	Desmond Howard	.40
131	Ty Detmer	.40
132	Erric Pegram	.40
133	Yancey Thigpen	.40
134	Danny Wuerffel	7.00
135	Charlie Jones	.40
136	Chris Warren	.40
137	Isaac Bruce	1.00
138	Errict Rhett	.75
139	Gus Frerotte	.40
140	Frank Sanders	.40
141	Todd Collins	.40
142	Jake Plummer	1.50
143	Darnay Scott	.40
144	Rashaan Salaam	.75
145	Terrell Davis	8.00
146	Scott Mitchell	.40
147	Junior Seau	.75
148	Warren Moon	.40
149	Wesley Walls	.40
150	Daryl Johnston	.40
151	Brett Favre	14.00
152	Emmitt Smith	12.00
153	Dan Marino	12.00
154	Larry Centers	.40
155	Michael Jackson	.40
156	Kerry Collins	5.00
157	Curtis Conway	.75
158	Peter Boulware	.75
159	Carl Pickens	.40
160	Shannon Sharpe	.40
161	Brett Perriman	.40
162	Eddie George	10.00
163	Mark Brunell	7.00
164	Tamarick Vanover	.75
165	Cris Carter	.40
166	Corey Dillon	3.00
167	Curtis Martin	8.00
168	Amani Toomer	.40
169	Jeff George	.40
170	Kordell Stewart	7.00
171	Garrison Hearst	.40
172	Tony Banks	3.00
173	Mike Alstott	.75
174	Jim Druckenmiller	7.00
175	Chris Chandler	.40
176	Bam Morris	.40
177	Billy Joe Hobert	.40
178	Ernie Mills	.40
179	Ki-Jana Carter	.40
180	Deion Sanders	3.00
181	Ricky Watters	.75
182	Shawn Springs	1.00
183	Barry Sanders	7.00
184	Antonio Freeman	1.00
185	Marvin Harrison	3.00
186	Elvis Grbac	.40
187	Terry Glenn	6.00
188	Willie Roaf	.40
189	Keyshawn Johnson	3.00
190	Orlando Pace	2.00
191	Jerome Bettis	.75
192	Tony Martin	.40
193	Jerry Rice	7.00
194	Joey Galloway	1.00
195	Terry Allen	.40
196	Eddie Kennison	3.00
197	Thurman Thomas	.75
198	Darrell Russell	.75
199	Rob Moore	.40
200	John Elway	4.00

1997 Playoff Absolute Playoff Honors

This three-card set, which was inserted 1:7,200 packs, was a continuation from the 1996 Playoff Prime and Contenders sets. The felt-like cards feature a player photo superimposed over a checkered background on the front. The Playoff Honors' logo appears in one of the upper corners of the card, with the player's name printed in a lower corner. The cards carry a prefix of "PF."

	MT
Complete Set (3):	650.00
Common Player:	125.00
PF07 Jerry Rice	300.00
PF08 Reggie White	125.00
PF09 John Elway	250.00

1997 Playoff Absolute Leather Quads

The 18-card set, which was produced on leather, was inserted 1:144 packs. Each card included four players, with two appearing on each side. The player photos are superimposed over the leather background. The players' names are printed vertically in green along the left and right borders. "Leather Quad" is printed in white over a black stripe which runs diagonally between the two players' photos. The Playoff logo and "1997" are printed in green at the bottom center on both sides of the cards. The card numbers appear in the top center inside a green oval on both sides of the cards.

	MT
Complete Set (18):	1200.00
Common Player:	20.00
LQ1 Brett Favre, Jerry Rice, Dan Marino, Emmitt Smith	300.00
LQ2 Barry Sanders, Terrell Davis, Eddie George, Curtis Martin	175.00
LQ3 Kordell Stewart, Herman Moore, Elvis Grbac, Chris Warren	75.00
LQ4 Troy Aikman, Leeland McElroy, Cris Carter, Zach Thomas	75.00
LQ5 Drew Bledsoe, Jamal Anderson, Michael Jackson, Jim Harbaugh	75.00
LQ6 John Elway, Reggie White, Warren Moon, Terrell Owens	60.00
LQ7 Kerry Collins, Rashaan Salaam, Shannon Sharpe, Ricky Watters	75.00
LQ8 Mark Brunell, Eric Moulds, Mario Bates, Larry Centers	75.00
LQ9 Karim Abdul-Jabbar, Robert Brooks, Jerome Bettis, Carl Pickens	60.00
LQ10 Steve Young, Tim Biakabutuka, Jeff George, Tony Martin	50.00
LQ11 Terry Glenn, Jeff Blake, Mike Alstott, Curtis Conway	50.00
LQ12 Joey Galloway, Antonio Freeman, Anthony Johnson, Rick Mirer	40.00
LQ13 Steve McNair, Marshall Faulk, Jimmy Smith, Isaac Bruce	50.00
LQ14 Deion Sanders, Tony Banks, Vinny Testaverde, Rodney Hampton	40.00
LQ15 Marvin Harrison, Lawrence Phillips, Thurman Thomas, Chris Chandler	20.00
LQ16 Keyshawn Johnson, Napoleon Kaufman, Gus Frerotte, Greg Hill	20.00
LQ17 Eddie Kennison, Terry Allen, Scott Mitchell, Errict Rhett	20.00
LQ18 Warrick Dunn, Orlando Pace, Jim Druckenmiller, Darrell Russell	80.00

1997 Playoff Absolute Pennants

Inserted one per box, the pennants measure 3-1/2" x 5". Each of the 192 pennants in the set have a felt-like feel to them. The pennant fronts have the player's name printed inside a rectangle in the upper left, while a cut-out color action photo of the player is included in the center of the pennant. The Playoff Pennants 1997 logo is on the right of the front. The vertical backs have the player's name, appropriate logos and pennant number in a stripe at the top. The player's headshot is included inside a circle in the center of the back, which also has a felt-like feel to it. The Playoff Pennants logo is on the bottom of the back.

#	Player	MT
	Common Player:	5.00
1	Marcus Allen	10.00
2	Eric Bieniemy	5.00
3	Jason Dunn	5.00
4	Jim Harbaugh (QBC)	5.00
5	Michael Westbrook	5.00
6	Tiki Barber	30.00
7	Frank Reich (QBC)	5.00
8	Irving Fryar	5.00
9	Courtney Hawkins	5.00
10	Eric Zeier	5.00
11	Kent Graham	5.00
12	Trent Dilfer (QBC)	10.00
13	Neil O'Donnell (QBC)	5.00
14	Reidel Anthony	45.00
15	Jeff Hostetler (QBC)	5.00
16	Lawrence Phillips	10.00
17	Dave Brown (QBC)	5.00
18	Mike Tomczak	5.00
19	Jake Reed	5.00
20	Anthony Miller	5.00
21	Eric Metcalf	5.00
22	Sedrick Shaw	20.00
23	Anthony Johnson	5.00
24	Mario Bates	5.00
25	Dorsey Levens	10.00
26	Stan Humphries	5.00
27	Ben Coates	5.00
28	Tyrone Wheatley	5.00
29	Adrian Murrell	5.00
30	William Henderson	5.00
31	Warrick Dunn	75.00
32	LeShon Johnson	5.00
33	James Stewart	5.00
34	Edgar Bennett	5.00
35	Raymont Harris	5.00
36	Leroy Butler	5.00
37	Darren Woodson	5.00
38	Darnell Autry	20.00
39	Johnnie Morton	5.00
40	William Floyd	10.00
41	Terrell Fletcher	5.00
42	Leonard Russell	5.00
43	Henry Ellard	5.00
44	Terrell Owens	40.00
45	John Friesz	5.00
46	Antowain Smith	25.00
47	Charles Johnson	5.00
48	Rickey Dudley	5.00
49	Lake Dawson	5.00
50	Bert Emanuel	5.00
51	Zach Thomas	15.00
52	Earnest Byner	5.00
53	Yatil Green	25.00
54	Chris Spielman	5.00
55	Muhsin Muhammad	5.00
56	Bobby Engram	5.00
57	Eric Bjornson	5.00
58	Willie Green	5.00
59	Derrick Mayes	5.00
60	Chris Sanders	5.00
61	Jimmy Smith	5.00
62	Tony Gonzalez	20.00
63	Rich Gannon	5.00
64	Stanley Pritchett	5.00
65	Brad Johnson	10.00
66	Rodney Peete (QBC)	5.00
67	Sam Gash	5.00
68	Chris Galloway	5.00
69	Chris T. Jones	5.00
70	Will Blackwell	10.00
71	Mark Bruener	5.00
72	Terry Kirby	5.00
73	Brian Blades	5.00
74	Craig Heyward	5.00
75	Jamie Asher	5.00
76	Terance Mathis	5.00
77	Troy Davis	40.00
78	Bruce Smith	5.00
79	Simeon Rice	5.00
80	Fred Barnett	5.00
81	Jerry Rice	75.00
82	James Jett	5.00

83	Mark Carrier	5.00
84	Shawn Jefferson	5.00
85	Ken Dilger	5.00
86	Rae Carruth	25.00
87	Keenan McCardell	10.00
88	Michael Irvin (QBC)	10.00
89	Mark Chmura	10.00
90	Derrick Alexander	5.00
91	Andre Reed	5.00
92	Ed McCaffrey	5.00
93	Erik Kramer (QBC)	5.00
94	Albert Connell	5.00
95	Frank Wycheck	5.00
96	Zach Crockett	5.00
97	Jim Everett (QBC)	5.00
98	Michael Haynes	5.00
99	Jeff Graham	5.00
100	Brent Jones	5.00
101	Troy Aikman (QBC)	75.00
102	Byron Hanspard	25.00
103	Robert Brooks	10.00
104	Joey Galloway	15.00
105	Drew Bledsoe (QBC)	75.00
106	Eddie Kennison	40.00
107	Steve Young (QBC)	50.00
108	Leeland McElroy	10.00
109	Jamal Anderson	15.00
110	David LaFleur	20.00
111	Vinny Testaverde	5.00
112	Eric Moulds	5.00
113	Tim Biakabutuka	10.00
114	Rick Mirer (QBC)	5.00
115	Jeff Blake (QBC)	15.00
116	Jim Schwantz	5.00
117	Herman Moore	15.00
118	Ike Hilliard	45.00
119	Reggie White	10.00
120	Steve McNair (QBC)	65.00
121	Marshall Faulk	10.00
122	Natrone Means	10.00
123	Greg Hill	5.00
124	O.J. McDuffie	5.00
125	Robert Smith	5.00
126	Bryant Westbrook	10.00
127	Ray Zellars	5.00
128	Rodney Hampton	5.00
129	Wayne Chrebet	5.00
130	Desmond Howard	5.00
131	Ty Detmer	5.00
132	Erric Pegram	5.00
133	Yancey Thigpen	5.00
134	Danny Wuerffel	50.00
135	Charlie Jones	5.00
136	Chris Warren	5.00
137	Isaac Bruce	15.00
138	Errict Rhett	10.00
139	Gus Frerotte (QBC)	5.00
140	Frank Sanders	5.00
141	Todd Collins	10.00
142	Jake Plummer	20.00
143	Darnay Scott	5.00
144	Rashaan Salaam	10.00
145	Terrell Davis	75.00
146	Scott Mitchell (QBC)	5.00
147	Junior Seau (QBC)	10.00
148	Warren Moon (QBC)	5.00
149	Wesley Walls	5.00
150	Daryl Johnston	5.00
151	Brett Favre (QBC)	160.00
152	Emmitt Smith (QBC)	150.00
153	Dan Marino (QBC)	150.00
154	Larry Centers	5.00
155	Michael Jackson	5.00
156	Kerry Collins (QBC)	75.00
157	Curtis Conway	10.00
158	Peter Boulware	5.00
159	Carl Pickens	10.00
160	Shannon Sharpe	5.00
161	Brett Perriman	5.00
162	Thurman Thomas	10.00
163	Mark Brunell (QBC)	75.00
164	Tamarick Vanover	10.00
165	Cris Carter	10.00
166	Corey Dillon	25.00
167	Curtis Martin	75.00
168	Amani Toomer	5.00
169	Jeff George (QBC)	5.00
170	Darrell Russell	5.00
171	Garrison Hearst	5.00
172	Tony Banks (QBC)	35.00
173	Rob Moore	5.00
174	Jim Druckenmiller	50.00
175	Chris Chandler	5.00
176	Bam Morris	5.00
177	Billy Joe Hobert	5.00
178	Ernie Mills	5.00
179	Ki-Jana Carter	10.00
180	Deion Sanders	35.00
181	Ricky Watters	10.00
182	Shawn Springs	20.00
183	Barry Sanders (QBC)	75.00

184	Antonio Freeman	15.00
185	Marvin Harrison	35.00
186	Elvis Grbac (QBC)	5.00
187	John Elway (QBC)	50.00
188	Willie Roaf	5.00
189	Keyshawn Johnson	35.00
190	Orlando Pace	15.00
191	Jerome Bettis	10.00
192	Tony Martin	5.00

1997 Playoff Absolute Autographed Pennants

Measuring 3-1/2" x 5", one of the eight signed pennants were randomly inserted in boxes of Playoff Absolute.

		MT
Complete Set (8):		600.00
Common Player:		40.00
A1	Kordell Stewart	125.00
A2	Eddie George	175.00
A3	Karim Abdul-Jabbar	75.00
A4	Mike Alstott	40.00
A5	Terry Glenn	125.00
A6	Napoleon Kaufman	40.00
A7	Terry Allen	40.00
A8	Tim Brown	40.00

1997 Playoff Absolute Reflex

The 200-card set is a parallel of the base set printed on mirror board. The card fronts have "Reflex" printed at the top, with the player's photo superimposed over a silver mirror background. "Playoff '97" is printed vertically along the left border, while his name is printed vertically along the right border. The cards were inserted 1:288 packs.

		MT
Common Player:		30.00
1	Brett Favre	750.00
2	Dorsey Levens	30.00
3	Antonio Freeman	60.00
4	Robert Brooks	30.00
5	Mark Chmura	30.00
6	Reggie White	60.00
7	Drew Bledsoe	350.00
8	Curtis Martin	350.00
9	Ben Coates	30.00
10	Terry Glenn	300.00
11	Kerry Collins	300.00
12	Tim Biakabutuka	60.00
13	Anthony Johnson	30.00
14	Wesley Walls	30.00
15	Muhsin Muhammad	30.00
16	Mark Brunell	350.00
17	Natrone Means	60.00
18	Jimmy Smith	30.00
19	John Elway	300.00
20	Terrell Davis	350.00
21	Anthony Miller	30.00
22	Shannon Sharpe	30.00
23	Steve Young	300.00
24	Garrison Hearst	30.00
25	Jerry Rice	350.00
26	Troy Aikman	350.00
27	Deion Sanders	200.00
28	Emmitt Smith	700.00
29	Michael Irvin	60.00
30	Kordell Stewart	300.00
31	Jerome Bettis	60.00
32	Charles Johnson	30.00
33	Ty Detmer	30.00
34	Ricky Watters	60.00
35	Irving Fryar	30.00
36	Todd Collins	60.00
37	Thurman Thomas	60.00
38	Bruce Smith	30.00
39	Eric Moulds	30.00
40	Brad Johnson	30.00
41	Robert Smith	60.00
42	Cris Carter	60.00
43	Elvis Grbac	30.00
44	Greg Hill	30.00
45	Marcus Allen	60.00
46	Gus Frerotte	30.00
47	Terry Allen	30.00
48	Michael Westbrook	30.00
49	Jim Harbaugh	30.00
50	Marshall Faulk	60.00

51	Marvin Harrison	125.00
52	Jeff Blake	75.00
53	Ki-Jana Carter	60.00
54	Carl Pickens	30.00
55	Junior Seau	60.00
56	Tony Martin	30.00
57	Dan Marino	700.00
58	Karim Abdul-Jabbar	175.00
59	Stanley Pritchett	30.00
60	Zach Thomas	60.00
61	Steve McNair	300.00
62	Eddie George	350.00
63	Chris Sanders	30.00
64	Rick Mirer	30.00
65	Rashaan Salaam	60.00
66	Curtis Conway	30.00
67	Bobby Engram	30.00
68	Kent Graham	30.00
69	Leeland McElroy	30.00
70	Larry Centers	30.00
71	Frank Sanders	30.00
72	Jeff George	30.00
73	Napoleon Kaufman	60.00
74	Desmond Howard	30.00
75	Tim Brown	30.00
76	John Friesz	30.00
77	Chris Warren	30.00
78	Joey Galloway	75.00
79	Tony Banks	125.00
80	Lawrence Phillips	60.00
81	Isaac Bruce	75.00
82	Eddie Kennison	125.00
83	Errict Rhett	60.00
84	Mike Alstott	60.00
85	Rodney Hampton	30.00
86	Amani Toomer	30.00
87	Scott Mitchell	30.00
88	Barry Sanders	350.00
89	Herman Moore	60.00
90	Vinny Testaverde	30.00
91	Bam Morris	30.00
92	Michael Jackson	30.00
93	Chris Chandler	30.00
94	Eric Metcalf	30.00
95	Jamal Anderson	60.00
96	Jim Everett	30.00
97	Mario Bates	30.00
98	Wayne Chrebet	30.00
99	Adrian Murrell	30.00
100	Keyshawn Johnson	125.00
101	William Henderson	30.00
102	Edgar Bennett	30.00
103	LeRoy Butler	30.00
104	Derrick Mayes	30.00
105	Sedrick Shaw	00.00
106	Sam Gash	30.00
107	Shawn Jefferson	30.00
108	Mark Carrier	30.00
109	Rae Carruth	100.00
110	Ernie Mills	30.00
111	James Stewart	30.00
112	Keenan McCardell	30.00
113	Willie Green	30.00
114	Ed McCaffrey	30.00
115	William Floyd	30.00
116	Terrell Owens	125.00
117	Terry Kirby	30.00
118	Brent Jones	30.00
119	Jim Schwantz	30.00
120	Jim Druckenmiller	175.00
121	Darren Woodson	30.00
122	Eric Bjornson	30.00
123	David LaFleur	60.00
124	Daryl Johnston	30.00
125	Mike Tomczak	30.00
126	Will Blackwell	60.00
127	Mark Bruener	30.00
128	Erric Pegram	30.00
129	Yancey Thigpen	30.00
130	Jason Dunn	30.00
131	Chris T. Jones	30.00
132	Rodney Peete	30.00
133	Antowain Smith	80.00
134	Chris Spielman	30.00
135	Andre Reed	30.00
136	Billy Joe Hobert	30.00
137	Jake Reed	30.00
138	Tamarick Vanover	30.00
139	Lake Dawson	30.00
140	Tony Gonzalez	60.00
141	Rich Gannon	30.00
142	Henry Ellard	30.00
143	Jamie Asher	30.00
144	Albert Connell	30.00
145	Ken Dilger	30.00
146	Zack Crockett	30.00
147	Eric Bieniemy	30.00
148	Darnay Scott	30.00
149	Corey Dillon	100.00
150	Stan Humphries	30.00
151	Terrell Fletcher	30.00

152	Leonard Russell	30.00
153	Charlie Jones	30.00
154	Yatil Green	100.00
155	Fred Barnett	30.00
156	O.J. McDuffie	30.00
157	Frank Wycheck	30.00
158	Raymont Harris	30.00
159	Darnell Autry	60.00
160	Erik Kramer	30.00
161	LeShon Johnson	30.00
162	Simeon Rice	30.00
163	Jake Plummer	60.00
164	Rob Moore	30.00
165	Jeff Hostetler	30.00
166	Rickey Dudley	30.00
167	James Jett	30.00
168	Darrell Russell	30.00
169	Brian Blades	30.00
170	Warren Moon	30.00
171	Shawn Springs	60.00
172	Craig Heyward	30.00
173	Orlando Pace	75.00
174	Courtney Hawkins	30.00
175	Trent Dilfer	60.00
176	Reidel Anthony	150.00
177	Warrick Dunn	225.00
178	Tiki Barber	120.00
179	Dave Brown	30.00
180	Tyrone Wheatley	30.00
181	Chris Calloway	30.00
182	Ike Hilliard	125.00
183	Frank Reich	30.00
184	Johnnie Morton	30.00
185	Bryant Westbrook	60.00
186	Brett Perriman	30.00
187	Eric Zeier	30.00
188	Earnest Byner	30.00
189	Derrick Alexander	30.00
190	Peter Boulware	30.00
191	Bert Emanuel	30.00
192	Terance Mathis	30.00
193	Byron Hanspard	80.00
194	Troy Davis	100.00
195	Michael Haynes	30.00
196	Ray Zellars	30.00
197	Danny Wuerffel	175.00
198	Willie Roaf	30.00
199	Neil O'Donnell	30.00
200	Jeff Graham	30.00

1997 Playoff Absolute Unsung Heroes

The 30-card set honors the players selected as the 1996 Playoff/Players Inc. Unsung Heroes, which were voted on by the fans and players. In its third year, the set includes a color photo of the player superimposed over a silver background on the right side of the front. His name is printed in the upper right. A black-and-white close-up photo, which is an enlarged version of the color photo, is printed on the left side of the card, with "1997" printed over the top of it. The Unsung Heroes logo is printed at the bottom. The backs are numbered inside a red box in the upper left. The player's name, bio and write-up are printed on the left side over a green background. Along the right side of the back is a color headshot of the player. The cards were inserted 1:12 packs.

		MT
	Complete Set (30):	20.00
	Common Player:	.50
1	Larry Centers	.50
2	Jessie Tuggle	.50
3	Stevon Moore	.50
4	Mark Pike	.50
5	Anthony Johnson	1.00
6	Anthony Carter	.50
7	Eric Bieniemy	.50
8	Jim Schwantz	.50
9	Tyrone Braxton	.50
10	Bennie Blades	.50
11	Don Beebe	.50
12	Barron Wortham	.50
13	Jason Belser	.50
14	Mickey Washington	.50
15	Dave Szott	.50
16	Zach Thomas	4.00
17	Chris Walsh	.50
18	Sam Gash	.50
19	Willie Roaf	.50
20	Charles Way	.50
21	Wayne Chrebet	1.00
22	Russell Maryland	.50
23	Michael Zordich	.50
24	Tim Lester	.50
25	Harold Green	.50
26	Rodney Harrison	.50
27	Gary Plummer	.50
28	Winston Moss	.50
29	Robb Thomas	.50
30	Darrick Brownlow	.50

1997 Playoff 1st & 10

The 250-card set features a color photo of a player superimposed over a purple "First and 10" background on the front. The player's name is printed in light purple in the upper center and right, while "Nineteen Ninety Seven" appears vertically along the lower left border. The First and 10 logo appears in the lower right. The backs have the card number in the upper right, while the player's number, position, name, highlights, bio and stats all are printed along the left side over a purple "First and 10" background. The player's head shot is printed on the right. In addition, a Kickoff parallel 250-card set was inserted 1:9 packs. The card fronts are identical to the base cards except they are printed on translucent lucite and a gold-foil Kickoff logo is stamped in the upper left. The only printing on the backs are the Players Inc., Play Football and the Playoff 1997 copyright tag line.

		MT
	Complete Set (250):	30.00
	Common Player:	.10
	Kickoff Cards:	10x-20x
	Wax Box:	55.00
1	Marcus Allen	.20
2	Eric Bieniemy	.10
3	Jason Dunn	.10
4	Jim Harbaugh	.10
5	Michael Westbrook	.10
6	*Tiki Barber*	1.00
7	Frank Reich	.10
8	Irving Fryar	.10
9	Courtney Hawkins	.10
10	Eric Zeier	.10
11	Kent Graham	.10
12	Trent Dilfer	.10
13	Neil O'Donnell	.10
14	*Reidel Anthony*	1.00
15	Jeff Hostetler	.10
16	Lawrence Phillips	.20
17	Dave Brown	.10
18	Mike Tomczak	.10
19	Jake Reed	.10
20	Anthony Miller	.10
21	Eric Metcalf	.10
22	*Sedrick Shaw*	.50
23	Anthony Johnson	.10
24	Mario Bates	.10
25	Dorsey Levens	.25
26	Stan Humphries	.10
27	Ben Coates	.10
28	Tyrone Wheatley	.10
29	Adrian Murrell	.10
30	William Henderson	.10
31	*Warrick Dunn*	2.50
32	LeShon Johnson	.10
33	James Stewart	.10
34	Edgar Bennett	.10
35	Raymont Harris	.10
36	Leroy Butler	.10
37	Darren Woodson	.10
38	*Darnell Autry*	.75
39	Johnnie Morton	.10
40	William Floyd	.10
41	Terrell Fletcher	.10
42	Leonard Russell	.10
43	Henry Ellard	.10
44	Terrell Owens	.50
45	John Friesz	.10
46	*Antowain Smith*	1.00
47	Charles Johnson	.10
48	Rickey Dudley	.10
49	Lake Dawson	.10
50	Bert Emanuel	.10
51	Zach Thomas	.25
52	Earnest Byner	.10
53	*Yatil Green*	.75
54	Chris Spielman	.10
55	Muhsin Muhammad	.10
56	Bobby Engram	.10
57	Eric Bjornson	.10
58	Willie Green	.10
59	Derrick Mayes	.10
60	Chris Sanders	.10
61	Jimmy Smith	.10
62	*Tony Gonzalez*	.50
63	Rich Gannon	.10
64	Stanley Pritchett	.10
65	Brad Johnson	.10
66	Rodney Peete	.10
67	Sam Gash	.10
68	Chris Calloway	.10
69	Chris T. Jones	.10
70	*Will Blackwell*	.20
71	Mark Bruener	.10
72	Terry Kirby	.10
73	Brian Blades	.10
74	Craig Heyward	.10
75	Jamie Asher	.10
76	Terance Mathis	.10
77	*Troy Davis*	1.00
78	Bruce Smith	.10
79	Simeon Rice	.10
80	Fred Barnett	.10
81	Tim Brown	.10
82	James Jett	.10
83	Mark Carrier	.10
84	Shawn Jefferson	.10
85	Ken Dilger	.10
86	*Rae Carruth*	1.00
87	Keenan McCardell	.10
88	Michael Irvin	.20
89	Mark Chmura	.10
90	Derrick Alexander	.10
91	Andre Reed	.10
92	Ed McCaffrey	.10
93	Erik Kramer	.10
94	Albert Connell	.10
95	Frank Wycheck	.10
96	Zack Crockett	.10
97	Jim Everett	.10
98	Michael Haynes	.10
99	Jeff Graham	.10
100	Brent Jones	.10
101	Troy Aikman	1.00
102	*Byron Hanspard*	.75
103	Robert Brooks	.10
104	Karim Abdul-Jabbar	.75
105	Drew Bledsoe	1.00
106	Napoleon Kaufman	.10
107	Steve Young	.50
108	Leeland McElroy	.10
109	Jamal Anderson	.20
110	*David LaFleur*	.50
111	Vinny Testaverde	.10
112	Eric Moulds	.20
113	Tim Biakabutuka	.20
114	Rick Mirer	.10
115	Jeff Blake	.20
116	Jim Schwantz	.10
117	Herman Moore	.20
118	*Ike Hilliard*	1.00
119	Reggie White	.20
120	Steve McNair	.50
121	Marshall Faulk	.20
122	Natrone Means	.20
123	Greg Hill	.10
124	O.J. McDuffie	.10
125	Robert Smith	.10
126	*Bryant Westbrook*	.20
127	Ray Zellars	.10
128	Rodney Hampton	.10
129	Wayne Chrebet	.10
130	Desmond Howard	.10
131	Ty Detmer	.10
132	Erric Pegram	.10
133	Yancey Thigpen	.10
134	*Danny Wuerffel*	1.50
135	Charlie Jones	.10
136	Chris Warren	.10
137	Isaac Bruce	.25
138	Errict Rhett	.20
139	Gus Frerotte	.10
140	Frank Sanders	.10
141	Todd Collins	.10
142	*Jake Plummer*	.50
143	Darnay Scott	.10
144	Rashaan Salaam	.20
145	Terrell Davis	1.50
146	Scott Mitchell	.10
147	Junior Seau	.20
148	Warren Moon	.10
149	Wesley Walls	.10
150	Daryl Johnston	.10
151	Brett Favre	2.25
152	Emmitt Smith	2.00
153	Dan Marino	2.00
154	Larry Centers	.10
155	Michael Jackson	.10
156	Kerry Collins	1.00
157	Curtis Conway	.20
158	*Peter Boulware*	.20
159	Carl Pickens	.10
160	Shannon Sharpe	.10
161	Brett Perriman	.10
162	Eddie George	1.50
163	Mark Brunell	1.00
164	Tamarick Vanover	.20
165	Cris Carter	.10
166	*Corey Dillon*	.75
167	Curtis Martin	1.25
168	Amani Toomer	.10
169	Jeff George	.10
170	Kordell Stewart	.75
171	Garrison Hearst	.10
172	Tony Banks	.50
173	Mike Alstott	.20
174	*Jim Druckenmiller*	1.50
175	Chris Chandler	.10
176	Bam Morris	.10
177	Billy Joe Hobert	.10
178	Ernie Mills	.10
179	Ki-Jana Carter	.10
180	Deion Sanders	.50
181	Ricky Watters	.20
182	*Shawn Springs*	.30
183	Barry Sanders	1.00
184	Antonio Freeman	.30
185	Marvin Harrison	.50
186	Elvis Grbac	.10
187	Terry Glenn	1.00
188	Willie Roaf	.10
189	Keyshawn Johnson	.50
190	*Orlando Pace*	.30
191	Jerome Bettis	.20
192	Tony Martin	.10
193	Jerry Rice	1.00
194	Joey Galloway	.30
195	Terry Allen	.10
196	Eddie Kennison	.50
197	Thurman Thomas	.20
198	*Darrell Russell*	.20
199	Rob Moore	.10
200	John Elway	.50
201	Quinn Early	.10
202	Kevin Greene	.10
203	Robert Green	.10
204	Tony Carter	.10
205	Michael Timpson	.10
206	Kevin Smith	.10
207	Herschel Walker	.10
208	Steve Atwater	.10
209	Tyrone Braxton	.10
210	Willie Davis	.10
211	Lamont Warren	.10
212	Sean Dawkins	.10
213	Dale Carter	.10
214	Kimble Anders	.10
215	Derrick Thomas	.10
216	Chris Penn	.10
217	Irving Spikes	.10
218	Amp Lee	.10
219	Qadry Ismail	.10
220	Dave Meggett	.10
221	Tyrone Hughes	.10
222	Haywood Jeffires	.10
223	Torrance Small	.10
224	Danny Kanell	.10
225	Thomas Lewis	.10
226	Kyle Brady	.10
227	Harvey Williams	.10
228	Bobby Hoying	.10
229	Charlie Garner	.10
230	Andre Hastings	.10
231	Heath Shuler	.10
232	J.J. Stokes	.10
233	Ken Norton	.10
234	Steve Walsh	.10
235	Harold Green	.10
236	Reggie Brooks	.10
237	Robb Thomas	.10
238	Brian Mitchell	.10
239	Bill Brooks	.10
240	Leslie Shepherd	.10
241	Jay Graham	.10
242	*Kevin Lockett*	.20
243	Derrick Mason	.10
244	*Marc Edwards*	.20
245	*Joey Kent*	.40
246	*Pat Barnes*	.50
247	Sherman Williams	.10
248	Ray Brown	.10
249	Stephen Davis	.10
250	Lamar Smith	.10

1997 Playoff 1st & 10 Chip Shots

Similar to a poker chip, the 250 plastic Chip Shot tokens were inserted one per pack. The fronts have the player's name at the top, while his photo is in the center. The Playoff logo and team name are printed at the bottom, with the token number appearing on the left and right sides of the front. The backs have "Chip Shot" printed at the top, with the Playoff logo in the center. "'97" is printed on the left and right of the token. "NFL" appears at the bottom.

		MT
	Complete Set (250):	200.00
	Common Player:	.25
1	Marcus Allen	.50
2	Eric Bieniemy	.25
3	Jason Dunn	.25
4	Jim Harbaugh	.25
5	Michael Westbrook	.25
6	*Tiki Barber*	1.50
7	Frank Reich	.25
8	Irving Fryar	.25
9	Courtney Hawkins	.25
10	Eric Zeier	.25
11	Kent Graham	.25
12	Trent Dilfer	.25
13	Neil O'Donnell	.25
14	*Reidel Anthony*	3.00
15	Jeff Hostetler	.25
16	Lawrence Phillips	.50
17	Dave Brown	.25
18	Mike Tomczak	.25
19	Jake Reed	.25
20	Anthony Miller	.25
21	Eric Metcalf	.25
22	*Sedrick Shaw*	.75
23	Anthony Johnson	.25
24	Mario Bates	.25
25	Dorsey Levens	.25
26	Stan Humphries	.25
27	Ben Coates	.25
28	Tyrone Wheatley	.25
29	Adrian Murrell	.25
30	William Henderson	.25
31	*Warrick Dunn*	6.00
32	LeShon Johnson	.25
33	James Stewart	.25
34	Edgar Bennett	.25
35	Raymont Harris	.25
36	Leroy Butler	.25
37	Darren Woodson	.25
38	*Darnell Autry*	1.50

#	Player	MT
39	Johnnie Morton	.25
40	William Floyd	.25
41	Terrell Fletcher	.25
42	Leonard Russell	.25
43	Henry Ellard	.25
44	Terrell Owens	3.00
45	John Friesz	.25
46	*Antowain Smith*	1.50
47	Charles Johnson	.25
48	Rickey Dudley	.25
49	Lake Dawson	.25
50	Bert Emanuel	.25
51	Zach Thomas	.75
52	Earnest Byner	.25
53	*Yatil Green*	3.00
54	Chris Spielman	.25
55	Muhsin Muhammad	.25
56	Bobby Engram	.25
57	Eric Bjornson	.25
58	Willie Green	.25
59	Derrick Mayes	.25
60	Chris Sanders	.25
61	Jimmy Smith	.25
62	*Tony Gonzalez*	.75
63	Rich Gannon	.25
64	Stanley Pritchett	.25
65	Brad Johnson	.25
66	Rodney Peete	.25
67	Sam Gash	.25
68	Chris Calloway	.25
69	Chris T. Jones	.25
70	*Will Blackwell*	.50
71	Mark Bruener	.25
72	Terry Kirby	.25
73	Brian Blades	.25
74	Craig Heyward	.25
75	Jamie Asher	.25
76	Torrance Mathis	.25
77	*Troy Davis*	3.00
78	Bruce Smith	.25
79	Simeon Rice	.25
80	Fred Barnett	.25
81	Tim Brown	.25
82	James Jett	.25
83	Mark Carrier	.25
84	Shawn Jefferson	.25
85	Ken Dilger	.25
86	*Rae Carruth*	2.50
87	Keenan McCardell	.25
88	Michael Irvin	.50
89	Mark Chmura	.25
90	Derrick Alexander	.25
91	Andre Reed	.25
92	Ed McCaffrey	.25
93	Erik Kramer	.25
94	Albert Connell	.25
95	Frank Wycheck	.25
96	Zack Crockett	.25
97	Jim Everett	.25
98	Michael Haynes	.25
99	Jeff Graham	.25
100	Brent Jones	.25
101	Troy Aikman	5.00
102	*Byron Hanspard*	2.00
103	Robert Brooks	.25
104	Karim Abdul-Jabbar	3.00
105	Drew Bledsoe	5.00
106	Napoleon Kaufman	.25
107	Steve Young	0.00
108	Leeland McElroy	.25
109	Jamal Anderson	.50
110	*David LaFleur*	.75
111	Vinny Testaverde	.25
112	Eric Moulds	.50
113	Tim Biakabutuka	.50
114	Rick Mirer	.25
115	Jeff Blake	.50
116	Jim Schwantz	.25
117	Herman Moore	.50
118	*Ike Hilliard*	3.00
119	Reggie White	.50
120	Steve McNair	4.00
121	Marshall Faulk	.50
122	Natrone Means	.50
123	Greg Hill	.25
124	O.J. McDuffie	.25
125	Robert Smith	.25
126	*Bryant Westbrook*	.50
127	Ray Zellars	.25
128	Rodney Hampton	.25
129	Wayne Chrebet	.25
130	Desmond Howard	.25
131	Ty Detmer	.25
132	Erric Pegram	.25
133	Yancey Thigpen	.25
134	*Danny Wuerffel*	5.00
135	Charlie Jones	.25
136	Chris Warren	.25
137	Isaac Bruce	.75
138	Errict Rhett	.50
139	Gus Frerotte	.25
140	Frank Sanders	.25
141	Todd Collins	.25
142	*Jake Plummer*	.75
143	Darnay Scott	.25
144	Rashaan Salaam	.50
145	Terrell Davis	6.00
146	Scott Mitchell	.25
147	Junior Seau	.50
148	Warren Moon	.25
149	Wesley Walls	.25
150	Daryl Johnston	.25
151	Brett Favre	10.00
152	Emmitt Smith	8.00
153	Dan Marino	8.00
154	Larry Centers	.25
155	Michael Jackson	.25
156	Kerry Collins	5.00
157	Curtis Conway	.50
158	*Peter Boulware*	.50
159	Carl Pickens	.25
160	Shannon Sharpe	.25
161	Brett Perriman	.25
162	Eddie George	6.00
163	Mark Brunell	5.00
164	Tamarick Vanover	.50
165	Cris Carter	.25
166	*Corey Dillon*	2.50
167	Curtis Martin	6.00
168	Amani Toomer	.25
169	Jeff George	.25
170	Kordell Stewart	5.00
171	Garrison Hearst	.25
172	Tony Banks	2.00
173	Mike Alstott	.50
174	*Jim Druckenmiller*	5.00
175	Chris Chandler	.25
176	Bam Morris	.25
177	Billy Joe Hobert	.25
178	Ernie Mills	.25
179	Ki-Jana Carter	.25
180	Deion Sanders	2.50
181	Ricky Watters	.50
182	*Shawn Springs*	.50
183	Barry Sanders	5.00
184	Antonio Freeman	1.50
185	Marvin Harrison	2.50
186	Elvis Grbac	.25
187	Terry Glenn	5.00
188	Willie Roaf	.25
189	Keyshawn Johnson	2.50
190	*Orlando Pace*	.50
191	Jerome Bettis	.50
192	Tony Martin	.25
193	Jerry Rice	5.00
194	Joey Galloway	1.00
195	Terry Allen	.25
196	Eddie Kennison	2.50
197	Thurman Thomas	.50
198	*Darrell Russell*	.50
199	Rob Moore	.25
200	John Elway	3.00
201	Quinn Early	.25
202	Kevin Greene	.25
203	Robert Green	.25
204	Tony Carter	.25
205	Michael Timpson	.25
206	Kevin Smith	.25
207	Herschel Walker	.25
208	Steve Atwater	.25
209	Tyrone Braxton	.25
210	Willie Davis	.25
211	Lamont Warren	.25
212	Sean Dawkins	.25
213	Dale Carter	.25
214	Kimble Anders	.25
215	Derrick Thomas	.25
216	Chris Penn	.25
217	Irving Spikes	.25
218	Amp Lee	.25
219	Qadry Ismail	.25
220	Dave Meggett	.25
221	Tyrone Hughes	.25
222	Haywood Jeffires	.25
223	Torrance Small	.25
224	Danny Kanell	.25
225	Thomas Lewis	.25
226	Kyle Brady	.25
227	Harvey Williams	.25
228	Bobby Hoying	.25
229	Charlie Garner	.25
230	Andre Hastings	.25
231	Heath Shuler	.25
232	J.J. Stokes	.25
233	Ken Norton	.25
234	Steve Walsh	.25
235	Harold Green	.25
236	Reggie Brooks	.25
237	Robb Thomas	.25
238	Brian Mitchell	.25
239	Bill Brooks	.25
240	Leslie Shepherd	.25
241	Jay Graham	.25
242	*Kevin Lockett*	.50
243	Derrick Mason	.25
244	*Marc Edwards*	.50
245	*Joey Kent*	.75
246	*Pat Barnes*	.75
247	Sherman Williams	.25
248	Ray Brown	.25
249	Stephen Davis	.25
250	Lamar Smith	.25

1997 Playoff 1st & 10 Hot Pursuit

Inserted 1:180 packs, the 100-card set has the player photo superimposed on an orange background on the front. The Hot Pursuit logo is in the top center, while "Playoff '97" is printed vertically along the left border and the player's name is printed vertically along the right border. The card fronts did include a Playoff peelable protective coating. The backs featured a full-bleed photo of the player, with the card number in the upper right.

#	Player	MT
	Common Player:	20.00
1	Brett Favre	400.00
2	Dorsey Levens	20.00
3	Antonio Freeman	60.00
4	Robert Brooks	20.00
5	Mark Chmura	20.00
6	Reggie White	40.00
7	Drew Bledsoe	200.00
8	Curtis Martin	225.00
9	Ben Coates	20.00
10	Terry Glenn	180.00
11	Kerry Collins	200.00
12	Tim Biakabutuka	40.00
13	Anthony Johnson	20.00
14	Wesley Walls	20.00
15	Muhsin Muhammad	20.00
16	Mark Brunell	200.00
17	Natrone Means	40.00
18	Jimmy Smith	20.00
19	John Elway	150.00
20	Terrell Davis	225.00
21	Anthony Miller	20.00
22	Shannon Sharpe	20.00
23	Steve Young	150.00
24	Garrison Hearst	20.00
25	Jerry Rice	200.00
26	Troy Aikman	200.00
27	Deion Sanders	100.00
28	Emmitt Smith	375.00
29	Michael Irvin	40.00
30	Kordell Stewart	200.00
31	Jerome Bettis	40.00
32	Charles Johnson	20.00
33	Ty Detmer	20.00
34	Ricky Watters	40.00
35	Irving Fryer	20.00
36	Todd Collins	20.00
37	Thurman Thomas	40.00
38	Bruce Smith	20.00
39	Eric Moulds	20.00
40	Brad Johnson	20.00
41	Robert Smith	20.00
42	Cris Carter	20.00
43	Elvis Grbac	20.00
44	Greg Hill	20.00
45	Marcus Allen	40.00
46	Gus Frerotte	20.00
47	Terry Allen	20.00
48	Michael Westbrook	20.00
49	Jim Harbaugh	20.00
50	Marshall Faulk	40.00
51	Marvin Harrison	75.00
52	Jeff Blake	50.00
53	Ki-Jana Carter	20.00
54	Carl Pickens	20.00
55	Junior Seau	40.00
56	Tony Martin	20.00
57	Dan Marino	375.00
58	Karim Abdul-Jabbar	150.00
59	Stanley Pritchett	20.00
60	Zach Thomas	60.00
61	Steve McNair	175.00
62	Eddie George	225.00
63	Chris Sanders	20.00
64	Rick Mirer	20.00
65	Rashaan Salaam	40.00
66	Curtis Conway	20.00
67	Bobby Engram	20.00
68	Kent Graham	20.00
69	Leeland McElroy	20.00
70	Larry Centers	20.00
71	Frank Sanders	20.00
72	Jeff George	20.00
73	Napoleon Kaufman	20.00
74	Desmond Howard	20.00
75	Tim Brown	20.00
76	John Friesz	20.00
77	Chris Warren	20.00
78	Joey Galloway	60.00
79	Tony Banks	75.00
80	Lawrence Phillips	20.00
81	Isaac Bruce	50.00
82	Eddie Kennison	75.00
83	Errict Rhett	40.00
84	Mike Alstott	20.00
85	Rodney Hampton	20.00
86	Amani Toomer	20.00
87	Scott Mitchell	20.00
88	Barry Sanders	200.00
89	Herman Moore	40.00
90	Vinny Testaverde	20.00
91	Bam Morris	20.00
92	Michael Jackson	20.00
93	Chris Chandler	20.00
94	Eric Metcalf	20.00
95	Jamal Anderson	50.00
96	Jim Everett	20.00
97	Mario Bates	20.00
98	Wayne Chrebet	20.00
99	Adrian Murrell	20.00
100	Keyshawn Johnson	75.00

1997 Playoff 1st & 10 Xtra Point

The 10-card set was inserted 1:432 packs. The card fronts featured the Extra Point logo in the upper left, and a player photo in the center. Both were surrounded by felt. The player's name is printed inside a white stripe along the right border. The card backs, which featured a prefix of "XP," have the player photo surrounded by felt. The card's number is printed inside an oval in the upper right.

#	Player	MT
	Complete Set (10):	1000.00
	Common Player:	50.00
XP1	Kordell Stewart	125.00
XP2	Dan Marino	200.00
XP3	Brett Favre	250.00
XP4	Emmitt Smith	200.00
XP5	John Elway	100.00
XP6	Eddie George	150.00
XP7	Karim Abdul-Jabbar	75.00

		MT
XP8	Terry Glenn	100.00
XP9	Curtis Martin	125.00
XP10	Joey Galloway	50.00

1997 Playoff 1st & 10 Extra Point Autograph

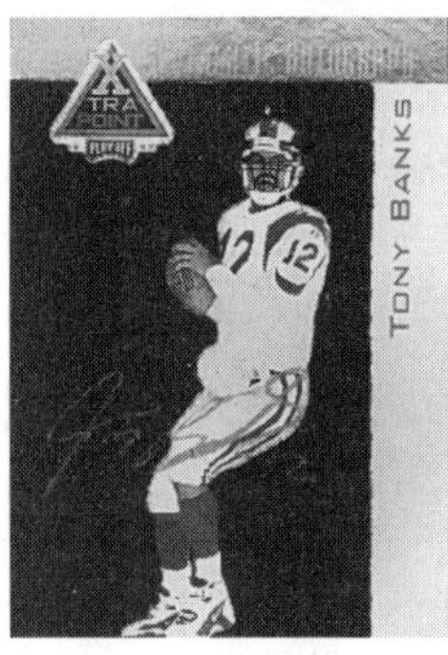

Inserted 1:444 packs, the autographed cards are signed by either Tony Banks or Terrell Davis. The cards have a gold-foil stripe at the top front with "Authentic Autograph" embossed on it. The Extra Point logo appears in the upper left. Black felt surrounds the photo of the respective player. The autograph is signed on the felt and into the photo. The player's name is listed inside a white stripe on the right border of the front. The backs, which are numbered with an "XPA" prefix, have a photo bordered in black. The number appears in an oval in the upper right.

		MT
Complete Set (2):		300.00
Common Player:		125.00
XPA1	Tony Banks	125.00
XPA2	Terrell Davis	200.00

1997 Press Pass

The 55-card set features full-bleed fronts, with the player's name, position and Press Pass logo at the bottom in gold foil. The backs have a player photo on the left over a "groovy" multicolored background. The player's name, bio, highlights and stats, are printed on the right side. Red Zone is a red-foil parallel which was inserted 1:1 hobby packs. Torquers, which is a blue-foil parallel, was inserted 1:1 mass market packs. In addition, a 50-card all-foil die-cut "set within a set" was inserted 1:1 pack.

		MT
Complete Set (50):		15.00
Common Player:		.10
Combine Cards:		2x
Red Zone Cards:		2x
1	Orlando Pace	1.00
2	Warrick Dunn	2.00

3	Danny Wuerffel	2.00
4	Darnell Autry	.75
5	Troy Davis	1.25
6	Jake Plummer	.75
7	Corey Dillon	.50
8	Reidel Anthony	1.25
9	Byron Hanspard	.75
10	Tiki Barber	.75
11	Ike Hilliard	1.25
12	Rae Carruth	1.00
13	Yatil Green	1.25
14	Peter Boulware	.10
15	Jim Druckenmiller	1.50
16	Pat Barnes	.20
17	Trevor Pryce	.10
18	Kevin Lockett	.10
19	Koy Detmer	.20
20	Bryant Westbrook	.40
21	Darrell Russell	.20
22	Tony Gonzalez	.30
23	Shawn Springs	.50
24	Chris Canty	.10
25	David LaFleur	.50
26	Dwayne Rudd	.10
27	Bob Sapp	.10
28	Mike Vrabel	.10
29	Antowain Smith	.50
30	Keith Poole	.10
31	Sedrick Shaw	.10
32	Tremain Mack	.10
33	Matt Russell	.10
34	Reinard Wilson	.10
35	Marc Edwards	.10
36	Greg Jones	.10
37	Michael Booker	.10
38	James Farrior	.10
39	Danny Wuerffel	.75
40	Troy Davis	.50
41	Corey Dillon	.10
42	Jake Plummer	.30
43	Peter Boulware, Reinard Wilson	.10
44	Eddie Robinson	.20
45	Bobby Bowden	.75
46	Steve Spurrier	1.00
47	Gary Barnett	.10
49	Checklist Tom Osborne	.50
50	Checklist Jarrett Irons	.10

1997 Press Pass Big 12

Inserted 1:12 packs, the 12-card set features a player photo superimposed over an etched foil background. The player's name, chase set name and Press Pass logo are printed at the bottom of the card front. The backs include a player photo over a "sun ray" background. The player's name and highlights are printed inside a box along the right side. The cards are numbered "of 12," with a prefix of "B".

		MT
Complete Set (12):		45.00
Common Player:		2.00
B1	Orlando Pace	5.00
B2	Peter Boulware	2.00
B3	Shawn Springs	4.00
B4	Warrick Dunn	12.00
B5	Dwayne Rudd	2.00
B6	Rae Carruth	6.00
B7	Bryant Westbrook	4.00
B8	Darrell Russell	2.00
B9	Yatil Green	6.00
B10	David LaFleur	4.00
B11	Jim Druckenmiller	8.00
B12	Reidel Anthony	6.00

1997 Press Pass Can't Miss

The six-card foil set was inserted on a progressive scale. Card No. 1 was inserted 1:720, while No. 2 was seeded at 1:360. The rest were as follows: No. 3 1:180, No. 4 1:90, No. 5 1:45 and No. 6 1:36. The player's photo is superimposed over a foil background. A football field and X's and O's also appear on the front. The Can't Miss logo and the player's name are printed at the bottom. The backs have a photo of each of the six players. The numbers have a prefix of "CM".

		MT
Complete Set (6):		225.00
Common Player:		10.00
CM1	Warrick Dunn	100.00
CM2	Jim Druckenmiller	60.00
CM3	Yatil Green	45.00
CM4	Orlando Pace	30.00
CM5	Rae Carruth	20.00
CM6	Peter Boulware	10.00

1997 Press Pass Head-Butt

Inserted 1:18 packs, the nine-card set features the player's photo superimposed over the player's college helmet. The Head Butt logo is in gold foil at the bottom, while the player's name is printed inside a gold-foil stripe at the bottom center. The backs have the player's photo printed over his college helmet. The bottom of the card back has the player's name and his highlights. The card numbers carry a prefix of "HB". A die-cut parallel version are randomly seeded 1:36 packs.

		MT
Complete Set (9):		60.00
Common Player:		3.00
Die Cuts:		2x
HB1	Warrick Dunn	16.00
HB2	Orlando Pace	8.00
HB3	Troy Davis	10.00
HB4	Reidel Anthony	10.00
HB5	Rae Carruth	10.00
HB6	Yatil Green	10.00
HB7	Corey Dillon	3.00
HB8	Danny Wuerffel	12.00
HB9	Darnell Autry	8.00

1997 Press Pass Marquee Matchups

Inserted 1:18 packs, the nine-card set features two players on the front, with their names printed at the bottom in prism foil. "Marquee Matchup" is printed in black inside a prism stripe at the bottom of the front. The backs have two player photos, their names and highlights. The card numbers are prefixed by "MM".

		MT
Complete Set (9):		40.00
Common Player:		2.00
MM1	Jim Druckenmiller, Danny Wuerffel	12.00
MM2	Warrick Dunn, Corey Dillon	10.00
MM3	Darnell Autry, Troy Davis	8.00
MM4	Byron Hanspard, Tiki Barber	6.00
MM5	Reidel Anthony, Bryant Westbrook	5.00
MM6	Orlando Pace, Peter Boulware	4.00
MM7	Rae Carruth, Ike Hilliard	5.00
MM8	Yatil Green, Shawn Springs	5.00
MM9	David LaFleur, Tony Gonzalez	2.00

1997 Pro Line DC III

The 100-card, regular-sized, die-cut set includes two subsets: Rewind and DC Top Ten. The first 67 cards in the set are die-cut in a circular pattern with a rectangle base. Cards 68-89 are die-cut with wave outlines on the sides (Rewind) while cards 90-100 are horizontal with the top die-cut in the shape of a football. All cards have gold foil.

		MT
Complete Set (100):		50.00
Common Player:		.20
Wax Box:		85.00
1	Emmitt Smith	5.00
2	Rod Woodson	.20
3	Eddie George	3.50
4	Ty Detmer	.20
5	Zach Thomas	1.00
6	Kevin Greene	.20
7	Michael Jackson	.20
8	Isaac Bruce	1.00
9	Joey Galloway	1.50
10	Bryant Young	.20

11	Terrell Davis	3.00
12	Mark Brunell	2.00
13	Marvin Harrison	1.50
14	Jake Reed	.20
15	Terry Allen	.20
16	Kordell Stewart	2.00
17	Reggie White	.40
18	Michael Irvin	.40
19	Tony Martin	.20
20	Barry Sanders	2.50
21	Tony Boselli	.20
22	Carl Pickens	.20
23	Simeon Rice	.20
24	Adrian Murrell	.20
25	Lamar Lathon	.20
26	Thurman Thomas	.40
27	Tim Brown	.20
28	Karim Abdul-Jabbar	2.00
29	Brad Johnson	.20
30	Keenan McCardell	.20
31	Keyshawn Johnson	1.50
32	Ricky Watters	.40
33	Michael McCrary	.20
34	Brett Favre	5.00
35	Steve McNair	2.00
36	Herman Moore	.40
37	Tony Banks	1.00
38	Deion Sanders	1.75
39	Kerry Collins	2.50
40	Shannon Sharpe	.20
41	Drew Bledsoe	2.50
42	Jim Everett	.20
43	Jamal Anderson	.40
44	Irving Fryar	.20
45	Terry Glenn	2.50
46	Jerry Rice	2.50
47	Curtis Martin	3.50
48	Curtis Conway	.20
49	Jerome Bettis	.40
50	Vinny Testaverde	.20
51	Mike Alstott	.75
52	Anthony Johnson	.20
53	Dan Marino	5.00
54	Junior Seau	.20
55	Steve Young	1.75
56	Troy Aikman	2.50
57	Jimmy Smith	.20
58	Cris Carter	.20
59	Gus Frerotte	.20
60	Marcus Allen	.40
61	Rodney Hampton	.20
62	Bruce Smith	.20
63	Leroy Butler	.20
64	Jeff Blake	.75
65	Antonio Freeman	.20
66	John Elway	1.75
67	Checklist	.20
68	Barry Sanders	1.00
69	Troy Aikman	1.00
70	Jerome Bettis	.20
71	Mark Brunell	1.00
72	Junior Seau	.20
73	John Elway	.75
74	Chad Brown	.20
75	Irving Fryar	.20
76	Drew Bledsoe	1.00
77	Jerry Rice	1.00
78	Larry Centers	.20
79	Terrell Davis	1.50
80	Carl Pickens	.20
81	Emmitt Smith	2.00
82	Kerry Collins	1.00
83	Eddie Kennison	.20
84	Kordell Stewart	1.00
85	Natrone Means	.20
86	Curtis Martin	1.50
87	Dorsey Levens	.20
88	Desmond Howard	.20
89	Checklist Brett Favre MVP	2.00
90	Brett Favre	2.00
91	Terrell Davis	1.50
92	Kevin Greene	.20
93	Terry Allen	.20
94	Barry Sanders	1.00
95	John Elway	.75
96	Ricky Watters	.20
97	Reggie White	.20
98	Jerome Bettis	.20
99	Jerry Rice	1.00
100	Checklist Brett Favre CL	2.00

1997 Pro Line DC III Perennial/Future All-Pros

The 20-card, regular-sized, die-cut set was inserted every 24 packs of Pro Line III DC football. The cards feature the same die-cut design as the Rewind subset in the base set, except the cards in Perennial/Future All-Pros are vertical, making the wave cut design on the card's top and bottom. The cards feature bronze foil on the top and bottom and the backs are numbered as "x of 20." The backs have a color action shot imaged over a white background with a black-and-white closeup behind a brief statistical analysis.

		MT
Complete Set (20):		475.00
Common Player:		7.00
AP1	Emmitt Smith	60.00
AP2	Brett Favre	60.00
AP3	Jerry Rice	30.00
AP4	Steve Young	25.00
AP5	Barry Sanders	30.00
AP6	Reggie White	15.00
AP7	Ricky Watters	7.00
AP8	Lawrence Phillips	7.00
AP9	Kerry Collins	30.00
AP10	Mark Brunell	30.00
AP11	John Elway	25.00
AP12	Dan Marino	60.00
AP13	Drew Bledsoe	30.00
AP14	Curtis Martin	45.00
AP15	Terrell Davis	35.00
AP16	Karim Abdul-Jabbar	20.00
AP17	Marvin Harrison	15.00
AP18	Keyshawn Johnson	15.00
AP19	Terry Glenn	20.00
AP20	Eddie George	30.00

1997 Pro Line DC III Road to the Super Bowl

The 30-card, regular-sized, die-cut set was inserted every 12 packs of Pro Line III DC. The cards feature the same die-cut design as the DC Top Ten subset in the base set.

		MT
Complete Set (30):		400.00
Common Player:		5.00
SB1	Ricky Watters	10.00
SB2	Ty Detmer	5.00
SB3	Emmitt Smith	50.00
SB4	Troy Aikman	25.00
SB5	Kerry Collins	25.00
SB6	Kevin Greene	5.00
SB7	Steve Young	20.00
SB8	Jerry Rice	25.00
SB9	Brett Favre	50.00
SB10	Reggie White	10.00
SB11	Cris Carter	5.00
SB12	Brad Johnson	5.00
SB13	Drew Bledsoe	25.00
SB14	Curtis Martin	35.00
SB15	Bruce Smith	5.00
SB16	Thurman Thomas	5.00
SB17	Jim Harbaugh	5.00
SB18	Marshall Faulk	15.00
SB19	Mark Brunell	25.00
SB20	Natrone Means	5.00
SB21	John Elway	20.00
SB22	Terrell Davis	30.00
SB23	Kordell Stewart	25.00
SB24	Jerome Bettis	10.00
SB25	Eddie George	30.00
SB26	Dan Marino	50.00
SB27	Terry Glenn	20.00
SB28	Antonio Freeman	10.00
SB29	Anthony Johnson	5.00
SB30	Kevin Hardy	5.00

1997 Pro Line

The 300-card set featured a full-bleed photo at the top on the card front, with a stripe at the bottom that included the player's name, team and position. The team's logo is included inside a circle at the bottom center. The Pro Line logo is in the upper left.

		MT
Complete Set (300):		30.00
Common Player:		.05
Wax Box:		50.00
1	Larry Centers	.05
2	Kent Graham	.05
3	LeShon Johnson	.05
4	Leeland McElroy	.10
5	Rob Moore	.05
6	Simeon Rice	.05
7	Frank Sanders	.05
8	Eric Swann	.05
9	Aeneas Williams	.05
10	Jamal Anderson	.15
11	Cornelius Bennett	.05
12	Ray Buchanan	.05
13	Bert Emanuel	.05
14	Terance Mathis	.05
15	Eric Metcalf	.05
16	Jessie Tuggle	.05
17	Derrick Alexander	.05
18	Earnest Byner	.05
19	Michael Jackson	.05
20	Antonio Langham	.05
21	Ray Lewis	.05
22	Bam Morris	.05
23	Jonathan Ogden	.05
24	Vinny Testaverde	.05
25	Eric Moulds	.10
26	Todd Collins	.05
27	Quinn Early	.05
28	Phil Hansen	.05
29	Darick Holmes	.10
30	Bryce Paup	.05
31	Andre Reed	.05
32	Bruce Smith	.05
33	Chris Spielman	.05
34	Matt Stevens	.05
35	Steve Tasker	.05
36	Thurman Thomas	.10
37	Mark Carrier	.05
38	Kerry Collins	1.00
39	Tim Biakabutuka	.25
40	Eric Davis	.05
41	Kevin Greene	.05
42	Anthony Johnson	.05
43	Lamar Lathon	.05
44	Sam Mills	.05
45	Wesley Walls	.05
46	Muhsin Muhammad	.10
47	Mark Carrier	.05
48	Curtis Conway	.10
49	Bryan Cox	.05
50	Bobby Engram	.05
51	Raymont Harris	.05
52	Walt Harris	.05
53	Rick Mirer	.05
54	Rashaan Salaam	.10
55	Alonzo Spellman	.05
56	Ashley Ambrose	.05
57	Jeff Blake	.15
58	Ki-Jana Carter	.10
59	John Copeland	.05
60	James Francis	.05
61	Tony McGee	.05
62	Carl Pickens	.10

63	Darnay Scott	.05
64	Steve Tovar	.05
65	Dan Wilkinson	.05
66	Troy Aikman	1.00
67	Eric Bjornson	.05
68	Michael Irvin	.10
69	Daryl Johnston	.05
70	Nate Newton	.05
71	Deion Sanders	.40
72	Emmitt Smith	2.00
73	Kevin Smith	.05
74	Kevin Williams	.05
75	Darren Woodson	.05
76	Mark Tuinei	.05
77	Steve Atwater	.05
78	Terrell Davis	1.25
79	John Elway	.75
80	Ed McCaffrey	.05
81	Anthony Miller	.05
82	John Mobley	.05
83	Michael Dean Perry	.05
84	Shannon Sharpe	.05
85	Alfred Williams	.05
86	Reggie Brown	.05
87	Luther Elliss	.05
88	Scott Mitchell	.05
89	Herman Moore	.15
90	Johnnie Morton	.05
91	Brett Perriman	.05
92	Robert Porcher	.05
93	Barry Sanders	1.00
94	Henry Thomas	.05
95	Edgar Bennett	.05
96	Robert Brooks	.10
97	Gilbert Brown	.05
98	LeRoy Butler	.05
99	Mark Chmura	.05
100	Brett Favre	2.25
101	Santana Dotson	.05
102	Antonio Freeman	.20
103	Dorsey Levens	.20
104	Wayne Simmons	.05
105	Reggie White	.10
106	Willie Davis	.05
107	Eddie George	1.50
108	Darryll Lewis	.05
109	Steve McNair	.50
110	Marcus Robertson	.05
111	Chris Sanders	.05
112	Al Smith	.05
113	Tony Bennett	.05
114	Quentin Coryatt	.05
115	Ken Dilger	.05
116	Sean Dawkins	.05
117	Marshall Faulk	.20
118	Jim Harbaugh	.05
119	Marvin Harrison	.50
120	Jeff Herrod	.05
121	Tony Boselli	.05
122	Tony Brackens	.05
123	Mark Brunell	1.00
124	Kevin Hardy	.05
125	Jeff Lageman	.05
126	Keenan McCardell	.05
127	Natrone Means	.10
128	Eddie Robinson	.05
129	Jimmy Smith	.05
130	James Stewart	.05
131	Marcus Allen	.10
132	Dale Carter	.05
133	Mark Collins	.05
134	Lake Dawson	.05
135	Greg Hill	.05
136	Sean LaChapelle	.05
137	Chris Penn	.05
138	Derrick Thomas	.05
139	Tamarick Vanover	.10
140	Elvis Grbac	.05
141	Karim Abdul-Jabbar	.75
142	Fred Barnett	.05
143	Terrell Buckley	.05
144	Daryl Gardener	.05
145	Randal Hill	.05
146	Dan Marino	2.00
147	O.J. McDuffie	.05
148	Jerris McPhail	.05
149	Zach Thomas	.20
150	Cris Carter	.05
151	Dixon Edwards	.05
152	Leroy Hoard	.05
153	Qadry Ismail	.05
154	Brad Johnson	.05
155	John Randle	.05
156	Jake Reed	.05
157	Robert Smith	.05
158	Orlando Thomas	.05
159	DeWayne Washington	.05
160	Drew Bledsoe	1.00
161	Tedy Bruschi	.05
162	Willie Clay	.05
163	Ben Coates	.05

164	Terry Glenn	1.00
165	Shawn Jefferson	.05
166	Ty Law	.05
167	Curtis Martin	1.25
168	Willie McGinest	.05
169	Chris Slade	.05
170	Eric Allen	.05
171	Mario Bates	.05
172	Jim Everett	.05
173	Michael Haynes	.05
174	Wayne Martin	.05
175	Torrance Small	.05
176	Dave Brown	.05
177	Chris Calloway	.05
178	Rodney Hampton	.05
179	Danny Kanell	.05
180	Thomas Lewis	.05
181	Jason Sehorn	.05
182	Amani Toomer	.05
183	Charles Way	.05
184	Tyrone Wheatley	.05
185	Wayne Chrebet	.05
186	Hugh Douglas	.05
187	Aaron Glenn	.05
188	Jeff Graham	.05
189	Keyshawn Johnson	.50
190	Mo Lewis	.05
191	Adrian Murrell	.05
192	Neil O'Donnell	.05
193	Tim Brown	.05
194	Rickey Dudley	.10
195	Jeff George	.10
196	Napoleon Kaufman	.05
197	Russell Maryland	.05
198	Terry McDaniel	.05
199	Chester McGlockton	.05
201	Pat Swilling	.05
200	Desmond Howard	.05
202	Ty Detmer	.05
203	Jason Dunn	.05
204	Ray Farmer	.05
205	Irving Fryar	.05
206	Chris T. Jones	.05
207	Bobby Taylor	.05
208	William Thomas	.05
209	Hollis Thomas	.05
210	Kevin Turner	.05
211	Ricky Watters	.10
212	Jerome Bettis	.10
213	Andre Hastings	.05
214	Charles Johnson	.05
215	Levon Kirkland	.05
216	Carnell Lake	.05
217	Greg Lloyd	.05
218	Darren Perry	.05
219	Kordell Stewart	.75
220	Rod Woodson	.05
221	Andre Coleman	.05
222	Marco Coleman	.05
223	Leonard Russell	.05
224	Stan Humphries	.05
225	Shawn Lee	.05
226	Tony Martin	.05
227	Chris Mims	.05
228	Junior Seau	.10
229	Chris Doleman	.05
230	William Floyd	.05
231	Merton Hanks	.05
232	Brent Jones	.05
233	Terry Kirby	.05
234	Ken Norton	.05
235	Terrell Owens	.75
236	Jerry Rice	1.00
237	Bryant Young	.05
238	Steve Young	.75
239	Garrison Hearst	.05
240	Brian Blades	.05
241	Chad Brown	.05
242	John Friesz	.05
243	Joey Galloway	.30
244	Cortez Kennedy	.05
245	Chris Warren	.05
246	Darryl Williams	.05
247	Tony Banks	.30
248	Isaac Bruce	.15
249	Kevin Carter	.05
250	Eddie Kennison	.50
251	Todd Lyght	.05
252	Leslie O'Neal	.05
253	Anthony Parker	.05
254	Roman Phifer	.05
255	Lawrence Phillips	.10
256	Mike Alstott	.15
257	Derrick Brooks	.05
258	Trent Dilfer	.10
259	Jackie Harris	.05
260	Hardy Nickerson	.05
261	Errict Rhett	.10
262	Warren Sapp	.05
263	Terry Allen	.05
264	Jamie Asher	.05

265	Henry Ellard	.05
266	Gus Frerotte	.05
267	Sean Gilbert	.05
268	Darrell Green	.05
269	Ken Harvey	.05
270	Brian Mitchell	.05
271	Michael Westbrook	.05
272	*Koy Detmer*	.50
273	*Yatil Green*	1.00
274	*Troy Davis*	1.50
275	*Darrell Russell*	.05
276	*Warrick Dunn*	2.50
277	*David LaFleur*	.50
278	*Tony Gonzalez*	.50
279	*Jake Plummer*	.50
280	*Antowain Smith*	.50
281	*Peter Boulware*	.05
282	*Shawn Springs*	.50
283	*Bryant Westbrook*	.10
284	*Rae Carruth*	.75
285	*Corey Dillon*	1.00
286	*Byron Hanspard*	.75
287	*Greg Jones*	.05
288	*Trevor Pryce*	.05
289	*Michael Booker*	.05
290	*Orlando Pace*	.40
291	*James Farrior*	.05
292	*Walter Jones*	.05
293	*Reinard Wilson*	.05
294	*Ike Hilliard*	1.50
295	*Kenard Lang*	.05
296	*Reidel Anthony*	1.50
297	Checklist #1 Brett Favre CL	.75
298	Checklist #2 Kerry Collins CL	.30
299	Checklist #3 Drew Bledsoe CL	.30
300	Checklist #4 Terrell Davis CL	.50

1997 Pro Line Board Members

This 15-card set was inserted 1:112 packs. It includes an inside look at the NFL Players that Score Board has signed to exclusive spokesman contracts.

		MT
Complete Set (15):		275.00
Common Player:		7.00
B1	Troy Aikman	25.00
B2	Kerry Collins	25.00
B3	Terrell Davis	25.00
B4	Brett Favre	50.00
B5	Gus Frerotte	7.00
B6	Emmitt Smith	40.00
B7	Kordell Stewart	25.00
B8	Steve Young	20.00
B9	Eddie George	30.00
B10	Terry Glenn	25.00
B11	Troy Davis	20.00
B12	Darrell Russell	7.00
B13	Peter Boulware	7.00
B14	Warrick Dunn	30.00
B15	Rae Carruth	15.00

1997 Pro Line Brett Favre

This 10-card set, which was inserted 1:28 packs, is an interactive insert series that focuses on Brett Favre. All 10 cards could be redeemed for autographed memorabil-

ia. All sets redeemed won either an autographed jersey or a Super Bowl XXXI autographed plaque.

		MT
Complete Set (10):		150.00
Common Player:		10.00
1	Brett Favre	10.00
2	Brett Favre	10.00
3	Brett Favre	10.00
4	Brett Favre	10.00
5	Brett Favre	10.00
6	Brett Favre	10.00
7	Brett Favre	10.00
8	Brett Favre	10.00
9	Brett Favre	10.00
10	Brett Favre	75.00

1997 Pro Line Rivalries

The 20-card set, which is numbered with an "R" prefix, was inserted 1:35 packs. The double-front cards provide insight into the top games of the 1997 campaign.

		MT
Complete Set (20):		275.00
Common Player:		4.00
R1	John Elway, Derrick Thomas	15.00
R2	Jeff Blake, Vinny Testaverde	4.00
R3	Emmitt Smith, Ricky Watters	35.00
R4	Jim Harbaugh, Thurman Thomas	4.00
R5	Barry Sanders, Reggie White	20.00
R6	Desmond Howard, Junior Seau	4.00
R7	Dan Marino, Hugh Douglas	35.00
R8	Jerome Bettis, Carl Pickens	4.00
R9	Mark Brunell, Kordell Stewart	25.00
R10	Karim Abdul-Jabbar, Bruce Smith	10.00
R11	Rashaan Salaam, Brad Johnson	4.00
R12	Steve Young, Kerry Collins	20.00
R13	Brett Favre, Troy Aikman	40.00
R14	Drew Bledsoe, Marshall Faulk	20.00
R15	Steve McNair, Ki-Jana Carter	15.00
R16	Jerry Rice, Terrell Davis	25.00
R17	Deion Sanders, Dave Brown	15.00
R18	Darrell Russell, Orlando Pace	4.00
R19	Warrick Dunn, Bryant Westbrook	20.00
R20	Yatil Green, Reidel Anthony	15.00

1997 Score

The 330-card set features a player photo in the center on the front, with the team and the player's position printed at the top. The Score logo is in the upper left of the photo, while goalposts appear on the center of each side of the photo. The player's name is printed at the bottom. The base set is paralleled by a Showcase Series and Artist's Proof version.

		MT
Complete Set (330):		15.00
Common Player:		.05
Showcase Series:		4x-8x
Artist's Proofs:		20x-40x
Wax Box:		32.00
1	John Elway	.50
2	Drew Bledsoe	.75
3	Brett Favre	1.75
4	Emmitt Smith	1.50
5	Kerry Collins	.75
6	Jerry Rice	.75
7	Kordell Stewart	.75
8	Barry Sanders	.75
9	Dan Marino	1.50
10	Steve Young	.50
11	Erik Kramer	.05
12	Warren Moon	.10
13	Chris Calloway	.05
14	Doug Evans	.05
15	Darren Woodson	.05
16	Alonzo Spellman	.05
17	Greg Hill	.05
18	Aaron Craver	.05
19	Jeff Hostetler	.05
20	William Thomas	.05
21	Marco Coleman	.05
22	Wayne Simmons	.05
23	Donnell Woolford	.05
24	Vinny Testaverde	.10
25	Ed McCaffrey	.05
26	Jim Everett	.05
27	Gilbert Brown	.05
28	Jason Dunn	.05
29	Stanley Pritchett	.05
30	Joey Galloway	.15
31	Amani Toomer	.05
32	Chris Penn	.05
33	Aeneas Williams	.05
34	Bobby Taylor	.05
35	Bryan Still	.05
36	Ty Law	.05
37	Shannon Sharpe	.05
38	Marty Carter	.05
39	Sam Mills	.05
40	William Floyd	.05
41	Brad Johnson	.05
42	Sean Dawkins	.05
43	Michael Irvin	.10
44	Jeff George	.10
45	Brent Jones	.05
46	Mark Brunell	.75
47	Rob Moore	.05
48	Hardy Nickerson	.05
49	Chris Chandler	.05
50	Willie Anderson	.05
51	Isaac Bruce	.15
52	Natrone Means	.10
53	Tony Banks	.15

#	Player		#	Player		#	Player	
54	Marshall Faulk	.15	155	Rodney Thomas	.05	256	Robert Brooks	.05
55	Michael Westbrook	.05	156	Mark Seay	.05	257	Zach Thomas	.15
56	Bruce Smith	.05	157	Derrick Alexander	.05	258	Alvin Harper	.05
57	Jamal Anderson	.15	158	Lamar Lathon	.05	259	Wayne Chrebet	.05
58	Jackie Harris	.05	159	Anthony Miller	.05	260	Bill Romanowski	.05
59	Sean Gilbert	.05	160	Shawn Wooden	.05	261	Willie Green	.05
60	Ki-Jana Carter	.05	161	Antonio Freeman	.15	262	Dale Carter	.05
61	Eric Moulds	.10	162	Cortez Kennedy	.05	263	Chris Slade	.05
62	James Stewart	.05	163	Rickey Dudley	.10	264	J.J. Stokes	.05
63	Jeff Blake	.10	164	Tony Carter	.05	265	Tim Brown	.05
64	O.J. McDuffie	.05	165	Kevin Williams	.05	266	Eric Davis	.05
65	Neil Smith	.05	166	Reggie White	.10	267	Mark Carrier	.05
66	Kevin Smith	.05	167	Tim Bowens	.05	268	Tony Martin	.05
67	Terry Allen	.05	168	Roy Barker	.05	269	Tyrone Wheatley	.05
68	Sean LaChapelle	.05	169	Adrian Murrell	.05	270	Eugene Robinson	.05
69	Rashaan Salaam	.10	170	Anthony Johnson	.05	271	Curtis Conway	.05
70	Jeff Graham	.05	171	Terry Glenn	.75	272	Michael Timpson	.05
71	Mark Carrier	.05	172	Jeff Lewis	.05	273	*Orlando Pace*	.50
72	Allen Aldridge	.05	173	Dorsey Levens	.10	274	*Tiki Barber*	1.00
73	Keenan McCardell	.05	174	Willie Jackson	.05	275	*Byron Hanspard*	.75
74	Willie McGinest	.05	175	Willie Clay	.05	276	*Warrick Dunn*	2.00
75	Napoleon Kaufman	.10	176	Richmond Webb	.05	277	*Rae Carruth*	1.00
76	Jerris McPhail	.05	177	Shawn Lee	.05	278	*Bryant Westbrook*	.30
77	Eric Swann	.05	178	Joe Aska	.05	279	*Antowain Smith*	1.00
78	Kimble Anders	.05	179	Rod Woodson	.05	280	*Peter Boulware*	.05
79	Charles Johnson	.05	180	Jim Schwantz	.05	281	*Reidel Anthony*	1.50
80	Bryan Cox	.05	181	Alfred Williams	.05	282	*Troy Davis*	1.50
81	Johnnie Morton	.05	182	Ferric Collons	.05	283	*Jake Plummer*	.50
82	Andre Rison	.05	183	Ken Norton Jr.	.05	284	*Chris Canty*	.05
83	Corey Miller	.05	184	Rick Mirer	.10	285	*Dwayne Rudd*	.05
84	Troy Drayton	.05	185	Leeland McElroy	.05	286	*Ike Hilliard*	1.50
85	Jim Harbaugh	.05	186	Rodney Hampton	.05	287	*Reinard Wilson*	.05
86	Wesley Walls	.05	187	Ted Popson	.05	288	*Corey Dillon*	.75
87	Bryce Paup	.05	188	Fred Barnett	.05	289	*Tony Gonzalez*	.50
88	Curtis Martin	1.00	189	Junior Seau	.10	290	*Darnell Autry*	.50
89	Michael Sinclair	.05	190	Michael Barrow	.05	291	*Kevin Lockett*	.20
90	Chris T. Jones	.05	191	Corey Widmer	.05	292	*Darrell Russell*	.05
91	Jake Reed	.05	192	Rodney Peete	.05	293	*Jim Druckenmiller*	1.75
92	LeRoy Butler	.05	193	Rod Smith	.05	294	*Scott Mitchell*	.05
93	Reggie Tongue	.05	194	Muhsin Muhammad	.15	295	*Joey Kent*	.30
94	Bert Emanual	.05	195	Keith Jackson	.05	296	*Shawn Springs*	.50
95	Stan Humphries	.05	196	Jimmy Smith	.05	297	*James Farrior*	.05
96	Neil O'Donnell	.05	197	Dave Meggett	.05	298	*Sedrick Shaw*	.50
97	Troy Vincent	.05	198	Lawrence Phillips	.10	299	*Marcus Harris*	.05
98	Mike Alstott	.15	199	Chad Brown	.05	300	*Danny Wuerffel*	1.75
99	Chad Cota	.05	200	Darrin Smith	.05	301	*Marc Edwards*	.20
100	Marvin Harrison	.30	201	Larry Centers	.05	302	*Michael Booker*	.05
101	Terrell Owens	.30	202	Kevin Greene	.05	303	*David LaFleur*	.50
102	Dave Brown	.05	203	Sherman Williams	.05	304	*Mike Adams*	.05
103	Harvey Williams	.05	204	Chris Sanders	.05	305	*Pat Barnes*	.75
104	Desmond Howard	.05	205	Shawn Jefferson	.05	306	*George Jones*	.05
105	Carl Pickens	.05	206	Thurman Thomas	.10	307	*Yatil Green*	1.00
106	Kent Graham	.05	207	Keyshawn Johnson	.30	308	Drew Bledsoe	.30
107	Michael Bates	.05	208	Bryant Young	.05	309	Troy Aikman	.30
108	Terrell Davis	1.00	209	Tim Diakabutuka	.15	310	Terrell Davis	.40
109	Marcus Allen	.10	210	Troy Aikman	.75	311	Jim Everett	.05
110	Ray Zellars	.05	211	Quentin Coryatt	.05	312	John Elway	.20
111	Chris Warren	.05	212	Karim Abdul-Jabbar	.50	313	Barry Sanders	.30
112	Phillippi Sparks	.05	213	Brian Blades	.05	314	Jim Harbaugh	.05
113	Craig Erickson	.05	214	Ray Farmer	.05	315	Steve Young	.20
114	Eddie George	1.00	215	Simeon Rice	.05	316	Dan Marino	.75
115	Daryl Johnston	.05	216	Tyrone Braxton	.05	317	Michael Irvin	.05
116	Ricky Watters	.10	217	Jerome Woods	.05	318	Emmitt Smith	.75
117	Tedy Bruschi	.05	218	Charles Way	.05	319	Jeff Hostetler	.05
118	Mike Mamula	.05	219	Garrison Hearst	.05	320	Mark Brunell	.30
119	Ken Harvey	.05	220	Bobby Engram	.10	321	Jeff Blake	.05
120	John Randle	.05	221	Billy Davis	.05	322	Scott Mitchell	.05
121	Mark Chmura	.05	222	Ken Dilger	.05	323	Boomer Esiason	.05
122	Sam Gash	.05	223	Robert Smith	.05	324	Jerome Bettis	.05
123	John Kasay	.05	224	John Friesz	.05	325	Warren Moon	.05
124	Barry Minter	.05	225	Charlie Garner	.05	326	Neil O'Donnell	.05
125	Raymont Harris	.05	226	Jerome Bettis	.10	327	Jim Kelly	.05
126	Derrick Thomas	.05	227	Darnay Scott	.05	328	Checklist Dan Marino	.75
127	Trent Dilfer	.10	228	Terance Mathis	.05	329	Checklist John Elway	.20
128	Carnell Lake	.05	229	Brian Williams	.05	330	Checklist Drew Bledsoe	.30
129	Brian Dawkins	.05	230	Cris Carter	.05			
130	Tyronne Drakeford	.05	231	Michael Haynes	.05			
131	Daryl Gardener	.05	232	Cedric Jones	.05			
132	Fred Strickland	.05	233	Danny Kanell	.05			
133	Kevin Hardy	.05	234	Deion Sanders	.30			
134	Winslow Oliver	.05	235	Steve Atwater	.05			
135	Herman Moore	.15	236	Jonathan Ogden	.05			
136	Keith Byars	.05	237	Lake Dawson	.05			
137	Harold Green	.05	238	Eric Allen	.05			
138	Ty Detmer	.05	239	Eddie Kennison	.30			
139	Lamar Thomas	.05	240	Irving Fryar	.05			
140	Elvis Grbac	.05	241	Michael Strahan	.05			
141	Edgar Bennett	.05	242	Steve McNair	.40			
142	Cornelius Bennett	.05	243	Terrell Buckley	.05			
143	Tony Tolbert	.05	244	Merton Hanks	.05			
144	James Hasty	.05	245	Jessie Armstead	.05			
145	Ben Coates	.05	246	Dana Stubblefield	.05			
146	Errict Rhett	.10	247	Brett Perriman	.05			
147	Jason Seahorn	.05	248	Mark Collins	.05			
148	Michael Jackson	.05	249	Willie Roaf	.05			
149	John Mobley	.05	250	Gus Frerotte	.05			
150	Walt Harris	.05	251	William Fuller	.05			
151	Terry Kirby	.05	252	Tamarick Vanover	.10			
152	Devin Wyman	.05	253	Scott Mitchell	.05			
153	Ray Crockett	.05	254	Eric Metcalf	.05			
154	Quinn Early	.05	255	Herschel Walker	.05			

This 16-card set includes the Franchise players from various NFL teams, including Emmitt Smith and Barry Sanders.

		MT
Complete Set (16):		200.00
Common Player:		4.00
1	Emmitt Smith	30.00
2	Barry Sanders	15.00
3	Brett Favre	35.00
4	Drew Bledsoe	15.00
5	Jerry Rice	15.00
6	Troy Aikman	15.00
7	Dan Marino	30.00
8	John Elway	10.00
9	Steve Young	10.00
10	Eddie George	18.00
11	Keyshawn Johnson	4.00
12	Terrell Davis	15.00
13	Marshall Faulk	4.00
14	Kerry Collins	15.00
15	Deion Sanders	8.00
16	Joey Galloway	4.00

1997 Score New Breed

This 18-card set features a player photo superimposed over a holographic background on the card front. "The New Breed" is printed at the top. A football's brown pebble grain is on the top and bottom border of the front. The Score logo is in the lower left, while his name, position and team are printed to the right of the logo. The backs are numbered "of 18" in the upper left corner.

		MT
Complete Set (18):		75.00
Common Player:		.75
1	Eddie George	8.00
2	Terrell Davis	8.00
3	Curtis Martin	8.00
4	Tony Banks	.75
5	Lawrence Phillips	.75
6	Terry Glenn	5.00
7	Jerome Bettis	.75
8	Karim Abdul-Jabbar	4.00
9	Napoleon Kaufman	.75
10	Isaac Bruce	.75
11	Keyshawn Johnson	.75
12	Rickey Dudley	.75
13	Eddie Kennison	3.00
14	Marvin Harrison	3.00
15	Emmitt Smith	10.00
16	Barry Sanders	6.00
17	Kerry Collins	6.00
18	Brett Favre	12.00

1997 Score Franchise

1997 Score The Specialist

The 18-card chase set features a holographic front, with the player over a background which repeats "The Specialist" many times. The player's name is printed in red at the bottom center. The cards are numbered "of 18" on the back.

		MT
Complete Set (18):		75.00
Common Player:		.75
1	Brett Favre	12.00

2	Drew Bledsoe	6.00
3	Mark Brunell	6.00
4	Kerry Collins	6.00
5	John Elway	4.00
6	Barry Sanders	6.00
7	Troy Aikman	6.00
8	Jerry Rice	6.00
9	Dan Marino	10.00
10	Neil O'Donnell	.75
11	Scott Mitchell	.75
12	Jim Harbaugh	.75
13	Emmitt Smith	10.00
14	Steve Young	4.00
15	Dave Brown	.75
16	Jeff Blake	2.00
17	Jim Everett	.75
18	Kordell Stewart	6.00

1997 Score Board NFL $3 Phone Cards

Each three-card pack of Score Board's 1997 NFL Phone Cards contained two $3 cards and one other denomination card: $5, $10, $25, $1000 and Test/Proof Cards, which also carry phone time. All cards have rounded edges and the $25 card is die-cut. Phone time is provided in conjunction with Sprint. Each of the 50 $3 cards is sequentially numbered to 9,435.

		MT
Complete Set (50):		50.00
Common Player:		1.00
1	Jim Kelly	1.00
2	Kerry Collins	2.00
3	Jeff George	1.00
4	Troy Aikman	2.00
5	John Elway	1.50
6	Herman Moore	1.00
7	Barry Sanders	2.00
8	Brett Favre	4.00
9	Jim Harbaugh	1.00
10	Steve Bono	1.00
11	Dan Marino	4.00
12	Drew Bledsoe	2.00
13	Jim Everett	1.00
14	Neil O'Donnell	1.00
15	Ricky Watters	1.00
16	Junior Seau	1.00
17	Chris Chandler	1.00
18	Errict Rhett	1.00
19	Joey Galloway	1.50
20	Steve Young	1.50
21	Kordell Stewart	2.00
22	Rodney Hampton	1.00
23	Curtis Martin	3.00
24	Mark Brunell	1.50

25	Steve McNair	1.50
26	Deion Sanders	1.50
27	Carl Pickens	1.00
28	Michael Irvin	1.00
29	Tamarick Vanover	1.50
30	Trent Dilfer	1.00
31	Chris Warren	1.00
32	Stan Humphries	1.00
33	J.J. Stokes	1.00
34	Tim Biakabutuka	1.50
35	Keyshawn Johnson	1.50
36	Simeon Rice	1.00
37	Jonathan Ogden	1.00
38	Rashaan Salaam	1.00
39	Bobby Engram	1.00
40	Reggie White	1.00
41	Isaac Bruce	1.50
42	Eddie George	3.00
43	Marvin Harrison	2.00
44	Kevin Hardy	1.00
45	Karim Abdul-Jabbar	2.50
46	Duane Clemons	1.00
47	Terry Glenn	3.00
48	Marcus Allen	1.00
49	Rickey Dudley	1.00
50	Lawrence Phillips	1.50

1997 Score Board NFL $5 Phone Cards

The 20-card set, sequentially numbered to 4,929, was inserted every three packs of 1997 NFL Phone Cards.

		MT
Complete Set (20):		75.00
Common Player:		2.00
1	Kerry Collins	3.00
2	Troy Aikman	3.00
3	Reggie White	2.00
4	Mark Brunell	2.50
5	Dan Marino	6.00
6	Kordell Stewart	3.00
7	Junior Seau	2.00
8	Steve Young	2.50
9	John Elway	2.50
10	Terrell Davis	4.00
11	Steve McNair	2.50
12	Drew Bledsoe	3.00
13	Joey Galloway	2.50
14	Deion Sanders	2.50
15	Kevin Hardy	2.00
16	Keyshawn Johnson	2.50
17	Marvin Harrison	3.00
18	Tim Biakabutuka	2.50
19	Eddie George	5.00
20	Terry Glenn	5.00

1997 Score Board NFL $10 Phone Cards

The 10-card set has rounded edges and was inserted every 12 packs of Score Board's 1997 NFL Phone Card release. The cards are sequentially numbered to 1,130.

		MT
Complete Set (10):		60.00
Common Player:		4.00
1	Dan Marino	12.00
2	Jim Harbaugh	4.00
3	Troy Aikman	6.00
4	Curtis Martin	8.00
5	Kordell Stewart	6.00
6	Steve Young	4.00
7	Barry Sanders	6.00
8	Keyshawn Johnson	5.00
9	Lawrence Phillips	5.00
10	Eddie George	8.00

1997 Score Board NFL $25 Die-Cut Phone Cards

The 10-card, die-cut set was inserted every 36 packs of the 1997 Phone Cards release. The cards are sequentially numbered to 377.

		MT
Complete Set (10):		140.00
Common Player:		10.00
1	Jim Kelly	10.00
2	Troy Aikman	15.00
3	John Elway	12.00
4	Kerry Collins	15.00
5	Barry Sanders	15.00
6	Drew Bledsoe	15.00
7	Keyshawn Johnson	10.00
8	Deion Sanders	12.00
9	Dan Marino	30.00
10	Brett Favre	30.00

1997 Score Board NFL Experience

The 100-card, regular-sized set was sold in six-card packs. The card fronts feature a color action photo with the player's name and position printed on the bottom edge. The team's logo appears in the lower left corner. The card backs include another photo, a short highlight and a trivia question with answer. The base cards are printed on vintage-style cards. Inserts include Foundations, Teams Of The 90's and NFL Vintage cards.

		MT
Complete Set (100):		12.00
Common Player:		.05
Wax Box:		35.00
1	Emmitt Smith	1.50
2	Kordell Stewart	.75
3	Antonio Freeman	.05
4	William Thomas	.05
5	Simeon Rice	.25
6	Drew Bledsoe	.75
7	Elvis Grbac	.05
8	Ken Dilger	.05
9	John Elway	.50
10	Curtis Conway	.05
11	Adrian Murrell	.05
12	Karim Abdul-Jabbar	.75
13	Terry Allen	.05
14	Lawrence Phillips	.50
15	Barry Sanders	.75
16	Shannon Sharpe	.05
17	Troy Aikman	.75
18	Kevin Greene	.05
19	Cris Carter	.05
20	Jim Kelly	.05
21	Eric Metcalf	.05
22	Joey Galloway	.50
23	Eddie George	1.00

24	Scott Mitchell	.05
25	Neil O'Donnell	.05
26	Ben Coates	.05
27	Andre Reed	.05
28	Michael Jackson	.05
29	Keith Jackson	.05
30	J.J. Stokes	.20
31	Rickey Dudley	.25
32	Ricky Watters	.10
33	Marcus Allen	.10
34	Brett Favre	1.25
35	Kevin Hardy	.05
36	Jim Everett	.05
37	Zach Thomas	.25
38	Lamar Lathon	.05
39	LeShon Johnson	.05
40	Bruce Smith	.05
41	Junior Seau	.05
42	Tony Banks	.50
43	Brian Mitchell	.05
44	Chris T. Jones	.05
45	Ty Detmer	.05
46	Robert Brooks	.05
47	Derrick Thomas	.05
48	Dan Wilkinson	.05
49	Michael Sinclair	.05
50	Dave Brown	.05
51	Carl Pickens	.05
52	Jim Harbaugh	.05
53	Wayne Chrebet	.05
54	Warren Moon	.05
55	Steve Young	.50
56	Sean Gilbert	.05
57	Jerome Bettis	.10
58	Dan Marino	1.50
59	Terrell Davis	.75
60	Mark Brunell	.20
61	Kent Graham	.05
62	Rashaan Salaam	.25
63	Tony Martin	.05
64	Robert Smith	.05
65	Thurman Thomas	.10
66	Marshall Faulk	.40
67	Dale Carter	.05
68	Stan Humphries	.05
69	Isaac Bruce	.40
70	Warren Sapp	.05
71	Kerry Collins	.75
72	Jamal Anderson	.40
73	Chris Chandler	.05
74	Herman Moore	.20
75	Rodney Hampton	.05
76	Tim Brown	.05
77	Keenan McCardell	.05
78	Anthony Miller	.05
79	Jake Reed	.05
80	Earnest Byner	.05
81	Chris Warren	.05
82	Deion Sanders	.50
83	Mike Tomczak	.05
84	Curtis Martin	1.00
85	John Friesz	.05
86	Gus Frerotte	.05
87	Vinny Testaverde	.05
88	Jason Dunn	.05
89	James Stewart	.05
90	Steve Bono	.05
91	Levon Kirkland	.05
92	Merton Hanks	.05
93	Marvin Harrison	.60
94	Reggie Brooks	.05
95	Reggie White	.10
96	Jeff Blake	.30
97	Terry Glenn	.75
98	Jerry Rice	.75
99	Keyshawn Johnson	.75
100	Checklist	.05

1997 Score Board NFL Experience Foundations

The 30-card, regular-sized set was inserted every 12 packs of Score Board's 1997 NFL Experience. The cards feature a key player on each of the league's 30 franchises. The cards are die-cut to put the card front player shot onto a pedestal foundation. The card backs feature another player photo, imaged over a pedestal blueprint, and are numbered with an "F" prefix.

		MT
Complete Set (30):		150.00
Common Player:		2.00
F1	Ray Lewis	2.00
F2	Bruce Smith	2.00
F3	Jeff Blake	6.00
F4	Terrell Davis	10.00
F5	Steve McNair	8.00
F6	Marshall Faulk	8.00
F7	Mark Brunell	5.00
F8	Derrick Thomas	2.00
F9	Karim Abdul-Jabbar	10.00
F10	Curtis Martin	15.00
F11	Keyshawn Johnson	8.00
F12	Tim Brown	2.00
F13	Kordell Stewart	10.00
F14	Junior Seau	2.00
F15	Joey Galloway	10.00
F16	Simeon Rice	2.00
F17	Jessie Tuggle	2.00
F18	Kerry Collins	10.00
F19	Rashaan Salaam	5.00
F20	Emmitt Smith	20.00
F21	Barry Sanders	10.00
F22	Brett Favre	15.00
F23	Cris Carter	2.00
F24	Jim Everett	2.00
F25	Amani Toomer	2.00
F26	Ricky Watters	2.00
F27	Tony Banks	5.00
F28	Jerry Rice	10.00
F29	Warren Sapp	2.00
F30	Terry Allen	2.00

1997 Score Board NFL Experience Teams of the 90's

The 15-card, regular-sized set highlights players who have starred in Super Bowls of the 1990s. The cards were inserted in every 100 packs of Score Board's 1997 NFL Experience. The cards are die-cut into the shape of an oval ring. The card fronts feature the player over a common Super Bowl ring while the backs have another player shot with a short bio.

		MT
Complete Set (15):		300.00
Common Player:		15.00
T1	Emmitt Smith	120.00
T2	Bruce Smith	15.00
T3	Steve Young	50.00
T4	Thurman Thomas	15.00
T5	Kordell Stewart	60.00
T6	Ricky Watters	15.00
T7	Ken Norton	15.00
T8	Jeff Hostetler	15.00
T9	Jim Kelly	15.00
T10	Troy Aikman	60.00
T11	Jerry Rice	60.00
T12	Mark Rypien	15.00
T13	Stan Humphries	15.00
T14	Deion Sanders	40.00
T15	Andre Reed	15.00

1997 Score Board NFL Rookies

The 100-card set features the player's name at the top, while the team's logos that drafted him are included in a black stripe in the upper left corner. The '97 Rookies Score Board logo is in the lower center. The team's name is printed inside a black half oval at the bottom. The black stripe that runs along the left side of the back includes the various logos, player's name, bio and card number. To the right of the stripe is the player's photo, highlights and stats. The set was paralleled by the Dean's List, which was inserted 1:5 packs. Vintage rookie cards and autographed rookie cards of current and ex-NFL players were also randomly inserted.

		MT
Complete Set (100):		10.00
Common Player:		.05
Dean's List:		2x-3x
1	Jake Plummer	.50
2	Tony Gonzalez	.20
3	Trevor Pryce	.05
4	Greg Jones	.05
5	Koy Detmer	1.25
6	Rae Carruth	.75
7	Peter Boulware	.05
8	Warrick Dunn	2.00
9	Antowain Smith	.30
10	Troy Davis	1.00
11	David LaFleur	.30
12	Yatil Green	1.00
13	Michael Booker	.05
14	Shawn Springs	.30
15	Bryant Westbrook	.30
16	Byron Hanspard	.50
17	Darrell Russell	.05
18	Corey Dillon	.05
19	Tyrus McCloud	.05
20	Reinard Wilson	.05
21	Adam Meadows	.05
22	Tremain Mack	.05
23	Ricky Parker	.05
24	George Jones	.05
25	Terry Battle	.05
26	Will Blackwell	.05
27	Jerald Sowell	.05
28	Isaac Byrd	.05
29	Chris Naeole	.05
30	Kevin Lockett	.05
31	Freddie Jones	.05
32	Pat Barnes	.05
33	Torrian Gray	.05
34	Brian Manning	.05
35	Dedric Ward	.05
36	Pete Monty	.05
37	Sam Madison	.05
38	Sedrick Shaw	.05
39	Mike Logan	.05
40	Albert Connell	.05
41	Canute Curtis	.05
42	Ronde Barber	.05
43	Orlando Pace	.75
44	Edward Perry	.05
45	Tiki Barber	.50
46	Kevin Jackson	.05
47	Jerry Wunsch	.05
48	Michael Hamilton	.05
49	Darnell Autry	.50
50	Jim Druckenmiller	1.25
51	James Farrior	.05
52	Derrick Mason	.05
53	Ty Howard	.05
54	Jason Taylor	.05
55	Reidel Anthony	1.00
56	Bert Berry	.05
57	Marc Edwards	.05
58	James Hamilton	.05
59	Ike Hilliard	1.00
60	Tommy Knight	.05
61	Walter Jones	.05
62	Chad Levitt	.05
63	Pratt Lyons	.05
64	Greg Clark	.05
65	Ryan Phillips	.05
66	Jason Martin	.05
67	Scott Sanderson	.05
68	Alshermond Singleton	.05
69	Duce Staley	.05
70	Jared Tomich	.05
71	Ross Verba	.05
72	Derrick Rodgers	.05
73	Mike Vrabel	.05
74	John Allred	.05
75	Bob Sapp	.05
76	Brad Otton	.05
77	Tarik Glenn	.05
78	Chad Scott	.05
79	Nathan Davis	.05
80	Henri Crockett	.05
81	Tarik Saleh	.05
82	Seth Payne	.05
83	Pete Chryplewicz	.05
84	Reidel Anthony	.50
85	Reinard Wilson	.05
86	Byron Hanspard	.20
87	Shawn Springs	.20
88	David LaFleur	.20
89	Troy Davis	.50
90	Warrick Dunn	1.00
91	Peter Boulware	.05
92	Rae Carruth	.20
93	Tony Gonzalez	.10
94	Jake Plummer	.25
95	Orlando Pace	.25
96	Ike Hilliard	.50
97	Kevin Jackson	.05
98	Jim Druckenmiller	.60
99	Shawn Springs	.20
100	Warrick Dunn	1.00

1997 Score Board NFL Rookies Varsity Club

Inserted 1:36 packs, the 30-card set features the school pennant and team logo of the player's college or university.

		MT
Complete Set (30):		140.00
Common Player:		2.00
V1	Tiki Barber	10.00
V2	Sedrick Shaw	2.00
V3	Kevin Lockett	2.00
V4	Byron Hanspard	10.00
V5	David LaFleur	6.00
V6	Warrick Dunn	25.00
V7	Yatil Green	15.00
V8	Corey Dillon	6.00
V9	Orlando Pace	10.00
V10	Tony Gonzalez	4.00
V11	Darrell Russell	2.00
V12	Jake Plummer	10.00
V13	Peter Boulware	2.00
V14	Shawn Springs	6.00
V15	Bryant Westbrook	6.00
V16	Rae Carruth	12.00
V17	Antowain Smith	6.00
V18	Reidel Anthony	15.00
V19	Michael Booker	2.00
V20	Freddie Jones	2.00
V21	Pat Barnes	2.00
V22	Troy Davis	15.00
V23	Walter Jones	2.00
V24	Reinard Wilson	2.00
V25	George Jones	2.00
V26	Terry Battle	2.00
V27	Tommy Knight	2.00
V28	Tremain Mack	2.00
V29	Jim Druckenmiller	20.00
V30	Ike Hilliard	15.00

1997 Score Board NFL Rookies NFL War Room

The 20-card set was inserted 1:100 packs. It includes comments from NFL insiders on players that were selected on draft day.

		MT
Complete Set (20):		300.00
Common Player:		10.00
W1	Yatil Green	45.00
W2	Antowain Smith	20.00
W3	Tony Gonzalez	20.00
W4	Corey Dillon	10.00
W5	Jake Plummer	30.00
W6	Peter Boulware	10.00
W7	Orlando Pace	30.00
W8	Darrell Russell	10.00
W9	Reinard Wilson	10.00
W10	Shawn Springs	20.00
W11	Bryant Westbrook	20.00
W12	Rae Carruth	40.00
W13	Warrick Dunn	80.00
W14	David LaFleur	20.00
W15	Byron Hanspard	30.00
W16	Michael Booker	10.00
W17	Reidel Anthony	45.00
W18	Troy Davis	45.00
W19	Chris Naeole	10.00
W20	Jim Druckenmiller	60.00

1997 SkyBox Impact

The 250-card set contains 207 player cards, three checklists and 40 rookies. The cards feature the player's photo superimposed over a jagged background, with the player's name printed in 3-D block letters at the top. The player's first and last name and team are printed at the bottom right in gold foil, while the Impact logo is in the lower left. The backs include the player's name, position, quote, Impact stats, bio, stats, photo and team helmet over a team-colored football background. A Rave parallel set was randomly seeded. SkyBox produced less than 150 Rave sets.

		MT
Complete Set (250):		20.00
Common Player:		.05
Circa Raves:		70x-140x
Wax Box:		50.00
1	Carl Pickens	.05
2	Ray Lewis	.05

3	Darrell Green	.05
4	Brett Favre	1.75
5	Todd Collins	.05
6	Errict Rhett	.10
7	John Elway	.50
8	Troy Aikman	.75
9	Steve McNair	.75
10	Kordell Stewart	.75
11	Drew Bledsoe	.75
12	Kerry Collins	.75
13	Dan Marino	1.50
14	Ricky Watters	.10
15	Marvin Harrison	.30
16	Simeon Rice	.05
17	Qadry Ismail	.05
18	Andre Coleman	.05
19	Keyshawn Johnson	.30
20	Barry Sanders	.75
21	Rickey Dudley	.10
22	Emmitt Smith	1.50
23	Erik Kramer	.05
24	Tony Boselli	.05
25	Steve Young	.50
26	Rod Woodson	.05
27	Eddie George	1.00
28	Curtis Martin	1.00
29	Amani Toomer	.05
30	Terrell Davis	1.00
31	Jim Everett	.05
32	Marcus Allen	.10
33	Karim Abdul-Jabbar	.50
34	Thurman Thomas	.10
35	Cortez Kennedy	.05
36	Jerome Bettis	.10
37	Kevin Carter	.05
38	Gilbert Brown	.05
39	Bert Emanuel	.05
40	Kyle Brady	.05
41	Trent Dilfer	.10
42	Garrison Hearst	.05
43	Kevin Greene	.05
44	Bryan Cox	.05
45	Desmond Howard	.05
46	Larry Centers	.05
47	Quentin Coryatt	.05
48	Michael Jackson	.05
49	John Randle	.05
50	Mark Brunell	.75
51	William Thomas	.05
52	Glyn Milburn	.05
53	Mike Alstott	.10
54	Chris Spielman	.05
55	Junior Seau	.10
56	Brian Blades	.05
57	Lamar Lathon	.05
58	Derrick Thomas	.05
59	Dave Brown	.05
60	Frank Wycheck	.05
61	Chris Slade	.05
62	Neil Smith	.05
63	Ashley Ambrose	.05
64	Alex Molden	.05
65	Edgar Bennett	.05
66	Alvin Harper	.05
67	Jamal Anderson	.15
68	Eddie Kennison	.30
69	Ken Norton	.05
70	Zach Thomas	.20
71	Leeland McElroy	.10
72	Terry Allen	.05
73	Raymont Harris	.05
74	Ken Dilger	.05
75	Jason Dunn	.05
76	Robert Smith	.05
77	William Roaf	.05
78	Bruce Smith	.05
79	Vinny Testaverde	.05
80	Jerry Rice	.75
81	Tim Brown	.05
82	James Stewart	.05
83	Andre Reed	.05
84	Herman Moore	.15
85	Stan Humphries	.05
86	Chris Warren	.05
87	Tyrone Wheatley	.05
88	Michael Irvin	.10
89	Dan Wilkinson	.05
90	Tony Banks	.20
91	Chester McGlockton	.05
92	Reggie White	.10
93	Elvis Grbac	.05
94	Willie Davis	.05
95	Greg Lloyd	.05
96	Ben Coates	.05
97	Rashaan Salaam	.10
98	Eric Swann	.05
99	Hugh Douglas	.05
100	Henry Ellard	.05
101	Rod Smith	.05
102	Tim Biakabutuka	.10
103	Chad Brown	.05

104	Kevin Hardy	.05
105	Chris T. Jones	.05
106	Antonio Freeman	.20
107	Lamont Warren	.05
108	Derrick Alexander	.05
109	Brett Perriman	.05
110	Antonio Langham	.05
111	Eric Moulds	.05
112	O.J. McDuffie	.05
113	Eric Metcalf	.05
114	Ray Zellars	.05
115	Marco Coleman	.05
116	Terry Kirby	.05
117	Darren Woodson	.05
118	Charles Johnson	.05
119	Sam Mills	.05
120	Rodney Hampton	.05
121	Rick Mirer	.10
122	Derrick Brooks	.05
123	Greg Hill	.05
124	John Mobley	.05
125	Chris Sanders	.05
126	Kent Graham	.05
127	Michael Westbrook	.05
128	Harvey Williams	.05
129	Keenan McCardell	.05
130	Neil O'Donnell	.05
131	LeRoy Butler	.05
132	Willie McGinest	.05
133	Ki-Jana Carter	.05
134	Robert Jones	.05
135	Jim Harbaugh	.05
136	Wesley Walls	.05
137	Jackie Harris	.05
138	Jermaine Lewis	.05
139	Jake Reed	.05
140	John Friesz	.05
141	Jerris McPhail	.05
142	Charlie Garner	.05
143	Bryce Paup	.05
144	Tony Martin	.05
145	Shannon Sharpe	.05
146	Terrell Owens	.50
147	Curtis Conway	.10
148	Jamie Asher	.05
149	Lawrence Phillips	.10
150	Deion Sanders	.30
151	Frank Sanders	.05
152	Joey Galloway	.20
153	Mel Gray	.05
154	Robert Brooks	.10
155	Jeff George	.05
156	Michael Haynes	.05
157	Chris Chandler	.05
158	Adrian Murrell	.05
159	Tamarick Vanover	.05
160	Marshall Faulk	.10
161	Thomas Lewis	.05
162	Ty Detmer	.05
163	Darnay Scott	.05
164	Bam Morris	.05
165	Scott Mitchell	.05
166	Brad Johnson	.05
167	Dave Meggett	.05
168	Bobby Engram	.05
169	Natrone Means	.10
170	Erric Pegram	.05
171	Leonard Russell	.05
172	Muhsin Muhammad	.05
173	Aeneas Williams	.05
174	Fred Barnett	.05
175	William Floyd	.05
176	Kimble Anders	.05
177	Darick Holmes	.05
178	Willie Green	.05
179	Rodney Thomas	.05
180	Derrick Alexander	.05
181	Sean Dawkins	.05
182	Dorsey Levens	.10
183	Napoleon Kaufman	.05
184	Mario Bates	.05
185	Yancey Thigpen	.05
186	Johnnie Morton	.05
187	Gus Frerotte	.05
188	Terance Mathis	.05
189	Tyrone Hughes	.05
190	Wayne Chrebet	.05
191	Tony Brackens	.05
192	Hardy Nickerson	.05
193	Daryl Johnston	.05
194	Irving Fryar	.05
195	Jeff Blake	.15
196	Charles Way	.05
197	Brian Mitchell	.05
198	Brent Jones	.05
199	Mark Chmura	.05
200	Terry Glenn	.75
201	Cris Carter	.05
202	Steve Atwater	.05
203	Rob Moore	.05
204	Anthony Johnson	.05

205	Warren Moon	.10
206	Darrien Gordon	.05
207	Isaac Bruce	.15
208	*Reidel Anthony*	1.50
209	*Darnell Autry*	.50
210	*Tiki Barber*	1.50
211	*Pat Barnes*	.75
212	*Terry Battle*	.10
213	*Michael Booker*	.10
214	*Peter Boulware*	.20
215	*Chris Canty*	.10
216	*Rae Carruth*	1.00
217	*Troy Davis*	1.50
218	*Corey Dillon*	1.00
219	*Jim Druckenmiller*	2.00
220	*Warrick Dunn*	2.50
221	*James Farrior*	.10
222	*Tarik Glenn*	.10
223	*Tony Gonzalez*	.50
224	*Yatil Green*	1.25
225	*Byron Hanspard*	1.00
226	*Ike Hilliard*	1.50
227	*Kenny Holmes*	.10
228	*Walter Jones*	.10
229	*Tom Knight*	.10
230	*David LaFleur*	.40
231	*Kenard Lang*	.10
232	*Kevin Lockett*	.10
233	*Tremain Mack*	.10
234	*Sam Madison*	.10
235	*Chris Naeole*	.10
236	*Orlando Pace*	.40
237	*Jake Plummer*	.75
238	*Dwayne Rudd*	.10
239	*Darrell Russell*	.25
240	*Jamie Sharper*	.10
241	*Sedrick Shaw*	.75
242	*Antowain Smith*	1.25
243	*Shawn Springs*	.75
244	*Bryant Westbrook*	.20
245	*Reinard Wilson*	.10
246	*Danny Wuerffel*	2.00
247	*Renaldo Wynn*	.10
248	Checklist	.05
249	Checklist	.05
250	Checklist	.05

1997 SkyBox Impact Boss

Inserted 1:6 packs, the 20-card set features the player's photo, name and team name embossed on the front. The backs have the player's name, team, position and highlights on the left side, while the Boss logo runs vertically along the right border. The cards are numbered "of 20" in the upper right corner. The Super Boss parallel set was inserted 1:36 packs. The cards are identical to the base Boss, except the cards are printed on foil. The Super Boss logo appears in the lower left of the card front. The Super Boss cards also have an "SB" suffix with the card numbers on the back.

		MT
Complete Set (20):		40.00
Common Player:		1.00
Super Boss Cards:		2x-4x
1	Karim Abdul-Jabbar	2.00
2	Troy Aikman	3.00
3	Tim Biakabutuka	1.00
4	Mark Brunell	3.00
5	Rae Carruth	2.00
6	Kerry Collins	3.00
7	Corey Dillon	2.00

8	Jim Druckenmiller	3.00
9	Warrick Dunn	4.00
10	Brett Favre	6.00
11	Eddie George	4.00
12	Marvin Harrison	1.50
13	Keyshawn Johnson	1.50
14	Eddie Kennison	1.50
15	Dan Marino	5.00
16	Curtis Martin	4.00
17	Steve McNair	3.00
18	Orlando Pace	1.00
19	Barry Sanders	3.00
20	Steve Young	2.00

1997 SkyBox Impact Excelerators

The 12-card set was inserted 1:48 packs. The die-cut cards have the player's photo superimposed over a black and silver background, with a shield in the center. Excelerators is printed in red in the center of the background, while the player's name is printed in silver over the center of the player photo. The SkyBox logo is at the bottom center of the front. The backs have a player photo in the center, with his name and highlights printed inside the shield. The card numbers are printed "of 12."

		MT
Complete Set (12):		100.00
Common Player:		3.00
1	Mark Brunell	15.00
2	Rae Carruth	10.00
3	Terrell Davis	20.00
4	Joey Galloway	3.00
5	Marvin Harrison	6.00
6	Keyshawn Johnson	3.00
7	Eddie Kennison	6.00
8	Steve McNair	12.00
9	Jerry Rice	15.00
10	Emmitt Smith	30.00
11	Shawn Springs	6.00
12	Kordell Stewart	15.00

1997 SkyBox Impact Instant Impact

The 15-card set was inserted 1:24 packs. The player's last name is printed in black at the top inside a white stripe. The Impact logo is printed in silver in the lower right of the photo. A black stripe at the bottom includes "Instant Impact," player's name and team in silver foil. The team's helmet is located in the bottom center. The backs have the card number "of 15" printed at the top, while his highlights are printed in the center of the card. The black stripe on the bottom repeats the information from the front, without the silver foil.

		MT
Complete Set (15):		75.00
Common Player:		1.50
1	Reidel Anthony	10.00
2	Darnell Autry	4.00
3	Tiki Barber	10.00
4	Peter Boulware	1.50
5	Troy Davis	10.00
6	Jim Druckenmiller	12.00
7	Warrick Dunn	15.00
8	Yatil Green	8.00
9	Ike Hilliard	10.00
10	Orlando Pace	3.00
11	Darrell Russell	1.50
12	Sedrick Shaw	5.00
13	Shawn Springs	5.00
14	Bryant Westbrook	1.50
15	Danny Wuerffel	12.00

1997 SkyBox Impact Rave Reviews

Inserted 1:288 packs, the 12-card set includes a player photo superimposed over a holofoil background of numbers. The Rave Reviews logo is printed above the player's name in the lower left corner. "Rave Review" is printed in holofoil vertically along the right border. The backs have the player's name at the top, with a quote from Ronnie Lott along the left border. The player's photo is on the right. Lott's photo and description, along with the card number "of 12" are printed in the lower left.

		MT
Complete Set (12):		600.00
Common Player:		25.00
1	Terrell Davis	60.00
2	John Elway	40.00
3	Brett Favre	120.00
4	Joey Galloway	25.00
5	Eddie George	60.00
6	Terry Glenn	50.00
7	Dan Marino	100.00
8	Curtis Martin	60.00
9	Jerry Rice	60.00
10	Barry Sanders	60.00
11	Deion Sanders	25.00
12	Emmitt Smith	100.00

1997 SkyBox Impact Total Impact

Inserted 1:36 retail packs, the 10-card set is printed on plastic over a white background.

		MT
Complete Set (10):		75.00
Common Player:		5.00
1	Karim Abdul-Jabbar	7.00
2	Troy Aikman	12.00
3	Drew Bledsoe	12.00
4	Isaac Bruce	5.00
5	Kerry Collins	10.00
6	John Elway	10.00
7	Terry Glenn	10.00
8	Lawrence Phillips	5.00
9	Deion Sanders	8.00
10	Kordell Stewart	12.00

1997 Topps

The 415-card set features a colored border on the left of the card front. In that border are the Topps' logo in gold foil in the lower left and the player's name in the upper left. The team's logo is in the upper right. A white border surrounds the three remaining sides. The backs have the player's name, team, position, bio, stats and highlights. A "Minted in Canton" parallel, which features a special gold-foil stamp, was randomly seeded in packs.

		MT
Complete Set (415):		40.00
Common Player:		.05
Minted Canton Cards:		5x-10x
Wax Box:		40.00
1	Brett Favre	2.50
2	Lawyer Milloy	.05
3	Tim Biakabutuka	.10
4	Clyde Simmons	.05
5	Deion Sanders	.50
6	Anthony Miller	.05
7	Marquez Pope	.05
8	Mike Tomczak	.05
9	William Thomas	.05
10	Marshall Faulk	.20
11	John Randle	.05
12	Jim Kelly	.10
13	Steve Bono	.05
14	Rod Stephens	.05
15	Stan Humphries	.05
16	Terrell Buckley	.05
17	Ki-Jana Carter	.10
18	Marcus Robertson	.05
19	Corey Harris	.05
20	Rashaan Salaam	.10
21	Rickey Dudley	.05
22	Jamir Miller	.05
23	Martin Mayhew	.05
24	Jason Sehorn	.05
25	Isaac Bruce	.20
26	Johnnie Morton	.05
27	Antonio Langham	.05
28	Cornelius Bennett	.05
29	Joe Johnson	.05
30	Keyshawn Johnson	.40
31	Willie Green	.05
32	Craig Newsome	.05
33	Brock Marion	.05
34	Corey Fuller	.05
35	Ben Coates	.05
36	Ty Detmer	.05
37	Charles Johnson	.05
38	Willie Jackson	.05
39	Tyronne Drakeford	.05
40	Gus Frerotte	.05
41	Robert Blackmon	.05
42	Andre Coleman	.05
43	Mario Bates	.05
44	Chris Calloway	.05
45	Terry McDaniel	.05
46	Anthony Davis	.05
47	Stanley Pritchett	.05
48	Ray Buchanan	.05
49	Chris Chandler	.05
50	Ashley Ambrose	.05
51	Tyrone Braxton	.05
52	Pepper Johnson	.05
53	Frank Sanders	.05
54	Clay Matthews	.05
55	Bruce Smith	.05
56	Jermaine Lewis	.05
57	Mark Carrier	.05
58	Jeff Graham	.05
59	Keith Lyle	.05
60	Trent Dilfer	.10
61	Trace Armstrong	.05
62	Jeff Herrod	.05
63	Tyrone Wheatley	.05
64	Torrance Small	.05
65	Chris Warren	.05
66	Terry Kirby	.05
67	Erric Pegram	.05
68	Sean Gilbert	.05
69	Greg Biekert	.05
70	Ricky Watters	.10
71	Chris Hudson	.05
72	Tamarick Vanover	.10
73	Orlando Thomas	.05
74	Jimmy Spencer	.05
75	John Mobley	.05
76	Henry Thomas	.05
77	Santana Dotson	.05
78	Boomer Esiason	.05
79	Bobby Hebert	.05
80	Kerry Collins	1.00
81	Bobby Engram	.05
82	Kevin Smith	.05
83	Rick Mirer	.10
84	Ted Johnson	.05
85	Derrick Alexander	.05
86	Hugh Douglas	.05
87	Rodney Harrison	.05
88	Roman Phifer	.05
89	Warren Moon	.10
90	Thurman Thomas	.10
91	Michael McCrary	.05
92	Dana Stubblefield	.05
93	Andre Hastings	.05
94	William Fuller	.05
95	Jeff Hostetler	.05
96	Danny Kanell	.05
97	Mark Fields	.05
98	Eddie Robinson	.05
99	Daryl Gardener	.05
100	Drew Bledsoe	1.00
101	Winslow Oliver	.05
102	Raymont Harris	.05
103	LeShon Johnson	.05
104	Byron Morris	.05
105	Herman Moore	.20
106	Keith Jackson	.05
107	Chris Penn	.05
108	Robert Griffith	.05
109	Jeff Burris	.05
110	Troy Aikman	1.00
111	Allen Aldridge	.05
112	Mel Gray	.05
113	Aaron Bailey	.05
114	Michael Strahan	.05
115	Adrian Murrell	.05
116	Chris Mims	.05
117	Robert Jones	.05
118	Derrick Brooks	.05
119	Tom Carter	.05
120	Carl Pickens	.05
121	Tony Brackens	.05
122	O.J. McDuffie	.05
123	Napoleon Kaufman	.05
124	Chris T. Jones	.05
125	Kordell Stewart	.75
126	Ray Zellars	.05
127	Jessie Tuggle	.05
128	Greg Kragen	.05
129	Brett Perriman	.05
130	Steve Young	.50
131	Willie Clay	.05
132	Kimble Anders	.05
133	Eugene Daniel	.05
134	Jevon Langford	.05
135	Shannon Sharpe	.05
136	Wayne Simmons	.05
137	Leeland McElroy	.05
138	Mike Caldwell	.05
139	Eric Moulds	.10
140	Eddie George	1.00
141	Jamal Anderson	.30
142	Michael Timpson	.05
143	Tony Tolbert	.05
144	Robert Smith	.05
145	Mike Alstott	.10
146	Gary Jones	.05
147	Terrance Shaw	.05
148	Carlton Gray	.05
149	Kevin Carter	.05
150	Darrell Green	.05
151	David Dunn	.05
152	Ken Norton	.05
153	Chad Brown	.05
154	Pat Swilling	.05
155	Irving Fryar	.05
156	Michael Haynes	.05
157	Shawn Jefferson	.05
158	Steve Grant	.05
159	James Stewart	.05
160	Derrick Thomas	.05
161	Tim Bowens	.05
162	Dixon Edwards	.05
163	Michael Barrow	.05
164	Antonio Freeman	.10
165	Terrell Davis	1.25
166	Henry Ellard	.05
167	Daryl Johnston	.05
168	Bryan Cox	.05
169	Chad Cota	.05
170	Vinny Testaverde	.05
171	Andre Reed	.05
172	Larry Centers	.05
173	Craig Heyward	.05
174	Glyn Milburn	.05
175	Hardy Nickerson	.05
176	Corey Miller	.05
177	Bobby Houston	.05
178	Marco Coleman	.05
179	Winston Moss	.05
180	Tony Banks	.30
181	Jeff Lageman	.05
182	Jason Belser	.05
183	James Jett	.05
184	Wayne Martin	.05
185	David Meggett	.05
186	Terrell Owens	.50
187	Willie Williams	.05
188	Eric Turner	.05
189	Chuck Smith	.05
190	Simeon Rice	.05
191	Kevin Greene	.05
192	Lance Johnston	.05
193	Marty Carter	.05
194	Ricardo McDonald	.05
195	Michael Irvin	.10
196	George Koonce	.05
197	Robert Porcher	.05
198	Mark Collins	.05
199	Louis Oliver	.05
200	John Elway	.50
201	Jake Reed	.05
202	Rodney Hampton	.05
203	Aaron Glenn	.05
204	Mike Mamula	.05
205	Terry Allen	.05
206	John Lynch	.05
207	Todd Lyght	.05
208	Dean Wells	.05
209	Aaron Hayden	.05
210	Blaine Bishop	.05
211	Bert Emanuel	.05
212	Mark Carrier	.05
213	Dale Carter	.05
214	Jimmy Smith	.05
215	Jim Harbaugh	.05
216	Jeff George	.05
217	Anthony Newman	.05
218	Ty Law	.05
219	Brent Jones	.05
220	Emmitt Smith	2.00
221	Bennie Blades	.05
222	Alfred Williams	.05
223	Eugene Robinson	.05
224	Fred Barnett	.05
225	Errict Rhett	.20
226	Leslie O'Neal	.05

227	Michael Sinclair	.05
228	Marvcus Patton	.05
229	Darrien Gordon	.05
230	Jerome Bettis	.10
231	Troy Vincent	.05
232	Ray Mickens	.05
233	Lonnie Johnson	.05
234	Charles Way	.05
235	Chris Sanders	.05
236	Bracey Walker	.05
237	Dave Krieg	.05
238	Kent Graham	.05
239	Ray Lewis	.05
240	Cris Carter	.05
241	Elvis Grbac	.05
242	Eric Davis	.05
243	Harvey Williams	.05
244	Eric Allen	.05
245	Bryant Young	.05
246	Terrell Fletcher	.05
247	Darren Perry	.05
248	Ken Harvey	.05
249	Marvin Washington	.05
250	Marcus Allen	.10
251	Darrin Smith	.05
252	James Francis	.05
253	Michael Jackson	.05
254	Ryan McNeil	.05
255	Mark Chmura	.10
256	Keenan McCardell	.05
257	Tony Bennett	.05
258	Irving Spikes	.05
259	Jason Dunn	.05
260	Joey Galloway	.25
261	Eddie Kennison	.40
262	Lonnie Marts	.05
263	Thomas Lewis	.05
264	Tedy Bruschi	.05
265	Steve Atwater	.05
266	Dorsey Levens	.20
267	Kurt Schulz	.05
268	Rob Moore	.05
269	Walt Harris	.05
270	Steve McNair	.75
271	Bill Romanowski	.05
272	Sean Dawkins	.05
273	Don Beebe	.05
274	Fernando Smith	.05
275	Willie McGinest	.05
276	Levon Kirkland	.05
277	Tony Martin	.05
278	Warren Sapp	.05
279	Lamar Smith	.05
280	Mark Brunell	1.00
281	Jim Everett	.05
282	Victor Green	.05
283	Mike Jones	.05
284	Charlie Garner	.05
285	Karim Abdul-Jabbar	.75
286	Michael Westbrook	.10
287	Lawrence Phillips	.10
288	Amani Toomer	.05
289	Neil Smith	.05
290	Barry Sanders	1.00
291	Willie Davis	.05
292	Bo Orlando	.05
293	Alonzo Spellman	.05
294	Eric Hill	.05
295	Wesley Walls	.05
296	Todd Collins	.05
297	Stevon Moore	.05
298	Eric Metcalf	.05
299	Darren Woodson	.05
300	Jerry Rice	1.00
301	Scott Mitchell	.05
302	Ray Crockett	.05
303	Jim Schwantz	.05
304	Steve Tovar	.05
305	Terance Mathis	.05
306	Earnest Byner	.05
307	Chris Spielman	.05
308	Curtis Conway	.10
309	Chris Dishman	.05
310	Marvin Harrison	.40
311	Sam Mills	.05
312	Brent Alexander	.05
313	Shawn Wooden	.05
314	DeWayne Washington	.05
315	Terry Glenn	1.00
316	Winfred Tubbs	.05
317	Dave Brown	.05
318	Neil O'Donnell	.05
319	Anthony Parker	.05
320	Junior Seau	.10
321	Brian Mitchell	.05
322	Regan Upshaw	.05
323	Darryl Williams	.05
324	Chris Doleman	.05
325	Rod Woodson	.05
326	Derrick Witherspoon	.05
327	Chester McGlockton	.05

328	Mickey Washington	.05
329	Greg Hill	.05
330	Reggie White	.10
331	John Copeland	.05
332	Doug Evans	.05
333	Lamar Lathon	.05
334	Mark Maddox	.05
335	Natrone Means	.10
336	Corey Widmer	.05
337	Terry Wooden	.05
338	Merton Hanks	.05
339	Cortez Kennedy	.05
340	Tyrone Hughes	.05
341	Tim Brown	.05
342	John Jurkovic	.05
343	Carnell Lake	.05
344	Stanley Richard	.05
345	Darryll Lewis	.05
346	Dan Wilkinson	.05
347	Broderick Thomas	.05
348	Brian Williams	.05
349	Eric Swann	.05
350	Dan Marino	2.00
351	Anthony Johnson	.05
352	Joe Cain	.05
353	Quinn Early	.05
354	Seth Joyner	.05
355	Garrison Hearst	.05
356	Edgar Bennett	.05
357	Brian Washington	.05
358	Kevin Hardy	.05
359	Quentin Coryatt	.05
360	Tim McDonald	.05
361	Brian Blades	.05
362	Courtney Hawkins	.05
363	Ray Farmer	.05
364	Jesse Armstead	.05
365	Curtis Martin	1.25
366	Zach Thomas	.30
367	Frank Wycheck	.05
368	Darnay Scott	.05
369	Percy Ellsworth	.05
370	Desmond Howard	.05
371	Aeneas Williams	.05
372	Bryce Paup	.05
373	Michael Bates	.05
374	Brad Johnson	.05
375	Jeff Blake	.25
376	Donnell Woolford	.05
377	Mo Lewis	.05
378	Phillippi Sparks	.05
379	Michael Bankston	.05
380	LeRoy Butler	.05
381	Tyrone Poole	.05
382	Wayne Chrebet	.05
383	Chris Slade	.05
384	Checklist 1	.05
385	Checklist 2	.05
386	*Will Blackwell*	.75
387	*Tom Knight*	.10
388	*Darnell Autry*	1.50
389	*Bryant Westbrook*	.50
390	*David LaFleur*	1.25
391	*Antowain Smith*	3.00
392	*Kevin Lockett*	.75
393	*Rae Carruth*	2.25
394	*Renaldo Wynn*	.10
395	*Jim Druckenmiller*	4.00
396	*Kenny Holmes*	.10
397	*Shawn Springs*	1.00
398	*Troy Davis*	3.50
399	*Dwayne Rudd*	.10
400	*Orlando Pace*	1.25
401	*Byron Hanspard*	1.75
402	*Corey Dillon*	2.00
403	*Walter Jones*	.10
404	*Reidel Anthony*	3.00
405	*Peter Boulware*	.10
406	*Reinard Wilson*	.10
407	*Pat Barnes*	1.25
408	*Yatil Green*	2.50
409	*Joey Kent*	.75
410	*Ike Hilliard*	3.00
411	*Jake Plummer*	2.00
412	*Darrell Russell*	.10
413	*James Farrior*	.10
414	*Tony Gonzalez*	1.50
415	*Warrick Dunn*	7.00

1997 Topps Hall of Fame Autograph

This four-card insert featured autographs from the four current Hall of Fame inductees and carried an "HF" prefix on the card back. The Haynes and Webster cards were inserted one per 436 hobby packs (1:120 jumbo), Mara was inserted one per 872 hobby packs (1:240 jumbo) and the Shula card was seeded one per 290 hobby packs (1:80 jumbo).

		MT
	Complete Set (4):	200.00
	Common Player:	25.00
1	Don Shula	80.00
2	Wellington Mara	75.00
3	Mike Webster	25.00
4	Mike Haynes	30.00

1997 Topps Career Best

This chase set includes Dan Marino, two cards of Marcus Allen, Reggie White and Jerry Rice.

		MT
	Complete Set (5):	50.00
	Common Player:	7.00
1	Dan Marino	25.00
2	Marcus Allen	7.00
3	Marcus Allen	7.00
4	Reggie White	7.00
5	Jerry Rice	12.00

1997 Topps Hall Bound

This 15-card set was inserted 1:36 hobby packs. The embossed cards were produced on die-cut mirrorboard.

	MT
Complete Set (15):	100.00
Common Player:	3.00
HB1 Jerry Rice	12.00
HB2 Rod Woodson	3.00
HB3 Marcus Allen	3.00
HB4 Reggie White	3.00
HB5 Emmitt Smith	20.00
HB6 Junior Seau	3.00
HB7 Troy Aikman	12.00
HB8 Bruce Smith	3.00
HB9 John Elway	8.00
HB10 Brett Favre	25.00
HB11 Thurman Thomas	3.00
HB12 Deion Sanders	6.00
HB13 Dan Marino	20.00
HB14 Steve Young	8.00
HB15 Barry Sanders	12.00

1997 Topps High Octane

Inserted 1:36 packs, the 15-card chase set includes "High Octane" at the top front of the cards, with the player's photo superimposed over a uniluster back. The team's logo is in the lower left, with the player's name in the lower right. The backs, which are numbered with an "HO" prefix, have the player's bio on the upper left, with his photo in the upper right. Four bar graphs are included in the center, with his highlights in the lower left.

	MT
Complete Set (15):	120.00
Common Player:	3.00
HO1 Brett Favre	25.00
HO2 Jerome Bettis	3.00
HO3 Jerry Rice	12.00
HO4 Junior Seau	3.00
HO5 Emmitt Smith	20.00
HO6 Herman Moore	3.00
HO7 Shannon Sharpe	3.00
HO8 Curtis Martin	12.00
HO9 Eddie George	12.00
HO10 Barry Sanders	12.00
HO11 John Elway	8.00
HO12 Steve Young	8.00
HO13 Drew Bledsoe	12.00
HO14 Troy Aikman	12.00
HO15 Dan Marino	20.00

1997 Topps Mystery Finest

The Mystery Finest chase set features 20 Pro Bowl players pictured three different ways, in their team's away jersey (bronze card, 1:36 packs), the team's home uniform (silver card, 1:108) and their Pro Bowl jersey (gold card, 1:324). Bronze Refractor parallels are found 1:144, silver Refractors are located 1:432 and a Gold Refractor is seeded 1:1,296 packs.

	MT
Complete Set (20):	130.00
Common Player:	3.00
Bronze Refractors:	2x-3x
Silver Cards:	2x
Silver Refractors:	5x
Gold Cards:	8x
Gold Refractors:	12x-24x
M1 Barry Sanders	12.00
M2 Mark Brunell	12.00
M3 Terrell Davis	12.00
M4 Isaac Bruce	6.00
M5 Jerry Rice	12.00
M6 Drew Bledsoe	12.00
M7 Carl Pickens	3.00
M8 Steve Young	8.00
M9 Cris Carter	3.00
M10 John Elway	8.00
M11 Junior Seau	3.00
M12 Herman Moore	3.00
M13 Vinny Testaverde	3.00
M14 Jerome Bettis	3.00
M15 Troy Aikman	12.00
M16 Reggie White	3.00
M17 Kerry Collins	12.00
M18 Curtis Martin	12.00
M19 Shannon Sharpe	3.00
M20 Brett Favre	25.00

1997 Topps Season's Best

The 25-card chase set was seeded 1:16 packs. The set honors players in five different categories, rushing leaders (Thunder and Lightning), passing experts (Air Command), receiving specialists (Special Delivery), sack masters (Demolition Men) and all-purpose yardage gainers (Magicians).

		MT
Complete Set (25):		75.00
Common Player:		.75
1	Mark Brunell	8.00
	(Air Command)	
2	Vinny Testaverde	.75
	(Air Command)	
3	Drew Bledsoe	8.00
	(Air Command)	
4	Brett Favre (Air Command)	16.00
5	Jeff Blake (Air Command)	1.50
6	Barry Sanders	8.00
	(Thunder & Lightning)	
7	Terrell Davis	8.00
	(Thunder & Lightning)	
8	Jerome Bettis	1.50
	(Thunder & Lightning)	
9	Ricky Watters	.75
	(Thunder & Lightning)	
10	Eddie George	10.00
	(Thunder & Lightning)	
11	Brian Mitchell (Magicians)	.75
12	Tyrone Hughes (Magicians)	.75
13	Eric Metcalf (Magicians)	.75
14	Glyn Milburn (Magicians)	.75
15	Ricky Watters (Magicians)	.75
16	Kevin Greene	.75
	(Demolition Men)	
17	Lamar Lathon	.75
	(Demolition Men)	
18	Bruce Smith	.75
	(Demolition Men)	
19	Michael Sinclair	.75
	(Demolition Men)	
20	Derrick Thomas	.75
	(Demolition Men)	
21	Jerry Rice	8.00
	(Special Delivery)	
22	Herman Moore	.75
	(Special Delivery)	
23	Carl Pickens	.75
	(Special Delivery)	
24	Cris Carter	.75
	(Special Delivery)	
25	Brett Perriman	.75
	(Special Delivery)	

1997 Topps Underclassmen

Inserted 1:24 retail packs, the 10-card set is comprised of first and second-year players. The "Underclassmen" logo is at the top center, with the player's photo superimposed over a multicolored holographic background. The player's name is printed in holographic foil at the bottom center. The backs, which are numbered with an "N" prefix, have the player's photo, name, bio, highlights and stats.

		MT
Complete Set (10):		75.00
Common Player:		2.50
U1	Kerry Collins	10.00
U2	Karim Abdul-Jabbar	10.00
U3	Simeon Rice	2.50
U4	Keyshawn Johnson	5.00
U5	Eddie George	15.00
U6	Eddie Kennison	5.00
U7	Terry Glenn	12.00
U8	Kevin Hardy	2.50
U9	Steve McNair	8.00
U10	Kordell Stewart	10.00

1997 Finest

The 175-card Series I set has a numbering format that features card Nos. 1-100 labeled as Common, cards Nos. 101-150 as Uncommon and Nos. 151-175 as Rare. Each card also has a different number corresponding to its theme. The Finest themes are Masters, Bulldozers, Hitmen, Dynamos and Field Generals. The numbering box on each card back indicates both sets of numbers, and which type of card it is, either Common, Uncommon or Rare. The card's theme is printed at the top of each card. Uncommon cards were seeded 1:4 packs, while Rare cards were inserted 1:24. Embossed Uncommon cards were seeded 1:16, while Embossed Die-Cut Rare cards were inserted 1:96. Embossed Die-Cut Rare cards were found 1:96.

		MT
Comp. Bronze Ser.1 (100):		25.00
Common Bronze Player:		.25
Comp. Silver Ser.1 (50):		250.00
Common Silver Player:		2.00
Embossed Silvers:		3x
Comp. Gold Ser.1 (25):		500.00
Common Gold Player:		7.50
Embossed Die-Cut Golds:		3x
Wax Box Series 1:		100.00
1	Mark Brunell	3.00
2	Chris Slade	.25
3	Chris Doleman	.25
4	Chris Hudson	.25
5	Karim Abdul-Jabbar	2.00
6	Darren Perry	.25
7	Daryl Johnston	.25
8	Rob Moore	.25
9	Robert Smith	.25
10	Terry Allen	.25
11	Jason Dunn	.25
12	Henry Thomas	.25
13	Rod Stephens	.25
14	Ray Mickens	.25
15	Ty Detmer	.25
16	Fred Barnett	.25
17	Derrick Alexander	.25
18	Marcus Robertson	.25
19	Robert Blackmon	.25
20	Isaac Bruce	.75
21	Chester McGlockton	.25
22	Stan Humphries	.25
23	Lonnie Marts	.25
24	Jason Sehorn	.25
25	Bobby Engram	.25
26	Brett Perriman	.25
27	Stevon Moore	.25
28	Jamal Anderson	.50
29	Wayne Martin	.25
30	Michael Irvin	.50
31	Thomas Smith	.25
32	Tony Brackens	.25
33	Eric Davis	.25
34	James Stewart	.25
35	Ki-Jana Carter	.25
36	Ken Norton	.25
37	William Thomas	.25
38	Tim Brown	.25
39	Lawrence Phillips	.50
40	Ricky Watters	.50
41	Tony Bennett	.25
42	Jesse Armstead	.25
43	Trent Dilfer	.25
44	Rodney Hampton	.25
45	Sam Mills	.25
46	Rodney Harrison	.25
47	Rob Fredrickson	.25
48	Eric Hill	.25
49	Bennie Blades	.25
50	Eddie George	5.00
51	Dave Brown	.25
52	Raymont Harris	.25
53	Steve Tovar	.25
54	Thurman Thomas	.50
55	Leeland McElroy	.25
56	Brian Mitchell	.25
57	Eric Allen	.25
58	Vinny Testaverde	.25
59	Marvin Washington	.25
60	Junior Seau	.25
61	Bert Emanuel	.25
62	Kevin Carter	.25
63	Mark Carrier	.25
64	Andre Coleman	.25
65	Chris Warren	.25
66	Aeneas Williams	.25
67	Eugene Robinson	.25
68	Darren Woodson	.25
69	Anthony Johnson	.25
70	Terry Glenn	2.50
71	Troy Vincent	.25
72	John Copeland	.25
73	Warren Sapp	.25
74	Bobby Hebert	.25
75	Jeff Hostetler	.25
76	Willie Davis	.25
77	Mickey Washington	.25
78	Cortez Kennedy	.25
79	Michael Strahan	.25
80	Jerome Bettis	.50
81	Andre Hastings	.25
82	Simeon Rice	.25
83	Cornelius Bennett	.25
84	Napoleon Kaufman	.25
85	Jim Harbaugh	.25
86	Aaron Hayden	.25
87	Gus Frerotte	.25
88	Jeff Blake	.50
89	Anthony Miller	.25
90	Deion Sanders	1.75
91	Curtis Conway	.25
92	William Floyd	.25
93	Eric Moulds	.25
94	Mel Gray	.25
95	Andre Rison	.25
96	Eugene Daniel	.25
97	Jason Belser	.25
98	Mike Mamula	.25
99	Jim Everett	.25
100	Checklist	.25
101	Drew Bledsoe S	12.00
102	Shannon Sharpe S	2.00
103	Ken Harvey S	2.00
104	Isaac Bruce S	5.00
105	Terry Allen S	2.00
106	Lawyer Milloy S	2.00
107	Ashley Ambrose S	2.00
108	Alfred Williams S	2.00
109	Hugh Douglas S	2.00
110	Junior Seau S	4.00
111	Kordell Stewart S	12.00
112	Adrian Murrell S	2.00
113	Byron Morris S	2.00
114	Terrell Buckley S	2.00
115	Dan Marino S	25.00
116	Willie Clay S	2.00
117	Neil Smith S	2.00
118	Blaine Bishop S	2.00
119	John Mobley S	2.00
120	Herman Moore S	4.00
121	Keyshawn Johnson S	6.00
122	Boomer Esiason S	2.00
123	Marshall Faulk S	5.00
124	Keith Jackson S	2.00
125	Ricky Watters S	4.00
126	Carl Pickens S	4.00
127	Cris Carter S	2.00
128	Mike Alstott S	4.00
129	Simeon Rice S	2.00
130	Troy Aikman S	12.00
131	Tamarick Vanover S	4.00
132	Marquez Pope S	2.00
133	Winslow Oliver S	2.00
134	Edgar Bennett S	2.00
135	David Meggett S	2.00
136	Marcus Allen S	4.00
137	Jerry Rice S	12.00
138	Steve Atwater S	2.00
139	Tim McDonald S	2.00
140	Barry Sanders S	12.00
141	Eddie George S	18.00
142	Wesley Walls S	2.00
143	Jerome Bettis S	4.00
144	Kevin Greene S	2.00
145	Terrell Davis S	15.00
146	Gus Frerotte S	2.00
147	Joey Galloway S	6.00
148	Vinny Testaverde S	2.00
149	Hardy Nickerson S	2.00
150	Brett Favre S	25.00
151	Desmond Howard G	7.50
152	Keyshawn Johnson G	15.00
153	Tony Banks G	15.00
154	Chris Spielman G	7.50
155	Reggie White G	15.00
156	Zach Thomas G	15.00
157	Carl Pickens G	7.50
158	Karim Abdul-Jabbar G	20.00
159	Chad Brown G	7.50
160	Kerry Collins G	40.00
161	Marvin Harrison G	15.00
162	Steve Young G	25.00
163	Deion Sanders G	20.00
164	Trent Dilfer G	7.50
165	Barry Sanders G	40.00
166	Cris Carter G	7.50
167	Keenan McCardell G	7.50
168	Terry Glenn G	30.00
169	Emmitt Smith G	80.00
170	John Elway G	25.00
171	Jerry Rice G	40.00
172	Troy Aikman G	40.00
173	Curtis Martin G	50.00
174	Darrell Green G	7.50
175	Mark Brunell G	40.00

1997 Finest Refractors

Each of the 175 base cards has a parallel Refractor. Refractor Common cards were inserted 1:12 packs, while Refractor Uncommon were seeded 1:18. Refractor Rare could be found 1:288 packs. In addition, Refractors of the Embossed and Embossed Die-Cut cards were also randomly seeded. An Embossed Uncommon Refractor was inserted 1:192 packs, while an Embossed Die-Cut Refractor was seeded 1:1,152 packs.

		MT
Comp. Bronze Ser.1 (100):		375.00
Common Bronze Player:		3.00
Comp. Silver Ser.1 (50):		1300.00
Common Silver Player:		10.00
Embossed Silver Refractors:		3x
Comp. Gold Ser.1 (25):		2500.
Common Gold Player:		40.00
Embossed DC Gold Refractors:		3x
1	Mark Brunell	50.00
2	Chris Slade	3.00
3	Chris Doleman	3.00
4	Chris Hudson	3.00
5	Karim Abdul-Jabbar	30.00
6	Darren Perry	3.00
7	Daryl Johnston	3.00
8	Rob Moore	3.00
9	Robert Smith	3.00
10	Terry Allen	3.00
11	Jason Dunn	3.00
12	Henry Thomas	3.00
13	Rod Stephens	3.00
14	Ray Mickens	3.00

15	Ty Detmer	3.00
16	Fred Barnett	3.00
17	Derrick Alexander	3.00
18	Marcus Robertson	3.00
19	Robert Blackmon	3.00
20	Isaac Bruce	10.00
21	Chester McGlockton	3.00
22	Stan Humphries	3.00
23	Lonnie Marts	3.00
24	Jason Sehorn	3.00
25	Bobby Engram	3.00
26	Brett Perriman	3.00
27	Stevon Moore	3.00
28	Jamal Anderson	6.00
29	Wayne Martin	3.00
30	Michael Irvin	6.00
31	Thomas Smith	3.00
32	Tony Brackens	3.00
33	Eric Davis	3.00
34	James Stewart	3.00
35	Ki-Jana Carter	3.00
36	Ken Norton	3.00
37	William Thomas	3.00
38	Tim Brown	3.00
39	Lawrence Phillips	6.00
40	Ricky Watters	6.00
41	Tony Bennett	3.00
42	Jesse Armstead	3.00
43	Trent Dilfer	3.00
44	Rodney Hampton	3.00
45	Sam Mills	3.00
46	Rodney Harrison	3.00
47	Rob Fredrickson	3.00
48	Eric Hill	3.00
49	Bennie Blades	3.00
50	Eddie George	50.00
51	Dave Brown	3.00
52	Raymont Harris	3.00
53	Steve Tovar	3.00
54	Thurman Thomas	6.00
55	Leeland McElroy	3.00
56	Brian Mitchell	3.00
57	Eric Allen	3.00
58	Vinny Testaverde	3.00
59	Marvin Washington	3.00
60	Junior Seau	3.00
61	Bert Emanuel	3.00
62	Kevin Carter	3.00
63	Mark Carrier	3.00
64	Andre Coleman	3.00
65	Chris Warren	3.00
66	Aeneas Williams	3.00
67	Eugene Robinson	3.00
68	Darren Woodson	3.00
69	Anthony Johnson	3.00
70	Terry Glenn	40.00
71	Troy Vincent	3.00
72	John Copeland	3.00
73	Warren Sapp	3.00
74	Bobby Hebert	3.00
75	Jeff Hostetler	3.00
76	Willie Davis	3.00
77	Mickey Washington	3.00
78	Cortez Kennedy	3.00
79	Michael Strahan	3.00
80	Jerome Bettis	6.00
81	Andre Hastings	3.00
82	Simeon Rice	3.00
83	Cornelius Bennett	3.00
84	Napoleon Kaufman	3.00
85	Jim Harbaugh	3.00
86	Aaron Hayden	3.00
87	Gus Frerotte	3.00
88	Jeff Blake	6.00
89	Anthony Miller	3.00
90	Deion Sanders	25.00
91	Curtis Conway	3.00
92	William Floyd	3.00
93	Eric Moulds	3.00
94	Mel Gray	3.00
95	Andre Rison	3.00
96	Eugene Daniel	3.00
97	Jason Belser	3.00
98	Mike Mamula	3.00
99	Jim Everett	3.00
100	Checklist	3.00
101	Drew Bledsoe S	80.00
102	Shannon Sharpe S	10.00
103	Ken Harvey S	10.00
104	Isaac Bruce S	30.00
105	Terry Allen S	10.00
106	Lawyer Milloy S	10.00
107	Ashley Ambrose S	10.00
108	Alfred Williams S	10.00
109	Hugh Douglas S	10.00
110	Junior Seau S	20.00
111	Kordell Stewart S	80.00
112	Adrian Murrell S	10.00
113	Byron Morris S	10.00
114	Terrell Buckley S	10.00
115	Dan Marino S	150.00

116	Willie Clay S	10.00
117	Neil Smith S	10.00
118	Blaine Bishop S	10.00
119	John Mobley S	10.00
120	Herman Moore S	20.00
121	Keyshawn Johnson S	40.00
122	Boomer Esiason S	10.00
123	Marshall Faulk S	30.00
124	Keith Jackson S	10.00
125	Ricky Watters S	20.00
126	Carl Pickens S	20.00
127	Cris Carter S	10.00
128	Mike Alstott S	20.00
129	Simeon Rice S	10.00
130	Troy Aikman S	80.00
131	Tamarick Vanover S	20.00
132	Marquez Pope S	10.00
133	Winslow Oliver S	10.00
134	Edgar Bennett S	10.00
135	David Meggett S	10.00
136	Marcus Allen S	20.00
137	Jerry Rice S	80.00
138	Steve Atwater S	10.00
139	Tim McDonald S	10.00
140	Barry Sanders S	80.00
141	Eddie George S	90.00
142	Wesley Walls S	10.00
143	Jerome Bettis S	20.00
144	Kevin Greene S	10.00
145	Terrell Davis S	100.00
146	Gus Frerotte S	10.00
147	Joey Galloway S	40.00
148	Vinny Testaverde S	10.00
149	Hardy Nickerson S	10.00
150	Brett Favre S	150.00
151	Desmond Howard G	40.00
152	Keyshawn Johnson G	80.00
153	Tony Banks G	80.00
154	Chris Spielman G	40.00
155	Reggie White G	80.00
156	Zach Thomas G	80.00
157	Carl Pickens G	40.00
158	Karim Abdul-Jabbar G	100.00
159	Chad Brown G	40.00
160	Kerry Collins G	200.00
161	Marvin Harrison G	80.00
162	Steve Young G	125.00
163	Deion Sanders G	100.00
164	Trent Dilfer G	40.00
165	Barry Sanders G	200.00
166	Cris Carter G	40.00
167	Keenan McCardell G	40.00
168	Terry Glenn G	150.00
169	Emmitt Smith G	400.00
170	John Elway G	125.00
171	Jerry Rice G	200.00
172	Troy Aikman G	200.00
173	Curtis Martin G	250.00
174	Darrell Green G	40.00
175	Mark Brunell G	200.00

1997 Stadium Club

The 170-card Series I set included a full-bleed photo on the front, with the Stadium Club logo at the top and a "wave" on the bottom that included the player's name and position. The backs included an action shot, with the player's name, bio and highlights on the left side in a "ripped out" area. The stats appear in a box in the lower right, along with one highlight. There are three parallel sets. Printing Plates (cyan, yellow, magenta and black plates of each card for a total of 640 cards) were inserted in Home Team Advan-

tage packs. One-of-a-Kind parallel cards were seeded 1:48 packs, while First Day Issue parallel cards were found 1:24 retail packs.

		MT
Complete Set (170):		25.00
Common Player:		.10
One Of A Kind Stars:		30x-60x
One Of A Kind Rookies:		15x-30x
Wax Box:		65.00
1	Junior Seau	.20
3	Marcus Allen	.20
5	*Darnell Autry*	.75
7	Darrell Green	.10
9	Steve Atwater	.10
11	Tony Brackens	.10
13	Henry Ellard	.10
15	*Jim Druckenmiller*	2.50
17	Terrell Davis	1.25
19	Derrick Thomas	.10
21	Deion Sanders	.50
23	Jake Reed	.10
25	Jerome Bettis	.20
27	Terry Allen	.10
29	Steve McNair	.75
31	Thurman Thomas	.20
33	Karim Abdul-Jabbar	.75
35	Jerry Rice	1.25
37	Errict Rhett	.20
39	Tim Brown	.10
41	Jim Harbaugh	.10
43	Kevin Greene	.10
45	Troy Aikman	1.25
47	Shannon Sharpe	.10
49	Mark Brunell	1.25
51	*Byron Hanspard*	1.00
53	Wayne Chrebet	.10
55	Barry Sanders	1.25
57	Ricky Watters	.20
59	Chris Warren	.10
61	*Peter Boulware*	.10
63	Eddie Kennison	.50
65	Brett Favre	3.00
67	Larry Centers	.10
69	Stevon Moore	.10
71	Bryce Paup	.10
73	Rashaan Salaam	.20
75	Drew Bledsoe	1.25
77	Joe Bowden	.10
79	Zach Thomas	.30
81	Daryl Johnston	.10
83	James Stewart	.10
85	*Shawn Springs*	1.00
87	Levon Kirkland	.10
89	Terrell Fletcher	.10
91	Jessie Tuggle	.10
93	Wayne Martin	.10
95	Mark Collins	.10
97	Napoleon Kaufman	.10
99	Ty Detmer	.10
101	William Floyd	.10
103	Robert Blackmon	.10
105	Warren Sapp	.10
107	Brian Mitchell	.10
109	Derrick Alexander	.10
111	James Farrior	.10
113	Marty Carter	.10
115	Wesley Walls	.10
117	Roman Phifer	.10
119	Henry Thomas	.10
121	Ty Law	.10
123	Kevin Williams	.10
125	Antonio Freeman	.30
127	*Pat Barnes*	.75
129	Irving Fryar	.10
131	Rodney Harrison	.10
133	Neil O'Donnell	.10
135	Jason Belser	.10
137	Seth Joyner	.10
139	Santana Dotson	.10
141	Terance Mathis	.10
143	John Mobley	.10
145	Herman Moore	.20
147	Chris Sanders	.10
149	Darrell Russell	.10
151	Tamarick Vanover	.10
153	Lamar Lathon	.10
155	Derrick Brooks	.10
157	Tim McDonald	.10
159	Terry McDaniel	.10
161	Phillippi Sparks	.10
163	*Bryant Westbrook*	.20
165	Jimmy Smith	.10
167	Frank Sanders	.10
169	Phil Hansen	.10
171	Mark Carrier	.10
173	Erik Kramer	.10
175	Tom Knight	.10
177	Robert Smith	.10
179	Chris Slade	.10

181	Mario Bates	.10
183	Mike Mamula	.10
185	Stan Humphries	.10
187	Kevin Carter	.10
189	Cortez Kennedy	.10
191	*Corey Dillon*	1.50
193	Bobby Hebert	.10
195	Ray Lewis	.10
197	Brian Williams	.10
199	*Jake Plummer*	1.00
201	Ashley Ambrose	.10
203	Mo Lewis	.10
205	Carnell Lake	.10
207	Dana Stubblefield	.10
209	*Ike Hilliard*	2.00
211	Hardy Nickerson	.10
213	Marcus Robertson	.10
215	Kent Graham	.10
217	*Will Blackwell*	.50
219	Eric Moulds	.20
221	Anthony Johnson	.10
223	Darrin Smith	.10
225	Marvin Harrison	.50
227	Joe Aska	.10
229	William Fuller	.10
231	Brian Blades	.10
233	Ken Harvey	.10
235	Simeon Rice	.10
237	Bert Emanuel	.10
239	Chris Calloway	.10
241	Alonzo Spellman	.10
243	*Antowain Smith*	1.25
245	Ray Crockett	.10
247	Glyn Milburn	.10
249	O.J. McDuffie	.10
251	Jim Everett	.10
253	Jessie Armstead	.10
255	Ken Norton	.10
257	Courtney Hawkins	.10
259	Todd Lyght	.10
261	Aaron Glenn	.10
263	*Troy Davis*	2.00
265	Darrien Gordon	.10
267	John Randle	.10
269	Mickey Washington	.10
271	Steve Grant	.10
273	Derrick Witherspoon	.10
275	Ben Coates	.10
277	Jim Schwantz	.10
279	Ryan McNeil	.10
281	Craig Newsome	.10
283	Michael Bankston	.10
285	Byron Morris	.10
287	*David LaFleur*	.75
289	Eric Davis	.10
291	Steve Tovar	.10
293	Alfred Williams	.10
295	Charles Johnson	.10
297	Merton Hanks	.10
299	Keith Jackson	.10
301	Tony Banks	.30
303	Bobby Engram	.10
305	Lawyer Milloy	.10
307	*Joey Kent*	.50
309	DeWayne Washington	.10
311	Ki-Jana Carter	.10
313	Don Beebe	.10
315	Tyrone Wheatley	.10
317	Quinn Early	.10
319	Tim Bowens	.10
321	Ken Dilger	.10
323	Jevon Langford	.10
325	*Orlando Pace*	.75
327	Mike Tomczak	.10
329	Andre Reed	.10
331	Qadry Ismail	.10
333	Dave Brown	.10
335	Jamal Anderson	.20
337	Tyrone Hughes	.10
339	*Rae Carruth*	1.25

1997 Stadium Club Aerial Assault

The 10-card set was inserted 1:12 packs. A player photo is superimposed over a holographic background of the United States, with the team's city targeted. "Aerial Assault" is printed at the top left, while the Stadium Club logo and the player's name are in the lower right. The backs, which are numbered with an "AA" prefix, has the player photo on the left, with the player's name, team and 1996 passing stats all to the right.

	MT
Complete Set (10):	40.00
Common Player:	1.50
AA1 Dan Marino	10.00
AA2 Mark Brunell	5.00
AA3 Troy Aikman	5.00
AA4 Ty Detmer	1.50
AA5 John Elway	3.00
AA6 Drew Bledsoe	5.00
AA7 Steve Young	3.00
AA8 Vinny Testaverde	1.50
AA9 Kerry Collins	5.00
AA10Brett Favre	12.00

1997 Stadium Club Bowman's Best Previews

The 15-card set was a sneak peek at the 1997 set. The cards were inserted at a 1:24 rate. The foil cards have a Bowman's Best logo in the upper left, with the player's name and team logo in the lower right. The backs, which are numbered with a "BBP" prefix, have the player photo on the left, with his name, bio, stats and highlights on the right. A Refractor parallel version was seeded 1:96 packs, while an Atomic Refractor version was found 1:192 packs.

	MT
Complete Set (15):	110.00
Common Player:	3.00
Refractors:	2x-3x
Atomic Refractors:	3x-6x
BBP1Dan Marino	20.00
BBP2Terry Allen	3.00
BBP3Jerome Bettis	3.00
BBP4Kevin Greene	3.00
BBP5Junior Seau	3.00
BBP6Brett Favre	25.00
BBP7Isaac Bruce	6.00
BBP8Michael Irvin	3.00
BBP9Kerry Collins	12.00
BBP10Karim Abdul-Jabbar	10.00
BBP11Keenan McCardell	3.00
BBP12Ricky Watters	3.00
BBP13Mark Brunell	12.00
BBP14Jerry Rice	12.00
BBP15Drew Bledsoe	12.00

1997 Stadium Club Co-Signers

Seventy-two NFL players autographed these two-sided cards. There are 108 Co-Signers matchups, with roughly half in Series I and half in Series II.

		MT
1	Karim Abdul-Jabbar, Eddie George	400.00
4	Fred Barnett, Lake Dawson	75.00
5	Blaine Bishop, Darrell Green	75.00
6	Jeff Blake, Gus Frerotte	150.00
7	Steve Bono, Cris Carter	125.00
8	Tim Brown, Isaac Bruce	150.00
9	Wayne Chrebet, Mickey Washington	75.00
11	Eric Davis, Jason Sehorn	75.00
14	Stephen Grant, Marvcus Patton	75.00
17	Merton Hanks, Aeneas Williams	75.00
19	Brent Jones, Wesley Walls	75.00
20	Carnell Lake, Tim McDonald	75.00
21	Thomas Lewis, Keith Lyle	75.00
22	Leeland McElroy, Jeff Lageman	75.00
25	Stevon Moore, William Thomas	75.00
27	Simeon Rice, Winslow Oliver	75.00
28	Bill Romanowski, Gary Plummer	75.00
30	Chris Slade, Kevin Greene	75.00
34	Steve Tovar, Ellis Johnson	75.00
36	Darren Woodson, Aaron Glenn	75.00
39	Jeff Blake, Derrick Thomas	75.00
41	Cris Carter, Marvin Harrison	125.00
44	Lake Dawson, Ray Mickens	50.00
48	Eddie George, Terrell Davis	250.00
49	Aaron Glenn, Eric Davis	50.00
50	Kent Graham, Steve Tovar	50.00
51	Darrell Green, Carnell Lake	50.00
52	Kevin Greene, Steve Atwater	50.00
54	Kevin Hardy, Merton Hanks	50.00
55	Desmond Howard, Tim Brown	80.00
56	Eddie Kennison, Brent Jones	100.00
57	Levon Kirkland, Simeon Rice	50.00
58	Jeff Lageman, Adrian Murrell	75.00
59	Keith Lyle, Wayne Chrebet	50.00
60	David Meggett, Herschel Walker	50.00
61	Herman Moore, Isaac Bruce	125.00
65	Thomas Randolph, Fred Barnett	50.00
67	Chris Spielman, Stevon Moore	50.00
69	Mike Tomczak, Trace Armstrong	50.00
72	Darren Woodson, Jason Sehorn	50.00
74	Isaac Bruce, Desmond Howard	75.00
75	Terrell Davis, Karim Abdul-Jabbar	250.00
77	Derrick Thomas, Gus Frerotte	40.00
78	Thurman Thomas, Eddie George	150.00
79	Steve Atwater, Chris Slade	25.00
80	Merton Hanks, Kevin Greene	25.00
81	Marvin Harrison, Steve Bono	75.00
82	Anthony Johnson, David Meggett	25.00
84	Herschel Walker, Rodney Hampton	25.00
85	Aeneas Williams, Kevin Hardy	25.00
87	Brent Jones, Curtis Conway	25.00
89	Tim McDonald, Darrell Green	25.00
90	Adrian Murrell, Leeland McElroy	40.00
91	Winslow Oliver, Levon Kirkland	25.00
92	Simeon Rice, Jeff Lageman	25.00
93	Wesley Walls, Eddie Kennison	50.00
98	Ray Mickens, Thomas Randolph	25.00
100	Marvcus Patton, Alonzo Spellman	25.00
104	Wayne Chrebet, Thomas Lewis	25.00
106	Ellis Johnson, Kent Graham	25.00

1997 Stadium Club Grid Kids

Inserted 1:36 packs, 20 1997 NFL Draft picks are showcased in their game uniforms in the set.

	MT
Complete Set (20):	150.00
Common Player:	4.00
GK1 Orlando Pace	8.00
GK2 Darrell Russell	4.00
GK3 Shawn Springs	8.00
GK4 Peter Boulware	4.00
GK5 Bryant Westbrook	8.00
GK6 Darnell Autry	8.00
GK7 Ike Hilliard	16.00
GK8 James Farrior	4.00
GK9 Jake Plummer	10.00
GK10Tony Gonzalez	10.00
GK11Yatil Green	14.00
GK12Corey Dillon	10.00
GK13Dwayne Rudd	4.00
GK14Renaldo Wynn	4.00
GK15David LaFleur	8.00
GK16Antowain Smith	10.00
GK17Jim Druckenmiller	20.00
GK18Rae Carruth	10.00
GK19Tom Knight	4.00
GK20Byron Hanspard	10.00

1997 Stadium Club Offensive Strikes

Inserted 1:12 packs, the top five running backs and wide receivers from 1996 are featured in this set. The cards are borderless foilboard.

	MT
Complete Set (10):	45.00
Common Player:	1.50
AF1 Jerry Rice (Air Force)	5.00
AF2 Carl Pickens (Air Force)	1.50
AF3 Shannon Sharpe (Air Force)	1.50
AF4 Herman Moore (Air Force)	1.50
AF5 Terry Glenn (Air Force)	5.00
GC1 Barry Sanders (Ground Control)	5.00
GC2 Curtis Martin (Ground Control)	5.00
GC3 Emmitt Smith (Ground Control)	10.00
GC4 Terrell Davis (Ground Control)	5.00
GC5 Eddie George (Ground Control)	8.00

1997 Stadium Club Triumvirate

Exclusive to retail packs, the laser-cut cards featured a trio of leading NFL offensive teammates fused together. There are six different complete cards made up of three players per, each player card is seeded at a 1:36 pack ratio. Refractor versions were found 1:96, while Atomic Refractor versions were seeded 1:192.

	MT
Complete Set (18):	200.00
Common Player:	5.00
Refractors:	2x-4x
Atomic Refractors:	3x-6x
T1A Emmitt Smith	30.00
T1B Troy Aikman	15.00
T1C Michael Irvin	5.00
T2A Curtis Martin	15.00
T2B Drew Bledsoe	15.00
T2C Terry Glenn	10.00
T3A Barry Sanders	15.00
T3B Scott Mitchell	5.00
T3C Herman Moore	5.00
T4A William Floyd	5.00
T4B Steve Young	10.00
T4C Jerry Rice	15.00
T5A Terrell Davis	15.00
T5B John Elway	10.00
T5C Shannon Sharpe	5.00
T6A Edgar Bennett	5.00
T6B Brett Favre	30.00
T6C Antonio Freeman	8.00

1997 Topps Stars

The 125-card set includes 100 NFL stars and 25 1997 NFL draft picks. Each card features diffraction and matte gold-foil stamping. The Always Mint parallel set was seeded 1:18 packs. Topps Stars was offered exclusively to Topps Home Team Advantage members.

		MT
Complete Set (125):		60.00
Common Player:		.10
Foil Stars:		15x-30x
Foil Rookies:		10x-20x
Wax Box:		60.00
1	Brett Favre	6.00
2	Michael Jackson	.10
3	Simeon Rice	.10
4	Thurman Thomas	.20
5	Karim Abdul-Jabbar	2.00
6	Marvin Harrison	1.25
7	John Elway	1.75
8	Carl Pickens	.20
9	Rod Woodson	.10
10	Kerry Collins	2.00
11	Cortez Kennedy	.10
12	William Fuller	.10
13	Michael Irvin	.20
14	Tyrone Braxton	.10
15	Steve Young	1.50
16	Keith Lyle	.10
17	Blaine Bishop	.10
18	Jeff Hostetler	.10
19	Levon Kirkland	.10
20	Barry Sanders	2.50
21	Deion Sanders	1.25
22	Jamal Anderson	.50
23	Eric Davis	.10
24	Hardy Nickerson	.10
25	LeRoy Butler	.10
26	Mark Brunell	2.50
27	Aeneas Williams	.10
28	Curtis Martin	2.50
29	Wayne Chrebet	.10
30	Jerry Rice	2.50
31	Jake Reed	.10
32	Wayne Martin	.10
33	Derrick Alexander	.10
34	Isaac Bruce	.50
35	Terrell Davis	2.50
36	Jerome Bettis	.20
37	Keenan McCardell	.10
38	Derrick Thomas	.10
39	Jason Sehorn	.10
40	Keyshawn Johnson	1.25
41	Jeff Blake	.30
42	Terry Allen	.10
43	Ben Coates	.10
44	William Thomas	.10
45	Bryce Paup	.10
46	Bryant Young	.10
47	Eric Swann	.10
48	Tim Brown	.10
49	Tony Martin	.10
50	Eddie George	3.00
51	Sam Mills	.10
52	Terry McDaniel	.10
53	Darren Woodson	.10
54	Ashley Ambrose	.10
55	Drew Bledsoe	2.50
56	Larry Centers	.10
57	Ty Detmer	.10
58	Merton Hanks	.10
59	Charles Johnson	.10
60	Dan Marino	5.00
61	Joey Galloway	.75
62	Junior Seau	.20
63	Brett Perriman	.10
64	Wesley Walls	.10
65	Chad Brown	.10
66	Henry Ellard	.10
67	Keith Jackson	.10
68	John Randle	.10
69	Chester McGlockton	.10
70	Emmitt Smith	5.00
71	Vinny Testaverde	.10
72	Steve Atwater	.10
73	Irving Fryar	.10
74	Gus Frerotte	.10
75	Terry Glenn	2.00
76	Anthony Johnson	.10
77	Jimmy Smith	.10
78	Terrell Buckley	.10
79	Kimble Anders	.10
80	Cris Carter	.20
81	David Meggett	.10
82	Shannon Sharpe	.10
83	Adrian Murrell	.20
84	Herman Moore	.50
85	Bruce Smith	.10
86	Lamar Lathon	.10
87	Ken Harvey	.10
88	Curtis Conway	.20
89	Alfred Williams	.10
90	Troy Aikman	2.50
91	Carnell Lake	.10
92	Michael Sinclair	.10
93	Ricky Watters	.20
94	Kevin Greene	.10
95	Reggie White	.20
96	Tyrone Hughes	.10
97	Dale Carter	.10
98	Rob Moore	.10
99	Tony Tolbert	.10
100	Willie McGinest	.10
101	*Orlando Pace*	1.00
102	*Yatil Green*	2.00
103	*Antowain Smith*	2.00
104	*David LaFleur*	1.25
105	*Jake Plummer*	1.75
106	*Will Blackwell*	.75
107	*Dwayne Rudd*	.20
108	*Corey Dillon*	2.00
109	*Pat Barnes*	1.50
110	*Peter Boulware*	.20
111	*Tony Gonzalez*	1.00
112	*Renaldo Wynn*	.20
113	*Darrell Russell*	.20
114	*Bryant Westbrook*	.20
115	*James Farrior*	.20
116	*Joey Kent*	1.25
117	*Rae Carruth*	2.00
118	*Jim Druckenmiller*	5.00
119	*Byron Hanspard*	2.00
120	*Ike Hilliard*	2.50
121	*Kevin Lockett*	.20
122	*Tom Knight*	.20
123	*Shawn Springs*	1.50
124	*Troy Davis*	3.50
125	*Darnell Autry*	1.50

1997 Topps Stars Future Pro Bowlers

Inserted 1:12 packs, the 15-card set features a player photo superimposed over a backdrop of Pro Bowl 1997 logos. The Topps Stars logo is in the upper left, while the Future Pro Bowlers logo is in the lower left. The player's name is to the right of the logo. The cards are numbered on the back with a prefix of "FPB".

		MT
Complete Set (15):		70.00
Common Player:		3.00
FPB1	Ike Hilliard	10.00
FPB2	Tom Knight	3.00
FPB3	David LaFleur	5.00
FPB4	Byron Hanspard	8.00
FPB5	Kevin Lockett	3.00
FPB6	Rae Carruth	6.00
FPB7	Jim Druckenmiller	15.00
FPB8	Darnell Autry	6.00
FPB9	Joey Kent	6.00
FPB10	Peter Boulware	3.00
FPB11	Orlando Pace	3.00
FPB12	Troy Davis	12.00
FPB13	Antowain Smith	8.00
FPB14	Bryant Westbrook	3.00
FPB15	Yatil Green	8.00

1997 Topps Stars Hall of Fame Rookie Reprints

The 10-card set was inserted 1:64 packs, while autographed versions were found 1:128 packs.

		MT
Complete Set (10):		50.00
Common Player:		5.00
Autographs:		3x-6x
1	George Blanda	5.00

2	Dick Butkus	10.00
3	Len Dawson	5.00
4	Jack Ham	5.00
5	Sam Huff	5.00
6	Deacon Jones	5.00
7	Ray Nitschke	5.00
8	Gale Sayers	10.00
9	Randy White	5.00
10	Kellen Winslow	5.00

1997 Topps Stars Pro Bowl Memories

The 10-card set was inserted 1:24 packs. The cards are laser cut through the middle with stars, which start small on the left and grow larger as the stars move to the right. The Pro Bowl logo is in the upper left, while "Pro Bowl Memories" and the player's name are printed vertically along the right border in the middle. The Topps Stars logo is in the lower right. The backs are numbered with a "PBM" prefix.

		MT
Complete Set (10):		75.00
Common Player:		3.00
PBM1	Barry Sanders	10.00
PBM2	Jeff Blake	6.00
PBM3	Ken Harvey	3.00
PBM4	Brett Favre	20.00
PBM5	Jerry Rice	10.00
PBM6	John Elway	8.00
PBM7	Marshall Faulk	3.00
PBM8	Steve Young	8.00
PBM9	Mark Brunell	10.00
PBM10	Troy Aikman	10.00

1997 Topps Stars Pro Bowl Stars

The 30-card set was inserted 1:24 packs. The card fronts feature a player photo superimposed over a uniluster background of the Pro Bowl 1997 logo and the NFC or AFC logo. The Topps Stars logo is in the upper left, while the Pro Bowl logo is in the lower left, with the player's name and position to the right. The backs are numbered with a prefix of "PB".

		MT
Complete Set (30):		400.00
Common Player:		6.00
PB1	Brett Favre	80.00
PB2	Mark Brunell	40.00
PB3	Kerry Collins	35.00
PB4	Drew Bledsoe	40.00
PB5	Barry Sanders	40.00
PB6	Terrell Davis	40.00
PB7	Terry Allen	6.00
PB8	Jerome Bettis	6.00
PB9	Ricky Watters	6.00
PB10	Curtis Martin	40.00
PB11	Emmitt Smith	70.00
PB12	Kimble Anders	6.00
PB13	Jerry Rice	40.00
PB14	Carl Pickens	6.00
PB15	Herman Moore	10.00
PB16	Tony Martin	6.00
PB17	Isaac Bruce	10.00
PB18	Tim Brown	6.00
PB19	Wesley Walls	6.00
PB20	Shannon Sharpe	6.00
PB21	Dana Stubblefield	6.00
PB22	Reggie White	10.00
PB23	Bruce Smith	6.00
PB24	Bryant Young	6.00
PB25	Junior Seau	6.00
PB26	Kevin Greene	6.00
PB27	Derrick Thomas	6.00
PB28	Chad Brown	6.00
PB29	Deion Sanders	25.00
PB30	Rod Woodson	6.00

1997 Upper Deck

The 300-card set includes subsets of Star Rookies (35 cards), Star Rookie Flashback (10 cards) and Game Dated Moments (30 cards). The base cards have the player's name printed vertically along the left border, with the Upper Deck logo and player's position in the lower left corner. The team's name is to the right of the Upper Deck logo on the card front.

		MT
Complete Set (300):		40.00
Common Player:		.10
1	*Orlando Pace*	.75
2	*Darrell Russell*	.10
3	*Shawn Springs*	1.00
4	*Bryant Westbrook*	.30
5	*Ike Hilliard*	1.75
6	*Peter Boulware*	.10
7	*Tom Knight*	.10
8	*Yatil Green*	1.50
9	*Tony Gonzalez*	1.00
10	*Reidel Anthony*	2.00
11	*Warrick Dunn*	3.00
12	*Kenny Holmes*	.10
13	*Jim Druckenmiller*	2.50
14	*James Farrior*	.10
15	*David LaFleur*	1.00
16	*Antowain Smith*	1.50
17	*Rae Carruth*	1.25
18	*Dwayne Rudd*	.10
19	*Jake Plummer*	1.00
20	*Reinard Wilson*	.10
21	*Byron Hanspard*	1.25
22	*Will Blackwell*	.50
23	*Troy Davis*	2.00
24	*Corey Dillon*	1.25
25	*Joey Kent*	.75
26	*Renaldo Wynn*	.10
27	*Pat Barnes*	1.00
28	*Kevin Lockett*	.10
29	*Darnell Autry*	1.00
30	*Walter Jones*	.10
31	Trevor Pryce	.10
32	Dan Marino SRF	2.00
33	Steve Young SRF	1.00
34	John Elway SRF	1.00

35	Jerry Rice SRF	1.00
36	Tim Brown SRF	.10
37	Deion Sanders SRF	.50
38	Troy Aikman SRF	1.00
39	Barry Sanders SRF	1.00
40	Emmitt Smith SRF	2.00
41	Junior Seau SRF	.10
42	Neil Smith	.10
43	Brett Perriman	.10
44	Jim Everett	.10
45	Qadry Ismail	.10
46	Dana Stubblefield	.10
47	Bryant Young	.10
48	Ken Norton Jr.	.10
49	Terrell Owens	.75
50	Jerry Rice	1.25
51	Steve Young	.75
52	Terry Kirby	.10
53	Chris Doleman	.10
54	Lee Woodall	.10
55	Merton Hanks	.10
56	Garrison Hearst	.10
57	Rashaan Salaam	.20
58	Raymont Harris	.10
59	Curtis Conway	.10
60	Bobby Engram	.10
61	Bryan Cox	.10
62	Walt Harris	.10
63	Tyrone Hughes	.10
64	Rick Mirer	.10
65	Jeff Blake	.20
66	Carl Pickens	.10
67	Darnay Scott	.10
68	Tony McGee	.10
69	Ki-Jana Carter	.10
70	Ashley Ambrose	.10
71	Dan Wilkinson	.10
72	Chris Spielman	.10
73	Todd Collins	.10
74	Andre Reed	.10
75	Quinn Early	.10
76	Eric Moulds	.10
77	Darrick Holmes	.10
78	Thurman Thomas	.20
79	Bruce Smith	.10
80	Bryce Paup	.10
81	John Elway	.75
82	Terrell Davis	1.25
83	Anthony Miller	.10
84	Shannon Sharpe	.10
85	Alfred Williams	.10
86	John Mobley	.10
87	Tory James	.10
88	Steve Atwater	.10
89	Darrien Gordon	.10
90	Mike Alstott	.10
91	Errict Rhett	.20
92	Trent Dilfer	.10
93	Courtney Hawkins	.10
94	Warren Sapp	.10
95	Regan Upshaw	.10
96	Hardy Nickerson	.10
97	Donnie Abraham	.10
98	Larry Centers	.10
99	Aeneas Williams	.10
100	Kent Graham	.10
101	Rob Moore	.10
102	Frank Sanders	.10
103	Leeland McElroy	.10
104	Eric Swann	.10
105	Simeon Rice	.10
106	Seth Joyner	.10
107	Stan Humphries	.10
108	Tony Martin	.10
109	Charlie Jones	.10
110	Andre Coleman ERR.#103	.10
111	Terrell Fletcher	.10
112	Junior Seau	.20
113	Eric Metcalf	.10
114	Chris Penn	.10
115	Marcus Allen	.20
116	Greg Hill	.10
117	Tamarick Vanover	.10
118	Lake Dawson	.10
119	Derrick Thomas	.10
120	Dale Carter	.10
121	Elvis Grbac	.10
122	Aaron Bailey	.10
123	Jim Harbaugh	.10
124	Marshall Faulk	.20
125	Sean Dawkins	.10
126	Marvin Harrison	.50
127	Ken Dilger	.10
128	Tony Bennett	.10
129	Jeff Herrod	.10
130	Chris Gardocki	.10
131	Cary Blanchard	.10
132	Troy Aikman	1.25
133	Emmitt Smith	2.50
134	Sherman Williams	.10
135	Michael Irvin	.20

136	Eric Bjornson	.10
137	Herschel Walker	.10
138	Tony Tolbert	.10
139	Deion Sanders	.50
140	Daryl Johnston	.10
141	Dan Marino	2.50
142	O.J. McDuffie	.10
143	Troy Drayton	.10
144	Karim Abdul-Jabbar	.75
145	Stanley Pritchett	.10
146	Fred Barnett	.10
147	Zach Thomas	.20
148	Sean Wooden	.10
149	Ty Detmer	.10
150	Derrick Witherspoon	.10
151	Ricky Watters	.20
152	Charlie Garner	.10
153	Chris T. Jones	.10
154	Irving Fryar	.10
155	Mike Mamula	.10
156	Troy Vincent	.10
157	Bobby Taylor	.10
158	Chris Boniol	.10
159	Devin Bush	.10
160	Bert Emanuel	.10
161	Jamal Anderson	.20
162	Terance Mathis	.10
163	Cornelius Bennett	.10
164	Ray Buchanan	.10
165	Chris Chandler	.10
166	Dave Brown	.10
167	Danny Kanell	.10
168	Rodney Hampton	.10
169	Tyrone Wheatley	.10
170	Amani Toomer	.10
171	Chris Calloway	.10
172	Thomas Lewis	.10
173	Phillipi Sparks	.10
174	Mark Brunell	1.25
175	Keenan McCardell	.10
176	Willie Jackson	.10
177	Jimmy Smith	.10
178	Pete Mitchell	.10
179	Natrone Means	.20
180	Kevin Hardy	.10
181	Tony Brackens	.10
182	James O. Stewart	.10
183	Wayne Chrebet	.10
184	Keyshawn Johnson	.50
185	Adrian Murrell	.10
186	Neil O'Donnell	.10
187	Hugh Douglas	.10
188	Mo Lewis	.10
189	Marvin Washington	.10
190	Aaron Glenn	.10
191	Barry Sanders	1.25
192	Scott Mitchell	.10
193	Herman Moore	.20
194	Johnnie Morton	.10
195	Glyn Milburn	.10
196	Reggie Brown	.10
197	Jason Hanson	.10
198	Steve McNair	.75
199	Eddie George	1.75
200	Ronnie Harmon	.10
201	Chris Sanders	.10
202	Willie Davis	.10
203	Frank Wycheck	.10
204	Darryll Lewis	.10
205	Blaine Bishop	.10
206	Robert Brooks	.10
207	Brett Favre	3.00
208	Edgar Bennett	.10
209	Dorsey Levens	.20
210	Derrick Mayes	.10
211	Antonio Freeman	.30
212	Mark Chmura	.10
213	Reggie White	.20
214	Gilbert Brown	.10
215	LeRoy Butler	.10
216	Craig Newsome	.10
217	Kerry Collins	1.00
218	Wesley Walls	.10
219	Muhsin Muhammad	.10
220	Anthony Johnson	.10
221	Tshimanga Biakabutuka	.20
222	Kevin Greene	.10
223	Sam Mills	.10
224	John Kasay	.10
225	Michael Barrow	.10
226	Drew Bledsoe	1.25
227	Curtis Martin	1.25
228	Terry Glenn	1.25
229	Ben Coates	.10
230	Shawn Jefferson	.10
231	Willie McGinest	.10
232	Ted Johnson	.10
233	Lawyer Milloy	.10
234	Ty Law	.10
235	Willie Clay	.10
236	Tim Brown	.10

237	Rickey Dudley	.10
238	Napoleon Kaufman	.10
239	Chester McGlockton	.10
240	Rob Fredrickson	.10
241	Terry McDaniel	.10
242	Desmond Howard	.10
243	Jeff George	.10
244	Isaac Bruce	.20
245	Tony Banks	.50
246	Lawrence Phillips ERR.#247	.20
247	Kevin Carter	.10
248	Roman Phifer	.10
249	Keith Lyle	.10
250	Eddie Kennison	.50
251	Craig Heyward	.10
252	Vinny Testaverde	.10
253	Derrick Alexander	.10
254	Michael Jackson	.10
255	Bam Morris	.10
256	Eric Green	.10
257	Ray Lewis	.10
258	Antonio Langham	.10
259	Michael McCreary	.10
260	Gus Frerotte	.10
261	Terry Allen	.10
262	Brian Mitchell	.10
263	Michael Westbrook	.10
264	Sean Gilbert	.10
265	Rich Owens	.10
266	Ken Harvey	.10
267	Jeff Hostetler	.10
268	Michael Haynes	.10
269	Mario Bates	.10
270	Eric Allen ERR.#273	.10
271	Ray Zellars	.10
272	Joe Johnson	.10
273	Renaldo Turnbull	.10
274	Heath Shuler	.10
275	Daryl Hobbs	.10
276	John Friesz	.10
277	Brian Blades	.10
278	Joey Galloway	.30
279	Chris Warren	.10
280	Lamar Smith	.10
281	Cortez Kennedy	.10
282	Chad Brown	.10
283	Warren Moon	.10
284	Jerome Bettis	.20
285	Charles Johnson	.10
286	Kordell Stewart	1.00
287	Erric Pegram	.10
288	Norm Johnson	.10
289	Levon Kirkland	.10
290	Greg Lloyd	.10
291	Carnell Lake	.10
292	Brad Johnson	.10
293	Cris Carter	.10
294	Jake Reed	.10
295	Robert Smith	.10
296	Derrick Alexander	.10
297	John Randle	.10
298	Dixon Edwards	.10
299	Orlanda Thomas	.10
300	DeWayne Washington	.10

1997 Upper Deck Game Jersey

The 10-card set includes a piece of the player's jersey. The cards were inserted 1:2,500 packs.

		MT
	Complete Set (10):	2800.00
	Common Player:	150.00
GM1	Warren Moon	150.00
GM2	Joey Galloway	225.00
GM3	Terrell Davis	350.00
GM4	Brett Favre	600.00
GM5	Brett Favre	600.00
GM6	Reggie White	200.00
GM7	John Elway	275.00
GM8	Troy Aikman	350.00
GM9	Carl Pickens	150.00
GM10	Herman Moore	150.00

1997 Upper Deck MVP

The 20-card set featured the players on gold Light F/X Cel Chrome cards. Upper Deck produced 100 of each card.

		MT
	Complete Set (20):	400.00
	Common Player:	10.00
MP1	Jerry Rice	35.00
MP2	Carl Pickens	10.00
MP3	Terrell Davis	35.00
MP4	Mike Alstott	10.00
MP5	Vinny Testaverde	10.00
MP6	Junior Seau	10.00
MP7	Marcus Allen	10.00
MP8	Troy Aikman	35.00
MP9	Dan Marino	60.00
MP10	Ricky Watters	10.00
MP11	Mark Brunell	35.00
MP12	Barry Sanders	35.00
MP13	Eddie George	45.00
MP14	Brett Favre	70.00
MP15	Kerry Collins	30.00
MP16	Drew Bledsoe	35.00
MP17	Napoleon Kaufman	10.00
MP18	Isaac Bruce	10.00
MP19	Terry Allen	10.00
MP20	Jerome Bettis	10.00

1997 Upper Deck Star Crossed

The 27-card set was inserted 1:27 packs. The player's photo is superimposed over an etched-foil starry background on the Light F/X cards. The cards are numbered on the back with an "SC" prefix.

		MT
	Complete Set (27):	200.00
	Common Player:	2.00
	Trade Card:	160.00
SC1	Dan Marino	20.00
SC2	Mark Brunell	12.00
SC3	Kerry Collins	10.00
SC4	Jerry Rice	12.00
SC5	Kevin Greene	2.00
SC6	Curtis Martin	12.00
SC7	Isaac Bruce	4.00
SC8	Eddie George	15.00
SC9	Deion Sanders	8.00
SC10	Troy Aikman	12.00
SC11	John Elway	10.00
SC12	Steve Young	10.00
SC13	Barry Sanders	12.00
SC14	Jerome Bettis	4.00
SC15	Herman Moore	2.00
SC16	Keyshawn Johnson	4.00
SC17	Simeon Rice	2.00
SC18	Bruce Smith	2.00
SC19	Drew Bledsoe	12.00
SC20	Kordell Stewart	12.00
SC21	Brett Favre	25.00
SC22	Emmitt Smith	20.00
SC23	Terrell Davis	12.00
SC24	Carl Pickens	2.00
SC25	Terry Glenn	10.00
SC26	Reggie White	1.00
SC27	Rod Woodson	2.00

1997 Upper Deck Team Mates

The 60-card set was inserted 1:4 packs. The die-cut cards feature the player's photo superimposed over a silver etched foil background. The die-cut cards fit together to show the two teammates from each team. The player's name, team, position and Upper Deck logo are printed in gold foil at the bottom. The cards are numbered on the back with a "TM" prefix.

	MT
Complete Set (60):	45.00
Common Player:	.25
TM1 Simeon Rice	.25
TM2 Eric Swann	.25
TM3 Jamal Anderson	.50
TM4 Terance Mathis	.25
TM5 Vinny Testaverde	.25
TM6 Michael Jackson	.25
TM7 Thurman Thomas	.50
TM8 Bruce Smith	.25
TM9 Kerry Collins	1.50
TM10 Anthony Johnson	.25
TM11 Bobby Engram	.25
TM12 Rashaan Salaam	.50
TM13 Carl Pickens	.25
TM14 Jeff Blake	.50
TM15 Troy Aikman	2.00
TM16 Emmitt Smith	4.00
TM17 John Elway	1.25
TM18 Terrell Davis	2.00
TM19 Herman Moore	.50
TM20 Barry Sanders	2.00
TM21 Brett Favre	5.00
TM22 Reggie White	.50
TM23 Eddie George	3.00
TM24 Steve McNair	1.00
TM25 Marshall Faulk	.50
TM26 Jim Harbaugh	.25
TM27 Mark Brunell	2.00
TM28 Keenan McCardell	.25
TM29 Marcus Allen	.50
TM30 Derrick Thomas	.25
TM31 Dan Marino	4.00
TM32 Karim Abdul-Jabbar	1.50
TM33 Cris Carter	.25
TM34 Jake Reed	.25
TM35 Curtis Martin	2.00
TM36 Drew Bledsoe	2.00
TM37 Mario Bates	.25
TM38 Ray Zellars	.25
TM39 Keyshawn Johnson	.50
TM40 Adrian Murrell	.25
TM41 Tyrone Wheatley	.25
TM42 Rodney Hampton	.25
TM43 Napoleon Kaufman	.25
TM44 Tim Brown	.25
TM45 Ricky Watters	.50
TM46 Chris T. Jones	.25
TM47 Kordell Stewart	1.50
TM48 Jerome Bettis	.50
TM49 Junior Seau	.50
TM50 Tony Martin	.25
TM51 Steve Young	1.25
TM52 Jerry Rice	2.00
TM53 Joey Galloway	.50
TM54 Chris Warren	.25
TM55 Eddie Kennison	.75
TM56 Tony Banks	.75
TM57 Mike Alstott	.25
TM58 Errict Rhett	.50
TM59 Terry Allen	.25
TM60 Gus Frerotte	.25

1997 Upper Deck
Black Diamond

The 180-card, regular-sized set was released in six-card packs. The set was tiered in three levels: 90 single diamond, 60 double diamonds (1:4) and 30 triple diamonds (1:30). A parallel gold version was issued for each card: single diamond (1:15), double diamonds (1:46) and triple diamonds (limited to a production of 50). One insert set was included, Title Quest.

	MT
Complete Set (180):	400.00
Comp. Single Diamond (90):	20.00
Comp. Double Diamond (60):	80.00
Comp. Triple Diamond (30):	320.00
Common Diamond (1-90):	.10
Common Double Diamond (91-150):	.75
Common Triple Diamond (151-180):	4.00
Wax Box:	100.00
1 Alfred Williams	.10
2 Alvin Harper	.10
3 Andre Hastings	.10
4 Andre Reed	.10
5 Anthony Johnson	.10
6 Anthony Miller	.10
7 Bam Morris	.10
8 Bobby Hebert	.10
9 Bobby Taylor	.10
10 Boomer Esiason	.10
11 Brett Perriman	.10
12 Brian Blades	.10
13 Bryan Cox	.10
14 Bryant Young	.10
15 Bryce Paup	.10
16 Carnell Lake	.10
17 Cedric Jones	.10
18 Chad Brown	.10
19 Charlie Garner	.10
20 Chris Chandler	.10
21 Cornelius Bennett	.10
22 Cortez Kennedy	.10
23 Cris Carter	.10
24 Dale Carter	.10
25 Daryl Gardner	.10
26 Derrick Alexander	.10
27 Derrick Mayes	.10
28 Don Beebe	.10
29 Eric Allen	.10
30 Eric Moulds	.10
31 Errict Rhett	.20
32 Frank Sanders	.10
33 Glyn Milburn	.10
34 Henry Ellard	.10
35 Jamal Anderson	.75
36 James O. Stewart	.10
37 Jason Dunn	.10
38 Jerry Rice	2.00
39 Jim Everett	.10
40 Jim Kelly	.10
41 Joey Galloway	1.00
42 John Carney	.10
43 John Elway	1.50
44 John Randle	.10
45 Karim Abdul-Jabbar	2.00
46 Keenan McCardell	.10
47 Ken Dilger	.10
48 Ken Norton	.10
49 Ki-Jana Carter	.10
50 Kordell Stewart	2.00
51 Lawrence Phillips	.10
52 Leslie O'Neal	.10
53 Mark Chmura	.10
54 Marshall Faulk	.25
55 Michael Haynes	.10
56 Michael Irvin	.20
57 Michael Jackson	.10
58 Michael Westbrook	.10
59 Mike Tomczak	.10
60 Napoleon Kaufman	.10
61 Neil O'Donnell	.10
62 Neil Smith	.10
63 O.J. McDuffie	.10
64 Orlanda Thomas	.10
65 Rashaan Salaam	.20
66 Regan Upshaw	.10
67 Rick Mirer	.10
68 Rob Moore	.10
69 Ronnie Harmon	.10
70 Sam Mills	.10
71 Sean Dawkins	.10
72 Shawn Jefferson	.10
73 Stan Humphries	.10
74 Stepfret Williams	.10

75 Stephen Davis	.10
76 Steve Atwater	.10
77 Terance Mathis	.10
78 Terrell Fletcher	.10
79 Terry Glenn	2.50
80 Terry McDaniel	.10
81 Tony McGee	.10
82 Trent Dilfer	.10
83 Troy Drayton	.10
84 Ty Detmer	.10
85 Tyrone Hughes	.10
86 Walt Harris	.10
87 Wayne Chrebet	.10
88 Wesley Walls	.10
89 Willie Davis	.10
90 Willie McGinest	.10
91 Adrian Murrell	.75
92 Alex Molden	.75
93 Alex Van Dyke	.75
94 Andre Coleman	.75
95 Ben Coates	.75
96 Bobby Engram	.75
97 Bruce Smith	.75
98 Charles Johnson	.75
99 Chris Sanders	.75
100 Chris T. Jones	.75
101 Chris Warren	.75
102 Darnay Scott	.75
103 Dave Brown	.75
104 Derrick Thomas	.75
105 Drew Bledsoe	7.00
106 Edgar Bennett	.75
107 Emmitt Smith	14.00
108 Eric Bjornson	.75
109 Eric Metcalf	.75
110 Garrison Hearst	.75
111 Gus Frerotte	.75
112 Hardy Nickerson	.75
113 Herman Moore	1.50
114 Hugh Douglas	.75
115 Irving Fryar	.75
116 J.J. Stokes	.75
117 Jake Reed	.75
118 Jeff Hostetler	.75
119 Jeff Lewis	.75
120 Jim Harbaugh	.75
121 Johnnie Morton	.75
122 Jonathan Ogden	.75
123 Kevin Carter	.75
124 Kevin Greene	.75
125 Kevin Hardy	.75
126 Leeland McElroy	.75
127 Mike Alstott	1.50
128 Muhsin Muhammad	2.50
129 Natrone Means	.75
130 Quentin Coryatt	.75
131 Ray Lewis	.75
132 Ray Zellars	.75
133 Rickey Dudley	.75
134 Ricky Watters	.75
135 Robert Smith	.75
136 Scott Mitchell	.75
137 Sean Gilbert	.75
138 Shannon Sharpe	.75
139 Simeon Rice	.75
140 Stanley Pritchett	.75
141 Steve McNair	4.00
142 Steve Young	5.00
143 Tamarick Vanover	1.50
144 Terry Allen	.75
145 Thurman Thomas	.75
146 Tony Banks	3.00
147 Tony Martin	.75
148 Tyrone Wheatley	.75
149 Vinny Testaverde	.75
150 Zach Thomas	4.00
151 Amani Toomer	4.00
152 Barry Sanders	25.00
153 Bobby Hoying	4.00
154 Brett Favre	50.00
155 Carl Pickens	4.00
156 Curtis Conway	4.00
157 Curtis Martin	25.00
158 Dan Marino	50.00
159 Deion Sanders	10.00
160 Eddie George	40.00
161 Eddie Kennison	10.00
162 Elvis Grbac	4.00
163 Isaac Bruce	6.00
164 Jeff Blake	8.00
165 Jerome Bettis	4.00
166 Junior Seau	4.00
167 Kerry Collins	20.00
168 Keyshawn Johnson	10.00
169 Larry Centers	4.00
170 Marcus Allen	4.00
171 Mark Brunell	25.00
172 Marvin Harrison	10.00
173 Reggie White	4.00
174 Rodney Hampton	4.00
175 Terrell Davis	25.00

176 Tim Brown	4.00
177 Todd Collins	4.00
178 Troy Aikman	25.00
179 Tim Biakabutuka	4.00
180 Warren Moon	4.00

1997 Upper Deck
Black Diamond Gold

Gold parallel cards were available for all 180 cards in the 1997 Black Diamond set. The only difference between regular and gold versions is that the silver foil that is used on regular-issue cards is replaced by gold foil. Gold version of Single Black Diamond cards (1-90) were seeded one per 15 packs, while gold versions of Double Black Diamond cards (91-150) were inserted every 46 packs and gold Triple Black Diamond cards (151-180) were limited to 50 each.

	MT
Complete Set (180):	2900.00
Comp. Single Diamond (90):	150.00
Comp. Double Diamond (60):	250.00
Comp. Triple Diamond (30):	2500.00
Gold Single Diamonds:	4x-8x
Gold Double Diamonds:	2x-4x
Gold Triple Diamonds:	5x-10x

1997 Upper Deck
Black Diamond Title Quest

The 20-card, regular-sized, die-cut set was inserted into packs of 1997 Black Diamond football and was limited to a production of 100. The card fronts feature a square color action shot with a gold border.

	MT
Complete Set (20):	3000.00
Common Player:	40.00
1 Dan Marino	350.00
2 Jerry Rice	200.00
3 Drew Bledsoe	200.00
4 Emmitt Smith	350.00
5 Troy Aikman	200.00
6 Steve Young	150.00
7 Brett Favre	350.00
8 John Elway	150.00
9 Barry Sanders	200.00
10 Jerome Bettis	75.00
11 Deion Sanders	100.00
12 Karim Abdul-Jabbar	125.00
13 Terrell Davis	225.00
14 Marshall Faulk	75.00
15 Curtis Martin	225.00
16 Eddie George	250.00
17 Steve McNair	125.00
18 Terry Glenn	150.00
19 Joey Galloway	40.00
20 Keyshawn Johnson	40.00

1997 SPx

The 50-card, regular-sized, die-cut set was available in one-card packs. The card fronts a hologram panorama-type headshot on the right half of the horizontal card with a color action shot on the left half. The cards are die-cut in the shape of an "X" on the right side.

	MT
Complete Set (50):	130.00
Common Player:	1.00
Wax Box:	100.00
1 Jerry Rice	6.00
2 Steve Young	4.00
3 Karim Abdul-Jabbar	8.00
4 Dan Marino	12.00
5 Bobby Engram	2.00
6 Rashaan Salaam	2.00
7 Marvin Harrison	5.00
8 Jim Harbaugh	1.00
9 Marshall Faulk	3.00
10 Eric Moulds	2.00
11 Thurman Thomas	2.00
12 Tamarick Vanover	2.00
13 Steve Bono	1.00
14 Warren Moon	1.00
15 Cris Carter	1.00
16 Carl Pickens	1.00
17 Ki-Jana Carter	1.00
18 Jeff Blake	2.00
19 Tim Biakabutuka	3.00
20 Kerry Collins	6.00
21 Leeland McElroy	2.00
22 Simeon Rice	1.00
23 John Elway	5.00
24 Terrell Davis	8.00
25 Jeff Lewis	1.00
26 Terry Glenn	10.00
27 Curtis Martin	10.00
28 Drew Bledsoe	6.00
29 Lawrence Phillips	3.00
30 Isaac Bruce	3.00
31 Eddie Kennison	4.00
32 Keyshawn Johnson	5.00
33 Stepfret Williams	1.00
34 Emmitt Smith	12.00
35 Troy Aikman	6.00
36 Deion Sanders	4.00
37 Joey Galloway	3.00
38 Rick Mirer	1.00
39 Rickey Dudley	2.00
40 Jeff Hostetler	1.00
41 Junior Seau	1.00
42 Derrick Mayes	1.00
43 Brett Favre	12.00
44 Edgar Bennett	1.00
45 Barry Sanders	6.00
46 Herman Moore	2.00
47 Kordell Stewart	6.00
48 Jerome Bettis	2.00
49 Eddie George	12.00
50 Steve McNair	4.00

1997 SPx Gold

This 50-card set featured the same die-cut design as the base set, but instead of the border being printed in team colors it was printed in gold. Gold parallels were inserted every nine packs.

	MT
Complete Set (50):	375.00
Gold Cards:	3x

1997 SPx Holofame

The 10-card, regular-sized set was inserted every 75 packs of Upper Deck's 1997 SPx football.

	MT
Complete Set (20):	600.00
Common Player:	10.00
1 Jerry Rice	45.00
2 Emmitt Smith	90.00
3 Karim Abdul-Jabbar	35.00
4 Brett Favre	90.00
5 Curtis Martin	60.00
6 Eddie Kennison	20.00
7 Troy Aikman	45.00
8 Steve Young	35.00
9 Tim Biakabutuka	10.00
10 Reggie White	10.00
11 Terry Glenn	40.00
12 Lawrence Phillips	10.00
10 Dan Marino	90.00
14 Deion Sanders	25.00
15 Terrell Davis	50.00
16 Marvin Harrison	25.00
17 Eddie George	50.00
18 Marshall Faulk	10.00
19 Keyshawn Johnson	10.00
20 Barry Sanders	45.00

1997 SPx ProMotion

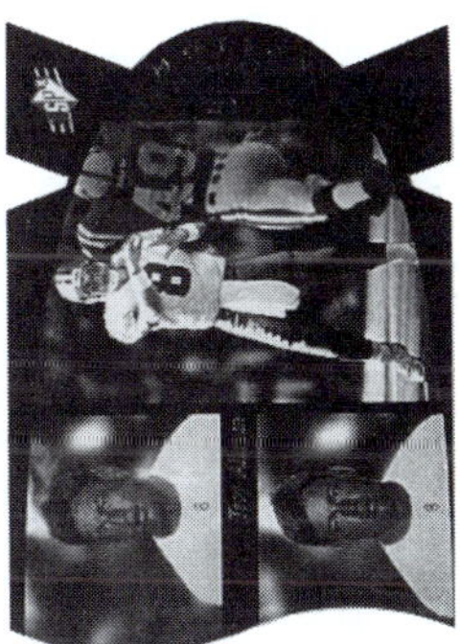

The six-card, regular-sized set was inserted every 433 packs of Upper Deck's 1997 SPx football.

	MT
Complete Set (6):	500.00
Common Player:	70.00
1 Dan Marino	150.00
2 Joe Montana	100.00
3 Troy Aikman	85.00
4 Barry Sanders	85.00
5 Karim Abdul-Jabbar	70.00
6 Eddie George	100.00

1997 SPx ProMotion Autographs

This insert included autographed versions of each of the six ProMotion inserts. Cards were autographed on the front and sequentially numbered to 100 on the back.

	MT
Complete Set (6):	3500.00
Common Player:	300.00
1 Dan Marino	1000.
2 Joe Montana	700.00
3 Troy Aikman	600.00
4 Barry Sanders	600.00
5 Karim Abdul-Jabbar	300.00
6 Eddie George	600.00

1997 Collector's Choice

The 310-card set features white borders on the front. The player's name and team are printed inside a stripe at the top, while his position is located inside a rectangle at the upper right. The Collector's Choice logo is printed in the lower left of the front. The backs have a photo on the left, with the player's bio, "Did you know?" and stats along the right side. The cards feature a dual numbering sys-

tem that helps collectors put players from their favorite team together. The base set also features a 45-card Rookie Class subset and a 40-card Names of the Game subset.

	MT
Complete Set (310):	25.00
Common Player:	.05
Wax Box:	40.00
1 Orlando Pace	.50
2 Darrell Russell	.05
3 Shawn Springs	.50
4 Peter Boulware	.05
5 Bryant Westbrook	.10
6 Tom Knight	.05
7 Ike Hilliard	1.50
8 James Farrior	.05
9 Chris Naeole	.05
10 Michael Booker	.05
11 Warrick Dunn	2.00
12 Tony Gonzalez	.50
13 Reinard Wilson	.05
14 Yatil Green	1.00
15 Reidel Anthony	1.50
16 Kenard Lang	.05
17 Kenny Holmes	.05
18 Tarik Glenn	.05
19 Dwayne Rudd	.05
20 Renaldo Wynn	.05
21 David LaFleur	.20
22 Antowain Smith	1.00
23 Jim Druckenmiller	1.75
24 Rae Carruth	1.00
25 Jared Tomich	.05
26 Chris Canty	.05
27 Jake Plummer	.50
28 Troy Davis	1.50
29 Sedrick Shaw	.50
30 Jamie Sharper	.05
31 Tiki Barber	1.00
32 Byron Hanspard	.75
33 Darnell Autry	.50
34 Corey Dillon	.75
35 Joey Kent	.30
36 Nathan Davis	.05
37 Will Blackwell	.30
38 Kim Herring	.05
39 Pat Barnes	.75
40 Kevin Lockett	.20
41 Trevor Pryce	.05
42 Matt Russell	.05
43 Greg Jones	.05
44 Antonio Anderson	.05
45 George Jones	.10
46 Steve Young	.20
47 Jerry Rice	.35
48 Curtis Conway	.05
49 Jeff Blake	.05
50 Carl Pickens	.05
51 Bruce Smith	.05
52 John Elway	.20
53 Terrell Davis	.50
54 Shannon Sharpe	.05
55 Junior Seau	.05
56 Darren Bennett	.05
57 Jim Harbaugh	.05
58 Marshall Faulk	.05
59 Emmitt Smith	.75
60 Troy Aikman	.35
61 Deion Sanders	.20
62 Dan Marino	.75
63 Ricky Watters	.05
64 Mark Brunell	.35
65 Keenan McCardell	.05
66 Keyshawn Johnson	.20
67 Barry Sanders	.35
68 Herman Moore	.05
69 Eddie George	.50
70 Steve McNair	.25
71 Brett Favre	1.00
72 Reggie White	.05
73 Edgar Bennett	.05
74 Kerry Collins	.35
75 Kevin Greene	.05
76 Drew Bledsoe	.35
77 Terry Glenn	.40
78 Curtis Martin	.50
79 Jeff Hostetler	.05
80 Napoleon Kaufman	.05
81 Isaac Bruce	.05
82 Terry Allen	.05
83 Joey Galloway	.05
84 Kordell Stewart	.20
85 Jerome Bettis	.05
86 Dana Stubblefield	.05
87 Merton Hanks	.05
88 Terrell Owens	.50
89 Brent Jones	.05
90 Ken Norton Jr.	.05
91 Jerry Rice	.75
92 Terry Kirby	.05
93 Bryant Young	.05
94 Raymont Harris	.05
95 Jeff Jaeger	.05
96 Curtis Conway	.10
97 Walt Harris	.05
98 Bobby Engram	.10
99 Donnell Woolford	.05
100 Rashaan Salaam	.10
101 Jeff Blake	.10
102 Tony McGee	.05
103 Ashley Ambrose	.05
104 Dan Wilkinson	.05
105 Jevon Langford	.05
106 Darnay Scott	.05
107 David Dunn	.05
108 Eric Moulds	.05
109 Darrick Holmes	.05
110 Thurman Thomas	.10
111 Quinn Early	.05
112 Jim Kelly	.10
113 Bryce Paup	.05
114 Bruce Smith	.05
115 Todd Collins	.05
116 Tory James	.05
117 Anthony Miller	.05
118 Terrell Davis	1.00
119 Tyrone Braxton	.05
120 John Mobley	.05
121 Bill Romanowski	.05
122 Vaughn Hebron	.05
123 Mike Alstott	.15
124 Errict Rhett	.10
125 Trent Dilfer	.10
126 Courtney Hawkins	.05
127 Hardy Nickerson	.05
128 Donnie Abraham	.05
129 Regan Upshaw	.05
130 Kent Graham	.05
131 Rob Moore	.05
132 Simeon Rice	.05
133 LeShon Johnson	.05
134 Frank Sanders	.05
135 Leeland McElroy	.05
136 Seth Joyner	.05
137 Andre Coleman	.05
138 Stan Humphries	.05
139 Charlie Jones	.05
140 Junior Seau	.10
141 Rodney Harrison	.05
142 Darrien Gordon	.05
143 Terrell Fletcher	.05
144 Tamarick Vanover	.10
145 Greg Hill	.05
146 Marcus Allen	.10
147 Lake Dawson	.05
148 Dale Carter	.05
149 Kimble Anders	.05
150 Chris Penn	.05
151 Sean Dawkins	.05
152 Ken Dilger	.05
153 Marvin Harrison	.40
154 Jeff Herrod	.05
155 Jim Harbaugh	.05
156 Cary Blanchard	.05
157 Aaron Bailey	.05
158 Deion Sanders	.40
159 Jim Schwantz	.05
160 Michael Irvin	.10
161 Herschel Walker	.05
162 Emmitt Smith	1.50
163 Chris Boniol	.05
164 Eric Bjornson	.05
165 Karim Abdul-Jabbar	.60
166 O.J. McDuffie	.05
167 Troy Drayton	.05
168 Zach Thomas	.40
169 Irving Spikes	.05
170 Shane Burton	.05
171 Stanley Pritchett	.05
172 Ty Detmer	.05
173 Chris T. Jones	.05
174 Troy Vincent	.05
175 Brian Dawkins	.05
176 Irving Fryar	.05
177 Charlie Garner	.05
178 Bobby Taylor	.05
179 Jamal Anderson	.10
180 Terance Mathis	.05
181 Craig Heyward	.05
182 Cornelius Bennett	.05
183 Jessie Tuggle	.05
184 Devin Bush	.05
185 Dave Brown	.05
186 Danny Kanell	.05
187 Rodney Hampton	.05
188 Tyrone Wheatley	.05
189 Amani Toomer	.05
190 Phillipi Sparks	.05
191 Thomas Lewis	.05

192	Jimmy Smith	.05
193	Pete Mitchell	.05
194	Natrone Means	.10
195	Mark Brunell	.75
196	Kevin Hardy	.05
197	Tony Brackens	.05
198	Aaron Beasley	.05
199	Chris Hudson	.05
200	Wayne Chrebet	.05
201	Keyshawn Johnson	.40
202	Adrian Murrell	.05
203	Neil O'Donnell	.05
204	Hugh Douglas	.05
205	Mo Lewis	.05
206	Glenn Foley	.05
207	Aaron Glenn	.05
208	Johnnie Morton	.05
209	Reggie Brown	.05
210	Barry Sanders	.75
211	Glyn Milburn	.05
212	Bennie Blades	.05
213	Steve McNair	.40
214	Frank Wycheck	.05
215	Chris Sanders	.05
216	Blaine Bishop	.05
217	Willie Davis	.05
218	Darryll Lewis	.05
219	Marcus Robertson	.05
220	Robert Brooks	.10
221	Antonio Freeman	.30
222	Keith Jackson (Retired)	.05
223	Mark Chmura	.05
224	Brett Favre	1.75
225	Sean Jones	.05
226	Reggie White	.10
227	LeRoy Butler	.05
228	Craig Newsome	.05
229	Wesley Walls	.05
230	Mark Carrier	.05
231	Muhsin Muhammad	.05
232	John Kasay	.05
233	Anthony Johnson	.05
234	Kerry Collins	.75
235	Kevin Greene	.05
236	Sam Mills	.05
237	Ben Coates	.05
238	Terry Glenn	.75
239	Willie McGinest	.05
240	Ted Johnson	.05
241	Lawyer Milloy	.05
242	Drew Bledsoe	.75
243	Willie Clay	.05
244	Chris Slade	.05
245	Tim Brown	.05
246	Daryl Hobbs	.05
247	Rickey Dudley	.05
248	Joe Aska	.05
249	Chester McGlockton	.05
250	Rob Fredrickson	.05
251	Terry McDaniel	.05
252	Tony Banks	.25
253	Lawrence Phillips	.10
254	Isaac Bruce	.15
255	Eddie Kennison	.40
256	Kevin Carter	.05
257	Roman Phifer	.05
258	Keith Lyle	.05
259	Vinny Testaverde	.05
260	Derrick Alexander	.05
261	Ray Lewis	.05
262	Jermaine Lewis	.05
263	Bam Morris	.05
264	Stevon Moore	.05
265	Antonio Langham	.05
266	Brian Mitchell	.05
267	Henry Ellard	.05
268	Leslie Shepherd	.05
269	Michael Westbrook	.05
270	Jamie Asher	.05
271	Ken Harvey	.05
272	Gus Frerotte	.05
273	Michael Haynes	.05
274	Ray Zellars	.05
275	Jim Everett	.05
276	Tyrone Hughes (Bears)	.05
277	Joe Johnson	.05
278	Eric Allen	.05
279	Brady Smith	.05
280	Mario Bates	.05
281	Torrance Small	.05
282	John Friesz	.05
283	Brian Blades	.05
284	Chris Warren	.05
285	Joey Galloway	.25
286	Michael Sinclair	.05
287	Lamar Smith	.05
288	Mike Pritchard	.05
289	Jerome Bettis	.10
290	Charles Johnson	.05
291	Mike Tomczak	.05
292	Levon Kirkland	.05

293	Carnell Lake	.05
294	Erric Pegram	.05
295	Kordell Stewart	.50
296	Greg Lloyd	.05
297	Dixon Edwards	.05
298	Cris Carter	.05
299	Brad Johnson	.05
300	Qadry Ismail	.05
301	John Randle	.05
302	Orlanda Thomas	.05
303	DeWayne Washington	.05
304	Jake Reed	.05
305	Derrick Alexander	.05
306	Eddie George	1.25
307	Dan Marino	1.50
308	Curtis Martin	1.00
309	Troy Aikman	.75
310	Marcus Allen	.10

1997 Collector's Choice Crash the Game

This 30-card chase set was inserted 1:5 packs. If the player featured on the front scored on the date shown on the card, the collector wins a redemption card of the player.

		MT
Complete Set (30):		25.00
Common Player:		.50
Each player has three cards with three different dates.		
1	Troy Aikman	1.50
2	Dan Marino	3.00
3	Steve Young	1.25
4	Brett Favre	3.50
5	Drew Bledsoe	1.50
6	Jeff Blake	1.00
7	Mark Brunell	1.00
8	John Elway	1.25
9	Vinny Testaverde	.50
10	Steve McNair	1.25
11	Jerry Rice	1.50
12	Terry Glenn	1.50
13	Michael Jackson	.50
14	Tony Martin	.50
15	Isaac Bruce	1.00
16	Cris Carter	1.00
17	Shannon Sharpe	.50
18	Rae Carruth	1.00
19	Ike Hilliard	1.25
20	Yatil Green	.75
21	Terry Allen	.50
22	Emmitt Smith	3.00
23	Karim Abdul-Jabbar	1.00
24	Barry Sanders	1.50
25	Terrell Davis	1.50
26	Jerome Bettis	1.00
27	Ricky Watters	1.00
28	Curtis Martin	1.25
29	Byron Hanspard	1.00
30	Warrick Dunn	2.00

1997 Collector's Choice Stick-Ums

Inserted in 1:3 packs, the 30-sticker set featured a photo of the player on the front, the Stick-ums logo, his name and team helmet which could be peeled off. The sticker number is printed in the upper left of the back. Directions on how to use the stickers are on the left of the back, while the checklist is on the right. Each of the stickers' numbers included an "S" prefix.

		MT
Complete Set (30):		15.00
Common Player:		.25
S1	Kerry Collins	1.00
S2	Troy Aikman	1.25
S3	Steve Young	.75
S4	Ricky Watters	.50
S5	Cris Carter	.25
S6	Terry Allen	.25
S7	Bobby Engram	.50
S8	Simeon Rice	.25
S9	Mike Alstott	.25
S10	Rodney Hampton	.25
S11	Eddie Kennison	.50
S12	Jamal Anderson	.50
S13	Jim Everett	.25
S14	Curtis Martin	1.25
S15	Keenan McCardell	.25
S16	Kordell Stewart	1.00
S17	John Elway	.75
S18	Terrell Davis	1.25
S19	Thurman Thomas	.50
S20	Marshall Faulk	.50
S21	Marcus Allen	.50
S22	Tony Martin	.25
S23	Dan Marino	2.00
S24	Karim Abdul-Jabbar	1.00
S25	Carl Pickens	.25
S26	Eddie George	1.50
S27	Joey Galloway	.50
S28	Napoleon Kaufman	.25
S29	Vinny Testaverde	.25
S30	Keyshawn Johnson	.50

1997 Collector's Choice Turf Champions

The 90-card chase set was broken up into four tiers. Tier One and Two both contain 30 cards, while Tier Three has 20. Tier Four includes 10. The Tiers were inserted as follows: One (every pack), Two (1:21), Three (1:71) and Four (1:145). The holofoil cards have a green-marble border at the top and bottom. The Collector's Choice logo is in the upper left, with the Turf Champions' logo in the lower left. The player's name, position and team are listed at the bottom center. The backs, which are numbered with a "TC" prefix, have the player's highlights printed over a green area on the left, with his achievement printed vertically in the center. The right has a photo and quote.

		MT
Complete Set (90):		650.00
Complete Tier 1 (30):		10.00
Complete Tier 2 (30):		100.00
Complete Tier 3 (20):		250.00
Complete Tier 4 (10):		300.00
Common Player (1-30):		.20
Common Player (31-60):		2.00
Common Player (61-80):		5.00
Common Player (81-90):		6.00
TC1	Kerry Collins	1.00
TC2	Scott Mitchell	.20
TC3	Jim Schwantz	.20
TC4	Orlando Pace	.40
TC5	Troy Davis	1.25
TC6	Vinny Testaverde	.20
TC7	Raghib Ismail	.20
TC8	Henry Ellard	.20
TC9	Kevin Turner	.20
TC10	Bobby Engram	.20
TC11	Keyshawn Johnson	.40
TC12	Trent Dilfer	.20
TC13	Elvis Grbac	.20
TC14	Trev Alberts	.20
TC15	Kevin Hardy	.20
TC16	Warren Sapp	.20
TC17	Chris Hudson	.20
TC18	Antonio Langham	.20
TC19	Jonathan Ogden	.20
TC20	Bruce Smith	.20
TC21	Marcus Allen	.40
TC22	Desmond Howard	.20
TC23	Eric Metcalf	.20
TC24	Terance Mathis	.20
TC25	LeShon Johnson	.20
TC26	Kevin Greene	.20
TC27	Alex Van Dyke	.20
TC28	Jeff Jaeger	.20
TC29	Jason Elam	.20
TC30	Thomas Lewis	.20
TC31	Rick Mirer	4.00
TC32	Warren Moon	4.00
TC33	Jim Kelly	4.00
TC34	Junior Seau	4.00
TC35	Jeff Hostetler	2.00
TC36	Neil O'Donnell	2.00
TC37	Jeff Blake	4.00
TC38	Kordell Stewart	14.00
TC39	Terry Glenn	12.00
TC40	Simeon Rice	2.00
TC41	Jimmy Smith	2.00
TC42	Natrone Means	4.00
TC43	Tony Martin	2.00
TC44	Charles Johnson	2.00
TC45	Napoleon Kaufman	4.00
TC46	Dale Carter	2.00
TC47	Brett Perriman	2.00
TC48	Cortez Kennedy	2.00
TC49	Bryce Paup	2.00
TC50	Greg Lloyd	2.00
TC51	Bryant Young	2.00
TC52	Steve McNair	14.00
TC53	Garrison Hearst	2.00
TC54	John Copeland	2.00
TC55	Eric Curry	2.00
TC56	Reggie White	4.00
TC57	Rod Woodson	2.00
TC58	Andre Rison	2.00
TC59	Herschel Walker	2.00
TC60	John Kasay	2.00
TC61	Emmitt Smith	60.00
TC62	Dan Marino	60.00
TC63	Michael Irvin	10.00
TC64	Drew Bledsoe	30.00
TC65	Mark Brunell	30.00
TC66	Jim Harbaugh	5.00
TC67	Herman Moore	10.00
TC68	Rashaan Salaam	10.00
TC69	Ty Detmer	5.00
TC70	Cris Carter	5.00
TC71	Chris Warren	5.00
TC72	Thurman Thomas	5.00
TC73	Ricky Watters	10.00
TC74	Tim Brown	5.00
TC75	Marshall Faulk	10.00
TC76	Jerome Bettis	10.00
TC77	Karim Abdul-Jabbar	20.00
TC78	Deion Sanders	14.00
TC79	Ben Coates	5.00
TC80	Andre Reed	5.00
TC81	Brett Favre	75.00
TC82	Troy Aikman	35.00
TC83	Barry Sanders	35.00
TC84	Jerry Rice	35.00
TC85	Steve Young	20.00
TC86	John Elway	20.00
TC87	Terrell Davis	35.00
TC88	Carl Pickens	6.00
TC89	Curtis Martin	35.00
TC90	Eddie George	35.00

1997 The Year in Hockey Cards

New technologies and autographs. That sums up the positive aspects of the year in hockey cards for 1997.

While the new insert cards released in 1997 were certainly exciting, there were too many men on the ice in the hockey card market of 1997. An already soft market was further diluted by too many hockey products, with no fewer than 25 hockey sets released for the 1996-97 season, and at least as many scheduled in 1997-98. And this despite Topps' exit from the market in 1996.

The major card manufacturer development in 1997 was the exit of Fleer/SkyBox and entrance of Pacific, which created some interest with Wayne Gretzky and friends appearing on their first Gold Crown Die-Cuts ($40) and Cramer's Choice ($250) cards. Pacific's first pro hockey venture, Crown Collection, was out of the gate fast at $2.50/pack, $65/box and the 350-card set at $35.

Mario Lemieux's retirement and immediate induction into the Hall of Fame also sparked some interest. Lemieux's 1985-86 O-Pee-Chee #9 cards remains strong at $375, while his 1985-86 Topps #9 is at $175.

The hottest inserts of the year were Upper Deck's Game Jerseys, actual pieces of game-used jerseys cut into pieces and placed onto a card. Game Jersey cards, inserted at 1:2,500 packs, helped make 1996-97 Upper Deck a big hit, with packs worth $2.50 and boxes at $65. Mario Lemieux's Game Jersey card was valued at $500 by the end of the year, with Jaromir Jagr at $450 and Steve Yzerman and Eric Lindros both at $400. The 390-card set ($40) includes top draft pick Joe Thornton's rookie card, which is going for $8 despite the fact that Thornton didn't score a goal until early December. Game-dated photos and excellent photography helped the Upper Deck product succeed.

Autographs helped Pinnacle's Be A Player product, the first fully licensed hockey cards to feature autographs. Packs were moving for $7 apiece and boxes at $110 as collectors searched for signatures like Lindros'

Hot insert cards make this year's products winners, including Pacific's In The Cage Die-Cut, top, and Upper Deck Game Jerseys.

Link 2 History (#L7B, $150) and Yzerman's Link 2 History (#L9B, $120). An Eric Lindros die cut autograph, limited to Lindros' uniform number of 88 cards per series, was red hot at $600. There was also a Mark Messier autograph, limited to 11 cards in each series, vaulted to $1,200 by the end of the year. There is a Lemieux version of the die-cut card, unautographed but still priced at $600

for each of the 66 cards in each series.

Another hot insert set that helped drive its card set to success was 1996-97 Flair's Blue Ice insert. A total of 250 serially numbered sets were produced, with Gretzky cards priced at $325 and Yzerman, Lindros and Jagr all over $150. Flair was going for $4/pack and $75/box, and the 125-card set was sold for $125.

With the Detroit Red Wings winning the Stanley Cup championship in a four-game sweep over Philadelphia, the Detroit players received a huge boost from a pricing standpoint. The major gainers in the rookie card department included most of the Red Wings, who enjoy a solid fan base in the Detroit area and state of Michigan. The end of the Red Wings' 42-year drought was the story of the NHL season, and helped rejuvenate Detroit-area hockey collecting.

Among the major gainers were Yzerman's 1984-85 O-Pee-Chee #67 card, jumping from $60 to $80 for a future Hall of Famer who has scored more than 500 goals. Brendan Shanahan, a 47-goal scorer, enjoyed a huge increase on his 1988-89 OPC #122, from $15 to $50, and that card's sister, Shanahan's Topps 1988-89 #122, vaulted from $10 to $25. Sergei Fedorov's rookie card (1990-91 Upper Deck #525) increased to $10, then slowed down by the end of the year as Fedorov was a holdout. Coach Scotty Bowman became the first coach to lead three NHL teams to a Stanley Cup championship (Montreal, Pittsburgh and Detroit) and won his seventh title overall. The Hall of Fame coach first appeared on a 1974-75 Topps card (#261, $9) and O-Pee-Chee card (#261, $18). Goaltender Mike Vernon, who also led Calgary to the Cup in 1989, won the Conn Smythe Trophy as playoff MVP and saw his cards jump to $12 for his 1987-88 OPC and $4 for his 1988-89 OPC, although his exit at the end of the season tamed the excitement for his cards.

Among the other rookie card gainers was Paul Kariya, whose 1992-93 Upper Deck #586 doubled to $15 when he scored 44 goals and 55 assists, and his cards didn't suffer much of a setback when Kariya declined to sign with the Mighty Ducks until mid-December of the 1997-98 season. Jagr, expected to take the reigns from Lemieux as the NHL's top player, saw his 1990-91 OPC Premier #50 card increase 50 percent, from $20 to $30. Jagr had only an "average" season in 1996-97 with 47 goals and 48 assists, but that followed a phenomenal year in 1995-96 when the Czechoslovakian player notched 62 goals and 87 assists.

Goaltender Dominik Hasek won the Vezina and Hart Trophies, the first time a goaltender won both since Jacque Plante collected the two trophies in the 1961-62 season. His 1991-92 Parkhurst #263 hovered around $5, with his 1991-92 Upper Deck #335 at $4. A pair of Hasek's inserts were highly sought-after, his 1995-96 Upper Deck Be A Player Autograph #192 ($35) and his 1996-97 Flair Blue Ice #8 ($90). A poor start to the 1997-98 season didn't have much of a negative effect on Hasek's cards.

While Eric Lindros received most of the publicity, one of the up-and-coming stars in the NHL is John LeClair, Lindros' teammate on the Flyers. LeClair had 50 goals and 47 assists, but his cards remained afford-able. His 1991-92 Bowman #344 is at just $2, with his 1991-92 Parkhurst #84 and 1991-92 Upper Deck #345 at $2.50. LeClair's 1995-96 Upper Deck Be A Player Autograph #130 is at $40.

Keith Tkachuk was the NHL's surprising lead-ing goal-scorer with 52 on the year. The rugged forward was also helped by the franchise's move to Phoenix from Winnipeg, as he gained a spiffy new uniform and attention from fans

Mario Lemieux, shown at top in his Canadian Ice Scrapbook insert, made his exit in 1997, while making their debuts were top draft pick Joe Thornton, middle, along with new hockey trading card manufac-turer Pacific, bottom.

in the States. His 1991-92 Parkhurst #424 is at $3, as is his 1991-92 Upper Deck #698.

Boston's Sergei Samsonov, a Russian player expected to turn into a star after being drafted in the first round in 1997, had his 1994-95 Upper Deck SP #189 card double from $3 to $6, but his play wasn't indicative of that type of increase as he had only three goals in his first 30 games.

One of the year's hottest products was 1996-97 Donruss Canadian Ice, distributed only in Canada, with only 1,200 cases produced. Packs sold for $3, boxes for $90 and the 150-card set went for $30. Gold Press Proofs (150 numbered sets) were the hottest insert, with Gretzky's card at $400. Lemieux autographed cards were also inserted (1,200 total) and those sold for $250.

Pinnacle's 1996-97 Select Certified was a hot product thanks to Mirror insert cards. Pinnacle announced a production run of only 30 Gold Mirror cards apiece, sending prices into the atmosphere. Gretzky was selling for $2,500, Lemieux at $2,000, Jagr for $1,500 and Yzerman at $1,100. Other collectors went after Mirror Blue (1:200) and Mirror Red (1:100) cards, helping push packs to $5 apiece and boxes to $100. Mirror Blue pricing includes Gretzky in the $1,000 range, Lemieux around $700, Jagr $600 and Yzerman $450. For Mirror Reds, Gretzky leads the way at $500, Lemieux $350, Jagr $275 and Yzerman $225. The 120-card base set could be found for $50.

1996-97 Upper Deck Ice was one solid trading card product that didn't rely on anything but quality. The base set was popular with those rare set builders, possibly because the cards were printed entirely on clear plastic. The 150-card set went for $125, with packs at $4 and boxes at $80.

The year had its share of winning products, led by rare insert cards. The quality of hockey cards certainly increased during the year, and with Pacific now in the fold, that trend should continue. Hopefully, there won't be too much of a good thing this season.

TOP TEN

INSERT SINGLES

THE FOLLOWING LIST OF CARDS HAVE GENERATED THE MOST DEMAND WITHIN THE HOBBY OVER THE LAST YEAR. THE RANKINGS ARE DETERMINED BY COLLECTORS AND DEALERS FROM THE HOBBY.

No. 1 — WAYNE GRETZKY
'97-98 Pinnacle Certified Mirror Gold #100
The "Great One's" Mirror Gold insert is the No. 1 card in hockey, as dealers report strong demand for this card from die-hard Gretzky collectors. The overall odds of getting this 1:299-pack insert is a whopping 1:38,870 packs, which is why dealers are selling this one for $2,200-$2,500.

No. 2 — MARIO LEMIEUX
'96-97 Upper Deck Game Jersey #GJ6
Lemieux's induction into the Hall of Fame was a fitting end to a highlight-filled career. This Game Jersey is one of his most sought-after, for $500.

No. 3 — ERIC LINDROS
'97-98 Pinnacle Certified Mirror Gold #31
Lindros started the season as a man possessed to get back into the Stanley Cup Finals. Early reports for this scarce insert have it going for $1,200-$1,500.

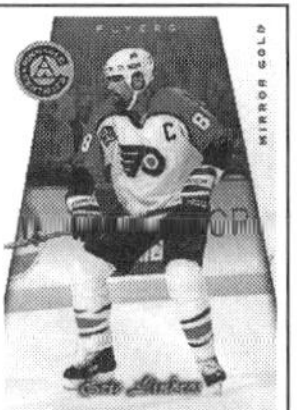

No. 4 — JAROMIR JAGR
'96-97 Upper Deck Game Jersey #GJ4
Game Jerseys remain in high demand, as serious collectors chase their favorite superstars. This red-hot Jagr is one of the most desirable, at $450.

No. 5 — WAYNE GRETZKY
'96-97 Select Certified Mirror Gold #4
Although this one drops four spots this month, any die-hard Gretzky collector would love to pick one up. Limited to 30 singles, it's priced at $2,500.

No. 6 — MARIO LEMIEUX/ERIC LINDROS
'96-97 Donruss Elite Hart to Hart Autograph
This dynamic duo would be a welcome addition to any front line. Collectors can expect to pay $400 for this card.

No. 7 — STEVE YZERMAN
'94-95 Upper Deck Be A Player Autograph #R115
Yzerman's leadership skills shined during the Red Wings' drive to the Stanley Cup title, which is why this autograph is in high demand at $325.

No. 8 — BRENDAN SHANAHAN
'94-95 Upper Deck Be A Player Autograph #86
Shanahan's toughness will once again be a necessary ingredient if the Red Wings are to win back-to-back championships. This one is priced at $200.

No. 9 — MARIO LEMIEUX
'96-97 Select Certified Mirror Gold #10
It's a shame Super Mario won't be entertaining fans with his wizardry, but his accomplishments will never be forgotten. This one books for $2,000.

No. 10 — WAYNE GRETZKY
'97-98 Pacific Crown Die-Cut #15
Pacific's innovative ideas have been a welcome addition to the hockey card market. This one remains in high demand and carries a $40 price tag.

TOP TEN

INSERT SETS

THE FOLLOWING LIST OF SETS HAVE GENERATED THE MOST DEMAND WITHIN THE HOBBY OVER THE LAST YEAR. THE RANKINGS ARE DETERMINED BY COLLECTORS AND DEALERS FROM THE HOBBY.

No. 1 — 1997-98 PINNACLE CERTIFIED MIRROR GOLD
Collectors love scarcity and shiny inserts, and the Mirror Golds satisfy those needs to perfection. Hockey dealers report strong pack sales, with collectors hoping to find one of these elusive 1:299 pack inserts. Commons sell for around $75 to $100.

No. 2 — 1996-97 FLEER FLAIR BLUE ICE
Many singles in this serially numbered set are on the rise. Steve Yzerman jumps to $150, Jaromir Jagr and Eric Lindros to $175 and Gretzky to $325.

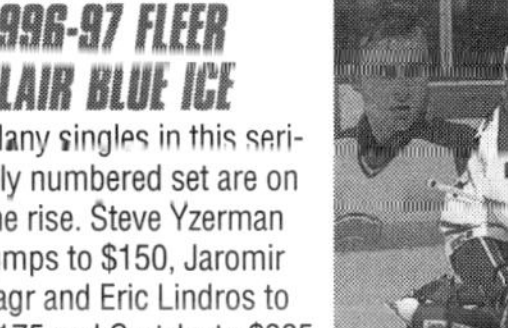

No. 3 — 1996-97 UPPER DECK GAME JERSEYS
Although Game Jerseys aren't No. 1, demand remains high for these elusive 1:2,500 pack inserts. Jagr and Lemieux are hot.

No. 4 — 1997-98 DONRUSS CANADIAN ICE DOMINION SERIES
Limited to 150 sets, these tough-to-find parallel inserts are in high demand. The Gretzky is a mover at $400.

No. 5 — 1996-97 SELECT CERTIFIED MIRROR GOLD
With some of the 1997-98 products hitting the market, demand has slipped a little. The Gretzky single, however, remains red-hot.

No. 6 — 1997-98 PACIFIC CRAMER'S CHOICE
The scarcest Pacific insert set is drawing collector interest. Seeded 1:721 packs, these die-cuts are tough to find but worth the chase. Gretzky moves for around $250.

No. 7 — 1996-97 SELECT CERTIFIED MIRROR BLUE
Seeded 1:200 packs, the Gretzky is the top pull at about $1,000. Other top singles include Lemieux ($800), Yzerman ($450) and Jagr ($600).

No. 8 — 1996-97 PINNACLE BE A PLAYER LINK 2 HISTORY AUTOGRAPHS
Autographs of Lindros ($125), Yzerman ($120), Selanne ($80) and Shanahan ($80) have helped spur demand.

No. 9 — 1997-98 PACIFIC CROWN DIE-CUT
Crown Die-Cuts feature the hot design used in the baseball and football releases. Seeded 1:37 packs, the 20-card set books for $160.

No. 10 — 1997-98 DONRUSS CANADIAN ICE PROVINCIAL SERIES
Limited to only 750 serially numbered sets, it's no surprise that these are in demand. The Gretzky moves for around $100.

REGULAR-ISSUE SINGLES

THE FOLLOWING LIST OF CARDS HAVE GENERATED THE MOST DEMAND WITHIN THE HOBBY OVER THE LAST YEAR. THE RANKINGS ARE DETERMINED BY COLLECTORS AND DEALERS FROM THE HOBBY.

No. 1 — SERGEI SAMSONOV
'94-95 Upper Deck SP #189
The No. 8 overall pick in the 1997 NHL entry draft has stepped right into the Boston Bruins' starting lineup and made an immediate impact. His size (5'8") is the only concern for this exciting player who, once he adapts to the NHL game, should be dominating. Activity has been rising for this one, as it climbs to $5.

No. 2 — JOE THORNTON
'96-97 Upper Deck #370
A pre-season wrist injury slowed his progress a bit, but the future is bright for the No. 1 overall pick in the NHL entry draft. Dealers report getting around $8 for this rookie card.

No. 3 — JOE THORNTON
'96-97 Upper Deck Ice #116
One of the best rookies to hit the NHL since Eric Lindros, Thornton has collectors paying $15 for this one.

No. 4 — JAROMIR JAGR
'90-91 OPC Premier #50
Jagr is the new franchise player in Pittsburgh, with his electrifying moves and strong skating. He's the most exciting performer in the NHL, and his rookie card is a good buy at $30.

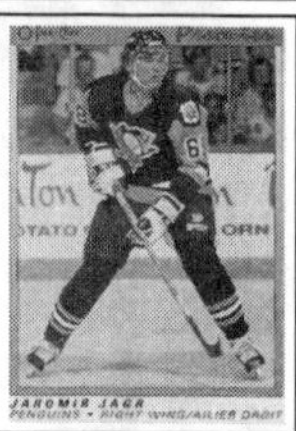

No. 5 — STEVE YZERMAN
'84-85 OPC #67
Yzerman is gearing up for a repeat Stanley Cup performance with the Red Wings. Dealers are getting a strong $80 for this rookie card.

No. 6 — PATRICK MARLEAU
'96-97 Upper Deck #384
The No. 2 overall pick by the San Jose Sharks is a budding superstar. He may have more offensive flair than Thornton, which is why dealers are getting around $2.50 for this one.

No. 7 — JOE THORNTON
'96-97 Upper Deck Black Diamond #160
Due to its $60 price tag, dealers are reporting less activity for this Triple Diamond card. But Bruins fans hope Thornton can add an offensive punch.

No. 8 — RYAN SMYTH
'94-95 Upper Deck SP #142
Edmonton Oiler fans are counting on Smyth to match his 39 goals and 22 assists from last year. This rookie card remains steady and currently carries a $3 price tag.

No. 9 — JOE SAKIC
'89-90 Topps #113
Sakic was the overlooked superstar when he played for the Quebec Nordiques. But a 1995-96 championship with the Avalanche changed that. Grab this rookie card now for $12.

No. 10 — PAUL KARIYA
'92-93 Upper Deck #586
Kariya's holdout couldn't have ended sooner for Mighty Duck fans. He's one of the most exciting players in the NHL, and his rookie remains priced at $15.

REGULAR-ISSUE SETS

THE FOLLOWING LIST OF SETS HAVE GENERATED THE MOST DEMAND WITHIN THE HOBBY OVER THE LAST YEAR. THE RANKINGS ARE DETERMINED BY COLLECTORS AND DEALERS FROM THE HOBBY.

No. 1 — 1997-98 PINNACLE CERTIFIED
Inserts are the driving force in today's market, which explains why Pinnacle Certified catapults to the No. 1 position this month. Inserts include Mirror Red (1:99), Mirror Blue (1:199), Mirror Gold (1:299), Certified Team Golds (1:129) and the Rookie Redemption Program inserts (1:19). Packs are moving for $5, boxes for $100, and the 130-card base set lists for $40.

No. 2 — 1997-98 DONRUSS CANADIAN ICE
The Provincial and Dominion parallel inserts, along with autographs of Shanahan ($175), Mike Vernon ($50) and Lindros ($150), make this product a winner.

No. 3 — 1996-97 SELECT CERTIFIED
Although the new Certified is out, last year's Certified remains a hot item. Packs are moving for $5, with boxes in the $100 range. The 120-card set books for $50.

No. 4 — 1996-97 FLEER FLAIR
The Blue Ice serially numbered inserts are especially active, with many singles on the rise. The 125-card set carries a $125 price tag.

No. 5 — 1996-97 UPPER DECK
The Game Jersey inserts, along with a stellar base card design, has helped spur pack sales. Packs are retailing for $2.50, with boxes at $65.

No. 6 — 1997-98 PACIFIC CROWN
Behind its strong lineup of innovative inserts, Pacific Crown has climbed to No. 6 in our Top Tens. Packs are retailing for around $2.50, with the set at $40.

No. 7 — 1997-98 DONRUSS
Donruss is again loaded with individually numbered inserts, a big hit with collectors. Dealers report selling packs for $2, with hobby boxes selling for $40. The 230-card set debuts at $25.

No. 8 — 1996-97 UPPER DECK ICE
Although Upper Deck Ice's popularity is fading slightly, the base set continues to be a big hit with set builders. The 150-card set currently carries a $125 price tag.

No. 9 — 1996-97 PINNACLE BE A PLAYER
Autographs are all the rage these days in the hobby, so it's no surprise that Be A Player is a winner. Dealers are getting around $7-$8 for packs.

No. 10 — 1996-97 DONRUSS CANADIAN ICE
Distributed exclusively in Canada and limited to 1,200 numbered cases, Canadian Ice remains a steady seller. Packs sell for $3 and the set for $30.

1996-97 Pinnacle Be a Player

The 240-card set was printed in regular-issue and autographed versions. Of the 240 cards, 19 cards were dedicated to rookies and 20 represented "Link To History" die-cut cards. The set was sold in two series. The front of the cards feature "Be A Player" printed in a black stripe in the upper right, while "Pinnacle" is printed vertically along the left. The player's name, position and team are printed at the bottom of the card fronts. The "Link To History" cards are noted on the front left.

	MT
Complete Set (220):	30.00
Complete Series 1 Set (110):	15.00
Complete Series II Set (110):	15.00
Common Player:	.15
Wax Box:	110.00
1 Todd Gill	.15
2 Dave Andreychuk	.15
3 Igor Kravchuk	.15
4 Tom Fitzgerald	.15
5 Jeremy Roenick	1.00
6 Peter Popovic	.15
7 Andy Moog	.40
8 Steven Rice	.15
9 Darren Langdon	.15
10 Mark Fitzpatrick	.15
11 Alexei Zhamnov	.15
12 Luc Robitaille	.30
13 Michal Pivonka	.15
14 Kevin Hatcher	.15
15 Stephane Yelle	.15
16 Bill Ranford	.25
17 Jamie Baker	.15
18 Sean Burke	.50
19 Al Iafrate	.15
20 Mark Recchi	.15
21 Rod Brind'Amour	.30
22 Doug Gilmour	.75
23 Mike Wilson	.15
24 Barry Potomski	.15
25 Mike Gartner	.15
26 Jason Wiemer	.15
27 Scott Lachance	.15
28 Joe Murphy	.15
29 Bill Guerin	.15
30 Byron Dafoe	.15
31 Esa Tikkanen	.15
32 Ken Baumgartner	.15
33 Valeri Kamensky	.30
34 J.J. Daigneault	.15
35 Ulf Dahlen	.15
36 Jason Allison	.15
37 Ted Donato	.15
38 Pat Verbeek	.15
39 Miroslav Satan	.15
40 Eric Desjardins	.15
41 Dave Karpa	.15
42 Jeff Hackett	.40
43 Doug Brown	.15
44 Gord Murphy	.15
45 Kelly Hrudey	.30
46 Kelly Miller	.15
47 Tie Domi	.15
48 Alexei Yashin	.40
49 German Titov	.15
50 Stephane Richer	.15
51 Corey Hirsch	.15
52 Brad May	.15
53 Joe Nieuwendyk	.15
54 Sylvain Lefebvre	.15
55 Brian Leetch	.50
56 Petr Svoboda	.15
57 Dave Manson	.15

58 Jason Woolley	.15
59 Scott Niedermayer	.15
60 Kelly Chase	.15
61 Guy Hebert	.50
62 Shayne Corson	.15
63 Jon Casey	.25
64 Rob Zettler	.15
65 Mikael Andersson	.15
66 Tony Amonte	.40
67 Johan Garpenlov	.15
68 Denny Lambert	.15
69 Jim McKenzie	.15
70 Darren Turcotte	.15
71 Eric Weinrich	.15
72 Troy Mallette	.15
73 Donald Audette	.15
74 Philippe Boucher	.15
75 Shawn Chambers	.15
76 Joel Otto	.15
77 Tommy Salo	.15
78 Olaf Kolzig	.15
79 Adrian Aucoin	.15
80 Alek Stojanov	.15
81 Robert Reichel	.15
82 Marc Bureau	.15
83 Alexander Godynyuk	.15
84 Bill Berg	.15
85 Marc Bergevin	.15
86 Kevin Kaminski	.15
87 Uwe Krupp	.15
88 Boris Mironov	.15
89 Bob Bassen	.15
90 Darryl Shannon	.15
91 Mikael Renberg	.40
92 Mike Stapleton	.15
93 David Roberts	.15
94 Peter Zezel	.15
95 Mathieu Dandonault	.15
96 Bobby Dollas	.15
97 Don Sweeney	.15
98 Niklas Andersson	.15
99 Pat Jablonski	.15
100 John Slaney	.15
101 Kevin Todd	.15
102 Jamie Pushor	.15
103 Andreas Johansson	.15
104 Corey Schwab	.15
105 Todd Simpson	.15
106 Landon Wilson	.15
107 Daniel Goneau	.15
108 David Wilkie	.15
109 Andreas Dackell	.15
110 Marek Malik	.15
111 Mark Messier	1.50
112 Francois Leroux	.15
113 Michal Sykora	.15
114 Rob Zamuner	.15
115 Craig Berube	.15
116 Mike Ricci	.15
117 Adam Burt	.15
118 Alexander Karpovtsev	.15
119 Shawn McEachern	.15
120 Shawn Antoski	.15
121 Dave Reid	.15
122 Todd Warriner	.15
123 Markus Naslund	.15
124 Martin Rucinsky	.15
125 Bob Carpenter	.15
126 Dean MacAmmond	.15
127 Trevor Kidd	.25
128 Martin Lapointe	.15
129 Enrico Ciccone	.15
130 Dixon Ward	.15
131 Jason Muzzatti	.15
132 Bryan Smolinski	.15
133 Norm Maciver	.15
134 Fredrik Olausson	.15
135 Daniel Lacroix	.15
136 Mike Peluso	.15
137 Andrei Nikolishin	.15
138 Rhett Warrener	.15
139 Ray Ferraro	.15
140 Glenn Healy	.15
141 Steve Duchesne	.15
142 Tony Granato	.15
143 Cory Cross	.15
144 Jon Klemm	.15
145 Sami Kapanen	.15
146 Grant Marshall	.15
147 Matthew Barnaby	.15
148 Lyle Odelein	.15
149 Joe Dziedzic	.15
150 Sergei Gonchar	.15
151 Doug Zmolek	.15
152 Sean O'Donnell	.15
153 Scott Thornton	.15
154 Steve Heinze	.15
155 Garry Valk	.15
156 Jeff Finley	.15
157 Trent Klatt	.15
158 Jeff Beukeboom	.15

159 Theoren Fleury	.30
160 Dana Murzyn	.15
161 Tommy Albelin	.15
162 Bryan McCabe	.15
163 Shaun Van Allen	.15
164 Rick Tabaracci	.15
165 Kevin Miller	.15
166 Mariusz Czerkawski	.15
167 Gerald Diduck	.15
168 Brad McCrimmon	.15
169 Stephane Matteau	.15
170 Scott Daniels	.15
171 Scott Mellanby	.15
172 Sandy Moger	.15
173 Steve Konowalchuk	.15
174 Doug Weight	.30
175 Darren McCarty	.15
176 Darryl Sydor	.15
177 Dave Ellett	.15
178 Bob Boughner	.15
179 Derek Armstrong	.15
180 Gary Suter	.15
181 Donald Brashear	.15
182 Chris Tamer	.15
183 Darrin Shannon	.15
184 Stanislav Neckar	.15
185 Brent Severyn	.15
186 Steve Rucchin	.15
187 Jeff Norton	.15
188 Steven Finn	.15
189 Kjell Samuelsson	.15
190 Jeff Friesen	.15
191 Shawn Burr	.15
192 Paul Laus	.15
193 Jeff Odgers	.15
194 Keith Jones	.15
195 Richard Matvichuk	.15
196 Adam Foote	.15
197 Bob Errey	.15
198 Ryan Smyth	.75
199 Mark Janssens	.15
200 Claude Lapointe	.15
201 Brian Noonan	.15
202 Damian Rhodes	.15
203 Dale Hawerchuk	.25
204 Bill Lindsay	.15
205 Brian Skrudland	.15
206 Curtis Joseph	1.00
207 Jon Rohloff	.15
208 Doug Bodger	.15
209 Steve Sullivan	.15
210 Ricard Persson	.15
211 Dwayne Roloson	.15
212 Mike Dunham	.15
213 *Marcel Cousineau*	.75
214 Eric Fichaud	.15
215 Matt Johnson	.15
216 Fredrik Modin	.15
217 Denis Pederson	.15
218 Kevin Hodson	1.00
219 Drew Bannister	.15
220 *Mike Grier*	1.50

1996-97 Pinnacle Be a Player Autographs

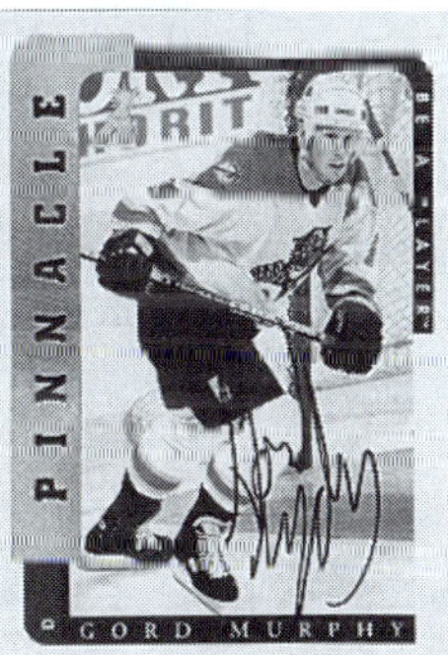

This chase set includes signed versions of the 240 base cards. Gold and black foil distinguishes this version from the common. Autographed cards were inserted one per pack. An autographed silver-foil parallel was inserted 1:7 packs.

	MT
Complete Set (220):	1000.
Common Autograph:	4.00
Foils:	2x
1 Todd Gill	4.00
2 Dave Andreychuk	15.00
3 Igor Kravchuk	4.00
4 Tom Fitzgerald	4.00
5 Jeremy Roenick	35.00
6 Peter Popovic	4.00
7 Andy Moog	20.00
8 Steven Rice	4.00
9 Darren Langdon	4.00
10 Mark Fitzpatrick	4.00
11 Alexei Zhamnov	4.00
12 Luc Robitaille	15.00
13 Michal Pivonka	4.00
14 Kevin Hatcher	10.00
15 Stephane Yelle	8.00
16 Bill Ranford	20.00
17 Jamie Baker	4.00
18 Sean Burke	20.00
19 Al Iafrate	8.00
20 Mark Recchi	10.00
21 Rod Brind'Amour	15.00
22 Doug Gilmour	25.00
23 Mike Wilson	4.00
24 Barry Potomski	4.00
25 Mike Gartner	10.00
26 Jason Wiemer	4.00
27 Scott Lachance	4.00
28 Joe Murphy	10.00
29 Bill Guerin	4.00
30 Byron Dafoe	8.00
31 Esa Tikkanen	8.00
32 Ken Baumgartner	4.00
33 Valeri Kamensky	15.00
34 J.J. Daigneault	4.00
35 Ulf Dahlen	4.00
36 Jason Allison	4.00
37 Ted Donato	4.00
38 Pat Verbeek	10.00
39 Miroslav Satan	10.00
40 Eric Desjardins	4.00
41 Dave Karpa	4.00
42 Jeff Hackett	15.00
43 Doug Brown	4.00
44 Gord Murphy	4.00
45 Kelly Hrudey	15.00
46 Kelly Miller	4.00
47 Tie Domi	4.00
48 Alexei Yashin	20.00
49 German Titov	4.00
50 Stephane Richer	8.00
51 Corey Hirsch	10.00
52 Brad May	4.00
53 Joe Nieuwendyk	10.00
54 Sylvain Lefebvre	4.00
55 Brian Leetch	25.00
56 Petr Svoboda	4.00
57 Dave Manson	4.00
58 Jason Woolley	4.00
59 Scott Niedermayer	10.00
60 Kelly Chase	4.00
61 Guy Hebert	15.00
62 Shayne Corson	4.00
63 Jon Casey	15.00
64 Rob Zettler	4.00
65 Mikael Andersson	4.00
66 Tony Amonte	15.00
67 Johan Garpenlov	4.00
68 Denny Lambert	4.00
69 Jim McKenzie	4.00
70 Darren Turcotte	4.00
71 Eric Weinrich	1.00
72 Troy Mallette	4.00
73 Donald Audette	4.00
74 Philippe Boucher	4.00
75 Shawn Chambers	4.00
76 Joel Otto	4.00
77 Tommy Salo	4.00
78 Olaf Kolzig	4.00
79 Adrian Aucoin	4.00
80 Alek Stojanov	4.00
81 Robert Reichel	4.00
82 Marc Bureau	4.00
83 Alexander Godynyuk	4.00
84 Bill Berg	4.00
85 Marc Bergevin	4.00
86 Kevin Kaminski	4.00
87 Uwe Krupp	4.00
88 Boris Mironov	4.00
89 Bob Bassen	4.00
90 Darryl Shannon	4.00
91 Mikael Renberg	15.00
92 Mike Stapleton	4.00
93 David Roberts	4.00
94 Peter Zezel	4.00
95 Mathieu Dandonault	4.00
96 Bobby Dollas	4.00
97 Don Sweeney	4.00
98 Niklas Andersson	4.00
99 Pat Jablonski	4.00
100 John Slaney	4.00
101 Kevin Todd	4.00
102 Jamie Pushor	10.00

103	Andreas Johansson	4.00
104	Corey Schwab	4.00
105	Todd Simpson	4.00
106	Landon Wilson	4.00
107	Daniel Goneau	10.00
108	David Wilkie	4.00
109	Andreas Dackell	4.00
110	Marek Malik	4.00
111	Mark Messier	70.00
112	Francois Leroux	4.00
113	Michal Sykora	4.00
114	Rob Zamuner	4.00
115	Craig Berube	4.00
116	Mike Ricci	10.00
117	Adam Burt	4.00
118	Alexander Karpovtsev	4.00
119	Shawn McEachern	4.00
120	Shawn Antoski	4.00
121	Dave Reid	4.00
122	Todd Warriner	4.00
123	Markus Naslund	4.00
124	Martin Rucinsky	4.00
125	Bob Carpenter	4.00
126	Dean McAmmond	4.00
127	Trevor Kidd	10.00
128	Martin Lapointe	8.00
129	Enrico Ciccone	4.00
130	Dixon Ward	4.00
131	Jason Muzzatti	4.00
132	Bryan Smolinski	4.00
133	Norm Maciver	4.00
134	Fredrik Olausson	4.00
135	Daniel Lacroix	4.00
136	Mike Peluso	4.00
137	Andrei Nikolishin	4.00
138	Rhett Warrener	4.00
139	Ray Ferraro	4.00
140	Glenn Healy	10.00
141	Steve Duchesne	4.00
142	Tony Granato	8.00
143	Cory Cross	4.00
144	Jon Klemm	4.00
145	Sami Kapanen	4.00
146	Grant Marshall	4.00
147	Matthew Barnaby	4.00
148	Lyle Odelein	4.00
149	Joe Dziedzic	4.00
150	Sergei Gonchar	4.00
151	Doug Zmolek	4.00
152	Sean O'Donnell	4.00
153	Scott Thornton	4.00
154	Steve Heinze	4.00
155	Garry Valk	4.00
156	Jeff Finley	4.00
157	Trent Klatt	4.00
158	Jeff Beukeboom	4.00
159	Theoren Fleury	10.00
160	Dana Murzyn	4.00
161	Tommy Albelin	4.00
162	Bryan McCabe	4.00
163	Shaun Van Allen	4.00
164	Rick Tabaracci	4.00
165	Kevin Miller	4.00
166	Mariusz Czerkawski	4.00
167	Gerald Diduck	4.00
168	Brad McCrimmon	4.00
169	Stephane Matteau	10.00
170	Scott Daniels	4.00
171	Scott Mellanby	4.00
172	Sandy Moger	4.00
173	Steve Konowalchuk	4.00
174	Doug Weight	12.00
175	Darren McCarty	8.00
176	Darryl Sydor	4.00
177	Dave Ellett	4.00
178	Bob Boughner	4.00
179	Derek Armstrong	4.00
180	Gary Suter	8.00
181	Donald Brashear	4.00
182	Chris Tamer	4.00
183	Darrin Shannon	4.00
184	Stanislav Neckar	4.00
185	Brent Severyn	4.00
186	Steve Rucchin	4.00
187	Jeff Norton	4.00
188	Steven Finn	4.00
189	Kjell Samuelsson	4.00
190	Jeff Friesen	10.00
191	Shawn Burr	8.00
192	Paul Laus	4.00
193	Jeff Odgers	4.00
194	Keith Jones	4.00
195	Richard Matvichuk	4.00
196	Adam Foote	8.00
197	Bob Errey	4.00
198	Ryan Smyth	20.00
199	Mark Janssens	4.00
200	Claude Lapointe	4.00
201	Brian Noonan	4.00
202	Damian Rhodes	4.00
203	Dale Hawerchuk	20.00

204	Bill Lindsay	4.00
205	Brian Skrudland	4.00
206	Curtis Joseph	30.00
207	Jon Rohloff	4.00
208	Doug Bodger	4.00
209	Steve Sullivan	4.00
210	Ricard Persson	4.00
211	Dwayne Roloson	4.00
212	Mike Dunham	4.00
213	Marcel Cousineau	6.00
214	Eric Fichaud	12.00
215	Matt Johnson	4.00
216	Fredrik Modin	4.00
217	Denis Pederson	4.00
218	Kevin Hodson	35.00
219	Drew Bannister	4.00
220	Mike Grier	25.00

1996-97 Pinnacle Be a Player Lemieux Die Cut

This series includes 132 cards, 66 from each series. The Dufex cards interlock.

	MT
Common Lemieux (DC66):	600.00

1996-97 Pinnacle Be a Player Lindros Die Cut

The 176 cards, 88 from each series, are autographed by Eric Lindros. The Dufex cards interlock.

	MT
Common Lindros (AU88):	600.00

1996-97 Pinnacle Be a Player Messier Die Cut

The 22 cards, 11 from each series, are autographed by Mark Messier. The Dufex cards interlock.

	MT
Common Messier (AU11):	1000.00

1996-97 Pinnacle Be a Player Link 2 History

The 20 Link 2 History cards are die-cut and are noted on the front left. An autographed edition and signed foil versions were also randomly seeded.

		MT
Complete Set (20):		50.00
Common Player:		.75
L1B	Teemu Selanne	4.00
L1A	Jarome Iginla	2.00
L2B	Peter Forsberg	8.00
L2A	Harry York	1.50
L3B	Brendan Shanahan	5.00
L3A	Sergei Berezin	3.00
L4A	Ethan Moreau	1.00
L4B	Pavel Bure	5.00
L5B	Jason Arnott	1.00

L5A	Rem Murray	1.50
L6B	Paul Kariya	8.00
L6A	Jamie Langenbrunner	.75
L7B	Eric Lindros	10.00
L7A	Jim Campbell	1.00
L8B	Pat LaFontaine	1.50
L8A	Jonas Hoglund	.75
L9B	Steve Yzerman	6.00
L9A	Wade Redden	.75
L10A	Patrick Lalime	4.00
L10B	John Vanbiesbrouck	6.00

1996-97 Pinnacle Be a Player Link 2 History Autographs

		MT
Complete Set (20):		900.00
Common Player:		15.00
Foils:		2x-3x
L1B	Teemu Selanne	80.00
L1A	Jarome Iginla	40.00
L2B	Peter Forsberg	125.00
L2A	Harry York	25.00
L3B	Brendan Shanahan	80.00
L3A	Sergei Berezin	25.00
L4A	Ethan Moreau	15.00
L4B	Pavel Bure	80.00
L5B	Jason Arnott	25.00
L5A	Rem Murray	15.00
L6B	Paul Kariya	125.00
L6A	Jamie Langenbrunner	15.00
L7B	Eric Lindros	150.00
L7A	Jim Campbell	15.00
L8B	Pat LaFontaine	25.00
L8A	Jonas Hoglund	15.00
L9B	Steve Yzerman	120.00
L9A	Wade Redden	15.00
L10A	Patrick Lalime	60.00
L10B	John Vanbiesbrouck	80.00

1996-97 Pinnacle Be a Player Stacking the Pads

The 15-card set is a tribute to the goalies. The Dufex cards were inserted 1:35 packs.

		MT
Complete Set (15):		350.00
Common Goalie:		15.00
1	Patrick Lalime	30.00
2	Chris Osgood	25.00
3	Ron Hextall	15.00
4	John Vanbiesbrouck	50.00
5	Martin Brodeur	40.00
6	Felix Potvin	25.00
7	Nikolai Khabibulin	15.00
8	Jim Carey	25.00
9	Grant Fuhr	20.00
10	Mike Richter	25.00
11	Dominik Hasek	35.00
12	Andy Moog	15.00
13	Patrick Roy	80.00
14	Curtis Joseph	20.00
15	Jocelyn Thibault	20.00

1996-97 Pinnacle Be a Player Biscuit in the Basket

The 25-card set was printed with Dufex technology. The cards were inserted 1:17 packs.

		MT
Complete Set (25):		500.00
Common Player:		6.00
1	Wayne Gretzky	75.00
2	Mario Lemieux	60.00
3	Eric Lindros	45.00
4	Theoren Fleury	6.00
5	Peter Forsberg	45.00
6	Keith Tkachuk	12.00
7	Sergei Fedorov	30.00
8	Mike Modano	6.00
9	Jaromir Jagr	45.00
10	Brendan Shanahan	30.00
11	Teemu Selanne	30.00
12	Mats Sundin	12.00
13	Steve Yzerman	35.00
14	Brett Hull	20.00
15	Zigmund Palffy	12.00
16	Joe Sakic	35.00
17	John LeClair	12.00
18	Pavel Bure	30.00
19	Mark Messier	20.00
20	Paul Kariya	45.00
21	Jason Arnott	6.00
22	Saku Koivu	15.00
23	Daniel Alfredsson	6.00
24	Alexander Mogilny	12.00
25	Owen Nolan	6.00

1996-97 Donruss

Donruss' 1996-97 240-card hockey set includes cards for 35 top rookie prospects and several inserts. The regular card front has a full-bleed color photo. The brand logo is in the left corner, with a team color-coordinated band coming off it which includes the player's name in it. The team logo is in a circle toward the bottom of the card. The horizontal card back has the player's name and position toward the upper left corner, with a card number in the upper right. A photo is on the right side, flanked on the left by NHL career stats and a brief player profile. A color stripe running along the bottom has biographical information. A parallel rendition of the regular set, Gold Press Proofs, was also made. These cards are die-cut and are sequentially numbered to 2,000. Insert sets include Hit List, Dominators, Between the Pipes, Silver Elite (a parallel Gold Elite set was also made; printed in gold foil, these cards are sequentially numbered to 1,500), Rated Rookies and Go Top Shelf (magazine exclusive).

		MT
Complete Set (240):		18.00
Common Player:		.10
Gold Press Proofs:		25x to 40x
Wax Box:		30.00
1	Joe Sakic	.75
2	Jeremy Roenick	.35
3	Kirk McLean	.10

#	Player	Price
4	Zarley Zalapski	.10
5	Jyrki Lumme	.10
6	Owen Nolan	.10
7	Luc Robitaille	.10
8	Bob Probert	.10
9	Ken Baumgartner	.10
10	Rick Tabaracci	.10
11	Alexei Zhitnik	.10
12	Al MacInnis	.10
13	Brian Leetch	.15
14	Valeri Kamensky	.10
15	Todd Gill	.10
16	Mark Messier	.40
17	Pierre Turgeon	.10
18	Mathieu Schneider	.10
19	Vyacheslav Kozlov	.10
20	Milos Holan	.10
21	Yanic Perreault	.10
22	Mike Modano	.15
23	Claude Lemieux	.10
24	Rob Niedermayer	.10
25	Eric Desjardins	.10
26	Alexander Semak	.10
27	Mark Recchi	.15
28	Viacheslav Fetisov	.10
29	Kevin Hatcher	.10
30	Mats Sundin	.25
31	Jeff Reese	.10
32	Alexander Selivanov	.10
33	Jim Carey	.40
34	Darren Puppa	.10
35	Vincent Damphousse	.10
36	John LeClair	.20
37	Jon Casey	.15
38	Chris Terreri	.10
39	Larry Murphy	.10
40	Geoff Sanderson	.10
41	Adam Oates	.15
42	Sandy McCarthy	.10
43	Jaromir Jagr	1.25
44	Roman Oksiuta	.10
45	Zigmund Palffy	.25
46	Doug Gilmour	.20
47	Cliff Ronning	.10
48	Curtis Leschyshyn	.10
49	Scott Mellanby	.10
50	Sergei Fedorov	.75
51	Denis Savard	.10
52	Mike Vernon	.20
53	Todd Marchant	.10
54	Geoff Courtnall	.10
55	Shayne Corson	.10
56	Dimitri Khristich	.10
57	Scott Stevens	.10
58	German Titov	.10
59	Darren Turcotte	.10
60	Michal Pivonka	.10
61	Ron Hextall	.20
62	Ed Belfour	.25
63	Chris Pronger	.10
64	Brian Bellows	.10
65	Pavel Bure	.75
66	Adam Graves	.10
67	Tom Barrasso	.20
68	Stu Barnes	.10
69	Norm MacIver	.10
70	Jesse Belanger	.10
71	Chris Chelios	.15
72	Tommy Soderstrom	.10
73	Nelson Emerson	.10
74	Kenny Jonsson	.10
75	Bill Lindsay	.10
76	Petr Nedved	.10
77	Robert Svehla	.15
78	Tomas Sandstrom	.10
79	Jeff Friesen	.10
80	Tony Amonte	.10
81	Sylvain Lefebvre	.10
82	Greg Adams	.10
83	Vladimir Konstantinov	.10
84	Roman Hamrlik	.10
85	Doug Weight	.10
86	Shaun Van Allen	.10
87	Bill Ranford	.10
88	Jeff Hackett	.10
89	Alexei Zhamnov	.10
90	Dale Hawerchuk	.10
91	Sergei Zubov	.10
92	Dan Quinn	.10
93	Wayne Gretzky	2.50
94	Todd Harvey	.10
95	Chris Osgood	.60
96	Felix Potvin	.50
97	Richard Matvichuk	.10
98	Wendel Clark	.10
99	Bryan Smolinski	.10
100	Rob Blake	.10
101	Jocelyn Thibault	.30
102	Trevor Linden	.10
103	Craig MacTavish	.10
104	Sandis Ozolinsh	.15

#	Player	Price
105	Oleg Tverdovsky	.10
106	Garry Galley	.10
107	Derek Plante	.10
108	Stephane Richer	.10
109	Dave Andreychuk	.10
110	Curtis Joseph	.25
111	Greg Johnson	.10
112	Patrick Roy	1.50
113	Pat LaFontaine	.15
114	Uwe Krupp	.10
115	Ulf Dahlen	.10
116	Brian Bradley	.10
117	Grant Fuhr	.20
118	Brian Skrudland	.10
119	Nicklas Lidstrom	.10
120	Steve Chiasson	.10
121	Sean Burke	.20
122	Rick Tocchet	.10
123	Martin Rucinsky	.10
124	Alexei Yashin	.10
125	Mikael Renberg	.10
126	Teppo Numminen	.10
127	Randy Burridge	.10
128	Radek Bonk	.10
129	Scott Young	.10
130	Gary Suter	.10
131	Mario Lemieux	2.00
132	Ray Bourque	.15
133	Martin Gelinas	.10
134	Keith Tkachuk	.40
135	Benoit Hogue	.10
136	Ken Wregget	.10
137	Eric Lindros	1.50
138	Keith Primeau	.10
139	Peter Forsberg	.75
140	Paul Coffey	.15
141	Mike Ridley	.10
142	Paul Kariya	1.00
143	Jason Arnott	.10
144	Joe Murphy	.10
145	Adam Deadmarsh	.10
146	John MacLean	.10
147	Peter Bondra	.15
148	Martin Brodeur	.40
149	Ron Francis	.20
150	Dino Ciccarelli	.10
151	Joe Juneau	.10
152	Matthew Barnaby	.10
153	Mark Tinordi	.10
154	Craig Janney	.10
155	Rod Brind'Amour	.10
156	Damian Rhodes	.10
157	Teemu Selanne	.50
158	James Patrick	.10
159	Theoren Fleury	.10
160	Trevor Kidd	.10
161	Kirk Muller	.10
162	Andrew Cassels	.10
163	Brent Fedyk	.10
164	Guy Hebert	.20
165	Jason Dawe	.10
166	Andy Moog	.20
167	Igor Larionov	.10
168	Brian Savage	.10
169	Kris Draper	.10
170	Dave Gagner	.10
171	Steve Yzerman	.75
172	Nikolai Khabibulin	.20
173	Chris Gratton	.10
174	Dave Lowry	.10
175	Travis Green	.10
176	Alexei Kovalev	.10
177	Mike Ricci	.10
178	Brendan Shanahan	.40
179	Corey Hirsch	.15
180	Bill Guerin	.10
181	Alexander Mogilny	.25
182	Steve Duchesne	.10
183	Ray Ferraro	.10
184	Mike Richter	.35
185	Yuri Khmylev	.10
186	Stephane Fiset	.15
187	John Vanbiesbrouck	.75
188	Scott Niedermayer	.10
189	Brad May	.10
190	Shawn McEachern	.10
191	Joe Mullen	.10
192	Dominik Hasek	.30
193	Steve Thomas	.10
194	Russ Courtnall	.10
195	Joe Nieuwendyk	.10
196	Petr Klima	.10
197	Brett Hull	.40
198	Bernie Nicholls	.10
199	Dale Hunter	.10
200	Pat Verbeek	.10
201	Phil Housley	.10
202	Todd Krygier	.10
203	Zdeno Ciger	.10
204	Alexandre Daigle	.10
205	Cam Neely	.10

#	Player	Price
206	Mike Gartner	.10
207	Garth Snow	.10
208	Pat Falloon	.10
209	Kelly Hrudey	.15
210	Ray Sheppard	.10
211	Ted Donato	.10
212	Glenn Healy	.10
213	Radek Dvorak	.15
214	Niclas Andersson	.10
215	Miroslav Satan	.15
216	Roman Vopat	.10
217	Bryan McCabe	.10
218	Jamie Langenbrunner	.10
219	Kyle McLaren	.15
220	Stephane Yelle	.10
221	Byron Dafoe	.10
222	Grant Marshall	.10
223	Ryan Smyth	.15
224	Ville Peltonen	.10
225	Deron Quint	.10
226	Brian Holzinger	.10
227	Jose Theodore	.20
228	*Ethan Moreau*	.35
229	Steve Sullivan	.10
230	*Kevin Hodson*	.50
231	Cory Stillman	.10
232	Ralph Intranuovo	.10
233	Vitali Yachmenev	.10
234	Marcus Ragnarsson	.10
235	Nolan Baumgartner	.10
236	Chad Kilger	.15
237	Niklas Sundstrom	.10
238	Checklist	.10
239	Checklist	.10
240	Checklist	.10

1996-97 Donruss Between the Pipes

These retail exclusive cards showcase the league's top 10 goalies. Cards, sequentially numbered to 4,000, are die-cut and incorporate red foil printing into the card design. The front has the red foil along the top and right borders, plus for the Donruss logo in an upper corner and the set logo. The center of the card has an action photo of the player, as seen through a net-like pattern, part of which is die-cut. The player's name and position run along the left side of the card. The back side reverses the red foil border, with the player's name, team, position and card number at the top, underlined by a red line. A color photo is in the middle, flanked on the left by a brief writeup. Career and 1995-96 stats are listed toward the bottom, in three colored bands. The serial number, 1 of 4,000, etc., is along the bottom.

		MT
Complete Set (10):		150.00
Common Goalie:		8.00
1	Patrick Roy	50.00
2	Martin Brodeur	25.00
3	Jim Carey	15.00
4	John Vanbiesbrouck	30.00
5	Chris Osgood	15.00
6	Ed Belfour	10.00
7	Jocelyn Thibault	10.00
8	Curtis Joseph	8.00
9	Nikolai Khabibulin	8.00
10	Felix Potvin	15.00

1996-97 Donruss Dominators

These cards, exclusive to 1996-97 Donruss hobby packs, showcase three of the game's premier players on the front of each card. Sequentially numbered to 5,000, the inserts are printed on laminated holographic foil stock for the front. The three players on the front are superimposed against a background which says "Dominators." A team logo appears beneath the photo. The card back, numbered 1 of 10 etc., has three mug shots of the players, with their names and stats underneath. The serial number, 1 of 5,000 etc., is at the bottom.

		MT
Complete Set (10):		160.00
Common Player:		8.00
1	Jim Carey, Martin Brodeur, John Vanbiesbrouck	20.00
2	Nikolai Khabibulin, Chris Osgood, Jocelyn Thibault	16.00
3	Chris Chelios, Paul Coffey, Ray Bourque	8.00
4	Mario Lemieux, Jaromir Jagr, Ron Francis	35.00
5	Eric Lindros, Wayne Gretzky, Jason Arnott	40.00
6	Doug Gilmour, Wendel Clark, Pierre Turgeon	8.00
7	Alexander Mogilny, Pavel Bure, Trevor Linden	16.00
8	Paul Kariya, Teemu Selanne, Keith Tkachuk	25.00
9	Mike Modano, Jeremy Roenick, Sergei Fedorov	16.00
10	Eric Daze, Saku Koivu, Ed Jovanovski	12.00

1996-97 Donruss Go Top Shelf

Ten of the NHL's top scorers are featured on these 1996-97 Donruss hockey insert cards. The cards were magazine exclusive. The horizontal front has a color action photo circled by an oval which swirls off into a foiled insert set logo and player's name. The Donruss logo is also in foil. The horizontal back has a team logo in the upper left corner, with a card number (1 of 10, etc.) in a white box in the opposite corner. A brief recap of the player's accomplishments is on the right, next to the team logo. Three rectangles are along the left, containing statistical and biographical information. The player photo is on the right, again inside an oval. The serial number (1 of 2,000) is along the bottom.

		MT
Complete Set (10):		450.00
Common Player:		15.00
1	Mario Lemieux	90.00
2	Teemu Selanne	35.00
3	Joe Sakic	50.00
4	Alexander Mogilny	20.00
5	Jaromir Jagr	65.00
6	Brett Hull	35.00
7	Jeremy Roenick	25.00
8	Paul Kariya	65.00
9	Eric Lindros	65.00
10	Peter Forsberg	50.00

1996-97 Donruss Hit List

These 20 die-cut insert cards take hockey fans up close and personal for a look at some of the most physical players in the sport. The cards are sequentially numbered to 10,000 and feature an internal die-cut H inside a circle with the player's name and position printed in foil along the perimeter. The team name is along an arch at the bottom. Donruss, stamped in foil, and "Hit List" are written at the top. The back, numbered sequentially 1 of 1,000, etc., has a photo on the right side, with the die-cut circle and a team logo underneath. The circle has biographical information in it. A colored panel along the left side has a description of the player's talents and skills.

		MT
Complete Set (20):		150.00
Common Player:		5.00
1	Eric Lindros	30.00
2	Wendel Clark	5.00
3	Ed Jovanovski	10.00
4	Jeremy Roenick	10.00
5	Doug Weight	5.00
6	Chris Chelios	5.00
7	Brendan Shanahan	10.00
8	Mark Messier	10.00
9	Scott Stevens	5.00
10	Keith Tkachuk	10.00
11	Trevor Linden	5.00
12	Eric Daze	8.00
13	John LeClair	8.00
14	Peter Forsberg	25.00
15	Doug Gilmour	6.00
16	Roman Hamrlik	5.00
17	Owen Nolan	5.00
18	Claude Lemieux	5.00
19	Saku Koivu	8.00
20	Theoren Fleury	5.00

1996-97 Donruss Rated Rookies

This set features the NHL's brightest young prospects - the next generation of superstars. The card front has a color action photo of the player, with his name and Donruss at the top of the card in silver foil. The Rated Rookie logo is centered at the bottom of the card, with the player's team name below in silver foil. The card back has "Rated Rookie" and a card number (1 of 10, etc.) along the top, with a color mug shot below. The player's name is above the shot; a team logo and his name are below. Then, biographical information and a career summary follow. The background is a Rated Rookies symbol.

		MT
Complete Set (10):		30.00
Common Player:		2.50
1	Eric Daze	5.00
2	Petr Sykora	5.00
3	Valeri Bure	2.50
4	Jere Lehtinen	2.50
5	Jeff O'Neill	2.50
6	Saku Koivu	8.00
7	Ed Jovanovski	6.00
8	Eric Fichaud	2.50
9	Todd Bertuzzi	2.50
10	Daniel Alfredsson	5.00

1996-97 Donruss Silver Elite

These 1996-97 Donruss insert cards honor some of the NHL's finest superstars using full silver foil print technology. The cards are sequentially numbered to 10,000. A special gold-foil parallel version of the Silver Donruss Elite insert set was also produced - Gold Donruss Elite. The cards were sequentially numbered to 1,500.

		MT
Complete Set (10):		125.00
Common Player:		6.00
Gold Elites:		2x to 4x
1	Pavel Bure	10.00
2	Wayne Gretzky	35.00
3	Doug Weight	6.00
4	Brett Hull	8.00
5	Mark Messier	8.00
6	Brendan Shanahan	10.00
7	Joe Sakic	15.00
8	Sergei Fedorov	10.00
9	Eric Lindros	25.00
10	Patrick Roy	30.00

1996-97 Canadian Ice

The 1996-97 Donruss Canadian Ice Hockey set features 150 cards with the entire production limited to 1,200 individually numbered cases. The bases cards feature a color action shot with "Canadian Ice" written is a semi-circle along the top edge. The player's name and team appear inset a gray half circle along the bottom edge. The card backs feature a player closeup within a small circle with bio and stat information given. Insert sets are Les Gardiens, O Canada, Mario Lemieux Autograph and Mario Lemieux Scrapbook.

		MT
Complete Set (150):		30.00
Common Player:		.15
Wax Box:		95.00
1	Jaromir Jagr	2.50
2	Jocelyn Thibault	.35
3	Paul Kariya	2.50
4	Derian Hatcher	.15
5	Wayne Gretzky	4.00
6	Peter Forsberg	2.00
7	Eric Lindros	2.50
8	Adam Oates	.25
9	Paul Coffey	.15
10	Chris Osgood	.75
11	Pat LaFontaine	.25
12	Mats Sundin	.25
13	Rob Niedermayer	.15
14	Doug Weight	.15
15	Al MacInnis	.15
16	Damian Rhodes	.15
17	Stephane Fiset	.35
18	Mike Gartner	.15
19	Patrick Roy	3.00
20	Eric Daze	.30
21	Ray Bourque	.25
22	Keith Tkachuk	.50
23	Mark Recchi	.15
24	Peter Bondra	.15
25	Mike Modano	.35
26	Mike Richter	.40
27	Keith Primeau	.15
28	Todd Bertuzzi	.15
29	Wendel Clark	.15
30	Scott Young	.15
31	Mario Lemieux	3.00
32	Valeri Kamensky	.15
33	Kirk McLean	.15
34	Daniel Alfredsson	.40
35	Ed Jovanovski	.25
36	Kelly Hrudey	.15
37	Trevor Kidd	.15
38	Joe Juneau	.15
39	Steve Yzerman	2.00
40	Saku Koivu	1.00
41	Alexei Kovalev	.15
42	Rob Blake	.15
43	Shayne Corson	.15
44	Roman Hamrlik	.15
45	Stephane Yelle	.15
46	Martin Brodeur	1.00
47	Kirk Muller	.15
48	Pat Verbeek	.15
49	Jari Kurri	.15
50	Michal Pivonka	.15
51	Ron Hextall	.30
52	Trevor Linden	.15
53	Vincent Damphousse	.15
54	Owen Nolan	.15
55	Sergei Fedorov	1.00
56	Chris Chelios	.25
57	Jeremy Roenick	.40
58	Zigmund Palffy	.50
59	Pavel Bure	1.50
60	Dominik Hasek	.75
61	Alexei Yashin	.25
62	Chris Gratton	.15
63	Joe Nieuwendyk	.15
64	Luc Robitaille	.15
65	Brett Hull	.50
66	Sean Burke	.25
67	Felix Potvin	.40
68	Jason Arnott	.15
69	Valeri Bure	.15
70	Tom Barrasso	.25
71	Vyacheslav Kozlov	.15
72	Petr Sykora	.15
73	Corey Hirsch	.25
74	Joe Sakic	1.75
75	Bill Ranford	.25
76	Yanic Perreault	.15
77	Mikael Renberg	.15
78	Theoren Fleury	.15
79	Jim Carey	.75
80	Vitali Yachmenev	.15
81	Martin Rucinsky	.15
82	Jeff O'Neill	.15
83	Marcus Ragnarsson	.15
84	John Vanbiesbrouck	1.75
85	Teemu Selanne	.75
86	Larry Murphy	.15
87	Mark Messier	.50
88	Alexei Zhamnov	.15
89	Ryan Smyth	.20
90	Andy Moog	.25
91	Alexander Mogilny	.40
92	Kris Draper	.15
93	Ron Francis	.25
94	Mike Vernon	.25
95	Nikolai Khabibulin	.35
96	Mariusz Czerkawski	.15
97	Mathieu Schneider	.15
98	Stephane Richer	.15
99	Mike Ricci	.15
100	John LeClair	.25
101	Brendan Shanahan	.75
102	Daren Puppa	.15
103	Scott Stevens	.15
104	Alexandre Daigle	.15
105	Dimitri Khristich	.15
106	Bernie Nicholls	.15
107	Scott Mellanby	.15
108	Brian Leetch	.15
109	Grant Fuhr	.35
110	Pierre Turgeon	.15
111	Jere Lehtinen	.15
112	Doug Gilmour	.25
113	Ed Belfour	.35
114	Geoff Sanderson	.15
115	Claude Lemieux	.15
116	Curtis Joseph	.35
117	Igor Larionov	.15
118	Jamie Pushor	.20
119	*Sergei Berezin*	.60
120	Eric Fichaud	.20
121	Wade Redden	.20
122	Hnat Domenichelli	.20
123	*Rem Murray*	.50
124	Jarome Iginla	.50
125	*Richard Zednik*	.40
126	*Daniel Goneau*	.40
127	*Ethan Moreau*	.40
128	Janne Niinimaa	.15
129	*Tomas Holmstrom*	.40
130	*Fredrik Modin*	.40
131	Bryan Berard	.40
132	Jim Campbell	.25
133	Chris O'Sullivan	.15
134	*Andreas Dackell*	.20
135	Daymond Langkow	.15
136	*Kevin Hodson*	.75
137	Jamie Langenbrunner	.15
138	*Mattias Timander*	.15
139	Tuomas Gronman	.15
140	Jonas Hoglund	.15
141	*Mike Grier*	.75
142	Terry Ryan	.15
143	Darcy Tucker	.15
144	Brandon Convery	.15
145	Anders Eriksson	.15
146	Christian Dube	.15
147	*Dainius Zubrus*	2.00
148	Grant Fuhr (Checklist)	.15
149	Paul Coffey (Checklist)	.15
150	Ray Bourque (Checklist)	.15

1996-97 Canadian Ice Gold Press Proofs

The 150-card parallel insert set was limited in production to 150 sets. The cards are identical to the base set of 1996-97 Donruss Canadian Ice. The cards feature gold foil.

	MT
Complete Set (150):	5000.
Common Player:	8.00
Veteran Stars:	75x to 125x
Young Stars & RC's:	50x to 75x

1996-97 Canadian Ice Red Press Proofs

The 150-card parallel insert set was limited in production to 750 sets and parallels in design the base cards from the 1996-97 Donruss Canadian Ice set with red foil.

	MT
Complete Set (150):	1500.
Common Player:	2.50
Veteran Stars:	20x to 30x
Young Stars & RC's:	15x to 20x

1996-97 Canadian Ice Les Gardiens

Numbered seuentially to 1,500, Les Gardiens were randomly inserted into packs of 1996-97 Donruss Canadian Ice Hockey. The set features 10 goalies who grew up in the province of Quebec.

		MT
Complete Set (10):		300.00
Common Player:		15.00
1	Patrick Roy	90.00
2	Jocelyn Thibault	40.00
3	Felix Potvin	40.00
4	Martin Brodeur	50.00
5	Stephane Fiset	25.00
6	Eric Fichaud	15.00
7	Dominic Roussel	15.00
8	Emmanuel Fernandez	20.00
9	Martin Biron	30.00
10	Jose Theodore	30.00

1996-97 Canadian Ice Mario Lemieux Scrapbook

The 25-card insert set, randomly found in packs of 1996-97 Donruss Canadian Ice Hockey, was limited in production to 1,966 sets. The cards feature a color photo on gold-foil board with a brief highlight in both English and French on the back.

		MT
Complete Set (25):		275.00
Common Lemieux:		12.00
Lemieux Autograph:		250.00
1	Mario Lemieux	12.00
2	Mario Lemieux	12.00
3	Mario Lemieux	12.00
4	Mario Lemieux	12.00
5	Mario Lemieux	12.00
6	Mario Lemieux	12.00
7	Mario Lemieux	12.00
8	Mario Lemieux	12.00
9	Mario Lemieux	12.00
10	Mario Lemieux	12.00
11	Mario Lemieux	12.00
12	Mario Lemieux	12.00
13	Mario Lemieux	12.00
14	Mario Lemieux	12.00
15	Mario Lemieux	12.00
16	Mario Lemieux	12.00
17	Mario Lemieux	12.00
18	Mario Lemieux	12.00
19	Mario Lemieux	12.00
20	Mario Lemieux	12.00
21	Mario Lemieux	12.00
22	Mario Lemieux	12.00
23	Mario Lemieux	12.00
24	Mario Lemieux	12.00
25	Mario Lemieux	12.00

1996-97 Canadian Ice O Canada

The 16-card, die-cut set features top NHL players from small Canadian towns. The Canadian flag is featured in the background and the entire set is sequentially numbered to 2,000

		MT
Complete Set (16):		300.00
Common Player:		8.00
1	Joe Sakic	30.00
2	Paul Kariya	50.00
3	Mark Messier	20.00
4	Jarome Iginla	20.00
5	Theoren Fleury	8.00
6	Ed Belfour	15.00
7	Wayne Gretzky	80.00
8	Chris Gratton	8.00
9	Doug Gilmour	12.00
10	Kirk Muller	8.00
11	Eric Lindros	50.00
12	Brendan Shanahan	25.00
13	Mario Lemieux	60.00
14	Eric Daze	10.00
15	Geoff Sanderson	8.00
16	Terry Ryan	8.00

1996-97 Donruss Elite

The 150-card set features the player's name written in cursive at the top of the card front. The Donruss Elite logo is at the bottom center, with the team name beneath the logo. Elite Stars is a 150-card parallel set that features silver-poly, foil laminate die-cut cards.

		MT
Complete Set (150):		40.00
Common Player:		.15
Wax Box:		55.00
1	Paul Kariya	2.50
2	Ron Hextall	.25
3	Andy Moog	.25
4	Brett Hull	.75
5	Felix Potvin	.75
6	Jocelyn Thibault	.50
7	Eric Lindros	2.50
8	Jaromir Jagr	2.50
9	Sergei Fedorov	1.00
10	Wayne Gretzky	4.00
11	Peter Bondra	.25
12	Peter Forsberg	2.00
13	Stephane Fiset	.15
14	Owen Nolan	.15
15	Rob Niedermayer	.15
16	Martin Brodeur	1.00
17	Ray Bourque	.25
18	Todd Bertuzzi	.15
19	Jim Carey	.50
20	Chris Chelios	.25
21	Chris Osgood	1.00
22	Mark Messier	.75
23	Roman Hamrlik	.15
24	Kevin Hatcher	.15
25	Doug Weight	.15
26	Mark Recchi	.15
27	Jeremy Roenick	.40
28	Derian Hatcher	.15
29	Grant Fuhr	.40
30	Scott Stevens	.15
31	Adam Oates	.25
32	Scott Mellanby	.15
33	Mikael Renberg	.15
34	Corey Hirsch	.15
35	Michal Pivonka	.15
36	Stephane Richer	.15
37	Dominik Hasek	1.00
38	Steve Yzerman	2.00
39	Jeff O'Neill	.15
40	Ron Francis	.15
41	Alexei Yashin	.15
42	Pat Verbeek	.15
43	Geoff Courtnall	.15
44	Doug Gilmour	.40
45	Trevor Kidd	.15
46	Jason Arnott	.15
47	Niklas Sundstrom	.15
48	Rob Blake	.15
49	Nikolai Khabibulin	.25
50	Igor Larionov	.15
51	Sean Burke	.25
52	Zigmund Palffy	.60
53	Jeff Friesen	.15
54	Theoren Fleury	.15
55	Mats Sundin	.50
56	Alexander Mogilny	.40
57	John LeClair	.60
58	Shayne Corson	.15
59	Teemu Selanne	1.00
60	Kelly Hrudey	.15
61	Keith Tkachuk	.60
62	Joe Nieuwendyk	.15
63	Tom Barrasso	.25
64	Aaron Gavey	.15
65	Alexei Zhamnov	.15
66	Patrick Roy	3.00
67	Al MacInnis	.15
68	Trevor Linden	.15
69	Bill Guerin	.15
70	Dimitri Khristich	.15
71	Eric Daze	.35
72	Paul Coffey	.25
73	Keith Primeau	.15
74	John Vanbiesbrouck	1.75
75	Bernie Nicholls	.15
76	Yanic Perreault	.15
77	Jere Lehtinen	.15
78	Luc Robitaille	.15
79	Todd Gill	.15
80	Saku Koivu	1.00
81	Vyacheslav Kozlov	.15
82	Ed Jovanovski	.35
83	Brendan Witt	.15
84	Alexandre Daigle	.15
85	Jari Kurri	.15
86	Mike Vernon	.25
87	Jeff Beukeboom	.15
88	Mathieu Schneider	.15
89	Niklas Andersson	.15
90	Joe Juneau	.15
91	Ed Belfour	.35
92	Curtis Joseph	.50
93	Rod Brind'Amour	.15
94	Vitali Yachmenev	.15
95	Alexander Selivanov	.15
96	Mike Richter	.60
97	Bill Ranford	.15
98	Wendel Clark	.15
99	Viacheslav Fetisov	.15
100	Daniel Alfredsson	.30
101	Pat LaFontaine	.15
102	Joe Murphy	.15
103	Pavel Bure	1.25
104	Craig Janney	.15
105	Radek Dvorak	.15
106	Cory Stillman	.15
107	Adam Graves	.15
108	Aki Berg	.15
109	Mario Lemieux	3.00
110	Claude Lemieux	.15
111	Sergei Zubov	.15
112	Pierre Turgeon	.15
113	Damian Rhodes	.15
114	Daren Puppa	.15
115	Alexei Zhitnik	.15
116	Mike Modano	.30
117	Kenny Jonsson	.15
118	Valeri Kamensky	.15
119	Valeri Bure	.15
120	Joe Sakic	1.75
121	Kirk McLean	.15
122	Petr Sykora	.15
123	Mike Gartner	.15
124	Ryan Smyth	.20
125	Brian Leetch	.15
126	Brendan Shanahan	.75
127	Geoff Sanderson	.15
128	Corey Schwab	.15
129	Anders Eriksson	.15
130	*Harry York*	.40
131	Jarome Iginla	.60
132	Eric Fichaud	.25
133	*Patrick Lalime*	2.50
134	Daymond Langkow	.15
135	*Mattias Timander*	.15
136	*Ethan Moreau*	.50
137	Christian Dube	.15
138	*Sergei Berezin*	.75
139	Jose Theodore	.40
140	Wade Redden	.15
141	*Dainius Zubrus*	2.00
142	Jim Campbell	.30
143	*Daniel Goneau*	.50
144	*Jamie Langenbrunner*	.15
145	*Rem Murray*	.50
146	Jonas Hoglund	.15
147	Bryan Berard	.25
148	Chris Osgood	.40
149	Eric Lindros	1.00
150	Jason Arnott	.15

1996-97 Donruss Elite Stars

This is a 150-card parallel of the base set. The silver-poly, foil laminate cards are die-cut.

	MT
Complete Set (150):	1600.
Common Player:	4.00
Stars:	20x to 35x
Yng. Stars & RC's	8x to 15x

1996-97 Donruss Elite Aspirations

This 25-card chase set features sequential numbering to 3,000.

		MT
Complete Set (25):		160.00
Common Player:		4.00
1	Eric Daze	8.00
2	Daniel Alfredsson	10.00
3	Petr Sykora	4.00
4	Todd Bertuzzi	4.00
5	Saku Koivu	25.00
6	Ed Jovanovski	8.00
7	Jim Campbell	5.00
8	Valeri Bure	4.00
9	Jeff O'Neill	4.00
10	Jere Lehtinen	4.00
11	Terry Ryan	4.00
12	Jonas Hoglund	4.00
13	Daymond Langkow	4.00
14	Eric Fichaud	6.00
15	Dainius Zubrus	20.00
16	Janne Niinimaa	12.00
17	Sergei Berezin	10.00
18	Daniel Goneau	6.00
19	Jarome Iginla	15.00
20	Ethan Moreau	6.00
21	Jamie Langenbrunner	4.00
22	Rem Murray	6.00
23	Bryan Berard	10.00
24	Wade Redden	4.00
25	Christian Dube	4.00

1996-97 Donruss Elite Lemieux Hart

This six-card set commemorates Mario Lemieux's Hart Memorial Trophy. Donruss produced 1,996 numbered sets. The first 166 cards of each of the six cards in the set will be autographed.

	MT
Complete Set (6):	150.00
Common Lemieux:	30.00
Lemieux Autograph:	260.00
Lemieux/Lindros Combo Autograph:	450.00

1996-97 Donruss Elite Lindros Hart

This six-card set honors Eric Lindros. The cards are sequentially numbered to 1,995. The first 188 cards of each of the six cards in the set will be autographed.

	MT
Complete Set (6):	120.00
Common Lindros:	25.00
Lindros Autograph:	240.00

1996-97 Donruss Elite Painted Warriors

The 10-card set honors the NHL's top goalies on clear plastic, die-cut cards. Donruss produced 2,500 of each card.

		MT
Complete Set (10):		200.00
Common Goalie:		10.00
1	Patrick Roy	75.00
2	Mike Richter	15.00
3	Jim Carey	20.00
4	John Vanbiesbrouck	40.00
5	Jocelyn Thibault	10.00
6	Felix Potvin	20.00
7	Ed Belfour	15.00
8	Martin Brodeur	45.00
9	Nikolai Khabibulin	10.00
10	Stephane Fiset	10.00

1996-97 Donruss Elite Perspective

The 12-card set takes an upclose look at the NHL's veteran elite players on die-cut cards. Donruss produced 500 of each card.

		MT
Complete Set (12):		800.00
Common Player:		20.00
1	Wayne Gretzky	240.00
2	Mark Messier	50.00
3	Steve Yzerman	100.00
4	Mario Lemieux	175.00
5	Paul Coffey	30.00
6	Doug Gilmour	35.00
7	Brendan Shanahan	60.00
8	Jaromir Jagr	125.00
9	Brett Hull	50.00
10	Pat LaFontaine	20.00
11	Chris Chelios	30.00
12	Grant Fuhr	30.00

1996-97 Donruss Elite Status

The 12-card chase set features top players on micro-etched foil cards. Donruss produced 750 of each card.

		MT
Complete Set (12):		650.00
Common Player:		15.00
1	Pavel Bure	70.00
2	Keith Tkachuk	30.00
3	Sergei Fedorov	40.00
4	Doug Weight	15.00
5	Paul Kariya	120.00
6	Owen Nolan	15.00
7	Peter Forsberg	100.00
8	Eric Lindros	120.00
9	Alexander Mogilny	25.00
10	Teemu Selanne	70.00
11	Joe Sakic	90.00
12	Jeremy Roenick	30.00

1996-97 Fleer

Fleer's 1996-97 hockey set has 156 cards, featuring 135 regular cards, 12 Sporting News League Leaders cards and three checklists. Six insert sets were produced, including five based on NHL post-season awards - Art Ross, Calder, Pearson, Vezina, Norris Trophy - and Rookie Sensations. The regular set includes a card which shows the reunion of Wayne Gretzky with Mark Messier in New York. Gretzky is shown wearing his Rangers jersey at his introductory press conference. Each regular card front has an up-close photo of the player, with the player silhouetted with a black outline to make him stand out against a ghosted background. The team logo is in a small white circle in the lower right corner; the player's name appears in the lower left-hand corner in a gold foil oval. Horizontal backs have information from the hockey experts at The Sporting News, plus a photo (on the left), yearly statistics and biographical information.

		MT
Complete Set (150):		15.00
Common Player:		.05
Wax Box:		40.00
1	Guy Hebert	.05
2	Paul Kariya	.75
3	Teemu Selanne	.40
4	Ray Bourque	.10
5	Kyle McLaren	.05
6	Adam Oates	.10
7	Bill Ranford	.05
8	Rick Tocchet	.05
9	Jason Dawe	.05
10	Dominik Hasek	.25
11	Pat LaFontaine	.15
12	Theoren Fleury	.05
13	Trevor Kidd	.05
14	German Titov	.05
15	Ed Belfour	.20
16	Chris Chelios	.10
17	Eric Daze	.25
18	Jeremy Roenick	.25
19	Gary Suter	.05
20	Peter Forsberg	.75
21	Valeri Kamensky	.05
22	Claude Lemieux	.05
23	Sandis Ozolinsh	.05
24	Patrick Roy	1.25
25	Joe Sakic	.60
26	Derian Hatcher	.05
27	Mike Modano	.15
28	Sergei Zubov	.05
29	Paul Coffey	.10
30	Sergei Fedorov	.50
31	Vladimir Konstantinov	.05
32	Slava Kozlov	.05
33	Chris Osgood	.40
34	Keith Primeau	.05
35	Steve Yzerman	.50
36	Jason Arnott	.10
37	Curtis Joseph	.25
38	Doug Weight	.05
39	Ed Jovanovski	.20
40	Scott Mellanby	.05
41	Rob Niedermayer	.05
42	Ray Sheppard	.05
43	Robert Svehla	.05
44	John Vanbiesbrouck	.50
45	Sean Burke	.10
46	Andrew Cassels	.05
47	Geoff Sanderson	.05
48	Brendan Shanahan	.35
49	Ray Ferraro	.05
50	Dimitri Khristich	.05
51	Vitali Yachmenev	.05
52	Valeri Bure	.10
53	Vincent Damphousse	.05
54	Saku Koivu	.25
55	Mark Recchi	.05
56	Jocelyn Thibault	.25
57	Pierre Turgeon	.10
58	Martin Brodeur	.40
59	Phil Housley	.05
60	Scott Niedermayer	.05
61	Scott Stevens	.05
62	Steve Thomas	.05
63	Todd Bertuzzi	.05
64	Travis Green	.05
65	Kenny Jonsson	.05
66	Zigmund Palffy	.25
67	Adam Graves	.05
68	Wayne Gretzky	2.00
69	Alexei Kovalev	.05
70	Brian Leetch	.10
71	Mark Messier	.25
72	Niklas Sundstrom	.05
73	Daniel Alfredsson	.20
74	Radek Bonk	.05
75	Steve Duchesne	.05
76	Damian Rhodes	.05
77	Alexei Yashin	.05
78	Rod Brind'Amour	.05
79	Eric Desjardins	.10
80	Ron Hextall	.15
81	John LeClair	.15
82	Eric Lindros	1.00
83	Mikael Renberg	.05
84	Tom Barrasso	.15
85	Ron Francis	.10
86	Jaromir Jagr	1.00
87	Mario Lemieux	1.50
88	Petr Nedved	.05
89	Bryan Smolinski	.05
90	Nikolai Khabibulin	.15
91	Teppo Numminen	.05
92	Keith Tkachuk	.30
93	Oleg Tverdovsky	.05
94	Alexei Zhamnov	.10
95	Shayne Corson	.05
96	Grant Fuhr	.15
97	Brett Hull	.35
98	Al MacInnis	.05
99	Chris Pronger	.05
100	Owen Nolan	.05
101	Marcus Ragnarsson	.05
102	Chris Terreri	.05
103	Brian Bradley	.05
104	Roman Hamrlik	.05
105	Daren Puppa	.05
106	Alexander Selivanov	.05
107	Doug Gilmour	.10
108	Larry Murphy	.05
109	Felix Potvin	.40
110	Mats Sundin	.15
111	Pavel Bure	.60
112	Trevor Linden	.05
113	Kirk McLean	.05
114	Alexander Mogilny	.25
115	Peter Bondra	.05
116	Jim Carey	.50
117	Sergei Gonchar	.05
118	Joe Juneau	.05
119	Michal Pivonka	.05
120	Brendan Witt	.05

121	Nolan Baumgartner	.05
122	Martin Biron	.05
123	Jason Bonsignore	.05
124	Andrew Brunette	.05
125	Jason Doig	.05
126	Peter Ferraro	.05
127	Eric Fichaud	.05
128	Ladislav Kohn	.05
129	Jamie Langenbrunner	.05
130	Daymond Langkow	.05
131	Jay McKee	.05
132	Wayne Primeau	.05
133	Jamie Storr	.05
134	Jose Theodore	.05
135	Roman Vopat	.05
136	Rookie Scoring	.10
137	Points	.20
138	Goals	.20
139	Assists	.20
140	Points by defenseman	.05
141	Power-play goals	.20
142	Game-winning goals	.15
143	Plus/Minus	.10
144	Goals against	.10
145	Games won	.15
146	Shutouts	.15
147	Save Percentage	.05
148	Checklist	.05
149	Checklist	.05
150	Checklist	.05

1996-97 Fleer Art Ross

These cards feature 25 players competing for the NHL scoring title. Cards were randomly seeded one per every six packs of 1996-97 Fleer hockey. Each card front has a color action photo on it, breaking out of a puck. "Art Ross Trophy," the Fleer logo and the player's last name are stamped in silver. The player's team name is in a rectangle in the lower left corner. The back has a panel along the left which includes a brief career summary, plus the player's name and team name. The right side has a color photo, card number (1 of 25, etc.) and a picture of the Norris Trophy.

		MT
Complete Set (25):		50.00
Common Player:		.50
1	Pavel Bure	4.00
2	Sergei Fedorov	4.00
3	Theoren Fleury	.50
4	Peter Forsberg	6.00
5	Ron Francis	.50
6	Wayne Gretzky	10.00
7	Brett Hull	2.50
8	Jaromir Jagr	6.00
9	Valeri Kamensky	.50
10	Paul Kariya	6.00
11	Pat LaFontaine	.75
12	John LeClair	.75
13	Mario Lemieux	8.00
14	Eric Lindros	6.00
15	Mark Messier	2.50
16	Alexander Mogilny	.75
17	Petr Nedved	.50
18	Adam Oates	.50
19	Jeremy Roenick	1.50
20	Joe Sakic	4.00
21	Teemu Selanne	3.00
22	Keith Tkachuk	1.50
23	Pierre Turgeon	.50
24	Doug Weight	.50
25	Steve Yzerman	4.00

1996-97 Fleer Calder

Ten rookies who will be competing for the NHL's Rookie of the Year Award are featured on these 1996-97 Fleer inserts. The cards were seeded one per every 90 packs. Each front has a color action photo, with "Calder Candidates" written along the right side in rainbow colors. The player's name and position are banners in the lower left corner. The horizontal card back has a photo on the left, with a card number (1 of 10, etc.) in the upper left. The right side of the card has the player's name and team name at the top, with a team logo in the middle. A Sporting News summary is underneath, along the right side.

		MT
Complete Set (10):		85.00
Common Player:		6.00
1	Andrew Brunette	10.00
2	Jason Doig	8.00
3	Peter Ferraro	12.00
4	Eric Fichaud	15.00
5	James Iginla	8.00
6	Jamie Langenbrunner	10.00
7	Daymond Langkow	12.00
8	Jamie Storr	12.00
9	Jose Theodore	20.00
10	Roman Vopat	8.00

1996-97 Fleer Pearson

Ten NHL superstars competing for the NHL MVP (Pearson) Award are spotlighted on these 1996-97 Fleer hockey insert cards. The cards were seeded one per every 144 packs. Each card front has a color photo in the center against a background of team emblems. The player's name and a team logo are in a silver-foiled panel at the top; "Pearson Award" is written in a panel along the bottom. The horizontal card back has a close-up shot on one side. The card number (1 of 10, etc.) and player's name are in the upper right corner. A brief summary of the player's MVP skills is listed below, with "Pearson Award" and a team logo underneath.

1996-97 Fleer Vezina

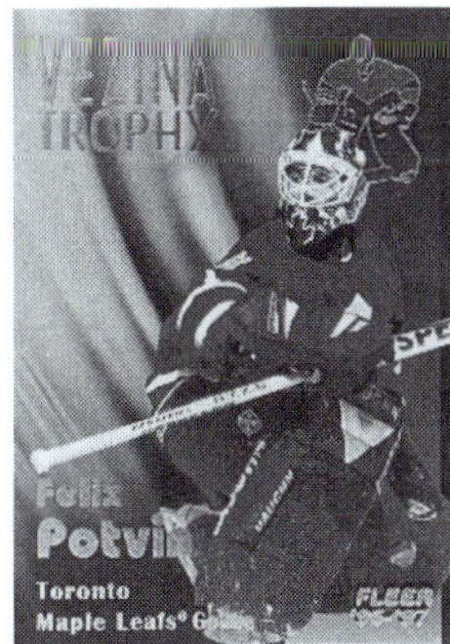

Ten top netminders competing for the league's top goalie award are featured on these 1996-97 Fleer hockey cards. They were seeded one per every 60 packs. Each card front has a color action photo, with a goalie and "Vezina Trophy" stamped in gold foil at the top. The player's name is below the photo in gold, flanked by a gold Fleer logo in the lower left corner and the player's team name and position in the lower right corner. The horizontal card back has a goalie character and the Vezina Trophy on one side, flanked by a close-up shot of the player. In between the two is a summary of the player's talents. His name and a team logo are underneath the photo. A card number (1 of 10, etc.) is in the upper left corner.

		MT
Complete Set (10):		100.00
Common Goalie:		6.00
1	Ed Belfour	8.00
2	Sean Burke	6.00
3	Jim Carey	12.00
4	Dominik Hasek	15.00
5	Ron Hextall	6.00
6	Chris Osgood	15.00
7	Felix Potvin	12.00
8	Daren Puppa	6.00
9	Patrick Roy	40.00
10	John Vanbiesbrouck	20.00

1996-97 Fleer Rookie Sensations

		MT
Complete Set (10):		450.00
Common Player:		25.00
1	Pavel Bure	30.00
2	Sergei Fedorov	30.00
3	Peter Forsberg	40.00
4	Wayne Gretzky	90.00
5	Jaromir Jagr	50.00
6	Paul Kariya	50.00
7	Mario Lemieux	80.00
8	Eric Lindros	60.00
9	Patrick Roy	75.00
10	Joe Sakic	30.00

Rookie Sensation cards, which are a hobby exclusive product, showcase 10 top rookies from the 1995-96 season. The cards were random inserts in 1996-97 Fleer hockey, one per every 20 packs. The front has a color action photo, with the player's name at the top and "Rookie Sensations" running down the left side. The Fleer logo is along the bottom, with a team logo in the lower right corner. A card number (1 of 10, etc.) is above the photo. The horizontal back has a color photo in the lower left corner, with the player's name and a summary of the player's talents below. "Rookie Sensations" is written along the top. The background is ice blue, with a line drawing of the player.

		MT
Complete Set (10):		35.00
Common Player:		2.50
1	Daniel Alfredsson	8.00
2	Todd Bertuzzi	2.50
3	Valeri Bure	4.00
4	Eric Daze	6.00
5	Sergei Gonchar	2.50
6	Ed Jovanovski	6.00
7	Saku Koivu	10.00
8	Marcus Ragnarsson	2.50
9	Petr Sykora	6.00
10	Vitali Yachmenev	2.50

1996-97 Fleer Norris

The 10 Norris Trophy inserts, seeded every 36 packs (retail only), highlight the hottest defensemen, such as Brian Leetch, Paul Coffey and Ray Bourque.

		MT
Complete Set (10):		60.00
Common Player:		5.00
1	Ray Bourque	12.00
2	Chris Chelios	12.00
3	Paul Coffey	12.00
4	Eric Desjardins	5.00
5	Phil Housley	5.00
6	Vladimir Konstantinov	5.00
7	Brian Leetch	12.00
8	Teppo Numminen	5.00
9	Larry Murphy	5.00
10	Sandis Ozolinsh	8.00

1996-97 Flair

The 125-card set includes 100 player cards and 25 Wave of the Future cards. The card fronts have etched silver foil with an action photo of the player silhouetted over a larger head shot image in the background. Cards of players chosen for the All-Star Game contain a special All-Star designation. Wave of the Future cards feature first-year players with a single photo and silver etched foil.

		MT
Complete Set (125):		130.00
Common Player:		.25
Common Wave of the Future:		2.00
Complete Wave of the Future (101-125):		75.00
Wax Box:		70.00
1	Guy Hebert	.40
2	Paul Kariya	3.50
3	Teemu Selanne	2.00
4	Ray Bourque	.25
5	Adam Oates	.25
6	Bill Ranford	.25
7	Jozef Stumpel	.25
8	Dominik Hasek	2.00
9	Pat LaFontaine	.25
10	Alexei Zhitnik	.25
11	Theoren Fleury	.25
12	Dave Gagner	.25
13	Trevor Kidd	.25
14	Tony Amonte	.25
15	Chris Chelios	.40
16	Eric Daze	.40
17	Alexei Zhamnov	.25
18	Peter Forsberg	3.00
19	Sandis Ozolinsh	.25
20	Patrick Roy	4.50
21	Joe Sakic	3.00
22	Derian Hatcher	.25
23	Mike Modano	.40
24	Andy Moog	.40
25	Pat Verbeek	.25
26	Sergei Fedorov	1.50
27	Slava Fetisov	.25
28	Nicklas Lidstrom	.25
29	Chris Osgood	1.50
30	Brendan Shanahan	1.50
31	Steve Yzerman	3.00
32	Jason Arnott	.25
33	Curtis Joseph	.50
34	Boris Mironov	.25
35	Ryan Smyth	.40
36	Doug Weight	.25
37	Ed Jovanovski	.50
38	Ray Sheppard	.25
39	Robert Svehla	.25
40	John Vanbiesbrouck	3.00
41	Andrew Cassels	.25
42	Jason Muzzatti	.25
43	Keith Primeau	.25
44	Geoff Sanderson	.25
45	Rob Blake	.25
46	Dimitri Khristich	.25
47	Vincent Damphousse	.25
48	Saku Koivu	1.50
49	Mark Recchi	.25
50	Martin Rucinsky	.25
51	Jocelyn Thibault	.50
52	Martin Brodeur	1.50
53	Bill Guerin	.25
54	Scott Stevens	.25
55	Scott Lachance	.25
56	Zigmund Palffy	.75
57	Tommy Salo	.25
58	Bryan Smolinski	.25
59	Wayne Gretzky	6.00
60	Brian Leetch	.25
61	Mark Messier	1.00
62	Mike Richter	.75
63	Daniel Alfredsson	.40
64	Damian Rhodes	.25
65	Alexei Yashin	.25
66	Paul Coffey	.25
67	Dale Hawerchuk	.25
68	Ron Hextall	.40
69	John LeClair	1.00
70	Eric Lindros	4.50
71	Nikolai Khabibulin	.40
72	Jeremy Roenick	.60
73	Keith Tkachuk	.60
74	Oleg Tverdovsky	.25
75	Ron Francis	.25
76	Kevin Hatcher	.25
77	Jaromir Jagr	3.50
78	Mario Lemieux	4.50
79	Petr Nedved	.25
80	Grant Fuhr	.50
81	Brett Hull	1.00

82	Al MacInnis	.25
83	Ed Belfour	.50
84	Tony Granato	.25
85	Owen Nolan	.25
86	Dino Ciccarelli	.25
87	John Cullen	.25
88	Roman Hamrlik	.25
89	Wendel Clark	.25
90	Doug Gilmour	.40
91	Felix Potvin	.75
92	Mats Sundin	.50
93	Pavel Bure	2.00
94	Corey Hirsch	.25
95	Trevor Linden	.25
96	Alexander Mogilny	.50
97	Peter Bondra	.25
98	Jim Carey	1.50
99	Dale Hunter	.25
100	Chris Simon	.25
101	Mattias Timander (Wave of the Future)	2.00
102	*Vaclav Varada* (Wave of the Future)	2.00
103	Jarome Iginla (Wave of the Future)	6.00
104	Ethan Moreau (Wave of the Future)	6.00
105	Jamie Langenbrunner (Wave of the Future)	2.00
106	Roman Turek (Wave of the Future)	2.00
107	Tomas Holmstrom (Wave of the Future)	2.00
108	Kevin Hodson (Wave of the Future)	8.00
109	Mats Lindgren (Wave of the Future)	2.00
110	Mike Grier (Wave of the Future)	8.00
111	Rem Murray (Wave of the Future)	4.00
112	Jose Theodore (Wave of the Future)	6.00
113	David Wilkie (Wave of the Future)	2.00
114	Bryan Berard (Wave of the Future)	4.00
115	Eric Fichaud (Wave of the Future)	3.00
116	Daniel Goneau (Wave of the Future)	3.00
117	Andres Dackell (Wave of the Future)	2.00
118	Wade Redden (Wave of the Future)	2.00
119	Dainius Zubrus (Wave of the Future)	15.00
120	Janne Niinimaa (Wave of the Future)	4.00
121	Patrick Lalime (Wave of the Future)	10.00
122	Harry York (Wave of the Future)	4.00
123	Jim Campbell (Wave of the Future)	3.00
124	Sergei Berezin (Wave of the Future)	6.00
125	*Jaroslav Svejkovsky* (Wave of the Future)	6.00

1996-97 Flair Blue Ice

This 125-card parallel set was inserted 1:20 packs. Fleer stated there were no more than 250 sequentially numbered sets. The cards feature blue foil.

		MT
Complete Set (125):		3500.
Common Player:		10.00
Semistars & Goalies:		20.00
Stars:		35x to 50x
Wave of the Futures (101-125):		5x to 7x
1	Guy Hebert	20.00
2	Paul Kariya	175.00
3	Teemu Selanne	90.00
4	Ray Bourque	20.00
5	Adam Oates	15.00
6	Bill Ranford	10.00
7	Jozef Stumpel	10.00
8	Dominik Hasek	90.00
9	Pat LaFontaine	15.00
10	Alexei Zhitnik	10.00
11	Theoren Fleury	15.00
12	Dave Gagner	10.00
13	Trevor Kidd	10.00
14	Tony Amonte	15.00
15	Chris Chelios	20.00
16	Eric Daze	20.00
17	Alexei Zhamnov	10.00
18	Peter Forsberg	150.00
19	Sandis Ozolinsh	10.00
20	Patrick Roy	200.00
21	Joe Sakic	125.00
22	Derian Hatcher	10.00
23	Mike Modano	20.00
24	Andy Moog	20.00
25	Pat Verbeek	10.00
26	Sergei Fedorov	60.00
27	Slava Fetisov	10.00
28	Nicklas Lidstrom	10.00
29	Chris Osgood	60.00
30	Brendan Shanahan	60.00
31	Steve Yzerman	150.00
32	Jason Arnott	10.00
33	Curtis Joseph	30.00
34	Boris Mironov	10.00
35	Ryan Smyth	20.00
36	Doug Weight	10.00
37	Ed Jovanovski	20.00
38	Ray Sheppard	10.00
39	Robert Svehla	10.00
40	John Vanbiesbrouck	125.00
41	Andrew Cassels	10.00
42	Jason Muzzatti	10.00
43	Keith Primeau	15.00
44	Geoff Sanderson	10.00
45	Rob Blake	10.00
46	Dimitri Khristich	10.00
47	Vincent Damphousse	10.00
48	Saku Koivu	50.00
49	Mark Recchi	15.00
50	Martin Rucinsky	10.00
51	Jocelyn Thibault	30.00
52	Martin Brodeur	75.00
53	Bill Guerin	10.00
54	Scott Stevens	10.00
55	Scott Lachance	10.00
56	Zigmund Palffy	25.00
57	Tommy Salo	10.00
58	Bryan Smolinski	10.00
59	Wayne Gretzky	325.00
60	Brian Leetch	15.00
61	Mark Messier	60.00
62	Mike Richter	35.00
63	Daniel Alfredsson	20.00
64	Damian Rhodes	10.00
65	Alexei Yashin	20.00
66	Paul Coffey	20.00
67	Dale Hawerchuk	10.00
68	Ron Hextall	20.00
69	John LeClair	40.00
70	Eric Lindros	175.00
71	Nikolai Khabibulin	20.00
72	Jeremy Roenick	25.00
73	Keith Tkachuk	30.00
74	Oleg Tverdovsky	10.00
75	Ron Francis	15.00
76	Kevin Hatcher	10.00
77	Jaromir Jagr	175.00
78	Mario Lemieux	225.00
79	Petr Nedved	10.00
80	Grant Fuhr	25.00
81	Brett Hull	50.00
82	Al MacInnis	10.00
83	Ed Belfour	20.00
84	Tony Granato	10.00
85	Owen Nolan	10.00
86	Dino Ciccarelli	10.00
87	John Cullen	10.00
88	Roman Hamrlik	10.00
89	Wendel Clark	10.00
90	Doug Gilmour	20.00
91	Felix Potvin	30.00
92	Mats Sundin	20.00
93	Pavel Bure	75.00
94	Corey Hirsch	10.00
95	Trevor Linden	10.00

96	Alexander Mogilny	20.00
97	Peter Bondra	15.00
98	Jim Carey	50.00
99	Dale Hunter	10.00
100	Chris Simon	10.00
101	Mattias Timander (Wave of the Future)	10.00
102	Vaclav Varada (Wave of the Future)	10.00
103	Jarome Iginla (Wave of the Future)	30.00
104	Ethan Moreau (Wave of the Future)	30.00
105	Jamie Langenbrunner (Wave of the Future)	10.00
106	Roman Turek (Wave of the Future)	10.00
107	Tomas Holmstrom (Wave of the Future)	10.00
108	Kevin Hodson (Wave of the Future)	50.00
109	Mats Lindgren (Wave of the Future)	10.00
110	Mike Grier (Wave of the Future)	40.00
111	Rem Murray (Wave of the Future)	20.00
112	Jose Theodore (Wave of the Future)	30.00
113	David Wilkie (Wave of the Future)	10.00
114	Bryan Berard (Wave of the Future)	10.00
115	Eric Fichaud (Wave of the Future)	15.00
116	Daniel Goneau (Wave of the Future)	15.00
117	Andres Dackell (Wave of the Future)	10.00
118	Wade Redden (Wave of the Future)	10.00
119	Dainius Zubrus (Wave of the Future)	75.00
120	Janne Niinimaa (Wave of the Future)	30.00
121	Patrick Lalime (Wave of the Future)	50.00
122	Harry York (Wave of the Future)	20.00
123	Jim Campbell (Wave of the Future)	15.00
124	Sergei Berezin (Wave of the Future)	40.00
125	Jaroslav Svejkovsky (Wave of the Future)	50.00

1996-97 Flair Center Ice Spotlight

Inserted 1:30 packs, the 10-card chase set features the NHL's top offensive stars.

		MT
Complete Set (10):		150.00
Common Player:		6.00
1	Pavel Bure	12.00
2	Sergei Fedorov	12.00
3	Peter Forsberg	20.00
4	Brett Hull	10.00
5	Jaromir Jagr	25.00
6	Paul Kariya	25.00
7	Joe Sakic	20.00
8	Teemu Selanne	15.00
9	Mats Sundin	6.00
10	Steve Yzerman	20.00

1996-97 Flair Hot Gloves

Inserted 1:40 packs, the 12-card set is die-cut to resemble a goaltender's catching glove.

		MT
Complete Set (12):		300.00
Common Player:		10.00
1	Ed Belfour	15.00
2	Martin Brodeur	40.00
3	Jim Carey	20.00
4	Dominik Hasek	35.00
5	Curtis Joseph	20.00
6	Patrick Lalime	35.00
7	Chris Osgood	20.00
8	Felix Potvin	15.00
9	Mike Richter	15.00
10	Patrick Roy	70.00
11	Jocelyn Thibault	15.00
12	John Vanbiesbrouck	50.00

1996-97 Flair Hot Numbers

Inserted 1:72 packs, the 10-card set includes cards of NHL superstars who wear a double number on their jerseys.

		MT
Complete Set (10):		260.00
Common Player:		12.00
1	Ray Bourque	12.00
2	Paul Coffey	12.00
3	Eric Daze	12.00
4	Wayne Gretzky	80.00
5	Ed Jovanovski	15.00
6	Saku Koivu	25.00
7	Mario Lemieux	60.00
8	Eric Lindros	50.00
9	Mark Messier	25.00
10	Owen Nolan	12.00

1996-97 Flair Now & Then

Inserted 1:400 packs, the three-card set showcases players in both their WHA uniforms and their current-year jerseys.

		MT
Complete Set (3):		500.00
Common Player:		150.00
	Wayne Gretzky, Mark Messier, Mike Garner	250.00
	Mario Lemieux, Patrick Roy, Kirk Muller	200.00

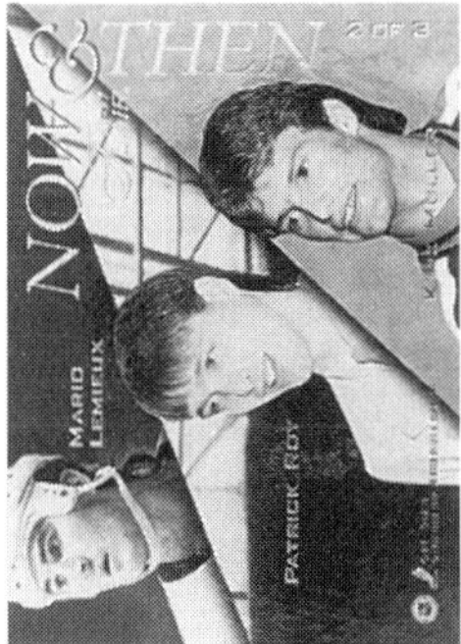

Eric Lindros, Peter Forsberg, Scott Niedermayer		150.00

1996-97 Metal Universe

The 200-card, standard-size set features 168 player cards, including 30 rookies and two checklists. The background for each card has a futuristic, metallized design with the player's color image over it. The card backs feature a color player closeup with brief stat and bio information. Inserts in Metal Universe are Lethal Weapons, Cool Steel, Ice Carvings and Armor Plate.

		MT
Complete Set (200):		35.00
Common Player:		.15
Wax Box:		50.00
1	Guy Hebert	.25
2	Paul Kariya	2.50
3	Jari Kurri	.15
4	Roman Oksiuta	.15
5	Steve Rucchin	.15
6	Teemu Selanne	1.00
7	Ray Bourque	.25
8	Kyle McLaren	.15
9	Adam Oates	.25
10	Bill Ranford	.15
11	Rick Tocchet	.15
12	Donald Audette	.15
13	Jason Dawe	.15
14	Dominik Hasek	1.00
15	Pat LaFontaine	.25
16	Derek Plante	.15
17	Wayne Primeau	.15
18	Theoren Fleury	.15
19	Dave Gagner	.15
20	Trevor Kidd	.25
21	James Patrick	.15
22	Robert Reichel	.15
23	German Titov	.15
24	Tony Amonte	.25
25	Ed Belfour	.30
26	Chris Chelios	.25
27	Eric Daze	.30
28	Gary Suter	.15
29	Alexei Zhamnov	.15
30	Adam Deadmarsh	.15
31	Adam Foote	.15
32	Peter Forsberg	2.00
33	Valeri Kamensky	.15
34	Uwe Krupp	.15
35	Claude Lemieux	.15
36	Sandis Ozolinsh	.15
37	Patrick Roy	3.00
38	Joe Sakic	1.50
39	Derian Hatcher	.15
40	Mike Modano	.40
41	Andy Moog	.25
42	Joe Nieuwendyk	.15
43	Pat Verbeek	.15
44	Sergei Zubov	.15
45	Sergei Fedorov	1.00
46	Vladimir Konstantinov	.15
47	Slava Kozlov	.15
48	Nicklas Lidstrom	.25
49	Chris Osgood	.60
50	Brendan Shanahan	.75
51	Steve Yzerman	2.00
52	Jason Arnott	.15
53	Curtis Joseph	.40
54	Andrei Kovalenko	.15
55	Miroslav Satan	.15
56	Doug Weight	.25
57	Radek Dvorak	.15
58	*Per Gustafsson*	.15
59	Ed Jovanovski	.25
60	Scott Mellanby	.15
61	Rob Niedermayer	.15
62	Ray Sheppard	.15
63	Robert Svehla	.15
64	John Vanbiesbrouck	1.50
65	Jeff Brown	.15
66	Sean Burke	.25
67	Paul Coffey	.25
68	Nelson Emerson	.15
69	Jeff O'Neill	.15
70	Keith Primeau	.15
71	Geoff Sanderson	.15
72	Aki-Petteri Berg	.15
73	Rob Blake	.15
74	Stephane Fiset	.25
75	Dimitri Khristich	.15
76	Petr Klima	.15
77	Ed Olczyk	.15
78	Vitali Yachmenev	.15
79	Vincent Damphousse	.15
80	Saku Koivu	1.00
81	Mark Recchi	.15
82	Stephane Richer	.15
83	Jocelyn Thibault	.40
84	Pierre Turgeon	.25
85	Dave Andreychuk	.15
86	Martin Brodeur	1.00
87	Scott Niedermayer	.15
88	Scott Stevens	.15
89	Petr Sykora	.15
90	Steve Thomas	.15
91	Todd Bertuzzi	.15
92	Travis Green	.15
93	Kenny Jonsson	.15
94	Bryan McCabe	.15
95	Zigmund Palffy	.60
96	Wayne Gretzky	3.50
97	Alexei Kovalov	.15
98	Brian Leetch	.25
99	Mark Messier	1.00
100	Mike Richter	.40
101	Luc Robitaille	.15
102	Niklas Sundstrom	.15
103	Daniel Alfredsson	.25
104	Radek Bonk	.15
105	Alexandre Daigle	.15
106	Steve Duchesne	.15
107	Damian Rhodes	.15
108	Alexei Yashin	.30
109	Rod Brind'Amour	.15
110	Eric Desjardins	.15
111	Dale Hawerchuk	.20
112	Ron Hextall	.25
113	John LeClair	.50
114	Eric Lindros	2.50
115	Mikael Renberg	.15
116	Mike Gartner	.15
117	Craig Janney	.15
118	Nikolai Khabibulin	.25
119	Dave Manson	.15
120	Teppo Numminen	.15
121	Jeremy Roenick	.50
122	Keith Tkachuk	.75
123	Oleg Tverdovsky	.15
124	Tom Barrasso	.25
125	Ron Francis	.25
126	Kevin Hatcher	.15
127	Jaromir Jagr	2.50
128	Mario Lemieux	3.00
129	Petr Nedved	.15
130	Shayne Corson	.15
131	Grant Fuhr	.40
132	Brett Hull	.75
133	Al MacInnis	.15
134	Joe Murphy	.15
135	Chris Pronger	.15
136	Kelly Hrudey	.25
137	Al Iafrate	.15
138	Bernie Nicholls	.15
139	Owen Nolan	.25
140	Marcus Ragnarsson	.15
141	Darren Turcotte	.15
142	Brian Bradley	.15
143	Dino Ciccarelli	.15
144	Chris Gratton	.15
145	Roman Hamrlik	.15
146	Daren Puppa	.15
147	Alexander Selivanov	.15
148	Wendel Clark	.15
149	Doug Gilmour	.30
150	Kirk Muller	.15
151	Larry Murphy	.15
152	Felix Potvin	.50
153	Mathieu Schneider	.15
154	Mats Sundin	.40
155	Pavel Bure	1.50
156	Russ Courtnall	.15
157	Trevor Linden	.15
158	Kirk McLean	.25
159	Alexander Mogilny	.40
160	Esa Tikkanen	.15
161	Peter Bondra	.25
162	Jim Carey	.50
163	Sergei Gonchar	.15
164	Phil Housley	.15
165	Calle Johansson	.15
166	Joe Juneau	.15
167	Michal Pivonka	.15
168	Brendan Witt	.15
169	Nolan Baumgartner	.15
170	Bryan Berard	.30
171	*Sergei Berezin*	.60
172	*Curtis Brown*	.15
173	*Jan Caloun*	.15
174	*Andreas Dackell*	.20
175	Hnat Domenichelli	.15
176	Christian Dube	.15
177	Anders Eriksson	.15
178	*Peter Ferraro*	.15
179	Eric Fichaud	.15
180	*Daniel Goneau*	.40
181	*Mike Grier*	.75
182	Jarome Iginla	.50
183	Steve Kelly	.15
184	Jamie Langenbrunner	.15
185	Daymond Langkow	.15
186	*Jay McKee*	.15
187	*Ethan Moreau*	.50
188	*Rem Murray*	.50
189	Janne Niinimaa	.60
190	Wade Redden	.15
191	*Ruslan Salei*	.25
192	Jamie Storr	.15
193	*Darren Van Impe*	.15
194	*Roman Vopat*	.15
195	*David Wilkie*	.15
196	*Landon Wilson*	.15
197	*Richard Zednik*	.40
198	*Dainius Zubrus*	1.50
199	Checklist	.15
200	Checklist	.15

1996-97 Metal Universe Armor Plate

The 12-card insert set, seeded every 72 packs, features the game's top goaltenders on a horizontal card design. The front background resembles a metal plate of sorts, with the horizontal card backs featuring a player closeup and profile. The cards are numbered as "x of 12."

		MT
Complete Set (12):		200.00
Common Player:		10.00
1	Ed Belfour	12.00
2	Martin Brodeur	25.00
3	Jim Carey	15.00
4	Dominik Hasek	25.00
5	Ron Hextall	10.00
6	Chris Osgood	20.00
7	Felix Potvin	20.00
8	Daren Puppa	10.00
9	Damian Rhodes	10.00
10	Mike Richter	20.00
11	Patrick Roy	60.00
12	John Vanbiesbrouck	35.00

1996-97 Metal Universe Armor Plate Super Powers

The 12-card insert set parallels the more common Armor Plate inserts, except at a higher pull ratio (1:720).

	MT
Complete Set (12):	700.00
Common Player:	30.00

1996-97 Metal Universe Cool Steel

The 12-card Cool Steel insert, found every 48 hobby packs, features the game's best stars on card fronts which resemble the look of brushed steel.

		MT
Complete Set (12):		160.00
Common Player:		5.00
1	Chris Chelios	5.00
2	Peter Forsberg	25.00
3	Ron Francis	5.00
4	Dominik Hasek	15.00
5	Ed Jovanovski	8.00
6	Vladimir Konstantinov	5.00
7	Eric Lindros	30.00
8	Mark Messier	15.00
9	Patrick Roy	40.00
10	Brendan Shanahan	15.00
11	Keith Tkachuk	12.00
12	John Vanbiesbrouck	20.00

1996-97 Metal Universe Cool Steel Super Powers

The 12-card insert set parallels the Cool Steel insert, except with holographic foil card stock. The Super Powers version is seeded every 480 hobby packs.

	MT
Complete Set (12):	450.00
Common Player:	15.00

1996-97 Metal Universe Ice Carvings

The retail-only insert set, seeded every 24 packs, features ice carving-like images on the front behind a color player image. The 12-card set is numbered as "x of 12" with the backs featuring a player closeup with a profile.

		MT
Complete Set (12):		140.00
Common Player:		6.00
1	Martin Brodeur	12.00
2	Pavel Bure	12.00
3	Jim Carey	8.00
4	Paul Coffey	6.00
5	Sergei Fedorov	12.00
6	Jaromir Jagr	25.00
7	Paul Kariya	25.00
8	Pat LaFontaine	6.00
9	Brian Leetch	6.00
10	Mario Lemieux	30.00
11	Alexander Mogilny	6.00
12	Joe Sakic	18.00

1996-97 Metal Universe Ice Carvings Super Powers

The 12-card insert set parallels the Ice Carvings set from Metal Universe and is found every 240 retail packs.

	MT
Complete Set (12):	400.00
Common Player:	15.00
Super Powers:	2x to 4x

1996-97 Metal Universe Lethal Weapons

Inserted every 12 packs of 1996-97 Metal Universe, the 20-card set highlights the game's top scorers. "Lethal Weapon" is printed along the left edge with the card backs containing a full player closeup with a few player highlights. The cards are numbered as "x of 20."

		MT
Complete Set (20):		100.00
Common Player:		2.00
1	Peter Bondra	2.00
2	Pavel Bure	6.00
3	Sergei Fedorov	6.00
4	Peter Forsberg	10.00
5	Ron Francis	2.00
6	Wayne Gretzky	20.00
7	Brett Hull	4.00
8	Jaromir Jagr	12.00
9	Paul Kariya	12.00
10	John LeClair	4.00
11	Mario Lemieux	15.00
12	Eric Lindros	12.00
13	Mark Messier	5.00
14	Alexander Mogilny	3.00
15	Adam Oates	2.00
16	Joe Sakic	8.00
17	Teemu Selanne	6.00
18	Brendan Shanahan	6.00
19	Keith Tkachuk	4.00
20	Doug Weight	2.00

1996-97 Metal Universe Lethal Weapons Super Powers

The 20-card insert set, seeded every 120 packs of Metal Universe, parallels the more common (1:12) Lethal Weapons inserts.

	MT
Complete Set (20):	300.00
Common Player:	8.00
Super Powers:	2x to 4x

1996-97 Fleer NHL Picks

Fleer and Topps combined for this 180-card set, which features 90 selections made by each company during the NHL Picks Fantasy Draft held in July during the National Sports Collectors Convention. The Fleer cards have the even numbers; Topps has odds. Each regular Fleer card has a color photo in the middle, with a black frame around it. The outside border is white. The Fleer logo is in an upper corner; the player's team logo is in the lower left corner. The player's name is along the bottom in the lower right corner. The horizontal card back has a career recap in the upper left corner, next to a color photo on the opposite side. The player's name and biographical information are in a rectangle on the bottom half of the card, along with 1995-96 stats and projected numbers for 1996-97, courtesy of Stats Inc. The card number is in the lower right corner. Five insert sets were made - Fabulous 50, Jagged Edge, Dream Lines, Fantasy Force and Captain's Choice. An official NHL/NHLPA Draft Game registration form, found in every pack, allows collectors the chance to draft a fantasy hockey team and win prizes based on the players' performances.

		MT
Complete Set (90):		8.00
Common Player:		.05
Wax Box:		28.00
2	Joe Sakic	.50

		MT
4	Eric Lindros	1.00
6	Paul Kariya	.75
8	Wayne Gretzky	1.50
10	Chris Osgood	.40
12	Brian Leetch	.10
14	Ray Bourque	.05
16	Ron Francis	.05
18	Keith Tkachuk	.20
20	Paul Coffey	.05
22	Phil Housley	.05
24	Theoren Fleury	.05
26	Sergei Zubov	.05
28	Adam Oates	.05
30	John LeClair	.10
32	Pierre Turgeon	.05
34	Nicklas Lidstrom	.05
36	Vincent Damphousse	.05
38	Pat LaFontaine	.05
40	Brendan Shanahan	.20
42	Robert Svehla	.05
44	Peter Bondra	.05
46	Mikael Renberg	.05
48	Alexei Yashin	.05
50	Zigmund Palffy	.20
52	Larry Murphy	.05
54	Rod Brind'Amour	.05
56	Alexei Zhamnov	.05
58	Jason Arnott	.05
60	Craig Janney	.05
62	Jason Wooley	.05
64	Jeff Brown	.05
66	Tomas Sandstrom	.05
68	Doug Gilmour	.10
70	Travis Green	.05
72	Teppo Numminen	.05
74	Petr Sykora	.10
76	Saku Koivu	.20
78	Daniel Alfredsson	.20
80	Ron Hextall	.05
82	Jocelyn Thibault	.20
84	Mike Richter	.20
86	Nikolai Khabibulin	.05
88	John Vanbiesbrouck	.30
90	Adam Graves	.05
92	Kenny Jonsson	.05
94	Jyrki Lumme	.05
96	Zdeno Ciger	.05
98	Ed Jovanovski	.15
100	Greg Johnson	.05
102	Pat Falloon	.05
104	Andrew Cassels	.05
106	German Titov	.05
108	Joe Juneau	.05
110	Igor Larionov	.05
112	Norm Maciver	.05
114	Chris Pronger	.05
116	Scott Niedermayer	.05
118	Vladimir Malakhov	.05
120	Dale Hawerchuk	.05
122	Jason Dawe	.05
124	Valeri Bure	.05
126	Marcus Ragnarsson	.05
128	Stephane Richer	.05
130	Wendel Clark	.05
132	Bryan Smolinski	.05
134	Dimitri Khristich	.05
136	Benoit Hogue	.05
138	Kirk Muller	.05
140	Peter Ferraro	.05
142	Vitali Yachmenev	.05
144	Jere Lehtinen	.05
146	Brandon Convery	.05
148	Darcy Tucker	.05
150	Curtis Brown	.05
152	Alexei Zhitnik	.05
154	John Slaney	.05
156	Bruce Driver	.05
158	Jeff O'Neill	.05
160	Patrice Brisebois	.05
162	Gord Murphy	.05
164	Doug Bodger	.05
166	Marty McSorley	.05
168	Nolan Baumgartner	.05
170	Mike Gartner	.05
172	Andrei Nikolishin	.05
174	Alexei Yegorov	.05
176	Dave Reid	.05
178	Marty Murray	.05
180	Anders Eriksson	.05

1996-97 Fleer NHL Picks Captain's Choice

Ten team captains, such as Mario Lemieux and Steve Yzerman, are showcased on these special cards. The cards are the rarest of Fleer's

NHL Picks inserts; they are seeded one per every 300 packs. The card front has a color photo of the captain, with the same photo in black-and-white as a background. The Fleer logo is in an upper corner; the player's name, "Captain's Choice" and a scripted letter "C" are in the lower right corner.

		MT
Complete Set (10):		325.00
Common Player:		10.00
1	Eric Lindros	75.00
2	Steve Yzerman	40.00
3	Mario Lemieux	90.00
4	Wayne Gretzky	100.00
5	Mark Messier	20.00
6	Joe Sakic	40.00
7	Keith Tkachuk	20.00
8	Doug Gilmour	10.00
9	Trevor Linden	10.00
10	Brendan Shanahan	20.00

1996-97 Fleer NHL Picks Dream Lines

These 1996-97 Fleer NHL Picks theme cards feature three players per card who form a "dream line" with lethal ability. The stars pictured each have something in common, such as Sweet 16 (Brett Hull, Pat Verbeek and Pat LaFontaine, who each wear #16). Cards were seeded one per every 70 packs.

		MT
Complete Set (10):		150.00
Common Line:		4.00
1	Wayne Gretzky, Mario Lemieux, Eric Lindros	45.00
2	Jeremy Roenick, Chris Chelios, Mike Richter	8.00
3	Daniel Alfredsson, Trevor Froschauer, Martin Brodeur	15.00
4	Sergei Fedorov, Alexander Mogilny, Pavel Bure	20.00
5	Teemu Selanne, Paul Kariya, Keith Tkachuk	25.00
6	Jaromir Jagr, Dominik Hasek, Roman Hamrlik	25.00
7	John LeClair, Brendan Shanahan, Mike Modano	8.00
8	Patrick Roy, Ed Belfour, John Vanbiesbrouck	30.00

9	Joe Sakic, Valeri Kamensky, Sandis Ozolinsh	20.00
10	Bret Hull, Pat Verbeek, Pat LaFontaine	15.00

1996-97 Fleer NHL Picks Fabulous 50

The best 50 players in the NHL are featured on these 1996-97 Fleer NHL Picks inserts. Cards were seeded one per pack. The front has a color photo on it, with a black border around it which says "Fabulous Fifty" all around it. There's a Fleer logo in an upper corner, and a team logo in the lower left corner. The player's name is in the bottom right corner. The card back is black, with a ghosted image of the player in the background. A career summary is written over the image. The image is bordered on all sides by the words "Fabulous Fifty." The player's name is at the top. A card number, 1 of 50, etc., is in the lower right corner.

		MT
Complete Set (50):		20.00
Common Player:		.15
(1)	Jaromir Jagr	2.50
(2)	Mario Lemieux	3.50
(3)	Peter Forsberg	2.50
(4)	Teemu Selanne	1.00
(5)	Alexander Mogilny	.40
(6)	Patrick Roy	3.00
(7)	Jim Carey	1.00
(8)	Pavel Bure	1.50
(9)	Sergei Fedorov	1.50
(10)	Chris Chelios	.25
(11)	Sandis Ozolinsh	.15
(12)	Doug Weight	.15
(13)	Mark Messier	.75
(14)	Martin Brodeur	1.00
(15)	Brett Hull	.75
(16)	Steve Yzerman	1.50
(17)	Kevin Hatcher	.15
(18)	Roman Hamrlik	.15
(19)	Petr Nedved	.15
(20)	Valeri Kamensky	.15
(21)	Joe Sakic	1.50
(22)	Eric Lindros	3.00
(23)	Paul Kariya	2.50
(24)	Wayne Gretzky	4.00
(25)	Ron Francis	.15
(26)	Keith Tkachuk	.30
(27)	Theoren Fleury	.15
(28)	Adam Oates	.25
(29)	John LeClair	.30
(30)	Pierre Turgeon	.15
(31)	Brian Leetch	.25
(32)	Chris Osgood	.75
(33)	Jeremy Roenick	.60
(34)	Alexei Zhamnov	.15
(35)	Owen Nolan	.15
(36)	Ray Bourque	.15
(37)	Paul Coffey	.15
(38)	Daniel Alfredsson	.40
(39)	John Vanbiesbrouck	.75
(40)	Ed Jovanovski	.40
(41)	Mike Modano	.25
(42)	Eric Daze	.40
(43)	Sergei Gonchar	.15
(44)	Brendan Shanahan	.50
(45)	Peter Bondra	.15
(46)	Alexei Yashin	.15
(47)	Ron Hextall	.15
(48)	Zigmund Palffy	.35
(49)	Joe Nieuwendyk	.15
(50)	Trevor Linden	.15

1996-97 Fleer NHL Picks Fantasy Force

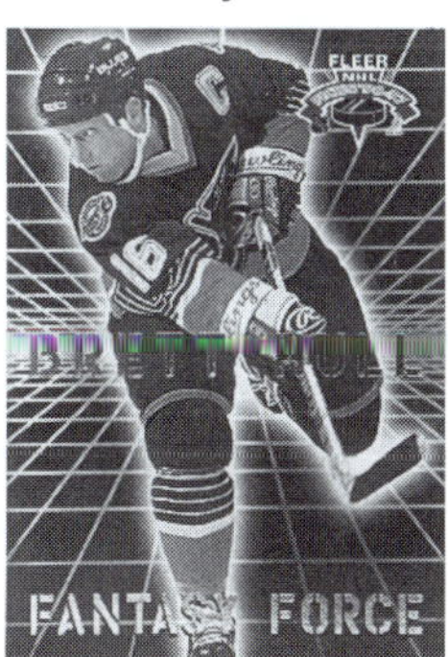

These 1996-97 Fleer NHL Picks inserts feature 10 players who can make or break a fantasy league team, such as Jaromir Jagr or Brett Hull. The card front has a color action photo of the player against a checkerboard, grid-like background. The player's name runs across the middle; "Fantasy Force" is along the bottom. The Fleer logo is in an upper corner.

		MT
Complete Set (10):		60.00
Common Player:		3.00
1	John LeClair	6.00
2	Chris Osgood	8.00
3	Ron Hextall	3.00
4	Eric Daze	4.00
5	Jaromir Jagr	20.00
6	Brett Hull	8.00
7	Ron Francis	3.00
8	Martin Brodeur	12.00
9	Sergei Fedorov	10.00
10	Petr Nedved	3.00

1996-97 Fleer NHL Picks Jagged Edge

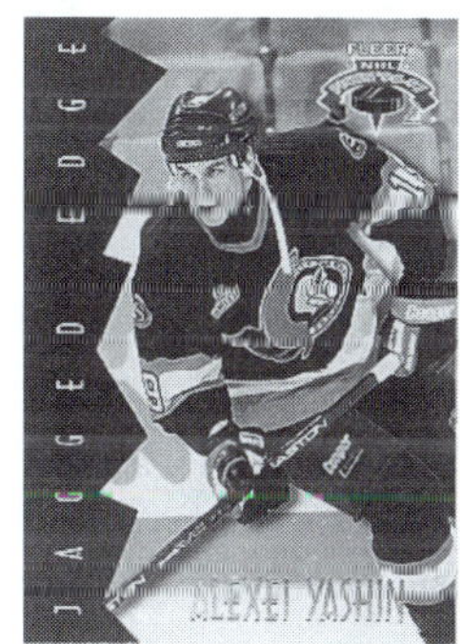

These 1996-97 Fleer NHL Picks insert cards spotlight 20 players with a flair for the dramatic. The cards were seeded one per every 18 packs; #s 1-10 were in hobby packs, while 11-20 were in retail packs. The card front has a color photo on it, with a colored jagged edge on one side in the team's primary color. The background also uses a team color. The Fleer logo is at the top; the player's name at the bottom is in gold foil. The back has a color photo on one side, with a jagged edge down the middle that separates it from a writeup about the player's career.

The player's name is in the upper right corner; the card number, 1 of 20, etc., is in the lower right corner.

		MT
Complete Set (20):		25.00
Common Player:		1.00
1	Daniel Alfredsson	2.00
2	Theoren Fleury	1.00
3	Alexander Mogilny	1.50
4	Doug Weight	1.00
5	Theoren Fleury	1.00
6	Paul Kariya	8.00
7	Saku Koivu	2.50
8	Sandis Ozolinsh	1.00
9	Petr Nedved	1.00
10	Jeremy Roenick	1.75
11	Mike Modano	1.25
12	Jim Carey	3.00
13	Ed Jovanovski	1.50
14	Alexei Zhamnov	1.00
15	Adam Oates	1.25
16	Ron Francis	1.00
17	Brian Leetch	1.25
18	Paul Coffey	1.00
19	Eric Daze	1.50
20	Zigmund Palffy	1.50

1996-97 Ultra

The 180-card 1996-97 Fleer Ultra set contains 148 player cards, 30 rookies and two checklists. A gold-stamped parallel version of the 178 player cards is inserted every 20 packs. The card fronts feature a full-bleed color shot with the player's name written in foil script on the lower quadrant. The backs contain complete statistics with a player image over a ghosted player image. Inserts in the set are Ultra Rookies, Ultra Power, Ultra Power Red/Blue Line, Clear The Ice and Mr. Momentum.

		MT
Complete Set (100):		25.00
Common Player:		.10
Gold Medallions:		2x to 5x
Wax Box:		50.00
1	Guy Hebert	.20
2	Paul Kariya	2.00
3	Jari Kurri	.10
4	Roman Oksiuta	.10
5	*Ruslan Salei*	.20
6	Teemu Selanne	.50
7	*Darren Van Impe*	.10
8	Ray Bourque	.15
9	Kyle McLaren	.10
10	Adam Oates	.15
11	Bill Ranford	.15
12	Rick Tocchet	.10
13	Donald Audette	.10
14	*Curtis Brown*	.10
15	Jason Dawe	.10
16	Dominik Hasek	.50
17	Pat LaFontaine	.15
18	*Jay McKee*	.10
19	Derek Plante	.10
20	Wayne Primeau	.10
21	Theoren Fleury	.10
22	Dave Gagner	.10
23	Jonas Hoglund	.10
24	Jarome Iginla	.50
25	Trevor Kidd	.15
26	Robert Reichel	.10
27	German Titov	.10
28	Tony Amonte	.10

29	Ed Belfour	.25
30	Chris Chelios	.20
31	Eric Daze	.20
32	*Ethan Moreau*	.40
33	Gary Suter	.10
34	Adam Deadmarsh	.10
35	Peter Forsberg	1.50
36	Valeri Kamensky	.10
37	Claude Lemieux	.10
38	Sandis Ozolinsh	.10
39	Patrick Roy	2.50
40	Joe Sakic	1.00
41	*Landon Wilson*	.10
42	Derian Hatcher	.10
43	Jamie Langenbrunner	.10
44	Mike Modano	.20
45	Andy Moog	.20
46	Joe Nieuwendyk	.10
47	Pat Verbeek	.10
48	Sergei Zubov	.10
49	Anders Eriksson	.10
50	Sergei Fedorov	.75
51	Vladimir Konstantinov	.10
52	Slava Kozlov	.10
53	Nicklas Lidstrom	.10
54	Chris Osgood	.75
55	Brendan Shanahan	.60
56	Steve Yzerman	1.25
57	Jason Arnott	.10
58	*Mike Grier*	.75
59	Curtis Joseph	.25
60	*Rem Murray*	.40
61	Jeff Norton	.10
62	Miroslav Satan	.10
63	Doug Weight	.10
64	Radek Dvorak	.10
65	Ed Jovanovski	.20
66	Scott Mellanby	.10
67	Rob Niedermayer	.10
68	Ray Sheppard	.10
69	Robert Svehla	.10
70	John Vanbiesbrouck	1.00
71	*Steve Washburn*	.10
72	Jeff Brown	.10
73	Sean Burke	.20
74	Paul Coffey	.10
75	Hnat Domenichelli	.10
76	Keith Primeau	.10
77	Geoff Sanderson	.10
78	Rob Blake	.10
79	Stephane Fiset	.20
80	Dimitri Khristich	.10
81	Mattias Norstrom	.10
82	Ed Olczyk	.10
83	Jamie Storr	.10
84	Jan Vopat	.10
85	Vitali Yachmenev	.10
86	Shayne Corson	.10
87	Vincent Damphousse	.10
88	Saku Koivu	.60
89	Mark Recchi	.10
90	Stephane Richer	.10
91	Jocelyn Thibault	.35
92	*David Wilkie*	.10
93	Dave Andreychuk	.10
94	Martin Brodeur	.60
95	Scott Niedermayer	.10
96	Scott Stevens	.10
97	Petr Sykora	.10
98	Steve Thomas	.10
99	Bryan Berard	.20
100	Todd Bertuzzi	.10
101	Eric Fichaud	.20
102	Travis Green	.10
103	Kenny Jonsson	.10
104	Zigmund Palffy	.25
105	Christian Dube	.10
106	*Daniel Goneau*	.25
107	Wayne Gretzky	3.00
108	Alexei Kovalev	.10
109	Brian Leetch	.10
110	Mark Messier	.50
111	Mike Richter	.35
112	Luc Robitaille	.10
113	Niklas Sundstrom	.10
114	Daniel Alfredsson	.20
115	Radek Bonk	.10
116	*Andreas Dackell*	.15
117	Alexandre Daigle	.10
118	Steve Duchesne	.10
119	Wade Redden	.10
120	Damian Rhodes	.10
121	Alexei Yashin	.10
122	Rod Brind'Amour	.10
123	Eric Desjardins	.10
124	Ron Hextall	.20
125	John LeClair	.20
126	Eric Lindros	2.00
127	Janne Niinimaa	.10
128	Mikael Renberg	.10
129	*Dainius Zubrus*	1.50

130	Mike Gartner	.10
131	Craig Janney	.10
132	Nikolai Khabibulin	.20
133	Dave Manson	.10
134	Teppo Numminen	.10
135	Jeremy Roenick	.40
136	Keith Tkachuk	.40
137	Oleg Tverdovsky	.10
138	Tom Barrasso	.15
139	Ron Francis	.10
140	Kevin Hatcher	.10
141	Jaromir Jagr	2.00
142	*Patrick Lalime*	1.50
143	Mario Lemieux	2.50
144	Jim Campbell	.25
145	Grant Fuhr	.25
146	Brett Hull	.50
147	Al MacInnis	.10
148	Pierre Turgeon	.10
149	*Harry York*	.30
150	Kelly Hrudey	.20
151	Al Iafrate	.10
152	Bernie Nicholls	.10
153	Owen Nolan	.10
154	Darren Turcotte	.10
155	Brian Bradley	.10
156	Dino Ciccarelli	.10
157	Roman Hamrlik	.10
158	Daymond Langkow	.10
159	Daren Puppa	.10
160	Alexander Selivanov	.10
161	*Sergei Berezin*	.50
162	Wendel Clark	.10
163	Doug Gilmour	.20
164	Larry Murphy	.10
165	Felix Potvin	.40
166	Mats Sundin	.25
167	Pavel Bure	1.00
168	Trevor Linden	.10
169	Kirk McLean	.10
170	Alexander Mogilny	.30
171	Esa Tikkanen	.10
172	Peter Bondra	.10
173	*Andrew Brunette*	.10
174	Jim Carey	.50
175	Sergei Gonchar	.10
176	Phil Housley	.10
177	Joe Juneau	.10
178	Michal Pivonka	.10
179	Checklist	.10
180	Checklist	.10

1996-97 Ultra Gold Medallion

Inserted every 20 packs, the cards parallel the 178 base player cards with gold-foil stamping.

	MT
Complete Set (180):	150.00
Common Player:	.25
Gold Medallions:	2x to 5x

1996-97 Ultra Clear the Ice

The 10 Clear The Ice cards are inserted every 350 packs and feature the game's top goalies on plastic card stock.

		MT
Complete Set (10):		550.00
Common Player:		20.00
1	Jim Carey	30.00
2	Peter Forsberg	80.00
3	Dominik Hasek	50.00
4	Jaromir Jagr	100.00
5	John LeClair	25.00
6	Eric Lindros	100.00
7	Mark Messier	40.00
8	Patrick Roy	125.00
9	Brendan Shanahan	50.00
10	Keith Tkachuk	25.00

1996-97 Ultra Mr. Momentum

The 10-card, retail-only set features top players on gold-foil cards, seeded every 36 retail packs. The cards also feature computer generated special effects.

		MT
Complete Set (10):		250.00
Common Player:		10.00
1	Peter Bondra	10.00
2	Pavel Bure	25.00
3	Ron Francis	10.00
4	Brett Hull	15.00
5	Jaromir Jagr	50.00
6	Pat LaFontaine	10.00
7	Eric Lindros	50.00
8	Mark Messier	20.00
9	Mats Sundin	12.00
10	Steve Yzerman	40.00

1996-97 Ultra Power

Sixteen Power inserts were seeded every 16 packs of 1996-97 Fleer Ultra hockey. The cards combine UV coating, silver-foil stamping and gold sparkles.

		MT
Complete Set (16):		150.00
Common Player:		3.00
1	Ray Bourque	3.00
2	Chris Chelios	4.00
3	Paul Coffey	3.00
4	Sergei Fedorov	15.00
5	Wayne Gretzky	40.00
6	Roman Hamrlik	3.00
7	Ed Jovanovski	5.00
8	Paul Kariya	30.00
9	Vladimir Konstantinov	3.00
10	Brian Leetch	3.00
11	Mario Lemieux	35.00
12	Nicklas Lidstrom	3.00
13	Alexander Mogilny	6.00
14	Adam Oates	3.00
15	Joe Sakic	20.00
16	Teemu Selanne	15.00

1996-97 Ultra Power Blue Line

The Power Blue Line inserts parallel eight of the 16 Power inserts with serial numbering. Inserted only in hobby packs, the Power Red Line inserts make up the other eight parallels.

		MT
Complete Set (8):		80.00
Common Player:		8.00
1	Ray Bourque	15.00
2	Chris Chelios	15.00
3	Paul Coffey	12.00
4	Roman Hamrlik	8.00

5	Ed Jovanovski	25.00
6	Vladimir Konstantinov	8.00
7	Brian Leetch	12.00
8	Nicklas Lidstrom	8.00

1996-97 Ultra Power Red Line

The Power Red Line inserts parallel eight of the 16 Power inserts with serial numbering. Inserted only in hobby packs, the Power Blue Line inserts make up the other eight parallels.

		MT
Complete Set (8):		300.00
Common Player:		15.00
1	Sergei Fedorov	30.00
2	Wayne Gretzky	100.00
3	Paul Kariya	65.00
4	Mario Lemieux	80.00
5	Alexander Mogilny	20.00
6	Adam Oates	15.00
7	Joe Sakic	50.00
8	Teemu Selanne	35.00

1996-97 Ultra Rookies

The 20-card insert set features the leagues top rookies from the 1996-97 NHL season. Inserted every nine packs, the cards are printed with enhanced metallic ink, gold-foil stamping and UV coating.

		MT
Complete Set (20):		40.00
Common Player:		1.50
1	Bryan Berard	4.00
2	Sergei Berezin	3.00
3	Curtis Brown	1.50
4	Jim Campbell	3.00
5	Christian Dube	1.50
6	Anders Eriksson	3.00
7	Eric Fichaud	4.00
8	Daniel Goneau	1.50
9	Mike Grier	5.00
10	Jarome Iginla	8.00
11	Jamie Langenbrunner	1.50
12	Jay McKee	1.50
13	Ethan Moreau	4.00
14	Rem Murray	2.50
15	Janne Niinimaa	4.00
16	Wayne Primeau	1.50
17	Wade Redden	1.50
18	Jamie Storr	1.50
19	David Wilkie	1.00
20	Landon Wilson	1.00

1996-97 Leaf

Released in November of 1996, Leaf Hockey contained 250 base cards with several insert sets: Leather And Laces (Prod: 5,000), Sweaters (Away - 5,000, Home - 1,000), Fire On Ice (2,500 retail), Shut Down (2,500 hobby) and the parallel Gold Press Proofs, gold-foil versions of the base cards limited to 1,500 sets. The Best Of... is a magazine-only insert. The main set includes a 10-card subset entitled Gold Leaf Rookies which feature silver foil. Leaf Hockey came 10 cards to a pack with an original SRP of $2.99.

		MT
Complete Set (240):		25.00
Common Player:		.10
Wax Box:		45.00
1	Sergei Fedorov	.75
2	Bill Ranford	.10
3	Oleg Tverdovsky	.10
4	Brad May	.10
5	Chris Pronger	.10
6	Martin Brodeur	.60
7	Yanic Perreault	.10
8	Garry Galley	.10
9	Shawn McEachern	.10
10	Brian Bellows	.10
11	Ron Francis	.10
12	Mike Modano	.25
13	Steve Yzerman	1.25
14	Joe Mullen	.10
15	Pavel Bure	.75
16	Dino Ciccarelli	.10
17	Claude Lemieux	.10
18	Stephane Richer	.10
19	Dominik Hasek	.75
20	Adam Graves	.10
21	Joe Juneau	.10
22	Rob Niedermayer	.10
23	Zigmund Palffy	.50
24	Dave Andreychuk	.10
25	Steve Thomas	.10
26	Tom Barrasso	.20
27	Eric Desjardins	.10
28	Curtis Joseph	.40
29	Russ Courtnall	.10
30	Stu Barnes	.10
31	Mark Tinordi	.10
32	Gary Suter	.10
33	Greg Johnson	.10
34	Joe Nieuwendyk	.10
35	Norm MacIver	.10
36	Craig Janney	.10
37	Mark Recchi	.10
38	Patrick Roy	2.00
39	Petr Klima	.10
40	Ken Wregget	.10
41	Rod Brind'Amour	.10
42	Viacheslav Fetisov	.10
43	Kirk McLean	.10
44	Pat LaFontaine	.10
45	Brett Hull	.50
46	Chris Chelios	.20
47	Damian Rhodes	.10
48	Kevin Hatcher	.10
49	Uwe Krupp	.10
50	Bernie Nicholls	.10
51	Tommy Soderstrom	.10

		MT
52	Teemu Selanne	.75
53	Mats Sundin	.30
54	Jeff Hackett	.10
55	Ulf Dahlen	.10
56	Dale Hunter	.10
57	Robert Kron	.10
58	Brian Bradley	.10
59	Pat Verbeek	.10
60	Kenny Jonsson	.10
61	Theoren Fleury	.10
62	Alexander Selivanov	.10
63	Nikolai Khabibulin	.20
64	Grant Fuhr	.20
65	Phil Housley	.10
66	Bill Lindsay	.10
67	Trevor Kidd	.10
68	Jim Carey	.40
69	Brian Skrudland	.10
70	Todd Krygier	.10
71	Petr Nedved	.10
72	Kirk Muller	.10
73	Darren Puppa	.10
74	Doug Gilmour	.20
75	Nicklas Lidstrom	.10
76	Zdeno Ciger	.10
77	Robert Svehla	.10
78	Andrew Cassels	.10
79	Vincent Damphousse	.10
80	Alexandre Daigle	.10
81	Tomas Sandstrom	.10
82	Brent Fedyk	.10
83	John LeClair	.20
84	Mario Lemieux	2.50
85	Sean Burke	.20
86	Cam Neely	.10
87	Jeff Friesen	.10
88	Guy Hebert	.20
89	Jon Casey	.20
90	Rick Tocchet	.10
91	Mike Gartner	.10
92	Tony Amonte	.10
93	Jason Dawe	.10
94	Chris Terreri	.10
95	Zarley Zalapski	.10
96	Martin Rucinsky	.10
97	Garth Snow	.10
98	Sylvain Lefebvre	.10
99	Andy Moog	.20
100	Larry Murphy	.10
101	Alexei Yashin	.10
102	Pat Falloon	.10
103	Greg Adams	.10
104	Igor Larionov	.10
105	Geoff Sanderson	.10
106	Jaromir Jagr	1.50
107	Alexei Zhamnov	.10
108	Mikael Renberg	.10
109	Kelly Hrudey	.20
110	Vladimir Konstantinov	.10
111	Brian Savage	.10
112	Adam Oates	.20
113	Teppo Numminen	.10
114	Ray Sheppard	.10
115	Michael Nylander	.10
116	Jozef Stumpel	.10
117	Ed Olczyk	.10
118	Roman Hamrlik	.10
119	Kris Draper	.10
120	Chris Gratton	.10
121	Randy Burridge	.10
122	Ray Bourque	.20
123	Jyrki Lumme	.10
124	Dale Hawerchuk	.10
125	Dave Lowry	.10
126	Curtis Leschyshyn	.10
127	Martin Gelinas	.10
128	Owen Nolan	.10
129	Radek Bonk	.10
130	Sergei Zubov	.10
131	Travis Green	.10
132	Scott Mellanby	.10
133	Keith Tkachuk	.40
134	Luc Robitaille	.10
135	Alexei Kovalev	.10
136	Doug Weight	.10
137	Benoit Hogue	.10
138	Cory Stillman	.10
139	Joe Sakic	1.00
140	Wayne Gretzky	3.00
141	Mike Ricci	.10
142	Kyle McLaren	.10
143	Deron Quint	.10
144	Ville Peltonen	.10
145	Todd Harvey	.10
146	Brendan Shanahan	.60
147	Mike Vernon	.20
148	Eric Lindros	1.75
149	Rick Tabaracci	.10
150	Stephane Yelle	.10
151	Chris Osgood	.50
152	Corey Hirsch	.10

		MT
153	Todd Marchant	.10
154	Keith Primeau	.10
155	Alexei Zhitnik	.10
156	Felix Potvin	.50
157	Vitali Yachmenev	.10
158	Geoff Courtnall	.10
159	Peter Forsberg	1.00
160	Radek Dvorak	.10
161	Bryan McCabe	.10
162	Alexander Mogilny	.35
163	Shayne Corson	.10
164	Paul Coffey	.20
165	Brian Leetch	.20
166	Wendel Clark	.10
167	Aaron Gavey	.10
168	Dimitri Khristich	.10
169	Grant Marshall	.10
170	Valeri Kamensky	.10
171	Ryan Smyth	.15
172	Niklas Sundstrom	.10
173	Cliff Ronning	.10
174	Al MacInnis	.10
175	Scott Stevens	.10
176	Paul Kariya	1.50
177	Rob Blake	.10
178	Mike Richter	.40
179	Jason Arnott	.10
180	Mark Messier	.50
181	Scott Young	.10
182	Jocelyn Thibault	.35
183	Marcus Ragnarsson	.10
184	Darren Turcotte	.10
185	Joe Murphy	.10
186	Pierre Turgeon	.20
187	Trevor Linden	.10
188	Stephane Fiset	.20
189	Miroslav Satan	.10
190	Mathieu Schneider	.10
191	Jeremy Roenick	.40
192	Craig MacTavish	.10
193	John Vanbiesbrouck	1.00
194	Ron Hextall	.20
195	John MacLean	.10
196	Viacheslav Kozlov	.10
197	Sandis Ozolinsh	.10
198	Scott Niedermayer	.10
199	Ed Belfour	.25
200	Peter Bondra	.20
201	Jere Lehtinen	.10
202	Eric Daze	.30
203	Chad Kilger	.10
204	Saku Koivu	.50
205	Todd Bertuzzi	.10
206	Petr Sykora	.20
207	Valeri Bure	.10
208	Ed Jovanovski	.40
209	Jeff O'Neill	.10
210	Daniel Alfredsson	.40
211	Byron Dafoe	.10
212	Brian Holzinger	.10
213	Martin Biron	.10
214	Anders Eriksson	.15
215	Landon Wilson	.10
216	Alexei Yegorov	.10
217	Jan Caloun	.10
218	David Sacco	.10
219	David Nemirovsky	.10
220	Anders Myrvold	.10
221	Tommy Salo	.10
222	Jan Vopat	.10
223	Steve Staios	.10
224	Patrick Labrecque	.10
225	Jamie Langenbrunner	.10
226	Denis Pederson	.10
227	Marek Malik	.10
228	Geoff Sarjeant	.10
229	Chris Ferraro	.10
230	Zdenek Nedved	.10
231	Wayne Primeau	.10
232	Daymond Langkow	.10
233	Marko Kiprusoff	.10
234	Niklas Sundblad	.10
235	Jamie Ram	.10
236	Jamie Rivers	.10
237	Steve Washburn	.10
238	Teemu Selanne CL	.30
239	Steve Yzerman CL	.50
240	Eric Lindros CL	.75

1996-97 Leaf Press Proofs

This 240-card parallel set featured each base card on a gold foil, die-cut design. Each Press Proof is numbered "1 of 1,500" sets produced on the back.

	MT
Complete Set (240):	1200.
Common Player:	4.00
Press Proof Stars 25x to 40x base cards	
Press Proofs Yng Stars & RC's	
	15x to 25x

1996-97 Leaf Fire on Ice

Available exclusively through retail packs, the 15-card Fire On Ice insert set was limited to a production total of 2,500. The cards are printed on foil-laminated, micro-etched card stock and are sequentially numbered.

		MT
Complete Set (15):		400.00
Common Player:		12.00
1	Mario Lemieux	75.00
2	Alexander Mogilny	15.00
3	Joe Sakic	40.00
4	Paul Kariya	60.00
5	Wayne Gretzky	100.00
6	Doug Weight	12.00
7	Zigmund Palffy	25.00
8	Eric Lindros	60.00
9	Teemu Selanne	25.00
10	Doug Gilmour	12.00
11	Jeremy Roenick	15.00
12	Steve Yzerman	50.00
13	Ed Jovanovski	12.00
14	Mike Modano	15.00
15	Mark Messier	25.00

1996-97 Leaf Gold Leaf Rookies

The 10-card subset features some of the NHL's top prospects on silver-foil card stock. The cards are not considered inserts as they were part of the base 250-card set.

		MT
Complete Set (10):		50.00
Common Player:		3.00
1	Ethan Moreau	8.00
2	Kevin Hodson	10.00
3	Jose Theodore	15.00
4	Peter Ferraro	3.00
5	Ralph Intranuovo	3.00
6	Nolan Baumgartner	3.00
7	Brandon Convery	3.00
8	Darcy Tucker	3.00
9	Eric Fichaud	8.00
10	Steve Sullivan	3.00

1996-97 Leaf Leather & Laces

Limited to a production total of 5,000, the 20-card insert set features leather-embossed technology and each card is sequentially numbered.

		MT
Complete Set (20):		300.00
Common Player:		6.00
1	Joe Sakic	25.00
2	Keith Tkachuk	12.00
3	Brett Hull	15.00
4	Paul Coffey	6.00

		MT
5	Jaromir Jagr	40.00
6	Peter Forsberg	30.00
7	Zigmund Palffy	6.00
8	Wayne Gretzky	60.00
9	Pavel Bure	20.00
10	Eric Lindros	40.00
11	Alexander Mogilny	10.00
12	Trevor Linden	6.00
13	Jeremy Roenick	12.00
14	Doug Gilmour	6.00
15	Mike Modano	8.00
16	Sergei Fedorov	18.00
17	Brendan Shanahan	18.00
18	Pierre Turgeon	6.00
19	Ed Jovanovski	6.00
20	Saku Koivu	15.00

1996-97 Leaf Shut Down

The hobby-only insert set features 15 of the league's top goaltenders on a canvas-like card stock. Production of each card was limited to 2,500 and each card is individually numbered.

		MT
Complete Set (15):		275.00
Common Player:		10.00
1	Patrick Roy	70.00
2	John Vanbiesbrouck	45.00
3	Jocelyn Thibault	15.00
4	Ed Belfour	15.00
5	Curtis Joseph	12.00
6	Martin Brodeur	35.00
7	Damian Rhodes	10.00
8	Felix Potvin	25.00
9	Nikolai Khabibulin	10.00
10	Jim Carey	20.00
11	Mike Richter	20.00
12	Corey Hirsch	10.00
13	Chris Osgood	25.00
14	Ron Hextall	10.00
15	Daren Puppa	10.00

1996-97 Leaf Sweaters

The 15-card insert set highlights the road uniforms of the top players on nylon-jersey card stock. Production of each card was limited to 5,000 with the more scarce Home Sweaters limited to 1,000 each.

		MT
Complete Set (15):		275.00
Common Player:		8.00
1	Mario Lemieux	40.00
2	Patrick Roy	40.00
3	Eric Lindros	30.00
4	John Vanbiesbrouck	25.00
5	Paul Kariya	30.00
6	Martin Brodeur	20.00
7	Eric Daze	8.00
8	Mark Messier	15.00
9	Jim Carey	15.00
10	Brendan Shanahan	20.00
11	Sergei Fedorov	20.00
12	Brett Hull	15.00
13	Pavel Bure	20.00
14	Daniel Alfredsson	10.00
15	Saku Koivu	15.00

1996-97 Leaf Home Sweaters

The 15-card insert set features the home jerseys of some of the best NHL players on embossed nylon-jersey card stock. The cards parallel the more common Away Sweaters and are numbered to just 1,000.

	MT
Complete Set (15):	1000.
Common Player:	30.00
Home Sweaters 3x Sweater prices	

1996-97 Leaf The Best of...

Available just through pre-priced magazine packs, The Best Of... highlights nine NHL record breakers on plastic stock with holographic foil. The cards are individually numbered to 1,500.

		MT
Complete Set (9):		325.00
Common Player:		20.00
1	Jaromir Jagr	80.00
2	Eric Daze	20.00
3	Eric Lindros	80.00
4	Chris Osgood	35.00
5	Keith Tkachuk	40.00
6	Nikolai Khabibulin	20.00
7	Doug Weight	20.00
8	Peter Forsberg	70.00
9	Jocelyn Thibault	25.00

1996-97 Leaf Limited

The 90-card Leaf Limited set was released in January of 1997 in five-card packs with a retail of $4.99. The base cards are printed on foil board with the color player image centered. A silver-foil stripe is found on each side with the top edges fading to one of the player's team colors. Another set of silver stripes are found inside which fade to the bottom to another team color. The player's name is printed in script along the bottom edge. The card backs feature a color photo with bio and highlight information given.

		MT
Complete Set (90):		60.00
Common Player:		.25
Wax Box:		100.00
1	Chris Chelios	.25
2	Brendan Shanahan	1.00
3	Keith Tkachuk	1.50
4	Roman Hamrlik	.25
5	Adam Oates	.25
6	Chris Osgood	2.00
7	Wayne Gretzky	8.00
8	Alexander Mogilny	.60
9	Patrick Roy	6.00
10	Saku Koivu	2.00
11	Jaromir Jagr	4.00
12	Wendel Clark	.25
13	Mike Modano	.50
14	Ed Jovanovski	.50
15	John LeClair	.25
16	Jim Carey	1.50
17	Paul Kariya	4.00
18	Paul Coffey	.25
19	Todd Bertuzzi	.25
20	Owen Nolan	.25
21	Dominik Hasek	2.00
22	Bill Ranford	.25
23	Scott Stevens	.25
24	Brett Hull	1.00
25	Trevor Kidd	.25
26	Viacheslav Fetisov	.25
27	Luc Robitaille	.25
28	Mats Sundin	.25
29	Peter Forsberg	3.00
30	John Vanbiesbrouck	3.00
31	Alexei Yashin	.25
32	Pavel Bure	2.50
33	Pat Verbeek	.25
34	Vitali Yachmenev	.25
35	Ron Hextall	.50
36	Michal Pivonka	.25
37	Eric Daze	.40
38	Pierre Turgeon	.25
39	Petr Nedved	.25
40	Steve Yzerman	3.00
41	Mike Richter	1.00
42	Marcus Ragnarsson	.25
43	Jason Arnott	.25
44	Jocelyn Thibault	.75
45	Alexander Selivanov	.25
46	Claude Lemieux	.25
47	Eric Lindros	4.00
48	Grant Fuhr	.50
49	Ray Bourque	.25
50	Scott Mellanby	.25
51	Craig Janney	.25
52	Ron Francis	.25
53	Ed Belfour	.60
54	Petr Sykora	.25
55	Damian Rhodes	.25
56	Joe Sakic	3.00
57	Zigmund Palffy	.75
58	Daren Puppa	.25
59	Pat LaFontaine	.25
60	Nikolai Khabibulin	.50
61	Sergei Fedorov	2.00
62	Valeri Bure	.25
63	Peter Bondra	.25
64	Teemu Selanne	2.00
65	Mark Messier	1.00
66	Shayne Corson	.25
67	Theo Fleury	.25
68	Jeff O'Neill	.25
69	Eric Fichaud	.25
70	Doug Gilmour	.25
71	Doug Weight	.25
72	Stephane Fiset	.25
73	Daniel Alfredsson	.50
74	Trevor Linden	.25
75	Joe Nieuwendyk	.25
76	Brian Bradley	.25
77	Jere Lehtinen	.25
78	Rob Niedermayer	.25
79	Mikael Renberg	.25
80	Felix Potvin	.75
81	Valeri Kamensky	.25
82	Brian Leetch	.25
83	Jeff Friesen	.25
84	Vincent Damphousse	.25
85	Mario Lemieux	6.00
86	Jeremy Roenick	.75
87	Martin Brodeur	2.50
88	Vyacheslav Kozlov	.25
89	Corey Hirsch	.25
90	Curtis Joseph	.75

1996-97 Leaf Limited Gold

The 1996-97 Leaf Limited Gold inserts, seeded every 13 packs, parallel the 90-card base Leaf Limited set in design, except for the gold-foil card stock. A "Limited Gold" stamp appears along the top of the card face.

		MT
Complete Set (90):		500.00
Common Player:		4.00
Unlisted Golds:		6x to 12x
1	Chris Chelios	5.00
2	Brendan Shanahan	12.00
3	Keith Tkachuk	20.00
4	Roman Hamrlik	3.00
5	Adam Oates	5.00
6	Chris Osgood	30.00
7	Wayne Gretzky	100.00
8	Alexander Mogilny	15.00
9	Patrick Roy	75.00
10	Saku Koivu	25.00
11	Jaromir Jagr	60.00
12	Wendel Clark	3.00
13	Mike Modano	10.00
14	Ed Jovanovski	8.00
15	John LeClair	5.00
16	Jim Carey	25.00
17	Paul Kariya	60.00
18	Paul Coffey	5.00
19	Todd Bertuzzi	3.00
20	Owen Nolan	3.00
21	Dominik Hasek	8.00
22	Bill Ranford	5.00
23	Scott Stevens	3.00
24	Brett Hull	15.00
25	Trevor Kidd	3.00
26	Viacheslav Fetisov	3.00
27	Luc Robitaille	3.00
28	Mats Sundin	8.00
29	Peter Forsberg	50.00
30	John Vanbiesbrouck	50.00
31	Alexei Yashin	3.00
32	Pavel Bure	40.00
33	Pat Verbeek	3.00
34	Vitali Yachmenev	3.00
35	Ron Hextall	5.00
36	Michal Pivonka	3.00
37	Eric Daze	6.00
38	Pierre Turgeon	5.00
39	Petr Nedved	3.00
40	Steve Yzerman	50.00
41	Mike Richter	15.00
42	Marcus Ragnarsson	3.00
43	Jason Arnott	3.00
44	Jocelyn Thibault	10.00
45	Alexander Selivanov	3.00
46	Claude Lemieux	3.00
47	Eric Lindros	60.00
48	Grant Fuhr	5.00
49	Ray Bourque	3.00
50	Scott Mellanby	3.00
51	Craig Janney	3.00
52	Ron Francis	5.00
53	Ed Belfour	5.00
54	Petr Sykora	3.00
55	Damian Rhodes	3.00
56	Joe Sakic	50.00
57	Zigmund Palffy	8.00
58	Daren Puppa	3.00
59	Pat LaFontaine	5.00
60	Nikolai Khabibulin	5.00
61	Sergei Fedorov	30.00
62	Valeri Bure	3.00
63	Peter Bondra	5.00
64	Teemu Selanne	20.00
65	Mark Messier	20.00
66	Shayne Corson	3.00
67	Theo Fleury	3.00
68	Jeff O'Neill	3.00
69	Eric Fichaud	3.00
70	Doug Gilmour	5.00
71	Doug Weight	3.00
72	Stephane Fiset	5.00
73	Daniel Alfredsson	5.00
74	Trevor Linden	3.00
75	Joe Nieuwendyk	3.00
76	Brian Bradley	3.00
77	Jere Lehtinen	3.00
78	Rob Niedermayer	3.00
79	Mikael Renberg	3.00
80	Felix Potvin	15.00
81	Valeri Kamensky	3.00
82	Brian Leetch	5.00
83	Jeff Friesen	3.00
84	Vincent Damphousse	3.00
85	Mario Lemieux	75.00
86	Jeremy Roenick	10.00
87	Martin Brodeur	30.00
88	Vyacheslav Kozlov	3.00
89	Corey Hirsch	5.00
90	Curtis Joseph	8.00

1996-97 Leaf Limited Bash the Boards

The 10-card Bash The Boards set, randomly inserted in 1996-97 Leaf Limited Hockey, feature a polycarbonate see-through card design which emulates the plexiglass boards of a hockey arena. The player's color image appears over the all-plastic card with the player's name appearing near the bottom over the red and black "Bash The Boards" logo. The backs

feature a small head shot with a brief highlight. The cards are sequentially numbered as "x/3,500." A parallel of Bash The Boards exists with Limited Edition, which feature a die-cut shatter hole on the corner of the plexiglass. These cards are numbered to 350.

		MT
Complete Set (10):		150.00
Common Player:		8.00
Limited Editions:		2.5x to 4x
1	Eric Lindros	50.00
2	Mark Messier	15.00
3	Owen Nolan	8.00
4	Doug Gilmour	12.00
5	Keith Tkachuk	15.00
6	Claude Lemieux	8.00
7	Ed Jovanovski	8.00
8	Peter Forsberg	40.00
9	Brendan Shanahan	25.00
10	Eric Daze	8.00

1996-97 Leaf Limited Rookies

The 10-card Leaf Limited Rookies are printed with silver hologram foil and are seeded in every 10 packs of 1996-97 Leaf Limited Hockey.

		MT
Complete Set (10):		70.00
Common Player:		3.00
1	Ethan Moreau	12.00
2	Jarome Iginla	25.00
3	Bryan Berard	10.00
4	Hnat Domenichelli	3.00
5	Wade Redden	6.00
6	Dainius Zubrus	25.00
7	Sergei Berezin	10.00
8	Jamie Langenbrunner	3.00
9	Tomas Holmstrom	3.00
10	Jonas Hoglund	3.00

1996-97 Leaf Limited Stubble

The 20-card Stubble inserts, sequentially numbered to 1,500, feature a close-up of the player with his name and "Stubble" printed in fuzzy letters to simulate the player's facial hair. The player's name is printed along the left border with "Stubble" appearing in the lower right corner.

		MT
Complete Set (20):		600.00
Common Player:		15.00
1	Patrick Roy	80.00
2	Eric Lindros	60.00
3	Wayne Gretzky	100.00
4	Paul Coffey	15.00
5	Jim Carey	30.00
6	Ed Belfour	25.00
7	Mario Lemieux	80.00
8	Mike Modano	25.00
9	Todd Bertuzzi	15.00
10	Pavel Bure	40.00
11	Martin Brodeur	40.00
12	Petr Nedved	15.00
13	Alexander Mogilny	20.00
14	Steve Yzerman	50.00
15	Brett Hull	30.00
16	Joe Sakic	45.00
17	Scott Mellanby	15.00
18	Trevor Linden	15.00
19	Rob Niedermayer	15.00
20	Wendel Clark	15.00

1996-97 Leaf Preferred

The 1996-97 Leaf Preferred Hockey set contains 150 cards, including 30 rookies. The base cards feature a silver-foil stripe along the left edge with "Leaf Preferred" and the player's position embossed within the stripe. The backs contain bio and stat information. A parallel version of each of the 150 cards exist with gold foil and limited to 250 sets. Other inserts are Silver Steel, Gold Steel, Steel Power, Masked Marauders, Silver Vanity Plates and Gold Vanity Plates.

		MT
Complete Set (150):		30.00
Common Player:		.10
Wax Box:		65.00
1	Patrick Roy	2.50
2	Alexander Mogilny	.40
3	Bill Ranford	.10
4	Jeremy Roenick	.40
5	Travis Green	.10
6	Owen Nolan	.10
7	Paul Kariya	2.00
8	Pat Verbeek	.10
9	Jeff O'Neill	.10
10	Nikolai Khabibulin	.25
11	Pat LaFontaine	.20
12	Rob Niedermayer	.10
13	Luc Robitaille	.10
14	Mats Sundin	.40
15	Cory Stillman	.10
16	Ray Ferraro	.10
17	Alexei Yashin	.20
18	Brian Bradley	.10
19	Chris Chelios	.20
20	Jason Arnott	.10
21	Petr Sykora	.10
22	Jaromir Jagr	2.00
23	Jim Carey	.50
24	Claude Lemieux	.10
25	Vincent Damphousse	.10
26	Shayne Corson	.10
27	Joe Nieuwendyk	.10
28	Kenny Jonsson	.10
29	Peter Bondra	.40
30	Ed Belfour	.25
31	Brendan Shanahan	.75
32	Eric Desjardins	.10
33	Corey Hirsch	.10
34	Viacheslav Fetisov	.10
35	Craig Janney	.10
36	Felix Potvin	.50
37	Joe Sakic	1.50
38	Scott Stevens	.10
39	Kelly Hrudey	.10
40	Adam Oates	.25
41	John Vanbiesbrouck	1.50
42	Brian Leetch	.20
43	Alexander Selivanov	.10
44	Mike Modano	.25
45	Saku Koivu	.75
46	Tom Barrasso	.20
47	Jere Lehtinen	.10
48	Daniel Alfredsson	.25
49	Joe Juneau	.10
50	Chris Osgood	.75
51	Dave Andreychuk	.10
52	Marcus Ragnarsson	.10
53	Valeri Kamensky	.10
54	Doug Weight	.20
55	Mike Richter	.40
56	Teemu Selanne	.75
57	Stephane Fiset	.10
58	Mikael Renberg	.10
59	Trevor Linden	.10
60	Bernie Nicholls	.10
61	Eric Daze	.20
62	Ron Francis	.20
63	Sergei Zubov	.10
64	Rod Brind'Amour	.10
65	Sergei Fedorov	.75
66	Mark Messier	.60
67	Theoren Fleury	.20
68	Ed Jovanovski	.20
69	Daren Puppa	.10
70	Pierre Turgeon	.20
71	Oleg Tverdovsky	.10
72	Ryan Smyth	.25
73	Jocelyn Thibault	.25
74	Brendan Witt	.10
75	Igor Larionov	.10
76	Stephane Richer	.10
77	Ron Hextall	.20
78	Mike Ricci	.10
79	Dimitri Khristich	.10
80	Derian Hatcher	.10
81	Martin Brodeur	1.00
82	Petr Nedved	.10
83	Ray Bourque	.20
84	Keith Primeau	.10
85	Sean Burke	.20
86	Antti Tormanen	.10
87	Wendel Clark	.10
88	Valeri Bure	.10
89	Keith Tkachuk	.50
90	Roman Hamrlik	.10
91	Dominik Hasek	.75
92	Ray Sheppard	.10
93	Todd Bertuzzi	.10
94	Pavel Bure	.75
95	Alexei Zhamnov	.10
96	Alexei Kovalev	.10
97	Jeff Friesen	.10
98	Scott Young	.10
99	Vitali Yachmenev	.10
100	Michael Pivonka	.10
101	Paul Coffey	.20
102	Steve Yzerman	1.50
103	Zigmund Palffy	.50
104	Doug Gilmour	.25
105	John LeClair	.50
106	Brett Hull	.50
107	Yanic Perreault	.10
108	Bill Guerin	.10
109	Damian Rhodes	.10
110	Peter Forsberg	1.50
111	Scott Mellanby	.10
112	Wayne Gretzky	3.00
113	Mario Lemieux	2.50
114	Todd Harvey	.10
115	Mark Recchi	.10
116	Trevor Kidd	.10
117	Eric Lindros	2.00
118	Jarome Iginla	.60
119	Eric Fichaud	.20
120	*Mattias Timander*	.10
121	Hnat Domenichelli	.10
122	Chris O'Sullivan	.10
123	*Sergei Berezin*	.50
124	Jonas Hoglund	.10
125	Anders Eriksson	.10
126	Corey Schwab	.10
127	Janne Niinimaa	.50
128	*Dainius Zubrus*	1.50
129	Bryan Berard	.30
130	Wade Redden	.10
131	Wayne Primeau	.10
132	Brandon Convery	.10
133	*Richard Zednik*	.30
134	Darcy Tucker	.10
135	Christian Dube	.10
136	*Rem Murray*	.25
137	Kevin Hodson	.60
138	Steve Washburn	.10
139	*Ethan Moreau*	.40
140	Daymond Langkow	.10
141	Terry Ryan	.10
142	Curtis Brown	.10
143	Steve Sullivan	.10
144	Jamie Langenbrunner	.10
145	*Daniel Goneau*	.25
146	Anson Carter	.10
147	Jim Campbell	.20
148	Keith Tkachuk CL	.25
149	Eric Daze CL	.10
150	Mike Modano CL	.15

1996-97 Leaf Preferred Press Proofs

The 150-card insert set parallels the base Leaf Preferred set, except with gold foil. Randomly inserted into packs, the gold versions are limited in production to 250 sets.

	MT
Complete Set (150):	2000.
Common Player:	4.00
Veteran Stars:	50x to 75x
Yng Stars & RC's:	25x to 40x

1996-97 Leaf Preferred Masked Marauders

The 12-card insert set, sequentially numbered to 2,500, features the top goalies on silver holographic foil board.

		MT
Complete Set (12):		250.00
Common Goalie:		10.00
1	Jim Carey	15.00
2	Martin Brodeur	40.00
3	John Vanbiesbrouck	40.00
4	Patrick Roy	80.00
5	Felix Potvin	20.00
6	Chris Osgood	20.00
7	Dominik Hasek	30.00
8	Jocelyn Thibault	15.00
9	Nikolai Khabibulin	10.00

		MT
10	Corey Hirsch	10.00
11	Mike Richter	15.00
12	Ed Belfour	15.00

1996-97 Leaf Preferred Steel

Sixty-three of the top players are featured on this silver metal card, which is inserted at a rate of one per pack. A gold version also exists. The card fronts have a color player image with a Leaf Preferred logo in the upper right corner. The backs feature another color player image over the Preferred logo with career statistics on the bottom.

		MT
Complete Set (63):		75.00
Common Player:		1.00
1	Sergei Fedorov	3.00
2	Martin Brodeur	4.00
3	Corey Hirsch	1.00
4	Ray Bourque	1.00
5	Saku Koivu	3.00
6	Ron Francis	1.00
7	Chris Chelios	1.50
8	Scott Mellanby	1.00
9	Ron Hextall	1.00
10	Doug Gilmour	1.50
11	Joe Sakic	5.00
12	Petr Sykora	1.00
13	Marcus Ragnarsson	1.00
14	Pat Verbeek	1.00
15	Stephane Fiset	1.00
16	Alexei Yashin	1.00
17	Daren Puppa	1.00
18	Eric Lindros	8.00
19	Jason Arnott	1.00
20	Todd Bertuzzi	1.00
21	Jim Carey	2.00
22	Pat LaFontaine	1.00
23	Brian Leetch	1.50
24	Trevor Linden	1.00
25	Eric Daze	1.00
26	Pierre Turgeon	1.00
27	Tom Barrasso	1.00
28	Mike Modano	1.50
29	Brendan Shanahan	3.00
30	Nikolai Khabibulin	1.50
31	Claude Lemieux	1.00
32	Zigmund Palffy	2.50
33	Mats Sundin	2.00
34	Paul Kariya	7.00
35	Daniel Alfredsson	1.50
36	Patrick Roy	10.00
37	Jaromir Jagr	8.00
38	Vyacheslav Kozlov	1.00
39	John LeClair	2.50
40	Bill Ranford	1.00
41	Vitali Yachmenev	1.00
42	Mark Messier	2.50
43	Valeri Bure	1.00
44	Roman Hamrlik	1.00
45	Joe Nieuwendyk	1.00
46	Mike Richter	2.00
47	Theoren Fleury	1.00
48	Wendel Clark	1.00
49	Doug Weight	1.00
50	Damian Rhodes	1.00
51	Alexander Mogilny	1.50
52	Dominik Hasek	3.00
53	Eric Fichaud	1.00
54	Adam Oates	1.00
55	Jocelyn Thibault	1.50
56	Petr Nedved	1.00
57	Paul Coffey	1.00
58	Mikael Renberg	1.00
59	Jeremy Roenick	2.00
60	Peter Forsberg	6.00
61	Rob Niedermayer	1.00
62	Owen Nolan	1.00
63	Jere Lehtinen	1.00

1996-97 Leaf Preferred Steel Gold

The 63-card set parallels the Steel version, except on gold metal. Both silver and gold metal cards were inserted at a rate of one per pack.

	MT
Complete Set (63):	800.00
Common Player:	6.00
Golds:	6x to 10x

1996-97 Leaf Preferred Steel Power

Twelve of the top goal scorers in the league are featured on this micro-etched, die-cut card. Limited in production to 4,000 of each card.

		MT
Complete Set (12):		375.00
Common Player:		15.00
1	Joe Sakic	30.00
2	Mario Lemieux	50.00
3	Pavel Bure	20.00
4	Mark Messier	15.00
5	Wayne Gretzky	75.00
6	Peter Forsberg	35.00
7	Sergei Fedorov	20.00
8	Jaromir Jagr	40.00
9	Brett Hull	15.00
10	Teemu Selanne	25.00
11	Paul Kariya	40.00
12	Eric Lindros	40.00

1996-97 Leaf Preferred Vanity Plates

Fourteen of the league's top players are highlighted on this set which features steel cards and resembles a personalized license plate. As with the Silver and Gold Steel cards, Vanity Plates are randomly inserted at a rate of one per pack.

		MT
Complete Set (12):		175.00
Common Player:		5.00
1	Wayne Gretzky	40.00
2	John Vanbiesbrouck	18.00
3	Chris Osgood	10.00
4	Steve Yzerman	20.00
5	Brett Hull	10.00
6	Mario Lemieux	30.00
7	Eric Lindros	30.00
8	Ed Jovanovski	5.00
9	Pavel Bure	15.00
10	Felix Potvin	10.00
11	Teemu Selanne	15.00
12	Keith Tkachuk	10.00

1996-97 Leaf Preferred Vanity Plates Gold

The Gold Vanity Plates parallel the design of the Silver Vanity Plates, but at a more scarce pull rate. The metal card design simulates a personalized license plate.

	MT
Complete Set (12):	500.00
Common Player:	12.00
Golds:	1.5x to 3x

1996-97 Pinnacle

Pinnacle's 250-card set included 35 rookies and five checklist cards. The base cards feature a foil stripe along the bottom with a pyramid-like design containing a hockey player icon. Some of the cards have the foil design along the left side in a horizontal design. The card backs have statistics from the 1995-96 season with another player close-up along the top half. A brief description is also given. Insert sets seeded among the 10-card hobby packs are: Masks, Team Pinnacle, By The Numbers and Masks Die-Cut. Rink Collection and Artist's Proof are parallel inserts.

		MT
Complete Set (250):		20.00
Common Player:		.10
Wax Box:		50.00
1	Wayne Gretzky	3.00
2	Mark Messier	.50
3	Kevin Hatcher	.10
4	Scott Stevens	.10
5	Derek Plante	.10
6	Theoren Fleury	.10
7	Brian Rolston	.10
8	Teppo Numminen	.10
9	Adam Graves	.10
10	Jason Dawe	.10
11	Sergei Nemchinov	.10
12	Jeff Brown	.10
13	Alexei Zhamnov	.10
14	Paul Coffey	.10
15	Kevin Miller	.10
16	Mike Vernon	.20
17	Brian Bradley	.10
18	Jeff Friesen	.10
19	Phil Housley	.10
20	Ray Whitney	.10
21	Sergei Fedorov	.60
22	Pierre Turgeon	.15
23	Rick Tocchet	.10
24	Uwe Krupp	.10
25	Steve Yzerman	1.25
26	Tom Chorske	.10
27	Pat LaFontaine	.20
28	Nicklas Lidstrom	.10
29	Ray Ferraro	.10
30	Brian Noonan	.10
31	Dino Ciccarelli	.10
32	Rob Niedermayer	.10
33	Stephane Richer	.10
34	Chris Chelios	.20
35	Mike Gartner	.10
36	German Titov	.10
37	Sean Burke	.10
38	Robert Svehla	.10
39	Dave Gagner	.10
40	Sergei Gonchar	.10
41	Bernie Nicholls	.10
42	Yanic Perreault	.10
43	Adam Deadmarsh	.10
44	Dale Hawerchuk	.10
45	Alexei Kovalev	.10
46	Esa Tikkanen	.10
47	Valeri Kamensky	.10
48	Craig Janney	.10
49	John LeClair	.20
50	Radek Bonk	.10
51	David Oliver	.10
52	Todd Harvey	.10
53	Steve Thomas	.10
54	Tony Amonte	.10
55	Mikael Renberg	.10
56	Brendan Shanahan	.60
57	Tom Fitzgerald	.10
58	Chris Pronger	.10
59	Donald Audette	.10
60	Nelson Emerson	.10
61	Joe Mullen	.10
62	Marty McInnis	.10
63	Martin Rucinsky	.10
64	Mark Recchi	.10
65	Vladimir Konstantinov	.10
66	Rick Tabaracci	.10
67	Marty McSorley	.10
68	Pat Verbeek	.10
69		.10
70	Travis Green	.10
71	Chris Tancill	.10
72	Vincent Damphousse	.10
73	Benoit Hogue	.10
74	Igor Larionov	.10
75	Russ Courtnall	.10
76	Mike Hough	.10
77	Alexander Selivanov	.10
78	Peter Forsberg	1.00
79	Petr Klima	.10
80	Adam Creighton	.10
81	Dave Lowry	.10
82	Andrew Cassels	.10
83	Martin Gelinas	.10
84	Bob Probert	.10
85	Calle Johansson	.10
86	Mario Lemieux	2.50
87	Alexander Mogilny	.35
88	Guy Hebert	.20
89	Bill Ranford	.20
90	Kirk McLean	.10
91	Kenny Jonsson	.10
92	Martin Brodeur	.60
93	Keith Jones	.10
94	Ed Belfour	.25
95	Tom Barrasso	.20
96	Felix Potvin	.50
97	Daren Puppa	.10
98	Jeremy Roenick	.40
99	Chris Osgood	.60
100	Zigmund Palffy	.40
101	Ron Hextall	.20
102	Jaromir Jagr	1.50
103	Chris Terreri	.10
104	Shayne Corson	.10
105	Jim Carey	.40
106	Dominik Hasek	.75
107	Eric Lindros	1.50
108	Petr Nedved	.10
109	Peter Bondra	.20
110	Jeff Hackett	.10
111	Trevor Linden	.10
112	Mike Richter	.35
113	Claude Lemieux	.10
114	Keith Tkachuk	.40
115	Pat Falloon	.10
116	Brent Fedyk	.10
117	Todd Marchant	.10
118	Jason Arnott	.10
119	Zarley Zalapski	.10
120	Kelly Hrudey	.20
121	Alexei Yashin	.10
122	Sergei Zubov	.10
123	Rod Brind'Amour	.10
124	Mathieu Schneider	.10
125	Bryan Smolinski	.10
126	Scott Mellanby	.10
127	Doug Gilmour	.20
128	Brett Hull	.50
129	Vyacheslav Kozlov	.10
130	Adam Oates	.20
131	Steve Konowalchuk	.10
132	Robert Kron	.10
133	Alexandre Daigle	.10
134	Brian Savage	.10
135	Stu Barnes	.10
136	Cam Neely	.10
137	Steve Rucchin	.10
138	Patrick Roy	2.00
139	Roman Oksiuta	.10
140	Greg Johnson	.10
141	Chris Gratton	.10

142	Jocelyn Thibault	.30
143	Ron Francis	.20
144	Mats Sundin	.20
145	Oleg Tverdovsky	.10
146	Geoff Courtnall	.10
147	Kirk Muller	.10
148	Zdeno Ciger	.10
149	John MacLean	.10
150	Damian Rhodes	.10
151	Michael Nylander	.10
152	Andrei Kovalenko	.10
153	Al MacInnis	.10
154	Mike Modano	.20
155	Teemu Selanne	.75
156	Tomas Sandstrom	.10
157	Bobby Dollas	.10
158	Doug Weight	.10
159	Sandis Ozolinsh	.10
160	Joe Juneau	.10
161	Nikolai Khabibulin	.20
162	Murray Craven	.10
163	Cliff Ronning	.10
164	Curtis Joseph	.30
165	Darren Turcotte	.10
166	Andy Moog	.20
167	Mariusz Czerkawski	.10
168	Keith Primeau	.10
169	Eric Desjardins	.10
170	Bill Guerin	.10
171	Glenn Anderson	.10
172	Mike Ridley	.10
173	Michal Pivonka	.10
174	Trevor Kidd	.10
175	Pavel Bure	.75
176	Todd Gill	.10
177	Dave Andreychuk	.10
178	Roman Hamrlik	.10
179	Andrei Nikolishin	.10
180	Alexei Zhitnik	.10
181	Grant Fuhr	.20
182	Dave Reid	.10
183	Joe Nieuwendyk	.10
184	Paul Kariya	1.50
185	Jyrki Lumme	.10
186	Owen Nolan	.10
187	Geoff Sanderson	.10
188	Alexander Semak	.10
189	Larry Murphy	.10
190	Dimitri Khristich	.10
191	Shane Churla	.10
192	Bill Lindsay	.10
193	Brian Leetch	.10
194	Greg Adams	.10
195	Gary Suter	.10
196	Wendel Clark	.10
197	Scott Young	.10
198	Randy Burridge	.10
199	Ray Bourque	.20
200	Petr Sykora	.10
201	Joe Sakic	1.00
202	Saku Koivu	.40
203	John Vanbiesbrouck	1.00
204	Ed Jovanovski	.30
205	Daniel Alfredsson	.30
206	Vitali Yachmenevlos	.10
207	Marcus Ragnarsson	.10
208	Todd Bertuzzi	.10
209	Valeri Bure	.10
210	Jeff O'Neill	.10
211	Corey Hirsch	.10
212	Eric Daze	.30
213	David Sacco	.10
214	Jan Vopat	.10
215	Sean Haggerty	.10
216	Steve Shields	.10
217	Jose Theodore	.10
218	Peter Ferraro	.10
219	Anders Eriksson	.10
220	Wayne Primeau	.10
221	Denis Pederson	.10
222	Jay McKee	.10
223	Darcy Tucker	.10
224	Martin Biron	.10
225	Marek Malik	.10
226	Steve Sullivan	.10
227	Curtis Brown	.10
228	Eric Fichaud	.10
229	Jan Caloun	.10
230	Niklas Sundblad	.10
231	Roman Vopat	.10
232	Steve Washburn	.10
233	Chris Ferraro	.10
234	Marko Kiprusoff	.10
235	Larry Courville	.10
236	David Nemirovsky	.10
237	Ralph Intranuovo	.10
238	*Kevin Hodson*	.50
239	*Ethan Moreau*	.35
240	Daymond Langkow	.10
241	Brandon Convery	.10
242	Cale Hulse	.10
243	Zdenek Nedved	.10
244	Tommy Salo	.10
245	Nolan Baumgartner	.10
246	Patrick Labrecque	.10
247	Jamie Langenbrunner	.10
248	Pavel Bure CL	.50
249	Peter Forsberg CL	.50
250	Teemu Selanne CL	.25

1996-97 Pinnacle Rink Collection

The 250-card parallel insert set was seeded every seven packs of 1996-97 Pinnacle Hockey. The cards feature Dufex printing with the card backs being identical to the base cards.

	MT
Complete Set (250):	350.00
Common Player:	1.50
Rink Collections:	15x to 25x

1996-97 Pinnacle Artist's Proofs

The Artist's Proof inserts parallel the base cards of 1996-97 Pinnacle Hockey. Inserted every 47 packs, the cards differentiate themselves from the base cards by a holographic foil stamp on the card face. The backs are identical to the base cards.

	MT
Complete Set (250):	1800.
Common Player:	4.00
Artist's Proofs:	50x to 75x

1996-97 Pinnacle Premium Stock

The 250-card Premium Stock Pinnacle issue was a parallel version of the 1996-97 Pinnacle Hockey set, produced on thicker card stock and sold exclusively to hobby outlets.

	MT
Complete Set (250):	50.00
Common Player:	.25
Premium Stocks:	1.5x to 2x

1996-97 Pinnacle By the Numbers

The 15-card, standard-size insert set was seeded every 23 packs of 1996-97 Pinnacle Hockey. The card fronts feature the player's image on foil cardboard with the player's jersey and team colors in the background. "By The Numbers" and the player's name is printed along the bottom edge. The card backs also feature the player's jersey with a brief highlights printed over. The cards are numbered as "x of 15."

		MT
Complete Set (15):		100.00
Common Player:		4.00
1	Teemu Selanne	10.00
2	Brendan Shanahan	10.00
3	Sergei Fedorov	10.00
4	Ed Jovanovski	4.00
5	Doug Weight	4.00
6	Brett Hull	8.00
7	Doug Gilmour	4.00
8	Jaromir Jagr	15.00
9	Wayne Gretzky	25.00
10	Daniel Alfredsson	6.00
11	Eric Daze	4.00
12	Mark Messier	8.00
13	Jocelyn Thibault	6.00
14	Eric Lindros	15.00
15	Pavel Bure	10.00

1996-97 Pinnacle By the Numbers Premium Stock

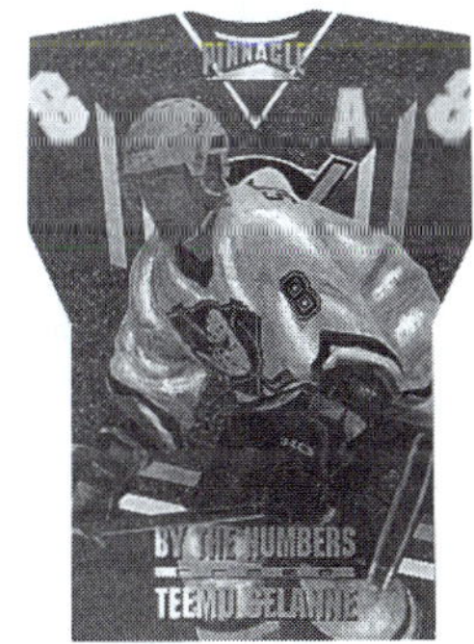

The Premium Stock version of the By The Numbers insert set directly parallels in design the base insert, seeded every 23 packs, except it's on

thicker card stock. The Premium Stock version was available only through hobby outlets.

	MT
Complete Set (15):	200.00
Common Player:	10.00
Premium Stocks:	2x

1996-97 Pinnacle Masks

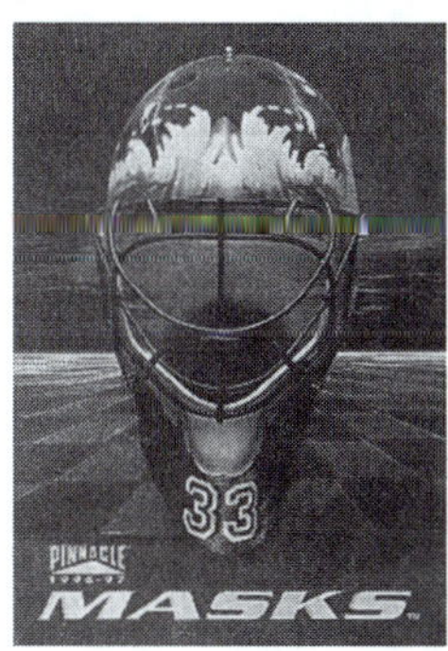

The 10-card Masks insert set was seeded every 90 packs of 1996-97 Pinnacle Hockey. The card fronts feature a close-up image of the goaltender's mask with a team-colored design in the background. "Masks" is printed in gold foil along the bottom. The backs contain a short highlight and a color action shot with the cards being numbered as "x of 10."

		MT
Complete Set (10):		320.00
Common Mask:		20.00
1	Patrick Roy	100.00
2	Mike Richter	30.00
3	Curtis Joseph	30.00
4	Corey Hirsch	20.00
5	Martin Brodeur	60.00
6	John Vanbiesbrouck	60.00
7	Nikolai Khabibulin	20.00
8	Ron Hextall	20.00
9	Jocelyn Thibault	30.00
10	Jim Carey	30.00

1996-97 Pinnacle Masks Die-Cut

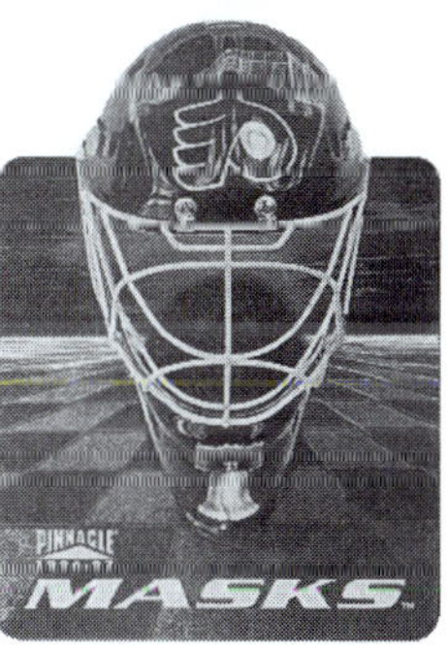

The 10-card, die-cut set parallels the base 10-card Masks insert set seeded very 90 packs of 1996-97 Pinnacle Hockey, except that the cards are die-cut around the top of the mask along the top edge of the card. Die-cut versions are more scarce, as they're inserted every 300 packs.

	MT
Complete Set (10):	500.00
Common Die-Cut Mask:	30.00
Die-Cuts:	1x to 1.5x

1996-97 Pinnacle Team Pinnacle

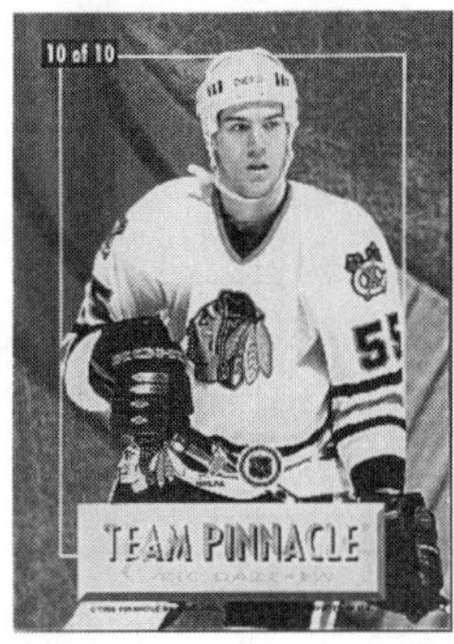

The 10-card Team Pinnacle insert set, seeded every 90 packs of 1996-97 Pinnacle Hockey, features a double-front card design which puts one player from each conference on opposite sides. The cards are printed with Dufex technology.

		MT
Complete Set (10):		300.00
Common Player:		15.00
1	Wayne Gretzky, Joe Sakic	60.00
2	Mario Lemieux, Peter Forsberg	50.00
3	Eric Lindros, Jeremy Roenick	30.00
4	Mark Messier, Doug Weight	20.00
5	Brendan Shanahan, Paul Kariya	40.00
6	Jaromir Jagr, Brett Hull	40.00
7	Ed Jovanovski, Paul Coffey	15.00
8	John Vanbiesbrouck, Patrick Roy	50.00
9	Martin Brodeur, Chris Osgood	30.00
10	Saku Koivu, Eric Daze	25.00

1996-97 Pinnacle Trophies

The 10-card insert set from 1996-97 Pinnacle Hockey was available only through seven-card magazine packs. Each card features a trophy winner from the 1995-96 season, including a card honoring the then-Stanley Cup champion Colorado Avalanche.

		MT
Complete Set (10):		300.00
Common Player:		10.00
1	Mario Lemieux	80.00
2	Paul Kariya	60.00
3	Sergei Fedorov	30.00
4	Daniel Alfredsson	20.00
5	Jim Carey	25.00
6	Chris Osgood, Mike Vernon	30.00
7	Kris King	10.00
8	Chris Chelios	15.00
9	Joe Sakic	50.00
10	Colorado Avalanche	30.00

1996-97 Pinnacle Mint Collection

Mint Collection combined cards and collectible coins in a 30-card set. Each pack contained two die-cut cards, one regular-issue card and two coins. Both the cards and coins featured one of the 30 different players, with the coins fitting inside the die-cut cards. Cards arrived in four different versions - die-cut (with a hole through it), bronze, silver and gold. Regular-issue cards, which were considered bronze, featured bronze colored foil in a circular shape. These were seeded one per pack. Silver Team cards were seeded one per 15 packs, while Gold Team cards were seeded one per 48 packs. Bronze, silver and gold coins were available at similar rates.

		MT
Complete Set (30):		20.00
Common Player:		.25
Bronze Cards:		1.5 to 2x
Silver Cards:		4x to 8x
Gold Cards:		10x to 20x
Wax Box:		55.00
1	Mario Lemieux	2.00
2	Dominik Hasek	.50
3	Eric Lindros	1.50
4	Jaromir Jagr	1.50
5	Paul Kariya	1.50
6	Peter Forsberg	1.00
7	Pavel Bure	1.00
8	Sergei Fedorov	.75
9	Saku Koivu	.60
10	Daniel Alfredsson	.25
11	Joe Sakic	1.00
12	Steve Yzerman	1.00
13	Teemu Selanne	.75
14	Brett Hull	.50
15	Jeremy Roenick	.40
16	Mark Messier	.50
17	Mats Sundin	.25
18	Brendan Shanahan	.50
19	Keith Tkachuk	.35
20	Paul Coffey	.25
21	Patrick Roy	2.00
22	Chris Chelios	.25
23	Martin Brodeur	.75
24	Felix Potvin	.50
25	Chris Osgood	.50
26	John Vanbiesbrouck	1.00
27	Jocelyn Thibault	.50
28	Jim Carey	.60
29	Jarome Iginla	.40
30	Jim Campbell	.25

1996-97 Pinnacle Mint Collection Coins

Thirty different coins were issued in Mint Collection packs at a rate of two coins per pack. The coins featured a head shot of a player on them and fit into the die-cut cards. Brass coins were the most common, with nickel-silver coins seeded every 15 packs and gold-plated coins seeded every 48 packs. In addition, there was also a chance to get redemption cards for solid silver and gold coins of each of the 30 players.

		MT
Complete Set (30):		55.00
Common Brass Coin:		1.00
Nickel Coins:		2x to 4x
Gold Plated Coins:		6x to 10x
Wax Box:		
1	Mario Lemieux	7.00
2	Dominik Hasek	2.50
3	Eric Lindros	5.00
4	Jaromir Jagr	5.00
5	Paul Kariya	5.00
6	Peter Forsberg	4.00
7	Pavel Bure	3.00
8	Sergei Fedorov	2.50
9	Saku Koivu	1.00
10	Daniel Alfredsson	1.00
11	Joe Sakic	3.50
12	Steve Yzerman	4.00
13	Teemu Selanne	2.50
14	Brett Hull	1.50
15	Jeremy Roenick	1.25
16	Mark Messier	1.50
17	Mats Sundin	1.00
18	Brendan Shanahan	1.50
19	Keith Tkachuk	1.00
20	Paul Coffey	1.00
21	Patrick Roy	7.00
22	Chris Chelios	1.00
23	Martin Brodeur	2.50
24	Felix Potvin	1.50
25	Chris Osgood	1.50
26	John Vanbiesbrouck	3.50
27	Jocelyn Thibault	1.50
28	Jim Carey	2.00
29	Jarome Iginla	1.00
30	Jim Campbell	1.00

1996-97 Summit

Pinnacle's 1996 Summit set features 200 cards, including 25 Rookies and three checklists. Each regular card has a colored photo inside a jagged circle; the rest of the background is half net, half gray. The Summit logo is in an upper corner; the player's name and team logo are stamped in gold foil at the bottom of the card. The back has a closeup shot at the top, with the player's position in the lower corner. The player's name and team name are along the right side, with a team logo underneath. The bottom half of the card has 1995 and 1996 stats and averages, broken down versus conferences and the NHL. A card number is in the upper left corner. Each card in the set is also reprinted as two parallel versions - Summit Ice (all prismatic-foil card

stock) and Artist's Proof (Artist's Proof logo is stamped on each card). The cards were seeded one per every six and one per every 35 packs. Three insert sets were also produced - High Voltage (a parallel version of these cards, Mirage, was also made), In The Crease, and Untouchables.

		MT
Complete Set (200):		35.00
Common Player:		.10
Summit Ice Stars:		10x to 15x
Summit Ice Young Stars & RCs:		5x to 10x
Artist's Proofs Stars:		50x to 75x
AP's Young Stars and RCs:		30x to 50x
Premium Stocks:		2x to 4x
Wax Box:		50.00
1	Joe Sakic	1.00
2	Dominik Hasek	.75
3	Paul Coffey	.15
4	Todd Gill	.10
5	Pat Verbeek	.10
6	John LeClair	.20
7	Joe Juneau	.10
8	Scott Mellanby	.10
9	Scott Stevens	.10
10	Ron Francis	.15
11	Larry Murphy	.10
12	Sandis Ozolinsh	.10
13	Luc Robitaille	.15
14	Grant Fuhr	.20
15	Adam Oates	.15
16	Keith Primeau	.10
17	Mark Recchi	.15
18	Brian Bradley	.10
19	Zdeno Ciger	.10
20	Zigmund Palffy	.40
21	Damian Rhodes	.10
22	Russ Courtnall	.10
23	Mike Modano	.20
24	Geoff Sanderson	.10
25	Michal Pivonka	.10
26	Randy Burridge	.10
27	Dimitri Khristich	.10
28	Mike Gartner	.10
29	Derian Hatcher	.10
30	Mathieu Schneider	.10
31	Steve Thomas	.10
32	Mario Lemieux	2.50
33	Darryl Sydor	.10
34	Alexei Yashin	.10
35	Brett Hull	.50
36	Trevor Kidd	.10
37	Alexei Zhamnov	.10
38	Uwe Krupp	.10
39	Brian Skrudland	.10
40	Igor Larionov	.10
41	Nikolai Khabibulin	.20
42	Pavel Bure	1.00
43	Chris Chelios	.20
44	Andrew Cassels	.10
45	Owen Nolan	.10
46	Todd Harvey	.10
47	Jari Kurri	.10
48	Olaf Kolzig	.10
49	Greg Johnson	.10
50	Dominic Roussel	.10
51	Mats Sundin	.30
52	Robert Svehla	.10
53	Sandy Moger	.10
54	Darren Turcotte	.10
55	Teppo Numminen	.10
56	Benoit Hogue	.10
57	Scott Niedermayer	.10
58	Alexander Selivanov	.10
59	Valeri Kamensky	.10
60	Ken Wregget	.15
61	Travis Green	.10
62	Peter Bondra	.15
63	Vladimir Konstantinov	.10
64	Craig Janney	.10
65	Joe Nieuwendyk	.10
66	John Vanbiesbrouck	1.00
67	Wayne Gretzky	3.00
68	Kirk McLean	.10
69	Alexei Zhitnik	.10
70	Mike Ricci	.10
71	Jeff Beukeboom	.10
72	Felix Potvin	.50
73	Mikael Renberg	.10
74	Jamie Baker	.10
75	Guy Hebert	.20
76	Steve Yzerman	1.25
77	Daren Puppa	.10
78	Scott Young	.10
79	Martin Gelinas	.10
80	Dave Gagner	.10
81	Tomas Sandstrom	.10

82	Alexei Kovalev	.10
83	Ray Whitney	.10
84	Vyacheslav Kozlov	.10
85	Jaromir Jagr	1.50
86	Joe Murphy	.10
87	Patrick Roy	2.00
88	Ray Sheppard	.10
89	Chris Terreri	.10
90	Pierre Turgeon	.15
91	Theoren Fleury	.10
92	Doug Weight	.10
93	Tom Barrasso	.20
94	Jim Carey	.60
95	Greg Adams	.10
96	Brian Leetch	.20
97	Ed Belfour	.25
98	Stephane Fiset	.10
99	Stephane Richer	.10
100	Ron Hextall	.20
101	Mike Vernon	.20
102	Jocelyn Thibault	.35
103	Jason Arnott	.10
104	Keith Tkachuk	.40
105	Sergei Fedorov	1.00
106	Alexandre Daigle	.10
107	Alexander Mogilny	.25
108	German Titov	.10
109	Sean Burke	.15
110	Arturs Irbe	.10
111	Mark Messier	.50
112	Nicklas Lidstrom	.10
113	Claude Lemieux	.10
114	Martin Brodeur	.75
115	Bernie Nicholls	.10
116	Paul Kariya	1.50
117	Eric Lindros	1.50
118	Doug Gilmour	.20
119	Sergei Zubov	.10
120	Adam Graves	.10
121	Phil Housley	.10
122	Bob Bassen	.10
123	Rod Brind'Amour	.10
124	Dave Andreychuk	.10
125	Corey Hirsch	.10
126	Kelly Hrudey	.10
127	Pat LaFontaine	.15
128	Viacheslav Fetisov	.10
129	Oleg Tverdovsky	.10
130	Andy Moog	.20
131	Stu Barnes	.10
132	Roman Hamrlik	.10
133	Teemu Selanne	.75
134	Trevor Linden	.10
135	Chris Osgood	.50
136	Vincent Damphousse	.10
137	Shayne Corson	.10
138	Jeremy Roenick	.40
139	Brendan Shanahan	.50
140	Wendel Clark	.10
141	Ray Bourque	.15
142	Peter Forsberg	1.25
143	John MacLean	.10
144	Jeff Friesen	.10
145	Mike Richter	.35
146	Dave Reid	.10
147	Rob Niedermayer	.10
148	Petr Nedved	.10
149	Sylvain Lefebvre	.10
150	Curtis Joseph	.05
151	Eric Daze	.30
152	Saku Koivu	.40
153	Jere Lehtinen	.10
154	Todd Bertuzzi	.10
155	Chad Kilger	.15
156	Stephane Yelle	.10
157	Bryan McCabe	.10
158	Aaron Gavey	.10
159	Kyle McLaren	.10
160	Valeri Bure	.10
161	Antti Tormanen	.10
162	Brendan Witt	.10
163	Ed Jovanovski	.25
164	Aki-Petteri Berg	.15
165	Marcus Ragnarsson	.10
166	Miroslav Satan	.10
167	Daniel Alfredsson	.35
168	Jeff O'Neill	.20
169	Radek Dvorak	.15
170	Petr Sykora	.20
171	Vitali Yachmenev	.10
172	Niklas Andersson	.10
173	Nolan Baumgartner	.10
174	Brandon Convery	.10
175	Ralph Intranuovo	.10
176	Darcy Tucker	.10
177	Sean Haggerty	.10
178	Eric Fichaud	.10
179	Martin Biron	.10
180	Steve Sullivan	.10
181	Peter Ferraro	.10
182	Jose Theodore	.10

183	*Kevin Hodson*	.75
184	*Ethan Moreau*	.40
185	Curtis Brown	.10
186	Daymond Langkow	.10
187	Jan Caloun	.10
188	Landon Wilson	.10
189	Tommy Salo	.15
190	Anders Eriksson	.10
191	David Nemirovsky	.10
192	Jamie Langenbrunner	.10
193	Roman Vopat	.10
194	Todd Hlushko	.10
195	Alexei Yegorov	.10
196	Jamie Pushor	.30
197	Anders Myrvold	.10
198	Checklist	.10
199	Checklist	.10
200	Checklist	.10

1996-97 Summit High Voltage

Sixteen of the NHL's most electrifying performers are featured on these sequentially-numbered 1996 Pinnacle Summit inserts. The cards, limited to 1,500 each, use Pinnacle's Spectrotech technology. A higher level rendition of High Voltage was also created as a parallel set. These cards, called Mirage, feature a floating hologram design and were limited to 600 each. Cards were available in retail, hobby and magazine packs.

		MT
Complete Set (16):		500.00
Common Player:		12.00
Mirages:		1.5x to 2x
1	Mark Messier	20.00
2	Joe Sakic	40.00
3	Paul Kariya	50.00
4	Daniel Alfredsson	12.00
5	Wayne Gretzky	90.00
6	Peter Forsberg	40.00
7	Eric Daze	12.00
8	Mario Lemieux	70.00
9	Eric Lindros	50.00
10	Jeremy Roenick	15.00
11	Alexander Mogilny	15.00
12	Teemu Selanne	35.00
13	Sergei Fedorov	30.00
14	Saku Koivu	20.00
15	Jaromir Jagr	50.00
16	Brett Hull	30.00

1996-97 Summit In the Crease

The NHL's top netminders are featured on this 16-card insert set from Pinnacle's 1996-97 Summit set. The cards use a spot embossed, gold-foil stamped print technology. Each card is sequentially numbered to 6,000 and, due to the embossing, has a sense of depth to it. Cards were seeded in retail and hobby packs.

		MT
Complete Set (16):		200.00
Common Goalie:		8.00
Premium Stock:		2x to 3x
1	Patrick Roy	50.00
2	Mike Richter	20.00
3	Ed Belfour	12.00
4	Daren Puppa	8.00
5	Curtis Joseph	12.00
6	Jim Carey	20.00
7	Damian Rhodes	8.00
8	Martin Brodeur	25.00
9	Felix Potvin	20.00
10	John Vanbiesbrouck	30.00
11	Jocelyn Thibault	18.00
12	Nikolai Khabibulin	10.00
13	Chris Osgood	20.00
14	Dominik Hasek	20.00
15	Corey Hirsch	8.00
16	Ron Hextall	10.00

1996-97 Summit Untouchables

These 1996-97 Pinnacle Summit inserts were exclusive to five-card magazine packs. The cards honor 12 skaters who amassed 100 or more points and six goaltenders who notched 30 wins during the 1995-96 season. Each micro-etched card is limited to 1,000; each is sequentially numbered.

		MT
Complete Set (18):		800.00
Common Player:		15.00
1	Mario Lemieux	100.00
2	Jaromir Jagr	80.00
3	Joe Sakic	50.00
4	Ron Francis	15.00
5	Peter Forsberg	60.00
6	Eric Lindros	80.00
7	Paul Kariya	80.00
8	Teemu Selanne	40.00
9	Alexander Mogilny	20.00
10	Sergei Fedorov	40.00
11	Doug Weight	15.00
12	Wayne Gretzky	125.00
13	Chris Osgood	25.00
14	Jim Carey	20.00
15	Patrick Roy	100.00
16	Martin Brodeur	40.00
17	Felix Potvin	30.00
18	Ron Hextall	15.00

1996-97 Zenith

Zenith was a 150-card set that was printed on thick, gold foil card stock. Card fronts featured the player over a dark background, with the Pinnacle Zenith logo in the upper right corner and the player's name in the lower right. Backs featured broken down 1995-96 stats on the left, with another shot of the player on the right. Inserts in this product include: Artist's Proofs parallel cards, Z-Team Assailants and Championship Salute.

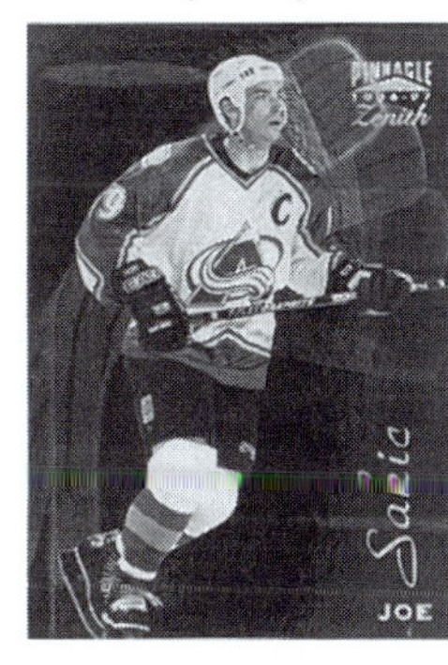

		MT
Complete Set (150):		50.00
Common Player:		.25
Wax Box:		90.00
1	Mike Modano	.50
2	Martin Brodeur	1.50
3	Pavel Bure	1.50
4	Ray Bourque	.40
5	Steve Yzerman	3.00
6	Keith Tkachuk	1.00
7	Jim Carey	1.00
8	Valeri Kamensky	.25
9	Valeri Bure	.25
10	Ron Francis	.40
11	Trevor Kidd	.40
12	Doug Weight	.25
13	Wayne Gretzky	6.00
14	Todd Gill	.25
15	Dominik Hasek	1.50
16	Scott Mellanby	.25
17	John LeClair	.75
18	Al MacInnis	.25
19	Derian Hatcher	.25
20	Stephane Fiset	.50
21	Alexander Selivanov	.25
22	Vyacheslav Kozlov	.25
23	Alexei Yashin	.25
24	Wendel Clark	.25
25	Ed Belfour	.50
26	Travis Green	.25
27	Joe Juneau	.25
28	Teemu Selanne	1.50
29	Jeff O'Neill	.25
30	Jeremy Roenick	.75
31	Felix Potvin	1.00
32	Bernie Nicholls	.25
33	Steve Thomas	.25
34	Alexander Mogilny	.75
35	Patrick Roy	4.00
36	Luc Robitaille	.25
37	Owen Nolan	.25
38	Sergei Zubov	.25
39	Pierre Turgeon	.25
40	Nikolai Khabibulin	.50
41	Adam Oates	.40
42	Stephane Richer	.25
43	Daren Puppa	.40
44	Joe Sakic	2.00
45	Ed Jovanovski	.40
46	Ron Hextall	.50
47	Doug Gilmour	.60
48	Paul Coffey	.40
49	Craig Janney	.25
50	Brendan Witt	.25
51	Jere Lehtinen	.25
52	Vitali Yachmenev	.25
53	Damian Rhodes	.25
54	Petr Nedved	.25
55	Theoren Fleury	.25
56	Petr Sykora	.50
57	Kelly Hrudey	.40
58	Saku Koivu	1.50
59	Brian Bradley	.25
60	Arturs Irbe	.25
61	Eric Lindros	4.00
62	Michal Pivonka	.25
63	Joe Nieuwendyk	.25
64	Mats Sundin	.75
65	Jason Arnott	.25
66	Mike Richter	.75
67	Brett Hull	.75
68	Chris Chelios	.50
69	Jocelyn Thibault	.50
70	Oleg Tverdovsky	.25

71	Peter Bondra	.40
72	Bill Ranford	.40
73	Scott Stevens	.25
74	Jaromir Jagr	4.00
75	Corey Hirsch	.40
76	Peter Forsberg	3.00
77	Brendan Shanahan	1.50
78	Antti Tormanen	.25
79	Marcus Ragnarsson	.25
80	Sergei Fedorov	1.50
81	Todd Bertuzzi	.25
82	Grant Fuhr	.50
83	Pat LaFontaine	.40
84	Rob Niedermayer	.25
85	Brian Leetch	.40
86	Yanic Perreault	.25
87	Dino Ciccarelli	.25
88	Dimitri Khristich	.25
89	Jeff Friesen	.25
90	Paul Kariya	4.00
91	John Vanbiesbrouck	2.00
92	Roman Hamrlik	.25
93	Pat Verbeek	.25
94	Mark Messier	1.00
95	Trevor Linden	.25
96	Igor Larionov	.25
97	Zigmund Palffy	1.00
98	Tom Barrasso	.40
99	Eric Daze	.40
100	Vincent Damphousse	.25
101	Keith Primeau	.25
102	Claude Lemieux	.25
103	Daniel Alfredsson	.50
104	Ryan Smyth	.75
105	Chris Osgood	1.00
106	Bill Guerin	.25
107	Shayne Corson	.25
108	Alexei Zhamnov	.25
109	Mikael Renberg	.25
110	Andy Moog	.50
111	Larry Murphy	.25
112	Curtis Joseph	.75
113	Cory Stillman	.25
114	Mario Lemieux	5.00
115	Scott Young	.25
116	Eric Fichaud	.25
117	Jonas Hoglund	.25
118	*Tomas Holmstrom*	.50
119	Jarome Iginla	1.00
120	*Richard Zednik*	.50
121	*Andreas Dackell*	.30
122	Anson Carter	.25
123	*Dainius Zubrus*	2.50
124	Janne Niinimaa	.75
125	Jason Allison	.25
126	Bryan Berard	.40
127	*Sergei Berezin*	.75
128	Wade Redden	.25
129	Jim Campbell	.40
130	Darcy Tucker	.25
131	*Harry York*	.60
132	Brandon Convery	.25
133	*Ethan Moreau*	.75
134	*Mattias Timander*	.25
135	Christian Dube	.25
136	Kevin Hodson	1.50
137	Anders Eriksson	.25
138	Chris O'Sullivan	.25
139	Jamie Langenbrunner	.25
140	Steve Sullivan	.25
141	Daymond Langkow	.25
142	Landon Wilson	.25
143	Scott Bailey	.25
144	Terry Ryan	.25
145	Curtis Brown	.25
146	*Rem Murray*	.50
147	Jamie Pushor	.25
148	*Daniel Goneau*	.50
149	Mike Prokopec	.25
150	*Brad Smyth*	.30

1996-97 Zenith Artist's Proofs

Each card in Zenith Hockey's 150-card set was also printed in a parallel Artist's Proofs set. The cards are identified by a gold Artist's Proof logo on the front, and were inserted every 48 packs.

	MT
Complete Set (150):	3000.
Common Player:	4.00
Veteran Stars:	30x to 50x
Yng. Stars & RC's:	15x to 30x

1996-97 Zenith Assailants

This insert captured 15 of the top shooters in the NHL. Assailants were seeded every 10 packs of Zenith.

		MT
	Complete Set (15):	80.00
	Common Player:	4.00
1	Alexei Yashin	4.00
2	Mike Modano	8.00
3	Jason Arnott	4.00
4	Mikael Renberg	4.00
5	Saku Koivu	15.00
6	Todd Bertuzzi	4.00
7	Zigmund Palffy	10.00
8	Eric Lindros	30.00
9	Pat LaFontaine	4.00
10	John LeClair	6.00
11	Theoren Fleury	4.00
12	Pierre Turgeon	4.00
13	Petr Nedved	4.00
14	Owen Nolan	4.00
15	Valeri Bure	4.00

1996-97 Zenith Champion Salute

This 15-card insert was printed on gold foil stock and included a championship ring in the lower left corner. Regular versions were seeded every 23 packs, while Diamond versions, which contain an actual diamond chip, were seeded one per 350 packs.

		MT
	Complete Set (15):	240.00
	Common Player:	6.00
1	Mark Messier	12.00
2	Wayne Gretzky	45.00
3	Grant Fuhr	6.00
4	Paul Coffey	6.00
5	Mario Lemieux	35.00
6	Jaromir Jagr	30.00
7	Ron Francis	6.00
8	Joe Sakic	25.00
9	Peter Forsberg	25.00
10	Claude Lemieux	6.00
11	Patrick Roy	35.00
12	Chris Chelios	6.00
13	Doug Gilmour	6.00
14	Mike Richter	12.00
15	Martin Brodeur	18.00

1996-97 Zenith Z-Team

This 18-card insert featured the top players in the NHL on gold highlighted plastic. Z-Team inserts were seeded every 71 packs.

		MT
	Complete Set (18):	750.00
	Common Player:	20.00
1	Eric Lindros	100.00
2	Paul Kariya	100.00
3	Teemu Selanne	50.00
4	Brendan Shanahan	35.00
5	Sergei Fedorov	40.00
6	Steve Yzerman	75.00
7	Brett Hull	40.00
8	Pavel Bure	65.00
9	Alexander Mogilny	30.00
10	Jeremy Roenick	30.00
11	Jocelyn Thibault	40.00
12	Keith Tkachuk	25.00
13	Daniel Alfredsson	20.00
14	Eric Daze	20.00
15	Jim Carey	40.00
16	Felix Potvin	30.00
17	John Vanbiesbrouck	80.00
18	Chris Osgood	40.00

1996-97 Certified

The 120-card hobby-exclusive set also included 30 Rookies and two checklists. The base set included a player photo superimposed over a foil background. The player's name is printed vertically along the right border. The Certified logo is in the upper right. The backs include the player photo in the upper left, with the card number, player's name, position and bio to the right. Listed below are the player's stats vs. the team's 1995-96 oppenents.

		MT
	Complete Set (120):	50.00
	Common Player:	.20
	Wax Box:	100.00
1	Eric Lindros	3.00
2	Mike Modano	.40
3	Jocelyn Thibault	.75
4	Wayne Gretzky	5.00
5	Ray Bourque	.40
6	Martin Brodeur	1.50
7	Rob Niedermayer	.20
8	Stephane Fiset	.20
9	Pat LaFontaine	.20
10	Mario Lemieux	4.00
11	Ed Belfour	.50
12	Ron Francis	.20
13	Luc Robitaille	.20
14	Paul Kariya	3.00
15	Doug Gilmour	.50
16	Joe Sakic	2.50
17	Nikolai Khabibulin	.40
18	Valeri Bure	.20
19	Brett Hull	1.00
20	Chris Osgood	1.00
21	Trevor Kidd	.20
22	Kirk McLean	.20
23	Zigmund Palffy	.75
24	Keith Tkachuk	.75
25	Andy Moog	.40
26	Bill Guerin	.20
27	Chris Chelios	.40
28	Damian Rhodes	.20
29	Jim Carey	.75
30	Ed Jovanovski	.40
31	Felix Potvin	1.00
32	Teemu Selanne	1.50
33	John LeClair	.75
34	Pavel Bure	1.50
35	Grant Fuhr	.50
36	Mark Messier	1.25
37	Vincent Damphousse	.20
38	Jason Arnott	.20
39	Mike Richter	1.00
40	Keith Primeau	.20
41	Steve Yzerman	2.50
42	Trevor Linden	.20
43	Jaromir Jagr	3.00
44	Sean Burke	.40
45	Alexei Zhitnik	.20
46	Dimitri Khristich	.20
47	Daniel Alfredsson	.50
48	Roman Hamrlik	.20
49	Pat Verbeek	.20
50	Doug Weight	.20
51	Adam Graves	.20
52	Michal Pivonka	.20
53	Claude Lemieux	.20
54	Scott Stevens	.20
55	Sergei Fedorov	1.50
56	Owen Nolan	.20
57	Niklas Andersson	.20
58	Cory Stillman	.20
59	John Vanbiesbrouck	2.00
60	Craig Janney	.20
61	Jeff Friesen	.20
62	Igor Larionov	.20
63	Ron Hextall	.40
64	Saku Koivu	1.00
65	Wendel Clark	.20
66	Curtis Joseph	.75
67	Valeri Kamensky	.20
68	Adam Oates	.20
69	Daren Puppa	.20
70	Alexander Mogilny	.75
71	Corey Hirsch	.20
72	Brendan Shanahan	1.00
73	Shayne Corson	.20
74	Dominik Hasek	1.25
75	Theoren Fleury	.20
76	Brian Leetch	.40
77	Jeremy Roenick	.75
78	Peter Bondra	.40
79	Eric Daze	.40
80	Todd Bertuzzi	.20
81	Patrick Roy	4.00
82	Pierre Turgeon	.20
83	Alexei Yashin	.20
84	Scott Mellanby	.20
85	Mats Sundin	.75
86	Jari Kurri	.20
87	Kelly Hrudey	.20
88	Joe Nieuwendyk	.20
89	Paul Coffey	.40
90	Jeff O'Neill	.20
91	*Kai Nurminen*	.20
92	Anders Eriksson	.20
93	Jarome Iginla	.75
94	Anson Carter	.20
95	Christian Dube	.20
96	*Harry York*	.50
97	*Tomas Holmstrom*	.50
98	*Sergei Berezin*	1.50
99	*Mattias Timander*	.20
100	Wade Redden	.20
101	*Mike Grier*	1.00
102	Jonas Hoglund	.20
103	Eric Fichaud	.20
104	Janne Niinimaa	.20
105	Tuomas Gronman	.20
106	Jim Campbell	.20
107	*Daniel Goneau*	.50
108	*Patrick Lalime*	2.50
109	*Ruslan Salei*	.40
110	*Richard Zednik*	.50
111	Chris O'Sullivan	.20
112	*Fredrik Modin*	.60
113	*Brad Smyth*	.30

		MT
114	Bryan Berard	.20
115	Jamie Langenbrunner	.20
116	*Ethan Moreau*	.75
117	Daymond Langkow	.20
118	*Andreas Dackell*	.25
119	*Rem Murray*	.60
120	*Dainius Zubrus*	2.00

1996-97 Certified Red

This parallel of the base set was a red-tinted mylar rendition of the silver regular-issue card. This set was seeded 1:8 packs.

	MT
Complete Set (120):	500.00
Common Player:	2.00
Stars:	4x to 8x
Yng. Stars & RC's	2x to 4x

1996-97 Certified Blue

This parallel of the base set included blue foil and was inserted 1:50 packs.

	MT
Complete Set (120):	3000.
Common Player:	8.00
Stars:	30x to 50x
Yng. Stars & RC's:	15x to 30x

1996-97 Certified Artist's Proofs

This parallel of the base set was inserted 1:48 packs.

	MT
Complete Set (120):	3000.
Common Player:	8.00
Stars:	30x to 50x
Yng Stars & RC's:	15x to 30x

1996-97 Certified Mirror Red

Inserted 1:100 packs, this parallel of the base set included red holographic foil.

	MT
Common Player:	25.00
Stars:	60x to 100x
Yng. Stars & RC's:	30x to 60x

1996-97 Certified Mirror Blue

Inserted 1:200 packs, this parallel included blue holographic foil.

	MT
Common Player:	50.00
Stars:	125x to 200x
Yng. Stars & RC's:	75x to 125x

1996-97 Certified Mirror Gold

Inserted 1:300 packs, the parallel includes gold holographic foil on the front. Pinnacle stated that fewer than 30 of each card was produced.

	MT
Common Player:	100.00
Stars:	300x to 500x
Yng. Stars:	150x to 250x

1996-97 Certified Cornerstones

The 15-card set features franchise players on Dufex cards, which were inserted 1:38 packs.

		MT
Complete Set (15):		375.00
Common Player:		10.00
1	Eric Lindros	40.00
2	Mario Lemieux	50.00
3	Jaromir Jagr	40.00
4	Wayne Gretzky	65.00
5	Mark Messier	20.00
6	Brett Hull	20.00
7	Pavel Bure	30.00
8	Saku Koivu	20.00
9	Joe Sakic	35.00
10	Keith Tkachuk	15.00
11	Paul Kariya	40.00
12	Teemu Selanne	25.00
13	Sergei Fedorov	25.00
14	Steve Yzerman	35.00
15	Peter Forsberg	35.00

1996-97 Certified Freezers

This 15-card set showcased the league's top goalies on the cards, which boasted the silver prime frost technology on the front. The cards were inserted 1:41 packs.

		MT
Complete Set (15):		250.00
Common Goalie:		10.00
1	Martin Brodeur	35.00
2	Patrick Roy	60.00
3	Jim Carey	20.00
4	John Vanbiesbrouck	45.00
5	Dominik Hasek	30.00
6	Ed Belfour	15.00
7	Curtis Joseph	20.00
8	Felix Potvin	20.00
9	Daren Puppa	10.00
10	Chris Osgood	20.00
11	Mike Richter	20.00
12	Jocelyn Thibault	20.00
13	Ron Hextall	10.00
14	Nikolai Khabibulin	10.00
15	Damian Rhodes	10.00

1996-97 SkyBox Impact

SkyBox returns for its second season with its 1996-97 Impact set, featuring 118 established veterans and 20 rookies with legitimate Calder Trophy credentials. There are also 20 Power Play Magazine subset cards, with front designs that actually look like tiny magazine covers, and two checklists. The set features the Phoenix Coyotes in their new uniforms, plus cards for the Stanley Cup Champion Colorado Avalanche, which have a special logo on them. Each regular card has a full-bleed color action photo on it, with a thin frame on the left and bottom sides of the card. The Impact logo is in the top left corner; the player's position is in a puck in the lower left corner. The player's name is stamped in gold foil in the lower right corner. The horizontal back has a color photo on the left, against a ghosted background. A "Point of View" by Denis Potvin is below the photo. The other side has the player's name and card number at the top, with his position, biographical information and a team logo below, then followed by complete career stats. The insert sets include Countdown to Impact, BladeRunners, NHL on Fox, and VersaTeam. A John LeClair SkyPin exchange card was also seeded in every 180th pack; it could be redeemed for a John LeClair preview card from SkyBox's new SkyPin trading card line. Each pack also has a SkyBox/Fox Game card in it; cards could be redeemed for prizes from Fox, the NHL and SkyBox.

		MT
Complete Set (150):		15.00
Common Player:		.05
Wax Box:		25.00
1	Guy Hebert	.15
2	Paul Kariya	1.00
3	Roman Oksiuta	.05
4	Teemu Selanne	.25
5	Ray Bourque	.10
6	Kyle McLaren	.05
7	Adam Oates	.10
8	Bill Ranford	.10
9	Rick Tocchet	.05
10	Dominik Hasek	.25
11	Pat LaFontaine	.10
12	Mike Peca	.05
13	Theoren Fleury	.05
14	Trevor Kidd	.05
15	German Titov	.05
16	Tony Amonte	.05
17	Ed Belfour	.15
18	Chris Chelios	.10
19	Eric Daze	.25
20	Gary Suter	.05
21	Alexei Zhamnov	.05
22	Peter Forsberg	.75
23	Valeri Kamensky	.05
24	Uwe Krupp	.05
25	Claude Lemieux	.05
26	Sandis Ozolinsh	.05
27	Patrick Roy	1.25
28	Joe Sakic	.75
29	Derian Hatcher	.05
30	Mike Modano	.15
31	Joe Nieuwendyk	.05
32	Sergei Zubov	.05
33	Paul Coffey	.10
34	Sergei Fedorov	.60
35	Vladimir Konstantinov	.05
36	Slava Kozlov	.05
37	Nicklas Lidstrom	.05
38	Chris Osgood	.35
39	Keith Primeau	.05
40	Steve Yzerman	.75
41	Jason Arnott	.05
42	Curtis Joseph	.20
43	Doug Weight	.05
44	Radek Dvorak	.10
45	Ed Jovanovski	.20
46	Scott Mellanby	.05
47	Rob Niedermayer	.05
48	Ray Sheppard	.05
49	Robert Svehla	.05
50	John Vanbiesbrouck	.60
51	Jeff Brown	.05
52	Sean Burke	.05
53	Andrew Cassels	.05
54	Geoff Sanderson	.05
55	Brendan Shanahan	.30
56	Byron Dafoe	.05
57	Ray Ferraro	.05
58	Dimitri Khristich	.05
59	Vitali Yachmenev	.05
60	Valeri Bure	.05
61	Vincent Damphousse	.05
62	Saku Koivu	.25
63	Mark Recchi	.05
64	Martin Rucinsky	.05
65	Jocelyn Thibault	.20
66	Pierre Turgeon	.10
67	Dave Andreychuk	.05
68	Martin Brodeur	.50
69	Bill Guerin	.05
70	Scott Niedermayer	.05
71	Scott Stevens	.05
72	Petr Sykora	.05
73	Steve Thomas	.05
74	Todd Bertuzzi	.05
75	Travis Green	.05
76	Kenny Jonsson	.05
77	Zigmund Palffy	.25
78	Adam Graves	.05
79	Wayne Gretzky	1.50
80	Alexei Kovalev	.05
81	Brian Leetch	.10
82	Mark Messier	.30
83	Mike Richter	.15
84	Ulf Samuelsson	.05
85	Niklas Sundstrom	.05
86	Daniel Alfredsson	.20
87	Radek Bonk	.05
88	Alexandre Daigle	.05
89	Steve Duchesne	.05
90	Damian Rhodes	.05
91	Alexei Yashin	.05
92	Rod Brind'Amour	.05
93	Eric Desjardins	.05
94	Dale Hawerchuk	.05
95	Ron Hextall	.15
96	John LeClair	.15
97	Eric Lindros	1.00

98	Mikael Renberg	.05
99	Tom Barrasso	.15
100	Ron Francis	.10
101	Jaromir Jagr	1.00
102	Mario Lemieux	1.25
103	Petr Nedved	.05
104	Bryan Smolinski	.05
105	Nikolai Khabibulin	.15
106	Teppo Numminen	.05
107	Keith Tkachuk	.25
108	Jeremy Roenick	.25
109	Oleg Tverdovsky	.05
110	Shayne Corson	.05
111	Geoff Courtnall	.05
112	Grant Fuhr	.15
113	Brett Hull	.30
114	Al MacInnis	.05
115	Chris Pronger	.05
116	Jeff Friesen	.05
117	Owen Nolan	.05
118	Marcus Ragnarsson	.05
119	Chris Terreri	.05
120	Brian Bradley	.05
121	Chris Gratton	.05
122	Roman Hamrlik	.05
123	Daren Puppa	.05
124	Alexander Seilvanov	.05
125	Wendel Clark	.05
126	Doug Gilmour	.15
127	Kirk Muller	.05
128	Larry Murphy	.05
129	Felix Potvin	.25
130	Mats Sundin	.15
131	Pavel Bure	.75
132	Russ Courtnall	.05
133	Trevor Linden	.05
134	Kirk McLean	.05
135	Alexander Mogilny	.20
136	Peter Bondra	.10
137	Jim Carey	.35
138	Sylvain Cote	.05
139	Sergei Gonchar	.05
140	Phil Housley	.05
141	Joe Juneau	.05
142	Michal Pivonka	.05
143	Brendan Witt	.05
144	*Nolan Baumgartner*	.05
145	Martin Biron	.15
146	*Jason Bonsignore*	.05
147	*Andrew Brunette*	.05
148	Jason Doig	.05
149	Peter Ferraro	.05
150	Eric Fichaud	.05
151	*Ladislav Kohn*	.05
152	Jamie Langenbrunner	.05
153	Daymond Langkow	.05
154	*Jay McKee*	.05
155	*Marty Murray*	.05
156	*Wayne Primeau*	.05
157	*Jamie Rivers*	.05
158	*Jamie Storr*	.15
159	*Jose Theodore*	.05
160	*Roman Vopat*	.05
161	*Steve Sullivan*	.05
162	*Jamie Pushor*	.20
163	*Alexei Yegorov*	.05
164	Daniel Alfredsson (Power Play)	.15
165	Niklas Andersson (Power Play)	.05
166	Todd Bertuzzi (Power Play)	.05
167	Valeri Bure (Power Play)	.05
168	Eric Daze (Power Play)	.20
169	Saku Koivu (Power Play)	.20
170	Miroslav Satan (Power Play)	.05
171	Petr Sykora (Power Play)	.05
172	Cory Stillman (Power Play)	.05
173	Vitali Yachmenev (Power Play)	.05
174	Checklist	.05
175	Checklist	.05

1996-97 SkyBox Impact BladeRunners

These 1996-97 SkyBox Impact inserts offer a frozen glimpse of some of the fastest men on ice. The cards were seeded one per every three packs. The front has a player photo against an icy background. "BladeRunners" is written in a banner at the top; a connecting banner down the left side has the player's name stamped in gold foil. The Impact logo is in the lower left corner. The back also has an icy background, with a mug shot in the upper left corner, flanked by the player's name, position, team logo and card number (1 of 25, etc.). "BladeRunners" is written in two banners running down the sides of the card; a rectangle in the middle has an analysis of the skills which define the player's quickness.

		MT
Complete Set (25):		30.00
Common Player:		.25
1	Brian Bradley	.25
2	Chris Chelios	.50
3	Peter Forsberg	6.00
4	Ron Francis	.25
5	Mike Gartner	.25
6	Doug Gilmour	.50
7	Phil Housley	.25
8	Brett Hull	2.00
9	Valeri Kamensky	.25
10	Pat LaFontaine	.25
11	John LeClair	.75
12	Claude Lemieux	.25
13	Nicklas Lidstrom	.25
14	Mark Messier	2.00
15	Alexander Mogilny	.75
16	Petr Nedved	.25
17	Adam Oates	.40
18	Zigmund Palffy	1.50
19	Jeremy Roenick	1.00
20	Teemu Selanne	3.00
21	Brendan Shanahan	2.50
22	Keith Tkachuk	1.50
23	Pierre Turgeon	.50
24	Doug Weight	.25
25	Steve Yzerman	6.00

1996-97 SkyBox Impact Countdown to Impact

These cards, seeded one in every 30 1996-97 SkyBox Impact hobby packs only, focus on the true superstars of the game. Each card front has a ghosted action shot, with part of it in full color, highlighted by an oval which has "Countdown To Impact" in gold foil around it. The Impact logo is in the upper right corner; the player's name is stamped in gold foil in the bottom left corner. The back is also ghosted, except for an oval which spotlights on the player's face. This area is in full color. The card number (1 of 10, etc.)

is in the lower left corner. The back also has an icy background, with a mug shot in the upper left corner, flanked by the player's name, position, team logo and card number (1 of 25, etc.). "BladeRunners" is written in two banners running down the sides of the card; a rectangle in the middle has an analysis of the skills which define the player's quickness.

and player's name are at the top of the card. A summary of the player's talents is underneath the color photo.

		MT
Complete Set (10):		250.00
Common Player:		10.00
1	Pavel Bure	15.00
2	Sergei Fedorov	15.00
3	Wayne Gretzky	50.00
4	Jaromir Jagr	35.00
5	Ed Jovanovski	10.00
6	Paul Kariya	35.00
7	Mario Lemieux	40.00
8	Eric Lindros	35.00
9	Patrick Roy	40.00
10	Joe Sakic	20.00

1996-97 SkyBox Impact NHL on Fox

These 20 1996-97 SkyBox Impact cards, seeded one per every 10 packs, are a joint venture with Fox Broadcasting to combine action and graphics. The horizontal card front has a color action photo of the player against a background of the earth. The player's name, an NHL on Fox logo and "Coolest Game On Earth" are also on the front. The horizontal back also uses the earth as a background, with a color photo of the player on it. The card number (1 of 14, etc.) is in the upper right corner. The left side of the card has a thermometer and a writeup of the player's skills.

		MT
Complete Set (20):		30.00
Common Player:		1.00
1	Daniel Alfredsson	3.00
2	Todd Bertuzzi	1.00
3	Ray Bourque	1.50
4	Valeri Bure	1.50
5	Chris Chelios	3.00
6	Paul Coffey	3.00
7	Eric Daze	2.00
8	Eric Desjardins	1.00
9	Sergei Gonchar	1.00
10	Phil Housley	1.00
11	Ed Jovanovski	2.00
12	Vladimir Konstantinov	1.00
13	Saku Koivu	10.00
14	Brian Leetch	3.00
15	Larry Murphy	1.00
16	Teppo Numminen	1.00
17	Sandis Ozolinsh	1.50
18	Marcus Ragnarsson	1.00
19	Petr Sykora	1.50
20	Vitali Yachmenev	1.00

1996-97 SkyBox Impact VersaTeam

These 1996-97 SkyBox Impact inserts, seeded one per every 20 packs, offer a look at a rare breed - the NHL's best multi-skilled players. The horizontal card front has a color photo in the middle, with the same image in black-and-white behind it. The player's name is in silver foil along the left

side of the card. An Impact logo is in the upper right corner; the VersaTeam logo is in the lower left corner. The back, numbered 1 of 10, etc., has the same photo on each side, but one image is upside down. The middle has a black panel down the middle which has "VersaTeam" written through it. Above and below are summaries of the player's offensive and defensive skills.

		MT
Complete Set (10):		350.00
Common Player:		15.00
1	Pavel Bure	20.00
2	Sergei Fedorov	20.00
3	Peter Forsberg	40.00
4	Wayne Gretzky	80.00
5	Jaromir Jagr	50.00
6	Paul Kariya	50.00
7	Mario Lemieux	60.00
8	Eric Lindros	50.00
9	Joe Sakic	30.00
10	Teemu Selanne	15.00

1996-97 SkyBox Impact Zero Heroes

The retail-only insert set highlights 10 of the top goalies in the league with each goaltender making a stop in front of a brick wall design. "Zero Heroes" is printed along the left edge with the horizontal backs containing a player closeup and descriptive text. The cards are numbered as "x of 10."

		MT
Complete Set (10):		175.00
Common Goalie:		5.00
1	Ed Belfour	10.00
2	Sean Burke	5.00
3	Jim Carey	20.00
4	Dominik Hasek	20.00
5	Ron Hextall	10.00
6	Chris Osgood	20.00
7	Felix Potvin	20.00
8	Daren Puppa	5.00
9	Patrick Roy	60.00
10	John Vanbiesbrouck	35.00

1996-97 Topps NHL Picks

Topps' only hockey set of the year is this set, created by Topps and Fleer during the NHL Picks Fantasy Draft held in July during the National Sports Collectors Convention. Each company selected 90 players, both rookies and veterans; Topps' cards have the odd numbers. Each card front has a color action shot with a white frame around it. The player's team name is in the upper left corner. The NHL Picks logo is in the lower right corner, with the Topps logo stamped in gold foil. The player's name runs along the bottom in gold, too. Each card back has complete career stats, biographical information, informative text, a closeup shot and a section called "Topps Fantasy Points Prediction," which predicts the season totals for goals, assists, wins and shutouts for the player. Insert sets include Fantasy Team, Ice D, The 500 Club, Rookie Stars and Top Shelf. Canadian packs only (1 in 4) also include cards from an O-Pee-Chee set which parallels the regular issue. An official NHL/NHLPA Draft Game registration form, found in every pack, allows collectors the chance to draft a fantasy hockey team and win prizes based on the players' performances.

		MT
Complete Set (90):		10.00
Common Player:		.05
OPC Stars:		5x to 10x
Wax Box:		40.00
1	Jaromir Jagr	.75
3	Mario Lemieux	1.25
5	Peter Forsberg	.75
7	Teemu Selanne	.50
9	Alexander Mogilny	.20
11	Patrick Roy	1.00
13	Jim Carey	.40
15	Pavel Bure	.75
17	Sergei Fedorov	.50
19	Chris Chelios	.10
21	Sandis Ozolinsh	.05
23	Doug Weight	.05
25	Mark Messier	.25
27	Martin Brodeur	.50
29	Brett Hull	.25
31	Steve Yzerman	.75
33	Kevin Hatcher	.05
35	Roman Hamrlik	.05
37	Petr Nedved	.05
39	Valeri Kamensky	.05
41	Gary Suter	.05
43	Mats Sundin	.15
45	Trevor Linden	.05
47	Jeremy Roenick	.25
49	Al MacInnis	.05
51	Mike Modano	.15
53	Mathieu Schneider	.05
55	Michal Pivonka	.05
57	Owen Nolan	.05
59	Martin Rucinsky	.05
61	Joe Nieuwendyk	.05
63	Mark Recchi	.05
65	Geoff Sanderson	.05
67	Vyacheslav Kozlov	.05
69	Pat Verbeek	.05
71	Brian Bradley	.05
73	Steve Duchesne	.05
75	Steve Thomas	.05
77	Eric Daze	.20
79	Alexei Kovalev	.05
81	Kevin Stevens	.05
83	Curtis Joseph	.15
85	Bill Ranford	.05
87	Luc Robitaille	.10
89	Claude Lemieux	.05
91	Sergei Gonchar	.05
93	Eric Desjardins	.05
95	Garry Galley	.05
97	Oleg Tverdovsky	.05
99	Rob Niedermayer	.05
101	Scott Mellanby	.05
103	Adam Deadmarsh	.05
105	Cliff Ronning	.05
107	Russ Courtnall	.05
109	Keith Primeau	.05
111	Rick Tocchet	.05
113	Scott Young	.05
115	Scott Stevens	.05
117	Al Iafrate	.05
119	Ray Ferraro	.05
121	Todd Bertuzzi	.10
123	Alexander Selivanov	.05
125	Steve Chiasson	.05
127	Dave Andreychuk	.05
129	Ray Sheppard	.05
131	Bernie Nicholls	.05
133	Tony Amonte	.05
135	Nelson Emerson	.05
137	Cam Neely	.05
139	Shayne Corson	.05
141	Bill Guerin	.05
143	Joe Murphy	.05
145	Cory Stillman	.05
147	Radek Bonk	.05
149	Geoff Courtnall	.05
151	Chad Kilger	.15
153	Sylvain Cote	.05
155	Glen Wesley	.05
157	Jeff Norton	.05
159	Rob Blake	.05
161	Calle Johansson	.05
163	Uwe Krupp	.05
165	James Patrick	.05
167	Dmitri Mironov	.05
169	Vladimir Konstantinov	.05
171	Mattias Norstrom	.05
173	David Wilkie	.05
175	Bryan McCabe	.05
177	Barry Richter	.05
179	Ed Belfour	.20

1996-97 Topps NHL Picks Fantasy Team

This 1996-97 Topps NHL Picks insert set contains players who make up a dream team of any NHL general manager. The cards, printed with a Dot Matrix type foil, were seeded one per every 24 packs. The front has a foiled background, with "Fantasy Team" written along the borders. The middle has a color action photo of the player, whose name appears below a set logo in the lower right corner. The horizontal back has stats and a brief recap of the player's accomplishments on the left side; the right side has a color photo, plus a card number (using an "FT" prefix) in the upper right corner. "Fantasy Team" is written along the bottom, as are the player's name, position and team name.

		MT
Complete Set (22):		175.00
Common Player:		2.00
FT1	Patrick Roy	20.00
FT2	Chris Osgood	6.00
FT3	Martin Brodeur	8.00
FT4	Ray Bourque	2.00
FT5	Brian Leetch	3.00
FT6	Chris Chelios	3.00
FT7	Paul Coffey	2.00
FT8	Ed Jovanovski	3.00
FT9	Roman Hamrlik	2.00
FT10	Wayne Gretzky	30.00
FT11	Paul Kariya	15.00
FT12	Brett Hull	6.00
FT13	Pavel Bure	10.00
FT14	Jaromir Jagr	15.00
FT15	Mario Lemieux	25.00
FT16	Peter Forsberg	12.00
FT17	Sergei Fedorov	10.00
FT18	Jeremy Roenick	4.00
FT19	Alexander Mogilny	4.00
FT20	Joe Sakic	12.00
FT21	Teemu Selanne	5.00
FT22	Eric Lindros	20.00

1996-97 Topps NHL Picks Ice D

Five top defensemen and 10 top goalies are featured on these 1996-97 Topps NHL Picks inserts. The cards, seeded one per every 24 packs, are numbered on the back with an "ID" prefix. The card front has an icy metallic-foiled background, with "Ice" written along the left side and a "D" in the middle with a color photo over it. The brand logo is in the upper right corner, with the player's name below, running down the side. The card back has the player's name and position in the upper left corner; the card number is in the upper right corner. The left side of the card has the player's name and a recap of the player's achievements; the other side has a color photo.

		MT
Complete Set (15):		90.00
Common Player:		1.50
ID1	Brian Leetch	1.50
ID2	Ray Bourque	1.50
ID3	Chris Chelios	2.00
ID4	Scott Stevens	1.50
ID5	Ed Jovanovski	2.50
ID6	Martin Brodeur	10.00
ID7	Patrick Roy	18.00
ID8	Chris Osgood	6.00
ID9	Jim Carey	6.00
ID10	Dominik Hasek	8.00
ID11	Ron Hextall	1.50
ID12	John Vanbiesbrouck	15.00
ID13	Mike Richter	5.00
ID14	Felix Potvin	5.00
ID15	Grant Fuhr	1.50

1996-97 Topps NHL Picks Rookie Stars

Seeded one per pack, these 1996-97 Topps NHL Picks inserts feature 18 of hockey's best and brightest stars. The card front has a color action photo, with "95-96 Rookie Stars" written along the left side. The NHL Picks logo is in the upper right corner; the player's name is stamped in gold along the bottom. The horizontal back has a color photo on the left, below the card number (using an "RS" prefix) in the upper corner. The right side of the card has the player's name, position, career recap and a comparison of the player's rookie season stats against those of an established NHL veteran. The background of the card is a ghosted action shot.

		MT
Complete Set (18):		8.00
Common Player:		.25
RS1	Daniel Alfredsson	1.50
RS2	Jere Lehtinen	.25
RS3	Vitali Yachmenev	.25
RS4	Eric Daze	1.00
RS5	Saku Koivu	2.00
RS6	Petr Sykora	.75
RS7	Marcus Ragnarsson	.25
RS8	Valeri Bure	.50
RS9	Cory Stillman	.25
RS10	Todd Bertuzzi	.40
RS11	Ed Jovanovski	1.00
RS12	Miroslav Satan	.25
RS13	Kyle McLaren	.25
RS14	Byron DaFoe	.25
RS15	Eric Fichaud	.50
RS16	Corey Hirsch	.25
RS17	Jeff O'Neill	.50
RS18	Niklas Sundstrom	.25

1996-97 Topps NHL Picks The 500 Club

This set features active NHL players who have scored 500 goals in their career, including four who accomplished the feat last season - Mario Lemieux, Steve Yzerman, Mark Messier and Dale Hawerchuk. The cards, seeded one per every 36 packs, are printed on rainbow diffraction foilboard for the background's front. A color action photo is in the center, with the "Five Hundred Club" and the player's name on the left side. The NHL Picks logo is in the lower right corner. All of this is within a thin red border around the card. The horizontal back has a close-up shot of the player on the left, with his name and position underneath, followed by a list of the player's milestone goals. The right side of the card lists the 23 players who have scored 500 goals; the name of the player featured is highlighted. "The Five Hundred Club" is written along the top; the card number, using an "FC" prefix, is in the upper left corner.

	MT
Complete Set (8):	60.00
Common Player:	4.00
FC1 Wayne Gretzky	30.00
FC2 Mike Gartner	4.00
FC3 Jari Kurri	4.00
FC4 Dino Ciccarelli	4.00
FC5 Mario Lemieux	25.00
FC6 Mark Messier	8.00
FC7 Steve Yzerman	12.00
FC8 Dale Hawerchuk	4.00

1996-97 Topps NHL Picks Top Shelf

Top scorers are highlighted with red foil stamping for the player's name on these 1996-97 Topps NHL Picks inserts. The center of the card has a color action shot, with a bull's-eye logo and a puck in the upper left corner. "Top Shelf" is written along the top, with a brand logo underneath. The background of the front is a net. The horizontal back has the player's name, team name and card number (using a "TS" prefix) along the left side. A photo is next to this, flanked by a bar graph of statistics comparing the featured player to the league and team averages in those departments.

	MT
Complete Set (15):	70.00
Common Player:	.75
TS1 John LeClair	1.00
TS2 Wayne Gretzky	15.00
TS3 Eric Lindros	10.00
TS4 Paul Kariya	8.00
TS5 Mark Messier	4.00
TS6 Jaromir Jagr	8.00
TS7 Peter Forsberg	6.00
TS8 Teemu Selanne	5.00
TS9 Alexander Mogilny	1.50
TS10 Brett Hull	4.00
TS11 Sergei Fedorov	6.00
TS12 Joe Sakic	6.00
TS13 Mats Sundin	1.00
TS14 Theoren Fleury	.75
TS15 Steve Yzerman	6.00

1996-97 Upper Deck

Upper Deck's 1996-97 Series I issue has 210 cards, including subsets for Star Rookies (15), Through the Glass (13) and two checklists. Each regular card front has a color photo on it, with silver foil stamping along the left side. The player's name and position are in a band between the foil and the photo. A team logo is in the lower left corner in an arch. The Upper Deck logo is stamped in silver foil in the upper right corner. A date from when the photo was taken, along with an expla-

nation of the photo, also appears on the front, along the bottom. The card back has a photo on the left, with the player's name, position, card number and biographical information in the upper corner. Career stats are below the photo. Along the right side of the photo, over a ghosted image of the player, are a brief career recap and highlights. The player's team name is at the top; an Upper Deck logo is at the bottom. Five insert sets were produced - Superstar Showdown, Game Jerseys and three versions of Lord Stanley's Heroes (quarterfinals, semifinals and finals). Upper Deck also continues its Meet the Stars program, which has 90 trivia cards seeded one per every three packs. If a collector correctly answers the question, he can win one of the many prizes available, including the chance to meet Wayne Gretzky. The 210-card Series II release featured 180 player cards with a 10-card On-Ice Insight subset and a 20-card CHA Draft Class subset. Inserts in Series II are the Game Jerseys (1:2,500), Hart Hopefuls (bronze - limited to 5,000, silver - 1,000 and 100 gold), Power Performers (1:13) and Generation Next (1:4).

		MT
Complete Set (390):		60.00
Complete Series I Set (210):		20.00
Complete Series II Set (180):		40.00
Common Player:		.10
Series I Wax Box:		55.00
Series II Wax Box:		60.00
1	Paul Kariya	1.50
2	Guy Hebert	.20
3	J.F. Jomphe	.10
4	Joe Sacco	.10
5	Jason York	.10
6	Alex Hicks	.10
7	Mikhail Shtalenkov	.10
8	Bill Ranford	.20
9	Kyle McLaren	.10
10	Rick Tocchet	.10
11	Jon Rohloff	.10
12	Jozef Stumpel	.10
13	Cam Neely	.10
14	Ray Bourque	.20
15	Pat LaFontaine	.10
16	Brian Holzinger	.10
17	Alexei Zhitnik	.10
18	Donald Audette	.10
19	Jason Dawe	.10
20	Wayne Primeau	.10
21	Mike Peca	.10
22	Theoren Fleury	.10
23	Sandy McCarthy	.10
24	Zarley Zalapski	.10
25	Trevor Kidd	.20
26	Steve Chiasson	.10
27	Michael Nylander	.10
28	Ronnie Stern	.10
29	Eric Daze	.30
30	Jeff Hackett	.10
31	Chris Chelios	.20
32	Tony Amonte	.10
33	Bob Probert	.10
34	Eric Weinrich	.10
35	Jeremy Roenick	.35
36	Mike Ricci	.10
37	Sandis Ozolinsh	.10
38	Patrick Roy	2.00
39	Uwe Krupp	.10

40	Stephane Yelle	.10
41	Adam Deadmarsh	.10
42	Scott Young	.10
43	Mike Modano	.20
44	Derian Hatcher	.10
45	Todd Harvey	.10
46	Brent Fedyk	.10
47	Grant Marshall	.10
48	Jamie Langenbrunner	.10
49	Jere Lehtinen	.10
50	Steve Yzerman	1.00
51	Igor Larionov	.10
52	Vladimir Konstantinov	.10
53	Chris Osgood	.75
54	Jamie Pushor	.10
55	Darren McCarty	.10
56	Nicklas Lidstrom	.10
57	Jason Arnott	.10
58	Doug Weight	.10
59	Todd Marchant	.10
60	David Oliver	.10
61	Luke Richardson	.10
62	Jason Bonsignore	.10
63	John Vanbiesbrouck	1.00
64	Stu Barnes	.10
65	Martin Straka	.10
66	Ed Jovanovski	.25
67	Robert Svehla	.10
68	Gord Murphy	.10
69	Tom Fitzgerald	.10
70	Jeff O'Neill	.10
71	Jason Muzzatti	.10
72	Sean Burke	.10
73	Jeff Brown	.10
74	Andrew Cassels	.10
75	Geoff Sanderson	.10
76	Dimitri Khristich	.10
77	Vitali Yachmenev	.10
78	Kevin Stevens	.10
79	Yanic Perreault	.10
80	Craig Johnson	.10
81	John Slaney	.10
82	Saku Koivu	.40
83	Jocelyn Thibault	.30
84	Vladimir Malakhov	.10
85	Turner Stevenson	.10
86	Vincent Damphousse	.10
87	Mark Recchi	.10
88	Patrice Brisebois	.10
89	Dave Andreychuk	.10
90	Bill Guerin	.10
91	Martin Brodeur	.60
92	Scott Niedermayer	.10
93	Petr Sykora	.10
94	Stephane Richer	.10
95	John MacLean	.10
96	Eric Fichaud	.10
97	Zigmund Palffy	.30
98	Alexander Semak	.10
99	Bryan McCabe	.10
100	Darby Hendrickson	.10
101	Kenny Jonsson	.10
102	Marty McInnis	.10
103	Alexei Kovalev	.10
104	Ulf Samuelsson	.10
105	Jeff Beukeboom	.10
106	Marty McSorley	.10
107	Niklas Sundstrom	.10
108	Wayne Gretzky	3.00
109	Mike Richter	.35
110	Alexei Yashin	.10
111	Randy Cunneyworth	.10
112	Damian Rhodes	.10
113	Daniel Alfredsson	.30
114	Antti Tormanen	.10
115	Ted Drury	.10
116	Janne Laukkanen	.10
117	Sean Hill	.10
118	John LeClair	.20
119	Ron Hextall	.20
120	Dale Hawerchuk	.10
121	Rod Brind'Amour	.10
122	Pat Falloon	.10
123	Eric Desjardins	.10
124	Joel Otto	.10
125	Alexei Zhamnov	.10
126	Nikolai Khabibulin	.20
127	Craig Janney	.10
128	Deron Quint	.10
129	Oleg Tverdovsky	.10
130	Chad Kilger	.10
131	Teppo Numminen	.10
132	Tom Barrasso	.20
133	Ron Francis	.10
134	Petr Nedved	.10
135	Ken Wregget	.10
136	Joe Dziedzic	.10
137	Tomas Sandstrom	.10
138	Dmitri Mironov	.10
139	Shayne Corson	.10
140	Grant Fuhr	.20

141	Al MacInnis	.10
142	Steve Leach	.10
143	Murray Baron	.10
144	Chris Pronger	.10
145	Jamie Rivers	.10
146	Owen Nolan	.10
147	Chris Terreri	.10
148	Marcus Ragnarsson	.10
149	Shean Donovan	.10
150	Ray Whitney	.10
151	Michal Sykora	.10
152	Viktor Kozlov	.10
153	Roman Hamrlik	.10
154	Bill Houlder	.10
155	Mikael Andersson	.10
156	Petr Klima	.10
157	Jason Wiemer	.10
158	Rob Zamuner	.10
159	Paul Ysebaert	.10
160	Mats Sundin	.20
161	Larry Murphy	.10
162	Doug Gilmour	.10
163	Todd Warriner	.10
164	Dimitri Yuskevich	.10
165	Kirk Muller	.10
166	Jamie Macoun	.10
167	Alexander Mogilny	.20
168	Corey Hirsch	.10
169	Trevor Linden	.10
170	Markus Naslund	.10
171	Martin Gelinas	.10
172	Jyrki Lumme	.10
173	Bret Hedican	.10
174	Jim Carey	.60
175	Sergei Gonchar	.10
176	Joe Juneau	.10
177	Brendan Witt	.10
178	Dale Hunter	.10
179	Steve Konowalchuk	.10
180	Peter Bondra	.20
181	Jarome Iginla (Star Rookie)	.50
182	Ralph Intranuovo (Star Rookie)	.10
183	Anders Eriksson (Star Rookie)	.15
184	Andrew Brunette (Star Rookie)	.10
185	Steve Sullivan (Star Rookie)	.10
186	Brandon Convery (Star Rookie)	.10
187	*Ethan Moreau* (Star Rookie)	.40
188	Marko Kiprusoff (Star Rookie)	.10
189	Jason McBain (Star Rookie)	.10
190	Mark Kolesar (Star Rookie)	.10
191	Greg DeVries (Star Rookie)	.10
192	Alexei Yegorov (Star Rookie)	.10
193	Sebastian Bordeleau (Star Rookie)	.10
194	Nick Stadjuhar (Star Rookie)	.10
195	Jan Caloun (Star Rookie)	.10
196	Dino Ciccarelli (Through the Glass)	.10
197	Ron Hextall (Through the Glass)	.10
198	Murray Baron (Through the Glass)	.10
199	Patrick Roy (Through the Glass)	1.00
200	Wayne Gretzky (Through the Glass)	1.50
201	Tie Domi (Through the Glass)	.10
202	Glenn Healy (Through the Glass)	.10
203	Keith Primeau (Through the Glass)	.10
204	Joe Sakic (Through the Glass)	.50
205	Jeremy Roenick (Through the Glass)	.20
206	Sergei Fedorov (Through the Glass)	.40
207	Claude Lemieux (Through the Glass)	.10
208	Theoren Fleury (Through the Glass)	.10
209	Checklist	.10
210	Checklist	.10
211	Teemu Selanne	.50
212	Jari Kurri	.10
213	Darren Van Impe	.10
214	Steve Rucchin	.10
215	*Ruslan Salei*	.20
216	Adam Oates	.15
217	Don Sweeney	.10
218	Steve Staios	.10

219	Barry Richter	.10
220	*Mattias Timander*	.10
221	Ted Donato	.10
222	Dominik Hasek	.50
223	Derek Plante	.10
224	*Vaclav Varada*	.10
225	Andrei Trefilov	.10
226	Curtis Brown	.10
227	German Titov	.10
228	Robert Reichel	.10
229	Cory Stillman	.10
230	Chris O'Sullivan	.10
231	Corey Millen	.10
232	Jonas Hoglund	.10
233	Alexei Zhamnov	.10
234	Ed Belfour	.25
235	Gary Suter	.10
236	Kevin Miller	.10
237	Tuomas Gronman	.10
238	*Enrico Ciccone*	.10
239	Peter Forsberg	1.00
240	Joe Sakic	1.00
241	Valeri Kamensky	.10
242	Landon Wilson	.10
243	Claude Lemieux	.10
244	Eric Lacroix	.10
245	Joe Nieuwendyk	.10
246	Sergei Zubov	.10
247	Benoit Hogue	.10
248	Arturs Irbe	.10
249	Pat Verbeek	.10
250	Sergei Fedorov	.75
251	Vyacheslav Kozlov	.10
252	Brendan Shanahan	.60
253	*Kevin Hodson*	.60
254	Greg Johnson	.10
255	*Tomas Holmstrom*	.40
256	Curtis Joseph	.35
257	Dean McAmmond	.10
258	Ryan Smyth	.15
259	*Mike Grier*	.60
260	Miroslav Satan	.10
261	*Rem Murray*	.40
262	Rob Niedermayer	.10
263	Ray Sheppard	.10
264	Dave Lowry	.10
265	Scott Mellanby	.10
266	Rhett Warrener	.10
267	*Per Gustafsson*	.10
268	Paul Coffey	.10
269	Nelson Emerson	.10
270	Kevin Dineen	.10
271	Keith Primeau	.10
272	Hnat Domenichelli	.10
273	Ray Ferraro	.10
274	Stephane Fiset	.10
275	*Kai Nurminen*	.10
276	Dan Bylsma	.10
277	Mattias Norstrom	.10
278	Rob Blake	.10
279	Jose Theodore	.40
280	Martin Rucinsky	.10
281	Darcy Tucker	.10
282	David Wilkie	.10
283	Valeri Bure	.10
284	Steve Thomas	.10
285	Brian Rolston	.10
286	Scott Stevens	.10
287	Shawn Chambers	.10
288	Denis Pederson	.10
289	Lyle Odelein	.10
290	Travis Green	.10
291	Todd Bertuzzi	.10
292	Niclas Andersson	.10
293	Darius Kasparaitus	.10
294	Bryan Berard	.20
295	*Daniel Goneau*	.25
296	Christian Dube	.10
297	Adam Graves	.10
298	Sergei Nemchinov	.10
299	Mark Messier	.50
300	Brian Leetch	.20
301	Radek Bonk	.10
302	Alexandre Daigle	.10
303	*Andreas Dackell*	.15
304	Steve Duchesne	.10
305	Wade Redden	.10
306	Eric Lindros	1.50
307	Mikael Renberg	.10
308	Shjon Podein	.10
309	*Dainius Zubrus*	1.50
310	Janne Niinimaa	.50
311	Karl Dykhuis	.10
312	Jeremy Roenick	.40
313	Keith Tkachuk	.40
314	Shane Doan	.10
315	Cliff Ronning	.10
316	Mike Gartner	.10
317	Dave Manson	.10
318	Shawn Antoski	.10
319	Kevin Hatcher	.10

320	Jaromir Jagr	1.50
321	Mario Lemieux	2.00
322	Bryan Smolinski	.10
323	Stefan Bergqvist	.10
324	Brett Hull	.50
325	Joe Murphy	.10
326	Stephane Matteau	.10
327	Geoff Courtnall	.10
328	Jim Campbell	.25
329	*Harry York*	.30
330	Kelly Hrudey	.10
331	Al Iafrate	.10
332	Jeff Friesen	.10
333	Darren Turcotte	.10
334	Bernie Nicholls	.10
335	Ville Peltonen	.10
336	Dino Ciccarelli	.10
337	Chris Gratton	.10
338	Daren Puppa	.10
339	Alexander Selivanov	.10
340	*Daymond Langkow*	.10
341	Felix Potvin	.40
342	Wendel Clark	.10
343	Mathieu Schneider	.10
344	Dave Ellet	.10
345	*Fredrik Modin*	.30
346	*Sergei Berezin*	.50
347	Pavel Bure	1.00
348	Kirk McLean	.10
349	Mike Sillinger	.10
350	Russ Courtnall	.10
351	Scott Walker	.10
352	Esa Tikkanen	.10
353	Pat Peake	.10
354	Olaf Kolzig	.10
355	Michal Pivonka	.10
356	*Richard Zednik*	.30
357	Phil Housley	.10
358	Anson Carter	.10
359	Eric Daze (On Ice Insight)	.20
360	Felix Potvin (On Ice Insight)	.20
361	Wayne Gretzky (On Ice Insight)	1.50
362	Ed Jovanovski (On Ice Insight)	.20
363	Mike Modano (On Ice Insight)	.20
364	Peter Bondra (On Ice Insight)	.10
365	Patrick Roy (On Ice Insight)	1.00
366	Ray Bourque (On Ice Insight)	.15
367	Roman Hamrlik (On Ice Insight)	.10
368	John LeClair (On Ice Insight)	.15
369	*Adam Colagiacomo*	.50
370	*Joe Thornton*	8.00
371	*Patrick Desrochers*	.50
372	Pierre-Luc Therrien	.10
373	*Nick Boynton*	.75
374	Andrew Ference	.10
375	Jean-Francois Fortin	.10
376	Daniel Tetrault	.10
377	Luc Theoeret	.10
378	Mike Van Ryn	.10
379	*Scott Barney*	.40
380	Harold Druken	.10
381	Dylan Gyori	.10
382	Chris Heron	.10
383	Chad Hinz	.10
384	*Patrick Marleau*	1.00
385	Serge Payer	.10
386	Jeremy Reich	.10
387	*Daniel Tkaczuk*	1.50
388	*Jason Ward*	1.00
389	Checklist 211-298	.10
390	Checklist 299-388	.10

1996-97 Upper Deck Game Jerseys

Each of these cards includes an actual piece of a jersey worn by the featured player during a game. The cards were seeded one per every 2,000 1996-97 Upper Deck Series I packs and every 2,500 for Series II. The cards are numbered with the "GJ" prefix.

		MT
	Complete Set (13):	3400.
	Complete Series 1 Set (5):	1200.
	Complete Series II Set (10):	2200.
	Common Player:	125.00
GJ1	Steve Yzerman	400.00
GJ2	Brett Hull	200.00
GJ3	Doug Gilmour	150.00

GJ4	Jaromir Jagr	450.00
GJ5	Ray Bourque	150.00
GJ6	Mario Lemieux	500.00
GJ7	John Vanbiesbrouck	300.00
GJ8	Eric Lindros	450.00
GJ9	Mike Modano	150.00
GJ10	Pavel Bure	250.00
GJ11	Mark Messier	200.00
GJ12	Theoren Fleury	125.00
GJ13	Mats Sundin	125.00

1996-97 Upper Deck GenerationNext

The 40-card insert set was seeded every four packs of Series II and features a dual-front design. The horizontal art on each side features a color player cut out with a silver background and "Generation Next" printed prominently in gold foil. The cards are numbered with the "X" prefix.

		MT
	Complete Set (40):	100.00
	Common Player:	1.50
X1	Paul Kariya, Wayne Gretzky	18.00
X2	Peter Forsberg, Trevor Linden	10.00
X3	Joe Sakic, Rob Niedermayer	8.00
X4	Chris O'Sullivan, Eric Weinrich	1.50
X5	Jocelyn Thibault, Patrick Roy	12.00
X6	Brett Hull, Daniel Alfredsson	4.00
X7	Chris Osgood, John Vanbiesbrouck	10.00
X8	Ray Bourque, Roman Hamrlik	1.50
X9	Paul Coffey, Sandis Ozolinsh	1.50
X10	Doug Gilmour, Sergei Fedorov	5.00
X11	Chris Chelios, Ed Jovanovski	2.50
X12	Jason Arnott, Jeremy Roenick	3.00
X13	Doug Weight, Steve Yzerman	8.00
X14	Brendan Shanahan, Todd Bertuzzi	5.00
X15	Keith Tkachuk, Wendel Clark	2.50
X16	Saku Koivu, Teemu Selanne	5.00
X17	Jaromir Jagr, Zigmund Palffy	10.00
X18	Ed Belfour, Martin Brodeur	6.00
X19	Eric Daze, Owen Nolan	2.00
X20	Valeri Kamensky, Vitali Yachmenev	1.50
X21	Jarome Iginla, Mike Modano	3.00
X22	Anders Eriksson, Nicklas Lidstrom	1.50
X23	Brian Leetch, Bryan Berard	2.50
X24	Jari Kurri, Niklas Sundstrom	1.50
X25	Adam Deadmarsh, Scott Mellanby	1.50
X26	Peter Bondra, Petr Sykora	1.50
X27	Curtis Joseph, Eric Fichaud	4.00
X28	Dominik Hasek, Roman Turek	5.00
X29	Alexander Mogilny, Valeri Bure	3.00
X30	Daymond Langkow, Theoren Fleury	1.50
X31	Bernie Nicholls, Sergei Berezin	2.00
X32	Chris Gratton, Rick Tocchet	1.50
X33	Felix Potvin, Grant Fuhr	3.00
X34	Keith Primeau, Kevin Stevens	1.50
X35	Rob Blake, Wade Redden	1.50
X36	Chris Pronger, Scott Stevens	1.50
X37	Gary Suter, Kyle McLaren	1.50
X38	Jonas Hoglund, Mats Sundin	1.50
X39	Larry Murphy, Sergei Zubov	1.50
X40	Adam Oates, Joe Juneau	1.50

1996-97 Upper Deck Hart Hopefuls Bronze

The 20-card insert set was randomly inserted in Series II packs. The set is based on 20 players who were the candidates for the Hart Memorial Trophy. Three versions of the inserts were available - bronze, silver and gold with production numbers of each reported at 5,000, 1,000 and 100, respectively.

		MT
	Complete Set (20):	300.00
	Common Player:	6.00
HH1	Wayne Gretzky	40.00
HH2	Mark Messier	10.00
HH3	Eric Lindros	25.00
HH4	Sergei Fedorov	12.00
HH5	Saku Koivu	12.00
HH6	John Vanbiesbrouck	15.00
HH7	Peter Forsberg	20.00
HH8	Keith Tkachuk	10.00
HH9	Paul Kariya	25.00
HH10	Martin Brodeur	15.00
HH11	Patrick Roy	30.00
HH12	Alexander Mogilny	8.00
HH13	Brett Hull	10.00
HH14	Pavel Bure	15.00
HH15	Teemu Selanne	12.00
HH16	Mario Lemieux	30.00
HH17	Jeremy Roenick	8.00
HH18	Jaromir Jagr	25.00
HH19	Steve Yzerman	20.00
HH20	Joe Sakic	15.00

1996-97 Upper Deck Hart Hopefuls Silver

The 20 silver Hart Hopefuls parallel the bronze versions from Series II packs and were limited in production to 1,000.

	MT
Complete Set (20):	1000.
Common Player:	25.00
Silvers:	2x to 4x

1996-97 Upper Deck Hart Hopefuls Gold

The gold Hart Hopefuls parallel the bronze and silver inserts from Series II packs and were limited in production to 100. Unlike the bronze and silver versions, the gold cards have cel chrome technology.

	MT
Complete Set (20):	7000.
Common Player:	125.00
Golds:	15x to 25x Bronze prices

1996-97 Upper Deck Lord Stanley's Heroes Quarterfinals

There are three versions of this 1996-97 Upper Deck Series I insert - quarterfinals, semifinals and finals. The quarterfinals cards are the most common; they are seeded one per every 37 packs and are limited to 5,000 each. They are printed on Cel technology. The semifinal versions (one per 185) are limited to 1,000 each. They are printed on Cel technology and are die-cut at the top. The rarest versions, the finals, are limited to 100 each and are seeded one per every 1,850 packs. They are printed on cel chrome technology and have a perimeter die cut. Each of these versions is numbered using an "LS" prefix. The reverse image of the photo in the front shows through in color on the back. It is flanked on both sides by a brief summary of the player's accomplishments. The card number is in the upper left corner; the limited edition number (one of 5,000) is above the photo. A tan band runs across the middle of the card; "Future Stanley Cup Hero" is written inside. The player's team name and position are written below this line.

	MT
Complete Set (20):	300.00
Common Player:	5.00
LS1 Wayne Gretzky	40.00
LS2 Mark Messier	10.00
LS3 Mario Lemieux	30.00
LS4 Jaromir Jagr	25.00
LS5 Martin Brodeur	15.00
LS6 Patrick Roy	30.00
LS7 Joe Sakic	15.00
LS8 Peter Forsberg	20.00
LS9 Theoren Fleury	5.00
LS10 Paul Coffey	5.00
LS11 Doug Gilmour	5.00
LS12 Paul Kariya	25.00
LS13 Eric Lindros	25.00
LS14 Sergei Fedorov	12.00
LS15 Eric Daze	6.00
LS16 Teemu Selanne	12.00
LS17 Keith Tkachuk	10.00
LS18 Pavel Bure	15.00
LS19 Mats Sundin	5.00
LS20 Saku Koivu	10.00

1996-97 Upper Deck Lord Stanley's Heroes Semifinals

Inserted every 185 packs of Series I, the semifinals inserts feature a die-cut design, but otherwise parallel the other Lord Stanley inserts. Production of the Semifinals inserts was 1,000.

	MT
Complete Set (20):	1000.
Common Player:	25.00
Semifinals 2x to 4x Quarterfinals prices	

1996-97 Upper Deck Lord Stanley's Heroes Finals

Each card in the insert set is die-cut into the shape of the Stanley Cup with card crash numbered and limited to 100.

	MT
Complete Set (20):	8000.
Common Player:	150.00
Finals 15x to 25x Quarterfinals prices	

1996-97 Upper Deck Power Performers

The 30-card insert set, seeded every 13 Series II packs, features the favorite thugs of hockey on a die-cut relief design. The card fronts have a reflective foil background with the color player image. An action shot is found along the left border while the backs contain three action shots along the right side with player text on the left half. The cards are numbered with the "P" prefix.

	MT
Complete Set (30):	80.00
Common Player:	3.00
P1 Brendan Shanahan	12.00
P2 Mikael Renberg	3.00
P3 John LeClair	6.00
P4 Keith Primeau	3.00
P5 Adam Graves	3.00
P6 Jason Arnott	3.00
P7 Todd Bertuzzi	3.00
P8 Ed Jovanovski	5.00
P9 Scott Stevens	3.00
P10 Chris Gratton	3.00
P11 Bill Guerin	3.00
P12 Vladimir Konstantinov	3.00
P13 Mike Grier	6.00
P14 Theoren Fleury	3.00
P15 Chris Chelios	5.00
P16 Trevor Linden	3.00
P17 Claude Lemieux	3.00
P18 Owen Nolan	3.00
P19 Jarome Iginla	8.00
P20 Joe Nieuwendyk	3.00
P21 Kevin Hatcher	3.00
P22 Dino Ciccarelli	3.00
P23 Adam Deadmarsh	3.00
P24 Chris Pronger	3.00
P25 Mike Ricci	3.00
P26 Rod Brind'Amour	3.00
P27 Derian Hatcher	3.00
P28 Mats Sundin	5.00
P29 Doug Gilmour	5.00
P30 Todd Harvey	3.00

1996-97 Upper Deck Superstar Showdown

These 1996-97 Upper Deck Series I inserts feature 60 players in 30 different one-on-one matchups. The metallic card front has a color photo in the center. One side is die-cut to form an interlocking piece with another card. These two cards, when placed together, form the Superstar Showdown. The players' names are written along the outsides in gold foil. The card back, numbered using an "SS" prefix and an a or b suffix, shows a sepia-toned image of the photo from the front. The player's team name runs along the outer border, just above the words "Superstar Showdown." A recap of the player's skills is written over his photo. Cards were seeded one per every four packs.

	MT
Complete Set (60):	125.00
Common Player:	.75
SS1a Pavel Bure	5.00
SS1b Paul Kariya	8.00
SS2a Patrick Roy	10.00
SS2b John Vanbiesbrouck	6.00
SS3a Eric Lindros	8.00
SS3b Ed Jovanovski	1.00
SS4a Theoren Fleury	.75
SS4b Doug Gilmour	.75
SS5a Wayne Gretzky	15.00
SS5b Mario Lemieux	10.00
SS6a Keith Tkachuk	3.00
SS6b Brendan Shanahan	4.00
SS7a Ray Bourque	.75
SS7b Brian Leetch	.75
SS8a Peter Forsberg	6.00
SS8b Sergei Fedorov	5.00
SS9a Mark Messier	3.00
SS9b Keith Primeau	.75
SS10a Teemu Selanne	4.00
SS10b Alexander Mogilny	1.00
SS11a Felix Potvin	3.00
SS11b Jocelyn Thibault	1.50
SS12a Martin Brodeur	4.00
SS12b Eric Fichaud	.75
SS13a Roman Hamrlik	.75
SS13b Jaromir Jagr	8.00
SS14a Jim Carey	2.00
SS14b Saku Koivu	2.00
SS15a Jeremy Roenick	1.50
SS15b Brett Hull	3.00
SS16a Joe Sakic	5.00
SS16b Steve Yzerman	6.00
SS17a Doug Weight	.75
SS17b Pat LaFontaine	.75
SS18a Daniel Alfredsson	1.50
SS18b Eric Daze	.75
SS19a Mike Modano	1.00
SS19b Jason Arnott	.75
SS20a Paul Coffey	.75
SS20b Sandis Ozolinsh	.75
SS21a Zigmund Palffy	2.50
SS21b Petr Sykora	.75
SS22a Ed Belfour	1.00
SS22b Ron Hextall	.75
SS23a Mats Sundin	1.00
SS23b Mikael Renberg	.75
SS24a Vitali Yachmenev	.75
SS24b Alexei Zhamnov	.75
SS25a Oleg Tverdovsky	.75
SS25b Kyle McLaren	.75
SS26a Dominik Hasek	2.50
SS26b Petr Nedved	.75
SS27a Chris Chelios	1.00
SS27b Chris Pronger	.75
SS28a Scott Niedermayer	.75
SS28b Rob Niedermayer	.75
SS29a Marty McSorley	.75
SS29b Bob Probert	.75
SS30a Bill Ranford	.75
SS30b Chris Osgood	2.50

1996-97 Collector's Choice

Upper Deck's 1996-97 Collector's Choice set features at least 10 of the top stars from each NHL team, plus a 20-card subset entitled Scotty Bowman's Winning Formula. These cards are players from his ideal team and include his comments about each. Each regular card front has a color action photo on it, framed with a white border. The brand logo is in the upper right corner; the player's name, team name and team logo are in a banner, using team colors, along the left side of the card. The back has a color photo at the top, with a card number and biographical information above it; career statistics and a career recap are below. The player's name, team name and position are along the right side. The bottom portion of the card has a trivia question and answer. Wayne Gretzky, an Upper Deck spokesman, is featured in his New York Rangers uniform on four cards. Fans who correctly answered the trivia question on the Meet the Stars insert (90, seeded one per every four packs) could redeem it for Gretzky memorabilia or be eligible for a chance to meet him. Other inserts include Stick-Ums stickers, Upper Deck MVP (two versions, gold and silver) and You Crash the Game. A Young Guns Trade Card was also seeded one per every 33 packs. This card could be redeemed for a 15-card set featuring the top rookies from the 1996-97 season.

		MT
Complete Set (348):		18.00
Common Player:		.05
Young Guns Trade Card:		7.50
Wax Box:		30.00
1	Paul Kariya	.60
2	Teemu Selanne	.30
3	Steve Rucchin	.05
4	Mikhail Shtalenkov	.05
5	Guy Hebert	.05
6	Shaun Van Allen	.05
7	Anatoli Semenov	.05
8	J.F. Jomphe	.05
9	Alex Hicks	.05
10	Roman Oksiuta	.05
11	Todd Ewen	.05
12	Adam Oates	.10
13	Ray Bourque	.10
14	Don Sweeney	.05
15	Kyle McLaren	.10
16	Cam Neely	.10
17	Bill Ranford	.10
18	Rick Tocchet	.05
19	Ted Donato	.05
20	Shawn McEachern	.05
21	Jon Rohloff	.05
22	Joe Mullen	.05
23	Pat LaFontaine	.10
24	Brian Holzinger	.05
25	Wayne Primeau	.05
26	Alexei Zhitnik	.05
27	Derek Plante	.05
28	Randy Burridge	.05
29	Brad May	.05
30	Dominik Hasek	.25
31	Jason Dawe	.05
32	Mike Peca	.05
33	Matthew Barnaby	.05
34	Trevor Kidd	.05
35	Theoren Fleury	.05
36	Cale Hulse	.05
37	Bob Sweeney	.05
38	Michael Nylander	.05
39	German Titov	.05
40	Cory Stillman	.05
41	Zarley Zalapski	.05
42	Jocelyn Lemieux	.05
43	Sandy McCarthy	.05
44	Gary Roberts	.05
45	Eric Daze	.20
46	Jeremy Roenick	.30
47	Chris Chelios	.10
48	Joe Murphy	.05
49	Tony Amonte	.05
50	Bernie Nicholls	.05
51	Eric Weinrich	.05
52	Gary Suter	.05
53	Jeff Shantz	.05
54	Jeff Hackett	.05
55	Ed Belfour	.20
56	Uwe Krupp	.05
57	Claude Lemieux	.05
58	Adam Deadmarsh	.05
59	Stephane Fiset	.05
60	Sandis Ozolinsh	.05
61	Stephane Yelle	.05
62	Valeri Kamensky	.05
63	Peter Forsberg	.60
64	Joe Sakic	.50
65	Patrick Roy	1.25
66	Chris Simon	.05
67	Todd Harvey	.05
68	Joe Nieuwendyk	.05
69	Mike Modano	.10
70	Derian Hatcher	.05
71	Kevin Hatcher	.05
72	Benoit Hogue	.05
73	Guy Carbonneau	.05
74	Jamie Langenbrunner	.05
75	Jere Lehtinen	.05
76	Craig Ludwig	.05
77	Grant Marshall	.05
78	Greg Johnson	.05
79	Steve Yzerman	.50
80	Sergei Fedorov	.50
81	Vyacheslav Kozlov	.05
82	Vladimir Konstantinov	.05
83	Igor Larionov	.05
84	Chris Osgood	.35
85	Paul Coffey	.10
86	Nicklas Lidstrom	.05
87	Keith Primeau	.05
88	Dino Ciccarelli	.05
89	Darren McCarty	.05
90	Curtis Joseph	.25
91	Doug Weight	.05
92	Jason Arnott	.05
93	Mariusz Czerkawski	.05
94	Kelly Buchberger	.05
95	Zdeno Ciger	.05
96	David Oliver	.05
97	Todd Marchant	.05
98	Miroslav Satan	.10
99	Bryan Marchment	.05
100	Louie DeBrusk	.05
101	John Vanbiesbrouck	.20
102	Scott Mellanby	.05
103	Rob Niedermayer	.05
104	Robert Svehla	.10
105	Ed Jovanovski	.20
106	Johan Garpenlov	.05
107	Jody Hull	.05
108	Bill Lindsay	.05
109	Terry Carkner	.05
110	Stu Barnes	.05
111	Ray Sheppard	.05
112	Brendan Shanahan	.25
113	Geoff Sanderson	.05
114	Andrei Nikolishin	.05
115	Andrew Cassels	.05
116	Nelson Emerson	.05
117	Jason Muzzatti	.05
118	Marek Malik	.05
119	Sean Burke	.05
120	Jeff Brown	.05
121	Jeff O'Neill	.10
122	Kelly Chase	.05
123	Dimitri Khristich	.05
124	Kevin Stevens	.05
125	Vitali Yachmenev	.05
126	Yanic Perreault	.05
127	Kevin Todd	.05
128	Aki Berg	.10
129	Craig Johnson	.05
130	Mattias Norstrom	.05
131	Ray Ferraro	.05
132	Steven Finn	.05
133	Pierre Turgeon	.10
134	Saku Koivu	.20
135	Mark Recchi	.10
136	Jocelyn Thibault	.25
137	Andrei Kovalenko	.05
138	Vincent Damphousse	.05
139	Vladimir Malakhov	.05
140	Brian Savage	.05
141	Valeri Bure	.05
142	Patrice Brisebois	.05
143	Martin Rucinsky	.05
144	Martin Brodeur	.35
145	Steve Thomas	.05
146	Bill Guerin	.05
147	Petr Sykora	.20
148	Scott Stevens	.05
149	Scott Niedermayer	.05
150	Phil Housley	.05
151	Brian Rolston	.05
152	Neal Broten	.05
153	Dave Andreychuk	.05
154	Randy McKay	.05
155	Eric Fichaud	.05
156	Zigmund Palffy	.20
157	Travis Green	.05
158	Darby Hendrickson	.05
159	Kenny Jonsson	.05
160	Marty McInnis	.05
161	Bryan McCabe	.05
162	Darius Kasparaitis	.05
163	Alexander Semak	.05
164	Todd Bertuzzi	.10
165	Niclas Andersson	.05
166	Mark Messier	.20
167	Mike Richter	.25
168	Niklas Sundstrom	.05
169	Brian Leetch	.10
170	Wayne Gretzky	3.00
171	Luc Robitaille	.10
172	Marty McSorley	.05
173	Jari Kurri	.05
174	Adam Graves	.10
175	Sergei Nemchinov	.05
176	Alexei Kovalev	.05
177	Daniel Alfredsson	.15
178	Randy Cunneyworth	.05
179	Alexei Yashin	.05
180	Alexandre Daigle	.05
181	Radek Bonk	.10
182	Steve Duchesne	.05
183	Ted Drury	.05
184	Antti Tormanen	.05
185	Stan Neckar	.05
186	Damian Rhodes	.05
187	Janne Laukkanen	.05
188	Eric Lindros	1.00
189	Mikael Renberg	.05
190	John LeClair	.15
191	Ron Hextall	.10
192	Rod Brind'Amour	.05
193	Joel Otto	.05
194	Pat Falloon	.05
195	Eric Desjardins	.05
196	Dale Hawerchuk	.05
197	Chris Therien	.05
198	Dan Quinn	.05
199	Oleg Tverdovsky	.05
200	Chad Kilger	.15
201	Keith Tkachuk	.20
202	Igor Korolev	.05
203	Alexei Zhamnov	.10
204	Nikolai Khabibulin	.05
205	Shane Doan	.05
206	Deron Quint	.05
207	Craig Janney	.05
208	Norm Maclver	.05
209	Teppo Numminen	.05
210	Mario Lemieux	1.25
211	Jaromir Jagr	1.00
212	Ron Francis	.10
213	Tom Barrasso	.10
214	Sergei Zubov	.05
215	Tomas Sandstrom	.05
216	Joe Dziedzic	.05
217	Richard Park	.05
218	Bryan Smolinski	.05
219	Petr Nedved	.05
220	Ken Wregget	.05
221	Dmitri Mironov	.05
222	Wayne Gretzky	1.75
223	Brett Hull	.30
224	Grant Fuhr	.10
225	Shayne Corson	.05
226	Chris Pronger	.05
227	Craig MacTavish	.05
228	Al MacInnis	.05
229	Geoff Courtnall	.05
230	Stephane Matteau	.05
231	Tony Twist	.05
232	Brian Noonan	.05
233	Owen Nolan	.05
234	Shean Donovan	.05
235	Darren Turcotte	.05
236	Marcus Ragnarsson	.05
237	Viktor Kozlov	.05
238	Jeff Friesen	.05
239	Chris Terreri	.05
240	Ray Whitney	.05
241	Ville Peltonen	.05
242	Andrei Nazarov	.05
243	Ulf Dahlen	.05
244	Roman Hamrlik	.05
245	Chris Gratton	.05
246	Petr Klima	.05
247	Daren Puppa	.05
248	Rob Zamuner	.05
249	Aaron Gavey	.05
250	Brian Bradley	.05
251	Paul Ysebaert	.05
252	Igor Ulanov	.05
253	Alexander Selivanov	.05
254	Shawn Burr	.05
255	Mats Sundin	.10
256	Doug Gilmour	.15
257	Felix Potvin	.30
258	Wendel Clark	.05
259	Kirk Muller	.05
260	Dave Gagner	.05
261	Tie Domi	.05
262	Mathieu Schneider	.05
263	Dimitri Yuskevich	.05
264	Don Beaupre	.05
265	Larry Murphy	.05
266	Pavel Bure	.50
267	Alexander Mogilny	.15
268	Trevor Linden	.05
269	Jyrki Lumme	.05
270	Cliff Ronning	.05
271	Kirk McLean	.05
272	Corey Hirsch	.05
273	Esa Tikkanen	.05
274	Gino Odjick	.05
275	Markus Naslund	.05
276	Russ Courtnall	.05
277	Joe Juneau	.05
278	Jim Carey	.50
279	Peter Bondra	.10
280	Michal Pivonka	.05
281	Steve Konowalchuk	.05
282	Pat Peake	.05
283	Brendan Witt	.05
284	Stefan Ustorf	.05
285	Keith Jones	.05
286	Sergei Gonchar	.05
287	Sylvain Cote	.05
288	Dale Hunter	.05
289	Paul Kariya (Bowman's Winning Formula)	.40
290	Wayne Gretzky (Bowman's Winning Formula)	1.00
291	Eric Lindros (Bowman's Winning Formula)	.50
292	Steve Yzerman (Bowman's Winning Formula)	.25
293	Mario Lemieux (Bowman's Winning Formula)	.75
294	Jaromir Jagr (Bowman's Winning Formula)	.50
295	Keith Tkachuk (Bowman's Winning Formula)	.10
296	Mark Messier (Bowman's Winning Formula)	.15
297	Jeremy Roenick (Bowman's Winning Formula)	.20
298	Peter Forsberg (Bowman's Winning Formula)	.50
299	Joe Sakic (Bowman's Winning Formula)	.25
300	Theo Fleury (Bowman's Winning Formula)	.05
301	Chris Chelios (Bowman's Winning Formula)	.05
302	Vladimir Konstantinov (Bowman's Winning Formula)	.05
303	Brian Leetch (Bowman's Winning Formula)	.05
304	(Bowman's Winning Formula)	.05
305	Scott Stevens (Bowman's Winning Formula)	.05
306	Martin Brodeur (Bowman's Winning Formula)	.25
307	Patrick Roy (Bowman's Winning Formula)	.60
308	Scotty Bowman (Bowman's Winning Formula)	.05
309	Anaheim (Three Star Selection)	.05
310	Boston (Three Star Selection)	.05
311	Buffalo (Three Star Selection)	.05
312	Calgary (Three Star Selection)	.05
313	Chicago (Three Star Selection)	.05
314	Colorado (Three Star Selection)	.05
315	Dallas (Three Star Selection)	.05
316	Detroit (Three Star Selection)	.05
317	Edmonton (Three Star Selection)	.05
318	Florida (Three Star Selection)	.05
319	Hartford (Three Star Selection)	.05
320	Los Angeles (Three Star Selection)	.05
321	Montreal (Three Star Selection)	.05
322	New Jersey (Three Star Selection)	.05
323	NY Islanders (Three Star Selection)	.05
324	NY Rangers (Three Star Selection)	.05
325	Ottawa (Three Star Selection)	.05
326	Philadelphia (Three Star Selection)	.05
327	Phoenix (Three Star Selection)	.05
328	Pittsburgh (Three Star Selection)	.05
329	St. Louis (Three Star Selection)	.05
330	San Jose (Three Star Selection)	.05
331	Tampa Bay (Three Star Selection)	.05
332	Toronto (Three Star Selection)	.05
333	Vancouver (Three Star Selection)	.05
334	Washington (Three Star Selection)	.05
335	Eastern Conference (Three Star Selection)	.05
336	Western Conference (Three Star Selection)	.05
337	Chad Kilger (Captain Tomorrow)	.05
338	Todd Bertuzzi (Captain Tomorrow)	.05
339	Petr Sykora (Captain Tomorrow)	.15
340	Ed Jovanovski (Captain Tomorrow)	.15
341	Kyle McLaren (Captain Tomorrow)	.05
342	Brian Holzinger (Captain Tomorrow)	.05

		MT
343	Jeff O'Neill (Captain Tomorrow)	.05
344	Daniel Alfredsson (Captain Tomorrow)	.05
345	Brendan Witt (Captain Tomorrow)	.05
346	Daymond Langkow (Captain Tomorrow)	.05
347	Checklist	.05
348	Checklist	.05

1996-97 Collector's Choice Hockey Stick'ums

The premiere edition of these re-stickable action stickers were seeded one per every three packs of 1996-97 Upper Deck Collector's Choice. Each front has a color action sticker, and stickers for the brand logo, insert set logo and player's first and last name. The back, numbered using an "S" pre-fix, has a player checklist. Each Collector's Choice hobby box also includes a Rink Scene poster which can be used to create scenes and display the stickers.

		MT
Complete Set (30):		10.00
Common Player:		.25
S1	Wayne Gretzky	2.00
S2	Brett Hull	.40
S3	Peter Forsberg	.75
S4	Patrick Roy	1.25
S5	Cam Neely	.25
S6	Jeremy Roenick	.40
S7	Mario Lemieux	1.50
S8	Jaromir Jagr	1.00
S9	Eric Lindros	1.50
S10	Mark Messier	.40
S11	Felix Potvin	.50
S12	Brendan Shanahan	.35
S13	Teemu Selanne	.50
S14	Paul Kariya	.75
S15	Mike Modano	.25
S16	Pavel Bure	.60
S17	Jim Carey	.50
S18	Roman Hamrlik	.25
S19	Pierre Turgeon	.25
S20	Theoren Fleury	.25
S21	Pat LaFontaine	.25
S22	Steve Yzerman	.50
S23	Sergei Fedorov	.50
S24	Martin Brodeur	.50
S25	Owen Nolan	.25
S26	Ice Machine	.25
S27	Champions	.25
S28	Slap Shot!	.25
S29	Stripes	.25
S30	Goal!	.25

1996-97 Collector's Choice MVP

The top stars and rookies from each of the 26 NHL teams are featured on these inserts. There are two versions - a gold-foiled version (seeded one per every 35 packs) and a silver one (one per pack). Each card front has a color photo on it, with the background shaded according to the corresponding version. The left border also uses the appropriate foil along it, with the player's name stamped in the opposite foil. The Upper Deck logo at the top and "MVP" along the bottom also use the opposite colored foil than the version the card is. The back of the card is shaded according to the appropriate gold or silver version. A photo is in a square on the right side, with a banner above and below. The card number, using a UD prefix, "MVP," the player's name, position and team name are on the left toward the top. A brief player profile is underneath this information along the left side. Stats from 1993-on, plus career totals, are along the bottom.

		MT
Complete Set (45):		25.00
Common Player:		.25
UD1	Wayne Gretzky	6.00
UD2	Ron Francis	.25
UD3	Peter Forsberg	3.00
UD4	Alexander Mogilny	.50
UD5	Joe Sakic	2.00
UD6	Claude Lemieux	.25
UD7	Teemu Selanne	1.25
UD8	Marty McSorley	.25
UD9	Doug Weight	.25
UD10	Paul Kariya	3.00
UD11	Theoren Fleury	.25
UD12	John Vanbiesbrouck	2.00
UD13	Sergei Fedorov	2.00
UD14	Steve Yzerman	2.00
UD15	Adam Oates	.50
UD16	Keith Tkachuk	.75
UD17	Mike Modano	.40
UD18	Jeremy Roenick	1.00
UD19	Patrick Roy	4.00
UD20	Felix Potvin	1.25
UD21	Martin Brodeur	1.25
UD22	Pavel Bure	2.00
UD23	Peter Bondra	.25
UD24	Chris Osgood	1.50
UD25	Roman Hamrlik	.25
UD26	Brendan Shanahan	1.00
UD27	Ray Bourque	.25
UD28	Paul Coffey	.25
UD29	Brett Hull	1.25
UD30	Brian Leetch	.25
UD31	Chris Chelios	.25
UD32	Larry Murphy	.25
UD33	Nicklas Lidstrom	.25
UD34	Ed Jovanovski	.50
UD35	Sandis Ozolinsh	.25
UD36	Scott Stevens	.25
UD37	Eric Daze	.40
UD38	Saku Koivu	.75
UD39	Daniel Alfredsson	.50
UD40	Pat LaFontaine	.25
UD41	Cam Neely	.25
UD42	Owen Nolan	.25
UD43	Jaromir Jagr	3.50
UD44	Mats Sundin	.25
UD45	Doug Gilmour	.50

1996-97 Collector's Choice MVP Golds

	MT
Complete Set (45):	150.00
Common Player:	1.00
Golds:	3x to 6x

1996-97 Collector's Choice You Crash the Game

If the player on the front of this 1996-97 Collector's Choice insert scores in the game listed, the card could be redeemed for a special F/X version of the card. The card front has a color photo of the player, with the brand logo, his name, his team name/position/team name at the top. Two versions of this insert were made; gold ones were seeded one per every 49 packs. These use gold foil stamping on the front for the game and Crash logo. The back, numbered using a "C" prefix, has the player's name at the top and the contest rules underneath. Regular versions were seeded one per every five packs.

		MT
Complete Set (88):		60.00
Common Player:		1.00
C1	Wayne Gretzky	7.00
C2	Doug Gilmour	1.00
C3	Alexander Mogilny	1.50
C4	Peter Bondra	1.00
C5	Mario Lemieux	5.00
C6	Jaromir Jagr	4.00
C7	Joe Sakic	2.50
C8	Vitali Yachmenev	1.00
C9	Doug Weight	1.00
C10	Steve Yzerman	2.50
C11	Alexei Zhamnov	1.00
C12	John LeClair	1.00
C13	Daniel Alfredsson	1.00
C14	Pat Verbeek	1.00
C15	Saku Koivu	1.50
C16	Steve Thomas	1.00
C17	Pavel Bure	3.00
C18	Vyacheslav Kozlov	1.00
C19	Teemu Selanne	2.00
C20	Eric Daze	1.50
C21	Adam Oates	1.00
C22	Ray Bourque	1.00
C23	Jason Arnott	1.00
C24	Paul Kariya	3.00
C25	Mikael Renberg	1.00
C26	Keith Tkachuk	1.00
C27	Brian Leetch	1.00
C28	Eric Lindros	4.00
C29	Mats Sundin	1.00
C30	Mark Messier	2.00

1996-97 Collector's Choice You Crash the Game Gold

	MT
Complete Set (88):	150.00
Common Player:	1.50
Golds:	1.5x to 3x

1996-97 Upper Deck Black Diamond

Black Diamond was a hobby exclusive product that consisted of all 180 cards printed on Light F/X technology. The set was broken down into three groups: Single Black Diamond (1-90), Double Black Diamond (91-150) and Triple Black Diamond (151-180) with the cards being distinguished by the number of black diamonds in the lower right corner Single Black Diamonds were considered the base cards, while Double Black Diamonds were inserted every four packs and Triple Black Diamonds were inserted every 30 packs. Inserts included parallel gold versions of each card and a 20-card Run for the Cup insert.

		MT
Complete Set (180):		700.00
Complete Single Diamond (90):		15.00
Common Diamond (1-90):		.10
Complete Double Diamond (60):		75.00
Common Double Diamond (91-150):		1.00
Complete Triple Diamond (30):		600.00
Common Triple Diamond (151-180):		6.00
Gold Diamonds (1-90):		5x to 10x
Gold Double Diamonds (91-150):		4x to 8x
Gold Triple Diamonds:		6x to 8x
Wax Box:		80.00
1	Roman Turek	.50
2	Viacheslav Fetisov	.10
3	Mike Dunham	.10
4	Mike Fountain	.10
5	Keith Primeau	.10
6	Zigmund Palffy	.75
7	Curtis Leschyshyn	.10
8	Vladimir Tsyplakov	.10
9	Adam Graves	.10
10	Ian Laperriere	.10
11	Bill Lindsay	.10
12	Brian Leetch	.25
13	Martin Lapointe	.10
14	Stephane Richer	.10
15	Mike Grier	1.50
16	Vladimir Konstantinov	.10
17	Rem Murray	.40
18	Ed Jovanovski	.20
19	Chris O'Sullivan	.10
20	Steve Rucchin	.10
21	Jay Pandolfo	.10
22	Aaron Gavey	.10
23	Greg Adams	.10
24	Steve Heinze	.10
25	Vincent Damphousse	.10
26	Anders Eriksson	.10
27	Alexei Kovalev	.10
28	Tie Domi	.10
29	Joel Otto	.10
30	Bill Ranford	.10
31	Tommy Salo	.10
32	Rob Ray	.10
33	Kris Draper	.10
34	Ed Belfour	.50
35	Mike Richter	.75
36	Nikolai Khabibulin	.40
37	Eric Desjardins	.10
38	Sasha Lakovic	.40
39	Keith Jones	.10
40	Per Gustafsson	.10
41	Jocelyn Thibault	.75
42	Mike Gartner	.10
43	Vitali Yachmenev	.10
44	Jonas Hoglund	.10
45	Craig Janney	.10
46	Daymond Langkow	.10
47	Mattias Timander	.10
48	Scott Young	.10
49	Mikael Renberg	.10
50	Nicklas Lidstrom	.10
51	Andrei Kovalenko	.10
52	Adam Foote	.10
53	Guy Hebert	.40
54	Kevin Hatcher	.10
55	Drew Bannister	.10
56	Sergei Zubov	.10
57	Larry Murphy	.10

58	Denis Savard	.10
59	Bernie Nicholls	.10
60	Jozef Stumpel	.10
61	Darius Kasparaitis	.10
62	Kelly Hrudey	.10
63	Marcel Cousineau	.10
64	Brian Skrudland	.10
65	Byron Dafoe	.10
66	Ray Sheppard	.10
67	Chris Simon	.10
68	*Dainius Zubrus*	3.00
69	*Ethan Moreau*	.40
70	Theoren Fleury	.10
71	Damian Rhodes	.10
72	Kevin Dineen	.10
73	Kenny Jonsson	.10
74	Ray Ferraro	.10
75	Jaromir Jagr	3.00
76	Wayne Primeau	.10
77	Chris Gratton	.10
78	*Patrik Elias*	.30
79	Christian Dube	.10
80	Jason Podollan	.10
81	Adam Deadmarsh	.10
82	Todd Krygier	.10
83	Derek Plante	.10
84	Todd Bertuzzi	.10
85	Stephane Fiset	.10
86	Trent Klatt	.10
87	Hnat Domenichelli	.10
88	Mike Rathje	.10
89	Alexander Mogilny	.60
90	Joe Juneau	.10
91	Alexandre Daigle	1.00
92	Jeff O'Neill	1.00
93	Doug Gilmour	1.50
94	*Sergei Berezin*	3.00
95	Petr Nedved	1.00
96	Phil Housley	1.00
97	Jason Arnott	1.00
98	Sandis Ozolinsh	1.00
99	Mike Modano	1.50
100	Mark Messier	6.00
101	Ron Francis	1.00
102	Oleg Tverdovsky	1.00
103	Valeri Kamensky	1.00
104	Brian Bellows	1.00
105	Eric Fichaud	1.00
106	Alexei Zhamnov	1.00
107	Wendel Clark	1.00
108	Dimitri Khristich	1.00
109	Mike Ricci	1.00
110	John LeClair	2.00
111	Owen Nolan	1.00
112	Bill Guerin	1.00
113	Vyacheslav Kozlov	1.00
114	Brendan Shanahan	8.00
115	Trevor Linden	1.00
116	Daniel Goneau	1.00
117	Rod Brind'Amour	1.00
118	Brian Holzinger	1.00
119	Shayne Corson	1.00
120	Bryan Smolinski	1.00
121	Tony Granato	1.00
122	Mariusz Czerkawski	1.00
123	Andrew Cassels	1.00
124	Scott Stevens	1.00
125	Mike Ridley	1.00
126	Jamie Langenbrunner	1.00
127	Scott Mellanby	1.00
128	Grant Fuhr	1.50
129	Felix Potvin	2.50
130	*Marc Denis*	2.50
131	Corey Hirsch	1.00
132	Chris Osgood	2.50
133	Peter Bondra	1.50
134	Martin Brodeur	8.00
135	Pierre Turgeon	1.00
136	Pat Verbeek	1.00
137	Scott Niedermayer	1.00
138	Geoff Sanderson	1.00
139	Jason Dawe	1.00
140	Rob Niedermayer	1.00
141	Daniel Alfredsson	1.00
142	Jim Campbell	1.00
143	Roman Hamrlik	1.00
144	Rob Blake	1.00
145	Chris Chelios	1.50
146	Teemu Selanne	8.00
147	Adam Oates	1.50
148	Dino Ciccarelli	1.00
149	Mark Recchi	1.00
150	Chris Pronger	1.00
151	Paul Coffey	6.00
152	Jim Carey	15.00
153	Keith Tkachuk	15.00
154	Janne Niinimaa	12.00
155	Sergei Fedorov	25.00
156	Dominik Hasek	25.00
157	Eric Lindros	50.00
158	Curtis Joseph	12.00

159	Alexei Yashin	6.00
160	Joe Thornton	60.00
161	Bryan Berard	10.00
162	Steve Yzerman	40.00
163	Mats Sundin	15.00
164	Jarome Iginla	15.00
165	John Vanbiesbrouck	30.00
166	Mario Lemieux	60.00
167	Jeremy Roenick	15.00
168	Patrick Lalime	20.00
169	Joe Sakic	35.00
170	Brett Hull	20.00
171	Peter Forsberg	40.00
172	Doug Weight	6.00
173	Tony Amonte	6.00
174	Patrick Roy	60.00
175	Paul Kariya	40.00
176	Pavel Bure	30.00
177	Ray Bourque	10.00
178	Saku Koivu	20.00
179	Wade Redden	6.00
180	Wayne Gretzky	80.00

1996-97 Upper Deck Black Diamond Gold

Gold versions of all 180 cards in Black Diamond were available and featured Gold Light F/X technology. Single Black Diamond golds were inserted every 15 packs, Double Black Diamond golds were inserted every 46 packs and Triple Black Diamond golds were individually numbered to 50 with no insertion rate given.

	MT
Complete Gold Diamond Set (90):	300.00
Common Single Gold:	4.00
Single Golds:	5x to 10x
Complete Double Gold Diamond Set (60):	500.00
Common Double Gold:	8.00
Double Golds:	4x to 8x
Complete Triple Gold Diamond Set (30):	6000.
Common Triple Gold:	75.00
Triple Golds:	6x to 8x

1996-97 Upper Deck Black Diamond Run for the Cup

This 20-card insert featured top stars on a die-cut cel card with gold foil etching. Run for the Cup was limited to 100 individually numbered sets.

	MT
Complete Set (20):	6000.
Common Player:	75.00
RC1 Wayne Gretzky	750.00
RC2 Saku Koivu	225.00
RC3 Mario Lemieux	600.00
RC4 Patrick Roy	600.00
RC5 Jaromir Jagr	450.00
RC6 John Vanbiesbrouck	300.00
RC7 Peter Forsberg	400.00
RC8 Paul Kariya	400.00
RC9 Steve Yzerman	350.00
RC10 Joe Sakic	300.00
RC11 Mark Messier	175.00
RC12 Sergei Fedorov	250.00
RC13 Mats Sundin	100.00
RC14 Pavol Bure	250.00
RC15 Ed Jovanovski	75.00
RC16 Mike Modano	75.00
RC17 Curtis Joseph	100.00
RC18 Teemu Selanne	250.00
RC19 Jarome Iginla	125.00
RC20 Eric Lindros	500.00

1996-97 Upper Deck Ice

Upper Deck Ice was a 150-card, retail-only product that was printed entirely on clear plastic. The first 75 cards were called Ice Performers, #76-105 were called Ice Phenoms, #106-115 were called Ice Legends and 116-150 made up the World Junior Championship subset. The first 115 cards were also available in parallel versions, while there was also one insert set called Stanley Cup Foundation that was available in a parallel Stanley Cup Dynasty Foundation.

		MT
	Complete Set (150):	125.00
	Common Player:	.40
	Wax Box:	85.00
1	Kevin Todd	.40
2	Adam Oates	.60
3	Bill Ranford	.40
4	Rick Tocchet	.40
5	Dominik Hasek	2.50
6	Richard Smehlik	.40
7	Derek Plante	.40
8	Joel Bouchard	.40
9	Theoren Fleury	.40
10	Chris Chelios	.60
11	Ed Belfour	.75
12	Eric Weinrich	.40
13	Tony Amonte	.40
14	Greg Adams	.40
15	Jamie Langenbrunner	.40
16	Sergei Zubov	.40
17	Pat Verbeek	.40
18	Chris Osgood	1.50
19	Rem Murray	.75
20	Jason Arnott	.40
21	Curtis Joseph	.75
22	Bill Lindsay	.40
23	Ray Sheppard	.40
24	Martin Straka	.40
25	*Jean-Sebastien Giguere*	2.00
26	Sean Burke	.60
27	Keith Primeau	.40
28	Geoff Sanderson	.40
29	Rob Blake	.40
30	Ian Laperriere	.40
31	Byron Dafoe	.40
32	Vincent Damphousse	.40
33	Darcy Tucker	.40
34	Brian Savage	.40
35	Bill Guerin	.40
36	Scott Niedermayer	.40
37	Steve Thomas	.40
38	Valeri Zelepukin	.40
39	Bryan Smolinski	.40
40	Derek King	.40
41	Mike Richter	1.00
42	Daniel Goneau	.75
43	Brian Leetch	.60
44	Adam Graves	.40
45	Damian Rhodes	.40
46	Mikael Renberg	.40
47	Eric Desjardins	.40
48	Rod Brind'Amour	.40
49	Janne Niinimaa	1.50
50	Dale Hawerchuk	.40
51	Jeremy Roenick	.75
52	Mike Gartner	.40
53	Cliff Ronning	.40
54	*Patrick Lalime*	3.00
55	Ron Francis	.40
56	Petr Nedved	.40
57	Bernie Nicholls	.40
58	Jeff Friesen	.40
59	Owen Nolan	.40
60	Marty McSorley	.40
61	Pierre Turgeon	.40
62	Grant Fuhr	.60
63	Chris Pronger	.40
64	Jim Campbell	.60
65	Chris Gratton	.40
66	Dino Ciccarelli	.40
67	Felix Potvin	1.50
68	Tie Domi	.40
69	Doug Gilmour	.60

70	Trevor Linden	.40
71	Corey Hirsch	.40
72	Jim Carey	1.50
73	Chris Simon	.40
74	Mark Tinordi	.40
75	Sergei Gonchar	.40
76	Paul Kariya	5.00
77	Teemu Selanne	3.00
78	Jarome Iginla	1.00
79	Eric Daze	.40
80	Sandis Ozolinsh	.60
81	Peter Forsberg	5.00
82	Mike Modano	.60
83	Anders Eriksson	.40
84	Sergei Fedorov	3.00
85	Brendan Shanahan	3.00
86	Mike Grier	1.00
87	Doug Weight	.40
88	Ed Jovanovski	.40
89	Saku Koivu	2.00
90	Jose Theodore	.75
91	Jocelyn Thibault	1.00
92	Martin Brodeur	2.50
93	Bryan Berard	.40
94	Zigmund Palffy	1.00
95	Daniel Alfredsson	.40
96	Alexei Yashin	.40
97	Wade Redden	.40
98	John LeClair	1.00
99	Oleg Tverdovsky	.40
100	Keith Tkachuk	1.50
101	Jaromir Jagr	5.00
102	Roman Hamrlik	.40
103	*Sergei Berezin*	1.50
104	Alexander Mogilny	.60
105	Pavel Bure	2.00
106	Ray Bourque	.60
107	Patrick Roy	6.00
108	Joe Sakic	4.00
109	Steve Yzerman	4.00
110	John Vanbiesbrouck	3.50
111	Mark Messier	1.50
112	Wayne Gretzky	9.00
113	Eric Lindros	5.00
114	Mario Lemieux	6.00
115	Brett Hull	1.50
116	*Joe Thornton (World Juniors)*	15.00
117	*Marc Denis (World Juniors)*	4.00
118	Martin Biron (World Juniors)	.40
119	Jason Doig (World Juniors)	.40
120	*Daniel Briere (World Juniors)*	3.00
121	Trevor Letowski (World Juniors)	.40
122	*Boyd Devereaux (World Juniors)*	2.50
123	*Dwayne Hay (World Juniors)*	1.00
124	*Hugh Hamilton (World Juniors)*	.40
125	*Brad Isbister (World Juniors)*	.40
126	*Shane Willis (World Juniors)*	1.00
127	*Trent Whitfield (World Juniors)*	1.00
128	*Jesse Wallin (World Juniors)*	1.00
129	Alyn McCauley (World Juniors)	1.50
130	*Cameron Mann (World Juniors)*	.40
131	Jeff Ware (World Juniors)	1.00
132	*Cory Sarich (World Juniors)*	1.00
133	*Richard Jackman (World Juniors)*	1.50
134	Brad Larsen (World Juniors)	.40
135	*Peter Schaefer (World Juniors)*	2.50
136	Christian Dube (World Juniors)	.75
137	Chris Phillips (World Juniors)	1.50
138	Sergei Samsonov (World Juniors)	3.00
139	Alexei Morozov (World Juniors)	3.00
140	*Sergei Fedotov (World Juniors)*	.40
141	Denis Khlopotnov (World Juniors)	1.00
142	*Andrei Markov (World Juniors)*	.40
143	Andrei Petrunin (World Juniors)	.40
144	*Roman Lyasenko (World Juniors)*	.40
145	Joe Corvo (World Juniors)	1.00
146	Erik Rasmussen (World Juniors)	.40
147	*Michael York (World Juniors)*	.40

148	Brian Boucher (World Juniors)	1.50
149	*Paul Mara* (World Juniors)	1.50
150	Marty Reasoner (World Juniors)	1.00

1996-97 Upper Deck Ice Performers

This 115-card parallel set reprinted the cards from the base set in gold, silver and bronze Light F/X designs. Cards 1-75 were printed in bronze, called Ice Performers and inserted one per nine packs. Cards 76-105 were printed in silver, called Ice Phenoms and inserted one per 47 packs. Cards 106-115 were printed in gold, called Ice Legends and inserted one per 325 packs.

		MT
Complete Set (115):		1500.
Complete Ice Performers Set (1-75):		175.00
Common Ice Performer:		3.00
Complete Ice Phenoms Set (76-105):		500.00
Common Ice Phenom:		8.00
Complete Ice Legend Set (106-115):		1100.00
Common Ice Legend:		30.00
1	Kevin Todd	2.50
2	Adam Oates	3.00
3	Bill Ranford	2.50
4	Rick Tocchet	2.50
5	Dominik Hasek	20.00
6	Richard Smehlik	2.50
7	Derek Plante	2.50
8	Joel Bouchard	2.50
9	Theoren Fleury	2.50
10	Chris Chelios	3.00
11	Ed Belfour	4.00
12	Eric Weinrich	2.50
13	Tony Amonte	2.50
14	Greg Adams	2.50
15	Jamie Langenbrunner	2.50
16	Sergei Zubov	2.50
17	Pat Verbeek	2.50
18	Chris Osgood	5.00
19	Rem Murray	4.00
20	Jason Arnott	2.50
21	Curtis Joseph	5.00
22	Bill Lindsay	2.50
23	Ray Sheppard	2.50
24	Martin Straka	2.50
25	Jean-Sebastien Giguere	3.00
26	Sean Burke	3.00
27	Keith Primeau	2.50
28	Geoff Sanderson	2.50
29	Rob Blake	2.50
30	Ian Laperriere	2.50
31	Byron Dafoe	2.50
32	Vincent Damphousse	2.50
33	Darcy Tucker	2.50
34	Brian Savage	2.50
35	Bill Guerin	2.50
36	Scott Niedermayer	2.50
37	Steve Thomas	2.50
38	Valeri Zelepukin	2.50
39	Bryan Smolinski	2.50
40	Derek King	2.50
41	Mike Richter	6.00
42	Daniel Goneau	3.00
43	Brian Leetch	3.00
44	Adam Graves	2.50
45	Damian Rhodes	2.50
46	Mikael Renberg	2.50
47	Eric Desjardins	2.50
48	Rod Brind'Amour	2.50

49	Janne Niinimaa	5.00
50	Dale Hawerchuk	2.50
51	Jeremy Roenick	4.00
52	Mike Gartner	2.50
53	Cliff Ronning	2.50
54	Patrick Lalime	25.00
55	Ron Francis	2.50
56	Petr Nedved	2.50
57	Bernie Nicholls	2.50
58	Jeff Friesen	2.50
59	Owen Nolan	2.50
60	Marty McSorley	2.50
61	Pierre Turgeon	2.50
62	Grant Fuhr	4.00
63	Chris Pronger	2.50
64	Jim Campbell	3.00
65	Chris Gratton	2.50
66	Dino Ciccarelli	2.50
67	Felix Potvin	5.00
68	Tie Domi	2.50
69	Doug Gilmour	3.00
70	Trevor Linden	2.50
71	Corey Hirsch	2.50
72	Jim Carey	6.00
73	Chris Simon	2.50
74	Mark Tinordi	2.50
75	Sergei Gonchar	2.50
76	Paul Kariya	75.00
77	Teemu Selanne	50.00
78	Jarome Iginla	10.00
79	Eric Daze	4.00
80	Sandis Ozolinsh	8.00
81	Peter Forsberg	75.00
82	Mike Modano	10.00
83	Anders Eriksson	8.00
84	Sergei Fedorov	50.00
85	Brendan Shanahan	50.00
86	Mike Grier	15.00
87	Doug Weight	8.00
88	Ed Jovanovski	8.00
89	Saku Koivu	35.00
90	Jose Theodore	15.00
91	Jocelyn Thibault	20.00
92	Martin Brodeur	40.00
93	Bryan Berard	8.00
94	Zigmund Palffy	15.00
95	Daniel Alfredsson	8.00
96	Alexei Yashin	8.00
97	Wade Redden	8.00
98	John LeClair	15.00
99	Oleg Tverdovsky	8.00
100	Keith Tkachuk	20.00
101	Jaromir Jagr	75.00
102	Roman Hamrlik	8.00
103	Sergei Berezin	8.00
104	Alexander Mogilny	15.00
105	Pavel Bure	40.00
106	Ray Bourque	30.00
107	Patrick Roy	240.00
108	Joe Sakic	150.00
109	Steve Yzerman	150.00
110	John Vanbiesbrouck	150.00
111	Mark Messier	75.00
112	Wayne Gretzky	300.00
113	Eric Lindros	200.00
114	Mario Lemieux	240.00
115	Brett Hull	75.00

1996-97 Upper Deck Ice Stanley Cup Foundation

Teammates on 10 different teams were showcased in this insert set. Cards were printed on a horizontal format, with one player on the right and one on the left. Stanley Cup Foundations were inserted one per 96 packs, with rarer, die-cut versions, called Dynasty Foundations, inserted one per 960 packs.

		MT
Complete Set (10):		450.00
Common Card:		15.00
S1	Wayne Gretzky, Mark Messier	100.00
S2	Steve Yzerman, Brendan Shanahan	65.00
S3	John Vanbiesbrouck, Ed Jovanovski	40.00
S4	Saku Koivu, Jocelyn Thibault	30.00
S5	Patrick Roy, Joe Sakic	75.00
S6	Paul Kariya, Teemu Selanne	65.00
S7	Mario Lemieux, Jaromir Jagr	80.00
S8	Keith Tkachuk, Jeremy Roenick	25.00
S9	Pavel Bure, Alexander Mogilny	20.00
S10	Eric Lindros, John LeClair	65.00

1996-97 Upper Deck Ice Stanley Cup Foundation Dynasty

This rarer version of Stanley Cup Foundation inserts was seeded one per 960 packs. The cards were die-cut and called Stanley Cup Dynasty Foundation.

		MT
Complete Set (10):		2000.
Common Card:		60.00
Dynasties:		3x to 5x

1996-97 SP

Released in March of 1997, Upper Deck SP Hockey has a 188 cards in its base set, including 20 Premier Prospects subset cards. The base cards feature gold foil with the SP logo along the right border in a holographic foil. The card backs contain another color player shot with brief bio and stat information. Inserts in SP Hockey are Inside Info, SPx Force, Autographed SPx Force, NHL Game Film, Clearcut Winner and Holoview Collection.

		MT
Complete Set (188):		40.00
Common Player:		.15
Wax Box:		90.00
1	Paul Kariya	2.50
2	Teemu Selanne	1.00
3	Jari Kurri	.15
4	Darren Van Impe	.15
5	Guy Hebert	.25
6	Steve Rucchin	.15
7	Ray Bourque	.25
8	Kyle McLaren	.15
9	Bill Ranford	.15
10	Don Sweeney	.15
11	Adam Oates	.25
12	Rick Tocchet	.15
13	Ted Donato	.15
14	Curtis Brown	.15
15	Pat LaFontaine	.25
16	Derek Plante	.15
17	Dominik Hasek	1.00
18	Brian Holzinger	.15
19	Alexei Zhitnik	.15
20	Theoren Fleury	.15
21	Trevor Kidd	.15

22	Steve Chiasson	.15
23	Jarome Iginla	.60
24	German Titov	.15
25	Zarley Zalapski	.15
26	Eric Daze	.35
27	Chris Chelios	.25
28	Ed Belfour	.30
29	Gary Suter	.15
30	Alexei Zhamnov	.15
31	*Ethan Moreau*	.50
32	Tony Amonte	.25
33	Peter Forsberg	2.00
34	Joe Sakic	1.75
35	Patrick Roy	3.00
36	Adam Deadmarsh	.15
37	Mike Ricci	.15
38	Adam Foote	.15
39	Claude Lemieux	.15
40	Mike Modano	.40
41	Pat Verbeek	.15
42	Todd Harvey	.15
43	Sergei Zubov	.15
44	Andy Moog	.25
45	Derian Hatcher	.15
46	Jamie Langenbrunner	.15
47	Steve Yzerman	1.75
48	Sergei Fedorov	1.00
49	Vyacheslav Kozlov	.15
50	Brendan Shanahan	.75
51	Chris Osgood	.75
52	Nicklas Lidstrom	.15
53	Vladimir Konstantinov	.15
54	Curtis Joseph	.40
55	Jason Arnott	.15
56	Ryan Smyth	.40
57	Doug Weight	.25
58	Andrei Kovalenko	.15
59	Mariusz Czerkawski	.15
60	Ed Jovanovski	.25
61	John Vanbiesbrouck	1.75
62	Rob Niedermayer	.15
63	Robert Svehla	.15
64	Brian Skrudland	.15
65	Scott Mellanby	.15
66	Ray Sheppard	.15
67	Jeff O'Neill	.15
68	Keith Primeau	.15
69	Geoff Sanderson	.15
70	Sean Burke	.25
71	Kevin Dineen	.15
72	Andrew Cassels	.15
73	Kevin Stevens	.15
74	Rob Blake	.15
75	Ed Olczyk	.15
76	Mattias Norstrom	.15
77	Stephane Fiset	.15
78	Vitali Yachmenev	.15
79	Saku Koivu	1.00
80	Valeri Bure	.15
81	Jocelyn Thibault	.75
82	David Wilkie	.15
83	Stephane Richer	.15
84	Shayne Corson	.15
85	Mark Recchi	.15
86	Martin Brodeur	1.00
87	Bobby Holik	.15
88	Petr Sykora	.15
89	Scott Stevens	.15
90	Scott Niedermayer	.15
91	Bill Guerin	.15
92	Eric Fichaud	.30
93	Kenny Jonsson	.15
94	Travis Green	.15
95	Derek King	.15
96	Todd Bertuzzi	.15
97	Zigmund Palffy	.60
98	Mark Messier	.75
99	Wayne Gretzky	4.00
100	Mike Richter	.60
101	Brian Leetch	.25
102	Luc Robitaille	.15
103	Adam Graves	.15
104	Alexei Kovalev	.15
105	Radek Bonk	.15
106	Alexandre Daigle	.15
107	Daniel Alfredsson	.30
108	Alexei Yashin	.15
109	*Andreas Dackell*	.20
110	Damian Rhodes	.15
111	Petr Svoboda	.15
112	John LeClair	.60
113	Eric Desjardins	.15
114	Eric Lindros	3.00
115	Mikael Renberg	.15
116	Ron Hextall	.40
117	*Dainius Zubrus*	2.00
118	Keith Tkachuk	.75
119	Jeremy Roenick	.40
120	Nikolai Khabibulin	.25
121	Oleg Tverdovsky	.15
122	Teppo Numminen	.15

123	Mike Gartner	.15
124	Cliff Ronning	.15
125	Mario Lemieux	3.00
126	Jaromir Jagr	2.50
127	Ron Francis	.15
128	Petr Nedved	.15
129	Darius Kasparaitis	.15
130	Kevin Hatcher	.15
131	Joe Mullen	.15
132	Joe Murphy	.15
133	Grant Fuhr	.40
134	*Harry York*	.40
135	Chris Pronger	.15
136	Brett Hull	.75
137	Pierre Turgeon	.15
138	Owen Nolan	.15
139	Bernie Nicholls	.15
140	Tony Granato	.15
141	Kelly Hrudey	.15
142	Darren Turcotte	.15
143	*Jeff Friesen*	.15
144	Roman Hamrlik	.15
145	Chris Gratton	.15
146	Daymond Langkow	.15
147	Dino Ciccarelli	.15
148	Alexander Selivanov	.15
149	Brian Bradley	.15
150	Wendel Clark	.15
151	Mats Sundin	.50
152	Doug Gilmour	.40
153	Felix Potvin	.75
154	Larry Murphy	.15
155	Mathieu Schneider	.15
156	Kirk Muller	.15
157	Pavel Bure	1.25
158	Alexander Mogilny	.40
159	Corey Hirsch	.15
160	Jyrki Lumme	.15
161	Russ Courtnall	.15
162	Mike Fountain	.15
163	Peter Bondra	.25
164	Jim Carey	.60
165	Sergei Gonchar	.15
166	Joe Juneau	.15
167	Phil Housley	.15
168	Jason Allison	.15
169	Ruslan Salei	.30
170	*Mattias Timander*	.15
171	*Vaclav Varada*	.15
172	Jonas Hoglund	.15
173	Jason Podollan	.15
174	Jose Theodore	.40
175	*Roman Turek*	.50
176	Anders Eriksson	.15
177	*Mike Grier*	1.00
178	*Rem Murray*	.50
179	*Per Gustafsson*	.15
180	Jay Pandolfo	.15
181	*Kai Nurminen*	.15
182	Bryan Berard	.15
183	Christian Dube	.15
184	*Daniel Goneau*	.50
185	Wade Redden	.15
186	Janne Niinimaa	.25
187	Jim Campbell	.25
188	*Sergei Berezin*	.75

1996-97 SP Clearcut Winner

The 20-card insert set features a chiseled out-of-ice design with a transparent hologram on each front. Clearcut Winner inserts are seeded every 91 packs.

		MT
	Complete Set (20):	800.00
	Common Player:	15.00
CW1	Wayne Gretzky	140.00
CW2	Saku Koivu	35.00
CW3	Mario Lemieux	110.00
CW4	Sergei Fedorov	35.00
CW5	Paul Kariya	90.00
CW6	Patrick Roy	110.00
CW7	Jeremy Roenick	20.00
CW8	Brendan Shanahan	35.00
CW9	John Vanbiesbrouck	60.00
CW10	Doug Weight	15.00
CW11	Mark Messier	35.00
CW12	Mats Sundin	20.00
CW13	Paul Coffey	15.00
CW14	Theoren Fleury	15.00
CW15	Steve Yzerman	75.00
CW16	Pavel Bure	40.00
CW17	Adam Deadmarsh	15.00
CW18	Chris Chelios	20.00
CW19	Joe Sakic	60.00
W20	Eric Daze	15.00

1996-97 SP Holoview Collection

The 30-card insert set, seeded every nine packs, highlight the top players in a die-cut design.

		MT
	Complete Set (30):	100.00
	Common Player:	2.50
HC1	Wayne Gretzky	25.00
HC2	Eric Daze	3.00
HC3	Doug Gilmour	3.00
HC4	Jason Arnott	2.50
HC5	Sergei Fedorov	10.00
HC6	Chris Chelios	3.00
HC7	Alexei Kovalev	2.50
HC8	Pat LaFontaine	2.50
HC9	Daniel Alfredsson	4.00
HC10	Chris Pronger	2.50
HC11	Jocelyn Thibault	8.00
HC12	Chris Gratton	2.50
HC13	Alexei Yashin	2.50
HC14	Peter Bondra	3.00
HC15	Saku Koivu	10.00
HC16	Valeri Bure	2.50
HC17	Joe Juneau	2.50
HC18	Tony Amonte	4.00
HC19	Brian Holzinger	2.50
HC20	Mats Sundin	6.00
HC21	Chris Osgood	8.00
HC22	Roman Hamrlik	2.50
HC23	Ray Bourque	4.00
HC24	Doug Weight	2.50
HC25	Mike Modano	4.00
HC26	Niklas Sundstrom	2.50
HC27	Mike Richter	7.00
HC28	Zigmund Palffy	7.00
HC29	Adam Oates	2.50
HC30	Dominik Hasek	10.00

1996-97 SP Inside Info

Inserted in each sealed box of 1996-97 Upper Deck SP Hockey, the eight Inside Info cards give collectors a card within a card as a smaller card can be pulled out from the side of the larger card. A parallel gold version was seeded in sealed boxes every two cases.

		MT
	Complete Set (8):	60.00
	Common Player:	4.00
IN1	Wayne Gretzky	25.00
IN2	Keith Tkachuk	6.00
IN3	Brendan Shanahan	8.00
IN4	Teemu Selanne	8.00

IN5	Ray Bourque	4.00
IN6	Joe Sakic	12.00
IN7	Felix Potvin	6.00
IN8	Steve Yzerman	12.00

1996-97 SP Inside Info Gold

The Inside Info Gold inserts parallel the design of the base Inside Info cards, but with gold foil. Inside Info Gold inserts were seeded in sealed boxes of SP hockey at an average of every two cases.

	MT
Complete Set (8):	350.00
Common Player:	20.00
Golds:	4x to 6x

1996-97 SP NHL Game Film

The 20-card insert set, seeded every 30 packs, feature actual piece of NHL game film.

		MT
	Complete Set (20):	300.00
	Common Player:	5.00
GF1	Wayne Gretzky	50.00
GF2	Peter Forsberg	30.00
GF3	Patrick Roy	40.00
GF4	Brett Hull	15.00
GF5	Keith Tkachuk	10.00
GF6	Eric Lindros	35.00
GF7	Felix Potvin	12.00
GF8	John Vanbiesbrouck	30.00
GF9	Paul Kariya	35.00
GF10	Mark Messier	15.00
GF11	Ed Belfour	10.00
GF12	Alexander Mogilny	10.00
GF13	Jim Carey	15.00
GF14	Ed Jovanovski	10.00
GF15	Theoren Fleury	5.00
GF16	Doug Gilmour	8.00
GF17	John LeClair	10.00
GF18	Pat LaFontaine	5.00
GF19	Paul Coffey	5.00
GF20	Daniel Alfredsson	5.00

1996-97 SP SPx Force

The four-card insert set, randomly inserted into packs of Upper Deck SP, features the top centers, wingers, goalies and rookies on each card. Production of each card was limited to 100 of the multi-image Holoview set.

		MT
	Complete Set (5):	700.00
	Common Player:	80.00
SPX1	Eric Lindros, Mario Lemieux, Peter Forsberg, Wayne Gretzky	250.00
SPX2	Brett Hull, Jaromir Jagr, Pavel Bure, Teemu Selanne	150.00
SPX3	Chris Osgood, Dominik Hasek, Martin Brodeur, Mike Richter	125.00
SPX4	Anders Eriksson, Bryan Berard, Jarome Iginla, Sergei Berezin	80.00
SPX5	Jarome Iginla, Jaromir Jagr, Wayne Gretzky, Martin Brodeur	200.00

1006-07 SP SPx Foroo Autographs

The four-card insert set exactly parallels in design the SPx Force inserts, with the exception being the autograph of one of the four players on each card. As with the SPx Force cards, just 100 hand-numbered sets were randomly inserted.

		MT
	Complete Set (4):	2500.
	Common Autograph:	150.00
1S	Wayne Gretzky Auto.	1500.
2S	Jaromir Jagr Auto.	700.00
3S	Martin Brodeur Auto.	350.00
4S	Jarome Iginla Auto.	150.00

1996-97 SPx

Upper Deck's 1996-97 SPX regular set includes 50 of the game's top players. Each card features three layers - a four-color litho photo in the foreground, a holoview or hologram portrait in the middle, and a hologram background. The player's name is stamped in gold foil at the top of the horizontally-designed card; his team name and position are below. The SPX logo is in gold foil in the upper left corner. The background of the card uses his team's colors. The horizontal card back has a square with a small portrait of the player in the center. His name and team name are above the photo; his career totals are below. The left side of the card has a player profile and card number, the right side has biographical information. All cards are die-cut. A gold parallel series of the regular cards was also made; these cards were seeded one per every seven packs. A 10-card insert set was also made - Holoview Heroes. Three other single inserts were also made. Wayne Gretzky is featured on a tribute card which showcases his career with holographic images of Gretzky in his Kings and Blues uniforms, along with a litho of Gretzky from his days as an Edmonton Oiler. These cards, numbered with a "GT" prefix, were seeded one per every 95 packs. A signed version, numbered with a "GS" prefix was seeded one per every 1,297 packs. The card, enhanced so it could be signed by a permanent pen, has a certificate of authenticity on the back and includes the Upper Deck trademark hologram. Four of the league's hottest young stars are found on an insert - Great Futures - which is numbered using a "GF" prefix. The Holoview card, seeded one per every 75 packs, allows the players to wink, smile and show all sorts of facial expressions when it is flicked.

		MT
Complete Set (50):		75.00
Common Player:		1.00
Gold Set (50):		250.00
Golds:		2x to 4x
Gretzky Tribute (GT1):		25.00
Gretzky Signed Tribute (GS1):		400.00
Great Futures (Gf1):		20.00
Wax Box:		75.00
1	Paul Kariya	6.00
2	Teemu Selanne	3.00
3	Ray Bourque	1.50
4	Cam Neely	1.00
5	Theoren Fleury	1.00
6	Chris Chelios	1.50
7	Jeremy Roenick	1.50
8	Peter Forsberg	5.00
9	Joe Sakic	5.00
10	Patrick Roy	8.00
11	Mike Modano	1.50
12	Joe Nieuwendyk	1.00
13	Sergei Fedorov	3.00
14	Steve Yzerman	5.00
15	Paul Coffey	1.00
16	Chris Osgood	2.00
17	Doug Weight	1.00
18	Pat LaFontaine	1.50
19	Brendan Shanahan	3.00
20	Vitali Yachmenev	1.00
21	Saku Koivu	3.00
22	Pierre Turgeon	1.00
23	Petr Sykora	1.00
24	Scott Stevens	1.00
25	Martin Brodeur	4.00
26	Brian Leetch	1.50
27	Mark Messier	2.50
28	Mike Richter	1.50
29	Zigmund Palffy	2.00
30	Todd Bertuzzi	1.00
31	Alexei Yashin	1.00
32	Daniel Alfredsson	1.50
33	Eric Lindros	8.00
34	John LeClair	2.00
35	Keith Tkachuk	2.00
36	Alexei Zhamnov	1.00
37	Mario Lemieux	8.00
38	Jaromir Jagr	6.00
39	Wayne Gretzky	12.00
40	Brett Hull	2.50
41	Owen Nolan	1.00
42	Roman Hamrlik	1.00
43	Mats Sundin	1.50
44	Felix Potvin	2.00
45	Doug Gilmour	1.50
46	Pavel Bure	3.00
47	Alexander Mogilny	1.50
48	Jim Carey	1.50
49	Peter Bondra	1.00
50	Eric Daze	1.50

1996-97 SPx Holoview Heroes

This 1996-97 Upper Deck SPX insert set features 10 players the company predicts will make the Hockey Hall of Fame. The front is basically similar to the style used for the regular cards, except Holoview Heroes is below the oval. The player's team is in the lower left corner; his position is in the lower right corner. The horizontal card back has an oval with a small portrait shot of the player in the center. His team name and position are below. The sides of the oval include a player summary. The player's name is above the oval, centered at the top of the card; Holoview Heroes is at the bottom. A card number, using an "HH" prefix, is in the upper left corner.

		MT
Complete Set (10):		150.00
Common Player:		6.00
HH1	Ray Bourque	6.00
HH2	Patrick Roy	30.00
HH3	Steve Yzerman	20.00
HH4	Paul Coffey	6.00
HH5	Mark Messier	10.00
HH6	Mario Lemieux	30.00
HH7	Wayne Gretzky	45.00
HH8	Brett Hull	10.00
HH9	Doug Gilmour	8.00
HH10	Grant Fuhr	8.00

1997-98 Canadian Ice

Donruss Canadian Ice was a 150-card set that was tailored toward the Stanley Cup as well as Canadian collectors. The cards featured full-bleed photos of each player with a reddish-black strip across the top that includes the player's name and his team. The Donruss logo is printed in the lower left with a Canadian Ice logo in the upper left. Rookie subset cards are distinguished by a large silver foil "Rookie" logo in the upper right. Inserts include: Provincial and Dominion parallel sets, Stanley Cup Scrapbook, National Pride and Les Gardiens.

		MT
Complete Set (150):		20.00
Common Player:		.10
1	Patrick Roy	2.50
2	Paul Kariya	2.00
3	Eric Lindros	2.00
4	Steve Yzerman	1.50
5	Wayne Gretzky	3.00
6	Peter Forsberg	1.50
7	John Vanbiesbrouck	1.25
8	Jaromir Jagr	2.00
9	Jim Campbell	.10
10	Dominik Hasek	1.00
11	Ray Bourque	.20
12	Jarome Iginla	.10
13	Mike Modano	.30
14	Ed Jovanovski	.10
15	Jocelyn Thibault	.25
16	Keith Tkachuk	.50
17	Brett Hull	.40
18	Pavel Bure	1.00
19	Saku Koivu	.75
20	Curtis Joseph	.30
21	Eric Daze	.15
22	Keith Primeau	.10
23	Theoren Fleury	.10
24	Pierre Turgeon	.15
25	Peter Bondra	.20
26	Ed Belfour	.25
27	Pat Verbeek	.10
28	Chris Osgood	.50
29	Ray Sheppard	.10
30	Stephane Fiset	.20
31	Wade Redden	.10
32	Trevor Linden	.10
33	Zigmund Palffy	.60
34	Tony Amonte	.20
35	Derek Plante	.10
36	Jonas Hoglund	.10
37	Guy Hebert	.20
38	Garth Snow	.20
39	Chris Gratton	.20
40	Mats Sundin	.40
41	Geoff Sanderson	.10
42	Martin Brodeur	1.00
43	Jozef Stumpel	.10
44	Ron Francis	.20
45	Alexander Mogilny	.25
46	Bill Ranford	.20
47	Kirk Muller	.10
48	Ron Hextall	.20
49	Doug Gilmour	.20
50	Mark Messier	.50
51	Joe Nieuwendyk	.10
52	Ryan Smyth	.25
53	Mark Recchi	.10
54	Mike Gardner	.10
55	Al MacInnis	.10
56	Felix Potvin	.50
57	Rob Blake	.10
58	Dimitri Khristich	.10
59	Jim Carey	.50
60	Trevor Kidd	.20
61	Martin Gelinas	.10
62	Oleg Tverdovsky	.10
63	Ron Tugnutt	.10
64	Paul Coffey	.20
65	Travis Green	.10
66	Andrew Cassels	.10
67	Brendan Shanahan	1.00
68	Luc Robitaille	.10
69	Pat LaFontaine	.10
70	Daymond Langkow	.10
71	Petr Nedved	.10
72	Sergei Fedorov	1.00
73	Anson Carter	.10
74	Teemu Selanne	1.00
75	Nikolai Khabibulin	.20
76	Ken Wregget	.10
77	Dino Ciccarelli	.10
78	Adam Oates	.20
79	Kirk McLean	.10
80	Wendel Clark	.10
81	Jeff Friesen	.10
82	Valeri Kamensky	.10
83	Ethan Moreau	.10
84	Matthew Barnaby	.10
85	Andy Moog	.20
86	Doug Weight	.10
87	Mike Dunham	.10
88	Brian Leetch	.20
89	Mike Peca	.10
90	Chris Pronger	.10
91	Alexei Zhamnov	.10
92	Bryan Berard	.20
93	John LeClair	.40
94	Steve Sullivan	.10
95	Grant Fuhr	.20
96	Mikael Renberg	.10
97	Adam Graves	.10
98	Ray Ferraro	.10
99	Sean Burke	.20
100	Jeremy Roenick	.30
101	Jeff Hackett	.10
102	Joe Sakic	1.25
103	Jamie Langenbrunner	.10
104	Stephane Richer	.10
105	Dave Andreychuk	.10
106	Tommy Salo	.10
107	Mike Richter	.40
108	Owen Nolan	.10
109	Corey Hirsch	.10
110	Daren Puppa	.10
111	Darcy Tucker	.10
112	Daniel Alfredsson	.20
113	Rod Brind'Amour	.10
114	Scott Stevens	.10
115	Vincent Damphousse	.10
116	Mathieu Schneider	.10
117	Jason Arnott	.10
118	Mike Vernon	.20
119	Sandis Ozolinsh	.10
120	Chris Chelios	.20
121	Mike Grier	.20
122	Alexandre Daigle	.10
123	Roman Hamrlik	.10
124	Derian Hatcher	.10
125	Damian Rhodes	.10
126	Adam Deadmarsh	.10
127	Alexei Yashin	.10
128	Terry Ryan	.10
129	Jeff Ware	.10
130	Steve Kelly	.10
131	Hnat Domenichelli	.10
132	Steve Shields	.10
133	Paxton Schafer	.10
134	Vadim Sharifijanov	.10
135	*Vaclav Prospal*	.10
136	Mike Fountain	.10
137	Christian Malto	.10
138	Tomas Vokoun	.10
139	Vladimir Vorobiev	.10
140	Domenic Pittis	.10
141	Vaclav Varada	.10
142	*D.J. Smith*	.10
143	Jaroslav Svejkovsky	.10
144	Jason Holland	.10
145	Marc Denis	.75
146	Jean-Sebastien Giguere	.30
147	Marcel Cousineau	.10
148	Dave Andreychuk	.10
149	Mike Gartner	.10
150	Stanley Cup Team Photo	.10

1997-98 Canadian Ice Dominion

This 150-card set mirrors the regular-issue Canadian Ice set, but is printed in gold foilboard and individually numbered to 150. The words "Dominion Series" are also printed up the left side in gold foil.

	MT
Common Player:	8.00
Stars:	75x to 125x
Yng. Stars & RC's:	40x to 75x

1997-98 Canadian Ice Provincial

This 150-card set parallels the regular-issue Canadian Ice set, but reprints each card on silver foilboard with individual numbering to 750. The words "Provincial Series" are also printed up the left side in silver foil.

	MT
Complete Set (150):	1200.00
Common Player:	3.00
Provincials:	15x to 30x

1997-98 Canadian Ice Stanley Cup Scrapbook

Stanley Cup Scrapbook was a 33-card insert set that featured players from each round of the playoffs. There were 16 Quarterfinals cards numbered to 2,000, eight Conference Semifinals cards numbered to 1,500, six Conference Finals cards numbered to 1,000, two Stanley Cup Finals cards numbered to 750 and one Stanley Cup Champions card numbered to 250. All 750 Stanley Cup Finals cards are autographed by either Mike Vernon or Eric Lindros, while all 250 Stanley Cup Champions cards are autographed by Brendan Shanahan.

		MT
Complete Set (33):		1100.00
Common Player:		10.00
1	Mike Modano	15.00
2	Curtis Joseph	15.00
3	Joe Sakic	30.00
4	Chris Chelios	10.00
5	Chris Osgood	20.00
6	Brett Hull	20.00
7	Jeremy Roenick	15.00
8	Teemu Selanne	20.00
9	Jaromir Jagr	50.00
10	Garth Snow	10.00
11	Alexei Yashin	10.00
12	Steve Shields	10.00
13	Doug Gilmour	10.00
14	Jose Theodore	15.00
15	Mike Richter	10.00
16	John Vanbiesbrouck	30.00
17	Ryan Smyth	15.00
18	Peter Forsberg	50.00
19	Steve Yzerman	50.00
20	Paul Kariya	60.00
21	Janne Niinimaa	15.00
22	Dominik Hasek	25.00
23	Mark Messier	20.00
24	Martin Brodeur	25.00
25	Slava Kozlov	20.00
26	Sergei Fedorov	40.00
27	Patrick Roy	90.00
28	Wayne Gretzky	120.00
29	John LeClair	20.00
30	Paul Coffey	20.00
31	Mike Vernon (750 auto.)	50.00
32	Eric Lindros (750 auto.)	150.00
33	Brendan Shanahan (250 auto.)	175.00

1997-98 Canadian Ice National Pride

This 30-card insert set highlighted the NHL's most prominent native Canadian players. Each National Pride insert was printed on die-cut plastic in the shape of a maple leaf and individually numbered to 1,997.

		MT
Complete Set (30):		350.00
Common Player:		10.00
1	Wayne Gretzky	80.00
2	Mark Messier	20.00
3	Paul Kariya	50.00
4	Steve Yzerman	40.00
5	Brendan Shanahan	25.00
6	Chris Osgood	20.00
7	Adam Oates	10.00
8	Eric Lindros	50.00

9	Doug Gilmour	10.00
10	Ryan Smyth	15.00
11	Ray Bourque	10.00
12	Jason Arnott	10.00
13	Jarome Iginla	10.00
14	Geoff Sanderson	10.00
15	Alexandre Daigle	10.00
16	Trevor Linden	10.00
17	Joe Sakic	30.00
18	Mark Recchi	10.00
19	Theoren Fleury	10.00
20	Ron Francis	10.00
21	Daymond Langkow	10.00
22	Ed Belfour	15.00
23	Paul Coffey	10.00
24	Pierre Turgeon	10.00
25	Claude Lemieux	10.00
26	Ron Hextall	10.00
27	Curtis Joseph	15.00
28	Mike Vernon	10.00
29	Vincent Damphousse	10.00
30	Owen Nolan	10.00

1997-98 Canadian Ice Les Gardiens

Les Gardiens was a 12-card insert set that highlighted top goaltenders on a gold foil card. Each card in the set was individually numbered to 1,500.

		MT
Complete Set (12):		275.00
Common Player:		15.00
1	Patrick Roy	80.00
2	Felix Potvin	30.00
3	Martin Brodeur	50.00
4	Jean-Sebastien Giguere	15.00
5	Stephane Fiset	15.00
6	Jose Theodore	15.00
7	Jocelyn Thibault	20.00
8	Eric Fichaud	15.00
9	Patrick Lalime	25.00
10	Marcel Cousineau	15.00
11	Philippe DeRouville	15.00
12	Marc Denis	25.00

1997-98 Pacific Crown

The 351-card set features the player's name in gold foil along the bottom on vertical cards and on the left on horizontal cards. The team's logo is to the right of the name over a gold-foil burst. The Pacific Crown logo appears in one of the upper corners in gold. The backs have all the basic information and a photo over a blue ice background. Copper foil parallels appear 1:1 U.S. hobby packs, while Emerald Green foil parallels appear 1:1 Canadian packs. Silver parallels were inserted 1:1 retail packs. Red parallels were inserted in Treat Entertainment U.S. packs.

		MT
Complete Set (350):		35.00
Common Player:		.05
Coppers:		2x to 3x
Emerald Greens:		3x to 6x
Silvers:		2x to 3x
1	Ray Bourque	.15
2	Brian Leetch	.20
3	Claude Lemieux	.05
4	Mike Modano	.30
5	Zigmund Palffy	.60
6	Nikolai Khabibulin	.20
7	Chris Chelios	.20

8	Teemu Selanne	1.00
9	Paul Kariya	2.00
10	John LeClair	.40
11	Mark Messier	.50
12	Jarome Iginla	.15
13	Petr Nedved	.05
14	Brendan Shanahan	1.00
15	Dino Ciccarelli	.05
16	Brett Hull	.40
17	Wendel Clark	.05
18	Peter Bondra	.15
19	Steve Yzerman	1.50
20	Ed Belfour	.20
21	Peter Forsberg	1.50
22	Mike Gartner	.05
23	Jim Carey	.50
24	Mike Vernon	.20
25	Vincent Damphousse	.05
26	Adam Graves	.15
27	Ron Hextall	.20
28	Keith Tkachuk	.50
29	Felix Potvin	.50
30	Martin Brodeur	1.00
31	Rod Brind'Amour	.05
32	Pierre Turgeon	.15
33	Patrick Roy	2.50
34	John Vanbiesbrouck	1.25
35	Andy Moog	.15
36	Sergei Berezin	.05
37	Adam Oates	.20
38	Joe Sakic	1.25
39	Dominik Hasek	1.00
40	Patrick Lalime	.50
41	Bobby Dollas	.05
42	Kyle McLaren	.05
43	Wayne Primeau	.05
44	Stephane Richer	.05
45	Theoren Fleury	.05
46	Kevin Miller	.05
47	Adam Deadmarsh	.05
48	Darryl Sydor	.05
49	Igor Larionov	.05
50	Radek Dvorak	.05
51	Andrei Kovalenko	.05
52	Keith Primeau	.15
53	Ray Ferraro	.05
54	David Wilkie	.05
55	Bobby Holik	.05
56	Tommy Salo	.05
57	Jeff Beukeboom	.05
58	Daniel Alfredsson	.20
59	Mikael Renberg	.15
60	Norm Maciver	.05
61	Darius Kasparaitis	.05
62	Geoff Courtnall	.05
63	Jeff Friesen	.05
64	Brian Bradley	.05
65	Tie Domi	.05
67	Martin Gelinas	.05
68	Jaromir Jagr	2.00
69	Steve Konowalchuk	.05
70	Brian Bellows	.05
71	Jozef Stumpel	.05
72	Darryl Shannon	.05
73	Todd Simpson	.05
74	Ulf Dahlen	.05
75	Sandis Ozolinsh	.05
76	Sergei Zubov	.05
77	Paul Coffey	.20
78	Nicklas Lidstrom	.15
79	Jason Arnott	.05
80	Ray Sheppard	.05
81	Sean Burke	.20
82	Vladimir Tsyplakov	.05
83	Darcy Tucker	.05
84	Dave Andreychuk	.05
85	Scott Lachance	.05
86	Niklas Sundstrom	.05
87	Ron Tugnutt	.15
88	Eric Lindros	2.00
89	Alexander Mogilny	.25
90	Kris King	.05

91	Sergei Fedorov	1.00
92	Ed Olczyk	.05
93	Doug Gilmour	.25
94	Ryan Smyth	.05
95	Scott Pellerin	.05
96	Pavel Bure	1.00
97	Jeremy Roenick	.30
98	Todd Gill	.05
99	Wayne Gretzky	3.00
100	Roman Hamrlik	.05
101	Rob Zettler	.05
102	Sergei Nemchinov	.05
103	Sergei Gonchar	.05
104	Steve Rucchin	.05
105	Landon Wilson	.05
106	Anatoli Semenov	.05
107	Corey Millen	.05
108	Eric Daze	.15
109	Mike Ricci	.05
110	Jamie Langenbrunner	.05
111	Viacheslav Fetisov	.05
112	Rem Murray	.05
113	Tom Fitzgerald	.05
114	Robert Kron	.05
115	Kevin Stevens	.05
116	Valeri Bure	.15
117	Bill Guerin	.05
118	Bryan McCabe	.05
119	Alexei Kovalev	.15
120	Alexei Yashin	.15
121	Eric Desjardins	.05
122	Teppo Numminen	.05
123	Ron Francis	.15
124	Chris Pronger	.10
125	Viktor Kozlov	.05
126	Corey Schwab	.05
127	Fredrik Modin	.05
128	Markus Naslund	.05
129	Dale Hunter	.05
130	Warren Rychel	.05
131	Anson Carter	.05
132	Miroslav Satan	.20
133	Trevor Kidd	.20
134	Sergei Krivokrasov	.05
135	Adam Foote	.05
136	Brent Gilchrist	.05
137	Chris Osgood	.50
138	Doug Weight	.05
139	Martin Straka	.05
140	Jeff O'Neill	.05
141	Byron Dafoe	.05
142	Brian Savage	.05
143	Lyle Odelein	.05
144	Niklas Andersson	.05
145	Luc Robitaille	.15
146	Damian Rhodes	.15
147	Garth Snow	.15
148	Craig Janney	.05
149	Fredrik Olausson	.05
150	Joe Murphy	.15
151	Owen Nolan	.15
152	Shawn Burr	.05
153	Dimitri Yushkevich	.05
154	Trevor Linden	.15
155	Joe Juneau	.05
156	Sean Pronger	.05
157	Jeff Odgers	.05
158	Brian Holzinger	.05
159	Dave Gagner	.05
160	Jeff Hackett	.15
161	Eric Lacroix	.05
162	Pat Verbeek	.05
163	Darren McCarty	.05
164	Mike Grier	.25
165	Per Gustafsson	.05
166	Andrew Cassels	.05
167	Vitali Yachmenev	.05
168	Jocelyn Thibault	.25
169	John MacLean	.05
170	Travis Green	.05
171	Ulf Samuelsson	.05
172	Bruce Gardiner	.05
173	Janne Niinimaa	.20
174	Jim Johnson	.05
175	Stu Barnes	.05
176	Harry York	.05
177	Al Iafrate	.05
178	Paul Ysebaert	.05
179	Mathieu Schneider	.05
180	Corey Hirsch	.05
181	Mark Tinordi	.05
182	Kevin Todd	.05
183	Tim Sweeney	.05
184	Donald Audette	.05
185	Jonas Hoglund	.05
186	Brent Sutter	.05
187	Scott Young	.05
188	Arturs Irbe	.10
189	Vladimir Konstantinov	.05
190	Mats Lindgren	.05
191	David Nemirovsky	.05

192	Sami Kapanen	.05
193	Rob Blake	.05
194	Sebastian Bordeleau	.05
195	Steve Thomas	.05
196	Bryan Smolinski	.05
197	Mike Richter	.40
198	Randy Cunneyworth	.05
199	Pat Falloon	.05
200	Cliff Ronning	.05
201	Ken Wregget	.05
202	Al McInnis	.05
203	Tony Granato	.05
204	Rob Zamuner	.05
205	Mats Sundin	.40
206	Mike Ridley	.05
207	Sylvain Cote	.05
208	Joe Sacco	.05
209	Ted Donato	.05
210	Matthew Barnaby	.05
211	Cory Stillman	.05
212	Gary Suter	.05
213	Valeri Kamensky	.05
214	Derian Hatcher	.05
215	Jamie Pushor	.05
216	Mariusz Czerkawski	.05
217	Kirk Muller	.05
218	Kevin Dineen	.05
219	Dimitri Khristich	.05
220	Martin Rucinsky	.05
221	Denis Pederson	.05
222	Bryan Berard	.20
223	Alexander Karpovtsev	.05
224	Shawn McEachern	.05
225	Dale Hawerchuk	.05
226	Bob Corkum	.05
227	Kevin Hatcher	.05
228	Grant Fuhr	.25
229	Darren Turcotte	.05
230	Patrick Poulin	.05
231	Jamie Macoun	.05
232	Jyrki Lumme	.05
233	Bill Ranford	.20
234	Dmitri Mironov	.05
235	Mattias Timander	.05
236	Alexei Zhitnik	.05
237	Hnat Domenichelli	.05
238	Murray Craven	.05
239	Mike Keane	.05
240	Benoit Hogue	.05
241	Martin Lapointe	.05
242	Curtis Joseph	.30
243	Robert Svehla	.05
244	Glen Wesley	.05
245	Stephane Fiset	.20
246	Shayne Corson	.05
247	Scott Niedermayer	.05
248	Steve Webb	.05
249	Esa Tikkanen	.05
250	Alexandre Daigle	.05
251	Trent Klatt	.05
252	Oleg Tverdovsky	.05
253	Dave Roche	.05
254	Tony Twist	.05
255	Bernie Nicholls	.05
256	Rick Tabaracci	.05
257	Todd Warriner	.05
258	Kirk McLean	.15
259	Phil Housley	.05
260	Guy Hebert	.20
261	Steve Heinze	.05
262	Derek Plante	.05
263	German Titov	.05
264	Tony Amonte	.15
265	Uwe Krupp	.05
266	Joe Nieuwendyk	.05
267	Vyacheslav Kozlov	.05
268	Kelly Buchberger	.05
269	Rob Niedermayer	.05
270	Geoff Sanderson	.05
271	Jan Vopat	.05
272	Saku Koivu	.75
273	Scott Stevens	.05
274	Eric Fichaud	.25
275	Russ Courtnall	.05
276	Wade Redden	.05
277	Petr Svoboda	.05
278	Andreas Dackell	.05
279	Jason Woolley	.05
280	Stephane Matteau	.05
281	Stephen Guolla	.05
282	John Cullen	.05
283	Steve Sullivan	.05
284	Bret Hedican	.05
285	Michal Pivonka	.05
286	Darren Van Impe	.05
287	Rob DiMaio	.05
288	Garry Galley	.05
289	Kent Manderville	.05
290	Bob Probert	.05
291	Keith Jones	.05
292	Guy Carbonneau	.05

293	Tomas Sandstrom	.05
294	Daniel McGillis	.05
295	Brian Skrudland	.15
296	Stu Grimson	.05
297	Doug Zmolek	.05
298	Mark Recchi	.10
299	Valeri Zelepukin	.05
300	Derek Armstrong	.05
301	Eric Cairns	.05
302	Steve Duchesne	.15
303	Dainius Zubrus	.35
304	Deron Quint	.05
305	Joe Dziedzic	.05
306	Mike Peluso	.05
307	Andrei Nazarov	.05
308	Chris Gratton	.15
309	Mike Craig	.05
310	Lonny Bohonos	.05
311	Rick Tocchet	.05
312	Ted Drury	.05
313	Jean-Yves Roy	.05
314	Jason Dawe	.05
315	Jamie Allison	.05
316	Alexei Zhamnov	.10
317	Aaron Miller	.05
318	Todd Krygier	.05
319	Tomas Holmstrom	.05
320	Todd Marchant	.05
321	Scott Mellanby	.05
322	Marek Malik	.05
323	Dan Bylsma	.05
324	Stephane Quintal	.05
325	Ken Daneyko	.05
326	Robert Reichel	.05
327	Daniel Goneau	.05
328	Sergei Zholtok	.05
329	Kjell Samuelsson	.05
330	Shane Doan	.05
331	Radek Bonk	.05
332	Jim Campbell	.05
333	Marty McSorley	.05
334	Brantt Myhres	.05
335	Mike Johnson	.05
336	Mike Sillinger	.05
337	Kelly Hrudey	.15
338	Joel Bouchard	.05
339	Brian Noonan	.05
340	Dean Chynoweth	.05
341	Mike Peca	.05
342	Jeff Toms	.05
343	Denis Savard	.05
344	Stephane Yelle	.05
345	Grant Ledyard	.05
346	Ronnie Stern	.05
347	Petr Klima	.05
348	Johan Garpenlov	.05
349	Nelson Emerson	.05
350	Matt Johnson	.05
351	Ken Belanger	.05

1997-98 Pacific Crown Ice Blue

The 351-card set was inserted 1:73 packs. It is believed there were 67 sets printed.

	MT
Common Player:	20.00
Stars:	12x to 25x
Young Stars & RC's:	8x to 12x

1997-98 Pacific Crown Card-Supials

The 40-card set includes a player photo superimposed over a holofoil background. A circle at the top of the card is multicolored. Below the circle is the team name repeated from left to right. The team logo is in the lower right corner. The backs include the player's highlights, along with a slot where a mini-card can be stored.

		MT
Complete Set (20):		120.00
Common Player:		2.00
1	Paul Kariya	20.00
2	Teemu Selanne	10.00
3	Jarome Iginla	4.00
4	Peter Forsberg	15.00
5	Claude Lemieux	2.00
6	Mike Modano	4.00
7	Sergei Fedorov	10.00
8	Vladimir Konstantinov	2.00
9	John Vanbiesbrouck	15.00
10	Martin Brodeur	12.00
11	Doug Gilmour	3.00
12	Zigmund Palffy	8.00
13	Mark Messier	8.00
14	John LeClair	6.00
15	Jeremy Roenick	5.00
16	Keith Tkachuk	6.00
17	Ron Francis	2.00
18	Brett Hull	6.00
19	Felix Potvin	8.00
20	Pavel Bure	10.00

1997-98 Pacific Crown Cramer's Choice

The 10-card set was inserted 1:721 packs. The card fronts feature a player photo superimposed over a holofoil background, which is shaped like a pyramid. The bottom of the card front has the player's name, position, "Cramer's Choice Award" and Pacific logo printed in red over a gold-foil background. The backs include a player photo, name, position and highlights.

		MT
Complete Set (10):		1200.
Common Player:		50.00
1	Paul Kariya	150.00
2	Dominik Hasek	75.00
3	Jarome Iginla	50.00
4	Peter Forsberg	125.00
5	Patrick Roy	200.00
6	Steve Yzerman	125.00
7	Wayne Gretzky	250.00
8	Mark Messier	75.00
9	Eric Lindros	200.00
10	Jaromir Jagr	150.00

1997-98 Pacific Crown Gold Crown

The 20-card chase set was seeded 1:37 packs. The card fronts featured a player photo superimposed over a holofoil background, with a gold-foil die-cut crown at the top. The player's name is printed inside a gold-foil banner at the bottom, with the team's logo inside a shield above the player's name. The backs include the player's name, team, position, highlights and photos.

		MT
Complete Set (20):		160.00
Common Player:		2.50
1	Paul Kariya	15.00

2	Teemu Selanne	8.00
3	Dominik Hasek	8.00
4	Mike Peca	2.50
5	Jarome Iginla	2.50
6	Chris Chelios	4.00
7	Peter Forsberg	12.00
8	Patrick Roy	20.00
9	Joe Sakic	10.00
10	Brendan Shanahan	8.00
11	Steve Yzerman	12.00
12	Ryan Smyth	4.00
13	John Vanbiesbrouck	10.00
14	Martin Brodeur	8.00
15	Wayne Gretzky	25.00
16	Mark Messier	6.00
17	Eric Lindros	20.00
18	Jaromir Jagr	15.00
19	Brett Hull	5.00
20	Pavel Bure	8.00

1997-98 Pacific Crown In the Cage

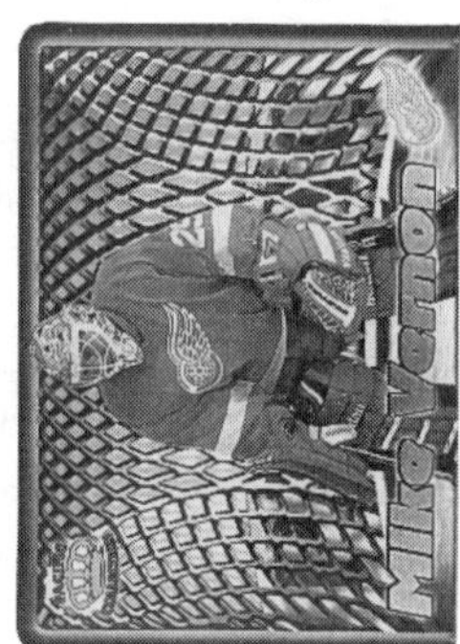

This 20-card set was inserted 1:145 packs. The card fronts feature a photo of the goaltender superimposed over a laser-cut net background. The player's name is printed in gold foil at the bottom, with the team logo printed in the lower right.

		MT
Complete Set (20):		325.00
Common Goalie:		10.00
1	Guy Hebert	10.00
2	Dominik Hasek	35.00
3	Trevor Kidd	10.00
4	Jeff Hackett	10.00
5	Patrick Roy	75.00
6	Andy Moog	15.00
7	Chris Osgood	20.00
8	Mike Vernon	10.00
9	Curtis Joseph	15.00
10	John Vanbiesbrouck	50.00
11	Jocelyn Thibault	15.00
12	Martin Brodeur	40.00
13	Mike Richter	15.00
14	Ron Hextall	10.00
15	Garth Snow	10.00
16	Nikolai Khabibulin	10.00
17	Patrick Lalime	20.00
18	Grant Fuhr	15.00
19	Ed Belfour	15.00
20	Felix Potvin	20.00

1997-98 Pacific Crown Slap Shots

The 36-card set featured three cards per number. In other words, the cards were numbered 1A, 1B and 1C, etc. The card fronts featured the player photo superimposed over a blue background. The right border was a jagged die-cut with blue foil. To the left of the die-cut is one of three pieces of a hockey stick. The Pacific Crown logo is printed in the upper left inside an icicle. The cards were inserted 1:73 packs.

		MT
Complete Set (36):		600.00
Common Player:		8.00
1A	Paul Kariya	50.00
1B	Jari Kurri	8.00
1C	Teemu Selanne	25.00
2A	Peter Forsberg	40.00
2B	Joe Sakic	35.00
2C	Claude Lemieux	8.00
3A	Brendan Shanahan	25.00
3B	Sergei Fedorov	25.00
3C	Steve Yzerman	40.00
4A	Mark Recchi	8.00
4B	Vincent Damphousse	8.00
4C	Stephane Richer	8.00
5A	Wayne Gretzky	75.00
5B	Mark Messier	20.00
5C	Brian Leetch	10.00
6A	Rod Brind'Amour	8.00
6B	Eric Lindros	60.00
6C	John LeClair	15.00
7A	Keith Tkachuk	15.00
7B	Jeremy Roenick	12.00
7C	Mike Gartner	8.00
8A	Petr Nedved	8.00
8B	Ron Francis	8.00
8C	Jaromir Jagr	50.00
9A	Geoff Courtnall	8.00
9B	Pierre Turgeon	8.00
9C	Brett Hull	15.00
10A	Wendel Clark	8.00
10B	Mats Sundin	12.00
10C	Sergei Berezin	8.00
11A	Pavel Bure	25.00
11B	Trevor Linden	8.00
11C	Alexander Mogilny	12.00
12A	Joe Juneau	8.00
12B	Adam Oates	10.00
12C	Peter Bondra	8.00

1997-98 Pacific Crown Cel Cards

This 26-card chase set was inserted 1:73 packs. The cards included the checklist for each team.

	MT
Complete Set (26):	300.00
Common Player:	5.00

1	Teemu Selanne	15.00
2	Ray Bourque	5.00
3	Dominik Hasek	15.00
4	Jarome Iginla	5.00
5	Keith Primeau	5.00
6	Chris Chelios	6.00
7	Patrick Roy	40.00
8	Mike Modano	6.00
9	Steve Yzerman	25.00
10	Curtis Joseph	8.00
11	John Vanbiesbrouck	20.00
12	Rob Blake	5.00
13	Stephane Richer	5.00
14	Martin Brodeur	15.00
15	Zigmund Palffy	10.00
16	Wayne Gretzky	50.00
17	Alexandre Daigle	5.00
18	Eric Lindros	40.00
19	Jeremy Roenick	8.00
20	Jaromir Jagr	30.00
21	Brett Hull	10.00
22	Owen Nolan	5.00
23	Dino Ciccarelli	5.00
24	Felix Potvin	10.00
25	Pavel Bure	15.00
26	Peter Bondra	5.00

1997-98 Collector's Choice

Collector's Choice consisted of 320 cards, with an average of 10 cards from each NHL team. This base brand featured action shots of players surrounded by a white border. There were two subsets: 36 National Heroes and nine Chippy's Checklists. There were also three insert sets in Collector's Choice, including Stick-Ums, three different You Crash the Game cards and StarQuest.

	MT
Complete Set (320):	20.00
Common Player:	.05

1	Guy Hebert	.15
2	Sean Pronger	.05
3	Dmitri Mironov	.05
4	Darren Van Impe	.05
5	Joe Sacco	.05
6	Ted Drury	.05
7	Steve Rucchin	.05
8	Teemu Selanne	.50
9	Paul Kariya	1.25
10	Jari Kurri	.05
11	Kevin Todd	.05
12	Ray Bourque	.15
13	Anson Carter	.05
14	Ted Donato	.05
15	Kyle McLaren	.05
16	Jason Allison	.05
17	Jim Carey	.40
18	Jozef Stumpel	.05
19	Jean-Yves Roy	.05
20	Steve Heinze	.05
21	Sheldon Kennedy	.05
22	Dominik Hasek	.50
23	Rob Ray	.05
24	Derek Plante	.05
25	Brian Holzinger	.05
26	Mike Peca	.05
27	Matthew Barnaby	.05
28	Donald Audette	.05
29	Alexei Zhitnik	.05
30	Rumun Ndur	.05
31	Pat LaFontaine	.05
32	Jason Dawe	.05
33	Hnat Domenichelli	.05
34	Jarome Iginla	.15
35	Chris O'Sullivan	.05
36	Todd Simpson	.05
37	Trevor Kidd	.15
38	Dave Gagner	.05
39	German Titov	.05
40	Theoren Fleury	.10
41	Dwayne Roloson	.05
42	Marty McInnis	.05
43	Jonas Hoglund	.05
44	Tony Amonte	.15
45	Gary Suter	.05
46	Chris Chelios	.15
47	Jeff Hackett	.10
48	Ulf Dahlen	.05
49	Bob Probert	.05
50	Kevin Miller	.05
51	Ethan Moreau	.05
52	Eric Weinrich	.05
53	Eric Daze	.15
54	Peter Forsberg	.75
55	Joe Sakic	.75
56	Patrick Roy	1.50
57	Adam Deadmarsh	.05
58	Valeri Kamensky	.05
59	Keith Jones	.05
60	Sandis Ozolinsh	.05
61	Mike Ricci	.05
62	Claude Lemieux	.05
63	Mike Keane	.05
64	Adam Foote	.05
65	Mike Modano	.20
66	Pat Verbeek	.05
67	Andy Moog	.15
68	Joe Nieuwendyk	.05
69	Jamie Langenbrunner	.05
70	Derian Hatcher	.05
71	Greg Adams	.05
72	Darryl Sydor	.05
73	Dave Reid	.05
74	Jere Lehtinen	.05
75	Todd Harvey	.05
76	Brendan Shanahan	.50
77	Mike Knuble	.05
78	Steve Yzerman	1.00
79	Sergei Fedorov	.60
80	Chris Osgood	.35
81	Nicklas Lidstrom	.10
82	Vladimir Konstantinov	.05
83	Darren McCarty	.05
84	Kirk Maltby	.05
85	Vyacheslav Kozlov	.05
86	Martin Lapointe	.05
87	Doug Weight	.05
88	Mike Grier	.20
89	Curtis Joseph	.25
90	Andrei Kovalenko	.05
91	Rem Murray	.05
92	Ryan Smyth	.25
93	Mariusz Czerkawski	.05
94	Todd Marchant	.05
95	Jason Arnott	.05
96	Luke Richardson	.05
97	Dean McAmmond	.05
98	Kirk Muller	.05
99	Ray Sheppard	.05
100	Scott Mellanby	.05
101	Ed Jovanovski	.15
102	John Vanbiesbrouck	.75
103	Radek Dvorak	.05
104	Robert Svehla	.05
105	Rob Niedermayer	.05
106	David Nemirovsky	.05
107	Steve Washburn	.05
108	Bill Lindsay	.05
109	Kevin Dineen	.05
110	Keith Primeau	.10
111	Sean Burke	.20
112	Derek King	.05
113	Andrew Cassels	.05
114	Glen Wesley	.05
115	Nelson Emerson	.05
116	Geoff Sanderson	.05
117	Jeff O'Neill	.05
118	Kent Manderville	.05
119	Dimitri Khristich	.05
120	Ian Laperriere	.05
121	Aki Berg	.05
122	Vladimir Tsyplakov	.05
123	Vitali Yachmenev	.05
124	Roman Vopat	.05
125	Rob Blake	.05
126	Kai Nurminen	.05
127	Jeff Shevalier	.05
128	Byron Dafoe	.05
129	Saku Koivu	.50
130	Vincent Damphousse	.05
131	Brian Savage	.05
132	Valeri Bure	.15
133	Mark Recchi	.10
134	Jocelyn Thibault	.25
135	Jose Theodore	.15
136	Dave Manson	.05
137	Shayne Corson	.05
138	Stephane Richer	.05
139	Doug Gilmour	.20
140	Scott Stevens	.05
141	Martin Brodeur	.50
142	Dave Andreychuk	.05
143	Bobby Holik	.05
144	Brian Rolston	.05
145	Jay Pandolfo	.05
146	John MacLean	.05
147	Bill Guerin	.05
148	Scott Niedermayer	.05
149	Denis Pederson	.05
150	Zigmund Palffy	.40
151	Robert Reichel	.05
152	Bryan Smolinski	.05
153	Eric Fichaud	.15
154	Todd Bertuzzi	.05
155	Bryan Berard	.15
156	Niclas Andersson	.05
157	Bryan McCabe	.05
158	Tommy Salo	.05
159	Kenny Jonsson	.05
160	Travis Green	.05
161	Mike Richter	.30
162	Brian Leetch	.20
163	Adam Graves	.15
164	Vladimir Vorobiev	.05
165	Niklas Sundstrom	.05
166	Russ Courtnall	.05
167	Wayne Gretzky	2.00
168	Mark Messier	.40
169	Alexander Karpovtsev	.05
170	Luc Robitaille	.05
171	Ulf Samuelsson	.05
172	Daniel Alfredsson	.15
173	Alexei Yashin	.15
174	Alexandre Daigle	.05
175	Andreas Dackell	.05
176	Wade Redden	.05
177	Sergei Zholtok	.05
178	Damian Rhodes	.05
179	Steve Duchesne	.05
180	Shawn McEachern	.05
181	Ron Tugnutt	.05
182	John LeClair	.30
183	Janne Niinimaa	.25
184	Mikael Renberg	.15
185	*Vaclav Prospal*	.05
186	Eric Lindros	1.50
187	Dainius Zubrus	.30
188	Ron Hextall	.15
189	Paul Coffey	.15
190	Dale Hawerchuk	.05
191	Trent Klatt	.05
192	Rod Brind'Amour	.10
193	Nikolai Khabibulin	.20
194	Keith Tkachuk	.40
195	Jeremy Roenick	.25
196	Mike Gartner	.15
197	Murray Baron	.05
198	Oleg Tverdovsky	.05
199	Cliff Ronning	.05
200	Teppo Numminen	.05
201	Craig Janney	.05
202	Deron Quint	.05
203	Joe Dziedzic	.05
204	Ron Francis	.15
205	Jaromir Jagr	1.25
206	Greg Johnson	.05
207	Kevin Hatcher	.05
208	Patrick Lalime	.35
209	Petr Nedved	.05
210	Ken Wregget	.10
211	Darius Kasparaitis	.05
212	Stu Barnes	.05
213	Ed Olczyk	.05
214	Owen Nolan	.15
215	Jeff Friesen	.05
216	Ed Belfour	.25
217	Viktor Kozlov	.05
218	Tony Granato	.05
219	Darren Turcotte	.05
220	Stephen Guolla	.05
221	Marty McSorley	.05
222	Marcus Ragnarsson	.05
223	Al Iafrate	.05
224	Brett Hull	.35
225	Grant Fuhr	.25
226	Pierre Turgeon	.15
227	Geoff Courtnall	.05
228	Jim Campbell	.05
229	Harry York	.05
230	Tony Twist	.05
231	Joe Murphy	.05
232	Pavol Demitra	.05
233	Chris Pronger	.05
234	Al MacInnis	.05
235	Daren Puppa	.05
236	Chris Gratton	.15
237	Dino Ciccarelli	.05
238	Rob Zamuner	.05

239	Rick Tabaracci	.05
240	Roman Hamrlik	.05
241	Alexander Selivanov	.05
242	Patrick Poulin	.05
243	Daymond Langkow	.05
244	Shawn Burr	.05
245	Mats Sundin	.20
246	Wendel Clark	.05
247	Sergei Berezin	.05
248	Steve Sullivan	.05
249	Fredrik Modin	.05
250	Darby Hendrickson	.05
251	Jason Podollan	.05
252	Felix Potvin	.30
253	Tie Domi	.05
254	Todd Warriner	.05
255	Pavel Bure	.50
256	Alexander Mogilny	.20
257	Martin Gelinas	.05
258	Corey Hirsch	.05
259	Trevor Linden	.10
260	Mike Sillinger	.05
261	Markus Naslund	.05
262	Jyrki Lumme	.05
263	Gino Odjick	.05
264	Mike Ridley	.05
265	Dave Roberts	.05
266	Adam Oates	.15
267	Bill Ranford	.10
268	Joe Juneau	.05
269	Chris Simon	.05
270	Peter Bondra	.15
271	Dale Hunter	.05
272	Rick Tocchet	.05
273	Sergei Gonchar	.05
274	Steve Konowalchuk	.05
275	Phil Housley	.05
276	Angela James (National Heroes)	.05
277	Nancy Drolet (National Heroes)	.05
278	Leslie Reddon (National Heroes)	.05
279	Hayley Wickenheiser (National Heroes)	.05
280	Vicky Sunohara (National Heroes)	.05
281	Cassie Campbell (National Heroes)	.05
282	Geraldine Heaney (National Heroes)	.05
283	Judy Diduck (National Heroes)	.05
284	France St. Louis (National Heroes)	.05
285	Danielle Goyette (National Heroes)	.05
286	Therese Brisson (National Heroes)	.05
287	Stacy Wilson (National Heroes)	.05
288	Danielle Dube (National Heroes)	.05
289	Jayna Hefford (National Heroes)	.05
290	Luce Letendre (National Heroes)	.05
291	Lori Dupuis (National Heroes)	.05
292	Rebecca Fahey (National Heroes)	.05
293	Fiona Smith (National Heroes)	.05
294	Laura Schuler (National Heroes)	.05
295	Karen Nystrom (National Heroes)	.05
296	Joe Thornton (National Heroes)	2.00
297	Peter Schaefer (National Heroes)	.25
298	Daniel Tkaczuk (National Heroes)	.20
299	Alyn McCauley (National Heroes)	.05
300	Shane Willis (National Heroes)	.15
301	Chris Phillips (National Heroes)	.15
302	Marc Denis (National Heroes)	.20
303	Jason Ward (National Heroes)	.15
304	Patrick Marleau (National Heroes)	1.25
305	Brad Isbister (National Heroes)	.10
306	Cameron Mann (National Heroes)	.10
307	*Daniel Cleary* (National Heroes)	.40

308	Brad Larsen (National Heroes)	.05
309	Nick Boynton (National Heroes)	.20
310	Scott Barney (National Heroes)	.15
311	Boyd Devereaux (National Heroes)	.15
312	Wayne Gretzky (Chippy's Checklist)	.75
313	Steve Yzerman (Chippy's Checklist)	.40
314	Jaromir Jagr (Chippy's Checklist)	.50
315	Jarome Iginla (Chippy's Checklist)	.05
316	Patrick Roy (Chippy's Checklist)	.60
317	John Vanbiesbrouck (Chippy's Checklist)	.35
318	Paul Kariya (Chippy's Checklist)	.50
319	Doug Weight (Chippy's Checklist)	.05
320	Mats Sundin (Chippy's Checklist)	.15

1997-98 Collector's Choice Star Quest

This 90-card set was broken up into four tiers and differentiated by the number of Stars on the front bottom right corner. Tier one includes 45 players inserted one per pack; tier two includes 20 players inserted one per 21; tier three includes 15 players inserted one per 71 packs; and tier four includes 10 players inserted one per 145 packs. The focus of each tier is to include more elite players than the former tier, with the top players being in tier four.

	MT
Complete Set (90):	400.00
Common Star Quest 1	.15
Common Star Quest 2	1.50
Common Star Quest 3	4.00
Common Star Quest 4	6.00
SQ1 Bryan Berard	.30
SQ2 Robert Svehla	.15
SQ3 Petr Nedved	.15
SQ4 Steve Sullivan	.15
SQ5 Nicklas Lidstrom	.15
SQ6 Wade Redden	.15
SQ7 Jason Arnott	.15
SQ8 Martin Gelinas	.15
SQ9 Mikael Renberg	.15
SQ10 Jeff Friesen	.15
SQ11 Chris Chelios	.30
SQ12 Jarome Iginla	.15
SQ13 Vyacheslav Kozlov	.15
SQ14 Brian Holzinger	.15
SQ15 Eric Daze	.15
SQ16 Pat Verbeek	.15
SQ17 Jozef Stumpel	.15
SQ18 Rob Niedermayer	.15
SQ19 Sergei Fedorov	1.00
SQ20 Brian Leetch	.25
SQ21 Bill Guerin	.15
SQ22 Dino Ciccarelli	.15
SQ23 Adam Oates	.25
SQ24 Mike Grier	.25
SQ25 Alexandre Daigle	.15
SQ26 Janne Niinimaa	.30
SQ27 Dimitri Khristich	.15
SQ28 Oleg Tverdovsky	.15
SQ29 Felix Potvin	.40

SQ30 Mike Richter	.40
SQ31 Curtis Joseph	.30
SQ32 Vincent Damphousse	.15
SQ33 Ron Francis	.15
SQ34 Andy Moog	.25
SQ35 Nikolai Khabibulin	.25
SQ36 Ed Belfour	.30
SQ37 Scott Mellanby	.15
SQ38 Sandis Ozolinsh	.15
SQ39 Travis Green	.15
SQ40 Patrick Lalime	.50
SQ41 Niklas Sundstrom	.15
SQ42 Guy Hebert	.25
SQ43 Vitali Yachmenev	.15
SQ44 Roman Hamrlik	.15
SQ45 Adam Deadmarsh	.15
SQ46 Alexei Zhamnov	2.00
SQ47 Saku Koivu	6.00
SQ48 Sergei Berezin	1.50
SQ49 Mark Messier	6.00
SQ50 Martin Brodeur	8.00
SQ51 Daniel Alfredsson	1.50
SQ52 John LeClair	3.00
SQ53 Chris Osgood	4.00
SQ54 Todd Marchant	1.50
SQ55 Keith Primeau	1.50
SQ56 Pierre Turgeon	1.50
SQ57 Jim Carey	4.00
SQ58 Peter Bondra	2.00
SQ59 Pavel Bure	10.00
SQ60 Ray Sheppard	1.50
SQ61 Chris Gratton	1.50
SQ62 Derek Plante	1.50
SQ63 Joe Sakic	10.00
SQ64 Theoren Fleury	1.50
SQ65 Tony Amonte	1.50
SQ66 Zigmund Palffy	10.00
SQ67 Steve Yzerman	25.00
SQ68 Jaromir Jagr	35.00
SQ69 Alexander Mogilny	8.00
SQ70 Doug Gilmour	6.00
SQ71 Peter Forsberg	20.00
SQ72 Alexei Yashin	4.00
SQ73 Geoff Sanderson	4.00
SQ74 Doug Weight	4.00
SQ75 Mark Recchi	4.00
SQ76 Brett Hull	8.00
SQ77 Ray Bourque	6.00
SQ78 Owen Nolan	4.00
SQ79 Jeremy Roenick	8.00
SQ80 Teemu Selanne	15.00
SQ81 Dominik Hasek	18.00
SQ82 Mike Modano	8.00
SQ83 Mats Sundin	10.00
SQ84 John Vanbiesbrouck	25.00
SQ85 Paul Kariya	40.00
SQ86 Patrick Roy	50.00
SQ87 Keith Tkachuk	18.00
SQ88 Eric Lindros	40.00
SQ89 Brendan Shanahan	18.00
SQ90 Wayne Gretzky	65.00

1997-98 Collector's Choice Stick-Ums

This 30-card insert features some of the top players in the NHL on re-stickable Stick-Ums. Cards from this insert are seeded one per three packs.

	MT
Complete Set (30):	15.00
Common Player:	.25
S1 Wayne Gretzky	3.00
S2 John Vanbiesbrouck	1.25
S3 Martin Brodeur	.75
S4 Rob Blake	.25
S5 Saku Koivu	.50

S6 Geoff Sanderson	.25
S7 Chris Chelios	.35
S8 Mike Modano	.35
S9 Paul Kariya	2.00
S10 Eric Lindros	2.50
S11 Daniel Alfredsson	.25
S12 Jarome Iginla	.40
S13 Jeremy Roenick	.40
S14 Brendan Shanahan	.75
S15 Jaromir Jagr	2.00
S16 Zigmund Palffy	.50
S17 Mats Sundin	.40
S18 Teemu Selanne	.75
S19 Joe Sakic	1.00
S20 Ed Belfour	.35
S21 Peter Forsberg	1.00
S22 Dino Ciccarelli	.25
S23 Patrick Roy	2.50
S24 Doug Gilmour	.40
S25 Pavel Bure	.75
S26 Brett Hull	.40
S27 Ray Bourque	.25
S28 Adam Oates	.25
S29 Steve Yzerman	1.00
S30 Dominik Hasek	.75

1997-98 Collector's Choice You Crash the Game

This 90-card set featured 30 different players with three "Crash teams" for each individual player. If the player scored against the team indicated on the front of the card, the card could be redeemed for a premium card of the winning player. The three cards for any player are identical with the exception of the team he has to score against, which is printed in the bottom right corner. You Crash the Game cards were seeded one per five packs.

	MT
Complete Set (30):	20.00
Common Player:	.25
C1 Wayne Gretzky	5.00
C2 Mike Modano	.40
C3 Doug Weight	.25
C4 Brendan Shanahan	1.25
C5 Ray Sheppard	.25
C6 Keith Primeau	.25
C7 Ray Bourque	.40
C8 Teemu Selanne	1.25
C9 Paul Kariya	3.00
C10 Tony Amonte	.25
C11 Saku Koivu	.75
C12 Donald Audette	.25
C13 Doug Gilmour	.40
C14 Theoren Fleury	.25
C15 Alexei Yashin	.25
C16 Zigmund Palffy	1.00
C17 Dimitri Khristich	.25
C18 Joe Sakic	2.00
C19 Steve Yzerman	2.50
C20 Eric Lindros	4.00
C21 Peter Forsberg	2.00
C22 Dino Ciccarelli	.25
C23 Mats Sundin	.40
C24 Pavel Bure	1.50
C25 Peter Bondra	.25
C26 Brett Hull	.75
C27 Keith Tkachuk	.75
C28 Jaromir Jagr	3.00
C29 Jarome Iginla	.25
C30 Owen Nolan	.25

1997 The Year in Racing Cards

The consolidation that had been predicted for the racing card market ever since its rapid growth began in 1994 came to fruition in 1997. By the time the year had come to a close, three manufacturers had filed for bankruptcy and another was purchased by a competitor.

Maxx, which pioneered the modern era of racing cards back in 1988, began the year in bankruptcy protection and its assets were eventually liquidated. While no buyers for the company were found, Upper Deck agreed to purchase the Maxx name, logo and trademark.

Another racing card company was dissolved when Finish Line Racing filed for bankruptcy protection in July. Finish Line had not produced a racing card set in nearly a year but had produced one racing phone card set during '97.

Fleer/SkyBox, which entered the racing card market in 1994, spent all of '97 operating under bankruptcy protection. While the company did release a handful of racing card sets during the year, it also continued to lose millions of dollars, making it unlikely that Fleer/SkyBox would return to the racing card market in 1998.

Not all the card companies were cutting back, however. Wheels issued a public stock offering back in April and then went on a buying spree over the next few months, purchasing Diamond Sports Group, Green's Racing, Emerald Sports, High Performance Sports Marketing and one of its top competitors in the racing card field, Press Pass. All of those acquisitions were a signal that Wheels was diversifying beyond just racing cards, offering a variety of NASCAR-licensed merchandise. Ironically, Wheels itself was purchased in December by Racing Champions, a leading manufacturer of die-cast products.

With manufacturers fighting for their fair share of the racing card market, collectors were treated to a number of innovative ideas in 1997. Press Pass, the company that pioneered the concept of race-used materials adhered to a tracing card, expanded on that theme in 1997. The Double Burners insert set from the Press Pass Premium release featured both race-used tires and firesuits built into the cards. The cards were found just 1:432 packs, with the Jeff Gordon and Dale Earnhardt versions finishing out the year valued at $250 each.

'97 Winston Cup champ Jeff Gordon remaines the hottest name in the racing card market

Press Pass also brought back its Sheet Metal cards in its VIP Racing set – utilizing sheet metal from cars onto laminated cards – and also introduced Action Vision, a 12-card set utilizing motion technology developed by the Kodak Company to show racing footage on a card. The Action Vision cards were sold in one-card packs for $7.99 each.

Upper Deck also joined in the race-used equipment game by offering an insert known as Piece of the Action. Swatches of race-worn firesuits, gloves and boots from Gordon, Rusty Wallace and Dale Jarrett were found on cards inserted 1:699 packs of the company's Victory Circle product. Meanwhile, the Piece of the Action inserts in Upper Deck's Road to the Cup set featured pieces of a driver's set, window net or safety harness. Values for these cards ranged from $300 for Gordon to $100 for Jarrett.

Pinnacle Brands came up with the most unique product in terms of packaging – Precision Racing was sold in cans that looked like containers of motor oil. Each $9.99 can featured a pack of cards and a beverage can cooler inside.

The one thing that remained constant in 1997 was the demand for Jeff Gordon's cards. The popular young driver dominated the NASCAR circuit in '97, winning the season-long Winston Cup driving title. His cards were the most popular in every set issued during the year. Long-time favorite and seven-time Winston Cup champ Dale Earnhardt also remained a top seller with collectors, as did veteran drivers Rusty Wallace and Dale Jarrett.

As 1998 began, four companies were committed to issuing cards of NASCAR drivers in the coming year. This downsizing may be a blessing for collectors, who had been overwhelmed by the number of racing card sets released during the previous two years. It may also be a blessing for the remaining companies, who can each enjoy a bigger piece of the racing card pie.

INSERT SINGLES

THE FOLLOWING LIST OF CARDS HAVE GENERATED THE MOST DEMAND WITHIN THE HOBBY OVER THE LAST YEAR. THE RANKINGS ARE DETERMINED BY COLLECTORS AND DEALERS FROM THE HOBBY.

No. 1 — JEFF GORDON
'97 Press Pass Premium Autograph #2
After winning his second NASCAR Winston Cup points championship in three years, Gordon continues to fuel demand for his cards. Demand for this scarce 1:72-pack autograph continues to be the strongest in the racing card hobby, as dealers report moving this one in the $250 neighborhood.

1997 PRESS PASS PREMIUM MIRROR JEFF BURTON #13

No. 2 — DALE EARNHARDT
'97 Press Pass Premium Autograph #4
Although his success on the track hasn't met his own or fans' expectations, Earnhardt continues to be a top-seller. This autograph books for $250.

No. 3 — JEFF GORDON
'96 Upper Deck Road to the Cup Autograph #H1
No Winston Cup driver is hotter on the track than Gordon, which has translated into strong sales for his cards. This autograph retails in the $200 range.

No. 4 — JEFF GORDON
'97 Wheels Jurassic Park Thunder Lizard #TL1
Only Wheels could think of putting lizard skin on a card. This 1:90-pack insert debuts at No. 4 and moves for $90.

No. 5 — DALE EARNHARDT
'97 Wheels Jurassic Park Thunder Lizard #TL8
The Intimidator isn't winning like he once did, but that hasn't stopped collectors from buying this one for $90.

No. 6 — JEFF GORDON
'97 Press Pass Premium Double Burner #DB2
The race-used concept has worked wonders for Press Pass. Dealers report moving this one in the $240 range.

No. 7 — JEFF GORDON
'97 Upper Deck Victory Circle Piece Of The Action #FS1
Any racing card collector would love to own a piece of Gordon's race-worn uniform, which is why this one is hot, selling for around $250.

No. 8 — JEFF GORDON
'97 Wheels Viper Diamondback Authentic #DBA1
Authentic snakeskin on a race card? It works for collectors. It's inserted 1:90 packs, and collectors aren't thinking twice about paying $80 for it.

No. 9 — DALE EARNHARDT
'97 Wheels Viper Diamondback Authentic #DBA8
Found 1:900 packs, this card has die-hard Earnhardt collectors doing a lot of pack-searching. The Intimidator's card goes for around $80.

No. 10 — DALE EARNHARDT
'97 Press Pass Premium Double Burner #DB1
While Earnhardt is searching for a way into the Winner's Circle, collectors are hunting for this rare $250 insert.

REGULAR-ISSUE SETS

THE FOLLOWING LIST OF SETS HAVE GENERATED THE MOST DEMAND WITHIN THE HOBBY OVER THE LAST YEAR. THE RANKINGS ARE DETERMINED BY COLLECTORS AND DEALERS FROM THE HOBBY.

No. 1 — 1997 WHEELS JURASSIC PARK
Wheels teamed with Universal Studios to release this dinosaur-themed product. Inserts include Thunder Lizards (1:90 packs), which feature actual lizard skin on each card, T-Rex (1:60), Pteranodon (1:30), Carnivore (1:15) and Raptors (1:6). Packs are moving for $3, with boxes in the $60-65 range. What will Wheels think of next? Stay tuned.

1997 PINNACLE MINT COLLECTION

No. 2 — 1997 PRESS PASS VIP
VIP drops from the pole position, but collectors continue to search for the Autographs (1:60) and Sheet Metal (1:384) inserts. Packs sell for $4.

No. 3 — 1997 WHEELS VIPER
For the second time, Wheels incorporates the snake theme with success. Packs are selling strong for $4, with boxes going for $70.

No. 4 — 1997 UPPER DECK ROAD TO THE CUP
Road to the Cup features Piece of the Action (1:117) and autographs of Gordon, Labonte and Wallace. Packs sell for $2.50, and boxes for $65.

No. 5 — 1997 PRESS PASS ACTIONVISION
Singles of Gordon are moving around $12-$15, with commons selling for $8. Packs are selling at $8-$9, with boxes and the 12-card set selling for $120.

No. 6 — 1997 PINNACLE ACTION PACKED
Action Packed continues to have a strong following in the racing card market, thanks to its unique design. Packs move for $3 and boxes for $60.

No. 7 — 1997 PRESS PASS PREMIUM
Collectors continue to chase the Double Burners and Autographs. Packs move for $4, with boxes at $75. The 45-card set books for $25.

No. 8 — 1997 UPPER DECK VICTORY CIRCLE
Collectors continue to chase the elusive Piece of the Actions, seeded 1:699 packs, along with Driver's Seat. Dealers are getting $2.50 per pack.

No. 9 — 1997 UPPER DECK SP
The Super Series three-flag inserts of Gordon and Earnhardt, along with their SP^X Force Autographs, are the main draw. Packs go for $3.50.

No. 10 — 1997 PRESS PASS
Racing card collectors love to chase the Burning Rubber inserts. Dealers report getting $2 per pack, with 24-count boxes moving for $40. The 140-card set carries a price tag of $20.

1996 Fleer Flair NASCAR

The 100-card set available in five-card packs features a double thick card with the driver's name and Flair logo in gold foil stamping. Each card has three photos, two on the front and one on the back. The 100-card set features NASCAR and Busch Grand National drivers along with owners, crew chiefs and cars.

		MT
Complete Set (100):		50.00
Common Card:		.25
Common Driver:		.50
Wax Box:		90.00
1	John Andretti	.50
2	Johnny Benson	.50
3	Brett Bodine	.50
4	Geoff Bodine	.50
5	Jeff Burton	.50
6	Ward Burton	.50
7	Derrike Cope	.50
8	Ricky Craven	.50
9	Wally Dallenbach, Jr.	.50
10	Dale Earnhardt	5.00
11	Bill Elliott	2.00
12	Jeff Gordon	5.00
13	Steve Grissom	.50
14	Bobby Hamilton	.50
15	Ernie Irvan	3.00
16	Dale Jarrett	2.50
17	Bobby Labonte	.25
18	Terry Labonte	3.00
19	Dave Marcis	.50
20	Sterling Marlin	.75
21	Mark Martin	3.00
22	Rick Mast	.50
23	Jeremy Mayfield	.50
24	Ted Musgrave	.50
25	Joe Nemechek	.50
26	Kyle Petty	.75
27	Robert Pressley	.50
28	Ricky Rudd	.50
29	Ken Schrader	.50
30	Lake Speed	.50
31	Jimmy Spencer	.50
32	Hut Stricklin	.50
33	Kenny Wallace	.50
34	Mike Wallace	.50
35	Rusty Wallace	3.00
36	Michael Waltrip	.50
37	Glenn Allen Jr.	.50
38	Rodney Combs	.50
39	David Green	.50
40	Randy LaJoie	.50
41	Chad Little	.50
42	Curtis Markham	.50
43	Mike McLaughlin	.50
44	Patty Moise	.50
45	Phil Parsons	.50
46	Jeff Purvis	.25
47	Bobby Allison	.50
48	Richard Childress	.25
49	Joe Gibbs	.25
50	Rick Hendrick	.25
51	Richard Petty	.75
52	Jack Roush	.25
53	Ray Evernham	.25
54	Todd Parrott	.25
55	Robin Pemberton	.25
56	David Smith	.25
57	Andretti #37 Ford	.25
58	Benson #30 Pontiac	.25
59	B. Bodine #11 Ford	.25
60	G. Bodine #7 Ford	.25
61	J. Burton #99 Ford	.25
62	W. Burton #22 Pontiac	.25
63	Cope #12 Ford	.25
64	Craven #41 Chevrolet	.25
65	Dallenbach #15 Ford	.25
66	Earnhardt #3 Chevrolet	3.00
67	Elliott #94 Ford	1.00
68	Gordon #24 Chevrolet	3.00
69	Grissom #29 Chevrolet	.25
70	Hamilton #43 Pontiac	.25
71	Irvan #28 Ford	1.50
72	Jarrett #88 Ford	1.25
73	B. Labonte #18 Chevrolet	.25
74	T. Labonte #5 Chevrolet	1.25
75	Marcis #71 Chevrolet	.25
76	Marlin #4 Chevrolet	1.00
77	Martin #6 Ford	1.50
78	Mast #1 Pontiac	.25
79	Mayfield #98 Ford	.25
80	Musgrave #16 Ford	.25
81	Nemechek #87 Chevrolet	.25
82	Petty #42 Pontiac	.25
83	Pressley #33 Chevrolet	.25
84	Rudd #10 Ford	.25
85	Schrader #25 Chevrolet	.25
86	Speed #9 Ford	.25
87	Spencer #23 Ford	.25
88	Stricklin #8 Ford	.25
89	K. Wallace #81 Ford	.25
90	M. Wallace #90 Ford	.25
91	R. Wallace #2 Ford	1.50
92	Waltrip #21 Ford	.25
93	Early Races	.25
94	Daytona 500	.25
95	Steve Grissom	.25
96	Bobby Labonte	.25
97	Terry Labonte	1.50
98	Mark Martin	1.50
99	Checklist	.25
100	Checklist	.25

1996 Fleer Flair NASCAR Autographs

The autographs are only available with redemption cards which were seeded 1:100 packs. The 12-card set featured many of the top NASCAR drivers including Jeff Gordon and Dale Earnhardt.

		MT
Complete Set (12):		800.00
Common Driver:		20.00
1	Ricky Craven	20.00
2	Dale Earnhardt	200.00
3	Bill Elliott	80.00
4	Jeff Gordon	200.00
5	Ernie Irvan	50.00
6	Dale Jarrett	50.00
7	Bobby Labonte	25.00
8	Terry Labonte	80.00
9	Sterling Marlin	30.00
10	Mark Martin	80.00
11	Ted Musgrave	20.00
12	Rusty Wallace	80.00

1996 Fleer Flair NASCAR Center Spotlight

Seeded 1:5 packs the 10-card set features the cars of NASCAR's leading drivers in a horizontal format.

		MT
Complete Set (10):		40.00
Common Driver:		1.50
1	Johnny Benson	1.50
2	Dale Earnhardt	12.00
3	Bill Elliott	5.00
4	Jeff Gordon	12.00
5	Steve Grissom	1.50
6	Bobby Hamilton	1.50
7	Terry Labonte	7.00
8	Mark Martin	7.00
9	Ricky Rudd	1.50
10	Rusty Wallace	7.00

1996 Fleer Flair NASCAR Hot Numbers

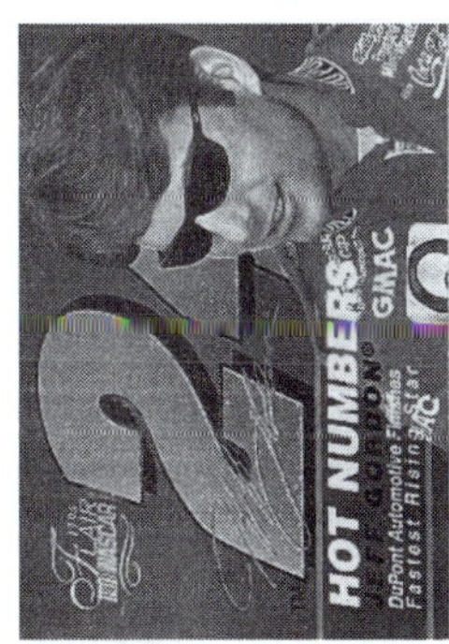

The 10-card set features holofoil stamping and embossed printing to showcase drivers favored by fans. The inserts were seeded 1:24 packs.

		MT
Complete Set (10):		160.00
Common Driver:		6.00
1	Dale Earnhardt	35.00
2	Bill Elliott	15.00
3	Jeff Gordon	35.00
4	Ernie Irvan	20.00
5	Dale Jarrett	20.00
6	Bobby Labonte	6.00
7	Terry Labonte	20.00
8	Mark Martin	20.00
9	Ricky Rudd	6.00
10	Rusty Wallace	20.00

1996 Fleer Flair NASCAR Power Performance

These 1:12 pack inserts feature the top-10 early season point leaders on a horizontal die-cut design.

		MT
Complete Set (10):		100.00
Common Driver:		3.50
1	Ricky Craven	3.50
2	Dale Earnhardt	25.00
3	Bill Elliott	10.00
4	Jeff Gordon	25.00
5	Dale Jarrett	15.00
6	Terry Labonte	15.00
7	Sterling Marlin	5.00
8	Mark Martin	15.00
9	Ricky Rudd	3.50
10	Rusty Wallace	15.00

1996 Fleer Ultra NASCAR Update

The 100-card Update set features a large Ultra logo as the backdrop on every card, with the bottom front of every card highlighting the team, driver and sponsor for each driver card. Available in 10-card packs the set features drivers, cars and Busch Grand National drivers.

		MT
Complete Set (100):		18.00
Common Player:		.10
Wax Box:		45.00
1	John Andretti	.10
2	Johnny Benson	.10
3	Brett Bodine	.10
4	Geoff Bodine	.10
5	Jeff Burton	.10
6	Ward Burton	.10
7	Derrike Cope	.10
8	Ricky Craven	.10
9	Wally Dallenbach, Jr.	.10
10	Dale Earnhardt	2.50
11	Bill Elliott	.75
12	Jeff Gordon	2.50
13	Steve Grissom	.10
14	Bobby Hamilton	.10
15	Ernie Irvan	.60
16	Dale Jarrett	.75
17	Bobby Labonte	.10
18	Terry Labonte	.75
19	Dave Marcis	.10
20	Sterling Marlin	.35
21	Mark Martin	1.25
22	Rick Mast	.10
23	Jeremy Mayfield	.10
24	Ted Musgrave	.10
25	Joe Nemechek	.10
26	Kyle Petty	.10
27	Robert Pressley	.10
28	Ricky Rudd	.10
29	Ken Schrader	.10
30	Hut Stricklin	.10
31	Kenny Wallace	.10
32	Rusty Wallace	1.25
33	Michael Waltrip	.10
34	Glenn Allen Jr.	.10
35	Rodney Combs	.10
36	David Green	.10
37	Randy LaJoie	.10
38	Chad Little	.10
39	Curtis Markham	.10
40	Mike McLaughlin	.10
41	Patty Moise	.10
42	Phil Parsons	.10
43	Jeff Purvis	.10
44	Dale Jarrett (Daytona)	.75
45	Dale Earnhardt (Rockingham, Atlanta)	2.50
46	Jeff Gordon (Richmond, Darlington)	2.50
47	#37 Ford Andretti	.10
48	#30 Pontiac Benson	.10
49	#11 Ford B. Bodine	.10
50	#7 Ford G. Bodine	.10
51	#99 Ford J. Burton	.10
52	#22 Pontiac W. Burton	.10
53	#12 Ford Cope	.10
54	#41 Chevrolet Craven	.10
55	#15 Ford Dallenbach	.10
56	#3 Chevrolet Earnhardt	1.00
57	#94 Ford Elliott	.30
58	#24 Chevrolet Gordon	1.00
59	#29 Chevrolet Grissom	.10
60	#43 Pontiac Hamilton	.10
61	#28 Ford Irvan	.30
62	#88 Ford Jarrett	.30
63	#18 Chevrolet B. Labonte	.10
64	#5 Chevrolet T. Labonte	.40
65	#71 Chevrolet Marcis	.10
66	#4 Chevrolet Marlin	.25
67	#6 Ford Martin	.50
68	#1 Pontiac Mast	.10
69	#98 Ford Mayfield	.10
70	#16 Ford Musgrave	.10
71	#87 Chevrolet Nemechek	.10

72	#42 Pontiac Petty	.10
73	#33 Chevrolet Pressley	.10
74	#10 Ford Rudd	.10
75	#25 Chevrolet Schrader	.10
76	#8 Ford Stricklin	.10
77	#81 Ford K. Wallace	.10
78	#2 Ford R. Wallace	.50
79	#21 Ford M. Waltrip	.10
80	Bill Elliott (McDonalds Car)	.10
81	Terry Labonte/Ripken (Ironman Car)	.30
82	Bobby Hamilton (25th Anniversary)	.10
83	Brett Bodine (Gold Car)	.10
84	Wally Dallenbach, Jimmy Means (Hayes Modem)	.10
85	Jeff Burton, Buddy Parrott (Exide Batteries)	.10
86	Dale Jarrett, Todd Parrott (Quality Care)	.40
87	Hut Stricklin, Philippe Lopez (Circuit City)	.10
88	Michael Waltrip (#21 Team)	.10
89	Morgan Shepherd (#75 Team/Remington Arms)	.10
90	Kenny Wallace (Square D)	.10
91	Ernie Irvan (Return)	.30
92	Rick Mast (Hooters)	.10
93	Geoff Bodine (QVC)	.10
94	Ricky Rudd, Richard Broome	.10
95	Brett Bodine, Donnie Richeson	.10
96	Dale Earnhardt, David Smith	1.00
97	Steve Grissom, Bill Ingle (Hanna Barbera)	.10
98	Johnny Benson	.10
99	Checklist	.10
100	Checklist	.10

1996 Fleer Ultra NASCAR Update Autographs

Autographs were only available by sending in the redemption cards in Ultra Update, which were seeded 1:100 packs. There were 10-autographs in the set.

		MT
Complete Set (12):		600.00
Common Autograph:		10.00
2	Dale Earnhardt	180.00
3	Bill Elliott	50.00
4	Jeff Gordon	180.00
5	Ernie Irvan	40.00
6	Dale Jarrett	40.00
8	Terry Labonte	60.00
9	Sterling Marlin	25.00
10	Mark Martin	60.00
12	Rusty Wallace	60.00

1996 Fleer Ultra NASCAR Update Proven Power

The 15-card set features 100% foil treatment, which showcase the point leaders from the 1995 and 1996 Winston Cup seasons. The inserts were seeded 1:72 packs.

		MT
Complete Set (15):		240.00
Common Driver:		10.00
1	Ricky Craven	10.00
2	Dale Earnhardt	45.00

3	Bill Elliott	20.00
4	Jeff Gordon	45.00
5	Bobby Hamilton	10.00
6	Dale Jarrett	15.00
7	Bobby Labonte	10.00
8	Terry Labonte	18.00
9	Sterling Marlin	12.00
10	Mark Martin	25.00
11	Jeremy Mayfield	10.00
12	Ted Musgrave	10.00
13	Ricky Rudd	10.00
14	Ken Schrader	10.00
15	Rusty Wallace	25.00

1996 Fleer Ultra NASCAR Update Rising Star

This five-card set salutes the hottest new drivers on the Winston Cup Circuit. Seeded 1:4 packs, the cards feature gold foil enhancing along with a themo-embossed black ink that's supposed to feel like tire rubber.

		MT
Complete Set (5):		8.00
Common Driver:		2.00
1	John Andretti	2.00
2	Johnny Benson	2.00
3	Jeff Burton	2.00
4	Ricky Craven	3.00
5	Jeremy Mayfield	2.00

1996 Fleer Ultra NASCAR Update Winner!

This 18-card set honors one winner from every track during the 1995 season. The 1:3 pack inserts feature a portrait of the winning driver, the track and date he won along with a photo of the winner's car.

		MT
Complete Set (18):		25.00
Common Driver:		.75
1	Atlanta J. Gordon	4.00
2	Bristol T. Labonte	1.50
3	Charlotte B. Labonte	.75
4	Darlington J. Gordon	4.00
5	Daytona S. Marlin	1.00
6	Dover K. Petty	.75
7	Indianapolis D. Earnhardt	4.00
8	Martinsville R. Wallace	2.00
9	Michigan B. Labonte	.75
10	New Hampshire J. Gordon	4.00
11	North Wilkesboro M. Martin	2.00
12	Phoenix R. Rudd	.75
13	Pocono D. Jarrett	1.50

14	Richmond T. Labonte	1.50
15	Rockingham W. Burton	.75
16	Sears Point D. Earnhardt	4.00
17	Talladega S. Marlin	1.00
18	Watkins Glen M. Martin	2.00

1996 Pinnacle

The 96-card set features the Pinnacle logo in the upper left hand corner on the card front with gold-foil stamping in the shape of a triangle on the bottom. The backs feature the driver's lifetime stats along with a brief commentary. They were available in eight-card packs.

		MT
Complete Set (96):		20.00
Common Driver:		.10
Gordons: 66-73		1.50
Wax Box:		60.00
1	Rick Mast	.10
2	Rusty Wallace	1.50
3	Dale Earnhardt	3.00
4	Sterling Marlin	.30
5	Terry Labonte	1.00
6	Mark Martin	1.50
7	Geoff Bodine	.10
8	Hut Strickland	.10
9	Lake Speed	.10
10	Ricky Rudd	.10
11	Brett Bodine	.10
12	Derrike Cope	.10
13	Dale Jarrett	.75
14	Joe Nemechek	.10
15	Wally Dallenbach	.10
16	Ted Musgrave	.10
17	Darrell Waltrip	.10
18	Bobby Labonte	.10
19	Kenny Wallace	.10
20	Bobby Hillin, Jr.	.10
21	Michael Waltrip	.10
22	Ward Burton	.10
23	Jimmy Spencer	.10
24	Jeff Gordon	3.00
25	Ken Schrader	.10
26	Morgan Shepherd	.10
27	Bill Elliott	1.50
28	Ernie Irvan	1.00
29	Bobby Hamilton	.10
30	Johnny Benson	.10
31	Kyle Petty	.10
32	Ricky Craven	.10
33	Robert Pressley	.10
34	John Andretti	.10
35	Jeremy Mayfield	.10
36	R. Mast Car	.10
37	R. Wallace Car	.75
38	D. Earnhardt Car	1.50
39	S. Marlin Car	.20
40	T. Labonte Car	.50
41	M. Martin Car	.75
42	G. Bodine Car	.10
43	R. Rudd Car	.10
44	D. Cope Car	.10
45	T. Musgrave Car	.10
46	D. Waltrip Car	.10
47	B. Labonte Car	.10
48	M. Waltrip Car	.10
49	W. Burton Car	.10
50	J. Spencer Car	.10
51	J. Gordon Car	1.50
52	E. Irvan Car	.50
53	J. Benson Car	.10
54	R. Pressley Car	.10
55	J. Andretti Car	.10
56	R. Craven Car	.10
57	K. Petty Car	.10
58	#43 Petty Enterprises	.10

59	#71 Marcis Auto Racing	.10
60	M. Shepherd Car	.10
61	B. Hillin Car	.10
62	K. Wallace	.10
63	J. Nemechek Car	.10
64	D. Jarrett Car	.20
65	H. Stricklin Car	.10
66	Jeff Gordon	1.50
67	Jeff Gordon	1.50
68	Jeff Gordon	1.50
69	Jeff Gordon	1.50
70	Jeff Gordon	1.50
71	Jeff Gordon	1.50
72	Jeff Gordon	1.50
73	Jeff Gordon	1.50
74	Sterling Marlin	.20
75	Sterling Marlin	.20
76	Sterling Marlin	.20
77	Sterling Marlin	.20
78	Hall of Fame Car	.10
79	Bobby Labonte	.25
80	Jimmy Makar	.10
81	Hall of Fame Car	.10
82	Elmo Langley	.10
83	Doyle Ford	.10
84	Buster Auton	.10
85	Jeff Gordon	1.50
86	Rusty Wallace	.75
87	Sterling Marlin	.20
88	Ernie Irvan	.50
89	Rusty Wallace	.75
90	Joe Gibbs Racing	.10
91	R. Childress Racing	.10
92	R. Hendrick Racing	.10
93	Morgan-McClure Motorsports	.10
94	Penske Racing	.10
95	Jeff Gordon CL	1.00
96	Mark Martin CL	.50

1996 Pinnacle Winston Cup Collection

A 96-card parallel to the base set, these 1:9 pack inserts utilize Dufex printing.

		MT
Complete Set (96):		150.00
Common Driver:		.75
Winston Cup Collections:		4x to 8x

1996 Pinnacle Artist's Proofs

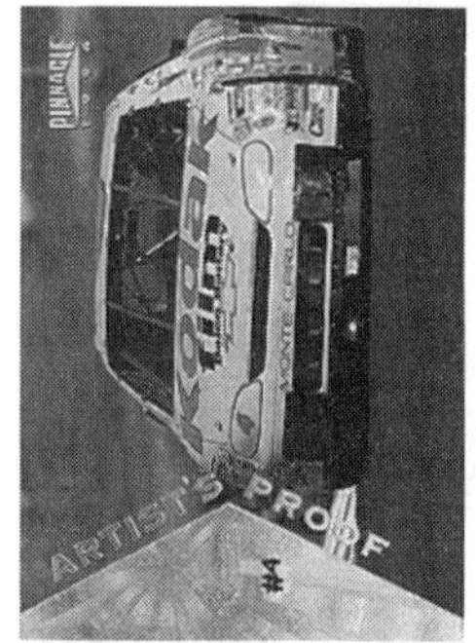

A parallel to the base set, Artist's Proofs are distinctive by the Artist's Proof logo along with Rainbow foil stamping. They were seeded 1:47 packs.

	MT
Complete Set (96):	500.00
Common Driver:	3.00
Artist's Proofs:	15x to 25x

1996 Pinnacle Bill's Back

This 2-card tribute Bill Elliot's return to racing following his potentially career ending crash. This special set is printed on all-foil Dufex card stock and is seeded 1:300 packs.

		MT
Complete Set (2):		100.00
Common Elliott:		50.00
1	Bill Elliott	50.00
2	Bill Elliott	50.00

1996 Pinnacle Cut Above

The 15-card set highlights the top drivers on the Winston Cup Circuit, utilizing a die-cut, foil stamped card stock. They are seeded 1:24 packs.

		MT
Complete Set (15):		125.00
Common Driver:		5.00
1	Jeff Gordon	25.00
2	Bill Elliott	12.00
3	Terry Labonte	12.00
4	Ernie Irvan	10.00
5	Dale Earnhardt	25.00
6	Ricky Rudd	5.00
7	Dale Jarrett	10.00
8	Rusty Wallace	12.00
9	Bobby Labonte	5.00
10	Mark Martin	12.00
11	Ricky Craven	5.00
12	Robert Pressley	5.00
13	Ted Musgrave	5.00
14	Sterling Marlin	6.00
15	John Andretti	5.00

1996 Pinnacle Driver's Suit Cloth

The 2-card set is printed on pieces of actual driver uniforms from Bill Elliott and Johnny Benson Jr. They are inserted 1:270 packs.

		MT
Complete Set (2):		250.00
Common Driver:		75.00
1	Bill Elliott	175.00
2	Johnny Benson	75.00

1996 Pinnacle Team Pinnacle

Featuring 12 of the top drivers on the NASCAR circuit, Team Pinnacle inserts appear in 1:90 packs. They picture a driver on the front with their owner or crew chief pictured on the flipside. The inserts utilize Dufex technology.

		MT
Complete Set (12):		150.00
Common Driver:		10.00
1	Jeff Gordon	90.00
2	Rusty Wallace	50.00
3	Dale Earnhardt	90.00
4	Dale Jarrett	30.00
5	Terry Labonte	50.00
6	Mark Martin	50.00
7	Bill Elliott	40.00
8	Sterling Marlin	20.00
9	Ricky Rudd	10.00
10	Jeff Gordon	90.00
11	Dale Earnhardt	90.00
12	Dale Jarrett	30.00

1996 Pinnacle Speedflix

The 100-card set features a printing process that allows multiple images of the driver to exist on the same card. The set also includes subsets of Dale Earnhardt, Jeff Gordon, Mark Martin, Ernie Irvan, Rusty Wallace, Bill Elliott and Ricky Rudd.

		MT
Complete Set (100):		20.00
Common Driver:		.10
Earnhardt's & Gordon's 60-75:		1.00
Irvan's (76-79) & Elliott's (88-91):		.25
Martin's (80-83) & Wallace's (84-87):		.50
Artist's Proofs:		12x to 20x
Complete Artist's Proof Set (100):		275.00
Wax Box:		30.00
1	Rusty Wallace	1.00
2	Dale Earnhardt	2.00
3	Sterling Marlin	.25
4	Terry Labonte	.50
5	Mark Martin	1.00
6	Bill Elliott	.50
7	Jeff Burton	.10
8	John Andretti	.10
9	Ricky Rudd	.10
10	Brett Bodine	.10
11	Bobby Hamilton	.10
12	Ted Musgrave	.10
13	Darrell Waltrip	.10
14	Bobby Labonte	.10
15	Michael Waltrip	.10
16	Ernie Irvan	.50
17	Jeff Gordon	2.00
18	Ken Schrader	.10
19	Dale Jarrett	.40
20	Johnny Benson	.10
21	Rick Mast	.10
22	Geoff Bodine	.10
23	Ward Burton	.10
24	Kenny Wallace	.10
25	Jeff Gordon	2.00
26	Dale Earnhardt	2.00
27	Rusty Wallace	1.00
28	Sterling Marlin	.25
29	Mark Martin	1.00
30	Ricky Rudd	.10
31	Darrell Waltrip	.10
32	Bobby Labonte	.10
33	Dale Jarrett	.40
34	Michael Waltrip	.10
35	Ken Schrader	.10
36	Bill Elliott	.50
37	Ernie Irvan	.50
38	Ted Musgrave	.10
39	Terry Labonte	.50
40	Bobby Hillin, Jr.	.10
41	John Andretti	.10
42	Bobby Hamilton	.10
43	Steve Grissom	.10
44	Kenny Wallace	.10
45	Penske (Racing South #2)	.10
46	Richard Childress (Racing #3)	.10
47	Morgan, McClure (Motorsports #4)	.10
48	Hendrick (Motorsports #5)	.10
49	Roush (Racing #6)	.10
50	Rudd (Performance Racing #10)	.10
51	Elliott, Hardy (Racing #94)	.10
52	BDR Racing #11	.10
53	Hendrick (Motorsports #24)	.10
54	Joe Gibbs (Racing #18)	.10
55	Terry Labonte	.30
56	Dale Jarrett	.25
57	Michael Waltrip	.10
58	Kenny Wallace	.10
59	Mark Martin	.60
60	Dale Earnhardt	1.00
61	Dale Earnhardt	1.00
62	Dale Earnhardt	1.00
63	Dale Earnhardt	1.00
64	Dale Earnhardt	1.00
65	Dale Earnhardt	1.00
66	Dale Earnhardt	1.00
67	Dale Earnhardt	1.00
68	Jeff Gordon	1.00
69	Jeff Gordon	1.00
70	Jeff Gordon	1.00
71	Jeff Gordon	1.00
72	Jeff Gordon	1.00
73	Jeff Gordon	1.00
74	Jeff Gordon	1.00
75	Jeff Gordon	1.00
76	Ernie Irvan	.25
77	Ernie Irvan	.25
78	Ernie Irvan	.25
79	Ernie Irvan	.25
80	Mark Martin	.50
81	Mark Martin	.50
82	Mark Martin	.50
83	Mark Martin	.50
84	Rusty Wallace	.50
85	Rusty Wallace	.50
86	Rusty Wallace	.50
87	Rusty Wallace	.50
88	Bill Elliott	.25
89	Bill Elliott	.25
90	Bill Elliott	.25
91	Bill Elliott	.25
92	Ricky Rudd	.10
93	Ricky Rudd	.10
94	Ricky Rudd	.10
95	Ricky Rudd	.10
96	Rockingham (Winners)	.10
97	Richmond (Winners)	.10
98	Atlanta (Winners)	.10
99	Jeff Gordon CL	.75
100	Dale Earnhardt CL	.75

1996 Pinnacle Speedflix Clear Shots

These inserts were available only in jumbo packs seeded 1:31 packs. The 12-card set features two-frame animation printed on clear vinyl stock for a see-through effect.

		MT
Complete Set (12):		60.00
Common Driver:		4.00
1	Dale Earnhardt	15.00
2	Jeff Gordon	15.00
3	Sterling Marlin	4.00
4	Rusty Wallace	8.00
5	Bobby Labonte	4.00
6	Terry Labonte	6.00
7	Dale Jarrett	6.00
8	Mark Martin	8.00
9	Bill Elliott	6.00
10	Ernie Irvan	6.00
11	Ted Musgrave	4.00
12	Johnny Benson	4.00

1996 Pinnacle Speedflix In Motion

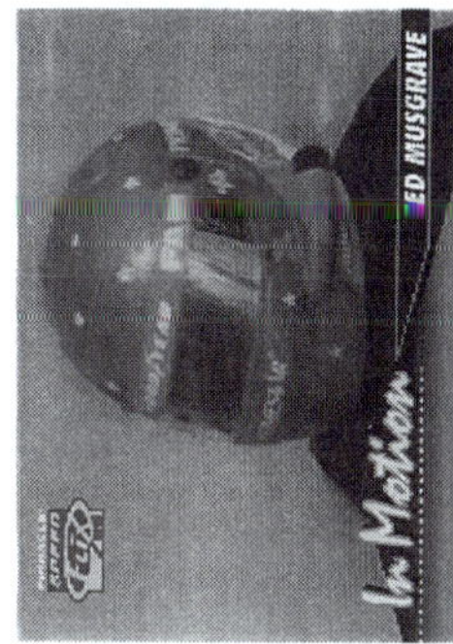

This 10-card set features Optiview technology, by photographing drivers' helmets on a turnstile, they provide a full 360-degree look at the headgear of the drivers in the set. They are inserted 1:48 packs.

		MT
Complete Set (10):		90.00
Common Driver:		8.00
1	Dale Earnhardt	20.00
2	Jeff Gordon	20.00
3	Sterling Marlin	6.00
4	Rusty Wallace	14.00
5	Bobby Labonte	8.00
6	Terry Labonte	10.00
7	Ernie Irvan	10.00
8	Mark Martin	14.00
9	Ricky Rudd	8.00
10	Bill Elliott	10.00

1996 Pinnacle Speedflix ProMotion

This 12-card insert set shows a driver climbing out of his car. They are inserted 1:9 packs.

		MT
Complete Set (12):		30.00
Common Driver:		1.50
1	Dale Earnhardt	10.00
2	Jeff Gordon	10.00
3	Sterling Marlin	1.50
4	Rusty Wallace	5.00
5	Bobby Labonte	1.50
6	Terry Labonte	3.00
7	Dale Jarrett	2.50
8	Mark Martin	5.00
9	Bill Elliott	3.00
10	Darrell Waltrip	1.50
11	Ricky Rudd	1.50
12	Ted Musgrave	1.50

1996 Pinnacle Zenith

The 100-card set features 18-point stock along with subsets highlighting Jeff Gordon and Dale Earnhardt, the Pinnacle Zenith logo is gold foil stamped on the upper right hand corner of the driver's cards. Available in six-card packs, inserts include Champion Salutes, Artist's Proofs, Highlights and Seven Wonders.

		MT
Complete Set (100):		50.00
Common Driver:		.25
Earnhardt's (65-69):		2.00
Gordon's (73-80):		2.00
Wax Box:		75.00
1	Dale Earnhardt	5.00
2	Jeff Gordon	5.00
3	Sterling Marlin	.50
4	Terry Labonte	2.50
5	Ricky Rudd	.25
6	Mark Martin	2.50
7	Bill Elliott	2.50
8	Ernie Irvan	1.50
9	Rusty Wallace	2.50
10	Dale Jarrett	1.50
11	Geoff Bodine	.25
12	Derrike Cope	.25
13	Michael Waltrip	.25
14	Brett Bodine	.25
15	Ted Musgrave	.25
16	Hut Stricklin	.25
17	Rick Mast	.25
18	Darrell Waltrip	.25
19	Bobby Labonte	.25
20	Jeff Burton	.25
21	Jeremy Mayfield	.25
22	Ken Schrader	.25
23	Johnny Benson	.25
24	Dave Marcus	.25
25	John Andretti	.25
26	Robert Pressley	.25
27	Kyle Petty	.25
28	Ricky Craven	.25
29	Bobby Hamilton	.25
30	Joe Nemechek	.25
31	Morgan Shepherd	.25
32	Bobby Hillin, Jr.	.25
33	Jimmy Spencer	.25
34	Ward Burton	.25
35	Dale Earnhardt	5.00
36	Jeff Gordon	5.00
37	Sterling Marlin	.50
38	Mark Martin	2.50
39	Terry Labonte	2.50
40	Bobby Labonte	.25
41	Darrell Waltrip	.25
42	Ernie Irvan	1.50
43	Dale Jarrett	1.50
44	Bobby Hamilton	.25
45	Bill Elliott	2.50
46	Joe Nemechek	.25
47	Dave Marcus	.25
48	Kyle Petty	.25
49	Michael Waltrip	.25
50	Dale Earnhardt	2.50
51	Jeff Gordon	2.50
52	Mark Martin	1.25
53	Ricky Rudd	.25
54	Terry Labonte	1.25
55	Kyle Petty	.25
56	Bobby Hillin, Jr.	.25
57	Ted Musgrave	.25
58	Ken Schrader	.25
59	John Andretti	.25
60	Dale Jarrett	.75
61	Johnny Benson	.25
62	Michael Waltrip	.25
63	Bobby Labonte	.25
64	Ernie Irvan	.75
65	Dale Earnhardt	2.00
66	Dale Earnhardt	2.00
67	Dale Earnhardt	2.00
68	Dale Earnhardt	2.00
69	Dale Earnhardt	2.00
70	Terry Labonte	1.00
71	Ricky Craven	.25
72	Ricky Craven	.25
73	Jeff Gordon	2.00
74	Jeff Gordon	2.00
75	Jeff Gordon	2.00
76	Jeff Gordon	2.00
77	Jeff Gordon	2.00
78	Jeff Gordon	2.00
79	Jeff Gordon	2.00
80	Jeff Gordon	2.00
81	Kenny Wallace	.25
82	Kenny Wallace	.25
83	Kenny Wallace	.25
84	Kenny Wallace	.25
85	Kenny Wallace	.25
86	Robert Yates	.25
87	Ernie Irvan	.75
88	Larry McReynolds	.25
89	Dale Jarrett	.75
90	Todd Parrott	.25
91	Jeff Gordon	2.00
92	Jeff Gordon	2.00
93	Terry Labonte	1.00
94	Rusty Wallace	1.00
95	Sterling Marlin	.40
96	Rusty Wallace	1.00
97	Dale Jarrett	.75
98	Jeff Gordon	2.00
99	Jeff Gordon	2.00
100	Bill Elliott	1.00

1996 Pinnacle Zenith Artist's Proofs

The 100-card parallel set is printed on gold rainbow holographic foil and are inserted at a 1:24 pack rate.

	MT
Complete Set (100):	750.00
Common Driver:	5.00
Artist's Proofs:	15x to 30x

1996 Pinnacle Zenith Champion Salute

Champion Salute is a 26-card tribute to the last 25 years of NASCAR Winston Cup racing. Each card spotlights all of the past champions and tops off the salute with a real diamond chip along with a photograph of an actual NASCAR championship ring. They are seeded 1:90 packs.

		MT
Complete Set (26):		1000.
Common Driver:		20.00
1	Jeff Gordon	140.00
2	Dale Earnhardt	90.00
3	Alan Kulwicki	20.00
4	Dale Earnhardt	90.00
5	Dale Earnhardt	90.00
6	Rusty Wallace	60.00
7	Bill Elliott	60.00
8	Dale Earnhardt	90.00
9	Dale Earnhardt	90.00
10	Darrell Waltrip	20.00
11	Terry Labonte	60.00
12	Bobby Allison	20.00
13	Darrell Waltrip	20.00
14	Darrell Waltrip	20.00
15	Dale Earnhardt	90.00
16	Richard Petty	40.00
17	Cale Yarborough	40.00
18	Cale Yarborough	40.00
19	Cale Yarborough	40.00
20	Richard Petty	40.00
21	Richard Petty	40.00
22	Benny Parsons	20.00
23	Richard Petty	40.00
24	Richard Petty	40.00
25	Richard Childress	20.00
26	Don Hawk	20.00

1996 Pinnacle Zenith Highlights

The 15-card die-cut set features the top NASCAR drivers and personal information about each driver. The insertion rate for Highlights is 1:11 packs.

		MT
Complete Set (15):		100.00
Common Driver:		4.00
1	Dale Earnhardt	20.00
2	Jeff Gordon	20.00
3	Sterling Marlin	5.00
4	Mark Martin	12.00
5	Ricky Rudd	4.00
6	Darrell Waltrip	4.00
7	Geoff Bodine	4.00
8	Bobby Labonte	4.00
9	Terry Labonte	12.00
10	Michael Waltrip	4.00
11	Ken Schrader	4.00
12	Jimmy Spencer	4.00
13	Kyle Petty	4.00
14	Ernie Irvan	8.00
15	Bill Elliott	12.00

1996 Pinnacle Zenith Seven Wonders

Honoring Dale Earnhardt's 1994 Winston Cup Championship, the Seven Wonders card contains multiple diamonds and is hand numbered. It is seeded 1:6,156 packs.

	MT
Seven Wonders	750.00

1996 Upper Deck SP

Available in seven-card packs the 84-card set features Dale Earnhardt for the first time in an Upper Deck racing product. The set features a photo of the driver along with his sponsor in Silver-foil stamping on the bottom front. The backs show the driver's stats from the 1995 season along with a brief commentary. Inserts include Holoviews, Holoview Die-Cuts, Driving Force, Richard Petty Tribute, Racing Legends and Driving Ace's, which feature Gordon and Earnhardt and is seeded 1:257 packs.

		MT
Complete Set (84):		25.00
Common Driver:		.20
Driving Aces (Earnhardt & Gordon):		150.00
Wax Box:		60.00
1	Rick Mast	.20
2	Rusty Wallace	2.00
3	Dale Earnhardt	4.00
4	Sterling Marlin	.50
5	Terry Labonte	2.00
6	Mark Martin	2.00
7	Geoff Bodine	.20
8	Hut Stricklin	.20
9	Lake Speed	.20
10	Ricky Rudd	.20
11	Brett Bodine	.20
12	Derrike Cope	.20
13	Bill Elliott	2.00
14	Bobby Hamilton	.20
15	Wally Dallenbach	.20
16	Ted Musgrave	.20
17	Darrell Waltrip	.20
18	Bobby Labonte	.20
19	Loy Allen	.20
20	Morgan Shepherd	.20
21	Michael Waltrip	.20
22	Ward Burton	.20
23	Jimmy Spencer	.20
24	Jeff Gordon	4.00
25	Ken Schrader	.20
26	Kyle Petty	.20
27	Bobby Hillin	.20
28	Ernie Irvan	1.50
29	Steve Grissom	.20
30	Johnny Benson	.20
31	Dave Marcis	.20
32	Jeremy Mayfield	.20
33	Robert Pressley	.20
34	Jeff Burton	.20
35	Joe Nemechek	.20
36	Dale Jarrett	1.50
37	John Andretti	.20
38	Kenny Wallace	.20
39	Mike Wallace	.20
40	Dick Trickle	.20
41	Ricky Craven	.20
42	Chad Little	.20
43	Jeff Gordon	2.00
44	Sterling Marlin	.35
45	Mark Martin	1.00
46	Rusty Wallace	1.00
47	Terry Labonte	1.00
48	Ted Musgrave	.20
49	Bill Elliott	1.00
50	Ricky Rudd	.20
51	Bobby Labonte	.20
52	Morgan Shepherd	.20
53	Michael Waltrip	.20
54	Dale Jarrett	.75
55	Bobby Hamilton	.20
56	Derrike Cope	.20
57	Geoff Bodine	.20

58	Ken Schrader	.20
59	John Andretti	.20
60	Darrell Waltrip	.20
61	Brett Bodine	.20
62	Kenny Wallace	.20
63	Ward Burton	.20
64	Lake Speed	.20
65	Ricky Craven	.20
66	Jimmy Spencer	.20
67	Steve Grissom	.20
68	Joe Nemechek	.20
69	Ernie Irvan	.75
70	Kyle Petty	.20
71	Johnny Benson	.20
72	Jeff Burton	.20
73	Dave Marcis	.20
74	Jeremy Mayfield	.20
75	Michael Waltrip (RPM)	.20
76	Dale Jarrett (RPM)	.75
77	Johnny Benson (RPM)	.20
78	Ricky Craven (RPM)	.20
79	Rusty Wallace (RPM)	1.00
80	Jeff Gordon (RPM)	2.00
81	Terry Labonte (RPM)	1.00
82	Sterling Marlin (RPM)	.35
83	Mark Martin (RPM)	1.00
84	Ernie Irvan (RPM)	.75

1996 Upper Deck SP Driving Force

This die-cut set highlights ten of the hottest up-and-coming drivers in racing. The fronts feature a close-up photo along with a photo of his helmet with the backs offering a bit of commentary for each driver. They are seeded 1:30 packs.

		MT
Complete Set (10):		65.00
Common Driver:		8.00
DF1	Johnny Benson	8.00
DF2	Jeremy Mayfield	8.00
DF3	Brett Bodine	8.00
DF4	Robert Pressley	8.00
DF5	Jeff Burton	8.00
DF6	Ricky Craven	8.00
DF7	Wally Dallenbach	8.00
DF8	Bobby Labonte	8.00
DF9	Kenny Wallace	8.00
DF10	Bobby Hamilton	8.00

1996 Upper Deck SP Holoview Maximum Effects

This set features Upper Deck's Holoview technology, which allows the collector to see his favorite driver in motion. The horizontal inserts have a color photo of the driver on back along with a brief commentary. They are seeded 1:6 packs.

	MT
Complete Set (25):	100.00
Common Driver:	3.00
ME1 Jeff Gordon	15.00
ME2 Rusty Wallace	9.00
ME3 Dale Earnhardt	15.00
ME4 Sterling Marlin	4.00
ME5 Terry Labonte	9.00
ME6 Mark Martin	9.00
ME7 Geoff Bodine	3.00
ME8 Johnny Benson	3.00
ME9 Derrike Cope	3.00
ME10 Ricky Rudd	3.00
ME11 Ricky Craven	3.00
ME12 John Andretti	3.00
ME13 Ken Schrader	3.00
ME14 Ernie Irvan	7.00
ME15 Steve Grissom	3.00
ME16 Ted Musgrave	3.00
ME17 Darrell Waltrip	3.00
ME18 Bobby Labonte	3.00
ME19 Kyle Petty	3.00
ME20 Bobby Hamilton	3.00
ME21 Kenny Wallace	3.00
ME22 Dale Jarrett	7.00
ME23 Bill Elliott	9.00
ME24 Jeremy Mayfield	3.00
ME25 Jeff Burton	3.00

1996 Upper Deck SP Holoview Maximum Effects Die-Cut

Identical to the regular Holoview Maximum Effects other than they are die-cut. The 25-card set inserts are seeded 1:73 packs.

	MT
Complete Set (25):	500.00
Common Driver:	12.00
Die-Cuts:	4x to 8x

1996 Upper Deck SP Petty/STP 25th Anniversary Tribute

This nine-card insert set pays tribute to the "King". The die-cut inserts provide a historical perspective on the great career of Petty, chronicling his 25-year Anniversary relationship with STP. They were inserted 1:47 packs.

	MT
Complete Set (10):	175.00
Common Petty:	20.00
RP1 Richard Petty	20.00
RP2 Richard Petty	20.00
RP3 Richard Petty	20.00
RP4 Richard Petty	20.00
RP5 Richard Petty	20.00
RP6 Richard Petty	20.00
RP7 Richard Petty	20.00
RP8 Richard Petty	20.00
RP9 Richard Petty	20.00
RP10 Richard Petty	20.00

1996 Upper Deck SP Racing Legends Collection

This five-card set is a continuation from a 10-card series in both '96 Upper Deck and '96 Upper Deck Road to the Cup. They are numbered with a prefix "RL" with the five cards finishing the series RL21-RL25. They are inserted 1:15 packs.

	MT
Complete Set (5):	60.00
Common Driver:	5.00
RL21 Rusty Wallace	15.00
RL22 Bill Elliott	15.00
RL23 Mark Martin	15.00
RL24 Jeff Gordon	25.00
RL25 Header	5.00

1996 Upper Deck SPx

Available in one-card packs, the 25-card base set utilizes Upper Deck's Holoview technology. The card fronts along with the Holoview have a color photo of the driver as well as his car number. The backs feature the driver's stats along with another photo of the driver and a brief commentary.

		MT
Complete Set (25):		45.00
Common Driver:		1.00
Wax Box:		90.00
1	Jeff Gordon	10.00
2	Rusty Wallace	5.00
3	Dale Earnhardt	10.00
4	Sterling Marlin	1.50
5	Terry Labonte	5.00
6	Mark Martin	5.00
7	Jeff Burton	1.00
8	Bobby Hamilton	1.00
9	Lake Speed	1.00
10	Ricky Rudd	1.00
11	Brett Bodine	1.00
12	Derrike Cope	1.00
13	Jeremy Mayfield	1.00
14	Ricky Craven	1.00
15	Johnny Benson	1.00
16	Ted Musgrave	1.00
17	Darrell Waltrip	1.00
18	Bobby Labonte	1.00
19	Steve Grissom	1.00
20	Kyle Petty	1.00
21	Michael Waltrip	1.00
22	Ernie Irvan	4.00
23	Dale Jarrett	4.00
24	Bill Elliott	5.00
25	Ken Schrader	1.00

1996 Upper Deck SPx Gold

A parallel to the 25-card base set and the same as the regular cards other than the border is draped in gold. They are seeded 1:7 packs.

	MT
Complete Set (25):	200.00
Common Driver:	3.00
Golds:	4x

1996 Upper Deck SPx Elite

The five-card die-cut insert set highlights five of the most elite drivers in racing. Seeded 1:23 packs, the inserts utilize Holoview technology along with a color photo of the driver on the front. The backs have a picture of the driver and his car.

		MT
Complete Set (5):		125.00
Common Driver:		10.00
E1	Jeff Gordon	50.00
E2	Dale Jarrett	15.00
E3	Terry Labonte	20.00
E4	Rusty Wallace	30.00
E5	Ernie Irvan	20.00

1996 Upper Deck SPx Jeff Gordon Tribute

Upper Deck's Tribute to the hottest new star in the Winston Cup Circuit. Numbered T1 and is seeded 1:71 packs. Also available is an autographed version seeded 1:395 packs.

	MT
Jeff Gordon (T1):	40.00
Jeff Gordon Autograph:	250.00

1996 Upper Deck SPx Terry Labonte Commemorative

This commemorative insert honors Labonte's record breaking accomplishment of 514 consecutive starts. Numbered C1 this one is seeded 1:47 packs. The Autographed version numbered C1A is identical other than the autograph and is inserted 1:395 packs.

	MT
Terry Labonte Commem. (C1):	20.00
Terry Labonte Autograph Redemption:	125.00

1996 Wheels Crown Jewels

This product was limited to 1,500 numbered cases. Of the 1,500 cases, 375 cases have each card stamped with a Treasure Chest logo. The 78-card base set features the driver with the Crown Jewels logo in the upper right-hand corner. The card backs feature career stats, a picture of the driver's car and a brief commentary.

	MT
Complete Set (80):	20.00
Common Player:	.15
Sapphires:	2x
Emeralds:	3x-4x
TC's	2x & Tributes 3x
after corresponding multiplier has been applied for parallels	
Wax Box:	80.00
1 Dale Earnhardt	3.00
2 Jeff Gordon	3.00
3 Terry Labonte	1.50
4 Mark Martin	1.50
5 Sterling Marlin	.30
6 Rusty Wallace	1.50
7 Bill Elliott	1.50
8 Bobby Labonte	.15
9 Dale Jarrett	.50
10 Bobby Hamilton	.15
11 Ted Musgrave	.15
12 Darrell Waltrip	.15
13 Kyle Petty	.15
14 Ken Schrader	.15
15 Michael Waltrip	.15
16 Derrike Cope	.15
17 Jeff Burton	.15
18 Ricky Craven	.15
19 Steve Grissom	.15
20 Robert Pressley	.15
21 Joe Nemechek	.15
22 Brett Bodine	.15
23 Jimmy Spencer	.15
24 Ward Burton	.15
25 Jeremy Mayfield	.15
26 Daytona Jarrett	.20
27 Rockingham Earnhardt	1.50
28 Richmond Gordon	1.50
29 Atlanta Earnhardt	1.50
30 Darlington Gordon	1.50
31 Bristol Gordon	1.50
32 N. Wilkesboro T. Labonte	.75
33 Martinsville Wallace	.75

34 Talladega Marlin	.20
35 Sonoma Wallace	.75
36 Travis Carter	.15
37 Bobby Allison	.15
38 Robert Yates	.15
39 Larry Hedrick	.15
40 Cale Yarborough	.15
41 Bill Ingle	.15
42 David Smith	.15
43 Todd Parrott	.15
44 Charlie Pressley	.15
45 Donnie Wingo	.15
46 Eddie Wood	.15
47 Len Wood	.15
48 Donnie Richeson	.15
49 Nemechek, Buce	.15
50 Craven, Pressley	.15
51 B. Bodine, D. Richeson	.15
52 Cope, Fennig	.15
53 Grissom, Ingle	.15
54 Jarrett, Parrott	.15
55 Martin, Hmiel	.50
56 R. Wallace, R. Pemberton	.50
57 B. Labonte, Makar	.15
58 Earnhardt, Smith	1.00
59 RCR #3	.15
60 SABCO #42	.15
61 Allison (#12)	.15
62 Penske (#2)	.15
63 Elliott (#94)	.15
64 Yates (#88)	.15
65 Hendrick (#5)	.15
66 Gibbs (#18)	.15
67 Nemco #87	.15
68 Diamond Ridge #29	.15
69 David Green	.15
70 Randy LaJoie	.15
71 Curtis Markham	.15
72 Phil Parsons	.15
73 Chad Little	.15
74 Jason Keller	.15
75 Jeff Green	.15
76 Mark Martin	1.50
77 Steve Grissom	.15
78 Bobby Labonte	.15
79 Checklist	.15
80 Checklist	.15

1996 Wheels Crown Jewels Birthstones of the Champions

This six-card set honors the reigning champions with a die-cut design, paying tribute to their birthdays by putting their actual birthstone on the card. They are seeded 1:192 packs.

	MT
Complete Set (6):	475.00
Common Driver:	15.00
BC1 Dale Earnhardt	150.00
BC2 Jeff Gordon	150.00
BC3 Rusty Wallace	75.00
BC4 Darrell Waltrip	15.00
BC5 Bill Elliott	75.00
BC6 Terry Labonte	75.00

1996 Wheels Crown Jewels Garnet Dual Jewels

A series of eight double-sided cards, each featuring a driver and gemstone on each side. Each of the eight cards will be available in three versions Garnet (1:48 packs), Amethyst (1:96) and Sapphire (1:192).

	MT
Complete Set (8):	200.00
Common Driver:	10.00
Amethyst:	1.5x-2x
Sapphire:	3x-4x
DJ1 Earnhardt, Gordon	75.00
DJ2 Jarrett, Wallace	40.00
DJ3 T. Labonte, B. Labonte	40.00
DJ4 Elliott, Martin	40.00
DJ5 D. Waltrip, M. Waltrip	10.00
DJ6 Hamilton, Petty	10.00
DJ7 R. Wallace, K. Wallace	40.00
DJ8 W. Burton, J. Burton	10.00

1996 Wheels Crown Jewels Earnhardt "7 Gems"

This card salutes Earnhardt's seven Winston Cup Championships with seven different gemstones on the card. The gemstones are Ruby, Topaz, Citrine, Peridot, Sapphire, Amethyst and Emerald. This one can be found 1:384 packs.

	MT
Dale Earnhardt (G7):	250.00

1997 Action Packed

The regular-sized embossed base set has a raised close-up photo of the driver on the front with the Action Packed logo on the bottom left portion of the card, written vertically on the left side of the card is the driver's name. The backs have biographical information, statistics and a photo that runs from top to bottom on the right half of the card.

	MT
Complete Set (86):	20.00
Common Driver:	.20
Wax Box:	60.00
1 Bobby Hamilton	.20
2 Rusty Wallace	1.00
3 Dale Earnhardt	2.50
4 Sterling Marlin	.20

5 Terry Labonte	1.00
6 Mark Martin	1.00
7 Jeremy Mayfield	.20
8 Jeff Gordon	2.50
9 Ernie Irvan	.75
10 Ricky Rudd	.20
11 Bill Elliott	1.00
12 Jimmy Spencer	.20
13 Dale Jarrett	.75
14 Ward Burton	.20
15 Michael Waltrip	.20
16 Ted Musgrave	.20
17 Darrell Waltrip	.20
18 Bobby Labonte	.20
19 John Andretti	.20
20 Robert Pressley	.20
21 Chad Little	.20
22 Geoff Bodine	.20
23 Morgan Shepherd	.20
24 Mike Skinner	.20
25 Ricky Craven	.20
26 Robby Gordon	.20
27 Mark Martin Car	.50
28 Jeremy Mayfield	.20
29 Jeff Gordon Car	1.00
30 Ernie Irvan Car	.40
31 Ricky Rudd	.20
32 Bill Elliott Car	.50
33 Jimmy Spencer	.20
34 Dale Jarrett Car	.40
35 Ward Burton	.20
36 Michael Waltrip	.20
37 Ted Musgrave	.20
38 Darrell Waltrip	.20
39 Bobby Labonte	.20
40 John Andretti	.20
41 Robert Pressley	.20
42 Chad Little	.20
43 Morgan Shepherd	.20
44 Rusty Wallace Car	.50
45 Dale Earnhardt Car	1.00
46 Sterling Marlin	.20
47 Terry Labonte Car	.50
48 Geoff Bodine	.20
49 Bobby Hamilton	.20
50 Mike Skinner	.20
51 Ricky Craven	.20
52 Robby Gordon	.20
53 Terry Labonte	.50
54 Dale Jarrett	.40
55 Randy LaJoie	.20
56 David Green	.20
57 Randy LaJoie	.20
58 Bill Elliott, Jackie Joyner	.20
59 Michael Waltrip	.20
60 Hut Stricklin	.20
61 Johnny Benson	.20
62 Carl Hill	.20
63 Dale Jarrett	.40
64 Bill Elliott	.50
65 Elmo Langley	.20
66 Harry Hyde	.20
67 Richard Petty	.40
68 Johnny Benson	.20
69 Rusty Wallace	.50
70 David Green	.20
71 Michael Waltrip	.20
72 Dale Jarrett	.40
73 Rusty Wallace	.50
74 Michael Waltrip	.20
75 Robby Gordon	.20
76 Sterling Marlin	.20
77 Ernie Irvan	.40
78 Dale Jarrett	.40
79 David Green	.20
80 Ernie Irvan	.40
81 Johnny Benson	.20
82 Robin Pemberton	.20
83 Terry Labonte	.50
84 Dale Earnhardt	1.00
85 Checklist Darrell Waltrip	.20
86 Checklist Bobby Hamilton	.20

1997 Action Packed First Impressions

This 86-card parallel rendition of the regular base set, utilizes all-silver foil card stock. The card fronts and backs are otherwise identical to the base cards. These are found on the average of one per seven packs.

	MT
Complete Set (86):	120.00
First Impressions:	3x to 6x

1997 Action Packed 24kt. Gold

The 14-card set features the top drivers on the Winston Cup circuit, each card is printed on genuine 24kt gold foil card stock. These are found on the average of every 86 packs.

		MT
Complete Set (14):		400.00
Common Driver:		15.00
1	Rusty Wallace	50.00
2	Dale Earnhardt	100.00
3	Jeff Gordon	100.00
4	Ernie Irvan	40.00
5	Terry Labonte	50.00
6	Johnny Benson	15.00
7	David Green	15.00
8	Dale Jarrett	40.00
9	Sterling Marlin	15.00
10	Michael Waltrip	15.00
11	Mark Martin	50.00
12	Bobby Hamilton	15.00
13	Ted Musgrave	15.00
14	Randy LaJoie	15.00

1997 Action Packed Chevy Madness

This six-card set is the first part of a continuing series that is included in Pinnacle Racer's Choice and Pinnacle Racing. The set features only drivers of Monte Carlo's and is silver foil stamped with micro-etching. The fronts have a photo of a car with the driver's name written above, Chevy Madness runs across the bottom and the Action Packed logo is in the upper right corner. By collecting all-six collectors would win a one-year membership to the Pinnacle Racing Club, these were seeded one per ten packs.

		MT
Complete Set (6):		18.00
Common Driver:		1.50
1	Dale Earnhardt	10.00
2	Darrell Waltrip	1.50
3	Dave Marcis	1.50
4	Jeff Gordon	10.00
5	Sterling Marlin	1.50
6	Steve Grissom	1.50

1997 Action Packed Fifth Anniversary

Action Pack commemorates its fifth anniversary with a special 12-card set, honoring 12 active and retired legends of racing. The cards are printed on silver foil stock with Prime First accents. These are seeded one per 128 packs.

		MT
Complete Set (12):		400.00
Common Driver:		15.00
1	Richard Petty	25.00
2	Cale Yarborough	15.00
3	Bobby Allison	15.00
4	Ned Jarrett	15.00
5	Benny Parsons	15.00
6	Dale Earnhardt	100.00
7	Rusty Wallace	50.00
8	Jeff Gordon	100.00
9	Terry Labonte	50.00
10	Dale Jarrett	40.00
11	Mark Martin	50.00
12	Bill Elliott	50.00

1997 Action Packed Fifth Anniversary Autographs

Five drivers each signed 1,000 cards to commemorate Action Packed's fifth anniversary. The card design is identical to the Fifth Anniversary inserts, with the checklist including Richard Petty, Cale Yarborough, Bobby Allison, Ned Jarrett, and Benny Parsons. The odds of getting an autograph are one per 165 packs.

		MT
Complete Set (5):		180.00
Common Autograph:		40.00
1	Richard Petty	60.00
2	Cale Yarborough	40.00
3	Bobby Allison	40.00
4	Ned Jarrett	40.00
5	Benny Parsons	40.00

1997 Action Packed Ironman Champion

This two-card set pays tribute to Terry Labonte's 1996 Winston Cup Points Championship. The cards feature embossed stamping with silver foil and micro-etching highlights. They are seeded one per 192 packs.

	MT
Complete Set (2):	80.00
Common Player:	30.00
Terry Labonte	50.00
T. Labonte/B. Labonte	30.00

1997 Action Packed Rolling Thunder

Action Packed chronicled the performances of 14 of NASCAR's top drivers as they competed on the Japanese circuit. The cards features the standard embossed highlights on full silver card stock. They were seeded one per 23 packs.

		MT
Complete Set (14):		80.00
Common Driver:		3.00
1	Mark Martin	10.00
2	Dale Earnhardt	20.00
3	Jeff Gordon	20.00
4	Ernie Irvan	8.00
5	Terry Labonte	10.00
6	Kyle Petty	3.00
7	Darrell Waltrip	3.00
8	Mike Skinner	3.00
9	Ricky Craven	3.00
10	Dale Jarrett	8.00
11	Sterling Marlin	3.00
12	Steve Grissom	3.00
13	Bill Elliott	10.00
14	Ricky Rudd	3.00

1997 Fleer Ultra NASCAR

The 100-card set features a borderless design with the driver's name and his/her sponsor in gold foil stamping. Also included is a Winston Cup Champion autographed insert of Terry Labonte seeded 1:180 packs. The 1996 NASCAR Rookie of the Year Johnny Benson also had an insert seeded at 1:72 packs.

		MT
Complete Set (100):		18.00
Common Driver:		.10
T. Labonte Auto. (C1):		50.00
J. Benson ROY (R1):		15.00
Wax Box:		70.00
1	John Andretti	.10
2	Johnny Benson	.10
3	Brett Bodine	.10
4	Geoff Bodine	.10
5	Jeff Burton	.10
6	Ward Burton	.10
7	Derrike Cope	.10
8	Ricky Craven	.10
9	Wally Dallenbach	.10
10	Dale Earnhardt	4.00
11	Bill Elliott	2.00
12	Jeff Gordon	4.00
13	Bobby Hamilton	.10
14	Bobby Hillin	.10
15	Ernie Irvan	1.50
16	Dale Jarrett	.75
17	Bobby Labonte	.10
18	Terry Labonte	2.00
19	Dave Marcis	.10
20	Sterling Marlin	.40
21	Mark Martin	2.00
22	Rick Mast	.10
23	Jeremy Mayfield	.10
24	Ted Musgrave	.10
25	Joe Nemechek	.10
26	Kyle Petty	.10
27	Robert Pressley	.10
28	Ricky Rudd	.10
29	Ken Schrader	.10
30	Morgan Shepherd	.10
31	Lake Speed	.10
32	Jimmy Spencer	.10
33	Hut Stricklin	.10
34	Dick Trickle	.10
35	Kenny Wallace	.10
36	Rusty Wallace	2.00
37	Michael Waltrip	.10
38	14 Car-Marvel	.10
39	Terry Labonte Car	1.00
40	Dale Jarrett Car	.25
41	Jeff Gordon Car	2.00
42	Mark Martin Car	1.00
43	Dale Earnhardt Car	2.00
44	10 Car-Tide	.10
45	4 Car-Kodak	.10
46	Rusty Wallace Car	1.00
47	43 Car-STP	.10
48	Bill Elliott Car	1.00
49	18 Car-Interstate Batteries	.10
50	37 Car-KMart/Little Caesars	.10
51	30 Car-Pennzoil	.10
52	16 Car-Family Channel	.10
53	41 Car-Kodiak	.10
54	Ernie Irvan Car	.75
55	21 Car-Citgo	.10
56	99 Car-Exide Batteries	.10
57	23 Car-Smokin' Joe's	.10
58	Bobby Allison	.10
59	Richard Childress	.10
60	Joe Gibbs	.10
61	Rick Hendrick	.10
62	Richard Petty	.40
63	Jack Roush	.10
64	Robert Yates	.10
65	Cale Yarborough	.10
66	Steve Hmiel (Crew Chiefs)	.10
67	Mike Beam (Crew Chiefs)	.10
68	David Smith (Crew Chiefs)	.10
69	Eddie Wood, Len Wood (Crew Chiefs)	.10
70	Ray Evernham (Crew Chiefs)	.10
71	Todd Parrott (Crew Chiefs)	.10
72	Larry McReynolds (Crew Chiefs)	.10
73	Tires (Tech Talk)	.10
74	Fuel Cell (Tech Talk)	.10
75	Roof Flaps (Tech Talk)	.10
76	Motor (Tech Talk)	.10
77	Seat (Tech Talk)	.10
78	Rear Spoiler (Tech Talk)	.10
79	Generator (Tech Talk)	.10
80	Jack Stob (Tech Talk)	.10
81	Track Bar Hole (Tech Talk)	.10
82	Todd Bodine	.10
83	David Green	.10
84	Jeff Green	.10
85	Jason Keller	.10
86	Randy LaJoie	.10
87	Chad Little	.10
88	Curtis Markham	.10
89	Phil Parsons	.10
90	Larry Pearson	.10
91	Jeff Purvis	.10
92	Mike McLaughlin	.10
93	Patty Moise	.10
94	Glenn Allen Jr.	.10
95	Kevin LePage	.10
96	Rodney Combs	.10
97	Tim Fedewa	.10
98	Dennis Setzer	.10
99	Checklist A	.10
100	Checklist B	.10

1997 Fleer Ultra NASCAR AKA

The 10-card set helps capture the true personalities of racing fans favorite drivers. The inserts are produced on thicker card stock and use the same concept as Fleer/SkyBox used with their E-Motion lines in other sports. They are seeded 1:24 packs.

		MT
Complete Set (10):		125.00
Common Driver:		5.00
A1	Dale Earnhardt	35.00
A2	Jeff Gordon	35.00
A3	Terry Labonte	15.00
A4	Dale Jarrett	10.00
A5	Bill Elliott	15.00
A6	Mark Martin	15.00
A7	Bobby Labonte	5.00
A8	Ernie Irvan	10.00
A9	Rusty Wallace	15.00
A10	Ricky Craven	5.00

1997 Fleer Ultra NASCAR Inside/Out

This fifteen-card set puts you behind the wheel with NASCAR's biggest superstars. The cards feature die-cut window nets, with a picture of the driver and his car, the backs feature a brief commentary about the driver. They are seeded 1:6 packs.

	MT
Complete Set (15):	50.00
Common Driver:	1.00
DC1 Dale Earnhardt	15.00
DC2 Jeff Gordon	15.00
DC3 Terry Labonte	8.00
DC4 Dale Jarrett	5.00
DC5 Bill Elliott	8.00
DC6 Sterling Marlin	2.50
DC7 Mark Martin	8.00
DC8 Ernie Irvan	6.00
DC9 Rusty Wallace	8.00
DC10 Benson	1.00
DC11 Ricky Rudd	1.00
DC12 Bobby Labonte	1.00
DC13 Ricky Craven	1.00
DC14 Bobby Hamilton	1.00
DC15 Michael Waltrip	1.00

1997 Pinnacle Mint Collection

The 30-card, regular sized set comes in three-card packs and contains two coin cards and one regular-issue card. The die-cut coin cards feature a closeup shot. The cards have a circular cutout in the upper right quadrant where the where the included brass, silver or gold coins fit. The regular-issue cards feature a foil team emblem (where the hole is on the coin cards) in brass (common), silver (1:20) or gold (1:48).

		MT
Complete Set (30):		18.00
Common Player:		.25
Bronze Cards:		2x
Silver Cards:		4x to 8x
Gold Cards:		10x to 20x
Wax Box:		55.00
1	Terry Labonte	.75
2	Jeff Gordon	2.00
3	Dale Jarrett	.50
4	Dale Earnhardt	2.00
5	Mark Martin	.75
6	Ricky Rudd	.25
7	Rusty Wallace	.75

8	Sterling Marlin	.25
9	Bobby Hamilton	.25
10	Ernie Irvan	.50
11	Bobby Labonte	.25
12	Johnny Benson	.25
13	Michael Waltrip	.25
14	Jimmy Spencer	.25
15	Ted Musgrave	.25
16	Geoff Bodine	.25
17	Bill Elliott	.75
18	John Andretti	.25
19	Ward Burton	.25
20	Randy LaJoie	.25
21	Dale Earnhardt Car	1.00
22	Ricky Rudd Car	.25
23	Dale Jarrett Car	.40
24	Jeff Gordon Car	1.00
25	Terry Labonte Car	.50
26	Mark Martin Car	.50
27	Bobby Labonte Car	.25
28	Ernie Irvan Car	.40
29	Bill Elliott Car	.50
30	Johnny Benson Car	.25

1997 Pinnacle Mint Collection Coins

The 30-piece set was included twice in every three-card pack of Mint Collection Racing. Two other variations of the brass coin were available: silver (1:20) and 24kt gold (1:48). The coin face has an image of the driver's face on the front.

		MT
Complete Set (30):		50.00
Common Brass Coin:		1.00
Nickel Coins:		2x to 4x
Gold Plated Coins:		6x to 10x
1	Terry Labonte	4.00
2	Jeff Gordon	8.00
3	Dale Jarrett	2.50
4	Dale Earnhardt	8.00
5	Mark Martin	4.00
6	Ricky Rudd	1.00
7	Rusty Wallace	4.00
8	Sterling Marlin	1.50
9	Bobby Hamilton	1.00
10	Ernie Irvan	3.00
11	Bobby Labonte	1.00
12	Johnny Benson	1.00
13	Michael Waltrip	1.00
14	Jimmy Spencer	1.00
15	Ted Musgrave	1.00
16	Geoff Bodine	1.00
17	Bill Elliott	4.00
18	John Andretti	1.00
19	Ward Burton	1.00
20	Randy LaJoie	1.00
21	Dale Earnhardt Car	4.00
22	Ricky Rudd Car	1.00
23	Dale Jarrett Car	1.50
24	Jeff Gordon Car	4.00
25	Terry Labonte Car	2.00
26	Mark Martin Car	2.00
27	Bobby Labonte Car	1.00
28	Ernie Irvan Car	1.50
29	Bill Elliott Car	2.00
30	Johnny Benson Car	1.00

1997 Pinnacle Racer's Choice

The regular sized 106-card set features one photo of the driver on the card front with his/her name at the top middle portion of the card, with white borders. The card backs have a close-up photo along with career statistics.

		MT
Complete Set (106):		12.00
Common Driver:		.05
Wax Box:		30.00
1	Morgan Shepherd	.05
2	Rusty Wallace	.50
3	Dale Earnhardt	1.00
4	Sterling Marlin	.05
5	Terry Labonte	.50
6	Mark Martin	.50
7	Geoff Bodine	.05
8	Hut Stricklin	.05
9	Chad Little	.05
10	Ricky Rudd	.05
11	Brett Bodine	.05
12	Derrike Cope	.05
13	Jeremy Mayfield	.05
14	Robby Gordon	.05
15	Steve Grissom	.05
16	Ted Musgrave	.05
17	Darrell Waltrip	.05
18	Bobby Labonte	.05
19	John Andretti	.05
20	Bobby Hamilton	.05
21	Michael Waltrip	.05
22	Ward Burton	.05
23	Jimmy Spencer	.05
24	Jeff Gordon	1.00
25	Ricky Craven	.05
26	Kyle Petty	.05
27	Dale Earnhardt	1.00
28	Ernie Irvan	.40
29	Joe Nemechek	.05
30	Johnny Benson	.05
31	Mike Skinner	.05
32	Dale Jarrett	.40
33	Ken Schrader	.05
34	Bill Elliott	.50
35	David Green	.05
36	Morgan Shepherd	.05
37	Rusty Wallace Car	.25
38	Dale Earnhardt Car	.50
39	Sterling Marlin	.05
40	Terry Labonte Car	.25
41	Mark Martin Car	.25
42	Geoff Bodine	.05
43	Hut Stricklin	.05
44	Chad Little	.05
45	Ricky Rudd	.05
46	Brett Bodine	.05
47	Derrike Cope	.05
48	Jeremy Mayfield	.05
49	Robby Gordon	.05
50	Steve Grissom	.05
51	Ted Musgrave	.05
52	Darrell Waltrip	.05
53	Bobby Labonte	.05
54	John Andretti	.05
55	Bobby Hamilton	.05
56	Michael Waltrip	.05
57	Ward Burton	.05
58	Jimmy Spencer	.05
59	Jeff Gordon Car	.50
60	Ricky Craven	.05
61	Kyle Petty	.05
62	Dale Earnhardt Car	.50
63	Ernie Irvan Car	.20
64	Joe Nemechek	.05
65	Johnny Benson	.05
66	Mike Skinner	.05
67	Dale Jarrett Car	.20
68	Ken Schrader	.05
69	Bill Elliott Car	.25
70	David Green	.05
71	Gary Nelson	.05
72	Robert Yates	.05
73	Robin Pemberton	.05
74	Kyle Petty	.05
75	Geoff Bodine	.05
76	Earl Barban	.05
77	Jeremy Mayfield	.05
78	Steve Grissom	.05
79	Mike Skinner	.05
80	Richard Childress	.05
81	Chocolate Meyers	.05
82	Ward Burton	.05
83	Chad Little	.05
84	Buddy Parrott	.05
85	Jimmy Cox	.05
86	Richard Petty	.05
87	Mike Skinner	.05
88	David Green	.05
89	Robby Gordon	.05
90	Dale Earnhardt	.75
91	Rusty Wallace	.30
92	Sterling Marlin	.05
93	Terry Labonte	.30
94	Mark Martin	.30
95	Ricky Rudd	.05
96	Ted Musgrave	.05
97	Johnny Benson	.05
98	Bobby Labonte	.05
99	Bobby Hamilton	.05
100	Michael Waltrip	.05
101	Ward Burton	.05
102	Ricky Craven	.05
103	Ernie Irvan	.25
104	Dale Earnhardt	.75
105	Dale Jarrett	.25
106	Dale Earnhardt CL	.50

1997 Pinnacle Racer's Choice Showcase Series

The 106-card parallel of the regular set was produced on full silver foil card stock, featuring a gold facsimile driver signature. They are seeded one per seven packs.

		MT
Complete Set (106):		30.00
Showcase Series:		2x to 3x

1997 Pinnacle Racer's Choice Busch Clash

The 14-card set honors the drivers for their consistent performances over the course of the 1996 season, qualifying them for the Busch Clash. The odds are one per 47 packs.

		MT
Complete Set (14):		60.00
Common Driver:		2.00
1	Dale Earnhardt	15.00
2	Terry Labonte	8.00
3	Johnny Benson	2.00
4	Ward Burton	2.00
5	Mark Martin	8.00
6	Ricky Craven	2.00
7	Ernie Irvan	5.00
8	Jeff Gordon	15.00
9	Ted Musgrave	2.00
10	Jeremy Mayfield	2.00
11	Dale Earnhardt	15.00
12	Dale Jarrett	5.00
13	Bobby Labonte	2.00
14	Rusty Wallace	8.00

1997 Pinnacle Racer's Choice Chevy Madness

The second level of the Chevy Madness sweepstakes, covering numbers 7-12. By collecting all six of these Monte Carlo exclusive driver cards, collectors would receive five Chevy Madness oversized cards consisting of Jeff Gordon, Dale Earnhardt, Ricky Craven, Robby Gordon and Terry Labonte. By collecting the other nine cards, found in Action Packed and Pinnacle, collectors would be put in a drawing for a Chevy pick-up truck. These are seeded one per 17 packs.

		MT
Complete Set (6):		18.00
Common Driver:		1.00
7	Jeff Gordon	8.00
8	Dale Earnhardt	8.00
9	Ricky Craven	1.00
10	Robby Gordon	1.00
11	Jeff Green	1.00
12	Terry Labonte	4.00

1997 Pinnacle Racer's Choice High Octane

The 15-card set has the top car and driver combinations on the Winston Cup circuit, which are printed on silver foil card stock. High Octanes are seeded one per 23 packs. A Glow in the Dark parallel version also exists, that features the name of the race the driver pictured will compete in. If the driver wins that race, collectors could send in their winning card to receive the entire Glow in the Dark set. Glow in the Darks are seeded one per 71 packs.

		MT
Complete Set (15):		125.00
Common Driver:		4.00
Complete Glow in the Dark Set (15):		250.00
Glow in the Darks:		1.5x to 2x
1	Terry Labonte	15.00
2	Dale Earnhardt	30.00
3	Jeff Gordon	30.00
4	Dale Jarrett	10.00
5	Mark Martin	15.00
6	Rusty Wallace	15.00
7	Bill Elliott	15.00
8	Bobby Labonte	4.00
9	Ernie Irvan	10.00
10	Kyle Petty	4.00
11	Ricky Rudd	4.00
12	Johnny Benson	4.00
13	Ward Burton	4.00
14	Ted Musgrave	4.00
15	Dale Earnhardt	30.00

1997 Press Pass

The 140-card set is available in eight-card packs, with each card UV coated with gold foil stamping. The full-bleed fronts have a photo of the driver with the logo and name gold foil stamped. The backs have a picture of the driver in his car along with biographical information and career stats. In addition to driver cards, subsets include, Winston Cup Cars, Busch Drivers, '96 Champions, '97 Preview, '96 Highlights, Back-to-Back and Triple Threat.

		MT
Complete Set (140):		18.00
Common Driver:		.10
Lasers & Torquers:		1.5x to 3x
Wax Box:		65.00
1	Terry Labonte	1.00
2	Jeff Gordon	2.00
3	Dale Jarrett	.40
4	Dale Earnhardt	2.00
5	Mark Martin	1.00
6	Ricky Rudd	.10
7	Rusty Wallace	1.00
8	Sterling Marlin	.20
9	Bobby Hamilton	.10
10	Ernie Irvan	.75
11	Bobby Labonte	.10
12	Ken Schrader	.10
13	Jeff Burton	.10
14	Michael Waltrip	.10
15	Ted Musgrave	.10
16	Geoff Bodine	.10
17	Rick Mast	.10
18	Morgan Shepherd	.10
19	Ricky Craven	.10
20	Johnny Benson	.10
21	Hut Stricklin	.10
22	Jeremy Mayfield	.10
23	Kyle Petty	.10
24	Kenny Wallace	.10
25	Darrell Waltrip	.10
26	Bill Elliott	1.00
27	Robert Pressley	.10

#		MT
28	Ward Burton	.10
29	Joe Nemechek	.10
30	Mike Skinner	.10
31	#2 Rusty Wallace Car	.50
32	#3 Dale Earnhardt Car	1.00
33	#4 Sterling Marlin Car	.15
34	#5 Terry Labonte Car	.50
35	#6 Mark Martin Car	.50
36	#10 Ricky Rudd Car	.10
37	#18 Bobby Labonte Car	.10
38	#21 Michael Waltrip Car	.10
39	#24 Jeff Gordon Car	1.00
40	#28 Ernie Irvan Car	.40
41	#41 Ricky Craven Car	.10
42	#42 Kyle Petty Car	.10
43	#43 Bobby Hamilton Car	.10
44	#88 Dale Jarrett Car	.20
45	#94 Bill Elliott Car	.50
46	Mike Bliss	.10
47	Rick Carelli	.10
48	Ron Hornaday Jr.	.10
49	Butch Miller	.10
50	Joe Ruttman	.10
51	Bill Sedgwick	.10
52	Mike Skinner	.10
53	Rusty Wallace	1.00
54	Darrell Waltrip	.10
55	Johnny Benson Car	.10
56	Dale Earnhardt Car	1.00
57	Jeff Gordon Car	1.00
58	Ernie Irvan Car	.40
59	Dale Jarrett Car	.40
60	Terry Labonte Car	.50
61	Sterling Marlin Car	.15
62	Rusty Wallace Car	.50
63	Michael Waltrip Car	.10
64	Todd Bodine	.10
65	Rodney Combs	.10
66	Ricky Craven	.10
67	Jeff Fuller	.10
68	David Green	.10
69	Jeff Green	.10
70	Dale Jarrett	.40
71	Jason Keller	.10
72	Terry Labonte	1.00
73	Randy LaJoie	.10
74	Chad Little	.10
75	Mark Martin	1.00
76	Mike McLaughlin	.10
77	Larry Pearson	.10
78	Michael Waltrip	.10
79	Michael Waltrip	.10
80	Dale Jarrett	.40
81	Bobby Labonte	.10
82	Terry Labonte	.75
83	Ricky Craven	.10
84	Rusty Wallace	.75
85	Ken Schrader	.10
86	Mike Wallace	.10
87	Jeremy Mayfield	.10
88	Chad Little	.10
89	Mark Martin	.75
90	Kenny Wallace	.10
91	Robby Gordon	.10
92	Jimmy Johnson	.10
93	Michael Waltrip, David Pearson	.10
94	Dale Jarrett	.40
95	Dale Earnhardt Car	1.00
96	Jeff Gordon	1.00
97	Terry Labonte	.50
98	Sterling Marlin	.15
99	Rusty Wallace	.50
100	Michael Waltrip	.10
101	Ernie Irvan	.40
102	Dale Jarrett	.40
103	Geoff Bodine	.10
104	Jeff Gordon Car	1.00
105	North Wilkesboro	.10
106	Terry Labonte	.50
107	Ricky Rudd	.10
108	Bobby Hamilton	.10
109	Terry Labonte, Bobby Labonte	.10
110	Terry Labonte	.50
111	Randy LaJoie	.10
112	Mark Martin	.50
113	Ron Hornaday Jr.	.10
114	Kelly Tanner	.10
115	Joe Kosiski	.10
116	Lyndon Amick	.10
117	Dave Dion	.10
118	Tony Hirschman	.10
119	Chris Raudman	.10
120	Mike Cope	.10
121	Kyle Petty	.10
122	Rusty Wallace (#2 Car)	.50
123	Michael Waltrip	.10
124	Dale Jarrett	.40
125	Chad Little	.10
126	Joe Nemechek	.10
127	Steve Grissom	.10
128	Robby Gordon	.10
129	Mike Wallace	.10
130	Bill Elliott Car	.50
131	Ken Schrader	.10
132	Wally Dallenbach	.10
133	Derrike Cope	.10
134	Jeff Gordon	1.00
135	Jeff Gordon	1.00
136	Jeff Gordon	1.00
137	Jeff Gordon	1.00
138	Jeff Gordon	1.00
139	Checklist	.10
140	Checklist	.10

1997 Press Pass Lasers

The 140-card parallel set is identical to the regular base cards other than they have silver foil stamping and are also hobby only. They are seeded one per pack.

	MT
Complete Set (140):	40.00
Lasers:	1.5x to 3x

1997 Press Pass Oil Slicks

This parallel 140-card set features black foil stamping. Press Pass announced only producing 100 sets. They were hobby exclusive and were seeded at a rate of one per 36 packs.

	MT
Complete Set (140):	750.00
Common Driver:	5.00
Oil Slicks:	20x to 40x

1997 Press Pass Torquers

The 140-card parallel set is identical to the regular cards other than the electric blue foil stamping. They are available only in retail packs and are seeded one per pack.

	MT
Complete Set (140):	40.00
Torquers:	1.5x to 3x

1997 Press Pass Banquet Bound

The 10-card set features the top drivers from the Winston Cup circuit, on an all Holofoil card design. The card fronts have one photo of the driver, while the backs have a small inset photo along with biographical information and career stats. They were seeded one per 12 packs.

	MT
Complete Set (10):	50.00
Common Driver:	1.50
BB1 Terry Labonte	8.00
BB2 Jeff Gordon	15.00
BB3 Dale Jarrett	4.00
BB4 Dale Earnhardt	15.00
BB5 Mark Martin	8.00
BB6 Ricky Rudd	1.50
BB7 Rusty Wallace	8.00
BB8 Sterling Marlin	2.00
BB9 Bobby Hamilton	1.50
BB10 Ernie Irvan	5.00

1997 Press Pass Burning Rubber

The seven card set is printed on an all acetate die-cut design, with the race-used tire forming the bottom half of the car in the shape, not surprisingly, of a tire. The card backs congratulate the collector for pulling the card and give the date and the race the tire is from. They are hand numbered to 400 and seeded at a rate of one per 480 packs.

	MT
Complete Set (7):	900.00
Common Driver:	60.00
1 Rusty Wallace	140.00
2 Dale Earnhardt	250.00
3 Terry Labonte	140.00
4 Michael Waltrip	60.00
5 Jeff Gordon	250.00
6 Ernie Irvan	120.00
7 Dale Jarrett	100.00

1997 Press Pass Clear Cut

Winston Cup drivers who won races during the '96 season are captured on a clear die-cut acetate design. With each card front having a shot of the driver and his car. These were seeded one per 18 packs.

	MT
Complete Set (10):	80.00
Common Player:	3.00
1 Dale Earnhardt	25.00
2 Jeff Gordon	25.00
3 Ernie Irvan	10.00
4 Dale Jarrett	10.00
5 Bobby Labonte	4.00
6 Terry Labonte	12.00
7 Mark Martin	12.00
8 Ricky Rudd	3.00
9 Rusty Wallace	12.00
10 Michael Waltrip	3.00

1997 Press Pass Cup Chase '97

The 20-card interactive set is printed on an all foil NitroKrome design, with the fronts having a photo of the driver surrounded by an outline of a trophy cup. Ten races were chosen, if the driver on the card finished first, second or third the card can be redeemed for a limited gold NitroKrome die-cut of the driver. At the end of the season, the 1997 Winston Cup Champion's Cup Chase card can be redeemed for the entire 20-card gold NitroKrome die-cut set. They were seeded one per 24 packs. All claims have to be postmarked by 1-31-98.

	MT
Complete Set (20):	150.00
Common Driver:	3.00
1 Johnny Benson	3.00
3 Ward Burton	3.00
4 Ricky Craven	3.00
5 Dale Earnhardt	30.00
6 Bill Elliott	15.00
7 Jeff Gordon	30.00
8 Bobby Hamilton	3.00
9 Ernie Irvan	12.00
10 Dale Jarrett	8.00
11 Bobby Labonte	3.00
12 Terry Labonte	15.00
13 Sterling Marlin	4.00
14 Mark Martin	15.00
15 Kyle Petty	3.00
16 Ricky Rudd	3.00
17 Ken Schrader	3.00
18 Rusty Wallace	15.00
19 Michael Waltrip	3.00
20 Field Card	5.00

1997 Press Pass Victory Lane

The nine-card set features the top Winston Cup drivers on a holofoil card design. Cards 1A-9A are hobby only, while cards 1B-9B are retail only. They are seeded one per 18 packs.

	MT
Complete Set (18):	100.00
Common Driver:	2.00
1A Dale Earnhardt	20.00
1B Earnhardt's Car	12.00
2A Jeff Gordon	20.00
2B Gordon's Car	12.00
3A Ernie Irvan	8.00
3B Irvan's Car	5.00
4A Dale Jarrett	6.00
4B Jarrett's Car	3.00
5A Terry Labonte	10.00
5B T. Labonte's Car	6.00
6A Sterling Marlin	3.00
6B Marlin's Car	2.50
7A Ricky Rudd	2.00
7B Rudd's Car	2.00
8A Rusty Wallace	10.00
8B Wallace's Car	6.00
9A Michael Waltrip	2.00
9B Waltrip's Car	2.00

1997 Press Pass ActionVision

The 12-card set uses Kodak's KODAMOTION technology, to capture several seconds of film on the card. Available in one-card packs, ActionVision features the top names in NASCAR Winston Cup racing.

	MT
Complete Set (12):	125.00
Common Card (1-12):	8.00
Wax Box:	125.00
1 Terry Labonte	12.00
2 Gordon Victory Lane	16.00
3 Earnhardt Qualifying	16.00
4 Jarrett Victory Lane	10.00
5 Gordon/Wallace/Labonte	14.00
6 Gordon/Labonte/Craven	14.00
7 Wallace Pit Stop	10.00
8 Earnhardt Pit Stop	14.00
9 Labonte Pit Stop	10.00
10 Gordon Pit Stop	14.00
11 Jarrett Pit Stop	8.00
12 Elliott Talladega	12.00

1997 Press Pass ActionVision Precious Metal

A continuation from Press Pass VIP, these are numbered (6-9) and have actual race-used pieces of sheet metal embedded into an individually numbered card, seeded at a rate of one per 160 packs.

	MT
Complete Set (4):	700.00
Common Driver (6-9):	125.00
6 Dale Earnhardt	350.00
7 Dale Jarrett	175.00
8 Ernie Irvan	125.00
9 Mark Martin	200.00

1997 Press Pass Premium

The 45-card base set is printed on 24 point card stock with gold foil stamping. The fronts feature two photos while the backs have career stats and personal information.

	MT
Complete Set (45):	25.00
Common Driver:	.25
Wax Box:	90.00
1 Terry Labonte	2.00
2 Jeff Gordon	4.00
3 Dale Jarrett	1.00
4 Dale Earnhardt	4.00
5 Mark Martin	2.00
6 Ricky Rudd	.25
7 Rusty Wallace	2.00
8 Sterling Marlin	.60
9 Bobby Hamilton	.25
10 Ernie Irvan	1.50
11 Bobby Labonte	.25
12 Ken Schrader	.25
13 Jeff Burton	.25
14 Michael Waltrip	.25
15 Ted Musgrave	.25
16 Ricky Craven	.25
17 Johnny Benson	.25
18 Wally Dallenbach	.25
19 Jeremy Mayfield	.25
20 Kyle Petty	.40
21 Bill Elliott	2.00
22 Ward Burton	.25
23 Joe Nemechek	.25
24 Chad Little	.25
25 Darrell Waltrip	.25
26 Robby Gordon	.25
27 Mike Skinner, Robby Gordon, David Green	.25
28 #2 Miller Lite R. Wallace	.75
29 #3 GM Goodwrench D. Earnhardt	1.50
30 #5 Kellogg's T. Labonte	.75
31 #6 Valvoline M. Martin Car	.75
32 #10 Tide Rudd	.25
33 #24 DuPont Auto. Fin. J. Gordon	1.50
34 #43 STP K. Petty	.25
35 #88 Quality Care D. Jarrett	.50
36 #94 McDonald's B. Elliott	.75
37 Bill Elliott	1.00
38 Jeff Gordon	2.00
39 Ernie Irvan	.75
40 Dale Jarrett	.50
41 Bobby Labonte	.25
42 Sterling Marlin	.40
43 Mark Martin	1.00
44 Rusty Wallace	1.00
45 Checklist	.25

1997 Press Pass Premium Emerald Proofs

The parallel set is metallic green on silver foil stock. Press Pass made a total of 380 sets, which are inserted at a rate of 1:45 packs.

	MT
Complete Set (45):	400.00
Common Driver:	4.00
Emerald Proofs:	15x to 25x

1997 Press Pass Premium Mirrors

This parallel set has an all-foil, reflective silver look on extra thick laminated card stock. They were inserted one per pack.

	MT
Complete Set (45):	40.00
Common Driver:	.40
Mirrors:	1.5x to 2x

1997 Press Pass Premium Oil Slicks

The toughest of all their parallel sets, these were on custom made foil and were individually numbered to 100 sets. They were seeded 1:96 packs.

	MT
Complete Set (45):	700.00
Common Driver:	6.00
Oil Slicks:	20x to 40x

1997 Press Pass Premium Autographs

The autographs are identical to the base card other than the drivers' signature. Autographs are seeded 1:72 packs.

	MT
Complete Set (23):	600.00
Common Autograph:	10.00
1 Terry Labonte	100.00
2 Jeff Gordon	200.00
4 Dale Earnhardt	200.00
5 Steve Hmiel	10.00
9 Bobby Hamilton	15.00
11 Ken Schrader	15.00
13 Michael Waltrip	15.00
14 Ted Musgrave	15.00
15 Geoff Bodine	15.00
17 Johnny Benson	15.00
19 Kyle Petty	20.00
22 Joe Nemechek	10.00
23 Wally Dallenbach	15.00
24 Robby Gordon	15.00
26 Jason Keller	10.00
27 Jeff Green	10.00
28 Mike McLaughlin	10.00
30 Jeff Fuller	10.00
31 Todd Bodine	15.00
32 Rodney Combs	10.00
33 Randy LaJoie	10.00
35 Larry McReynolds	10.00

1997 Press Pass Premium Crystal Ball

Printed on Holofoil card stock, the fronts feature the driver positioned inside a crystal ball like inset. They are

seeded 1:18 packs. A die-cut version also exists and is cut like a crystal ball, they were seeded 1:36 packs.

	MT
Complete Set (12):	120.00
Common Driver:	6.00
Die-Cuts:	1.5x to 2x
CB1 Ricky Craven	6.00
CB2 D. Earnhardt Car	25.00
CB3 Bill Elliott	15.00
CB4 Jeff Gordon	30.00
CB5 Ernie Irvan	12.00
CB6 Dale Jarrett	10.00
CB7 Bobby Labonte	6.00
CB8 Terry Labonte	15.00
CB9 Sterling Marlin	8.00
CB10 Mark Martin	15.00
CB11 Ricky Rudd	6.00
CB12 Rusty Wallace	15.00

1997 Press Pass Premium Double Burners

Double Burners incorporate race-used firesuit and tire onto one card. The horizontal fronts feature a photo of the driver along with a swatch of firesuit and a circular piece of rubber. They are seeded 1:432 packs.

	MT
Complete Set (5):	700.00
Common Driver:	50.00
DB1 Dale Earnhardt	250.00
DB2 Jeff Gordon	250.00
DB3 Terry Labonte	140.00
DB4 Rusty Wallace	140.00
DB5 Michael Waltrip	50.00

1997 Press Pass Premium Lap Leaders

The 12-card insert set combines thick card stock and clear acetate to help form a sort of crystal vision look. These were seeded 1:12 packs.

	MT
Complete Set (12):	75.00
Common Driver:	4.00
LL1 Dale Earnhardt	20.00
LL2 Bill Elliott	10.00
LL3 Jeff Gordon	20.00
LL4 Ernie Irvan	8.00
LL5 Dale Jarrett	6.00

		MT
LL6	Bobby Labonte	4.00
LL7	Terry Labonte	10.00
LL8	Mark Martin	10.00
LL9	Kyle Petty	4.00
LL10	Ricky Rudd	4.00
LL11	Rusty Wallace	10.00
LL12	Michael Waltrip	4.00

1997 Press Pass VIP

The 50-card set comes in seven-card packs and includes driver cards from Winston Cup, Busch Grand National and Truck racing. The card fronts are gold-foil stamped with two photos of the driver. The backs have a close-up of the driver along with 1996 stats.

		MT
Complete Set (50):		12.00
Common Driver:		.20
Explosives:		2x
Oil Slicks:		20x to 40x
Wax Box:		70.00
1	Johnny Benson	.20
2	Geoff Bodine	.20
3	Jeff Burton	.20
4	Ward Burton	.20
5	Ricky Craven	.20
6	Dale Earnhardt	3.00
7	Bill Elliott	1.25
8	Jeff Gordon	3.00
9	Robby Gordon	.20
10	Bobby Hamilton	.20
11	Ernie Irvan	1.00
12	Dale Jarrett	1.00
13	Bobby Labonte	.40
14	Terry Labonte	1.25
15	Sterling Marlin	.20
16	Mark Martin	1.25
17	Ted Musgrave	.20
18	Joe Nemechek	.20
19	Kyle Petty	.30
20	Ricky Rudd	.20
21	Ken Schrader	.20
22	Mike Skinner	.20
23	Rusty Wallace	1.25
24	Darrell Waltrip	.20
25	Michael Waltrip	.20
26	David Green	.20
27	Chad Little	.20
28	Todd Bodine	.20
29	Tim Fedewa	.20
30	Jeff Fuller	.20
31	Jeff Green	.20
32	Jason Keller	.20
33	Randy LaJoie	.20
34	Kevin LePage	.20
35	Mark Martin	.75
36	Mike McLaughlin	.20
37	Rich Bickle	.20
38	Mike Bliss	.20
39	Rick Carelli	.20
40	Ron Hornaday Jr.	.20
41	Kenny Irwin Jr.	.20
42	Tammy Jo Kirk	.20
43	Butch Miller	.20
44	Joe Ruttman	.20
45	Jack Sprague	.20
46	Jeff Burton	.20
47	Dale Jarrett	.50
48	Mark Martin	.75
49	Bruton Smith, Eddie Gossage	.20
50	Checklist	.20

1997 Press Pass VIP Explosives

This 50-card parallel set uses gold foil micro etching to enhance the card fronts. Explosive is printed underneath the VIP logo in the upper left quadrant. The card backs are identical to the base cards, these are found one per pack.

	MT
Complete Set (50):	40.00
Explosives:	2x

1997 Press Pass VIP Oil Slicks

This 50-card parallel set is printed on custom made foil and are hobby only. Oil Slicks is printed on the front and each card is individually numbered to 100. They were seeded one per 64 packs.

	MT
Complete Set (50):	600.00
Oil Slicks:	20x to 40x

1997 Press Pass VIP Autographs

A continuation from Press Pass Premium series, Autographs are inserted one per 60 packs with many of the top drivers included in the set. VIP base cards are signed with all of the signatures on the card front.

		MT
Complete Set (35):		900.00
Common Autograph:		10.00
1	Terry Labonte	100.00
2	Jeff Gordon	200.00
3	Dale Jarrett	70.00
4	Dale Earnhardt	200.00
5	Steve Hmiel	10.00
6	Ricky Rudd	20.00
7	Rusty Wallace	100.00
8	Sterling Marlin	20.00
9	Bobby Hamilton	15.00
10	Bobby Labonte	20.00
11	Ken Schrader	15.00
12	Jeff Burton	15.00
13	Michael Waltrip	15.00
14	Ted Musgrave	15.00
16	Ricky Craven	20.00
18	Jeremy Mayfield	15.00
19	Kyle Petty	20.00
20	Bill Elliott	75.00
21	Wood Brothers	10.00
24	Robby Gordon	15.00
25	David Green	10.00
26	Jason Keller	10.00
27	Jeff Green	10.00
28	Mike McLaughlin	10.00
29	Chad Little	15.00
30	Jeff Fuller	10.00
31	Todd Bodine	15.00
33	Randy LaJoie	15.00
34	Ray Evernham	10.00
36	Gary DeHart	10.00
37	Mike Beam	10.00
38	Darrell Waltrip	20.00
39	Ward Burton	15.00
40	Mike Skinner	15.00

1997 Press Pass VIP Head Gear

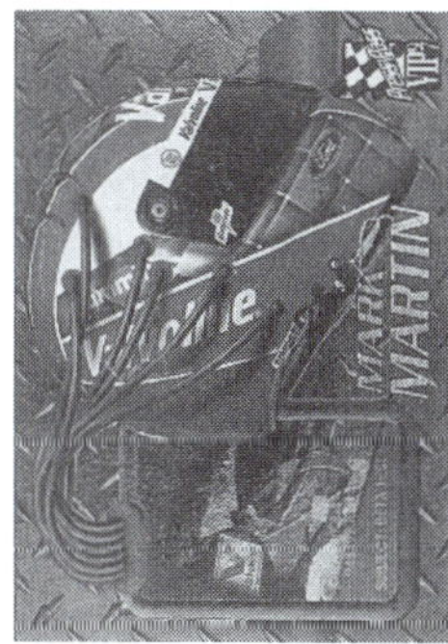

This nine-card set uses foil NitroKrome technology on an embossed design, with one image of the driver's helmet featured on the card front and a small inset photo of the driver in his helmet at the side of the image. The backs name the maker of the driver's helmet along with the helmet designer. These were seeded 1:16 packs. A die-cut version also exists that is shaped like the drivers' helmet. They were inserted 1:40 packs.

		MT
Complete Set (9):		100.00
Common Driver:		5.00
Die-Cuts:		2x
HG1	Dale Earnhardt	25.00
HG2	Bill Elliott	15.00
HG3	Jeff Gordon	25.00
HG4	Ernie Irvan	10.00
HG5	Mark Martin	15.00
HG6	Kyle Petty	5.00
HG7	Ricky Rudd	5.00
HG8	Rusty Wallace	15.00
HG9	Michael Waltrip	5.00

1997 Press Pass VIP Ring of Honor

Clear acetate inside of an oval track with gold foil stamping of the driver's name and track where he won highlight the card fronts. The backs

have a brief commentary on the drivers' win, they were seeded one per ten packs. Die-cut versions are identical other than they are cut around the oval track. They were seeded one per 30 packs.

		MT
Complete Set (12):		75.00
Common Driver:		3.00
Die-Cuts:		2x
RH1	Rusty Wallace Car	12.00
RH2	Dale Earnhardt Car	18.00
RH3	Sterling Marlin Car	3.00
RH4	Terry Labonte Car	12.00
RH5	Mark Martin Car	12.00
RH6	Ricky Rudd Car	3.00
RH7	Bobby Labonte Car	3.00
RH8	Jeff Gordon Car	18.00
RH9	Ernie Irvin Car	8.00
RH10	Bobby Hamilton Car	3.00
RH11	Dale Jarrett Car	8.00
RH12	Bill Elliott Car	12.00

1997 Press Pass VIP Sam Bass

Race Artist Sam Bass for the second straight year created six original artworks for this six-card set. Top Winston Cup drivers are featured including Earnhardt and Gordon. They were seeded one per 30 packs, a gold version also exists which is identical other than the gold treatment, they were inserted one per 120 packs.

		MT
Complete Set (6):		100.00
Common Driver:		8.00
Golds:		2x to 3x
KT1	Dale Earnhardt	30.00
KT2	Jeff Gordon	30.00
KT3	Dale Jarrett	15.00
KT4	Bobby Labonte	8.00
KT5	Terry Labonte	20.00
KT6	Rusty Wallace	20.00

1997 Press Pass VIP Sheet Metal

Authentic race-used sheet metal from Winston Cup drivers are incorporated into a thick laminated card. Each card is individually numbered and comes with a certificate of authenticity. They were seeded one per 384 packs.

	MT
Complete Set (5):	750.00
Common Driver:	75.00
SM1 Jeff Gordon	300.00
SM2 Bobby Labonte	75.00
SM3 Bill Elliott	160.00
SM4 Terry Labonte	160.00
SM5 Rusty Wallace	160.00

1997 Score Board IQ

Score Board produced 995 numbered cases of racing IQ, with each pack containing two cards. The horizontal formatted 50-card set features black and silver foil stamping with the driver's name written across the bottom. The backs have a close-up photo of the driver along with biographical information and a brief career summary.

		MT
Complete Set (50):		45.00
Common Driver:		.50
1	Dale Earnhardt	6.00
2	Jeff Gordon	6.00
3	Terry Labonte	3.00
4	Dale Jarrett	2.00
5	Michael Waltrip	.50
6	Mark Martin	3.00
7	Mike Skinner	.50
8	Bobby Labonte	.50
9	Robby Gordon	.50
10	Rick Mast	.50
11	Geoff Bodine	.50
12	Sterling Marlin	.75
13	Jeff Burton	.75
14	Jimmy Spencer	.50
15	Darrell Waltrip	.50
16	Ken Schrader	.50
17	Kyle Petty	.50
18	Bobby Hamilton	.50
19	Ernie Irvan	2.00
20	Steve Grissom	.50
21	Ted Musgrave	.50
22	Jeremy Mayfield	.50
23	Ricky Rudd	.75
24	Ricky Craven	.75
25	Hut Stricklin	.50
26	Jeff Gordon	6.00
27	Dale Earnhardt	6.00
28	Dale Jarrett	2.00
29	Terry Labonte	3.00
30	Richard Childress	.50
31	Rick Hendrick	.50
32	Richard Petty	1.00
33	Robert Yates	.50
34	Joe Gibbs	.50
35	Ray Everham	.50
36	Larry McReynolds	.50
37	Jeff Gordon	6.00
38	Dale Earnhardt	6.00
39	Car #2 Penske Racing South	.50
40	Earnhardt's Car	3.00
41	Car #4 Morgan-McClure Racing	.50
42	Car #6 Roush Racing	.50
43	Car #18 Joe Gibbs Racing	.50
44	Car #21 Wood Brothers Racing	.50
45	Gordon's Car	3.00
46	Car #28 Robert Yates Racing	.50
47	Car #40 Team Sabco	.50
48	Car #43 Petty Enterprises	.50
49	Car #88 Robert Yates Racing	.50
50	Checklist	.50

1997 Score Board IQ $10 Phone Cards

The 10-card set captures the top drivers on foil stamping. The $10 phone cards are inserted at an average of one per ten packs.

	MT
Complete Set (10):	75.00
Common Driver:	8.00
PC1 Dale Earnhardt	15.00
PC2 #2 Miller Car	10.00
PC3 Bobby Labonte	8.00
PC4 #3 Goodwrench Car	12.00
PC5 Sterling Marlin	8.00
PC6 Mark Martin	10.00
PC7 Bill Elliott	12.00
PC8 Dale Jarrett	10.00
PC9 Ricky Rudd	8.00
PC10 Ernie Irvan	10.00

1997 Score Board IQ Remarques

Each card features a reprint of an original Sam Bass art work along with an unfinished area, where Bass personally hand draws the finishing touches on the first 100 of each of the ten cards in the set. The remaining 470 cards will be autographed by Bass. The inserts are printed on canvas stock and are sequentially numbered to 570. They are inserted one per 65 packs.

	MT
Complete Set (10):	400.00
Common Driver:	20.00
SB1 Dale Earnhardt	125.00
SB2 Jeff Gordon	125.00
SB3 Richard Childress	20.00
SB4 Ernie Irvan	40.00
SB5 #2 MGD Car	50.00
SB6 Darrell Waltrip	20.00
SB7 Richard Petty	30.00
SB8 Bobby Labonte	20.00
SB9 Alan Kulwicki	20.00
SB10 Terry Labonte	60.00

1997 Score Board SB

The complete regular sized 100-card set includes drivers, owners, crew chiefs. The full bleed card fronts feature one photo and his/her name written across the bottom. The backs contain statistics and biographical information updated through the end of the 1996 season and a photo. Each pack contains six cards.

		MT
Complete Set (100):		10.00
Common Driver:		.05
Wax Box:		35.00
1	Dale Earnhardt	1.00
2	Jeff Gordon	1.00
3	Terry Labonte	.50
4	Dale Jarrett	.40
5	Robby Gordon	.05
6	Mark Martin	.50
7	Ricky Rudd	.10
8	Richard Petty	.15
9	Ken Schrader	.05
10	Ernie Irvan	.40
11	Sterling Marlin	.15
12	Bobby Labonte	.05
13	Ted Musgrave	.05
14	Bobby Hamilton	.05
15	Jimmy Spencer	.05
16	Michael Waltrip	.05
17	Jeff Burton	.05
18	Rick Mast	.05
19	Geoff Bodine	.05
20	Ricky Craven	.05
21	Morgan Shepherd	.05
22	Johnny Benson	.05
23	Jeremy Mayfield	.05
24	Wally Dallenbach, Jr.	.05
25	Brett Bodine	.05
26	Lake Speed	.05
27	Ned Jarrett	.05
28	Darrell Waltrip	.05
29	Hut Stricklin	.05
30	Richard Petty	.15
31	Kyle Petty	.15
32	Robert Yates	.05
33	Roger Penske	.05
34	Robin Pemberton	.05
35	Ray Evernham	.05
36	Larry McReynolds	.05
37	Mike Wallace	.05
38	Derrick Cope	.05
39	Jeff Green	.05
40	Dale Jarrett	.40
41	Dale Earnhardt	1.00
42	Mark Martin	.50
43	Ricky Rudd	.05
44	Wood Brothers	.05
45	Chad Little	.05
46	Car #2 (Penske Racing South)	.05
47	Dale Earnhardt Car	.50
48	Car #4 (Morgan-McClure Racing)	.05
49	Car #6 (Roush Racing)	.05
50	Checklist 1	.05
51	Car #17 Darrell Waltrip	.05
52	Car #18 Joe Gibbs	.05
53	Car #21 (Wood Brothers Racing)	.05
54	Car #28 (Robert Yates Racing)	.05
55	Car #43 (Petty Enterprises)	.05
56	Dale Jarrett Car	.25
57	Sterling Marlin	.10
58	Ken Schrader	.05
59	Richard Childress	.05
60	Wood Brothers	.05
61	Tony Glover	.05
62	Steve Hmiel	.05
63	The Rainbow Warriors	.05
64	Jimmy Makar	.05
65	Larry McClure	.05
66	Ernie Irvan	.40
67	Dr. Jerry Punch	.05
68	Shelton Pittman	.05
69	Jack Roush	.05
70	Geoff Bodine	.05
71	Robert Pressley	.05
72	John Andretti	.05
73	Ward Burton	.05
74	Dick Trickle	.05
75	Dave Marcis	.05
76	Kenny Wallace	.05
77	Todd Bodine	.05
78	Gary Dehart	.05
79	Ron Hornaday	.05
80	David Green	.05
81	Randy Dorton	.05
82	The Kellogg's Crew	.05
83	Johnny Benson	.05
84	Jeremy Mayfield	.05
85	Ricky Craven	.05
86	#25 Hendrick Team	.05
87	Bobby Labonte	.05
88	Jimmy Johnson	.05
89	Jimmy Spencer	.05
90	Darrell Waltrip	.05
91	Morgan Shepherd	.05
92	Dale Earnhardt	1.00
93	Dale Jarrett	.40
94	Rick Hendrick	.05
95	Mark Martin	.50
96	Ricky Rudd	.05
97	Ernie Irvan	.40
98	Sterling Marlin	.15
99	Kyle Petty	.10
100	Checklist 2	.05

1997 Score Board SB Autographed Cards

Five top Winston Cup drivers autographed an average of 500 cards to be inserted into SB. Each card is hand numbered with "Authentic Autograph" stamped on the bottom left corner on the front of the card. Autographs are found on the average of one per 576 packs.

	MT
Complete Set (5):	600.00
Common Autograph:	25.00
AU1 Dale Earnhardt	250.00
AU2 Jeff Gordon	250.00
AU3 Terry Labonte	75.00
AU4 Dale Jarrett	50.00
AU5 Robby Gordon	25.00

1997 Score Board SB Race Chat

The card fronts of the 10-card set have a close-up photo of the driver on silver foil stamping. The backs give an up-close-and-personal look at the driver by getting quotes from the driver's owner, crew chief and the driver himself. These are seeded one per 36 packs.

	MT
Complete Set (10):	60.00
Common Driver:	4.00
RC1 Dale Earnhardt	25.00
RC2 Ricky Craven	4.00
RC3 Ernie Irvan	8.00
RC4 Dale Jarrett	8.00
RC5 Sterling Marlin	5.00
RC6 Mark Martin	12.00
RC7 Johnny Benson	4.00
RC8 Ricky Rudd	4.00
RC9 Bobby Labonte	4.00
RC10 Kyle Petty	5.00

1997 Score Board SB '96 W.C. Rewind

The 31-card insert set commemorates a major event which occurred at each of the 30 races during the '96 season. The 31st card, which will be hand numbered to 1,996, pays tribute to the 1996 Winston Cup Champion. They were inserted at an average rate of one per eight packs.

	MT
Complete Set (31):	50.00
Common Driver:	1.50
WC1 Dale Jarrett	2.50
WC2 Dale Earnhardt Car	5.00
WC3 Ted Musgrave	1.50
WC4 Johnny Benson	1.50
WC5 Ward Burton	1.50
WC6 Mark Martin	5.00
WC7 Robert Pressley	1.50
WC8 Ricky Craven	1.50
WC9 Sterling Marlin	1.50
WC10 Wally Dallenbach	1.50
WC11 Dale Jarrett	2.50
WC12 Bobby Labonte	1.50
WC13 Todd Bodine	1.50
WC14 Bobby Hamilton	1.50
WC15 Dave Marcis	1.50
WC16 Ernie Irvan	3.00
WC17 Ricky Rudd	1.50
WC18 Jeremy Mayfield	1.50
WC19 Dale Jarrett	2.50
WC20 Geoff Bodine	1.50
WC21 Jeff Burton	1.50
WC22 Mark Martin	5.00
WC23 Hut Stricklin	1.50
WC24 Ernie Irvan	3.00
WC25 Bobby Labonte	1.50
WC26 Bobby Hamilton	1.50
WC27 Ted Misgrave	1.50
WC28 Ricky Craven	1.50
WC29 Ricky Rudd	1.50
WC30 Bobby Hamilton	1.50
WC31 The Kellog's Team	1.50

1997 SkyBox NASCAR Profile

The 80-card base set available in five-card packs is printed on 24-point card stock with a matte finish and spot UV coating. The card fronts have a close up shot of the driver with an image of his car in the background.

	MT
Complete Set (80):	40.00
Common Driver:	.25
Wax Box:	90.00
1 John Andretti	.25
2 Johnny Benson	.25
3 Derrike Cope	.25
4 Ricky Craven	.25
5 Dale Earnhardt	5.00
6 Bill Elliott	2.50
7 Jeff Gordon	5.00
8 Robby Gordon	.25
9 Steve Grissom	.25
10 David Green	.25
11 Bobby Hamilton	.25
12 Bobby Hillan	.25
13 Ernie Irvan	2.00
14 Dale Jarrett	2.00
15 Bobby Labonte	.25
16 Terry Labonte	2.50
17 Dave Marcis	.25
18 Sterling Marlin	.25
19 Mark Martin	2.50
20 Rick Mast	.25
21 Jeremy Mayfield	.25
22 Ted Musgrave	.25
23 Joe Nemechek	.25
24 Ricky Rudd	.25
25 Ken Schrader	.25
26 Morgan Shepherd	.25
27 Hut Stricklin	.25
28 Dick Trickle	.25
29 Kenny Wallace	.25
30 Rusty Wallace	2.50
31 Michael Waltrip	.25
32 Richard Childress	.25
33 Richard Petty	.50
34 Rick Hendrick	.25
35 Robert Yates	.25
00 Joe Gibbs	.25
37 Cale Yarborough	.25
38 Jack Roush	.25
39 Ray Evernham	.25
40 Larry McReynolds	.25
41 Gary Dehart	.25
42 Todd Parrott	.25
43 Marc Reno	.25
44 Steve Hmiel	.25
45 Robin Pemberton	.25
46 Todd Bodine	.25
47 Jason Keller	.25
48 Randy LaJoie	.25
49 Phil Parsons	.25
50 Steve Parks	.25
51 Buckshot Jones	.25
52 Jeff Fuller	.25
53 Tracy Leslie	.25
54 Elton Sawyer	.25
55 Jeff Green	.25
56 Mike McLaughlin	.25
57 Ron Barfield	.25
58 Glenn Allen Jr.	.25
59 Kevin Lapage	.25
60 Rodney Combs	.25
61 Tim Fedewa	.25
62 R. Wallace Car	1.25
63 D. Earnhardt Car	2.50
64 S. Marlin Car	.25
65 T. Labonte Car	1.25
66 M. Martin Car	1.25
68 B. Labonte Car	.25
69 M. Waltrip Car	.25
70 J. Gordon Car	2.50
71 E. Irvan Car	1.00
72 K. Schrader Car	.25
73 36 Car	.25
74 37 Car	.25
75 40 Car	.25
76 B. Hamilton Car	.25
77 D. Jarrett Car	1.00
78 B. Elliott Car	1.25
79 97 Car	.25
80 Checklist	.25

1997 SkyBox NASCAR Profile Breakthrough

Nine of the top young drivers are showcased with a variety of foil stampings, gloss lamination and embossing, to give the cards a cutting edge look. These were inserted one per four packs.

	MT
Complete Set (9):	30.00
Common Driver:	2.50
J. Gordon	18.00
R. Gordon	4.00
R. Barfield	2.50
Benson	2.50
Steve Parks	2.50
Craven	2.50
B. Labonte	4.00
Mayfield	2.50
Green	2.50

1997 SkyBox NASCAR Profile Pace Setters

Nine top Winston Cup drivers who have attained milestones to put them in the record books are featured in this set. The card fronts have metallic ink on a matte finish and UV coating. These were seeded one per ten packs.

	MT
Complete Set (9):	100.00
Common Player:	5.00
E1 D. Earnhardt	25.00
E2 T. Labonte	15.00
E3 B. Elliott	15.00
E4 R. Rudd	5.00
E5 J. Gordon	25.00
E6 D. Jarrett	12.00
E7 M. Waltrip	5.00
E8 R. Wallace	15.00
E9 M. Martin	15.00

1997 SkyBox NASCAR Profile Team

This nine-card set features etched foil and gloss film laminate to highlight the card fronts, which have a group shot of the driver, crew chief and owners from each of the biggest winners on the circuit. They were seeded one per 100 packs.

	MT
Complete Set (9):	500.00
Common Driver:	15.00
T1 T. Labonte	60.00
T2 J. Gordon	125.00
T3 D. Jarrett	50.00
T4 D. Earnhardt	125.00
T5 M. Martin	60.00
T6 R. Rudd	15.00
T7 E. Irvan	50.00
T8 B. Elliott	60.00
T9 R. Wallace	60.00

1997 Upper Deck Collector's Choice

The 155-card set features a simple white bordered design with the Collectors Choice logo on the top right portion of the base cards and the make of the car on the mid-top left portion. The backs feature year by year stats, including wins and earnings for each year and also a brief commentary on each driver. The set also has a 50-card Maximum MPH subset that has information about some of the top driver's cars. Collector's Choice was available in 10-card packs.

	MT
Complete Set (155):	15.00
Common Driver:	.05
Wax Box:	35.00
1 Rick Mast	.05
2 Rusty Wallace	.75
3 Dale Earnhardt	1.50
4 Sterling Marlin	.20
5 Terry Labonte	.75
6 Mark Martin	.75
7 Geoff Bodine	.05
8 Hut Stricklin	.05
9 Lake Speed	.05
10 Ricky Rudd	.05
11 Brett Bodine	.05
12 Derrike Cope	.05
13 Bill Elliott	.75
14 Bobby Hamilton	.05
15 Wally Dallenbach	.05
16 Ted Musgrave	.05
17 Darrell Waltrip	.05
18 Bobby Labonte	.05
19 Loy Allen	.05
20 Morgan Shepherd	.05
21 Michael Waltrip	.05
22 Ward Burton	.05
23 Jimmy Spencer	.05
24 Jeff Gordon	1.50
25 Ken Schrader	.05
26 Kyle Petty	.05
27 Bobby Hillin	.05
28 Ernie Irvan	.50
29 Jeff Purvis	.05
30 Johnny Benson	.05
31 Dave Marcis	.05
32 Jeremy Mayfield	.05
33 Robert Pressley	.05
34 Jeff Burton	.05
35 Joe Nemechek	.05
36 Dale Jarrett	.25
37 John Andretti	.05
38 Kenny Wallace	.05
39 Elton Sawyer	.05
40 Dick Trickle	.05
41 Ricky Craven	.05
42 Chad Little	.05
43 Todd Bodine	.05
44 David Green	.05
45 Randy LaJoie	.05
46 Larry Pearson	.05
47 Jason Keller	.05
48 Hermie Sadler	.05
49 Mike McLaughlin	.05
50 Tim Fedewa	.05
51 Rick Mast	.05
52 Rusty Wallace	.40
53 Ricky Craven	.05
54 Sterling Marlin	.15
55 Terry Labonte	.40
56 Mark Martin	.40
57 Geoff Bodine	.05
58 Hut Stricklin	.05
59 Lake Speed	.05
60 Ricky Rudd	.05
61 Brett Bodine	.05
62 Derrike Cope	.05
63 Bill Elliott	.40
64 Bobby Hamilton	.05
65 Wally Dallenbach	.05
66 Ted Musgrave	.05
67 Darrell Waltrip	.05
68 Bobby Labonte	.05
69 Loy Allen	.05
70 Morgan Shepherd	.05
71 Michael Waltrip	.05
72 Ward Burton	.05
73 Jimmy Spencer	.05
74 Jeff Gordon	.75
75 Ken Schrader	.05
76 Kyle Petty	.05
77 Bobby Hillin	.05
78 Ernie Irvan	.25
79 Jeff Purvis	.05
80 Johnny Benson	.05
81 Dave Marcis	.05
82 Jeremy Mayfield	.05
83 Robert Pressley	.05
84 Jeff Burton	.05
85 Joe Nemechek	.05
86 Dale Jarrett	.15
87 John Andretti	.05
88 Kenny Wallace	.05
89 Elton Sawyer	.05
90 Dick Trickle	.05
91 Chad Little	.05
92 Todd Bodine	.05
93 David Green	.05
94 Randy LaJoie	.05
95 Larry Pearson	.05
96 Jason Keller	.05
97 Hermie Sadler	.05
98 Mike McLaughlin	.05
99 Tim Fedewa	.05
100 Patty Moise	.05
101 Jeff Gordon	.75
102 Rusty Wallace	.40
103 Sterling Marlin	.15
104 Terry Labonte	.40
105 Mark Martin	.40
106 Ricky Rudd	.05
107 Ted Musgrave	.05
108 Michael Waltrip	.05
109 Dale Jarrett	.15
110 Ernie Irvan	.25
111 Bill Elliott	.40
112 Ken Schrader	.05
113 Bobby Labonte	.05

114	Kyle Petty	.05
115	Ricky Craven	.05
116	Bobby Hamilton	.05
117	Johnny Benson	.05
118	Jeremy Mayfield	.05
119	Darrell Waltrip	.05
120	Junior Johnson	.05
121	Glen Wood	.05
122	Benny Parsons	.05
123	Bobby Allison	.05
124	Ned Jarrett	.05
125	Cale Yarborough	.05
126	Richard Petty	.25
127	Jeff Gordon	.75
128	Jeff Gordon	.75
129	Jeff Gordon	.75
130	Terry Labonte	.40
131	Terry Labonte	.40
132	Terry Labonte	.40
133	Ken Schrader	.05
134	Ken Schrader	.05
135	Ken Schrader	.05
136	Mark Martin	.40
137	Mark Martin	.40
138	Mark Martin	.40
139	Ted Musgrave	.05
140	Ted Musgrave	.05
141	Ted Musgrave	.05
142	Jeff Burton	.05
143	Jeff Burton	.05
144	Jeff Burton	.05
145	Rusty Wallace	.40
146	Ricky Craven	.05
147	Ricky Rudd	.05
148	Bill Elliott	.40
149	Joe Nemechek	.05
150	Brett Bodine	.05
151	Darrell Waltrip	.05
152	Geoff Bodine	.05
153	Dave Marcis	.05
154	Jeff Gordon	.75
155	Rusty Wallace	.40

1997 Upper Deck Collector's Choice Speedecals

This 48-card sticker insert set seeded 1:3 packs, includes car photos and photos of driver's helmets.

		MT
Complete Set (48):		18.00
Common Driver:		.25
S1	Rick Mast	.25
S2	Joe Nemechek	.25
S3	Rusty Wallace	1.00
S4	Rusty Wallace	1.00
S5	Bill Elliott	1.00
S6	Bill Elliott	1.00
S7	Sterling Marlin	.35
S8	Sterling Marlin	.35
S9	Terry Labonte	.75
S10	Terry Labonte	.75
S11	Mark Martin	1.00
S12	Mark Martin	1.00
S13	Bobby Hamilton	.25
S14	Derrike Cope	.25
S15	Ricky Craven	.25
S16	Ricky Craven	.25
S17	Lake Speed	.25
S18	Morgan Shepherd	.25
S19	Ricky Rudd	.25
S20	Ricky Rudd	.25
S21	Kyle Petty	.25
S22	Kyle Petty	.25
S23	Johnny Benson	.25
S24	Johnny Benson	.25
S25	Ernie Irvan	.60
S26	Kenny Wallace	.25

S27	Jeff Burton	.25
S28	Jeff Burton	.25
S29	Ken Schrader	.25
S30	Dave Marcis	.25
S31	Ted Musgrave	.25
S32	Ted Musgrave	.25
S33	Darrell Waltrip	.25
S34	Darrell Waltrip	.25
S35	Bobby Labonte	.25
S36	Bobby Labonte	.25
S37	Dale Jarrett	.50
S38	Dale Jarrett	.50
S39	Jeremy Mayfield	.25
S40	Jeremy Mayfield	.25
S41	Michael Waltrip	.25
S42	Michael Waltrip	.25
S43	Ward Burton	.25
S44	Wally Dallenbach	.25
S45	Wally Dallenbach	.25
S46	Jimmy Spencer	.25
S47	Jeff Gordon	2.00
S48	Jeff Gordon	2.00

1997 Upper Deck Collector's Choice Triple Force

This 30-card set is broken down into three-card puzzles that feature an event during the season when the die-cuts are put together. Triple Force inserts are found on the average of 1:11 packs.

		MT
Complete Set (30):		60.00
Common Player:		1.50
1A	Dale Jarrett	3.00
2A	Ernie Irvan	4.00
3A	Dale Jarrett	3.00
1B	Ted Musgrave	1.50
2B	Jeff Burton	1.50
3B	Mark Martin	5.00
1C	Johnny Benson	1.50
2C	Ricky Craven	1.50
3C	Jeremy Mayfield	1.50
1D	Terry Labonte	4.00
2D	Terry Labonte	4.00
3D	Terry Labonte	4.00
1E	Jimmy Spencer	1.50
2E	Dale Jarrett	3.00
3E	Michael Waltrip	1.50
1F	Jeff Gordon	10.00
2F	Terry Labonte	4.00
3F	Ken Schrader	1.50
1G	Terry Labonte	4.00
2G	Jeff Gordon	10.00
3G	Jeff Gordon	10.00
1H	Bobby Hamilton	1.50
2H	Rusty Wallace	5.00
3H	Geoff Bodine	1.50
1I	Ricky Craven	1.50
2I	Ernie Irvan	4.00
3I	Dale Jarrett	3.00
1J	Mark Martin	5.00
2J	Rusty Wallace	5.00
3J	Johnny Benson	1.50

1997 Upper Deck Collector's Choice Upper Deck 500

This 90-card interactive set can be played as a game with the first player to reach 500 laps declared the winner. Lap cards have different lap amounts that you use to accumulate laps as well as hazard cards that take laps away. These are inserted one per pack.

		MT
Complete Set (90):		10.00
Common Driver:		.05
UD1	Dale Earnhardt	1.50
UD2	Rusty Wallace	.75
UD3	Rusty Wallace	.75
UD4	Robin Pemberton	.05
UD5	Sterling Marlin	.15
UD6	Sterling Marlin	.15
UD7	Terry Labonte	.75
UD8	Terry Labonte	.75
UD9	Mark Martin	.75
UD10	Mark Martin	.75
UD11	Steve Hmiel	.05
UD12	Geoff Bodine	.05
UD13	Geoff Bodine	.05
UD14	Hut Stricklin	.05
UD15	Hut Stricklin	.05
UD16	Lake Speed	.05
UD17	Lake Speed	.05
UD18	Ricky Rudd	.05
UD19	Ricky Rudd	.05
UD20	Brett Bodine	.05
UD21	Brett Bodine	.05
UD22	Derrike Cope	.05
UD23	Derrike Cope	.05
UD24	Bobby Allison	.05
UD25	Bill Elliott	.75
UD26	Bill Elliott	.75
UD27	Bobby Hamilton	.05
UD28	Bobby Hamilton	.05
UD29	Richard Petty	.25
UD30	Wally Dallenbach	.05
UD31	Wally Dallenbach	.05
UD32	Ted Musgrave	.05
UD33	Ted Musgrave	.05
UD34	Darrell Waltrip	.05
UD35	Darrell Waltrip	.05
UD36	Bobby Labonte	.20
UD37	Bobby Labonte	.20
UD38	Loy Allen	.05
UD39	Loy Allen	.05
UD40	Morgan Shepherd	.05
UD41	Morgan Shepherd	.05
UD42	Michael Waltrip	.05
UD43	Michael Waltrip	.05
UD44	Ward Burton	.05
UD45	Ward Burton	.05
UD46	Jimmy Spencer	.05
UD47	Jimmy Spencer	.05
UD48	Jeff Gordon	1.50
UD49	Jeff Gordon	1.50
UD50	Ray Evernham	.05
UD51	Rick Hendrick	.05
UD52	Ken Schrader	.05
UD53	Ken Schrader	.05
UD54	Kyle Petty	.05
UD55	Kyle Petty	.05
UD56	Bobby Hillin	.05
UD57	Bobby Hillin	.05
UD58	Ernie Irvan	.50
UD59	Ernie Irvan	.50
UD60	Jeff Purvis	.05
UD61	Jeff Purvis	.05
UD62	Johnny Benson	.05
UD63	Johnny Benson	.05
UD64	Dave Marcis	.05
UD65	Dave Marcis	.05
UD66	Jeremy Mayfield	.05
UD67	Jeremy Mayfield	.05
UD68	Cale Yarborough	.05
UD69	Robert Pressley	.05
UD70	Robert Pressley	.05
UD71	Jeff Burton	.05
UD72	Jeff Burton	.05
UD73	Joe Nemechek	.05
UD74	Joe Nemechek	.05
UD75	Dale Jarrett	.50
UD76	Dale Jarrett	.50
UD77	John Andretti	.05
UD78	John Andretti	.05
UD79	Kenny Wallace	.05
UD80	Kenny Wallace	.05
UD81	Elton Sawyer	.05
UD82	Elton Sawyer	.05
UD83	Dick Trickle	.05
UD84	Dick Trickle	.05
UD85	Ricky Craven	.05
UD86	Ricky Craven	.05
UD87	Chad Little	.05
UD88	Chad Little	.05
UD89	Rick Mast	.05
UD90	Rick Mast	.05

1997 Upper Deck Collector's Choice Victory Circle

These inserts feature the top active drivers according to career victories when the product was released. Each insert documents the total number of career victories on the front of each card. There are 10 cards in the set with the insertion ratio stated at 1:50 packs.

		MT
Complete Set (10):		100.00
Common Driver:		4.00
VC1	Darrell Waltrip	4.00
VC2	Dale Earnhardt	30.00
VC3	Rusty Wallace	15.00
VC4	Bill Elliott	15.00
VC5	Mark Martin	15.00
VC6	Geoff Bodine	4.00
VC7	Terry Labonte	12.00
VC8	Ricky Rudd	4.00
VC9	Ernie Irvan	10.00
VC10	Jeff Gordon	30.00

1997 Upper Deck Road to the Cup

The 150-card regular sized set is broken down into six subsets: Heroes of the Hardtop (1-45), Power Plants (46-89), Inside Track (90-104), Haulin' (105-120), Alternators (121-142) and Thunder Struck (143-150). Driver cards feature silver foil stamping with the card fronts having one large photo of the driver. The backs have a small inset photo, with biographical information, statistics and a brief commentary.

		MT
Complete Set (150):		25.00
Common Driver:		.10
1	Terry Labonte	1.25
2	Jeff Gordon	2.50
3	Dale Jarrett	.75
4	Dale Earnhardt	2.50
5	Mark Martin	1.25
6	Ricky Rudd	.10
7	Rusty Wallace	1.25
8	Sterling Marlin	.10
9	Bobby Hamilton	.10
10	Ernie Irvan	.75
11	Bobby Labonte	.25

12	Bill Elliott	1.25
13	Kyle Petty	.20
14	Ken Schrader	.10
15	Jeff Burton	.10
16	Michael Waltrip	.10
17	Jimmy Spencer	.10
18	Ted Musgrave	.10
19	Geoff Bodine	.20
20	Rick Mast	.10
21	Morgan Shepherd	.10
22	Ricky Craven	.10
23	Johnny Benson	.10
24	Hut Stricklin	.10
25	Lake Speed	.10
26	Brett Bodine	.10
27	Wally Dallenbach	.10
28	Jeremy Mayfield	.10
29	Kenny Wallace	.10
30	Darrell Waltrip	.10
31	John Andretti	.10
32	Robert Pressley	.10
33	Ward Burton	.10
34	Joe Nemechek	.10
35	Derrike Cope	.10
36	Dick Trickle	.10
37	Dave Marcis	.10
38	Steve Grissom	.10
39	Mike Wallace	.10
40	Chad Little	.10
41	Gary Bradberry	.10
43	David Green	.10
44	Rick Mast	.10
45	J. Gordon Car	1.50
46	Terry Labonte (Power Plants)	.50
47	Jeff Gordon (Power Plants)	1.00
48	Dale Jarrett (Power Plants)	.40
49	Mark Martin (Power Plants)	.50
50	Ricky Rudd (Power Plants)	.10
51	Rusty Wallace (Power Plants)	.50
52	Sterling Marlin (Power Plants)	.10
53	Bobby Hamilton (Power Plants)	.10
54	Ernie Irvan (Power Plants)	.25
55	Bobby Labonte (Power Plants)	.20
56	Bill Elliott (Power Plants)	.50
57	Kyle Petty (Power Plants)	.10
58	Ken Schrader (Power Plants)	.10
59	Jeff Burton (Power Plants)	.10
60	Michael Waltrip (Power Plants)	.10
61	Jimmy Spencer (Power Plants)	.10
62	Ted Musgrave (Power Plants)	.10
63	Geoff Bodine (Power Plants)	.10
64	Rick Mast (Power Plants)	.10
65	Morgan Shepherd (Power Plants)	.10
66	Ricky Craven (Power Plants)	.10
67	Johnny Benson (Power Plants)	.10
68	Hut Stricklin (Power Plants)	.10
69	Lake Speed (Power Plants)	.10
70	Brett Bodine (Power Plants)	.10
71	Wally Dallenbach (Power Plants)	.10
72	Jeremy Mayfield (Power Plants)	.10
73	Kenny Wallace (Power Plants)	.10
74	Darrell Waltrip (Power Plants)	.10
75	John Andretti (Power Plants)	.10
76	Robert Pressley (Power Plants)	.10
77	Ward Burton (Power Plants)	.10
78	Joe Nemechek (Power Plants)	.10
79	Derrike Cope (Power Plants)	.10
80	Dick Trickle (Power Plants)	.10
81	Dave Marcis (Power Plants)	.10
82	Steve Grissom (Power Plants)	.10
83	Mike Wallace (Power Plants)	.10
84	Chad Little (Power Plants)	.10
85	Gary Bradberry (Power Plants)	.10
86	Terry Labonte (Power Plants)	1.00

87	Jeff Gordon (Power Plants)	2.00
88	Dale Jarrett (Power Plants)	.75
89	Mark Martin (Power Plants)	1.00
90	Terry Labonte (Inside Track)	.20
91	Rusty Wallace (Inside Track)	1.00
92	Dale Jarrett (Inside Track)	.20
93	Mark Martin (Inside Track)	.20
94	Ernie Irvan (Inside Track)	.75
95	Rusty Wallace (Inside Track)	.20
96	Bill Elliott (Inside Track)	1.00
97	Bobby Hamilton (Inside Track)	.10
98	Ernie Irvan (Inside Track)	.20
99	Bobby Labonte (Inside Track)	.20
100	Bill Elliott (Inside Track)	.20
101	Kyle Petty (Inside Track)	.10
102	Ricky Craven (Inside Track)	.10
103	Darrell Waltrip (Inside Track)	.10
104	(Inside Track)	.10
105	Terry Labonte (Haulin')	.20
106	Jeff Gordon (Haulin')	.20
107	Jeff Gordon (Haulin')	1.00
108	Dale Earnhardt (Haulin')	.10
109	Mark Martin (Haulin')	.10
110	Ricky Rudd (Haulin')	.10
111	Rusty Wallace (Haulin')	.15
112	Sterling Marlin (Haulin')	.10
113	Bobby Hamilton (Haulin')	.10
114	Ernie Irvan (Haulin')	.15
115	Bobby Labonte (Haulin')	.20
116	Bill Elliott (Haulin')	.15
117	Kyle Petty (Haulin')	.10
118	Ricky Craven (Haulin')	.10
119	Derrike Cope (Haulin')	.10
120	(Haulin')	.10
121	Dale Earnhardt (Alternators)	1.00
122	Sterling Marlin (Alternators)	.10
123	Bobby Hamilton (Alternators)	.10
124	Rusty Wallace (Alternators)	1.00
125	Kyle Petty (Alternators)	.10
126	Ken Schrader (Alternators)	.10
127	Ernie Irvan (Alternators)	.60
128	Rick Mast (Alternators)	.10
129	Morgan Shepherd (Alternators)	.10
130	Ricky Craven (Alternators)	.10
131	Lake Speed (Alternators)	.10
132	Brett Bodine (Alternators)	.10
133	Wally Dallenbach (Alternators)	.10
134	Robert Pressley (Alternators)	.10
135	Joe Nemechek (Alternators)	.10
136	Derrike Cope (Alternators)	.10
137	Steve Grissom (Alternators)	.10
138	Mike Wallace (Alternators)	.10
139	Chad Little (Alternators)	.10
140	(Alternators)	.10
141	David Green (Alternators)	.10
142	(Alternators)	.10
143	Mark Martin (Thunder Struck)	.20
144	Ernie Irvan (Thunder Struck)	.20
145	Geoff Bodine (Thunder Struck)	.10
146	Darrell Waltrip (Thunder Struck)	.10
147	Mark Martin (Thunder Struck)	1.00
148	(Thunder Struck)	.10
149	David Green (Thunder Struck)	.10
150	(Thunder Struck)	.10

1997 Upper Deck Road to the Cup Cup Quest

This set has three different levels featuring three different cards of each of the ten drivers in the series. The Green versions have silver Light F/X technology and are numbered to 5,000. The White version has gold Light F/X and is individually numbered to 1,000. The Checkered version features a die-cut cel card that is hand numbered to 100.

	MT
Complete Set (10).	100.00
Common Green Driver:	5.00
Complete White Set (10):	250.00
White Cup Quests:	1.5x to 2x
Complete Checkered Cup Set (10):	1500.
Checkered Cup Quests:	8x to 15x
CQ1 Terry Labonte	20.00
CQ2 Jeff Gordon	40.00
CQ3 Dale Earnhardt	40.00
CQ4 Dale Jarrett	15.00
CQ5 Rusty Wallace	20.00
CQ6 Ernie Irvan	15.00
CQ7 Mark Martin	20.00
CQ8 Sterling Marlin	6.00
CQ9 Bobby Hamilton	5.00
CQ10 Ricky Rudd	6.00

1997 Upper Deck Road to the Cup Million Dollar Memoirs

The 20-card set features five of the top Winston Cup circuit drivers. The card fronts have a large photo of the driver's car, with a miniture photo of the driver in the upper right quadrant. The driver's name and Million Dollar Memoirs are gold foil stamped. Each driver in the set has four different cards, they are seeded one per 20 packs.

	MT
Complete Set (20):	175.00
Common Driver:	8.00
T. Labonte (MM1-MM4):	10.00
J. Gordon (MM5-MM7):	20.00
R. Wallace (MM8-MM12):	10.00
D. Jarrett (MM13-MM16):	8.00
B. Elliott (MM17-MM20):	10.00

1997 Upper Deck Road to the Cup Million Dollar Autos.

This 20-card set is identical to the regular Million Dollar Memoirs set other than the driver's signature, which appears in most instances across the bottom portion on the front of the card.

	MT
Complete Set (20):	1100.
Common Driver:	60.00
T. Labonte (MM1-MM4):	75.00
J. Gordon (MM5-MM7):	150.00
R. Wallace (MM8-MM12):	75.00
D. Jarrett (MM13-MM16):	60.00
B. Elliott (MM17-MM20):	75.00

1997 Upper Deck Road to the Cup Hot Seat

Each of the nine cards in this set contain an actual piece of the driver's seat, window net or safety harness. There are three different cards for each of the three drivers, insertion odds are one per 1,117 packs.

	MT
Complete Set (9):	1200.
Common Driver:	100.00
Jeff Gordon Cards:	300.00
Dale Jarrett Cards:	100.00
Rusty Wallace Cards:	150.00

1997 Upper Deck Road to the Cup Predictor Plus

Each of the 30 cards in the set has three scratch bars, which reveals the goal the driver on the front of the card must achieve or exceed during the race indicated on the front of the card. By scratching only one, the collector can win a single Cel card of the driver pictured. If the collector wishes to scratch two bars he/she has the opportunity to win a set of 30 die-cut Cel cards, the third level is an entire set of Road to the Cup and the 30-card Cel set. Cards with one or more unobtained goals revealed are void. All claims must be postmarked by 1-30-98. Insertion odds are one per 11 packs.

		MT
Complete Set (30):		00.00
Common Driver:		1.50
Prices for Unscratched cards:		
1	Terry Labonte	8.00
2	Jeff Gordon	15.00
3	Dale Jarrett	6.00
4	Sterling Marlin	1.50
5	Ricky Craven	1.50
6	Ernie Irvan	6.00
7	Rusty Wallace	8.00
8	Dale Earnhardt	15.00
9	Terry Labonte	8.00
10	Bill Elliott	8.00
11	Jeff Gordon	15.00
12	Geoff Bodine	1.50
13	Dale Jarrett	6.00
14	Rusty Wallace	8.00
15	Jeremy Mayfield	1.50
16	Mark Martin	8.00
17	Ken Schrader	1.50
18	Jimmy Spencer	1.50
19	Ted Musgrave	1.50
20	Darrell Waltrip	1.50
21	Jeff Burton	1.50
22	Ward Burton	1.50
23	Ricky Rudd	1.50
24	Johnny Benson	1.50
25	Kyle Petty	1.50
26	Bobby Hamilton	1.50
27	Terry Labonte	8.00
28	Jeff Gordon	15.00
29	Bobby Labonte	1.50
30	Bill Elliott	8.00

1997 Upper Deck Road to the Cup Premiere Position

The 48-card regular sized die-cut set features 48 drivers who won the pole position in one of 24 races in 1996 and early 1997. The die-cuts match-up so the pole position winner combines with the winner of the race. These are seeded one per five packs.

	MT
Complete Set (48):	120.00
Common Player:	1.00
PP1 Ernie Irvan	3.00
PP2 Dale Jarrett	3.00
PP3 Terry Labonte	4.00
PP4 Ricky Rudd	1.00
PP5 Terry Labonte	4.00
PP6 Jeff Gordon	8.00
PP7 Johnny Benson	1.00
PP8 Bobby Hamilton	1.00
PP9 Ward Burton	1.00
PP10 Jeff Gordon	8.00
PP11 Mark Martin	4.00
PP12 Jeff Gordon	8.00
PP13 Ricky Craven	1.00
PP14 Rusty Wallace	4.00
PP15 Ernie Irvan	3.00
PP16 Sterling Marlin	1.00
PP17 Jeff Gordon	8.00
PP18 Dale Jarrett	3.00
PP19 Jeff Gordon	8.00
PP20 Jeff Gordon	8.00
PP21 Jeff Gordon	8.00
PP22 Terry Labonte	4.00
PP23 Derrike Cope	1.00
PP24 Rusty Wallace	4.00
PP25 Jeremy Mayfield	1.00
PP26 Jeff Gordon	8.00
PP27 Jeff Burton	1.00
PP28 Dale Jarrett	3.00
PP29 Dale Jarrett	3.00
PP30 Jeff Gordon	8.00
PP31 Rusty Wallace	4.00
PP32 Jeff Gordon	8.00
PP33 Ted Musgrave	1.00
PP34 Jeff Gordon	8.00
PP35 Dale Jarrett	3.00
PP36 Ricky Rudd	1.00
PP37 Bobby Labonte	1.00
PP38 Bobby Hamilton	1.00
PP39 Bobby Labonte	1.00
PP40 Bobby Labonte	1.00
PP41 Mike Skinner	1.00
PP42 Jeff Gordon	8.00
PP43 Geoff Bodine	1.00
PP44 Jeff Gordon	8.00
PP45 Geoff Bodine	1.00
PP46 Rusty Wallace	4.00
PP47 Dale Jarrett	3.00
PP48 Dale Jarrett	3.00

1997 Upper Deck SP

The regular-sized card set has a close-up shot of the driver on the front with silver-foil stamping. The backs have two shots of the driver, one in his car the other a mini close-up photo. The backs also have a brief commentary along with personal information and stats of the driver.

	MT
Complete Set (126):	125.00
Complete Single Flag Set (84):	20.00
Common Single Flag:	.20
Complete Double Flag Set (21):	30.00
Common Double Flags (85-105):	.75
Complete Triple Flag Set (21):	75.00
Common Triple Flags (106-126):	1.50
Wax Box:	75.00
1 Morgan Shepard	.20
2 Rusty Wallace	1.50
3 Dale Earnhardt	4.00
4 Sterling Marlin	.35
5 Terry Labonte	1.50
6 Mark Martin	1.50
7 Geoff Bodine	.20
8 Hut Stricklin	.20
9 Lake Speed	.20
10 Ricky Rudd	.20
11 Brett Bodine	.20
12 Dale Jarrett	1.00
13 Bill Elliott	1.50
14 Bobby Hamilton	.20
15 Wally Dallenbach	.20
16 Ted Musgrave	.20
17 Darrell Waltrip	.20
18 Bobby Labonte	.35
19 Loy Allen	.20
20 Rick Mast	.20
21 Michael Waltrip	.20
22 Ward Burton	.20
23 Jimmy Spencer	.20
24 Jeff Gordon	4.00
25 Ricky Craven	.20
26 Kyle Petty	.35
27 Bobby Hillin	.20
28 Ernie Irvan	1.00
29 Robert Pressley	.20
30 Johnny Benson	.20
31 Dave Marcis	.20
32 Jeremy Mayfield	.20
33 Ken Schrader	.20
34 Jeff Burton	.20
35 Chad Little	.20
36 Derrike Cope	.20
37 John Andretti	.20
38 Kenny Wallace	.20
39 Dick Trickle	.20
40 Robby Gordon	.20
41 Todd Bodine	.20
42 Joe Nemechek	.20
43 Morgan Shepard	.20
44 Rusty Wallace	.75
45 Dale Earnhardt	2.00
46 Sterling Marlin	.20
47 Terry Labonte	.75
48 Mark Martin	.75
49 Geoff Bodine	.20
50 Hut Stricklin	.20
51 Lake Speed	.20
52 Ricky Rudd	.20
53 Brett Bodine	.20
54 Dale Jarrett	.50
55 Bill Elliott	.75
56 Bobby Hamilton	.20
57 Wally Dallenbach	.20
58 Ted Musgrave	.20
59 Darrell Waltrip	.20
60 Bobby Labonte	.20
61 Loy Allen	.20
62 Rick Mast	.20
63 Michael Waltrip	.20
64 Ward Burton	.20
65 Jimmy Spencer	.20
66 Jeff Gordon	2.00
67 Ricky Craven	.20
68 Kyle Petty	.20
69 Bobby Hillin	.20
70 Ernie Irvan	.50
71 Robert Pressley	.20
72 Johnny Benson	.20
73 Dave Marcis	.20
74 Jeremy Mayfield	.20
75 Ken Schrader	.20
76 Jeff Burton	.20
77 Chad Little	.20
78 Derrike Cope	.20
79 John Andretti	.20
80 Kenny Wallace	.20
81 Dick Trickle	.20
82 Robby Gordon	.20
83 Todd Bodine	.20
84 Joe Nemechek	.20
85 Rusty Wallace	4.00
86 Sterling Marlin	.75
87 Terry Labonte	4.00
88 Mark Martin	4.00
89 Geoff Bodine	.75
90 Lake Speed	.75
91 Ricky Rudd	.75
92 Dale Jarrett	3.00
93 Bill Elliott	4.00
94 Bobby Hamilton	.75
95 Wally Dallenbach	.75
96 Ted Musgrave	.75
97 Darrell Waltrip	.75
98 Bobby Labonte	.75
99 Michael Waltrip	.75
100 Ward Burton	.75
101 Jimmy Spencer	.75
102 Jeff Gordon	10.00
103 Ricky Craven	.75
104 Kyle Petty	.75
105 Ernie Irvan	3.00
106 Johnny Benson	1.50
107 Jeremy Mayfield	1.50
108 Ken Schrader	1.50
109 Jeff Burton	1.50
110 Derrike Cope	1.50
111 John Andretti	1.50
112 Kenny Wallace	1.50
113 Rusty Wallace	12.00
114 Sterling Marlin	2.00
115 Terry Labonte	12.00
116 Mark Martin	12.00
117 Ricky Rudd	1.50
118 Dale Jarrett	8.00
119 Bill Elliott	12.00
120 Bobby Labonte	2.00
121 Jimmy Spencer	1.50
122 Jeff Gordon	25.00
123 Kyle Petty	2.00
124 Ernie Irvan	8.00
125 Ricky Craven	1.50
126 Ken Schrader	1.50

1997 Upper Deck SP Race Film

This 10-card set uses actual race film to highlight NASCAR's hottest drivers and their accomplishments. The set is individually numbered to 400 sets.

	MT
Complete Set (10):	800.00
Common Driver:	25.00
RD1 Jeff Gordon	175.00
RD2 Rusty Wallace	100.00
RD3 Dale Earnhardt	175.00
RD4 Sterling Marlin	25.00
RD5 Terry Labonte	100.00
RD6 Mark Martin	100.00
RD7 Dale Jarrett	75.00
RD8 Ernie Irvan	75.00
RD9 Bill Elliott	100.00
RD10 Ricky Rudd	25.00

1997 Upper Deck SP SPx Force Autographs

	MT
Complete Set (4):	600.00
Common Driver:	80.00
SF1 Jeff Gordon	350.00
SF2 Rusty Wallace	125.00
SF3 Ricky Craven	80.00
SF4 Terry Labonte	125.00

1997 Upper Deck Victory Circle

This 120-card set includes the date the photo was taken to chronicle some of the racing moments from the season. The base cards include a close-up of the driver, with the driver's name and the make of his car written vertically on the left-hand side of the card. The card backs feature a brief commentary, career highlights and stats from the prior season.

	MT
Complete Set (120):	18.00
Common Driver:	.10
Wax Box:	70.00
1 Rick Mast	.10
2 Rusty Wallace	1.50
3 Dale Earnhardt	3.00
4 Sterling Marlin	.20
5 Terry Labonte	1.50
6 Mark Martin	1.50
7 Geoff Bodine	.10
8 Hut Stricklin	.10
9 Lake Speed	.10
10 Ricky Rudd	.10
11 Brett Bodine	.10
12 Derrike Cope	.10
13 Bill Elliott	1.50
14 Bobby Hamilton	.10
15 Wally Dallenbach	.10
16 Ted Musgrave	.10
17 Darrell Waltrip	.10
18 Bobby Labonte	.10
19 Loy Allen	.10
20 Morgan Shepherd	.10
21 Michael Waltrip	.10
22 Ward Burton	.10
23 Jimmy Spencer	.10
24 Jeff Gordon	3.00
25 Ken Schrader	.10
26 Kyle Petty	.10
27 Bobby Hillin	.10
28 Ernie Irvan	1.00
29 Jeff Purvis	.10
30 Johnny Benson	.10
31 Dave Marcis	.10
32 Jeremy Mayfield	.10
33 Robert Pressley	.10
34 Jeff Burton	.10
35 Joe Nemechek	.10
36 Dale Jarrett	.50
37 John Andretti	.10
38 Kenny Wallace	.10
39 Elton Sawyer	.10
40 Dick Trickle	.10
41 Ricky Craven	.10
42 Chad Little	.10
43 Todd Bodine	.10
44 David Green	.10
45 Randy LaJoie	.10
46 Larry Pearson	.10
47 Jason Keller	.10
48 Hermie Sadler	.10
49 Mike McLaughlin	.10
50 Tim Fedewa	.10
51 Rick Mast	.10
52 Rusty Wallace	1.50
53 Ricky Craven	.10
54 Sterling Marlin	.20
55 Terry Labonte	1.50
56 Mark Martin	1.50
57 Geoff Bodine	.10
58 Hut Stricklin	.10
59 Lake Speed	.10
60 Ricky Rudd	.10
61 Brett Bodine	.10
62 Derrike Cope	.10
63 Bill Elliott	1.50
64 Bobby Hamilton	.10
65 Wally Dallenbach	.10
66 Ted Musgrave	.10
67 Darrell Waltrip	.10
68 Bobby Labonte	.10
69 Loy Allen	.10
70 Morgan Shepherd	.10
71 Michael Waltrip	.10
72 Ward Burton	.10

73	Jimmy Spencer	.10
74	Jeff Gordon	3.00
75	Ken Schrader	.10
76	Kyle Petty	.10
77	Bobby Hillin	.10
78	Ernie Irvan	1.00
79	Jeff Purvis	.10
80	Johnny Benson	.10
81	Dave Marcis	.10
82	Jeremy Mayfield	.10
83	Robert Pressley	.10
84	Jeff Burton	.10
85	Joe Nemechek	.10
86	Dale Jarrett	.50
87	John Andretti	.10
88	Kenny Wallace	.10
89	Elton Sawyer	.10
90	Dick Trickle	.10
91	Chad Little	.10
92	Todd Bodine	.10
93	David Green	.10
94	Randy LaJoie	.10
95	Larry Pearson	.10
96	Jason Keller	.10
97	Hermie Sadler	.10
98	Mike McLaughlin	.10
99	Tim Fedewa	.10
100	Patty Moise	.10
101	Dale Jarrett	.50
102	Ricky Rudd	.10
103	Rusty Wallace	1.50
104	Sterling Marlin	.20
105	Geoff Bodine	.10
106	John Andretti	.10
107	Jeremy Mayfield	.10
108	Terry Labonte	1.50
109	Mark Martin	1.50
110	Derrick Cope	.10
111	Jeff Gordon	3.00
112	Ricky Craven	.10
113	Ted Musgrave	.10
114	Joe Nemechek	.10
115	Bill Elliott	1.50
116	Kenny Wallace	.10
117	Darrell Waltrip	.10
118	Bobby Labonte	.10
119	North Wilkesboro Speedway	.10
120	North Wilkesboro Speedway	.10

1997 Upper Deck Victory Circle A Piece of the Action

These 1:699 contain an authentic piece of race-worn uniform from the drivers, including pieces of glove, suit and shoe.

	MT
Complete Set (9)	1000.
Common Driver:	60.00
J. Gordon: FS1-FS3	250.00
R. Wallace: FS4-FS6	125.00
D. Jarrott: FS7-FS9	60.00
FS1 Jeff Gordon	250.00
FS2 Jeff Gordon	250.00
FS3 Jeff Gordon	250.00
FS4 Rusty Wallace	125.00
FS5 Rusty Wallace	125.00
FS6 Rusty Wallace	125.00
FS7 Dale Jarrett	75.00
FS8 Dale Jarrett	75.00
FS9 Dale Jarrett	75.00

1997 Upper Deck Victory Circle Championship Reflections

This 10-card set features the top 10 finishers in points standing from the 1996 season. The card fronts have a metallic look with the driver encircled in an oval. The backs have a brief commentary along with a small inset photo of the driver.

	MT
Complete Set (10):	18.00
Common Driver:	1.00
CR1 Terry Labonte	2.50
CR2 Jeff Gordon	5.00
CR3 Dale Jarrett	2.00
CR4 Dale Earnhardt	5.00
CR5 Mark Martin	2.50
CR6 Ricky Rudd	1.00
CR7 Rusty Wallace	2.50
CR8 Sterling Marlin	1.25
CR9 Bobby Hamilton	1.00
CR10 Ernie Irvan	2.00

1997 Upper Deck Victory Circle Crowning Achievement

This five-card die-cut insert set features the 1996 Winston Cup Points champion, Terry Labonte. Seeded 1:35 packs, each features a close-up photo from Labonte's championship season.

	MT
Complete Set (5):	35.00
Common Labonte:	8.00
CA1 Terry Labonte	8.00
CA2 Terry Labonte	8.00
CA3 Terry Labonte	8.00
CA4 Terry Labonte	8.00
CA5 Terry Labonte	8.00

1997 Upper Deck Victory Circle Driver's Seat

This 10-card set features a cel technology that provides a view of what it's like in the driver's seat. These are seeded 1:69 packs.

	MT
Complete Set (10):	175.00
Common Driver:	6.00
DS1 Dale Earnhardt	50.00
DS2 Jeff Gordon	50.00
DS3 Terry Labonte	25.00
DS4 Ken Schrader	6.00
DS5 Sterling Marlin	8.00
DS6 Mark Martin	25.00
DS7 Rusty Wallace	25.00
DS8 Bobby Labonte	6.00
DS9 Ernie Irvan	20.00
DS10 Dale Jarrett	15.00

1997 Upper Deck Victory Circle Generation Excitement

This five-card set highlights NASCAR's hottest up-and-coming drivers. These are seeded 1:11 packs.

	MT
Complete Set (5):	15.00
Common Driver:	2.00
GE1 Jeff Gordon	10.00
GE2 Bobby Hamilton	2.00
GE3 Johnny Benson	2.00
GE4 Ricky Craven	2.00
GE5 Bobby Labonte	2.00

1997 Upper Deck Victory Circle Predictor

This 10-card interactive set allows the collector to win when the driver depicted on the card achieves the goal listed on the card during any one race throughout the season. They have a die-cut design and are seeded 1:21 packs.

	MT
Complete Set (10):	50.00
Common Driver:	3.00
PE1 Jeff Gordon	15.00
PE2 Rusty Wallace	8.00
PE3 Dale Jarrett	5.00
PE4 Sterling Marlin	4.00
PE5 Terry Labonte	8.00
PE6 Mark Martin	8.00
PE7 Bobby Labonte	3.00
PE8 Ernie Irvan	6.00
PE9 Bill Elliott	8.00
PE10 Ricky Rudd	3.00

1997 Upper Deck Victory Circle Victory Lap

This 10-card hobby only insert set features a die-cut design that looks like a checkered flag. All of the drivers in the set took a trip to victory lane, with the date they won highlighted at the top of the card. These are seeded 1:109 packs.

	MT
Complete Set (10):	250.00
Common Driver:	10.00
VL1 Dale Earnhardt	80.00
VL2 Jeff Gordon	80.00
VL3 Bobby Labonte	10.00
VL4 Dale Jarrett	25.00
VL5 Ernie Irvan	30.00
VL6 Sterling Marlin	15.00
VL7 Ricky Rudd	10.00
VL8 Geoff Bodine	10.00
VL9 Bobby Hamilton	10.00
VL10 Rusty Wallace	40.00

1997 Wheels Predator

This 66-card set is printed on 20-point card stock and UV coated with silver foil stamping. The card fronts feature a close-up photo, while the backs identify the driver's car and his career stats. First Slash versions of the base set as well as the inserts come from the first 375 cases printed.

	MT
Complete Set (66):	20.00
Common Driver:	.15
Complete First Slash Set (66):	40.00
First Slash:	1x to 2x
Grizzlies:	5x to 8x
Red Wolf:	10x to 20x
Wax Box:	60.00
1 Jeff Gordon	3.00
2 Terry Labonte	1.25
3 Dale Earnhardt	3.00
4 Dale Jarrett	.75
5 Mark Martin	1.25
6 Rusty Wallace	1.25
7 Sterling Marlin	.40
8 David Green	.15
9 Jeff Burton	.15
10 Bobby Hamilton	.15
11 Michael Waltrip	.15
12 Bobby Labonte	.25
13 Ricky Craven	.25
14 Johnny Benson	.15
15 Jeremy Mayfield	.15
16 Hut Stricklin	.15
17 Kyle Petty	.25
18 Darrell Waltrip	.15
19 John Andretti	.15
20 Bill Elliott	1.25
21 Robert Pressley	.15
22 Joe Nemechek	.15
23 Derrick Cope	.15
24 Ward Burton	.15
25 Chad Little	.15
26 Mike Skinner	.15
27 Jimmy Spencer	.15
28 Dave Marcis	.15
29 Wally Dallenbach	.15
30 Kenny Wallace	.15
31 Brett Bodine	.15
32 Ted Musgrave	.15
33 Robby Gordon	.25
34 Randy LaJoie	.15
35 Jeff Fuller	.15
36 Jason Keller	.15
37 Mike McLaughlin	.15
38 Bobby Labonte	.15
39 Dale Jarrett	.50
40 Michael Waltrip	.15
41 Mark Martin	1.00
42 Steve Park	.15
43 Glenn Allen	.15
44 Gordon (Martinsville)	2.00
45 T. Labonte (Charlotte)	.75
46 Hamilton (Phoenix)	.15
47 B. Labonte (Atlanta)	.15
48 Ray Evernham	.15
49 Gary DeHart	.15
50 Todd Parrott	.15
51 Steve Hmiel	.15
52 Robin Pemberton	.15
53 Jimmy Makar	.15

54	Jeff Hammond	.15
55	Larry McReynolds	.15
56	Kevin Hamlin	.15
57	David Smith	.15
58	Richard Childress	.15
59	Joe Gibbs	.15
60	Rick Hendrick	.15
61	Robert Yates	.15
62	Johnny Benson ('96 Champions)	.15
63	Randy LaJoie ('96 Champions)	.15
64	Bill Elliott ('96 Champions)	1.00
65	Ron Hornaday ('96 Champions)	.15
66	Checklist ('96 Champions)	.15

1997 Wheels Predator American Eagle

This 10-card set features double foil stamping and multi-level embossing and features the American Eagle as the insert set's theme, they were seeded 1:30 packs.

	MT
Complete Set (10):	100.00
Common Driver:	6.00
First Slash:	1x to 1.5x
AE1 Dale Earnhardt	30.00
AE2 Jeff Gordon	30.00
AE3 Rusty Wallace	12.00
AE4 Terry Labonte	12.00
AE5 Dale Jarrett	10.00
AE6 Sterling Marlin	6.00
AE7 Mark Martin	12.00
AE8 Bobby Labonte	6.00
AE9 Bill Elliott	12.00
AE10 Darrell Waltrip	6.00

1997 Wheels Predator Eye of the Tiger

This foil enhanced, micro-etched card showcases eight of the most feared drivers in the NASCAR circuit. The fronts feature an image of a tiger in the top left corner of the card, they were inserted 1:10 packs.

	MT
Complete Set (8):	30.00
Common Driver:	2.00
First Slash:	1x to 1.5x
ET1 Dale Earnhardt	10.00
ET2 Jeff Gordon	10.00
ET3 Rusty Wallace	5.00
ET4 Terry Labonte	5.00
ET5 Dale Jarrett	3.50
ET6 Mark Martin	5.00
ET7 Bobby Labonte	2.00
ET8 Sterling Marlin	2.00

1997 Wheels Predator Gatorbacks

Multi-level embossing on simulated crocodile hide are the features of this 10-card set, that is otherwise identical to the Gatorback Authentics. These were inserted 1:40 packs.

	MT
Complete Set (10):	125.00
Common Driver:	8.00
First Slash:	1x to 1.5x
GB1 Dale Earnhardt	40.00
GB2 Jeff Gordon	40.00
GB3 Mike Skinner	8.00
GB4 Dale Jarrett	14.00
GB5 Rusty Wallace	20.00
GB6 Bobby Labonte	8.00
GB7 Mark Martin	20.00
GB8 Sterling Marlin	8.00
GB9 Darrell Waltrip	8.00
GB10 Bill Elliott	20.00

1997 Wheels Predator Gatorback Authentic

This 10-card set has double foil stamping and micro-etching, that is highlighted by a piece of actual crocodile skin imported from Australia on the card front. These were seeded 1:120 packs.

	MT
Complete Set (10):	500.00
Common Driver:	20.00
First Slash:	1.5x to 2x
GBA1 Dale Earnhardt	125.00
GBA2 Jeff Gordon	125.00
GBA3 Mike Skinner	20.00
GBA4 Dale Jarrett	45.00
GBA5 Rusty Wallace	75.00
GBA6 Bobby Labonte	20.00
GBA7 Mark Martin	75.00
GBA8 Sterling Marlin	20.00
GBA9 Darrell Waltrip	20.00
GBA10 Bill Elliott	70.00

1997 Wheels Predator Golden Eagle

This 10-card set is identical to the American Eagle set other than it's gold foil stamping. These were inserted 1:40 packs.

	MT
Complete Set (10):	140.00
Common Driver:	8.00
GE1 Dale Earnhardt	40.00
GE2 Jeff Gordon	40.00
GE3 Rusty Wallace	20.00
GE4 Terry Labonte	20.00
GE5 Dale Jarrett	14.00
GE6 Sterling Marlin	8.00
GE7 Mark Martin	20.00
GE8 Bobby Labonte	10.00
GE9 Bill Elliott	20.00
GE10 Darrell Waltrip	8.00

1997 Wheels Predator Jeff Gordon First Slash Promos

This 1:30 pack Jeff Gordon insert has two versions-Black Wolf (First Slash) and Red Wolf (Retail).

	MT
Black Wolf (First Slash):	15.00
Red Wolf (Retail):	10.00

1997 Wheels Predator Terry Labonte Double Eagle

This insert salutes Terry Labonte's Winston Cup Championship seasons in 1984 and 1996. Two versions exist, Gold (First Slash) and Silver (Hobby). These were inserted 1:180 packs.

	MT
Golden Double Eagle (GD1):	35.00
Silver Double Eagle (SD1):	25.00

1997 Wheels Race Sharks

Printed on 36-point stock, UV coated, and foil stamped with an image of a shark in the background the 45-card set consists of all the top NASCAR drivers. The card backs include a photo of the driver's car along with a brief commentary of the driver.

	MT
Complete Set (45):	20.00
Common Driver:	.15
First Bite Complete Set (45):	40.00
First Bites:	1x to 2x
Wax Box:	75.00
1 Dale Earnhardt	3.00
2 Jeff Gordon	3.00
3 Dale Jarrett	1.00
4 Terry Labonte	1.50
5 Rusty Wallace	1.50
6 Mark Martin	1.50
7 Sterling Marlin	.25
8 Bill Elliott	1.50
9 Bobby Labonte	.15
10 Bobby Hamilton	.15
11 Darrell Waltrip	.15
12 Michael Waltrip	.15
13 Mike Wallace	.15
14 Kyle Petty	.15
15 Ken Schrader	.15
16 Ricky Craven	.15
17 Derrike Cope	.15
18 Jeff Burton	.15
19 Ward Burton	.15
20 Robert Pressley	.15
21 Joe Nemechek	.15
22 Brett Bodine	.15
23 Jimmy Spencer	.15
24 Chad Little	.15
25 Bobby Labonte	.15
26 Terry Labonte	.75
27 Mark Martin	.75
28 Jeff Green	.15
29 David Green	.15
30 Dale Jarrett	.50
31 Joe Gibbs	.15
32 Richard Childress	.15
33 Bobby Allison	.15
34 Dale Jarrett	.50
35 Jeff Gordon	2.00
36 Jeff Gordon	2.00
37 Rusty Wallace	1.00
38 Sterling Marlin	.25
39 Rusty Wallace	1.00
40 Jeff Gordon	2.00
41 Dale Jarrett	.50
42 Rusty Wallace	2.00
43 Jeff Gordon	2.00
44 Checklist	.15
45 Checklist	.15

1997 Wheels Race Sharks Hammerhead

This 45-card parallel set to the base set features 36-point card stock, UV coating and foil stamping. They are seeded 1:8 packs with 1,350 total sets produced.

	MT
Complete Set (45):	200.00
Common Card:	2.00
Hammerheads:	5x to 10x

1997 Wheels Race Sharks Tiger Shark

This is a parallel to the 45-card base set. Seeded 1:16 packs, each card is double foil stamped and micro-etched. 675 sets were produced.

	MT
Complete Set (45):	400.00
Common Card:	3.00
Tiger Sharks:	15x to 25x

1997 Wheels Race Sharks Great White

This 10-card set features a real shark's tooth embedded in each insert. Featuring the top drivers in NASCAR, these are seeded 1:96 packs.

	MT
Complete Set (10):	400.00
Common Driver:	12.00
GW1 Dale Earnhardt	100.00
GW2 Jeff Gordon	100.00
GW3 Terry Labonte	50.00
GW4 Dale Jarrett	25.00
GW5 Rusty Wallace	50.00
GW6 Mark Martin	50.00
GW7 Bobby Labonte	12.00
GW8 Bill Elliott	50.00
GW9 Sterling Marlin	15.00
GW10 Ricky Craven	12.00

1997 Wheels Race Sharks Shark Tooth Signature

This 25-card autographed set is comprised of autographs by various Winston Cup and Busch Grand National drivers, crew chiefs and owners. Autographs are inserted 1:24 packs.

	MT
Complete Set (25):	650.00
ST1 Dale Earnhardt	200.00
ST2 Jeff Gordon	200.00
ST3 Dale Jarrett	60.00
ST4 Terry Labonte	100.00
ST5 Sterling Marlin	30.00
ST6 Bill Elliott	100.00
ST7 Ricky Craven	10.00
ST8 Robert Pressley	10.00
ST9 Jeff Burton	10.00
ST10 Ward Burton	10.00
ST11 Bobby Labonte	10.00
ST12 Joe Nemechek	10.00
ST13 Chad Little	10.00
ST14 David Green	10.00
ST15 Jeff Green	10.00
ST16 Joe Gibbs	10.00
ST17 Todd Parrott	10.00
ST18 Jeff Hammond	10.00
ST19 Charlie Pressley	10.00
ST20 Joey Knuckles	10.00
ST21 David Smith	10.00
ST22 Brad Parrott	10.00
ST23 Eddie Dickerson	10.00
ST24 Randy Dorton	10.00
ST25 Jimmy Johnson	10.00

1997 Wheels Race Sharks Shark Attack

This 10-card set features top Winston Cup drivers and is highlighted by foil stamping, micro-etching and features a simulated shark's tooth embossed on each card. These are inserted 1:48 packs. Also included were Preview Shark Attacks, which were inserted as boxtoppers in Crown Jewel Elite Boxes, the cards were unnumbered.

	MT
Complete Set (10):	125.00
Common Driver:	8.00
SA1 Dale Earnhardt	50.00
SA2 Jeff Gordon	50.00
SA3 Dale Jarrett	15.00
SA4 Rusty Wallace	25.00
SA5 Terry Labonte	25.00
SA6 Sterling Marlin	8.00
SA7 Michael Waltrip	8.00
SA8 Kyle Petty	8.00
SA9 Ward Burton	8.00
SA10 Jeff Burton	8.00

1997 Wheels Viper

The 82-card regular sized set, available in five card packs are printed on a thick card stock, with the driver's name and Viper logo stamped with chrome foil. The full bleed card fronts have one photo of the driver while the backs give a brief wrap-up of each driver's career. First Strike parallel versions also exist with First Strike stamped across the front of the card, otherwise the card designs are identical.

	MT
Complete Set (82):	20.00
Common Driver:	.20
1 Jeff Gordon	3.00
2 Dale Jarrett	1.00
3 Terry Labonte	1.50
4 Mark Martin	1.50
5 Rusty Wallace	1.50
6 Bobby Labonte	.30
7 Sterling Marlin	.20
8 Jeff Burton	.20
9 Ted Musgrave	.20
10 Michael Waltrip	.20
11 David Green	.20
12 Ricky Craven	.20
13 Johnny Benson	.20
14 Jeremy Mayfield	.20
15 Bobby Hamilton	.20
16 Kyle Petty	.20
17 Darrell Waltrip	.20
18 Wally Dallenbach	.20
19 Bill Elliott	1.50
20 Robert Pressley	.20
21 Joe Nemechek	.20
22 Derrike Cope	.20
23 Ward Burton	.20
24 Chad Little	.20
25 Mike Skinner	.20
26 Brett Bodine	.20
27 Hut Stricklin	.20
28 Dave Marcis	.20
29 Ken Schrader	.20
30 Steve Grissom	.20
31 Robby Gordon	.20
32 Kenny Wallace	.20
33 Bobby Hillin, Jr.	.20
34 Jimmy Spencer	.20
35 Dick Trickle	.20
36 John Andretti	.20
37 Steve Park	.20
38 Jeff Burton	.20
39 Michael Waltrip	.20
40 Dale Jarrett	.75
41 Mike McLaughlin	.20
42 Todd Bodine	.20
43 Bobby Labonte	.20
44 Jeff Fuller	.20
45 Kyle Petty	.20
46 Jason Keller	.20
47 Mark Martin	1.00
48 Randy LaJoie	.20
49 Joe Nemechek	.20
50 Glenn Allen	.20
51 Jeff Gordon	1.50
52 Rusty Wallace	.75
53 Dale Jarrett	.50
54 Jeff Burton	.20
55 Dale Jarrett	.50
56 Jeff Hammond	.20
57 Andy Petree	.20
58 Robbie Loomis	.20
59 Mike Beam	.20
60 Buddy Parrott	.20
61 Roger Penske	.20
62 Bill Davis	.20
63 Travis Carter	.20
64 Chuck Rider	.20
65 Felix Sabates	.20
66 Larry Hedrick	.20
67 R. Wallace Car	.75
68 D. Earnhardt Car	1.50
69 T. Labonte Car	.75
70 M. Martin Car	.75
71 B. Bodine Car	.20
72 B. Labonte Car	.20
73 J. Spencer Car	.20
74 J. Gordon Car	1.50
75 Car #31 Chevrolet	.20
76 Car #40 Chevrolet	.20
77 J. Nemechek Car	.20
78 K. Petty Car	.20
79 D. Jarrett Car	.50
80 B. Elliott Car	.75
81 Checklist	.20
82 Checklist	.20

1997 Wheels Viper Black Racer

This 82-card parallel set has the driver's name and logo printed with gold foil stamping with a shimmering steel etched serpent encircling each driver. Black Racers can be found on the average of one per six packs.

	MT
Complete Set (82):	150.00
Common Driver:	2.00
Black Racers:	5x to 10x

1997 Wheels Viper Anaconda

The 13-card set features a super-sized snake stamped with black and gold metal foil, printed with a 3-D background. Found exclusively in Western and Eastern hobby boxes, they are seeded one per 48 packs.

	MT
Complete Set (13):	260.00
Common Driver:	10.00
A1 Terry Labonte	30.00
A2 Jeff Gordon	60.00
A3 Dale Jarrett	20.00
A4 Bobby Labonte	10.00
A5 Dale Earnhardt	60.00
A6 Rusty Wallace	30.00
A7 Darrell Waltrip	10.00
A8 Joe Nemechek	10.00
A9 Jeremy Mayfield	10.00
A10 Bill Elliott	30.00
A11 Jeff Burton	10.00
A12 Mark Martin	30.00
A13 Kyle Petty	10.00

1997 Wheels Viper Cobra

The 10-card set features micro-etching with gold and black foil stamping. The card fronts have a photo of the driver beside a picture of a cobra ready to strike. They are seeded one per 24 packs.

	MT
Complete Set (10):	80.00
Common Driver:	4.00
C1 Dale Earnhardt	20.00
C2 Jeff Gordon	20.00
C3 Bobby Labonte	4.00
C4 Terry Labonte	10.00
C5 Rusty Wallace	10.00
C6 Bill Elliott	10.00
C7 Sterling Marlin	4.00
C8 Mark Martin	10.00
C9 Dale Jarrett	8.00
C10 Kyle Petty	4.00

1997 Wheels Viper Diamondback

The 10-card set is printed on 24-point card stock and has simulated snake skin on the card front. Above the simulated snake skin is a close-up photo of the driver, the card backs have a brief description of the driver's early 1997 season results.

	MT
Complete Set (10):	140.00
Common Driver:	8.00
DB1 Jeff Gordon	40.00
DB2 Dale Jarrett	15.00
DB3 Bobby Labonte	8.00
DB4 Rusty Wallace	20.00
DB5 Bill Elliott	20.00
DB6 Jeff Burton	8.00
DB7 Mark Martin	20.00
DB8 Dale Earnhardt	40.00
DB9 Mike Skinner	8.00
DB10 Robby Gordon	8.00

1997 Wheels Viper Diamondback Authentic

Diamondback Authentic inserts are identical in design to the regular Diamondback other than these have actual Diamondback Rattlesnake skin. Like the regular Diamondbacks the card fronts use gold and metallic black foil stamping. These are seeded one per 96 packs.

	MT
Complete Set (10):	320.00
Common Driver:	15.00
DBA1 Jeff Gordon	80.00
DBA2 Dale Jarrett	30.00
DBA3 Bobby Labonte	15.00
DBA4 Rusty Wallace	40.00
DBA5 Bill Elliott	40.00
DBA6 Jeff Burton	15.00
DBA7 Mark Martin	40.00
DBA8 Dale Earnhardt	80.00
DBA9 Mike Skinner	15.00
DBA10 Robby Gordon	15.00

1997 Wheels Viper King Cobra

The oversized 10-card set features gold and black foil stamping, printed on a textured 3-D surface and die-cut design. Found exclusively in Western and Eastern First Strike boxes, they can be found on the average of every two boxes.

	MT
Complete Set (10):	160.00
Common Driver:	8.00
KC1 Dale Earnhardt	40.00
KC2 Jeff Gordon	40.00
KC3 Bobby Labonte	8.00
KC4 Terry Labonte	20.00
KC5 Rusty Wallace	20.00
KC6 Bill Elliott	20.00
KC7 Sterling Marlin	8.00
KC8 Mark Martin	20.00
KC9 Dale Jarrett	15.00
KC10 Kyle Petty	8.00

1997 Wheels Viper Sidewinder

The 16-card die-cut set features a close-up shot of the driver with name and logo in gold foil stamping. The right half portion of the card front is bordered by black spikes. These are found on the average of one every six packs.

	MT
Complete Set (16):	40.00
Common Driver:	2.00
S1 Terry Labonte	6.00
S2 Jeff Gordon	12.00
S3 Johnny Benson	2.00
S4 Ward Burton	2.00
S5 Bobby Hamilton	2.00
S6 Ricky Craven	2.00
S7 Michael Waltrip	2.00
S8 Bobby Labonte	2.00
S9 Dale Jarrett	4.00
S10 Bill Elliott	6.00
S11 Rusty Wallace	6.00
S12 Jimmy Spencer	2.00
S13 Sterling Marlin	2.00
S14 Kyle Petty	2.00
S15 Ken Schrader	2.00
S16 Robby Gordon	2.00

1997 Wheels Viper Snake Eyes

The 12-card set features a serpent in the background, lurking over the driver's shoulders. The logo and driver's name are stamped in red and silver foil on a full bleed card design. These are seeded one per 12 packs.

	MT
Complete Set (12):	60.00
Common Driver:	3.00
SE1 Dale Earnhardt	15.00
SE2 Jeff Gordon	15.00
SE3 Dale Jarrett	6.00
SE4 Bobby Labonte	3.00
SE5 Jimmy Spencer	3.00
SE6 Bill Elliott	8.00
SE7 Terry Labonte	8.00
SE8 Rusty Wallace	8.00
SE9 Jeff Burton	3.00
SE10 Mark Martin	8.00
SE11 Brett Bodine	3.00
SE12 Sterling Marlin	3.00

MULTI-SPORT/FIGURINES

1996-97 All Sport PPF Plus

All Sport PPF Plus is the second series to All Sport PPF. The base cards are standard size and numbered from 101 to 200. There is also a gold parallel that was inserted 1:5 packs. Each card is the same as the base card except for the gold block on the bottom that reads "PPF Gold" and the players name is in gold above it. Vintage cards of Mickey Mantle, Joe Namath, Bill Russell, Bobby Orr and many others were directly inserted into packs at a rate of two per box. Score Board also inserted Vintage Memorabilia Redemption cards for rare memorabilia items autographed by Ruth, Cobb, Robinson, Lombardi and other deceased legends. They were inserted 1:9 cases.

	MT
Complete Set (100):	15.00
Common Player:	.05
Gold Cards:	6x
101 Hakeem Olajuwon	.20
102 Alonzo Mourning	.10
103 Rasheed Wallace	.05
104 Glenn Robinson	.10
105 Tyus Edney	.05
106 Joe Smith	.10
107 Jason Kidd	.20
108 Shareef Abdur-Rahim	.75
109 Kerry Kittles	.30
110 Lorenzen Wright	.05
111 Samaki Walker	.05
112 Todd Fuller	.05
113 Steve Nash	.10
114 Jamie Feick	.05
115 Walter McCarty	.05
116 Jeff McInnis	.05
117 Derek Fisher	.10
118 Moochie Norris	.05
119 Joseph Blair	.05
120 Steve Hamer	.05
121 Randy Livingston	.05
122 Ron Riley	.05
123 Mark Pope	.05
124 Drew Barry	.05
125 Brian Evans	.05
126 Emmitt Smith	.50
127 Drew Bledsoe	.25
128 Steve McNair	.25
129 Marshall Faulk	.10
130 Keyshawn Johnson	.25
131 Lawrence Phillips	.10
132 Leeland McElroy	.05
133 Tony Banks	.50
134 Derrick Mayes	.05
135 Jonathan Ogden	.05
136 Pete Kendall	.05
137 Tim Biakabutuka	.10
138 Jamin Stephens	.05
139 Ray Lewis	.05
140 Marco Battaglia	.05
141 John Mobley	.05
142 Marvin Harrison	.50
143 Duane Clemons	.05
144 Lance Johnstone	.05
145 Eddie Kennison	.50
146 Bobby Hoying	.05
147 John Michels	.05
148 Reggie Brown	.05
149 Walt Harris	.05
150 Checklist 1 Kobe Bryant	.50
151 Marcus Jones	.05
152 Je'Rod Cherry	.05
153 Brian Dawkins	.05
154 Johnny McWilliams	.05
155 Brian Roche	.05
156 Muhsin Muhammad	.05
157 Lawyer Milloy	.05
158 Jermain Mayberry	.05
159 DeRon Jenkins	.05
160 Barry Bonds	.10
161 Jay Payton	.05
162 Jose Cruz, Jr.	1.50
163 Richard Hidalgo	.05
164 Bartolo Colon	.05
165 Matt Drews	.05
166 Kerry Wood	.30
167 Ben Grieve	.30
168 Wes Helms	.30
169 Livan Hernandez	.30
170 Dainius Zubrus	.50
171 Joe Thornton	.75
172 Daniel Briere	.05
173 Radek Dvorak	.05
174 Richard Jackman	.05
175 Robert Dome	.05
176 Sergei Samsonov	.50
177 Jarome Iginla	.05
178 Daniel Cleary	.05
179 Allen Iverson	1.00
180 Antonio McDyess	.10
181 Scottie Pippen	.20
182 Dikembe Mutombo	.05
183 Damon Stoudamire	.20
184 Stephon Marbury	1.00
185 Kobe Bryant	1.50
186 Marcus Camby	.50
187 Steve Young	.20
188 Kerry Collins	.20
189 Kevin Hardy	.05
190 Kordell Stewart	.25
191 Joey Galloway	.10
192 Simeon Rice	.05
193 Eddie George	1.50
194 Todd Walker	.05
195 Rey Ordonez	.05
196 Todd Greene	.05
197 Andrei Zyuzin	.05
198 Ed Jovanovski	.05
199 Emmitt Smith	.50
200 Checklist 2 (Eddie George)	.75

1996-97 All Sport PPF Plus Revivals

Each of the ten cards in this set are printed on vintage-style stock to give the look and feel of an old-time card. The fronts have a color photo of the player on half of the card and the other half has a picture of the player in black and white. They were inserted 1:35 packs.

	MT
Complete Set (10):	60.00
Common Player:	5.00
RV1 Allen Iverson	10.00
RV2 Stephon Marbury	8.00
RV3 Alonzo Mourning	5.00
RV4 Shareef Abdur-Rahim	6.00
RV5 Kerry Kittles	5.00
RV6 Emmitt Smith	8.00
RV7 Keyshawn Johnson	5.00
RV8 Eddie George	10.00
RV9 Marvin Harrison	5.00
RV10 Barry Bonds	5.00

1997 Autographed Collection

Autographed Collection was a 50-card set that was oriented toward autographed cards and memorabilia. The product contained memorabilia redemption cards (one per 16 packs), autgraphed cards, Certified Autographs, Game Breakers and Gold Game Breakers. Regular-issue cards featured a color shot of the player on the left side, with the same shot, but tighter, on the right. The player's name, position, team and Score Board logo were printed in silver foil across the bottom. The set included players from baseball, basketball, football and hockey.

	MT
Complete Set (50):	12.00
Common Player:	.10
1 Damon Stoudamire	.30
2 Scottie Pippen	.30
3 Jason Kidd	.20
4 Hakeem Olajuwon	.30
5 Alonzo Mourning	.20
6 Antonio McDyess	.10
7 Allen Iverson	1.50
8 Rasheed Wallace	.10
9 Glenn Robinson	.20
10 Marcus Camby	.75
11 Shareef Abdur-Rahim	1.00
12 Stephon Marbury	1.25
13 Kobe Bryant	1.50
14 Ray Allen	.50
15 Antoine Walker	1.00
16 Kerry Kittles	.50
17 John Wallace	.30
18 Emmitt Smith	.50
19 Kordell Stewart	.30
20 Lawrence Phillips	.10
21 Kerry Collins	.20
22 Drew Bledsoe	.30
23 Marshall Faulk	.10
24 Steve Young	.20
25 Joey Galloway	.10
26 Keyshawn Johnson	.50
27 Eddie George	2.00
28 Karim Abdul-Jabbar	.75
29 Terry Glenn	1.50
30 Marvin Harrison	.75
31 Tim Biakabutuka	.10
32 Leeland McElroy	.10
33 Simeon Rice	.10
34 Kevin Hardy	.10
35 Rickey Dudley	.10
36 Zach Thomas	.10
37 Bobby Engram	.10
38 Barry Bonds	.10
39 Vladimir Guerrero	.50
40 Rey Ordonez	.20
41 Jermaine Dye	.10
42 Todd Walker	.20
43 Billy Wagner	.20
44 Karim Garcia	.20
45 Joe Thornton	.75
46 Daniel Cleary	.10
47 Robert Dome	.10
48 Alexandre Volchkov	.10
49 Adam Colagiacomo	.10
50 Andrei Zyuzin	.10

1997 Autographed Collection Autographs

Autographed versions of cards were inserted every seven packs of Autographed Collection. The cards were autographed on the front and contained blue foil instead of the silver used on regular-issue cards. There were also Certified Autographs, which were hand-numbered on the front and had gold foil stamping on the front.

	MT
Complete Set (49):	800.00
Common Player:	8.00
Karim Abdul-Jabbar	50.00
Shareef Abdur-Rahim	60.00
Ray Allen	40.00
Drew Barry	8.00
Marco Battaglia	8.00
Michael Cheever	8.00
Daniel Cleary	8.00
Adam Colagiacomo	8.00
Chris Darkins	8.00
Tony Delk	8.00
Robert Dome	8.00
Donnie Edwards	8.00
Ray Farmer	8.00
Karim Garcia	30.00
Vladimir Guerrero	50.00
Kevin Hardy	8.00
Othella Harrington	8.00
Jimmy Herndon	8.00
Bobby Hoying	8.00
Dietrich Jells	8.00
DeRon Jenkins	8.00
Andre Johnson	8.00
Lance Johnstone	8.00
Danny Kanell	8.00
Kerry Kittles	40.00
Travis Knight	15.00
Jeff Lowis	8.00
Stephon Marbury	80.00
Derrick Mayes	8.00
Walter McCarty	8.00
Leeland McElroy	8.00
Ray Mickens	8.00
Roman Oben	8.00
Jason Odom	8.00
Rey Ordonez	15.00
Vitaly Potapenko	8.00
Roy Rogers	15.00
Sergei Samsonov	40.00
Jermain Stephens	8.00
Matt Stevens	8.00
Joe Thornton	50.00
Billy Wagner	8.00
Antoine Walker	60.00
Todd Walker	30.00
John Wallace	15.00

Jerome Williams	8.00
Lorenzen Wright	8.00
Dainius Zubrus	8.00
Andrei Zyuzin	8.00

1997 Autographed Collection Gold Autographs

Certified Autographs featured gold foil stamping across the bottom instead of the silver foil on regular-issue cards or the blue foil used on regular autographs. Certified Autographs also contained hand-numbering on the front and a Certified Autograph seal in the lower right corner. Under 350 of each card exist and they were inserted one per 16 packs.

	MT
Complete Set (49):	1400.00
Common Player:	15.00
Karim Abdul-Jabbar	100.00
Shareef Abdur-Rahim	125.00
Ray Allen	80.00
Drew Barry	15.00
Marco Battaglia	15.00
Michael Cheever	15.00
Daniel Cleary	15.00
Adam Colagiacomo	15.00
Chris Darkins	15.00
Tony Delk	15.00
Robert Dome	15.00
Donnie Edwards	15.00
Ray Farmer	15.00
Karim Garcia	60.00
Vladimir Guerrero	100.00
Kevin Hardy	15.00
Othella Harrington	15.00
Jimmy Herndon	15.00
Bobby Hoying	15.00
Dietrich Jells	15.00
DeRon Jenkins	15.00
Andre Johnson	15.00
Lance Johnstone	15.00
Danny Kanell	15.00
Kerry Kittles	75.00
Travis Knight	30.00
Jeff Lewis	15.00
Derrick Mayes	15.00
Walter McCarty	15.00
Leeland McElroy	15.00
Ray Mickens	15.00
Roman Oben	15.00
Jason Odom	15.00
Rey Ordonez	30.00
Vitaly Potapenko	30.00
Roy Rogers	30.00
Sergei Samsonov	75.00
Jermain Stephens	15.00
Matt Stevens	15.00
Zack Thomas	30.00
Joe Thornton	100.00
Billy Wagner	15.00
Antoine Walker	125.00
Todd Walker	60.00
John Wallace	30.00
Jerome Williams	15.00
Lorenzen Wright	15.00
Dainius Zubrus	15.00
Andrei Zyuzin	15.00

1997 Autographed Collection Game Breakers

This 30-card insert highlighted some of the top players in Autographed Collection. Regular Game Breakers cards were printed on silver foil and inserted one per 10 packs, while Gold versions used gold foil and were inserted one per 50 packs. The card numbers on the back include a "GB" prefix.

	MT
Complete Set (30):	200.00
Common Player:	2.50
Gold Cards:	4x
GB1 Damon Stoudamire	6.00
GB2 Scottie Pippen	6.00
GB3 Jason Kidd	5.00
GB4 Ray Allen	12.00
GB5 Alonzo Mourning	5.00
GB6 Joe Smith	5.00
GB7 Allen Iverson	25.00
GB8 Rasheed Wallace	2.50
GB9 Antoine Walker	20.00
GB10 Marcus Camby	15.00
GB11 Shareef Abdur-Rahim	20.00
GB12 Stephon Marbury	20.00
GB13 Kobe Bryant	30.00
GB14 Emmitt Smith	12.00
GB15 Kordell Stewart	8.00
GB16 Kevin Hardy	2.50
GB17 Kerry Collins	6.00
GB18 Drew Bledsoe	8.00
GB19 Marshall Faulk	5.00
GB20 Steve Young	5.00
GB21 Lawrence Phillips	2.50
GB22 Keyshawn Johnson	8.00
GB23 Eddie George	25.00
GB24 Karim Abdul-Jabbar	12.00
GB25 Terry Glenn	20.00
GB26 Marvin Harrison	10.00
GB27 Tim Biakabutuka	2.50
GB28 Rey Ordonez	2.50
GB29 Joe Thornton	10.00
GB30 Alexandre Volchkov	2.50

1997 Talk N' Sports

This 50-card set featured Score Board's Frontier phone cards, with five different denominations. Regular-issue cards contain a jagged gray-black area on the bottom with the player's name. Team, position and a Talk N' Sports logo are included in a strip up the right side of the card. The product includes $1, $10, $20, $50 and $1,000 phone cards, an Essentials insert and a Honus Wagner Redemption card, redeemable for the T206 Wagner. Score Board produced 1,500 sequentially numbered cases.

	MT
Complete Set (50):	10.00
Common Player:	.10
1 Brett Favre	.50
2 Marshall Faulk	.20
3 Steve Young	.20
4 Troy Aikman	.30
5 Kordell Stewart	.30
6 Kerry Collins	.30
7 Keyshawn Johnson	.20
8 Eddie George	1.00
9 Terry Glenn	.75
10 Kevin Hardy	.10
11 Emmitt Smith	.50
12 Karim Abdul-Jabbar	.20
13 Tony Banks	.20
14 Zach Thomas	.20
15 Mike Alstott	.20
16 Matt Stevens	.10
17 Troy Davis	.50
18 Warrick Dunn	1.50
19 Yatil Green	.50
20 Rae Carruth	.30
21 Darrell Russell	.10
22 Peter Boulware	.10
23 Shawn Springs	.10
24 Clyde Drexler	.30
25 Scottie Pippen	.30
26 Hakeem Olajuwon	.30
27 Alonzo Mourning	.20
28 Joe Smith	.20
29 Antonio McDyess	.10
30 Allen Iverson	.75
31 Kerry Kittles	.20
32 Stephon Marbury	.60
33 Marcus Camby	.30
34 Ray Allen	.20
35 Shareef Abdur-Rahim	.50
36 Kobe Bryant	1.00
37 Antoine Walker	.50
38 Glenn Robinson	.20
39 Dikembe Mutombo	.10
40 Barry Bonds	.20
41 Jay Payton	.20
42 Todd Walker	.20
43 Jose Cruz, Jr.	1.25
44 Kerry Wood	.30
45 Wes Helms	.10
46 Dainius Zubrus	.10
47 Sergei Samsonov	.10
48 Jay McKee	.10
49 Marcus Nilsson	.10
50 Joe Thornton	.10

1997 Talk N' Sports $1 Phone Cards

This 50-card phone card insert mirrors the regular-issue set checklist. Each card contains $1 of phone time, with one phone card being inserted into each pack.

	MT
Complete Set (50):	75.00
Common Player:	.75
1 Brett Favre	2.00
2 Marshall Faulk	1.50
3 Steve Young	1.50
4 Troy Aikman	1.50
5 Kordell Stewart	1.50
6 Kerry Collins	1.50
7 Keyshawn Johnson	.75
8 Eddie George	3.00
9 Terry Glenn	2.50
10 Kevin Hardy	.75
11 Emmitt Smith	2.00
12 Karim Abdul-Jabbar	2.00
13 Tony Banks	1.50
14 Zach Thomas	.75
15 Mike Alstott	1.50
16 Matt Stevens	.75
17 Troy Davis	2.00
18 Warrick Dunn	4.00
19 Yatil Green	1.50
20 Rae Carruth	1.50
21 Darrell Russell	.75
22 Peter Boulware	.75
23 Shawn Springs	.75
24 Clyde Drexler	1.50
25 Scottie Pippen	1.50
26 Hakeem Olajuwon	1.50
27 Alonzo Mourning	.75
28 Joe Smith	1.50
29 Antonio McDyess	.75
30 Allen Iverson	2.50
31 Kerry Kittles	1.50
32 Stephon Marbury	2.50
33 Marcus Camby	2.00
34 Ray Allen	1.50
35 Shareef Abdur-Rahim	2.00
36 Kobe Bryant	2.50
37 Antoine Walker	2.00
38 Glenn Robinson	.75
39 Dikembe Mutombo	.75
40 Barry Bonds	1.50
41 Jay Payton	.75
42 Todd Walker	1.50
43 Jose Cruz, Jr.	4.00
44 Kerry Wood	1.50
45 Wes Helms	.75
46 Dainius Zubrus	2.00
47 Sergei Samsonov	2.00
48 Jay McKee	.75
49 Marcus Nilsson	.75
50 Joe Thornton	2.50

1997 Talk N' Sports Essentials

This 10-card set was inserted one per 20 packs and utilized cel-card technology. The cards contained a large cel "e" in the upper left corner and the word "Essentials" across the bottom. The backs were numbered with an "E" prefix.

	MT
Complete Set (10):	125.00
Common Player:	10.00
1 Brett Favre	30.00
2 Scottie Pippen	15.00
3 Barry Bonds	10.00
4 Cal Ripken Jr.	15.00
5 Clyde Drexler	10.00
6 Kobe Bryant	25.00
7 Eddie George	25.00
8 Troy Davis	10.00
9 Darrell Russell	10.00
10 Dainius Zubrus	10.00

1997 Talk N' Sports $10 Phone Cards

This interactive set gave collectors a chance to win autographed bats by answering trivia questions. In addition, one collector could win an autographed Babe Ruth baseball. Trivia Catch $10 phone cards were inserted into every 12th pack and sequentially numbered to 3,960. There were also 50 Instant Win cards randomly inserted.

	MT
Complete Set (10):	150.00
Common Player:	15.00
1 Brett Favre	30.00
2 Hakeem Olajuwon	15.00
3 Keyshawn Johnson	15.00
4 Steve Young	20.00
5 Kordell Stewart	20.00
6 Cal Ripken Jr.	25.00
7 Eddie George	20.00
8 Troy Aikman	15.00
9 Clyde Drexler	15.00
10 Scottie Pippen	15.00

1997 Talk N' Sports $20 Phone Cards

Ten different $20 phone cards were inserted into packs of Talkn' Sports. The cards were inserted every 36 packs and sequentially numbered to 1,440.

		MT
Complete Set (10):		220.00
Common Player:		20.00
1	Brett Favre	50.00
2	Scottie Pippen	25.00
3	Barry Bonds	20.00
4	Cal Ripken Jr.	35.00
5	Clyde Drexler	20.00
6	Kobe Bryant	40.00
7	Eddie George	40.00
8	Troy Davis	25.00
9	Darrell Russell	20.00
10	Dainius Zubrus	20.00

1997 Visions Signings

The 50-card set is made up of the top players from each of the four major sports. Each card has a parallel gold card that is inserted 1:2 packs. The big attraction to this product was the Autographed Memorabilia Redemption Cards that were inserted 1:16 packs. Collectors could redeem cards for autographed basketballs, baseballs, footballs, helmets, pucks, jerseys, photos, plaques or Sports Illustrated magazines. Score Board also gave away a T206 Wagner. They inserted five specially marked cards, each redeemable for an original Honus Wagner card and a chance to win the coveted T206 Wagner.

		MT
Complete Set (50):		15.00
Common Player:		.10
Gold Cards:		3x
1	Barry Bonds	.20
2	Hakeem Olajuwon	.20
3	Glenn Robinson	.10
4	Steve Young	.20
5	Jose Cruz	2.00
6	Ben Grieve	1.00
7	Kerry Wood	.50
8	Erick Dampier	.10
9	Tony Delk	.10
10	Steve Nash	.10
11	Jerry Stackhouse	.20
12	Lorenzen Wright	.10
13	Vitaly Potapenko	.10
14	Allen Iverson	1.00
15	Marcus Camby	.50
16	Shareef Abdur-Rahim	.75
17	Stephon Marbury	1.00
18	Ray Allen	.20
19	Antoine Walker	.75
20	John Wallace	.20
21	Kobe Bryant	1.25
22	Jermaine O'Neal	.10
23	Clyde Drexler	.20
24	Scottie Pippen	.20
25	Rasheed Wallace	.10
26	Joe Smith	.20
27	Antonio McDyess	.20
28	Alonzo Mourning	.20
29	Eddie George	1.25
30	Warrick Dunn	2.00
31	Darrell Russell	.10
32	Peter Boulware	.10
33	Shawn Springs	.10
34	Yatil Green	.30
35	David LaFleur	.10
36	Bryant Westbrook	.10
37	Rae Carruth	.75
38	Brett Favre	.75
39	Emmitt Smith	.75
40	Dainius Zubrus	.75
41	Joe Thornton	.75
42	Daniel Cleary	.10
43	Sergei Samsonov	.75
44	Wes Helms	.10
45	Richard Hidalgo	.10
46	Jay Payton	.10
47	Leeland McElroy	.10
48	Troy Davis	.50
49	Tony Gonzalez	.00
50	Byron Hanspard	.30

1997 Visions Signings Autographs

The Autograph set is made up of 48 players from four different sports. They were inserted 1:5 packs. Each card is autographed on the front with most stating that you have received an authentic autograph on the back. Not every card is signed on a Visions Signing card. Some are signed on other Score Board products.

		MT
Complete Set (48):		700.00
Common Player:		8.00
	Jonathan Aitken	8.00
	Jerome Allen	8.00
	Tony Banks	40.00
	Dante Calabria	8.00
	Erick Dampier	8.00
	Tony Delk	8.00
	Tyus Edney	8.00
	Brian Evans	8.00
	Derek Fisher	15.00
	Ben Grieve	45.00
	Vladimir Guerrero	40.00
	Steve Hamer	8.00
	Kevin Hardy	8.00
	Othella Harrington	8.00
	Wes Helms	30.00
	Richard Hidalgo	8.00
	DeRon Jenkins	8.00
	Andre Johnson	8.00
	Danny Kanell	8.00
	Pete Kendall	8.00
	Jason Kidd	40.00
	Travis Knight	25.00
	Carnell Lake	8.00
	Jeff Lewis	8.00
	Walter McCarty	8.00
	Leeland McElroy	15.00
	Ray Mickens	8.00
	Jermaine O'Neal	15.00
	Jay Payton	25.00
	Gary Plummer	8.00
	Vitaly Potapenko	8.00
	Efthimis Retzias	8.00
	Roy Rogers	15.00
	Malik Rose	8.00
	Sergei Samsonov	40.00
	Steve Taneyhill	8.00
	Kurt Thomas	8.00
	Zack Thomas	30.00
	Joe Thornton	40.00
	Amani Toomer	8.00
	Regan Upshaw	8.00
	John Wallace	15.00
	Bryant Westbrook	15.00
	Jerome Williams	8.00
	Stepfret Williams	8.00
	Paul Wilson	20.00
	Kerry Wood	25.00
	Lorenzen Wright	8.00

1997 Visions Signings Artistry

The Artistry set is made up of primarily basketball and football #1 picks. Each card front has a color pho-

to of the player along with a smaller black-and-white photo on the front. The card backs also have a color photo with a brief write-up about the player. They were inserted 1:6 packs.

		MT
Complete Set (20):		100.00
Common Player:		3.00
A1	Jose Cruz	12.00
A2	Allen Iverson	10.00
A3	Marcus Camby	5.00
A4	Shareef Abdur-Rahim	7.00
A5	Stephon Marbury	8.00
A6	Ray Allen	4.00
A7	Antoine Walker	6.00
A8	Kobe Bryant	12.00
A9	Clyde Drexler	3.00
A10	Scottie Pippen	4.00
A11	Alonzo Mourning	3.00
A12	Eddie George	10.00
A13	Warrick Dunn	12.00
A14	Darrell Russell	3.00
A15	Peter Boulware	3.00
A16	Shawn Springs	3.00
A17	Yatil Green	5.00
A18	Brett Favre	10.00
A19	Emmitt Smith	10.00
A20	Dainius Zubrus	5.00

1997 Visions Signings Artistry Autographs

The Artistry Autographs are the same as the Artistry set except for the autograph that appears on the fronts of each card. Only eight players signed for this set that is inserted 1:25 packs.

		MT
Complete Set (8):		900.00
Common Player:		30.00
	Peter Boulware	30.00
	Jose Cruz	150.00
	Warrick Dunn	150.00
	Brett Favre	300.00
	Stephon Marbury	125.00
	Alonzo Mourning	125.00
	Antoine Walker	80.00
	Dainius Zubrus	60.00

BASEBALL

1997 Kenner Starting Lineups

The 1997 release features the rookies of Scott Brosius, Johnny Damon, Steve Finley, Todd Hundley, Jason Isringhausen, John Jaha, Jason Kendall, Tino Martinez, Brian McRae, Jose Mesa, Rey Ordonez, Chan Ho Park, Henry Rodriguez, Ismael Valdes and Bernie Williams.

	MT
Complete Set (48):	700.00
Roberto Alomar	12.00
Brady Anderson	25.00
Jeff Bagwell	12.00
Derek Bell	12.00
Albert Belle	12.00
Dante Bichette	12.00
Barry Bonds	12.00
Scott Brosius	12.00
Ellis Burks	14.00
Roger Clemens	14.00
Johnny Damon	12.00
Steve Finley	14.00
Tom Glavine	15.00
Rusty Greer	12.00
Ken Griffey Jr.	16.00
Todd Hundley	20.00
Jason Isringhausen	12.00
John Jaha	10.00
Randy Johnson	15.00
Chipper Jones	40.00
Brian Jordan	12.00
Wally Joyner	10.00
Jason Kendall	14.00
Ryan Klesko	15.00
Javier Lopez	15.00
Tino Martinez	40.00
Brian McRae	10.00
Jose Mesa	10.00
Paul Molitor	12.00
Raul Mondesi	12.00
Hideo Nomo	20.00
Rey Ordonez	18.00
Chan Ho Park	15.00
Mike Piazza	14.00
Manny Ramirez	20.00
Cal Ripken Jr	16.00
Alex Rodriguez	30.00
Henry Rodriguez	14.00
Ivan Rodriguez	12.00
Ryne Sandberg	12.00
Reggie Sanders	10.00
John Smoltz	25.00
J.T. Snow	10.00
Frank Thomas	14.00
Ismael Valdes	15.00
Devon White	10.00
Bernie Williams	25.00
Matt Williams	10.00

1997 Kenner Starting Lineups Extended

	MT
Complete Set (14):	200.00
Albert Belle	12.00
Ricky Bottalico	12.00
Ken Caminiti	12.00
Tony Clark	20.00
Roger Clemens	15.00
Dennis Eckersley	12.00
Derek Jeter	18.00
Andruw Jones	35.00
Mark McGwire	20.00
Mike Mussina	15.00
Andy Pettitte	20.00
Alex Rodriguez	20.00
Deion Sanders	12.00
Matt Williams	12.00

1997 Kenner 12" Figures

	MT
Complete Set (4):	150.00
Ken Griffey Jr.	50.00
Greg Maddux	40.00
Mike Piazza	40.00
Cal Ripken Jr.	40.00

1997 Kenner Classic Doubles

	MT
Complete Set (10):	300.00
Hank Aaron, J. Robinson	25.00
Barry Bonds, Bobby Bonds	25.00
Don Drysdale, Hideo Nomo	25.00
Ken Griffey Sr., Ken Griffey Jr.	40.00
R. Johnson, Nolan Ryan	35.00
Greg Maddux, C. Young	40.00
Mickey Mantle, Roger Maris	45.00
Roger Maris, Mark McGwire	30.00
Cal Ripken Jr., B. Robinson	35.00
Babe Ruth, F. Thomas	35.00

1997 Kenner Cooperstown Collection

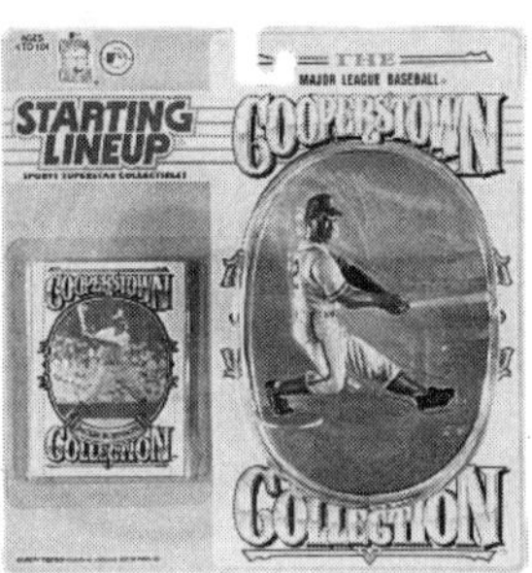

	MT
Complete Set (11):	125.00
Johnny Bench	10.00
Rollie Fingers	10.00
Josh Gibson	10.00
Walter Johnson	10.00
Dotty Kamenshek	15.00
Mickey Mantle	35.00
Brooks Robinson	10.00
Jackie Robinson	60.00
Duke Snider	10.00
Hoyt Wilhelm	10.00
Carl Yastrzemski	10.00

1997 Kenner Stadium Stars

	MT
Complete Set (7):	175.00
Hank Aaron	25.00
Fergie Jenkins	25.00
Al Kaline	25.00
Mickey Mantle	50.00
Babe Ruth	40.00
Mike Schmidt	25.00
Carl Yastrzemski	25.00

1997 Kenner Freeze Frames

	MT
Complete Set (6):	225.00
Dante Bichette	25.00
Juan Gonzalez	30.00
Ken Griffey Jr.	50.00

Chipper Jones	50.00
Mike Piazza	40.00
Frank Thomas	40.00

1997 Corinthian Headliners

	MT
Complete Set (29):	150.00
Common Player:	4.00
Roberto Alomar	4.00
Albert Belle	5.00
Wade Boggs	4.00
Barry Bonds	6.00
Jose Canseco	4.00
Lenny Dykstra	4.00
Andres Galarraga	4.00
Ken Griffey Jr.	12.00
Tony Gwynn	5.00
Orel Hershiser	4.00
Randy Johnson	4.00
Chipper Jones	10.00
David Justice	4.00
Eric Karros	4.00
Barry Larkin	4.00
Kenny Lofton	4.00
Fred McGriff	4.00
Mark McGwire	4.00
Paul Molitor	5.00
Raul Mondesi	4.00
Hideo Nomo	5.00
Paul O'Neill	4.00
Mike Piazza	6.00
Cal Ripken Jr.	10.00
Ryne Sandberg	4.00
Gary Sheffield	5.00
Frank Thomas	10.00
Mo Vaughn	4.00
Matt Williams	4.00

BASKETBALL

1996 Kenner Starting Lineup

The 35-player set featured three different hair versions of Bulls star Dennis Rodman (green, orange, yellow) and rookie pieces of Kevin Garnett, Juwon Howard, Jerry Stackhouse and Damon Stoudamire.

	MT
Complete Set (34):	600.00
Set price only includes regular G. Hill and Rodman green.	
Vin Baker	20.00
Charles Barkley	14.00
Clyde Drexler	14.00
Sean Elliott	10.00
Patrick Ewing	12.00
Kevin Garnett	75.00
Anfernee Hardaway	25.00
Grant Hill	20.00
Grant Hill special	30.00
Tyrone Hill	12.00
Juwan Howard	40.00
Larry Johnson	15.00
Eddie Jones	30.00
Jason Kidd	15.00
Karl Malone	15.00
Jamal Mashburn	12.00
Antonio McDyess	25.00
Reggie Miller	15.00

Alonzo Mourning	12.00
Hakeem Olajuwon	15.00
Shaquille O'Neal	20.00
Gary Payton	30.00
Scottie Pippen	15.00
Dino Radja	15.00
Bryant Reeves	18.00
Pooh Richardson	12.00
Mitch Richmond	12.00
Cliff Robinson	10.00
David Robinson	12.00
Glenn Robinson	14.00
Dennis Rodman green	45.00
Dennis Rodman orange	40.00
Dennis Rodman yellow	40.00
Joe Smith	25.00
Rik Smits	15.00
Jerry Stackhouse	25.00
Damon Stoudamire	25.00

1996-97 Kenner Starting Lineup Extended

Kenner's first attempt at an extended basketball set featured two rookies (Kobe Bryant and Allen Iverson) and several top players in retro uniforms, including Grant Hill and Shaquille O'Neal.

	MT
Complete Set (8):	180.00
Charles Barkley	20.00
Kobe Bryant	50.00
Grant Hill	30.00
Allen Iverson	60.00
Larry Johnson	15.00
Dikembe Mutombo	15.00
Shaquille O'Neal	30.00
Damon Stoudamire	25.00

1996 Kenner Dream Team III

The 1996 Olympic set was released in two, five-player boxes. The first box contained Penny Hardaway, Shaquille O'Neal, Scottie Pippen, David Robinson and John Stockton, while the second set consisted of Grant Hill, Karl Malone, Reggie Miller, Hakeem Olajuwon and Glenn Robinson.

	MT
Complete Set (2):	60.00
Five player boxes:	30.00

1997 Corinthian Headliners

The inaugural Headliners set contains 39 players with four different hair variations for Dennis Rodman -- green, red, yellow and orange. The figures were available in single packs, four-packs and 10-packs.

	MT
Complete Set (25):	130.00
Common Player:	4.00
Charles Barkley	5.00
Shawn Bradley	4.00
Horace Grant	4.00
Anfernee Hardaway	8.00
Grant Hill	10.00
Juwan Howard	5.00
Larry Johnson	4.00
Shawn Kemp	6.00
Luc Longley	4.00
Karl Malone	5.00
Jamal Mashburn	4.00
Reggie Miller	5.00
Alonzo Mourning	4.00
Dikembe Mutombo	4.00
Hakeem Olajuwon	5.00
Scottie Pippen	6.00
Mitch Richmond	4.00
Clifford Robinson	4.00
David Robinson	5.00
Glenn Robinson	5.00
Dennis Rodman - Green	15.00
Dennis Rodman - Orange	12.00
Dennis Rodman - Red	8.00
Dennis Rodman - Yellow	8.00
Jerry Stackhouse	5.00
John Starks	4.00
Damon Stoudamire	5.00

FOOTBALL

1997 Kenner Starting Lineup

	MT
Complete Set (43):	550.00
Karim Abdul-Jabbar	25.00
Troy Aikman	15.00
Jamal Anderson	12.00
Jerome Bettis	10.00
Jeff Blake	10.00
Drew Bledsoe	16.00
Terry Bradshaw Hill's	30.00
Mark Brunell	20.00
Dale Carter	10.00
Larry Centers	10.00
Mark Chmura	20.00
Kerry Collins	15.00
Brian Cox	10.00
Terrell Davis	35.00
Quinn Early	10.00
John Elway	15.00
Brett Favre	30.00
Eddie George	40.00
Jeff George	10.00
Elvis Grbac	12.00
Kevin Greene	10.00
Marvin Harrison	15.00
Jim Harbaugh	10.00
Brad Johnson	15.00
Keyshawn Johnson	15.00
Daryl Johnston	18.00
Dan Marino	16.00
Curtis Martin	45.00
Tony Martin	12.00
Herman Moore	20.00
Jerry Rice	15.00
Willie Roaf	10.00
Deion Sanders	14.00
Bruce Smith	10.00
Emmitt Smith	20.00

	MT
Emmitt Smith Alb.	25.00
Phillipi Sparks	10.00
Kordell Stewart	25.00
Vinny Testaverde	10.00
Eric Turner	10.00
Chris Warren	10.00
Ricky Watters	10.00
Michael Westbrook	18.00
Reggie White	14.00
Steve Young	14.00

1996 Corinthian Headliners

The 40-piece inaugural football set from Corinthian Marketing features top players such as Brett Favre, Emmitt Smith, Troy Aikman and Dan Marino and is available in single blister card packages.

	MT
Complete Set (40):	225.00
Common Player:	5.00
Troy Aikman	10.00
Marcus Allen	5.00
Drew Bledsoe	10.00
Tim Brown	5.00
Cris Carter	5.00
Kerry Collins	8.00
John Elway	6.00
Marshall Faulk	5.00
Brett Favre	12.00
Jeff George	5.00
Kevin Greene	5.00
Charles Haley	5.00
Jim Harbaugh	6.00
Jeff Hostetler	5.00
Stan Humphries	5.00
Daryl Johnston	5.00
Jim Kelly	6.00
Leon Lett	5.00
Greg Lloyd	5.00
Dan Marino	12.00
Steve McNair	8.00
Natrone Means	5.00
Rick Mirer	5.00
Nate Newton	5.00
Jay Novacek	5.00
Neil O'Donnell	5.00
Jerry Rice	8.00
Rashaan Salaam	6.00
Barry Sanders	8.00
Deion Sanders	6.00
Junior Seau	5.00
Heath Shuler	5.00
Bruce Smith	5.00
Emmitt Smith	12.00
Kordell Stewart	15.00

	MT
Ricky Watters	5.00
Reggie White	5.00
Kevin Williams	5.00
Darren Woodson	5.00
Steve Young	6.00

HOCKEY

1996 Kenner Starting Lineup American

	MT
Complete Set (22):	300.00

Barrasso and LaFontaine are not included in set price.

	MT
Tom Barrasso Hills special	20.00
Brian Bradley	12.00
Jim Carey	30.00
Paul Coffey	15.00
Sergei Fedorov	12.00
Ron Francis	12.00
Dominik Hasek	30.00
Paul Kariya	25.00
John LeClair	15.00
Brian Leetch	12.00
Eric Lindros	15.00
Al MacInnis	12.00
Scott Mellanby	12.00
Mark Messier	16.00
Mike Modano	12.00
Adam Oates	12.00
Mikael Renberg	15.00
Stephane Richer	12.00
Jeremy Roenick	14.00
Patrick Roy	45.00
Joe Sakic	20.00
Brendan Shanahan	15.00
Mats Sundin	14.00

1996 Kenner Starting Lineup Canadian

	MT
Complete Set (15):	225.00
Brian Bradley	12.00
Jim Carey	30.00
Sergei Fedorov	12.00
Ron Francis	12.00
Paul Kariya	25.00
John LeClair	15.00
Brian Leetch	12.00
Eric Lindros	15.00
Al MacInnis	12.00
Scott Mellanby	12.00
Mark Messier	18.00
Mikael Renberg	15.00
Patrick Roy	45.00
Joe Sakic	20.00
Mats Sundin	14.00

1996 Kenner Timeless Legends Canadian

	MT
Complete Set (6):	100.00
Jean Beliveau	20.00
Phil Esposito	20.00
Tony Esposito	20.00
Gordie Howe	20.00
Bobby Hull	20.00
Maurice Richard	20.00

1997 Corinthian Headliners

	MT
Complete Set (28):	130.00
Common Player:	4.00
Ray Bourque	5.00
Martin Brodeur	5.00
Pavel Bure	6.00
Chris Chelios	5.00

	MT
Paul Coffey	4.00
Sergei Fedorov	6.00
Peter Forsberg	5.00
Grant Fuhr	4.00
Wayne Gretzky	10.00
Brett Hull	5.00
Jaromir Jagr	8.00
Jari Kurri	6.00
Pat LaFontaine	4.00
Brian Leetch	5.00
Claude Lemieux	5.00
Mario Lemieux	8.00
Eric Lindros	8.00
Mark Messier	6.00
Jeremy Roenick	8.00
Patrick Roy	8.00
Joe Sakic	6.00
Teemu Selanne	6.00
Brendan Shanahan	5.00
Mats Sundin	5.00
Keith Tkachuk	5.00
Pierre Turgeon	4.00
John Vanbiesbrouck	6.00
Steve Yzerman	5.00

MULTI-SPORTS

1996 Kenner Timeless Legends

	MT
Complete Set (9):	90.00
Nadia Comaneci	15.00
Florence Griffith-Joyner	15.00
Bruce Jenner	15.00
Michael Johnson	15.00
Jackie Joyner-Kersey	15.00
Olga Korbut	15.00
Dan O'Brien	15.00
Jesse Owens	15.00
Jim Thorpe	15.00

MVP Player Checklists

Ken Griffey Jr.: American League MVP

Set	Card No.	Value
1984-91 O'Connell & Son Ink Mini Prints	237	1.00
1988 ProCards Vermont Mariners	—	25.00
1988-1989 Star	1-11	10.00
1988-1989 Star	1-11	25.00
1988-92 Star Ad Cards	(8)	10.00
1988-92 Star Ad Cards	(9)	10.00
1988-92 Star Ad Cards	(9g)	10.00
1988-89 Star Nova Edition	(7)	100.00
1988-89 Star Nova Edition	(7)	250.00
1988-89 Star Promos	(17)	10.00
1988-89 Star Promos	(18)	25.00
1988-89 Star Silver Edition	(1)	60.00
1988-89 Star Silver Edition	(1)	30.00
1989 Baseball Cards Magazine Repli-cards	63	4.00
1989 Bowman	220	5.00
1989 Classic Travel Update I (Orange)	131	3.00
1989 Classic Travel Update II (Purple)	193	3.00
1989 Donruss	33	4.50
1989 Donruss Baseball's Best	192	4.00
1989 Donruss Rookies	3	5.00
1989 Fleer	548	6.00
1989 Fleer Glossy Tin	548	45.00
1989 Mother's Cookies Mariners	3	25.00
1989 Mother's Cookies/Ken Griffey, Jr.	1	5.00
1989 Mother's Cookies/Ken Griffey, Jr.	2	5.00
1989 Mother's Cookies/Ken Griffey, Jr.	3	5.00
1989 Mother's Cookies/Ken Griffey, Jr.	4	5.00
1989 Phoenix Magnetables	(57)	4.00
1989 Score Traded	100T	6.00
1989 Score Young Superstars Series II	18	3.00
1989 Scoremasters	30	2.00
1989-91 Sports Illustrated For Kids	158	8.00
1989 Star Silver Edition	(5)	50.00
1989 Star Silver Edition	(5p)	60.00
1989 Topps Heads Up! Test Issue	4	250.00
1989 Topps Major League Debut	46	5.00
1989 Topps Traded	41T	4.00
1989 Upper Deck	1	90.00
1990 All American Baseball Team	17	3.50
1990 Baseball Cards Magazine Repli-cards	37	3.00
1990 Bazooka	18	2.50
1990 Bowman	481	2.00
1990 Classic Baseball	20	2.00
1990 Classic Series III	1	1.50
1990 Donruss	4	.50
1990 Donruss	365	2.00
1990 Donruss Best A.L.	1	1.50
1990 Donruss Diamond Kings Supers	4	4.00
1990 Donruss Learning Series	8	9.00
1990 Fleer	513	2.00
1990 Fleer Award Winners	17	3.50
1990 Fleer Baseball All Stars	14	2.00
1990 Fleer Baseball All Stars (Canadian)	14	6.00
1990 Fleer Box Panels	10	2.50
1990 Fleer Canadian	513	12.00
1990 Fleer League Leaders	14	1.50
1990 Fleer League Leaders (Canadian)	14	8.00
1990 Fleer MVP	14	2.00
1990 Fleer MVP (Canadian)	14	8.00
1990 Fleer Soaring Stars	6	12.00
1990 Jumbo Sunflower Seeds	(2)	3.00
1990 Kenner Starting Lineups Extended	(4)	125.00
1990 Kenner Starting Lineups	(33a)	125.00
1990 King-B	16	3.00
1990 Leaf	245	30.00
1990 Leaf Previews	4	400.00
1990 Major League Baseball Photocards	(38)	2.00
1990 Mother's Cookies Mariners	3	12.00
1990 O-Pee-Chee	336	1.75
1990 Panini Stickers	155	1.50
1990 Post Cereal	23	.75
1990 Score	560	2.00
1990 Score Rising Stars	3	3.00
1990 Sportflics	7	3.00
1990-91 Star	1-11	6.00
1990-91 Star	1-11	6.00
1990-91 Star	1-11	4.00
1990-91 Star	1-11	4.00
1990-91 Star Gold Edition	(7)	25.00
1990-91 Star Gold Edition	(7)	50.00
1990-91 Star Nova Edition	(9)	75.00
1990-91 Star Nova Edition	(9)	100.00
1990-91 Star Platinum Edition	(10)	30.00
1990-91 Star Platinum Edition	(10)	40.00
1990-91 Star Promos	(14)	6.00
1990-91 Star Promos	(15)	6.00
1990-91 Star Promos	(16)	6.00
1990-91 Star Promos	(17)	6.00
1990-91 Star Promos	(18)	6.00
1990-91 Star Silver Edition	(11)	24.00
1990-91 Star Silver Edition	(11)	30.00
1990 Star Sophomore Stars	1	10.00
1990 Star Sophomore Stars	2	10.00
1990 Topps	336	2.00
1990 Topps All-Star Glossy Set of 60	20	1.75
1990 Topps Big Baseball	250	2.00
1990 Topps Coins	16	.90
1990 Topps Double Headers	(29)	4.00
1990 Topps Glossy Rookies	11	3.00
1990 Topps Heads Up!	5	2.00
1990-93 Topps Magazine	3	3.00
1990-93 Topps Magazine	27	1.50
1990 Topps Stickercards	49	1.00
1990 Toys "R" Us Rookies	13	2.00
1990 U.S. Playing Card All-Stars	J	.75
1990 Upper Deck	24	.40
1990 Upper Deck	156	6.00
1990 Wonder Stars	18	2.50
1991 Alrak Griffey Gazette	(1)	1.00
1991 Alrak Griffey Gazette	(2)	1.00
1991 Alrak Griffey Gazette	(3)	1.00
1991 Alrak Griffey Gazette	(4)	1.00
1991 Arena Holograms	2	10.00
1991 Barry Colla	1-12	9.00
1991 Baseball Cards Magazine Repli-cards	37	3.00
1990-92 Baseball Cards Presents Repli-cards	5	3.00
1990-92 Baseball Cards Presents Repli-cards	10	4.00
1990-92 Baseball Cards Presents Repli-cards	4	3.00
1991-1992 Bleacher Promos	(1)	3.00
1991 Bowman	246a	2.00
1991 Card Guard Griffey Promo		1.00
1991 Cardboard Dreams	6	1.00
1991 Classic	3	1.00
1991 Classic Collector's Edition	120	1.00
1991 Classic Series II	1	1.00
1991 Classic Series III	30	1.00
1991 Country Hearth Mariners	15	15.00
1991 Country Hearth Mariners	28	3.00
1991 Cracker Jack Topps 1st Series	36	2.00
1991 Donruss	49	.50
1991 Donruss	77	1.50
1991 Donruss	392	.40
1991 Donruss Previews	4	300.00
1991 Fleer	450	1.50
1991 Fleer	710	.50
1991 Fleer All Stars	7	6.00
1991 Foot Locker Slam Fest	(1)	1.50
1991 Foot Locker Slam Fest	1-1	1.50
1991 Foot Locker Slam Fest	1	3.00
1991 Holsum Bakeries Superstars Discs	9	16.00
1991 Jimmy Dean	2	1.50
1991 Jumbo Sunflower Seeds	11	2.75
1991 Kenner Headline Collection	(3)	50.00
1991 Kenner Starting Lineups Extended	(4)	30.00
1991 Kenner Starting Lineups	(22a)	25.00
1991 Leaf	372	3.50
1991 MooTown Snackers	4	1.25
1991 Mother's Cookies/Griffeys	1	3.00
1991 Mother's Cookies/Griffeys	3	1.00
1991 Mother's Cookies/Griffeys	4	1.00
1991 O-Pee-Chee	392	.40
1991 O-Pee-Chee	790	1.50
1991 O-Pee-Chee/Premier	56	2.00
1991 Panini Stickers	189	2.00
1991 Panini Stickers - Canadian	172	.45
1991 Panini Stickers - Canadian	233	1.00
1991 Panini Top 15 Stickers (Canadian)	116	1.00
1991 Pepsi-Cola Griffeys	1	2.00
1991 Pepsi-Cola Griffeys	2	2.00
1991 Pepsi-Cola Griffeys	3	2.00
1991 Pepsi-Cola Griffeys	4	2.00
1991 Pepsi-Cola Griffeys	5	.50
1991 Pepsi-Cola Griffeys	6	.50
1991 Petro Canada All-Star Fanfest Standups	23	4.00
1991 Playball U.S.A. Ken Griffey, Jr.	91-32	.50
1991 Playball U.S.A. Ken Griffey, Jr.	91-33	.50
1991 Playball U.S.A. Ken Griffey, Jr.	91-34	.50
1991 Playball U.S.A. Ken Griffey, Jr.	91-35	.50
1991 Playball U.S.A. Ken Griffey, Jr.	91-36	.50
1991 Playball U.S.A. Ken Griffey, Jr.	91-37	.50
1991 Playball U.S.A. Ken Griffey, Jr.	91-38	.50
1991 Post Cereal	11	1.00
1991 Post Cereal - Canadian	26	4.00
1991 Score	2	1.25
1991 Score	396	.40
1991 Score	697	.50
1991 Score	841	.50
1991 Score	858	.50
1991 Score	892	1.50
1991 Score Cooperstown	3	6.00
1991 Score Superstars	5	1.00
1991-92 Sports Cards Portrait Cards	15	5.00
1991 Sports Educational Workbook	4	1.00
1991 Stadium Club	270	15.00
1991 Stadium Club Charter Members	(10)	2.00
1991-92 Stadium Club Charter Member	19	7.50
1991 Star All-Stars	(7)	30.00
1991 Star All-Stars	(7)	35.00
1991 Star Diamond Series	(6)	20.00
1991 Star Diamond Series	(6)	25.00
1991 Star Gold Edition	(7)	25.00
1991 Star Gold Edition	(7)	30.00
1991 Star Home Run Series	(5)	25.00
1991 Star Home Run Series	(5)	30.00
1991 Star Millennium Edition	(5)	25.00
1991 Star Millennium Edition	(5)	30.00
1991 Star Nova Edition	(6)	50.00
1991 Star Nova Edition	(6)	50.00
1991 Star Platinum Edition	(8)	30.00
1991 Star Platinum Edition	(8)	50.00
1991 Star Silver Edition	(6)	25.00
1991 Star Silver Edition	(6)	30.00
1991 Star Stellar Edition	(5)	30.00
1991 Star Stellar Edition	(5)	35.00
1991 Studio	112	4.00
1991 Topps	392	.40
1991 Topps	790	1.50
1991 Topps All-Star Glossy Set of 22	7	.90
1991 Topps Superstar Stand-Ups	17	12.00
1991 U.S. Playing Card All-Stars	A	.75
1991 Ultra	336	4.00
1991 Ultra Gold	4	4.00
1991 Upper Deck	555	2.50
1991 Upper Deck Final Edition	79	.40
1991 Upper Deck Final Edition	87	.75
1992 Alrak Griffey's Golden Moments	1	2.50
1992 Alrak Griffey's Golden Moments	2	2.50
1992 Alrak Griffey's Golden Moments	3	2.50
1992 Alrak Griffey's Golden Moments	4	2.50
1992 Alrak Griffey's Golden Moments	5	2.50
1992 Alrak Griffey's Golden Moments	6	2.50
1992 Alrak Griffey's Golden Moments	7	2.50
1992 Alrak Griffey's Golden Moments	8	2.50
1992 Alrak Griffey's Golden Moments	9	2.50
1992 Alrak Griffey's Golden Moments	10	2.50
1992 Arena Kid Griff Holograms	1	1.50
1992 Arena Kid Griff Holograms	2	1.50
1992 Arena Kid Griff Holograms	3	1.50
1992 Arena Kid Griff Holograms	4	1.50
1992 Arena Kid Griff Holograms	5	1.50
1992 Baseball Cards Magazine Repli-cards	36	3.00
1992 Ben's Bakery Super Hitters Discs	10	4.50
1992 Bleachers Ken Griffey, Jr.	1	6.00
1992 Bleachers Ken Griffey, Jr.	2	6.00
1992 Bleachers Ken Griffey, Jr.	3	6.00
1992 Bowman	100	18.00
1992 Classic Best	1	200.00
1992 Classic Best	200	1.50
1992 Classic Best Blue Bonus	12	4.00
1992 Classic Best Red Bonus	12	5.00
1992 Classic Collector's Edition	186	1.00
1992 Classic Series I	40	.60
1992 Classic Series II	44	.50
1992 Classic Show Promos 20	10	5.00
1992 Colla All-Stars	11	1.50
1992 Cracker Jack Donruss Series 1	12	4.00
1992 Diet Pepsi All-Stars	(27)	3.00
1992 Diet Pepsi Collector Series	26	2.50
1992 Donruss	24	.75
1992 Donruss	165	1.50
1992 Donruss Elite	13	160.00
1992 Donruss McDonald's	22	1.00
1992 Donruss Previews	7	90.00
1992 Fleer	279	1.50
1992 Fleer	709	1.00
1992 Fleer All-Stars	23	9.00
1992 Fleer Team Leaders	15	25.00
1992 Fleer Update	H1	25.00
1992 Fleer 7-Eleven	4	2.00
1992 Flopps Promos	(3)	12.00
1992 French's Mustard	14	2.00
1992 Front Row Draft Picks	—	15.00
1992 High 5 Decals	(69)	6.00
1992 Jimmy Dean	11	1.50
1992 Jumbo Sunflower Seeds	14	2.00
1992 Kenner Headline Collection	(3)	30.00
1992 Kenner Starting Lineups	(19a)	25.00
1992 Kenner Starting Lineups	(19b)	30.00
1992 Leaf	392	3.00
1992 Leaf Gold Edition	392	12.00
1992 Leaf Gold Previews	24	18.00
1992 Leaf Previews	24	22.00
1992 Lime Rock Griffey Baseball Holograms	2	3.00
1992 Lime Rock Griffey Baseball Holograms	2	12.00
1992 Lime Rock Griffey Baseball Holograms	2	60.00
1992 Lime Rock Griffey Baseball Holograms	2	12.00
1992 McDonald's Baseball's Best	8	2.50
1992 McDonald's Ken Griffey, Jr.	1	4.00
1992 McDonald's Ken Griffey, Jr.	2	4.00
1992 McDonald's Ken Griffey, Jr.	3	4.00
1992 MooTown Snackers	7	1.00
1992 Mother's Cookies Mariners	2	7.50
1992 Mr. Turkey	12	3.00
1992 O-Pee-Chee	50	.75
1992 O-Pee-Chee/Premier	167	1.50
1992 Paccar/Alrak Ken Griffey Jr.	(1)	2.00
1992 Paccar/Alrak Ken Griffey Jr.	(2)	2.00
1992 Paccar/Alrak Ken Griffey Jr.	(3)	2.00
1992 Paccar/Alrak Ken Griffey Jr.	(4)	2.00
1992 Paccar/Alrak Ken Griffey Jr.	(5)	2.00
1992 Panini Stickers	60	1.00
1992 Panini Stickers	277	1.00
1992 Pinnacle	283	.75
1992 Pinnacle	549	4.00
1992 Pinnacle Slugfest	7	12.00
1992 Pinnacle Team Pinnacle	9	25.00
1992 Pinnacle Team 2000	47	5.00
1992 Post Cereal	20	1.50
1992 Score	1	1.50
1992 Score	436	.60
1992 Score Impact Players	28	3.00
1992 Score Procter & Gamble	7	1.00
1992 Score Promos	1	12.00
1992 Score Superstars	1	1.00
1992 Silver Star Hologram Promo Cards	(4)	2.00
1992 Sports Cards Inserts	51	2.50
1992-98 Sports Illustrated For Kids	173	8.00

	Card No.	Value
1992-98 Sports Illustrated For Kids	572	4.00
1992 Stadium Club	400	6.00
1992 Stadium Club	603	2.75
1992 Stadium Club East Coast National	603	40.00
1992 Stadium Club Master Photos	(7)	8.00
1992 Stadium Club Members Only	(16)	3.00
1992 Stadium Club Special (SkyDome)	70	2.50
1992 Star '92	N	25.00
1992 Star '92		25.00
1992 Star Gold Edition	(4)	30.00
1992 Star Gold Edition	(4)	35.00
1992 Star Millenium Edition	(4)	35.00
1992 Star Millenium Edition	(4)	35.00
1992 Star Nova Edition	(5)	40.00
1992 Star Nova Edition	(5)	40.00
1992 Star Platinum Edition	(5)	25.00
1992 Star Platinum Edition	(5)	30.00
1992 Star Silver Edition	(4)	20.00
1992 Star Silver Edition	(4)	25.00
1992 Star Stellar Edition	(5)	30.00
1992 Star Stellar Edition	(5)	35.00
1992 Star The Kid	1-5	25.00
1992 Studio	232	3.00
1992 Topps	50	1.50
1992 Topps Kids	122	.50
1992 Topps Triple Header Photo Balls	(13)	7.50
1992 Triple Play	152	1.25
1992 Triple Play Gallery of Stars	8	7.00
1992 Triple Play Previews	1	150.00
1992 U.S. Playing Card Aces	J	.75
1992 U.S. Playing Card All-Stars	AS	.75
1992 Ultra	123	4.00
1992 Ultra All-Stars	6	10.00
1992 Ultra Award Winners	22	12.00
1992 Upper Deck	85	1.00
1992 Upper Deck	424	1.50
1992 Upper Deck	650	.50
1992 Upper Deck FanFest	24	1.50
1992 Upper Deck MVP Holograms	22	3.50
1992 Upper Deck Ted Williams' Best	15	6.00
1992 7-11 Slurpee Superstar Action Coins	26	3.00
1993 Alrak Ken Griffey Jr., Triple Play	(1)	3.00
1993 Alrak Ken Griffey, Jr.	(1)	1.50
1993 Alrak Ken Griffey, Jr.	(2)	1.50
1993 Alrak Ken Griffey, Jr.	(3)	1.50
1993 Alrak Ken Griffey, Jr.	(4)	1.50
1993 Bleachers Promos	(2)	3.00
1993 Bowman	375	5.00
1993 Bowman	703	1.00
1993 Classic	30	.90
1993 Colla All-Stars	3	1.50
1993 DiamondMarks	(107)	3.00
1993 DiamondMarks Inserts	(3)	35.00
1993 DiamondMarks Promos	(4)	40.00
1993 Donruss	553	2.00
1993 Donruss Diamond Kings	1	5.00
1993 Donruss Elite Dominators	12	150.00
1993 Donruss Long Ball Leaders	9	20.00
1993 Donruss Masters of the Game	8	6.00
1993 Donruss MVP's	20	6.00
1993 Donruss Previews	20	15.00
1993 Duracell Power Players	15	.75
1993 Finest	110	35.00
1993 Finest Jumbo All-Stars	110	75.00
1993 Finest Refractors	110	1800.00
1993 Flair	270	10.00
1993 Fleer	307	1.50
1993 Fleer All-Stars	7	10.00
1993 Fleer Atlantic	11	2.00
1993 Fleer Fruit of the Loom	25	8.00
1993 Fleer Team Leaders AL	10	25.00
1993 Golden Moments Ken Griffey, Jr.	(1)	5.00
1993 Golden Moments Ken Griffey, Jr.	(2)	5.00
1993 Highland Mint Mint-Cards	(13s)	275.00
1993 Highland Mint Mint-Cards	(13b)	66.00
1993 Highland Mint Mint-Cards	(13g)	475.00
1993 Hostess Twinkies	25	5.00
1993 Humpty Dumpty	15	6.00
1993 Jimmy Dean	11	1.50
1993 Kenner Stadium Stars	3	45.00
1993 Kenner Starting Lineups	(14)	20.00
1993 King-B	2	3.00
1993 Kraft Pop-Up Action	(8)	3.00
1993 Leaf	319	4.00
1993 Leaf Gold All-Stars	7	7.00
1993 Leaf Update Gold All-Stars	8	6.00
1993 Metz Bakeries	(18)	1.50
1993 Mother's Cookies Mariners	4	5.00
1993 O-Pee-Chee	91	4.00
1993 O-Pee-Chee/Prem Foil Star Performers	9	55.00
1993 O-Pee-Chee/Prem Star Performers	9	1.50
1993 Pacific	286	2.00
1993 Pacific Jugadores Calientes	7	6.00
1993 Panini Stickers	63	1.50
1993 Pinnacle	110	3.50
1993 Pinnacle Cooperstown	22	1.00
1993 Pinnacle Cooperstown Dufex	22	300.00
1993 Pinnacle Home Run Club	13	3.00
1993 Pinnacle Slugfest	28	15.00
1993 Post Cereal	7	1.00
1993 Post Cereal - Canadian	9	4.00
1993 Score	1	1.75
1993 Score	504	.75
1993 Score	536	.75
1993 Score Gold Dream Team	5	5.00
1993 Score The Franchise	12	30.00
1993 Select	2	3.50
1993 Select Chase Stars	19	50.00
1993 Select Stat Leaders	15	1.00
1993 Stadium Club	591	2.00
1993 Stadium Club	707	3.50
1993 Stadium Club First Day Production	591	75.00
1993 Stadium Club First Day Production	707	125.00
1993 Stadium Club II Inserts	4	4.00
1993 Stadium Club Master Photos	(26)	9.00
1993 Stadium Club Members Only	(11)	4.00
1993 Stadium Club Special Master Photos	(3)	3.00
1993 Stadium Club Special (Murphy)	56	3.00
1993 Stadium Club Team Sets	1	2.50
1993 Studio	96	3.00
1993 Studio Superstars on Canvas	1	12.00
1993 SP	4	10.00
1993 SP Platinum Power	9	60.00
1993 Topps	179	1.50
1993 Topps	405	.40
1993 Topps Black Gold	33	3.50
1993 Topps Full Shot Super	2	16.00
1993 Topps Gold	179	4.00
1993 Topps Gold	405	.90
1993 Topps Promo Sheet	(6)	3.00
1993 Topps Promos	179	1.50
1993 Toys "R" Us Master Photos	(b)	1.50
1993 Toys "R" Us Topps Stadium Club	1	1.50
1993 Triple Play	1	1.00
1993 Triple Play Action Baseball	24	.40
1993 Triple Play Nicknames	5	6.00
1993 Triple Play Promos	1	75.00
1993 Ultra	619	4.00
1993 Ultra All-Stars	17	14.00
1993 Ultra Award Winners	16	14.00
1993 Ultra Performers	3	8.00
1993 Upper Deck	55	.50
1993 Upper Deck	355	2.00
1993 Upper Deck	355a	6.00
1993 Upper Deck	355b	25.00
1993 Upper Deck	525	.20
1993 Upper Deck Clutch Performers	11	6.00
1993 Upper Deck Diamond Gallery	13	6.00
1993 UD Fun Packs All-Star Scratch-Off	8	5.00
1993 Upper Deck Fun Packs	16	3.00
1993 Upper Deck Fun Packs	24	1.00
1993 Upper Deck Fun Packs	30	1.00
1993 Upper Deck Fun Packs	111	1.00
1993 Upper Deck Fun Packs	114	2.00
1993 Upper Deck Fun Packs	224	.50
1993 Upper Deck Future Heroes	59	6.00
1993 Upper Deck Highlights	9	40.00
1993 Upper Deck Home Run Heroes	9	5.00
1993 Upper Deck Iooss Collection	13	5.00
1993 Upper Deck Iooss Collection Supers	13	9.00
1993 Upper Deck On Deck	13	6.00
1993 Upper Deck Triple Crown	4	10.00
1993 Upper Deck 5th Anniversary	1	7.50
1993 Upper Deck 5th Anniversary Supers	1	9.00
1994 Bowman	5	3.00
1994 Bowman Superstar Sampler	5	35.00
1994 Bowman's Best	96	7.50
1994 Bowman's Best	40	10.00
1994 Bowman's Best Refractors	96	35.00
1994 Bowman's Best Refractors	40	100.00
1994 Church's Chicken Show Stoppers	3	9.00
1994 UD CC	117	1.50
1994 UD CC	317	.30
1994 UD CC	324	.30
1994 UD CC	340	.50
1994 UD CC	634	.75
1994 UD CC Home Run All-Stars	2HA	3.00
1994 UD CC Promos	50	6.00
1994 UD CC Promos	—	5.00
1994 Dairy Queen Ken Griffey, Jr.	1	1.00
1994 Dairy Queen Ken Griffey, Jr.	2	1.00
1994 Dairy Queen Ken Griffey, Jr.	3	1.00
1994 Dairy Queen Ken Griffey, Jr.	4	1.00
1994 Dairy Queen Ken Griffey, Jr.	5	1.00
1994 Dairy Queen Ken Griffey, Jr.	6	1.00
1994 Dairy Queen Ken Griffey, Jr.	7	1.00
1994 Dairy Queen Ken Griffey, Jr.	8	1.00
1994 Dairy Queen Ken Griffey, Jr.	9	1.00
1994 Dairy Queen Ken Griffey, Jr.	10	1.00
1994 Denny's Grand Slam	13	3.00
1994 Donruss	4	3.00
1994 Donruss Decade Dominators	6	8.00
1994 Donruss Decade Dominators Supers	6	8.00
1994 Donruss Decade Dominators	9	8.00
1994 Donruss Decade Dominators Supers	9	8.00
1994 Donruss Diamond Kings	14	9.00
1994 Donruss Diamond Kings Supers	14	7.50
1994 Donruss Elite	45	60.00
1994 Donruss Long Ball Leaders	5	12.00
1994 Donruss MVP's	26	8.00
1994 Donruss Promos	7	15.00
1994 Donruss Special Edition - Gold	4	5.00
1994 Donruss Spirit of the Game	3	8.00
1994 Donruss Spirit of the Game Super	3	9.00
1994 Finest	232	12.00
1994 Finest Bronze	2	35.00
1994 Finest Refractors	232	125.00
1994 Finest Superstar Jumbos	232	35.00
1994 Finest Superstar Sampler	232	35.00
1994 Flair	103	5.00
1994 Flair Hot Glove	3	75.00
1994 Flair Outfield Power	6	15.00
1994 Fleer	286	3.00
1994 Fleer All-Stars	10	4.00
1994 Fleer Atlantic	13	1.50
1994 Fleer Golden Moments	4	10.00
1994 Fleer Golden Moments Super	4	15.00
1994 Fleer Lumber Co.	5	6.00
1994 Fleer Team Leaders	12	5.00
1994 Fleer/Extra Bases	166	3.00
1994 Fleer/Extra Bases Game Breakers	14	4.00
1994 Kenner Starting Lineups	(23)	20.00
1994 King-B	6	3.00
1994 Kraft Pop Ups	5	1.50
1994 Leaf	368	3.00
1994 Leaf Gamers	1	55.00
1994 Leaf Gold Stars	4	80.00
1994 Leaf MVP Contenders	7a	35.00
1994 Leaf MVP Contenders	7b	60.00
1994 Leaf Power Brokers	5	10.00
1994 Leaf Promos	3	12.00
1994 Leaf Slide Show	9	20.00
1994 Leaf Statistical Standouts	6	8.00
1994 Leaf/Limited	66	15.00
1994 Leaf/Limited Gold	11	75.00
1994 Mother's Cookies Mariners	4	4.00
1994 O-Pee-Chee	22	3.00
1994 O-Pee-Chee All-Star Redemption	8	5.00
1994 O-Pee-Chee Jumbo All-Stars	8	20.00
1994 O-Pee-Chee Jumbo All-Stars Factory	8	10.00
1994 Oscar Mayer Superstar Pop-Ups	6	5.00
1994 Pacific Crown	570	2.50
1994 Pacific Crown Homerun Leaders	2	18.00
1994 Pacific Crown Jewels of the Crown	8	18.00
1994 Pacific Crown Promos	4	8.00
1994 Panini Stickers	118	1.00
1994 Pinnacle	100	3.00
1994 Pinnacle Power Surge	23	1.50
1994 Pinnacle Run Creators	3	20.00
1994 Pinnacle Team Pinnacle	6	66.00
1994 Pinnacle The Naturals	3	2.50
1994 Pinnacle Tribute	17	20.00
1994 Post Cereal	15	.80
1994 Post Cereal - Canadian	10	2.50
1994 Pro Mint	(5)	17.50
1994 Score	3	1.50
1994 Score	628	1.00
1994 Score Gold Stars	32	50.00
1994 Score Samples	3	25.00
1994 Score Samples	3	125.00
1994 Score The Cycle	17	65.00
1994 Select	1	3.50
1994 Select Crown Contenders	10	20.00
1994 Signature Rookies Draft Picks Flip	1	2.00
1994 Signature Rookies Draft Picks Flip	1	150.00
1994 Signature Rookies Draft Picks Flip	1	10.00
1994 Signature Rookies Draft Picks Flip	1	200.00
1994 Signature Rookies Draft Picks Flip	3	2.00
1994 Signature Rookies Draft Picks Flip	3	150.00
1994 Signature Rookies Draft Picks Flip	3	10.00
1994 Signature Rookies Draft Picks Flip	3	200.00
1994 Sportflics FanFest All-Stars	AS7	12.00
1994 Sportflics 2000	143	3.00
1994 Sportflics 2000	181	1.50
1994 Sportflics 2000 Rookie/Traded Going	GG4	25.00
1994 Stadium Club	85	3.00
1994 Stadium Club	262	1.50
1994 Stadium Club	529	1.50
1994 Stadium Club Dugout Dirt	7	4.00
1994 Stadium Club Finest	5	10.00
1994 Stadium Club Finest Jumbo	5	30.00
1994 Stadium Club First Day Production	85	90.00
1994 Stadium Club First Day Production	262	50.00
1994 Stadium Club First Day Production	529	50.00
1994 Stadium Club Members Only Baseball	17	4.00
1994 Stadium Club Superstar Sampler	85	25.00
1994 Studio	101	3.00
1994 Studio Editor's Choice	3	15.00
1994 Studio Gold Stars	4	70.00
1994 Studio Silver Stars	4	20.00
1994 SuperSlam	(60)	12.00
1994 SP	105	5.00
1994 SP Holoview Blue	12	30.00
1994 SP Holoview Red	12	250.00
1994 Taco Time Ken Griffey Jr. Promos	(1)	5.00
1994 Taco Time Ken Griffey, Jr.	1	1.50
1994 Taco Time Ken Griffey, Jr.	1SP	1.50
1994 Taco Time Ken Griffey Jr. Promos	(2)	5.00
1994 Taco Time Ken Griffey, Jr.	2	1.50
1994 Taco Time Ken Griffey, Jr.	2SP	1.50
1994 Taco Time Ken Griffey, Jr.	3	1.50
1994 Taco Time Ken Griffey, Jr.	3SP	1.50
1994 Taco Time Ken Griffey, Jr.	4	1.50
1994 Taco Time Ken Griffey, Jr.	4SP	1.50
1994 Taco Time Ken Griffey, Jr.	5	1.50
1994 Taco Time Ken Griffey, Jr.	5SP	1.50
1994 Taco Time Ken Griffey, Jr.	6	1.50
1994 Tombstone Pizza	21	2.50
1994 Topps	388	.40
1994 Topps	400	1.50
1994 Topps	606	.75
1994 Topps Bilingual	388	.75
1994 Topps Bilingual	400	5.00
1994 Topps Bilingual	606	3.50
1994 Topps Black Gold	8	4.00
1994 Topps Gold	388	1.50
1994 Topps Gold	400	4.00
1994 Topps Gold	606	3.00
1994 Topps Traded Finest Inserts	5	8.00
1994 Triple Play	127	1.50
1994 Triple Play Bomb Squad	8	8.00
1994 Triple Play Medalists	11	2.00
1994 Triple Play Promos	4	4.00
1994 U.S. Playing Card Aces	Q	.90
1994 Ultra	120	3.00
1994 Ultra All-Stars	8	6.00
1994 Ultra Award Winners	6	6.00
1994 Ultra Home Run Kings	2	22.00
1994 Ultra On-Base Leaders	6	65.00
1994 Upper Deck	53	2.00
1994 Upper Deck	224	3.00
1994 Upper Deck	224a	4.00
1994 Upper Deck	292	2.00
1994 Upper Deck	MM1	400.00
1994 Upper Deck	KG1	250.00
1994 Upper Deck	GM1	1000.00
1994 Upper Deck Diamond Collection	4W	50.00
1994 Upper Deck Jumbo Checklists	1CL	3.00
1994 Upper Deck Jumbo Checklists	2CL	3.00
1994 Upper Deck Jumbo Checklists	3CL	3.00
1994 Upper Deck Jumbo Checklists	4CL	3.00
1994 Upper Deck Mantle's Long Shots	10MM	12.00
1994 Upper Deck Next Generation	6	30.00
1994 Upper Deck SP Insert	3	32.00
1994 Upper Deck SP Insert	3	35.00
1994 Upper Deck Team Scratch-Off	3	.75
1994 Upper Deck Team Scratch-Off	15	.35
1994 Upper Deck/All-Stars	1	4.00
1994 Upper Deck/All-Stars Gold	1	15.00
1994 Upper Deck/All-Stars	48	4.00
1994 Upper Deck/All-Stars Gold	48	10.00
1994 Upper Deck/All-Stars	48a	3.00
1994 Upper Deck/Fun Packs	24	2.50
1994 Upper Deck/Fun Packs	24a	3.00
1994 Upper Deck/Fun Packs	182	1.00
1994 Upper Deck/Fun Packs	103	1.00
1994 Upper Deck/Fun Packs	200	2.50
1994 Upper Deck/Fun Packs	216	1.00
1994 Upper Deck/Fun Packs	224	2.50
1994 Upper Deck/Fun Packs	229	1.00
1994 Upper Deck/Fun Packs	235	1.00
1994 Z Silk Cachets	(4)	15.00
1995 Bazooka	31	2.00
1995 Bazooka Red Hot Inserts	RH7	4.00
1995 Bowman	321	4.00
1995 Bowman's Best	12	5.00
1995 Bowman's Best	49	8.00
1995 Bowman's Best Refractors - Jumbo	49	40.00

Description	Card No.	Value
1995 Bowman's Best Refractors	12	25.00
1995 Bowman's Best Refractors	49	80.00
1995 Cardtoons	67	3.75
1995 Cardtoons Big Bang Bucks	BB8	6.00
1995 Certified	70	4.00
1995 Certified Checklists	1	.25
1995 Certified Gold Team	1	50.00
1995 Classic Phone Card Promos	(4)	12.00
1995 Classic Phone Cards	(23)	7.50
1995 UD CC	62	1.00
1995 UD CC	70	2.00
1995 UD CC	88	1.00
1995 UD CC "Crash" Winners	CR8	6.00
1995 UD CC "You Crash the Game"	CG8	.75
1995 UD CC "You Crash the Game"	CG8	.75
1995 UD CC "Crash" Winners	CR8	15.00
1995 UD CC "You Crash the Game"	CG8	3.00
1995 UD CC "You Crash the Game"	CG8	5.00
1995 UD CC "You Crash the Game"	CG8	3.00
1995 UD CC Gold Signature	62	40.00
1995 UD CC Gold Signature	70	80.00
1995 UD CC Gold Signature	88	40.00
1995 UD CC Silver Signature	62	4.00
1995 UD CC Silver Signature	70	8.00
1995 UD CC Silver Signature	88	3.00
1995 UD CC/SE	26	1.00
1995 UD CC/SE Gold	26	50.00
1995 UD CC/SE Silver	26	9.00
1995 UD CC/SE	125	3.00
1995 UD CC/SE Gold	125	100.00
1995 UD CC/SE Silver	125	15.00
1995 UD CC/SE	125a	3.00
1995 Conlon Collection In the Zone	1	3.50
1995 Conlon Collection In the Zone	2	3.00
1995 Conlon Collection In the Zone	3	2.50
1995 Conlon Collection In the Zone	4	2.00
1995 Conlon Collection In the Zone	5	2.00
1995 Conlon Collection In the Zone	6	2.50
1995 Conlon Collection In the Zone	7	3.00
1995 Conlon Collection In the Zone	8	3.00
1995 Denny's Classic Hits	11	3.00
1995 Donruss	340	3.00
1995 Donruss All-Stars	AL8	35.00
1995 Donruss Bomb Squad	1	5.00
1995 Donruss Diamond Kings	27	10.00
1995 Donruss Dominators	8	8.00
1995 Donruss Elite	54	75.00
1995 Donruss Long Ball Leaders	3	6.00
1995 Donruss Press Proofs	340	125.00
1995 Finest	118	10.00
1995 Finest Bronze League Leaders	4	40.00
1995 Finest Power Kings	10	50.00
1995 Finest Refractors	118	350.00
1995 Flair	81	5.00
1995 Flair Hot Gloves	3	65.00
1995 Flair Hot Numbers	4	16.00
1995 Flair Outfield Power	7	10.00
1995 Fleer	269	2.50
1995 Fleer All-Fleer 9	7	2.50
1995 Fleer All-Stars	7	3.50
1995 Fleer League Leaders	2	5.00
1995 Fleer Lumber Company	6	12.00
1995 Fleer Team Leaders	12	40.00
1995 Fleer Update Diamond Tribute	6	2.50
1995 Fleer Update Headliners	11	3.00
1995 Fleer Update Smooth Leather	3	9.00
1995 Fleer-Panini Stickers	86	.50
1995 Fleer-Panini Stickers	123	.35
1995 Fleer/ Ultra Gold Medallion	101	12.00
1995 Kenner Stadium Stars	(3)	30.00
1995 Kenner Starting Lineups	(24)	20.00
1995 Kraft Singles Superstars	5	2.00
1995 Leaf	211	8.00
1995 Leaf Gold Stars	4	40.00
1995 Leaf Great Gloves	6	3.00
1995 Leaf Heading For The Hall	2	50.00
1995 Leaf Slideshow	8a	15.00
1995 Leaf Slideshow	8b	15.00
1995 Leaf Statistical Standouts	2	125.00
1995 Leaf Statistical Standouts Promos	2	60.00
1995 Leaf 300 Club	10	30.00
1995 Leaf/Limited	118	6.00
1995 Leaf/Limited Bat Patrol	5	5.00
1995 Leaf/Limited Gold	6	5.00
1995 Leaf/Limited Lumberjacks	4	80.00
1995 Leaf/Opening Day	5	3.00
1995 Megacards Ken Griffey, Jr. Wish List	1-25	.50
1995 Mother's Cookies Mariners	4	6.00
1995 National Packtime	6	1.50
1995 Pacific	398	2.50
1995 Pacific Gold Crown Die-cut	16	40.00
1995 Pacific Mariners Memories	1	.25
1995 Pacific Mariners Memories	6	.25
1995 Pacific Mariners Memories	9	.25
1995 Pacific Mariners Memories	32	6.00
1995 Pacific Marquee Prism	21	20.00
1995 Pacific Prism	126	15.00
1995 Pinnacle	128	3.00
1995 Pinnacle	304	1.50
1995 Pinnacle	447	1.00
1995 Pinnacle	450	2.00
1995 Pinnacle Gate Attraction	1	20.00
1995 Pinnacle Red Hot	2	15.00
1995 Pinnacle Team Pinnacle	7	40.00
1995 Pinnacle White Hot	2	30.00
1995 Pinnacle/FanFest	11	3.00
1995 Post Cereal	4	2.00
1995 Post Cereal - Canadian	1	4.00
1995 Premier Mint Gold Signature Cards	(2)	40.00
1995 Score	437	2.00
1995 Score	551	1.00
1995 Score Double Gold Champions	2	20.00
1995 Score Dream Team Gold	7	30.00
1995 Score Hall of Gold	1	10.00
1995 Score Platinum Redemption Team	437	30.00
1995 Score Platinum Redemption Team	551	20.00
1995 Score Score Rules	1	12.00
1995 Score Score Rules Supers	1	60.00
1995 Select	89	3.00
1995 Select	243	1.25
1995 Select	250	.50
1995 Select Big Sticks	BS2	25.00
1995 SkyBox E-Motion	77	4.00
1995 SkyBox E-Motion Masters	3	15.00
1995 SkyBox E-Motion N-Tense	6	40.00
1995 Sportflix	1	2.50
1995 Sportflix	168	1.00
1995 Sportflix Double Take	9	20.00
1995 Sportflix ProMotion	1	18.00
1995 Sportflix 3D Detonators	3	10.00
1995 Sportflix 3D Hammer Team	1	4.00
1995 Sportflix/UC3	73	3.00
1995 Sportflix/UC3	124	1.50
1995 Sportflix/UC3 Cyclone Squad	2	4.00
1995 Sportflix/UC3 In Motion	2	6.00
1995 Stadium Club	241	3.00
1995 Stadium Club	521	1.25
1995 Stadium Club Clear Cut	18	24.00
1995 Stadium Club Crunch Time	9	8.00
1995 Stadium Club Members Only Baseball	19	2.00
1995 Stadium Club Power Zone	7	15.00
1995 Stadium Club Ring Leaders	14	35.00
1995 Stadium Club Super Skills	11	25.00
1995 Stadium Club Super Team Division	241	12.00
1995 Stadium Club Virtual Reality	120	7.50
1995 Stadium Club VR Extremist	VRE2	30.00
1995 Studio	5	3.00
1995 Studio Gold	5	4.00
1995 Studio Platinum	5	15.00
1995 Summit	1	3.00
1995 Summit	174	1.50
1995 Summit	195	.75
1995 Summit Big Bang	BB1	50.00
1995 SP	100(P)	6.00
1995 SP	190	4.00
1995 SP Championship Die Cuts	183	3.50
1995 SP Championship Die Cuts	185	8.00
1995 SP Griffey Gold Signature	190	125.00
1995 SP Platinum Power	PP12	5.00
1995 SP Special F/X	18	150.00
1995 SP SuperbaFoil	190	20.00
1995 SP/Championship	183	1.75
1995 SP/Championship	185	3.00
1995 SP/Championship Dest: Fall Classic	1	25.00
1995 SP/Championship Dest: Fall Classic	1	40.00
1995 Test Set	31	2.00
1995 Tombstone Pizza	9	4.00
1995 Topps	388	1.00
1995 Topps	397	2.50
1995 Topps Cyberstats	199	8.00
1995 Topps League Leaders	31	5.00
1995 Topps Opening Day	3	8.00
1995 Topps Pre-production	6	9.00
1995 Topps Pre-production	6	35.00
1995 Topps Total Bases Finest	3	10.00
1995 Topps Traded and Rookies	2	1.00
1995 Topps Traded/Rookies Power Boosters	2	30.00
1995 Topps Traded and Rookies	160	.50
1995 Topps/DIII	43	6.00
1995 Topps/Embossed	51	3.00
1995 Ultra	101	3.00
1995 Ultra All-Stars	7	5.00
1995 Ultra Award Winners	6	5.00
1995 Ultra Hitting Machines	6	6.00
1995 Ultra Home Run Kings	1	10.00
1995 Ultra Power Plus	2	16.00
1995 Upper Deck	100	3.00
1995 Upper Deck	100a	3.00
1995 Upper Deck	110	1.50
1995 Upper Deck	136	1.50
1995 Upper Deck Hobby Predictors	H3	10.00
1995 Upper Deck Retail Predictors	R4	10.00
1995 Upper Deck Retail Predictors	R45	10.00
1995 Upper Deck Retail Predictors	R52	10.00
1995 Upper Deck Special Edition	255	10.00
1995 Upper Deck/GTS Phone Cards	MLB04	6.00
1995 Zenith	61	4.00
1995 Zenith All-Star Salute	15	10.00
1995 Zenith Z-Team	2	50.00
1995 1995 Topps/Stadium Club 1st Day	241	3.00
1996 Bazooka	1	2.00
1996 Bowman	79	4.00
1996 Bowman's Best	71	6.00
1996 Bowman's Best Cuts	1	25.00
1996 Bowman's Best Cuts Refractors	1	60.00
1996 Bowman's Best Mirror Image	7	40.00
1996 Bowman's Best Preview	30	30.00
1996 Bowman's Best Preview Refractors	30	70.00
1996 Certified	47	5.00
1996 Certified	136	3.00
1996 Certified Artist's Proofs	47	110.00
1996 Certified Artist's Proofs	136	60.00
1996 Certified Interleague Preview	1	60.00
1996 Certified Interleague Preview Samples	1	25.00
1996 Certified Mirror Blue	47	100.00
1996 Certified Mirror Blue	136	525.00
1996 Certified Mirror Gold, Blue, Red	47	3200.00
1996 Certified Mirror Gold, Blue, Red	136	2000.00
1996 Certified Mirror Red	47	450.00
1996 Certified Mirror Red	136	275.00
1996 Certified Red, Blue	47	45.00
1996 Certified Red, Blue	136	25.00
1996 Certified Select Few	3	30.00
1996 Circa	78	3.00
1996 Circa	198	1.00
1996 Circa Access	12	20.00
1996 Circa Boss	20	15.00
1996 Circa Rave	78	500.00
1996 Circa Rave	198	175.00
1996 UD CC	310	2.00
1996 UD CC	370	1.25
1996 UD CC	415	.50
1996 UD CC Crash the Game Redemp	CR26	15.00
1996 UD CC Crash the Game	26a	6.00
1996 UD CC Crash the Game	26b	6.00
1996 UD CC Crash the Game	26c	6.00
1996 UD CC Gold Signature	310	40.00
1996 UD CC Gold Signature	415	3.00
1996 UD CC Promo	100	8.00
1996 UD CC Silver Signature	310	10.00
1996 UD CC Silver Signature	415	.70
1996 Donruss	338	3.00
1996 Donruss	490	1.50
1996 Donruss Elite	70	60.00
1996 Donruss Freeze Frame	2	35.00
1996 Donruss Hit List	2	40.00
1996 Donruss Long Ball Leaders	6	60.00
1996 Donruss Power Alley	10	50.00
1996 Donruss Power Alley Die-Cuts	10	275.00
1996 Donruss Round Trippers	6	60.00
1996 Donruss Samples	4	9.00
1996 Donruss Showdown	3	50.00
1996 E-Motion XL	113	7.00
1996 E-Motion XL D-Fense	4	15.00
1996 E-Motion XL Legion of Boom	4	60.00
1996 E-Motion XL N-Tense	4	25.00
1996 Finest	24	6.00
1996 Finest	135	90.00
1996 Finest	305	25.00
1996 Finest Refractors	24	75.00
1996 Finest Refractors	135	400.00
1996 Finest Refractors	305	140.00
1996 Flair	160	10.00
1996 Flair Diamond Cuts	5	45.00
1996 Flair Hot Gloves	4	150.00
1996 Flair Powerline	4	10.00
1996 Fleer	238	2.50
1996 Fleer Checklists	2	2.00
1996 Fleer Lumber Company	4	5.00
1996 Fleer Post-Season Glory	2	4.00
1996 Fleer Team Leaders	12	12.00
1996 Fleer Update	U223	1.50
1996 Fleer Update Diamond Tribute	3	50.00
1996 Fleer Update Headliners	7	8.00
1996 Fleer Update Smooth Leather	4	5.00
1996 Fleer Update Soaring Stars	4	10.00
1996 Fleer Zone	3	55.00
1996 Fleer-Panini Stickers	223	1.50
1996 Kenner Starting Lineups	(20)	20.00
1996 Leaf	41	3.00
1996 Leaf All-Star MVP Contenders Gold	18	24.00
1996 Leaf All-Star MVP Contenders	18	8.00
1996 Leaf Gold Leaf Stars	4	100.00
1996 Leaf Hats Off	5	50.00
1996 Leaf Picture Perfect	7	40.00
1996 Leaf Picture Perfect Promos	7	70.00
1996 Leaf Statistical Standouts	4	100.00
1996 Leaf Total Bases	9	30.00
1996 Leaf Total Bases Promos	9	70.00
1996 Leaf/Limited	11	8.00
1996 Leaf/Limited Lumberjacks	1	45.00
1996 Leaf/Limited Lumberjacks Samples	1	35.00
1996 Leaf/Limited Pennant Craze	4	100.00
1996 Leaf/Limited Pennant Craze Samples	4	25.00
1996 Leaf/Preferred	1	4.00
1996 Leaf/Preferred Leaf Steel	52	15.00
1996 Leaf/Preferred Leaf Gold Promos	52	100.00
1996 Leaf/Preferred Staremaster	6	100.00
1996 Leaf/Preferred Steel Power	3	50.00
1996 Leaf/Signature Series	10	5.00
1996 Metal Universe	107	3.00
1996 Metal Universe Heavy Metal	4	12.00
1996 Metal Universe Mother Lode	3	18.00
1996 Metal Universe Titanium	3	30.00
1996 Mother's Cookies Mariners	4	4.00
1996 Pacific Crown Collection	410	2.50
1996 Pacific Crown Cramer's Choice	CC8	250.00
1996 Pacific Crown Gold Crown Die-Cuts	DC13	50.00
1996 Pacific Crown Hometown of Players	HP11	18.00
1996 Pacific Crown Milestones	M9	25.00
1996 Pacific Crown October Moments	OM6	30.00
1996 Pacific Prism	131	15.00
1996 Pacific Prism Fence Busters	6	40.00
1996 Pacific Prism Red Hot Stars	7	40.00
1996 Pinnacle	82	3.00
1996 Pinnacle	134	1.50
1996 Pinnacle	255	1.50
1996 Pinnacle	301.8	1.50
1996 Pinnacle	394	1.25
1996 Pinnacle	399	.75
1996 Pinnacle Essence of the Game	7	25.00
1996 Pinnacle First Rate	1	30.00
1996 Pinnacle Pinnacle Power	3	25.00
1996 Pinnacle Skylines	1	40.00
1996 Pinnacle Slugfest	2	35.00
1996 Pinnacle Starburst	41	40.00
1996 Pinnacle Starburst	61	20.00
1996 Pinnacle Starburst	155	20.00
1996 Pinnacle Starburst	185	20.00
1996 Pinnacle Team Pinnacle	6	25.00
1996 Pinnacle Team Spirit	2	50.00
1996 Pinnacle/Aficionado Magic Numbers	1	50.00
1996 Pinnacle/Aficionado Rivals	1	25.00
1996 Pinnacle/Aficionado Slick Picks	3	20.00
1996 Pinnacle/Aficionado Rivals	4	20.00
1996 Pinnacle/Aficionado Rivals	5	25.00
1996 Pinnacle/Aficionado Rivals	7	25.00
1996 Pinnacle/Aficionado Rivals	9	20.00
1996 Pinnacle/Aficionado Rivals	10	25.00
1996 Pinnacle/Aficionado	75	5.00
1996 Pinnacle/FanFest	3	3.00
1996 Pinnacle/Summit Above & Beyond	86	40.00
1996 Pinnacle/Summit Above & Beyond	158	20.00
1996 Pinnacle/Summit Above & Beyond	197	20.00
1996 Pizza Hut	(3)	4.00
1996 Score	282	2.50
1996 Score All-Stars	3	25.00
1996 Score Big Bats	2	25.00
1996 Score Diamond Aces	14	30.00
1996 Score Dream Team	7	25.00
1996 Score Dugout Collection	7	6.00
1996 Score Gold Stars	1	10.00
1996 Score Numbers Game	3	10.00
1996 Score Power Pace	12	25.00
1996 Score Reflexions	2	40.00
1996 Score Titantic Taters	4	25.00
1996 Select	6	2.50
1996 Select	151	1.25
1996 Select	197	1.00
1996 Select Claim to Fame	3	50.00
1996 Select En Fuego	1	30.00
1996 Select Team Nucleus	9	15.00
1996 Sportflix	18	3.00
1996 Sportflix	98	1.50
1996 Sportflix	142	1.50
1996 Sportflix Double Take	4	25.00
1996 Sportflix Hit Parade	1	10.00

	Card No.	Value
1996 Sportflix Power Surge	2	17.50
1996 Sportflix ProMotion	6	10.00
1996 Stadium Club	105	3.00
1996 Stad Club Ext Player - Silver Winner	EW8	20.00
1996 Stadium Club Ext Player - Bronze	105	25.00
1996 Stadium Club Ext Player - Gold	105	100.00
1996 Stadium Club Extreme Player - Silver	105	50.00
1996 Stadium Club Mega Heroes	2	30.00
1996 Stadium Club Power Packed	PP6	30.00
1996 Stadium Club Prime Cuts	PC3	25.00
1996 Stadium Club TSC Awards	5	18.00
1996 Studio	116	3.00
1996 Studio Hit Parade	2	25.00
1996 Studio Masterstrokes	7	40.00
1996 Studio Masterstrokes Samples	7	12.50
1996 Studio Stained Glass Stars	2	20.00
1996 Summit	86	3.00
1996 Summit	158	1.00
1996 Summit	197	1.50
1996 Summit Ballparks	5	35.00
1996 Summit Big Bang	2	150.00
1996 Summit Big Bang Mirage	2	150.00
1996 Summit Hitters, Inc.	4	40.00
1996 Summit Positions	8	35.00
1996 SP	170	4.00
1996 SP	170p	20.00
1996 SP	188	2.00
1996 SP Baseball Heroes	81	60.00
1996 SP Baseball Heroes	90	60.00
1996 SP FanFest Promos	1	12.00
1996 SP Marquee Matchups Blue	MM1	8.00
1996 SP Marquee Matchups Red	MM1	30.00
1996 SP SpecialFX	10	20.00
1996 SP SpecialFX Red	10	100.00
1996 SPx	55	12.00
1996 SPx	55p	15.00
1996 SPx Bound for Glory	1	30.00
1996 SPx Ken Griffey Jr. Comm	KG1	25.00
1996 Team Metal Ken Griffey Jr	1	2.50
1996 Team Metal Ken Griffey Jr.	2	2.50
1996 Team Metal Ken Griffey Jr.	3	2.50
1996 Team Metal Ken Griffey Jr.	4	2.50
1996 Team Out! Game	(32)	6.00
1996 Team Out! Game	(101)	.40
1996 Topps	205	2.50
1996 Topps	230	1.00
1996 Topps A.L. West Champion Mariners	205	2.50
1996 Topps A.L. West Champion Mariners	230	1.00
1996 Topps Big Topps	(3)	4.00
1996 Topps Classic Confrontations	1	1.50
1996 Topps Mystery Finest	M16	20.00
1996 Topps Profiles-AL	5	6.00
1996 Topps Wrecking Crew	WC9	20.00
1996 Topps 5-Star Mystery Finest	M25	20.00
1996 Topps/Chrome	70	8.00
1996 Topps/Chrome	90	4.00
1996 Topps/Chrome Wrecking Crew	WC9	25.00
1996 Topps/Gallery	146	4.00
1996 Topps/Gallery Expressionists	3	30.00
1996 Topps/Gallery Photo Gallery	PG10	30.00
1996 Topps/Laser	42	10.00
1996 Topps/Laser Power Cuts	14	70.00
1996 Topps/Laser Stadium Stars	4	100.00
1996 Topps/R&N China Stadi Porcelains	(1)	30.00
1996 Ultra	176	3.00
1996 Ultra	579	1.50
1996 Ultra Call to the Hall	2	18.00
1996 Ultra Checklists	3	3.00
1996 Ultra Diamond Producers	3	18.00
1996 Ultra Hitting Machines	4	150.00
1996 Ultra Home Run Kings	6	40.00
1996 Ultra Home Run Kings Exchange	6	4.00
1996 Ultra Power Plus	3	10.00
1996 Ultra Prime Leather	6	12.00
1996 Ultra Promotional Samples	(1)	15.00
1996 Ultra R-E-S-P-E-C-T	2	15.00
1996 Ultra Rawhide	4	10.00
1996 Ultra Thunderclap	11	90.00
1996 Upper Deck	200	3.00
1996 Upper Deck	376	1.50
1996 Upper Deck All-Star Supers	200	4.00
1996 Upper Deck Diamond Destiny	DD35	15.00
1996 Upper Deck Gameface	GF1	4.00
1996 Upper Deck Hobby Predictor	H4	10.00
1996 Upper Deck Hot Commodities	HC1	30.00
1996 Upper Deck Lovero Collection	VJ10	8.00
1996 Upper Deck Power Driven	PD7	10.00
1996 Upper Deck Retail Predictor	R4	10.00
1996 Upper Deck Retail Predictor	R15	10.00
1996 Upper Deck Retail Predictor	R24	10.00
1996 Upper Deck Run Producers	RP7	50.00
1996 Zenith	1	4.00
1996 Zenith	135	2.00
1996 Zenith Diamond Club	3	30.00
1996 Zenith Mozaics	5	25.00
1996 Zenith Z-Team	1	100.00
1996 Zenith Z-Team Samples	1	25.00
1997 Bowman	16	4.00
1997 Bowman Chrome	12	7.00
1997 Bowman International Best	BBI2	15.00
1997 Bowman's Best	1	8.00
1997 Bowman's Best Cuts	BC6	20.00
1997 Bowman's Best Jumbos	1	17.50
1997 Bowman's Best Mirror Image	MI5	30.00
1997 Bowman's Best Preview	2	20.00
1997 Circa	24	3.00
1997 Circa	395	1.50
1997 Circa Boss	6	8.00
1997 Circa Icons	2	25.00
1997 Circa Limited Access	5	20.00
1997 Circa Rave	24	350.00
1997 Circa Rave	395	150.00
1997 Circa Rave Reviews	4	100.00
1997 UD CC	230	2.00
1997 UD CC	244	.50
1997 UD CC	245	.50
1997 UD CC	246	.50
1997 UD CC	247	.50
1997 UD CC	248	.50
1997 UD CC	249	.50
1997 UD CC	334	1.00
1997 UD CC All-Star Connection	5	2.50
1997 UD CC Big Shots	1	10.00
1997 UD CC Big Show	43	4.00
1997 UD CC Clearly Dominant	CD1	12.00
1997 UD CC Clearly Dominant	CD2	12.00
1997 UD CC Clearly Dominant	CD3	12.00
1997 UD CC Clearly Dominant	CD4	12.00
1997 UD CC Clearly Dominant	CD5	12.00
1997 UD CC Hot List Jumbos	334	9.00
1997 UD CC New Frontier	NF11	35.00
1997 UD CC Premier Power	PP3	15.00
1997 UD CC Stick'Ums	24	3.00
1997 UD CC Toast of the Town	T27	12.00
1997 UD CC Team Sets	SM2	2.00
1997 UD CC You Crash the Game	CG28	5.00
1997 Corinthian Headliners		12.00
1997 Donruss	21	2.50
1997 Donruss	399	1.50
1997 Donruss	439	1.00
1997 Donruss	450	1.00
1997 Donruss Armed and Dangerous	1	30.00
1997 Donruss Diamond Kings	1	30.00
1997 Donruss Elite	5	4.00
1997 Donruss Elite Inserts	7	80.00
1997 Donruss Elite Leather & Lumber	1	200.00
1997 Donruss Elite Promos	7	45.00
1997 Donruss Limited	1	5.00
1997 Donruss Limited	18	100.00
1997 Donruss Limited	19	100.00
1997 Donruss Limited Exposure	1	75.00
1997 Donruss Limited Exposure	18	700.00
1997 Donruss Limited Exposure	19	800.00
1997 Donruss Limited Fabric of the Game		140.00
1997 Donruss Limited Fabric of the Game		125.00
1997 Donruss Longball Leaders	6	25.00
1997 Donruss Preferred	2	80.00
1997 Donruss Preferred	175	2.00
1997 Donruss Preferred Precious Metals	2	700.00
1997 Donruss Preferred Staremasters	9	125.00
1997 Donruss Preferred Tins	2	2.00
1997 Donruss Preferred Tin Boxes	2	12.00
1997 Donruss Preferred X-Ponential Power	7A	50.00
1997 Donruss Team Sets	136	3.00
1997 Donruss Team Sets MVP	13	75.00
1997 Donruss Update Dominators	2	15.00
1997 Donruss Update Franchise Features	1	75.00
1997 Donruss Update Power Alley	2	120.00
1997 Finest	139	25.00
1997 Finest	238	5.00
1997 Finest	342	80.00
1997 Finest Refractors	139	160.00
1997 Finest Refractors	238	80.00
1997 Finest Refractors	342	450.00
1997 Flair Showcase	24	10.00
1997 Flair Showcase Diamond Cuts	5	45.00
1997 Flair Showcase Hot Gloves	4	125.00
1997 Flair Showcase Legacy Collection	24	600.00
1997 Fleer	206	3.00
1997 Fleer	492	1.00
1997 Fleer	701	1.50
1997 Fleer	745	1.00
1997 Fleer Bleacher Blasters	4	15.00
1997 Fleer Diamond Tribute	4	120.00
1997 Fleer Goudey Greats	2	5.00
1997 Fleer Headliners	6	2.00
1997 Fleer Lumber Company	9	35.00
1997 Fleer Night & Day	4	75.00
1997 Fleer Soaring Stars	4	8.00
1997 Fleer Sports Illustrated Great Shots		1.00
1997 Fleer Sports Illustrated	28	2.00
1997 Fleer Sports Illustrated	157	4.00
1997 Fleer Sports Illustrated	172	2.00
1997 Fleer Sports Illustrated	178	2.00
1997 Fleer Team Leaders	12	20.00
1997 Fleer Zone	7	40.00
1997 Kenner Classic Doubles	(4)	40.00
1997 Kenner Freeze Frames	(3)	50.00
1997 Kenner 12" Figures	(1)	50.00
1997 Leaf	193	1.50
1997 Leaf	204	3.00
1997 Leaf	371	1.50
1997 Leaf Banner Season	2	60.00
1997 Leaf Dress for Success	12	40.00
1997 Leaf Fractal Matrix	193	40.00
1997 Leaf Fractal Matrix Die-Cut	193	300.00
1997 Leaf Fractal Matrix	204	350.00
1997 Leaf Fractal Matrix Die-Cut	204	100.00
1997 Leaf Fractal Matrix	371	70.00
1997 Leaf Fractal Matrix Die-Cut	371	175.00
1997 Leaf Get-A-Grip	1	40.00
1997 Leaf Knot-Hole Gang	2	30.00
1997 Leaf Knot-Hole Gang Samples	2	20.00
1997 Leaf Leagues of the Nation	6	60.00
1997 Leaf Statistical Standouts	3	125.00
1997 Leaf Warning Track	1	50.00
1997 Leaf 22kt Gold Stars	3	70.00
1997 Metal Universe	145	3.00
1997 Metal Universe Blast Furnace	6	30.00
1997 Metal Universe Magnetic Field	4	10.00
1997 Metal Universe Mother Lode	4	120.00
1997 Metal Universe Titanium	3	18.00
1997 New Pinnacle	1	3.00
1997 New Pinnacle Interleague Encounter	3	125.00
1997 New Pinnacle Keeping the Pace	4	125.00
1997 New Pinnacle Spellbound	1-6KG	25.00
1997 Pacific Crown	186	3.00
1997 Pacific Crown Card-Supials	17	30.00
1997 Pacific Crown Cramer's Choice Awards	5	250.00
1997 Pacific Crown Fireworks Die-Cuts	11	50.00
1997 Pacific Crown Gold Crown Die-Cuts	16	40.00
1997 Pacific Crown Triple Crown Die-Cuts	9	100.00
1997 Pacific Invincible	63	15.00
1997 Pacific Invincible Gate Attractions	14	60.00
1997 Pacific Inv Gems of the Diamond	86	4.00
1997 Pacific Inv Sluggers & Hurlers	SH-6a	100.00
1997 Pacific Invincible Sizzling Lumber	6A	50.00
1997 Pinnacle	193	3.00
1997 Pinnacle Artist's Proofs	193	250.00
1997 Pinnacle Cardfrontations	14	35.00
1997 Pinnacle Certified	53	5.00
1997 Pinnacle Certified	136	2.50
1997 Pinnacle Certified Lasting Impression	2	40.00
1997 Pinnacle Certified Team	13	40.00
1997 Pinnacle Home/Away	2	30.00
1997 Pinnacle Inside	19	4.00
1997 Pinnacle Inside Cans	1	2.50
1997 Pinnacle Inside Dueling Dugouts	6	50.00
1997 Pinnacle Inside Fortysomething	12	80.00
1997 Pinnacle Mint Collection	1	7.50
1997 Pinnacle Mint Collection Coins	1	10.00
1997 Pinnacle Passport to the Majors	2	25.00
1997 Pinnacle Shades	1	25.00
1997 Pinnacle Team Pinnacle	7	50.00
1997 Pinnacle X-Press	7	2.50
1997 Pinnacle X-Press	139	1.00
1997 Pinnacle X-Press Far & Away	14	20.00
1997 Pinnacle X-Press Melting Pot	6	100.00
1997 Pinnacle X-Press Metal Works	1	25.00
1997 Pinnacle X-Press Swing for Fences	1	1.00
1997 Pinnacle/FanFest	FF11	4.00
1997 R & N China Co. Keeper Series	(1)	30.00
1997 Score	156	2.00
1997 Score	499	1.00
1997 Score	548	.75
1997 Score Blastmasters	6	25.00
1997 Score Heart of the Order	8	20.00
1997 Score Pitcher Perfect	3	15.00
1997 Score Stand & Deliver	5	50.00
1997 Score Stellar Season	6	20.00
1997 Score Team Collection	6	4.00
1997 Score The Franchise	1	30.00
1997 Score The Franchise Samples	1	25.00
1997 Score The Highlight Zone	2	20.00
1997 Score Titanic Taters	3	25.00
1997 Select	47	3.00
1997 Select	145	1.50
1997 Select	150	.75
1997 Select Samples	47	9.00
1997 Select Tools of the Trade	1	25.00
1997 SkyBox E-X2000	40	10.00
1997 SkyBox E-X2000 A Cut Above	2	120.00
1997 SkyBox E-X2000 Essential Credentials	40	600.00
1997 SkyBox E-X2000 Hall or Nothing	2	40.00
1997 Stadium Club	50	3.00
1997 Stadium Club	385	6.00
1997 Stadium Club Firebrand	F5	30.00
1997 Stadium Club Members Only Baseball	20	3.00
1997 Stadium Club Patent Leather	PL4	35.00
1997 Stadium Club Pure Gold	PG15	60.00
1997 Stadium Club TSC Matrix	50	40.00
1997 Studio	16	3.00
1997 Studio	163	1.00
1997 Studio Hard Hats	3	35.00
1997 Studio Master Strokes	3	70.00
1997 Studio Master Strokes 8x10	3	25.00
1997 Studio Portrait Collection	P1	159.00
1997 Studio Portrait Collection	M3	299.00
1997 Studio Portraits	1	5.00
1997 SP	165	4.00
1997 SP	183	4.00
1997 SP Autographed Inserts	4	2000.00
1997 SP Autographed Inserts	PP9	25.00
1997 SP Autographed Inserts	105	800.00
1997 SP Autographed Inserts	190	1100.00
1997 SP Autographed Inserts	170	400.00
1997 SP Baseball Heroes	91	40.00
1997 SP Baseball Heroes	92	40.00
1997 SP Baseball Heroes	93	40.00
1997 SP Baseball Heroes	94	40.00
1997 SP Baseball Heroes	95	40.00
1997 SP Baseball Heroes	96	40.00
1997 SP Baseball Heroes	97	40.00
1997 SP Baseball Heroes	98	40.00
1997 SP Baseball Heroes	99	40.00
1997 SP Baseball Heroes	100	40.00
1997 SP Game Film	GF10	200.00
1997 SP Inside Info	1	30.00
1997 SP Marquee Matchups	MM1	10.00
1997 SP Special FX	1	25.00
1997 SP SPx Force	1	200.00
1997 SP SPx Force Autographs	1	1000.00
1997 SPx	45	6.00
1997 SPx Bound for Glory	19	70.00
1997 SPx Cornerstones of the Game	1	150.00
1997 Topps	300	2.50
1997 Topps All-Stars	AS13	15.00
1997 Topps Chrome Jumbos	101	15.00
1997 Topps Gold	(1)	20.00
1997 Topps Hobby Masters	HM1	15.00
1997 Topps Inter-League Match Ups	ILM3	15.00
1997 Topps Porcelain	300	25.00
1997 Topps Screenplays		20.00
1997 Topps Screenplays Inserts	6	80.00
1997 Topps Season's Best	8	8.00
1997 Topps Series 2 Supers	2	15.00
1997 Topps Stars	4	4.00
1997 Topps Stars AS Game Memories	ASM5	25.00
1997 Topps Stars 1997 All-Stars	AS16	40.00
1997 Topps Sweet Strokes	SS6	10.00
1997 Topps Team Timber	TT1	15.00
1997 Topps/Chrome	101	8.00
1997 Topps/Chrome All-Stars	AS13	35.00
1997 Topps/Chrome Diamond Duos	DD3	25.00
1997 Topps/Chrome Season's Best	8	30.00
1997 Topps/Gallery	79	5.00
1997 Topps/Gallery of Heroes	GH4	40.00
1997 Topps/Gallery Peter Max	1	20.00
1997 Topps/Gallery Photo Gallery	PG4	35.00
1997 Topps/Gallery Private Issue	79	200.00
1997 Totally Certified Platinum Red	53	30.00
1997 Totally Certified Platinum Blue	53	60.00
1997 Totally Certified Platinum Gold	53	1400.00
1997 Totally Certified Platinum Red	136	15.00
1997 Totally Certified Platinum Blue	136	30.00
1997 Totally Certified Platinum Gold	136	700.00
1997 Ultra	121	3.00
1997 Ultra Baseball "Rules"!	2	25.00
1997 Ultra Checklists	3	2.00
1997 Ultra Diamond Producers	3	140.00
1997 Ultra Double Trouble	9	4.00
1997 Ultra Fielder's Choice	6	80.00
1997 Ultra Hitting Machines	2	30.00
1997 Ultra Homerun Kings	4	25.00
1997 Ultra II Checklists	2	2.00
1997 Ultra II Power Plus	1	7.00
1997 Ultra Leather Shop	1	5.00
1997 Ultra Power Plus	4	18.00

	Card No.	Value
1997 Ultra RBI Kings	7	15.00
1997 Ultra Starring Role	2	140.00
1997 Ultra The Fame Game	1	10.00
1997 Ultra Thunderclap	8	15.00
1997 Ultra Top 30	2	2.50
1997 Upper Deck	150	1.50
1997 Upper Deck	175	3.00
1997 Upper Deck	385	1.50
1997 Upper Deck	424	12.00
1997 Upper Deck Amazing Greats	AG1	80.00
1997 Upper Deck Game Jersey	GJ1	600.00
1997 Upper Deck Home Team Heroes	1	5.00
1997 Upper Deck Hot Commodities	HC5	15.00
1997 Upper Deck Long Distance Conn	LD3	35.00
1997 Upper Deck Power Package	PP1	30.00
1997 Upper Deck Power Package Jumbos	PP1	15.00
1997 Upper Deck Predictor Prize Cards	P26	30.00
1997 Upper Deck Predictor	26	5.00
1997 Upper Deck Run Producers	RP1	60.00
1997 Upper Deck UD3	3	5.00
1997 Upper Deck UD3 Marquee Attraction	MA1	100.00
1997 Upper Deck UD3 Superb Signatures	2	500.00
1997 Upper Deck/Pepsi Mariners	P2	10.00
1997 Wheaties All Stars	(1)	3.00
1997 Wheaties All Stars	(9)	2.50
1997 Wheaties All Stars	(22)	2.50
1997 Zenith	20	6.00
1997 Zenith V-2	1	100.00
1997 Zenith Z-Team	1	150.00
1997 Zenith 8x10	4	10.00
1998 Topps Etch-A-Sketch	ES3	12.00
1998 Topps Flashback	FB2	25.00
1998 Topps Hallbound	HB9	18.00
1998 Topps Inter-League Mystery Finest	ILM10	20.00
1998 Ultra	1	3.00
1998 Ultra	246	1.50
1998 Ultra Artistic Talents	1	8.00
1998 Ultra Big Shots	1	4.00
1998 Ultra Diamond Producers	1	125.00
1998 Ultra Double Trouble	1	4.00
1998 Ultra Fall Classics	1	15.00
1998 Ultra Power Plus	1	25.00
1998 Ultra Prime Leather	1	75.00
1998 Upper Deck	10	1.50
1998 Upper Deck	140	1.50
1998 Upper Deck	225	3.00
1998 Upper Deck	245	1.50
1998 Upper Deck Amazing Greats	AG1	60.00
1998 UD Griffey's HR Chronicles	KG1-30	60.00
1998 Upper Deck National Pride	NP39	60.00
1998 Upper Deck 10th Anniversary	48	12.00
1989 Topps Major League Debut	133	1.00
1990 Baseball Cards Magazine Repli-cards	35	1.50
1990 Best Greensboro Hornets	15	3.00

Larry Walker: National League MVP

	Card No.	Value
1990 Bowman	117	1.50
1990 Classic Series II	16	.75
1990 Donruss	578	1.50
1990 Donruss Best N.L.	91	.15
1990 Fleer	363	1.25
1990 Fleer Canadian	363	4.00
1990 Fleer Soaring Stars	3	3.00
1990 Leaf	325	15.00
1990 O-Pee-Chee	757	.40
1990 ProCards Greensboro Hornets	2667	2.00
1990 Score	631	1.00
1990 Score Young Superstars Set II	9	.50
1990 Star Co. Greensboro Hornets	25	1.00
1990 Topps	757	1.00
1990 Topps Big Baseball	296	.15
1990-93 Topps Magazine	95	.50
1990 Upper Deck	466	1.50
1990 Upper Deck	702	.40
1991 Bazooka	19	.50

	Card No.	Value
1991 Bowman	442	.25
1991 Donruss	359	.25
1991 Fleer	250	.25
1991 Leaf	241	.30
1991 O-Pee-Chee	339	.20
1991 Panini Stickers	65	.20
1991 Panini Stickers - Canadian	145	.20
1991 Score	241	.20
1991 Score Rising Stars	21	.20
1991 Stadium Club	93	.75
1991 Stadium Club Promos	(48)	40.00
1991 Topps	339	.20
1991 Topps Glossy Rookies	32	.45
1991 Toys "R" Us Rookies	31	.30
1991 Ultra Update	93	4.00
1991 Upper Deck	536	.20
1992 Bowman	648	2.00
1992-93 Canadian Card News Repli-cards	5	.50
1992-93 Canadian Card News Repli-cards	22	.75
1992 Classic Series II	39	.15
1992 Donruss	259	.20
1992 Donruss Durivage Montreal Expos	18	6.00
1992 Fleer	493	.20
1992 High 5 Decals	(120)	.50
1992 Leaf	201	.25
1992 Leaf Gold Edition	201	.75
1992 O-Pee-Chee	531	.20
1992 Panini Stickers	206	.12
1992 Pinnacle	194	.25
1992 Pinnacle Team 2000	21	.40
1992 Score	199	.15
1992 Score Impact Players	29	.25
1992 Stadium Club	256	.40
1992 Studio	59	.20
1992 Topps	531	.15
1992 Triple Play	89	.15
1992 U.S. Playing Card All-Stars	3H	.10
1992 Ultra	525	.35
1992 Upper Deck	249	.15
1993 Bowman	100	.75
1993 Classic	97	.15
1993 DiamondMarks	(40)	.40
1993 Donruss	540	.25
1993 Donruss Diamond Kings	6	1.50
1993 Donruss Elite	30	25.00
1993 Donruss Elite Supers	12	20.00
1993 Donruss Long Ball Leaders	18	2.50
1993 Donruss MVP's	9	1.00
1993 Donruss Previews	6	5.00
1993 Finest	97	4.00
1993 Finest Jumbo All-Stars	97	10.00
1993 Finest Refractors	97	350.00
1993 Flair	87	.75
1993 Fleer	81	.20
1993 Fleer	715	.10
1993 Fleer All-Stars	6	1.00
1993 Fleer Fruit of the Loom	64	1.50
1993 Hostess Twinkies	30	.15
1993 Humpty Dumpty	42	.90
1993 Kenner Starting Lineups	(44)	25.00
1993 Leaf	392	.20
1993 McDonald's Expos	7	3.00
1993 Milk Bone Super Stars	(15)	1.25
1993 O-Pee-Chee	384	.25
1993 O-Pee-Chee/Premier	39	.15
1993 Pacific	190	.15
1993 Panini Stickers	231	.20
1993 Pinnacle	3	.25
1993 Pinnacle	299	.15
1993 Pinnacle Home Run Club	14	.50
1993 Pinnacle Promos	3	15.00
1993 Pinnacle Slugfest	13	1.00
1993 Pinnacle Team Pinnacle	10	8.00
1993 Post Cereal - Canadian	13	.65
1993 Score	5	.15
1993 Score The Franchise	20	2.00
1993 Select	27	.30
1993 Sports Card Pocket Price Guide	34	.50
1993 Stadium Club	299	.20
1993 Stadium Club	320	.30
1993 Stadium Club First Day Production	299	10.00
1993 Stadium Club First Day Production	320	10.00
1993 Stadium Club Special Master Photos	(11)	.75
1993 Stadium Club Special (Murphy)	94	.30
1993 Studio	123	.20
1993 SP	107	.75
1993 Topps	95	.15
1993 Topps	406	.20
1993 Topps Black Gold	22	.40
1993 Topps Gold	95	.25
1993 Topps Gold	406	.35
1993 Topps Promo Sheet	(9)	1.00

	Card No.	Value
1993 Toys "R" Us Topps Stadium Club	23	.15
1993 Triple Play	42	.12
1993 Triple Play Action Baseball	6	.12
1993 Ultra	71	.35
1993 Ultra All-Stars	8	1.00
1993 Ultra Award Winners	9	1.50
1993 Upper Deck	144	.20
1993 Upper Deck	481	.15
1993 Upper Deck Fun Packs	98	.20
1993 Upper Deck Home Run Heroes	16	.75
1993 Upper Deck Triple Crown	10	1.50
1994 Bowman	500	.50
1994 Bowman Superstar Sampler	500	3.00
1994 Bowman's Best	76	1.50
1994 Bowman's Best Refractors	76	15.00
1994 Collector's Choice	286	.20
1994 Denny's Grand Slam	28	.50
1994 Donruss	371	.25
1994 Donruss Special Edition - Gold	91	.50
1994 Finest	216	1.00
1994 Finest Refractors	216	10.00
1994 Finest Superstar Jumbos	216	3.00
1994 Finest Superstar Sampler	216	5.00
1994 Flair	404	.60
1994 Fleer	554	.30
1994 Fleer/Extra Bases	312	.25
1994 Leaf	397	.20
1994 Leaf Clean-Up Crew	1	3.00
1994 Leaf/Limited	127	.75
1994 O-Pee-Chee	253	.25
1994 O-Pee-Chee All-Star Redemption	19	1.50
1994 O-Pee-Chee Jumbo All-Stars	19	4.00
1994 O-Pee-Chee Jumbo All-Stars Factory	19	4.00
1994 Pacific Crown	392	.20
1994 Panini Stickers	213	.15
1994 Pinnacle	310	.25
1994 Post Cereal - Canadian	8	.50
1994 Score	376	.15
1994 Score Dream Team	9	6.00
1994 Score Gold Stars	27	2.50
1994 Select	18	.25
1994 Select Skills	9	4.00
1994 Sportflics 2000	77	.25
1994 Stadium Club	280	.25
1994 Stadium Club First Day Production	280	10.00
1994 Stadium Club Superstar Sampler	280	3.00
1994 Studio	80	.25
1994 SP	86	.40
1994 Topps	230	.15
1994 Topps Bilingual	230	.20
1994 Topps Gold	230	.25
1994 Triple Play	99	.20
1994 Ultra	526	.25
1994 Ultra Award Winners	17	.60
1994 Upper Deck	274	.20
1994 Upper Deck	370	.20
1994 Upper Deck/All-Stars	28	.40
1994 Upper Deck/All-Stars Gold	28	2.50
1994 Upper Deck/Fun Packs	136	.20
1995 Bazooka	93	.25
1995 Bowman	290	.60
1995 Bowman's Best	63	1.00
1995 Bowman's Best Refractors	63	15.00
1995 Certified	89	.50
1995 Certified Samples	89	9.00
1995 Classic Phone Cards	(60)	3.00
1995 Collector's Choice	238	.20
1995 Collector's Choice Gold Signature	238	4.00
1995 Collector's Choice Redemption Cards	579	.60
1995 Collector's Choice Silver Signature	238	.40
1995 Collector's Choice Trade Cards	TC1	.75
1995 Collector's Choice/SE	96	.25
1995 Collector's Choice/SE Gold	96	6.00
1995 Collector's Choice/SE Silver	96	.25
1995 Donruss	492	.20
1995 Donruss Press Proofs	492	5.00
1995 Finest	215	.60
1995 Finest Refractors	215	12.00
1995 Finest Update	274	.75
1995 Finest Update Refractors	274	40.00
1995 Flair	348	.40
1995 Fleer	361	.25
1995 Fleer Update	U171	.40
1995 Fleer-Panini Stickers	75	.15
1995 Fleer/ Ultra Gold Medallion	409	.60
1995 Leaf	305	.30
1995 Leaf/Limited	91	.75
1995 Leaf/Limited Bat Patrol	4	.50
1995 Leaf/Limited Gold	10	.75
1995 Leaf/Opening Day	8	.50
1995 Pacific	273	.20
1995 Pacific Marquee Prism	30	2.00

	Card No.	Value
1995 Pacific Prism	89	.75
1995 Pinnacle	372	.25
1995 Pinnacle/FanFest	28	.50
1995 Police/Fire Safety Rockies	33	2.00
1995 Score	346a	.15
1995 Score	346b	.50
1995 Score Hall of Gold	71a	.50
1995 Score Hall of Gold	71b	.75
1995 Score Platinum Redemption Team	346	7.50
1995 Select	224	.25
1995 SkyBox E-Motion	126	.40
1995 Sportflix	139	.25
1995 Sportflix/UC3	90	.30
1995 Sportflix/UC3	145	.20
1995 Stadium Club	148	.20
1995 Stadium Club	618	.25
1995 Stadium Club Crunch Time	10	1.50
1995 Stadium Club Members Only Baseball	44	.35
1995 Stadium Club Super Skills	15	2.50
1995 Stadium Club Virtual Reality	77	.60
1995 Studio	58	.25
1995 Summit	45	.30
1995 SP	50	.40
1995 SP Championship Die Cuts	39	.50
1995 SP Championship Die Cuts	42	.50
1995 SP Platinum Power	PP7	.75
1995 SP SuperbaFoil	50	1.25
1995 SP/Championship	39	.25
1995 SP/Championship	42	.35
1995 Test Set	93	.30
1995 Topps	422	.20
1995 Topps Cyberstats	221	.40
1995 Topps Pre-production	1	1.00
1995 Topps Pre-production	1	4.00
1995 Topps Traded and Rookies	20	.20
1995 Upper Deck	82	.20
1995 Upper Deck	415	.25
1995 Upper Deck Retail Predictors	R34	1.00
1995 Upper Deck Retail Predictors	R47	1.00
1995 Upper Deck Special Edition	4	.40
1995 Upper Deck Special Edition	240	.75
1995 Zenith	67	.75
1995 Zenith Z-Team	11	8.00
1995 1995 Topps/Stadium Club 1st Day	148	.45
1996 Bazooka	26	.25
1996 Bowman	17	.60
1996 Bowman's Best	83	.75
1996 Bowman's Best Mirror Image	5	10.00
1996 Bowman's Best Preview	21	3.00
1996 Bowman's Best Preview Refractors	21	12.00
1996 Certified	85	.60
1996 Certified Artist's Proofs	85	8.00
1996 Certified Mirror Blue	85	175.00
1996 Certified Mirror Gold, Blue, Red	85	650.00
1996 Certified Mirror Red	85	85.00
1996 Certified Red, Blue	85	6.00
1996 Circa	124	.40
1996 Circa Rave	124	80.00
1996 Collector's Choice	326	.20
1996 Collector's Choice	540	.15
1996 Collector's Choice	753	.10
1996 Collector's Choice Crash the Game	16a	.65
1996 Collector's Choice Crash the Game	16b	.65
1996 Collector's Choice Crash the Game	16c	.65
1996 Collector's Choice Gold Signature	326	4.00
1996 Collector's Choice Gold Signature	540	5.00
1996 Collector's Choice Gold Signature	753	2.50
1996 Collector's Choice Silver Signature	326	.50
1996 Collector's Choice Silver Signature	540	.50
1996 Collector's Choice Silver Signature	753	.25
1996 Donruss	342	.30
1996 Donruss Diamond Kings	11	10.00
1996 Donruss Long Ball Leaders	7	12.00
1996 E-Motion XL	179	.40
1996 Finest	13	4.00
1996 Finest	302	4.00
1996 Finest Refractors	13	25.00
1996 Finest Refractors	302	30.00
1996 Flair	253	.75
1996 Fleer	377	.30
1996 Fleer Baseball '96	16	.30
1996 Fleer-Panini Stickers	86	.40
1996 Kenner Starting Lineups	(50)	14.00
1996 Leaf	63	.30
1996 Leaf/Limited	86	.75
1996 Leaf/Preferred	80	.40
1996 Leaf/Preferred Leaf Steel	37	1.50
1996 Leaf/Preferred Leaf Gold Promos	37	10.00
1996 Leaf/Signature Series	77	.30
1996 Metal Universe	159	.40
1996 Pacific Crown Collection	65	.25
1996 Pacific Prism	140	1.50

	Card No.	Value
1996 Pinnacle	150	.15
1996 Pinnacle	219	.30
1996 Pinnacle Pinnacle Power	19	4.00
1996 Pinnacle Starburst	77	1.00
1996 Pinnacle Starburst	119	1.50
1996 Pinnacle/Aficionado First Pitch Previews	68	4.00
1996 Pinnacle/Aficionado	68	.50
1996 Pinnacle/Aficionado First Pitch Previews	152	3.00
1996 Pinnacle/Aficionado	152	.30
1996 Pinnacle/Summit Above & Beyond	61	3.00
1996 Police/Fire Safety Rockies	33	.60
1996 Score	13	.25
1996 Score	374	.15
1996 Score All-Stars	17	3.00
1996 Score Big Bats	15	3.00
1996 Score Diamond Aces	12	3.00
1996 Score Dugout Collection	99	.40
1996 Score Gold Stars	27	1.00
1996 Score Numbers Game	20	1.00
1996 Score Power Pace	8	3.00
1996 Score Reflexions	9	3.00
1996 Score Titantic Taters	13	3.00
1996 Select	98	.25
1996 Select Team Nucleus	4	4.00
1996 Sportflix	72	.20
1996 Sportflix	114	.15
1996 Sportflix Power Surge	18	1.50
1996 Stadium Club	319	.30
1996 Stadium Club Extreme Player - Bronze	319	1.50
1996 Stadium Club Extreme Player - Gold	319	4.00
1996 Stadium Club Extreme Player - Silver	319	3.00
1996 Stadium Club Members Only	45	.25
1996 Stadium Club Power Streak	PS11	4.00
1996 Studio	78	.30
1996 Summit	61	.35
1996 SP	80	.40
1996 SPx	23	1.50
1996 Team Out! Game	(86)	.40
1996 Topps	5	.20
1996 Topps	363	.25
1996 Topps Power Boosters	5	3.00
1996 Topps Profiles-NL	10	1.00
1996 Topps/Chrome	5	.75
1996 Topps/Chrome	147	.75
1996 Topps/Gallery	179	.50
1996 Topps/Gallery Photo Gallery	PG14	3.00
1996 Topps/Laser	112	1.00
1996 Topps/Laser Power Cuts	16	12.00
1996 Ultra	194	.35
1996 Ultra Home Run Kings	11	6.00
1996 Ultra Home Run Kings Exchange	11	1.00
1996 Ultra Power Plus	11	1.50
1996 Upper Deck	60	.35
1996 Upper Deck	421	.20
1996 Upper Deck Power Driven	PD19	5.00
1996 Upper Deck Retail Predictor	R38	1.00
1996 Zenith	57	.50
1996 Zenith Mozaics	12	3.00
1997 Bowman	275	4.00
1997 Bowman Chrome	92	.75
1997 Bowman International Best	BBI7	2.00
1997 Bowman's Best	67	.75
1997 Circa	377	.35
1997 Circa Rave	377	60.00
1997 Collector's Choice	U8	.20
1997 Collector's Choice Big Shots	6	1.00
1997 Collector's Choice Team Sets	CR4	.30
1997 Donruss	48	.30
1997 Donruss	410	.15
1997 Donruss Armed and Dangerous	7	5.00
1997 Donruss Limited	87	7.50
1997 Donruss Limited	126	20.00
1997 Donruss Limited	133	.75
1997 Donruss Limited	169	20.00
1997 Donruss Limited Exposure	87	12.00
1997 Donruss Limited Exposure	126	25.00
1997 Donruss Limited Exposure	133	5.00
1997 Donruss Limited Exposure	169	50.00
1997 Donruss Limited Fabric of the Game		30.00
1997 Donruss Preferred	10	2.50
1997 Donruss Team Sets	92	.30
1997 Donruss Team Sets MVP	16	4.00
1997 Finest	106	5.00
1997 Finest	335	15.00
1997 Finest Refractors	106	30.00
1997 Finest Refractors	335	60.00
1997 Flair Showcase	76	1.00
1997 Flair Showcase Legacy Collection	76	100.00
1997 Fleer	319	.30
1997 Fleer Sports Illustrated	111	.30
1997 Leaf	238	.25
1997 Leaf	385	.10
1997 Leaf Fractal Matrix	238	15.00
1997 Leaf Fractal Matrix Die-Cut	238	40.00
1997 Leaf Fractal Matrix	385	4.00
1997 Leaf Fractal Matrix Die-Cut	385	20.00
1997 Leaf Leagues of the Nation	6	60.00
1997 Metal Universe	76	.40
1997 New Pinnacle	9	.35
1997 Pacific Crown	291	.25
1997 Pinnacle Certified	24	.50
1997 Pinnacle Inside	114	.40
1997 Pinnacle Passport to the Majors	24	3.00
1997 Pinnacle X-Press	1	.20
1997 Pinnacle X-Press	138	.15
1997 Pinnacle X-Press Melting Pot	4	15.00
1997 Pinnacle X-Press Swing for Fences	31	.10
1997 Police/Fire Safety Rockies	33	1.50
1997 Score	170	.25
1997 Score Team Collection	8	.50
1997 Select	97	.40
1997 Stadium Club	251	.35
1997 Stadium Club TSC Matrix	251	2.00
1997 Studio	105	.35
1997 SP	67	.50
1997 SPx	25	1.00
1997 Topps	461	.30
1997 Topps Screenplays Inserts	1	25.00
1997 Topps Stars	1	.40
1997 Topps Stars AS Game Memories	ASM9	6.00
1997 Topps Stars 1997 All-Stars	AS13	6.00
1997 Topps/Chrome	162	.50
1997 Topps/Gallery	72	.40
1997 Topps/Gallery Private Issue	72	20.00
1997 Totally Certified Platinum Red	24	5.00
1997 Totally Certified Platinum Blue	24	10.00
1997 Totally Certified Platinum Gold	24	200.00
1997 Ultra	320	.35
1997 Upper Deck	182	.35
1997 Upper Deck	353	.25
1997 Zenith	11	1.00
1997 Zenith Z-Team	2	25.00
1998 Fleer	33	—
1998 Topps	2	.25
1998 Topps Inter-League Mystery Finest	ILM9	4.00
1998 Ultra	90	.30
1998 Upper Deck	11	.20
1998 Upper Deck Amazing Greats	AG6	8.00
1998 Upper Deck National Pride	NP2	5.00
1998 Upper Deck 10th Anniversary	52	1.50
1986-87 Fleer	68	60.00
1987-88 Fleer	68	15.00
1988-89 Fleer	114	4.00

Karl Malone: NBA MVP

	Card No.	Value
1988-89 Fleer Stickers	8	1.50
1988 Fournier NBA Estrellas	16	2.00
1988-89 Jazz Smokey	(4)	25.00
1988 Kenner Starting Lineups Bk	(45)	750.00
1988-89 Panini European Stickers	179	7.50
1988-89 Panini European Stickers	276	5.00
1989 Converse	(10)	3.00
1989-90 Fleer	155	1.00
1989-90 Fleer	163	.50
1989-90 Fleer	165	.20
1989-90 Fleer Stickers	1	.50
1989-90 Hoops	30	.25
1989-90 Hoops	116	.15
1989 Jazz Old Home	10	25.00
1989 Magnetables	(19)	2.50
1989-90 Panini European Stickers	176	10.00
1989-90 Panini European Stickers	257	6.00
1989 Panini Spanish Stickers	179	10.00
1989 Panini Spanish Stickers	276	5.00
1990-91 Fleer	188	.25
1990-91 Fleer All-Stars	7	.75
1990-91 Hoops	21	.25
1990-91 Hoops	292	.25
1990-91 Hoops	380	.10
1990-91 Hoops	383	.05
1990 Hoops Action Photos	(11)	1.00
1990-91 Hoops All-Star Panels	(2)	8.00
1990-91 Hoops CollectABooks	5	.75
1990 Hoops Superstars	94	.75
1990-91 Hoops Team Night Sheets	25	4.00
1990-91 Jazz Star	1	2.50
1990 Kenner Starting Lineups Bk	(9)	60.00
1990-91 Panini Stickers	49	.03
1990-91 SkyBox	282	.30
1990 SkyBox Promo Cards	282	60.00
1990 Star Gold	7	35.00
1990 Star Karl Malone	1	1.00
1990 Star Karl Malone	2	1.00
1990 Star Karl Malone	3	1.00
1990 Star Karl Malone	4	1.00
1990 Star Karl Malone	5	1.00
1990 Star Karl Malone	6	1.00
1990 Star Karl Malone	7	1.00
1990 Star Karl Malone	8	1.00
1990 Star Karl Malone	9	1.00
1990 Star Karl Malone	10	1.00
1990 Star Karl Malone	11	1.00
1990 Star Nova	4	75.00
1990 Star Platinum	7	35.00
1990 Star Promos	(10)	7.50
1990 Star Silver	7	25.00
1990 Star Slam	5	35.00
1991-92 Fleer	201	.15
1991-92 Fleer	219	.10
1991-92 Fleer Pro Visions	5	.50
1991-92 Fleer Schoolyard	5	3.00
1991-92 Fleer Tony's Pizza	2	7.00
1991-92 Fleer Wheaties Sheets	2	6.00
1991-92 Hoops	211	.25
1991-92 Hoops	267	.10
1991-92 Hoops	306	1.00
1991-92 Hoops	499	.10
1991-92 Hoops	580	.50
1991 Hoops McDonald's	44	.75
1991 Hoops McDonald's	56	.50
1991-92 Hoops MVP All-Stars	10	2.00
1991 Hoops Prototypes 00	005	30.00
1991 Hoops Prototypes 00	009	20.00
1991 Hoops Superstars	96	.75
1991-92 Hoops Team Night Sheets	(26)	4.00
1991-92 Kellogg's College Greats	6	.50
1991-92 Panini Stickers	85	.75
1991-92 Panini Stickers	91	.40
1991-92 Panini Stickers	191	.40
1991-92 Pro Set Prototypes	5	125.00
1991-92 SkyBox	283	.40
1991-92 SkyBox	430	.10
1991-92 SkyBox	484	.20
1991-92 SkyBox	535	.75
1991 SkyBox Mini	46	1.50
1991-92 Upper Deck	31	.25
1991-92 Upper Deck	51	.10
1991-92 Upper Deck	355	.25
1991-92 Upper Deck	466	.25
1991-93 5 Majeur	(37)	5.00
1992-93 Fleer	225	.25
1992-93 Fleer	268	.10
1992-93 Fleer All Utaro	17	0.00
1992-93 Fleer Drake's	52	2.00
1992-93 Fleer Team Leaders	26	14.00
1992-93 Fleer Tony's Pizza	S2	3.00
1992-93 Hoops	227	.25
1992-93 Hoops	311	.10
1992-93 Hoops	320	.75
1992-93 Hoops	343	.10
1992-93 Hoops Supreme Court	6SC	2.00
1992 Hoops 100 Superstars	95	3.00
1992-93 Jazz Chevron	5	5.00
1992 Kellogg's Team USA Posters	(2)	4.00
1992 Kenner Olympic Bk	(6)	10.00
1992 Kenner Starting Lineups Bk	(18)	20.00
1992-93 Panini Stickers	100	.25
1992-93 Panini Stickers	104	.40
1992-93 SkyBox	242	.50
1992-93 SkyBox Golden USA Basketball	535	.75
1992-93 SkyBox Olympic Team	4	2.00
1992-93 SkyBox Thunder and Lightning	8	10.00
1992 SkyBox USA Basketball	46	.15
1992 SkyBox USA Basketball	47	.15
1992 SkyBox USA Basketball	48	.15
1992 SkyBox USA Basketball	49	.15
1992 SkyBox USA Basketball	50	.15
1992 SkyBox USA Basketball	51	.15
1992 SkyBox USA Basketball	52	.15
1992 SkyBox USA Basketball	53	.15
1992 SkyBox USA Basketball	54	.15
1992 SkyBox/Nestle	(22)	4.00
1992-93 Stadium Club	13	.50
1992-93 Stadium Club	205	.30
1992-93 Stadium Club Beam Team	17	7.00
1992-93 Stadium Club Members Only	13	3.00
1992-93 Stadium Club Members Only	205	1.50
1992-93 Stadium Club Members Only	BT17	5.00
1992-93 Topps	20	.20
1992-93 Topps	123	.10
1992-93 Topps	199	.10
1992-93 Topps Archives	66	.30
1992-93 Topps Beam Team	4	.75
1992-93 Ultra	182	.50
1992-93 Ultra	217	.20
1992-93 Ultra All-NBA Team	1	3.00
1992-93 Upper Deck	44	.10
1992-93 Upper Deck	66	.25
1992-93 Upper Deck	112	.25
1992-93 Upper Deck	434	.10
1992-93 Upper Deck	489	.15
1992-93 Upper Deck	508	.15
1992-93 Upper Deck All-Division Team	AD12	1.00
1992-93 Upper Deck All-NBA	AN4	3.00
1992-93 Upper Deck All-Star Weekend	16	.75
1992-93 Upper Deck All-Star Weekend	39	.50
1992-93 Upper Deck European	18	1.00
1992 Upper Deck European	18	.50
1992-93 Upper Deck European	98	1.00
1992 Upper Deck European	98	1.00
1992-93 Upper Deck Italian Basketball	14	.40
1992-93 Upper Deck Italian Basketball	46	3.00
1992-93 Upper Deck Italian Basketball	248	1.00
1992-93 Upper Deck McDonald's	P40	.40
1992-93 Upper Deck MVP Holograms	20	1.25
1992-93 Upper Deck Sheets	(1)	8.00
1992-93 Upper Deck 15000-Point Club	PC16	6.00
1993-94 Finest	112	1.00
1993-94 Finest	215	2.00
1993-94 Finest Main Attraction	26	4.00
1993-94 Finest Refractors	112	8.00
1993-94 Finest Refractors	215	25.00
1993-94 Fleer	211	.25
1993-94 Fleer All-Stars	19	3.00
1993-94 Fleer NBA Superstars	10	.75
1993-94 Fleer Towers of Power	13	3.00
1993-94 Hoops	218	.25
1993-94 Hoops	275	.15
1993-94 Hoops	283	.50
1993-94 Hoops Face to Face	7	2.00
1993-94 Hoops Prototypes	(3)	2.00
1993-94 Hoops Scoops	HS26	.15
1993-94 Hoops Supreme Court	SC6	.50
1993-94 Jam Session	227	.40
1993-94 Jam Session Slam Dunk Heroes	4	.75
1993-94 Jazz Old Home	7	8.00
1993 Kenner Starting Lineups Bk	(17)	20.00
1993-94 Panini Stickers	119	.50
1993-94 SkyBox	178	.30
1993-94 SkyBox	319	.10
1993-94 SkyBox Showdown Series	SS7	.50
1993-94 SkyBox USA Tip-Off	4	4.00
1993-94 Stadium Club	125	.40
1993-94 Stadium Club	174	.25
1993-94 Stadium Club	186	.20
1993-94 Stadium Club Beam Team	9	2.00
1993-94 Stadium Club First Day Cards	125	20.00
1993-94 Stadium Club First Day Cards	174	10.00
1993-94 Stadium Club First Day Cards	186	6.00
1993-94 Stad Club Frequent Flyer Upg	186	4.00
1993-94 Stadium Club Members Only	125	3.00
1993-94 Stadium Club Members Only	174	1.50
1993-94 Stadium Club Members Only	186	1.50
1993-94 Stadium Club Members Only	BT9	3.00
1993-94 Topps	119	.15
1993-94 Topps	279	.20
1993-94 Topps	389	.10
1993-94 Ultra	189	.30
1993-94 Ultra All-NBA Team	3	2.50
1993-94 Ultra Famous Nicknames	9	1.50
1993-94 Ultra Karl Malone	1	2.00
1993-94 Ultra Karl Malone	2	2.00
1993-94 Ultra Karl Malone	3	2.00
1993-94 Ultra Karl Malone	4	2.00
1993-94 Ultra Karl Malone	5	2.00
1993-94 Ultra Karl Malone	6	2.00
1993-94 Ultra Karl Malone	7	2.00
1993-94 Ultra Karl Malone	8	2.00
1993-94 Ultra Karl Malone	9	2.00
1993-94 Ultra Karl Malone	10	2.00
1993-94 Ultra Power in the Key	3	3.00

Set	Card No.	Value
1993-94 Ultra Rebound Kings	4	.75
1993-94 Ultra Scoring Kings	6	10.00
1993-94 Upper Deck	249	.10
1993-94 Upper Deck	274	.30
1993-94 Upper Deck	422	.10
1993-94 Upper Deck All-NBA	AN2	1.00
1993 Upper Deck European	14	.50
1993 Upper Deck European	46	.50
1993 Upper Deck European	88	.50
1993 Upper Deck European	248	1.00
1993 Upper Deck French McDonald's	18	2.50
1993-94 Upper Deck Holojams	H26	1.50
1993-94 Upper Deck Jordan's Flight Team	FT13	6.00
1993-94 Upper Deck Locker Talk	LT11	5.00
1993-94 Upper Deck McDonald's French	18	2.00
1993-94 Upper Deck Pro View	1	.25
1993-94 Upper Deck Pro View	94	.15
1993-94 Upper Deck SE	152	.30
1993-94 Upper Deck SE Electric Gold	152	15.00
1993-94 Upper Deck SE USA Trade	USA7	2.00
1993-94 Upper Deck SE West All Stars	15	5.00
1993-94 Upper Deck WalMart Jumbos	FT13	3.00
1994-95 UD CC	32	.20
1994-95 UD CC	191	.15
1994-95 UD CC	397	.10
1994-95 UD CC Gold Signature	32	12.00
1994-95 UD CC Gold Signature	191	6.00
1994-95 UD CC Gold Signature	397	4.00
1994-95 UD CC 1,000 Rebounds	R5	1.00
1994-95 UD CC 2,000 Points	S5	2.00
1994-95 E-Motion	95	1.00
1994-95 E-Motion	113	.75
1994-95 E-Motion N-Tense	N5	5.00
1994-95 Embossed	96	.75
1994-95 Finest	195	2.00
1994-95 Finest Cornerstone	4	7.00
1994-95 Finest Iron Men	5	4.00
1994-95 Finest Marathon Men	14	6.00
1994-95 Finest Refractors	195	40.00
1994-95 Flair	148	1.00
1994-95 Flair Scoring Power	3	3.00
1994-95 Fleer	224	.20
1994-95 Fleer Career Achievement Awards	2	4.00
1994-95 Fleer NBA All-Stars	18	1.25
1994-95 Fleer Towers of Power	4	2.00
1994-95 Fleer Triple Threats	4	.50
1994-95 Hoops	211	.25
1994-95 Hoops	242	.10
1994-95 Hoops Power Ratings	PR52	.50
1994-95 Hoops Sheets	(15)	3.00
1994-95 Hoops Supreme Court	48	.75
1994-95 Jam Session	187	.50
1994-95 Jam Session GameBreakers	3	1.00
1994 Kenner Starting Lineups Bk	(14)	15.00
1994-95 Panini Stickers	217	1.00
1994-95 SkyBox	165	.30
1994-95 SkyBox	182	.20
1994-95 SkyBox	308	.20
1994-95 SkyBox SkyTech Force	SF13	.75
1994-95 Stadium Club	161	.50
1994-95 Stadium Club	162	.25
1994-95 Stadium Club	361	.25
1994-95 Stadium Club Beam Team	26	5.00
1994-95 Stadium Club Clear Cut	26	5.00
1994-95 Stadium Club Dynasty and Destiny	2A	.50
1994-95 Stadium Club First Day Cards	161	15.00
1994-95 Stadium Club First Day Cards	162	7.00
1994-95 Stadium Club First Day Cards	361	8.00
1994-95 Stadium Club Members Only	161	1.50
1994-95 Stadium Club Members Only	162	.75
1994-95 Stadium Club Members Only	361	.75
1994-95 Stadium Club Members Only	BT26	1.50
1994-95 Stadium Club Members Only	CC26	1.50
1994-95 Stadium Club Members Only	DD2A	.75
1994-95 Stadium Club Members Only	SS18	1.50
1994-95 Stadium Club Super Skills	18	3.00
1994-95 SP	156	.40
1994-95 SP Championship	26	.20
1994-95 SP Championship	130	.40
1994-95 Topps	185	.10
1994-95 Topps	279	.20
1994-95 Topps	280	.10
1994-95 Topps Super Rebounders	7	.50
1994-95 Topps Super Scorers	5	.50
1994-95 Ultra	186	.50
1994-95 Ultra All-NBA Team	1	1.00
1994-95 Ultra Power	5	1.00
1994-95 Ultra Power in the Key	5	2.00
1994-95 Ultra Scoring Kings	3	8.00
1994-95 Upper Deck	12	.20
1994-95 Upper Deck	241	.40
1994 Upper Deck European	93	1.00
1994 Upper Deck European	178	2.00
1994-95 Upper Deck Predictors Retail	R6	2.00
1994-95 Upper Deck Predictors Retail	R25	3.00
1994-95 Upper Deck Special Edition	86	1.00
1995-96 UD CC	192	.10
1995-96 UD CC	235	.20
1995-96 UD CC	347	.10
1995-96 UD CC	402	.10
1995-96 UD CC Crash The Game	C8A	.60
1995-96 UD CC Crash The Game	C8B	.60
1995-96 UD CC Crash The Game	C8C	4.00
1995 UD CC Int. European Gold Signature	191	8.00
1995 UD CC Int. Japanese Gold Signature I	191	25.00
1995 UD CC Int. Japanese Silver Signature	191	2.00
1995 UD CC Int. Japanese II	178	.75
1995 UD CC Int. Japanese Gold Signature II	178	8.00
1995 UD CC Int. Japanese I	32	1.50
1995 UD CC Int. Japanese I	32	1.50
1995 UD CC Int. Spanish I	32	1.00
1995 UD CC Int. European Gold Signature	397	8.00
1995 UD CC Int. Spanish II	178	.50
1995 UD CC Int. European	191	.75
1995 UD CC Int. Japanese I	191	.75
1995 UD CC Int. Spanish I	191	.50
1995 UD CC Int. European	397	.75
1995-96 E-XL	83	.75
1995-96 E-XL Unstoppable	18	2.00
1995-96 Finest	209	1.00
1995-96 Finest Dish and Swish	DS27	30.00
1995-96 Finest Hot Stuff	HS9	2.00
1995-96 Finest Mystery	M12	1.50
1995-96 Finest Mystery Brdrls Refr/Gold	M12	30.00
1995-96 Finest Refractors	209	20.00
1995-96 Finest Veteran/Rookie	RV28	12.00
1995-96 Flair	138	1.00
1995-96 Flair	237	.50
1995-96 Flair Hardwood Leaders	26	.50
1995-96 Flair Hot Numbers	7	8.00
1995-96 Flair New Heights	6	5.00
1995-96 Fleer	188	.20
1995-96 Fleer	346	.10
1995-96 Fleer Double Doubles	7	.50
1995 Fleer European	226	1.00
1995 Fleer European Career Achievement	1	2.50
1995 Fleer European Triple Threats	4	1.50
1995-96 Fleer NBA All-Stars	7	.25
1995-96 Fleer Towers of Power	2	7.00
1995-96 Hoop Magazine/Mother's Cookies	27	4.00
1995-96 Hoops	160	.20
1995-96 Hoops	212	.10
1995-96 Hoops	240	.10
1995-96 Hoops	387	.10
1995-96 Hoops HoopStars	HS10	2.00
1995-96 Hoops Number Crunchers	17	.40
1995-96 Hoops Slamland	SL46	.25
1995-96 Jam Session	109	.30
1995-96 Jam Session Show Stoppers	S4	10.00
1995 Kenner Starting Lineups Bk	(13)	15.00
1995-96 Metal	110	.50
1995-96 Metal	214	.10
1995-96 Metal Maximum Metal	6	3.00
1995-96 Metal Metal Force	8	8.00
1995-96 Panini Stickers	138	.50
1995-96 Panini Stickers	193	1.00
1995-96 Panini Stickers	274	.50
1995-96 SkyBox	118	.25
1995-96 SkyBox	275	.15
1995-96 SkyBox Close-Ups	C8	2.00
1995-96 SkyBox USA Basketball	U3	1.50
1995-96 Stadium Club	127	.20
1995-96 Stadium Club	187	.30
1995-96 Stadium Club	354	.40
1995-96 Stadium Club Beam Team	8	3.00
1995 Stadium Club Members Only 50	25	.75
1995-96 Stadium Club Members Only I	127B	1.50
1995-96 Stadium Club Members Only I	127R	1.50
1995-96 Stadium Club Members Only I	BT8	1.50
1995-96 Stadium Club Members Only I	PZ4	3.00
1995-96 Stadium Club Nemeses	N5	8.00
1995-96 Stadium Club Power Zone	PZ4	5.00
1995-96 Stadium Club X-2	6	4.00
1995-96 SP	135	.60
1995-96 SP All-Stars	AS19	2.00
1995-96 SP Championship	107	.30
1995-96 Topps	9	.10
1995-96 Topps	32	.20
1995-96 Topps Gallery	14	.40
1995-96 Topps Gallery Expressionists	EX9	4.00
1995-96 Topps Pan For Gold	9	4.00
1995-96 Topps Power Boosters	9	4.00
1995-96 Topps Show Stoppers	10	4.00
1995-96 Topps World Class	WC2	2.00
1995-96 Ultra	185	.30
1995-96 Ultra	323	.20
1995-96 Ultra All-NBA	2	1.00
1995-96 Ultra Power	5	.50
1995-96 Ultra Scoring Kings	5	7.00
1995-96 Ultra U.S.A. Basketball	3	10.00
1995-96 Upper Deck	69	.30
1995-96 Upper Deck	142	.20
1995-96 Upper Deck	166	.20
1995-96 Upper Deck	318	.25
1995-96 Upper Deck All-Star Class	AS16	6.00
1995-96 Upper Deck Predictor Retail MVP	R8	1.00
1995-96 Upper Deck Predictor MVP	R8	2.00
1995-96 Upper Deck Special Edition	SE171	1.00
1996-97 Bowman's Best	55	.75
1996-97 Bowman's Best Cuts	BC1	4.00
1996-97 Bowman's Best Honor Roll	HR3	10.00
1996-97 UD CC	155	.15
1996-97 UD CC Crash the Game II	C27	2.00
1996 UD CC International II	101	1.25
1996 UD CC International II	137	.60
1996 UD CC International I	192	.60
1996 UD CC International II	192	.60
1996 UD CC International Japanese	192	.60
1996 UD CC International Japanese	235	1.25
1996 UD CC International Japanese	347	.60
1996 UD CC International Japanese	402	.60
1996-97 UD CC Mini-Cards	9	1.50
1996-97 UD CC Stick-Ums	S27	.50
1996-97 Finest	52	1.00
1996-97 Finest	116	5.00
1996-97 Finest	285	20.00
1996-97 Finest Refractors	52	20.00
1996-97 Finest Refractors	116	30.00
1996-97 Finest Refractors	285	100.00
1996-97 Flair Showcase	A28	.75
1996-97 Flair Showcase	B28	1.00
1996-97 Flair Showcase	C28	20.00
1996-97 Flair Showcase Hot Shots	13	12.00
1996-97 Flair Showcase Legacy	28	50.00
1996-97 Fleer	110	.20
1996-97 Fleer	146	.10
1996-97 Fleer	259	.25
1996-97 Fleer	284	.10
1996-97 Fleer Decade of Excellence	5	18.00
1996-97 Fleer Game Breakers	15	7.00
1996-97 Fleer Stackhouse's All-Fleer	7	1.00
1996-97 Fleer Total "O"	6	3.00
1996 Fleer USA	3	1.50
1996 Fleer USA	13	.50
1996 Fleer USA	23	1.50
1996 Fleer USA	33	.50
1996 Fleer USA	43	1.50
1996 Fleer USA Heroes	3	8.00
1996-97 Hoops	160	.20
1996-97 Hoops	189	.05
1996-97 Hoops	244	.20
1996-97 Hoops	338	.10
1996-97 Hoops Head to Head	HH10	3.00
1996-97 Hoops Hot List	11	6.00
1996-97 Hoops Starting Five	27	1.00
1996-97 Metal	101	.30
1996-97 Metal	141	.10
1996-97 Metal	225	.10
1996-97 Metal Cyber-Metal	CM8	2.00
1996-97 Metal Decade of Excellence	5	12.00
1996-97 Metal Maximum Metal	6	15.00
1996-97 Metal Molten Metal	20	8.00
1996-97 Metal Platinum Portraits	PP7	4.00
1996-97 Metal Power Tools	7	2.00
1996-97 SkyBox	119	.30
1996-97 SkyBox	TT8	.10
1996-97 SkyBox	249	.05
1996-97 SkyBox E-X2000	74	2.00
1996-97 SkyBox E-X2000 Net Assets	11	4.00
1996-97 SkyBox Golden Touch	7	20.00
1996-97 SkyBox Net Set	11	6.00
1996-97 SkyBox Rubies	119	15.00
1996-97 SkyBox Rubies	249	5.00
1996-97 SkyBox Thunder and Lightning	9	15.00
1996 SkyBox USA	3	.10
1996 SkyBox USA	13	.10
1996 SkyBox USA	23	.10
1996 SkyBox USA	33	.10
1996 SkyBox USA	43	.10
1996 SkyBox USA	56	.25
1996 SkyBox USA Bronze	B3	1.00
1996 SkyBox USA Gold	G3	10.00
1996 SkyBox USA Quads	Q3	.40
1996 SkyBox USA Silver	S3	4.00
1996-97 SkyBox Z-Force	90	.30
1996-97 SkyBox Z-Force	182	.20
1996-97 SkyBox Z-Force Slam Cam	SC7	20.00
1996-97 Stadium Club	87	.40
1996-97 Stadium Club	135	.30
1996-97 Stadium Club Finest Reprints	26	5.00
1996-97 Stadium Club Fusion	F28	6.00
1996-97 Stadium Club Mega Heroes	MH3	2.00
1996-97 Stadium Club Members Only	35	.30
1996-97 Stadium Club Moments	SM3	.40
1996-97 Stadium Club Player's Private Issue	14	20.00
1996-97 Stadium Club Top Crop	TC6	3.00
1996-97 SP	114	.30
1996-97 SPx	47	2.00
1996-97 Topps	105	.15
1996-97 Topps	178	.25
1996-97 Topps Chrome	105	1.00
1996-97 Topps Chrome	178	1.00
1996-97 Topps Chrome Pro Files	PF18	1.50
1996-97 Topps Chrome Refractors	105	30.00
1996-97 Topps Chrome Refractors	178	30.00
1996-97 Topps Chrome Season's Best	SB4	1.50
1996-97 Topps Hobby Masters	HM23	5.00
1996-97 Topps Holding Court	HC15	4.00
1996 Topps NBA Stars	26	.40
1996 Topps NBA Stars	76	.40
1996 Topps NBA Stars	126	.40
1996 Topps NBA Stars Imagine	I16	6.00
1996 Topps NBA Stars Reprints	26	5.00
1996-97 Topps Pro Files	PF18	2.00
1996-97 Topps Season's Best	SB4	2.00
1996-97 Ultra	112	.30
1996-97 Ultra	130	.10
1996-97 Ultra	253	.25
1996-97 Ultra	293	.10
1996-97 Ultra Board Game	10	1.00
1996-97 Ultra Court Masters	3	10.00
1996-97 Ultra Decade of Excellence	U5	10.00
1996-97 Ultra Platinum	112	30.00
1996-97 Ultra Platinum	130	20.00
1996-97 Ultra Platinum	253	30.00
1996-97 Ultra Platinum	293	14.00
1996-97 Ultra Scoring Kings	27	5.00
1996-97 Ultra Starring Role	6	10.00
1996-97 Upper Deck	304	.30
1996-97 Upper Deck	357	.10
1996-97 Upper Deck Fast Break	FB30	3.00
1996-97 Upper Deck Predictor	P19	6.00
1996-97 Upper Deck UD3	47	.25
1996-97 UD UD3 SuperStar Spotlight	S4	15.00
1996 Upper Deck USA	9	.20
1996 Upper Deck USA	10	.20
1996 Upper Deck USA	11	.20
1996 Upper Deck USA	12	.20
1996 Upper Deck USA	51	.20
1996 Upper Deck USA Follow Your Dreams	F3	1.00
1996 Upper Deck USA SP Career Highlights	S3	4.00
1997-98 UD CC	142	.20
1997 UD CC Crash the Game Scoring	CR27	—
1997-98 UD CC Stick-Ums	S27	.40
1997-98 UD CC StarQuest	SQ71	8.00
1997-98 UD CC You Crash the Game	C27	1.00
1997 Corinthian Headliners Bk		5.00
1997-98 Finest	90	1.00
1997-98 Finest	127	4.00
1997-98 Finest Refractors	90	25.00
1997-98 Finest Refractors	127	30.00
1997-98 Fleer	32	.25
1997-98 Fleer Decade of Excellence	6	8.00
1997-98 Fleer Flair Hardwood Leaders	27	1.50
1997-98 Fleer Game Breakers	11	15.00
1997-98 Fleer Key Ingredients	6	.50
1997-98 Hoops	150	.25
1997-98 Hoops Talkin' Hoops	TH27	.30
1997-98 Metal	97	.40
1997 PP Double Threat Auto Combos	—	—
1997 Press Pass Double Threat Nitrokrome	DT2	4.00
1997 Press Pass Double Threat Showdown	S2	8.00
1997 PP Double Threat Double-Threads	DD5	150.00
1997 PP Double Threat Light it Up	LU22	4.00
1997 Press Pass Double Threat	40	.20
1997-98 SkyBox	82	.30
1997-98 SkyBox Premium Players	14	8.00
1997-98 SkyBox Z-Force	32	.30
1997-98 Stadium Club	115	.40
1997-98 Stad Club Bowman's Best Prev	BBP5	6.00
1997-98 Stadium Club Co-Signers	CO1	275.00
1997-98 Stadium Club Co-Signers	CO8	150.00
1997-98 Stadium Club Co-Signers	CO12	100.00
1997-98 Stadium Club Triumvirate	T7B	10.00
1997 SPx	46	1.50
1997-98 Topps Bound for Glory	BG7	3.00
1997-98 Topps Rock Stars	RS7	4.00
1997-98 Topps Season's Best	SB16	4.00

	Card No.	Value
1997-98 Topps 40	18	1.50
1997-98 Ultra	12	.40
1997-98 Ultra Jam City	7	3.00
1997 Upper Deck	162	.10
1997 Upper Deck Diamond Dimensions	D25	—
1997-98 Upper Deck Diamond Vision	27	—
1997 Upper Deck High Dimensions	D25	16.00
1997 Upper Deck Teammates	T53	1.50
1991 AP Rookie Update	21	8.00
1991 Classic Fb	30	2.00
1991 Classic Four-Sport	129	2.00
1991 Pacific	551	3.00
1991 Pro Set	762	3.00

Brett Favre: NFL MVP

	Card No.	Value
1991 Pro Set Platinum	290	1.75
1991 Pro Set Spanish	262	1.25
1991 Score	611	3.00
1991 Stadium Club	94	70.00
1991 Star Pics Fb	65	2.50
1991 Ultra	283	3.50
1991 Ultra Update	1	25.00
1991 Upper Deck	13	4.00
1991 Upper Deck	627	.50
1991 Upper Deck	647	2.00
1991 Wild Card College Draft Picks	119	2.00
1992 Packers Police	5	6.00
1992 Pinnacle	303	5.00
1992 Pinnacle Team 2000	23	5.00
1992 Pro Set	505	1.25
1992 Pro Set Gold MVPs	20	3.00
1992 Pro Set Power	104	1.25
1992 Stadium Club	683	100.00
1992 Topps	696	2.50
1992 Upper Deck	484	2.00
1992 Upper Deck Coach's Report	5	10.00
1992 Wild Card Field Force	14	2.00
1992 Wild Card Stat Smashers	SS23	10.00
1993 AP	16	5.00
1993 AP Monday Night	38	3.00
1993 AP Monday Night Mint	38	175.00
1993 AP Quarterback Club	5	6.00
1993 AP Quarterback Club Braille	5B	10.00
1993 AP Rookies Previews	RU2	4.00
1993 AP 24K Gold	5	125.00
1993 Bowman	335	8.00
1993 Classic TONX	41	2.00
1993 Edge	70	2.00
1993 Dog Tags	62	2.50
1993 Fleer	100	2.00
1993 Fleer GameDay	100	3.00
1993 Fleer GameDay Game Breakers	2	4.00
1993 Fleer Team Leaders	1	20.00
1993 FACT Fleer Shell	10	5.00
1993-95 Highland Mint Topps	7	100.00
1993 McDonald's GameDay	6	2.00
1993 McDonald's GameDay	28	2.00
1993 Pacific	89	1.50
1993 Pacific Gold Prisms	5	30.00
1993 Pacific Prisms	31	12.00
1993 Pacific Silver Prism Inserts	5	16.00
1993 Pacific Triple Folder Superstars	9	2.00
1993 Pacific Triple Folders	21	1.50
1993 Packers Police	9	4.00
1993 Pinnacle	1	4.00
1993 Pinnacle Men of Autumn	37	4.00
1993 Pinnacle Samples	1	6.00
1993 Pinnacle Team 2001	7	8.00
1993 Playoff	168	5.00
1993 Playoff	285	2.00
1993 Playoff Brett Favre	1	20.00
1993 Playoff Brett Favre	2	20.00
1993 Playoff Brett Favre	3	20.00
1993 Playoff Brett Favre	4	20.00
1993 Playoff Brett Favre	5	20.00

	Card No.	Value
1993 Playoff Contenders	1	4.00
1993 Playoff Headliners Redemption	H1	14.00
1993 Pro Line Live	88	1.00
1993 Pro Line Live Autographs	88	175.00
1993 Pro Line Live LPs	LP10	8.00
1993 Pro Line Live Portraits	486	.75
1993 Pro Line Portraits Autographs	486	250.00
1993 Pro Set	152	2.00
1993 Pro Set Power	4	1.00
1993 Score	25	2.00
1993 Score Ore-Ida QB Club	9	6.00
1993 Select	43	8.00
1993 Select Young Stars	1	10.00
1993 SkyBox	122	4.00
1993 SkyBox Impact	108	2.00
1993 SkyBox Thunder and Lightning	2	12.00
1993 Sp	93	12.00
1993 Spectrum QB Club Tribute Sheets	5	8.00
1993 Stadium Club	210	4.00
1993 Stadium Club	498	1.50
1993 Stadium Club First Day Cards	210	125.00
1993 Stadium Club First Day Cards	498	14.00
1993 Stadium Club Super Teams	20	16.00
1993 Topps	250	2.00
1993 Topps Black Gold	39	8.00
1993 Topps FantaSports	11	20.00
1993 Ultra	146	5.00
1993 Ultra Stars	1	50.00
1993 Upper Deck	82	.50
1993 Upper Deck	360	2.00
1993 Upper Deck	439	.50
1993 Upper Deck Future Heroes	44	5.00
1993 Upper Deck Pro Bowl	14	30.00
1993 Wild Card	136	1.25
1993 Wild Card Field Force Superchrome	10	3.00
1993 Wild Card Field Force	112	2.50
1993 Wild Card Stat Smashers	107	3.00
1993 Wild Card Superchrome FF/RHR B/B	3	5.00
1994 AP	34	5.00
1994 AP	183	1.00
1994 AP CoaStars	8	5.00
1994 AP Fantasy Forecast	7	5.00
1994 AP Mammoth	MM9	16.00
1994 AP Monday Night Silver	9S	75.00
1994 AP Monday Night	29	2.00
1994 AP Quarterback Club	6	5.00
1994 AP Quarterback Challenge	FA6	5.00
1994 AP 24K Gold	6	110.00
1994 AP 24K Gold	54	75.00
1994 Bowman	295	5.00
1994 Classic NFL Experience	32	1.00
1994 UD CC	309	2.00
1994 UD CC Gold	309	80.00
1994 Edge	71	2.00
1994 Edge Excalibur Knights-NFL	5	10.00
1994 Edge Excalibur	23	3.00
1994 Finest	124	18.00
1994 Finest Refractors	124	230.00
1994 Fleer	168	2.00
1994 Fleer GameDay	147	2.00
1994 Fleer Pro Visions	4	3.00
1994-96 Highland Mint Silver Medallions	19	40.00
1994 Images	64	4.00
1994 Kenner Starting Lineups Fb	(6)	120.00
1994 National League Back to School	(9)	2.00
1994 Pacific	140	2.00
1994 Pacific Gems of the Crown	11	20.00
1994 Pacific Marquee Prisms	12	5.00
1994 Pacific Prisms	10	16.00
1994 Pacific Triple Folders	12	3.00
1994 Packers Police	7	3.00
1994 Pinnacle	36	3.00
1994 Pinnacle Performers	13	12.00
1994 Pinnacle Team Pinnacle	2	60.00
1994 Playoff	30	4.00
1994 Playoff Contenders	71	5.00
1994 Playoff Contenders Back-To-Backs	13	150.00
1994 Pro Line Live	47	1.50
1994 Pro Line Live	302	.10
1994 Pro Line Live Autographs	47	200.00
1994 Pro Line Live MVP Sweepstakes	9	30.00
1994 Pro Line Live Spotlight	PB10	4.00
1994 Pro Mags	72	5.00
1994 Pro Set National Promos	3	5.00
1994 Pro Tags	57	5.00
1994 Score	142	2.00
1994 Select	142	5.00
1994 SkyBox	58	4.00
1994 SkyBox Impact	92	2.00
1994 SkyBox Impact Ultimate Impact	15	20.00
1994 SkyBox SkyTech Stars	14	16.00
1994 Sp	163	5.00

	Card No.	Value
1994 Sp All-Pro Holoview Die-Cuts	15	200.00
1994 Sp All-Pro Holoviews	15	20.00
1994 Sp Die-Cuts	163	5.00
1994 Sportflics	27	3.00
1994 Sportflics	183	1.00
1994 Stadium Club	536	4.00
1994 Stadium Club	604	3.00
1994 Stadium Club Bowman Black	12	10.00
1994 Stadium Club First Day Cards	536	90.00
1994 Stadium Club First Day Cards	604	25.00
1994 Ted Williams Card Co. Auckland Coll	1	6.00
1994 Ted Williams Card Co. POG Cards	1	.75
1994 Ted Williams Card Co. Instant Replays	5	4.00
1994 Ted Williams Card Co. NFL	82	.50
1994 Ted Williams Card Co. NFL	83	.65
1994 Ted Williams Card Co. NFL	84	.65
1994 Ted Williams Card Co. NFL	85	.65
1994 Topps	530	2.00
1994 Topps 1000/3000	22	14.00
1994 Ultra	107	3.00
1994 Upper Deck	250	3.00
1994 Upper Deck Electric Gold	250	125.00
1994 Upper Deck Pro Bowl Samples	2	10.00
1994 Upper Deck Pro Bowl	9	35.00
1994 Upper Deck Retail Predictor	5	10.00
1994 Wild Card Field Force Chromium	10	35.00
1994 Wild Card Superchrome	136	9.00
1995 AP	15	3.00
1995 AP Armed Forces	5	20.00
1995 AP Monday Night Night Flights	6	10.00
1995 AP Monday Night Reverse Angle	8	7.00
1995 AP Monday Night 24KT Gold Team	9	35.00
1995 AP Monday Night	60	1.00
1995 AP Monday Night	109	.50
1995 AP Rocket Men	12	20.00
1995 AP Rookies & Stars 24K Gold Team	2	55.00
1995 AP Rookies & Stars Closing Seconds	6	17.00
1995 AP Rookies & Stars	60	2.00
1995 AP 24 Kt. Gold	9G	90.00
1995 Bowman	110	3.00
1995 Bowman's Best	V43	8.00
1995 Bowman's Best Refractors	V43	120.00
1995 Classic NFL Experience	35	1.00
1995 Cleo Quarterback Club Valentines	3	1.50
1995 UD CC	73	1.50
1995 UD CC Crash The Game	C6	3.00
1995 UD CC Update Stick-Ums	8	1.00
1995 UD CC Update Post Season Heroics	13	4.00
1995 UD CC Update	73	.40
1995 Edge	71	1.50
1995 Edge Edge Tech	21	12.00
1995 Edge Excalibur 22K Gold	33	100.00
1995 Edge Excalibur	102	4.00
1995 Edge Instant Replay	13	3.00
1995 Edge 12th Man Redempton	4	8.00
1995 Crown Pro Die-Cuts	7	4.00
1995 Finest	56	12.00
1995 Finest Refractors	56	150.00
1995 Flair	75	6.00
1995 Flair Hot Numbers	6	14.00
1995 Fleer	135	1.50
1995 Flickball Prototypes	4	2.00
1995 FACT Fleer Shell	12	3.00
1995-96 Highland Mint Bronze Medallions	3	14.00
1995 Images Limited/Live	7	3.00
1995 Images Limited/Live Icons	18	26.00
1995 Images Limited/Live Focused	F15	20.00
1995 Images Limited/Live Die Cuts	DC21	50.00
1995 Kenner Starting Lineups Fb	(10)	45.00
1995 Metal	70	3.00
1995 Metal Gold Blasters	6	12.00
1995 Metal Silver Flashers	16	8.00
1995 Pacific	180	2.00
1995 Pacific Crown Royale Pride of NFL	PN12	35.00
1995 Pacific Crown Royale	139	10.00
1995 Pacific Gems of the Crown	12	16.00
1995 Pacific Gridiron	38	8.00
1995 Pacific Prisms	142	12.00
1995 Pacific Triple Folder Teams	4	2.00
1995 Pacific Triple Folder Big Guns	6	10.00
1995 Pacific Triple Folders	38	1.50
1995 Packers Safety Fritsch	3	3.00
1995 Pinnacle	26	2.50
1995 Pinnacle	199	.75
1995 Pinnacle Artist's Proof	26	90.00
1995 Pinnacle Black 'N Blue	25	50.00
1995 Pinnacle Club Collection Arms Race	5	10.00
1995 Pinnacle Club Collection Aerial Assault	11	20.00
1995 Pinnacle Club Collection	91	.50
1995 Pinnacle Club Collection	92	.50
1995 Pinnacle Club Collection	93	.50
1995 Pinnacle Club Collection	94	.50

	Card No.	Value
1995 Pinnacle Club Collection	95	.50
1995 Pinnacle Club Collection	96	.50
1995 Pinnacle Club Collection	97	.50
1995 Pinnacle Club Collection	98	.50
1995 Pinnacle Club Collection	99	.50
1995 Pinnacle Dial Corporation	DC11	3.00
1995 Pinnacle Showcase	10	14.00
1995 Pinnacle Team Pinnacle	7	50.00
1995 Pinnacle/Dial	11	3.00
1995 Playoff Absolute Die Cut Helmets	6	70.00
1995 Playoff Absolute Quad Series	2	225.00
1995 Playoff Absolute-Prime	35	3.00
1995 Playoff Contenders	4	4.00
1995 Playoff Contenders Back-to-Back	3	125.00
1995 Playoff Contenders Hog Heaven	10	150.00
1995 Playoff Prime Fantasy Team	6	40.00
1995 Playoff Prime Minis	35	50.00
1995 Pro Line	3	1.50
1995 Pro Line Field Generals	9	50.00
1995 Pro Line Game of the Week	20	2.00
1995 Pro Line Game Breakers	GB9	20.00
1995 Pro Line Grand Gainers	G17	4.00
1995 Pro Line Impact	8	18.00
1995 Pro Line MVP Redemption	14	30.00
1995 Pro Line Pogs	C15	1.50
1995 Pro Line Series II	37	1.50
1995 Pro Mags	48	4.00
1995 Pro Mags By The Zone	4	4.00
1995 Score	64	1.50
1995 Score	224	.40
1995 Score Offense Inc.	8	12.00
1995 Score Pass Time	7	30.00
1995 Score Pin-Cards	16	5.00
1995 Select Certified	50	7.00
1995 Select Certified Checklists	4	1.50
1995 Select Certified Gold Team	9	70.00
1995 Select Certified Mirror Golds	50	60.00
1995 Select Certified Select Few	6	60.00
1995 SkyBox	46	2.00
1995 SkyBox	139	1.00
1995 SkyBox	141	.50
1995 SkyBox	142	1.00
1995 SkyBox	148	1.00
1995 SkyBox Impact	53	1.50
1995 SkyBox Impact	M1	25.00
1995 SkyBox Impact Countdown	9	15.00
1995 SkyBox Impact Power	IP15	8.00
1995 SkyBox Paydirt	PD10	8.00
1995 Sp	56	6.00
1995 Sp All-Pros	4	8.00
1995 Sp Championship	111	3.00
1995 Sp Championship Playoff Showcase	6	25.00
1995 Sp Holoview Die-Cuts	36	125.00
1995 Sp Holoviews	36	20.00
1995 Sportflix	76	1.50
1995 Sportflix	157	.50
1995 Sportflix Man 2 Man	11	15.00
1995 Stadium Club	191	4.00
1995 Stadium Club	320	3.00
1995 Stadium Club Ground Attack	2	15.00
1995 Stad Club Members Only Parallel	GA2	4.00
1995 Stad Club Members Only Parallel	NE4	4.00
1995 Stad Club Members Only Parallel	NM28	4.00
1995 Stadium Club Nemeses	4	25.00
1995 Stadium Club Nightmares	28	25.00
1995 Summit	32	3.00
1995 Summit	193	.50
1995 Summit	197	.30
1995 Summit Team Summit	10	80.00
1995 Topps	34	1.00
1995 Topps	345	1.00
1995 Topps Finest Inserts		16.00
1995-96 Topps Finest Pro Bowl Jumbos	5	14.00
1995-96 Finest Pro Bowl Jumbos Refractors	5	275.00
1995 Topps Yesteryear	15	20.00
1995 Topps 1000/3000 Boosters	34	20.00
1995 Ultra	112	3.00
1995 Ultra	490	1.00
1995 Ultra Magna Force	16	20.00
1995 Ultra Rising Stars	8	25.00
1995 Ultra Ultrabilities	9	10.00
1995 Upper Deck	39	3.00
1995 Upper Deck Retail Predictor	6	12.00
1995 Zenith	62	10.00
1995 Zenith Second Season	1	20.00
1995 Zenith Z-Team	9	70.00
1996 AP	18	3.00
1996 AP Artist's Proof	18	125.00
1996 AP Longest Yard	1	35.00
1996 AP Sculptor's Proof	4	150.00
1996 AP The Longest Yard	1	40.00
1996 AP 24kt Gold	1	80.00

	Card No.	Value
1996 Bowman's Best	70	8.00
1996 Bowman's Best Best Cuts	5	40.00
1996 Bowman's Best Mirror Images	2a	40.00
1996 Classic NFL Experience Sculpted	S9	20.00
1996 Classic NFL Experience	19	2.00
1996 Classic NFL 7-11 Phone Cards	—	4.00
1996 UD CC	57	.50
1996 UD CC	178	2.00
1996 UD CC A Cut Above	6	3.00
1996 UD CC Crash The Game	6	6.00
1996 UD CC MVPs	M17	
1996 UD CC Packers	GB1	1.50
1996 UD CC Packer Leaders	GB81	4.50
1996 UD CC Packers	GB31	1.50
1996 UD CC Packers	GB32	1.50
1996 UD CC Packers	GB33	1.50
1996 UD CC Packers	GB64	1.50
1996 UD CC Stick-Ums	S6	2.00
1996 UD CC Update Stick-Ums	S4	2.00
1996 UD CC Update You Make The Play	7	2.00
1996 UD CC Update You Make The Play	52	2.00
1996 UD CC Update	72	.75
1996 Edge	82	2.00
1996 Edge Advantage Edge Video	1	35.00
1996 Edge Advantage Game Ball	3	150.00
1996 Edge Advantage	13	2.50
1996 Edge President's Reserve Air Force One	1	30.00
1996 Edge President's Reserve Pro Bowl '96	3	16.00
1996 Edge President's Reserve TimeWarp	6	100.00
1996 Edge Pres Reserve Running Mates	13	90.00
1996 Edge President's Reserve	70	6.00
1996 Edge Quantum	10	40.00
1996 Edge Ripped	6	12.00
1996 Crown Pro Die-Cuts	8	5.00
1996 Donruss	72	2.00
1996 Donruss Elite	9	40.00
1996 Donruss Hit List	5	25.00
1996 Donruss Stop Action	3	50.00
1996 Donruss What If?	6	40.00
1996 Donruss Will to Win	2	30.00
1996 Finest	4	25.00
1996 Finest	132	85.00
1996 Finest Refractors	4	200.00
1996 Finest Refractors	132	625.00
1996 Fleer	51	2.00
1996 Fleer Statistically Speaking	4	20.00
1996 Flickball	24	2.00
1996 Flickball Commemoratives	C3	20.00
1996 Laser View	7	10.00
1996 Laser View	34	5.00
1996 Laser View Inscriptions		125.00
1996 Leaf	44	3.00
1996 Leaf Gold Leaf Stars	11	80.00
1996 Leaf Shirt Off My Back	10	60.00
1996 Leaf Statisical Standouts	15	80.00
1996 Metal	45	3.00
1996 Metal Goldflingers	5	14.00
1996 Metal Molten Metal	6	50.00
1996 Motion Vision	13	20.00
1996 Motion Vision	14	20.00
1996 Motion Vision Lmt Digital Replays	LDR7	60.00
1996 Motion Vision Lmt Digital Replays	LDR8	60.00
1996 NFL Properites 7-11	8	3.00
1996 NFL Properties Back-to-School	—	3.00
1996 Pacific	150	2.00
1996 Pacific Bomb Squad	5	45.00
1996 Pacific Card-Supials	14	40.00
1996 Pacific Cramer's Choice Awards	4	200.00
1996 Pacific Crown Roy Cramer's Choice	2	125.00
1996 Pacific Crown Roy Triple Crown Die-Cut	3	90.00
1996 Pacific Crown Royale Pro Bowl Die-Cut	4	100.00
1996 Pacific Crown Royale Field Force	9	100.00
1996 Pacific Crown Royale	54	10.00
1996 Pacific Crown Royale NFL Regime	110	2.50
1996 Pacific Dynagon	53	10.00
1996 Pacific Dynagon Dynamic Duos	DD3	40.00
1996 Pacific Dynagon Gold Tandems	4	150.00
1996 Pacific Dynagon Kings of the NFL	K5	100.00
1996 Pacific Gems of the Crown	23	20.00
1996 Pacific Gold Crown Die-Cuts	9	40.00
1996 Pacific Gridiron	45	8.00
1996 Pacific Gridiron Gems	18	6.00
1996 Pacific Gridiron Gold Crown Die-Cut	19	50.00
1996 Pacific Invincible	53	12.00
1996 Pacific Invincible Kick-Starters	6	75.00
1996 Pacific Invincible Pro Bowl	6	30.00
1996 Pacific Invincible Smash-Mouth	61	3.00
1996 Pacific Litho-Cel	39	14.00
1996 Pacific Litho-Cel Feature Performers	10	40.00
1996 Pacific Litho-Cel Game Time	13	3.00
1996 Pacific Litho-Cel Litho-Proof	14	160.00
1996 Pacific Litho-Cel Moments in Time	11	100.00
1996 Pacific Power Corps	8	12.00
1996 Pacific The Zone	12	100.00
1996 Packers Police	8	6.00
1996 Pinnacle	40	2.50
1996 Pinnacle	196	.30
1996 Pinnacle	199	.30
1996 Pinnacle	200	2.50
1996 Pinnacle Black 'N Blue	7	40.00
1996 Pinnacle Double Disguise	3	12.00
1996 Pinnacle Double Disguise	11	10.00
1996 Pinnacle Double Disguise	13	10.00
1996 Pinnacle Double Disguise	14	10.00
1996 Pinnacle Double Disguise	15	10.00
1996 Pinnacle Double Disguise	16	12.00
1996 Pinnacle Double Disguise	18	8.00
1996 Pinnacle Mint Cards	10	3.00
1996 Pinnacle Mint Coins	10	8.00
1996 Pinnacle Super Bowl Card Show	6	5.00
1996 Pinnacle Team Pinnacle	3	50.00
1996 Playoff Absolute	152	25.00
1996 Playoff Absolute Xtreme Team	5	40.00
1996 Playoff Absolute/Prime Metal XL	4	80.00
1996 Playoff Contenders Air Command	2	90.00
1996 Playoff Contenders Leather	1	100.00
1996 Playoff Contenders Leather Accents	1	600.00
1996 Playoff Contenders Open Field	1	20.00
1996 Playoff Contenders Pennants	1	90.00
1996 Playoff Illusions	100	10.00
1996 Playoff Illusions Optical Illusions	1	150.00
1996 Playoff Illusions Spectralusion Elite	100	20.00
1996 Playoff Prime	1	4.00
1996 Playoff Prime Boss Hogs	14	100.00
1996 Playoff Prime Playoff Honors	PH3	350.00
1996 Playoff Prime Surprise	PS2	200.00
1996 Playoff Prime X's and O's	1	50.00
1996 Playoff Trophy Contenders	1	3.00
1996 Playoff Trophy Contenders Playoff Zone	4	50.00
1996 Playoff Trophy Cont Mini Back-to-Backs	12	90.00
1996 Pro Line	6	2.00
1996 Pro Line Cels	C13	50.00
1996 Pro Line DC III	41	6.00
1996 Pro Line DC III All-Pros	AP8	80.00
1996 Pro Line DC III Road to Super Bowl	13	45.00
1996 Pro Line II Intense $3 Phone Cards	8	12.00
1996 Pro Line II Intense	88	2.00
1996 Pro Line Memorabilia Producers	6	10.00
1996 Pro Line Memorabilia Stretch Drive	12	18.00
1996 Pro Line Memorabilia	88	3.00
1996 Pro Line Rivalries	R9	20.00
1996 Score	119	1.50
1996 Score	245	.30
1996 Score	273	.30
1996 Score	275	.50
1996 Score Artist's Proofs	119	35.00
1996 Score Artist's Proofs	245	20.00
1996 Score Artist's Proofs	273	15.00
1996 Score Board NFL Lasers	1	2.50
1996 SB NFL Lasers Laser Images	I11	30.00
1996 SB NFL Lasers Sunday's Heroes	S12	50.00
1996 Score Dream Team	6	30.00
1996 Score Footsteps	9	15.00
1996 Score In the Zone	1	30.00
1996 Score Numbers Game	3	12.00
1996 Score Settle the Score	7	35.00
1996 Score Settle the Score	19	35.00
1996 Score Settle the Score	21	20.00
1996 Select	19	3.00
1996 Select	182	.50
1996 Select Artist's Proofs	10	70.00
1996 Select Artist's Proofs	182	35.00
1996 Select Certified	85	5.00
1996 Select Certified	117	2.00
1996 Select Certified Gold Team	11	60.00
1996 Select Certified Thumbs Up	7	60.00
1996 Select Four-midable	5	20.00
1996 Select Prime Cut	7	70.00
1996 Select Promos	19	4.00
1996 SkyBox	63	2.50
1996 SkyBox Autographs		250.00
1996 SkyBox Brett Favre MVP	1	40.00
1996 SkyBox Brett Favre MVP	2	40.00
1996 SkyBox Brett Favre MVP	3a	30.00
1996 SkyBox Brett Favre MVP	3b	40.00
1996 SkyBox Brett Favre MVP	3c	60.00
1996 SkyBox Brett Favre MVP	4	30.00
1996 SkyBox Brett Favre MVP	5	30.00
1996 SkyBox Impact	52	1.50
1996 SkyBox Impact	194	.25
1996 SkyBox Impact	195	.25
1996 SkyBox Impact	196	.25
1996 SkyBox Impact	197	.25
1996 SkyBox Impact	198	.25
1996 SkyBox Impact No Surrender	5	30.00
1996 SkyBox Impact Rookies Rookie Rewind	5	18.00
1996 SkyBox Impact Rookies	83	.75
1996 SkyBox SkyMotion	17	15.00
1996 SkyBox SkyMotion Team Galaxy	2	50.00
1996 SkyBox Thunder and Lightning	7	40.00
1996 Sp	33	5.00
1996 Sp Explosive	X4	250.00
1996 Sp Holoview	4	25.00
1996 Sp Spx Force	3	250.00
1996 Spx	17	15.00
1996 Stadium Club	174	2.00
1996 Stadium Club	250	2.50
1996 Stadium Club Dot Matrix	250	25.00
1996 Stadium Club Fusion	5A	30.00
1996 Stadium Club Laser Sites	1	25.00
1996 Stadium Club Members Only	20	5.00
1996 Stadium Club Photo Gallery	15	25.00
1996 Stadium Club Pro Bowl	1	30.00
1996 Summit	63	2.50
1996 Summit	192	1.00
1996 Summit	199	.30
1996 Summit Inspirations	5	30.00
1996 Summit Third and Long	6	80.00
1996 Summit Turf Team	2	50.00
1996 Tombstone Pizza Quarterback Club	9	1.25
1996 Topps	371	.75
1996 Topps	400	2.00
1996 Topps Broadway's Reviews	4	7.00
1996 Topps Chrome	131	2.25
1996 Topps Chrome	145	5.00
1996 Topps Chrome 40th Anniversary	7	20.00
1996 Topps Gilt Edge	1	4.00
1996 Topps Gilt Edge Definitive Edge	2	8.00
1996 Topps Hobby Masters	1	25.00
1996 Topps Laser	80	6.00
1996 Topps Laser Stadium Stars	5	80.00
1996 Topps Turf Warriors	5	20.00
1996 Topps 40th Anniversary	7	10.00
1996 Ultra	57	2.50
1996 Ultra Mr. Momentum	6	15.00
1996 Ultra Pulsating	2	16.00
1996 Ultra Sensations	39	2.50
1996 Ultra Sensations Creative Chaos	1	18.00
1996 Ultra Sensations Creative Chaos	2	18.00
1996 Ultra Sensations Creative Chaos	2	16.00
1996 Ultra Sensations Creative Chaos	2	14.00
1996 Ultra Sensations Creative Chaos	2	10.00
1996 Ultra Sensations Creative Chaos	2	11.00
1996 Ultra Sensations Creative Chaos	2	12.00
1996 Ultra Sensations Creative Chaos	2	13.00
1996 Ultra Sensations Creative Chaos	2	13.00
1996 Ultra Sensations Creative Chaos	2	10.00
1996 Ultra Sensations Creative Chaos	2	11.00
1996 Ultra Sensations Creative Chaos	3	14.00
1996 Ultra Sensations Creative Chaos	4	10.00
1996 Ultra Sensations Creative Chaos	5	11.00
1996 Ultra Sensations Creative Chaos	6	12.00
1996 Ultra Sensations Creative Chaos	7	13.00
1996 Ultra Sensations Creative Chaos	8	13.00
1996 Ultra Sensations Creative Chaos	9	10.00
1996 Ultra Sensations Creative Chaos	10	11.00
1996 Upper Deck	131	3.00
1996 Upper Deck Hot Properties	HT4	20.00
1996 Upper Deck Predictor	PH3	50.00
1996 Upper Deck Predictor	PR3	10.00
1996 Upper Deck Pro Bowl	PB2	20.00
1996 Upper Deck Proview	3	16.00
1996 Upper Deck Silver	191	3.00
1996 Upper Deck Silver	212	1.00
1996 Upper Deck Silver All-NFL	AN7	10.00
1996 Upper Deck Team Trio	41	6.00
1996 Upper Deck TV Cels	PH3	125.00
1996 Zenith	21	5.00
1996 Zenith	144	2.00
1996 Zenith Artist's Proofs	21	125.00
1996 Zenith Artist's Proofs	144	60.00
1996 Zenith Noteworthy '95	7	14.00
1996 Zenith Z-Team	9	100.00
1997 AP	17	4.00
1997 AP	111	2.00
1997 AP Crash Course	5	40.00
1997 AP 24K Team	1	90.00
1997 Bowman's Best	1	—
1997 Bowman's Best Cuts	BC5	—
1997 Bowman's Best Mirror Images	MI1	—
1997 UD CC	71	1.00
1997 UD CC	224	1.75
1997 UD CC Crash the Game	4	3.50
1997 UD CC Crash the Game Redemption	4	—
1997 UD CC Mini-Standee	ST20	—
1997 UD CC Star Quest	SQ82	—
1997 UD CC Turf Champions	TC81	75.00
1997 Edge Excalibur Game Gear	1	100.00
1997 Edge Excalibur Crusaders	1	50.00
1997 Edge Excalibur 22k Knights	3	25.00
1997 Edge Excalibur Marauders	3	25.00
1997 Edge Excalibur Over Lords	18	25.00
1997 Edge Excalibur Castle Cards	18	25.00
1997 Edge Excalibur	50	3.00
1997 Edge Extreme Fury	8	—
1997 Edge Extreme Forerunners	10	—
1997 Edge Extreme Game Gear Quads	11	—
1997 Edge Extreme Parallel 3	P60	—
1997 Edge Extreme Finesse	13	—
1997 Edge Extreme Force	14	—
1997 Edge Extreme	60	—
1997 Edge Extreme Parallel 1	P60	—
1997 Edge Masters Super Bowl Game Ball	1	300.00
1997 Edge Masters Radical Rivals	2	25.00
1997 Edge Masters Capture the Flag	3	—
1997 Edge Masters Night Games	6	20.00
1997 Edge Masters Nitro-Retail	94	5.00
1997 Edge Masters Capture the Flag	13	—
1997 Edge Masters Playoff Game Ball	14	110.00
1997 Edge Masters Playoff Game Ball	18	120.00
1997 Edge Masters Capture the Flag	22	—
1997 Edge Masters	94	2.00
1996 Corinthian Headliners Fb		12.00
1997 Donruss	2	1.75
1997 Donruss	227	1.00
1997 Donruss Elite	3	50.00
1997 Donruss Legends of the Fall	8	35.00
1997 Donruss Passing Grade	12	45.00
1997 Donruss Zoning Commission	1	—
1997 E-X2000	13	12.00
1997 E-X2000 A Cut Above	2	120.00
1997 Finest	150	25.00
1997 Finest	190	10.00
1997 Finest	340	80.00
1997 Finest Refractors	150	150.00
1997 Finest Refractors	190	85.00
1997 Finest Refractors	340	400.00
1997 Flair Showcase	A4	8.00
1997 Flair Showcase	B4	12.00
1997 Flair Showcase	C4	125.00
1997 Flair Showcase Hot Hands	HH4	125.00
1997 Flair Showcase Legacy	4	550.00
1997 Fleer	400	2.00
1997 Fleer All-Pro	7	30.00
1997 Fleer Goudey	105	2.00
1997 Fleer Goudey Gridiron Greats	105	—
1997 Fleer Goudey Heads Up	8	30.00
1997 Fleer Goudey II	4	2.25
1997 Fleer Goudey II Big Time Backs	5	30.00
1997 Fleer Goudey II Vintage Goudey	5	25.00
1997 Fleer Goudey Tittle Says	9	30.00
1997 Fleer Thrill Seekers	5	90.00
1997 Kenner Starting Lineups Fb	(17)	30.00
1997 Leaf	2	3.00
1997 Leaf	184	1.50
1997 Leaf Fractal Matrix	2	500.00
1997 Leaf Fractal Matrix Die-Cuts	2	120.00
1997 Leaf Fractal Matrix	184	25.00
1997 Leaf Fractal Matrix Die-Cuts	184	100.00
1997 Leaf Hardwear	2	40.00
1997 Leaf Letterman	1	150.00
1997 Leaf 1948 Leaf Reproductions	2	75.00
1997 Metal	156	2.50
1997 Metal Platinum Portraits	PP9	90.00
1997 Metal Titanium	TT2	60.00
1997 Motion Vision	11	20.00
1997 Motion Vision Limited Digital Replays	3	60.00
1997 Pacific Crown	145	2.00
1997 Pacific Crown Big Number Die-Cuts	8	40.00
1997 Pacific Crown Card Supials	11	30.00
1997 Pacific Crown Cramer's Choice	4	250.00
1997 Pacific Crown Gold Crown Die-Cut	12	45.00
1997 Pacific Crown The Zone Die-Cuts	7	55.00
1997 Pacific Dynagon	54	10.00
1997 Pacific Dynagon Best Kept Secrets	13	—
1997 Pacific Dynagon Careers	5	100.00
1997 Pacific Dynagon Player of the Week	13	30.00
1997 Pacific Dynagon Player of the Week	13	30.00
1997 Pacific Dynagon Royal Connections	7a	100.00
1997 Pacific Dynagon Tandems	12	150.00
1997 Pacific Hobby Cramer's Choice	6	250.00
1997 Pacific Hobby Exclusive Cel-Fusions	7	120.00
1997 Pacific Hobby Chalk Talk Laser-Cuts	7	150.00
1997 Pacific Hobby Pro Bowl Die-Cuts	8	100.00

	Card No.	Value
1997 Pacific Hobby Exclusive Firestone On	8	100.00
1997 Pacific Hobby Exclusive	51	12.00
1997 Pacific Invincible	53	12.00
1997 Pacific Invincible Canton, Ohio	5	100.00
1997 Pacific Invincible Moments in Time	7	100.00
1997 Pacific Invincible Pop Cards	6	12.00
1997 Pacific Invincible Smash Mouth	4	2.25
1997 Pacific Invincible Smash Mouth X-tra	4	2.25
1997 Pacific Philadelphia Milestones	7	35.00
1997 Pacific Philadelphia Heart of the Game	8	45.00
1997 Pacific Philadelphia Photoengravings	11	30.00
1997 Pacific Philadelphia Gold	66	4.00
1997 Pacific Philadelphia	111	3.00
1997 Pacific Philadelphia	330	1.50
1997 Pacific Revolution	52	—
1997 Pacific Revolution Air Mail Die-Cuts	12	—
1997 Pacific Revolution Prologue	9	
1997 Pacific Rev Ring Bearers Laser-Cuts	4	—
1997 Pacific Revolution Silks	8	—
1997 Pinnacle	1	2.50
1997 Pinnacle	183	1.25
1997 Pinnacle Artist's Proofs	1	75.00
1997 Pinnacle Certified	3	—
1997 Pinnacle Certified Epix	10	—
1997 Pinnacle Certified Team	1	—
1997 Pinnacle Epix	10	30.00
1997 Pinnacle Inscriptions V2	3	—
1997 Pinnacle Inscriptions	4	—
1997 Pinnacle Inscriptions Autographs		—
1997 Pinnacle Inscriptions	33	—
1997 Pinnacle Inside	7	3.00
1997 Pinnacle Inside Autographed Cards	1	—
1997 Pinnacle Inside Cans	1	3.00
1997 Pinnacle Inside Cans	26	3.00
1997 Pinnacle Inside Fourth & Goal	1	00.00
1997 Pinnacle Mint Cards	1	2.50
1997 Pinnacle Mint Cards	21	1.25
1997 Pinnacle Mint Coins	1	8.00
1997 Pinnacle Mint Coins	21	4.00
1997 Pinnacle Mint Commemorative Cards	2	10.00
1997 Pinnacle Mint Commemorative Coins	2	35.00
1997 Pinnacle Scoring Core	5	60.00
1997 Pinnacle Team Pinnacle	2	100.00
1997 Pinnacle Trophy Collection	1	30.00
1997 Pinnacle X-Press	3	2.25
1997 Pinnacle X-Press	138	1.00
1997 Pinnacle X-Press	148	.50
1997 Pinnacle X-Press Bombs Away	1	20.00
1997 Pinnacle X-Press Divide & Conquer	8	120.00
1997 Pinnacle X-Press Pursuit QBs	3	4.50
1997 Playoff Absolute	151	14.00
1997 Playoff Absolute Chip Shots	151	14.00
1997 Playoff Absolute Leather Quads	LQ1	300.00
1997 Playoff Absolute Pennants	151	160.00
1997 Playoff Absolute Reflex	1	750.00
1997 Playoff Contenders	51	—
1997 Playoff Contenders Clash	1	—
1997 Playoff Cont Die-Cut Leather Helmets	3	—
1997 Playoff Contenders Plaques	23	—
1997 Playoff Contenders Pennants	23	—
1997 Playoff Zone	1	3.00
1997 Playoff Zone Close-Up	1	12.00
1997 Playoff Zone Frenzy	1	25.00
1997 Playoff Zone Sharpshooters	1	35.00
1997 Playoff Zone Treasures	1	120.00
1997 Playoff 1st & 10	151	2.25
1997 Playoff 1st & 10 Chip Shots	151	10.00
1997 Playoff 1st & 10 Hot Pursuit	1	400.00
1997 Playoff 1st & 10 Xtra Point	XP3	250.00
1997 Pro Line	100	2.25
1997 Pro Line	297	.75
1997 Pro Line Board Members	B4	50.00
1997 Pro Line Brett Favre	1	10.00
1997 Pro Line Brett Favre	2	10.00
1997 Pro Line Brett Favre	3	10.00
1997 Pro Line Brett Favre	4	10.00
1997 Pro Line Brett Favre	5	10.00
1997 Pro Line Brett Favre	6	10.00
1997 Pro Line Brett Favre	7	10.00
[illegible]	8	10.00
[illegible]	9	10.00
[illegible]	0	75.00
[illegible]	4	5.00
[illegible]	9	2.00
[illegible]	90	2.00
[illegible]	00	2.00
[illegible]	P2	60.00
[illegible]	39	50.00
[illegible]	1	3.50
[illegible]	60	1.50
[illegible]	67	1.50

	Card No.	Value
1997 Pro Line Gems	70	1.50
1997 Pro Line Gems of the NFL	G6	50.00
1997 Pro Line Gems Championship Ring	CR1	175.00
1997 Pro Line Gems Through the Years	TY2	25.00
1997 Pro Line Rivalries	R13	40.00
1997 Score	3	1.75
1997 Score Board NFL $1000 Phone	5	—
1997 Score Board NFL $25 Die-Cut Phone	10	30.00
1997 Score Board NFL $3 Phone Cards	8	4.00
1997 Score Board NFL Exp Foundations	F22	15.00
1997 Score Board NFL Experience	34	1.25
1997 Score Board Players Club	1	—
1997 Score Board Players Club Play Backs	PB1	—
1997 Score Franchise	3	35.00
1997 Score New Breed	18	12.00
1997 Score The Specialist	1	12.00
1997 SkyBox	1	3.00
1997 SkyBox Autographics		750.00
1997 SkyBox Impact	4	1.75
1997 SkyBox Impact Boss	10	6.00
1997 SkyBox Impact Rave Reviews	3	120.00
1997 SkyBox Larger Than Life	9	125.00
1997 SkyBox Premium Players	6	120.00
1997 Spx	43	12.00
1997 Spx Holofame	4	90.00
1997 Stadium Club	65	3.00
1997 Stadium Club Aerial Assault	AA10	12.00
1997 Stad Club Bowman's Best Previews	BBP6	25.00
1997 Stadium Club Triumvirate II	T2B	30.00
1997 Stadium Club Triumvirate	T6B	30.00
1997 Studio	9	6.00
1997 Studio	30	3.00
1997 Studio Red Zone Masterpiece	9	40.00
1997 Studio Stained Glass Stars	9	100.00
1997 Talk N' Sports	1	.50
1997 Talk N' Sports $1 Phone Cards	1	2.00
1997 Talk N' Sports $1,000 Phone Cards	3	—
1997 Talk N' Sports $10 Phone Cards	1	30.00
1997 Talk N' Sports $20 Phone Cards	1	50.00
1997 Talk N' Sports Essentials	1	30.00
1997 Test copy of item 176-350	150	25.00
1997 Test copy of item 176-350	190	—
1997 Test copy of item 176-350	340	—
1997 Topps	1	2.50
1997 Topps Chrome	1	10.00
1997 Topps Chrome Draft Year	DR9	45.00
1997 Topps Chrome Season's Best	4	20.00
1997 Topps Gallery	100	5.00
1997 Topps Gallery Critics Choice	CC10	40.00
1997 Topps Gallery Gallery of Heroes	GH10	45.00
1997 Topps Gallery Peter Max	PM1	25.00
1997 Topps Gallery Photo Gallery	PG3	35.00
1997 Topps Hall Bound	HB10	25.00
1997 Topps High Octane	HO1	25.00
1997 Topps Mystery Finest	M20	25.00
1997 Topps Season's Best	4	16.00
1997 Topps Stars	1	6.00
1997 Topps Stars Pro Bowl Stars	PB1	80.00
1997 Topps Stars Pro Bowl Memories	PBM4	20.00
1997 Ultra	1	2.50
1997 Ultra Blitzkrieg	6	15.00
1997 Ultra Specialists	5	12.00
1997 Ultra Starring Role	9	100.00
1997 Ultra Stars	9	100.00
1997 Upper Deck	207	3.00
1997 Upper Deck Black Diam Title Quest	7	350.00
1997 Upper Deck Black Diamond	154	50.00
1997 Upper Deck Game Jersey	GM4	600.00
1997 Upper Deck Game Jersey	GM5	600.00
1997 Upper Deck MVP	MP14	70.00
1997 Upper Deck Star Crossed	SC21	25.00
1997 Upper Deck Team Mates	TM21	5.00
1997 Upper Deck UD3	32	6.00
1997 UD UD3 Marquee Attraction	MA8	110.00
1997 Visions Signings	30	.75
1997 Visions Signings Artistry Autographs		300.00
1997 Visions Signings Artistry	A18	10.00
1997 Zenith	1	1.00
1997 Zenith	139	2.00
1997 Zenith V2	12	50.00
1997 Zenith Z-Team	11	80.00
1991-92 Parkhurst	263	5.00
1991-92 Parkhurst	449	1.00
1991-92 Pro Set	529	1.00
1991-92 Pro Set Platinum	252	1.00
1991-92 Score American	316	1.25
1991-92 Score Canadian	346	1.25
1991-92 Upper Deck	335	4.00

Dominik Hasek: NHL MVP

	Card No.	Value
1991-92 Upper Deck Euro-Stars	14	3.00
1992-93 Bowman	428	4.00
1992-93 O-Pee-Chee	301	.50
1992-93 O-Pee-Chee Premier	50	.50
1992 Panini Stickers English	292	.15
1992-93 Score	373	.40
1992-93 Stadium Club	107	.75
1992-93 Topps	136	.30
1992-93 Upper Deck	92	.75
1992-93 Upper Deck	366	.40
1992-93 Upper Deck	506	.60
1992-93 Upper Deck All-Rookie Team	6	7.50
1992-93 Upper Deck Euro Stars	3	4.00
1992-93 Upper Deck Euro-Rookie Team	3	5.00
1993-94 Fleer PowerPlay	297	.50
1993 Kraft	2	1.50
1993-94 Leaf	256	.60
1993-94 Pinnacle	403	.60
1993-94 Score	281	.30
1993-94 Stadium Club	178	.40
1993-94 Topps Premier	320	.25
1993-94 Topps Premier	463	.35
1993-94 Ultra	274	.60
1993-94 Upper Deck	387	.75
1994-95 Donruss	94	.50
1994-95 Donruss Dominators	3	15.00
1994-95 Donruss Masked Marvels	3	5.00
1994-95 Finest	43	2.00
1994-95 Flair	17	1.00
1994-95 Flair Hot Numbers	3	10.00
1994-95 Fleer	20	.40
1994-95 Fleer Netminders	3	1.25
1994-95 Leaf	120	.50
1994-95 Leaf Crease Patrol	6	1.50
1994-95 Leaf Gold Stars	8	45.00
1994-95 Leaf Limited	102	2.00
1994-95 Leaf Limited Inserts	3	6.00
1994-95 O-Pee-Chee Premier	35	.15
1994-95 O-Pee-Chee Premier	80	.10
1994-95 O-Pee-Chee Premier	152	.10
1994-95 O-Pee-Chee Premier	156	.10
1994-95 O-Pee-Chee Premier	312	.30
1994-95 O-Pee-Chee Premier	440	.20
1994-95 Parkhurst	24	.40
1994-95 Parkhurst Vintage Parkhurst	1	.85
1994-95 Pinnacle	175	.50
1994-95 Pinnacle Artist's Proofs	175	40.00
1994-95 Pinnacle Goaltending Greats	1	10.00
1994-95 Pinnacle Hockey MVP's	(1)	25.00
1994-95 Pinnacle Rink Collection	175	8.00
1994-95 Pinnacle World Edition	6	8.00
1994-95 Score	78	.30
1994-95 Score Hockey Gold Line	78	2.00
1994-95 Select	52	.40
1994-95 Stadium Club	125	.35
1994-95 Stadium Club	179	.20
1994-95 Stadium Club	269	.20
1994-95 SP	14	1.00
1994-95 SP Die-Cut	14	1.50
1994-95 SP Premier	19	6.00
1994-95 SP Premier Die-Cut	19	20.00
1994-95 Topps Premier	35	.20
1994-95 Topps Premier	80	.15
1994-95 Topps Premier	152	.20
1994-95 Topps Premier	156	.15
1994-95 Topps Premier	312	.20
1994-95 Topps Premier	440	.20
1994-95 Ultra	22	.50
1994-95 Ultra Global Greats	2	12.00
1994-95 Ultra NHL Award Winners	6	2.00
1994-95 Ultra Premier Pad Men	1	12.00
1994-95 Upper Deck	233	.25
1994-95 Upper Deck	285	.50
1994-95 Upper Deck	545	.40
1994-95 Upper Deck Electric Ice	233	15.00
1994-95 Upper Deck Ross/Vezina Predictor	H31	3.00

	Card No.	Value
1994-95 Upper Deck SP Inserts	SP8	1.00
1995-96 Bowman	56	.50
1995-96 Certified	89	1.50
1995-96 Certified Mirror Gold	89	25.00
1995-96 UD CC	258	.40
1995-96 UD CC	367	.10
1995-96 UD CC	381	.10
1995-96 UD CC	394	.10
1995-96 Donruss	33	.40
1995-96 Donruss Between the Pipes	2	12.00
1995-96 Donruss Elite	30	.50
1995-96 Donruss Elite Stars	30	25.00
1995-96 E-Motion	16	1.00
1995-96 Finest	72	2.00
1995-96 Finest	90	12.00
1995-96 Finest Refractors	72	20.00
1995-96 Finest Refractors	90	60.00
1995 Kenner Starting Lineups Canadian	(7)	25.00
1995 Kenner Starting Lineups American	(9)	25.00
1995-96 Leaf	56	.50
1995-96 Leaf Gold Leaf Stars	1	25.00
1995-96 Leaf Limited	76	2.00
1995-96 Leaf Limited Stick Side	5	30.00
1995-96 Metal	15	.75
1995-96 Metal International Steel	7	2.50
1995-96 Parkhurst All-Stars	1	20.00
1995-96 Parkhurst Goal Patrol	4	14.00
1995-96 Parkhurst Trophy Winners	5	7.50
1995-96 Parkhurst Crown Collection Gold II	5	15.00
1995-96 Parkhurst Crown Collection Silver II	5	6.00
1995-96 Parkhurst Parkie's Trophy Picks	28	12.00
1995-96 Parkhurst	236	.35
1995-96 Parkhurst Emerald Ice	236	10.00
1995-96 Pinnacle	139	.75
1995-96 Pinnacle Artist's Proofs	139	40.00
1995-96 Pinnacle Clear Shots	15	12.00
1995-96 Pinnacle First Strike	14	14.00
1995-96 Pinnacle Rink Collection	139	10.00
1995-96 Score	200	.40
1995-96 Score	325	.20
1995-96 SkyBox Impact	16	.10
1995-96 SkyBox Impact Deflectors	1	4.00
1995-96 Stadium Club	60	.50
1995-96 Stadium Club Metalists	M10	12.00
1995-96 Stadium Club Nemeses	N6	12.00
1995-96 Summit	159	.75
1995-96 Summit Artist's Proofs	159	25.00
1995-96 Summit In The Crease	2	35.00
1995-96 SP	13	1.00
1995-96 Topps	2	.20
1995-96 Topps	302	.30
1995-96 Topps Hidden Gems	4HG	7.00
1995-96 Topps Mystery Finest	M19	6.00
1995-96 Topps Power Boosters	2	8.00
1995-96 Topps Profiles	PS14	4.00
1995-96 Topps Super Skills	75	.40
1995-96 Ultra	18	.60
1995-96 Ultra	370	.20
1995-96 Ultra Extra Ultraview	3	10.00
1995-96 Ultra Premier Pad Men	5	20.00
1995-96 Upper Deck	104	.50
1995-96 Upper Deck All-Star	AS20	15.00
1995-96 Upper Deck Be a Player	192	1.00
1995-96 UD Be a Player Autographs	192	35.00
1995-96 UD Be a Player Die-Cut Autos	192	70.00
1995-96 Upper Deck Freeze Frame	F11	12.00
1995-96 Upper Deck Hobby Predictor	H13	8.00
1995-96 Upper Deck Special Edition	SE98	1.50
1995-96 Zenith	109	2.00
1996-97 Canadian Ice	60	.75
1996-97 Certified	74	1.25
1996-97 Certified Freezers	5	30.00
1996-97 UD CC	30	.25
1996-97 Donruss	192	.30
1996-97 Donruss Elite	37	1.00
1996-97 Flair	8	2.00
1996-97 Flair Blue Ice	8	90.00
1996-97 Flair Hot Gloves	4	35.00
1996-97 Fleer	10	.25
1996-97 Fleer NHL Picks Dream Lines	6	25.00
1996-97 Fleer Vezina	4	15.00
1996 Kenner Starting Lineups American	(6)	30.00
1996-97 Leaf	19	.75
1996-97 Leaf Limited	21	2.00
1996-97 Leaf Limited Gold	21	8.00
1996-97 Leaf Preferred	91	.75
1996-97 Leaf Preferred Masked Marauders	7	30.00
1996-97 Leaf Preferred Steel	52	3.00
1996-97 Metal Universe	14	1.00
1996-97 Metal Universe Armor Plate	4	25.00
1996-97 Metal Universe Cool Steel	4	15.00
1996-97 Pinnacle	106	.75

Set	Card No.	Value
1996-97 Pinn Be a Player Stacking the Pads	11	35.00
1996-97 Pinnacle Mint Collection	2	.50
1996-97 Pinnacle Mint Collection Coins	2	2.50
1996-97 Score	18	.35
1996-97 Score Net Worth	4	15.00
1996-97 Score Sudden Death	3	6.00
1996-97 SkyBox Impact	10	.25
1996-97 SkyBox Impact Zero Heroes	4	20.00
1996 Stadium Club Members Only	42	1.00
1996-97 Summit	2	.75
1996-97 Summit In the Crease	14	20.00
1996-97 SP	17	1.00
1996-97 SP Holoview Collection	HC30	10.00
1996-97 SP SPx Force	SPX3	125.00
1996-97 Topps NHL Picks Ice D	ID10	8.00
1996-97 Ultra	16	.50
1996-97 Ultra Clear the Ice	3	50.00
1996-97 Upper Deck	222	.50
1996-97 Upper Deck Black Diamond	156	25.00
1996-97 Upper Deck GenerationNext	X28	5.00
1996-97 Upper Deck Ice	5	2.50
1996-97 Upper Deck Ice Performers	5	20.00
1996-97 UD Superstar Showdown	SS26a	2.50
1996-97 Zenith	15	1.50
1997-98 Canadian Ice	10	1.00
1997-98 Canadian Ice Cup Scrapbook	22	25.00
1997-98 UD CC	22	.50
1997-98 UD CC Stick-Ums	S30	.75
1997-98 UD CC Star Quest	SQ81	18.00
1997-98 Donruss	9	.75
1997-98 Donruss Between the Pipes	4	25.00
1997-98 Donruss Elite	11	30.00
1997-98 Donruss Limited	76	—
1997-98 Donruss Limited	86	—
1997-98 Donruss Limited	147	—
1997-98 Pacific Crown	39	1.00
1997-98 Pacific Crown Cel Cards	3	15.00
1997-98 Pacific Crown Cramer's Choice	2	75.00
1997-98 Pacific Crown Gold Crown	3	8.00
1997-98 Pacific Crown In the Cage	2	35.00
1997-98 Pacific Dynagon	10	3.00
1997-98 Pacific Dynagon	136	1.50
1997-98 Pacific Dynagon Best Kept Secrets	10	.75
1997-98 Pacific Dynagon Best Kept Secrets	104	.75
1997-98 Pacific Dynagon Dynamic Duos	3A	15.00
1997-98 Pacific Dynagon Stonewallers	3	30.00
1997-98 Pacific Dynagon Tandems	4	100.00
1997-98 Pacific Dynagon Tandems	21	20.00
1997-98 Pacific Invincible	12	4.00
1997-98 Pacific Inv Feature Performers	4	10.00
1997-98 Pacific Invincible New Regime	20	.50
1997-98 Pinnacle Certified	1	1.50
1997-98 Pinnacle Certified Epix	22	12.00
1997-98 Pinnacle Certified Team	4	12.00
1997-98 SPX	4	3.00
1997-98 SPX DuoView	DV	90.00
1997-98 Totally Certified Platinum Red	1	10.00
1997-98 Totally Certified Platinum Gold	1	200.00
1997-98 Totally Certified Platinum Blue	1	18.00
1997-98 Upper Deck Game Jersey	GJ3	250.00
1997-98 Upper Deck The Specialists	S18	15.00
1997-98 Upper Deck Three Star Selects	T2-A	2.50
1991 Traks	1	2.00
1992 Maxx	29	2.00
1992 Maxx	50	1.50
1992 Maxx Red/Black Update	U6	3.50
1992 Pro Set Winston Cup	128	2.00
1993 AP	32	8.00
1993 AP	61	4.00
1993 AP	63	4.00

Jeff Gordon: Winston Cup Champion

Set	Card No.	Value
1993 AP	86	4.00
1993 AP	87	2.00
1993 AP	93	4.00
1993 AP	150	4.00
1993 AP	153	4.00
1993 AP	173	3.00
1993 AP	205	3.00
1993 AP Gold	10	125.00
1993 AP Gold	12	100.00
1993 AP Gold	26	100.00
1993 AP Gold	29	100.00
1993 AP Gold	36	100.00
1993 AP Gold	55	100.00
1993 Finish Line	83	.10
1993 Finish Line	110	.10
1993 Maxx	24	1.50
1993 Maxx	168	1.00
1993 Maxx Premier Plus	24	5.00
1993 Maxx Premier Plus	39	2.00
1993 Press Pass	17	3.50
1993 Press Pass	18	3.50
1993 Press Pass	26	3.50
1993 Traks	39	.10
1993 Traks	151	.10
1994 AP	73	3.00
1994 AP	103	2.00
1994 AP	146	4.00
1994 AP	189	3.00
1994 AP	209	3.00
1994 AP 24K Gold	27G	100.00
1994 AP 24K Gold	189G	350.00
1994 Classic Assets	68	1.00
1994 Classic Assets	93	1.00
1994 Classic Assets $5 Foncards	(8)	15.00
1994 Classic Assets Die-Cut Cards	DC19	12.00
1994 Classic Assets $2 Foncards	(42)	5.00
1994 Finish Line	36	1.00
1994 Finish Line	75	1.00
1994 Finish Line Gold	11	3.50
1994 Finish Line Gold	28	3.50
1994 Finish Line Gold	60	3.50
1994 Finish Line Gold	65	1.00
1994 Finish Line Gold	88	3.50
1994 Finish Line Silver	36	5.00
1994 Finish Line Silver	75	5.00
1994 High Gear	73	2.50
1994 High Gear	97	2.50
1994 High Gear Day One	101	7.00
1994 High Gear Gold	73	15.00
1994 High Gear Gold	97	15.00
1994 Maxx	24	1.50
1994 Maxx	65	.75
1994 Maxx	201	1.00
1994 Maxx Premier	13	3.00
1994 Maxx Premier	24	4.00
1994 Maxx Premier	65	2.50
1994 Maxx Premier	260	3.00
1994 Maxx Premier Jumbos	8	5.00
1994 Maxx Premier Plus	13	2.00
1994 Maxx Premier Plus	24	5.00
1994 Maxx Premier Plus	46	4.00
1994 Maxx Rookies of the Year	16	15.00
1994 Maxx Select 25	14	7.50
1994 Press Pass	7	2.00
1994 Press Pass	124	2.50
1994 Press Pass Cup Chase	CC7	25.00
1994 Press Pass Optima XL	2	.20
1994 Press Pass Optima XL	6	3.00
1994 Press Pass Optima XL	26	3.00
1994 Press Pass Optima XL	38	1.50
1994 Press Pass Optima XL	56	1.50
1994 Press Pass Optima XL	62	1.50
1994 Press Pass Race Day	RD7	20.00
1994 Press Pass VIP	12	1.00
1994 Press Pass VIP	74	1.00
1994 Press Pass VIP 24K Gold	3	70.00
1994 Traks	10	.75
1994 Traks	24	1.50
1994 Traks	36	1.50
1994 Traks	86	1.50
1994 Traks	106	1.50
1994 Traks	171	1.50
1994 Traks First Run	10	1.50
1994 Traks First Run	24	4.00
1994 Traks First Run	36	4.00
1994 Traks First Run	86	4.00
1994 Traks First Run	106	4.00
1994 Traks First Run	171	4.00
1994 Traks Winners	8	15.00
1994 Traks Winners	21	15.00
1994 Traks Winners	22	15.00
1995 AP	9	3.00
1995 AP	36	2.50
1995 AP	50	2.50
1995 AP	66	2.50
1995 AP	70	2.50
1995 AP Country 24KT Team	1	60.00
1995 AP Country Team Rainbow	1	12.00
1995 AP Country 24KT Team	2	60.00
1995 AP Country 24KT Team	3	60.00
1995 AP Country 2nd Career Choice	5	5.00
1995 AP Country Team Rainbow	5	12.00
1995 AP Country	6	1.50
1995 AP Country Team Rainbow	8	12.00
1995 AP Country Team Rainbow	12	12.00
1995 AP Country	14	1.50
1995 AP Country	22	1.50
1995 AP Country	50	1.50
1995 AP Country	51	1.50
1995 AP Country	63	2.00
1995 AP Country	104	1.00
1995 AP Winston Cup Trucks That Haul	ST1	12.00
1995 AP Winston Cup 24K Gold	2G	75.00
1995 AP Winston Cup 24K Gold	4G	75.00
1995 AP Winston Cup 24K Gold	6G	75.00
1995 AP Winston Cup 24K Gold	19G	75.00
1995 AP Winston Cup 24K Gold	20G	75.00
1995 AP Winston Cup	24	2.00
1995 AP Winston Cup	40	1.00
1995 AP Winston Cup	47	2.00
1995 AP Winston Cup	49	2.00
1995 AP Winston Cup	51	2.00
1995 AP Winston Cup	60	1.00
1995 AP Winston Cup	61	1.00
1995 AP Winston Cup	62	1.00
1995 AP Winston Cup	63	1.00
1995 AP Winston Cup	64	1.00
1995 AP Winston Cup	65	1.00
1995 AP 24K Gold	2G	85.00
1995 Assets	3	3.50
1995 Assets	31	3.50
1995 Assets $100/$1000 Phone Cards		175.00
1995 Assets $5/$25 Phone Cards		20.00
1995 Assets Gold Signature	3	40.00
1995 Assets Gold Signature	31	40.00
1995 Assets Gold Signature	49	15.00
1995 Assets Racing Images Previews	RI4	35.00
1995 Assets 1 Minute/$2 Phone Cards		9.00
1995 Classic Five-Sport Fast Track	FT 3	12.00
1995 Classic Images	24	6.00
1995 Classic Images	48	6.00
1995 Classic Images	72	6.00
1995 Classic Images	99	1.00
1995 Classic Images Driven	D2	20.00
1995 Classic Images Hard Chargers	HC8	20.00
1995 Classic Images Owner's Pride	OP5	20.00
1995 Classic Images Race Reflections	JG1	12.00
1995 Classic Images Race Reflections	JG2	12.00
1995 Classic Images Race Reflections	JG3	12.00
1995 Classic Images Race Reflections	JG4	12.00
1995 Classic Images Race Reflections	JG5	12.00
1995 Classic Images Race Reflections	JG6	12.00
1995 Classic Images Race Reflections	JG7	12.00
1995 Classic Images Race Reflections	JG8	12.00
1995 Classic Images Race Reflections	JG9	12.00
1995 Classic Images Race Reflections	JG10	12.00
1995 Finish Line	24	2.00
1995 Finish Line	53	2.00
1995 Finish Line	105	2.00
1995 Finish Line Gold Signature	1	60.00
1995 Finish Line Printer's Proof	24	100.00
1995 Finish Line Printer's Proof	53	100.00
1995 Finish Line Printer's Proof	105	100.00
1995 Finish Line Silver Series	24	.25
1995 Finish Line Silver Series	53	.25
1995 Finish Line Silver Series	105	.25
1995 Finish Line Standout Drivers	7	15.00
1995 High Gear	6	2.00
1995 High Gear	91	1.00
1995 High Gear	98	.50
1995 High Gear Busch Clash	BC7	15.00
1995 High Gear Day One	6	4.00
1995 High Gear Day One	91	2.50
1995 High Gear Day One	98	1.00
1995 Maxx	24	2.00
1995 Maxx	72	.75
1995 Maxx	80	.75
1995 Maxx	105	.75
1995 Maxx	236	2.00
1995 Maxx	237	.75
1995 Maxx Over the Wall	1	14.00
1995 Pinnacle Zenith	23	5.00
1995 Pinnacle Zenith	64	3.00
1995 Pinnacle Zenith	78	3.00
1995 Pinnacle Zenith	79	3.00
1995 Pinnacle Zenith	80	3.00
1995 Pinnacle Zenith	81	3.00
1995 Pinnacle Zenith	82	3.00
1995 Pinnacle Zenith	83	3.00
1995 Pinnacle Zenith Helmets	3	110.00
1995 Pinnacle Zenith Tribute	2	100.00
1995 Pinnacle Zenith Winners	2	15.00
1995 Pinnacle Zenith Winners	4	15.00
1995 Pinnacle Zenith Winners	6	15.00
1995 Pinnacle Zenith Winners	15	15.00
1995 Pinnacle Zenith Winners	16	15.00
1995 Pinnacle Zenith Winners	23	15.00
1995 Pinnacle Zenith Winners	25	15.00
1995 Pinnacle Zenith Z-Team	2	100.00
1995 Press Pass	10	2.00
1995 Press Pass	102	1.50
1995 Press Pass	129	1.50
1995 Press Pass	136	1.50
1995 Press Pass Checkered Flags	3	12.00
1995 Press Pass Cup Chase Redemption	3	60.00
1995 Press Pass Cup Chase Redemption	4	60.00
1995 Press Pass Cup Chase	10	100.00
1995 Press Pass Optima XL Jeff Gordon	1	10.00
1995 Press Pass Optima XL Jeff Gordon	2	25.00
1995 Press Pass Optima XL Jeff Gordon	3	75.00
1995 Press Pass Optima XL Jeff Gordon	4	200.00
1995 Press Pass Optima XL Stealth	4	25.00
1995 Press Pass Optima XL	8	3.00
1995 Press Pass Optima XL Red Hots	8	6.00
1995 Press Pass Optima XL Cool Blues	8	6.00
1995 Press Pass Optima XL Die-Cut Proofs	8	20.00
1995 Press Pass Optima XL	31	2.00
1995 Press Pass Optima XL Red Hots	31	4.00
1995 Press Pass Optima XL Cool Blues	31	4.00
1995 Press Pass Optima XL Die-Cut Proofs	31	15.00
1995 Press Pass Optima XL	56	3.00
1995 Press Pass Optima XL Red Hots	56	6.00
1995 Press Pass Optima XL Cool Blues	56	6.00
1995 Press Pass Optima XL Die-Cut Proofs	56	20.00
1995 Press Pass Premium	8	4.00
1995 Press Pass Premium	33	4.00
1995 Press Pass Premium Hot Pursuit	3	35.00
1995 Press Pass Prime Time Phone Cards	2	26.00
1995 Press Pass Race Day	4	20.00
1995 Press Pass VIP	11	3.00
1995 Press Pass VIP	31	3.00
1995 Press Pass VIP	61	.75
1995 Press Pass VIP Fan's Choice	FC3	18.00
1995 Press Pass VIP Helmets	H4	35.00
1995 Press Pass VIP Reflections	R2	60.00
1995 Select	12	4.00
1995 Select	118	2.00
1995 Select	141	2.00
1995 Select	NNO	15.00
1995 Select Skills	SS3	35.00
1995 Traks	4	2.00
1995 Traks	26	2.00
1995 Traks	52	2.00
1995 Traks	58	2.00
1995 Traks	68	2.00
1995 Traks Challenger Series	1	90.00
1995 Traks Racing Machines	7	35.00
1995 Traks Series Stars	8	40.00
1995 Upper Deck	2	3.50
1995 Upper Deck	45	2.50
1995 Upper Deck	70	1.50
1995 Upper Deck	138	1.50
1995 Upper Deck	163	2.00
1995 Upper Deck	202	2.00
1995 Upper Deck	246	2.00
1995 Upper Deck	281	1.25
1995 Upper Deck Autographs	202	200.00
1995 Upper Deck Illustrations	I9	14.00
1995 Upper Deck Inserts	UD2	60.00
1995 Upper Deck Points Predictors	PP6	30.00
1995 Upper Deck Race Winner Predictors	P4	25.00
1995 Upper Deck SP	18	4.50
1995 Upper Deck SP	55	4.00
1995 Upper Deck SP	56	4.00
1995 Upper Deck SP	97	1.50
1995 Upper Deck SP	100	1.50
1995 Upper Deck SP Speed Merchants	SM24	20.00
1995 Wheels Crown Jewels Sig Gems	SG1	45.00
1995 Wheels Crown Jewels Dual Jewels	DJ1	40.00
1995 Wheels Crown Jewels	2	3.00
1995 Wheels Crown Jewels	68	2.00
1995 Wheels Crown Jewels	73	2.00
1996 AP Credentials	1	2.00
1996 AP Credentials	2	2.00
1996 AP Credentials	3	2.00
1996 AP Credentials	4	2.00
1996 AP Credentials	5	2.00
1996 AP Credentials Leaders of the Pack	5	25.00
1996 AP Credentials Leaders of the Pack	6	25.00

Card	Card No.	Value
1996 AP Credentials Leaders of the Pack	7	25.00
1996 AP Credentials Leaders of the Pack	8	25.00
1996 AP Credentials	20	1.25
1996 AP Credentials	99	1.00
1996 AP Credentials	105	.75
1996 Assets	2	2.50
1996 Assets $100 Cup Champion Phone	2	20.00
1996 Finish Line	1	2.00
1996 Finish Line	87	2.00
1996 Finish Line Black Gold Gordon/Elliott	SG1	15.00
1996 Finish Line Gold Signature	GS1	35.00
1996 Finish Line Jeff Gordon	JG1-10	7.50
1996 Finish Line Man & Machine	MM1	12.00
1996 Fleer Flair NASCAR	12	5.00
1996 Fleer Flair NASCAR Autographs	4	200.00
1996 Fleer Flair NASCAR Center Spotlight	4	12.00
1996 Fleer Flair NASCAR Hot Numbers	3	35.00
1996 Fleer Flair NASCAR Power Performance	4	25.00
1996 Fleer Ultra NASCAR	1	2.50
1996 Fleer Ultra NASCAR	2	2.50
1996 Fleer Ultra NASCAR	152	1.00
1996 Fleer Ultra NASCAR	157	.75
1996 Fleer Ultra NASCAR	168	1.00
1996 Fleer Ultra NASCAR	170	1.00
1996 Fleer Ultra NASCAR	172	1.00
1996 Fleer Ultra NASCAR	181	1.00
1996 Fleer Ultra NASCAR	182	1.00
1996 Fleer Ultra NASCAR	189	1.00
1996 Fleer Ultra NASCAR	191	1.00
1996 Fleer Ultra NASCAR	200	.10
1996 Fleer Ultra NASCAR Autographs	(11)	180.00
1996 Fleer Ultra NASCAR Champions Club	5	5.00
1996 Fleer Ultra NASCAR Flair Preview	1	20.00
1996 Fleer Ultra NASCAR Season Crowns	2	5.00
1996 Fleer Ultra NASCAR Season Crowns	4	5.00
1996 Fleer Ultra NASCAR Season Crowns	7	5.00
1996 Fleer Ultra NASCAR Season Crowns	10	5.00
1996 Fleer Ultra NASCAR Season Crowns	11	5.00
1996 Fleer Ultra NASCAR Thunder/Lightning	3	4.00
1996 Fleer Ultra NASCAR Thunder/Lightning	4	4.00
1996 Fleer Ultra NASCAR Upd Proven Power	4	45.00
1996 Fleer Ultra NASCAR Update Autographs	4	180.00
1996 Fleer Ultra NASCAR Update	12	2.50
1996 Fleer Ultra NASCAR Update	46	2.50
1996 Maxx	24	2.00
1996 Maxx Jeff Gordon Chase Champion	CTC1	15.00
1996 Pinnacle	24	3.00
1996 Pinnacle	66-73	1.50
1996 Pinnacle	85	1.50
1996 Pinnacle	95	1.00
1996 Pinnacle Checkered Flag	1	10.00
1996 Pinnacle Cut Above	1	25.00
1996 Pinnacle Racers Choice Up Close	1	10.00
1996 Pinnacle Racers Choice Top Ten	1-7	25.00
1996 Pinnacle Racers Choice	9	1.75
1996 Pinnacle Racers Choice	51	.75
1996 Pinnacle Racers Choice	52	.75
1996 Pinnacle Racers Choice	54	.75
1996 Pinnacle Racers Choice	55	.75
1996 Pinnacle Racers Choice	83	.75
1996 Pinnacle Racers Choice	90	.75
1996 Pinnacle Racers Choice	110	.75
1996 Pinnacle Speedflix	17	2.00
1996 Pinnacle Speedflix	25	2.00
1996 Pinnacle Speedflix	68	1.00
1996 Pinnacle Speedflix	69	1.00
1996 Pinnacle Speedflix	70	1.00
1996 Pinnacle Speedflix	71	1.00
1996 Pinnacle Speedflix	72	1.00
1996 Pinnacle Speedflix	73	1.00
1996 Pinnacle Speedflix	74	1.00
1996 Pinnacle Speedflix	75	1.00
1996 Pinnacle Speedflix	99	.75
1996 Pinnacle Speedflix Clear Shots	2	15.00
1996 Pinnacle Speedflix In Motion	2	20.00
1996 Pinnacle Speedflix ProMotion	2	10.00
1996 Pinnacle Team Pinnacle	1	90.00
1996 Pinnacle Team Pinnacle	10	90.00
1996 Pinnacle Zenith	2	5.00
1996 Pinnacle Zenith	36	5.00
1996 Pinnacle Zenith	51	2.50
1996 Pinnacle Zenith	73	2.00
1996 Pinnacle Zenith	74	2.00
1996 Pinnacle Zenith	75	2.00
1996 Pinnacle Zenith	76	2.00
1996 Pinnacle Zenith	77	2.00
1996 Pinnacle Zenith	78	2.00
1996 Pinnacle Zenith	79	2.00
1996 Pinnacle Zenith	80	2.00
1996 Pinnacle Zenith	91	2.00
1996 Pinnacle Zenith	92	2.00
1996 Pinnacle Zenith	98	2.00
1996 Pinnacle Zenith	99	2.00
1996 Pinnacle Zenith Champion Salute	1	140.00
1996 Pinnacle Zenith Highlights	2	20.00
1996 Press Pass	11	2.00
1996 Press Pass	93	2.00
1996 Press Pass	100	2.00
1996 Press Pass	111	.75
1996 Press Pass Burning Rubber	BR2	250.00
1996 Press Pass Cup Chase	CC11	35.00
1996 Press Pass F.Q.S.	FQS3A	20.00
1996 Press Pass Focused	F3	50.00
1996 Press Pass Jeff Gordon Insert	#0	10.00
1996 Press Pass M-Force	19	10.00
1996 Press Pass M-Force	40	10.00
1996 Press Pass M-Force Blacks	B7	100.00
1996 Press Pass M-Force Blacks	B12	100.00
1996 Press Pass M-Force Metallic Force	M5	300.00
1996 Press Pass M-Force Silvers	S14	35.00
1996 Press Pass Premium	1	4.00
1996 Press Pass Prem Burning Rubber	BR1	250.00
1996 Press Pass Premium Crystal Ball	CB5	45.00
1996 Press Pass Premium Hot Pursuit	HP3	35.00
1996 Press Pass VIP	10	4.00
1996 Press Pass VIP	30	4.00
1996 Press Pass VIP Autographs	—	200.00
1996 Press Pass VIP Head Gear	HG3	20.00
1996 Press Pass VIP Sam Bass	SB3	50.00
1996 Score Board Autographed Racing	2	2.00
1996 Score Board Auto Autographs		150.00
1996 Upper Deck Motor Predictor-WINS	HP1	15.00
1996 Upper Deck Motor Virtual Velocity	VV1	18.00
1996 Upper Deck Motorsports	22	2.50
1996 Upper Deck Motorsports	62	1.50
1996 Upper Deck Motorsports	102	1.50
1996 Upper Deck Motorsports	150	1.50
1996 UUD Road to Cup	RC1	3.00
1996 UUD Road to Cup 2-D Card	JG1	15.00
1996 UUD Road to Cup Leaders of Pack	LP1	30.00
1996 UUD Road to Cup Predictor-Points	PP1	12.00
1996 UUD Road to Cup Predictor-Top 3	T1	10.00
1996 UUD Road to Cup Authentic Sign	H1	200.00
1996 UUD Road to Cup Diary Champion	DC1	3.00
1996 UUD Road to Cup Diary Champion	DC2	3.00
1996 UUD Road to Cup Predictor-Top 3	T3	10.00
1996 UUD Road to Cup Diary of a Cham	DC3	3.00
1996 UUD Road to Cup Diary of a Champ	DC4	3.00
1996 UUD Road to Cup Diary of a Champ	DC5	3.00
1996 UUD Road to Cup Predictor-Top 3	T6	8.00
1996 UUD Road to Cup Diary of a Champ	DC6	3.00
1996 UUD Road to Cup Predictor-Top 3	T7	10.00
1996 UUD Road to Cup Diary of a Champ	DC7	3.00
1996 UUD Road to Cup Diary of a Champ	DC8	3.00
1996 UUD Road to Cup Diary of a Champ	DC9	3.00
1996 UUD Road to Cup Diary of a Champ	DC10	3.00
1996 UUD Road to Cup	RC51	1.50
1996 UUD Road to Cup	RC121	2.00
1996 UUD Road to Cup	RC124	2.00
1996 UUD Road to Cup	RC148	1.50
1996 Upper Deck SP	24	4.00
1996 Upper Deck SP	43	2.00
1996 Upper Deck SP	80	2.00
1996 UD SP Holoview Max Effects	ME1	15.00
1996 UD SP Racing Legends Collection	RL24	25.00
1996 Upper Deck SPx	1	10.00
1996 Upper Deck SPx Elite	E1	50.00
1996 Wheels Crown Jewels	2	3.00
1996 Wheels Crown Jewels Birthstones	BC2	150.00
1996 Wheels Knight Quest Knights	K11	75.00
1996 Wheels Knight Quest Armor	2	3.00
1996 Wheels Knight Quest Royalty	2	25.00
1996 Wheels Knight Quest Black Knight	2	75.00
1996 Wheels Knight Quest First Knights	FK3	35.00
1996 Wheels Knight Quest Prot of Crown	PC6	90.00
1996 Wheels Knight Quest Armor	21	3.00
1996 Wheels Knight Quest Royalty	21	25.00
1996 Wheels Knight Quest Black Knight	21	75.00
1996 Wheels Knight Quest Armor	30	3.00
1996 Wheels Knight Quest Royalty	30	25.00
1996 Wheels Knight Quest Black Knight	30	75.00
1996 Wheels Knight Quest Armor	31	3.00
1996 Wheels Knight Quest Royalty	31	25.00
1996 Wheels Knight Quest Black Knight	31	75.00
1996 Wheels Viper	2	3.00
1996 Wheels Viper	37	1.50
1996 Wheels Viper	39	1.50
1996 Wheels Viper Busch Clash	B5	15.00
1996 Wheels Viper Cobra	C2	35.00
1996 Wheels Viper Diamondback	D1	75.00
1996 Wheels Viper Diamondback Auth	DA1	175.00
1996 Wheels Viper King Cobra	KC2	50.00
1997 AP	8	2.50
1997 AP	29	1.00
1997 AP Chevy Madness	4	10.00
1997 AP Fifth Anniversary	8	100.00
1997 AP Rolling Thunder	3	20.00
1997 AP 24kt. Gold	3	100.00
1997 Fleer Ultra NASCAR	12	4.00
1997 Fleer Ultra NASCAR AKA	A2	35.00
1997 Fleer Ultra NASCAR Inside/Out	DC2	15.00
1997 Pinnacle	24	2.50
1997 Pinnacle	53	1.00
1997 Pinnacle Chevy Madness	15	20.00
1997 Pinnacle Mint Collection	2	2.00
1997 Pinnacle Mint Collection Coins	2	8.00
1997 Pinnacle Racer's Choice Chevy Madness	7	8.00
1997 Pinnacle Racer's Choice High Octane	3	30.00
1997 Pinnacle Racer's Choice Busch Clash	8	15.00
1997 Pinnacle Racer's Choice	24	1.00
1997 Pinnacle Racer's Choice	59	.50
1997 Pinnacle Spellbound	6R	30.00
1997 Pinnacle Team Pinnacle	1	125.00
1997 Press Pass	2	2.00
1997 Press Pass	57	1.00
1997 Press Pass	96	1.00
1997 Press Pass	134	1.00
1997 Press Pass	135	1.00
1997 Press Pass	136	1.00
1997 Press Pass	137	1.00
1997 Press Pass	138	1.00
1997 Press Pass ActionVision	2	16.00
1997 Press Pass ActionVision	10	14.00
1997 Press Pass Banquet Bound	BB2	15.00
1997 Press Pass Burning Rubber	5	250.00
1997 Press Pass Clear Cut	2	25.00
1997 Press Pass Cup Chase '97	7	30.00
1997 Press Pass Premium	2	4.00
1997 Press Pass Premium	33	1.50
1997 Press Pass Premium	38	2.00
1997 Press Pass Premium Autographs	2	200.00
1997 Press Pass Premium Crystal Ball	CB4	30.00
1997 Press Pass Prem Double Burners	DB2	250.00
1997 Press Pass Premium Lap Leaders	LL3	20.00
1997 Press Pass Victory Lane	2A	20.00
1997 Press Pass VIP	8	3.00
1997 Press Pass VIP Autographs	2	200.00
1997 Press Pass VIP Head Gear	HG3	25.00
1997 Press Pass VIP Sam Bass	KT2	30.00
1997 Press Pass VIP Sheet Metal	SM1	300.00
1997 Score Board Auto Checkered Flag	TF1	50.00
1997 Score Board Autographed	4	2.00
1997 Score Board Auto Mayne St.	KM4	1.00
1997 Score Board IQ	2	6.00
1997 Score Board IQ	26	6.00
1997 Score Board IQ	37	6.00
1997 Score Board IQ Remarques	SB2	125.00
1997 Score Board SB	2	1.00
1997 Score Board SB Autographed	AU2	250.00
1997 SkyBox NASCAR Profile	7	5.00
1997 SkyBox NASCAR Profile	70	2.50
1997 UD CC Victory Circle	VC10	30.00
1997 UD CC Triple Force	1F	10.00
1997 UD CC Triple Force	2G	10.00
1997 UD CC Triple Force	3G	10.00
1997 UD CC	24	1.50
1997/98 UD CC	24	—
1997 UD CC Speedecals	S47	2.00
1997 UD CC Speedecals	S48	2.00
1997 UD CC Upper Deck 500	UD48	1.50
1997 UD CC Upper Deck 500	UD49	1.50
1997/98 UD CC	60	—
1997/98 UD CC	73	—
1997 UD CC	74	.75
1997/98 UD CC	88	—
1997/98 UD CC	100	—
1997 UD CC	101	.75
1997 UD CC	127	.75
1997 UD CC	128	.75
1997 UD CC	129	.75
1997 UD CC	154	.75
1997 Upper Deck Diamond Vision	1	—
1997 UD Diamond Vision Of Champion	VC3	—
1997 Upper Deck Maxx	24	2.00
1997 Upper Deck Maxx	69	1.00
1997 UD Maxx Chase the Champion (Silver)	C1	6.00
1997 UD Maxx Chase the Champion (Gold)	C1	20.00
1997 Upper Deck Maxx Flag Firsts	FF24	10.00
1997 UD Maxx Rookies of the Year	MR6	15.00
1997 UD Road to Cup	2	2.50
1997 UD Road to Cup Cup Predictor Plus	2	15.00
1997 UD Road to Cup Cup Quest	CQ2	40.00
1997 UD Road to Cup Hot Seat	HS4	300.00
1997 UD Road to Cup Million Dollar	MM5	20.00
1997 UD Road to Cup Hot Seat	HS5	300.00
1997 UD Road to Cup Million Dollar Autos.	MM5	150.00
1997 UD Road to Cup Premiere Position	PP6	8.00
1997 UD Road to Cup Million Dollar	MM6	20.00
1997 UD Road to Cup Hot Seat	HS6	300.00
1997 UD Road to Cup Million Dollar Autos.	MM6	150.00
1997 UD Road to Cup Million Dollar	MM7	20.00
1997 UD Road to Cup Million Dollar Autos.	MM7	150.00
1997 UD Road to Cup Million Dollar	MM8	20.00
1997 UD Road to Cup Million Dollar Autos.	MM8	150.00
1997 UD Road to Cup Premiere Position	PP10	8.00
1997 UD Road to Cup Predictor Plus	11	15.00
1997 UD Road to Cup Premiere Position	PP12	8.00
1997 UD Road to Cup Premiere Position	PP17	8.00
1997 UD Road to Cup Premiere Position	PP19	8.00
1997 UD Road to Cup Premiere Position	PP20	8.00
1997 UD Road to Cup Premiere Position	PP21	8.00
1997 UD Road to Cup Premiere Position	PP26	8.00
1997 UUD Road to Cup Predictor Plus	28	15.00
1997 UUD Road to Cup Prem Position	PP30	8.00
1997 UUD Road to Cup Prem Position	PP32	8.00
1997 UUD Road to Cup Prem Position	PP34	8.00
1997 UUD Road to Cup Prem Position	PP42	8.00
1997 UUD Road to Cup Prem Position	PP44	8.00
1997 UUD Road to Cup	47	1.00
1997 UUD Road to Cup	87	2.00
1997 UUD Road to Cup	106	.20
1997 UUD Road to Cup	107	1.00
1997 Upper Deck SP	24	4.00
1997 Upper Deck SP	66	2.00
1997 Upper Deck SP	102	10.00
1997 Upper Deck SP	122	25.00
1997 Upper Deck SP Race Film	RD1	175.00
1997 Upper Deck SP Super Series	24	12.00
1997 Upper Deck SP Super Series	66	6.00
1997 Upper Deck SP Super Series	102	70.00
1997 Upper Deck SP Super Series	122	200.00
1997 Upper Deck SP SPx Force Auto	SF1	350.00
1997 Upper Deck SPx	24	6.00
1997 Upper Deck SPx Speedview Auto	1	300.00
1997 Upper Deck SPx Tag-Team	1	50.00
1997 Upper Deck SPx Tag-Team Auto	1	—
1997 Upper Deck SPx Tag-Team	5	40.00
1997 Upper Deck Victory Circle Predictor	PE1	15.00
1997 UD Victory Circle A Piece of Action	FS1	250.00
1997 UD Vict Circle Gen Excitement	GE1	10.00
1997 UD Victory Circle Champ Reflections	CR2	5.00
1997 UD Victory Circle Driver's Seat	DS2	50.00
1997 UD Victory Circle Victory Lap	VL2	80.00
1997 UD Victory Circle A Piece of Action	FS2	250.00
1997 UD Victory Circle A Piece of Action	FS3	250.00
1997 Upper Deck Victory Circle	24	3.00
1997 Upper Deck Victory Circle	74	3.00
1997 Upper Deck Victory Circle	111	3.00
1997 Wheels Jurassic Park	1	3.00
1997 Wheels Jurassic Park Thunder Lizard	TL1	90.00
1997 Wheels Jurassic Park Raptors	R2	8.00
1997 Wheels Jurassic Park Carnivore	C2	15.00
1997 Wheels Jurassic Park Pteranodon	P2	30.00
1997 Wheels Jurassic Park T-Rex	TR2	50.00
1997 Wheels Jurassic Park	48	2.00
1997 Wheels Jurassic Park	51	2.00
1997 Wheels Predator	1	3.00
1997 Wheels Predator American Eagle	AE2	30.00
1997 Wheels Predator Eye of the Tiger	ET2	10.00
1997 Wheels Pred Gatorback Authentic	GBA2	125.00
1997 Wheels Predator Gatorbacks	GB2	40.00
1997 Wheels Predator Golden Eagle	GE2	40.00
1997 Wheels Race Sharks	2	3.00
1997 Wheels Race Sharks Great White	GW2	100.00
1997 Wheels Race Sharks Shark Tooth Sig	ST2	200.00
1997 Wheels Race Sharks Shark Attack	SA2	50.00
1997 Wheels Viper	1	3.00
1997 Wheels Viper	51	1.50
1997 Wheels Viper	74	1.50
1997 Wheels Viper Anaconda	A2	60.00
1997 Wheels Viper Cobra	C2	20.00
1997 Wheels Viper Diamondback	DB1	40.00
1997 Wheels Viper Diamondback Auth	DBA1	80.00
1997 Wheels Viper King Cobra	KC2	40.00
1997 Wheels Viper Sidewinder	S2	12.00
1997 Wheels Viper Snake Eyes	SE2	15.00
1998 UD CC	24	1.50
1998 UD CC	60	.75
1998 UD CC	88	.75
1998 UD CC	98	.75
1998 UD CC StarQuest	SQ36	30.00
1998 UD CC StarQuest	SQ41	125.00

START YOUR OWN DYNASTY!

Know The Value Of Your Collectibles and Memorabilia!

Eugene Robinson: Diary of a Super Bowl Season
by Eugene Robinson

From the X's and O's on the field to the joys and sorrows off the field, Robinson's tale is one of work, dedication, focus and family. As spoken to Kevin Isaacson, author of the award-winning Packer book "Return to Glory," and Packer Profiles magazine editor Rocky Landsverk, "Eugene Robinson: Diary of a Super Bowl Season" is a season-long lesson on football and recitation on life.
Softcover • 6 x 9 • 256 pages • 40 b&w photos • 40 color photos • **SAFI • $19.95**
AVAIL. 3/98

Price Guide to Packers Memorabilia
by John Carpentier

This exhaustive price guide features 2,500 different Packer collectibles from the 1920s through the 1997 Super Bowl season. All items are identified and carry current market prices. As a bonus, there's an eight-page color section featuring rare and unusual memorabilia. Items listed include autographs, banks, banners, bobbing head dolls, trading cards, and more. Over 2,500 different items identified with current market prices.
Softcover • 6 x 9 • 304 pages • 350 b&w photos • 20 color photos • **GBMEM • $17.95**
AVAIL. 2/98

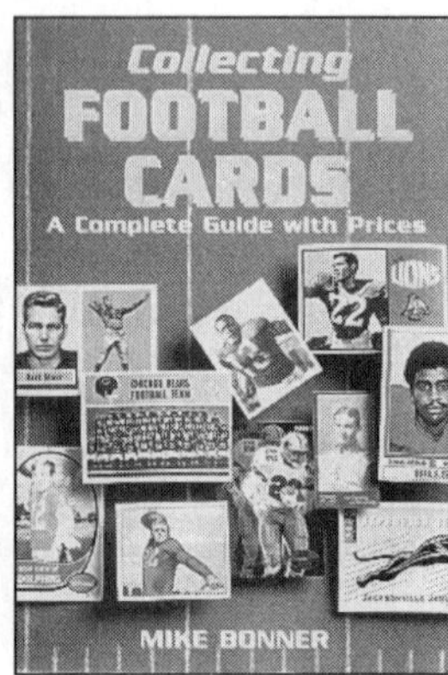

Collecting Football Cards
A Complete Guide with Prices
by Mike Bonner

Play the field confidently with this comprehensive price guide to football cards. You'll get a full history of football cards from the beginning in 1888. Learn which cards are hot, when to pass, and when to run with it. Hundreds of photos illustrate almost every set, plus the 100 most collectible cards.
Softcover • 8-1/4 x 10-7/8 • 224 pages • **FOCA • $15.95**

Return to Glory
by Kevin Isaacson

You'll help fan the flames of the incredible Packer comeback nearly 30 years after the NFL team's historic Super Bowl victories. Get the scoop on Brett Favre, Reggie White, and the controversial Sterling Sharpe. And you'll get up close and personal with Coach Mike Holmgren. Kevin Isaacson broke many of the stories that defined the Packers of the 1990s. Now he authors the Packer's amazing return to glory.
Softcover • 6 x 9 • 240 pages • 225 b&w photos • 16 color photos • **RTG • $16.95**

Getting Started in Card Collecting
by Sports Collectors Digest staff

The SCD staff shows you what to save, how to buy, where to purchase, how to store, when to sell and what to avoid. Give someone this book along with a couple of wax packs and you'll likely start a love affair with sport and entertainment card collecting.
Softcover • 5-1/2 x 8-1/2 • 208 pages • 100 b&w photos • **SR01 • $6.95**

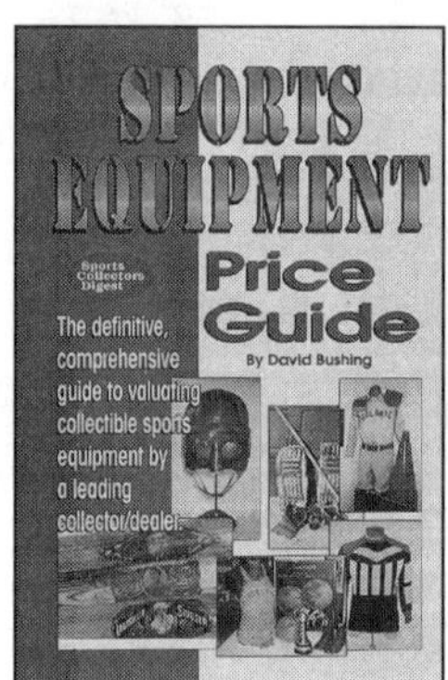

Sports Equipment Price Guide
by David Bushing

Get prices for baseball, football, basketball and hockey equipment used from 1860 to 1960, all in this new comprehensive guide to collectible sports equipment. David Bushing gives prices in three grades of condition for bats, gloves, uniforms, helmets, pucks, sticks and more.
Softcover • 6 x 9 • 336 pages • 500 b&w photos • **SEP01 • $16.95**

Credit Card Calls Toll-free

800-258-0929 Dept. SEB1

**Mon.-Fri., 7 am - 8 pm • Sat. 8 am.- 2 pm, CT
Visit and order from our secure web site: www.krause.com
Krause Publications • 700 E. State Street • Iola, WI 54990-0001**

SATISFACTION GUARANTEE

If for any reason you are not completely satisfied with your purchase, simply return it within 14 days and receive a full refund, less shipping.